PEARSON myeducationlab™

D1128964

Save Time.

Improve Results.

PEARSON myeducationlab

HOME   LEARN ABOUT   TOURS & TRAINING   SUPPORT

Returning Users

Already registered?

| Log In | ▶ |

Need help?

Register or Buy Access

New user? Start here!

| Students | ▶ |

| Instructors | ▶ |

Need help?

MyEducationLab, where you save time and improve results!

MyEducationLab offers you and your students a uniquely valuable teacher education tool. Working with many of you and our authors, we've created a website that provides the context of real classrooms and artifacts that research on teacher education shows is so important. Through authentic in-class video footage, interactive simulations, case studies, examples of teacher and student work, and more, MyEducationLab brings the classroom to life! Learn more...

ANNOUNCEMENTS

Courses for MyEducationLab are available! See Books Available for live dates and available courses.

Want a live product tour? Join us via WebEx to see MyEducationLab! See our Training page for dates and times.

Getting ready for the first day of class? Watch a video (.mov, 19 Mb) about registration, login, and features of MyEducationLab. More information on registration and login for students can be found on our Student Support page.

Previous MyLabSchool or TeacherPrep user? Log in using your existing login name and password!

PEARSON   Pearson product Copyright © 2008 Pearson Education, Inc. All rights reserved.   Legal Notice | Privacy Policy | Permissions

MyEducationLab is a suite of online tools designed to help you make the transition from student to teacher. This fun and easy-to-navigate site enhances this book with a variety of online learning resources—video footage of actual classrooms, sample lesson plans and activities, case studies, and more!

To take advantage of all that *MyEducationLab* has to offer, you will need an access code. If you do not already have an access code, you can buy one online at

www.myeducationlab.com

PEARSON

PEARSON
myeducationlab™

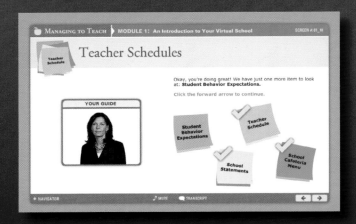

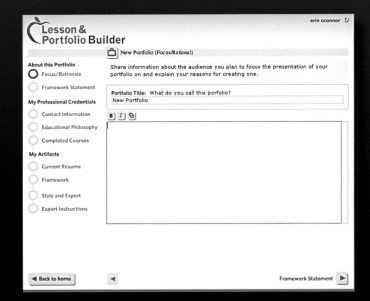

Videos and Practical Tools for Your Classroom and Career!
MyEducationLab helps bring the classroom to life with a wealth of resources to help you prepare for practice teaching and the job of teaching itself.

Managing To Teach

An interactive, virtual learning environment designed to help teachers-in-training develop effective classroom management skills. Users will watch videos of classroom scenarios, complete interactive assignments, assume the role of decision maker in simulated teaching experiences, and receive valuable feedback from the Program Guide on their classroom decisions. Based on the three cornerstones of effective classroom management—prior planning, establishing constructive behaviours, and exhibiting desired modes of behaviour—**Managing to Teach** is the *MyEducationLab* resource that soon-to-be teachers have been waiting for!

Canadian Link Library

A comprehensive aggregation of provincial- and board-level links that will provide you and other students across the country with valuable information about programs and standards that will start you on the right path to becoming a teacher!

Portfolio Builder and Sample Lesson Plans

Use the portfolio-building wizard to build a print or e-portfolio, and sample a rich array of lesson plans that can be used during your practicum or when you start teaching.

Educational Psychology

FOURTH CANADIAN EDITION

Educational Psychology

ANITA E. WOOLFOLK
The Ohio State University

PHILIP H. WINNE
Simon Fraser University

NANCY E. PERRY
University of British Columbia

with

JENNIFER SHAPKA
University of British Columbia

Pearson Canada

Toronto

Library and Archives Canada Cataloguing in Publication

Woolfolk, Anita

    Educational psychology / Anita E. Woolfolk, Philip H. Winne, Nancy
E. Perry. — 4th Canadian ed.

Includes bibliographical references and index.
ISBN 978-0-205-75926-2

    1. Educational psychology—Textbooks. I. Winne, Philip H.
II. Perry, Nancy E. (Nancy Ellen), 1962– III. Title.

LB1051.W73 2009   370.15   C2007-905485-4

Copyright © 2010, 2009, 2006, 2003, 2000 Pearson Education Canada, a division of Pearson Canada Inc., Toronto, Ontario. Pearson Allyn and Bacon. All rights reserved. This publication is protected by copyright and permission should be obtained from the publisher prior to any prohibited reproduction, storage in a retrieval system, or transmission in any form or by any means, electronic, mechanical, photocopying, recording, or likewise. For information regarding permission, write to the Permissions Department.

Original edition published by Pearson Education, Inc., Upper Saddle River, New Jersey, USA. Copyright © 2007 Pearson Education, Inc. This edition is authorized for sale only in Canada.

ISBN-13: 978-0-205-75926-2
ISBN-10: 0-205-75926-2

Vice President, Editorial Director: Gary Bennett
Editor-in-Chief: Ky Pruesse
Acquisitions Editor: David LeGallais
Marketing Manager: Loula March
Senior Developmental Editor: Jennifer Murray
Production Editors: Amanda Wesson, Kevin Leung
Copy Editor: Karen Alliston
Proofreader: Valerie Adams
Production Manager: Peggy Brown
Composition: Pixel Graphics Inc.
Photo and Permissions Research: Julie Pratt
Art Director: Julia Hall
Cover and Interior Design: Anthony Leung
Cover Image: Veer Inc.

For permission to reproduce copyrighted material, the publisher gratefully acknowledges the copyright holders listed on page 613, which is considered an extension of this copyright page.

Statistics Canada information is used with the permission of Statistics Canada. Users are forbidden to copy the data and redisseminate them, in an original or modified form, for commercial purposes, without permission from Statistics Canada. Information on the availability of the wide range of data from Statistics Canada can be obtained from Statistics Canada's Regional Offices, its World Wide Web site at http://www.statcan.ca, and its toll-free access number 1-800-263-1136.

1 2 3 4 5   13 12 11 10 09

Printed and bound in the United States of America.

In memory of my grandmother,
Anita Marie Wiekert,
1902–2002
She gave us all a century of wisdom.

—A.W.

In memory of missed parents,
Bill Perry and Jean and Hawley Winne,
And to family and friends who continue
To teach us the joys of life and learning

—P.H.W.
—N.E.P.

To my children, Kalla and Willem, who give me new
insights every day.

—J.S.

Brief Contents

Contents

Chapter 10 MOTIVATION IN LEARNING AND TEACHING   371

Preface

Many of you reading this book will be enrolled in an educational psychology course as part of your professional preparation for teaching, counselling, speech therapy, or psychology. Others, while not planning to become teachers, are reading this text because you are interested in what educational psychology has to say about teaching and learning in a variety of settings. The material presented here should be of interest to everyone who is concerned about education and learning, from the nursery school volunteer to the instructor in a community program for adults with learning disabilities. No background in psychology or education is necessary to understand this material. It is as free of jargon and technical language as possible, and many people have worked to make this edition clear, relevant, and interesting.

Since the original edition of *Educational Psychology* appeared, there have been many exciting developments in the field. This fourth Canadian edition incorporates new insights and current trends in Canada while retaining the best features of the previous work. The new edition continues to emphasize the educational implications and applications of research on child development, cognitive science, learning, teaching, and assessment. Theory and practice are not separated but are considered together; we show how information and ideas drawn from research in educational psychology can be applied to solve the everyday problems of teaching. To help you explore the connections between knowledge and practice, we have included many **examples, lesson segments, case studies, guidelines,** and **practical tips** from experienced teachers. Throughout the text, you will be challenged to think about the value and use of the ideas in each chapter, and you will see principles of educational psychology in action. Both professors and students find these features very helpful.

As you read *Educational Psychology*, you will notice that the authors are referred to by name as they share their personal experiences. Anita Woolfolk, Phil Winne, and Nancy Perry have been studying, researching, and practising the strategies, methods, and theories discussed in this text for many years. Jennifer Shapka also lends her expertise in this edition. We hope you enjoy the authors' stories and use them to gain insights into your own experiences.

New Content and Organization in This Edition

In this edition, we include the most currently available statistics about our population and the implications for education in a rapidly changing Canadian mosaic. We continue to highlight the latest research on uniquely Canadian issues concerning **programming for students with exceptional learning needs, multicultural education,** and **second-language learning.**

New Topics Hundreds of new citations have been added to this edition to bring prospective teachers the most current information. Topics include the following:

- History of educational psychology
- Scientifically based research
- The brain and teaching
- Physical development
- Bronfenbrenner's theory of development
- Neo-Piagetian approaches

- Cultural tools in learning
- The importance of teacher–student relationships
- Theory of mind
- Bullying and relational aggression
- Ethnic, racial, and gender identity
- New perspectives on moral reasoning
- Flynn effect
- Visual/verbal learning styles
- Autism and Asperger syndrome
- Fostering resilience
- Functional behavioural assessment
- Flashbulb memories
- Heuristics
- Concept mapping
- Teaching for self-regulation
- Problem-based learning
- Engagement in learning
- Managing computers in the classroom
- Culture and classroom management
- School-wide positive behavioural supports
- Assistive technology
- Lesson study
- Informal and authentic assessment
- High-stakes testing

The Plan of the Book

The introductory chapter begins with you and the questions you may be asking yourself about teaching. What is good teaching, and what does it take to become an excellent teacher? How can educational psychology help you to understand what good teaching is and, if you choose a career in teaching, become such a teacher?

Parts 1 and 2 focus on the learners. Part 1, "Student Development," looks at how students develop mentally, physically, emotionally, and socially, and how all these aspects fit together. Part 2, "Student Diversity," looks at various types of diversity in the classroom. How do students differ in their abilities and preferences for learning, and how can teachers accommodate these differences? What does it mean to create a culturally compatible classroom, one that makes learning accessible to all students?

Part 3, "Learning and Motivation," looks at learning and motivation from three major perspectives—behavioural, cognitive, and constructivist—with an emphasis on the last two. Learning theories have important but different implications for instruction at every level. Cognitive research is particularly vital right now and promises to be a wellspring of ideas for teaching in the immediate future.

Part 4, "Teaching, and Assessing Students' Learning," discusses the ever-present, linked issues of motivating, managing, teaching, and assessing today's students. The material in these chapters is based on the most recent research in real classrooms and includes information on both teacher-centred and student-centred approaches to teaching. The chapter on classroom assessment looks at many ways to assess and evaluate students' learning.

Aids to Understanding

At the beginning of each chapter you will find an **Overview** of the key topics with page numbers for quick reference. Then you are confronted with a question, "What Would You Do?" about a real-life classroom situation related to the information in the chapter. By the time you reach the Teachers' Casebook at the end of the chapter, you should have even more ideas about how to solve the problem raised, so be alert as you read. Each chapter begins with a preview and questions to focus your thinking about the upcoming pages.

Within the chapter, headings point out themes, questions, and problems as they arise, so you can look up information easily. These can also serve as a quick review of important points. When a new term or concept is introduced, it appears in boldface type along with a brief marginal definition. These **Key Terms** are also defined in the **Glossary** at the end of the book. After every major section of the chapter, **Check Your Knowledge** and **Apply to Practice** questions ask you to review and apply your learning. Can you answer these questions? If not, you might need to review the material. Throughout the book, graphs, tables, photos, and cartoons have been chosen to clarify and extend the text material—and to add to your enjoyment.

Each chapter ends with a **Summary** of the main ideas directed to the Check Your Knowledge questions in each main heading, as well as an alphabetical list of the key terms from the chapter, along with the page number where each term is discussed.

Text Features

As in previous editions, every chapter includes **Guidelines, Connect & Extend**, the **Teachers' Casebook**, and **Point/Counterpoint** elements on such issues as teaching standards, inclusion, and zero-tolerance policies in schools.

Guidelines. An important reason for studying educational psychology is to gain skills in solving classroom problems. Often texts give pages of theory and research findings, but little assistance in translating theory into practice. This text is different. Included in each chapter are several sets of guidelines, teaching tips, and practical suggestions based on the theory and research discussed in the chapter. Each suggestion is clarified by two or three specific examples. Although the guidelines cannot cover every possible situation, they do provide a needed bridge between knowledge and practice and should help you apply the text's information to new situations. In addition, every chapter after the first has one set of guidelines that provides ideas for working with families and the community—an area of growing importance today.

Connect & Extend. Connect & Extend features appear in the margins several times throughout each chapter, linking content to teaching, students' thinking, research, and the news. They are valuable components for promoting deep-level processing and transferring theory to authentic classroom settings.

Teachers' Casebook. At the end of each chapter, teachers from across Canada offer their own solutions to the problem presented at the beginning of each chapter. Teachers' Casebook: What Would They Do? gives you insight into the thinking of expert teachers; compare their solutions to the ones you devised. Their ideas truly show educational psychology at work in a range of everyday situations. The Teachers' Casebook brings to life the topics and principles discussed in each chapter.

Point/Counterpoint. There is a section in each chapter called Point/Counterpoint, a debate that examines two contrasting perspectives on an important question or controversy related to research or practice in educational psychology. Many of the topics considered in these Point/Counterpoint features have been in the news recently and are central to the discussions of educational reformers.

Becoming a Professional. At the end of each chapter, beginning with Chapter 2, is a section called Becoming a Professional that gives you guidance for developing a professional teaching portfolio and a resource file for your future classrooms.

What Would You Say? Two or three times in every chapter, you are asked how you would answer possible job interview questions based on the text material. These questions were suggested by practising principals and superintendents.

Reaching Every Student. This feature provides ideas for assessing, teaching, and motivating all students in today's classroom. Some describe teaching strategies to reach students with learning problems. Some explain ways of using technology to reach every student. Others present creative ways to teach complex concepts.

Student Supplements

MyEducationLab   Discover where the classroom comes to life! From video clips of teachers and students interacting to sample lessons and portfolio templates, MyEducationLab gives students the tools they will need to succeed in the classroom—with content easily integrated into existing courses. MyEducationLab gives students powerful insights into how real classrooms work and also gives them a rich array of tools that will support them on their journey from their first class to their first classroom.

Instructor Supplements

Instructor's Resource CD-ROM. This resource CD includes the following instructor supplements:

Instructor's Manual. This manual includes a variety of resources for instructors, including teaching outlines; cooperative, research, and field experience activities, supported by handouts; discussion questions; and suggested videos and websites.

PowerPoint Presentations. This instructor resource contains key points, lecture notes, and figures to accompany each chapter in the text.

Test Item File. This test bank contains over 2000 test questions, including multiple choice, fill-in-the-blank, true/false, short answer, and case studies.

MyTest. The test bank is also available as a MyTest, a powerful assessment generation program that helps instructors easily create and print quizzes, tests, exams, as well as homework or practice handouts. Questions and tests can all be authored online, allowing instructors ultimate flexibility and the ability to efficiently manage assessments at anytime, from anywhere. The MyTest can be accessed by visiting **www.pearsonmytest.com**.

These instructor supplements are also available for download from a password-protected section of Pearson Education Canada's online catalogue (vig.pearsoned.ca). Navigate to your book's catalogue page to view a list of the supplements that are available. See your local sales representative for details and access.

Feedback

You are invited to respond to any aspect of this text. We welcome your feedback. You may wish to criticize the solutions in the Teachers' Casebook, for example, or suggest topics or materials you think should be added to future editions. We would also like to know what you think of the text features and student supplements. Please send letters to

Acquisitions Editor, Education
Pearson Education Canada
26 Prince Andrew Place
Don Mills, ON M3C 2T8

Acknowledgments

Our work on this project benefited immensely from consultations with friends and colleagues. Especially, we thank Anita Woolfolk for supporting this Canadian adaptation of her excellent textbook and Nancy Hutchinson (Queen's University) for providing material for Chapters 4 and 5. Also, we thank teachers across this country who responded to the cases and who allowed us to describe their exemplary classroom practices. They are an inspiration to us.

The following Canadian reviewers contributed thoughtful comments:

Marlene Maldonado-Esteban, University of Windsor
Noella Piquette-Tomei, University of Lethbridge
Linda Lysynchuk, Laurentian University
Michael Harrison, University of Ottawa
Krista Pierce, Red Deer College
Jennifer A. Vadeboncoeur, University of British Columbia
Connie Edwards, University of Toronto
David Young, University of Western Ontario

Thanks to the entire team at Pearson Education Canada.

1 TEACHERS, TEACHING, AND EDUCATIONAL PSYCHOLOGY

Lawyers and Clients, 1993, Jacob Lawrence. Gouache on paper, 20 × 22 inches
© 2006 The Jacob and Gwendolyn Lawrence Foundation, Seattle/Artists Rights
Society (ARS), New York. Photo: The Jacob and Gwendolyn Lawrence Foundation/
Art Resource, New York.

Teachers' Casebook

What Would You Do?

It is your second year as a teacher at John A. Macdonald Public School (kindergarten–grade 8). One of your colleagues has been nominated for a Prime Minister's Award for Teaching Excellence. This person has been a role model to you in your first two years as a teacher, providing advice and encouragement. You would like to support her by writing a letter of recommendation highlighting her exemplary teaching practices, commitment, and leadership. The deadline for submissions is a week away. How will you prepare to write the letter?

Critical Thinking

- What do you need to know about teaching to complete this task?
- What are some indicators of excellent teaching?
- Do different philosophies of teaching provide different answers to this question?
- What points will you make in your letter, and how will you back them up?

Collaboration

Discuss the characteristics of good teaching with three or four members of your class. You might draw a concept map that graphically depicts good teaching. See Chapter 8 for some examples of concept maps.

If you are like many students, you begin this course with a mixture of anticipation and wariness. Perhaps you are required to take educational psychology as part of a program in teacher education, speech therapy, nursing, or counselling. You may have chosen this class as an elective because you are interested in education or psychology. Whatever your reason for enrolling, you probably have questions about teaching, schools, students—or even about yourself—that you hope this course may answer. The fourth Canadian edition of *Educational Psychology* has been written with questions such as these in mind.

In this first chapter, we begin not with educational psychology but with education—more specifically, with the state of teaching today. Teachers have been both criticized as ineffective and lauded as the best hope for young people. Do teachers make a difference in students' learning? What characterizes good teaching? Only when you are aware of the challenges teachers face can you appreciate the contributions of educational psychology. After a brief introduction to the world of the teacher, we turn to a discussion of educational psychology itself. How can principles identified by educational psychologists benefit teachers, therapists, parents, and others who are interested in teaching and learning? What exactly is the content of educational psychology, and where does this information come from?

By the time you have completed this chapter, you should be able to answer these questions:

- *Does teaching matter?*
- *What is good teaching?*
- *What do expert teachers know?*
- *Why should I study educational psychology?*
- *What roles do theory and research play in this field?*
- *What are the greatest concerns of beginning teachers?*

DO TEACHERS MAKE A DIFFERENCE?

For a while, some researchers reported findings suggesting that wealth and social status, not teaching, were the major factors determining who learned in schools (e.g., Coleman, 1966). In fact, much of the early research on teaching was conducted by educational psychologists who refused to accept these claims that teachers were powerless in the face of poverty and societal problems (Wittrock, 1986).

How could you decide if teaching makes a difference? You could look to your own experience. Were there teachers who had an impact on your life? Perhaps one of your teachers even influenced your decision to become an educator. But one of the purposes of educational psychology in general is to go beyond individual experiences and testimonies, powerful as they are, to systematically examine the impact of teaching on the lives of students by using carefully designed research studies. Several of these studies are described below.

Teacher–Student Relationships

Bridget Hamre and Robert Pianta (2001) followed 179 children in a small school district from when they entered kindergarten right through to the end of grade 8. The researchers concluded that the quality of the teacher–student relationship in kindergarten (defined in terms of level of conflict with the child, the child's dependency on the teacher, and the teacher's affection for the child) predicted a number of academic and behavioural outcomes through grade 8, particularly for students with high levels of behaviour problems. Even when the gender, ethnicity, cognitive ability, and behaviour ratings of the student were accounted for, the relationship with the teacher still predicted aspects of school success. According to these researchers, "The association between the quality of early teacher–child relationships and later school performance can be both strong and persistent" (p. 636).

Based on these results, it appears that students with significant behaviour problems in the early years are less likely to have problems later in school if their teachers are sensitive to their needs and provide frequent, consistent feedback. Interestingly, in another study, Paula Stanovich and Anne Jordan (1998), two researchers at the Ontario Institute for Studies in Education of the University of Toronto (OISE/UT), found that teachers who believed that it was their responsibility to include and instruct all the students in their classrooms (including students with disabilities and students who don't speak English as their first language) engaged in more academic interactions with their students and were more persistent in helping students to succeed in school.

Teacher Preparation and Quality

Linda Darling-Hammond (2000), a researcher at Stanford University, examined the ways in which teacher qualifications are related to student achievement using data from several U.S.-based sources, including a survey of policies in the 50 states, case study analyses, the 1993–1994 Schools and Staffing Surveys, and the National Assessment of Educational Progress (NAEP). Her findings indicated that the quality of teachers—as measured by whether the teachers were fully certified and had a major in their teaching field—was related to student performance. In fact, measures of teacher preparation and certification were by far the strongest predictors of student achievement in reading and mathematics, both before and after controlling for student poverty and English language proficiency. Look at Table 1.1. In the first row, all the correlations are positive and significant. This means that the higher the percentage of teachers with full certification and a major in their teaching field, the higher their students' achievement in math and in reading. All but one of the correlations in the second row are negative and significant. This

TABLE 1.1 Correlations between Teacher Quality Variables and Student Achievement, United States

	Grade 4 Math, 1992	Grade 4 Math, 1996	Grade 8 Math, 1996	Grade 4 Reading, 1992	Grade 4 Reading, 1994
Percentage of teachers well-qualified (with full certification and a major in their field)	.71**	.61**	.67**	.80**	.75**
Percentage of teachers out of field (with less than a minor in the field they teach)	–.48*	–.44*	–.42*	–.56*	–.33

*p < .05
**p < .01

Source: Darling-Hammond, L. (2000). Teacher quality and student achievement: A review of state policy evidence. *Educational Policy Analysis Archives*, 8, pp. 1-48. Retrieved January 27, 2005, from **http://epaa.asu.edu/epaa/v8n1**. Copyright © Educational Policy Analysis Archives. Adapted with permission of the EPAA.

indicates that the higher the percentage of teachers who are teaching outside of their field, the lower their students' achievement. So there is evidence that more qualified teachers make a difference in student learning. (Later in the chapter, we will look closely at how to interpret these statistics.)

Finally, researchers studied how students are affected by having several effective or ineffective teachers in a row (Sanders & Rivers, 1996). They looked at grade 5 students in two large metropolitan school systems in the state of Tennessee. Students who had highly effective teachers for grades 3, 4, and 5 on average scored at the 83rd percentile on a standardized mathematics achievement test in one district and at the 96th percentile in the other (99th percentile is the highest possible score). In contrast, students who had the least effective teachers three years in a row obtained scores at the 29th and 44th percentiles in the two districts respectively—a difference of over 50 percentile points in both cases! Students with average teachers or with a mix of teachers with low, average, and high effectiveness for the three years had math scores between these extremes. Sanders and Rivers concluded that the best teachers encouraged good to excellent gains in achievement for all students, but lower-achieving students were the first to benefit from good teaching. The effects of teaching were cumulative and residual—that is, better teaching in a later grade could make up in part for less effective teaching in earlier grades, but it could not erase all the deficits.

Check Your Knowledge

• What evidence is there that teachers make a difference?

Apply to Practice

• How can teachers establish healthy, positive relationships with students?

Connect & Extend

TO YOUR OWN PEDAGOGY
What are the goals of education, real and ideal? What does it mean to be an educated person? What makes a teacher effective? Describe the most effective teacher you ever had. How do you learn best? What do you hope to gain from this course? Your answers will provide the basis for developing a philosophy of teaching.

WHAT IS GOOD TEACHING?

What Would You Say?

It is your first interview for a teaching position. The principal takes out a pad of paper and pen, looks intently into your eyes, and says, "Tell me what you admired about your favourite teacher. What makes a good teacher?" What will you say?

Educators, psychologists, philosophers, novelists, journalists, filmmakers, mathematicians, scientists, historians, policymakers, and parents, to name only a few groups, have examined this question; there are hundreds of answers. And good teaching is not confined to classrooms—it occurs in homes and hospitals, museums and sales meetings, therapists' offices and summer camps. In this book we are primarily concerned with teaching in classrooms, but much of what you will learn applies to other settings as well.

Inside Three Classrooms

To begin our examination of good teaching, let's step inside the classrooms of several outstanding teachers. All the situations that follow are real.

A Multilingual Grade 1. Anne Lee-Hawman teaches grade 1 in Mississauga, Ontario. Of the 22 children in her classroom, half speak English as a second language (ESL). As is true for most linguistically diverse students in Canada, they spend 100 percent of their school day using English as opposed to their native language. This immersion, or submersion, approach to second-language learning contrasts with the bilingual approaches used in many American states.

The ESL teacher helps Anne integrate these children by working in Anne's classroom each day. Together they support students in small groups and make modifications to the curriculum that enable students who speak ESL to participate in all the activities of the classroom. One strategy they have found useful is to make information available through visual materials (e.g., pictures, diagrams, and word or concept maps). Anne also makes use of peer tutors and, whenever possible, offers one-on-one instruction to students who need it.

In addition to supporting students' acquisition of English, Anne encourages students and their parents to continue talking, reading, and writing in their first language at home. As well, she fosters an appreciation for diverse languages and cultures in her classroom by celebrating multicultural holidays and by having students compare and contrast their home/community experiences and practices during classroom discussions and sharing times.

Anne makes a point of learning as much as she can about her students' linguistic and cultural heritages. She recognizes how important it is for teachers to understand how issues of language and culture influence children's learning, so that they don't misinterpret children's motivation and behaviour. This year, five languages are represented in Anne's classroom: English, Hindi, Punjabi, Chinese, and Malaysian. She has a lot of learning to do.

A Suburban Grade 6. Ken teaches grade 6 in a suburban elementary school in Richmond, B.C. Students in the class represent a range of racial, ethnic, family income, and language backgrounds. Ken emphasizes "process writing." His students complete first drafts, discuss them with others in the class, revise, edit, and "publish" their work. The students also keep daily journals and often use these to share personal concerns with Ken. They tell him of problems at home, fights, and fears; he always takes the time to respond in writing. The study of science is also placed in the context of the real world. The students use a National Geographic Society computer network to link with other schools in order to identify acid rain patterns around the world. For social studies, the class played two simulation games that focused on the first half of the 1800s. They "lived" as trappers collecting animal skins and as pioneers heading west.

Throughout the year, Ken is very interested in the social and emotional development of his students—he wants them to learn about responsibility and fairness as well as science and social studies. This concern is evident in the way he develops his class rules at the beginning of the year. Rather than specifying dos and don'ts, Ken and his students generate a list of rights and responsibilities for their class. This list covers most of the situations that might need a "rule."

An Advanced Math Class. Hilda Borko and Carol Livingston (1989) describe how Randy, an expert secondary school mathematics teacher, worked with his

Connect & Extend

TO YOUR TEACHING DEVELOPMENT
Begin your own development by reading educational publications. One widely read periodical is *Education Week*, which you can access online at **www. edweek.com**. There is also a lot of useful information on the Canadian Education Association website: **www.cea-ace.ca**.

Connect & Extend

TO OTHER CHAPTERS
Ken's process writing, student publishing, and journal writing are examples of a "whole language" approach, discussed in **Chapter 12**. Ken's "Bill of Rights" is an example of an innovative approach to setting class rules, discussed in **Chapter 11**.

Connect & Extend

TO THE RESEARCH
Borko, H., & Livingston, C. (1989). Cognition and improvisation: Differences in mathematics instruction by expert and novice teachers. *American Educational Research Journal, 26,* 473–498.

students' confusion to construct a review lesson about strategies for doing integrals. When one student said that a particular section in the book seemed "haphazard," Randy led the class through a process of organizing the material. He asked the class for general statements about useful strategies for doing integrals. He clarified their suggestions, elaborated on some, and helped students improve others. He asked the students to relate their ideas to passages in the text. Even though he accepted all reasonable suggestions, he listed only the key strategies on the board. By the end of the period, the students had transformed the disorganized material from the book into an ordered and useful outline to guide their learning. They also had a better idea about how to read and understand difficult material.

One thing that's noticeable in all three of these classrooms is the teachers' commitment to their students. These teachers must deal with a wide range of student abilities and challenges: different languages, different home situations, and different abilities and disabilities. They must adapt instruction and assessment to students' needs. They must make the most abstract concepts, such as integrals, real and understandable for their particular students. Then there is the challenge of new technologies and techniques. The teachers must use them appropriately to accomplish important goals, not just to entertain the students. And the whole time these experts are navigating through the academic material, they are also taking care of the emotional needs of their students, propping up sagging self-esteem and encouraging responsibility. If we followed these individuals from the first day of class, we would see that they carefully plan and teach the basic procedures for living and learning in their classes. They can efficiently collect and correct homework, regroup students, give directions, distribute materials, collect lunch money, and deal with disruptions—and do all this while also making a mental note to find out why one of their students is so tired.

So, What Is Good Teaching?   Is good teaching science or art, teacher-centred lecture or student-centred discovery, the application of general theories or the invention of situation-specific practices? Is a good teacher a good explainer or a good questioner, a "sage on the stage" or a "guide by the side"? These debates have raged for years. In reality, both sides are probably right. That is, most people agree that teachers must be both theoretically knowledgeable and inventive. They must be able to use a range of strategies, and they must also be able to invent new strategies. They must have some basic research-based routines for managing classes, but they must also be willing and able to break from the routine when the situation calls for change. And teachers need both general theories and situation-specific insights. They need "understandings of students in general—patterns common to particular ages, culture, social class, geography, and gender; patterns in typical student conceptions of the subject matter" (Ball, 1997, p. 773), and they also need to know their own students. "Face to face with actual children who are particular ages and gender, culture and class, teachers must see individuals against a backdrop of sociological and psychological generalizations about groups" (p. 773). The theories you encounter in this text should be used as cognitive tools to help you examine, inspect, and interpret the claims you will hear and read throughout your career (Leinhardt, 2001).

Anne, Ken, and Randy are examples of expert teachers, the focus of much recent research in education and psychology. For another perspective on the question "What is good teaching?" let's examine this research on what expert teachers know.

Expert Knowledge

Connect & Extend

TO THE RESEARCH
Carter, K., Sabers, D., Cushing, K., Pinnegar, S., & Berliner, D. (1987). Processing and using information about students: A study of expert, novice, and postulant teachers. *Teaching and Teacher Education, 3,* 147–157.

expert teachers Experienced, effective teachers who have developed solutions for common classroom problems. Their knowledge of teaching process and content is extensive and well organized.

Expert teachers have elaborate *systems of knowledge* for understanding problems in teaching. For example, when a beginning teacher is faced with students' wrong answers on math or history tests, all of these answers may seem about the same—wrong. But for an expert teacher, wrong answers are part of a rich system of knowledge that could include how to recognize several types of wrong answers, the misunderstanding or lack of information behind each kind of mistake, the best way to reteach and correct the misunderstanding, materials and activities that have worked in the past, and several ways to test whether the reteaching was successful. In addition, expert teachers have clear goals and take individual differences into account when planning for their students. These teachers are **reflective** practitioners (Floden & Klinzing, 1990; Hogan, Rabinowitz, & Craven, 2003).

What do expert teachers know that allows them to be so successful? Lee Shulman (1987) has studied this question, and he has identified seven areas of professional knowledge. Expert teachers know

1. The academic subjects they teach.
2. General teaching strategies that apply in all subjects (such as the principles of classroom management, effective teaching, and evaluation that you will discover in this book).
3. The curriculum materials and programs appropriate for their subject and grade level.
4. Subject-specific knowledge for teaching: special ways of teaching certain students and particular concepts, such as the best ways to explain negative numbers to students with lower abilities.
5. The characteristics and cultural backgrounds of learners.
6. The settings in which students learn—pairs, small groups, teams, classes, schools, and the community.
7. The goals and purposes of teaching.

A key factor for expert teachers that may not be clear from the above list is the need to know yourself—your biases, strengths, and blind spots as well as your own cultural identity. Only by having a clear sense of yourself can you understand and respect the cultural identity of your students. Jay Dee and Allan Henkin (2002) note that teachers must be willing to explore beyond their own zone of comfort as members of the majority cultural status quo.

This is quite a list. Obviously, one course cannot give you all the information you need to teach. In fact, a whole program of courses won't make you an expert. That takes time and experience. But studying educational psychology can add to your professional knowledge because at the heart of educational psychology is a concern with learning wherever it occurs. To become a good teacher, you will need to know about your *students* (Part 1 of this book), *learning and motivation* (Part 2), and *teaching and assessing* (Part 3).

Check Your Knowledge

- What do expert teachers know?

Apply to Practice

- Analyze one of your current teachers in terms of Shulman's seven kinds of knowledge.

> **reflective** Thoughtful and inventive. Reflective teachers think back over situations to analyze what they did and why, and to consider how they might improve learning for their students.

Expert teachers know not only the content of the subjects they teach; they also know how to relate this content to the world outside the classroom and how to keep students involved in learning.

THE ROLE OF EDUCATIONAL PSYCHOLOGY

For as long as **educational psychology** has existed—about 100 years—there have been debates about what it really is. Some people believe educational psychology is simply knowledge gained from psychology and applied to the activities of the classroom. Others believe it involves applying the methods of psychology to study classroom and school life (Brophy, 2003; Wittrock, 1992). A look at history shows the close connections between educational psychology and teaching.

> **educational psychology** The discipline concerned with teaching and learning processes; applies the methods and theories of psychology and has its own as well.

Some Interesting History

In one sense, educational psychology is very old. Topics that Plato and Aristotle discussed—the role of the teacher, the relationship between teacher and student, methods of teaching, the nature and order of learning, the role of affect in learning—are still studied by educational psychologists today. In the 1500s, Juan Luis Vives had some very contemporary thoughts about the value of practice, the need to tap student interests and adapt instruction to individual differences, and the advantages of using self-comparisons rather than competitive social comparisons in evaluating students' work. In the 1700s, Comenius introduced visual aids in books and teaching and proclaimed that understanding, not memorizing, was the goal of teaching (Berliner, 1993). But let's fast forward to the formal study of psychology.

Connect & Extend

TO THE RESEARCH
The Spring 2001 issue of *Educational Psychologist, 36*(2), is devoted to "Educational Psychology: Yesterday, Today, and Tomorrow" with articles about self-regulated learning, classroom management, teacher expectancy effects, program development, and conceptions of learning.

From the beginning, psychology in North America was linked to teaching. In 1890, William James officially founded the field of psychology and developed a lecture series for teachers entitled *Talks to Teachers about Psychology*. These lectures were given in summer schools for teachers and then published in 1899. James's student, G. Stanley Hall, founded the American Psychological Association. His dissertation was about children's understandings of the world; teachers helped him collect data. Hall encouraged teachers to make detailed observations to study their students' development—as his mother had done when she was a teacher. Hall's student, John Dewey, founded the Laboratory School at the University of Chicago and is considered the father of the progressive education movement (Hilgard, 1996).

Another of William James's students, E. L. Thorndike, wrote the first educational psychology text in 1903 and founded the *Journal of Educational Psychology* in 1910. Thorndike began a shift from the classroom to the laboratory to study learning—a shift decried by both James and Hall. Thorndike's view proved to be too narrow as he sought laws of learning in laboratories that could be applied to teaching without actually evaluating their applications in real classrooms—but it still took 50 years to return to the psychological study of learning in classrooms (Hilgard, 1996).

Developments in teaching continued to be closely tied to psychology in the first half of the 20th century. It was not uncommon for psychologists such as Thorndike, Judd, or their students to be both presidents of the American Psychological Association and authors of materials for teaching or assessing school subjects. During this era, educational psychology was the "guiding science of the school" (Cubberly, 1919, p. 755). In the 1940s and 1950s, the study of educational psychology concentrated on individual differences, assessment, and learning behaviours. In the 1960s and 1970s, the focus of research shifted to the study of cognitive development and learning, with attention to how students learn concepts and remember. Recently, educational psychologists have investigated how culture and social factors affect learning and development (Pressley & Roehrig, 2003).

What is educational psychology today? The view generally accepted is that educational psychology is a distinct discipline with its own theories, research methods, problems, and techniques. Both in the past and today, educational psychologists study learning and teaching and, at the same time, strive to improve educational practice (Pintrich, 2000). But even with this long history of interest in teaching and learning, are the findings of educational psychologists really that helpful for teachers? After all, most teaching is just common sense, isn't it? Let's take a few minutes to examine these questions.

Is It Just Common Sense?

In many cases, the principles set forth by educational psychologists—after spending much thought, research, and money—sound pathetically obvious. People are tempted to say, and usually do say, "Everyone knows that!" Consider these examples:

Taking Turns.   What method should a teacher use in selecting students to participate in a primary-grade reading class?

Common Sense Answer. Teachers should call on students randomly so that everyone will have to follow the lesson carefully. If a teacher were to use the same order every time, the students would know when their turn was coming up.

Answer Based on Research.   Research by Ogden, Brophy, and Evertson (1977) indicates that the answer to this question is not so simple. In grade 1 reading classes, for example, going around the circle in order and giving each child a chance to read led to better overall achievement than calling on students randomly. The critical factor in going around the circle may be that each child has a chance to participate. Without a system for calling on everyone, many students can be overlooked or skipped. Research suggests there are better alternatives for teaching reading than going around the circle, but if teachers choose this alternative, they should make sure that everyone has the chance for practice and feedback (Tierney, Readence, & Dishner, 1990).

Classroom Management.   Students are engaged in an appropriate and educationally meaningful task, but still, some students are repeatedly out of their seats without permission, wandering around the room. What should the teacher do?

Connect & Extend

TO OTHER CHAPTERS
See **Chapter 10** for more information on the unintended messages of well-intended teacher actions.

Common Sense Answer.   Each time the wanderers get up, the teacher should remind students to remain in their seats. If the teacher does not remind them and lets them get away with breaking the rules, both the out-of-seat students and the rest of the class may decide the teacher is not really serious about the rule.

Answer Based on Research.   In a now-classic study, Madsen, Becker, Thomas, Koser, and Plager (1968) found that the more often a teacher told students to sit down when they were out of their seats, the more often the students got out of their seats without permission. When the teacher ignored students who were out of their seats and praised students who were sitting down, the rate of out-of-seat behaviour dropped greatly. When the teacher returned to the previous system of telling students to sit down, the rate of out-of-seat behaviour increased once again. It seems that—at least under some conditions—the more a teacher says, "Sit down!" the more the students stand up!

Skipping Grades.   Should a school encourage exceptionally bright students to skip grades or to enter university or college early?

Common Sense Answer. No! Very intelligent students who are a year or two younger than their classmates are likely to be social misfits. They are neither physically nor emotionally ready for dealing with older students and would be miserable in the social situations that are so important in school, especially in the later grades.

Answer Based on Research. Maybe. According to Samuel Kirk and his colleagues (1993), "from early admissions to school to early admissions to college, research studies invariably report that children who have been accelerated have adjusted as well as or better than have children of similar ability who have not been accelerated" (p. 105). Whether acceleration is the best solution for a student depends on many specific individual characteristics, including the intelligence and maturity of the student, and on the other available options. For some students, moving quickly through the material and working in advanced courses with older students is a very good idea.

Obvious Answers?   Lily Wong (1987) demonstrated that just seeing research results in writing can make them seem obvious. She selected 12 findings from research on teaching; one of them was the "taking turns" result noted above. She

Connect & Extend

TO THE RESEARCH
Read and discuss the article by Gage, N. L. (1991). The obvious-ness of social and educational research results. *Educational Researcher, 20*(1), 10–16. Focus Questions: What makes findings in educational research seem "obvious"? What is the danger in this kind of thinking?

presented six of the findings in their correct form and six in *exactly the opposite form* to college students and to experienced teachers. Both the college students and teachers rated about half of the *wrong* findings as "obviously" correct. In a follow-up study, other participants were shown the 12 findings and their opposites and were asked to pick which ones were correct. For 8 of the 12 findings, the participants chose the wrong result more often than the right one.

You may have thought that educational psychologists spend their time discovering the obvious. The examples above point out the danger of this kind of thinking. When a principle is stated in simple terms, it can sound simplistic. A similar phenomenon takes place when we see a gifted dancer or athlete perform; the well-trained performer makes it look easy. But we see only the results of the training, not all the work that went into mastering the individual movements. And bear in mind that any research finding—or its opposite—may sound like common sense. The issue is not what *sounds* sensible, but what is demonstrated when the principle is put to the test (Gage, 1991).

Using Research to Understand and Improve Teaching

Conducting research to test possible answers is one of two major tasks of educational psychology. The other task is combining the results of various studies into theories that attempt to present a unified view of such things as teaching, learning, and development.

descriptive studies Studies that collect detailed information about specific situations, often using observation, surveys, interviews, recordings, or a combination of these methods.

Descriptive Studies.   Educational psychologists design and conduct many different kinds of research studies in their attempts to understand teaching and learning. Some of these studies are "descriptive"—that is, their purpose is to describe events in a particular class or several classes. Reports of **descriptive studies** often include survey results, interview responses, samples of actual classroom dialogue, or observations of class activities.

ethnography A descriptive approach to research that focuses on life within a group and tries to understand the meaning of events to the people involved.

One descriptive approach, classroom **ethnography**, is borrowed from anthropology. Ethnographic methods involve studying naturally occurring events in the life of a group and trying to understand the meaning of these events to the people involved. For example, the description of an expert high school mathematics teacher in the opening pages of this chapter was taken from an ethnographic study by Hilda Borko and Carol Livingston (1989). The researchers made detailed in-class observations and analyzed these observations, along with audio recordings and information from interviews with the teachers, in order to describe differences between novice and expert teachers.

participant observation A method for conducting descriptive research in which the researcher becomes a participant in the situation in order to better understand life in that group.

In some descriptive research, researchers carefully analyze videotapes of classes to identify recurring patterns of teacher and student behaviour. In other studies, the researcher uses **participant observation** and works within the class or school to understand the actions from the perspectives of the teacher and the students. Researchers also may employ case studies. A **case study** investigates in depth how a teacher plans courses, for example, or how a student tries to learn specific material.

case study Intensive study of one person or one situation.

correlation Statistical description of how closely two variables are related.

Correlational Studies.   Often the results of descriptive studies include reports of correlations. We will take a minute to examine this concept, because you will encounter many correlations in the coming chapters. A **correlation** is a number that indicates both the strength and the direction of a relationship between two events or measurements. Correlations range from 1.00 to −1.00. The closer the correlation is to either 1.00 or −1.00, the stronger the relationship. For example, the correlation between height and weight is about .70 (a strong relationship); the correlation between height and number of languages spoken is about .00 (no relationship at all).

positive correlation A relationship between two variables in which the two increase or decrease together. Example: calorie intake and weight gain.

The sign of the correlation tells the direction of the relationship. A **positive correlation** indicates that the two factors increase or decrease together. As one gets larger, so does the other. Height and weight are positively correlated because greater height tends to be associated with greater weight. A **negative correlation** means that increases in one factor are related to decreases in the other. For example, the correlation between outside temperature and the weight of clothing worn is negative, since people tend to wear clothing of increasing weight as the temperature decreases.

It is important to note that correlations do not prove cause and effect (see Figure 1.1). Height and weight are correlated—taller people tend to weigh more than shorter people. But gaining weight obviously does not cause you to grow taller. Knowing a person's height simply allows you to make a general prediction about that person's weight. Educational psychologists identify correlations so that they can make predictions about important events in the classroom.

Experimental Studies. A second type of research—**experimentation**—allows educational psychologists to go beyond predictions and actually study cause and effect. Instead of just observing and describing an existing situation, the investigators introduce changes and note the results. First, a number of comparable groups of subjects are created. In psychological research, the term **subjects** generally refers to the people being studied—teachers or grade 8 students, for example—not to subjects such as math or science. One common way to make sure that groups of subjects are essentially the same is to assign each subject to a group using a random procedure. **Random** means that each subject has an equal chance to be in any group.

In one or more of these groups, the experimenters change some aspect of the situation to see if this change or "treatment" has an expected effect. The results in each group are then compared. Usually statistical tests are conducted to see if the differences between the groups are significant. When differences are described as **statistically significant**, it means that they probably did not happen simply by chance. A number of the studies we will examine attempt to identify cause-and-effect relationships by asking questions such as this: If teachers ignore students who are out of their seats without permission and praise students who are working hard at their desks (cause), will students spend more time working at their desks (effect)?

In many cases, both descriptive and experimental research occur together. The study by Ogden, Brophy, and Evertson (1977) described at the beginning of this section is a good example. In order to answer questions about the relationship between how students are selected to read in a primary-grade class and their achievement in reading, these investigators first observed students and teachers in a number of classrooms and then measured the reading achievement of the students. They found that having students read in a predictable order was associated, or correlated, with gains in reading scores. With a simple correlation such as this, however, the researchers could not be sure that the strategy was actually causing the effect. In the second part of the study, Ogden and her colleagues asked several

negative correlation A relationship between two variables in which a high value on one is associated with a low value on the other. Example: height and distance from top of head to the ceiling.

Connect & Extend

TO REAL LIFE
Perfect positive (1.00) correlation: the radius of a circle and its circumference. Perfect negative (−1.00) correlation: the number of minutes of daylight and the number of minutes of dark each day. Less than perfect positive correlation: the cost of a car and the cost of insuring it; child's IQ score and school grades: .39 (Sattler, 1992). Less than perfect negative correlation: cost of a theatre ticket and distance from the stage. Zero correlation: population of India and the winning percentage of the New York Yankees.

experimentation Research method in which variables are manipulated and the effects recorded.

subjects People or animals participating in a study.

random Without any definite pattern; following no rule.

statistically significant Not likely to be a chance occurrence.

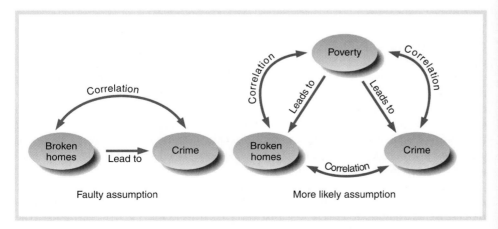

Figure 1.1 Correlations Do Not Show Causation

When research shows that broken homes and crime are correlated, it does not show causation. Poverty, a third variable, may be the cause of both crime and broken homes.

These students are conducting field observations and measurements as part of a science lesson. What will they learn using this approach? Can research shed light on this question?

single-subject experimental studies Systematic interventions to study effects with one person, often by applying and then withdrawing a treatment.

microgenetic studies Detailed observation and analysis of changes in a cognitive process as the process unfolds over several days or weeks.

Connect & Extend

TO WHAT YOU KNOW

Are the following studies descriptive (D) or experimental (E)?

1. Researchers observe teachers of classes that have high achievement in order to determine how these teachers are alike. 2. Teachers give three groups of impulsive children different types of training to determine which type of training is most effective in reducing impulsivity. 3. Researchers administer IQ tests to a group of boys and girls to determine if there is a relationship between gender and verbal ability. 4. Teachers use two different methods of instruction for two similar groups of math students to determine which method leads to higher scores on a math achievement test.

Answers: 1. D; 2. E; 3. D; 4. E.

teachers to call on each student in turn. They then compared reading achievement in these groups with achievement in groups where teachers used other strategies. This second part of the research was thus an experimental study.

Single-Subject Experimental Studies. The goal of **single-subject experimental studies** is to determine the effects of a therapy, teaching method, or other intervention. One common approach is to observe the individual for a baseline period (A) and assess the behaviour of interest; then try an intervention (B) and note the results; then remove the intervention and go back to baseline conditions (A); and finally reinstate the intervention (B). This form of single-subject design is called an ABAB experiment. For example, a teacher might record how much students are out of their seats without permission during a week-long baseline (A), and then, for the following week (B), ignore those who are up but praise those who are seated, recording how many are wandering out of their seats. Next, the teacher returns to the baseline conditions (A) and records results. Finally, the teacher reinstates the intervention (B) and observes whether it works again. Years ago, when this very intervention was tested, the praise-and-ignore strategy proved effective in increasing the time students spent in their seats (Madsen, Becker, Thomas, Koser, & Plager, 1968).

Microgenetic Studies. The goal of **microgenetic studies** is to intensively study cognitive processes in the midst of change—as the change is actually happening. For example, researchers might analyze how children learn a particular strategy for adding two-digit numbers over the course of several weeks. The microgenetic approach has three basic characteristics: (a) researchers observe the entire period of the change—from when it starts to the time it is relatively stable; (b) many observations are made, often using videotape recordings, interviews, and transcriptions of the exact words of the individuals being studied; (c) the behaviour that is observed is "put under a microscope," that is, examined moment by moment or trial by trial. The goal is to explain the underlying mechanisms of change—for example, what new knowledge or skills are developing to allow change to take place (Siegler & Crowley, 1991). This kind of research is expensive and time-consuming, so often only one or a few children are studied.

The Role of Time in Research. Another distinction is useful in understanding research—a distinction based on time. Many things that psychologists want to study, such as cognitive development, happen over several months or years. Ideally, researchers would study the development by observing their subjects over many years as changes occur. These are called **longitudinal studies**. They are informative, but time-consuming, expensive, and not always practical—keeping up with subjects over years as they grow up and move can be impossible. So instead, much research involves **cross-sectional studies**, which focus on groups of children at different ages. For example, to study how children's conceptions of "alive" change from ages 3 to 16, researchers can interview children of several different ages rather than following the same children for 14 years.

Teachers as Researchers. Research can also be a way to improve teaching in one classroom or one school. The same kind of careful observation, intervention, data gathering, and analysis that occurs in large research projects can be applied in any classroom to answer questions such as: Which writing prompts seem to encourage the best descriptive writing in my class? When does Kenyon seem to have the greatest difficulty concentrating on academic tasks? Would assigning task roles in science groups lead to more equitable participation of girls and boys in the work? This kind of problem-solving investigation is called **action research**. By focusing on a specific problem and making careful observations, teachers can learn a great deal about both their teaching and their students.

There has been a great debate about the importance of experimental research in applied settings, such as in education. Many feel that utilizing systematic, controlled experimental research designs and rigorous data analyses enhances the usefulness of educational research. Unfortunately, as you will see in the Point/ Counterpoint section, this isn't necessarily the case.

Theories for Teaching

A major goal for research in educational psychology is to understand teaching and learning. Reaching this goal is a slow process; there are very few landmark studies that answer a question once and for all. Human beings are too complicated. Instead, research in educational psychology examines limited aspects of a situation—perhaps a few variables at a time, or life in one or two classrooms. If enough studies are completed in a certain area and findings repeatedly point to the same

longitudinal studies Studies that document changes that occur in subjects over time, often many years.

cross-sectional studies Studies that focus on groups of subjects at different ages rather than following the same group for many years.

action research Systematic observations or tests of methods conducted by teachers or schools to improve teaching and learning for their students.

POINT > < COUNTERPOINT
WHAT KIND OF RESEARCH SHOULD GUIDE EDUCATION?

> Point *Research should be scientific; educational reforms should be based on solid evidence.*

According to Robert Slavin, "Education is on the brink of a scientific revolution that has the potential to profoundly transform policy, practice, and research" (Slavin, 2002, p. 15). He goes on to describe several educational reforms from the U.S. government that will provide money for programs, but only if they are based on scientific research. The best example of this kind of research, according to Grover Whitehurst, the director of the U.S. Office of Educational Research and Improvement, is randomized experiments. Slavin argues that once there is evidence from randomized trials or carefully controlled experiments, all aspects of the education system will begin to show steady improvements. He paints a bright future for educational reform guided by scientifically based research:

> It is possible that these policy reforms could set in motion a process of research and development on programs and practices affecting children everywhere. This process could create the kind of progressive, systematic improvement over time that has characterized successful parts of our economy and society throughout the 20th century, in fields such as medicine, agriculture, transportation, and technology. In each of these fields,

processes of development, rigorous evaluation, and dissemination have produced a pace of innovation and improvement that is unprecedented in history. . . . These innovations have transformed the world. Yet education has failed to embrace this dynamic, and as a result, education moves from fad to fad. Educational practice does change over time, but the change process more resembles the pendulum swings of taste characteristic of art or fashion (think hemlines) rather than the progressive improvements characteristic of science and technology. (p. 16)

The major reason for extraordinary advances in medicine and agriculture, according to Slavin, is that these fields base their practices on scientific evidence. Randomized clinical trials and replicated experiments are the sources of the evidence.

< Counterpoint *Experiments are not the only or even the best source of evidence.*

David Olson (2004), a professor emeritus at the Ontario Institute for Studies in Education of the University of Toronto, disagrees strongly with Slavin's position. He claims that we cannot use medicine as an analogy to education. "Treatments" in education are much more complex and unpredictable than administering one drug or another in medicine. And every educational program is changed by classroom

conditions and the way it is implemented. He argues:

> The difficulty in defining a treatment indicates a much deeper problem, namely, assumptions about causality. In medical trials, the treatment is assumed to have an invariant or law-like causal relation with the symptoms of the disease. In education, such simple causal relations do not obtain between teaching and learning; interactions are filtered through the goals, beliefs, and intentions of the teachers and learners. (p. 25)

David Berliner (2002) makes a similar point, arguing that "doing science and implementing scientific findings are so difficult in education because humans in schools are embedded in complex and changing networks of social interaction" and that "compared to designing bridges and circuits or splitting either atoms or genes, the science to help change schools and classrooms is harder to do because context cannot be controlled" (p. 20). Berliner concludes that a complex problem like education needs a whole range of methods for study: "Ethnographic research is crucial, as are case studies, survey research, time series, design experiments, action research, and other means to collect reliable evidence for engaging in unfettered argument about education issues. A single method is not what the government should be promoting for educational researchers" (Berliner, 2002, p. 20).

principle Established relationship between factors.

theory Integrated statement of principles that attempts to explain a phenomenon and make predictions.

conclusions, we eventually arrive at a **principle**. This is the term for an established relationship between two or more factors—between a certain teaching strategy, for example, and student achievement.

Another tool for building a better understanding of the teaching and learning processes is **theory**. The common-sense notion of theory (as in "Oh well, it was only a theory") is that it is a guess or a hunch. But the scientific meaning of theory is quite different. According to Keith Stanovich at the Ontario Institute for Studies in Education of the University of Toronto, "A theory in science is an interrelated set of concepts that is used to explain a body of data and to make predictions about the results of future experiments" (1992, p. 21). Given a number of established principles, educational psychologists have developed explanations for the relationships among many variables and even whole systems of relationships. There are theories to explain how language develops, how differences in intelligence occur, and, as noted earlier, how people learn.

Few theories explain and predict perfectly. In this book, you will see many examples of educational psychologists taking different theoretical positions and disagreeing on the overall explanations of such issues as learning and motivation. Since no one theory offers all the answers, it makes sense to consider what each has to offer.

So why, you may ask, is it necessary to deal with theories? Why not just stick to principles? The answer is that both are useful. Principles of classroom management, for example, will give you help with specific problems. A good theory of classroom management, on the other hand, will give you a new way of thinking about discipline problems; it will give you tools for creating solutions to many different problems and for predicting what might work in new situations. A major goal of this book is to provide you with the best and the most useful theories for teaching—those that have solid evidence behind them. Although you may prefer some theories over others, consider them all as ways of understanding the challenges teachers face.

Becoming a Good Beginning Teacher

Beginning teachers everywhere share many concerns, including maintaining classroom discipline, motivating students, accommodating differences among students, evaluating student work, dealing with parents, and getting along with other teachers (Conway & Clark, 2003; Veenman, 1984). Many teachers also experience what has been called "reality shock" when they take their first job because they really cannot ease into their responsibilities. On the first day of their first job, beginning teachers face the same tasks as teachers with years of experience. Student teaching, while a critical element, does not really prepare prospective teachers for starting off a school year with a new class. These concerns come with the job of being a beginning teacher (Borko & Putnam, 1996; Cooke & Pang, 1991). Here is some advice from Dave Brown, a fantastic teacher who started his career at a junior high school in Toronto and who is currently teaching middle school in Lethbridge, Alberta:

> I think one of the most difficult things new teachers face is the almost immediate realization that the environment they find themselves in after being hired is quite different from the one they experienced in their practicum, when they essentially had backup from the sponsor teacher should any negative situation arise. In contrast, many teaching positions are filled mere days before school starts. A new teacher may find that he or she is starting tomorrow, handed a schedule, and offered a "welcome aboard" along with an evening to prepare his or her program. Moreover, you may find that it is a tricky balancing act satisfying the needs of the school's administration, the curriculum, and most importantly, yourself.
>
> The assumption that a new teacher can be expected to come in on short notice and perform in a manner that makes the transition seamless for students, staff, and administration is unrealistic. In fact, most good administrators and staff members know this

and are very approachable and helpful. In addition, when I was thrust into my first position—covering a maternity leave—I quickly learned that it's important to know and rely on your strengths in delivering the material, and to be aware of what doesn't work for you. I think this is especially important as a beginning teacher since you are essentially test-driving your lessons for the first time.

With experience, hard work, and good support, most teachers have more time to experiment with new methods or materials. Finally, as confidence grows, seasoned teachers can focus on the students' needs. At this advanced stage, teachers judge their success by the successes of their students (Fuller, 1969; Pigge & Marso, 1997). It is often acknowledged that "the difference between a beginning teacher and an experienced one is that the beginning teacher asks, 'How am I doing?' and the experienced teacher asks, 'How are the children doing?'" (Codell, 2001, p. 191).

Check Your Knowledge

- What is educational psychology?
- What are descriptive studies?
- What are correlations and experimental studies?
- What are single-subject and microgenetic studies?
- What is action research?
- What is the difference between principles and theories?
- What are the concerns of beginning teachers?

Apply to Practice

- What would you say to someone who asserts, "Teaching is just common sense"?

THE CONTENTS OF THIS BOOK

Part 1 of this text focuses on the students' development. In Part 1, we examine the ways in which students change as they age. Because children may differ from adolescents and adults in their thinking, language, and images of themselves, they may require different kinds of teaching. Teachers must want to take into account the cognitive, physical, emotional, and social abilities and limitations of their students.

Part 2 discusses how children differ from one another in their abilities, previous learning, and learning preferences, and in the ways they have been prepared for schools by their cultural and community experiences. Classrooms today are becoming more and more diverse. Teachers are expected to work with students with learning disabilities and visual or hearing impairments, for example, and with students who have developmental disabilities or who are gifted or developmentally advanced. As well, in Canada, most classrooms today are multicultural, with students who speak different languages and come from a variety of cultural backgrounds. Teachers must be able to recognize, respect, and adapt to these individual and group differences and to create classroom communities that allow students to belong and to thrive.

Having introduced the students, in Part 3 we move to two of the most important topics in both educational psychology and the classroom: learning and motivation. Part 3 explores several approaches to the study of learning, including behavioural, cognitive, and sociocognitive as well as constructivist. We will see how these approaches can be applied in a number of practical ways, including strategies for teaching in various subject areas. An understanding of how students learn is the basis for teachers' professional knowledge about both general and specific teaching strategies. Also, we will examine theories of motivation and their applications to teaching. There is no learning without attention and engagement, so teachers and students must understand and incorporate the motivational factors that support active, engaged, independent learning.

Connect & Extend

TO REAL LIFE

A national survey of 750 Canadian elementary- and secondary-school teachers indicates that Canada's teachers are committed professionals and lifelong learners. The New Approaches to Lifelong Learning (NALL) study (2000), conducted by researchers at the Ontario Institute for Studies in Education of the University of Toronto and funded by the Social Sciences and Humanities Research Council of Canada, indicates that, on average, Canadian teachers work 47 to 55 hours each week, more than most other professional and managerial groups in Canada. How do teachers spend this time? The survey reveals that, on average, teachers spend about 28 hours each week on direct teaching activities and 19 hours on other school work. Outside class time, teachers are preparing courses, planning lessons, marking students' work, and meeting with students and parents. In addition, the survey found that the majority of teachers spend several hours each week engaged in extracurricular activities, such as coaching sports and running school clubs. Finally, the survey found that more than 90 percent of Canada's teachers participate in coursework, professional workshops, and informal learning activities that are connected with their current teaching duties and that keep them current with best practices in their field.

Discuss the validity of these results with the rest of your class. Do you think they are representative of the work teachers do? What are some potential biases? You might want to continue the discussion by noting the need to be "critical consumers" of research results, particularly those reported in the press.

Source: National survey finds heavy teacher workloads. Retrieved from **http://gleneagle.vr9.com/go/ resources/staff/ teacherworkloadstudy.html**.

Having covered the dual foundations of teaching—the students and the processes of learning and motivation—we can concentrate in Part 4 on actual practice. Here we examine how to organize and manage a classroom full of active learners. And because teachers deal with individuals as well as groups, we will spend some time discussing communication and interpersonal relationships. In this part of the book, we will look at instruction from two perspectives: a teacher-focused view that emphasizes the teacher's role in planning, providing, and monitoring instruction, and a student-centred view that emphasizes the students' active construction of understanding. Teachers owe it to their students to design powerful environments for learning, so teachers must understand how different approaches can influence students' learning.

Finally, we consider how to evaluate what has been taught. Because to learn is to become more knowledgeable and competent, teachers must have at their disposal ways to assess knowledge and competence in order to guide students and give them useful information so that they can guide themselves.

The goal of this book is to help you become an excellent beginning teacher, one who can both apply and improve many techniques. Even more important, we hope that this book will cause you to think about students and teaching in new ways, so that you will have the foundation for becoming an expert as you gain experience.

Check Your Knowledge

- How can this book help you?

Apply to Practice

- How do you plan to use the features in this text (described in the preface) to maximize your learning?

Do Teachers Make a Difference? (pp. 3–4)

What evidence is there that teachers make a difference?

Three studies speak to the power of teachers in the lives of students. The first found that the quality of the teacher–student relationship in kindergarten predicted several aspects of school success through grade 8. The second study of thousands of students and teachers across the United States found that teacher quality was the strongest predictor of student achievement in mathematics and reading. The third study examined mathematics achievement for students in two large school districts as they moved through grades 3, 4, and 5. Again, the quality of the teacher made a difference—students who had three high-quality teachers in a row were way ahead of students who spent one or more years with less competent teachers.

What Is Good Teaching? (pp. 4–7)

What do expert teachers know?

It takes time and experience to become an expert teacher. These teachers have a rich store of well-organized knowledge about the many specific situations of teaching. This includes knowledge about the subjects they teach, their students, general teaching strategies, subject-specific ways of teaching, settings for learning, curriculum materials, and the goals of education.

The Role of Educational Psychology (pp. 7–15)

What is educational psychology?

The goals of educational psychology are to understand and to improve the teaching and learning processes. Educational psychologists develop knowledge and meth-ods; they also use the knowledge and methods of psychology and other related disciplines to study learning and teaching in everyday situations.

What are descriptive studies?

Reports of descriptive studies often include survey results, interview responses, samples of actual classroom dialogue, or records of the class activities. Ethnographic methods involve studying the naturally occurring events in the life of a group and trying to understand the meaning of these events to the people involved. A case study investigates in depth how a teacher plans courses, for example, or how a student tries to learn specific material.

What are correlations and experimental studies?

Correlations allow you to predict events that are likely to occur in the classroom. A correlation is a number that indicates both the strength and the direction of a relationship between two events or measurements. The closer the correlation is to either 1.00 or −1.00, the stronger the relationship. Experimental studies can indicate cause-and-effect relationships and should help teachers implement useful changes. Instead of just observing and describing an existing situation, the investigators introduce changes and note the results.

What are single-subject and microgenetic studies?

In single-subject experimental studies, researchers examine the effects of treatments on one person, often by using a baseline/intervention/baseline/intervention, or ABAB, approach. Microgenetic studies take many detailed observations of subjects to track the progression of change from the very beginning until a process becomes stable.

What is action research?

When teachers or schools make systematic observations or test out methods to improve teaching and learning for their students, they are conducting action research.

What is the difference between principles and theories?

A principle is an established relationship between two or more factors—between a certain teaching strategy, for example, and student achievement. A theory is an interrelated set of concepts that is used to explain a body of data and to make predictions about the results of future experiments. The principles from research offer a number of possible answers to specific problems, and the theories offer perspectives for analyzing almost any situation that may arise.

What are the concerns of beginning teachers?

Learning to teach is a gradual process. The concerns and problems of teachers change as they progress. During the beginning years, attention tends to be focused on survival. Maintaining discipline, motivating students, evaluating students' work, and dealing with parents are universal concerns for beginning teachers. Even with these concerns, many beginning teachers bring creativity and energy to their teaching and improve every year. The more experienced teacher can move on to concerns about professional growth and effectiveness with a wide range of students.

The Contents of This Book (pp. 15–16)

How can this book help you?

Becoming a good teacher means being a good learner. Much of the information in this text will help you become a more expert learner if you take the ideas personally and apply them to your own life. Take advantage of the book's features-the tables of contents, overviews, What Would You Do? and Check Your Knowledge questions, organizational headings, Guidelines, key terms, Reaching Every Student boxes, Becoming a Professional boxes, and the Teachers' Casebook-to become an expert learner.

KEY TERMS

action research, p. 12
case study, p. 10
correlation, p. 10
cross-sectional studies, p. 12
descriptive studies, p. 10
educational psychology, p. 7
ethnography, p. 10
experimentation, p. 11

expert teachers, p. 6
longitudinal studies, p. 12
microgenetic studies, p. 12
negative correlation, p. 11
participant observation, p. 10
positive correlation, p. 10
principle, p. 14
random, p. 11

reflective, p. 7
single-subject experimental studies, p. 12
statistically significant, p. 11
subjects, p. 11
theory, p. 14

Teachers' Casebook

What Would They Do?

Here is how two practising teachers responded to the teaching situation presented at the beginning of this chapter about writing a letter of recommendation for a colleague who has been nominated for a Prime Minister's Award for Teaching Excellence.

Sally Bender
George Fitton School
Brandon, Manitoba

While, individually, we have our ideas about what an exemplary teacher is and should be, it is important to look at what the profession is saying about the same issue. Taking time to read the professional journals and other literature would help in determining what a letter describing a colleague's performance should include. The granting of such a prestigious award could well depend on your words.

To prepare for writing the letter, I would list qualities describing my colleague's commitment to the profession and to the children whose lives are touched by

excellent teaching practice. The list would include the following:

*   builds close relationships with students and the school community through respect and example;

*   creates a classroom that encourages and honours diversity in thinking and response;

*   provides ongoing opportunities for children to take responsibility and ownership for what happens in the classroom and beyond;

*   knows about child growth and development and uses that knowledge to drive the teaching and learning that occurs in the classroom;

*   manages the classroom with respect for the rights of the children and encourages them to take responsibility for their own actions at all times;

*   is flexible enough to respond to "teachable moments" by giving up the "teaching" agenda for the "learning" one;

- models patience, tolerance, and respect for all;
- shares learning and teaching practice with colleagues;
- works as a team member and shares responsibility;
- is enthusiastic, challenging, and responsive to all students and colleagues;
- has consistent expectations and evaluates regularly the learning that is taking place for all students;
- provides a positive and encouraging atmosphere where children are free to take risks while learning and to learn from and through their mistakes;
- sees learning as a process that results in better performance;
- is knowledgeable about learning styles and uses that knowledge when planning lessons and learning experiences for all children;
- provides opportunities for learning that begin with the child's experiences and develop from the child's perspective;
- plans activities where cooperation is a necessity, for it is a life skill;
- ensures a classroom environment that is rich in print and language-stimulating possibilities;
- provides a balance between teacher-directed and child-initiated experiences;
- encourages parent support through regular communication.

By determining the qualities that you value in your colleague, you will be better prepared to write the letter of recommendation to accompany the nomination for such a prestigious award.

Barb Popoff
Lord Baden-Powell Elementary
Coquitlam, British Columbia

Following are the qualities that I consider important in being an effective teacher.
An effective teacher

- demonstrates his or her love of teaching and working with children by providing a warm and caring environment for learning. In a positive learning environment, children take risks without feeling threatened or insecure. They feel safe making decisions about their learning. A happy environment balances hard work and fun.
- considers the self-esteem of children and provides opportunities for children to feel successful and to take pride in their accomplishments. Balancing encouragement, motivation, and constructive criticism allows self-esteem to grow within the structure of the curriculum.
- knows the children—their strengths and their needs. An effective teacher is flexible and can modify the curriculum or teaching lesson to fit the needs and/or strengths of the children. Such a learning environment accommodates children with learning problems, as well as those who need to be challenged.
- works cooperatively and collaboratively with colleagues. The teaching profession can be quite overwhelming, especially to a teacher just starting out. Advising, encouraging, and showing direction and support lessens the anxiety and confusion felt by beginning teachers.
- continues to develop professionally and seeks self-improvement by attending regular professional seminars and conferences. Growth and learning are lifelong, and new ideas and skills are an asset and an exciting part of teaching in any classroom.

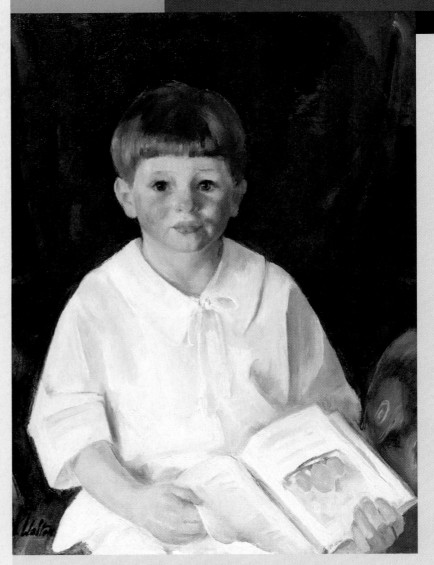

Young Boy in White Reading Book, 1918, Martha Walter. Oil on canvas. © David David Gallery/SuperStock.

Teachers' Casebook

What Would You Do?

The provincial curriculum guide calls for a unit on poetry, including lessons on *symbolism* in poems. You are concerned that many of your grade 5 students may not be ready to understand this abstract concept. To test the waters, you ask a few students to describe a symbol.

"It's sorta like a big metal thing that you bang together." Tracy waves her hands like a drum major.

"Yeah," Sean adds, "my sister plays one in the high school band."

You realize they are on the wrong track here, so you try again. "I was thinking of a different kind of symbol, like a ring as a symbol of marriage or a heart as a symbol of love, or..."

You are met with blank stares.

Trevor ventures, "You mean like the Olympic torch?"

"And what does that symbolize, Trevor?" you ask.

"I said, the torch." Trevor wonders how you could be so dense.

Critical Thinking

What do these students' reactions tell you about children's thinking? How would you approach this unit? What more would you do to "listen" to your students' thinking so that you could match your teaching to their level of thinking? How would you give your students concrete experience with symbolism? How will you decide if the students are not developmentally ready for this material?

Collaboration

With three or four other students in your educational psychology class, plan a lesson about symbolism in poetry that would be appropriate for students in this class. Pair up with another group and teach your lesson.

What is going on with Trevor? In this chapter, you will find out. We begin with a discussion of the general principles of human development and take a brief look at the human brain. Then we will examine the ideas of two of the most influential cognitive developmental theorists, Jean Piaget and Lev Vygotsky. Piaget's ideas have implications for teachers about what their students can learn and when the students are ready to learn it. We will consider important criticisms of his ideas as well. The work of Lev Vygotsky, a Russian psychologist, has become very influential. His theory highlights the important role that teachers and parents play in the cognitive development of children. Finally, we will explore language development and discuss the role of the school in developing and enriching language skills.

By the time you have completed this chapter, you should be able to answer these questions:

- *What are some general principles of human development?*

- *How does children's thinking differ at each of Piaget's four stages of development?*

- *What are the similarities and differences between Piaget's and Vygotsky's ideas about cognitive development?*

- *What are the implications of Piaget's and Vygotsky's theories for teaching students of different ages?*

- *How does language develop during the school years, and what happens if children are learning two languages at once?*

A DEFINITION OF DEVELOPMENT

development Orderly, adaptive changes that humans (or animals) go through from conception to death.

The term **development** in its most general psychological sense refers to certain changes that occur in human beings (or animals) between conception and death. The term is not applied to all changes, but rather to those that appear in orderly ways and remain for a reasonably long period of time. A temporary change caused by a brief illness, for example, is not considered a part of development. Psychologists also make a value judgment in determining which changes qualify as development. The changes, at least those that occur early in life, are generally assumed to be for the better and to result in behaviour that is more adaptive, more organized, more effective, and more complex (Mussen, Conger, & Kagan, 1984).

physical development Changes in body structure that take place as one grows.

social and emotional development Changes over time in the ways in which one relates to others and the self.

cognitive development Gradual, orderly changes by which mental processes become more complex and sophisticated.

maturation Genetically programmed, naturally occurring changes over time.

Human development can be divided into a number of different aspects. **Physical development,** as you might guess, deals with changes in the body. **Social and emotional development** refers to changes in the way an individual relates to others, as well as an individual's personality and emotional understanding. **Cognitive development** implies changes in thinking.

Many changes during development are simply matters of growth and maturation. **Maturation** refers to changes that occur naturally and spontaneously and that are, to a large extent, genetically programmed. Such changes emerge over time and are relatively unaffected by environment, except in cases of malnutrition or severe illness. Much of a person's physical development falls into this category. Other changes are brought about through learning, as individuals interact with their environment. Such changes make up a large part of a person's social development. What about the development of thinking and personality? Most psychologists agree that in these areas, both maturation and interaction with the environment (or nature and nurture, as they are sometimes called) are important, although they may disagree about the amount of emphasis to place on each.

General Principles of Development

Although there is disagreement about what is involved in development and about the way it takes place, there are a few general principles that almost all theorists would support.

1. *People develop at different rates.* In your own classroom, you will have a whole range of examples of different developmental rates. Some students will be larger, better coordinated, or more mature in their thinking and social relationships. Others will be much slower to mature in these areas. Except in rare cases of very rapid or very slow development, such differences are normal and to be expected in any large group of students.

2. *Development is relatively orderly.* People develop certain abilities before others. In infancy, they sit before they walk, babble before they talk, and see the world through their own eyes before they can begin to imagine how others see it. In school, they master addition before algebra, Bambi before Shakespeare, and so on. Theorists may disagree on exactly what comes before what, but they all seem to find a relatively logical progression.

3. *Development takes place gradually.* Very rarely do changes appear overnight. A student who cannot manipulate a pencil or answer a hypothetical question may well develop this ability, but the change is likely to take time.

The Brain and Cognitive Development

What Would You Say?

You are being interviewed for a job in a great district, one known for innovation. After a few minutes, the principal asks, "Do you know anything about this brain-based education? I've read a lot about that lately." How would you answer?

If you have taken an introductory psychology class, you have read about the brain and nervous system. You probably remember that there are several different areas of the brain and that certain areas are involved in particular functions. For example, the feathery looking cerebellum coordinates and orchestrates balance and smooth, skilled movements—from the graceful gestures of the dancer to the everyday action of eating without stabbing yourself in the nose with a fork. The cerebellum may also play a role in higher cognitive functions such as learning. The hippocampus is critical in recalling new information and recent experiences, while the amygdala directs emotions. The thalamus is involved in our ability to learn new information, particularly if it is verbal. The reticular formation plays a role in attention and arousal, blocking some messages and sending others on to higher brain centres for processing, and the corpus callosum moves information from one side of the brain to the other.

Some researchers have described the brain as a jungle of layers and loops, an interconnected and complex organic system (Edelman, 1992). The outer 0.3-centimetre-thick covering of the cerebrum is the wrinkled-looking cerebral cortex—the largest area of the brain. The cerebral cortex allows the greatest human accomplishments, such as complex problem solving and language. In humans, this area of the brain is much larger than it is in lower animals. The cortex is the last part of the brain to develop, so it is believed to be more susceptible to environmental influences than other areas of the brain (Berk, 2005; Meece, 2002; Wood, Wood, & Boyd, 2005). The cerebral cortex accounts for about 85 percent of the brain's weight in adulthood and contains the greatest number of **neurons**—the tiny structures that store and transmit information. Let's see how neurons develop.

The Developing Brain: Neurons. About one month after conception, brain development starts. In the tiny tube that is the very beginning of the human brain, neuron cells emerge at the amazing rate of 50 000 to 100 000 per second for the next three months or so. These cells send out long arm- and branch-like fibres to connect with other neuron cells and share information by releasing chemicals that jump across the tiny spaces, called **synapses**, between the fibre ends. By the time we are born, we have all the neurons we will ever have, about 100 to 200 billion, and each neuron has about 2500 synapses. However, the fibres that reach out from the neurons and the synapses between the fibre ends increase during the first years of life, perhaps into adolescence or longer.

By age two to three, each neuron has around 15 000 synapses; children this age have many more synapses than they will have as adults. In fact, they are *oversupplied* with the neurons and synapses that they will need to adapt to their environments. However, only those neurons that are used will survive, and unused neurons will be "pruned" (Bransford, Brown, & Cocking, 2000). This pruning is necessary and supports cognitive development. In fact, some forms of mental retardation are associated with a gene defect that interferes with pruning (Cook & Cook, 2005).

Two kinds of overproduction and pruning processes take place. One is called *experience-expectant* because synapses are overproduced in certain parts of the brain during certain developmental periods, awaiting (expecting) stimulation. For example, during the first months of life, the brain expects visual and auditory stimulation. If a normal range of sights and sounds occurs, then the visual and auditory areas of the brain develop. But children who are born completely deaf receive no auditory stimulation and, as a result, the auditory processing area of their brains becomes devoted to processing visual information. Similarly, the visual processing area of the brain for children blind from birth becomes devoted to auditory processing (Nelson, 2001; Siegler, 1998).

Experience-expectant overproduction and pruning processes are responsible for general development in large areas of the brain. This may explain why adults have difficulty with pronunciations that are not part of their native language. For example, native Japanese speakers do not distinguish the different sounds of "r" and "l." The capacity to hear these differences was available to Japanese infants, but the

Connect & Extend

TO THE NEWS
See the May 1, 2001, issue of *Maclean's* for the cover story, "How We Think." Montrealer Steven Pinker is challenging other fellow neuroscientists with provocative theories about how evolution has changed the human brain. He and other researchers are probing the mysteries of learning, emotions, and how the brain functions.

neurons Nerve cells that store and transfer information.

synapses The tiny space between neurons; chemical messages are sent across these gaps.

neurons and synapses involved in recognizing these differences may have been "pruned" because they were not used to learn Japanese. Therefore, learning these sounds as an adult requires intense instruction and practice (Bransford et al., 2000).

The second kind of synaptic overproduction and pruning is called *experience-dependent*. Here, synaptic connections are formed based on the individual's experiences. New synapses are formed in response to neural activity in very localized areas of the brain when the individual is not successful in processing information. Again, more synapses are produced than will be kept after "pruning." Experience-dependent processes are involved in individual learning, such as learning unfamiliar sound pronunciations in a second language you are studying.

Stimulation is important in both development (experience-expectant processes) and learning (experience-dependent processes). In fact, animal studies have shown that rats raised in stimulating environments (with toys, tasks for learning, other rats, and human handling) develop and retain 25 percent more synapses than rats who are raised with little stimulation. Both social stimulation (interactions with other rats) and physical/sensory stimulation (toys and tasks) are important; some studies showed that toys and tasks alone did not lead to increased brain development (Bransford et al., 2000). And age may matter, too. Stimulating environments may help in the pruning process in early life (experience-expectant period) and support increased synapse development in adulthood (experience-dependent period) (Cook & Cook, 2005).

Early stimulation is important for humans as well. It is clear that extreme deprivation can have negative effects on brain development, but extra stimulation will not necessarily improve development for young children who are getting adequate or typical amounts of stimulation (Byrnes & Fox, 1998; Kolb & Whishaw, 1998). So spending money on expensive toys or baby education programs probably provides more stimulation than is necessary. Pots and pans, blocks and books, sand and water all provide excellent stimulation—especially if accompanied by caring conversations with parents or teachers.

Even though the brain is developing rapidly during early childhood, learning continues over a lifetime. Early severe stimulus deprivation can have lasting effects, but because of brain **plasticity** or adaptability, some compensation can overcome deprivation or damage. Of course, many factors besides stimulus deprivation, such as the mother's intake of drugs (including alcohol and caffeine) during pregnancy, toxins in the infant's environment such as lead paint, or poor nutrition, can have direct and dramatic negative effects on brain development.

Another factor that influences thinking and learning is **myelination**, or the coating of neuron fibres with an insulating fatty covering. This process is something like coating bare electrical wires with rubber or plastic. This myelin coating makes message transmission faster and more efficient. Myelination happens quickly in the early years, but continues gradually into adolescence and is the reason the child's brain grows rapidly in size in the first few years of life.

The Developing Brain: Cerebral Cortex. Let's move from the neuron level to the brain itself. The cerebral cortex develops more slowly than other parts of the brain, and parts of the cortex mature at different rates. The part of the cortex that controls physical motor movement matures first, followed by the areas that control complex senses such as vision and hearing, and then the frontal lobe that controls higher-order thinking processes. The temporal lobes of the cortex that play major roles in emotions and language do not develop fully until the high school years and maybe later.

Neuroscientists are just beginning to understand how brain development is related to child and adolescent functioning, such as planning and decision making as well as risk taking and managing impulsive behaviours. Getting angry or wanting revenge when we are insulted are common human emotions. It is the job of the prefrontal cortex to control these impulses through reason, planning, or delay of gratification. But the impulse-inhibiting capacities of the brain are not present at

plasticity The brain's tendency to remain somewhat adaptable or flexible.

myelination The process by which neural fibres are coated with a fatty sheath called *myelin* that makes message transfer more efficient.

birth (as all new parents quickly discover). An immature prefrontal lobe explains some of the impulsiveness and temper tantrums of two-year-olds. Emotional regulation is more difficult at this age. Many studies show advances in the prefrontal cortex around three to four years old (Berger, 2006), but it takes at least two decades for the biological processes of brain development to produce a fully functional prefrontal cortex (Weinberger, 2001). Thus middle and high school students still lack the brain development to balance impulse with reason and planning. Weinberger suggests that parents have to "loan" their children a prefrontal cortex, by helping them set rules and limits and make plans, until the child's own prefrontal cortex can take over. Schools and teachers can also play major roles in cognitive and emotional development if they provide appropriate environments for these developing, but sometimes impulsive, brains (Meece, 2002).

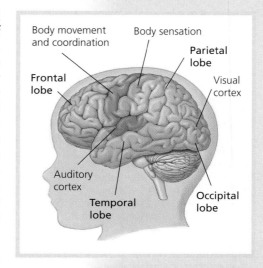

Figure 2.1 A View of the Cerebral Cortex

This is a simple representation of the left side of the human brain, showing the cerebral cortex. The cortex is divided into different areas, or lobes, each having a variety of regions with different functions. A few of the major functions are indicated here.

lateralization The specialization of the two hemispheres (sides) of the brain cortex.

Specialization and Integration.   Different areas of the cortex seem to have different functions, as shown in Figure 2.1. Even though different functions are found in different areas of the brain, these specialized functions are quite specific and elementary. To accomplish more complex functions such as speaking or reading, the various areas of the cortex must work together (Byrnes & Fox, 1998).

Another aspect of brain functioning that has implications for cognitive development is **lateralization,** or the specialization of the two hemispheres of the brain. We know that each half of the brain controls the opposite side of the body. Damage to the right side of the brain will affect movement of the left side of the body and vice versa. In addition, certain areas of the brain affect particular behaviour. For most of us, the left hemisphere of the brain is the major factor in language processing, and the right hemisphere handles most of the spatial-visual information and emotions (non-verbal information). For some left-handed people, the relationship may be reversed, but for most left-handers, and females on average, there is less hemispheric specialization altogether (Berk, 2002). In addition, females on average seem to show less hemispheric specialization than males (Berk 2005; O'Boyle & Gill, 1998). Before lateralization, damage to one part of the cortex can often be overcome as other parts of the cortex take over the function of the damaged area. But after lateralization, the brain is less able to compensate.

These differences in brain hemisphere performance, however, are more relative than absolute; one hemisphere is just more efficient than the other in performing certain functions. Nearly any task, particularly the complex skills and abilities that concern teachers, requires participation of many different areas of the brain. For example, the right side of the brain is better at figuring out the meaning of a story, but the left side is where grammar and syntax are understood, so both sides of the brain have to work together in reading. "The primary implication of these findings is that the practice of teaching to 'different sides of the brain' is not supported by the neuroscientific research" (Byrnes & Fox, 1998, p. 310). Thus, beware of educational approaches based on simplistic views of brain functioning—what Keith Stanovich (1998), a professor at the University of Toronto, has called "the left-brain–right-brain nonsense that has inundated education through workshops, inservices, and the trade publications" (p. 420). Remember, no mental activity is exclusively the work of a single part of the brain—so there is no such thing as a "right-brained student" unless that individual has had the left hemisphere removed, a rare and radical treatment for some forms of epilepsy.

Instruction and Brain Development.   Research from animal and human studies shows that both experiences and direct teaching cause changes in the organization and structure of the brain. For example, deaf individuals who use sign language have different patterns of electrical activity in their brains compared with deaf

Connect & Extend

TO THE WEB
See **www.nih.gov/news/pr/apr2004/nichd-19.htm** for a summary of the Shaywitz et al. study.

One clear connection between the brain and classroom learning is in the area of emotions and stress. Anxiety interferes with learning, whereas challenge, interest, and curiosity can support learning. If students feel unsafe and anxious, they are not likely to be able to focus attention on academics (Sylvester, 2003). But if students are not challenged or interested, learning suffers too. Keeping the level of challenge and support "just right" is a challenge for teachers. And helping students learn to regulate their own emotions and motivation is an important goal for education (see Chapter 3).

people who do not use sign language. Also, the intensive instruction and practice provided when someone suffers a stroke can help the person regain functioning by forming new connections and using new areas of the brain (Bransford et al., 2000). Bennett Shaywitz and his colleagues (2004) reported a dramatic demonstration of brain changes in children following instruction. The researchers studied 28 children aged six to nine who were good readers and 49 children who were poor readers. A process known as functional magnetic-resonance imaging (fMRI) showed differences in the brain activity of the two groups. The poor readers underused parts of their brains' left hemisphere and sometimes overused their right hemispheres. After over 100 hours of intensive instruction in letter-sound combinations, the brains of the poor readers started to function more like those of the good readers and continued this functioning a year later. Poor readers who got the standard school remediation did not show the brain function changes.

Implications for Teachers.   As you have seen, the brain and learning are intimately related, but what does this mean for teachers? Marcy Driscoll (2005) draws these implications:

1.   Many cognitive functions are differentiated—they are associated with different parts of the brain. Thus, learners are likely to have preferred modes of processing (visual, or verbal, for example) as well as different capabilities in these different modes. Using different modalities for instruction and activities that draw on different senses may support learning-for example, using maps and songs to teach geography.

2.   The brain is relatively plastic, so enriched active environments and flexible instructional strategies are likely to support cognitive development in young children and learning in adults.

3.   Some learning disorders may have a neurological basis, so neurological testing may assist in diagnosing, treating, and evaluating the effects of treatments.

Much has been written lately about brain-based education. Many of these publications for parents and teachers have useful ideas, but beware of suggestions that oversimplify the complexities of the brain.

We turn next to examine a theory of cognitive development offered by a biologist turned psychologist, Jean Piaget.

Check Your Knowledge

- What are the different kinds of development?
- What are three principles of development?
- What part of the brain is associated with higher mental functions?
- What is lateralization, and is it important for teaching?

Apply to Practice

- What aspect of development is involved in Trevor's understanding of symbolism at the opening of this chapter?

PIAGET'S THEORY OF COGNITIVE DEVELOPMENT

Swiss psychologist Jean Piaget devised a model describing how humans go about making sense of their world by gathering and organizing information (Piaget, 1954, 1963, 1970a, 1970b). According to Piaget (1954), certain ways of thinking that are quite simple for an adult are not so simple for a child. For example, Piaget asked a nine-year-old:

> What is your nationality?—*I am Swiss.*—How come?—*Because I live in Switzerland.*—Are you also a Genevan?—*No, that's not possible... I'm already Swiss, I can't also be Genevan.* (Piaget, 1965/1995, p. 252)

Imagine teaching this student geography. The student has trouble with classifying one concept (Geneva) as a subset of another (Switzerland). There are other differences between adult and child thinking. Children's concepts of time may be different from your own. They may think, for example, that they will someday catch up to a sibling in age, or they may confuse the past and the future.

Influences on Development

Cognitive development is much more than the addition of new facts and ideas to an existing store of information. According to Piaget, our thinking processes change radically, though slowly, from birth to maturity because we constantly strive to make sense of the world. How do we do this? Piaget identified four factors—biological maturation, activity, social experiences, and equilibration—that interact to influence changes in thinking (Piaget, 1970a). Let's briefly examine the first three factors. We'll return to a discussion of equilibration in the next section.

Jean Piaget was a Swiss psychologist whose insightful descriptions of children's thinking changed the way we understand cognitive development.

One of the most important influences on the way we make sense of the world is *maturation,* the unfolding of the biological changes that are genetically programmed in each human being at conception. Parents and teachers have little impact on this aspect of cognitive development, except to ensure that children get the nourishment and care they need to be healthy.

Activity is another influence. With physical maturation comes the increasing ability to act on the environment and learn from it. When a young child's coordination is reasonably developed, for example, the child may discover principles about balance by experimenting with a seesaw. Thus, as we act on the environment—as we explore, test, observe, and eventually organize information—we are likely to alter our thinking processes at the same time.

As we develop, we are also interacting with the people around us. According to Piaget, our cognitive development is influenced by *social transmission,* or learning from others. According to Piaget, by interacting with other individuals, we are exploring and building knowledge about our world. Of course, the amount people can learn from social transmission varies according to their stage of cognitive development.

Basic Tendencies in Thinking

Piaget's original work was in biology. As such, he felt that all species inherit two basic instincts, or "invariant functions." The first of these tendencies is toward **organization**—the combining, arranging, recombining, and rearranging of behaviour and thoughts into coherent systems. The second tendency is toward **adaptation**, or adjusting to the environment.

Organization. People are born with a tendency to organize their thinking and knowledge into psychological structures or schemes. These psychological structures are our systems for understanding and interacting with the world. Simple structures are continually combined and coordinated to become more sophisticated and thus more effective. Very young infants, for example, can either look at an object or grasp it when it comes in contact with their hands. They cannot coordinate looking and grasping at the same time. As they develop, however, infants organize these two separate behavioural structures into a coordinated higher-level structure of looking at, reaching for, and grasping the object. They can, of course, still use each structure separately (Ginsburg & Opper, 1988; Miller, 2002).

Piaget gave a special name to these structures: **schemes**. In his theory, schemes are the basic building blocks of thinking. They are organized systems of actions or thought that allow us to mentally represent or "think about" the objects and events

Connect & Extend

TO YOUR STUDENTS' THINKING

To experience some of the ways in which children differ from adults in their thinking, ask children of various ages the following questions:

- What does it mean to be alive?
- Can you name some things that are alive?
- Is the moon alive?
- Where do dreams come from?
- Where do they go?
- Which is farther, to go from the bottom of the hill all the way to the top or to go from the top of the hill all the way to the bottom?
- Can a person live in Winnipeg and Manitoba at the same time?
- Will you be just as old as your big brother someday?
- When is yesterday?
- Where does the sun go at night?

organization Ongoing process of arranging information and experience into mental systems or categories.

adaptation Adjustment to the environment.

schemes Mental systems or categories of perception and experience.

in our world. Schemes may be very small and specific—for example, the sucking-through-a-straw scheme or the recognizing-a-rose scheme. Or they may be more general—the drinking scheme or the categorizing-plants scheme. As a person's thinking processes become more organized and new schemes develop, behaviour also becomes more sophisticated and better suited to the environment.

Adaptation. In addition to the tendency to organize their psychological structures, people are born with the tendency to adapt to their environment. Two basic processes are involved in adaptation: assimilation and accommodation.

Assimilation takes place when people use their existing schemes to make sense of events in their world. Assimilation involves trying to understand something new by fitting it into what we already know. At times, we may have to distort the new information to make it fit. For example, the first time many children see a skunk, they call it a "kitty." They try to match the new experience with an existing scheme for identifying animals.

Accommodation occurs when a person must change existing schemes to respond to a new situation. If data cannot be made to fit any existing schemes, more appropriate structures must be developed. We adjust our thinking to fit the new information, instead of adjusting the information to fit our thinking. Children demonstrate accommodation when they add the scheme for recognizing skunks to their other systems for identifying animals.

People adapt to their increasingly complex environments by using existing schemes whenever these schemes work (assimilation) and by modifying and adding to their schemes when something new is needed (accommodation). In fact, both processes are required most of the time. Even using an established pattern such as sucking through a straw may require some accommodation, if you are used to a straw of a different size or length. If you have tried drinking juice from box packages, you know that you have to add a new skill to your sucking scheme—don't squeeze the box or you will shoot juice through the straw, straight up into the air and into your lap. Whenever new experiences are assimilated into an existing scheme, the scheme is enlarged and changed somewhat, so assimilation involves some accommodation.

There are also times when neither assimilation nor accommodation is used. If people encounter something that is too unfamiliar, they may ignore it. Experience is filtered to fit the kind of thinking a person is doing at a given time. For example, if you overhear a conversation in a foreign language, you probably will not try to make sense of the exchange unless you have some knowledge of the language.

Equilibration. According to Piaget, organizing, assimilating, and accommodating can be seen as a kind of complex balancing act. In his theory, the actual changes in thinking take place through the process of **equilibration**—the act of searching for a balance. Piaget assumed that people continually test the adequacy of their thinking processes in order to achieve that balance.

Briefly, the process of equilibration works as follows. If we apply a particular scheme to an event or situation and the scheme works, equilibrium exists. If the scheme does not produce a satisfying result, **disequilibrium** exists, and we become uncomfortable. This motivates us to keep searching for a solution through assimilation and accommodation, and thus our thinking changes and moves ahead.

Four Stages of Cognitive Development

What Would You Say?

Your interview with a principal seems to be going fairly well. Her next question is, "Students in some of our grade 11 classes are pretty concrete in their thinking, but others are quite advanced. How would you differentiate instruction?"

assimilation Fitting new information into existing schemes.

accommodation Altering existing schemes or creating new ones in response to new information.

equilibration Search for mental balance between cognitive schemes and information from the environment.

disequilibrium In Piaget's theory, the "out-of-balance" state that occurs when a person realizes that his or her current ways of thinking are not working to solve a problem or understand a situation.

Now we turn to the actual differences that Piaget hypothesized for children as they grow. Piaget's four stages of cognitive development are called sensorimotor, preoperational, concrete-operational, and formal-operational. Piaget believed that all people pass through the same four stages in exactly the same order. These stages are generally associated with specific ages, as shown in Table 2.1. When you see ages linked to stages, remember that these are only general guidelines, not labels for all children of a certain age. Piaget was interested in the kinds of thinking abilities people are able to use, not in labelling. There are individual differences in how people pass through these stages, which means that knowing a student's age is never a guarantee of knowing his or her level of cognitive development (Orlando & Machado, 1996). Also, as you will see later in this chapter, many people disagree with the ages Piaget has assigned to the various stages.

Infancy: The Sensorimotor Stage.　The earliest period is called the **sensorimotor** stage, because the child's thinking involves the major senses of seeing, hearing, moving, touching, and tasting. During this period, the infant develops **object permanence**, the understanding that objects in the environment exist whether the baby perceives them or not. As most parents discover, before infants develop object permanence, it is relatively easy to take something away from them.

The older infant who searches for the ball that has rolled out of sight is indicating an understanding that objects still exist even when they are not in view (Moore & Meltzoff, 2004). Recent research, however, suggests that infants as young as three to four months may know that the object still exists, but they do not have the memory skills to "hold on" to the location of the object or the motor skills to coordinate a search (Baillargeon, 1999; Flavell et al., 2002).

A second major accomplishment in the sensorimotor period is the beginning of logical, **goal-directed actions**. Think of the familiar container toy for babies. It is usually plastic, has a lid, and contains several colourful items that can be dumped out and replaced. A six-month-old baby is likely to become frustrated trying to get to the toys inside. An older child who has mastered the basics of the sensorimotor stage will probably be able to deal with the toys in an orderly fashion. Through

The ability to manipulate concrete objects helps children understand abstract relationships, such as the connection between symbols and quantity.

sensorimotor Involving the senses and motor activity.

object permanence The understanding that objects have a separate, permanent existence.

goal-directed actions Deliberate actions toward a goal.

TABLE 2.1 Piaget's Stages of Cognitive Development

Stage	Approximate Age	Characteristics
Sensorimotor	0–2 years	Begins to make use of imitation, memory, and thought. Begins to recognize that objects do not cease to exist when they are hidden. Moves from reflex actions to goal-directed activity.
Preoperational	2–7 years	Gradually develops use of language and ability to think in symbolic form. Is able to think operations through logically in one direction. Has difficulties seeing another person's point of view.
Concrete-operational	7–11 years	Is able to solve concrete (hands-on) problems in logical fashion. Understands laws of conservation and is able to classify and seriate. Understands reversibility.
Formal-operational	11–adult	Is able to solve abstract problems in logical fashion. Becomes more scientific in thinking. Develops concerns about social issues, identity.

Source: From Wadsworth, B. J. (1996). *Piaget's theory of cognitive and affective development* (5th ed.). Boston: Allyn & Bacon. Copyright © 1996 by Pearson Education. Adapted by permission of the publisher.

trial and error, the child will slowly build a "container toy" scheme: (1) get the lid off; (2) turn the container upside down; (3) shake if the items jam; (4) watch the items fall. Separate lower-level schemes have been organized into a higher-level scheme to achieve a goal.

The child is soon able to reverse this action by refilling the container. Learning to reverse actions is a basic accomplishment of the sensorimotor stage. As we will soon see, however, learning to reverse thinking—that is, learning to imagine the reverse of a sequence of actions—takes much longer.

Early Childhood to the Early Elementary Years: The Preoperational Stage.

By the end of the sensorimotor stage, the child can use many action schemes. As long as these schemes remain tied to physical actions, however, they are of no use in recalling the past, keeping track of information, or planning. For this, children need what Piaget called **operations**, or actions that are carried out and reversed mentally rather than physically. The stage after sensorimotor is called **preoperational**, because the child has not yet mastered these mental operations but is moving toward mastery.

According to Piaget, the first step from action to thinking is the internalization of action—that is, performing an action mentally rather than physically. The first type of thinking that is separate from action involves making action schemes symbolic. The ability to form and use symbols—words, gestures, signs, images, and so on—is thus a major accomplishment of the preoperational period and moves children closer to mastering the mental operations of the next stage. This ability to work with symbols, such as using the word "horse" or a picture of a horse or even pretending to ride a horse to represent a real horse that is not actually present, is called the **semiotic function**. In fact, the child's earliest use of symbols is in pretending. Children who are not yet able to talk will often use action symbols—pretending to drink from an empty cup or touching a comb to their hair, showing that they know what each object is for. This behaviour also shows that their schemes are becoming more general and less tied to specific actions. The eating scheme, for example, can be used in playing house. During the preoperational stage, there is also rapid development of that very important symbol system, language. Between the ages of two and four, most children enlarge their vocabulary from about 200 to 2000 words.

As the child moves through the preoperational stage, the developing ability to think about objects in symbolic form remains somewhat limited to thinking in one direction only, or using *one-way logic*. It is very difficult for the child to "think backwards," or imagine how to reverse the steps in a task. **Reversible thinking** is involved in many tasks that are difficult for the preoperational child, such as the conservation of matter.

Conservation is the principle that the amount or number of something remains the same even if the arrangement or appearance is changed, as long as nothing is added and nothing is taken away. You know that if you tear a piece of paper into several pieces, you will still have the same amount of paper. To prove this, you know that you can reverse the process by taping the pieces back together. A classic example of difficulty with conservation is found in the preoperational child's response to the following Piagetian task. Leah, a five-year-old, is shown two identical glasses, both short and wide in shape. Both have exactly the same amount of coloured water in them. She agrees that the amounts are "the same." The experimenter then pours the water

operations Actions that a person carries out by thinking them through instead of literally performing them.

preoperational The stage of development before a child masters logical mental operations.

semiotic function The ability to use symbols—language, pictures, signs, or gestures—to represent actions or objects mentally.

reversible thinking Thinking backward, from the end to the beginning.

conservation Principle that some characteristics of an object remain the same despite changes in appearance.

decentring Focusing on more than one aspect at a time.

Family Circus, March 12, 2002. Copyright © 2002 Bill Keane, Inc. Reprinted with special permission of King Features Syndicate.

from one of the glasses into a taller, narrower glass and asks, "Now, does one glass have more water, or are they the same?" Leah responds that the tall glass has more because "It goes up more here" (she points to higher level on taller glass).

Piaget's explanation for Leah's answer is that she is focusing, or centring, attention on the dimension of height. She has difficulty considering more than one aspect of the situation at a time, or **decentring**. The preoperational child cannot understand that increased diameter compensates for decreased height, since this would require taking into account two dimensions at once. Thus, children at the preoperational stage have trouble freeing themselves from their own perceptions of how the world appears.

This brings us to another important characteristic of the preoperational stage. Preoperational children, according to Piaget, are very **egocentric**; they tend to see the world and the experiences of others from their own viewpoints. Egocentric, as Piaget intended it, does not mean selfish; it simply means that children often assume that everyone else shares their feelings, reactions, and perspectives. Very young children centre on their own perceptions and on the way the situation appears to them. This is one reason it is difficult for these children to understand that your right hand is not on the same side as theirs when you are facing them.

Egocentrism is also evident in the child's language. You may have seen young children happily talking about what they are doing even though no one is listening. This can happen when the child is alone or, even more often, in a group of children—each child talks enthusiastically, without any real interaction or conversation. Piaget called this the **collective monologue**.

Research has shown that young children are not totally egocentric in every situation, however. Children as young as four change the way they talk to two-year-olds by speaking in simpler sentences, and even before the age of two a child shows a toy to an adult by turning the front of the toy to face the other person. So young children do seem quite able to take the needs and different perspectives of others into account, at least in certain situations (Flavell et al., 2002). And in fairness to young children, even adults can make assumptions that others feel or think as they do. For example, have you ever gotten a gift that the giver loved but was clearly inappropriate for you? The Guidelines box on page 32 gives ideas for working with preoperational thinkers.

Later Elementary to the Middle School Years: The Concrete-Operational Stage. Piaget coined the term **concrete operations** to describe this stage of "hands-on" thinking. The basic characteristics of the stage are the recognition of the logical stability of the physical world, the realization that elements can be changed or transformed and still conserve many of their original characteristics, and the understanding that these changes can be reversed.

Figure 2.2 on page 33 shows examples of the different tasks given to children to assess conservation and the approximate age ranges when most children can solve these problems. According to Piaget, a student's ability to solve conservation problems depends on an understanding of three basic aspects of reasoning: identity, compensation, and reversibility. With a complete mastery of **identity**, the student knows that if nothing is added or taken away, the material remains the same. With an understanding of **compensation**, the student knows that an apparent change in one direction can be compensated for by a change in another direction. That is, if the liquid rises higher in the glass, the glass must be narrower. And with an understanding of **reversibility**, the student can mentally cancel out the change that has been made.

Another important operation mastered at this stage is **classification**. Classification depends on a student's abilities to focus on a single characteristic of objects in a set and group the objects according to that characteristic. More advanced classification at this stage involves recognizing that one class fits into another. A city can be in a particular province and also in Canada. As children apply this advanced classification to locations, they often become fascinated with

Connect & Extend

TO YOUR STUDENTS' THINKING
To witness an example of young children's difficulties with reversibility and egocentric thinking, ask a child with only one sibling, "Do you have a brother (sister)?" The child should say, "Yes." Now ask, "Does your brother (sister) have a brother (sister)?" Young children have difficulty reversing the situation and putting themselves in their siblings' position, so they usually reply "No." Now face the child and ask the child to point to your right hand. Most young children assume that your right hand is on the same side as theirs, even when they are facing you.

egocentric Assuming that others experience the world the way you do.

collective monologue Form of speech in which children in a group talk but do not really interact or communicate.

Connect & Extend

TO YOUR TEACHING
By the time children reach the concrete-operational stage of cognitive development, they have some operations and strategies that they are able to employ. Considering these new skills, how might you go about teaching a child in this stage (a) a history lesson about Canada's role in the Second World War, and (b) the importance of the five food groups for nutrition?

concrete operations Mental tasks tied to concrete objects and situations.

identity The principle that a person or object remains the same over time.

compensation The principle that changes in one dimension can be offset by changes in another dimension.

reversibility A characteristic of Piagetian logical operations—the ability to think through a series of steps, then mentally reverse the steps and return to the starting point; also called reversible thinking.

classification Grouping objects into categories.

TEACHING THE PREOPERATIONAL CHILD

Use concrete props and visual aids whenever possible.

EXAMPLES

1. When you discuss concepts such as "part," "whole," or "one-half," use shapes on a felt board or cardboard "pizzas" to demonstrate.
2. Let children add and subtract with sticks, rocks, or coloured chips.

Make instructions relatively short, using actions as well as words.

EXAMPLES

1. When giving instructions about how to enter the room after recess and prepare for social studies, ask a child to demonstrate the procedure for the rest of the class by walking in quietly, going straight to his or her seat, and placing the text, paper, and a pencil on his or her desk.
2. Explain a game by acting out one of the parts.
3. Show children what their finished papers should look like. Use an overhead projector or display examples where children can see them easily.

Don't expect children to be consistent in their ability to see the world from someone else's point of view.

EXAMPLES

1. Avoid social studies lessons about worlds too far removed from the child's experience.
2. Avoid long lectures on sharing. Be clear about rules for sharing or use of materials, but avoid long explanations of the rationales for the rules.

Be sensitive to the possibility that children may have different meanings for the same word or different words for the same meaning. Children may also expect everyone to understand words they have invented.

EXAMPLES

1. If a child protests, "I won't take a nap. I'll just rest!" be aware that a nap may mean something like "changing into pyjamas and being in my bed at home."
2. Ask children to explain the meanings of their invented words.

Give children a great deal of hands-on practice with the skills that serve as building blocks for more complex skills such as reading comprehension.

EXAMPLES

1. Provide cut-out letters to build words.
2. Supplement paper-and-pencil tasks in arithmetic with activities that require measuring and simple calculations—cooking, building a display area for class work, dividing a batch of popcorn equally.

Provide a wide range of experiences in order to build a foundation for concept learning and language.

EXAMPLES

1. Take field trips to zoos, gardens, theatres, and concerts; invite storytellers to the class.
2. Give children words to describe what they are doing, hearing, seeing, touching, tasting, and smelling.

"complete" addresses, such as Lee Jary, 5116 Forest Hill Drive, Richmond Hill, Ontario, Canada, North America, Northern Hemisphere, Earth, Solar System, Milky Way, the Universe.

Classification is also related to reversibility. The ability to reverse a process mentally now allows the concrete-operational student to see that there is more than one way to classify a group of objects. The student understands, for example, that buttons can be classified by colour and then reclassified by size or by the number of holes.

seriation Arrangement of objects in sequential order according to one aspect, such as size, weight, or volume.

Seriation is the process of making an orderly arrangement from large to small or vice versa. This understanding of sequential relationships permits a student to construct a logical series in which A < B < C (A is less than B is less than C) and so on. Unlike the preoperational child, the concrete-operational child can grasp the notion that B can be larger than A but smaller than C.

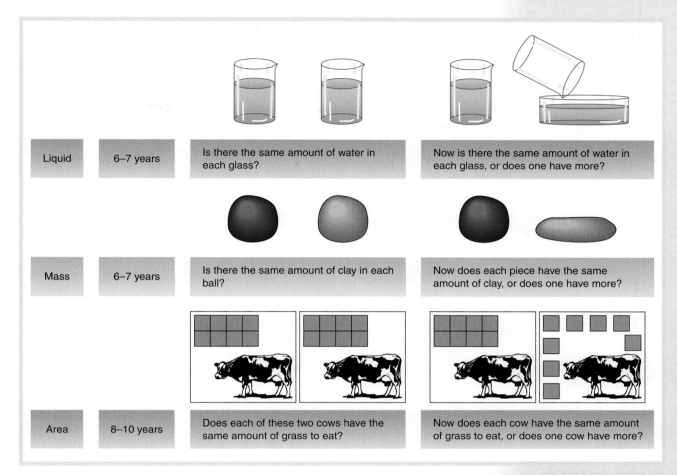

Liquid	6–7 years	Is there the same amount of water in each glass?	Now is there the same amount of water in each glass, or does one have more?
Mass	6–7 years	Is there the same amount of clay in each ball?	Now does each piece have the same amount of clay, or does one have more?
Area	8–10 years	Does each of these two cows have the same amount of grass to eat?	Now does each cow have the same amount of grass to eat, or does one cow have more?

Figure 2.2 Some Piagetian Conservation Tasks

In addition to the tasks shown here, other tasks involve the conservation of number, length, weight, and volume. These tasks are all achieved over the concrete-operational period.

Source: Berk, L. E. (1997). *Child development* (4th ed.). Boston: Allyn & Bacon. Copyright 1997. All rights reserved. Adapted by permission of Allyn & Bacon.

With the abilities to handle operations such as conservation, classification, and seriation, the student at the concrete-operational stage has finally developed a complete and very logical system of thinking. This system of thinking, however, is still tied to physical reality. The logic is based on concrete situations that can be organized, classified, or manipulated. For example, children at this stage can imagine several different arrangements for the furniture in their rooms before they move it. They do not have to solve the problem strictly through trial and error by actually making the arrangements. However, the concrete-operational child is not yet able to reason about hypothetical, abstract problems that involve the coordination of many factors at once. This kind of coordination is part of Piaget's next and final stage of cognitive development.

In any grade you teach, knowledge of concrete-operational thinking will be helpful. In the early grades, the students are moving toward this logical system of thought. In the middle grades, it is in full flower, ready to be applied and extended by your teaching. In the high school years, it may be used by students whose thinking has not fully developed to the next stage—the stage of formal operations. The Guidelines on page 34 should give you ideas for teaching children who can apply concrete operations.

High School and University: The Formal-Operational Stage. Some students remain at the concrete-operational stage throughout their school years, even throughout life. However, new experiences, usually those that take place in school, eventually present most students with problems that they cannot solve using concrete operations. What happens when a number of variables interact, as in a laboratory experiment? In such a situation, a mental system for controlling sets of variables and working through a set of possibilities is needed. These are the abilities that Piaget called **formal operations.**

formal operations Mental tasks involving abstract thinking and coordination of a number of variables.

TEACHING THE CONCRETE-OPERATIONAL CHILD

Continue to use concrete props and visual aids, especially when dealing with sophisticated material.

EXAMPLES

1. Use timelines in history and three-dimensional models in science.

2. Use diagrams to illustrate hierarchical relationships, such as branches of government and the agencies under each branch.

Continue to give students a chance to manipulate and test objects.

EXAMPLES

1. Set up simple scientific experiments like the following involving the relationship between fire and oxygen. What happens to a flame when you blow on it from a distance? (If you don't blow it out, the flame gets larger briefly, because it has more oxygen to burn.) What happens when you cover the flame with a jar?

2. Have students make candles by dipping wicks in wax, weave cloth on a simple loom, bake bread, set type by hand, or do other craft work that illustrates the daily occupations of people in the pioneer period.

Make sure that presentations and readings are brief and well organized.

EXAMPLES

1. Assign stories or books with short, logical chapters, moving to longer reading assignments only when students are ready.

2. Break up a presentation with a chance to practise the first steps before introducing the next.

Use familiar examples to explain more complex ideas.

EXAMPLES

1. Compare students' lives with those of characters in a story. For example, after reading *Island of the Blue Dolphins* (the true story of a girl who grew up alone on a deserted island), ask, "Have you ever had to stay alone for a long time? How did you feel?"

2. Teach the concept of area by having students measure two rooms in the school that are different sizes.

Give opportunities to classify and group objects and ideas on increasingly complex levels.

EXAMPLES

1. Give students slips of paper that each have one sentence written on them and ask the students to group the sentences into paragraphs.

2. Compare the systems of the human body to other kinds of systems: the brain to a computer, the heart to a pump. Break down stories into components, from the broad to the specific: author; story; characters, plot, theme; place, time; dialogue, description, actions.

Present problems that require logical, analytical thinking.

EXAMPLES

1. Use mind twisters, brain teasers, Mastermind, and riddles.

2. Discuss open-ended questions that stimulate thinking, such as, "Are the brain and the mind the same thing?" "How should the city deal with stray animals?" "What is the largest number?"

hypothetico-deductive reasoning A formal-operations problem-solving strategy in which an individual begins by identifying all the factors that might affect a problem and then deduces and systematically evaluates specific solutions.

At the level of formal operations, all the earlier operations and abilities continue in force; that is, formal thinking is reversible, internal, and organized in a system of interdependent elements. The focus of thinking shifts, however, from what *is* to what *might be*. Situations do not have to be experienced to be imagined. Ask a young child how life would be different if people did not sleep, and the child might say, "People have to sleep!" In contrast, the adolescent who has mastered formal operations can consider contrary-to-fact questions. In answering, the adolescent demonstrates the hallmark of formal operations—**hypothetico-deductive reasoning**. The formal thinker can consider a hypothetical situation (people do not sleep) and reason deductively (from the general assumption to specific implications, such as longer workdays, more money spent on lighting, or new entertainment industries). Formal operations also include inductive reasoning, or using specific observations to identify general principles. For example, the economist observes many specific changes in the stock market and attempts to identify general principles about economic cycles. Formal-operational thinkers can form hypotheses, set up mental experiments to test them, and isolate or control variables in order to complete a valid test of the hypotheses. This kind of reasoning is necessary for success in many advanced high school or university courses (Meece, 2002).

After elementary school, the ability to consider abstract possibilities is critical for much of mathematics and science. After elementary school, most math is concerned with hypothetical situations, assumptions, and givens: "Let $x = 10$," or "Assume $x^2 + y^2 = z^2$," or "Given two sides and an adjacent angle ..." Young children cannot reason based on symbols and abstractions, but this kind of reasoning is expected in the later grades (Bjorklund, 1989). Work in social studies and literature requires abstract thinking, too: "What did Woodrow Wilson mean when he called the First World War the 'war to end all wars'?" "What are some metaphors for hope and despair in Shakespeare's sonnets?" "What symbols of old age does T. S. Eliot use in *The Waste Land*?" "How do animals symbolize human character traits in Aesop's fables?"

The organized, scientific thinking of formal operations requires that students systematically generate different possibilities for a given situation. For example, if a child capable of formal operations is asked, "How many different meat/vegetable/salad meals can you make using three meats, three vegetables, and three salads?" the child can systematically identify the 27 possible combinations. A concrete thinker might name just a few meals, focusing on favourite foods or using each food only once. The underlying system of combinations is not yet available.

Another characteristic of this stage is **adolescent egocentrism**. Unlike egocentric young children, adolescents do not deny that other people may have different perceptions and beliefs; the adolescents simply become very focused on their own ideas. They analyze their own beliefs and attitudes. They reflect on others' thinking as well but often assume that everyone else is as interested as they are in their thoughts, feelings, and behaviour. This can lead to what Elkind (1981) calls the sense of an imaginary audience—the feeling that everyone is watching. Thus, adolescents believe that others are analyzing them (e.g., "Everyone noticed that I wore this shirt twice this week." "The whole class thought my answer was dumb!" "Everybody is going to love this CD."). You can see that social blunders or imperfections in appearance can be devastating if "everybody is watching." In fact, Schonert-Reichl (1994) at the University of British Columbia has linked adolescent egocentrism with adolescent depression. In particular, she found that girls from high-socioeconomic-status (SES) families tended to be overly self-conscious and more at risk for depression. In contrast, boys from high-SES families reported a heightened sense of omnipotence, uniqueness, and invulnerability. Luckily, this feeling of being "on stage" seems to peak in early adolescence, by age 14 or 15.

The ability to think hypothetically, consider alternatives, identify all possible combinations, and analyze one's own thinking has some interesting consequences for adolescents. Since they can think about worlds that do not exist, they often become interested in science fiction. Because they can reason from general principles to specific actions, they are often critical of people whose actions seem to contradict their principles. Adolescents can deduce the set of "best" possibilities and imagine ideal worlds (or ideal parents and teachers, for that matter). This explains why many students at this age develop interests in utopias, political causes, and social issues. They want to design better worlds, and their thinking allows them to do so. Adolescents can also imagine many possible futures for themselves and may try to decide which is best. Feelings about any of these ideals may be strong.

Do We All Reach the Fourth Stage? Most psychologists agree that there is a level of thinking more sophisticated than concrete operations. But the question of how universal formal-operational thinking actually is, even among adults, is a matter

adolescent egocentrism Assumption that everyone else is interested in one's thoughts, feelings, and concerns.

Try this test to see if your students can use formal operations by determining, in an organized way, the number of different possibilities that exist within a reasonably limited framework. Ask your students, "How many different outfits can be made with the following clothes: (1) three tops—polo shirt, dress shirt, and T-shirt; (2) three pairs of pants—jeans, shorts, slacks; and (3) three jackets—bomber, blazer, and jean jacket?" A student capable of formal operations would begin by laying out the possibilities systematically: first each jacket with the polo shirt and jeans, then each jacket with the polo shirt and slacks, then each jacket with the polo shirt and shorts, then on to the jackets with the dress shirt and shorts, and so forth. A student at the concrete-operational stage, however, would be much less systematic; he or she might start with favourite clothes and continue in order of preference. It would not be unusual for a student operating at the concrete level to mention only three outfits, using each garment only once.

neo-Piagetian theories More recent theories that integrate findings about attention, memory, and strategy use with Piaget's insights about children's thinking and the construction of knowledge.

of debate. The first three stages of Piaget's theory are forced on most people by physical realities. Objects really are permanent. The amount of water doesn't change when it is poured into another glass. Formal operations, however, are not so closely tied to the physical environment. They may be the product of practice in solving hypothetical problems and using formal scientific reasoning—abilities that are valued and taught in literate cultures, particularly in college and university. Even so, about 50 percent of undergraduate students fail Piaget's formal operational tasks (Berk, 2005).

Piaget himself (1974) suggested that most adults may be able to use formal-operational thought in only a few areas where they have the greatest experience or interest. Taking a college or university class fosters formal operational abilities in that subject, but not necessarily in others (Lehman & Nisbett, 1990). So expect many students in your junior high or high school class to have trouble thinking hypothetically, especially when they are learning something new. Sometimes, students find shortcuts for dealing with problems that are beyond their grasp; they may memorize formulas or lists of steps. These systems may be helpful for passing tests, but real understanding will take place only if students are able to go beyond this superficial use of memorization. The accompanying Guidelines box may help you support the development of formal operations with your students.

Information-Processing and Neo-Piagetian Views of Cognitive Development

As you will see in Chapter 7, there are explanations for why children have trouble with conservation and other Piagetian tasks. These explanations focus on the child's developing information-processing skills, such as attention, memory capacity, and learning strategies. As children mature and their brains develop, they are better able to focus their attention, process information more quickly, hold more information in memory, and use thinking strategies more easily and flexibly. Siegler (1998, 2000) proposes that as children grow older, they develop progressively better rules and strategies for solving problems and thinking logically. Teachers can help students develop their capacities for formal thinking by putting the students in situations that challenge their thinking and reveal the shortcomings of their logic. Siegler's approach is called *rule assessment* because it focuses on understanding, challenging, and changing the rules that students use for thinking.

Some developmental psychologists have formulated **neo-Piagetian theories** that retain Piaget's insights about children's construction of knowledge and the general trends in children's thinking, but add findings from information processing about the role of attention, memory, and strategies. For example, Robbie Case (1992, 1998), who was a professor at both Stanford University and the Ontario Institute for Studies in Education of the University of Toronto before his untimely death in 2000, devised an explanation of cognitive development suggesting that children develop in stages within specific domains such as numerical concepts, spatial concepts, social tasks, storytelling, reasoning about physical objects, and motor development. As children practise using the schemes in a particular domain (for example, using counting schemes in the number concept area), accomplishing the schemes takes less attention. The schemes become more automatic because the child does not have to "think so hard" about it. This frees up mental resources and memory to do more. The child now can combine simple schemes into more complex ones and invent new schemes when needed (assimilation and accommodation in action).

Within each domain such as numerical concepts or social skills, children move from grasping simple schemes during the early preschool years, to merging two schemes into a unit (between about ages four and six), to coordinating these scheme units into larger combinations, and finally, by about ages nine to eleven, to forming complex relationships that can be applied to many problems (Berk, 2005; Case, 1992, 1998). Children do progress through these qualitatively different

GUIDELINES
HELPING STUDENTS USE FORMAL OPERATIONS

Continue to use concrete-operational teaching strategies and materials.

EXAMPLES

1. Use visual aids, such as charts and illustrations, as well as somewhat more sophisticated graphs and diagrams.
2. Compare the experiences of characters in stories to students' experiences.

Give students the opportunity to explore many hypothetical questions.

EXAMPLES

1. Have students write position papers, then exchange these papers with the opposing side and have debates about topical social issues—the environment, the economy, national unity.
2. Ask students to write about their personal vision of a utopia, a description of a universe that has no gender differences, a description of Earth after humans are extinct, etc.

Give students opportunities to solve problems and reason scientifically.

EXAMPLES

1. Set up group discussions in which students design experiments to answer questions.
2. Ask students to justify two different positions on animal rights, with logical arguments for each position.

Whenever possible, teach broad concepts, not just facts, using materials and ideas relevant to the students' lives.

EXAMPLES

1. When discussing Native land claims, consider other issues that have divided Canadians (e.g., Quebec separation).
2. Use lyrics from popular songs to teach poetic devices, to reflect on social problems, and to stimulate discussion on the place of popular music in our culture.

stages within each domain, but Case argues that progress in one domain does not automatically affect movement in another. The child must have experience and involvement with the content and the ways of thinking within each domain in order to construct increasingly complex and useful schemes and coordinated conceptual understandings about the domain.

Some Limitations of Piaget's Theory

Although most psychologists agree with Piaget's insightful descriptions of *how* children think, many disagree with his explanations of *why* thinking develops as it does.

The Trouble with Stages. Some psychologists have questioned the existence of four separate stages of thinking, even though they agree that children do go through the changes that Piaget described (Miller, 2002). One problem with the stage model is the lack of consistency in children's thinking. For example, children can conserve number (the number of blocks does not change when they are rearranged) a year or two before they can conserve weight (a ball of clay does not change when you flatten it). Why can't they use conservation consistently in every situation? In fairness, we should note that in his later work, even Piaget put less emphasis on *stages* of cognitive development and gave more attention to how thinking *changes* through equilibration (Miller, 2002).

Another problem with the idea of separate stages is that, when "viewed from afar, many changes in children's thinking appear discontinuous; when viewed from close up, the same changes often appear as part of a continuous, gradual progression" (Siegler, 1998, p. 55). For example, rather than appearing all at once, object permanence may develop gradually as children's memories develop.

The longer you make the infants wait before searching, the older they have to be to succeed—so the problem may be with memory and not with knowing that things still exist when out of sight. Siegler notes that change can be both continuous and discontinuous, as described by a branch of mathematics called *catastrophe theory*. Changes that appear suddenly, such as the collapse of a bridge, are preceded by many slowly developing changes, such as gradual, continuous corrosion of the metal structures. Similarly, gradually developing changes in children can lead to large changes in abilities that seem abrupt (Fischer & Pare-Blagoev, 2000).

Some psychologists have pointed to research on the brain to support Piaget's stage model. Epstein (1978, 1980) observed changes in rates of growth in brain weight and skull size and changes in the electrical activity of the brain between infancy and adolescence. These growth spurts occur at about the same time as transitions between the stages described by Piaget. Evidence from animal studies indicates that infant rhesus monkeys show dramatic increases in synaptic (nerve) connections throughout the brain cortex at the same time that they master the kinds of sensorimotor problems described by Piaget (Berk, 2000). This may be true in human infants as well. Transition to the higher cognitive states in humans has also been related to changes in the brain, such as production of additional synaptic connections (Byrnes & Fox, 1998). Thus, there is some neurological evidence for stages.

Underestimating Children's Abilities. It now appears that Piaget underestimated the cognitive abilities of children, particularly younger ones. The problems he gave young children may have been too difficult and the directions too confusing. His subjects may have understood more than they could show on these problems. For example, work by Gelman and her colleagues (Gelman, 2001; Gelman & Cordes, 2001) shows that preschool children know much more about the concept of number than Piaget thought, even if they sometimes make mistakes or get confused. As long as preschoolers work with only three or four objects at a time, they can tell that the number remains the same, even if the objects are spread far apart or clumped close together. In other words, we may be born with a greater store of cognitive tools than Piaget suggested. Some basic understandings, such as the sense of number or understanding what other people know, may be part of our evolutionary equipment, ready for use in our cognitive development (Geary & Borklund, 2000).

Piaget's theory also does not explain how even young children can perform at an advanced level in certain areas where they have highly developed knowledge and expertise. For example, Marion Porath (1997; 1996), at the University of British Columbia, found the drawings of artistically gifted children and the story plots of verbally gifted children to be far more elaborate than those of children in a same-age control group. Similarly, an expert 9-year-old chess player can think abstractly about chess moves, whereas a novice 20-year-old player may have to resort to more concrete strategies to plan and remember moves (Siegler, 1998).

Cognitive Development and Culture. One final criticism of Piaget's theory is that it overlooks the important effects of the child's cultural and social group. Children in Western cultures may master scientific thinking and formal operations because this is the kind of thinking required in Western schools (Berk, 2005; Geary, 1998). Even basic concrete operations such as classification may not be so basic to people of other cultures. For example, when individuals from the Kpelle people of Africa were asked to sort 20 objects, they created groups that made sense to them—a hoe with a potato, a knife with an orange. The experimenter could not get the Kpelle to change their categories; they said this is how a wise man would do it. Finally, the experimenter asked in desperation, "Well, how would a fool do it?" Then the subjects promptly created the four neat classification piles the experimenter had expected—food, tools, and so on (Rogoff & Morelli, 1989).

- What are the main influences on cognitive development?
- What is a scheme?
- As children move from sensorimotor to formal-operational thinking, what are the major changes?
- How do neo-Piagetians and information-processing views explain changes in children's thinking over time?

Apply to Practice

- What are the characteristics of concrete-operational thinking? Is Trevor's thinking concrete?

There is another increasingly influential view of cognitive development. Proposed years ago by Lev Vygotsky and recently rediscovered, this theory ties cognitive development to culture.

VYGOTSKY'S SOCIOCULTURAL PERSPECTIVE

Psychologists today recognize that the child's culture shapes cognitive development by determining what and how the child will learn about the world. For example, young Zinacanteco Indian girls of southern Mexico learn complicated ways of weaving cloth through informal teachings of adults in their communities. In Brazil, without going to school, children who sell candy on the streets learn sophisticated mathematics in order to buy from wholesalers, sell, barter, and make a profit. Cultures that prize cooperation and sharing teach these skills early, whereas cultures that encourage competition nurture these abilities in their children (Bakerman et al., 1990; Ceci & Roazzi, 1994). The stages observed by Piaget are not necessarily "natural" for all children because to some extent they reflect the expectations and activities of the children's culture (Kozulin, 2003; Rogoff, 2003).

A major spokesperson for this **sociocultural theory** (also called *sociohistoric theory*) was a Russian psychologist who died more than 70 years ago. Lev Semenovich Vygotsky was only 38 when he died of tuberculosis, but during his life he produced more than 100 books and articles. Some of his translations are now available (Vygotsky, 1978, 1986, 1987, 1993, 1997). Vygotsky's work began when he was studying learning and development to improve his own teaching (Wink & Putney, 2002). He wrote about language and thought, the psychology of art, learning and development, and educating students with special needs. His work was banned in Russia for many years because he referenced Western psychologists. But in the past 30 years, with the rediscovery of his work, Vygotsky's ideas about language, culture, and cognitive development have become major influences in psychology and education and have provided alternatives to many of Piaget's theories (Kozulin, 2003; McCaslin & Hickey, 2001; Wink & Putney, 2002).

Vygotsky believed that human activities take place in cultural settings and cannot be understood apart from the settings. One of his key ideas was that our specific mental structures and processes can be traced to our interactions with others. These social interactions are more than simple influences on cognitive development—they actually create our cognitive structures and thinking processes (Palincsar, 1998). In fact, "Vygotsky conceptualized development as the transformation of socially shared activities into internalized processes" (John-Steiner & Mahn, 1996, p. 192). We will examine two themes in Vygotsky's writings that explain how social processes form learning and thinking: the social sources of individual thinking and the role of tools in learning and development, especially the tool of language (Wertsch & Tulviste, 1992; Driscoll, 2005).

Connect & Extend

TO THE RESEARCH
See the Spring 1995 *Educational Psychologist* for a special issue on Lev Vygotsky and contemporary educational psychology.

sociocultural theory Theory that emphasizes the role in development of cooperative dialogues between children and more knowledgeable members of society; children learn the culture of their community (ways of thinking and behaving) through these interactions.

Lev Vygotsky, shown here with his daughter, elaborated the sociocultural theory of development. His ideas about language, culture, and cognitive development have become major influences in the fields of psychology and education.

The Social Sources of Individual Thinking

Vygotsky assumed that "every function in a child's cultural development appears twice: first on the social level and later on the individual level; first between people (interpsychological) and then inside the child (intrapsychological)" (1978, p. 57). In other words, higher mental processes appear first between people as they are **co-constructed** during shared activities. Then the processes are internalized by the child and become part of that child's cognitive development. For example, children first use language in activities with others, to regulate the behaviour of the others ("No nap!" or "I wanna cookie"). Later, however, children can regulate their own behaviour using private speech ("Don't spill"), as you will see in a later section. So, for Vygotsky, social interaction was more than influence—it was the origin of higher mental processes such as problem solving. Consider this example:

> A six-year-old has lost a toy and asks her father for help. The father asks her where she last saw the toy; the child says, "I can't remember." He asks a series of questions—did you have it in your room? Outside? Next door? To each question, the child answers, "no." When he says "in the car?" she says "I think so" and goes to retrieve the toy. (Tharp & Gallimore, 1988, p. 14)

Who remembered? The answer is really neither the father nor the daughter, but the two together. The remembering and problem solving was co-constructed—between people—in the interaction. But the child may have internalized strategies to use next time something is lost. At some point, the child will be able to function independently to solve this kind of problem. So, as the strategy for finding the toy indicates, higher functions appear first between a child and a "teacher" before they exist within the individual child (Kozulin, 1990, 2003).

Here is another example of the social sources of individual thinking. Richard Anderson and his colleagues (2001) studied how grade 4 students in small-group classroom discussions appropriate (take for themselves and use) argument strategems that occur in the discussions. An argument strategem is a particular form such as "I think [POSITION] because [REASON]," where the student fills in the position and the reason. For example, a student might say, "I think that the wolves should be left alone because they are not hurting anyone." Another strategy form is "If [ACTION] then [BAD CONSEQUENCE]," as in "If they don't trap the wolves, then the wolves will eat the cows." Other forms manage participation, for example, "What do you think [NAME]?" or "Let [NAME] talk."

Anderson's research identified 13 forms of talk and argument that helped manage the discussion, get everyone to participate, present and defend positions, and handle confusion. The researchers found that the use of these different forms of talking and thinking *snowballed*—once a useful argument was employed by one student, it spread to other students, and the argument strategem form appeared more and more in the discussions. Open discussions—students asking and answering each other's questions—were better than teacher-dominated discussion for the development of these argument forms. Over time, these ways of presenting, attacking, and defending positions could be internalized as mental reasoning and decision making for the individual students.

Both Piaget and Vygotsky emphasized the importance of social interactions in cognitive development, but Piaget saw a different role for interaction. He believed that interaction encouraged development by creating disequilibrium—cognitive conflict—that motivated change. Thus, Piaget believed that the most helpful interactions were between peers because peers are on an equal basis and can challenge each other's thinking. Vygotsky (1978, 1986, 1987, 1993), on the other hand, suggested that children's cognitive development is fostered by interactions with people who are more capable or advanced in their thinking—people such as parents and teachers (Moshman, 1997; Palincsar, 1998). Of course, as we have seen above, students can learn from both adults and peers.

co-constructed Constructed through a social process in which people interact and negotiate (usually verbally) to create an understanding or to solve a problem; the final product is shaped by all participants.

Cultural Tools and Cognitive Development

Vygotsky believed that **cultural tools**, including real tools (such as printing presses, rulers, the abacus—today, we would add PDAs, computers, the internet) and symbolic tools (such as numbers and mathematical systems, Braille and sign language, maps, works of art, signs and codes, and language), play very important roles in cognitive development. For example, as long as the culture provides only Roman numerals for representing quantity, certain ways of thinking mathematically—from long division to calculus—are difficult or impossible. But with a number system that has a zero, fractions, positive and negative values, and an infinite number of numbers, much more is possible. The number system is a cultural tool that supports thinking, learning, and cognitive development. This symbol system is passed from adult to child through formal and informal interactions and teachings.

Vygotsky believed that all higher-order mental processes, such as reasoning and problem solving, are *mediated* by psychological tools, such as language, signs, and symbols. Adults teach these tools to children during day-to-day activities and the children internalize them. Then the psychological tools can help students advance their own development (Karpov & Haywood, 1998). In other words, as children engage in activities with adults or more capable peers, they exchange ideas and ways of thinking about or representing concepts—drawing maps, for example, as a way to represent spaces and places. Children internalize these co-created ideas. Thus, children's knowledge, ideas, attitudes, and values develop through appropriating or "taking for themselves" the ways of acting and thinking provided by their culture and by the more capable members of their group (Kozulin & Presseisen, 1995).

In this exchange of signs and symbols and explanations, children begin to develop a "cultural tool kit" to make sense of and learn about their world (Wertsch, 1991). The kit is filled with physical tools such as pencils or paint brushes directed toward the external world and psychological tools such as problem solving or memory strategies for acting mentally. Children do not just receive the tools transmitted to them by others, however. Children transform the tools as they construct their own representations, symbols, patterns, and understandings. As we learned from Piaget, children's constructions of meaning are not the same as those of adults. In the exchange of signs and symbols such as number systems, children create their own understandings (a skunk is a "kitty"). These understandings are gradually changed (a skunk is a skunk) as the children continue to

cultural tools The real tools (computers, scales, etc.) and symbol systems (numbers, language, graphs, etc.) that allow people in a society to communicate, think, solve problems, and create knowledge.

Vygotsky emphasized the tools that particular cultures provide to support thinking and the idea that children use the tools they're given to construct their own understanding of the physical and social worlds.

engage in social activities and try to make sense of their world (John-Steiner & Mahn, 1996; Wertsch, 1991).

In Vygotsky's theory, language is the most important symbol system in the tool kit, and it is the one that helps fill the kit with other tools.

The Role of Language and Private Speech

Language is critical for cognitive development. It provides a means for expressing ideas and asking questions, the categories and concepts for thinking, and the links between the past and the future (Das, 1995; Driscoll, 2005). When we consider a problem, we generally think in words and partial sentences. Vygotsky thought that

> the specifically human capacity for language enables children to provide for auxiliary tools in the solution of difficult tasks, to overcome impulsive action, to plan a solution to a problem prior to its execution, and to master their own behavior. (Vygotsky, 1978, p. 28)

If we study language across cultures, we see that different cultures need and develop different language tools.

Language and Cultural Diversity. In general, cultures develop words for the concepts that are important to them. For example: How many different shades of green or blue can you name? English-speaking countries have over 3000 words for colours. Such words are important in our lives for fashion and home design, artistic expression, films and television, and lipstick and eye shadow choices—to name only a few areas (Price & Crapo, 2002). Other cultures care less about colour. For example, the Hanunoo people of Midori Island in the Philippines or the Dani in New Guinea have fewer than five words for colours, even though they can recognize many colour variations. Inuit really don't have hundreds of words for snow, but the Ulgunigamiut Inuit do have more than 160 words for ice, because they have to recognize ice at different stages of freezing to hunt and live safely in their environment. Anita's mother grew up on a farm in Wisconsin and she can tell you many different words for horse: mare, foal, stallion, gelding, stud, colt, pony, workhorse, jumper. Cultures that care about feelings have many word tools to talk about emotion. Think of the variety of words in English for *anger* (e.g., *rage, resentment, disgust, pique, wrath, fury, exasperation, ire, hostility, animosity*).

Languages change over time to indicate changing cultural needs and values. The Shoshoni Native Americans have one word that means "to make a crunching sound walking on the sand." This word was valuable in the past to communicate about hunting, but today new words describing technical tools have been added to the Shoshoni language, as these people's lives move away from nomadic hunting. As we move into a technological age, think of all the hundreds of words that are related to information technologies, such as PDA, gigabyte, laptop, etc. (Price & Crapo, 2002).

Vygotsky placed more emphasis than Piaget on the role of learning and language in cognitive development. He believed that "thinking deepens on speech, on the means of thinking, and on the child's socio-cultural experience" (Vygotsky, 1987, p. 120). In fact, Vygotsky believed that language in the form of *private speech* (talking to yourself) guides cognitive development.

Private Speech: Vygotsky's and Piaget's Views Compared. If you have spent much time around young children, you know that they often talk to themselves as they play. Piaget called children's self-directed talk "egocentric speech." He assumed that this egocentric speech is another indication that young children can't see the world through the eyes of others. They talk about what matters to them, without taking into account the needs or interests of their listeners. As they mature, and especially as they have disagreements with peers, Piaget believed, children develop socialized speech. They learn to listen and exchange (or argue) ideas. Vygotsky had very different ideas about young children's **private speech**. He suggested that, rather than being a sign of cognitive immaturity, these mutterings play an important role in cognitive development by moving children toward self-regulation—the ability to plan, monitor, and guide one's own thinking and problem solving (see Chapter 8 for a detailed description of this highly effective form of learning).

private speech Children's self-talk, which guides their thinking and action; eventually, these verbalizations are internalized as silent inner speech.

Vygotsky believed that self-regulation developed in a series of stages. First, the child's behaviour is regulated by others, usually parents, using language and other signs such as gestures. For example, the parent says "No!" when the child reaches toward a candle flame. Next, the child learns to regulate the behaviour of others using the same language tools. The child says "No!" to another child who is trying to take away a toy, often even imitating the parent's voice tone. The child also begins to use private speech to regulate her own behaviour, saying "no" quietly to herself as she is tempted to touch the flame. Finally, the child learns to regulate her own behaviour by using silent inner speech (Karpov & Haywood, 1998). For example, in any preschool room, you might hear four- or five-year-olds saying, "No, it won't fit. Try it here. Turn. Turn. Maybe this one!" while they do puzzles. As these children mature, their self-directed speech goes underground, changing from spoken to whispered speech and then to silent lip movements. Finally, the children just "think" the guiding words. The use of private speech peaks at around nine years of age, although one study found that some students from ages 11 to 17 still spontaneously muttered to themselves during problem solving (McCafferty, 2004; Winsler, Carlton, & Barry, 2000; Winsler & Naglieri, 2003).

This series of steps is another example of how higher mental functions appear first between people as they communicate and regulate each other's behaviour—what McCaslin and Good (1996) refer to as co-regulating learning—and then appear again within the individual as a cognitive process. Through this process, the child is using language to accomplish important cognitive activities such as directing attention, solving problems, planning, forming concepts, and gaining self-control. Research supports Vygotsky's ideas (Berk & Spuhl, 1995; Emerson and Miyake, 2003). Children and adults tend to use more private speech when they are confused, having difficulties, or making mistakes (Duncan & Cheyne, 1999). Inner speech not only helps us solve problems but also allows us to regulate our behaviour. Have you ever thought to yourself something like, "Let's see, the first step is ..." or "Where did I use my glasses last?" or "If I work to the end of this page, then I can ..."? You were using inner speech to remind, cue, encourage, or guide yourself. In a really tough situation, such as taking an important test, you might even find that you return to muttering out loud.

Table 2.2 on the next page contrasts Piaget's and Vygotsky's theories of private speech. We should note that Piaget accepted many of Vygotsky's arguments and came to agree that language could be used in both egocentric and problem-solving ways (Piaget, 1962).

Self-Talk and Learning. Because private speech helps students regulate their thinking, it makes sense to allow and even encourage students to use private speech in school. Insisting on total silence when young students are working on difficult problems may make the work even harder for them. You may notice when muttering increases—this could be a sign that students need help. One approach, developed by Donald Meichenbaum at the University of Waterloo, is called *cognitive self-instruction*. It teaches students to use self-talk to guide learning. For example, students learn to give themselves reminders to go slowly and carefully. They "talk themselves through" tasks, saying such things as "Okay, what is it I have to do? ... Copy the picture with the different lines. I have to go slowly and carefully. Okay, draw the line down, down, good; then to the right, that's it; now ..." (Meichenbaum, 1977, p. 32).

TABLE 2.2 Differences between Piaget's and Vygotsky's Theories of Egocentric or Private Speech

	Piaget	Vygotsky
Developmental significance	Represents an inability to take the perspective of another and engage in reciprocal communication	Represents externalized thought; its function is to communicate with the self for the purpose of self-guidance and self-direction
Course of development	Declines with age	Increases at younger ages and then gradually loses its audible quality to become internal verbal thought
Relationship to social speech	Negative; least socially and cognitively mature children use more egocentric speech	Positive; private speech develops out of social interaction with others
Relationship to environmental contexts	—	Increases with task difficulty; private speech serves a helpful self-guiding function in situations where more cognitive effort is needed to reach a solution

Source: From Berk, L. E., & Garvin, R. A. (1984). Development of private speech among low-income Appalachian children. *Developmental Psychology, 20,* 272. Copyright © 1984 by the American Psychological Association. Adapted by permission.

The Zone of Proximal Development

According to Vygotsky, at any given point in development, there are certain problems that a child is on the verge of being able to solve. The child just needs some structure, clues, reminders, help with remembering details or steps, encouragement to keep trying, and so on. Some problems, of course, are beyond the child's capabilities, even if every step is explained clearly. The **zone of proximal development (ZPD)** is the area between the child's current developmental level "as determined by independent problem solving" and the level of development that the child could achieve "through adult guidance or in collaboration with more peers" (Vygotsky, 1978, p. 86).

zone of proximal development Phase at which a child can master a task if given appropriate help and support.

According to Vygotsky, much of children's learning is assisted or mediated by teachers and tools in their environment, and most of this guidance is communicated through language.

Private Speech and the Zone. We can see how Vygotsky's beliefs about the role of private speech in cognitive development fit with the notion of the zone of proximal development. Often, an adult helps a child to solve a problem or accomplish a task using verbal prompts and structuring. This scaffolding may be gradually reduced as the child takes over the guidance, perhaps first by giving the prompts as private speech and finally as inner speech. Let's move forward to a future day in the life of the girl in the earlier example who had lost her toy and *listen to* her thoughts when she realizes that a school book is missing. They might sound something like this:

> "Where's my math book? Used it in class. Thought I put it in my book bag after class. Dropped my bag on the bus. That dope Larry kicked my stuff, so maybe ..."

The girl can now systematically search for ideas about the lost book without help from anyone else.

The Role of Learning and Development

Piaget defined *development* as the active construction of knowledge and *learning* as the passive formation of associations (Siegler, 2000). He was interested in knowledge construction and believed that cognitive development has to come before learning—the child has to be cognitively "ready" to learn. He said that "learning is subordinated to development and not vice-versa" (Piaget, 1964, p. 17). Students can memorize, for example, that Geneva is in Switzerland but still insist that they cannot be Genevan and Swiss at the same time. True understanding will happen only when the child has developed the operation of *class inclusion*—the idea that one category can be included in another. In contrast, Vygotsky believed that learning was an active process that does not have to wait for readiness. In fact, "properly organized learning results in mental development and sets in motion a variety of developmental processes that would be impossible apart from learning" (Vygotsky, 1978, p. 90). He saw learning as a tool in development—learning pulls development up to higher levels, and social interaction is a key in learning (Glassman, 2001; Wink & Putney, 2002). Vygotsky's belief that learning pulls development to higher levels means that other people, including teachers, play a significant role in cognitive development.

Limitations of Vygotsky's Theory

Vygotsky's theory added important considerations by highlighting the role of culture and social processes in cognitive development, but he may have gone too far. As we have seen in this chapter, we may be born with a greater store of cognitive tools than either Piaget or Vygotsky suggested. Some basic understandings, such as the idea that adding increases quantity, may be part of our biological predispositions, ready for use to guide our cognitive development. Young children appear to figure out much about the world before they have the chance to learn from either their culture or teachers (Schunk, 2004). Also, Vygotsky did not detail the cognitive processes underlying developmental changes—which cognitive processes allow students to engage in more advanced and independent participation in social activities? The major limitation of Vygotsky's theory, however, is that it consists mostly of general ideas; Vygotsky died before he could expand and elaborate on his ideas and pursue his research. His students continued to investigate his ideas, but much of that work was suppressed until the 1950s and 1960s by Stalin's regime (Gredler, 2005; Kozulin, 1990, 2003). A final limitation might be that Vygotsky did not have time to detail the applications of his theories for teaching, even though he was very interested in instruction. So most of the applications described today have been created by others—and we don't even know if Vygotsky would agree with them.

Check Your Knowledge

- According to Vygotsky, what are the three main influences on development?
- Explain how interpsychological development becomes intrapsychological development.
- What are some differences between Piaget's and Vygotsky's perspectives on learning and development?

Apply to Practice

- Can you trace the origin of one of your problem-solving strategies to social interactions with parents or teachers? How did you learn?

IMPLICATIONS OF PIAGET'S AND VYGOTSKY'S THEORY FOR TEACHERS

Piaget did not make specific educational recommendations and Vygotsky did not have time to make a complete set of applications. But we can still glean some guidance from both of them.

Piaget: What Can We Learn?

Piaget was more interested in understanding children's thinking than in guiding teachers. He did express some general ideas about educational philosophy, however. He believed that the main goal of education should be to help children learn how to learn, and that education should "form not furnish" the minds of students (Piaget, 1969, p. 70). Piaget has taught us that we can learn a great deal about how children think by listening carefully, by paying close attention to their ways of solving problems. If we understand children's thinking, we will be better able to match teaching methods to children's abilities.

Understanding and Building on Students' Thinking.   The students in any class will vary greatly both in their level of cognitive development and in their academic knowledge. As a teacher, how can you determine whether students are having trouble because they lack the necessary thinking abilities or because they simply have not learned the basic facts? To do this, Robbie Case (1985b) suggested that you observe your students carefully as they try to solve the problems you have presented. What kind of logic do they use? Do they focus on only one aspect of the situation? Are they fooled by appearances? Do they suggest solutions systematically or by guessing and forgetting what they have already tried? Ask your students how they tried to solve the problem. Listen to their strategies. What kind of thinking is behind repeated mistakes or problems? Students are the best sources of information about their own thinking abilities (Confrey, 1990a).

An important implication of Piaget's theory for teaching is what J. M. Hunt years ago (1961) called "the problem of the match." Students must be neither bored by work that is too simple nor left behind by teaching they cannot understand. According to Hunt, disequilibrium must be kept "just right" to encourage growth. Setting up situations that lead to errors can help create an appropriate level of disequilibrium. When students experience some conflict between what they think should happen (a piece of wood should sink because it is big) and what actually happens (it floats!), they may rethink their understanding, and new knowledge may develop.

Many materials and lessons can be understood at several levels and can be "just right" for a range of cognitive abilities. Classics such as *Alice in Wonderland,* myths, and fairy tales can be enjoyed at both concrete and symbolic levels. It is also possible for students to be introduced to a topic together, then work individually on follow-up activities matched to their level. Tom Good and Jere Brophy (2003) describe activity cards for three or four ability levels. These cards provide different readings and assignments, but all are directed toward the overall class objectives. One of the cards should be a good "match" for each student. Often it makes sense to let students choose their own follow-up activities—with encouragement from the teacher to tackle challenges. Using multi-level lessons is called *differentiated instruction* (Tomlinson, 2005b).

Activity and Constructing Knowledge.   Piaget's fundamental insight was that individuals *construct* their own understanding; learning is a constructive process. At every level of cognitive development, you will also want to see that students are actively engaged in the learning process. In his words,

> Knowledge is not a copy of reality. To know an object, to know an event, is not simply to look at it and make a mental copy or image of it. To know an object is to act on it. To know is to modify, to transform the object, and to understand the process of this transformation, and as a consequence to understand the way the object is constructed. (Piaget, 1964, p. 8)

This active experience, even at the earliest school levels, should not be limited to the physical manipulation of objects. It should also include mental manipulation of ideas that arise out of class projects or experiments (Gredler, 2005). For example, after a social studies lesson on different jobs, a primary-grade teacher might show the students a picture of a woman and ask, "What could this person be?" After answers such as "teacher," "doctor," "secretary," "lawyer," "saleswoman," and so on, the teacher could suggest, "How about a daughter?" Answers such as "sister," "mother," "aunt," and "granddaughter" may follow. This should help the children switch dimensions in their classification and centre on another aspect of the situation. Next, the teacher might suggest "Canadian," "jogger," or "blonde." With older children, hierarchical classification might be involved: "It is a picture of a woman, who is a human being; a human being is a primate, which is a mammal, which is an animal, which is a life form."

All students need to interact with teachers and peers in order to test their thinking, to be challenged, to receive feedback, and to watch how others work out problems. Disequilibrium is often set in motion quite naturally when the teacher or another student suggests a new way of thinking about something. As a general rule, students should act, manipulate, observe, and then talk and/or write (to the teacher and each other) about what they have experienced. Concrete experiences provide the raw materials for thinking. Communicating with others makes students use, test, and sometimes change their thinking abilities.

The Value of Play. Maria Montessori once noted, and Piaget would agree, that "play is children's work." We saw that the brain develops with stimulation, and that play provides some of that stimulation at every age. Babies in the sensorimotor stage learn by exploring, sucking, pounding, shaking, throwing—acting on their environments. Preoperational preschoolers love pretend play and through pretending form symbols, use language, and interact with others. They are beginning to play simple games with predictable rules. During their elementary-school years, children also like fantasy, but they are beginning to play more complex games and sports and thus learn cooperation, fairness, negotiation, winning, and losing, as well as developing language. As children grow into adolescents, play continues to be part of their physical and social development (Meece, 2002).

Piaget taught us that children do not think like adults, but discussions about the implications of Piaget's theory often centre on the question of whether cognitive development can be accelerated. The Point/Counterpoint box on page 48 examines this question.

Vygotsky: What Can We Learn?

There are at least three ways in which cultural tools can be passed from one individual to another: imitative learning (where one person tries to imitate the other), instructed learning (where learners internalize the instructions of the teacher and use these instructions to self-regulate), and collaborative learning (where peers strive to understand each other and learning occurs in the process) (Tomasello, Kruger, & Ratner, 1993). Vygotsky was most concerned with instructed learning through direct teaching or through structuring experiences that support another's learning, but his theory supports the other forms of cultural learning as well. Thus, Vygotsky's ideas are relevant for educators who teach directly and who also create learning environments (Das, 1995; Wink & Putney, 2002). One major aspect of teaching in either situation is assisted learning.

The Role of Adults and Peers. Language plays another important role in development. Vygotsky believed that cognitive development occurs through the child's conversations and interactions with more capable members of the culture—adults or more able peers. These people serve as guides and teachers, providing the information and support necessary for the child to grow intellectually. The adult listens carefully to the child and provides just the right help to advance the child's understanding. Thus, the child is not alone in the world "discovering" the cognitive operations of conservation or classification. This discovery is *assisted* or *mediated* by family members, teachers, and peers. Most of this guidance is communicated

CAN COGNITIVE DEVELOPMENT BE ACCELERATED?

Ever since Piaget described his stages of cognitive development, people have asked if progress through the stages could be accelerated. More recently, the question has focused on whether we should accelerate learning for preschoolers and young children at risk of academic failure. Can learning be accelerated, and if so, is this a good idea?

> Point *Every child deserves a head start.*

Some of the strongest arguments in favour of "speeding up" cognitive development are based on the results of cross-cultural studies of children (studies that compare children growing up in different cultures). These results suggest that certain cognitive abilities are indeed influenced by the environment and education. Children of pottery-making families in one area of Mexico, for example, learn conservation of substance earlier than their peers in families that do not make pottery (Ashton, 1978). Furthermore, children in non-Western cultures appear to acquire conservation operations later than children in Western cultures. It seems likely that factors in the environment contribute to the rate of cognitive development.

But even if cognitive development can be accelerated, is this a good idea? Two of the most vocal (and heavily criticized) advocates of early academic training are Siegfried and Therese Engelmann (1981). In their book *Give Your Child a Superior Mind*, they suggest that children who learn academic skills as preschoolers will be smarter throughout their school years, are less likely to fail, and are more likely to enjoy school. They contend,

> Children respond to the environment. Their capacity to learn and what they learn depends on what the environment teaches.... Instead of relying on the traditional environment that is rich in learning opportunities for the child, we can take the environment a step further and mold it into a purposeful instrument that teaches and that guarantees your child will have a superior mind. (p. 10)

< Counterpoint *Acceleration is ineffective and may be harmful.*

The position of psychologists who attempt to apply Piaget's theory to education is that development should not be speeded up. This traditional view has been well summarized by Wadsworth (1978):

> The function of the teacher is not to accelerate the development of the child or speed up the rate of movement from stage to stage. The function of the teacher is to insure that development within each stage is thoroughly integrated and complete. (p. 117)

According to Piaget, cognitive development is based on the self-selected actions and thoughts of the student, not on the teacher's action. If you try to teach a student something the student is not ready to learn, he or she may learn to give the "correct" answer. But this will not really affect the way the student thinks about this problem. Therefore, why spend a long time teaching something at one stage when students will learn it by themselves much more rapidly and thoroughly at another stage?

Today, the pressure is on parents and preschool teachers to create "superkids," three-year-olds who read, write, and speak a second language. David Elkind (1991) asserts that pushing children can be harmful. He believes that preschool children who are given formal instruction in academic subjects often show signs of stress, such as headaches. These children may become dependent on adults for guidance. Early focus on "right" and "wrong" answers can lead to competition and loss of self-esteem. Elkind asserts,

> The miseducation of young children, so prevalent in the United States today, ignores well-founded and non-controversial differences between early education and formal education. As educators, our first task is to reassert this difference and insist on its importance. (p. 31)

scaffolding Support for learning and problem solving; the support could be clues, reminders, encouragement, breaking the problem down into steps, providing an example, or anything else that allows the student to grow in independence as a learner.

through language, at least in Western cultures. In some cultures, observing a skilled performance, not talking about it, guides the child's learning (Rogoff, 1990). Jerome Bruner called this adult assistance **scaffolding** (Wood, Bruner, & Ross, 1976). The term aptly suggests that children use this help for support while they build a firm understanding that will eventually allow them to solve the problems on their own. The accompanying Reaching Every Student feature gives an example of using scaffolding.

Assisted Learning.   Vygotsky's theory suggests that teachers need to do more than just arrange the environment so that students can discover on their own. He believed that children cannot and should not be expected to reinvent or rediscover knowledge already available in their cultures. Rather, they should be guided and assisted in their learning—so, Vygotsky saw teachers, parents, and other adults as central to the child's learning and development (Karpov & Haywood, 1998).

SCAFFOLDING LEARNING

Here is an example of how a teacher named Tamara supported her students' learning about math concepts and problem solving:

> Tamara announces, "To prepare for our museum trip, there's something very important I need to do: Write a check for our entrance fees." She tears a check from a checkbook and holds it up. "It's two dollars a person, and we have twenty-two children. How much would that be?"
>
> When none of the children responds, Tamara modifies her question: "How much for ten people to get into the museum? Let's have ten people stand up so we can see." Tamara asks Kara to tap ten people on the shoulder. After they form a line she continues, "Now, if each ticket costs two dollars and we have ten people, how much will it cost? How could we find out?"

> Several children chorus, "We can count by twos!"
>
> Tamara nods and says, "Let's count," as she taps each child in the line. When she reaches "twenty" she asks ten more people to stand. The children continue counting, reaching "forty."
>
> "Now, our last two people. Randy and Michael, please stand up."
>
> A child calls out, "Forty-four dollars in all. That's a lot!" Tamara writes the check, pointing out the dollar signs, followed by numerals 4-4. (Berk, 2001, pp. 186–187)

The scaffolding that Tamara provided—making the problem more concrete, breaking it into steps, using the students as "counters," using the familiar process of counting by twos—allowed her students to understand and solve this problem that they could not solve alone.

Assisted learning, or guided participation in the classroom, requires scaffolding—giving information, prompts, reminders, and encouragement at the right time and in the right amounts, and then gradually allowing the students to do more and more on their own. Teachers can assist learning by adapting materials or problems to students' current levels; demonstrating skills or thought processes; walking students through the steps of a complicated problem; doing part of the problem (for example, in algebra, the students set up the equation and the teacher does the calculations or vice versa); giving detailed feedback and allowing revisions; or asking questions that refocus students' attention (Rosenshine & Meister, 1992). Meichenbaum's cognitive self-instruction described earlier is an example of assisted learning. Cognitive apprenticeships, reciprocal teaching, and instructional conversations (described in Chapter 9) are other examples. Table 2.3 on the next page gives examples of strategies that can be used in any lesson.

assisted learning Learning by having strategic help provided in the initial stages; the help gradually diminishes as students gain independence.

Teaching with Technology. Vygotsky's sociocultural perspective has had a great influence on developing strategies for enhancing learning using computer technology. The advancement of information technology in our society has greatly increased the opportunity for social interaction. In fact, between talking or texting on cell phones, instant messaging, and emailing, today's children can be constantly connected to their peer groups (Rideout, Roberts, & Foehr, 2005). As noted earlier, Vygotsky felt that humans use tools, such as speech and writing, to learn from their social environments. Learning theorists have begun to view the computer, and in particular the social connectivity of this technology, as a tool that can be harnessed to create powerful learning environments. The underlying notion is that students will have unique opportunities to collaborate and share their ideas with other learners. Sometimes they also interact with these learners in face-to-face settings, while at other times they may know them only in an online capacity.

In fact, online courses are becoming more and more common at the postsecondary level. A frequently used instructional strategy that has been developed to supplement classroom learning is called a *webquest*. A webquest is an internet-based activity that focuses on a central question. The question is real, relevant, and frequently complex, inviting examination from multiple perspectives and requiring

Sometimes, the best teachers are other students who have just understood a particular concept. These "teachers" may be engaging in reciprocal teaching.

TABLE 2.3 Assisted Learning: Strategies to Scaffold Complex Learning

- *Using procedural facilitators.* These provide a "scaffold" to help students learn implicit skills. For example, a teacher might encourage students to use "signal words" such as *who, what, where, when, why,* and *how* to generate questions after reading a passage.

- *Modelling use of facilitators.* The teacher, in the above example, might model the generation of questions about the reading.

- *Thinking out loud.* This models the teacher's expert thought processes, showing students the revisions and choices the learner makes in using procedural facilitators to work on problems.

- *Anticipating difficult areas.* During the modelling and presentations phase of instruction, for example, the teacher anticipates and discusses potential student errors.

- *Providing prompt or cue cards.* Procedural facilitators are written on "prompt cards" that students

keep for reference as they work. As students practise, the cards gradually become unnecessary.

- *Regulating the difficulty.* Tasks involving implicit skills are introduced by beginning with simpler problems, providing for student practice after each step, and gradually increasing the complexity of the task.

- *Providing half-done examples.* Giving students half-done examples of problems and having them work out the conclusions can be an effective way to teach them how to ultimately solve problems on their own.

- *Utilizing reciprocal teaching.* This means having the teacher and students rotate the role of teacher. The teacher provides support to students as they learn to lead discussions and ask their own questions.

- *Providing checklists.* Students can be taught self-checking procedures to help them regulate the quality of their responses.

Source: From Association for Supervision and Curriculum Development. (1990). Effective teaching redux. *ASCD Update, 32*(6), 5. Reprinted by permission of the Association for Supervision and Curriculum Development. Copyright © 1990 by ASCD. All rights reserved.

higher-order thinking skills. To answer the question, students must draw on each other as well as from resources from the internet (Fiedler, 2002). Dr. Bernie Dodge, who developed webquests, maintains a website (**http://webquest.sdsu.edu**) with examples and guidelines for implementing these in your teaching.

The following Guidelines give more pointers for applying Vygotsky's ideas.

GUIDELINES
APPLYING VYGOTSKY'S IDEAS IN TEACHING

Tailor scaffolding to the needs of students.

EXAMPLES

1. When students are beginning new tasks or topics, provide models, prompts, sentence starters, coaching, and feedback. As the students grow in competence, give less support and more opportunities for independent work.

2. Give students choices about the level of difficulty or degree of independence in projects; encourage them to challenge themselves but to seek help when they are really stuck.

Make sure that students have access to powerful tools that support thinking.

EXAMPLES

1. Teach students to use learning and organizational strategies, research tools, language tools (diction-

aries or computer searches), spreadsheets, and word-processing programs.

2. Model the use of tools; show students how you use an appointment book or electronic notebook to make plans and manage time, for example.

Capitalize on dialogue and group learning.

EXAMPLES

1. Experiment with peer tutoring; teach students how to ask good questions and give helpful explanations.

2. Experiment with cooperative learning strategies described in Chapters 9 and 11, including using the internet to create communities of learners.

Check Your Knowledge

- What is the "problem of the match" described by Hunt?
- What is active learning? Why is Piaget's theory of cognitive development consistent with active learning?
- What is assisted learning, and what role does scaffolding play?

Apply to Practice

- In the situation at the beginning of the chapter, how would you use peer learning to move students toward an understanding of symbolism?

Clearly, language plays a major role in learning, inside and outside the classroom. Let's look at this human capability more closely.

THE DEVELOPMENT OF LANGUAGE

All children in every culture master the complicated system of their native language, unless severe deprivation or physical problems interfere. This knowledge is remarkable. At the least, sounds, meanings, words and sequences of words, volume, voice tone, inflection, and turn-taking rules must all be coordinated before a child can communicate effectively in conversations.

It is likely that many factors—biological and experiential—play a role in language development. We saw earlier that culture plays a major role in determining what language tools are necessary in the life of the people. The important point is that children develop language as they develop other cognitive abilities by actively trying to make sense of what they hear and by looking for patterns and making up rules to put together the jigsaw puzzle of language. In this process, humans may have built-in biases, rules, and constraints about language that restrict the number of possibilities considered. For example, young children seem to have a constraint specifying that a new label refers to a whole object, not just a part. Another built-in bias leads children to assume that the label refers to a class of similar objects. So the child learning about the rabbit is equipped naturally to assume that *rabbit* refers to the whole animal (not just its ears) and that other similar-looking animals are also rabbits (Markman, 1992). Reward and correction play a role in helping children learn correct language use, but the child's thinking in putting together the parts of this complicated system is very important (Flavell et al., 2002). Table 2.4 on the next page shows the milestones of language development, ages one to six, in Western cultures, along with ideas for encouraging development.

Diversity in Language: Dual Language Development

In 2001, 61 percent of Canada's immigrants reported speaking a language other than French or English in their homes (Statistics Canada, 2001). In Vancouver, the rate was even higher (73 percent). The addition of immigrant children in schools challenges teachers and school boards, who must find ways of helping these students learn.

It is important to know that learning a second language does not interfere with understanding in the first language. In fact, according to Jim Cummins at the University of Toronto, the more proficient the speaker is in the first language, the more quickly she or he will master a second language (Cummins, 1984, 1994). For most children who learn two languages simultaneously as toddlers, there is a period between ages two and three when they progress more slowly because they have not yet figured out that they are learning two different languages. They may mix up the grammar of the two. But researchers believe that by age four, if they have enough exposure to both languages, they get things straight and speak as well as native monolinguals, that is, people who speak only one language (Baker, 1993;

TABLE 2.4 Milestones in Language in the First Six Years and Ways to Encourage Development

Age Range	Milestone	Strategies to Encourage Development
By age 1	Says 1–2 words; recognizes name; imitates familiar sounds; understands simple instructions	• Respond to coos, gurgles, and babbling. • Tell nursery rhymes and sing songs. • Teach the names of everyday items and familiar people. • Play simple games such as peek-a-boo and pat-a-cake.
Between 1 and 2	Uses 5–20 words, including names, says 2-word sentences; vocabulary is growing; waves goodbye; makes "sounds" of familiar animals; uses words (like "more") to make wants known; understands "no"	• Reward and encourage early efforts at saying new words. • Talk about everything you're doing while you're with the child. • Talk simply, clearly, and slowly. • Look at the child when he or she talks to you. • Describe what the child is doing, feeling, hearing. • Let the child listen to children's records and tapes.
Between 2 and 3	Identifies body parts; calls self "me" instead of name; combines nouns and verbs; has a 450-word vocabulary; uses short sentences; matches 3–4 colours, knows "big" and "little"; likes to hear same story repeated; forms some plurals; answers "where" questions	• Help the child listen and follow instructions by playing simple games. • Repeat new words over and over. • Describe what you are doing, planning, thinking. • Have the child deliver simple messages for you. • Show the child you understand what he or she says by answering, smiling, and nodding your head. • Expand what the child says. Child: "More juice." You say, "Chris wants more juice."
Between 3 and 4	Can tell a story; sentence length of 4–5 words; vocabulary about 1000 words; knows last name, name of street, several nursery rhymes	• Talk about how objects are the same or different. • Help the child to tell stories using books and pictures. • Encourage play with other children. • Talk about places where you've been or will be going.
Between 4 and 5	Sentence length of 4–5 words; uses past tense; vocabulary of about 1500 words; identifies colours, shapes; asks many questions like "why?" and "who?"	• Help the child sort objects and things (e.g., things to eat, animals). • Teach the child how to use the telephone. • Let the child help you plan activities. • Continue talking about the child's interests. • Let the child tell and make up stories for you.
Between 5 and 6	Sentence length of 5–6 words; average 6-year-old has vocabulary of about 10 000 words; defines objects by their use; knows spatial relations (like "on top" and "far") and opposites; knows address; understands "same" and "different"; uses all types of sentences	• Praise children when they talk about feelings, thoughts, hopes, fears. • Sing songs, rhymes. • Talk with them as you would an adult.
At every age		• Listen and show your pleasure when the child talks to you. • Carry on conversations with the child. • Ask questions to get the child to think and talk. • Read books to the child every day, increasing in length as the child develops.

Source: Adapted from www.ldonline.org/ld_indepth/speech-language/lda_milestones.html and www.med.umich.edu/1libr/yourchild/devmile.htm.

Reich, 1986). Also, bilingual children may mix vocabularies of the two languages when they speak, but this is not a sign that they are confused, since their bilingual parents often intentionally mix vocabularies as well. It takes from three to five years to become truly competent in a second language (Berk, 2002; Bhatia & Richie, 1999).

It is also important to note that it is a misconception that young children learn a second language faster than adolescents or adults. In fact, older students go through the stages of language learning faster than young children. Adults have more learning strategies and greater knowledge of language in general to bring to bear in mastering a second language (Diaz-Rico & Weed, 2002). Age is a factor in learning language, but "not because of any critical period that limits the possibility of language learning by adults" (Marinova-Todd, Marshall, & Snow, 2000, p. 28). However, it appears that there is a critical period for learning accurate language pronunciation. The earlier people learn a second language, the more their pronunciation is near-native. After adolescence, it is difficult to learn a new language without speaking with an accent (Anderson & Graham, 1994). Kathleen Berger (2006) concludes that the best time to *teach* a second language is during early or middle childhood, but the best time to *learn* on your own through exposure (and to learn native pronunciation) is early childhood.

The more proficient speakers are in their first language, the faster they will learn a second language.

There is no cognitive penalty for students who learn and speak two languages. In fact, there are benefits. Higher degrees of bilingualism are correlated with increased cognitive abilities in such areas as concept formation, creativity, and cognitive flexibility. In addition, these students have more advanced metalinguistic awareness; for example, they are more likely to notice grammatical errors. These findings seem to hold as long as there is no stigma attached to being bilingual and as long as students are not expected to abandon their first language to learn the second (Berk, 2005; Bialystok, 1999; Galambos Goldin-Meadow, 1990; Garcia, 1992).

Despite the advantages of speaking two languages, many children and adults are losing their heritage languages. This is particularly problematic for many First Nation peoples whose intergenerational language transmission ceased as a result of the children being sent to residential schools during the first half of the 20th century. Dr. Nicole Rosen at the University of Lethbridge is currently attempting to document one such language, called Michif, which is spoken by a few hundred Métis in Saskatchewan and Manitoba. As part of these efforts, she is involved in a language revitalization project with the Manitoba Métis Federation. The revitalization process follows a multi-pronged approach, with language learning targeted to both adults and children and taking place in both school and the home (Rosen, 2004).

Language Development in the School Years

By about age five or six, most children have mastered the basics of their native language. What remains for the school-aged child to accomplish?

Pronunciation. The majority of grade 1 students have mastered most of the sounds of their native language, but a few may remain unconquered. The *j, v, th,* and *zh* sounds are the last to develop. About 10 percent of 8-year-olds still have some trouble with *s, z, v, th,* and *zh* (Rathus, 1988). Young children may understand and be able to use many words but prefer to use the words they can pronounce easily.

Grammar. Children master the basics of word order, or **syntax**, in their native language early. But the more complicated forms, such as the passive voice ("The car was hit by the truck"), take longer to master. By early elementary school, many

syntax The order of words in phrases or sentences.

children can understand the meaning of passive sentences, yet they do not use such constructions in their normal conversations. Other accomplishments during elementary school include first understanding and then using complex grammatical structures such as extra clauses, qualifiers, and conjunctions. In adolescence, students can understand and use more elaborate grammatical constructions—clauses, connecting words, longer sentences, and so on (Berk, 2005).

Vocabulary and Meaning.   The average six-year-old has a vocabulary of 8000 to 14 000 words, growing to about 40 000 by age 11. In fact, some researchers estimate that students in the early grades learn up to 20 words a day (Berger, 2003). School-aged children enjoy language games and jokes that play on words. In the early elementary years, some children may have trouble with abstract words such as *justice* or *economy*. They also may not understand the subjunctive case ("If I were a butterfly ...") because they lack the cognitive ability to reason about things that are not true ("But you aren't a butterfly ..."). They may take statements literally and thus misunderstand sarcasm or metaphor. Fairy tales are understood concretely simply as stories instead of as moral lessons, for example. Many children are in their preadolescent years before they are able to distinguish being kidded from being taunted or before they know that a sarcastic remark is not meant to be taken literally. By adolescence, students are able to use their developing cognitive abilities to learn abstract word meanings and use poetic, figurative language (Berger, 2003; Gardner, 1982).

pragmatics Knowledge about how to use language—when, where, how, and to whom to speak.

Pragmatics.   **Pragmatics** involves the appropriate use of language to communicate. For instance, children must learn the rules of turn-taking in conversation. Young children may appear to take turns in conversations, but if you listen in, you realize that they are not exchanging information, only talk time. In later elementary school, children's conversations start to sound like conversations. Contributions are usually on the same topic. Also, by middle childhood, students understand that an observation can be a command, as in, "I see too many children at the pencil sharpener." By adolescence, individuals are very adept at varying their language style to fit the situation. So they can talk to their peers in slang that makes little sense to adults, but marks the adolescent as a member of the group. Yet these same students can speak politely to adults (especially when making requests) and write persuasively about a topic in history. As students grow older, they become more adept at judging whether their communications are clear to their audiences (Berk, 2005).

metalinguistic awareness Understanding about one's own use of language.

Metalinguistic Awareness.   Around the age of five, students begin to develop **metalinguistic awareness**. This means that their understanding of language and how it works becomes explicit. They have knowledge about language itself. They are ready to study and extend the rules that have been implicit—understood but not consciously expressed. This process continues throughout life, as we all become better able to manipulate and comprehend language. In Chapter 12, we describe how teachers can develop the language and literacy abilities of their students.

Partnerships with Families

Especially in the early years, the students' home experiences are central in the development of language and literacy (Roskos & Neuman, 1993; Snow, 1993; Whitehurst et al., 1994). In homes that promote literacy, parents and other adults value reading as a source of pleasure, and there are books and other printed materials everywhere. Parents read to their children, take them to bookstores and libraries, limit the amount of television everyone watches, and encourage literacy-related play, such as setting up a pretend school or writing "letters" (Pressley, 1996; Roskos & Neuman, 1998; Sulzby & Teale, 1991). Of course, not all homes provide this literacy-rich environment, but teachers can help, as you can see in the accompanying Family and Community Partnerships box.

PROMOTING LITERACY

Communicate with families about the goals and activities of your program.

EXAMPLES

1. At the beginning of the school year, send home a description of the goals to be achieved in your class. Make sure it is in a clear and readable format.

2. As you start each unit, send home a newsletter describing what students will be studying. Give suggestions for home activities that support the learning.

Involve families in decisions about curriculum.

EXAMPLES

1. Have planning workshops at times when family members can attend; provide child care for younger siblings, but let children and families work together on projects.

2. Invite parents to come to class to read to students, take dictation of stories, tell stories, record or bind books, and demonstrate skills.

Provide home activities to be shared with family members.

EXAMPLES

1. Encourage family members to work with children to read and follow simple recipes, play language games, keep diaries or journals for the family, and visit the library. Get feedback from families or students about the activities.

2. Give families feedback sheets and ask them to help evaluate the child's school work.

3. Provide lists of good children's literature that is available locally—work with libraries, clubs, and religious institutions to identify sources.

Source: From Morrow, L. M. (1997). *Literacy development in the early years: Helping children read and write* (3rd ed., pp. 68–70). Boston: Allyn & Bacon. Copyright © 1997 by Allyn & Bacon. Adapted by permission.

Check Your Knowledge

- How are humans predisposed to develop language? What role does learning play?
- What are pragmatics and metalinguistic awareness?

Apply to Practice

- Name two things you could do to form literacy partnerships with your students' families.
- How could you elaborate on and extend Trevor's understanding of "symbolism" (described at the beginning of this chapter)?

SUMMARY

A Definition of Development (pp. 22–26)

What are the different kinds of development?

Human development can be divided into physical development (changes in the body), personal development (changes in an individual's personality), social development (changes in the way an individual relates to others), and cognitive development (changes in thinking).

What are three principles of development?

Theorists generally agree that people develop at different rates, that development is an orderly process, and that development takes place gradually.

What part of the brain is associated with higher mental functions?

The cortex is a crumpled sheet of neurons that serves three major functions: receiving signals from sense organs (such as visual or auditory signals), controlling vol-

untary movement, and forming associations. The part of the cortex that controls physical motor movement develops or matures first, followed by the areas that control complex senses such as vision and hearing, and then the frontal lobe that controls higher-order thinking processes.

What is lateralization and why is it important?

Lateralization is the specialization of the two sides, or hemispheres, of the brain. The brain begins to lateralize soon after birth. For most people, the left hemisphere is the major factor in language, and the right hemisphere is prominent in spatial and visual processing. Even though certain functions are associated with certain parts of the brain, the various parts and systems of the brain work together to learn and perform complex activities such as reading and to construct understanding.

Piaget's Theory of Cognitive Development
(pp. 26–39)

What are the main influences on cognitive development?

Piaget's theory of cognitive development is based on the assumption that people try to make sense of the world and actively create knowledge through direct experience with objects, people, and ideas. Maturation, activity, social transmission, and the need for equilibrium all influence the way thinking processes and knowledge develop. In response to these influences, thinking processes and knowledge develop through changes in the organization of thought (the development of schemes) and through adaptation—including the complementary processes of assimilation (incorporating new information into existing schemes) and accommodation (changing existing schemes).

What are schemes?

Schemes are the basic building blocks of thinking. They are organized systems of actions or thought that allow us to mentally represent or "think about" the objects and events in our world. Schemes may be very small and specific (grasping, recognizing a square), or they may be larger and more general (using a map in a new city). People adapt to their environment as they increase and organize their schemes.

As children move from sensorimotor to formal-operational thinking, what are the major changes?

Piaget believed that young people pass through four stages as they develop: sensorimotor, preoperational, concrete-operational, and formal-operational. In the sensorimotor stage, infants explore the world through their senses and motor activity and work toward mastering object permanence and performing goal-directed activities. In the preoperational stage, symbolic thinking and logical operations begin. Children in the stage of concrete operations can think logically about tangible situations and can demonstrate conservation, reversibility, classification, and seriation. The ability to perform hypothetico-deductive reasoning, coordinate a set of variables, and imagine other worlds marks the stage of formal operations.

How do neo-Piagetian and information-processing views explain changes in children's thinking over time?

Information-processing theories focus on attention, memory capacity, learning strategies, and other processing skills to explain how children develop rules and strategies for making sense of the world and solving problems. Neo-Piagetian approaches also look at attention, memory, and strategies and at how thinking develops in different domains such as numbers or spatial relations.

Vygotsky's Sociocultural Perspective
(pp. 39–45)

According to Vygotsky, what are three main influences on cognitive development?

Vygotsky believed that human activities must be understood in their cultural settings. He believed that our specific mental structures and processes can be traced to our interactions with others; that the tools of the culture, especially the tool of language, are key factors in development; and that the zone of proximal development is the area where learning and development are possible.

What are psychological tools and why are they important?

Psychological tools are signs and symbol systems such as numbers and mathematical systems, codes, and language that supports learning and cognitive development—they change the thinking process by enabling and shaping thinking. Many of these tools are passed from adult to child through formal and informal interactions and teachings.

Explain how interpsychological development becomes intrapsychological development.

Higher mental processes appear first between people as they are co-constructed during shared activities. As children engage in activities with adults or more capable peers, they exchange ideas and ways of thinking about or representing concepts. These co-created ideas are internalized by children. Thus children's knowledge, ideas, attitudes, and values develop through appropriating, or "taking for themselves," the ways of acting and thinking provided by their culture and by the more capable members of their group.

What are the differences between Piaget's and Vygotsky's perspectives on private speech and its role in development?

Vygotsky's sociocultural view asserts that cognitive development hinges on social interaction and the development of language. As an example, Vygotsky described the role of children's self-directed talk in guiding and monitoring thinking and problem solving, while Piaget suggested that private speech was an indication of the child's egocentrism.

Vygotsky, more than Piaget, emphasized the significant role played by adults and more able peers in children's learning. This adult assistance provides early support while students build the understanding necessary to solve problems on their own.

Implications of Piaget's and Vygotsky's Theories for Teachers
(pp. 45–51)

What is the "problem of the match" described by Hunt?

The "problem of the match" is that students must be neither bored by work that is too simple nor left behind by teaching they cannot understand. According to Hunt, disequilibrium must be carefully balanced to encourage growth. Situations that lead to errors can help create an appropriate level of disequilibrium.

What is active learning? Why is Piaget's theory of cognitive development consistent with active learning?

Piaget's fundamental insight was that individuals *construct* their own understanding; learning is a constructive process. At every level of cognitive development, students must be able to incorporate information into their own schemes. To do this, they must act on the information in some way. This active experience, even at the earliest school levels, should include both physical manipulation of objects and mental manipulation of ideas. As a general rule, students should act, manipulate, observe, and then talk and/or write about what they have experienced. Concrete experiences provide the raw materials for thinking. Communicating with others makes students use, test, and sometimes change their thinking abilities.

What is assisted learning, and what role does scaffolding play?

Assisted learning, or guided participation in the classroom, requires scaffolding—giving information, prompts, reminders, and encouragement at the right time and in the right amounts, and then gradually allowing the students to do more and more on their own. Teachers can assist learning by adapting materials or problems to students' current levels, demonstrating skills or thought processes, walking students through the steps of a complicated problem, doing part of the problem, giving detailed feedback and allowing revisions, or asking questions that refocus students' attention.

The Development of Language
(pp. 51–55)

How are humans predisposed to develop language? What role does learning play?

Children develop language as they develop other cognitive abilities by actively trying to make sense of what they hear, looking for patterns, and making up rules. In this process, built-in biases and rules may limit the search and guide the pattern recognition. Reward and correction play a role in helping children learn correct language use, but the child's thought processes are very important. Metalinguistic awareness begins around age five or six and grows throughout life.

What are pragmatics and metalinguistic awareness?

Pragmatics is knowledge about how to use language—when, where, how, and to whom to speak. Metalinguistic awareness begins around age five or six and grows throughout life.

KEY TERMS

accommodation, p. 28

adaptation, p. 27

adolescent egocentrism,
  p. 35

assimilation, p. 28

assisted learning, p. 49

classification, p. 31

co-constructed, p. 40

cognitive development,
  p. 22

collective monologue,
  p. 31

compensation, p. 31

concrete operations, p. 31

conservation, p. 30

cultural tools, p. 41

decentring, p. 30, 31

development, p. 22

disequilibrium, p. 28

egocentric, p. 31

equilibration, p. 28

formal operations, p. 33

goal-directed actions,
  p. 29

hypothetico-deductive
  reasoning, p. 34

identity, p. 31

lateralization, p. 25

maturation, p. 22

metalinguistic awareness,
  p. 54

myelination, p. 24

neo-Piagetian theories,
  p. 36

neurons, p. 23

object permanence, p. 29

operations, p. 30

organization, p. 27

physical development,
  p. 22

plasticity, p. 24

pragmatics p. 54

BECOMING A PROFESSIONAL

Reflecting on the Chapter

Can you apply the ideas from this chapter on cognitive development to solve the following problems of practice?

Preschool and Kindergarten

A group of vocal parents wants you to introduce workbooks to teach basic arithmetic in your class for four- and five-year-olds. They seem to think that "play" with blocks, water, sand, clay, and so on, is "wasted time." How would you respond?

Elementary and Middle School

Two very concerned parents want to have a conference with you about their son's "language problems." He is in grade 1 and has some trouble with pronunciation. How would you prepare for the conference?

Junior High and High School

The students in your class persist in memorizing definitions for many of the important abstract concepts in your class. They insist, "that's what you have to do to make a good grade in this class." Even though they can repeat the definitions precisely, they seem to have no conception of what the terms mean; they can't recognize examples of the concept in problems or give their own examples. It is almost as if they don't believe that there is any real hope of understanding the ideas. Pick one important, difficult concept in your field and design a lesson to teach it to students who believe only in memorization.

Check Your Understanding

- Be clear about the three basic principles of development.

- Make sure that you understand the elements of Piaget's theory (assimilation, accommodation, equilibration, schemes) and his four stages of cognitive development.

- From Vygotsky's theory, be familiar with the ideas of zone of proximal development and assisted learning. Also, be clear about how private speech supports cognitive development.

Your Teaching Portfolio

Think about your philosophy of teaching, a question you will be asked at most job interviews. What do you believe about matching teaching to students' current level of development? Are Piaget's ideas related to "readiness to learn"? What are the roles of direct teaching and discovery in students' learning? Do Piaget and Vygotsky lead you to different philosophies?

Add some ideas for parent involvement from this chapter to your portfolio.

Teaching Resources

Adapt Table 2.3, "Assisted Learning: Strategies to Scaffold Complex Learning" (page 50), for the grades and subjects you might teach and add it to your teaching resources file.

Teachers' Casebook

What Would They Do?

Here is how two practising teachers responded to the teaching situation presented at the beginning of this chapter about teaching abstract concepts such as "symbol."

Janet E. Gettings
Elementary Educator
Willoughby Elementary School
Langley, British Columbia
Faculty Adviser and Sessional Instructor,
University of British Columbia

The students of the class have indicated a need for scaffolded learning to enhance their understanding of the concept of symbolism.

To introduce the concept, I would build on the children's prior knowledge of homonyms by doing a quick review of commonly used word pairs, such as bear/bare, stare/stair, I/eye, pair/pear, two/to/too, followed by cymbal/symbol. With the latter example, I would explain that Tracy had defined "cymbal." I would then invite suggestions for "symbol," summarizing with a formal definition, such as "something that stands for or represents something else."

I would follow the discussion with a "Think, Pair, Share" activity. Students would be asked to think about symbols independently, then pair with a partner to share ideas. Next, the partners would be invited to go on a "detective search" of the room and their desks for symbols they could share with the class. For example, when I hang an umbrella on the door, students know they can stay in the classroom at lunch.

Another follow-up activity would be a modified game of Pictionary. The class would be divided into teams of five or six and take turns being artists. Each team would send a student to the teacher to view a phrase, which the student then has to represent pictorially. Sample phrases might include "the house had not been lived in for a long time," "her face reflected pain and sadness."

At this stage, the students might be ready to move to usage of symbolism in written language. Sections of a familiar novel that includes symbolic phrases to describe feelings and emotions could be shared. For example, the phrase "thunderclouds passed over her face" describes the feelings of a character in a story in language that students understand easily. I would engage the class in a discussion to share the author's message and intent.

Reading aloud humorous poetry, such as that of Jack Prelutsky, might be used to move toward the final goal of identifying the use of symbolism in poetry. Students could demonstrate their understanding by researching the use of symbolic language in the genre of poetry and by writing their own poems, incorporating symbolism into their products.

Mary Lightly
Terry Fox Secondary School
Port Coquitlam, British Columbia

In planning activities for the classroom, I try to be mindful of research on effective teaching. In particular, I draw on the work of Anita Archer at the University of Oregon and Barrie Bennet at the University of Toronto. Both these researchers have written texts that summarize current research, and both relate that research to actual classroom situations.

To develop the concept of symbol, I would first design activities in which students could engage independently or in small groups. For example, I might engage students in a matching activity that requires them to identify the symbolic meaning of concrete, or real-life, objects. I might create a worksheet that includes two lists: one list would include real-world objects, such as a dove or a heart (this list might be presented as pictures); the second list would include descriptions of the symbolic meaning for each object. Students would match the picture of the dove with peace, and the picture of the heart with love. I might ask students to generate their own symbols. For example, a red rose could symbolize passion, a sword could symbolize war. Students could colour their images and display them in the classroom as a reminder of how real-life objects can have symbolic meaning.

After introducing the concept in this manner, I would take the class through one or two concept attainment lessons, a strategy in which students are presented with "yes" and "no" examples of a concept, in this case examples and non-examples of symbols and/or symbolism. I would begin with very clear and simple examples and then increase the level of difficulty as students become more confident and skilled at recognizing symbols and symbolism.

It might take many trials and a variety of strategies, but eventually students would be ready to look for symbolic meaning in literature.

3 PERSONAL, SOCIAL, AND EMOTIONAL DEVELOPMENT

Pushball, Pavel Kusnetov. Art © Estate of Pavel Kusnetsov/RAO, Moscow/VAGA, New York. Photo: Art Resource/New York.

Teachers' Casebook

What Would You Do?

You have seen it before, but this year the situation in your middle school classroom seems especially vicious. A clique of popular girls has made life miserable for one of their former friends, Stephanie, who is now rejected. Stephanie committed the social sins of not fitting in—wearing the wrong clothes or not being pretty enough or not being interested in boys yet. To keep the status distinctions clear between themselves and Stephanie, the popular girls spread gossip about their former friend, often disclosing the intimate secrets revealed when Stephanie was still considered a close friend, which was only a few months ago. However, these girls are not using traditional way of spreading gossip—instead of passing notes or whispering in the hallways, they are using the internet to humiliate Stephanie. First they forwarded a long, heart-baring email from Stephanie to her former best friend Alison to the entire school. More recently, one of them used a cell phone to take a picture of Stephanie while she was changing after gym class and then emailed it around to the whole school. Stephanie has been absent for three days since this latest incident.

Critical Thinking

- How would you respond to the girls? Would you say anything to your other students? What?

- In your teaching, are there ways you can address the issues raised by this situation? Reflecting on your years in school, were your experiences more like those of Alison or Stephanie?

Collaboration

With three or four other students in your class, role-play a talk with Stephanie, Alison, or their families. Take turns playing the different roles in your group.

Schooling involves more than cognitive development. As you remember your years in school, what stands out—memories of academic knowledge or memories of feelings, friendships, and fears? In this chapter, we examine personal, social, and moral development.

We begin with a basic aspect of development that affects all the others—physical changes as students mature. Next we turn to the work of Erik Erikson and Urie Bronfenbrenner, whose comprehensive theories provide a framework for studying personal and social development. We then consider three major influences on children's personal and social development: families, peers, and schools. Families today have gone through many transitions, and these changes affect the roles of teachers. Next, we explore ideas about how we come to understand ourselves, by looking at self-concept and identity, including ethnic and sexual identity. Finally, we look at emotional and moral development. What factors determine our views about morality? What can teachers do to nurture honesty, cooperation, empathy, and self-esteem? We end the chapter by examining several risks that confront students today, such as child abuse, eating disorders, and drugs.

By the time you have completed this chapter, you should be able to answer these questions:

- *How does physical development affect personal and social development in adolescence?*

- *What are Erikson's stages of psychosocial development, and what are the implications of his theory for teaching?*

- *How does Bronfenbrenner's framework describe the social systems that influence development?*
- *What are the roles of peers, cliques, and friendships in students' lives?*
- *What can teachers do to deal with aggression and bullying in schools?*
- *How do relationships with teachers support student development?*
- *What are Kohlberg's stages of moral reasoning, and what are some of the challenges to his work?*
- *What encourages cheating and aggression in classrooms, and how can teachers respond to each problem?*

PHYSICAL DEVELOPMENT

For most children, at least in the early years, growing up means getting bigger, stronger, more coordinated. It also can be a frightening, disappointing, exciting, and puzzling time.

The Preschool Years

Preschool children are very active. Their gross-motor (large muscle) skills improve greatly over the years from ages two to five. Between ages two and about four or five, preschoolers' muscles grow stronger, their balance improves, and their centre of gravity moves lower, so they are able to run, jump, climb, and hop. Most of these movements develop naturally if the child has normal physical abilities and the opportunity to play. Children with physical problems, however, may need special training to develop these skills. For young children, as for many adolescents and adults, physical activity can be an end in itself. It is fun just to improve. Because they can't always judge when to stop, preschoolers may need interludes of rest scheduled after periods of physical exertion (Darcey & Travers, 2006).

Fine-motor skills such as tying shoes or fastening buttons, which require the coordination of small movements, also improve greatly during the preschool years (see Table 3.1 on page 65). Children should be given the chance to work with large paintbrushes, fat pencils and crayons, large pieces of drawing paper, large Legos, and soft clay or playdough to accommodate their developing skills. During this time, children will begin to develop a lifelong preference for their right or left hand. By age five, about 90 percent of students prefer their right hand for most skilled work, and 10 percent or so prefer their left hand, with more boys than girls being left-handed (Feldman, 2004). This is a genetically based preference, so don't try to make children switch.

The Elementary School Years

During the elementary-school years, physical development is fairly steady for most children. They become taller, leaner, and stronger, so they are better able to master sports and games. There is tremendous variation, however. A particular child can be much larger or smaller than average and still be perfectly healthy. Because children at this age are very aware of physical differences but are not the most tactful people, you may hear comments such as, "You're too little to be in grade 5. What's wrong with you?" or "How come you're so fat?"

Throughout elementary school, many of the girls are likely to be as large as or larger than the boys in their classes. Between the ages of 11 and 14, girls are, on the average, taller and heavier than boys of the same age (Cook & Cook, 2005). The size discrepancy can give the girls an advantage in physical activities, although some girls may feel conflict over this and, as a result, downplay their physical abilities.

Adolescence

Puberty marks the beginning of sexual maturity. It is not a single event, but a series of changes involving almost every part of the body. The sex differences in physical development observed during the later elementary years become even more pronounced at the beginning of puberty. Generally, girls begin puberty between ages 10 and 11, about two years ahead of boys, and reach their final height by age 16 or 17; most boys continue growing until about age 18, but both boys and girls can continue to grow slightly until about 25. Around 80 percent of North American girls have their first menstrual period between the ages of 11 and 14. One tension for adolescents is that they are physically and sexually mature years before they are psychologically or financially ready to shoulder the adult responsibilities of marriage and child-rearing.

The physical changes of adolescence have significant effects on the individual's identity. Psychologists have been particularly interested in the academic, social, and emotional differences they have found between adolescents who mature early and those who mature later. Early maturation seems to have certain special advantages for boys. The early maturers' taller, broader-shouldered body type fits the cultural stereotype for the male ideal. Early-maturing boys are more likely to enjoy high social status; they tend to be popular and to be leaders. But they also tend to engage in more delinquent behaviour (Cota-Robles, Neiss, & Rowe, 2002). On the other hand, boys who mature late may have a more difficult time. However, some studies show that in adulthood, males who matured later tend to be more creative, tolerant, and perceptive. Perhaps the trials and anxieties of maturing late teach some boys to be better problem solvers (Brooks-Gunn, 1988; Steinberg, 2005).

For girls, these effects are reversed. Maturing way ahead of classmates can be a definite disadvantage. Being larger than everyone else in the class is not a valued characteristic for girls in many cultures (Jones, 2004). A girl who begins to mature early probably will be the first in her peer group to start the changes of puberty. Early maturation is associated with emotional difficulties such as depression, anxiety, and eating disorders, especially in societies that define thin as attractive (Steinberg, 2005). Later-maturing girls seem to have fewer problems, but they may worry that something is wrong with them. All students can benefit from knowing that the "normal" range in rates of maturation is great and that there are advantages for both early and late maturers.

Adolescents going through the changes of puberty are very concerned about their bodies. This has always been true, but today, the emphasis on fitness and appearance makes adolescents even more likely to worry about how their bodies "measure up." Both boys and girls can become dissatisfied with their bodies during adolescence—boys because they do not match the muscular models they see and girls because they don't match the cultural ideals either. For girls, it also appears that conversations with friends about appearance can make dissatisfactions worse (Jones, 2004). For some, the concern becomes excessive. One consequence is eating disorders such as **bulimia** (binge eating) and **anorexia nervosa** (self-starvation), both of which are more common in females than in males. Bulimics often binge, eating a huge carton of ice cream or a whole cake. Then, to avoid gaining weight, they force themselves to vomit, or they use strong laxatives, to purge themselves of the extra calories. Bulimics tend to maintain a normal weight, but their digestive systems can be permanently damaged.

Anorexia is an even more dangerous disorder, for anorexics either refuse to eat or eat practically nothing while often exercising obsessively. In the process, they may lose 20 to 25 percent of their body weight, and some (about 20 percent) literally starve themselves to death. Anorexic students become very thin, and may appear pale, have brittle fingernails, and develop fine dark hairs all over their bodies. They are easily chilled because they have so little fat to insulate their bodies. They are often depressed, insecure, moody, and lonely. Girls may stop having their menstrual period. These eating disorders often begin in adolescence and are

puberty The physiological changes during adolescence that lead to the ability to reproduce.

bulimia Eating disorder characterized by overeating, then getting rid of the food by self-induced vomiting or laxatives.

anorexia nervosa Eating disorder characterized by very limited food intake.

becoming more common—about 1 percent of adolescents (mostly, but not all, girls) become anorexic (Rice & Dolgin, 2002). These students usually require professional help. Don't ignore the warning signs—less than one-third of people with eating disorders actually receive treatment (Stice & Shaw, 2004). A teacher may be the person who begins the chain of help for students with these tragic problems.

The Brain and Adolescent Development

Along with all the other changes in puberty come changes in the brain and neurological system that affect personal and social development. Throughout adolescence, changes in the brain increase students' computational skills as well as their ability to control behaviour in both low-stress and high-stress situations, to be more purposeful and organized, and to inhibit impulsive behaviour. But these abilities are not fully developed until the early 20s, so adolescents may "seem" like adults, at least in low-stress situations, but their brains are not fully developed. They may have trouble controlling emotions and avoiding risky behaviours. In fact, adolescents appear to need more intense emotional stimulation than either children or adults, so these young people are set up for taking risks or seeking thrills. Teachers can take advantage of their adolescent students' intensity by helping them devote their energy to areas such as politics, the environment, or social causes (Price, 2005) or by guiding them to explore emotional connections with characters in history or literature.

Other changes in the neurological system during adolescence affect sleep; students need about nine hours of sleep per night, but many students' biological clocks are reset so that it is difficult for them to fall asleep before midnight. Getting nine hours of sleep during the school week is therefore impossible, and as a result students can be continually sleep-deprived. Classes that keep students in their seats, taking notes for the full period, may literally put them to sleep. And with no time for breakfast, and little for lunch, these students' nutrition is often deprived as well (Sprenger, 2005).

We turn now to personal and social development. Two psychologists have proposed broad theories that help us understand development in context: Erik Erikson and Urie Bronfenbrenner.

Connect & Extend

TO THE RESEARCH
See the Autumn 2004 issue of *Theory Into Practice* on Developmental Psychology: Implications for Teaching (Vol. 43, No. 4). Guest Editor: Chris Andersen.

Check Your Knowledge

- Describe the changes in physical development in the preschool, elementary, and secondary grades.
- What are some of the consequences of early and late maturation for boys and girls?
- What are some of the signs of eating disorders?

Apply to Practice

- How might Stephanie's (described at the beginning of this chapter) developmental status influence her fitting in with the "popular" group?

ERIKSON: STAGES OF INDIVIDUAL DEVELOPMENT

Like Jean Piaget, Erik Erikson did not start out as a psychologist. In fact, Erikson never graduated from high school. He spent his early adult years studying art and travelling around Europe. A meeting with Sigmund Freud in Vienna led to an invitation from Freud to study psychoanalysis. Erikson then emigrated to the United States to practise his profession and to escape the threat of Hitler.

In his influential *Childhood and Society* (1963), Erikson offered a basic framework for understanding the needs of young people in relation to the society in which they grow, learn, and ultimately make their contributions. His later books,

Identity, Youth, and Crisis (1968) and *Identity and the Life Cycle* (1980), expanded on his ideas.

Erikson's **psychosocial** theory emphasized the emergence of the self, the search for identity, the individual's relationships with others, and the role of culture throughout life. Like Piaget, Erikson saw development as a passage through a series of stages, each with its particular goals, concerns, accomplishments, and dangers. The stages are interdependent: accomplishments at later stages depend on how conflicts are resolved in the earlier years. At each stage, Erikson suggests, the individual faces a **developmental crisis**. Each crisis involves a conflict between a positive alternative and a potentially unhealthy alternative. The way in which the individual resolves each crisis has a lasting effect on that person's self-image and view of society. An unhealthy resolution of problems in the early stages can have potential negative repercussions throughout life, although sometimes damage can be repaired at later stages. We will look briefly at all eight stages in Erikson's theory—or, as he called them, the "eight ages of man." Table 3.1 presents the stages in summary form.

Erik Erikson proposed a theory of psychosocial development that describes tasks to be accomplished at different stages of life.

psychosocial Describing the relation of the individual's emotional needs to the social environment.

developmental crisis A specific conflict whose resolution prepares the way for the next stage.

The Preschool Years: Trust, Autonomy, and Initiative

Erikson identifies *trust versus mistrust* as the basic conflict of infancy. In the first months of life, babies begin to find out whether they can depend on the world around them. According to Erikson, the infant will develop a sense of trust if its needs for food and care are met with comforting regularity and responsiveness from

TABLE 3.1   Erikson's Eight Stages of Psychosocial Development

Stages	Approximate Age	Important Event	Description
1. Basic trust versus basic mistrust	Birth to 12–18 months	Feeding	The infant must first form a loving, trusting relationship with the caregiver or develop a sense of mistrust.
2. Autonomy versus shame and doubt	18 months to 3 years	Toilet training	The child's energies are directed toward the development of physical skills, including walking, grasping, controlling the sphincter. The child learns control but may develop shame and doubt if not handled well.
3. Initiative versus guilt	3 to 6 years	Independence	The child continues to become more assertive and to take more initiative but may be too forceful, which can lead to feelings of guilt.
4. Industry versus inferiority	6 to 12 years	School	The child must deal with demands to learn new skills or risk a sense of inferiority, failure, or incompetence.
5. Identity versus role confusion	Adolescence	Peer relationships	The teenager must achieve identity in occupation, gender roles, politics, and religion.
6. Intimacy versus isolation	Young adulthood	Love relationships	The young adult must develop intimate relationships or suffer feelings of isolation.
7. Generativity versus stagnation	Middle adulthood	Parenting/mentoring	Each adult must find some way to satisfy and support the next generation.
8. Ego integrity versus despair	Late adulthood	Reflection on and acceptance of one's life	The culmination is a sense of acceptance of oneself as one is and a sense of fulfillment.

Source: Adapted from Lefton, L. A. (1994). *Psychology* (5th ed.). Needham Heights, MA: Allyn & Bacon. Copyright © 1994 by Allyn & Bacon. Reprinted by permission.

Connect & Extend

TO WHAT YOU KNOW
Relate this information to concepts you learned in Chapter 2. For example, what aspects of formal-operational thought are helpful (or perhaps necessary) in achieving identity formation? Can you think of people who seem to have established their identity but who do not seem to have achieved the formal-operational stage? Is identity formation necessarily a conscious process?

autonomy Independence.

initiative Willingness to begin new activities and explore new directions.

caregivers. In this first year, infants are in Piaget's sensorimotor stage and are just beginning to learn that they are separate from the world around them. This realization is part of what makes trust so important: infants must trust the aspects of their world that are beyond their control (Isabella & Belsky, 1991; Posada et al., 2002).

Erikson's second stage, *autonomy versus shame and doubt*, marks the beginning of self-control and self-confidence. Young children are capable of doing more and more on their own. They must begin to assume important responsibilities for self-care such as feeding, going to the toilet, and dressing. During this period parents must tread a fine line; they must be protective—but not overprotective. If parents do not maintain a reassuring, confident attitude and do not reinforce the child's efforts to master basic motor and cognitive skills, children may begin to feel shame; they may learn to doubt their abilities to manage the world on their own terms. Erikson believes that children who experience too much doubt at this stage will lack confidence in their own powers throughout life.

For Erikson, "initiative adds to **autonomy** the quality of undertaking, planning, and attacking a task for the sake of being active and on the move" (Erikson, 1963, p. 255). But with **initiative** comes the realization that some activities are forbidden. At times, children may feel torn between what they want to do and what they should (or should not) do. The challenge of this period is to maintain a zest for activity and at the same time understand that not every impulse can be acted on. Again, adults must tread a fine line, this time in providing supervision without interference. If children are not allowed to do things on their own, a sense of guilt may develop; they may come to believe that what they want to do is always "wrong." The following Guidelines suggest ways of encouraging initiative.

GUIDELINES
ENCOURAGING INITIATIVE IN PRESCHOOL CHILDREN

Encourage children to make and to act on choices.

EXAMPLES

1. Have a free-choice time when children can select an activity or game.
2. Try to avoid interrupting children who are very involved in what they are doing.
3. When children suggest an activity, try to follow their suggestions or incorporate their ideas into ongoing activities.
4. Offer positive choices: instead of saying, "You can't have the cookies now," ask, "Would you like the cookies after lunch or after naptime?"

Make sure that each child has a chance to experience success.

EXAMPLES

1. When introducing a new game or skill, teach it in small steps.
2. Avoid competitive games that highlight differences in children's abilities.

Encourage make-believe with a wide variety of roles.

EXAMPLES

1. Have costumes and props that go along with stories the children enjoy. Encourage the children to act out the stories or make up new adventures for favourite characters.
2. Monitor the children's play to be sure no one monopolizes playing "teacher," "Mommy," "Daddy," or other heroes.

Be tolerant of accidents and mistakes, especially when children are attempting to do something on their own.

EXAMPLES

1. Use cups and pitchers that make it easy to pour and hard to spill.
2. Recognize the attempt, even if the result is unsatisfactory.
3. If mistakes are made, show children how to clean up, repair, or redo.
4. Most important, help children to view errors as opportunities to learn and let them know that everyone makes mistakes (even adults, even you).

Elementary and Middle School Years: Industry versus Inferiority

Let's set the stage for the next phase. Between the ages of five and seven, when most children start school, cognitive development is proceeding rapidly. Children can process more information faster and their memory spans are increasing. They are moving from preoperational to concrete operational thinking. As these internal changes progress, the children are spending hours every weekday in the new physical and social world of school. They must now re-establish Erikson's stages of psychosocial development in the unfamiliar school setting. They must learn to *trust* new adults, act *autonomously* in this more complex situation, and *initiate* actions in ways that fit the new rules of school.

The new psychosocial challenge for the school years is what Erikson calls *industry versus inferiority*. Students are beginning to see the relationship between perseverance and the pleasure of a job completed. In modern societies, children's ability to move between the worlds of home, neighbourhood, and school and to cope with academics, group activities, and friends will lead to a growing sense of competence. Difficulty with these challenges can result in feelings of inferiority. Children must master new skills and work toward new goals while being compared with others and risking failure.

industry Eagerness to engage in productive work.

The way children cope with these challenges has implications for the rest of their school experience. Two of the best predictors of dropping out of school are low grade point average by grade 3 and being held back in one of the primary grades (Paris & Cunningham, 1996). "How well students do in the primary grades matters more for their future success than does their school performance at any other time" (Entwisle & Alexander, 1998, p. 354). And because schools tend to reflect middle-class values and norms, making the transition to school may be especially difficult for children who differ economically or culturally. The achievement test score differences among students from high- and low-socioeconomic groups in grade 1 are relatively small, but by grade 6, the differences have tripled.

The following Guidelines give ideas for encouraging industry.

GUIDELINES

ENCOURAGING INDUSTRY

Make sure that students have opportunities to set and work toward realistic goals.

EXAMPLES

1. Begin with short assignments, then move on to longer ones. Monitor student progress by setting up progress checkpoints.
2. Teach students to set reasonable goals. Write down goals and have students keep a journal of their progress toward them.

Give students a chance to show their independence and responsibility.

EXAMPLES

1. Tolerate honest mistakes.

2. Delegate to students tasks such as watering class plants, collecting and distributing materials, monitoring the computer lab, grading homework, keeping records of forms returned, and so on.

Provide support to students who seem discouraged.

EXAMPLES

1. Use individual charts and contracts that show student progress.
2. Keep samples of earlier work so that students can see their improvements.
3. Have awards for those who are most improved, most helpful, most hard-working.

Adolescence: The Search for Identity

identity The complex answer to the question, "Who am I?"

As students move into adolescence, their cognitive processes are expanding as they develop capabilities for abstract thinking and the capacity to understand the perspectives of others. Even greater physical changes are taking place as students approach puberty. So, with developing minds and bodies, young adolescents must confront the central issue of constructing an **identity** that will provide a firm basis for adulthood. The individual has been developing a sense of self since infancy. But adolescence marks the first time that a conscious effort is made to answer the now-pressing question: "Who am I?" The conflict defining this stage is *identity versus role confusion.* *Identity* refers to the organization of the individual's drives, abilities, beliefs, and history into a consistent image of self. It involves deliberate choices and decisions, particularly about work, values, ideology, and commitments to people and ideas (Marcia, 1987; Penuel & Wertsch, 1995). If adolescents fail to integrate all these aspects and choices, or if they feel unable to choose at all, role confusion threatens.

identity diffusion Uncentredness; confusion about who one is and what one wants.

Identity Statuses.   James Marcia suggests that there are four identity alternatives for adolescents, depending on whether they have *explored* options and made *commitments* (Marcia, 1991, 1994, 1999). The first, **identity diffusion**, occurs when individuals do not explore any options or commit to any actions. They reach no conclusions about who they are or what they want to do with their lives; they have no firm direction. Adolescents experiencing identity diffusion may be apathetic and withdrawn, with little hope for the future, or they may be openly rebellious. These adolescents often go along with the crowd, so they are more likely to abuse drugs (Archer & Waterman, 1990; Berger & Thompson, 1995; Kroger, 2000).

identity foreclosure Acceptance of other life choices without consideration of options.

Identity foreclosure is commitment without exploration. Foreclosed adolescents have not experimented with different identities or explored a range of options but simply committed themselves to the goals, values, and lifestyles of others, usually their parents but sometimes cults or extremist groups. Foreclosed adolescents tend to be rigid, intolerant, dogmatic, and defensive (Frank, Pirsch, & Wright, 1990).

moratorium Identity crisis; suspension of choices because of struggle.

Adolescents in the midst of struggling with choices are experiencing what Erikson called a **moratorium**. Erikson used this term to describe exploration with a delay in commitment to personal and occupational choices. This delay is very common, and probably healthy, for modern adolescents. Erikson believed that adolescents in complex societies have an *identity crisis* during moratorium. Today, the period is no longer referred to as a crisis because, for most people, the experience is a gradual exploration rather than a traumatic upheaval (Grotevant, 1998).

identity achievement Strong sense of commitment to life choices after free consideration of alternatives.

Identity achievement means that after exploring the realistic options, the individual has made choices and is committed to pursuing them. It appears that few students achieve this status by the end of high school; students who attend university or college may take a bit longer to decide. Because so many people today go on to university or other continuing education after high school, it is not uncommon for the explorations of moratorium to continue into the early 20s. About 80 percent of students change their majors at least once. And some adults may achieve a firm identity at one period in their lives, only to reject that identity and achieve a new one later. So identity, once achieved, may not be unchanging for everyone (Kroger, 2000; Nurmi, 2004).

Both moratorium and identity-achieved statuses are considered healthy. Schools that give adolescents experiences with community service, real-world work, internships, and mentoring help to foster identity formation (Cooper, 1998). The accompanying Guidelines give other ideas for supporting identity formation.

Beyond the School Years

The crises of Erikson's stages of adulthood all involve the quality of human relations. The first of these stages is *intimacy versus isolation.* Intimacy in this sense

SUPPORTING IDENTITY FORMATION

Give students many models for career choices and other adult roles.

EXAMPLES

1. Point out models from literature and history. Have a calendar with the birthdays of eminent women, minority leaders, or people who made a little-known contribution to the subject you are teaching. Briefly discuss the person's accomplishments on her or his birthday.

2. Invite guest speakers to describe how and why they chose their professions. Make sure all kinds of work and workers are represented.

Help students find resources for working out personal problems.

EXAMPLES

1. Encourage them to talk to school counsellors.
2. Discuss potential outside services.

Be tolerant of teenage fads as long as they don't offend others or interfere with learning.

EXAMPLES

1. Discuss the fads of earlier eras (neon hair, powdered wigs, love beads).
2. Don't impose strict dress or hair codes.

Give students realistic feedback about themselves.

EXAMPLES

1. When students misbehave or perform poorly, make sure they understand the consequences of their behaviour—the effects on themselves and others.

2. Give students model answers or show them other students' completed projects so that they can compare their work with good examples.

3. Since students are "trying on" roles, keep the roles separate from the person. You can criticize behaviour without criticizing the student.

refers to a willingness to relate to another person on a deep level, to have a relationship based on more than mutual need. Someone who has not achieved a sufficiently strong sense of identity tends to fear being overwhelmed or swallowed up by another person and may retreat into isolation.

The conflict at the next stage is *generativity versus stagnation.* **Generativity** extends the ability to care for another person and involves caring and guidance for the next generation and for future generations. While *generativity* frequently refers to having and nurturing children, it has a broader meaning. Productivity and creativity are essential features.

generativity Sense of concern for future generations.

The last of Erikson's stages is *integrity versus despair,* or coming to terms with death. Achieving **ego integrity** means consolidating your sense of self and fully accepting its unique and now unalterable history. Those unable to attain a feeling of fulfillment and completeness sink into despair.

ego integrity Sense of self-acceptance and fulfillment.

With Erikson's theory of psychosocial development as a framework, we can now examine several aspects of personal and social development that are issues throughout childhood and adolescence.

Check Your Knowledge

- Why is Erikson's theory considered a psychosocial perspective?
- What are Erikson's stages of psychosocial development?

Apply to Practice

- How might an adolescent experiencing identity foreclosure answer the question, "Why did you choose that major?"?
- How might Stephanie's difficulties fitting in with the popular group (described at the beginning of this chapter) influence her identity achievement?

BRONFENBRENNER: THE SOCIAL CONTEXT FOR DEVELOPMENT

bioecological model Bronfenbrenner's theory describing the nested social and cultural contexts that shape development. Every person develops within a *microsystem*, inside a *mesosystem*, embedded in an *exosystem*, all of which are a part of the *macrosystem* of the culture.

Erikson highlighted the role of social and cultural context in personal-social development, but Urie Bronfenbrenner went further to map the many interacting social contexts that affect development with his **bioecological model** of development (Bronfenbrenner, 1989; Bronfenbrenner & Evans, 2000). The *bio* aspect of the model recognizes that people bring their biological selves to the developmental process. The *ecological* part recognizes that the social contexts in which we develop are ecosystems because they are in constant interaction and influence each other. Look at Figure 3.1. Every person lives within a *microsystem*, inside a *mesosystem*, embedded in an *exosystem*, all of which are a part of the *macrosystem*—like a set of Russian painted dolls, nested one inside the other.

In the microsystem are the person's immediate relationships and activities. For a child, it might be the immediate family, friends, or teachers and the activities of play and school. Relationships in the microsystem are reciprocal—they flow in both directions. The child affects the parent and the parent influences the child, for example. The mesosystem is the set of interactions and relationships among all the elements of the microsystem—the family members interacting with each other or with the teacher. Again, all relationships are reciprocal—the teacher influences the parents and the parents affect the teacher, and these interactions affect the child. The exosystem includes all the social settings that affect the child, even though the child is not a direct member of the systems. Examples are the teachers' relations with administrators and the school board; parents' jobs; the community resources for health, employment, or recreation; or the family's religious affiliation. The macrosystem is the larger society—its values, laws, conventions, and traditions.

Figure 3.1 Urie Bronfenbrenner's Bioecological Model of Human Development

Every person develops within a microsystem (family, friends, school activities, teacher, etc.) inside a mesosystem (the interactions among all the microsystem elements), embedded in an exosystem (social settings that affect the child, even though the child is not a direct member—community resources, parents' workplace, etc.); all are part of the macrosystem (the larger society with its laws, customs, values, etc.).

Source: Adapted from K. S. Berger (2004), *The developing person through the lifespan.* New York: Worth, p. 3.

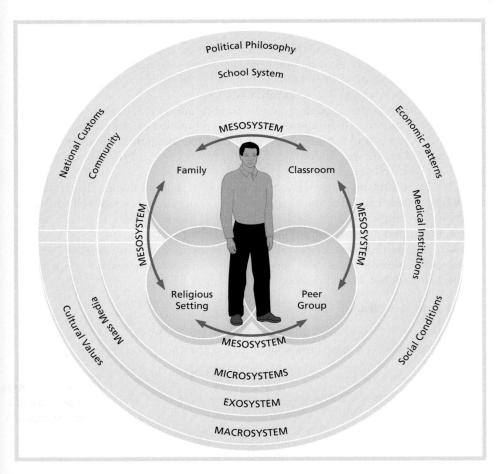

For another example, think of the teacher's own bioecological system. The teacher is influenced by the microsystem of the principal, colleagues, and students; the mesosystem of the interactions among those people; the exosystem of government educational policies, and the macrosystem of cultural norms and values (Woolfolk Hoy, Pape, & Davis, 2006).

Bronfenbrenner's theory has at least two lessons for teachers. First, influences in all social systems are reciprocal. Second, there are many dynamic forces that interact to create the context for individual development. Next, we look at three important social contexts—families, peers, and teachers.

Families

The most appropriate expectation to have about your students' families is no expectation at all. Increasingly, students today have only one or no sibling, or they may be part of **blended families**, with stepbrothers or stepsisters who move in and out of their lives. Some of your students may live with an aunt, with grandparents, with one parent, in foster or adoptive homes, or with an older brother or sister. The best advice is to avoid the phrases "your parents" and "your mother and father" and to speak of "your family" when talking to students. Divorce is one reason why family structures are so varied.

blended families Parents, children, and stepchildren merged into families through remarriages.

Divorce. According to Statistics Canada (2005), the 2003 divorce rates indicate that 38 percent of marriages will end in divorce. As many of us know from experiences in our own families, separation and divorce are stressful events for all participants, even under the best circumstances. The actual separation of the parents may have been preceded by years of conflict in the home or may come as a shock to all, including friends and children. During the divorce itself, conflict may increase as property and custody rights are being decided.

After the divorce, more changes may disrupt the children's lives. Today, as in the past, the mother is most often the custodial parent, even though the number of households headed by fathers has been increasing, to about 19 percent by 2001 (Statistics Canada, 2001). The parent who has custody may have to move to a less-expensive home, find new sources of income, go to work for the first time, or work longer hours. For the child, this can mean leaving behind important friendships in the old neighbourhood or school, just when support is needed the most. It may mean having just one parent, who has less time than ever to be with the children. About two-thirds of parents remarry and then half of them divorce again, so there are more adjustments ahead for the children (Nelson, 1993). In some divorces, there are few conflicts, ample resources, and the continuing support of friends and extended family. But divorce is never easy for anyone.

The first two years after the divorce seem to be the most difficult period for both boys and girls. During this time, children may have problems in school, lose or gain an unusual amount of weight, develop difficulties sleeping, and so on. They may blame themselves for the breakup of their family or hold unrealistic hopes for reconciliation (Hetherington, 1999). Long-term adjustment is also affected. Boys tend to show a higher rate of behavioural and interpersonal problems at home and in school than girls in general or boys from intact families do. Girls may have trouble in their dealings with males. They may become more sexually active or have difficulties trusting males. However, living with one fairly content, if harried, parent may be better than living in a conflict-filled situation with two unhappy parents. And adjustment to divorce is an individual matter; some children respond with increased responsibility, maturity, and coping skills (Amato, Loomis, & Booth, 1995; Berk, 2005). See the Guidelines on page 72 for ideas about how to help students in these situations.

Parenting Styles. If you spend time in teachers' lounges in schools, you may hear quite a bit of talk about students' parents, including some blame for students'

Connect & Extend

TO THE RESEARCH
For a concise discussion of the effects of divorce on children and suggestions for ways that teachers can help their students cope with divorce, see Rotenberg, K. J., Kim, L. S., & Herman-Stahl, M. (1998). The role of primary and secondary appraisals in the negative emotions and psychological adjustment of children of divorce. *Journal of Divorce and Remarriage, 29*, 43–66.

HELPING CHILDREN OF DIVORCE

Take note of any sudden changes in behaviour that might indicate problems at home.

EXAMPLES

1. Be alert to physical symptoms such as repeated headaches or stomach pains, rapid weight gain or loss, fatigue or excess energy.

2. Be aware of signs of emotional distress, including moodiness, temper tantrums, and difficulty in paying attention or concentrating.

3. Let parents know about the students' signs of stress.

Talk individually to students about their attitude or behaviour changes. This gives you a chance to find out about unusual stress such as divorce.

EXAMPLES

1. Be a good listener. Students may have no other adult willing to hear their concerns.

2. Let students know you are available to talk, and then let students who approach you set the agenda.

Watch your language to make sure you avoid stereotypes about "happy" (two-parent) homes.

EXAMPLES

1. Simply say "your families" instead of "your mothers and fathers" when addressing the class.

2. Avoid statements such as "We need volunteers for room mother" or "Your father can help you."

Help students maintain self-esteem.

EXAMPLES

1. Recognize a job well done.

2. Make sure the student understands the assignment and can handle the workload. This is not the time to pile on new and very difficult work.

3. The student may be angry at his or her parents but may direct the anger at teachers. Don't take the student's anger personally.

Find out what resources are available at your school.

EXAMPLES

1. Talk to the school psychologist, guidance counsellor, social worker, or principal about students who seem to need outside help.

2. Consider establishing a discussion group, led by a trained adult, for students going through a divorce.

Be sensitive to both parents' rights to information.

EXAMPLES

1. When parents have joint custody, both are entitled to receive information and attend parent–teacher conferences.

2. The non-custodial parent may still be concerned about the child's school progress. Check with your principal about provincial laws regarding the non-custodial parent's rights.

problems. Actually, most current research in child development says it's not that simple. As Bronfenbrenner's bioecolgial model tells us, there are many influences on children. But parents are still important (Berger, 2006).

parenting styles The ways of interacting with and disciplining children.

One well-known description of **parenting styles** is based on the research of Diane Baumrind (1991). Her early work focused on a careful longitudinal study of 100 (mostly European American, middle-class) preschool children. Through observation of children and parents and interviews with parents, Baumrind and the other researchers who built on her findings identified four styles based on the parents' high or low levels of warmth and control (Berger, 2006):

• *Authoritarian* parents (low warmth, high control) seem cold and controlling in their interactions with their children. The children are expected to be mature and to do what the parent says—"Because I said so!" There is not much talk about emotions. Punishments are strict, but not abusive. The parents love their children, but they are not openly affectionate.

- *Authoritative* parents (high warmth, high control) also set clear limits, enforce rules, and expect mature behaviour. But they are warmer with their children. They listen to concerns, give reasons for rules, and allow more democratic decision making. There is less strict punishment and more guidance. Parents help children think through the consequences of their actions (Hoffman, 2001).
- *Permissive* parents (high warmth, low control) are warm and nurturing, but they have few rules or consequences for their children and expect little in the way of mature behaviour because "they're just kids."
- *Rejecting/Neglecting* parents (low warmth, low control) don't seem to care at all and can't be bothered with controlling, communicating, or caring for their children.

Culture and Parenting. Authoritarian, authoritative, and permissive parents all love their children and are trying to do their best—they simply have different ideas about the best ways to parent. In broad strokes, there are differences in children associated with these three parenting styles. At least in North American, middle-class families, children of authoritative parents are more likely to be happy with themselves and to relate well to others, whereas children of authoritarian parents are more likely to be guilty or depressed, and children of permissive parents may have trouble interacting with peers—they are used to having their way. Of course, the extreme of permissiveness becomes indulgence. Indulgent parents cater to their children's every whim—perhaps it is easier than being the adult who must make unpopular decisions. Both indulgent and rejecting/neglecting parenting styles are harmful.

Cultures also differ in parenting styles. Research indicates that higher-control parenting is linked to better grades for Asian students (Glasgow et al., 1997). Parenting that is strict and directive, with clear rules and consequences, combined with high levels of warmth and emotional support, is associated with higher academic achievement and greater emotional maturity for inner-city children (Garner & Spears, 2000; Jarrett, 1995). Differences in cultural values and in the danger level of some urban neighbourhoods may make tighter parental control appropriate, and even necessary (Smetana, 2000). And it may be a misreading of the parents' actions to perceive their demand for obedience as "authoritarian" in cultures that have a greater respect for elders and a more group-centred rather than individualist philosophy (Nucci, 2001).

Peers

Peers and friendships are central to students' lives. When there has been a falling-out or an argument, when one child is not invited to a sleep-over, when rumours are started and pacts are made to ostracize someone (as with Alison and Stephanie at the beginning of the chapter), the results can be devastating. The immaturity and impulsiveness of the adolescent brain combined with the power of peer cultures can make these problems even more likely.

Peer Cultures. Recently, psychologists have studied the powerful role of peer culture in children's development. Peer cultures are groups of students who have a set of "rules"—how to dress, talk, style their hair. The group determines which activities, music, or other students are in or out of favour. For example, when Jessica, a popular high school student, was asked to explain the rules that her group lives by, she had no trouble:

> OK. No. 1: clothes. You cannot wear jeans any day but Friday, and you cannot wear a ponytail or sneakers more than once a week. Monday is fancy day—like black pants or maybe you bust out with a skirt. You have to remind people how cute you are in case they forgot over the weekend. No. 2: parties. Of course we sit down and discuss

which ones we're going to because there is no point in getting all dressed up for a party that's going to be lame. (Talbot, 2002, p. 28)

These peer cultures encourage conformity to the group rules. When another girl in Jessica's group wore jeans on Monday, Jessica confronted her: "Why are you wearing jeans today? Did you forget it was Monday?" (Talbot, 2002, p. 28). Jessica explained that the group had to suspend this "rebel" several times, not allowing her to sit with them at lunch.

To understand the power of peers, we have to look at situations where the values and interests of parents clash with those of peers, and then see whose influence dominates. In these comparisons, peers usually win. But not all aspects of peer cultures are bad or cruel. The norms in some groups are positive and support achievement in school. Peer cultures are more powerful in defining issues of style and socializing. Parents and teachers still are influential in matters of morality, career choice, and religion (Harris, 1998).

Beyond the immediate trauma of being "in" or "out" of the group, peer relationships play significant positive and negative roles in healthy personal and social development. Peer groups influence members' motivation and achievement in school (A. Ryan, 2001). In one study, grade 6 students without friends showed lower levels of academic achievement and positive social behaviours and were more emotionally distressed, even two years later, than students with at least one friend (Wentzel, Barry, & Caldwell, 2004). The characteristics of friends and the quality of the friendships matter, too. Having stable, supportive relationships with friends who are socially competent and mature enhances social development, especially during difficult times such as parents' divorce or transition to new schools (Hartup & Stevens, 1999). Children who are rejected by their peers are less likely to participate in classroom learning activities; they are more likely to drop out of school as adolescents and may even evidence more problems as adults. For example, rejected aggressive students are more likely to commit crimes as they grow older (Coie & Dodge, 1998; Coie et al., 1995; Fredricks, Blumenfeld, & Paris, 2004).

Who Is Likely to Have Problems with Peers? Children and adolescents are not always tolerant of differences. New students who are physically, intellectually, eth-

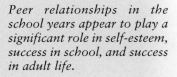

Peer relationships in the school years appear to play a significant role in self-esteem, success in school, and success in adult life.

nically, racially, economically, or linguistically different may be rejected in classes with established peer groups. Students who are aggressive, withdrawn, and inattentive-hyperactive are more likely to be rejected. But classroom context matters too, especially for aggressive or withdrawn students. In classrooms where the general level of aggression is high, being aggressive is less likely to lead to peer rejection. And in classrooms where solitary play and work are more common, being withdrawn is not as likely to lead to rejection. Thus, part of being rejected is being too different from the norm. Also, pro-social behaviours such as sharing, cooperating, and friendly interactions are associated with peer acceptance, no matter what the classroom context. Many aggressive and withdrawn students lack these social skills; inattentive-hyperactive students often misread social cues or have trouble controlling impulses, so their social skills suffer, too (Coplan et al., 2004; Stormshak et al., 1999). A teacher should be aware of how each student gets along with the group. Are there outcasts? Do some students play the bully role? Careful adult intervention can often correct such problems, especially at the late elementary and middle school levels.

What Would You Say?

As part of the interview process for a job in a high school, you are asked the following: "Tell me how you could tell if there might be violence among students in our school. What are the warning signs?"

Peer Aggression.   There are several forms of aggression. The most common form is **instrumental aggression**, which is intended to gain an object or privilege, such as shoving to get in line first or snatching a toy from another child. The intent is to get what one wants, not to hurt the other child, but the hurt may happen anyway. A second kind is **hostile aggression**—inflicting intentional harm. Hostile aggression can be either the **overt aggression** of threats or physical attacks (as in, "I'm gonna beat you up!") or **relational aggression**, which involves threatening or damaging social relationships (as in, "I'm never going to speak to you again!"). Boys are more likely to use overt aggression and girls, like Alison in the opening case, are more likely to use relational aggression (Berk, 2005). Aggression should not be confused with assertiveness, which means affirming or maintaining a legitimate right. As Helen Bee (1981) explains, "A child who says, 'That's my toy!' is showing assertiveness. If he bashes his playmate over the head to reclaim it, he has shown aggression" (p. 350).

Modelling plays an important role in the expression of aggression (Bandura, Ross, & Ross, 1963). According to the National Longitudinal Survey of Children and Youth (NLSCY) in Canada (Craig, Peters, & Konarski, 1998; Tremblay et al., 1996), there is a strong relationship between family membership and family functioning and aggressive behaviour. The survey found that children who are aggressive tend to have aggressive siblings and parents who, perhaps inadvertently, reinforce aggressive interactions between or among siblings (e.g., by not consistently praising pro-social behaviour and punishing anti-social behaviour). Furthermore, research indicates that children who grow up in homes filled with harsh and inconsistent punishment and daily interactions within the family that can be characterized as coercive or aggressive are more likely to use aggression to solve their own problems (Craig et al., 1998).

One very real source of aggressive models is found in almost every home in North America—television. In the United States, 82 percent of TV programs have at least some violence. The rate for children's programs is especially high—an average of 32 violent acts per hour, with cartoons being the worst. Furthermore, in more than 70 percent of the violent scenes, the violence goes unpunished (Mediascope, 1996; Waters, 1993).

Most children spend more time watching television than they do on any other activity except sleep (Timmer, Eccles, & O'Brien, 1988). On average, Canadian

instrumental aggression Strong actions aimed at claiming an object, place, or privilege—not intended to harm, but may lead to harm.

hostile aggression Bold, direct action that is intended to hurt someone else; unprovoked attack.

overt aggression A form of hostile aggression that involves physical attack.

relational aggression A form of hostile aggression that involves verbal attacks and other actions meant to harm social relationships.

Over time, children learn to internalize moral principles such as compassion and justice and adopt them for themselves.

Connect & Extend

TO THE RESEARCH
Galen, B. R., & Underwood, M. K. (1997). A developmental investigation of social aggression among children. *Developmental Psychology, 33,* 589–600.

children between the ages of 2 and 11 watch 15.5 hours of television each week (Statistics Canada, 1998a). People have asked the Canadian government to impose rules that restrict youth access to violent television programs and films (Tremblay et al., 1996). In fact, a Canadian researcher, Tim Collings, is responsible for the development of the V-chip that, when inserted in television sets, allows parents to block their children's access to certain TV programs.

Does watching violent TV increase aggression? Results of a recent longitudinal study indicate a clear "yes." Rowell Huesmann and colleagues examined the relationship between exposure to violence on television from ages 6 to 10 and aggressive behaviour in adulthood 15 years later for over 300 people. Their conclusion? "Childhood exposure to media violence predicts young adult aggressive behavior for both males and females.... These relations persist even when the effects of socioeconomic status, intellectual ability, and a variety of parenting factors are controlled" (Huesmann et al., 2003, p. 201). When the children identified with aggressive TV characters (they said they acted like those characters) and when they thought the violence on TV was like real life, they were more likely to be violent as adults.

You can reduce the negative effects of TV violence by stressing three points with your students: Most people do not behave in the aggressive ways shown on television; the violent acts on TV are not real, but are created by special effects and stunts; and there are better ways to resolve conflicts, and these are the ways most real people use to solve their problems (Huesmann et al., 2003). Also, avoid using TV viewing as a reward or punishment because that makes television even more attractive to children (Slaby et al., 1995).

Television is not the only source of violent models. Many popular films and video games also are filled with graphic depictions of violence, often performed by the "hero." Students growing up in the inner cities see gangs and drug deals. Newspapers, magazines, and radio are filled with stories of murders, rapes, and robberies.

Finally, the breakdown of the family has also been suggested as a possible source of aggressive behaviour on the part of children and youth (Tremblay et al., 1996; Craig et al., 1998). Stress, poverty, and problems with discipline have been associated with parental separation and have been linked to aggressive behaviour in children. Other proposed explanations include lax discipline in schools; the availability of drugs, alcohol, and guns; and the ineffectiveness of laws concerning juvenile offenders. However, the Canadian *Criminal Code* is getting tougher on young offenders. In December 1995, Bill C-37 was passed to permit tougher sentences for violent crimes, and adolescents who commit serious violent offences, such as murder, can now be tried in adult courts.

Bullying. Two Canadian researchers, Wendy Craig and Debra Pepler, are among the leading experts on one type of aggressive behaviour in schools—bullying. They characterize bullying as a form of social interaction in which a more dominant individual (the bully) exhibits aggressive behaviour that is intended to cause distress or harm to a less dominant individual (the victim) (Craig & Pepler, 1997, p. 42). Bullying can include relational forms of aggression (e.g., calling someone names or gossiping behind his or her back) as well as physical forms of aggression.

In one survey (Charach, Pepler, & Ziegler, 1995), 19 percent of students in Canadian schools reported being bullied twice a term, and 8 percent of students indicated that they experience aggression in school at least once each week. Craig and Pepler (1998) observed 65 elementary-school children playing in the schoolyard at recess and lunch. During 48 hours of observations, they observed a total of 314 bullying episodes, approximately 6.5 episodes every hour. They rated 84 percent of the episodes they observed as overt and occurring when peers and/or adults were present. According to their ratings, school staff intervened in only 25 percent of the episodes they witnessed. Clearly, aggressive behaviour in Canadian schools is a serious problem.

Aggressive children tend to believe that violence will be rewarded, and they use aggression to get what they want. They are more likely to believe that violent retaliation is acceptable: "It's okay to shove people when you're mad" (Craig et al., 1998; Egan, Monson, & Perry, 1998). Seeing violent acts go unpunished probably affirms and encourages these beliefs. In addition to being surrounded by violence and believing that violent "payback" is appropriate when you are insulted or harmed, some children, particularly boys, have difficulty reading the intentions of others (Porath, 2001; Zelli et al., 1999). They assume that another child "did it on purpose" when their block tower is toppled, they are pushed on the bus, or some other mistake is made. Retaliation follows and the cycle of aggression continues.

Helping children handle aggression can make a lasting difference in their lives. For example, one study in Finland found that teacher-rated aggression at the age of eight predicted school adjustment problems in early adolescence and long-term unemployment in adulthood (Kokko & Pulkkinen, 2000). Sandra Graham (1996) has successfully experimented with approaches that help aggressive African American boys in grades 5 and 6 become better judges of others' intentions. Strategies include engaging in role play, participating in group discussions of personal experiences, interpreting social cues from photographs, playing pantomime games, making videos, and writing endings to unfinished stories. The boys in the 12-session training group showed clear improvement in reading the intentions of others and responding with less aggression.

Relational Aggression. Insults, gossip, exclusion, taunts—all these are forms of relational aggression, sometimes called *social aggression* because the intent is to harm social connections. Tremblay et al. (1996) and Pepler and Sedighdeilami (1998) analyzed data from the NLSCY to examine patterns of aggressive behaviour relating to age (2–11 years), gender, and socioeconomic status (SES). As children mature, they become less likely to respond to problem situations with overt physical aggression but more likely to respond with less direct forms of relational aggression. Also, whereas boys at all ages are more physically aggressive than girls, they are less involved in relational aggression. This type of aggression can be even more damaging than overt physical aggression—both to the victim and to the aggressor. Victims, like Stephanie in this chapter's casebook, can be devastated. Relational aggressors can be viewed as even more problematic than physical aggressors by teachers and other students (Berger, 2003; Crick, Casas, & Mosher, 1997).

Trembley et al.'s analyses showed that boys and girls with low SES had the highest physical aggression scores, and that the differences between boys and girls were most pronounced among these children. Tremblay and his colleagues suggest that efforts to reduce all forms of aggression and increase pro-social behaviour should begin early.

Victims. While some students tend to be bullies, other children are victims. Studies from Europe and the United States indicate that about 10 percent of children are chronic victims—the constant targets for physical or verbal attacks. In Canada, data from the NLSCY indicate that 5 percent of school-aged children are victims (Craig, Peters, & Konarski, 1998). Victims tend to have low self-esteem, and they feel anxious, lonely, insecure, and unhappy. They often are prone to crying and withdrawal; when attacked, generally they don't defend themselves. Recent research suggests that victims may blame themselves for their situation. They believe that they are rejected because they have character flaws that they cannot change or control—no wonder they are depressed and helpless! The situation is worse for young adolescent victims whose peers seem to have little sympathy for them. Children who have been chronic victims through elementary and middle school are more depressed and more likely to attempt suicide as young adults (Graham, 1998; Hodges & Perry, 1999). In recent years, we have seen tragic consequences when tormented students turned guns on their tormentors in schools in Canada, the United States, and Europe.

There is a second kind of victim—highly emotional and hot-tempered students who seem to provoke aggressive reactions from their peers. Members of this group, who constitute about 10 to 15 percent of students, are rejected by almost all peers and have few friends (Pellegrini, Bartini, & Brooks, 1999). The Guidelines below may give you ideas for handling aggression and encouraging cooperation.

Cyberbullying. The use of the internet for communicating with others has become a part of everyday life for adolescents (Bargh, McKenna, & Fitzsimmons, 2002; Gross, Juvonen, & Gable, 2002; Roberts, Ridout, & Foehr, 2005). In 2005, 94 percent of Canadian youth reported having access to the internet from their homes (Media Awareness Network, 2005). While some research is showing that access to this media may help some individuals overcome shyness and enhance their social skills (Maczewski, 2002; Valkenburg, Schouten, & Peter, 2005), there is also evidence that it is being used as a venue for bullying activities. *Cyberbullying* has been defined as a form of intentional aggression where an individual, or a group of individuals, use information technologies, such as email, websites (developed specifically for the purpose of humiliating or degrading others), instant messaging (IM), and/or text messaging on cell phones to inflict harm on others by embarrassing them or gossiping about them (Ybarra & Mitchell, 2004). There is very little research on this topic, so it is not known whether the impact of cyberbullying is as devastating as schoolyard bullying. Also not known is whether the same individuals who bully in person are the ones who are more likely to bully online. But given the anonymous nature of the internet, and the sense of protection one might feel being behind a screen, it is possible that individuals may feel more free to bully online than in person.

GUIDELINES

DEALING WITH AGGRESSION AND ENCOURAGING COOPERATION

Present yourself as a non-aggressive model.

EXAMPLES

1. Do not use threats of aggression to win obedience.
2. When problems arise, model non-violent conflict-resolution strategies.

Ensure that your classroom has enough space and appropriate materials for every student.

EXAMPLES

1. Prevent overcrowding.
2. Make sure prized toys or resources are plentiful.
3. Remove or confiscate materials that encourage personal aggression, such as toy guns.

Make sure students do not profit from aggressive behaviour.

EXAMPLES

1. Comfort the victim of aggression and ignore the aggressor.

2. Use reasonable punishment, especially with older students.

Teach directly about positive social behaviour.

EXAMPLES

1. Incorporate lessons on social ethics/morality through reading selections and discussions.
2. Discuss the effects of anti-social actions such as stealing, bullying, and spreading rumours.

Provide opportunities for learning tolerance and cooperation.

EXAMPLES

1. Emphasize the similarities among people rather than the differences.
2. Set up group projects that encourage cooperation.

Teachers

The first and most important task of the teacher is to educate, but student learning suffers when there are problems with personal and social development, and teachers are the main adults in students' lives for many hours each week. Teachers have the opportunity to play a significant role in students' personal and social development. For students facing emotional or interpersonal problems, teachers are sometimes the best source of help. When students have chaotic and unpredictable home lives, they need a caring, firm structure in school. They need teachers who set clear limits, are consistent, enforce rules firmly but not punitively, respect students, and show genuine concern. As a teacher, you can be available to talk about personal problems without requiring that your students do so. One student teacher gave a boy in her class a journal entitled "Very Hard Thoughts" so that he could write about his parents' divorce. Sometimes, he talked to her about the journal entries, but at other times, he just recorded his feelings. The student teacher was very careful to respect the boy's privacy about his writings.

Academic and Personal Caring. When researchers ask students to describe a "good teacher," three qualities are at the centre of their descriptions. Good teachers have positive interpersonal relationships—they care about their students. Second, good teachers can keep the classroom organized and maintain authority without being rigid or "mean." Finally, good teachers are good motivators—they can make learning fun by being creative and innovative (Woolfolk Hoy & Weinstein, 2006). Pedro Noguera (2005) said that the students in a "last chance" high school told him they look for three things in a teacher: "They look first for people who care.... Second, they respect teachers who are strict and hold students accountable. Third, they like teachers who teach them something" (pp. 17–18). We will look at management in Chapter 11 and at motivation in Chapter 10, so for now let's focus on caring and teaching.

For the past 15 years, research has documented the value and importance of positive relationships with teachers for students at every grade level (Davis, 2003). Tamera Murdock and Angela Miller (2003) found that grade 8 students' perceptions that their teachers cared about them were significantly related to the students' academic motivation, even after taking into account the motivational influences of parents and peers. Students seek respect, affection, trust, a listening ear, patience, and humour in their relationships with teachers (Bosworth, 1995; Phelan et al., 1992; Wentzel, 1997). Frequently, students' decisions about whether to cooperate are based on their liking for the teacher.

As a student in a study by Stinson (1993) commented, "If I don't like 'em ... I'm not gonna do anything for 'em" (p. 221). Students define caring in two ways. One is academic caring—setting high but reasonable expectations and helping students reach those goals. The second is personal caring—being patient, respectful, humorous, willing to listen, and interested in students' issues and personal problems.

For higher-achieving students, academic caring is especially important, but for students who are placed at risk and often alienated from school, personal caring is critical (Cothran & Ennis, 2000; Woolfolk Hoy & Weinstein, 2006). In fact, in one study in a Texas high school, the Mexican and Mexican American students saw teacher caring as a prerequisite for their own caring about school; in other words, they needed to be *cared for* before they could *care about* school (Valenzuela, 1999). Unfortunately, in the same school, the mostly non-Latino teachers expected the students to care about school before they would invest their caring in the students. And for many teachers, caring about school meant behaving in more "middle-class" ways.

These contrasting student and teacher views can lead to a downward spiral of mistrust. Students withhold their cooperation until teachers "earn it" with their authentic caring. Teachers withhold caring until students "earn it" with respect for authority and cooperation. Marginalized students expect unfair treatment and behave defensively when they sense any unfairness. Teachers get tough and punish. Students feel correct in mistrusting, and become more guarded and defiant. Teachers feel correct in mistrusting and become more controlling and punitive, and so it goes. In short, caring means not giving up on students and their learning as well as demonstrating and teaching kindness in the classroom (Davis, 2003).

Teachers and Child Abuse. Certainly, one critical way to care about students is to protect their welfare and intervene in cases of abuse. Accurate information about the number of abused children in Canada is difficult to find because many cases go unreported. In 1996, children under 18 were victims in 22 percent of the violent crimes reported to the police, and family members were responsible for 20 percent of the physical assaults and 32 percent of the sexual assaults on children (Statistics Canada, 1998b). Parents are the most likely perpetrators in familial physical and sexual abuse cases, and fathers are responsible for 73 percent of physical assaults and 98 percent of sexual assaults on children within families. About half of all abusive parents could change their destructive behaviour patterns if they received help and support. Without assistance, probably only about 5 percent of abusing parents improve (Starr, 1979). Of course, parents are not the only people who abuse children. Siblings, other relatives, and even teachers have been responsible for the physical and sexual abuse of children. And today, there is another source of abuse—the internet. The Reaching Every Student feature presents a set of guidelines to give to students to protect them from internet predators.

REACHING EVERY STUDENT
SAFETY ON THE INTERNET

Provide these guidelines to your students so that they can protect themselves when using the internet.

1. Never give identifying data such as your name, address, phone number, school name, and so on to anyone on the internet unless you check with a parent or teacher first.

2. Never share your password with anyone, even a best friend.

3. Never tell anyone online where you will be or what you will be doing at a certain time without a parent's or teacher's permission.

4. Never give out your picture over the internet.

5. Choose a name that is not your own name for an email address.

6. Check with a parent or teacher before you enter a chat room.

7. Never agree to meet in person anyone whom you have met on the internet. If someone asks to meet you, tell a parent or a teacher.

8. If you receive pictures or messages that make you uncomfortable, tell an adult at home or school immediately.

9. If someone makes suggestive comments to you on the internet, stop talking to him or her immediately. Tell an adult at home or at school.

10. Never fill out a questionnaire or give a credit card number online without checking with a parent or teacher.

11. If you unintentionally come across nude or obscene pictures, tell someone immediately.

12. Never open or respond to an email message from someone you do not know.

13. Be open with parents or teachers about what you are accessing on the internet.

14. Be careful when anyone offers you anything free on the internet.

15. Do not do things online that you would hesitate to do in real life.

Source: From Crosson-Tower, C. (2002). *When children are abused: An educator's guide to intervention.* Boston: Allyn & Bacon. Copyright © 2002 by Pearson Education. Reprinted by permission of the publisher. See also Hughes, 1998; Monteleone, 1998; **http://encarta.msn.com/schoolhouse/safety.asp;** and **www.missingkids.com**.

As a teacher, you must alert your principal, or school counsellor, or a school social worker if you suspect abuse. Child protection is a provincial responsibility, so be sure you understand the laws in your province concerning this important role. In British Columbia, the *Child, Family, and Community Service Act* clearly states that *anyone* who has reason to believe that a child has been or is likely to be physically or sexually abused or exploited, or neglected, has a legal responsibility to report the matter to a child-protection social worker (British Columbia Ministry for Children and Families, 1998). In British Columbia, a child is any individual under the age of 19. Sometimes, people don't report their suspicions because they think they need proof. This is not true. All that is required is a reasonable belief that a child is in emotional or physical danger. Each year, thousands of children die because of abuse or neglect, in many cases because no one would "get involved" (Thompson & Wyatt, 1999). Table 3.2 lists possible indicators of abuse.

Connect & Extend

TO THE RESEARCH
Tocane, N., & Schumaker, K. (1999). Reported child sexual abuse in Canadian schools and recreational facilities: Implications for developing effective prevention strategies. *Children and Youth Service Review, 21,* 621–642.

TABLE 3.2 Indicators of Child Abuse

The following are some of the signs of abuse. Not every child with these signs is abused, but these indicators should be investigated.

	Physical Indicators	Behavioural Indicators	
Physical Abuse	• unexplained bruises (in various stages of healing), welts, human bite marks, bald spots • unexplained burns, especially cigarette burns or immersion burns (glove-like) • unexplained fractures, lacerations, or abrasions	• self-destructive • withdrawn and aggressive—behavioural extremes • uncomfortable with physical contact • arrives at school early or stays late, as if afraid	• peer problems, lack of involvement • massive weight change • chronic runaway (adolescents) • complains of soreness or moves uncomfortably • wears clothing inappropriate to weather, to cover body
Physical Neglect	• abandonment • unattended medical needs • consistent lack of supervision • consistent hunger, inappropriate dress, poor hygiene • lice, distended stomach, emaciation	• regularly displays fatigue or listlessness, falls asleep in class • steals food, begs from classmates • reports that no caretaker is at home	• frequently absent or tardy • self-destructive • school dropout (adolescents)
Sexual Abuse	• torn, stained, or bloodied underclothing • pain or itching in genital area • difficulty walking or sitting • bruises or bleeding in external genitalia • venereal disease • frequent urinary or yeast infections	• withdrawn, chronic depression • excessive seductiveness • role reversal, overly concerned for siblings • poor self-esteem, self-devaluation, lack of confidence	• suicide attempts (especially adolescents) • hysteria, lack of emotional control • sudden school difficulties • inappropriate sex play or premature understanding of sex • threatened by physical contact, closeness • promiscuity

Source: From Bear, T., Schenk, S., & Buckner, L. (1993). Supporting victims of child abuse. *Educational Leadership, 50*(4), 44. Reprinted with permission of the Association for Supervision and Curriculum Development. Copyright © 1993 by ASCD. All rights reserved.

Check Your Knowledge

- Describe Bronfenbrenner's bioecological model of development.
- What challenges face children whose parents are divorced?
- Why are peer relations important?
- What are peer cultures and how can aggression develop?

Apply to Practice

- As Stephanie's teacher, would you involve her family in dealing with her social problems? What about Alison's family?
- How might teachers support students who, like Stephanie, are victims of online bullying?

SELF-CONCEPT: UNDERSTANDING OURSELVES

What is self-concept? Is self-concept different from self-esteem or identity? You will see that developments in these areas follow patterns similar to those noted in Chapter 2 for cognitive development. Children's understandings of themselves are concrete at first, and then they become more abstract. Early views of self and friends are based on immediate behaviour and appearances. Children assume that others share their feelings and perceptions. Their thinking about themselves and others is simple, segmented, and rule-bound, not flexible or integrated into organized systems. In time, children are able to think abstractly about internal processes—beliefs, intentions, values, and motivations. With these developments in abstract thinking, knowledge of self, others, and situations can incorporate more abstract qualities (Berk, 2005; Harter, 2003).

Self-Concept and Self-Esteem

Psychologists' interests in all aspects of the self have grown steadily. In 1970, about 1 in every 20 publications in psychology was related to the self. By 2000, the ratio was 1 in every 7 (Tesser, Stapel, & Wood, 2002). In educational psychology, much research is focused on self-concept and self-esteem, particularly as they are related to educational outcomes.

The term *self-concept* is part of our everyday conversation. We talk about people who have a "low" self-concept or individuals whose self-concept is not "strong," as if self-concept were fluid levels in a car or a muscle to be developed. These are actually misuses of the term. In psychology, **self-concept** generally refers to individuals' knowledge and beliefs about themselves—their ideas, feelings, attitudes, and expectations (Pajares & Schunk, 2001). We could consider self-concept to be our attempt to explain ourselves to ourselves, to build a scheme (in Piaget's terms) that organizes our impressions, feelings, and attitudes about ourselves. But this model or scheme is not permanent, unified, or unchanging. Our self-perceptions vary from situation to situation and from one phase of our lives to another.

Self-concept and *self-esteem* are often used interchangeably, even though they have distinct meanings. Self-concept is a cognitive structure—a belief about who you are. In contrast, **self-esteem** is an affective reaction—an evaluation of who you are; for example, feeling good about your basketball skills. If people evaluate themselves positively—if they "like what they see"—we say that they have high self-esteem (Pintrich & Schunk, 2002). Sometimes self-esteem is considered one aspect of self-concept—the evaluative part. Self-esteem is influenced by whether the culture around you values your particular characteristics and capabilities (Bandura, 1997). In research, these two concepts are often closely related, so some writers use *self-concept* and *self-esteem* interchangeably. However, there is an important conceptual difference.

self-concept Individuals' knowledge and beliefs about themselves—their ideas, feelings, attitudes, and expectations.

self-esteem The value each of us places on our own characteristics, abilities, and behaviour.

The Structure of Self-Concept.   As can be seen from the model shown in Figure 3.1, an individual's self-concept is hierarchical in nature, with an overall sense of self-worth at the apex and other, more specific self-concepts fanning out below. Self-concepts represent all facets of life, including non-academic self-concepts about, for example, social relations or physical appearance, and academic self-concepts in English, mathematics, art, and other subjects. These self-concepts at the second level are themselves made up of more specific, separate conceptions of the self. For example, self-concepts about social relationships might be made up of concepts about relations with peers, teachers, other adults, and family (particularly parents) (Byrne & Shavelson, 1996; Vispoel, 1995; Yeung et al., 2000). These conceptions are based on many experiences and events, such as sports or academic performances, assessment of one's body, friendships, artistic abilities, contributions to community groups, and so on. For older adolescents and adults, the separate, specific self-concepts are not necessarily integrated into an overall self-concept, so self-concept is more situation-specific in adults (Byrne & Worth Gavin, 1996; Marsh & Ayotte, 2003).

How Self-Concept Develops.   The self-concept evolves through constant self-evaluation in different situations. Children and adolescents are continually asking themselves, in effect, "How am I doing?" They gauge the verbal and non-verbal reactions of significant people—parents and other family members in the early years and friends, schoolmates, and teachers later—to make judgments (Harter, 1998).

Young children tend to make self-concept appraisals based on their own improvement over time. A recent study followed 60 students in New Zealand from the time they started school until the middle of their third year (Chapman, Tunmer, & Prochnow, 2000). In the first two months of school, differences in reading self-concept began to develop, based on the ease or difficulty students had learning to read. Students who entered school with good knowledge about sounds and letters learned to read more easily and developed more positive reading self-concepts. Over time, differences in the reading performance of students with high and low reading self-concepts grew even greater. Thus, the early experiences with the important school task of reading had strong impact on self-concept.

During the middle-school years, as children's cognitive abilities develop, they become more self-conscious. At this age, self-concepts are tied to physical appearance and social acceptance as well as school achievement (Shapka & Keating,

Connect & Extend

TO THE RESEARCH
Byrne, B. M., & Worth Gavin, D. A. (1996). The Shavelson model revisited: Testing for structure of academic self-concept across pre-, early, and late adolescents. *Journal of Educational Psychology, 88,* 215–229.

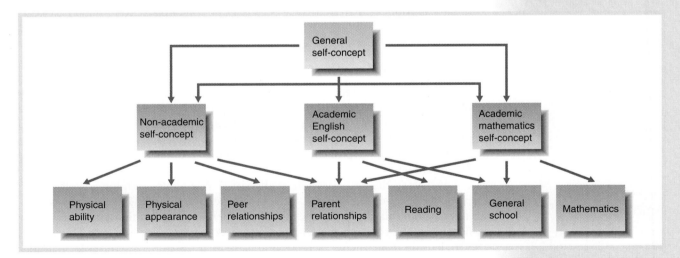

Figure 3.2   Structure of Self-Concept
Students have many separate but sometimes related concepts of themselves. The overall sense of self appears to be divided into at least three separate but slightly related self-concepts—English, mathematics, and non-academic.

Source: From Marsh, H. W., & Shavelson, R. J. (1985). Self-concept: Its multifaceted, hierarchical structure. *Educational Psychologist, 20,* 114. Adapted by permission of the publisher and authors.

2005), so these years can be exceedingly difficult for students such as Stephanie, described at the opening of this chapter (Wigfield, Eccles, & Pintrich, 1996). In academics, students compare their performance with their own standards—their performance in math with their performance in English and science, for example—to form self-concepts in these areas. But social comparisons are becoming more influential, too, at least in Western cultures. Students' self-concepts in math are shaped by how their performance compares with that of other students in their math classes and even by comments their classmates make about them (Altermatt et al., 2002; Pintrich & Schunk, 2002). Students who are strong in math in an average school feel better about their math skills than do students of equal ability in high-achieving schools. Marsh (1990) calls this the "Big-Fish-Little-Pond Effect (BFLP)." Research that surveyed over 100 000 15-year-olds around the world found the BFLP effect in every one of the 26 participating countries (Marsh & Hau, 2003). Participation in a gifted and talented program seems to have an opposite "Little-Fish-Big-Pond" effect: Students who participate in gifted programs, compared with similar students who remain in regular classes, tend to show *declines* in academic self-concepts over time, but no changes in non-academic self-concepts (Marsh & Craven, 2002).

Self-Concept and Achievement.   Many psychologists consider self-concept to be the foundation of both social and emotional development. Research has linked self-concept to a wide range of accomplishments—from performance in competitive sports to job satisfaction and achievement in school (Byrne, 2002; Davis-Kean & Sandler, 2001; Marsh & Hau, 2003; Shapka & Keating 2003). One important way self-concept affects learning in school is through course selection. Think back to high school. When you had a chance to choose courses, did you pick your worst subjects—those where you felt least capable? Probably not. Herbert Marsh and Alexander Yeung (1997) examined how 246 boys in early high school in Sydney, Australia, chose their courses. Academic self-concept for a particular subject (mathematics, science, etc.) was the most important predictor of course selection—more important than previous grades in the subject or overall self-concept. In fact, having a positive self-concept in a particular subject was an even bigger factor in selecting courses when self-concept in other subjects was low. The courses selected in high school put students on a path toward the future, so self-concepts about particular academic subjects can be life-changing influences. Some of Jennifer's work has also shown that self-concept is one of the biggest predictors of post-secondary enrolment, particularly in the area of math and science (Shapka & Keating, 2003).

School Life and Self-Esteem

We turn now to self-esteem—the students' evaluations and feelings about themselves. For teachers, there are at least two questions to ask about self-esteem: (1) How does self-esteem affect a student's behaviour in school? (2) How does life in school affect a student's self-esteem? As you can see from the accompanying Point/Counterpoint, the school's role in student's self-esteem has been hotly debated.

In answer to the first question, it appears that students with higher self-esteem are somewhat more likely to be successful in school (Marsh, 1990), although the strength of the relationship varies greatly, depending on the characteristics of the students and the research methods used (Ma & Kishor, 1997; Marsh & Holmes, 1990). In addition, higher self-esteem is related to more favourable attitudes toward school, more positive behaviour in the classroom, and greater popularity with other students (Cauley & Tyler, 1989; Metcalfe, 1981; Reynolds, 1980). Of course, as we discussed in Chapter 1, knowing that two variables are related (correlated) does not tell us that one is causing the other. It may be that high

Connect & Extend

TO THE RESEARCH
Boileau, L., Bouffard, T., & Vezeau, C. (2000). The examination of self, goals and their impact on school achievement in sixth grade students. *The Canadian Journal of Behavioural Science, 32,* 6–17.

WHAT SHOULD SCHOOLS DO TO ENCOURAGE STUDENTS' SELF-ESTEEM?

More than 2000 books about how to increase self-esteem have been published. Schools and mental health facilities continue to develop self-esteem programs (Slater, 2002). James Beane (1991) begins his article on the school's role in self-esteem, "Sorting Out the Self-Esteem Controversy," with this statement: "In the '90s, the question is not whether schools should enhance students' self-esteem, but how they proposed to do so" (p. 25). The attempts to improve students' self-esteem have taken three main forms: personal development activities such as sensitivity training, self-esteem programs where the curriculum focuses directly on improving self-esteem; and structural changes in schools that place greater emphasis on cooperation, student participation, community involvement, and ethnic pride.

> Point *The self-esteem movement has problems.*

Many of the self-esteem courses are commercial packages—costly for schools but without solid evidence that they make a difference for students (Crisci, 1986; Leming, 1981). As Beane notes, "Saying 'I like myself and others' in front of a group is not the same as actually feeling that way, especially if I am only doing it because I am supposed to. Being nice has a place in enhancing self-esteem, but it is not enough" (p. 26). Some people have accused schools of developing programs where the main objective is "to dole out huge heapings of praise, regardless of actual accomplishments" (Slater, 2002, p. 45).

Sensitivity training and self-esteem courses share a common conceptual problem. They assume that we encourage self-esteem by changing the individual's beliefs, making the young person work harder against the odds. But what if the student's environment is truly unsafe, debilitating, and unsupportive? Some people have overcome tremendous problems, but to expect everyone to do so "ignores the fact that having positive self-esteem is almost impossible for many young people, given the deplorable conditions under which they are forced to live by the inequities in our society" (Beane, 1991, p. 27). Worse yet, some psychologists are now contending that low self-esteem is not a problem, whereas high self-esteem may be. For example, they contend that people with high self-esteem are more willing to inflict pain and punishment on others (Slater, 2002).

< Counterpoint *The self-esteem movement has promise.*

Because many attempts have been superficial, commercial, and filled with pop psychology, the self-esteem movement has become an easy target for critics in magazine articles. But beyond the feel-good psychology of some aspects of the self-esteem movement is a basic truth: "Self-esteem is a central feature of human dignity and thus an inalienable human entitlement. As such, schools and other agencies have a moral obligation to help build it and avoid debilitating it" (Beane 1991, p. 28). If we view self-esteem accurately as a product of our thinking and our beliefs as well as our interactions with others, then we see a significant role for the school. Practices that allow authentic participation, cooperation, problem solving, and accomplishment should replace policies that damage self-esteem, such as tracking and competitive grading.

Beane (1991) suggests four principles to guide educators:

> First, being nice is surely a part of this effort, but it is not enough. Second, there is a place for some direct instruction regarding affective matters, but this is not enough either. Self-esteem and affect are not simply another school subject to be placed in set-aside time slots. Third, the negative affect of "get tough" policies is not a promising route to self-esteem and efficacy. This simply blames young people for problems that are largely not of their own making. Fourth, since self-perceptions are powerfully informed by culture, comparing self-esteem across cultures without clarifying cultural differences is distracting and unproductive. (pp. 29–30)

Psychologist Lauren Slater (2002) suggests that we rethink self-esteem and move toward honest self-appraisal that will lead to self-control:

> Maybe self-control should replace self-esteem as a primary peg to reach for.... Ultimately, self-control need not be experienced as a constriction; restored to its original meaning, it might be experienced as the kind of practiced prowess an athlete or artist demonstrates, muscles not tamed but trained, so that the leaps are powerful, the spine supple and the energy harnessed and shaped. (p. 47)

Sources: From Slater, L. (2002, February 3). The trouble with self-esteem. *The New York Times Magazine,* 44–47; Beane, J. A. (1991). Sorting out the self-esteem controversy. *Educational Leadership, 49*(1), 25–30. Copyright © 1991 by the Association for Supervision and Curriculum Development. Reprinted with permission. All rights reserved.

Research indicates that awards such as "author of the week" have less impact on students' self-esteem than feedback and evaluation from the teacher or interactions with other students in class.

achievement and popularity lead to self-esteem, or vice versa. In fact, it probably works both ways (Marsh, 1987; Pintrich & Schunk, 2002).

What about the second question of how school affects self-esteem—is school important? A study that followed 322 grade 6 students for two years would say yes. Hoge, Smit, and Hanson (1990) found that students' satisfaction with the school, their sense that classes were interesting and that teachers cared, and teacher feedback and evaluations all influenced students' self-esteem. In physical education, teachers' opinions were especially powerful in shaping students' conceptions of their athletic abilities. Being placed in a low-ability group or being held back in school seems to have a negative impact on students' self-esteem, but learning in collaborative and cooperative settings seems to have a positive effect (Covington, 1992; Deci & Ryan, 1985). Interestingly, special programs such as "student of the month" or admission to advanced math classes had little effect on self-esteem. (Relate this to the big-fish–little pond effect.)

More than 100 years ago, William James (1890) suggested that self-esteem is determined by how *successful* we are in accomplishing tasks or reaching goals we *value*. If a skill or accomplishment is not important, incompetence in that area doesn't threaten self-esteem. Susan Harter (1990) has found evidence that James was right. Children who believe an activity is important and who feel capable in that area have higher self-esteem than students who think the activity is important but question their competence. Students must have legitimate success on tasks that matter to them. The way individuals explain their successes or failures is also important. Students must attribute their successes to their own actions, not to luck or to special assistance, in order to build self-esteem.

Teachers' feedback, grading practices, evaluations, and communication of caring for students can make a difference in how students feel about their abilities in particular subjects. But the greatest increases in self-esteem probably come when students grow more competent in areas they value—including the social areas that become so important in adolescence. Thus, a teacher's greatest challenge is to help students achieve important understandings and skills. Given this responsibility, what can teachers do? The recommendations in Table 3.3 are a beginning.

TABLE 3.3 Suggestions for Encouraging Self-Esteem

1. Value and accept all pupils, for their attempts as well as their accomplishments.

2. Create a climate that is physically and psychologically safe for students.

3. Become aware of your own personal biases (everyone has some biases) and expectations.

4. Make sure that your procedures for teaching and grouping students are really necessary, not just a convenient way of handling problem students or avoiding contact with some students.

5. Make standards of evaluation clear; help students learn to evaluate their own accomplishments.

6. Model appropriate methods of self-criticism, perseverance, and self-reward.

7. Avoid destructive comparisons and competition; encourage students to compete with their own prior levels of achievement.

8. Accept a student even when you must reject a particular behaviour or outcome. Students should feel confident, for example, that failing a test or being reprimanded in class does not make them "bad" people.

9. Remember that positive self-concept grows from success in operating in the world and from being valued by important people in the environment.

10. Encourage students to take responsibility for their reactions to events; show them that they have choices in how to respond.

11. Set up support groups or "study buddies" in school and teach students how to encourage each other.

12. Help students set clear goals and objectives; brainstorm about resources they have for reaching their goals.

13. Highlight the value of different ethnic groups—their cultures and accomplishments.

Sources: Information from Canfield, J. (1990). Improving students' self-esteem. *Educational Leadership, 48*(1), 48–50; Kash, M. M., & Borich, G. (1978). *Teacher behavior and student self-concept.* Menlo Park, CA: Addison-Wesley; Marshall, H. H. (1989). The development of self-concept. *Young Children, 44*(5), 44–51.

Diversity and Perceptions of Self

What Would You Say?

As part of the interview process for a job in a middle school, you are asked the following: "What would you do to help all your students feel good about themselves?"

Younger children tend to have positive and optimistic views of themselves. In one study, more than 80 percent of the grade 1 students surveyed thought they were the best students in class. As they mature, students become more realistic, but many are not accurate judges of their own abilities (Paris & Cunningham, 1996). In fact, some students suffer from "illusions of incompetence"—they seriously underestimate their own competence (Phillips & Zimmerman, 1990). Gender and ethnic stereotypes can play roles here.

Gender and Self-Esteem. A recent study followed 761 middle-class, primarily European American students from grade 1 through high school (Jacobs et al., 2002). It is difficult to get longitudinal data, so this is a valuable study. In grade 1, girls and boys had comparable perceptions of their own abilities in language arts, but boys felt significantly more competent in math and sports. As you can see in Figure 3.3 on the next page, competence beliefs declined for both boys and girls across the grades, but boys fell faster in math so that by high school, math competence beliefs were about the same for boys and girls. In language arts, boys' competence ratings fell more sharply than those of girls after grade 1, but both levelled off during high school. In sports, competence ratings for both boys and girls dropped, but boys remained significantly more confident in their competence in sports throughout the entire 12 years.

Other studies have also found that girls tend to see themselves as more able than boys in reading and close friendships, and that boys are more confident about

Figure 3.3 Gender Differences in Changes in Self-Competence over the School Years

Source: Jacobs, J. E., Lanza, S., Osgood, D. W., Eccles, J. S., & Wigfield, A. (2002). Changes in children's self-competence and values: Gender and domain differences across grades 1 through 12. *Child Development, 73,* 516. Copyright © 2002 by the Society for Research in Child Development, University of Michigan Center for Growth & Human Development. Reprinted with permission of the SRCD.

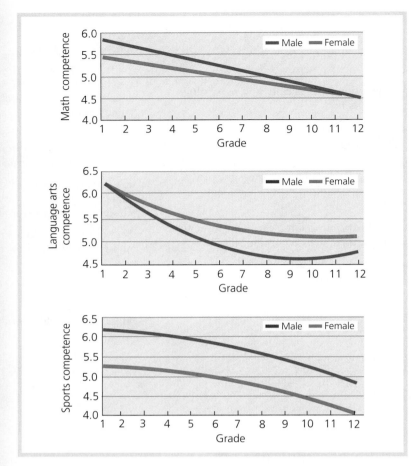

their abilities in math and athletics. Of course, some of these differences in self-confidence may reflect actual differences in achievement—girls tend to be better readers than boys, for example. It is likely that confidence and achievement are reciprocally related—each affects the other (Cole et al., 1999; Eccles, Wigfield, & Schiefele, 1998; Shapka & Keating, 2005). For most ethnic groups (except African Americans), males are more confident about their abilities in math and science. Differences between males and females are generally small, but consistent across studies (Kling et al., 1999; Shapka & Keating, 2003). Unfortunately, there are no long-term studies of other ethnic groups, so these patterns may be limited to European North Americans.

How do students feel about themselves in general during the school years? Jean Twenge and Keith Campbell (2001) analyzed over 150 samples of students from studies conducted between 1968 and 1994, looking at general self-esteem, not subject-specific competence. They found that self-esteem decreased slightly for both girls and boys in the transition to junior high. Then boys' general self-esteem increased dramatically during high school, while girls' self-esteem stayed about the same, leaving girls with significantly lower general self-esteem than boys by the end of high school. These results, together with Marsh and Yeung's (1997) findings that academic self-concept influences course selection, suggest that many students make decisions about courses that forever limit their options in life. Often, these decisions are not based on ability but instead on "illusions of incompetence."

Ethnicity and Perceptions of Self.   To this point, we have discussed self-esteem as a purely individual characteristic. A number of psychologists have suggested that there is another basis for self-worth and identity called the *collective self,* or the self as a member of a family, peer group, ethnic heritage, class, or team (Wright & Taylor, 1995). Perhaps our self-esteem is influenced by both individual qualities and by **collective self-esteem**—a sense of the worth of the groups to which we belong. When students are faced with daily reminders, subtle or blatant, that their ethnic or family group has less status and power, the basis for collective self-esteem can erode.

collective self-esteem The sense of the value of a group, such as an ethnic group, to which one belongs.

Some early research on children's perceptions seemed to indicate that children from ethnic minority groups internalized negative stereotypes. In a seminal study by Clark and Clark (1939), African American children, when confronted with a light-skinned and a dark-skinned doll, tended to choose the light-skinned doll as prettier and better on a number of dimensions. Similar findings were reported for Mexican American children (Weiland & Coughlin, 1979), Chinese American children (Aboud & Skerry, 1984), and Canadian Native children (Corenblum & Annis, 1987). However, many of these studies didn't ask the children *why* they preferred the light-skinned dolls. Some psychologists suggest that the children are simply indicating that they understand the power and status differences that surround them. The children do not think less of themselves—their self-esteem is high—but they know that majority-group members tend to have more wealth and power (Spencer & Markstrom-Adams, 1990).

For all students, pride in family and community is part of the foundation for a stable identity and collective self-esteem. Because ethnic-minority students are members of both a majority culture and a subculture, it is sometimes difficult for them to establish a clear identity. Values, learning styles, and communication patterns of the students' subculture may be inconsistent with the expectations of the school and the larger society. Embracing the values of mainstream culture may seem to require rejecting ethnic values. Ethnic-minority students have to "sift through two sets of cultural values and identity options" to achieve a firm identity, so they may need more time to explore possibilities (Markstrom-Adams, 1992, p. 177). In the process of establishing identity, individuals may pass through several stages (Frable, 1997):

- being unaware of, denying, or devaluing ethnic identity;
- being challenged by conflicts and discrimination to confront and examine ethnicity;
- becoming immersed in a particular ethnic or racial consciousness;
- appreciating ethnicity;
- integrating ethnicity into a full and complex bicultural identity.

Jim Cummins (1989), at the University of Toronto, encourages schools to make special efforts to foster **ethnic pride** so that these students do not get the message that differences are deficits. For example, Cummins suggests that schools display bilingual and multilingual signs, provide opportunities for students to use their first languages, and arrange for parents and community members who represent ethnic minorities to be involved in school events. Each of us has an ethnic heritage. When adolescents from ethnic majorities are knowledgeable and secure about their own heritage, they are also more respectful of the heritage of others. Thus, exploring the ethnic roots of all students should foster both self-esteem and acceptance of others (Rotherham-Borus, 1994).

ethnic pride A positive self-concept about one's racial or ethnic heritage.

There is a particular aspect of ethnic heritage and pride that affects schooling—language. In Chapter 5, we will examine language learning in greater depth. But while we are talking about self-esteem, consider the results of a study conducted by Stephen Wright and Donald Taylor (1995) on the impact of heritage language on personal and collective self-esteem. These researchers found that when Inuit children were educated in their heritage language for the first three years of school, they had more positive personal and collective self-esteem than the Inuit children in the same school who received second-language instruction (English or French) from kindergarten on. When schools value the language of all students, ethnic pride and collective self-esteem may be enhanced.

One very important group membership for all students is their family. A study by John Fantuzzo, Gwendolyn Davis, and Marika Ginsburg (1995) capitalized on

BUILDING SELF-ESTEEM

1. Work with families to co-create methods for family involvement. Offer a range of possible participation methods. Make sure the plans are realistic and fit the lives of the families.

2. Maintain regular contact between home and school through telephone calls or notes. If a family has no telephone, identify a contact person (relative or friend) who can take messages. If literacy is a problem, use pictures, symbols, and codes for written communication.

3. Make all communications positive, emphasizing growth, progress, and accomplishments.

4. With the family, design family–student celebrations of the student's efforts and successes (a movie, spe-cial meal, trip to the park or library, going out for ice cream or pizza).

5. On a regular basis, send home a note in word or picture form that describes the student's progress. Ask the family to indicate how they celebrated the success and to return the note.

6. Follow up with a telephone call to discuss progress, answer questions, solicit family suggestions, and express appreciation for the families' contributions.

7. Encourage families to visit the classroom.

Source: Adapted from Fantuzzo, J., Davis, G., & Ginsburg, M. (1995). Effects of parent involvement in isolation or in combination with peer tutoring on student self-concept and mathematics achievement. *Journal of Educational Psychology, 87,* 272–281.

Connect & Extend

TO THE RESEARCH

Lay, C., & Verkyten, M. (1999). Ethnic identity and its relation to personal self-esteem: A comparison of Canadian-born and foreign-born Chinese adolescents. *Journal of Social Psychology, 139,* 288–299.

Abstract

Ethnic identity and its relation to personal self-esteem were examined by comparing 31 Chinese adolescents (aged 13–18 years) who immigrated to Canada and 31 who were Canadian-born. The foreign-born adolescents were more likely to identify themselves as Chinese (rather than Chinese Canadian) and to include references to their ethnicity in response to an open-ended Who Am I Questionnaire, a variation of the 20 Statements Test (M. H. Kuhn & T. S. McPartland, 1954). For the foreign-born group only, aspects of collective self-esteem were positively related to personal self-esteem. The data were consistent with an interpretation involving collectivistic-individualistic distinctions, with the foreign-born sample being more collectivistic.

the power of families to improve students' self-esteem. The Family and Community Partnerships feature lists the strategies from their study that proved effective in increasing self-esteem and mathematics achievement for ethnic-minority students in grades 4 and 5.

Check Your Knowledge

- What are the similarities and differences between self-concept and self-esteem?
- How do self-concept and self-esteem change as children develop?
- Are there differences in self-concepts for boys and girls?

Apply to Practice

- How might Stephanie's experiences with peers influence her self-concept and self-esteem, given her age?

EMOTIONAL AND MORAL DEVELOPMENT

As we seek our own identity and form images of ourselves, we are also seeking and forming ways to understand the "significant others" around us. Children learn to see themselves as separate and to see others as separate people as well, with their own identities. How do we learn to interpret what others are thinking and feeling?

Emotional Competence

Understanding intentions and taking the perspective of others are elements in the development of emotional competence, or the ability to understand and manage emotional situations. Carolyn Saarni (2002) says that "we demonstrate emotional competence when we emerge from an emotion-eliciting encounter with a sense of having accomplished what we set out to do" (p. 3). Social and emotional competences are critical for both academic and personal development. In fact, a number of studies that followed students over several years in the United States and in Italy have found that pro-social behaviours and social competence in the early grades are related to academic achievement and popularity with peers as many as five years later (Elias & Schwab, 2006). Table 3.4 describes eight skills of emotional

TABLE 3.4 Emotional Competence Skills

Here are eight skills that make up emotional competence:

1. Awareness of your own emotions, including understanding that you can feel multiple emotions at the same time.

2. Ability to read emotions in others, even taking into account cultural differences in emotional expression.

3. Ability to talk about emotions with appropriate vocabulary.

4. Capacity for empathy and sympathy with others.

5. Knowing that outward emotional expression may not match inner feelings in yourself or in others.

6. Capacity to cope with negative emotions and manage stress in ways that are adaptive—not harmful to yourself or others.

7. Awareness that relationships are defined in part by how emotions are expressed within them and that different kinds of relationships (parent–child, employer–employee, close friends, acquaintances, etc.) involve different kinds of appropriate expressions.

8. Capacity for emotional self-efficacy—feeling that, overall, your emotions fit your own beliefs about emotional balance and your own moral sense.

Source: From Saarni, C. (2002). *The development of emotional competence.* New York: Guilford Publications. Copyright © 2002 by Guilford Publications, Inc. Adapted with permission of the publisher.

competence. How can teachers help students develop emotional competence? The Guidelines on page 92 give some ideas. In Chapter 11 we look at teaching strategies and programs that encourage self-regulation of emotions.

Theory of Mind and Intention

By two or three years old, children are beginning to develop a **theory of mind,** an understanding that other people are people too, with their own minds, thoughts, feelings, beliefs, desires, and perceptions (Flavell, Miller, & Miller, 2002). Children need a theory of mind to make sense of other people's behaviour. Why is Sarah crying? Does she feel sad because no one will play with her? You will see in Chapter 4 that one explanation for autism is that children with this condition lack a theory of mind to help them understand their own or other people's emotions and behaviours.

Around the age of two, children have a sense of intention, at least of their own intentions. They will announce, "I wanna peanut butter sandwich." They can say firmly, "I didn't break it on purpose!" By two and a half or three years of age, children extend the understanding of intention to others. Older preschoolers who get along well with their peers are able to separate intentional from unintentional actions and react accordingly. For example, they will not get angry when other children accidentally knock over their block towers.

With a developing theory of mind, children are increasingly able to understand that other people have different feelings and experiences, and therefore may have a different viewpoint or perspective. This **perspective-taking ability** develops over time until it is quite sophisticated in adults. Being able to understand how others might think and feel is important in fostering cooperation and moral development, reducing prejudice, resolving conflicts, and encouraging positive social behaviours in general (Gehlbach, 2004). Marion Porath (2001, 2003), at the University of British Columbia, has conducted research about young children's social understanding. Her findings indicate that preschool girls engage in more sophisticated reasoning about social situations than boys the same age do and are better able to interpret subtle social cues. Also, she finds children's understandings of others' intentions to be a significant predictor of children's ability to analyze classroom experiences. Other research indicates that aggressive children have more trouble

Connect & Extend

TO YOUR TEACHING/PORTFOLIO

For a full description of several programs and strategies that support social emotional learning, see Cohen, J. (Ed.) (1999). *Educating minds and hearts: Social emotional learning and the passage into adolescence.* New York: Teachers College Press.

theory of mind An understanding that other people are people too, with their own minds, thoughts, feelings, beliefs, desires, and perceptions.

perspective-taking ability Understanding that others have different feelings and experiences.

GUIDELINES
ENCOURAGING EMOTIONAL COMPETENCE

Create a climate of trust in your classroom.

EXAMPLES

1. Avoid listening to "tattle-tale" stories about students.
2. Follow through with fair consequences.
3. Avoid unnecessary comparisons and give students opportunities to improve their work.

Help students recognize and express their feelings.

EXAMPLES

1. Provide a vocabulary of emotions and note descriptions of emotions in characters or stories.
2. Be clear and descriptive about your own emotions.
3. Encourage students to write in journals about their own feelings. Protect the privacy of those who do so (see trust above).

Help students recognize emotions in others.

EXAMPLES

1. For young children, ask direct questions that help them realize what others might be feeling, such as

"Look at Chandra's face. How do you think she feels when you say those things?"
2. For older students, use readings, films, or role reversals to help them identify the emotions of others.

Provide strategies for coping with emotions.

EXAMPLES

1. Discuss or practise alternatives such as stopping to think how the other person feels, seeking help, or using anger-management strategies such as self-talk or leaving the scene.
2. Model strategies for students. Talk about how you handle anger, disappointment, or anxiety.

Help students recognize cultural differences in emotional expression.

EXAMPLES

1. Have students write about or discuss how they show emotions in their family.
2. Teach students to ask other people how they are feeling.

assessing intention. They are likely to attack anyone who topples their towers, even accidentally (Berk, 2002; Dodge & Somberg, 1987). As children mature, they are more able to assess and consider the intentions of others.

Robert Selman (1980) has developed a stage model to describe perspective-taking. As children mature and move toward formal-operational thinking, they take more information into account and realize that different people can react differently to the same situation. At some point between the ages of 10 and 15, most children develop the ability to analyze the perspectives of several people involved in a situation from the viewpoint of an objective bystander. Finally, older adolescents and adults can even imagine how different cultural or social values would influence the perceptions of the bystander. Even though children move through these stages, there can be great variation among children of the same age. Students who have difficulty taking the perspective of others may feel little remorse when they mistreat peers or adults. Some coaching in perspective-taking from the teacher might help if the mistreatment is not part of a deeper emotional or behavioural disorder (Berk, 2005).

Moral Development

moral reasoning The thinking process involved in judgments about questions of right and wrong.

Along with a more advanced theory of mind and an understanding of intention, children also are developing a sense of right and wrong. In this section we focus on children's **moral reasoning**, their *thinking* about right and wrong and their *active construction* of moral judgments. Some of the earliest moral issues in classrooms involve dividing and sharing materials or **distributive justice** (Damon, 1994). For young children (ages five to six), fair distribution is based on *equality;* thus, teachers often hear, "Tristan got more than I did—that's not fair!" In the next few years, children come to recognize that some people should get more based on *merit*—they worked harder or performed better. Finally, around age eight, children are able to take need into account and to reason based on *benevolence;* they can understand that some students may get more time or resources from the teacher because those students have special needs.

Another area that involves moral development is an understanding of rules. If you have spent time with young children, you know that there is a period when you can say, "Eating in the living room is not allowed!" and get away with it. For young children, rules simply exist. Piaget (1965) called this the state of **moral realism**. At this stage, the child of five or six believes that rules about conduct or rules about how to play a game are absolute and can't be changed. If a rule is broken, the child believes that the punishment should be determined by how much damage is done, not by the intention of the child or by other circumstances. So, accidentally breaking three cups is worse than intentionally breaking one, and in the child's eyes, the punishment for the three-cup offence should be greater.

As children interact with others, develop perspective-taking emotional abilities, and see that different people have different rules, there is a gradual shift to a **morality of cooperation**. Children come to understand that people make rules and people can change them. When rules are broken, both the damage done and the intention of the offender are taken into account.

Kohlberg's Theories of Moral Development. Lawrence Kohlberg's (1963, 1975, 1981) theory of moral development is based in part on Piaget's ideas, described earlier. Kohlberg has evaluated the moral reasoning of both children and adults by presenting them with **moral dilemmas**, or hypothetical situations in which people must make difficult decisions and give their reasons for their decision. The following is a classic example of one such dilemma:

> A man's wife is dying. There is one drug that could save her, but it is very expensive, and the druggist who invented it will not sell it at a price low enough for the man to buy it. Finally, the man becomes desperate and considers stealing the drug for his wife. What should he do and why?

Based on the individual's reasoning, Kohlberg proposed a detailed sequence of stages of moral reasoning, or judgments about right and wrong. He divided moral development into three levels: (1) preconventional, where judgment is based solely on a person's own needs and perceptions; (2) conventional, where the expectations of society and law are taken into account; and (3) postconventional, where judgments are based on abstract, more personal principles of justice that are not necessarily defined by society's laws. Look at Table 3.5 on page 94 to see how each of these three levels is then subdivided into stages.

At level 1 (the preconventional level), the child's answer might be, "It is wrong to steal because you might get caught." This answer reflects the child's basic egocentrism. The reasoning might be, "What would happen to me if I stole something? I might get caught and punished."

At level 2 (the conventional level), the subject is able to look beyond the immediate personal consequences and consider the views, and especially the approval, of others. Laws, religious or civil, are very important and are regarded as absolute and unalterable. One answer stressing adherence to rules is, "It is wrong to steal because it is against the law." Another answer, placing high value on loyalty to family and loved ones but still respecting the law, is, "It's right to steal because the man means well—he's trying to help his wife. But he will still have to pay the druggist when he can or accept the penalty for breaking the law."

At level 3 (the postconventional level), one answer might be, "It is not wrong to steal because human life must be preserved. The worth of a human life is greater

distributive justice Beliefs about how to divide materials or privileges fairly among members of a group; follows a sequence of development from equality to merit to benevolence.

moral realism Stage of development wherein children see rules as absolute.

morality of cooperation Stage of development wherein children realize that people make rules and people can change them.

moral dilemmas Situations in which no single choice is clearly and indisputably right.

TABLE 3.5 Kohlberg's Stage Theory of Moral Reasoning

Level 1: Preconventional Moral Reasoning	Level 2: Conventional Moral Reasoning	Level 3: Postconventional Moral Reasoning
Judgment is based on personal needs and others' rules.	Judgment is based on others' approval, family expectations, traditional values, the laws of society, and loyalty to country.	Stage 5 Social Contract Orientation
Stage 1 Punishment–Obedience Orientation		Good is determined by socially agreed-upon standards of individual rights.
Rules are obeyed to avoid punishment. A good or bad action is determined by its physical consequences.	Stage 3 Good Boy–Nice Girl Orientation	Stage 6* Universal Ethical Principle Orientation
Stage 2 Personal Reward Orientation	Good means "nice." It is determined by what pleases, aids, and is approved by others.	Good and right are matters of individual conscience and involve abstract concepts of justice, human dignity, and equality.
Personal needs determine right and wrong. Favours are returned along the lines of "you scratch my back; I'll scratch yours."	Stage 4 Law and Order Orientation	
	Laws are absolute. Authority must be respected and the social order maintained.	

*In later work, Kohlberg questioned whether stage 6 exists separately from stage 5.
Source: From Kohlberg, L. (1975). The cognitive-developmental approach to moral education. *Phi Delta Kappan, 56,* 671. Adapted by permission of the *Journal of Philosophy.*

than the worth of property." This response considers the underlying values that might be involved in the decision. Abstract concepts are no longer rigid, and, as the name of this level implies, principles can be separated from conventional values. A person reasoning on this level understands that what is considered right by the majority may not be considered right by an individual in a particular situation. Rational, personal choice is stressed.

Moral reasoning is related to both cognitive and emotional development. As we have seen, abstract thinking becomes increasingly important in the higher stages of moral development, as children move from decisions based on absolute rules to decisions based on abstract principles such as justice and mercy. The ability to see another's perspective, to judge intentions, and to imagine alternative bases for laws and rules also enters into judgments at the higher stages.

Criticisms of Kohlberg's Theory.   Even though there is evidence that the different levels of reasoning identified by Kohlberg do form a hierarchy, with each stage representing an advancement in reasoning over the one before (Boom, Brugman, & van der Heijden, 2001), the stage theory has been criticized. First, in reality, the stages do not seem to be separate, sequenced, and consistent. People often give reasons for moral choices that reflect several different stages simultaneously. Or a person's choices in one instance may fit one stage, while his or her decisions in a different situation may reflect another stage. When asked to reason about helping someone else versus meeting their own needs, both children and adolescents reason at higher levels than when they are asked to reason about breaking the law or risking punishment (Arnold, 2000; Eisenberg et al., 1987; Sobesky, 1983).

Second, in everyday life, making moral choices involves more reasoning. Emotions, competing goals, relationships, and practical considerations all affect choices. People may be able to reason at higher levels but may make choices at lower levels based on these other factors (Carpendale, 2000). Kohlberg emphasized cognitive reasoning about morality, but he overlooked other aspects of moral maturity, such as character and virtue, that operate to solve moral problems in everyday life (Walker & Pitts, 1998).

Another criticism is that Kohlberg's theory does not differentiate between social conventions and true moral issues until the higher stages of moral reasoning. Social conventions are the social rules and expectations of a particular group or society—for example, "It is rude to eat with your hands." Such behaviour is not morally wrong, just socially inappropriate; in some cultures or situations, it is acceptable to eat with your hands (in fact, try eating potato chips with a fork). True moral issues, on the other hand, involve the rights of individuals, the general welfare of the group, or the avoidance of harm. "Stealing" would be wrong, even if there were no "rule" against it; stealing is wrong, not rude. Children as young as three can distinguish between social conventions and moral issues. They know, for example, that being noisy in school would be fine if there were no rule requiring quiet, but that it would not be right to hit another child, even if there were no rule against it. So even very young children can reason based on moral principles that are not tied to social conventions and rules (Nucci, 1987; Smetana & Braeges, 1990; Turiel, 1983).

Another criticism of Kohlberg's stage theory is that stages 5 and 6 in moral reasoning are biased in favour of Western, male values that emphasize individualism. In cultures that are more family-centred or group-oriented, the highest moral value might involve putting the opinions of the group before decisions based on individual conscience. There has been much disagreement over the "highest" moral stage. Kohlberg himself questioned the applicability of stage 6. Few people other than trained philosophers reason naturally or easily at this level. Kohlberg (1984) suggested that for all practical purposes, stages 5 and 6 might be combined.

The Morality of Caring. One of the most hotly debated criticisms of Kohlberg's theory is that the stages are biased in favour of males and do not represent the way moral reasoning develops in women. Because the stage theory was based on a longitudinal study of men only, it is very possible that the moral reasoning of women and the stages of women's development are not adequately represented (Gilligan, 1982; Gilligan & Attanucci, 1988). Carol Gilligan (1982) has proposed a different sequence of moral development, an "ethic of care." Gilligan suggests that individuals move from a focus on self-interests to moral reasoning based on commitment to specific individuals and relationships, and then to the highest level of morality based on the principles of responsibility and care for all people.

The highest stage in Kohlberg's theory of moral development involves decisions based on universal principles of justice and fairness. Reasoning based on caring for others and maintaining relationships is scored at a lower level. Many of Kohlberg's early studies of moral reasoning found that most men progressed to stages 4 and 5 by adulthood, while most women "stayed" at stage 3. This makes it appear as if women are morally challenged. But recent studies find few significant differences between men and women, or boys and girls, in their level of moral reasoning as measured by Kohlberg's procedures (Eisenberg, Martin, & Fabes, 1996; Turiel, 1998).

In order to study moral reasoning as it actually happens in real life, and to get an idea about the basis for decisions, Walker and his colleagues (Walker, 1991; Walker et al., 1995) asked children, adolescents, and adults to describe a personal moral problem and analyze a traditional moral dilemma. For both types of problems, males and females revealed both a morality of caring and a concern with justice. Andrew Garrod and his colleagues (1990) used fables to study the moral reasoning of students in grades 1, 3, and 5 and found that both boys and girls tended to adopt a care orientation. There were no differences between the moral reasoning of boys and girls in grades 1 and 3. However, a few grade 5 boys (but no girls) suggested solutions involving violence or tricks. So justice and caring seem to be important bases for moral reasoning for both genders. Even though men and women both seem to value caring and justice, there is some evidence that in everyday life, women feel more guilty about violating caring norms by being inconsiderate or untrustworthy, for example, and men feel more guilty when they show

Connect & Extend

TO YOUR TEACHING
In a classroom discussion about stealing, the teacher finds that many students express the opinion that it is all right to steal if you don't get caught. How should a teacher respond? Would the race, culture, gender, or socioeconomic status of the student influence the teacher's response?

Carol Gilligan has challenged traditional conceptions of moral development with her work on the "ethic of care."

Connect & Extend

TO PROFESSIONAL JOURNALS

See the May 1995 issue of *Phi Delta Kappan* for a special section on schools and caring. Nel Noddings's article is included, as well as an article by Joyce Epstein about family–school partnerships to create caring schools.

violent behaviour, such as fighting or damaging property (Williams & Bybee, 1994). Women are somewhat more likely to use a care orientation, but both men and women *can* use both orientations (Skoe, 1998).

Caring for students and helping students learn to care has become a theme for many educators. For example, Nel Noddings (1995) urged that "themes of care" be used to organize the curriculum. Possible themes include "Caring for Self," "Caring for Family and Friends," and "Caring for Strangers and the World." Using the theme of "Caring for Strangers and the World," there could be units on crime, war, poverty, tolerance, ecology, or technology. Table 3.6 shows how a focus on crime and caring for strangers could be integrated into several high school classes.

Moral versus Conventional Domains and Implications for Teachers

For teachers, the most common "right and wrong" situations involve the moral and conventional domains. In the moral domain, beginning with a few basic ideas about right and wrong ("It is wrong to hurt others"), children move through the following stages: a sense that justice means equal treatment for all, an appreciation of equity and special needs, a more abstract integration of equity and equality along with a sense of caring in social relations, and finally, a sense as adults that morality involves beneficence and fairness and that moral principles are independent of the norms of any particular group.

In the conventional domain, children begin by believing that the regularities they see are real and right—men have short hair, women have longer hair, for example, so that is the way it should be. As they mature, children see the exceptions (men with ponytails, women with very short cuts) and realize that conventions are arbitrary. Next, children understand that rules, even though they are arbitrary, are made to maintain order and that people in charge make the rules. But by early adolescence, students begin to question these rules. Because they are arbitrary and made by others, maybe rules are "nothing but" social expectations. As they move through adolescence, there is another swing—from understanding

---

TABLE 3.6 Using "Caring for Strangers and the World" as a Teaching Theme

As part of a unit on "Caring for Strangers and the World," high school students examine the issue of crime in several classes. In every class, the study of aspects of crime would be continually tied to the theme of caring and to discussions of safety, responsibility, trust in each other and in the community, and commitment to a safer future.

Subject	Elements
Mathematics	Statistics: Gather data on the location and rates of crimes, ages of offenders, and costs of crime to society. Is there a correlation between severity of punishment and incidence of crime? What is the actual cost of a criminal trial?
English and social studies	Read *Oliver Twist*. Relate the characters to their social and historical context. What factors contributed to crime in 19th-century England?
	Read popular mysteries. Are they literature? Are they accurate depictions of the criminal justice system?
Science	Genetics: Are criminal tendencies heritable? Are there sex differences in aggressive behaviour? Are women less competent than men in moral reasoning (and why did some social scientists think so)? How would you test this hypothesis?
Arts	Is graffiti art really art?

Source: From Noddings, N. Teaching themes of care. *Phi Delta Kappan, 76,* 675–679. Copyright © 1995 Phi Delta Kappan. Reprinted by permission of Phi Delta Kappan and the author.

conventions as the appropriate way things have to operate in a social system to again seeing them as nothing but society's standards that have become set because they are used. Finally, adults realize that conventions are useful in coordinating social life, but changeable, too. So, compared with young children, older adolescents and adults are generally more accepting of others who think differently about conventions and customs.

Nucci (2001) offers several suggestions for creating a moral atmosphere in your classroom. First, it is important to establish a community of mutual respect and warmth with a fair and consistent application of the rules. Without that kind of community, all your attempts to create a moral climate will be undermined. Second, teachers' responses to students should be appropriate to the domain of the behaviour—moral or conventional. For example, here are some responses to *moral issues* (Nucci, 2001, p. 146):

1. When an act is inherently hurtful or unjust, emphasize the harm done to others: "John, that really hurt Jamal."

2. Encourage perspective-taking: "Chris, how would you feel if someone stole from you?"

Here are two responses to rule or *conventional issues*:

3. Restate the rule: "Lisa, you are not allowed to be out of your seat during announcements."

4. Command: "Howie, stop swearing!"

In all four cases, the teacher's response fits the domain. To create an inappropriate response, just switch responses 1 or 2 with 3 or 4. For example, "Jim, how would you feel if other people got out of their seat during announcements?" Jim might feel just fine. And it is a weak response to a moral transgression to say, "John, it is against the rules to hit." It is more than against the rules—it hurts and it is wrong.

In the third domain, personal, children must sort out what decisions and actions are their personal choices and what decisions are outside personal choice. This process is the foundation for developing moral concepts related to individual rights, fairness, and democracy. Here, different cultures may have very different understandings about individual choice, privacy, and the role of individuality in the larger society. For example, some research has shown that both the parents in cultures that emphasize individualism and the parents in cultures that emphasize group membership believe that children need to be given choices to develop their ability to make good decisions. But middle-class parents tend to encourage making choices earlier, before adolescence. For children living in poverty, making too many choices early may be a bad idea, given the very real dangers they face in their neighbourhoods (Nucci, 2001).

Moral Behaviour

As people move toward higher stages of moral reasoning, they also evidence more sharing, helping, and defending of victims of injustice. This relationship between moral reasoning and moral behaviour is not very strong, however (Berk, 2002). Many other factors besides reasoning affect behaviour. Three important influences on moral behaviour are modelling, internalization, and self-concept.

First, children who have been consistently exposed to caring, generous adult models will tend to be more concerned for the rights and feelings of others (Lipscomb, MacAllister, & Bregman, 1985). Most theories of moral behaviour assume that young children's moral behaviour is first controlled by others through direct instruction, supervision, rewards and punishments, and correction. But in time, children **internalize** the moral rules and principles of the authority figures who have guided them; that is, children adopt the external standards as their own. If

internalize To adopt external standards as one's own.

children are given reasons that they can understand when they are corrected—particularly reasons that highlight the effects of actions on others—then they are more likely to internalize moral principles. They learn to behave morally even when "no one is watching" (Berk, 2002; Hoffman, 2000).

Finally, we must integrate moral beliefs and values into our total sense of who we are, our self-concept.

The tendency for a person to behave morally is largely dependent on the extent to which moral beliefs and values are integrated in the personality, and in one's sense of self. The influence our moral beliefs have on our lives, therefore, is contingent on the personal importance that we as individuals attach to them—we must identify and respect them as our own (Arnold, 2000, p. 372).

The following Guidelines give ideas for supporting personal and moral development. Let's consider a moral issue that arises in classrooms—cheating.

GUIDELINES
SUPPORTING PERSONAL AND SOCIAL DEVELOPMENT

Help students examine the kinds of dilemmas they are currently facing or will face in the near future.

EXAMPLES

1. In elementary school, discuss sibling rivalries, teasing, stealing, prejudice, treatment of new students in the class, behaviour toward classmates with disabilities.
2. In high school, discuss cheating, letting friends drive when they are intoxicated, conforming to be more popular, protecting a friend who has broken a rule.

Help students see the perspectives of others.

EXAMPLES

1. Ask a student to describe his or her understanding of the views of another, and then have the other person confirm or correct the perception.
2. Have students exchange roles and try to "become" the other person in a discussion.

Help students make connections between expressed values and actions.

EXAMPLES

1. Follow a discussion of "What should be done?" with "How would you act? What would be your first step? What problems might arise?"
2. Help students see inconsistencies between their values and their own actions. Ask them to identify inconsistencies, first in others, then in themselves.

Safeguard the privacy of all participants.

EXAMPLES

1. Remind students that in a discussion they can "pass" and not answer questions.
2. Intervene if peer pressure is forcing a student to say more than he or she might like.
3. Don't reinforce a pattern of telling "secrets."

Make sure students are really listening to each other.

EXAMPLES

1. Keep groups small.
2. Be a good listener yourself.
3. Recognize students who pay careful attention to each other.

Make sure that your class reflects concern for moral issues and values as much as possible.

EXAMPLES

1. Make clear distinctions between rules based on administrative convenience (keeping the room orderly) and rules based on moral issues.
2. Enforce standards uniformly. Be careful about showing favouritism.

Source: Adapted with permission from Eiseman, J. W. (1981). What criteria should public school moral education programs meet? *The Review of Education, 7,* 226–227.

Cheating

Early research indicates that cheating seems to have more to do with the particular situation than with the general honesty or dishonesty of the individual (Burton, 1963). A student who cheats in math class is probably more likely to cheat in other classes, but may never consider lying to a friend or taking candy from the store. Many students will cheat if the pressure to perform well is great and the chances of being caught are slim. In one study, about 60 percent of middle-school students and 70 percent of high-school students believed that cheating was a serious problem in their school (Evans & Craig, 1990). In 1996, Steinberg reported that 66 percent of the adolescents in his study admitted to cheating on a test in the last year, and figures as high as 90 percent have been reported for college students (Jensen et al., 2001). But the sad fact is that cheating by all groups has increased over the past 20 years (Jensen et al., 2002; Murdock, Hale, & Weber, 2001).

There are some individual differences in cheating. Most studies of adolescent and university-age students find that males are more likely to cheat than females and lower-achieving students are more likely to cheat than higher achievers. Students focusing on performance goals (making good grades, looking smart) as opposed to learning goals, and students with a low sense of academic self-efficacy (a belief that they probably can't do well in school) are more likely to cheat.

Cheating is not all about individual differences—the situation plays a role as well. In one study, the level of cheating decreased when students moved from math classes that emphasized competition and grades to classes that emphasized understanding and mastery (Anderman & Midgley, 2004). Students are also particularly likely to cheat when they are behind or "cramming for tests" or when they believe that their teachers do not care about them. For example, Erica had this perspective:

> I am a high school honors student, and I think there are different degrees of cheating. I'm a dedicated student, but when my history teacher bombards me with 50 questions due tomorrow or when a teacher gives me a fill-in-the-blanks worksheet on a night when I have swim practice, church, aerobics—and other homework—I'm going to copy from a friend!... Since I only do this when I need to, it isn't a habit. Every kid does this when they're in a pinch. (Jensen et al., 2002, p. 210)

The implications for teachers are straightforward. To prevent cheating, try to avoid putting students in high-pressure situations. Make sure they are well prepared for tests, projects, and assignments so that they can do reasonably well without cheating. Focus on learning and not on grades. Encourage collaboration on assignments and experiment with open-book, collaborative, or take-home tests. Anita often tells her students what concepts will be on the test and encourages them to discuss the concepts and their applications before the test. You might also make extra help available for those who need it. Be clear about your policies in regard to cheating, and enforce them consistently. Help students resist temptation by monitoring them carefully during testing.

Check Your Knowledge

- What are the skills involved in emotional competence?
- What are the key differences among the preconventional, conventional, and postconventional levels of moral reasoning?
- Describe Gilligan's levels of moral reasoning.
- What influences moral behaviour?

Apply to Practice

- How can teachers encourage moral behaviour and caring?

Physical Development
(pp. 62–64)

Describe the changes in physical development in the preschool, elementary, and secondary grades.

During the preschool years, there is rapid development of children's gross- and fine-motor skills. Physical development continues throughout the elementary-school years, with girls often ahead of boys in size. With adolescence comes puberty and emotional struggles to cope with all the related changes.

What are some of the consequences of early and late maturation for boys and girls?

Females mature about two years ahead of males. Early-maturing boys are more likely to enjoy high social status; they tend to be popular and to be leaders. But they also tend to engage in more delinquent behaviour. Early maturation is not generally beneficial for girls.

What are some of the signs of eating disorders?

Anorexic students may appear pale, have brittle fingernails, and have fine dark hairs developing all over their bodies. They are easily chilled because they have so little fat to insulate their bodies. They often are depressed, insecure, moody, and lonely. Girls may stop having their menstrual period.

Erikson: Stages of Individual Development
(pp. 64–69)

Why is Erikson's theory considered a psychosocial perspective?

Erikson was interested in the ways individuals develop psychologically to become active and contributing members of society. He believed that all humans have the same basic needs and that each society must accommodate those needs. Erikson's emphasis on the relationship between society and the individual is a psychosocial theory of development—a theory that connects personal development (psycho) to the social environment (social).

What are Erikson's stages of psychosocial development?

Erikson believed that people go through eight life stages between infancy and old age, each of which involves a central crisis. Adequate resolution of each crisis leads to greater personal and social competence and a stronger foundation for solving future crises. In the first two stages, an infant must develop a sense of trust over mistrust and a sense of autonomy over shame and doubt. In early childhood, the focus of the third stage is on developing initiative and avoiding feelings of guilt. In the child's elementary-school years, the fourth stage involves achieving a sense of industry and avoiding feelings of inferiority. In the fifth stage, identity versus role confusion, adolescents consciously attempt to solidify their identity. According to Marcia, these efforts may lead to identity achievement, foreclosure, diffusion, or moratorium. Erikson's three stages of adulthood involve struggles to achieve intimacy, generativity, and integrity.

Bronfenbrenner: The Social Context for Development
(pp. 70–82)

Describe Bronfenbrenner's bioecological model of development.

This model takes into account both the biological aspects internal to the individual and the nested social and culturahl contexts that shape development. Every person develops within a *microsystem* (immediate relationships and activities) inside a *mesosystem* (relationships among microsystems), embedded in an *exosystem* (larger social settings such as communities); all of these are part of the *macrosystem* (culture).

What challenges face children whose parents are divorced?

During the divorce itself, conflict may increase as property and custody rights are being decided. After the divorce, the custodial parent may have to move to a less expensive home, find new sources of income, go to work for the first time, or work longer hours. For the child, this can mean leaving behind important friendships in the old neighbourhood or school just when support is needed the most, having only one parent (who has less time than ever to be with the children), or adjusting to new family structures when parents remarry.

Why are peer relations important?

Peer relationships play a significant role in healthy personal and social development. There is strong evidence that adults who had close friends as children have higher self-esteem and are more capable of maintaining intimate relationships than adults who had lonely childhoods. Adults who were rejected as children tend to have more problems, such as dropping out of school or committing crimes.

What are peer cultures and how can aggression develop?

Groups of students develop their own norms for appearance and social behaviour. Group loyalties can lead to rejection for some students, leaving them upset and unhappy. Peer aggression can be instrumental (intended to gain an object or privilege) or hostile (intended to inflict harm). Hostile aggression can be either overt threats or physical attacks or relational aggression, which involves threatening or damaging social relationships. Boys are more likely to use overt aggression and girls are more likely to use relational aggression.

Self-Concept: Understanding Ourselves
(pp. 82–90)

What are the similarities and differences between self-concept and self-esteem?

Both self-concept and self-esteem are beliefs about the self. Self-concept is our attempt to explain ourselves to ourselves, to build a scheme that organizes our impressions, feelings, and attitudes about ourselves. But this model is not fixed or permanent. Our self-perceptions vary from situation to situation and from one phase of our lives to another. Self-esteem is an affective reaction—an evaluation of who you are. If people evaluate themselves positively—if they "like what they see"—we say that they have high self-esteem. Self-concept and self-esteem are often used interchangeably, even though they have distinct meanings. Self-concept is a cognitive structure, while self-esteem is an affective evaluation.

How do self-concept and self-esteem change as children develop?

Self-concept (definition of self) and self-esteem (valuing of self) become increasingly complex, differentiated, and abstract as we mature. Self-concept evolves through constant self-reflection, social interaction, and experiences in and out of school. Students develop a self-concept by comparing themselves with personal (internal) standards and social (external) standards. The self-esteem of middle and junior high school students becomes more tied to physical appearance and social acceptance. High self-esteem is related to better overall school experience, both academically and socially. Gender and ethnic stereotypes are significant factors as well.

Are there differences in self-concepts for boys and girls?

From grades 1 to 12, competence beliefs decline for both boys and girls in math, language arts, and sports. By high school, boys and girls express about the same competence in math, girls are higher in language arts, and boys are higher in sports. In terms of general self-esteem, both boys and girls report declines in the transition to middle school, but boys' self-esteem goes up in high school while girls' self-esteem stays down.

Emotional and Moral Development
(pp. 90–99)

What are the skills involved in emotional competence?

Emotionally competent individuals are aware of their own emotions and the feeling of others—realizing that inner emotions can differ from outward expressions. They can talk about and express emotions in ways that are appropriate for their cultural group. They can feel empathy for others in distress and also cope with their own distressing emotions—they can handle stress. Emotionally competent individuals know that relationships are defined in part by how emotions are communicated within the relationship. All these skills come together to produce a capacity for emotional self-efficacy.

What are the key differences among the preconventional, conventional, and postconventional levels of moral reasoning?

Lawrence Kohlberg's theory of moral development includes three levels: (1) a preconventional level, where judgments are based on self-interest; (2) a conventional level, where judgments are based on traditional family values and social expectations; and (3) a postconventional level, where judgments are based on more abstract and personal ethical principles. Kohlberg has evaluated the moral reasoning of both children and adults by presenting them with moral dilemmas, or hypothetical situations in which people must make difficult decisions. Critics suggest that Kohlberg's view does not account for possible sex differences in moral reasoning or differences between moral reasoning and moral behaviour.

Describe Gilligan's levels of moral reasoning.

Carol Gilligan has suggested that because Kohlberg's theory of stages was based on a longitudinal study of men only, it is very possible that the moral reasoning of women and the stages of women's development are inadequately represented. She has proposed a different sequence of moral development, an "ethic of care." Gilligan believes that individuals move from a focus on self-interests to moral reasoning based on commitment to specific individuals and relationships, and then to the highest level of morality based on the principles of responsibility and care for all people. There is some evidence that in everyday life, women feel more guilty about violating caring norms, by being inconsiderate or untrustworthy, and men feel more guilty when they show violent behaviour, such as fighting or damaging property. Women are somewhat more likely to use a care orientation, but studies also show that both men and women *can* use both orientations.

What influences moral behaviour?

Others first control young children's moral behaviour through direct instruction, supervision, rewards and punishments, and correction. In time, children internalize the moral rules and principles of the authority figures who have guided them; that is, children adopt the external standards as their own. If children are given reasons that they can understand at the time they are being instructed on correct behaviour—particularly reasons that highlight the effects of actions on others—they are more likely to internalize moral principles. A second important influence on the development of moral behaviour is modelling. Children who have been consistently exposed to caring, generous adult models will tend to be more concerned for the rights and feelings of others. The world and the media provide many negative models of behaviour. Some schools have adopted programs to increase students' capacity to care for others. Cheating and aggression are two common behaviour problems in the schools that involve moral issues.

KEY TERMS

anorexia nervosa,   p. 63

autonomy,   p. 66

bioecological model,   p. 70

blended families,   p. 71

bulimia,   p. 63

collective self-esteem,   p. 89

developmental crisis,   p. 65

distributive justice,   p. 93

ego integrity,   p. 69

ethnic pride,   p. 89

generativity,   p. 69

hostile aggression,   p. 75

identity,   p. 68

identity achievement,   p. 68

identity diffusion,   p. 68

identity foreclosure,   p. 68

industry,   p. 67

initiative,   p. 66

instrumental aggression,   p. 75

internalize,   p. 97

moral dilemmas,   p. 93

moral realism,   p. 93

moral reasoning,   p. 92

morality of cooperation,   p. 93

moratorium,   p. 68

overt aggression,   p. 75

parenting styles,   p. 72

perspective-taking ability,
   p. 91

psychosocial,   p. 65

puberty,   p. 63

relational aggression,   p. 75

self-concept,   p. 82

self-esteem,   p. 82

theory of mind,   p. 91

BECOMING A PROFESSIONAL

Reflecting on the Chapter

Can you apply the ideas from this chapter on personal and social development to solve the following problems of practice?

Preschool and Kindergarten

Elise and Donis have always been two of the most cooperative students in your four-year-old group. But both will soon have new babies in their families, and as the time draws nearer, they are becoming more and more disruptive. What would you do?

Elementary and Middle School

You notice a fairly dramatic change in one of your students. This boy seems very tired and anxious, and he is not doing his homework. The situation has gone on for a few weeks now. How would you approach this problem?

Junior High and High School

Several of your junior high school students are afraid to go to gym class because a gang of students has been extorting money and personal possessions. What steps would you take to end this situation?

You hear from one of your students that a group of seniors has a small "business" selling university application essays. What would you do?

Check Your Understanding

- Be clear about the difference between self-esteem and self-concept.

- Make sure you understand the elements of Kohlberg's theory and his three stages of moral reasoning, as well as Gilligan's alternative theory.

- Understand the range of family structures today.

- Be familiar with indicators of child abuse and neglect and your legal responsibilities.

Your Teaching Portfolio

Think about your philosophy of teaching, a question you will be asked at most job interviews. What do you believe about teaching values and moral behaviour? How can you support the development of genuine and well-founded self-esteem in your students? (Consult Table 3.3 on page 87 for ideas.)

Add some ideas for parent involvement from this chapter to your portfolio.

Teaching Resources

Adapt Table 3.6, "Using 'Caring for Strangers and the World' as a Teaching Theme" on page 96, for the grades and subjects you might teach and add it to your teaching resources file.

Add Table 3.2, "Indicators of Child Abuse" on page 81, to your teaching resources file.

Teachers' Casebook

What Would They Do?

Here is how some practising teachers responded to the teaching situation presented at the beginning of this chapter about cliques in middle school and the difficulties some students face with fitting in.

Meagan Mano
The Prince Charles School
Napanee, Ontario

To determine my actions in dealing with social issues in development, I would consider who was affected and how students could avoid problem situations and effectively deal with them in the future.

The actions of Alison and her clique are a form of harassment. I would make sure that my health program was geared toward educating the class, especially this group of girls, on harassment. Topics covered would include identifying ways of dealing with harassment and resources that can support someone experiencing it. As part of my program, I would arrange for a guest speaker to talk about relationships and about decision-making skills.

Harassment is not the only issue, as the girls seem to have found themselves in cliques. Again, to reach all students, I would analyze different case scenarios using an age-related film that involved several different cliques. In groups, I would have the students discuss the feelings of the characters in the film and brainstorm the characteristics of a true friend.

Since the email was forwarded to the entire school, it is important that the issues of harassment and bullying be addressed in every classroom. I would discuss the situation with the staff. One approach to ensure that all students were being exposed to these issues would be to set up a school-based program informing students about social skills.

I would speak one-on-one with Stephanie and Alison about friendship. They should both understand that although they were friends in the past, choosing different friends now was acceptable. It is common to hang out with people that share the same interests— and interests change. Alison should be made aware that there are ways of dealing with people that do not involve ridiculing them. I would have both of the girls brainstorm (on their own) different ways in which they could have dealt with the situation. Their ideas would help guide the discussion in my health program.

Finally, I would speak with Alison's and Stephanie's parents to inform them of the situation and of how I plan to address it at school. I would also suggest some topics they could raise at home to follow up my own conversations with the two girls.

Kathleen Barter
Seycove Secondary School
North Vancouver, British Columbia

This situation of cyberbullying is, unfortunately, all too commonplace in school today. The biggest problem associated with cyberbullying is that often, as educators, we are unaware when it is occurring. And by the time we find out, the situation has often gone beyond the scope of the classroom teacher. Nevertheless, when a situation like this is exposed, teachers must respond to it in a timely manner. If the situation were not so severe, I would deal with the issue in a class discussion that focused on conflict resolution as a solution to bullying. Depending on the group and how many kids in the class know of the situation or were involved in it, I would do a lesson on ethics. I might find a short story about a bullying situation and have the students discuss responses and possible solutions. However, given the severity of the situation with Stephanie and Alison, this is a problem for the administrators in the school.

The administrators would start by using some conflict resolution strategies with the girls. They would speak separately to Stephanie and Alison and the group to get the story from each girl. Following the individual conversations, they would bring all the girls in together and have each girl speak about why she did the bullying or how she felt as a victim or as a bully. The administrator's challenge is to make the girls understand how Stephanie felt as a result of being bullied and how these girls would feel if they were the victims. The girls need to understand that Stephanie might not be interested in the same things they are, but that doesn't mean they have to malign their past friendship.

The administrative team would also decide at what point in these discussions the girls' parents would be called and asked to come into the school. As well, the girls need to understand very clearly that it is a criminal offence to photograph people against their knowledge. At this point perhaps the school's police liaison officer should also be brought in to talk to the girls.

4 ABILITIES AND DISABILITIES

School Bus, Diana Ong, © Diana Ong/SuperStock.

Teachers' Casebook

What Would You Do?

It is a new school year and you scan the list of students who will be registered in your classroom. It's a bit overwhelming. Since your district follows the policy of inclusion, you always expect to have students whose academic abilities, social skills, and motivation for learning vary widely. However, this year you will also have a student who is deaf, two students who are new to Canada and just learning to speak English, and a student who is severely learning disabled. In principle, you believe in the policy of inclusion, but your new class represents a challenge.

Critical Thinking

How will you design tasks and structure interactions with students to ensure that they *all* make progress and learn to their full potential?

What can you do to address the specific needs of students who are identified as having exceptional learning needs?

Collaboration

With two or three students in your class, make a plan for teaching and monitoring the progress of all your students.

To answer the questions above, you need to understand that learners can differ in their learning strengths and needs. So far, we have talked little about students as individuals. We have discussed principles of development that apply to everyone—stages, processes, conflicts, and tasks. Our development as human beings is similar in many ways, but not in every way. Even among members of the same family, there are marked contrasts in appearance, interests, abilities, and temperament. We examine how students can differ in this chapter and again in Chapter 5, where we discuss culture and community.

We begin our discussion of how learners can differ with a look at names and labels that have been applied to particular groups of students. Then we turn to an extended examination of intellectual abilities, which vary greatly from individual to individual and have proved very difficult to define and measure. Next, we examine a wide range of exceptionalities (e.g., gifts and talents, learning disabilities, sensory impairments) and the ways in which teachers can accommodate such diversity in their classrooms. Is ability grouping a good answer? How can teachers encourage creativity in all students? How can technology improve the education of students with exceptional learning needs?

Provincial policies for educating exceptional learners mean that you will have exceptional students in your class, whatever grade you teach. We include in this chapter a discussion of Canadian policies on inclusion and our roles as educators in upholding them.

By the time you have completed this chapter, you should be able to answer these questions:

- *What are the potential problems in categorizing and labelling students?*

- *What is your personal concept of intelligence?*

- *What is your stance on ability grouping?*

- *What are the implications of the Canadian Charter of Rights and Freedoms for your teaching?*

- *In your classroom, how will you plan your teaching to include a wide range of student interests and abilities?*

LANGUAGE AND LABELLING

exceptional students Students who have high abilities in particular areas or disabilities that impact learning and may require special education or other services.

Every child has a distinctive collection of strengths and challenges that relate to learning and development. In that sense, all children are "exceptional." Some **exceptional students** have high abilities in particular areas (e.g., music, art, math). Others have disabilities that impact learning and may require special education or other services. These students may have developmental delays, learning disabilities, communication disorders, emotional or behavioural disorders, physical disabilities, autism, traumatic brain injury, impaired hearing, impaired vision, or advanced abilities and talents. Even though we will use these terms throughout the chapter, a caution is in order: labelling students is a controversial issue.

A label does not tell which methods to use with individual students. For example, few specific "treatments" automatically follow from a "diagnosis" of a learning disability or high ability—many different teaching strategies and materials are appropriate. Further, the labels can become self-fulfilling prophecies. Everyone—teachers, parents, classmates, and even the students themselves—may see a label as a stigma that cannot be changed. Finally, labels are mistaken for explanations, as in, "Chris gets into fights because he has a behaviour disorder." "How do you know he has a behaviour disorder?" "Because he gets into fights."

On the other hand, some educators argue that having a label protects the child. For example, if classmates know that a student has a disability, they will be more willing to accept his or her behaviour. Labels still open doors to some special programs, useful information, special technology and equipment, or financial assistance. In truth, labels probably both stigmatize and help students. Therefore, they should be applied judiciously.

People-First Language

Today, many people object to such labels as "the developmentally delayed" or "the gifted student," because describing a complex person in this fashion implies that the condition labelled is the most important aspect of the person. Actually, the individual has many abilities, and to focus on the disability or high ability is to misrepresent the individual. An alternative is to use "people-first" language—to refer to "students with learning disabilities" or "students with gifts and talents." Here the emphasis is on the students first, not on the special challenges these students face. Table 4.1 (from Hutchinson, 2007, p. 41) provides more examples of people-first language.

Disabilities and Handicaps

disability The inability to do something specific, such as walk or hear.

handicap A disadvantage in a particular situation, sometimes caused by a disability.

One more distinction in language is important. A **disability** is just what the word implies—an inability to do something specific such as see or walk. A **handicap** is a disadvantage in certain situations. Some disabilities lead to handicaps, but not in all contexts. For example, being blind (a visual disability) is a handicap if you want to drive a car. But blindness is not a handicap when you are composing music or talking on the telephone. Stephen Hawking, a great physicist, had Lou Gehrig's disease and, after a time, could not walk or talk. He once said he was lucky that he became a theoretical physicist "because it is all in the mind. So my disability has not been a serious handicap." It is important that we do not create handicaps for people by the way we react to their disabilities. Some educators have suggested that we drop the word "handicap" altogether because the source of the word is demeaning. Handicap came from the phrase "cap-in-hand," used to describe people with disabilities who once were forced to beg just to survive (Hardman, Drew, & Egan, 2005).

TABLE 4.1 Using Person-First Language: Students with Disabilities

Terminology Guide Concerning Persons with Disabilities

Do not use or say	Do use or say
The blind; visually impaired	Person who is blind; person with a visual impairment
Confined to a wheelchair; wheelchair-bound	Person who uses a wheelchair; wheelchair user
Crippled	Person with a disability; person who has a spinal cord injury; etc.
The deaf	Person who is deaf (when referring to the entire deaf population and their culture, one can use "the deaf")
The hearing impaired	Person who is hard of hearing
Epileptic	Person who has epilepsy
Fit	Seizure
The handicapped	Person with a disability (unless referring to an environmental or attitudinal barrier)
Insane; mentally diseased	Person with a mental health disability; person who has schizophrenia; person who has depression
Mentally retarded	Person with a developmental disability
Normal	Person who is not disabled
Physically challenged	Person with a physical disability

Source: Adapted from the Office for Disability Issues, *A way with words: Guidelines and appropriate terminology for the portrayal of persons with disabilities* (Human Resources Development Canada, 1997). Copyright © 1997 by Human Resources Development Canada. Used with permission.

Check Your Knowledge

- What are the advantages of and problems with labels?
- What is people-first language?
- Distinguish between a disability and a handicap.

Apply to Practice

- Do your professors use person-first language?

In the next section, we consider a concept that has provided the basis for many labels—intelligence.

INDIVIDUAL DIFFERENCES IN INTELLIGENCE

Because the concept of intelligence is so important in education, so controversial, and so often misunderstood, we will spend quite a few pages discussing it. Let us begin with a basic question.

What Does Intelligence Mean?

The idea that people vary in what we call **intelligence** has been with us for a long time. Plato discussed similar variations over 2000 years ago. Most early theories about the nature of intelligence involved one or more of the following three themes: (1) the capacity to learn; (2) the total knowledge a person has acquired; and (3) the ability to adapt successfully to new situations and to the environment in general.

In the past century, there has been considerable controversy over the meaning of intelligence. Thirteen psychologists in 1921 and 24 psychologists in 1986 met

intelligence Ability or abilities to acquire and use knowledge for solving problems and adapting to the world.

Connect & Extend

TO THE RESEARCH
Here are a few current ideas about the meaning of intelligence:

- Goal-directed adaptive behaviour
- Ability to solve novel problems
- Ability to acquire and think with new conceptual systems
- Problem-solving ability
- Planning and other metacognitive skills
- Memory access speed
- What people think intelligence is
- What IQ tests measure
- Ability to learn from bad teaching

fluid intelligence Mental efficiency that is culture-free and non-verbal and is grounded in brain development.

crystallized intelligence Ability to apply culturally approved problem-solving methods.

to discuss intelligence. Both times, every psychologist had a different view about its nature (Neisser et al., 1996; Sternberg & Detterman, 1986). Both times, about half of the experts mentioned higher-level thinking processes, such as abstract reasoning and problem solving, as important aspects of intelligence. The 1986 definitions added metacognition and executive processes (monitoring your own thinking), the interaction of knowledge with mental processes, and the cultural context—what is valued by the culture—as elements of intelligence. But in 1921 and again in 1986, the psychologists disagreed about the structure of intelligence—whether it is a single ability or many separate abilities (Gustafsson & Undheim, 1996; Louis et al., 2000; Sattler, 2001; Sternberg, 2004).

Intelligence: One Ability or Many? Some theorists believe that intelligence is a basic ability that affects performance on all cognitively oriented tasks, from computing mathematical problems to writing poetry or solving riddles. Evidence for this position comes from study after study finding moderate to high positive correlations among all the different tests designed to measure separate intellectual abilities (Carroll, 1993; McNemar, 1964). What could explain these results? Charles Spearman (1927) suggested that there is one mental attribute, which he called *g* or general intelligence, that is used to perform any mental test, but that each test also requires some specific abilities in addition to *g*. For example, memory for a series of numbers probably involves both *g* and some specific ability for immediate recall of what is heard. Spearman assumed that individuals vary in both general intelligence and specific abilities, and that together these factors determine performance on mental tasks.

Another view that has stood the test of time is Raymond Cattell and John Horn's theory of fluid and crystallized intelligence (Cattell, 1963; Horn, 1998). **Fluid intelligence** is mental efficiency that is essentially culture-free and non-verbal. This aspect of intelligence increases until adolescence because it is grounded in brain development, then declines gradually with age. Fluid intelligence is sensitive to injuries. In contrast, **crystallized intelligence**, the ability to apply culturally approved problem-solving methods, can increase throughout the lifespan because it includes the learned skills and knowledge such as vocabulary, facts, and how to hail a cab, make a quilt, or study in university. By *investing fluid intelligence* in solving problems, we *develop our crystallized intelligence,* but many tasks in life, such as mathematical reasoning, draw on both fluid and crystallized intelligence (Finkel et al., 2003; Hunt, 2000).

The most widely accepted view today is that intelligence, like self-concept, has many facets and is a hierarchy of abilities, with general ability at the top and more specific abilities at lower levels of the hierarchy (Sternberg, 2000). Earl Hunt (2000) summarized the current thinking about the structure of intelligence this way:

> After almost a century of such research, that structure is pretty well-established. There is considerable agreement for the bottom two levels of a three-tiered lattice model of intelligence. At the bottom are elementary information-processing actions, and immediately above them are eight or so secondary abilities. These are more broadly defined capabilities, such as holding and accessing information in short- and long-term memory and, most importantly, the trio of "intellectual" abilities: crystallized intelligence ..., fluid intelligence ..., and visual-spatial reasoning ability [which] may be just the most visible of several abilities to manipulate information coded in a particular sensory modality. (p. 123)

Look at Figure 4.1 to see an example of this three-level view of intelligence. John Carroll (1997) identifies one general ability, a few broad abilities (such as fluid and crystallized abilities, learning and memory, visual and auditory perception, and processing speed), and at least 70 specific abilities (such as language development, memory span, and simple reaction time). General ability may be related to the maturation and functioning of the frontal lobe of the brain, while specific abilities may be connected to other parts of the brain (Byrnes & Fox, 1998).

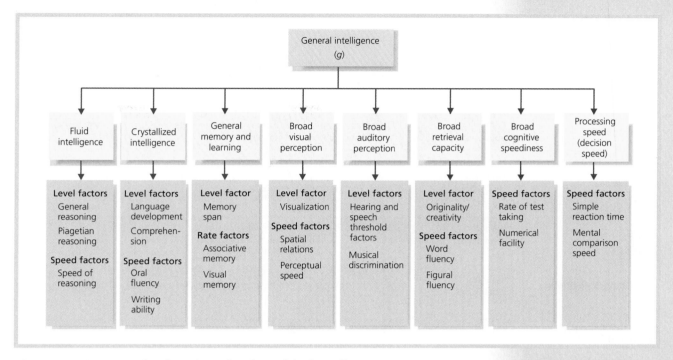

Figure 4.1 An Example of a Hierarchical Model of Intelligence

The specific abilities at the third level are just some of the possibilities. Carroll identified over 70 specific abilities.

Source: From Carroll, J. B. (1997). The three-stratum theory of cognitive abilities. In D. B. Flanagan & P. L. Harrison (Eds.), *Contemporary intellectual assessment: Theories, tests, and issues* (pp. 122–130). New York: Guilford Publications. Copyright © 1996 by Guilford Publications, Inc. Adapted with permission of the publisher.

Multiple Intelligences. In spite of the correlations among the various tests of different abilities, some psychologists insist that there are several separate mental abilities (Gardner, 1983; Guilford, 1988). According to Gardner's (1983, 2003) theory of **multiple intelligences**, there are at least eight separate intelligences: logical-mathematical, linguistic (verbal), musical, spatial, bodily-kinesthetic (movement), interpersonal (understanding others), intrapersonal (understanding self), and naturalist (observing and understanding natural and human-made patterns and systems) (see Figure 4.2 on page 110). Gardner stresses that there may be more kinds of intelligence—eight is not a magic number. Recently, he has speculated that there may be a spiritual intelligence and an existential intelligence, or the abilities to contemplate big questions about the meaning of life (Gardner, 2003). Gardner bases his notion of separate abilities on evidence that brain damage (from a stroke, for example) often interferes with functioning in one area, such as language, but does not affect functioning in other areas. Also, individuals may excel in one of these eight areas but have no remarkable abilities in the other seven.

What are these intelligences? Gardner (1998, 2003) contends that an intelligence is the ability to solve problems and create products or outcomes that are valued by a culture. Varying cultures and eras of history place different values on the eight intelligences. A naturalist intelligence is critical in farming cultures, whereas verbal and mathematical intelligences are important in technological cultures. In addition, Gardner believes that intelligence has a biological basis. Intelligence "is a biological and psychological potential; that potential is capable of being realized to a greater or lesser extent as a consequence of the experiential, cultural, and motivational factors that affect a person" (1998, p. 62).

Gardner's multiple intelligences theory has not received wide acceptance in the scientific community, even though many educators have embraced it. Some critics suggest that several of the intelligences are really talents (bodily-kinesthetic skill, musical ability) or personality traits (interpersonal ability). Other "intelligences"

multiple intelligences In Gardner's theory of intelligence, a person's eight separate abilities: logical-mathematical, linguistic, musical, spatial, bodily-kinesthetic, interpersonal, intrapersonal, and naturalist.

Intelligence	End states	Core components
Logical-mathematical	Scientist Mathematician	Sensitivity to, and capacity to discern, logical or numerical patterns; ability to handle long chains of reasoning.
Linguistic	Poet Journalist	Sensitivity to the sounds, rhythms, and meanings of words; sensitivity to the different functions of language.
Musical	Composer Violinist	Abilities to produce and appreciate rhythm, pitch, and timbre; appreciation of the forms of musical expressiveness.
Spatial	Navigator Sculptor	Capacities to perceive the visual-spatial world accurately and to perform transformations on one's initial perceptions.
Bodily-kinesthetic	Dancer Athlete	Abilities to control one's body movements and to handle objects skilfully.
Interpersonal	Therapist Salesman	Capacities to discern and respond appropriately to the moods, temperaments, motivations, and desires of other people.
Intrapersonal	Person with detailed, accurate self-knowledge	Access to one's own feelings and the ability to discriminate among them and draw on them to guide behaviour; knowledge of one's own strengths, weaknesses, desires, and intelligence.
Naturalist	Botanist Farmer Hunter	Abilities to recognize plants and animals, to make distinctions in the natural world, to understand systems and define categories (perhaps even categories of intelligence).

Figure 4.2 Eight Intelligences

Howard Gardner's theory of multiple intelligences suggests that there are eight kinds of human abilities. An individual might have strengths or weaknesses in one or several areas.

Source: From Gardner, H., & Hatch, T. (1989). Multiple intelligences go to school. *Educational Researcher, 18*(8), 6 (figure). Copyright © 1989 by the American Educational Research Association. Reprinted with permission of the publisher. Gardner. H. (2002). Are there additional intelligences? The case for the naturalist, spiritual, and existential intelligences. In J. Kane (Ed.), *Educational information and transformation*. Saddle River, NJ: Prentice-Hall, Inc.

are not new at all. Many researchers have identified verbal and spatial abilities as elements of intelligence. In addition, the eight intelligences are not independent; there are correlations among the abilities. In fact, logical-mathematical and spatial intelligences are highly correlated (Sattler, 2001). So these "separate abilities" may not be so separate after all. Recent evidence linking musical and spatial abilities has prompted Gardner to consider that there may be connections among the intelligences (Gardner, 1998).

Gardner (1998, 2003) has responded to critics by identifying a number of myths and misconceptions about multiple intelligences theory and schooling. One is that intelligences are the same as learning styles; Gardner doesn't believe that people actually have consistent learning styles. Another misconception is that multiple intelligences theory disproves the idea of *g*. Gardner does not deny the existence of a general ability, but he does question how useful *g* is as an explanation for human achievements.

Multiple Intelligences Go to School.   An advantage of the multiple intelligences perspective is that it expands teachers' thinking about abilities and avenues for teaching, but the theory has been misused. Some teachers embrace a simplistic version of Gardner's theory. They include every "intelligence" in every lesson, no matter how inappropriate. Table 4.2 lists some misuses and positive applications of Gardner's work.

Many teachers and schools have embraced Gardner's ideas. However, there is not yet strong research evidence that adopting a multiple intelligences approach will enhance learning. In one of the few carefully designed evaluations, Callahan, Tomlinson, and Plucker (1997) found no significant gains in either achievement or self-concept for students who participated in START, a multiple intelligences approach to identifying and promoting talent in students who were at risk of failing. Learning is still hard work, even if there are multiple paths to knowledge. Perry Klein (2002) argues that the multiple intelligences theory is too broad to tell teachers how to teach. "For instance, the knowledge that basketball relies on 'bodily-kinesthetic intelligence' tells a coach nothing about the skills her players need to learn" (p. 228).

TABLE 4.2 Misuses and Applications of Multiple Intelligences Theory

Recently, Howard Gardner described these negative and positive applications of his theory. The quotations are his words on the subject.

Misuses

1. **Trying to teach all concepts or subjects using all intelligences:** "There is no point in assuming that every subject can be effectively approached in at least seven ways, and it is a waste of effort and time to attempt to do this."

2. **Assuming that it is enough just to apply a certain intelligence, no matter how you use it:** For bodily-kinesthetic intelligence, for example, "random muscle movements have nothing to do with the cultivation of the mind."

3. **Using an intelligence as a background for other activities,** such as playing music while students solve math problems. "The music's function is unlikely to be different from that of a dripping faucet or humming fan."

4. **Mixing intelligences with other desirable qualities:** For example, interpersonal intelligence "is often distorted as a license for cooperative learning," and intrapersonal intelligence "is often distorted as a rationale for self-esteem programs."

5. **Direct evaluation or even grading of intelligences without regard for context:** "I see little point in grading individuals in terms of how 'linguistic' or how 'bodily-kinesthetic' they are."

Good Uses

1. **The cultivation of desired capabilities:** "Schools should cultivate those skills and capabilities that are valued in the community and in the broader society."

2. **Approaching a concept, subject matter, discipline in a variety of ways:** Schools try to cover too much. "It makes far more sense to spend a significant amount of time on key concepts, generative ideas, and essential questions and to allow students to become familiar with these notions and their implications."

3. **The personalization of education:** "The heart of the MI perspective—in theory and in practice—inheres in taking human difference seriously."

Source: Gardner, H. (1998). Reflections on multiple intelligences: Myths and messages. In A. Woolfolk (Ed.), *Readings in educational psychology* (2nd. ed., pp. 64–66). Boston: Allyn & Bacon. Copyright © 1998 by Phi Delta Kappan.

Howard Gardner's model of multiple intelligences broadened our view of intelligent behaviour to include such factors as linguistic and musical abilities.

Intelligence as a Process

As you can see, the theories of Spearman, Thurstone, Gardner, and Goleman tend to describe how individuals differ in the content of intelligence—the different abilities. Recent work in cognitive psychology has emphasized instead the thinking processes that may be common to all people. How do humans gather and use information to solve problems and behave intelligently? New views of intelligence are growing out of this work.

triarchic theory of intelligence A three-part description of the mental abilities (thinking processes, coping with new experiences, and adapting to context) that lead to more or less intelligent behaviour.

Robert Sternberg's (1985, 2004) **triarchic theory of intelligence** is a cognitive process approach to understanding intelligence. Successful intelligence includes "the skills and knowledge needed for success in life, according to one's own definition of success, within one's own sociocultural context" (Sternberg, 2004, p. 326). Sternberg prefers the term *successful intelligence* in order to stress that intelligence is more than what is measured by mental abilities tests—intelligence is about success in life. As you might guess from the name, this theory has three parts—analytic, creative, and practical. See Figure 4.3 for more details.

components In an information processing view, basic problem-solving processes underlying intelligence.

Analytic/componential intelligence involves the mental processes of the individual that lead to more or less intelligent behaviour. These processes are defined in terms of **components**—elementary information processes that are classified by the functions they serve and by how general they are. Metacomponents perform

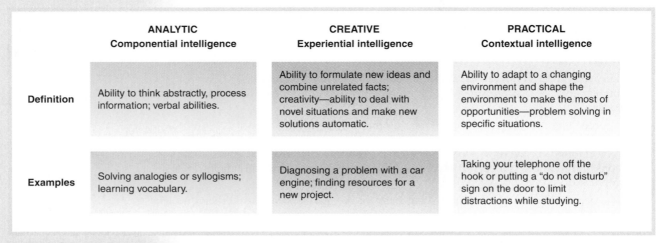

	ANALYTIC Componential intelligence	**CREATIVE** Experiential intelligence	**PRACTICAL** Contextual intelligence
Definition	Ability to think abstractly, process information; verbal abilities.	Ability to formulate new ideas and combine unrelated facts; creativity—ability to deal with novel situations and make new solutions automatic.	Ability to adapt to a changing environment and shape the environment to make the most of opportunities—problem solving in specific situations.
Examples	Solving analogies or syllogisms; learning vocabulary.	Diagnosing a problem with a car engine; finding resources for a new project.	Taking your telephone off the hook or putting a "do not disturb" sign on the door to limit distractions while studying.

Figure 4.3 Sternberg's Triarchic Theory of Intelligence
Sternberg suggests that intelligent behaviour is the product of applying thinking strategies, handling new problems creatively and quickly, and adapting to contexts by selecting and reshaping our environment.

higher-order functions such as planning, strategy selection, and monitoring. Executing the strategies selected is handled by performance components. The third function—gaining new knowledge—is performed by knowledge-acquisition components; one example is separating relevant from irrelevant information as you try to understand a new concept (Sternberg, 1985).

Some components are specific; that is, they are necessary for only one kind of task, such as solving analogies. Other components are very general and may be necessary in almost every cognitive task. For example, metacomponents are always operating to select strategies and keep track of progress. This may help explain the persistent correlations among all types of mental tests. People who are effective in selecting good problem-solving strategies, monitoring progress, and moving to a new approach when the first one fails are more likely to be successful on all types of tests. Metacomponents may be a modern-day version of Spearman's *g*.

The second part of Sternberg's triarchic theory, creative/experiential intelligence, involves coping with new experiences. Intelligent behaviour is marked by two characteristics: (1) **insight**, or the ability to deal effectively with novel situations, and (2) **automaticity**—the ability to become efficient and automatic in thinking and problem solving. So intelligence involves solving new problems as well as quickly turning new solutions into routine processes that can be applied without much cognitive effort.

The third part of Sternberg's theory, practical/contextual intelligence, highlights the importance of choosing to live and work in a context where success is likely, adapting to that context, and reshaping it if necessary. Here, culture is a major factor in defining successful choice, adaptation, and shaping. What works in one cultural group will not work in another. For example, abilities that make a person successful in a rural farm community may be useless in the inner city or at a country club in the suburbs. People who are successful often seek situations in which their abilities will be valuable, then work hard to capitalize on those abilities and compensate for any weaknesses. Thus, intelligence in this third sense involves practical matters, such as career choice or social skills. In a field study conducted in a Russian city, Elena Grigorenko and Robert Sternberg (2001) found that adults with higher practical and analytical intelligence coped better mentally and physically with the stresses caused by rapid changes in that part of the world.

Practical intelligence is made up mostly of action-oriented **tacit knowledge**. This tacit knowledge is more likely to be learned during everyday life than through formal schooling and "takes the form of 'knowing how' rather than 'knowing that'" (Sternberg et al., 1995, p. 916). Recently, however, Sternberg and his colleagues have designed a program for developing practical intelligence for school success by teaching students effective strategies for reading, writing, homework, and test taking (Sternberg 2002; Williams et al., 1996). As you will read shortly, adaptive skills (similar to practical skills) are considered when identifying individuals with developmental delays.

How Is Intelligence Measured?

Even though psychologists do not agree on what intelligence is, they do agree that the intelligence recorded in standard tests is related to learning in school. Why is this so? It has to do in part with the way intelligence tests were first developed.

Binet's Dilemma. In 1904, Alfred Binet was confronted with the following problem by the minister of public instruction in Paris: How can students who will need special teaching and extra help be identified early in their school careers, before they fail in regular classes? Binet was also a political activist, very concerned with the rights of children. He believed that having an objective measure of learning ability could protect students from poor families who might be forced to leave school because they were the victims of discrimination and assumed to be slow learners.

insight The ability to deal effectively with novel situations.

automaticity The result of learning to perform a behaviour or thinking process so thoroughly that the performance is automatic and does not require effort.

tacit knowledge Knowing *how* rather than knowing *that*—knowledge that is more likely to be learned during everyday life than through formal schooling.

Alfred Binet developed a systematic procedure for assessing learning aptitudes. His goal was to understand intelligence and use this knowledge to help children.

mental age In intelligence testing, a score based on average abilities for that age group.

intelligence quotient (IQ) Score comparing mental and chronological ages.

Binet and his collaborator Theophile Simon wanted to measure not merely school achievement but the intellectual skills that students needed to do well in school. After trying many different tests and eliminating items that did not allow discrimination between successful and unsuccessful students, Binet and Simon finally identified 58 tests, several for each age group from 3 to 13. Binet's tests allowed the examiner to determine a **mental age** of a child. A child who succeeded on the items passed by most six-year-olds, for example, was considered to have a mental age of six, whether the child was actually four, six, or eight years of age.

The concept of **intelligence quotient**, or **IQ**, was added after Binet's test was brought to North America and revised at Stanford University to give us the Stanford-Binet test. An IQ score was computed by comparing the mental-age score with the person's actual chronological age. The formula was

$$\text{intelligence quotient} = \text{mental age/chronological age} \times 100 \text{ chronological age}$$

The early Stanford-Binet test has been revised five times, most recently in 2003 (Roid, 2003). The practice of computing a mental age has been problematic because IQ scores calculated on the basis of mental age do not have the same meaning as children get older. To cope with this problem, the concept of **deviation IQ** was introduced. The deviation IQ score is a number that tells exactly how much above or below the average a person scored on the test, compared with others in the same age group.

deviation IQ Score based on statistical comparison of individuals' performance with the average performance of others in that age group.

Group versus Individual IQ Tests. The Stanford-Binet test is an individual intelligence test. It has to be administered to one student at a time by a trained psychologist and takes about two hours. Most of the questions are asked orally and do not require reading or writing. A student usually pays closer attention and is more motivated to do well when working directly with an adult.

Psychologists also have developed group tests that can be given to whole classes or schools. Compared with an individual test, a group test is much less likely to yield an accurate picture of any one person's abilities. When students take tests in a group, they may do poorly because they do not understand the instructions, because their pencils break, because other students distract them, or because they do not shine on paper-and-pencil tests. As a teacher, you should be wary of IQ scores based on group tests.

What Does an IQ Score Mean?

Most intelligence tests are designed so that they have certain statistical characteristics. For example, the average score is 100; 50 percent of the people from the general population who take the tests will score 100 or above, and 50 percent will score below 100. About 68 percent of the general population will earn IQ scores between 85 and 115. Only about 16 percent of the population will receive scores below 85, and only 16 percent will score above 115. Note, however, that these figures hold true for white, native-born Americans whose first language is Standard English. Whether IQ tests should be used with students from ethnic minorities is hotly debated. Canadian teachers also need to be aware that many of these tests contain content that is not familiar to our students (e.g., math problems using imperial measures) and compare Canadian students to an American reference group. The accompanying Guidelines will help you interpret IQ scores realistically.

The Flynn Effect: Are We Getting Smarter? Ever since IQ tests were introduced in the early 1900s, scores in 20 different industrialized countries and in some more traditional cultures have been rising (Daley et al., 2003). In fact, in a generation, the average score goes up about 18 points on standardized IQ tests—maybe you

INTERPRETING IQ SCORES

Check to see if the score is based on an individual or a group test. Be wary of group test scores.

EXAMPLES

1. Individual tests include the Wechsler Scales (WPPSI, WISC-III, WAIS-R), the Stanford-Binet, the McCarthy Scales of Children's Abilities, the Woodcock-Johnson Psycho-Educational Battery, and the Kaufman Assessment Battery for Children.

2. Group tests include the Lorge-Thorndike Intelligence Tests, the Analysis of Learning Potential, the Kuhlman-Anderson Intelligence Tests, the Otis-Lennon Mental Abilities Tests, and the School and College Ability Tests (SCAT).

Remember that IQ tests are only estimates of general aptitude for learning.

EXAMPLES

1. Ignore small differences in scores among students.

2. Bear in mind that even an individual student's scores may change over time for many reasons, including measurement error.

3. Be aware that a total score is usually an average of scores on several kinds of questions. A score in

the middle or average range may mean that the student performed at the average on every kind of question or that the student did quite well in some areas (for example, on verbal tasks) and rather poorly in other areas (for example, on quantitative tasks).

Remember that IQ scores reflect a student's past experiences and learning.

EXAMPLES

1. Consider these scores as predictors of school abilities, not measures of innate intellectual abilities.

2. If a student is doing well in your class, do not change your opinion or lower your expectations just because one score seems low.

3. Be wary of IQ scores for ethnic-minority students and for students whose first language is not English. Even scores on "culture-free" tests are lower for disadvantaged students.

4. Check to see if Canadian norms are available for the tests used. Use caution when interpreting a student's scores on American tests normed for American students.

really are smarter than your parents! This is called the **Flynn effect** after James Flynn, a political scientist who documented the phenomenon. Some explanations include better nutrition and medical care for children and parents, increasing complexity in the environment that stimulates thinking, smaller families who give more attention to their children, increased literacy of parents, more and better schooling, and better preparation for taking tests. One result of the Flynn effect is that the norms used to determine scores (more about norms in Chapter 13) have to be continually revised. In other words, to keep a score of 100 as the average, the test questions have to be made more difficult. This increasing difficulty has implications for any program that uses IQ scores as part of the entrance requirements. For example, some "average" students of the previous generation now might be identified as having intellectual disabilities because the test questions are harder (Kanaya, Scullin, & Ceci, 2003).

Flynn effect Because of better health, smaller families, increased complexity in the environment, and more and better schooling, IQ test scores are steadily rising.

Intelligence and Achievement. Intelligence test scores predict achievement in schools quite well, at least for large groups. For example, the correlation is about .4 to .5 between school grades and scores on a popular individual intelligence test, the revised Wechsler Intelligence Scale for Children (WISC-III). Correlations between standardized achievement test and intelligence test scores are higher, around .5 to .7 (Sattler, 2001). This isn't surprising because the tests were designed to predict school achievement. Remember, Binet threw out test items that did not discriminate between good and poor students.

Do people who score high on IQ tests achieve more in life? Here the answer is less clear. There is evidence that *g*, or general intelligence, correlates with

This boy is trying to arrange the red and white blocks so that they match the pattern in the booklet. His performance is timed. This subtest of the Wechsler Intelligence Scale for Children assesses spatial ability.

"real-world academic, social, and occupational accomplishments" (Ceci, 1991), but there is great debate about the size and meaning of these correlations (*Current Directions in Psychological Science*, 1993; McClelland, 1993). People with higher intelligence test scores tend to complete more years of school and to have higher-status jobs. However, when the number of years of education is held constant, IQ scores and school achievement are not highly correlated with income and success in later life. Other factors such as motivation, social skills, emotional intelligence, and luck may make the difference (Goleman, 1995; Neisser et al., 1996; Sternberg & Wagner, 1993).

Intelligence: Heredity or Environment? Nowhere, perhaps, has the nature-versus-nurture debate raged so hard as in the area of intelligence. Should intelligence be seen as a potential, limited by our genetic makeup? Or does intelligence simply refer to an individual's current level of intellectual functioning, as fed and influenced by experience and education? In fact, it is almost impossible to separate intelligence "in the genes" from intelligence "due to experience." Today, most psychologists believe that differences in intelligence are due to both heredity and environment, probably in about equal proportions for children (Petrill & Wilkerson, 2000). "Genes do not fix behaviour. Rather they establish a range of possible reactions to the range of possible experiences that the environment can provide" (Weinberg, 1989, p. 101). And environmental influences include everything from the health of a child's mother during pregnancy to the amount of lead in the child's home to the quality of teaching a child receives.

As a teacher, it is especially important for you to realize that cognitive skills, like any other skills, can always be improved. Intelligence is a current state of affairs, affected by past experiences and open to future changes. Even if intelligence is a limited potential, the potential is still quite large, and it presents a challenge to all teachers. For example, Japanese and Chinese students know much more mathematics than North American students do, but their intelligence test scores are quite similar. This superiority in math is probably related to differences in the way mathematics is taught and studied in these countries and to the self-motivation skills of many Asian students (Baron, 1998; Stevenson & Stigler, 1992).

Check Your Knowledge

- What is *g*?
- What is Gardner's view of intelligence and his position on *g*?
- What are the elements of Sternberg's theory of intelligence?
- How is intelligence measured, and what does an IQ score mean?

Apply to Practice

- What will you tell your students' parents about the meaning and uses of intelligence test scores?
- Give an original example of each of Gardner's eight intelligences.

Now that you have a sense of what intelligence means, let's consider how to handle cognitive ability differences in teaching.

ABILITY DIFFERENCES AND TEACHING

What Would You Say?

You are being interviewed for a job in a new middle school scheduled to open this fall. After about four minutes of small talk, the curriculum supervisor says to you, "We have been having some heated debates in this district about ability grouping and tracking. Where do you stand on those issues?"

In this section, we consider how you might handle differences in academic ability in your classes. Is ability grouping a solution to the challenge of ability differences? The expressed goal of ability grouping is to make teaching more appropriate for students. As we will see, this does not always happen.

Between-Class Ability Grouping

When whole classes are formed based on ability, the process is called **between-class ability grouping**, or tracking, a common practice in secondary schools and some elementary schools as well. Most high schools have "university prep" courses and "general" courses, or high-, middle-, and low-ability classes in a particular subject. Although this seems on the surface to be an efficient way to teach, research has consistently shown that segregation by ability may benefit students who are high-achieving, but it often causes problems for students who are low-achieving (Castle, Deniz, & Tortora, 2005; Garmon et al., 1995; Oakes & Wells, 1998; Robinson & Clinkenbeard, 1998).

Historically, students in low-ability classes have received lower-quality instruction. In these contexts, teachers tend to emphasize lower-level objectives and routine procedures, with less academic focus. Often, there are more management problems and, along with these problems, increased teacher stress and decreased enthusiasm. These differences in instruction and the teachers' negative attitudes may mean that low expectations are communicated to the students. Students' attendance may drop along with their self-esteem. The lower ability tracks often include a disproportionate number of students from minority groups and students who are economically disadvantaged, so ability grouping, in effect, becomes segregation in school. Possibilities for friendships become limited to students in the same ability range, and placements in classes can have long-term implications. For example, students in modified programs may not qualify for graduation diplomas, which can limit opportunities for careers and further education.

Increasingly, schools are looking for creative ways to teach *all* students in mixed ability groups, by providing extra help for those who struggle and enrichment for those who learn quickly (Corno, 1995; Oakes & Wells, 2002). We describe Canada's movement toward inclusive teaching and learning later in this chapter. Most teachers agree that this movement is a good idea, but they struggle to implement it in their classrooms, especially in secondary classrooms. Here are several ways to effectively teach mixed ability groups in secondary schools (Oakes & Wells, 2002):

- Offer honours assignment options or challenge pullout activities within each course.
- Require all students to take a common core of classes. Then allow self-selection into advanced classes after the core.
- Encourage students from minority groups to enrol in advanced placement courses.
- Provide additional times during breaks from classes when struggling students can get extra help.
- Provide tutoring before and after school.
- Staff a "homework help centre" with teachers, parents, and community volunteers.
- Instead of "dumbing down" content, teach students learning strategies for dealing with difficult material.

There are two exceptions to the general finding that between-class ability grouping leads to lower achievement. The first is found in honours or gifted classes, where students with high ability tend to perform better than comparable students in regular classes. The second exception is the **non-graded elementary school** and the related **Joplin Plan**. In a non-graded school, students of several ages (for example, six-, seven-, and eight-year-olds) are together in one class (an arrangement that is sometimes referred to as family grouping), but they are flexibly

between-class ability grouping System of grouping in which students are assigned to classes based on their measured ability or their achievements.

Connect & Extend

TO THE RESEARCH
A review of the research on ability grouping is Biemiller, A. (1993, December). Lake Wobegon revisited: On diversity and education. *Educational Researcher, 22*(9), 7–12, and Biemiller, A. (1993, December). Students differ: So address differences effectively. *Educational Researcher, 22*(9), 14–15.

non-graded elementary school/ Joplin Plan Arrangement wherein students are grouped by ability in particular subjects, regardless of their ages or grades.

grouped within the class for instruction based on achievement, motivation, or interest in different subjects. This cross-grade grouping seems to be effective for students of all abilities as long as the grouping allows teachers to give more direct instruction to the groups. Andrew Biemiller (1993), at the University of Toronto, agrees that flexibly grouping students to tailor instruction to their current skill levels is sometimes necessary if we want all students to gain or demonstrate expertise in particular areas. However, he also emphasizes the need for all students to participate in a variety of ability groupings. We need to be sensible about cross-age grouping. Mixing students from grades 3, 4, and 5 for math or reading class based on what they are ready to learn makes sense. Sending a grade 4 student to grade 2, where he is the only older student and stands out like a sore thumb, isn't likely to work well. Also, when cross-age classes are created just because there are too few students for one grade and not in order to better meet the students' learning needs, the results are not positive (Veenman, 1997).

Within-Class Ability Grouping

Differences like the ones mentioned above are common in most schools and classrooms. If you decided to simply forge ahead and teach the same material in the same way to your entire class, you would not be alone. One study found that in 46 different classrooms, 84 percent of the activities were the same for all students, whether they were high- or low-achieving (Westberg et al., 1993). Differences in students' prior knowledge are a major challenge for teachers, especially in subjects that build on previous knowledge and skills, such as math and science (Loveless, 1998).

Today, many elementary-school classes are grouped for reading, and some are grouped for math, even though there is no clear evidence that this **within-class ability grouping** is superior to other approaches. Thoughtfully constructed and well-taught ability groups in math and reading can be effective, but other approaches such as cooperative learning are available too. The point of any grouping strategy should be to provide appropriate challenge and support—that is, to reach learners within their zone of proximal development (Vygotsky, 1997).

Flexible Grouping. In **flexible grouping**, students are grouped and regrouped based on their learning needs. Assessment is continuous so that students are always working within their zone of proximal development. Arrangements might include small groups, partners, individuals, and even the whole class—depending on which grouping best supports each student's learning of the particular academic content. Flexible grouping approaches often include high-level instruction and high expectations for all students, no matter what their group placement. One five-year longitudinal study of flexible grouping in a high-needs urban elementary school (Castle, Deniz, & Tortora, 2005) found 10 percent to 57 percent increases in students who reached mastery level, depending on the subject area and grade level. Teachers received training and support in the assessment, grouping, and teaching strategies needed, and by the end of the study, 95 percent of the teachers were using flexible grouping. The teachers in the study believed that some of the gains came because students were more focused on learning and more confident.

If you ever decide to use ability grouping in your class, the accompanying Guidelines should make the approach more effective (Good & Brophy, 2003).

Check Your Knowledge

- What are the problems with between-class ability grouping?
- What alternatives are available to ability grouping in classes?
- What is the Flynn effect and what are its implications?

Apply to Practice

- If you have a wide range of academic abilities in your class, what are your options in grouping students for learning?

---

within-class ability grouping System of grouping in which students in a class are divided into two or three groups based on ability in an attempt to accommodate student differences.

flexible grouping Grouping and regrouping students based on learning needs.

GROUPING BY ACHIEVEMENT

Form and reform groups on the basis of students' current performance in the subject being taught.

EXAMPLES

1. Use scores on the most recent reading assessments to establish reading groups and rely on current math performance to form math groups.

2. Change group placement frequently when students' achievement or the goals of instruction change.

Discourage comparisons between groups and encourage students to develop a whole-class spirit.

EXAMPLES

1. Don't seat groups together outside the context of their reading or math group.

2. Avoid naming ability groups—save the names for mixed-ability or whole-class teams.

Group by ability for one or, at the most, two subjects.

EXAMPLES

1. Make sure there are many lessons and projects that mix members from the groups.

2. Experiment with learning strategies in which cooperation is stressed (described in Chapters 9 and 11).

3. Keep the number of groups small (two or three at most) so that you can provide as much direct teaching as possible—leaving students alone for too long leads to less learning.

Make sure that teachers, methods, and pace are adjusted to fit the needs of the group.

EXAMPLES

1. Organize and teach groups so that students who are low-achieving get appropriate extra instruction—not just the same material again.

2. Experiment with alternatives to grouping. There are alternatives to within-class grouping that appear more effective for some subjects. DeWayne Mason and Tom Good (1993) found that supplementing whole-class instruction in math with remediation and enrichment for students when they needed it worked better than dividing the class into two ability groups and teaching these groups separately.

LEARNING STYLES AND PREFERENCES

> **What Would You Say?**
>
> Describe a learning activity you have planned for a class and the ways in which you have accommodated individual learning styles or needs.

The way a person approaches learning and studying is his or her **learning style.** Although many different learning styles have been described, one theme that unites most of the styles is differences between deep and surface approaches to processing information in learning situations (Snow, Corno, & Jackson, 1996). Individuals who have a *deep-processing approach* to learning see the learning materials or activities as a means for understanding some underlying concepts or meanings. These students tend to learn for the sake of learning and are less concerned about how their performance is evaluated, so motivation plays a role as well. Students who take a *surface-processing approach* focus on memorizing the learning materials, not understanding them. These students tend to be motivated by rewards, grades, external standards, and the desire to be evaluated positively by others. Of course, specific situations can encourage deep or surface processing, but there is evidence that individuals have tendencies to approach learning situations in characteristic ways (Biggs, 2001; Coffield et al., 2004; Pintrich & Schrauben, 1992; Tait & Entwistle, 1998).

What Are Learning Preferences? Since the late 1970s, a great deal has been written about differences in students' learning preferences (Dunn, 1987; Dunn &

learning styles An individual's characteristic approaches to learning and studying, usually involving deep or superficial processing of information.

learning preferences Individual preferences for particular learning environments (e.g., quiet versus loud).

People have different preferences for how and where they like to learn. Students who are distracted by noise may work better in a quiet space, even if that place is on the floor in the hall.

Dunn, 1978, 1987; Gregorc, 1982; Keefe, 1982). Learning preferences often are called *learning styles,* but *preferences* is probably a more accurate label. **Learning preferences** are individual preferences for particular learning environments. They could be preferences for where, when, with whom, or with what lighting, food, or music you like to study. Think for a minute about how you learn best. Anita likes to study and write during large blocks of time, late at night. She usually makes some kind of commitment or deadline every week, so that she has to work under pressure in long stretches to finish the work. Then she takes a day off. Phil and Nancy like to write very early in the morning, but they also like to set goals.

Cautions about Learning Styles and Preferences.   There are a number of instruments for assessing students' learning preferences. Be aware, however, that many lack evidence of reliability and validity. In fact, research that has assessed children's learning styles and then tried to match instructional methods to them have failed to show any effect on learning (Stahl, 2002, p. 99). This led Snider (1990) to conclude that

> people are different, and it is good practice to recognize and accommodate individual differences. It is also good practice to present information in a variety of ways through more than one modality, but it is not wise to categorize learners and prescribe methods solely on the basis of tests with questionable technical qualities. The idea of learning styles is appealing, but a critical examination of this approach should cause educators to be skeptical. (p. 53)

So before you try to accommodate all your students' learning styles, remember that students, especially younger ones, may not be the best judges of how they should learn. Sometimes students, particularly students who have difficulty, prefer what is easy and comfortable; real learning can be hard and uncomfortable. Sometimes students prefer to learn in a certain way because they have no alternatives; it is the only way they know how to approach the task. These students may benefit from developing new—and perhaps more effective—ways to learn.

Check Your Knowledge

- Distinguish between learning styles and learning preferences.
- What are the advantages and disadvantages of matching teaching to individual learning styles?
- What learning style distinctions are the most well-supported by research?

Apply to Practice

- What are some reasonable accommodations teachers might make to assignments or the classroom environment to suit students' preferences for learning?

So far, we have focused mostly on teachers' responses to variability in students' abilities and learning preferences apart from specific exceptionalities. For the rest of the chapter, we will consider the needs of students whose high abilities and disabilities create particular challenges for teaching and learning.

STUDENTS WHO ARE GIFTED AND TALENTED

Consider this situation, a true story.

> Latoya was already an advanced reader when she entered 1st grade in a large urban school district. Her teacher noticed the challenging chapter books Latoya brought to school and read with little effort. After administering a reading assessment, the school's reading consultant confirmed that Latoya was reading at the 5th grade level. Latoya's parents reported with pride that she had started to read independently when she was 3 years old and "had read every book she could get her hands on." (Reis et al., 2002)

In her struggling urban school, Latoya received no particular accommodations, and by grade 5, she was still reading at just above the grade 5 level. Her grade 5 teacher had no idea that Latoya had ever been an advanced reader.

Latoya is not alone. There is a group of students with special needs that is often overlooked by the schools: students with gifts and talents. In the past, providing an enriched education for extremely bright or talented students was seen as undemocratic and elitist. Now there is a growing recognition that **gifted students** are being poorly served by most public schools. Lupart and Pyryt (1996) at the University of Calgary estimated that, in a sample of 373 students they identified as having gifts and talents, 21 percent were underachieving in school. Because Lupart and Pyryt applied a very narrow definition of giftedness (referring to intellectual/academic talent), they claim that their estimate is fairly low. A more accurate estimate, according to these researchers, is somewhere between 40 and 50 percent.

Who Are the Gifted?   There are many definitions of the term *gifted* because individuals can have many different gifts. Remember that Gardner (2003) identified eight separate kinds of "intelligences," and that Sternberg suggests a triarchic model. Recent provincial definitions reflect the research of Dan Keating (1990, 1991), formerly at the University of Toronto and now at the University of Michigan, and Dona Matthews (1996), at the University of Toronto. These scholars emphasize that gifts and talents are often located in specific domains (i.e., individuals typically are not advanced in all areas).

Children who are truly gifted are not the students who simply learn quickly with little effort. The work of gifted students is original, extremely advanced for their age, and potentially of lasting importance. These children may read fluently with little instruction by the age of three or four. They may play a musical instrument as would a skilful adult, turn a visit to the grocery store into a mathematical puzzle, and become fascinated with algebra when their friends are having trouble carrying in addition (Winner, 2000). Recent conceptions widen the view of giftedness to include attention to the children's culture, language, and other exceptionalities (Association for the Gifted, 2001).

What do we know about these remarkable individuals? A classic study of the characteristics of individuals with gifts was started decades ago by Lewis Terman and colleagues (1925, 1947, 1959). This huge project is following the lives of 1528 gifted males and females and will continue until the year 2010. The subjects were identified on the basis of teacher recommendations, and all have IQ scores in the top 1 percent of the population (140 or above on the Stanford-Binet individual test of intelligence).

Terman and colleagues found that these children were larger, stronger, and healthier than the norm. Often, they began walking sooner and were more athletic. They were more emotionally stable than their peers and became better-adjusted adults than the average. They had lower rates of delinquency, emotional difficulty, divorce, drug problems, and so on. Of course, the teachers in Terman's study who made the nominations may have selected students who were better adjusted initially.

What Problems Do the Gifted Face?   In spite of Terman's findings, it would be incorrect to say that every student with gifts and talents is superior in adjustment and emotional health. In fact, gifted adolescents, especially girls, are more likely to be depressed and to report social and emotional problems (Berk, 2002). Many problems confront children with gifts, including boredom and frustration in school as well as isolation (sometimes even ridicule) from peers. Schoolmates may be consumed with baseball or worried about failing math, while the gifted child is fascinated with Mozart, focused on a social issue, or totally absorbed in computers, drama, or geology. Children who are gifted may also find it difficult to accept their own emotions, because the mismatch between mind and emotion may be great. They may be impatient with friends, parents, and even teachers who do not share their interests or abilities. If their language is highly developed, they may be seen as show-offs when they are simply expressing themselves. If they are highly sensitive to expectations and feelings of others, these students may be very vulnerable to criticisms and taunts. Because they are goal-directed and focused, they may seem stubborn and uncooperative. Their keen sense of humour can be used as a weapon against teachers and other students. Adjustment problems seem to be greatest for

gifted student A very bright, creative, and talented student.

Connect & Extend

TO THE RESEARCH
Robert Hoge at Carleton University wrote a now classic paper about the controversies surrounding definitions of giftedness. See Hoge, R. D. (1988). Issues in the definition and measurement of the giftedness construct. *Educational Researcher, 27*(7), 12–16.

Current definitions of giftedness include the characteristics of above-average ability, creativity, and motivation to achieve. They also acknowledge that most individuals, rather than being "superhumans," are gifted in some areas and average in others.

children with the greatest gifts—those in the highest range of academic ability (i.e., above 180 IQ) (Keogh & MacMillan, 1996; Robinson & Clinkenbeard, 1998).

Identifying Gifted Students.   Identifying children's gifts is not always easy. Many parents provide early educational experiences for their children. A preschool or primary student coming to your class may read above grade level, play an instrument quite well, or whiz through every assignment. But even very advanced reading in the early grades does not guarantee that students will still be outstanding readers years later (Mills & Jackson, 1990). How do you separate students who are gifted from hard-working or parentally pressured students? In junior high and high school, some very able students deliberately earn lower grades, making their abilities even harder to recognize. Judy Lupart at the University of Alberta has conducted a longitudinal study with a national sample of girls who are gifted. Her data indicate that gifted girls are especially likely to hide their abilities (Lupart & Barva, 1998).

Recognizing Students' Special Abilities.   Teachers are successful only about 10 to 50 percent of the time in picking out children with gifts and talents in their classes (Fox, 1981). Here are a few questions to guide identification, suggested by Marilyn Friend (2006). Who can easily manipulate abstract symbol systems such as mathematics? Who can concentrate for long periods of time on personal interests? Who remembers easily? Who developed language and reading early (as did Latoya, described at the beginning of this section)? Who is curious and has many interests? Whose work is original and creative? These students may also prefer to work alone, have a keen sense of justice and fairness, be energetic and intense, form strong commitments to friends—often older students, and struggle with perfectionism.

Group achievement and intelligence tests tend to underestimate the IQs of very bright children. Group tests may be appropriate for screening, but they are not appropriate for making decisions about instruction. Many psychologists recommend a case study approach to identifying students with gifts and talents. This means gathering many kinds of information, including test scores, grades, examples of work, projects and portfolios, letters or ratings from teachers, self-ratings, and so on (Renzulli & Reis, 2003; Sisk, 1988). Especially for recognizing artistic talent, experts in the field can be called in to judge the merits of a child's creations. Science projects, exhibitions, performances, auditions, and interviews are all possibilities. Creativity tests may identify some children not picked up by other measures, particularly students from minority groups who may be at a disadvantage on the other types of tests (Maker, 1987). Remember, students with remarkable abilities in one area may have much less impressive abilities in others. In fact, many students in North American schools have both gifts and learning disabilities.

Teaching Gifted Students.   Some educators believe that students who are gifted should be accelerated—moved quickly through the grades or through particular subjects. Other educators prefer enrichment—giving the students additional, more sophisticated, and more thought-provoking work, but keeping them with their age mates in school. Actually, both may be appropriate (Torrance, 1986). Look at Table 4.3 to see examples of how content can be modified through acceleration, enrichment, sophistication, and novelty.

Many people object to acceleration, but most careful studies indicate that students who are truly gifted and who begin elementary school, junior high school, high school, college or university, or even graduate school early do as well as, and usually better than, other students who are progressing at the normal pace. Social and emotional adjustment does not appear to be impaired. Students who are gifted tend to prefer the company of older playmates and may be miserably bored if kept with children of their own age. Skipping grades may not be the best solution for a particular student, but it does not deserve the bad name it has received (Jones & Southern, 1991; Kulik & Kulik, 1984; Richardson & Benbow, 1990). An alternative to skipping grades is to accelerate students in one or two particular subjects but keep them with peers for most classes (Robinson & Clinkenbeard, 1998). However, for students who are extremely advanced intellectually (for example,

TABLE 4.3 Examples of How to Modify Content for Students with Gifts and Talents

Modification	Math	Science	Language Arts	Social Studies
Acceleration	Algebra in grade 5	Early chemistry and physics	Learning grammatical structure early	Early introduction to world history
Enrichment	Changing bases in number systems	Experimentation and data collection	Short story and poetry writing	Reading biographies for historical insight
Sophistication	Mastering the laws of arithmetic	Learning the laws of physics	Mastering the structural properties of plays, sonnets, and so on	Learning and applying the principles of economics
Novelty	Probability and statistics	Science and its impact on society	Rewriting Shakespeare's tragedies with happy endings	Creating future societies and telling how they are governed

Source: From Gallagher, J. J., & Gallagher, S. (1994). *Teaching the gifted child* (4th ed.). Boston: Allyn & Bacon. Copyright © 1994 by Pearson Education. Adapted by permission of the publisher.

those scoring 160 or higher on an individual intelligence test), the only practical solution may be to accelerate their education (Hardman, Drew, & Egan, 2005; Hunt & Marshall, 2002).

Teaching methods for students who are gifted should encourage abstract thinking (formal-operational thought), creativity, and independence, not just the learning of greater quantities of facts. One approach that does *not* seem promising with gifted students is cooperative learning in mixed ability groups. Gifted students tend to learn more when they work in groups with other high-ability peers (Fuchs et al., 1998; Robinson & Clinkenbeard, 1998). In working with students who are gifted and talented, teachers must be imaginative, flexible, and unthreatened by the capabilities of these students. The teacher must ask the following questions: What does this child need most? What is she ready to learn? Who can help me to challenge her? Answers might come from faculty members at nearby colleges and universities, from books, museums, planetariums, and aquariums, from retired professionals, or from older students. Strategies might be as simple as letting the child do math with the next grade. Increasingly, more flexible programs are being devised for students who are gifted: summer institutes; courses at nearby colleges and universities; classes with local artists, musicians, or dancers; independent research projects; selected classes in high school for younger students; honours classes; and special-interest clubs. Teachers at Vancouver's University Hill Secondary School asked 33 students at their school who were identified as gifted what they would like teachers to do to provide them with the "very best learning situation for [them]" (British Columbia Ministry of Education, 1996). Students' responses are summarized in Table 4.4 on page 124.

In the midst of providing challenge, don't forget the support. We have all seen the ugly sights of parents, coaches, or teachers forcing the joy out of talented children by demanding practice and perfection beyond the child's interest. Just as we should not force children to stop investing in their talent ("Oh Michelangelo, quit fooling around with those sketches and go outside and play"), we should also avoid destroying intrinsic motivation with heavy doses of pressure and external rewards.

Check Your Knowledge

- What are the characteristics of students who are gifted?
- Is acceleration a useful approach with gifted students?

Apply to Practice

- If you had two students in your class who were way ahead of the others in their understanding, how would you help them learn?

TABLE 4.4 Recommendations of Gifted Students

Thirty-three academically gifted students at Vancouver's University Hill Secondary School were asked: "If we as teachers could provide the very best learning situation for you, what would you have us do?" Responses included

- Let me go ahead and work at higher levels.
- Let us work with older kids. We can fit in.
- It's not an age difference but an attitude difference that's important here. Older kids are more accepting.
- Give us independent programs. Let us work ahead on our own.
- Know that everyone has talent—and need. Provide challenge (in our talent area).
- Have totally hands-on lessons. If we're studying elections, have a mock election.
- Use more videos, films, and telecommunications.
- Use humour.
- Provide independent study opportunities—let us study something we are interested in.

Source: From British Columbia Ministry of Education. (1996). *Gifted education: A resource guide for teachers* (p. 14). Victoria, BC: British Columbia Ministry of Education. Copyright © Province of British Columbia. All rights reserved. Reprinted with permission of the Province of British Columbia, **www.ipp.gov.bc.ca**.

HIGH-INCIDENCE DISABILITIES

Teachers are more likely to encounter students with certain disabilities. These higher-incidence groups include children with learning disabilities, communication disorders, developmental disabilities, and emotional or behavioural disorders. As you can see in Table 4.5, most provinces and territories have adopted inclusive policies that place students with disabilities in their neighbourhood schools within general education classrooms. As a result of these policies, you will have children from all these categories in your classes.

More than half of all students receiving some kind of special education services in Canada are diagnosed as having learning disabilities. This is by far the largest category of students with disabilities.

Learning Disabilities

How do you explain what is wrong with a student who struggles to read, write, spell, or learn math, even though she is not developmentally delayed, emotionally disturbed, or educationally deprived and has normal vision, hearing, and language capabilities? One explanation is that the student has a **learning disability**. This is a relatively new category for exceptional students, less than 50 years old, according to Bernice Wong (1996) at Simon Fraser University in British Columbia. Wong is a pioneer in the field of learning disabilities.

Even among experts, there is no fully agreed upon definition of learning disabilities (Wong, 1996), and there are slight differences in emphasis in the definitions used across Canada (Hutchinson, 2007). Many scholars believe that, in practice, too much emphasis is given to the discrepancy between students' IQ, as measured by an intelligence test, and their achievement in school. They would like to see equal, if not greater, emphasis placed on the psychological processing problems these students experience (e.g., phonological processing problems, memory problems, and problems with number sense). Linda Siegel, at the University of British Columbia, has written extensively about this topic (1989, 1999). And the official definition of learning disabilities, adopted by the Learning Disabilities Association of Canada on January 30, 2002, emphasizes processing problems as the primary characteristic of students with learning disabilities:

learning disability Problem with acquisition and use of language; may show up as difficulty with reading, writing, reasoning, or math.

TABLE 4.5 Summary of Provincial and Territorial Approaches to Education of Exceptional Learners

Province/Territory	IEP or Equivalent	Description of Policy	Review of Special Ed.
British Columbia	Individual Education Plan	Inclusive education	1990s
Yukon	Individual Education Plan	Inclusive philosophy	1990s
Alberta	Individualized Program Plan	Most appropriate placement	1990s, 2000
Northwest Territories	Individual Education Plan	Inclusive schooling	1990s
Nunavut	Individual Education Plan (of NT)	Inclusive schooling (of NT)	Created in 1999
Saskatchewan	Personal Program Plan	Inclusive settings	Ongoing
Manitoba	Individual Education Plan	Philosophy of inclusion	Ongoing
Ontario	Individual Education Plan and Identification, Placement, and Review Committee	Regular class first	1990s
Quebec	Individual Education Plan	Integration, neighbourhood schools	Ongoing
New Brunswick	Individual Education Plan	Inclusive education	1990s
Nova Scotia	Individual Program Plan	Regular instructional settings	1990s
Prince Edward Island	Individual Education Plan	Most enabling environment	Ongoing
Newfoundland and Labrador	Individual Support Services Plan	Regular classroom and s continuum of service	1990s

Source: Hutchinson, N. L. (2007). *Inclusion of exceptional learners in Canadian schools: A practical handbook for teachers* (2nd ed., p. 12). Toronto: Pearson Education. Reprinted with permission by Pearson Education Canada Inc.

"Learning Disabilities" refer to a number of disorders which may affect the acquisition, organization, retention, understanding or use of verbal or nonverbal information. These disorders affect learning in individuals who otherwise demonstrate at least average abilities essential for thinking and/or reasoning. As such, learning disabilities are distinct from global intellectual deficiency.

Learning disabilities result from impairments in one or more processes related to perceiving, thinking, remembering or learning. These include, but are not limited to: language processing; phonological processing; visual spatial processing; processing speed; memory and attention; and executive functions (e.g., planning and decision-making).

Learning disabilities range in severity and may interfere with the acquisition and use of one or more of the following:

- oral language (e.g., listening, speaking, understanding);
- reading (e.g., decoding, phonetic knowledge, word recognition, comprehension);
- written language (e.g., spelling and written expression); and
- mathematics (e.g., computation, problem solving).

Learning disabilities may also involve difficulties with organizational skills, social perception, social interaction and perspective taking.

Learning disabilities are lifelong. The way in which they are expressed may vary over an individual's lifetime, depending on the interaction between the demands of the environment and the individual's strengths and needs. Learning disabilities are suggested by unexpected academic under-achievement or achievement which is maintained only by unusually high levels of effort and support.

Learning disabilities are due to genetic and/or neurobiological factors or injury that alters brain functioning in a manner which affects one or more processes related to learning. These disorders are not due primarily to hearing and/or vision problems, socio-economic factors, cultural or linguistic differences, lack of motivation or ineffective teaching, although these factors may further complicate the challenges faced by individuals with learning disabilities. Learning disabilities may co-exist with various conditions including attentional, behavioural and emotional disorders, sensory impairments or other medical conditions.

Students with Learning Disabilities

Students with learning disabilities are not all alike. The most common characteristics are specific difficulties in one or more academic areas; poor coordination; problems paying attention; hyperactivity and impulsivity; problems organizing and interpreting visual and auditory information; disorders of thinking, memory, speech, and hearing; and difficulties making and keeping friends (Hallahan & Kauffman, 2006; Hunt & Marshall, 2002). Also, many students with other disabilities (such as attention-deficit/hyperactivity disorder, or ADHD) and many students without disabilities may have some of the same characteristics. To complicate the situation even more, not all students with learning disabilities will have these problems, and few will have all of these problems.

Most students with learning disabilities have difficulties reading. Table 4.6 lists some behaviours that might signal a reading problem. Most often, these difficulties are due to phonological processing problems and insufficiently developed skills relating to phonemic awareness (Stanovich, 1994). Math, both in terms of computation and problem solving, is the second most common problem for students with learning disabilities. As well, the writing of some students with learning disabilities is virtually unreadable, and their spoken language can be halting and disorganized.

Many researchers trace some of these problems to the students' inability to use effective learning strategies such as those we will discuss in Chapters 7 and 8. Students with learning disabilities often lack effective ways to approach academic tasks. They don't know how to focus on the relevant information, get organized, apply learning strategies and study skills, change strategies when one isn't working, or evaluate their learning. They appear to be passive learners, in part because they don't know how to learn. Working independently is especially trying, so

---

TABLE 4.6 Reading Habits and Errors of Students with Learning Disabilities

Do any of your students show these signs? They could be indicators of learning disabilities.

Poor Reading Habits	Word Recognition Errors	Comprehension Errors
• Frequently loses his or her place • Jerks head from side to side • Expresses insecurity by crying or refusing to read • Prefers to read with the book held within inches from face • Shows tension while reading; such as reading in a high-pitched voice, biting lips, and fidgeting	• Omitting a word (e.g., "He came to the park" is read, "He came to park") • Inserting a word (e.g., "He came to the [beautiful] park") • Substituting a word for another (e.g., "He came to the *pond*") • Reversing letters or words (e.g., *was* is read *saw*) • Mispronouncing words (e.g., *park* is read *pork*) • Transposing letters or words (e.g., "The dog ate fast" is read, "The dog fast ate") • Not attempting to read an unknown word by breaking it into familiar units • Slow, laborious reading, fewer than 20 to 30 words per minute	• Not recalling basic facts (e.g., cannot answer questions directly from a passage) • Not recalling sequence (e.g., cannot explain the order of events in a story) • Not recalling main theme (e.g., cannot give the main idea of a story)

Source: Adapted from Meece, J. L. (1997). *Child and adolescent development for educators* (p. 400). New York: McGraw-Hill. Copyright © 1997 by McGraw-Hill Companies. Adapted with permission.

homework and independent classroom work are often left incomplete (Hallahan et al., 2005).

Nancy Perry (see Perry et al., 2001) has argued that early diagnosis is important in order that students with learning disabilities get the remediation they need and do not become terribly frustrated and discouraged. Also, it is important to help students understand their disabilities. When students do not understand why they are having such trouble, they may become victims of learned helplessness. Students who experience **learned helplessness** believe that they cannot control or improve their own learning. This is a powerful belief. The students never exert the effort to discover that they can make a difference in their own learning, so they remain passive and helpless. This becomes a greater problem as students move through school and into life beyond school. These students need to understand their disability and the accommodations they need to advocate for themselves.

Students with learning disabilities may also try to compensate for their problems and develop bad learning habits in the process, or they may begin avoiding certain subjects out of fear of not being able to handle the work. Research by Nancy Heath (1996; Heath & Ross, 2000) at McGill University indicates that students with learning disabilities are at risk for social withdrawal and even depression. To prevent these things from happening, teachers must be sensitive to the emotional and motivational impact of students' academic difficulties.

Teaching Students with Learning Disabilities. There is also controversy over how best to help students with learning disabilities. A promising approach seems to be to emphasize study skills and methods for processing information in a given subject, such as reading or math. Many of the principles of cognitive learning described in Chapters 7 and 8 can be applied to help all students improve their attention, memory, and problem-solving abilities (Sawyer, Graham, & Harris, 1992). Strategic Content Learning, developed by Deborah Butler at the University of British Columbia, is one example of this approach (Butler, 1998; Wong et al., 2003). No set of teaching techniques will be effective for every learning disabled child. However, here are some general strategies for supporting students with learning disabilities (Hardman, Drew, & Egan, 2005):

Preschool Years
- Keep verbal instructions short and simple.
- Match the level of content carefully to the child's developmental level.
- Give multiple examples to clarify meaning.
- Allow more practice than usual, especially when material is new.

Elementary School Years
- Keep verbal instructions short and simple; have students repeat directions back to you to be sure they understand.
- Use mnemonics (memory strategies) in instruction to teach students how to remember.
- Repeat main points several times.
- Provide additional time for learning and practice—reteach when necessary.

Secondary School and Transition Years
- Directly teach self-monitoring strategies, such as cueing students to ask, "Was I paying attention?"
- Connect new material to knowledge students already have.
- Teach students to use external memory strategies and devices (tape-recording, note-taking, to-do lists, etc.).

learned helplessness The expectation, based on previous experiences involving lack of control, that all one's efforts will lead to failure.

Connect & Extend

TO OTHER CHAPTERS
The concept of learned helplessness will be discussed again in **Chapter 5** as one explanation for the lower achievement of children living in poverty and again in **Chapter 10** as a factor influencing motivation.

You may be thinking that these are good ideas for many students who need more support and direct teaching of study skills. You are right.

In teaching reading, a combination of teaching letter-sound (phonological) knowledge and word identification strategies appears to be effective. For example, Maureen Lovett at the University of Toronto and her colleagues (Lovett et al., 2000) taught students with severe reading disabilities to use the four different word identification strategies: (1) word identification by analogy, (2) seeking the part of the word that you know, (3) attempting different vowel pronunciations, and (4) "peeling off" prefixes and suffixes in a multisyllabic word. Teachers worked one-on-one with the students to learn and practise these four strategies, along with analysis of word sounds and blending sounds into words (phonological knowledge). Explicit and intensive teaching of skills and strategies is especially helpful for students with reading disabilities. However, reading instruction should not focus solely on low-level skills. Students with learning disabilities should also be learning and using higher-order comprehension skills and strategies. Joanna Williams and her colleagues (2002) describe a system for teaching students with severe learning disabilities how to identify themes in literary works. The Reaching Every Student box describes the approach.

REACHING EVERY STUDENT

HIGHER-ORDER COMPREHENSION AND SEVERE LEARNING DISABILITIES

Joanna Williams (2002) developed the Theme Identification Program to help middle school students with severe learning disabilities understand and use the abstract idea of themes in literature. Teachers taught 12 different lessons using 12 stories. In summary, the process for each lesson was as follows:

Prereading: The teacher defines the idea of theme and leads a discussion on the value of themes, drawing on students' personal experiences.

Reading: The teacher reads the story and inserts questions while reading to help students connect what they know to the story. At the end of the reading, the class discusses the main point in the story, and the teacher reads a summary highlighting the points.

Discussion using the Theme Scheme: The teacher and students discuss the important information using six organizing questions. The first four questions focus on the content of the story:

- Who was the main character?
- What was her or his problem?
- What did she or he do?
- What happened at the end of the story?

The last two questions encourage students to make judgments in order to identify a theme:

- Was what happened good or bad?
- Why was it good or bad?

Identification of the theme: The students then state the theme in a standard format:

- [The main character] learned that she (he) should (not) _____.
- We should (not) _____.
- The theme of the story is _____.

Application of theme: The students learn to ask three questions to generalize the theme:

- Can you name someone who should (not) _____?
- When is it important for (that person) to do (or not do) _____?
- In what situation will this help?

Multimodal activity: Every lesson after the first one includes a role play of the story theme where the students act out the characters in the story, an art activity to show the theme, or a music activity such as writing a rap song that communicates the theme.

Review: The class does a recap of the Theme Scheme and previews the next lesson.

For a summary of research about teaching higher-order skills to students with learning disabilities, see Swanson, H. L. (2001). Research on interventions for adolescents with learning disabilities: A meta-analysis of outcomes related to higher-order processing. *The Elementary School Journal, 101,* 332–348.

Hyperactivity and Attention Disorders

What Would You Say?

If a student is struggling to pay attention, manage time, and organize activities, what kinds of accommodation would you try? How would you talk to parents about these issues?

You have probably heard and may even have used the term **hyperactivity**. The notion is a modern one; there were no hyperactive children 50 to 60 years ago. Today, if anything, the term is applied too often and too widely. Actually, hyperactivity is not one particular condition, but two kinds of problems that may or may not occur together—attention disorders and impulsive-hyperactivity problems.

Characteristics of Hyperactivity and Attention Disorders.   Today, most psychologists agree that the main problem for children who are labelled hyperactive is directing and maintaining attention, not simply controlling their restlessness and physical activity. The American Psychiatric Association has established the diagnostic category of **attention-deficit/hyperactivity disorder (ADHD)** to identify children with this problem. Table 4.7 lists some indicators of ADHD used by this group.

Hyperactive children are not only more physically active and inattentive than other children; they also have difficulty responding appropriately and working steadily toward goals (even their own goals), and they may not be able to control

hyperactivity Behaviour disorder marked by atypical, excessive restlessness and inattentiveness.

attention-deficit/hyperactivity disorder (ADHD) Current term for disruptive behaviour disorders marked by overactivity, excessive difficulty sustaining attention, or impulsiveness.

TABLE 4.7 Indicators of ADHD: Attention-Deficit/Hyperactivity Disorder

Do any of your students show these signs? They could be indicators of ADHD.

Problems with *Inattention*

- Often does not give close attention to details or makes careless mistakes
- Has difficulty sustaining attention in tasks or play activities
- Does not seem to listen when spoken to directly
- Does not follow through on instructions and fails to finish school work (not due to oppositional behaviour or failure to understand instructions)
- Has difficulty organizing tasks or activities
- Avoids, dislikes, or is reluctant to engage in tasks that require sustained mental effort (such as school work or homework)
- Loses things necessary for tasks or activities
- Is easily distracted by extraneous stimuli
- Is forgetful in daily activities

Problems with *Impulse Control*

- Often blurts out answers before questions have been completed
- Has difficulty awaiting his or her turn
- Often interrupts or intrudes on others in conversations or games

Hyperactivity

- Fidgets with hands or feet or squirms in seat
- Often gets up from seat when remaining seated is expected
- Often runs about or climbs excessively in situations in which it is inappropriate (in adolescents may be limited to subjective feelings of restlessness)
- Often has difficulty playing or engaging in leisure activities quietly
- Talks excessively
- Often acts as if "driven by a motor" and cannot remain still

Source: Reprinted with permission from *Diagnostic and Statistical Manual of Mental Disorders*, Fourth Edition, Text Revision. (Copyright 2000). American Psychiatric Association.

their behaviour on command, even for a brief period. The problem behaviour is generally evident in all situations and with every teacher.

It is difficult to know how many children should be classified as hyperactive. The most common estimate is 3 to 5 percent of the elementary-school population in Canada (Hutchinson, 2007). About three to four times more boys than girls are identified as hyperactive, but the gap appears to be narrowing (Hallahan et al., 2005). Just a few years ago, most psychologists thought that ADHD diminished as children entered adolescence, but now experts agree that the problems can persist into adulthood (Hallowell & Ratey, 1994). Adolescence—with the increased stresses of puberty, transition to middle or high school, more demanding academic work, and more engrossing social relationships—can be an especially difficult time for students with ADHD (Taylor, 1998).

Treatment and Teaching for Students with ADHD. The most common intervention for students with ADHD is a controversial one—prescription of psychostimulant medications (e.g., Ritalin and Dexedrine). Concern has been expressed through the media that there is an increasing reliance on drug therapy for ADHD. Health Canada (1997, cited in Maté, 2000) reported a fivefold increase in the use of Ritalin from 1990 to 1997. Similarly, articles in *The Globe and Mail* and *Newsweek* magazine (published in the United States) have expressed concern over the rise in drug use and potential abuse to treat ADHD. However, controlled studies have consistently demonstrated the benefits of psychostimulant therapy in treating the vast majority of children with ADHD; the therapy helps in 70 to 90 percent of cases (Batschaw, 1997; Hutchinson, 2007). In general, students with ADHD who take stimulant medication engage in less stimulant-seeking behaviour and are more able to benefit from educational and social interventions (Hutchinson, 2007; Zentall, 1993). Of course, these drugs need to be carefully administered and their effects carefully monitored. Some children experience side effects such as loss of appetite or nausea, headaches, insomnia, and increased heart rate and blood pressure. For most children, these side effects are mild and can be controlled by adjusting the dosage. However, little is known about the long-term effects of drug therapy.

Gabor Maté is a Vancouver physician who has ADHD. In his book *Scattered Minds* (2000), he recommends a balanced view, one that relies on accurate and up-to-date information to weigh the potential costs and benefits of using medication to treat ADHD. Ultimately, parents need to decide, in consultation with a physician, whether to include medication in their child's intervention. See Table 4.8 for suggested questions parents and teachers should ask about medication for children with ADHD.

While stimulant medications can improve the attention and behaviour of students with ADHD, in and of themselves they will not improve students' learning and achievement in school. For learning to occur, medication needs to be paired with other effective interventions. The methods that have proven most successful for helping students with ADHD are based on behavioural principles of learning such as those described in Chapter 6. One promising approach is Positive Behaviour Support (PBS). According to Joe Lucyshyn (Lucyshyn et al., 2002) at the University of British Columbia, PBS, which is linked to applied behaviour analysis, helps families, educators, and psychologists identify and understand the full range of variables (e.g., personal, ecological) influencing problem behaviour. The goal of PBS is to foster more adaptive behaviour that supports learning. The bottom line is that even if students in your class are on medication, it is critical that they also learn the academic and social skills they will need to succeed. They need to learn how and when to apply learning strategies and study skills. Also, they need to be encouraged to persist when challenged by difficult tasks and to see themselves as having control over their learning and behaviour. Medication alone will not make this happen (Kneedler, 1984).

TABLE 4.8 Questions for Teachers and Parents to Ask about Medication for Children with ADHD

The most commonly prescribed medications for children and adolescents with ADHD are Ritalin (methylphenidate) and Dexedrine (dextroamphetamine). Parents and teachers should be well informed about these medications.

1. What is the medication? What information can I read about it?

2. Why is this medication prescribed for this adolescent? What changes should we expect to see at home? At school?

3. What behavioural program or behavioural therapy is being implemented in conjunction with this drug therapy?

4. How long will this medication be prescribed for this adolescent?

5. What are the side effects in the short term? In the long term?

6. What is the dosage? What is the schedule on which the medication will be taken?

7. How often will the adolescent be seen by the prescribing physician for re-evaluation?

8. Should the medication be stopped for a short period of time to see if it is still required? When?

9. Are there foods, beverages, or other substances that should not be consumed when one is taking this medication?

10. What kind of communication is necessary among home, school, and the adolescent to evaluate whether the medication is having the desired effect?

11. What procedures should be followed if the adolescent accidentally ingests an overdose?

12. Who explains all of this to the adolescent and what should the adolescent be told?

Source: Hutchinson, N. L. (2004). *Teaching exceptional children and adolescents: A Canadian casebook.* Toronto: Prentice Hall. Reprinted by permission.

The notion of being in control is part of a new strategy for dealing with ADHD, one that stresses personal agency (Nylund, 2000). Rather than focusing on the child's problems, Nylund's idea is to enlist the child's strengths to conquer the child's problems—to put the child in control. New metaphors for the situation are developed. Rather than seeing the problems as inside the child, Nylund helps everyone see ADHD, Trouble, Boredom, and other enemies of learning as outside the child—demons to be conquered or unruly spirits to be enlisted in the service of what *the child* wants to accomplish. The focus is on solutions. The steps of the SMART approach are

Separating the problem of ADHD from the child;
Mapping the influence of ADHD on the child and family;
Attending to the exceptions to the ADHD story;
Reclaiming special abilities of children diagnosed with ADHD;
Telling and celebrating the new story. (Nylund, 2000, p. xix)

As a teacher, you can look for times when the student is engaged—even short times. What is different about these times? Discover the student's strengths and allow yourself to be amazed by them. Make changes in your teaching that support the changes the student is trying to make. Nylund gives the following example. Nine-year-old Chris and his teacher, Ms. Baker, became partners in putting Chris in control of his concentration in school. Ms. Baker moved Chris's seat to the front of the room. The two designed a subtle signal to get Chris back on track, and Chris organized his messy desk. When Chris's concentration improved, Chris received the award shown in Figure 4.4 at a party in his honour. Chris described how he was learning to listen in class: "You just have to have a strong mind and tell ADHD and Boredom not to bother you" (Nylund, 2000, p. 166). Here are suggestions that came from students working with Nylund, telling how their teachers can help them gain control:

Figure 4.4 Conquering Boredom: Putting Students in Charge

Notice how the words in the certificate recognize the child as being in control of his own life.

Source: From Nylund, D. (2000). *Treating Huckleberry Finn: A new narrative approach to working with kids diagnosed ADD/ADHD.* San Francisco: Jossey-Bass. Copyright © 2000 by Jossey-Bass. This material is adapted by permission of John Wiley & Sons, Inc.

Improving Concentration

Chris

This certificate is awarded to Chris in recognition of his recent conquering of boredom! He now is taking control of the boredom and is disciplining his mind to pay attention in class!

Teacher _____

Date _____

Use lots of pictures (visual clues) to help me learn.
Recognize cultural and racial identity.
Know when to bend the rules.
Notice when I am doing well.
Don't tell the other kids that I am taking Ritalin.
Offer us choices.
Don't just lecture—it's boring!
Realize that I am intelligent.
Let me walk around the classroom.
Don't give tons of homework.
More recess!
Be patient.

Communication Disorders

Language is a complex learned behaviour. Language disorders may arise from many sources, because so many different aspects of the individual are involved in learning language. A child with a hearing impairment may not learn to speak normally. A child who hears inadequate language at home will learn inadequate language. Children who are not listened to, or whose perception of the world is distorted by emotional problems, will reflect these problems in their language development. Because speaking involves movements, any impairment of the motor functions involved with speech can cause language disorders. And because language development and thinking are so interwoven, any problems in cognitive functioning can affect ability to use language.

Speech Impairments. A student who cannot produce sounds effectively for speaking is considered to have a **speech impairment**. Winzer (2006), at the University of Lethbridge, estimates that between 5 and 8 percent of school-aged children have some form of speech impairment. Articulation problems and stuttering are the two most common problems, and about two-thirds of all children with communication disorders are boys (Winzer, 2006).

Articulation disorders include substituting one sound for another (*thunthine* for *sunshine*), distorting a sound (*shoup* for *soup*), adding a sound (*ideer* for *idea*), or omitting sounds (*po-y* for *pony*) (Smith, 1998). Keep in mind, however, that most children are six to eight years old before they can successfully pronounce all English sounds in normal conversation. The sounds of the consonants *l, r, y, s,* and *z* and the consonant blends *sh, ch, zh,* and *th* are the last to be mastered. Also, there are dialect differences based on geography that do not represent articulation problems. A student from Newfoundland might say *ideer* for *idea* but have no speech impairment.

Stuttering generally appears between the ages of three and four. Causes of stuttering are unclear, but might include emotional or neurological problems or learned behaviour. Whatever the cause, stuttering can lead to embarrassment and anxiety for the sufferer. If stuttering continues more than a year or so, the child should be referred to a speech therapist. Early intervention can make a big difference (Hardman et al., 2005).

Voicing problems, a third type of speech impairment, include speaking with an inappropriate pitch, quality, or loudness, or in a monotone (Hallahan & Kauffman, 2006). A student with any of these problems should be referred to a speech therapist. Recognizing the problem is the first step. Be alert for students whose pronunciation, loudness, voice quality, speech fluency, expressive range, or speaking rate is very different from that of their peers. Pay attention also to students who seldom speak. Are they simply shy, or do they have difficulties with language?

speech impairment Inability to produce sounds effectively for speaking.

articulation disorders Any of a variety of pronunciation difficulties.

stuttering Repetitions, prolongations, and hesitations that block flow of speech.

voicing problems Speech impairments involving inappropriate pitch, quality, loudness, or intonation.

All students benefit from learning alternative ways of communicating, for example, sign language systems. This encourages understanding and mutual respect among students of all abilities.

Language Disorders. Language differences are not necessarily language disorders. Students with language disorders are those who are markedly deficient in their ability to understand or express language, compared with other students of their own age and cultural group (Owens, 1999). Students who seldom speak, who use few words or very short sentences, or who rely only on gestures to communicate should be referred to a qualified school professional for observation or assessment. Table 4.9 gives ideas for promoting language development for all students.

TABLE 4.9 Encouraging Language Development

- Talk about things in which the child is interested.
- Follow the child's lead. Reply to the child's initiations and comments. Share his or her excitement.
- Don't ask too many questions. If you must, use questions such as "How did/do ...?" "Why did/do ...?" and "What happened?" that result in longer explanatory answers.
- Encourage the child to ask questions. Respond openly and honestly. If you don't want to answer a question, say so and explain why (e.g., "I don't think I want to answer that question; it's very personal").
- Use a pleasant tone of voice. You need not be a comedian, but you can be light and humorous. Children love it when adults are a little silly.
- Don't be judgmental or make fun of a child's language. If you are overly critical of the child's language or try to catch and correct all errors, he or she will stop talking to you.
- Allow enough time for the child to respond.
- Treat the child with courtesy by not interrupting when he or she is talking.
- Include the child in family and classroom discussions. Encourage participation and listen to the child's ideas.
- Be accepting of the child and of the child's language. Hugs and acceptance can go a long way.
- Provide opportunities for the child to use language and to have that language work for him or her to accomplish his or her goals.

Source: From Owens, R. E., Jr. (1999). *Language disorders: A functional approach to assessment and intervention* (3rd ed.). Boston: Allyn & Bacon. Copyright © 1999 by Pearson Education. Reprinted by permission.

Developmental Disabilities

developmental disabilities Significantly below-average intellectual and adaptive social behaviour evident before the age of 18.

The term **developmental disabilities** refers to disabilities that affect all aspects of development and is used widely in Canada to replace the term *mental retardation*, still used in the United States (Hutchinson, 2007). Students with developmental delays have significant limitations in cognitive abilities and adaptive behaviour. In general, these individuals learn at a far slower rate than other students, and they may reach a point at which their learning plateaus. Often, these individuals have difficulties maintaining skills without ongoing practice and generalizing skills learned in one context to another. Also, many of these students have difficulties carrying out tasks that involve combining or integrating multiple skills (e.g., doing the laundry).

Intelligence tests are typically used to identify developmental delays. An IQ score below 70 to 75 is one indicator of a developmental delay, but it is not enough evidence to diagnose a child as having a developmental disability. There must also be problems with adaptive behaviour, day-to-day independent living, and social functioning. This caution is especially important when interpreting the scores of students from different cultures. Defining developmental disabilities based on test scores alone can create what some critics call "six-hour retardates"—students who are seen as developmentally disabled only for that part of the day when they are in school.

Given the limitations of formal assessments, advocates for individuals with developmental disabilities are beginning to argue that it is better to focus efforts on identifying the amount and types of services these individuals require. In Canada, a distinction is made between two levels of developmental disabilities, mild and severe (Hutchinson, 2007). This distinction is made primarily on the basis of the level of support required for adaptive functioning. As a general education teacher, you may not have contact with children needing extensive or pervasive support, but you will probably work with children with mild developmental disabilities. In the early grades, these students may simply learn more slowly than their peers. They need more time and more practice to learn and have difficulty transferring learning from one setting to another or putting small skills together to accomplish a more complex task.

For many students with developmental disabilities between the ages of 9 and 13, learning goals include basic reading, writing, arithmetic, learning about the local environment, social behaviour, and personal interests. In junior and senior high school, the emphasis is on vocational and domestic skills, literacy for living (using the telephone book; reading signs, labels, and newspaper ads; completing a job application), job-related behaviours such as courtesy and punctuality; health self-care; and citizenship skills. Today, there is a growing emphasis on **transition programming**—preparing the student to live and work in the community. Nancy Hutchinson and her colleagues at Queen's University, Kingston, are researching the benefits of cooperative education and on-the-job training for high school students with developmental disabilities. Their research shows that these students benefit from workplace experiences that gradually increase demands for independence and productivity (Hutchinson et al., 2005). As you will see later in the chapter, schools need to design an IEP, or individualized educational program, for every child with disabilities. An ITP, or individualized transition plan, may be part of the IEP for students with retardation (Friend, 2005).

transition programming Gradual preparation of exceptional students to move from high school into further education or training, employment, or community involvement.

The accompanying Guidelines list suggestions for teaching students with below-average general intelligence.

Behavioural and Emotional Disorders

emotional and behavioural disorders Behaviours or emotions that deviate so much from the norm that they interfere with the child's own growth and development and/or the lives of others—inappropriate behaviours, unhappiness or depression, fears and anxieties, and trouble with relationships.

Teachers consistently describe students with **emotional and behavioural disorders** as the most challenging to teach in general education classrooms. Behaviour becomes a problem when it deviates so greatly from what is appropriate for the

TEACHING CHILDREN WITH BELOW-AVERAGE GENERAL INTELLIGENCE

1. Be clear about your instructional objectives and expectations. Use instructional approaches that match those expectations and, whenever possible, make adaptations that are appropriate for the student and that become a natural part of your instructional environment.

2. Use heterogeneous classroom groups to support and include students with moderate and severe disabilities. Using strategies such as peer tutoring, cooperative learning, and friend support systems fosters a sense of community in the classroom and helps students learn to value and respect one another.

3. Sometimes students with disabilities need specialized instruction about skills that are not a part of your regular curriculum. Identify optimal times for this instruction to occur (e.g., when students are working on independent projects) and, when appropriate, involve other students in the classroom.

4. Enlist natural support systems such as older students, parents, volunteers, and teaching assistants. These individuals can reinforce your instructional objectives and support students' development of appropriate social skills.

5. Involve the students' families whenever possible. Family members can provide valuable tips about how their children learn and reinforce your goals and objectives at home.

6. Take advantage of technology. For example, students who cannot use language to communicate can be supported by various forms of augmentative communication (e.g., electronic communication boards).

Source: Adapted from Friend, M., Bursuck, W., & Hutchinson, N. (1998). *Including exceptional students: A practical guide for classroom teachers.* Scarborough, ON: Allyn & Bacon Canada.

child's age group that it significantly interferes with the child's own growth and development and/or the lives of others. Clearly, deviation implies a difference from some standard, and standards of behaviour differ from one situation, age group, culture, and historical period to another. Thus, what passes for team spirit in the football bleachers might be seen as disturbed behaviour in a bank or restaurant. In addition, the deviation must be more than a temporary response to stressful events; it must be consistent across time and in different situations (Forness & Knitzer, 1992). Recently, Don Dworet of Brock University and Arthur Rathgeber of Nipissing University, both in Ontario, studied how behaviour disorders were defined across Canada (Dworet & Rathgeber, 1999). They found differences in definitions across provinces but agreement that these disorders lead to dysfunctional interactions between students and others in their classrooms, homes, and communities. Individuals' behaviour problems range in severity and in their effect on interpersonal relationships and personal adjustment.

Children who have *conduct disorders* are aggressive, destructive, disobedient, uncooperative, distractible, disruptive, and persistent. They have been corrected and punished for the same misbehaviour countless times. Often, these children are disliked by the adults and even by the other children in their lives. They can be bullies or the ones being bullied. The most successful strategies for helping these children include behaviour management approaches such as those described in Chapter 6 and PBS (described earlier in this chapter). These students need very clear rules and consequences, consistently enforced. Nancy Hutchinson (2007) at Queen's University recommends that students with behaviour disorders have the following supports in their classrooms to enhance their self-confidence, sense of responsibility and independence, and engagement in positive problem solving:

- structure, predictability, and consistency;
- immediate, frequent, and specific feedback with consequences;
- opportunities for academic success;

Connect & Extend

TO OTHER CHAPTERS
In **Chapter 11,** you will find ideas for dealing with mild to moderate behaviour problems.

- positive alternatives to current behaviours;
- positive school-to-home support systems;
- evidence that the student is making change for the better.

Early intervention and school-wide initiatives are also effective (Sprague & Walker, 2000). Importantly, most students with behaviour problems need challenging and cognitively engaging work. According to Hutchinson (2007), we should not lower our expectations or excuse these students from learning. Boredom often contributes to these students' difficulties in the classroom. The future is not promising for those who never learn to control their behaviour and who also fail academically, so waiting for the students to "outgrow" their problems is seldom effective (O'Leary & Wilson, 1987). In fact, doing nothing may result in the problem behaviours of the individual becoming more socialized. Students with behaviour problems are drawn to gangs and get involved in anti-social behaviour, such as stealing and vandalism, because their peer culture expects it.

Children who are extremely anxious, withdrawn, shy, depressed, and hypersensitive, or who cry easily and have little confidence, may have an *anxiety-withdrawal disorder*. These children have few social skills and consequently very few friends. The most successful approaches with them appear to involve the direct teaching of social skills (Gresham, 1981).

Many exceptional students—those with learning disabilities, developmental disabilities, or ADHD, for example—may also have emotional or behavioural problems as they struggle in school. In Chapter 12, we will consider how to help all students cope with social and emotional challenges that threaten both their own learning and the learning of others in the classroom.

No set of teaching techniques can be effective for every child. You should work with the special education teachers in your school to design appropriate instruction for individual students. Also, you will need to continue your professional development in this area throughout your teaching career. One way to do this is to read professional journals. Table 4.10 lists professional journals that may help you understand your students.

Let's consider an area where teachers may be able to detect problems and make a difference—suicide.

Suicide. According to the Bureau of Reproductive and Child Health (1999), suicide is a leading cause of death among Canada's youth (aged 10–19), second only

---

TABLE 4.10 Reading the Journals

Special Education Journals	General Education Journals
Education and Training in Mental Retardation	*Canadian Journal of Education*
Exceptional Children	*Education Canada*
Exceptionality Education Canada	*Educational Leadership*
Focus on Exceptional Children	*Journal of Reading*
Intervention in School and Clinic	*Phi Delta Kappan*
Journal of Learning Disabilities	*Reading Research Quarterly*
Journal of Special Education	*Reading Teacher*
Learning Disabilities Research and Practice	*Review of Educational Research*
Learning Disability Quarterly	
Remedial and Special Education	
Teaching Exceptional Children	

Source: Hutchinson, N. L. (2007). *Inclusion of exceptional learners in Canadian schools: A practical handbook for teachers* (2nd ed.) (p. 29). Toronto: Prentice Hall. Reprinted with permission by Pearson Education Canada Inc.

to motor vehicle crashes. The rate of suicide death is higher for boys than for girls. However, non-fatal, self-inflicted injuries, many of which are suicide attempts, are more common in girls. The rate of suicide in youth from minority groups (e.g., youth with disabilities and youth who are gay or lesbian) is more than three times higher than that in the general population. Similarly, the rate of suicide among First Nations youth is three to four times the rate among non–First Nations youth.

Suicide is often a response to life problems—problems that parents and teachers sometimes dismiss. There are many warning signs that trouble is brewing. Watch for changes in eating or sleeping habits, weight, grades, disposition, activity level, or interest in friends. Students at risk sometimes suddenly give away prized possessions such as stereos, CDs, clothing, or pets. They may seem depressed or hyperactive and may say things like, "Nothing matters any more," "You won't have to worry about me any more" or "I wonder what dying is like." They may start missing school or quit doing work. The situation is especially dangerous if the student not only talks about suicide but also has a plan for carrying out a suicide attempt.

If you suspect that there is a problem, talk to the student directly. One feeling shared by many people who attempt suicide is that no one really takes them seriously. "A question about suicide does not provoke suicide. Indeed, teens (and adults) often experience relief when someone finally cares enough to ask" (Range, 1993, p. 145). Be realistic, not poetic, about suicide. Ask about specifics, and take the student seriously. Also, be aware that teenage suicides often occur in clusters. After one student acts or when stories about a suicide are reported in the media, other teens are more likely to copy the suicide (Lewinsohn, Rohde, & Seeley, 1994; Rice & Dolgin, 2002). Table 4.11 lists common myths and facts about suicide.

Drug Abuse. Although drug abuse is not always associated with emotional or behavioural problems and people without these challenges may abuse drugs, many adolescents with emotional problems also abuse drugs. Modern society makes growing up a very confusing process. Celebrities who are attractive and popular with youth drink alcohol and smoke cigarettes with seemingly little concern for their health. We have over-the-counter drugs for almost every common ailment. Coffee wakes us up, and a pill helps us sleep. And then we tell our youth to "say no" to drugs.

For many reasons, not just because of these contradictory messages, drug use has become a problem for students. Accurate statistics are hard to find, but

---

TABLE 4.11 Myths and Facts about Suicide

Myth: People who talk about suicide don't kill themselves.

Fact: Eight out of 10 people who commit suicide tell someone that they're thinking about hurting themselves before they actually do it.

Myth: Only certain types of people commit suicide.

Fact: All types of people commit suicide—male and female, young and old, rich and poor, country people and city people. It happens in every racial, ethnic, and religious group.

Myth: When a person talks about suicide, you should change the subject to get his or her mind off it.

Fact: You should take them seriously. Listen carefully to what they are saying. Give them a chance to express their feelings. Let them know you are concerned. And help them get help.

Myth: Most people who kill themselves really want to die.

Fact: Most people who kill themselves are confused about whether they want to die. Suicide is often intended as a cry for help.

Source: From Bell, R. (1980). *Changing bodies, changing lives: A book for teens on sex and relationships.* New York: Random House, p. 142.

one survey conducted by Health Canada (2004/05) indicates that 21 percent of youths in grades 5 to 9 have tried tobacco. While this is alarming, given all the information available about the harmful effects of smoking, it represents a 50 percent reduction in the prevalence of youth smoking over 10 years. Data from the Canadian Centre on Substance Abuse (2007) found that 83 percent of 15- to 24-year-olds either were current drinkers or had consumed alcohol within the previous year. Marijuana is the most popular illicit drug. In fact, it is more popular than tobacco among youth, used by 17 percent of students in grades 7 to 9. Significantly, these behaviours are associated with peer groups. Two-thirds of youths who reported having been drunk once also indicated that their peers drank alcohol. Drug use among secondary-school students has been gradually declining or holding steady since 2001, with the exception of inhalants. Inhalants (glues, paint thinners, nail polish remover, aerosol sprays, etc.) are inexpensive and available. Also, students don't realize that they are risking injury or death when they use inhalants. One study found that the proportion of students in grades 8 and 10 who believe that inhalants are dangerous is actually declining (Johnston et al., 2004).

What can be done about drug use among our students? First, we should distinguish between experimentation and abuse. Many students try something at a party but do not become regular users. The best way to help students who have trouble saying no appears to be through peer programs that teach how to say no assertively. Also, the older students are when they experiment with drugs, the more likely they are to make responsible choices, so helping younger students say no is a clear benefit.

Check Your Knowledge

- What is a learning disability?
- What is ADHD, and how is it handled in school?
- What are the most common communication disorders?
- What defines intellectual disabilities?
- What are the best approaches for students with emotional and behavioural disorders?
- What are some warning signs of potential suicide?

Apply to Practice

- How would you teach the concept of "safety" to a student with a mild developmental disability?

LOW-INCIDENCE DISABILITIES

In this section, we discuss students with disabilities that are less common in the general population. Low-incidence disabilities include severe developmental disabilities, autism, and sensory impairments having to do with hearing and vision. They also include physical disabilities and chronic health concerns that can range from allergies and asthma to diabetes, cystic fibrosis, HIV/AIDS, and cancer. Over the course of your teaching career, it is likely that you will encounter only a few students with low-incidence disabilities. However, you can still make a difference in their lives. We don't have space to describe the full range of low-incidence disabilities. Instead, we focus on two types of chronic health concerns—cerebral palsy and seizure disorders—and on hearing and vision impairments. For more information about these and other disabilities, we refer you to the descriptions in Table 4.12 and the professional journals listed in Table 4.10 on page 136.

TABLE 4.12 Students with Low-Incidence Exceptionalities, Physical Disabilities, and Chronic Medical Conditions

Exceptionality	Description
Low-Incidence Exceptionalities	
Severe developmental disabilities	Severe limitation in both intellectual functioning and adaptive behaviour; focus is on the individual's need for support to function in the community
Autism	Impairments in verbal and non-verbal communication and reciprocal social interaction; restricted, repetitive patterns of behaviour; and intellectual disability
Asperger syndrome	Severe and sustained impairment in social interaction, and development of restricted, repetitive patterns of behaviour and interests
Hard of hearing and deaf	Hearing loss that has significantly affected development of speech and/or language and caused students to need adaptations to learn
Visual impairments	Blind or partially sighted students who need adaptations to learn through channels other than visual

Physical Disabilities and Chronic Medical Conditions

Nervous System Impairment	
Cerebral palsy	Disorders affecting body movement and muscle coordination resulting from damage to brain during pregnancy or first three years
Spina bifida	Neural tube defect that occurs during first four weeks of pregnancy causing vertebrae or spinal cord to fail to develop properly
Epilepsy	Neurological disorder involving sudden bursts of electrical energy in the brain
Tourette syndrome	Neurological disorder characterized by tics
Brain injury	Damage to brain tissue that prevents it from functioning properly
Fetal alcohol syndrome	Neurological disorder caused by significant prenatal exposure to alcohol
Musculoskeletal Conditions	
Muscular dystrophy	Genetically based muscle disorders that result in progressive muscle weakness
Juvenile arthritis	Continuous inflammation of joints in young people under 16

Chronic Health Impairments

Diabetes	Condition in which the body does not make enough insulin and has problems absorbing and storing sugars
Allergies	Sensitivity or abnormal immune response to normal substance, which can cause anaphylactic shock
Asthma	Chronic lung condition, characterized by difficulty breathing, in which airways are obstructed by inflammation, muscle spasms, and excess mucus
Cystic fibrosis	Incurable disorder caused by inherited genetic defect, affecting mainly the lungs and the digestive system
HIV/AIDS	Human immunodeficiency virus/acquired immune deficiency syndrome, a virus-caused illness resulting in the breakdown of the immune system; currently no known cure exists

cerebral palsy Condition involving a range of motor or coordination difficulties due to brain damage.

spasticity Overly tight or tense muscles, characteristic of some forms of cerebral palsy.

epilepsy Disorder marked by seizures and caused by abnormal electrical discharges in the brain.

generalized seizure A seizure involving a large portion of the brain.

partial seizure or absence seizure A seizure involving only a small part of the brain.

Students with Chronic Health Concerns

Some students must have special devices, such as braces, special shoes, crutches, or wheelchairs, to participate in school programs. If the school has the necessary architectural features, such as ramps, elevators, and accessible washrooms, and if teachers allow for the physical limitations of students, little needs to be done to alter the usual educational program.

Cerebral Palsy. Damage to the brain before or during birth or during infancy can cause a child to have difficulty moving and coordinating his or her body. The problem may be mild, so that the child simply appears a bit clumsy, or so severe that voluntary movement is practically impossible. The most common form of **cerebral palsy** is characterized by **spasticity** (overly tight or tense muscles). But many children with cerebral palsy have secondary handicaps (Kirk, Gallagher, & Anastasiow, 1993). In the classroom, these secondary handicaps are the greatest concern—and these are usually what the general education teacher can help with most. For example, many children with cerebral palsy also have hearing impairments, speech problems, or mild developmental disabilities. The strategies described in other sections of this chapter should prove helpful in such situations.

Seizure Disorders (Epilepsy). A seizure is a cluster of behaviour that occurs in response to abnormal neurochemical activities in the brain (Hardman, Drew, & Egan, 2005). The effects of the seizure depend on where the discharge of energy starts in the brain and how far it spreads. People with **epilepsy** have recurrent seizures, but not all seizures are the result of epilepsy; temporary conditions such as high fevers or infections can also trigger seizures. Seizures take many forms and differ with regard to the length, frequency, and movements involved. A partial seizure involves only a small part of the brain, whereas a **generalized seizure** includes much more of the brain.

Most generalized seizures (once called *grand mal*) are accompanied by uncontrolled jerking movements that ordinarily last from two to five minutes, possible loss of bowel or bladder control, and irregular breathing, followed by a deep sleep or coma. On regaining consciousness, the student may be very weary, confused, and in need of extra sleep. Most seizures can be controlled by medication. If a student has a seizure accompanied by convulsions in class, the teacher must take action so that the student will not be injured. The major danger to a student having a seizure is getting hurt by striking a hard surface during the violent jerking.

For this or any other medical emergency, it is important to stay calm and reassure the rest of the class. Do not try to restrain the child's movements; you can't stop the seizure once it starts. Lower the child gently to the floor, away from furniture or walls. Move hard objects away. Loosen scarves, ties, or anything that might make breathing difficult. Turn the child's head gently to the side and put a soft coat or blanket under the student's head. Never put anything in the student's mouth—it is not true that people having seizures can swallow their tongues. Don't attempt artificial respiration unless the student does not start breathing again after the seizure stops. Find out from the student's parents how the seizure is usually dealt with. If one seizure follows another and the student does not regain consciousness in between, if the student is pregnant, if the student has a medical ID that does not say "epilepsy, seizure disorder," if there are signs of injury, or if the seizure goes on for more than five minutes, get medical help right away (Friend, 2005). For more ideas and information, see **www.epilepsy.ca**.

Not all seizures are dramatic. Sometimes the student just loses contact briefly. The student may stare, fail to respond to questions, drop objects, and miss what has been happening for 1 to 30 seconds. These **partial seizures or absence seizures**, which were once called *petit mal*, can easily go undetected. If a child in your class appears to daydream frequently, does not seem to know what is going on at times, or cannot remember what has just happened when you ask, you should consult the school psychologist or nurse. The major problem for students with partial seizures is that they miss the continuity of the class interaction—these seizures can occur as often as 100 times a day. If their seizures are frequent, students will find the lessons confusing. Question these students to be sure they are understanding and following the lesson. Be prepared to repeat yourself periodically.

Students Who Are Deaf and Hard of Hearing

You will hear the term *hearing impaired* used to describe students who have difficulties hearing. The deaf community and researchers prefer the terms *deaf* and *hard of hearing*. The number of deaf students has been declining over the past three decades, but when the problem does occur, the consequences for learning are serious (Hunt & Marshall, 2002). Signs of hearing problems are turning one ear toward the speaker, favouring one ear in conversation, or misunderstanding conversation when the speaker's face cannot be seen. Other indications include not following directions, seeming distracted or confused at times, frequently asking people to repeat what they have said, mispronouncing new words or names, and being reluctant to participate in class discussions. Take note particularly of students who have frequent earaches, sinus infections, or allergies.

In the past, educators have debated whether oral or manual approaches are better for children who are deaf or hard of hearing. Oral approaches involve **speech reading** (also called lip reading) and training students to use whatever limited hearing they may have. Manual approaches include **sign language** and **finger spelling**. Research indicates that children who learn some manual method of communicating perform better in academic subjects and are more socially mature than students who are exposed only to oral methods. Today, the trend is to combine both approaches (Hallahan & Kauffman, 2006).

Another perspective suggests that people who are deaf are part of a different culture with a different language, values, social institutions, and literature. Hunt and Marshall (2002) quote one deaf professional: "How would women like to be referred to as male-impaired, or whites like to be called black-impaired? I'm not impaired; I'm deaf!" (p. 348). From this perspective, a goal is to help deaf children become bilingual and bicultural, to be able to function effectively in both cultures. Technological innovations such as teletypewriters in homes and public phones and the many avenues of communication possible through email and the internet have expanded communication possibilities for all people with hearing problems.

> **speech reading** Using visual cues to understand language.
>
> **sign language** Communication system of hand movements that symbolize words and concepts.
>
> **finger spelling** Communication system that "spells out" each letter with a hand position.

Students with Low Vision and Blindness

Approximately 1 in 1000 students in Canada is visually impaired (Hutchinson, 2007). Of these, approximately 80 percent are print users and 20 percent are potential Braille users. Students who have difficulty seeing often hold books either very close to or very far from their eyes. They may squint, rub their eyes frequently, or complain that their eyes burn or itch. The eyes may actually be swollen, red, or encrusted. Students with vision problems may misread material on the board, describe their vision as being blurred, be very sensitive to light, or hold their heads at an odd angle. They may become irritable when they have to work at a desk or lose interest if they have to follow an activity happening across the room (Hunt & Marshall, 2002). Any of these signs should be reported to a qualified school professional.

Mild vision problems can be overcome with corrective lenses. However, students with more significant visual impairments probably require special materials and equipment to function in general education classrooms. Most of these students have partial or **low vision**; that is, they have some useful vision between 20/70 and 20/200 (Friend et al., 1998). For example, a person with 20/70 vision can only see at six metres what individuals with normal vision see at 21.3 metres. An individual with 20/200 vision is considered legally and **educationally blind**. Students who are educationally blind must use hearing and touch as their primary learning channels (Kirk, Gallagher, & Anastasiow, 1993).

> **low vision** Vision limited to close objects.
>
> **educationally blind** Needing Braille materials in order to learn.

Special materials and equipment that help these students function in regular classrooms include large-print typewriters; software that converts printed material to speech or to Braille; personal organizers that have talking appointment books or address books (such as a PalmPilot); variable-speed tape recorders (which allow teachers to make time-compressed tape recordings that can be sped up in a way that changes the rate of speech without changing the voice pitch); special calculators; the abacus; three-dimensional maps, charts, and models; and special measuring devices. For students with visual problems, the quality of the print is often more important than the size, so watch out for hard-to-read handouts and blurry copies. Make yourself aware of local, provincial, and national resource centres (e.g., Special Education Technology, SET-BC, in British Columbia and the Canadian National Institute for the Blind, CNIB) that have resource materials and assistive technologies for students with sensory impairments.

The arrangement of your classroom is also an issue. Students with low vision or blindness need to know where things are, so consistency matters—a place for everything and everything in its place. Leave plenty of space for moving around the room and make sure to monitor possible obstacles and safety hazards, such as garbage cans in aisles and open cabinet doors. If you rearrange the room, give students with visual problems a chance to learn the new layout. Make sure that each student has a buddy for fire drills or other emergencies (Friend et al., 1998).

Autism Spectrum Disorders

autism/autism spectrum disorders Developmental disability significantly affecting verbal and non-verbal communication, social interaction, and imaginative creativity, generally evident before age three and ranging from mild to major.

You may be familiar with the term *autism*. According to the American Psychiatric Association (2000), **autism** is a developmental disability that significantly affects verbal and non-verbal communication, social interaction, and imaginative creativity, and is characterized by restrictive, repetitive, and stereotypic patterns of behaviour, interests, and activities. Generally, autism is evident before age three. We use the term **autism spectrum disorders** to emphasize that autism includes a range of disorders, from mild to major. From an early age, children with autism spectrum disorders may have difficulties in social relations. They do not form connections with others, avoid eye contact, or don't share feelings such as enjoyment or interest with others. Communication is impaired. About half of these students are non-verbal; they have very few or no language skills. Others make up their own language. They may obsessively insist on regularity and sameness in their environments—change is very disturbing. They may repeat behaviours and have restricted interests, watching the same DVD over and over, for example. They may be very sensitive to light, sound, touch, or other sensory information—sounds may be painful, for example. They may be able to memorize words or steps in problem solving, but not use them appropriately or be very confused when the situation changes or questions are asked in a different way (Friend, 2006).

Asperger syndrome is one of the disabilities included in the autistic spectrum. These children have many of the characteristics described above, but their greatest trouble is with social relations. Language is less affected. Their speech may be fluent, but unusual, mixing up "I" and "you" pronouns, for example (Friend, 2006; Hutchinson, 2007). Many students with autism also have moderate to severe intellectual disabilities, but those with Asperger syndrome usually have average to above average intelligence.

Theory of Mind. One current explanation for autism and Asperger syndrome is that children with these disorders lack a theory of mind—an understanding that they and other people have minds, thoughts, and emotions. They have difficulty explaining their own behaviours, appreciating that other people might have different feelings, and predicting how behaviours might affect emotions. So, for example, a student may not understand why classmates are bored by his constant repetition of stories or obscure facts about topics he finds fascinating. Or the student may stand too close or too far away when interacting, not realizing that she is making other people uncomfortable (Friend, 2006; Hutchinson, 2007; Wellman et al., 2002).

Interventions.   Early and intense interventions that focus on communication and social relations are particularly important for children with autism spectrum disorders. As they move into elementary school, some of these students will be in inclusive settings, others in specialized classes, and many in some combination of these two. Collaboration among teachers and the family is particularly important. Supports such as smaller classes, structured environments, providing a safe "home base" for times of stress, consistency in instruction, assistive technologies, and the use of visual supports may be part of a collaborative plan (Friend, 2006). Through adolescence and the transition to adulthood, life, work, and social skills are important educational goals.

If you decide that students in your class might benefit from special services, the first step is making a referral. How would you begin? Table 4.13 guides you through the referral process. In Chapter 12, when we discuss effective teaching, we will look at more ways to reach all your students.

Check Your Knowledge

- How can schools accommodate the needs of physically disabled students?
- How would you handle a seizure in class?
- What are some signs of hearing and visual impairment?

Apply to Practice

- What accommodations could you make in your classroom for students with hearing or vision problems?

TABLE 4.13 Making a Referral

1. Contact the student's parents. It is very important that you discuss the student's problems with the parents *before* you refer.

2. Before making a referral, check *all* the student's school records. Has the student ever
   - had a psychological evaluation?
   - qualified for special services?
   - been included in other special programs (e.g., for disadvantaged children; speech or language therapy)?
   - scored far below average on standardized tests?
   - been retained?

   Do the records indicate
   - good progress in some areas but poor progress in others?
   - any physical or medical problem?
   - that the student is taking medication?

3. Talk to the student's other teachers and professional support personnel about your concern for the student. Have other teachers also had difficulty with the student? Have they found ways of dealing successfully with the student? Document the strategies you have used in your class to meet the student's educational needs. Your documentation will provide evidence that will be helpful to or required by the team of professionals who will evaluate the student. Demonstrate your concern by keeping written records. Your notes should include items such as
   - exactly what you are concerned about;
   - why you are concerned about it;
   - dates, places, and times you have observed the problem;
   - precisely what you have done to try to resolve the problem;
   - who, if anyone, helped you devise the plans or strategies you have used;
   - evidence that the strategies have been successful or unsuccessful.

Remember that you should refer a student only if you can make a convincing case that the student may have a handicapping condition and probably cannot be served appropriately without special education. Referral for special education begins a time-consuming, costly, and stressful process that is potentially damaging to the student and has many legal ramifications.

Source: Pullen, P. L., & Kaufmann, J. M. (1987). *What should I know about special education? Answers for classroom teachers.* Austin, TX: Pro-Ed. Reprinted by permission.

EXCEPTIONAL EDUCATION AND INCLUSION

We have been discussing in detail the many needs of exceptional learners because, no matter what grade or subject you teach, you will encounter these students in your classroom. The trend toward including exceptional students in general education classrooms began in the early 1970s.

Exceptional Education Laws and Policies

Canada does not have a national office of education, unlike Britain and the United States. Each province has the authority to make its own laws concerning education, including exceptional education, and each province and territory has an **education or school act** that governs education in its elementary and secondary schools. As a teacher, you will need to become familiar with the laws and policies that govern education in your province or territory.

Inclusion is the current policy of the ministries of education in all of Canada's provinces and territories (Hutchinson, 2007). However, provinces vary in their definitions of inclusion. In British Columbia, for example, the principle of inclusion supports "equitable access to learning by all students and the opportunity for all students to pursue their goals in all aspects of their education" (British Columbia Special Education Branch, 1995, Section A, p. 2). However, the British Columbia Ministry of Education clarifies that **integration**—exceptional students' participation in activities with non-exceptional peers—is only one way to achieve inclusion, the preferred way. This definition of inclusion means that exceptional students may not spend 100 percent of every school day in general education activities or classrooms. The emphasis is on meeting the educational needs of all students, and this "does not preclude the appropriate use of resource rooms, self-contained classrooms, community-based training, or other specialized settings" (British Columbia Special Education Branch, 1995, Section A, p. 3). Consistent with British Columbia's policy in this regard, no jurisdiction uses the expression "full inclusion" and all provide alternatives to the general education classroom when that choice clearly does not meet the student's needs.

There is one national piece of legislation that has an impact on education across Canada—the *Canadian Charter of Rights and Freedoms*, which is part of the Constitution. Section 15.1 of the *Charter* outlines the equality provisions that apply to education:

> Every individual is equal before and under the law and has the right to equal protection and equal benefit of the law without discrimination and, in particular, without discrimination based on race, national or ethnic origin, colour, religion, sex, age, or mental or physical disability.

According to William MacKay (1986), a law professor at Dalhousie University in Nova Scotia, there are three dimensions of "equality rights"—non-discrimination, equal opportunity, and equal outcomes. For some students, having equal opportunities and achieving equal outcomes requires differential treatment—that is, a program that attends to and supports their exceptional learning needs.

Exceptional education in Canada has also been influenced by American legislation. In particular, Canadian practices in special education have embraced American practices of providing exceptional learners with a least restrictive placement and an individualized education program (IEP) and of protecting the rights of exceptional students and their families.

Least Restrictive Placement. In the United States, federal law requires that students be educated in the least restrictive environment possible. Typically, this is interpreted to mean that exceptional students should be educated in general educational settings whenever possible or in settings that provide as close a match as possible to general educational settings. This practice is referred to as **least restrictive placement**. While there is no law requiring least restrictive placement in Canada, the

---

education or school act Provincial or territorial legislation that governs education in elementary and secondary schools.

inclusion The practice of integrating exceptional students into regular education classrooms; the emphasis is on participation rather than placement.

integration The practice of having exceptional students participate in activities with their non-exceptional peers.

Canadian Charter of Rights and Freedoms Legislation that protects the rights of all Canadians and, in particular, Canadians who are members of minority groups, including Canadians with disabilities.

least restrictive placement The practice of placing exceptional students in the most regular educational settings possible while ensuring that they are successful and receive support appropriate to their special needs.

principle is embodied in our practices. Some provinces (e.g., Prince Edward Island) refer to placement in the "most enabling environment" rather than the least restrictive environment (Hutchinson, 2007). Consistent with Canada's goal of becoming an inclusive society, it is generally accepted that the most enabling environment for most learners most of the time is the general education classroom. But as you can see in the Point/Counterpoint feature, inclusion challenges our education systems.

Individualized Education Program.   Each student with exceptional learning needs must have an educational program tailored to his or her unique needs. The

POINT > < COUNTERPOINT

IS INCLUSION A REASONABLE APPROACH TO TEACHING EXCEPTIONAL STUDENTS?

Most educators agree with the principle of inclusion: "People with exceptionalities ought to be part of the mainstream of society and all its institutions from birth onward.... They [should] be ensured full social, educational, and economic participation in society and on their own terms as much as possible" (Hutchinson, 2007, p. 18). However, many teachers feel unprepared and unsupported in their efforts to meet the needs of these students in their classrooms. For this reason, inclusion is a controversial issue in schools in Canada.

> Point   *Inclusion makes sense.*

Supporters of full inclusion, such as Marsha Forest, believe that

> All children need to learn with and from other children.... All children need to belong and feel wanted.... All children need to have fun and enjoy noise and laughter in their lives.... All children need to take risks and fall and cry and get hurt.... All children need to be in real families and real schools and real neighborhoods. (cited in Michael Hardman, 1994, p. 403)

These opportunities are limited in special class placements. No matter how good the teaching, students with exceptionalities will never learn to cope with the world outside their special classroom if they are not allowed to live in that world. Furthermore, many researchers believe that special education has failed. For example, only 56 percent of students with disabilities earn a high school diploma and only 21

percent of these graduates go on to pursue any kind of post-secondary education. Segregation away from the mainstream, in special classes, robs these students of the opportunity to learn to participate fully in society, and it robs other students of the opportunity to develop understanding and acceptance of disabilities. The result is an increased likelihood that individuals who are exceptional will be stigmatized.

< Counterpoint   *Inclusion is not working.*

Just because a student is physically present in a class doesn't mean that student feels a sense of belonging. Students with high abilities and disabilities can be just as socially isolated and alone in a general education classroom as they would be in a "special" class across the hall or in another school. Children can be cruel, and they may not necessarily provide opportunities for their peers who are exceptional to "have fun and enjoy noise and laughter in their lives." And special education classes cannot be held solely responsible for low graduation and high dropout rates among students with disabilities. Ninety-two percent of all students with exceptionalities spend at least some of their time in general education classes already. Shouldn't these classes be held responsible too?

Finally, is it reasonable to expect general education teachers who are already overburdened with responsibilities for low-achieving students, students coping with family crises,

and students who speak little or no English to also handle the wide range of disabilities that could confront them? General educators are unprepared, unsupported, and unable to handle all these challenges at once. The idea that extra support and consultation will be provided is good in theory, but it has been lacking in practice.

Nancy Hutchinson (2007) agrees that effective inclusion has been an elusive goal in education. Perhaps it's because our social values precede our knowledge about how best to accomplish this goal, or we haven't put adequate human and financial resources into our efforts so far, or we haven't found creative ways to articulate general and special education programming. Paula Stanovich and Anne Jordan (Stanovich, 1999; Stanovich & Jordan, 1998), at the University of Toronto, have interviewed and observed many educators in order to identify what makes inclusion work. Their research indicates that teachers who believe in inclusion and are confident about their ability to implement practices that support all students are more effective in inclusive classrooms. Furthermore, their research indicates that teachers' beliefs and practices reflect, in large measure, those of the school administrator. One way to promote inclusion, then, is to ensure that school administrators support it. Another is to do more in teacher preparation programs and in-service development programs to prepare teachers to accommodate diversity among students in their classrooms.

individualized education program (IEP) Annually revised program for an exceptional student detailing present achievement level, goals, and strategies, drawn up by teachers, family members, specialists, and (if possible) the student.

individualized education program, or **IEP,** is written by a team that includes the student's teacher or teachers, a qualified school psychologist or special education supervisor, the parent(s) or guardian(s), and (when possible) the student. The program should be reviewed and updated each year and should address the following issues:

1. The student's present level of functioning.

2. Goals for the year and short-term measurable instructional objectives leading to those goals.

3. A list of specific services to be provided to the student and details of when those services will be initiated.

4. A description of how fully the student will participate in the general education program.

5. A schedule telling how the student's progress toward the objectives will be evaluated and approximately how long the services described in the plan will be needed.

6. Beginning at the age of 16 (and as young as 14 for some students), a statement of needed transitional services to move the student toward further education or work in adult life.

Figure 4.5 is an excerpt from the IEP of a nine-year-old girl with developmental disabilities. This section of the IEP focuses on one behaviour problem and on reading.

The Rights of Students and Parents/Guardians. As a teacher, you need to be aware of the expectations for the participation of parents and guardians in education in your province. Typically, parents and guardians are viewed as partners in the education of exceptional learners. They must approve any testing and special placements concerning their child, and they have the right to see all records kept by the school board that concern their child. They may obtain an independent evaluation, and they have the right to participate in planning their children's IEPs. Schools must maintain the confidentiality of students' records and ensure that testing practices do not discriminate against students from minority groups. Furthermore, schools should communicate with parents and guardians in their native languages (i.e., through interpreters and translators) and must have processes in place for them to appeal any decisions made by the school about their children. Finally, students are entitled to see all records that the school board keeps about them, and should, whenever possible, be involved in planning their educational programs.

Effective Teaching in Inclusive Classrooms

When you think about working with students who have exceptional learning needs, what are your concerns? Do you have enough training? Will you get the support you need from school administrators or specialists? Will working with these students take time away from your other responsibilities? These are common questions, and sometimes concerns are justified. But effective teaching for exceptional students does not require a unique set of skills. It is a combination of good teaching practices and sensitivity to all your students. As much as possible, all students need to be challenged academically and treated as full participants in the day-to-day life of classrooms.

To accomplish the first goal of academic learning, Larrivee (1985) concluded that teachers who effectively include students with exceptional learning needs in their classrooms do the following:

1. Use time efficiently by having smooth management routines, avoiding discipline problems, and planning carefully.

2. Ask questions at the right level of difficulty.

3. Give supportive, positive feedback to students, helping them figure out the right answer if they are wrong but on the right track.

Connect & Extend

TO THE RESEARCH
For a discussion of how teachers' and school administrators' attitudes toward exceptional learners and beliefs about inclusive education influence effective teaching practices, see Stanovich, P., & Jordan, A. (1998). Canadian teachers' and principals' beliefs about inclusive education as predictors of effective teaching in heterogeneous classrooms. *Elementary School Journal, 98,* 221–238.

Figure 4.5 An Excerpt from an Individualized Education Program (IEP)

Source: From Hallahan, Daniel P., & James M. Kauffmann, *Exceptional Learners*, 7th ed. Published by Allyn & Bacon, Boston, MA. Copyright © 1997 by Pearson Education. Reprinted by permission of the publisher.

This IEP was developed for a nine-year-old girl. This section of the plan focuses on following the teacher's directions and on reading.

Student: Amy North   Age: 9   Grade: 1   Date: Oct. 17, 1995

---

1. Unique Characteristics or Needs: Non-compliance

Frequently non-compliant with teacher's instructions.

1. Present Levels of Performance
Complies with about 50 percent of teacher requests/commands.

2. Special Education, Related Services, and Modifications
Implemented immediately, strong reinforcement for compliance with teacher's instructions (Example: "Sure I will!" plan including precision requests and reinforcer menu for points earned for compliance, as described in *The Tough Kid Book*, by Rhode, Jenson, and Reavis, 1992); within three weeks, training of parents by school psychologist to use precision requests and reinforcement at home.

3. Objectives (Including Procedures, Criteria, and Schedule)
Within one month, will comply with teacher requests/commands 90 percent of the time; compliance monitored weekly by the teacher.

4. Annual Goals
Will become compliant with teacher's requests/commands.

2. Unique Characteristics or Needs: Reading

2a. Very slow reading rate
2b. Poor comprehension
2c. Limited phonics skills
2d. Limited sight-word vocabulary

1. Present Levels of Performance
2a. Reads stories of approximately 100 words of first-grade level at approximately 40 words per min.
2b. Seldom can recall factual information about stories immediately after reading them.
2c. Consistently confuses vowel sounds, often misidentifies consonants, and does not blend sounds.
2d. Has sight-word vocabulary of approximately 150 words.

2. Special Education, Related Services, and Modifications
2a–2c.   Direct instruction 30 minutes daily in vowel discrimination, consonant identification, and sound blending: begin immediately, continue throughout schoolyear.

2a & 2d. Sight word drill 10 minutes daily in addition to phonics instruction and daily practice; 10 minutes practice in using phonics and sight-word skills in reading story at her level; begin immediately, continue for schoolyear.

3. Objectives (Including Procedures, Criteria, and Schedule)
2a. Within three months, will read stories on her level at 60 words per minute with two or fewer errors per story; within six months, 80 words with two or fewer errors; performance monitored daily by teacher or aide.

2b. Within three months, will answer oral and written comprehension questions requiring recall of information from stories she has just read with 90 percent accuracy (e.g., Who is in the story? What happened? When? Why?) and be able to predict probable outcomes with 80 percent accuracy; performance monitored daily by teacher or aide.

2c. Within three months, will increase sight-word vocabulary to 200 words, within six months to 250 words, assessed by flashcard presentation.

4. Annual Goals
2a–2c.   Will read fluently and with comprehension at beginning-second-grade level.

To accomplish the second goal of including exceptional learners in the day-to-day life of the classroom, Ferguson, Ferguson, and Bogdan (1987) give the following guidelines:

Connect & Extend

TO THE RESEARCH
Barber, L., & Brophy, K. (1993). Parents' views on school placement procedures for their children with special needs. *Journal on Developmental Disabilities, 2,* 100–111.

Abstract
Mothers from five Ontario families with a child with Down syndrome (aged 5–10 years) were interviewed regarding their experiences in meetings with the school and as part of a partnership process concerning the identification and placement of their children and their views of these experiences. Subjects felt that it was very important for parents to be major players in the placement process, and that schools need to take steps to ensure that parents are able to participate more fully in order that the best possible decisions are made for the child. Results also show that parents would like to see the nature of the procedure changed so that they feel more comfortable at meetings rather than intimidated. Recommendations for change are given.

resource room Classroom with special materials and a specially trained teacher.

cooperative teaching Collaboration between regular and special education teachers.

1. Create heterogeneous groups of students for instruction.
2. Instead of sending students out for special services such as speech therapy, remedial reading, and individualized instruction, try to integrate the special help into the class setting, perhaps during a time when the other students are working independently too.
3. Make sure that your language and behaviour with exceptional learners is a good model for everyone.
4. Teach about differences among people as part of the curriculum. Let students become familiar with accommodations for students with disabilities, such as hearing aids, sign language, communication boards, and so on.
5. Have students work together in cooperative groups or on special projects, such as role plays, biographical interviews, or lab assignments.
6. Try to keep the schedules and activity patterns of students with and without exceptional learning needs similar.

Resource Rooms, Collaborative Consultation, and Cooperative Teaching.   Many schools provide additional help for classroom teachers working with students who are exceptional. A **resource room** is a classroom with special materials and equipment and a specially trained teacher. Students may come to the resource room each day for several minutes or several hours and receive instruction individually or in small groups. During the rest of the day, the students are in general education classes.

The resource room can also be used as a tutorial centre. Individual students may spend an hour, a day, or a week there to receive direct and intensive instruction that their classroom teacher is unable to provide. Besides working with students directly, a resource teacher may work with them indirectly by giving the general education teacher ideas, materials, or actual demonstrations of teaching techniques.

Increasingly, special and general education teachers are working together, collaborating to assume equal responsibility for the education of students with exceptional learning needs. The collaboration may work through consultation, planning, and problem solving about how to teach specific students, or the special education teacher might work directly alongside the general education teacher in a class made up of students with and without exceptional learning needs. The latter is called **cooperative teaching**. The teachers assume different roles, depending on the age of the students and their needs. For example, in a secondary class, the general education teacher might be responsible for academic content, while the special educator teaches study skills and learning strategies. In another classroom, the general education teacher might deal with core content, while the special education teacher provides remediation, enrichment, or reteaching when necessary. The two teachers might also try team teaching, where each is responsible for different parts of the lesson.

When using cooperative teaching, it is important that students with and without disabilities are not segregated in the class, with the general education teacher always working with the "regular" students and the special education teacher always working with the "special" students. Recall that the one exception to this might be students who are gifted and talented. Sometimes, it is beneficial for them to work in homogeneous groups with their similarly gifted and talented peers. When Nancy was a resource teacher in a school district in British Columbia, she often collaborated with classroom teachers to plan and teach units of instruction. For example, she once taught research and writing strategies to a grade 7 class that included several students with learning disabilities and a student recovering from a brain injury. While she targeted the processes involved in doing research, the classroom teacher taught content relating to Egypt. Figure 4.6 shows different ways to implement cooperative teaching.

Including Families.   To create supportive learning environments for students having exceptional learning needs, collaboration should extend outside the classroom to the students' families. The Family and Community Partnerships box offers some ideas about working with families.

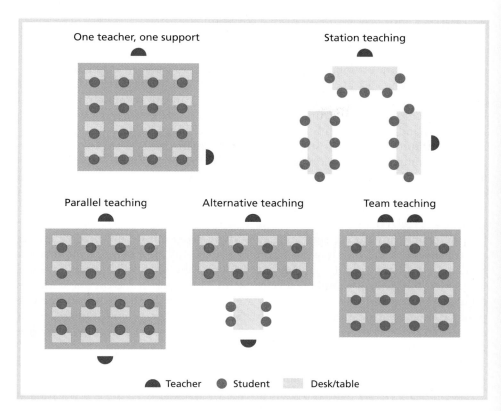

One teacher, one support

Station teaching

Parallel teaching

Alternative teaching

Team teaching

Teacher   Student   Desk/table

Figure 4.6 Cooperative and Co-Teaching Approaches

There are many ways for teachers to work together in inclusion classrooms.

Source: From Friend, M., & Bursuck, W. (1996). *Including students with special needs: A practical guide for classroom teachers.* Copyright © 1996 Published by Allyn and Bacon, Boston, MA. Copyright © 1996 by Pearson Education. Reprinted by permission of the publisher.

FAMILY AND COMMUNITY PARTNERSHIPS
PRODUCTIVE CONFERENCES

Plan and prepare for a productive conference.

EXAMPLES

1. Have a clear purpose and gather the needed information. If you want to discuss student progress, have work samples.
2. Send home a list of questions and ask families to bring the information to the conference.

Sample questions from Friend and Bursuck (1996, p. 101):

1. What is your child's favourite class activity?
2. Does your child worry about class activities? If so, which ones?
3. What are your priorities for your child's education this year?
4. What questions do you have about your child's education in my class this year?
5. How could we at school help make this the most successful year ever for your child?
6. Are there any topics you want to discuss at the conference that I might need to prepare for? If so, please let me know.
7. Would you like other individuals to participate in the conference? If so, please give me a list of their names.

8. Is there particular school information you would like me to have available? If so, please let me know.

During the conference, create and maintain an atmosphere of collaboration and respect.

EXAMPLES

1. Arrange the room for private conversation. Put a sign on your door to avoid interruptions. Meet around a conference table for better collaboration. Have tissues available.
2. Address family members formally, using the words *Mr.* and *Ms.*, not *Mom* or *Dad* or *Grandma*. Use students' names.
3. Listen to families' concerns and build on their ideas for their children.

After the conference, keep good records and follow up on decisions.

EXAMPLES

1. Make notes to yourself and keep them organized.
2. Summarize any actions or decisions in writing and send a copy to the family and any other teachers or professionals involved.
3. Communicate with families on other occasions, especially when there is good news to share.

Technology and Exceptional Students

assistive technology Devices, systems, and services that support and improve the capabilities of individuals with disabilities.

Connect & Extend

TO THE WEB

You can find out more about assistive technology at Closing the Gap (**www.closingthegap. com**).

universal design Considering the needs of all users in the design of new tools, learning programs, or websites.

Computers and other technology can support learning for students with disabilities so that the disabilities are less handicapping.

Assistive technology is any product, piece of equipment, or system that is used to increase, maintain, or improve the functional capabilities of individuals with disabilities (Goldman et al., 2006). Computers have improved the education of exceptional children in countless ways. Teachers can use computers for record keeping, program planning, and managing instruction. For students who require small steps and many repetitions to learn a new concept, computers are the perfect patient tutors, repeating steps and lessons as many times as necessary. A well-designed computer instructional program is engaging and interactive—two important qualities for students who have problems paying attention or a history of failure that has eroded motivation. For example, a math or spelling program might use images, sounds, and game-like features to maintain the attention of a student with ADHD. Interactive videodisc programs are being developed to teach hearing people how to use sign language. Many programs do not involve sound, so students with hearing impairments can get the full benefit from the lessons. Students who have trouble reading can use programs that will "speak" a word for them if they touch the unknown word with a light pen or the cursor. With this immediate access to help, the students are much more likely to get the reading practice they need to prevent falling further and further behind. Other devices actually convert printed pages and typed texts to spoken words or Braille for students who are blind.

For the student with a learning disability whose writing can't be read, word processors produce perfect penmanship so that the ideas can finally get on paper. Once the ideas are on paper, the student can reorganize and improve the writing without the agony of rewriting by hand (Hallahan & Kauffman, 2006; Hardman, et al., 2005).

With these tremendous advances in technology have come new barriers, however. Many computers have graphic interfaces. To manipulate the programs requires precise "mouse movements," as you may remember when you first learned to point and click. These manoeuvres are difficult for students with motor problems or visual impairments. And the information available on the internet is often unusable for students with visual problems. Researchers are trying to devise ways for people to access the information non-visually, but the adaptations are not perfected yet (Hallahan & Kauffman, 2006). One current trend is **universal design**—considering the needs of all users in the design of new tools, learning programs, or websites (Pisha & Coyne, 2001).

For gifted students, computers can be a connection with databases and computers in universities, museums, and research labs. Computer networks allow students to work on projects and share information with others across the country. It is also possible to have gifted students write programs for students and teachers. These are just a few examples of what technology can do. Check with the resource teachers in your district to find out what is available in your school.

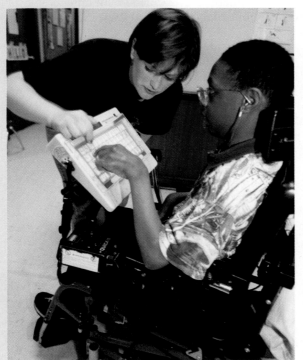

Check Your Knowledge

- What legislation affects special education across Canada?

Apply to Practice

- What is your position on inclusion?
- What should you do before referring a student for evaluation by special education professionals?

SUMMARY

Language and Labelling
(pp. 106–107)

What are the advantages of and problems with labels?

Labels and diagnostic classifications of students with exceptionalities can easily become both stigmas and self-fulfilling prophecies, but they can also open doors to special programs and help teachers develop appropriate instructional strategies.

What is people-first language?

People-first language ("students with developmental disabilities," "students with gifts and talents," etc.) is an alternative to labels that describe a complex person with one or two words, implying that the condition labelled is the most important aspect of the person. With person-first language, the emphasis is on the students first, not on the special challenges these students face.

Distinguish between a disability and a handicap.

A disability is an inability to do something specific, such as see or walk. A handicap is a disadvantage in certain situations. Some disabilities lead to handicaps, but not in all contexts. Teachers must avoid imposing handicaps on disabled learners.

Individual Differences in Intelligence
(pp. 107–116)

What is g?

Spearman suggested that there is one mental attribute, which he called g, or general intelligence, that is used to perform any mental test, but that each test also requires some specific abilities in addition to g. Spearman assumed that individuals vary in both general intelligence and specific abilities, and that together these factors determine performance on mental tasks. A current version of the general plus specific abilities theory is Carroll's work identifying a few broad abilities (such as learning and memory, visual perception, verbal fluency) and at least 70 specific abilities.

What is Gardner's view of intelligence and his position on g?

Gardner contends that an intelligence is a biological and psychological potential to solve problems and create products or outcomes that are valued by a culture. These intelligences are realized to a greater or lesser extent as a consequence of experiential, cultural, and motivational factors. There are at least eight separate intelligences: logical-mathematical, linguistic, musical, spatial, bodily-kinesthetic, interpersonal, intrapersonal, naturalist, and perhaps existential. Gardner does not deny the existence of a general ability, but he does question how useful g is as an explanation for human achievements.

What are the elements of Sternberg's theory of intelligence?

Sternberg's triarchic theory of intelligence is a cognitive process approach to understanding intelligence that has three parts: analytic, creative, and practical. Analytic/componential intelligence involves the mental processes that are defined in terms of components: metacomponents, performance components, and knowledge-acquisition components. Creative/experiential intelligence involves coping with new experiences through insight or automaticity. Practical/contextual intelligence involves choosing to live and work in a context where success is likely, adapting to that context, and reshaping it if necessary. Practical intelligence is made up mostly of action-oriented tacit knowledge learned during everyday life rather than through formal schooling.

How is intelligence measured, and what does an IQ score mean?

Intelligence is measured through individual tests (Stanford-Binet, Wechsler, Woodcock-Johnson, etc.) and group tests (Lorge-Thorndike, Analysis of Learning Potential, Otis-Lennon Mental Abilities Tests, School and College Ability Tests, etc.). Compared with an individual test, a group test is much less likely to yield an accurate picture of any one person's abilities. The average score is 100. About 68 percent of the general population will earn IQ scores between 85 and 115. Only about 16 percent of the population will receive scores below 85, and only 16 percent will score above 115. These figures hold true for white, native-born North Americans whose first language is Standard English. Intelligence test scores predict success in school, but they are less predictive of success in life when level of education is taken into account.

What is the Flynn effect and what are its implications?

Since the early 1900s, IQ scores have been rising. To keep 100 as the average for IQ test scores, questions have to be made more difficult. This increasing difficulty has implications for any program that uses IQ scores as part of the entrance requirements. For example, students who were not identified as having intellectual disabilities a generation ago might be identified as disabled now because the test questions are harder.

Ability Differences and Teaching
(pp. 116–119)

What are the problems with between-class ability grouping?

Academic ability groupings can have both disadvantages and advantages for students and teachers. For students who have low ability, however, between-class ability grouping generally has a negative effect on achievement, social adjustment, and self-esteem. Teachers of low achievement classes tend to emphasize lower-level objectives and routine procedures, with less academic focus. Often, there are more student behaviour problems and, along with these problems, increased teacher stress and decreased enthusiasm. Ability grouping can also promote segregation within school.

What are the alternatives available for grouping in classes?

Cross-age grouping by subject can be an effective way to deal with ability differences in a school. Within-class ability grouping, if handled sensitively and flexibly, can have positive effects, but alternatives such as cooperative learning may be better.

Learning Styles and Preferences
(pp. 119–120)

Distinguish between learning styles and learning preferences.

Learning styles are the characteristic ways a person approaches learning and studying. Learning preferences are individual preferences for particular learning modes and environments. Even though learning styles and learning preferences are not related to intelligence or effort, they can affect school performance.

What are the advantages and disadvantages of matching teaching to individual learning styles?

Results of some research indicate that students learn more when they study in their preferred setting and manner, but most research does not show a benefit. Many students would benefit from developing new—and perhaps more effective—ways to learn.

What learning style distinctions are the most well-supported by research?

One distinction that is repeatedly supported by the research is deep versus surface processing. Individuals who have a *deep-processing approach* see the learning activities as a means for understanding some underlying concepts or meanings. Students who take a *surface-processing* approach focus on memorizing the learning materials, not understanding them. A second distinction is Mayer's visualizer–verbalizer dimension, which has three facets: *cognitive spatial ability* (low or high), *cognitive style* (a visualizer versus a verbalizer), and *learning preference* (a verbal learner versus a visual learner).

Students Who Are Gifted and Talented
(pp. 120–124)

What are the characteristics of students who are gifted?

Students who are gifted learn easily and rapidly and retain what they have learned; use common sense and practical knowledge; know about many things that the other children don't; use a large number of words easily and accurately; recognize relations and comprehend meaning; are alert and keenly observant and respond quickly; are persistent and highly motivated on some tasks; and are creative or make interesting connections. Most students have gifts and talents in particular areas. Teachers should make special efforts to support students who are underrepresented in gifted programs—girls, students who also have learning disabilities, students from minority cultures, and students who are living in poverty.

Is acceleration a useful approach with gifted students?

Many people object to acceleration, but most careful studies indicate that truly gifted students who are accelerated do as well as, and usually better than, other students who are progressing at the normal pace. Students who are gifted tend to prefer the company of older playmates and may be bored if kept with children their own age. Skipping grades may not be the best solution for a particular student, but for students who are extremely advanced intellectually (with a score of 160 or higher on an individual intelligence test), the only practical solution may be to accelerate their education.

High-Incidence Disabilities
(pp. 124–138)

What is a learning disability?

Specific learning disabilities involve significant difficulties in the acquisition and use of listening, speaking, reading, writing, reasoning, or mathematical abilities. These difficulties are intrinsic to the individual, presumed to be the result of central nervous system dysfunction, and may occur throughout the lifespan. Students with learning disabilities may become victims of learned helplessness when they come to believe that they cannot control or improve their own learning and therefore cannot succeed. A focus on learning strategies often helps students with learning disabilities.

What is ADHD, and how is it handled in school?

Attention-deficit/hyperactivity disorder (ADHD) is the term used to describe individuals of any age with hyperactivity and attention difficulties. Use of medication to address ADHD is effective for 70 to 90 percent of individuals who suffer from the disorder; however, it is controversial. There can be negative side effects, such as headaches and nausea, but modifying the dosage can typically control these. Also, little is known about the long-term effects of drug therapy. As well, this type of therapy is not a panacea. The drugs alone will not lead to improvements in academic learning or peer relationships, two areas in which children with ADHD have great problems. Instructional methods that have proven most successful for helping students with ADHD are based on behavioural principles of learning such as those described in Chapter 6. One promising approach is Positive Behaviour Support.

What are the most common communication disorders?

Common communication disorders include speech impairments (articulation disorders, stuttering, and voicing problems) and oral language disorders. If these problems are addressed early, great progress is possible.

What defines intellectual disabilities?

Before age 18, students must score below about 70 on a standard measure of intelligence and must have problems with adaptive behaviour, day-to-day independent living, and social functioning.

What are the best approaches for students with emotional and behaviourial disorders?

Methods from applied behavioural analysis and direct teaching of social skills are two useful approaches. Students also may respond to structure and organization in the environment, schedules, activities, and rules.

What are some warning signs of potential suicide?

Students at risk of suicide may show changes in eating or sleeping habits, weight, grades, disposition, activity level, or interest in friends. They sometimes suddenly give away prized possessions such as stereos, CDs, clothing, or pets.

They may seem depressed or hyperactive and may start missing school or quit doing work. It is especially dangerous if the student not only talks about suicide, but also has a plan for carrying it out.

Low-Incidence Disabilities
(pp. 138–143)

How can schools accommodate the needs of physically disabled students?

If the school has the necessary architectural features, such as ramps, elevators, and accessible washrooms, and if teachers allow for the physical limitations of students, little needs to be done to alter the usual educational program. Identifying a peer to help with movements and transitions can be useful.

How would you handle a seizure in class?

Do not restrain the child's movements. Lower the child gently to the floor, away from furniture or walls. Move hard objects away. Turn the child's head gently to the side, put a soft coat or blanket under the student's head, and loosen any tight clothing. Never put anything in the student's mouth. Find out from the student's parents how the seizure is usually dealt with. If one seizure follows another and the student does not regain consciousness in between, if the student is pregnant, if the student has a medical ID that does not say "epilepsy, seizure disorder," if there are signs of injury, or if the seizure goes on for more than five minutes, get medical help right away.

What are some signs of hearing and visual impairment?

Signs of hearing problems are turning one ear toward the speaker,

favouring one ear in conversation, or misunderstanding conversation when the speaker's face cannot be seen. Other indications include not following directions, seeming distracted or confused at times, frequently asking people to repeat what they have said, mispronouncing new words or names, and being reluctant to participate in class discussions. Students who have frequent earaches, sinus infections, or allergies should be scrutinized particularly closely. Holding books very close or far away, squinting, rubbing eyes, misreading the chalkboard, and holding the head at an odd angle are possible signs of visual problems.

Exceptional Education and Inclusion
(pp. 144–150)

What legislation affects special education across Canada?

Each province and territory has an education or school act that governs education in its elementary and secondary schools. Inclusion is the current policy of all provinces and territories in Canada. Also, educating students in the least restrictive or most enabling environment, developing an individualized education plan (IEP) that meets the unique needs of each exceptional learner, and protecting the rights of students with exceptionalities and their families are principles shared by ministries of education across Canada. Only one piece of legislation has an impact on education across the country: the *Canadian Charter of Rights and Freedoms,* which is part of the Constitution.

BECOMING A PROFESSIONAL

Reflecting on the Chapter

Can you apply the ideas from this chapter on individual differences to solve the following problems of practice?

Preschool and Kindergarten

- A little girl in your kindergarten class seldom speaks. When she does, she usually says only a word or two. She seems to understand when others talk but almost never responds verbally. How would you approach this situation?

Elementary and Middle School

- The school psychologist tells you that one of your students is going to start taking medication designed to "calm him down." What would you want

to know? How would you respond?

- The principal tells you that she is assigning two more students to your class because you are "new, and have more training in inclusion than the older teachers." One student has developmental disabilities and has problems making friends. The other is blind. How will you respond to the principal's decision? How would you prepare your class and modify your teaching for these students?

Junior High and High School

- A student in your fifth-period class is failing. When you look at your grade book, you see that it is the written work that is giving the student trouble. Multiple-choice test scores and class participation are fine. But

his writing is hardly legible and very disorganized. Sentences are started and never finished. Ideas fly in and out like frightened birds. How would you identify the source of the problem?

- How would you adapt your teaching to accommodate a student who is hard of hearing in your biology lab class?

Check Your Understanding

- Be clear about the difference between a handicap and a disability.

- Know the mean of standardized IQ tests and the range in which most people score.

- Make sure you understand Gardner's theory of multiple intelligences.

- Be familiar with the effects of between-class ability grouping and some alternatives for in-class grouping.

- Be aware of some alternatives for teaching students who are gifted.

- Be familiar with Section 15.1 of the *Canadian Charter of Rights and Freedoms*, as well as the human rights legislation and the school act in your province or territory.

- Understand the differences between learning styles and learning preferences, and how you can make accommodations for these differences in the classroom.

Your Teaching Portfolio

- Use Table 4.9 "Encouraging Language Development" on page 133, to generate ideas for developing students' language and add these to your portfolio.

- For your portfolio, develop a lesson plan that appropriately uses Gardner's work on multiple intelligences.

- Add Table 4.13, "Making a Referral" on page 143, to your portfolio.

Teaching Resources

Add Tables 4.3, 4.6, 4.7, and 4.9 (pages 123, 126, 129, and 133) to your file of teaching resources.

Teachers' Casebook

What Would They Do?

Here is how two practising teachers responded to the teaching situation presented at the beginning of this chapter about interpreting and communicating assessment results.

Barb Cadel
Poplar Bank Public School
Newmarket, Ontario

When setting up a classroom and planning programming, I find it beneficial to think about using Universal Design for Learning. This way of thinking helps teachers design their classrooms to make the learning accessible for all students. Looking at learning as a continuum allows each student in the class, regardless of ability, to progress towards his or her learning goals in the most appropriate way, and to be assessed and evaluated fairly and accurately. Every student in every classroom is unique; recognizing this will help to ensure that every student will benefit. Assessing students learning preferences will also help in planning a program that will help each to learn.

The physical set-up of the classroom will be important to ensure that the student with a hearing impairment and the English language learners will have the supports they require. I post a visual schedule of the day, which includes words and pictures to help

all students understand what will happen during the course of the day. Labels throughout the classroom also assist with language development and allow students to "read the room."

The students with identifications of a hearing impairment and a learning disability will have Individual Education Plans (IEPs), which will outline the specific program accommodations and modifications they require to be successful in the classroom. The IEP will outline teaching, learning, and assessment strategies that will be beneficial to those students. It will also be important to have a sound understanding of any assistive technology any of the students may require (e.g., hearing aids, interpreter, computer technology).

When planning tasks and learning opportunities for the students, I would ensure that each student would be engaged each week working in a variety of groupings. Working in a small group will allow all students an opportunity to participate in meaningful discussion about their learning and to learn from and with each other. Tiered activities also provide all students with opportunities for success. With tiered instruction, the teacher plans a variety of activities around a central essential skill or concept that has varying degrees of complexity. All students will learn the basic skill or concept, but the students will achieve a variety of learning outcomes based on their learning strengths and needs.

It will also be important to consider the needs of all learners when planning assessments. Students should have the opportunity to be assessed in ways that allow them to best demonstrate their understanding; instead of traditional pen-and-paper tasks, many students will share their ideas orally, through art, drama, or music, using technology or through an appropriate graphic organizer.

By looking first at a student's strengths and focusing on what the student can do, a teacher can plan appropriate programs to benefit all students and help them to learn in the most appropriate way.

Karen Noel-Bentley
Choice School for Gifted Children
Vancouver, British Columbia

In a diverse classroom, it is important that all students feel like they belong and that they can learn. Every student has something to offer in a community of learners. In the first weeks of school, I would design activities that foster a sense of community and cooperation. I would give all students the opportunity to demonstrate their areas of interest and strength, celebrating their diversity while finding areas of common interest and aspirations. This would provide me with insight into their learning preferences and would facilitate an atmosphere of acceptance and camaraderie.

To accommodate the unique learning needs of my students with exceptionalities, I would try to learn more about their needs and what support is available before the start of the year. How does my deaf student communicate? Sign language? Lip reading? Is there technology available to facilitate communication? Is there an audiologist or doctor with whom I can collaborate to support my deaf student? Does my school have a teacher with expertise in teaching English as a Second Language? Is a pullout program offered for ESL at my school? Are there other students in my class who speak the same language as the students who are learning to speak English? What are the needs of my student with a learning disability? Will he or she be in the classroom every day, and for how long? Will a Special Education Assistant be involved? I would hope to be able to work as a team with these experts, involving them in planning and consulting with them as needed.

The best way to manage planning for a diverse class is to design complex tasks that involve opportunities to differentiate content, process, and product. When designing a task for my diverse class, I would

start with determining the big idea. What do all students need to learn? This is the main concept of the task, which all students would be expected to learn. What do most of the students need to learn? This would involve deeper learning that most students would be required to achieve, but would be optional for the students with exceptional learning needs. Finally, what do some students need to learn? This would include further enrichment for those students who are highly able and need advanced work to stay challenged. All students would be offered the choice to attempt a higher level of learning.

To differentiate the process of learning, I would consider what I know about how students in my class prefer to learn. For example, I would be sure to include a variety of visual and kinesthetic strategies that would be beneficial to my students with special needs, along with many other students who learn best visually or through direct manipulation. I would offer opportunities for cooperative learning, independent projects, and learning centres. Learning materials would include books, videos, manipulatives, and discussions. All students would be exposed to a variety of learning tactics and strategies and would be offered choices for how they would acquire their information.

To provide all students with opportunities to demonstrate their learning, I would differentiate the products required from the learning tasks. For example, my student with a learning disability may not be able to write, but he may be able to dictate his thoughts to a scribe, type them on a computer, or draw a picture. Choices for some tasks could include drawing a map, creating a puppet show, or writing a diary. I would conduct regular and ongoing assessments with all students, using techniques such as interviews and observation. The students would maintain portfolios, indicating growth in their learning and giving them control over content. A variety of products and assessment strategies would ensure that all students can demonstrate their learning in ways that meet their unique needs.

The choices offered in all phases of learning and assessment give students control and understanding of their own learning. All students benefit when they understand their own strengths and areas of need. Students with exceptional needs become part of a continuum of learners within the classroom community. When teachers plan for this continuum, they can adjust the edges of the continuum to accommodate the specific needs of individual learners without feeling overwhelmed.

5 CULTURE AND COMMUNITY

The Storyteller, 1995, Christian Pierre. Acrylic on canvas. © Christian Pierre/Super-Stock.

Teachers' Casebook

What Would You Do?

There are students from four different ethnic groups in the middle school "pod" you are working with this year. Also, there is a student with pretty severe emotional and behavioural problems and a student with cerebral palsy in the group. The boy with cerebral palsy is in a wheelchair and has some difficulties with language and hearing. Students from each of the four ethnic groups seem to stick together, never making friends with students from "outside." When you ask people to work together on projects, the divisions are strictly along ethnic lines. Many of the subgroups communicate in their native language—one you don't understand—and you assume that often the joke is on you because of the looks and laughs directed your way. Clarise, the emotionally disturbed student, is making matters worse by telling ethnic jokes to anyone who will listen in a voice loud enough to be overheard by half the class. There are rumours of an ambush after school to "teach Clarise a lesson." You agree that she—and the whole class for that matter—needs a lesson, but not of this kind.

Critical Thinking

How would you handle the situation? How would you teach the class to help the students feel more comfortable together? What are your first goals in working on this problem? How will these issues affect the grade levels you want to teach?

Collaboration

With four or five other members of your class, brainstorm as many reasonable ways as you can of addressing this situation. Come to consensus on the two best ways and present them to the class, with your rationale for why these are good choices.

Connect & Extend

TO THE RESEARCH
For an article on multicultural education, see Fowler, R. (1998). Intercultural education in Canada: Glimpses from the past, hopes for the future. In K. Cushner (Ed.), *International perspectives on intercultural education* (pp. 302–318). Mahwah, NJ: Lawrence Erlbaum Associates.

The face of Canadian classrooms is changing. The same can be said for many countries today. In a talk to the American Educational Research Association, Frank Pajares said, "The critical questions in education involve matters that cannot be settled by universal prescription. They demand attention to the cultural forces that shape our lives" (Pajares, 2000, p. 5).

In this chapter, we examine the many cultures that form the fabric of our society. We begin by tracing the schools' responses to different ethnic and cultural groups and consider the concept of multicultural education. With a broad conception of culture as a basis, we then examine three important dimensions of every student's identity: social class, ethnicity, and gender. Then, we turn to a consideration of language and bilingual education. The last section of the chapter presents three general principles for teaching every student.

By the time you have completed this chapter, you should be able to answer these questions:

- *What is the difference between the melting pot and multicultural education?*

- *What is culture, and what groups make up your own cultural identity?*

- *Why does the school achievement of low-income students often fall below that of middle- and upper-income students?*

- *What are some examples of conflicts and compatibilities between home and school cultures?*

- *What is the school's role in the development of sex differences?*

- *What are examples of culturally relevant pedagogy that fit the grades and subjects you will teach?*

- *How can you create a resilient classroom?*

TODAY'S MULTICULTURAL CLASSROOMS

Who are the students in Canadian classrooms today? Here are a few facts (Campaign 2000, 2006):

- In 2006, 17.7 percent of Canadians under the age of 18—that is, over one million children—were living in poverty.
- This proportion was more than double for children from Aboriginal, immigrant, and visible minority groups.
- Children with disabilities were also more likely to live in poverty.
- Over half of all low-income children were living with one parent, usually their mother.
- Many children faced problems that interfered with learning (e.g., being unhealthy, neglected, physically or emotionally abused, homeless, or living with alcoholic or drug-addicted parents).

Of the 1.8 million immigrants who arrived in Canada during the 1990s, 17 percent were school aged. Most of these children (69 percent) lived in Toronto, Vancouver, or Montreal, and more than half spoke a language other than French or English (Statistics Canada, 2001).

Such diversity presents unique challenges to schools and communities, but it presents opportunities too.

Individuals, Groups, and Society

Canada has always prided itself on being a multicultural society—a **mosaic** as opposed to a **melting pot**—although there are examples of grave intolerance in our past and present. Crealock and Bachor (1995) correctly point out that Aboriginal peoples have been in North America for tens of thousands of years and have always shown collective differences in tribal beliefs, values, and rituals (p. 511). English and French Canadians settled here in the 15th and 16th centuries. In the 19th and early 20th centuries, people came from Ireland, Russia, Poland, Ukraine, and Asia. More than 200 ethnic origins were reported in the 2001 census. Immigrants came from the countries cited above but also from many other areas, including Eastern Europe, Central Asia, the Middle East, Africa, and Central and South America.

As we indicated in Chapter 4, Canada aspires to be an inclusive society, and this is reflected in Canada's policy on multiculturalism. The *Canadian Multiculturalism Act* of 1989 reflects Canada's commitment to respecting and understanding our multiculturalism through the social, cultural, economic, and political institutions of our nation. Other laws that protect multiculturalism include the *Canadian Charter of Rights and Freedoms* (recall Section 15.1 from Chapter 4), the *Indian Act*, the *Immigration Act*, the *Employment Equity Act*, and the *Canadian Human Rights Act* (Crealock & Bachor, 1995). According to Nancy Hutchinson of Queen's University in Kingston, Ontario, schools have a unique role to play in the creation of an inclusive society because they have a legislated responsibility to prepare all children and adolescents (including those who are exceptional in some respect) to take on meaningful roles in life after school. Also, schools are responsible for preparing children and youth to participate in our democratic society, which implies promoting acceptance of all individuals as fellow citizens (Hutchinson, 2007, p. 142).

Multicultural Education

Multicultural education is "a field of study designed to increase educational equity for all students" (Banks & Banks, 1995, p. xii). Multicultural education is one response to the increasing diversity of the school population as well as to the

mosaic The idea that individuals can maintain their culture and identity while still being a respected part of the larger society.

melting pot A metaphor for the absorption and assimilation of immigrants into the mainstream of society so that ethnic differences vanish.

multicultural education Education that teaches the value of cultural diversity.

growing demand for equity for all groups. An examination of the alternative approaches to multicultural education is beyond the scope of an educational psychology text, but be aware that there is no general agreement about the "best" approach.

James Banks (2006) suggests that multicultural education has five dimensions, as shown in Figure 5.1. Many people are familiar only with the dimension of *content integration*, using examples and content from a variety of cultures when teaching a subject. Because they believe that multicultural education is simply a change in curriculum, some teachers assume that it is irrelevant for subjects such as science and mathematics. But if you consider the other four dimensions—helping students understand how knowledge is influenced by beliefs, reducing prejudice, creating social structures in schools that support learning and development for all students, and using teaching methods that reach all students—then you will see that this view of multicultural education is relevant to all subjects and all students.

Multicultural education rejects the idea of the melting pot and supports a society that values diversity—more a salad bowl of many contributions (Banks, 1997, 2006; Sleeter, 1995). Let's take a closer look at the differences that make up the mosaic of cultural diversity.

Canadian Cultural Diversity

In this text, we take a broad interpretation of culture and multicultural education, so we will examine social class, race, ethnicity, and gender as aspects of diversity. We begin with a look at the meaning of culture. Many people associate this concept with the "cultural events" section of the newspaper—art galleries, museums, Shakespeare plays, classical music, and so on. Culture has a much broader meaning: it embraces the whole way of life of a group of people.

Culture and Group Membership.   There are many definitions of **culture**. Most definitions include the knowledge, rules, traditions, attitudes, and values that guide behaviour in a particular group of people (Betancourt & Lopez, 1993; Pai & Alder, 2001). The group creates a culture—a program for living—and commu-

culture The knowledge, rules, traditions, attitudes, and values that guide the behaviour of a group of people and allow them to solve the problems of living in their environment.

Figure 5.1 Banks's Dimensions of Multicultural Education

Multicultural education is more than a change in the curriculum. To make education appropriate for all students, we must consider other dimensions as well. The way in which athletics and counselling programs are structured, the teaching method used, inclusion of lessons about prejudice, consideration of perspectives on knowledge—these and many more elements contribute to true multicultural education.

Source: From Banks, J. A. (2001). *Cultural diversity and education: Foundations, curriculum, and teaching* (4th ed.). Boston: Allyn & Bacon. Adapted with the permission of the author and the publisher.

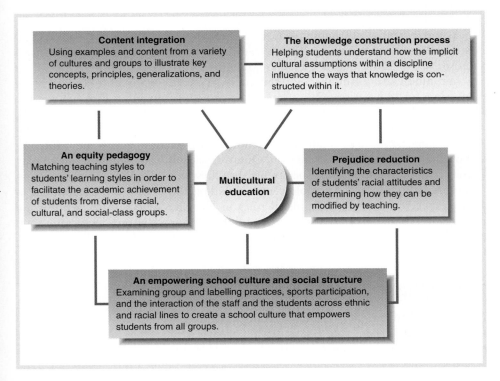

nicates the culture to members. Thus people are members of groups, not members of cultures. Groups can be defined along regional, ethnic, religious, racial, gender, social class, or other lines. Each of us is a member of many groups, so we all are influenced by many different cultures. Sometimes the influences are incompatible or even contradictory. For example, if you are a feminist but also a Roman Catholic, you may have trouble reconciling the two different cultures' beliefs about the ordination of women as priests. Your personal belief will be based, in part, on how strongly you identify with each group (Banks, 1994).

There are many different cultures, of course, in every modern country. In Canada, students living in the suburbs of Toronto certainly differ in a number of ways from students growing up in a Montreal high-rise apartment or on a farm in Quebec. In the United States, students growing up in a small rural town in the South are part of a cultural group that is very different from that of students in a large urban centre or students in a West Coast suburb. Within those small towns in the South or in Quebec, the child of a gas station attendant grows up in a different culture from the child of the town doctor or dentist. Individuals of African, Asian, Aboriginal, or European descent have distinctive histories and traditions. The experiences of males and females are different in most ethnic and economic groups. Everyone living within a particular country shares many common experiences and values, especially because of the influence of the mass media, but other aspects of their lives are shaped by differing cultural backgrounds.

Cautions about Interpreting Cultural Differences.   Before we examine the bases for cultural differences, two cautions are necessary. First, we will consider social class, ethnicity, and gender separately, because much of the available research focuses on only one of these variables. Of course, real children are not just Asian, or middle class, or female; they are complex beings and members of many groups.

The second caution comes from James Banks (1993a), who has written several books on multicultural education:

> Although membership in a gender, racial, ethnic, social-status, or religious group can provide us with important clues about an individual's behaviour, it cannot enable us to predict behaviour.... *Membership in a particular group does not determine behaviour but makes certain types of behaviour more probable.* (pp. 13–14)

Keep this in mind as you read about characteristics of economically disadvantaged students or Asian Canadians or males. The information we will examine reflects tendencies and probabilities. It does not tell you about a specific person. Remember that you will be teaching individual students. Each child is a unique product of many influences, a member of a variety of groups. For example, if a minority-group student in your class consistently arrives late, you should not assume that the student's behaviour reflects a cultural difference in beliefs about punctuality. It may be that the student has a job before school or must walk a long distance, or that he or she is simply not a morning person.

Check Your Knowledge

- Distinguish between the "melting pot" and multiculturalism.
- What is multicultural education?
- What is culture?

Apply to Practice

- What cultural groups affect your identity?

Connect & Extend

TO A SPECIFIC GROUP
For help with developing a clearer understanding of culturally related learning styles of Aboriginal students and with how to use these to students' advantage, see More, A. J. (1989). Native Indian students and their language styles: Research results and classroom applications. In B. Robinson (Ed.), *Culture, style and the educative process* (pp. 150–166). Springfield, IL: Charles C. Thomas.

ECONOMIC AND SOCIAL CLASS DIFFERENCES

Even though most researchers would agree that social class is one of the most meaningful cultural dimensions in people's lives, those same researchers have great difficulty defining social class (Liu et al., 2004). Different terms are used—social class, socioeconomic status (SES), economic background, wealth, poverty, or privilege. Some people consider only economic differences; others add considerations of power, influence, mobility, control over resources, and prestige.

Social Class and SES

In modern societies, levels of wealth, power, and prestige are not always consistent. Some people—for instance, university professors—are members of professions that are reasonably high in terms of social status, but provide little wealth or power. Other people have political power even though they are not wealthy, or they may be members of the social register in a town, even though their family money is long gone. Most people are generally aware of their social class—that is, they perceive that some groups are above them in social class and some are below. They may even show a kind of "classism" (like racism or sexism), believing that they are "better" than members of lower social classes and avoiding association with them.

socioeconomic status (SES) Relative standing in the society based on income, power, background, and prestige.

There is another way of thinking about class differences that is commonly used in research. Sociologists and psychologists combine variations in wealth, power, control over resources, and prestige into an index called **socioeconomic status**, or **SES**. In contrast to social class, most people are not conscious of their SES designation. SES is usually ascribed to people by researchers; different formulas for determining SES might lead to different assignments (Liu et al., 2004). No single variable, not even income, is an effective measure of SES. The National Longitudinal Survey of [Canada's] Children and Youth (NLSCY) considered family income, parents' occupations, and parents' education to arrive at an overall indicator of SES (Lipps & Frank, 1997). Five equally sized groups (or quintiles) were created to reflect five levels of SES: lower, lower-middle, middle, upper-middle, and highest.

Poverty and School Achievement

The United States has the highest rate of poverty for children (over 25 percent) of all developed nations, but Canada is not far behind. Moreover, a recent report on Canadian children in poverty indicates that the gap between the rich and poor in Canada keeps growing (Campaign 2000, 2006). According to the report, families in the highest (top 10 percent) income bracket earn more than 14 times what families in the lowest (bottom 10 percent) income bracket earn. The report also indicates that, on average, poor families would have to earn $10 400 more to reach the poverty line.

Margret Winzer (2006) at the University of Lethbridge rightly points out that poverty is a significant risk factor for children's physical, social-emotional, and intellectual development. For example, poor children are more likely to suffer the consequences of poor nutrition (e.g., they may be underweight or suffer from allergies), and their lives at home are more often filled with stress. At school, they are at risk for reading and writing difficulties, and they make up a large percentage of the students who repeat a grade, get referred for special education services, or drop out of school. Furthermore, some children are not just poor; they also are homeless. Estimates are that 1 percent of Canadians are homeless at some point in a year and that 25 percent of homeless people are children (Hutchinson, 2007). Children who are homeless may not attend school regularly because they lack transportation, clothes, and school supplies. They may be ashamed, hungry, or sick.

As we indicated earlier, children from minority cultures are more likely than those from majority cultures to be poor, and students from minority cultures who also have limited English proficiency have historically done poorly in school (Winzer, 2006). These students are more likely than their peers from majority cultures to experience social isolation, increasing academic failure as they move through school, disproportionate referrals for special education, lower scores on tests, high dropout rates, and lower rates of college and university attendance (Winzer & Mazurek, 1998).

Regarding SES and school achievement, it is well documented that high-SES students of all ethnic groups show higher average levels of achievement and stay in school longer than low-SES students (Gutman, Sameroff, & Cole, 2003; McLoyd, 1998). The relationship between high SES and higher levels of achievement is shown in Figure 5.2. However, when SES is measured solely in terms of parents' education, income, or occupation, the relationship between SES and achievement is weaker than when it is measured in terms that include family atmosphere variables such as parents' attitudes toward education, the aspirations of parents for their children, or the intellectual activities of the family (Laosa, 1984; Peng & Lee, 1992; White, 1982). This is an encouraging result. It indicates that lack of income may not be as important for school achievement as the activities that constitute a child's family life.

Poverty during a child's preschool years appears to have the greatest negative impact. Unfortunately, families with young children are the most likely to be poor because young parents have the lowest-paying jobs or no jobs at all (Bronfenbrenner et al., 1996). And the longer the child is in poverty, the stronger the impact on achievement. For example, even when we take into account parents' education, the chance that children will be retained in grades or placed in special education increases by 2 to 3 percent for every year the children live in poverty (Ackerman, Brown, & Izard, 2004; Sherman, 1994).

What are the effects of low socioeconomic status that might explain the lower school achievement of these students? Many factors maintain a cycle of poverty—no one cause is to blame (Evans, 2004). Poor health care for mother and child, dangerous or unhealthy environments, limited resources, family stress, interruptions in schooling, exposure to violence, overcrowding, homelessness, discrimination, and other factors lead to school failures, low-paying jobs—and another generation born in poverty. Garcia (1991), Evans (2004), and McLoyd (1998) describe other possible explanations. Let's take a closer look at each of them.

Health, Environment, and Stress.   Poor children breathe more polluted air and drink more contaminated water (Evans, 2004). Children who live in older houses with lead paint and lead-soldered pipes, which exist in many inner city areas, have

Connect & Extend

TO PROFESSIONAL JOURNALS
Teaching the children of poverty. (1991, special edition). *Phi Delta Kappan, 73*(4), 282–310.

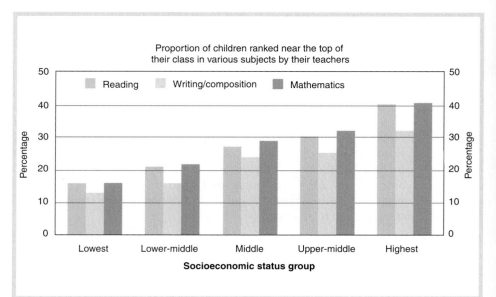

Figure 5.2 Proportion of Children at the Top of Their Class According to SES Quintiles

Children from highest socioeconomic status families are most likely to be near the top of their class.

Source: Adapted from Statistics Canada, *Education Quarterly Review, 1997*, cat. no. 81-003, vol. 4, no. 2, September 29, 1997, p. 55. From the *National Longitudinal Survey of Children and Youth, 1994–95: Initial Results from the School Component.*

greater concentrations of lead in their blood. Poor children are at least twice as likely as non-poor children to suffer lead poisoning, which is associated with lower school achievement and long-term neurological impairment (McLoyd, 1998). Families in poverty are less likely to access good prenatal and infant health care and nutrition. Poor mothers and adolescent mothers are more likely to have premature babies, and prematurity is associated with many cognitive and learning problems. Children in poverty are more likely to be exposed to legal drugs (nicotine, alcohol) and illegal drugs (cocaine, heroin) before birth. Children whose mothers take drugs during pregnancy can have problems with organization, attention, and language skills. Also, when parents have more physical and emotional problems, there tend to be more conflicts between parents and children because stress levels are high (Duncan & Brooks-Gunn, 2000).

Low Expectations—Low Self-Esteem. Because low-SES students may wear old clothes, speak ungrammatically, or be less familiar with books and school activities, teachers and other students may assume that these students are not bright. The teacher may avoid calling on them to protect them from the embarrassment of giving wrong answers or because they make the teacher uncomfortable. Thus, low expectations become institutionalized and the educational resources provided are inadequate (Borman & Overman, 2004). Ultimately, the children come to believe that they aren't very good at school work (Elrich, 1994).

Low expectations, along with a lower-quality educational experience, can lead to a sense of helplessness, as described in the previous chapter. That is, economically disadvantaged students (or any students who fail continually) may come to believe that doing well in school is impossible. In fact, about one-fourth of children from poor families drop out of school (Bennett, 1995). Without a high-school diploma, these students find few rewards awaiting them in the work world. Many available jobs barely pay a living wage. If the head of a family of three works full-time at the minimum wage, the family's income will still be below the poverty line. Low-SES children, particularly those who also encounter racial discrimination, "become convinced that it is difficult if not impossible for them to advance in the mainstream by doing well in school" (Goleman, 1988).

Peer Influences and Resistance Cultures. Some researchers have suggested that low-SES students may become part of a **resistance culture**. To members of this culture, making it in school means selling out and trying to act "middle class." In order to maintain their identity and their status within the group, low-SES students must reject the behaviour that would make them successful in school—studying, cooperating with teachers, even coming to class (Bennett, 1995; Ogbu, 1987, 1997). John Ogbu linked identification in a resistance culture to poor Hispanic American, Native American, and African American groups, but similar reactions have been noted for poor white students both in the United States and in England (Willis, 1977). This is not to say that all low-SES students resist achievement. Data from the Canadian NLSCY have demonstrated that some students, despite the enormous challenges they face, do well in school and in life. These students are said to be *resilient*. Judy Lupart and Vianne Timmons (2003) summarized a national study of how students "at risk" are identified across Canada and what provinces and schools are doing for these students. They concluded that students' at-risk status is not simply a characteristic of individuals; rather, it is the result of interactions among a "confluence of factors within social, economic, cultural, and community contexts" (p. 219). According to Lupart and Timmons, successful intervention programs are personalized and seek to eliminate the environmental conditions that contribute to students' problems.

Tracking Poor Teaching. Another explanation for the lower achievement of many low-SES students is that these students experience **tracking** and, therefore, have a different academic socialization—they are actually taught differently (Oakes, 1990). If they are tracked into "low-ability" or "general" classes, they may be taught to memorize and be passive. Their classes may be low-level and

resistance culture Group values and beliefs about refusing to adopt the behaviour and attitudes of the majority culture.

Connect & Extend

TO PROFESSIONAL JOURNALS
For a discussion of the possible clashes between school cultures and students' home cultures, see Crago, M. B., Eriks-Brophy, A., Pesco, D., & McAlpine, L. (1997). Culturally based miscommunication in the classroom. *Language, Speech and Hearing Services in Schools, 28,* 245–254.

tracking Assignment to different classes and academic experiences based on achievement.

teacher-dominated. Middle-class students are more likely to be encouraged to think and create in their classes (Anyon, 1980). When low-SES students receive an inferior education, their academic skills are inferior and their life chances are limited. In an interview with Marge Scherer (1993), Jonathan Kozol, a well-known author, former teacher, and advocate for children living in poverty in the United States, described the cruel predictive side of tracking:

> [T]racking is so utterly predictive. The little girl who gets shoved into the low reading group in 2nd grade is very likely to be the child who is urged to take cosmetology instead of algebra in the 8th grade, and most likely to be in vocational courses, not college courses, in the 10th grade, if she hasn't dropped out by then. (p. 8)

Even if they are not tracked, low-income students are more likely to attend schools with inadequate resources and less-effective teachers (Evans, 2004).

Home Environment and Resources. Families in poverty seldom have access to high-quality preschool care for their young children. Research has shown that such high-quality care enhances cognitive and social development (Duncan & Brooks-Gunn, 2000). Poor children read less and spend more time watching television; they have less access to books, computers, libraries, trips, and museums (Evans, 2004). These home and neighbourhood resources seem to have the greatest impact on children's achievement when school is not in session—during the summer or before students enter school. For example, Entwisle, Alexander, and Olson (1997) found that low-SES and high-SES students made comparable gains in reading and math when schools were open, but the low-SES students lost ground during summer while the high-SES students continued to improve academically. Another study found that lack of cognitive stimulation in the home accounted for one-third to one-half of the disadvantages in verbal, reading, and math skills of poor children in a national study (Korenman, Miller, & Sjaastad, 1995).

Again, not all low-income families lack resources. Many of these families provide rich learning environments for their children. When parents of any SES level support and encourage their children—by reading to them, providing books and educational toys, taking the children to the library, making time and space for learning—the children tend to become better, more enthusiastic readers (Morrow, 1983; Peng & Lee, 1992; Shields, Gordon, & Dupree, 1983).

Check Your Knowledge

- What is SES?
- What is the relationship between SES and school achievement?

Apply to Practice

- What changes might you need to make in your classroom to help low-SES students succeed?

When families stress the value of reading and learning, their children are usually at an advantage in school.

ETHNIC AND RACIAL DIFFERENCES

Ethnicity refers to "groups that are characterized in terms of a common nationality, culture, or language" (Betancourt & Lopez, 1993, p. 631). This shared sense of identity may be based on geography, religion, race, or language. We all have some ethnic heritage, whether our background is Italian, Jewish, Ukrainian, Hmong, Chinese, Japanese, Iranian, Cree, Inuit, German, Jamaican, or Irish—to name only a few. **Race**, on the other hand, is defined as "a category composed of men and women who share biologically transmitted traits that are defined as socially significant," such as skin colour or hair texture (Macionis, 2003, p. 354). Depending on the traits you measure and the theory you follow, there are between 3 and 300 races. In effect, race is a label that people apply to themselves and to others based on appearances. There are no biologically pure races (Betancourt &

ethnicity A cultural heritage shared by a group of people.

race A group of people who share common biological traits that are seen as self-defining by the people of the group.

Lopez, 1993). In fact, for any two humans chosen at random, an average of only .012 percent (about one-hundredth of one percent) of the alphabetic sequence of their genetic codes is different due to race (Myers, 2005). Still, race is a powerful construct. At the individual level, race is part of our identity—how we understand ourselves and interact with others. At the group level, race is involved with economic and political structures (Omi & Winant, 1994).

minority group A group of people who have been socially disadvantaged—not always a minority in actual numbers.

Sociologists sometimes use the term **minority group** to label a group of people that receives unequal or discriminatory treatment. Strictly speaking, however, the term refers to a numerical minority compared with the total population. Referring to particular racial or ethnic groups as "minorities" is technically incorrect in some situations, because in certain places the "minority" group is actually the majority—for example, students from Pacific Rim countries in some of the inner-city schools in Vancouver. So the practice of referring to people as "minorities" because of their racial or ethnic heritage has been criticized because it can be misleading.

The Changing Demographics: Cultural Differences

Table 5.1 shows how ethnically diverse Canada has become. It is estimated that by the year 2016, 20 percent of Canada's population will be members of a visible minority group (Winzer, 2006).

TABLE 5.1 Recent Immigrants by Country of Last Residence

	1993–1994	1994–1995	1995–1996	1996–1997	1997–1998
	Number of immigrants				
Total immigrants	234 457	220 123	216 988	224 870	194 351
Africa	13 460	14 598	14 862	14 226	14 649
Asia	146 629	135 509	133 912	148 198	115 475
India	19 450	15 802	19 511	20 764	17 572
Hong Kong	41 524	39 873	28 500	29 516	12 115
Vietnam	7 799	4 696	3 151	1 899	1 748
Philippines	20 919	16 745	14 165	11 775	7 799
Other Asian countries	56 937	58 393	68 585	84 244	76 241
Australasia	1 276	969	1 173	1 325	1 345
Europe	40 072	41 110	41 166	37 506	41 225
Great Britain	7 059	6 203	6 299	5 440	4 299
France	3 369	3 506	3 792	2 868	3 400
Germany	1 988	2 093	2 618	2 241	2 030
Netherlands	643	583	820	1 004	660
Greece	402	337	293	291	248
Italy	689	588	709	555	525
Portugal	989	746	837	708	635
Poland	4 791	2 869	2 231	1 867	1 678
Other European countries	20 142	24 185	23 567	22 532	27 750
United States, West Indies	19 070	15 397	15 465	13 872	12 292
United States	6 705	5 851	5 466	5 462	4 696
West Indies	12 365	9 546	9 999	8 410	7 596
Other North and Central American countries	4 545	3 212	3 070	3 459	3 166
South America	8 102	8 279	6 534	5 582	5 618
Other countries	1 303	1 049	806	702	581

Note: Data are given from July 1 of one year to June 30 of the next year.

Source: "Recent Immigrants by Country of Last Residence," adapted from the Statistics Canada CANSIM database, **http://cansim2.statcan.ca**, Table 051-0006. Available at **http://cansim2.statcan.ca/cgi-win/CNSMCGI.EXE.table051-006.**

Ricardo Garcia (1991) compares culture to an iceberg. One-third of the iceberg is visible; the rest is hidden and unknown. The visible signs of culture, such as costumes and marriage traditions, represent only a small portion of the differences among cultures. Many of the differences are below the surface—implicit, unstated, even unconscious biases and beliefs. Each cultural group teaches its members certain "lessons" about living (Casanova, 1987; Sheets, 2005).

Cultures differ in rules for conducting interpersonal relationships, for example. In some groups, listeners give a slight affirmative nod of the head and perhaps an occasional "uh-huh" to indicate that they are listening carefully. But members of other cultures listen without giving acknowledgment, or with eyes downcast, as a sign of respect. In some cultures, high-status individuals initiate conversations and ask the questions, and low-status individuals only respond. In other cultures, the pattern is reversed.

Cultural influences are widespread and pervasive. Some psychologists even suggest that culture defines intelligence. For example, physical grace is essential in Balinese social life, so the ability to master physical movements is a mark of intelligence in that culture. Manipulating words and numbers is important in Western societies, so in these cultures such skills are indicators of intelligence (Gardner, 1983).

How can you get to know the cultures of your students? The Family and Community Partnerships box on page 168 gives some ideas. Later in this chapter, we will explore other ways to make classrooms compatible with the home cultures of students.

Cultural Conflicts.   The ideas in the Family and Community Partnerships box are just a few areas where cultures may teach different lessons about living. The differences may be obvious, such as holiday customs, or they may be subtle, such as how to get your turn in conversations. The more subtle and unconscious the difference, the more difficult it is to change or even recognize (Casanova, 1987). Cultural conflicts are usually about below-the-surface differences, because when subtle cultural differences meet, misunderstandings are common. These conflicts can happen when the values and competencies of the dominant, mainstream culture are used to determine what is considered "normal" or appropriate behaviour in schools. In these cases, children who have been socialized in a different culture may be perceived as acting inappropriately, not following the rules, or being rude and disrespectful.

Rosa Hernandez Sheets (2005) describes a five-year-old Mexican American girl who tried to bring a bread roll, part of her school cafeteria lunch, home to give to her little brother every day. Her parents were proud of her for sharing, but the school officials made her throw the roll away, because it was against school rules to take food from the cafeteria. The girl was conflicted about following school rules versus honouring her family's cultural values. The teacher in this case solved the problem by talking to the cafeteria cook, getting the roll in a baggie, and putting the baggie in the girl's backpack to be taken home after school.

Cultural Compatibility.   Not all cultural differences lead to clashes, however. In a study by Jim Anderson (1995) at the University of British Columbia, Chinese Canadian, Indo-Canadian, and Euro-Canadian parents were asked to describe five things they were doing to promote the reading and writing development of their children (kindergarten through grade 2). Parents in all three groups indicated that they read to their children, engaged in some form of direct teaching (e.g., teaching children how to spell or how to decode difficult words), and tried to teach their children about the value and uses of literacy (e.g., implicitly through modelling or through direct teaching). What was evident across all responses was that children in all three groups experienced a wide array of literacy activities. What differed among groups was the relative emphasis placed on directly teaching literacy skills versus involving children in

The visible signs of cultural differences represent only a small portion of the differences among cultures. Many are "below the surface" and have more to do with beliefs and attitudes about life.

BUILDING LEARNING COMMUNITIES

Joyce Epstein (1995) describes six types of family–school–community partnerships. The following guidelines are based on her six categories:

Parenting partnerships: Help all families establish home environments to support children as students.

EXAMPLES

1. Offer workshops, videos, courses, family literacy fairs, and other informational programs to help parents cope with parenting situations that they identify as important.

2. Establish family support programs to assist with nutrition, health, and social services.

3. Find ways to help families share information with the school about the child's cultural background, talents, and needs. Learn from the families.

Communication: Design effective forms for school-to-home and home-to-school communication.

EXAMPLES

1. Make sure that communications fit the needs of families. Provide translations, visual support—whatever is needed to make communication effective.

2. Visit families in their territory after gaining their permission. Don't expect family members to come to school until a trusting relationship is established.

3. Balance messages about problems with communications of accomplishments and positive information.

Volunteering: Recruit and organize parent help and support.

EXAMPLES

1. Do an annual postcard survey to identify family talents, interests, times available, and suggestions for improvements.

2. Establish a structure (telephone tree, etc.) to keep all families informed. Make sure that families without telephones are included.

3. If possible, set aside a room for volunteer meetings and projects.

Learning at home: Provide information and ideas for families about how to help children with school work and learning activities.

EXAMPLES

1. Provide assignment schedules, homework policies, and tips on how to help with school work without doing the work.

2. Get family input into curriculum planning—have idea and activity exchanges.

3. Send home learning packets and enjoyable learning activities, especially over holidays and summers.

Decision-making partnerships: Include families in school decisions, developing family and community leaders and representatives.

EXAMPLES

1. Create family advisory committees for the school with parent representatives.

2. Make sure that all families are in a network with their representative.

Community partnerships: Identify and integrate resources and services from the community to strengthen school programs, family practices, and student learning and development.

EXAMPLES

1. Have students and parents research existing resources; build a database based on this research.

2. Identify service projects for students; explore service learning.

3. Identify community members who are school alumni and get them involved in school programs.

Source: From Epstein, J. L. (1995). School/family/community partnerships: Caring for the children we share. *Phi Delta Kappan, 76,* 704–705. Copyright © 1995 by Phi Delta Kappan. Reprinted by permission of Phi Delta Kappan and the author.

naturally occurring literacy events. Anderson suggests that some differences across cultures may not really matter if teachers understand these differences and are willing to accommodate them.

Ethnic and Racial Differences in School Achievement

A major concern in schools is that some ethnic groups consistently achieve below the average for all students (Byrnes, 2003; Uline & Johnson, 2005). For example, Aboriginal students are three times more likely to be labelled as learning disabled or as delinquent than are non-Aboriginal students, and 40 percent of Aboriginal students drop out of school between the ages of 14 and 18. Their attendance at university is less than half the national average (Crealock & Bachor, 1995).

Although there are consistent differences among ethnic groups on tests of cognitive abilities, most researchers agree that these differences are mainly the legacy of discrimination, the product of cultural mismatches, or a result of growing up in a low-SES environment. Because many students from minority groups are also economically disadvantaged, it is important to separate the effects of these two sets of influences on school achievement. When we compare students from different ethnic and racial groups who are all at the same SES level, their achievement differences diminish (Gleitman, Fridlund, & Reisberg, 1999). For example, in an analysis of National Assessment of Educational Progress (NAEP) mathematics test results, James Byrnes (2003) found that less than 5 percent of the variance in math test scores was associated with race, but about 50 percent of the variance came from differences in SES, motivation, and exposure to learning opportunities (course work, calculator use, homework, etc.).

The Legacy of Discrimination

What Would You Say?

As part of your interview for a job in a very diverse middle school, the lead teacher for one of the "pods" says to you, "Describe how your life experiences will contribute to our goal to create culturally relevant learning experiences for our students."

When we considered explanations for why low-SES students have trouble in school, we listed the low expectations and biases of teachers and fellow students. Many ethnic-minority students have similar experiences. Imagine that the children described below are your own. What would you do?

> Almost forty years ago, in the city of Topeka, Kansas, a minister walked hand in hand with his seven-year-old daughter to an elementary school four blocks from their home. Linda Brown wanted to enroll in the 2nd grade, but the school refused to admit her. Instead, public school officials required her to attend another school two miles away. This meant that she had to walk six blocks to a bus stop, where she sometimes waited half an hour for the bus. In bad weather, Linda Brown would be soaking wet by the time the bus came; one day she became so cold at the bus stop that she walked back home. Why, she asked her parents, could she not attend the school only four blocks away? (Macionis, 1991, p. 307)

In Canada, residential schools were built for First Nations children, who were then educated off the reserve.

> [The schools] were funded by the federal government who inspected the curriculum, and operated by the Christian churches who provided administrators, teachers, and additional funds.... The residential schools were not successful academically, vocationally, or socially, but they persisted into the 1960s.... In 1961, scholars at the University of British Columbia reported to the government ... that the schools represented a severe discontinuity in experience for the native youth. Nearly all dropped out before grade 12, few went to university, and many suffered social and emotional difficulties. (Crealock & Bachor, 1995, p. 518)

Linda Brown's parents filed a suit against the Board of Education of Topeka and challenged the school segregation policy. The outcome of that landmark case, *Brown* v. *Topeka Board of Education,* is the basis for the principle of free and appropriate education for *all* students. In contrast, Aboriginal communities have increasingly moved to create and control schools for their children and to inject more and more Aboriginal content into their curricula. Increasingly, Aboriginal bands are moving toward full responsibility for the education of children in their communities (Crealock & Bachor, 1995).

Connect & Extend

TO THE RESEARCH
In the Chinese tradition, achievement is seen as dependent more on concentration, effort, and persistence than on talent. Centuries ago, Xu Gan, a revered Chinese scholar, said, "Will is the teacher of study and talent is the follower of study. If a person has no talent, [achievement] is possible. But if a person has no will, it is not worth talking about study" (Hess, Chih-Mei, & McDevitt, 1987, p. 180).

Nine-year-old Linda Brown, the plaintiff in Brown v. Topeka Board of Education.

Years of research on the effects of desegregation have mostly shown that legally mandated integration is not a quick solution to the detrimental effects of centuries of racial inequality. Too often, minority-group students are resegregated in low-ability tracks even in integrated schools. Simply putting people in the same building does not mean that they will come to respect each other or even that they will experience the same quality of education (Ladson-Billings, 2004; Pettigrew, 1998). The University of British Columbia (UBC) and several other institutions across Canada have developed teacher education programs especially for preservice teachers of First Nations ancestry. The hope is that once students in the Native Indian Teacher Education Program (NITEP) at UBC complete their degrees, they will return to their band schools or teach in public schools and provide high-quality, culturally sensitive instruction to First Nations students. In the Reaching Every Student feature, we describe how one educator has given back to her community.

What is the legacy of unequal treatment and discrimination?

What Is Prejudice?   The word *prejudice* is closely related to the word *prejudge*. **Prejudice** is a rigid and irrational generalization—a prejudgment—about an entire category of people. Prejudice is made up of beliefs, emotions, and tendencies toward particular actions. For example, you are prejudiced against people who are overweight if you believe they are lazy (belief), feel disgusted (emotion), and refuse to date them (action) (Myers, 2005). Prejudice can be positive or negative; that is, you can have positive as well as negative irrational beliefs about a group, but the word usually refers to negative attitudes. Targets of prejudice can be based on race, ethnicity, religion, politics, geographic location, language, sexual orientation, gender, or appearance.

prejudice Prejudgment, or irrational generalization about an entire category of people.

The Development of Prejudice.   Racial prejudice is pervasive and it starts early. By about age 6, about 85 percent of students in a Canadian sample had significant pro-white, anti-black biases (Doyle & Aboud, 1995). Two popular beliefs are that young children are innocently colour-blind and that they will not develop biases unless their parents teach them to be prejudiced. Although these beliefs are appealing, they are not supported by research. Even without direct coaching from their

REACHING EVERY STUDENT
AWAKENING THE SPIRIT THROUGH LANGUAGE

Gwen Point learned *her* language from her grandmother, along with the stories and songs of her people. However, when she went to school, she learned about discrimination and shame. "I became ashamed of being Indian." At school, Point did not have the opportunity to speak Halq'eméylem. None of her teachers were Aboriginal, and there was no First Nations content in the curriculum. Point's grandmother told her to go to university and "come home and help your people," which is exactly what she did.

Point has had a distinguished career as an educator and advocate for Aboriginal culture. Especially, she has been instrumental in restoring the Halq'eméylem language, which was on the verge of extinction, to the Sto:lo community. In cooperation with Simon Fraser

University and the B.C. College of Teachers, Point developed a certificate program that allows adults to learn the language and prepare to teach it to students in public and First Nations schools. One graduate of the program says, "We give our children opportunities to learn the language. And by sharing the language with others, we help to build awareness and self-esteem."

Point believes that this is a remarkable shift "from not being allowed to speak our language. It's a validation of our people and our elders.... As a parent, grandparent, and educator, I can see it's helping our students."

Source: British Columbia College of Teachers. (2004, Winter). Aboriginal education initiatives: From parents clubs to teacher education. *Connected,* 9–11.

parents, many young children develop racial prejudice. Current explanations of the development of prejudice combine personal and social factors (Katz, 2003).

One source of prejudice is the human tendency to divide the social world into two categories—*us* and *them,* or the *in-group* and the *out-group*. These divisions may be made on the basis of race, religion, sex, age, ethnicity, or even athletic team membership. We tend to see members of the out-group as inferior and different from us, but similar to each other—"They all look alike" (Aboud, 2003; Lambert, 1995). Also, those who have more (more money, more social status, more prestige) may justify their privilege by assuming that they deserve to "have" because they are superior to the "have-nots." This can lead to blaming the victims: People who live in poverty or women who are raped are seen as causing their problems by their behaviour—"They got what they deserved." Emotions play a part as well. When things go wrong, we look for someone or some whole group to blame. For example, in the United States, after the tragic events of 9/11, some people vented their anger by attacking innocent Arab Americans (Myers, 2005).

But prejudice is more than a tendency to form in-groups, a self-justification, or an emotional reaction—it is also a set of cultural values. Children learn about valued traits and characteristics from their families, friends, teachers, and the world around them. And for years, most of the models presented in books, films, television, and advertising were middle- and upper-class European Americans. People of different ethnic and racial backgrounds were seldom the "heroes" (Ward, 2004). This is changing. In 2002, the Academy Awards for best actress and best actor went to African Americans, although Denzel Washington won for his portrayal of a villain. However, in 2005, Jamie Foxx won for his remarkable portrayal of Ray Charles—a hero.

Prejudice is difficult to combat because it can be part of our thinking processes. You saw in Chapter 2 that children develop schemes, or schemas, as they are referred to in Chapter 7—organized bodies of knowledge—about objects, events, and actions. We have schemas that organize our knowledge about drinking from a straw, people we know, the meaning of words, and so on. We can also form schemas about groups of people. If we were to ask you to list the traits most characteristic of university students, politicians, Asian Canadians, athletes, Buddhists, lesbians, or members of Greenpeace, you probably could generate a list. That list would show that you have a **stereotype**—a schema—that organizes what you know about the group (Wyler, 1988).

stereotype Schema that organizes knowledge or perceptions of a category.

As with any schema, we use our stereotype to make sense of the world. You will see in Chapter 7 that having a schema allows you to process information more quickly and efficiently, but it also allows you to distort information to make it fit your schema better (Macrae, Milne, & Bodenhausen, 1994). This is the danger in racial and ethnic stereotypes. We notice information that confirms or agrees with our stereotype—our schema—and miss or dismiss information that does not fit. For example, if a juror has a negative stereotype of Asian Canadians and is listening to evidence in the trial of an Asian Canadian, the juror may interpret the evidence more negatively. The juror may actually forget testimony in favour of the defendant but remember more damaging testimony. Information that fits the stereotype is even processed more quickly (Anderson, Klatzky, & Murray, 1990; Baron, 1998).

Continuing Discrimination.   Prejudice consists of beliefs and feelings (usually negative) about an entire category of people. The third element of prejudice is a tendency to act, called discrimination. **Discrimination** is unequal treatment of particular categories of people. Members of minority groups face prejudice and discrimination in subtle or blatant ways every day. One discouraging finding is that only 4 percent of the scientists, engineers, and mathematicians in the United States are either African American or Hispanic American—whereas more than 20 percent of the total population is from one of these groups. Even though their attitudes toward science and math are more favourable than the attitudes of white

discrimination Treating particular categories of people unequally.

students, black and Hispanic students begin to lose out in science and math as early as elementary school. They are chosen less often for gifted classes and acceleration or enrichment programs. They are more likely to be tracked into "basic skills" classes. As they progress through junior high, high school, and university or college, their paths take them farther and farther out of the pipeline that produces scientists. If they do persist and become scientists or engineers, as a group they—along with women—will still be paid proportionally less than whites for the same work (National Science Foundation, 1988).

Comparable figures for Canadians are not available. However, according to Canadian researchers Sandra Acker and Keith Oatley (1993), the "patterns of participation in mathematics, science, and technology are complex, and ... the role of schooling in deepening or mitigating disadvantage needs much closer examination" (p. 257). In their article on gender issues in science and technology, Acker and Oatley cite evidence indicating that educational inequality relating to ethnicity, gender, religion, and class background also occurs in Canada.

There is another problem caused by stereotypes and prejudice that can undermine academic achievement—stereotype threat.

Stereotype Threat

stereotype threat The extra emotional and cognitive burden that one's performance in an academic situation might confirm a stereotype that others hold.

Stereotype threat is an "apprehensiveness about confirming a stereotype" (Aronson, 2002, p. 282). The basic idea is that when stereotyped individuals are in situations where the stereotype applies, they bear an extra emotional and cognitive burden. The burden is the possibility of confirming the stereotype, either in the eyes of others or in their own eyes. Thus when girls are asked to solve complicated mathematics problems, for example, they are at risk of confirming widely held stereotypes that girls are inferior to boys in mathematics. It is not necessary that the individual even believe the stereotype. All that matters is that the person is *aware* of the stereotype and *cares about performing* well enough to disprove its unflattering implications (Aronson, Lustina, Good, Keough, Steele, & Brown, 1999). What are the results of stereotype threat? Recent research provides answers that should interest all teachers.

Short-Term Effects: Test Performance. In the short run, the fear that you might confirm a negative stereotype can induce test anxiety and undermine performance (Aronson, Steele, Salinas, & Lustina, 1999). In a series of experiments, Joshua Aronson, Claude Steele, and their colleagues demonstrated that when minority-group university students are put in situations that induce stereotype threat, their performance suffers (Aronson, 2002; Aronson & Salinas, 1998; Aronson, Steele, Salinas, & Lustina, 1999; Steele & Aronson, 1995). For example, African American and white undergraduate subjects in an experiment at Stanford University were told that the test they were about to take would precisely measure their verbal ability. A similar group of subjects was told that the purpose of the test was to understand the psychology of verbal problem solving and not to assess individual ability. As shown in Figure 5.3, when the test was presented as diagnostic of verbal ability, the African American students solved about half as many problems as the white students. In the non-threat situation, the two groups solved about the same number of problems.

All groups, not just minority-group students, can be susceptible to stereotype threat. In another study, the subjects were white male university students who were very strong in mathematics. One group was told that the test they were taking would help experimenters determine why Asian students performed so much better than white students on that particular test. Another group just took the test. The group that faced the stereotype threat of confirming that "Asians are better in math" scored significantly lower on the test (Aronson et al., 1999).

Being vulnerable to stereotype threat varies among individuals. In one study, Aronson and Inzlicht (2004) found that African American college students who

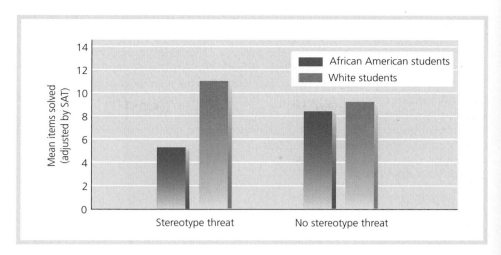

Figure 5.3 The Impact of Stereotype Threat on University Students' Standardized Test Performance

When African American university students were told that they were taking a test that would diagnose their verbal ability (stereotype threat), they solved about one-half as many problems as African American students who were not told the test would assess ability. The performance of white students was not affected by the threat conditions.

Source: Aronson, J., Steele, C. M., Salinas, M. F., & Lustina, M. J. (1999). The effect of stereotype threat on the standardized test performance of college students. In E. Aronson (Ed.), *Readings about the social animal* (8th ed.). New York: Freeman. © 1973, 1977, 1981, 1984, 1988, 1992, 1995, 1999 by Worth Publishers. Adapted by permission of the publisher.

were more vulnerable to stereotype threat were less accurate in assessing their performance on a test. In addition, their sense of academic competence varied more widely from day to day. And who is most vulnerable? Those who care the most and who are most deeply invested in high performance.

Why does stereotype threat affect test performance? One link is anxiety. Jason Osborne (2001) studied a large, representative national sample of white, African American, and Latino high school seniors who took achievement tests and tests of anxiety at the same time. The white students scored significantly higher, but anxiety played a role in those differences. Even after controlling for prior achievement in school, anxiety explained almost one-third of the racial differences in the scores. Anxiety and distraction appeared to be the main problems in the studies of college students, too. Minority-group students were more likely to be thinking about the stereotypes as they tried to work (Spencer, Steele, & Quinn, 1999).

Long-Term Effects. As we will see in Chapter 10, students often develop self-defeating strategies to protect their self-esteem about academics. They withdraw, claim to not care, exert little effort, or even drop out of school—they psychologically disengage from success in the domain and claim "math is for nerds" or "school is for losers." Once students define academics as "uncool," it is unlikely they will exert the effort needed for real learning. There is some evidence that black male students are more likely than black female students and white students to *disidentify* with academics—that is, to separate their sense of self-esteem from their academic achievement (Cokley, 2002; Major & Schmader, 1998; Steele, 1992). Other studies have questioned this connection, however. Historically, education has been valued among African American communities (Walker, 1996). One study found that African American adolescents who had strong Afrocentric beliefs also had higher achievement goals and self-esteem than adolescents who identified with the larger white culture (Spencer et al., 2001). The message for teachers is to help all students see academic achievement as part of their ethnic, racial, and gender identity.

Combatting Stereotype Threat. Stereotypes are pervasive and difficult to change. Rather than wait for changes, it may be better to acknowledge that these images exist, at least in the eyes of many, and give students ways of coping with the stereotypes. In Chapter 10, we will discuss test anxiety and ways to overcome the negative effects of anxiety. Many of those strategies are appropriate for helping students resist stereotype threat.

Aronson and Fried (2002) demonstrated the powerful effects of changing beliefs about intelligence. In their study, African American and white undergraduates at Stanford University were asked to write letters to at-risk middle school students to encourage them to persist in school. Some of the undergraduates were given evidence that intelligence is *improvable* and encouraged to communicate this information to their pen pals. Others were given information about multiple intelligences, but not told that these multiple abilities can be improved. The middle school students were not real, but the process of writing persuasive letters about improving intelligence had a powerful effect. The African American college students, and the white students to a lesser extent, who were encouraged to believe that intelligence can be improved had higher grade-point averages and reported greater enjoyment of and engagement in school when contacted at the end of the next school quarter. Thus, believing that intelligence can be improved might inoculate students against stereotype threat.

Check Your Knowledge

- Distinguish between ethnicity and race.
- How can ethnicity affect school performance?
- Distinguish among prejudice, discrimination, and stereotype threat.

Apply to Practice

- How could you as a teacher counteract stereotype threat for your students?

In the next section, we examine another difference that is the source of stereotypes—gender.

GIRLS AND BOYS: DIFFERENCES IN THE CLASSROOM

What Would You Say?

You are being interviewed for a job teaching grades 2 and 3 in an affluent district. After a few questions, the principal asks, "Do you believe that boys and girls learn differently?" How would you answer?

Anita was travelling on a train while proofreading this very page for a previous edition. The conductor stopped beside her seat. He said, "I'm sorry, dear, for interrupting your homework, but do you have a ticket?" He surely would not have made the same comment to the man across the aisle writing on his legal pad. Like racial discrimination, messages of sexism can be subtle. In this section, we examine the development of two related identities that can be the basis for discrimination—sexual identity and gender-role identity. We look at how men and women are socialized and consider the role of teachers in providing an equitable education for both sexes.

Sexual Identity

sexual identity A complex combination of beliefs and orientations about gender roles and sexual orientation.

The word *gender* usually refers to traits and behaviours that a particular culture judges to be appropriate for men and for women. In contrast, *sex* refers to biological differences (Brannon, 2002; Deaux, 1993). **Sexual identity** includes gender identity, gender-role behaviours, and sexual orientation (Patterson, 1995). *Gender identity* is a person's self-identification as male or female. Gender-role behaviours are those behaviours and characteristics that the culture associates with each gender, and *sexual* orientation involves the person's choice of a sexual partner. Relations among these three elements are complex. For example, a woman may identify herself as a female (gender identity), but behave in ways that are not consistent with the gender role (play football), and may be heterosexual, bisexual, or homosexual in her orientation. So sexual identity is a complicated construction of beliefs, attitudes, and behaviours.

Sexual Orientation. During adolescence, about 8 percent of boys and 6 percent of girls report engaging is some same-sex activity or feeling strong attractions to same-sex individuals. Males are more likely than females to experiment with same-sex partners as adolescents, but females are more likely to experiment later, often in university or college. Fewer adolescents actually have a homosexual or bisexual orientation—about 4 percent of adolescents identify themselves as gay (males who chose male partners), lesbian (females who chose female partners), or bisexual (people who have partners of both sexes). This number increases to about 8 percent for adults (Savin-Williams & Diamond, 2004; Steinberg, 2005).

Scientists debate the origins of homosexuality. Most of the research has been with men, so less is known about women. Evidence so far suggests that both biological and social factors are involved. For example, sexual orientation is more similar for identical twins than for fraternal twins, but not all identical twins have the same sexual orientation (Berk, 2005). There are quite a few models describing the development of sexual orientation. Most focus on how adolescents develop an identity as gay, lesbian, or bisexual. Generally, the models include the following or similar stages (Berk, 2005; Yarhouse, 2001):

- *Feeling different*—Beginning around age six, the child may be less interested in the activities of other children who are the same sex. Some children may find this difference troubling and fear being "found out." Others do not experience these anxieties.
- *Feeling confused*—In adolescence, as they feel attractions for the same sex, students may be confused, upset, lonely, unsure of what to do. They may lack role models and try to change to activities and dating patterns that fit heterosexual stereotypes.
- *Acceptance*—As young adults, many of these youth sort through sexual orientation issues and identify themselves as gay, lesbian, or bisexual. They may or may not make their sexual orientation public, but might share the information with a few friends.

The problem with phase models of identity development is that the identity achieved is assumed to be final. Actually, newer models emphasize that sexual orientation can be flexible, complex, and multifaceted; it can change over the lifetime. For example, people may have dated or married opposite-sex partners at one point in their lives, but have same-sex attractions or partners later in their lives, or vice versa (Garnets, 2002).

Parents and teachers are seldom the first people to hear about the adolescent's sexual identity concerns. But if a student does seek your counsel, Table 5.2 on page 176 has some ideas for reaching out.

Gender-Role Identity

Gender-role identity is the image each individual has of himself or herself as masculine or feminine in characteristics—a part of self-concept. Erikson and many other earlier psychologists thought that identifying your gender and accepting gender roles were straightforward; you simply realized that you were male or female and acted accordingly. But today, we know that some people experience conflicts about their gender identity. For example, transsexuals often report feeling trapped in the wrong body; they experience themselves as female, but their biological sex is male or vice versa (Berk, 2005; Yarhouse, 2001).

How do gender-role identities develop? As early as age two, children are aware of gender differences—they know whether they are girls or boys and that mommies are girls and daddies are boys. It is likely that biology plays a role. Very early, hormones affect activity level and aggression, with boys tending to prefer active, rough, noisy play. By age four, children have a beginning sense of gender roles—they believe that some toys are for boys (trucks, for example) and some are for

Connect & Extend

TO THE RESEARCH
See the Spring 2004 issue of *Theory Into Practice* on "Sexual Identities and Schooling" (Vol. 43, No. 2). Guest Editors: Mollie V. Blackburn and Randal Donelson.

gender-role identity Beliefs about characteristics and behaviour associated with one gender as opposed to the other.

TABLE 5.2 Reaching Out to Help Students Struggling with Sexual Identity

These ideas come from the *Attic Speakers Bureau*, a program of The Attic Youth Center in Philadelphia, where trained peer educators reach out to youth and youth-service providers in schools, organizations, and health-care facilities.

Reaching Out

If a lesbian, gay, bisexual, or transgender youth or a youth questioning his or her own sexual orientation should come to you directly for assistance, remember the following simple, 5-point plan:

LISTEN It seems obvious, but the best thing that you can do in the beginning is allow that individual to vent and express what is going on in his or her life.

AFFIRM Tell them, "You are not alone"—this is crucial. A lot of l/g/b/t/q youth feel isolated and lack peers with whom they can discuss issues around sexual orientation. Letting them know that there are others dealing with the same issues is invaluable. This statement is also important because it does not involve a judgment call on your part.

REFER You do not have to be the expert. A referral to someone who is trained to deal with these issues is a gift you are giving to that student, not a dismissal of responsibility.

ADDRESS Deal with harassers—do not overlook issues of verbal or physical harassment around sexual orientation. It is important to create and maintain an environment where all youth feel comfortable and welcome.

FOLLOW UP Be sure to check in with the individual to see if the situation has improved and if there is anything further you may be able to do.

There are also some things that you as an individual can do to better serve l/g/b/t/q youth and youth dealing with issues around sexual orientation:

- Work on your own comfortability around issues of sexual orientation and sexuality.
- Get training on how to present information on sexual orientation effectively.
- Dispel myths around sexual orientation by knowing facts and sharing that information.
- Work on setting aside your own personal biases to better serve students dealing with issues around sexual orientation and sexuality.

Source: From Figure 3. Copyright © The Attic Speakers Bureau and Carrie E. Jacobs, Ph.D. Reprinted with permission.

girls (dolls) and that some jobs are for girls (nurse) and others are for boys (police officer) (Berk, 2005). Play styles lead young children to prefer same-sex play partners with similar styles, so by age four, children spend three times as much play time with same-sex playmates as with opposite-sex playmates; by age six, the ratio is 11 to 1 (Benenson, 1993; Maccoby, 1998). Of course, these are averages and individuals do not always fit the average. In addition, many other factors—social and cognitive—affect gender-role identity.

Parents are more likely to react positively to assertive behaviour on the part of their sons and emotional sensitivity in their daughters (Brody, 1999; Fagot & Hagan, 1991). Through their interactions with family, peers, teachers, and the environment in general, children begin to form **gender schemas,** or organized networks of knowledge about what it means to be male or female. Gender schemas help children make sense of the world and guide their behaviour (see Figure 5.4). So a young girl whose schema for "girls" includes "girls play with dolls and not with trucks" or "girls can't be scientists" will pay attention to, remember, and interact more with dolls than trucks, and she may avoid science activities (Berk, 2005; Leaper, 2002; Liben & Signorella, 1993).

gender schemas Organized networks of knowledge about what it means to be male or female.

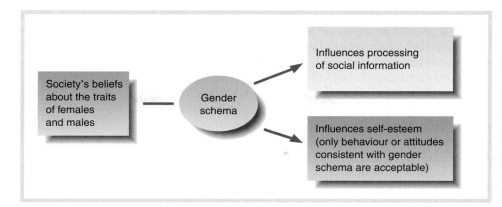

Figure 5.4 **Gender Schema Theory**

According to gender schema theory, children and adolescents use gender as an organizing theme to classify and understand their perceptions of the world.

Society's beliefs about the traits of females and males → Gender schema →
- Influences processing of social information
- Influences self-esteem (only behaviour or attitudes consistent with gender schema are acceptable)

Gender-Role Stereotyping in the Preschool Years. Different treatment of the sexes and gender-role stereotyping continue in early childhood. Researchers have found that boys are given more freedom to roam the neighbourhood, and they are not protected for as long a time as girls from potentially dangerous activities, such as playing with sharp scissors or crossing the street alone. Parents quickly come to the aid of their daughters but are more likely to insist that their sons handle problems themselves. Thus, independence and initiative seem to be encouraged more in boys than in girls (Block, 1983; Brannon, 2002; Fagot et al., 1985).

And then there are the toys! Walk through any store's toy section and see what is offered to girls and boys. Dolls and kitchen sets for girls and toy weapons for boys have been with us for decades, but what about even more subtle messages? Margot Mifflin went shopping for a toy for her four-year-old that was not gender-typed and found a Wee Waffle farm set. Then she discovered that "the farmer plugged into a round hole in the driver's seat of the tractor, but the mother—literally a square peg in a round hole—didn't" (Mifflin, 1999, p. 1). But we cannot blame the toy makers alone. Adults buying for children favour gender-typed toys and fathers tend to discourage young sons from playing with "girls'" toys (Brannon, 2002).

By age four or five, children have developed a gender schema that describes what clothes, games, toys, behaviours, and careers are "right" for boys and girls—and these ideas can be quite rigid (Brannon, 2002). Many student teachers are surprised when they hear young children talk about gender roles. Even in this era of great progress toward equal opportunity, a preschool girl is more likely to tell you she wants to become a nurse than to say she wants to be an engineer. After she had given a lecture on the dangers of sex stereotyping in schools, a colleague brought her young daughter to her college class. The students asked the little girl, "What do you want to be when you grow up?" The child immediately replied, "A doctor," and her professor/mother beamed with pride. Then the girl whispered to the students in the front row, "I really want to be a nurse, but my mommy won't let me." Actually, this is a common reaction for young children. Preschoolers tend to have more stereotyped notions of sex roles than older children, and all ages seem to have more rigid and traditional ideas about male occupations than about what females do (Berk, 2005).

Gender Bias in the Curriculum. During the elementary school years, children continue to learn about what it means to be male or female. Unfortunately, schools often foster these **gender biases** in a number of ways. Most of the textbooks produced for the early grades before 1970 portrayed both males and females in sexually stereotyped roles. Publishers have established guidelines to prevent these problems, but it still makes sense to check your teaching materials for stereotypes. For example, even though children's books now have an equal number of males and females as central characters, there still are more males in the titles and the

Gender schemas have often become barriers to success when girls and boys avoid activities not associated with their gender. By recognizing these potential barriers, teachers can help children make choices that are less gender-driven.

Connect & Extend

TO THE RESEARCH

Lytton, H., & Romney, D. M. (1991). Parents' sex-related differential socialization of boys and girls: A meta-analysis. *Psychological Bulletin, 109,* 267–296.

gender biases Different views of males and females, often favouring one gender over the other.

Connect & Extend

TO THE RESEARCH
Purcell, P., & Stewart, L. (1990). Dick and Jane in 1989. *Sex Roles, 22,* 177–185. This study replicates analyses of textbooks and children's books conducted in the 1970s. *Focus Question:* What evidence of sexism, if any, remains in textbooks today?

illustrations, and the characters (especially the boys) continue to behave in stereotypical ways. Boys are more aggressive and argumentative, and girls are more expressive and affectionate. Girl characters sometimes cross gender roles to be more active, but boy characters seldom show "feminine" expressive traits (Brannon, 2002; Evans & Davies, 2000). Videos, computer programs, and testing materials also often feature boys more than girls (Meece, 2002).

Another "text" that students read long before they arrive in your classroom is television. A content analysis of television commercials found that white male characters were more prominent than any other group. Even when only the actor's voice could be heard, men were 10 times more likely to narrate commercials. And this pattern of men as the "voice of authority" on television was not unique to North America. It also occurred in the United Kingdom, Continental Europe, Australia, and Asia. Women were more likely than men to be shown as dependent on men and often were depicted at home (Brannon, 2002). So, before and after going to school, students are likely to encounter texts that overpresent males.

Sex Discrimination in Classrooms. There has been quite a bit of research on teachers' treatment of male and female students. You should know, however, that most of these studies have focused on white students, so the results reported in this section hold mostly for white male and female students. One of the best-documented findings of the past 25 years is that teachers have more overall interactions and more negative interactions, but not more positive interactions, with boys than with girls (Jones & Dindia, 2004). This is true from preschool to university or college. Teachers ask more questions of males, give males more feedback (praise, criticism, and correction), and give more specific and valuable comments to boys. As girls move through the grades, they have less and less to say. By the time students reach university, men are twice as likely to initiate comments as women (Bailey, 1993; Sadker & Sadker, 1994). The effect of these differences is that from preschool through university, girls, on the average, receive 1800 fewer hours of attention and instruction than boys (Sadker, Sadker, & Klein, 1991). Of course, these differences are not evenly distributed. Some boys, generally high-achieving white students, receive more than their share, whereas high-achieving girls receive the least teacher attention.

The imbalances of teacher attention given to boys and girls are particularly dramatic in math and science classes. In one study, boys were questioned in science class 80 percent more often than girls (Baker, 1986). Teachers wait longer for boys to answer and give more detailed feedback to the boys (Meece, 2002; Sadker & Sadker, 1994). Boys also dominate the use of equipment in science labs, often dismantling the apparatus before the girls in the class have a chance to perform the experiments (Rennie & Parker, 1987).

Stereotypes are perpetuated in many ways, some obvious, some subtle. Boys with high scores on standardized math tests are more likely to be put in the high-ability math group than girls with the same scores. Guidance counsellors, parents, and teachers often do not protest at all when a bright girl says she doesn't want to take any more math or science courses, but when a boy of the same ability wants to forget about math or science, they will object. More women than men are teachers, but men tend to be the administrators, coaches, and advanced math and science teachers. In these subtle ways, students' stereotyped expectations for themselves are reinforced (Sadker & Sadker, 1994).

Sex Differences in Mental Abilities

Most studies find that from infancy through the preschool years there are few differences between boys and girls in overall mental and motor development or in specific abilities. During the school years and beyond, psychologists find no differences in general intelligence on the standard measures. However, scores on some tests of specific abilities show sex differences. For example, from elementary school through high school, girls score higher than boys on tests of reading and writing and get higher grades in general (Berk, 2002; Halpern, 2004). Females even attain the majority of university degrees (Halpern, 2004). By contrast, males tend to score higher on standardized math and science tests (tests which are not directly tied to curriculum), and show an advantage on visuospatial tests.

There is a caution, however. In most studies of sex differences, race and socio-economic status are not taken into account. When racial groups are studied separately, African American females outperform African American males in high school mathematics; there is little or no difference in the performance of Asian American girls and boys in math or science (Grossman & Grossman, 1994; Yee, 1992). And girls in general tend to get higher grades than boys in mathematics classes (Halpern, 2004). Also, international studies of 15-year-olds in 41 countries show no sex differences in mathematics for half of the countries tested. In fact, in Iceland, girls significantly outperformed boys on all the math tests, just as they usually do on their national math exams (Angier & Chang, 2005).

What is the basis for these differences? The answers are complex. In 2005, then-Harvard president Lawrence H. Summers ignited a wave of international protest and debate by suggesting to the university community that women are under-represented in the maths and sciences as a result of underlying differences in biologically based cognitive abilities. Many leading female scientists publicly condemned his views, arguing that the under-representation stems from social, structural, and cultural factors such as discriminatory practices, socialization processes, sex stereotyping, and family–work con-flicts. In general, for every biological explanation, there is an equally plausible explanation based on how we are socialized. For example, males on average are better on tests that require mental rotation of a figure in space, prediction of the trajectories of moving objects, and navigating. Some researchers argue that evolution has favoured these skills in males (Buss, 1995; Geary, 1995, 1999), but others relate these skills to males' more active play styles and to their participation in athletics (Linn & Hyde, 1989; Newcombe & Baenninger, 1990; Stumpf, 1995). The cross-cultural comparisons cited above suggest that much of the difference in mathematics scores comes from learning, not biol-ogy. And studies showing that adults rated a math paper attrib-uted to "John T. McKay" a full point higher on a 5-point scale than the same paper attributed to "Joan T. McKay" suggests that discrimination plays a role as well (Angier & Chang, 2005).

The historical disparity between male and female performance in science and tech-nical, or so-called "hard," subjects has diminished over the past few decades. How-ever, teachers must monitor classroom practices to encour-age all students equally in all subjects.

Eliminating Gender Bias

The average differences found between boys and girls are quite small (and tend to be getting smaller), but the variation within each gender is often much larger. This means that there are almost as many children who don't fit the stereotypes—that boys do better in math and girls do better in reading—as those who do fit it. Based on this, do we still need to be worried about gender differences? Occupational out-comes would suggest that these are still a concern. Based on 2001 census data, only 9 percent of engineers in Canada are women; and women are still paid, on average, 71 cents to every dollar a man is paid. For her doctoral thesis, Jennifer looked at the long-term impact of girls being taught in separate classes for math and science within an otherwise co-educational public high school. The all-girl classes outperformed—by far—all the co-ed students (both boys and girls). How-ever, despite this higher achievement, these girls had lower perceptions of their ability in math and science than the boys and were no more likely to study in the field of math or science at the post-secondary level. Jennifer concluded that

Connect & Extend

TO PROFESSIONAL JOURNALS

Sadker, D. (1998). Gender equity: Still knocking at the classroom door. *Educational Leadership, 56*(7), 22–27.

perceptions of ability are as much, if not more, a predictor of future engagement with a subject than actual achievement (Shapka & Keating, 2003). This means that we need to be concerned not only with how girls are doing in math, but how they see themselves in this discipline. To address this, each year Simon Fraser University in British Columbia hosts a one-day conference called "Women Do Math." Young women in grades 9 and 10 who attend the conference are involved in workshops and discussions that stress math-related career opportunities for women. The Guidelines below provide additional ideas for avoiding sexism in your teaching. Some are taken from Rop (1997/1998).

Some popular authors have argued that boys and girls learn differently and that schools tend to reward the passive, cooperatie behaviours of girls (Guran & Henley, 2001). Other people believe that schools "shortchange" girls and "fail to be fair" (American Association of University Women [AAUW], 1991; Sadker & Sadker, 1995). The Point/Counterpoint feature examines these issues.

GUIDELINES

AVOIDING SEXISM IN TEACHING

Check to see if textbooks and other materials you are using present an honest view of the options open to both males and females.

EXAMPLES

1. Are both males and females portrayed in traditional and non-traditional roles at work, at leisure, and at home?

2. Discuss your analyses with students and ask them to help you find gender-role biases in other materials—magazine advertisements, TV programs, or news reports, for example.

Watch for any unintended biases in your own classroom practices.

EXAMPLES

1. Do you group students by gender for certain activities? Is the grouping appropriate?

2. Do you call on one gender or the other for certain answers—boys for math and girls for poetry, for example?

Look for ways in which your school may be limiting the options open to male or female students.

EXAMPLES

1. What advice is given by guidance counsellors to students in course and career decisions?

2. Is there a good sports program for both girls and boys?

3. Are girls asked to take advanced placement courses in science and mathematics? Boys in English and foreign languages?

Use gender-free language as much as possible.

EXAMPLES

1. Do you speak of "police officer" and "letter carrier" instead of "policeman" and "mailman"?

2. Do you name a committee "head" or "chair" instead of a "chairman"?

Provide role models.

EXAMPLES

1. Assign professional journal articles written by female research scientists or mathematicians.

2. Have recent female high school graduates who are majoring in science, math, engineering, or other technical fields come to class to talk about university.

3. Create electronic mentoring programs for both male and female students to connect them with adults working in areas of interest to the students.

Make sure that all students have a chance to do complex, technical work.

EXAMPLES

1. Experiment with same-sex lab groups so that girls do not always end up as the secretaries or boys as the technicians.

2. Rotate jobs in groups or randomly assign responsibilities.

DO BOYS AND GIRLS LEARN DIFFERENTLY?

As we have seen, there are a number of documented sex differences in mental abilities. Do these translate into different ways of learning and thus different needs in the classroom?

> Point *Yes, boys and girls learn differently.*

Since at least the 1960s, there have been questions about whether schools serve boys well. Accusations that schools were trying to destroy "boys' culture" and forcing "feminine, frilly content" on boys caused some public concern (Connell, 1996).

> Discrimination against girls has ended, the argument runs. Indeed, thanks to feminism, girls have special treatment and special programs. Now, what about the boys? It is boys who are slower to learn to read, more likely to drop out of school, more likely to be disciplined, more likely to be in programs for children with special needs. In school it is girls who are doing better, boys who are in trouble—and special programs for boys that are needed. (Connell, 1996, p. 207)

In their book *Boys and Girls Learn Differently,* Michael Gurian and Patricia Henley (2001) make a similar argument that boys and girls need different teaching approaches. Reviewing the book, J. Steven Svoboda (2001) writes,

Our schools seem to be creating overt depression in girls and covert depression in boys. Through violence, male hormones and brains cry out for a different school promoting closer bonding, smaller classes, more verbalization, less male isolation, better discipline, and more attention to male learning styles. Most of all, boys need men in their schools. (90% of elementary teachers are female.) They need male teachers, male teaching assistants, male volunteers from the parents or grandparents, and older male students. Peer mentoring across grades helps everybody involved.

For girls, Gurian and Henley recommend developing their leadership abilities, encouraging them to enjoy healthy competition, providing extra access to technology, and helping them understand the impact of the media on their self-images.

< Counterpoint *No, differences are too small or inconsistent to have educational implications.*

Many of Gurian and Henley's claims about sex differences in learning are based on sex differences in the brain. But John Bruer (1999) cautions that

> Although males are superior to females at mentally rotating objects, this seems to be the only spatial task for which psychologists have found

such a difference. Moreover, when they do find gender differences, these differences tend to be very small. The scientific consensus among psychologists and neuroscientists who conduct these studies is that whatever gender differences exist may have interesting consequences for the scientific study of the brain, but they have no practical or instructional consequences.

In fact, there are boys who thrive in schools and boys who do not; girls who are strong in mathematics and girls who have difficulties; boys who excel in languages and those who do not. There is some evidence that the activities used to teach math may make a difference for girls. Elementary-age girls may do better in math if they learn in cooperative as opposed to competitive activities. Certainly, it makes sense to balance both cooperative and competitive approaches so that students who learn better each way have equal opportunities (Fennema & Peterson, 1988).

It also makes sense to offer a variety of ways to learn, so that all students have access to the important outcomes of your teaching. Your attitude and encouragement may make the difference for students, male or female, who need a persuasive boost to believe in themselves as writers, or mathematicians, or painters, or athletes.

Check Your Knowledge

- What are the stages for achieving a sexual orientation for gay and lesbian youth?
- What is gender-role identity and how do gender-role identities develop?
- Are there sex differences in mental abilities?

Apply to Practice

- How can teachers promote gender equity in classrooms?

LANGUAGE DIFFERENCES IN THE CLASSROOM

In the classroom, quite a bit happens through language. Communication is at the heart of teaching, and culture affects communication. In this section, we examine issues related to being bilingual (or multilingual).

Bilingualism

bilingualism The ability to speak two languages fluently.

Bilingualism is a topic that sparks heated debate and touches many emotions. One reason is the changing demographics discussed earlier in this chapter. Between 2004 and 2005, over 262 000 immigrants were admitted to Canada, and over 39 percent of these spoke neither of Canada's official languages. Toronto, Vancouver, and Montreal are the most ethnically diverse cities in Canada. In many Vancouver schools, for example, well over half the students enrolled are English language learners, and many are unfamiliar with the Roman alphabet or with Western traditions, history, and lifestyles (British Columbia Ministry of Education, 1998). As a result, teachers need to focus not only on teaching these students English but on orienting them to B.C. society as well. Some students are refugees from war-torn nations and need counselling support to adapt to school and life in Canada.

What Does Bilingualism Mean?   There are disagreements about the meaning of bilingualism. Some definitions focus exclusively on a language-based meaning: bilingual people speak two languages. But this limited definition minimizes the significant relationship between language and culture. Consider the following descriptions of two grade 6 students who had been in the United States for two years:

> ... there was the eager Ting, a child of Asian ancestry, who was quite simply indomitable; she treated her halting search for English words as, at worst, an inconvenience. She had an impressive repertoire of strategies, including the dogged pursuit of clarity. She constantly monitored for sense making, striving to make connections between the concepts to which the class was being introduced and the ideas with which she was familiar.
>
> Then there was the reticent Manuel, a child of Latino ancestry.... Manuel's responses in oral and written contexts, small- and large-group configurations, were sparse. Few activities or roles within the small-group problem solving contexts engaged him productively. He certainly was not a behavior problem; in fact, I would have welcomed a bit of acting out in the service of his establishing his place in this community. (Palincsar, 1996, p. 221)

Palincsar goes on to confirm what we already suspect—Ting made substantial academic gains while "Manuel's growth was modest." According to Jim Cummins (1989) at the University of Toronto, research regarding minority students' underachievement has consistently shown that those students who perform poorly in school and are over-represented in special education programs are members of minority groups who have historically been discriminated against by the dominant group. Furthermore, when students from these groups immigrate relatively late in their school experience (after the age of 10), their academic prospects are better. Cummins attributes this difference to the fact that the latecomers have not experienced the devaluation of their cultural identity in their home country. He claims that the extent to which students' language and culture are incorporated into the school program is a significant predictor of academic success and appears to have no negative impact on their learning English.

Becoming Bilingual.   Proficiency in a second language has two separate aspects: face-to-face communication (known as "contextualized language skills") and academic uses of language, such as reading and doing grammar exercises ("decontextualized language skills") (Snow, 1987). It takes students about two to three years

Connect & Extend

TO THE RESEARCH

Wright, S. C., Taylor, D. M., & Macarthur, J. (2000). Subtractive bilingualism and the survival of the Inuit language: Heritage versus second language education. *Journal of Educational Psychology, 92,* 63–84.

This study examined the impact of early heritage- and second-language education on heritage- and second-language development among Inuit, white, and mixed-heritage (Inuit/white) children.

in a good-quality program to be able to communicate face-to-face in a second language, but mastering decontextualized, academic language skills in the new language takes five to seven years. So students who seem in conversation to "know" a second language may still have great difficulty with complex school work in that language (Cummins, 1994; Ovando, 1989).

A number of misconceptions about becoming bilingual are summarized in Table 5.3. Here we emphasize that learning a second language does not interfere with understanding in the first language. Recall our reference in Chapter 2 to Jim Cummins's research, which indicates that the more proficient speakers are in their first language, the more quickly they master a second language (Cummins, 1984, 1994). By the age of four, bilingual children speak each language as well as native **monolinguals** (Baker, 1993; Reich, 1986).

monolinguals Individuals who speak only one language.

Recognizing Giftedness in Bilingual Students. To identify gifted bilingual students, you can use a case study or portfolio approach in order to collect a variety of evidence, including interviews with parents and peers, formal and informal assessments, samples of student work and performances, and student self-assessments. This checklist from Castellano and Diaz (2002) is a useful guide. Watch for students who

_____ Learn English quickly
_____ Take risks in trying to communicate in English
_____ Practise English skills by themselves
_____ Initiate conversations with native English speakers

TABLE 5.3 Myths about Bilingual Students

In the following table, L1 means the original language and L2 means the second language.

Myth	Truth
Learning a second language (L2) takes little time and effort.	Learning English as a second language takes two to three years for oral and five to seven years for academic language use.
All language skills (listening, speaking, reading, writing) transfer from L1 to L2.	Reading is the skill that transfers most readily.
Code-switching is an indication of a language disorder.	Code-switching indicates high-level language skills in both L1 and L2.
All bilinguals easily maintain both languages.	It takes great effort and attention to maintain high-level skills in both languages.
Children do not lose their first language.	Loss of L1 and underdevelopment of L2 are problems for second-language learners (semilingual in L1 and L2).
Exposure to English is sufficient for L2 learning.	To learn L2, students need to have a reason to communicate, access to English speakers, interaction, support, feedback, and time.
To learn English, students' parents need to speak only English at home.	Children need to use both languages in many contexts.
Reading in L1 is detrimental to learning English.	Literacy-rich environments in either L1 or L2 support development of necessary prereading skills.
Language disorders must be identified by tests in English.	Children must be tested in both L1 and L2 to determine language disorders.

Source: From Brice, A. E. (2002). *The Hispanic child: Speech, language, culture, and education.* Boston: Allyn & Bacon. Copyright © 2002 by Pearson Education. Adapted by permission of the publisher.

_____ Do not frustrate easily

_____ Are curious about new words or phrases and practise them

_____ Question word meanings; for example, "How can a bat be an animal and also something you use to hit a ball?"

_____ Look for similarities between words in their native language and English

_____ Are able to modify their language for less capable English speakers

_____ Use English to demonstrate leadership skills; for example, use English to resolve disagreements and to facilitate cooperative learning groups

_____ Prefer to work independently or with students whose level of English proficiency is higher than theirs

_____ Are able to express abstract verbal concepts with a limited English vocabulary

_____ Are able to use English in a creative way; for example, can make puns, poems, jokes, or original stories in English

_____ Become easily bored with routine tasks or drill work

_____ Have a great deal of curiosity

_____ Are persistent; stick to a task

_____ Are independent and self-sufficient

_____ Have a long attention span

_____ Become absorbed with self-selected problems, topics, and issues

_____ Retain, easily recall, and use new information

_____ Demonstrate social maturity, especially in the home or community

Bilingual Education

Virtually everyone agrees that all citizens should learn the official language of their country. But when and how should instruction in that language begin? Here the debate is bitter at times. Is it better to teach **English language learners** (ELL) to read first in their native language or should they begin reading instruction in English? Do these children need some oral lessons in English before reading instruction can be effective? Should other subjects, such as mathematics and social studies, be taught in the primary (home) language until the children are fluent in English? On these questions there are two basic positions, which have given rise to two contrasting teaching approaches: one that focuses on making the _transition_ to English as quickly as possible and the other that attempts to _maintain_ or improve the native language and use the native language as the primary teaching language until English skills are more fully developed.

Proponents of the _transition_ approach believe that English ought to be introduced as early as possible; they argue that valuable learning time is lost if students are taught in their native language. Most bilingual programs in Canada follow this line of thinking. Proponents of _native-language maintenance instruction,_ however, raise four important issues (Gersten, 1996b; Goldenberg, 1996; Hakuta & Garcia, 1989). First, children who are forced to try to learn math or science in an unfamiliar language are bound to have trouble. What if you had been forced to learn fractions or biology in a second language that you had studied for only a semester? Some psychologists believe students taught by this approach may become _semilingual;_ that is, they are not proficient in either language.

Second, students may get the message that their home languages (and therefore, their families and cultures) are second class. Third, the academic content (math, science, history, etc.) that students are taught in their native language is learned—they do not forget the knowledge and skills when they are able to speak English.

Fourth is what Kenji Hakuta (1986) calls a "paradoxical attitude of admiration and pride for school-attained bilingualism on the one hand and scorn and shame for home-brewed immigrant bilingualism on the other" (p. 229). Ironically, by the time students have mastered academic English and let their home language deteriorate, they reach secondary school and are encouraged to learn a second lan-

English language learners (ELL) Students whose primary or heritage language is not English.

Connect & Extend

TO PROFESSIONAL JOURNALS

Menkart, D. J. (1999). Deepening the meaning of heritage months. _Educational Leadership, 56_(7), 19–21. This article discusses how to get past foods and festivals to increase students' understandings of heritage.

Teachers in today's bilingual classrooms must help students learn skills to communicate in more than one culture.

guage. Hakuta (1986) suggests that the goals of the educational system could be the development of *all students* as functional bilinguals.

One approach to reaching this goal is to create classes that mix students who are learning a second language with students who are native speakers. The objective is for both groups to become fluent in both languages (Sheets, 2005). Anita's daughter spent a summer in such a program in Quebec and was ahead in every French class after that. For truly effective bilingual education, we will need many bilingual teachers. If you have a competence in another language, you might want to develop it fully for your teaching.

As noted earlier, the transition approach to learning English or French is the most common practice in Canadian schools. However, ministries and school boards are recognizing the educational, social, and economic benefits of maintaining students' first languages. They are encouraging parents and children to continue using their first languages outside the school setting, even to learn to read and write in those languages. In Ontario, the government funds native-language instruction and international-languages instruction, sometimes referred to as **Heritage Language Programs**. Through these programs, students have opportunities to receive some portion of instruction in their native languages. According to Ontario's Ministry of Education,

> ... it is crucial to value the first (non-English/non-French) language rather than giving the impression that it and, by extension, the student's native culture are unimportant or disposable. Support for the heritage (international) languages helps all students develop a stronger identity and appreciate the validity of all cultures and languages. (Ontario Ministry of Education and Training, 1999, p. 5)

Research on Bilingual Programs.   It is difficult to separate politics from practice in the debate about bilingual education. It is clear that high-quality bilingual education programs can have positive results. Students improve in the subjects that were taught in their native language, in their mastery of English, and in self-esteem as well (Crawford, 1997; Hakuta & Gould, 1987; Wright & Taylor, 1995). Similarly, English as a second language (ESL) programs seem to have positive effects on reading comprehension (Fitzgerald, 1995). But attention today is shifting from debate about general approaches to a focus on effective teaching strategies. As you will see many times in this book, a combination of clarity of learning goals and direct instruction in needed skills—including learning strategies and tactics, teacher- or peer-guided practice leading to independent practice, authentic and engaging tasks, opportunities for interaction and conversation that are academically focused, and warm encouragement from the teacher—seems to be effective (Chamot & O'Malley, 1996; Gersten, 1996b; Goldenberg, 1996). Table 5.4 on the next page provides a set of constructs for promoting learning and language acquisition that capture many of these methods for effective instruction.

Heritage Language Programs
Programs that offer opportunities for students to receive instruction in their own language.

Connect & Extend

TO PROFESSIONAL JOURNALS
Thomas, W. P., & Collier, V. P. (1998). Two languages are better than one. *Educational Leadership, 55*(4), 23–27. This article makes the case that native and non-native speakers of English benefit greatly from learning together in two languages.

TABLE 5.4 Ideas for Promoting Learning and Language Acquisition

Effective teaching for students in bilingual and ESL classrooms combines many strategies—direct instruction, mediation, coaching, feedback, modelling, encouragement, challenge, and authentic activities.

1. Structures, frameworks, scaffolds, and strategies
   - Provide support to students by "thinking aloud," building on and clarifying input of students
   - Use visual organizers, story maps, or other aids to help students organize and relate information

2. Relevant background knowledge and key vocabulary concepts
   - Provide adequate background knowledge to students and informally assess whether students have background knowledge
   - Focus on key vocabulary words and use consistent language
   - Incorporate students' primary language meaningfully

3. Mediation/feedback
   - Give feedback that focuses on meaning, not grammar, syntax, or pronunciation
   - Give frequent and comprehensible feedback
   - Provide students with prompts or strategies
   - Ask questions that press students to clarify or expand on initial statements
   - Provide activities and tasks that students can complete
   - Indicate to students when they are successful

   - Assign activities that are reasonable, avoiding undue frustration
   - Allow use of native language responses (when context is appropriate)
   - Be sensitive to common problems in second-language acquisition

4. Involvement
   - Ensure active involvement of all students, including low-performing students
   - Foster extended discourse

5. Challenge
   - Provide implicit challenge, e.g., cognitive challenge, use of higher-order questions
   - Provide explicit challenge, e.g., high but reasonable expectations

6. Respect for—and responsiveness to—cultural and personal diversity
   - Show respect for students as individuals, respond to things students say, show respect for culture and family, and possess knowledge of cultural diversity
   - Incorporate students' experiences into writing and language arts activities
   - Link content to students' lives and experiences to enhance understanding
   - View diversity as an asset, reject cultural deficit notions

Source: From Gersten, R. (1996). Literacy instruction for language minority students: The transition years. *The Elementary School Journal*, 96, 241–242. Copyright © 1996. Adapted by permission of the University of Chicago Press.

Check Your Knowledge

- What are the origins of language differences in the classroom?
- What is bilingual education?

Apply to Practice

- How can teachers accommodate different languages in their classrooms?

We have dealt with a wide range of differences in this chapter. How can teachers provide an appropriate education for all their students? One response is to make the classroom compatible with the students' cultural heritage. Such a classroom is described as being culturally compatible.

culturally inclusive classrooms Classrooms in which procedures, rules, grouping strategies, attitudes, and teaching methods do not cause conflicts with the students' culturally influenced ways of learning and interacting.

CREATING CULTURALLY INCLUSIVE CLASSROOMS

Sheets (2005) uses the term "culturally inclusive" to describe classrooms that provide culturally diverse students with equitable access to the teaching–learning process. The goal of creating **culturally inclusive classrooms** is to eliminate racism, sexism, classism, and prejudice while adapting the content and methods of instruction to meet the needs of all students. In the past, discussions of teaching low-income students from racial, ethnic, or language minority groups have focused on remediating problems or overcoming perceived deficits. But thinking today emphasizes teaching to the strengths and the resilience of these students. In this section, we look at two positive approaches—culturally relevant pedagogy and fostering resilience.

Diversity in Learning

Roland Tharp (1989) outlines several dimensions of classrooms that reflect the diversity of the students. The dimensions—social organization, cultural values and learning styles, and sociolinguistics—can be tailored to better fit the background of students.

Social Organization. Tharp (1989) states that "a central task of educational design is to make the organization of teaching, learning, and performance compatible with the social structures in which students are most productive, engaged, and likely to learn" (p. 350). Social structure or social organization in this context means the ways people interact to accomplish a particular goal. For example, the social organization of Hawaiian society depends heavily on collaboration and cooperation. Their culture values interdependence, compared with the majority North American culture, which tends to value autonomy and independence. In societies characterized as **collectivist** or **interdependent** (Triandis, 1989; Markus & Kitayama, 1991), it is more important to connect with others than to distinguish yourself. Children play together in groups of friends and siblings, with older children often caring for the younger ones. When cooperative working groups of four or five boys and girls were established in Hawaiian classrooms, student learning and participation improved (Okagaki, 2001). The teacher worked intensively with one group while the children in the remaining groups helped each other. Similarly, students raised in interdependent societies may feel awkard when they are rewarded for their performance, as many Aboriginal students do, because their cultures value non-competitiveness and emotional restraint. If you have students from several cultures, you may need to provide choices and variety in grouping to accommodate their needs for interdependence or independence.

collectivist/interdependent societies Societies in which it is more important to connect with others than distinguish yourself.

Connect & Extend

TO YOUR TEACHING
Barba, R. H. (1998). *Science in the multicultural classroom.* Toronto: Allyn & Bacon.
   Wallace, J., & Harper, H. (1998). *Taking action: Reworking gender in school contexts.* Toronto: OADE/OWD.
   Lipkin, A. (1999). *Understanding homosexuality, changing schools: A text for teachers, counselors, and administrators.* Boulder, CO: Westview Press.

Cultural Values and Learning Preferences. Rosa Hernandez Sheets (2005) describes three characteristics of teachers who design culturally inclusive classrooms. The teachers (1) recognize the various ways all their students display their capabilities; (2) respond to students' preferred ways of learning; and (3) understand that a particular group's cultural practices, values, and learning preferences may not apply to everyone in that group.

Results of research conducted by Jim Anderson and Lee Gunderson (1997) at the University of British Columbia showed cultural differences in the beliefs about learning to read and write. They interviewed more than 60 parents and 100 students from Chinese, Iranian, and Indo-Canadian communities and compared their beliefs and preferences concerning the teaching and learning of literate behaviour. Many North American teachers support an emergent model of reading, believing that learning to read and write are imprecise processes, that approximation and invention are part of the learning process, and that adult standards for correctness and conventions will not be met in the early stages of reading and writing. This was not the view of many of the parents Anderson and Gunderson interviewed. These parents believed that accuracy and precision were important from the beginning. They criticized practices such as invented spelling and recognizing children's early attempts at reading—"It's not real reading," they said. Parents from these communities also believed that teachers should engage in more direct instruction and that students should talk less, receive more homework, and be asked to memorize more facts.

These cultural values also were evident in students' behaviour. Consider Alice's preferences for reading and writing activities:

> Alice was an extraordinary third grader. She was an immigrant who in two years had become fluent in English; her intelligence had qualified her as an intellectually gifted student. Alice was most content at school when she was filling out pages in a workbook. She and her family believed that answering questions and filling in bubbles in multiple-choice workbook items were essential learning activities that represented the basic goal of literacy learning: to master a set of discrete skills. (Anderson & Gunderson, 1997, p. 514)

Anderson and Gunderson urge teachers to recognize that there are many ways to learn reading and writing and to encourage parents to support their children's literacy learning in ways that are familiar to them. At the same time, teachers can help parents understand our more meaning-based view of reading and writing through regular communication and involvement in the classroom. Also, teachers can engage students in a wide range of literacy activities in the classroom, including some that build on what students experience at home.

For Aboriginal Canadians, oral communication has historically been the primary method of teaching among Aboriginal groups, resulting in less attention to written forms of communication (Crealock & Bachor, 1995). In fact, some Aboriginal languages are only now being coded in a manner that will standardize their written forms and make them available to Aboriginal and non-Aboriginal Canadians. Traditionally, Aboriginals have not written books for children, and storybook reading has not been valued as a preschool activity to the extent it is in most Euro-Canadian families. This may put First Nations students at a disadvantage, since storybook reading is considered instrumental to building understandings and skills essential for reading success in school (International Reading Association & National Association for the Education of Young Children, 1998). Furthermore, Aboriginal cultures train and reward visual-motor and spatial skills, while the dominant culture trains and rewards verbal skills (Crealock & Bachor, 1995). According to Crealock and Bachor, many Aboriginal students have above-average spatial skills and high mechanical aptitude but never have these strengths reinforced in school. Ensuring that these students have opportunities to engage in activities such as map-making, or making patterns or clothes, is one way to recognize these strengths.

Cautions about Learning Style Research. In considering this research on learning styles, you should keep two points in mind. First, the validity of some of the learning styles research has been strongly questioned, as we saw in the previous chapter. Second, there is a heated debate today about whether identifying ethnic group differences in learning styles and preferences is a dangerous, racist, sexist exercise. In our society, we are quick to move from the notion of "difference" to the idea of "deficits" and stereotypes (Gordon, 1991; O'Neil, 1990). We have included the information about learning style differences because we believe that, used sensibly, this information can help you better understand your students.

It is dangerous and incorrect, however, to assume that every individual in a group shares the same learning style. The best advice for teachers is to be sensitive to individual differences in all your students and to make available alternative paths to learning. Never prejudge how a student will learn best on the basis of assumptions about the student's ethnicity or race. Get to know the individual.

Sociolinguistics. Sociolinguistics is the study of "the courtesies and conventions of conversation across cultures" (Tharp, 1989, p. 351). A knowledge of sociolinguistics will help you understand why communication sometimes breaks down in

Connect & Extend

TO PROFESSIONAL JOURNALS

O'Neil, J. (1990a). Link between style, culture proves divisive. *Educational Leadership, 48*(2), 8. *Focus Question:* Why do some educators argue against linking learning styles to cultural differences?

One goal of creating culturally compatible classrooms is to encourage mutual acceptance and respect among students from all backgrounds.

sociolinguistics The study of formal and informal rules for how, when, about what, to whom, and how long to speak in conversations within cultural groups.

classrooms. The classroom is a special setting for communicating; it has its own set of rules for when, how, to whom, about what subject, and in what manner to use language. Sometimes the sociolinguistic skills of students do not fit the expectations of teachers.

In order to be successful, students must know the communication rules; that is, they must understand the pragmatics of the classroom—when, where, and how to communicate. This is not such an easy task. As class activities change, rules change. Sometimes you have to raise your hand (during the teacher's presentation), but sometimes you don't (during story time on the rug). Sometimes it is good to ask a question (during discussion), but other times it isn't so good (when the teacher is reprimanding you). These differing activity rules are called **participation structures**, and they define appropriate participation for each class activity. Most classrooms have many different participation structures. To be competent communicators in the classroom, students sometimes have to read very subtle, nonverbal cues telling them which participation structures are currently in effect. For example, in one classroom, when the teacher stood in a particular area of the room, put her hands on her hips, and leaned forward at the waist, the children in the class were signalled to "stop and freeze," look at the teacher, and anticipate an announcement (Shultz & Florio, 1979).

participation structures The formal and informal rules for how to take part in a given activity.

Sources of Misunderstandings.   Some children are simply better than others at reading the classroom situation because the participation structures of the school match the structures they have learned at home. In North America, the communication rules for most school situations are similar to those in middle-class white homes, so children from these homes often appear to be more competent communicators. They know the unwritten rules. Students from different cultural backgrounds may have learned participation structures that conflict with the behaviour expected in school. For example, one study found that the home conversation style of Hawaiian children is to chime in with contributions to a story. In school, however, this overlapping style is seen as "interrupting." When the teachers in one school learned about these differences and made their reading groups more like their students' home conversation groups, the young Hawaiian children in their classes improved in reading (Au, 1980; Tharp, 1989).

The source of misunderstanding can be a subtle sociolinguistic difference, such as how long the teacher waits to react to a student's response. White and Tharp (1988) found that when Navajo students in one class paused in giving a response, their Anglo teacher seemed to think that they had finished speaking. As a result, the teacher often unintentionally interrupted students. In another study, researchers found that Pueblo Indian students participated twice as much in classes where teachers waited longer to react. Waiting longer also helps girls participate more freely in math and science classes (Grossman & Grossman, 1994).

It seems that even students who speak the same language as their teachers may still have trouble communicating, and thus learning school subjects, if their knowledge of pragmatics does not fit the school situation. What can teachers do? Especially in the early grades, you should make communication rules for activities clear and explicit. Do not assume that students know what to do. Use cues to signal students when changes occur. Explain and demonstrate appropriate behaviour. We have seen teachers ask students to "use your inside voice" or "whisper so you won't disturb others." One teacher said and then demonstrated, "If you have to interrupt me while I'm working with other children, stand quietly beside me until I can help you." Be consistent in responding to students. If students are supposed to raise their hands, don't call on those who break the rules. In these ways, you teach students how to communicate and learn in school.

Culturally Relevant Pedagogy

Several researchers have focused on teachers who are especially successful with students of colour and students in poverty (Delpit, 1995; Ladson-Billings, 1994, 1995; Moll, Amanti, Neff, & Gonzalez, 1992; Siddle Walker, 2001). The work of Gloria Ladson-Billings (1990, 1992, 1995) is a good example. For three years, she studied excellent teachers in a California school district that served an African American community. In order to select the teachers, she asked parents and principals for nominations. Parents nominated teachers who respected them, created enthusiasm for learning in their children, and understood their children's need to operate successfully in two different worlds—the home community and the white world beyond. Principals nominated teachers who had few discipline referrals, high attendance rates, and high standardized test scores. Ladson-Billings was able to examine in depth eight of the nine teachers who were nominated by *both parents and principals.*

culturally relevant pedagogy Excellent teaching for students from visible minorities that includes academic success and developing/maintaining cultural competence and critical consciousness to challenge the status quo.

Based on her research, Ladson-Billings developed a conception of teaching excellence that encompasses but goes beyond considerations of sociolinguistics and social organizations. She uses the term **culturally relevant pedagogy** to describe teaching that rests on three propositions.

Help Students Experience Academic Success. "Despite the current social inequities and hostile classroom environments, students must develop their academic skills. The ways in which those skills are developed may vary, but all students need literacy, numeracy, technological, social, and political skills in order to be active participants in a democracy" (Ladson-Billings, 1995, p. 160).

Develop/Maintain Students' Cultural Competence. As they become more academically skilled, students still retain their cultural competence. "Culturally relevant teachers utilize students' culture as a vehicle for learning" (Ladson-Billings, 1995, p. 161). For example, a teacher might use "non-offensive" rap music to teach literal and figurative meaning, rhyme, alliteration, and onomatopoeia in poetry. He or she might bring in a representative from a community to work with students on a project that has cultural significance (e.g., researching and experimenting with an art form that is linked with students' ethnic origins).

Help Students Develop a Critical Consciousness to Challenge the Status Quo. In addition to developing academic skills while encouraging cultural competence, excellent teachers help students "develop a broader sociopolitical consciousness that allows them to critique the social norms, values, mores, and institutions that produce and maintain social inequities" (Ladson-Billings, 1995, p. 162). For example, in one school students were upset that their textbooks were out of date. They mobilized to investigate the funding formulas that allowed students in other schools to have newer books, wrote letters to the newspaper editor to challenge these inequities, and updated their texts with current information from other sources.

Ladson-Billings (1995) noted that many people have said that her three principles "are just good teaching." She agrees that she is describing good teaching, but she questions "why so little of it seems to be occurring in classrooms populated by African American students" (p. 159).

Fostering Resilience

resilience The ability to adapt successfully in spite of difficult circumstances and threats to development.

In any given week, the 12 to 15 percent of school-age children who have urgent needs for social and emotional support are not getting help. Community and mental health services often don't reach the students who are at the highest risk. But many children at risk for academic failure not only survive—they thrive. They are resilient students. What can we learn from these students? What can teachers and schools do to encourage **resilience**?

Resilient Students.   People vary in their capacity to be resilient. Students who seem able to thrive in spite of serious challenges are actively engaged in school. They have good interpersonal skills, confidence in their own ability to learn, positive attitudes toward school, pride in their ethnicity, and high expectations (Borman & Overman, 2004; Lee, 2005). Also, students who have high intelligence or valued talents are more protected from risks. Being easy-going and optimistic is associated with resilience as well. Factors outside the student—interpersonal relationships and social support—matter, too. It helps to have a warm relationship with a parent who has high expectations and supports learning by organizing space and time at home for study. But even without such a parent, a strong bond with someone competent—a grandparent, aunt, uncle, teacher, mentor, or other caring adult—can serve the same supportive function. Involvement in school, community, or religious activities can provide more connections to concerned adults and also teach lessons in social skills and leadership (Berk, 2005).

Resilient Classrooms.   You can't choose personalities or parents for your students. Even if you could, stresses can build up for even the most resilient students. Beth Doll and her colleagues (2005) suggest that we have to change classrooms instead of kids because "alternative strategies will be more enduring and most successful when they are integrated into naturally occurring systems of support [like schools] that surround children" (p. 3). In addition, there is some evidence that changes in classrooms—such as reducing class size and forming supportive relationships with teachers—have a greater impact on the academic achievement of African American students compared with Latino and white students (Borman & Overman, 2004). So how can you create a classroom that supports resilience?

Borman and Overman (2004) identified two characteristics of schools associated with academic resilience: a safe, orderly environment, and positive teacher–student relationships. In their book on resilient classrooms, Doll and her colleagues (2005) draw on research in education and psychology on best practices for children in poverty and children with disabilities to describe the characteristics of resilient classrooms. There are two strands of elements that bind students to their classroom community. One strand emphasizes the self-agency of students— their capacity to set and pursue goals; the second strand emphasizes caring and connected relationships in the classroom and the school.

Self-Agency Strand

- *Academic self-efficacy*, a belief in your own ability to learn, is one of the most consistent predictors of academic achievement. As you will see in Chapters 9 and 10, self-efficacy emerges when students tackle challenging, meaningful tasks with the support needed to be successful and observe other students doing the same thing. Accurate and encouraging feedback from teachers also helps.
- *Behavioural self-control*, or student self-regulation, is essential for a safe and orderly learning environment. Chapters 6, 9, and 12 will give you ideas for helping students develop self-regulation knowledge and skills.
- *Academic self-determination*, making choices, setting goals, and following through, is the third element in the self-agency strand. As you will see in Chapter 10, students who are self-determined are more motivated and committed to learning.

Relationship Strand

- *Caring teacher–student relationships* are consistently associated with better school performance, especially for students who face serious challenges. We saw the power of caring teachers in Chapter 3 and will return to this theme in Chapter 11.

- *Effective peer relations*, as we saw in Chapter 3, also are critical in connecting students to school.
- *Effective home–school relationships* are the final element in building a caring, connected network for students. In the School Development program, James Comer has found that when parents stay involved, their children's grades and test scores improve (Comer, Haynes, & Joyner, 1996).

Constructing a Resilient Classroom.   In order to build student self-agency and relationships, the two strands of resilience, Doll and her colleagues (2005) provide student questionnaires for gathering data about your classroom. One teacher used this questionnaire and found that almost half of her students did not listen carefully or have any fun in class. They said the teacher was not fair and did not help, respect, or believe in them.

Bringing It All Together: Teaching Every Student

What Would You Say?

As the interview for the position in the diverse middle school continues, one of the interviewers says, "Describe the things you do for students to indicate you care for them." What would you say?

The goal of this chapter is to give you a sense of the diversity in today's and tomorrow's schools and to help you meet the challenges of teaching in a multicultural classroom. How will you understand and build on all the cultures of your students? How will you deal with many different languages? Here are a few general teaching principles to guide you in finding answers to these questions.

Know Your Students.   Nothing you read in a chapter on cultural differences will teach you enough to understand the lives of all your students. If you can take other courses or read about other cultures, we encourage you to do it. But reading and studying are not enough. You should get to know your students' families and communities. Elba Reyes, a successful bilingual teacher for children with special needs, describes her approach:

> Usually I find that if you really want to know a parent, you get to know them on their own turf. This is key to developing trust and understanding the parents' perspective. First, get to know the community. Learn where the local grocery store is and what the children do after school. Then schedule a home visit at a time that is convenient for the parents. (Bos & Reyes, 1996, p. 349)

Try to spend time with students and parents on projects outside school. Ask parents to help in class or to speak to your students about their jobs, hobbies, history, and heritage. In the elementary grades, don't wait until a student is in trouble to have the first meeting with a family member. Watch and listen to the ways your students interact in large and small groups. Have students write to you, and write back to them. Eat lunch with one or two students. Spend some non-teaching time with them.

Respect Your Students.   From knowledge ought to come respect for your students' learning strengths—for the struggles they face and the obstacles they overcome. For a child, genuine acceptance is a necessary condition for developing self-esteem. Pride and self-esteem are important accomplishments of the school years. Sometimes the self-image and occupational aspirations of minority-group children actually decline in their early years in public school, probably because of the emphasis on majority culture values, accomplishments, and history. By presenting the accomplishments of particular members of an ethnic group or by bringing that group's culture into the classroom (in the form of literature, art, music, or any cultural knowledge), teachers can help students maintain a sense of pride in their cultural group. This integration of culture must be more than the "tokenism" of sampling ethnic foods or wearing costumes. Students should learn about the socially and intellectually important contributions of the various groups. There are many excellent references that provide background information, history, and teaching strategies for different groups of students (e.g., Banks, 1997, 1999; Bennett, 1999; Ladson-Billings, 1995).

Teach Your Students. The most important thing you can do for your students is to teach them to read, write, speak, compute, think, and create. Too often, goals for low-SES or minority-group students have focused exclusively on basic skills. Students are taught words and sounds, but the meaning of the story is supposed to come later. Knapp, Turnbull, and Shields (1990) make these suggestions:

- Focus on meaning and understanding from beginning to end—for example, by orienting instruction toward comprehending reading passages, communicating important ideas in written text, or understanding the concepts underlying number facts.
- Balance routine skill learning with novel and complex tasks from the earliest stages of learning.
- Provide context for skill learning that establishes clear reasons for needing to learn the skills.
- Influence attitudes and beliefs about the academic content areas as well as skills and knowledge.
- Eliminate unnecessary redundancy in the curriculum (e.g., repeating instruction in the same mathematics skills year after year). (p. 5)

And finally, teach students directly about how to be students. In the early grades, this could mean directly teaching the courtesies and conventions of the classroom: how to get a turn to speak, how and when to interrupt the teacher, how to whisper, how to get help in a small group, how to give an explanation that is helpful. In the later grades, it may mean teaching the study skills that fit your subject. You can ask students to learn "how we do it in school" without violating the second principle above—respect your students. Ways of asking questions around the kitchen table at home may be different from ways of asking questions in school, but students can learn both ways, without deciding that either way is superior. The Guidelines on page 194 give more ideas.

Check Your Knowledge

- What are the elements of a culturally inclusive classroom?
- What is culturally relevant pedagogy?
- How can teachers create classroom environments in which all students can learn?

Apply to Practice

- How do participation structures affect students' access to learning in classrooms?
- How can you move "beyond the basics" in teaching all your students?

CULTURALLY RELEVANT TEACHING

Experiment with different grouping arrangements to encourage social harmony and cooperation.

EXAMPLES

1. Try "study buddies" and pairs.
2. Organize heterogeneous groups of four or five.
3. Establish larger teams for older students.

Provide a range of ways to learn material to accommodate a range of learning styles.

EXAMPLES

1. Give students verbal materials at different reading levels.
2. Offer visual materials—charts, diagrams, models.
3. Provide tapes for listening and viewing.
4. Set up activities and projects.

Teach classroom procedures directly, even ways of doing things that you thought everyone would know.

EXAMPLES

1. Tell students how to get the teacher's attention.
2. Explain when and how to interrupt the teacher if students need help.
3. Show which materials students can take and which require permission.
4. Demonstrate acceptable ways to disagree with or challenge another student.

Learn the meaning of different behaviour for your students.

EXAMPLES

1. Ask students how they feel when you correct or praise them. What gives them this message?

2. Talk to family and community members and other teachers to discover the meaning of expressions, gestures, or other responses that are unfamiliar to you.

Emphasize meaning in teaching.

EXAMPLES

1. Make sure that students understand what they read.
2. Try storytelling and other modes that don't require written materials.
3. Use examples that relate abstract concepts to everyday experiences; for instance, relate negative numbers to being overdrawn in your chequebook.

Get to know the customs, traditions, and values of your students.

EXAMPLES

1. Use holidays as a chance to discuss the origins and meaning of traditions.
2. Analyze different traditions for common themes.
3. Attend community fairs and festivals.

Help students detect racist and sexist messages.

EXAMPLES

1. Analyze curriculum materials for biases.
2. Make students "bias detectives," reporting comments from the media.
3. Discuss the ways in which students communicate biased messages about each other and what should be done when this happens.
4. Discuss expressions of prejudice such as anti-Semitism.

SUMMARY

Today's Multicultural Classrooms
(pp. 159–161)

Distinguish between the "melting pot" and multiculturalism.

Statistics point to increasing cultural diversity in Canadian society.

Canadian laws and policies support our multiculturalism and promote multicultural education, equal educational opportunity, and the celebration of cultural diversity. This is in contrast to the view that immigrants should lose their cultural distinctiveness and assimilate to the Canadian culture.

What is multicultural education?

James Banks suggests that multicultural education has five dimensions: integrating content, helping students understand how knowledge is influenced by beliefs, reducing prejudice, creating social structures in schools that support learning and development for all students, and using teaching methods that reach all students.

What is culture?

There are many conceptions of culture, but most include the knowledge, rules, traditions, attitudes, and values that guide behaviour in a particular group of people. Everyone is a member of many cultural groups, defined in terms of geographic region, nationality, ethnicity, race, gender, social class, and religion. Membership in a particular group does not determine behaviour or values but makes certain values and kinds of behaviour more likely. Wide variations exist within each group.

Economic and Social Class Differences
(pp. 162–165)

What is SES?

Socioeconomic status (SES) is a term used by sociologists for variations in wealth, power, and prestige. Socioeconomic status is determined by several factors—not just income—and often overpowers other cultural differences.

What is the relationship between SES and school achievement?

Socioeconomic status and academic achievement are closely related. High-SES students of all ethnic groups show higher average levels of achievement on test scores and stay in school longer than low-SES students. Poverty during a child's preschool years appears to have the greatest negative impact. And the longer the child is in poverty, the stronger the impact on achievement. Why is there a correlation between SES and school achievement? Low-SES students may suffer from inadequate health care, teachers' lowered expectations of them, learned helplessness, participation in resistance cultures, tracking, and understimulating, perhaps stressful home environments. However, some students from low-SES backgrounds are remarkably resilient.

Ethnic and Racial Differences
(pp. 165–174)

Distinguish between ethnicity and race.

Ethnicity (culturally transmitted behaviour) and race (biologically transmitted physical traits) are socially significant categories people use to describe themselves and others. Minority groups (either numerically or historically unempowered) are rapidly increasing in population.

How can ethnicity affect school performance?

Conflicts between groups can arise from differences in culture-based beliefs, values, and expectations. Students in some cultures learn attitudes and behaviour that are more consistent with school expectations. Differences among ethnic groups in cognitive and academic abilities are largely the legacy of racial segregation and continuing prejudice and discrimination.

Distinguish among prejudice, discrimination, and stereotype threat.

Prejudice is a rigid and irrational generalization—a prejudgment—about an entire category of people. Prejudice may target people from particular racial, ethnic, religious, political, geographic, or language groups, or it may be directed toward the gender or sexual orientation of the individual. Discrimination is unequal treatment of particular categories of people. Stereotype threat is the extra emotional and cognitive burden that your performance in an academic situation might confirm a stereotype that others hold about you.

Girls and Boys: Differences in the Classroom
(pp. 174–181)

What are the stages for achieving a sexual orientation for gay and lesbian youth?

Stages of achieving a sexual orien-

tation for gay and lesbian students can also follow a pattern from discomfort to confusion to acceptance. Some researchers contend that sexual identity is not always permanent and can change over the years.

What is gender-role identity and how do gender-role identities develop?

Gender-role identity is the image each individual has of himself or herself as masculine or feminine in characteristics—a part of self-concept. Biology (hormones) plays a role, as does the differential behaviour of parents and teachers toward male and female children. Through their interactions with family, peers, teachers, and the environment in general, children begin to form gender schemas, or organized networks of knowledge about what it means to be male or female. Research shows that gender-role stereotyping begins in the preschool years and continues through gender bias in the school curriculum and sex discrimination in the classroom. Teachers often unintentionally perpetuate these problems.

Are there sex differences in mental abilities?

Most studies find that there are few differences between boys and girls in overall mental and motor development or in specific abilities before children enter school. During the school years and beyond, psychologists find no differences in general intelligence on the standard measures, but some differences on tests that focus on specific abilities. For example, from elementary school through high school, girls score higher than boys on tests of reading and writing, and boys tend to do better on advanced tests of mathematical achievement.

Language Differences in the Classroom
(pp. 182–186)

What are the origins of language differences in the classroom?

Language differences among students can be due to students having different first languages or culture-based communication styles.

What is bilingual education?

While there is much debate over the best way to help students master a second language, studies show that it is best if students are not forced to abandon their first language. The more proficient students are in their first language, the faster they will master the second. Mastering academic language skills in any new language takes five to seven years.

Creating Culturally Inclusive Classrooms
(pp. 186–194)

What are the elements of a culturally inclusive classroom?

Culturally inclusive classrooms are free of racism, sexism, and ethnic prejudice. They provide equal educational opportunities for all students. Dimensions of classroom life that can be modified to that end include social organization, teaching and learning formats, and participation structures. Teachers, however, must avoid stereotypes based on cultural interpretations of learning preferences. They must not assume that every individual in a group approaches learning in the same way or has the same preferences.

Communication may break down in classrooms because of differences in sociolinguistic styles and skills. Teachers can directly teach appropriate participation structures and be sensitive to culture-based communication rules.

What is culturally relevant pedagogy?

Gloria Ladson-Billings developed a conception of teaching excellence that encompasses considerations of sociolinguistics and social organizations but goes beyond them. She uses the term *culturally relevant pedagogy* to describe teaching that rests on three propositions: students must experience academic success, develop/maintain their cultural competence, and develop a critical consciousness to challenge the status quo.

How can teachers create classroom environments in which all students can learn?

To help create compatible multicultural classrooms, teachers must know and respect all their students, have high expectations of them, and teach them what they need to know to succeed.

KEY TERMS

bilingualism, p. 182

collectivist/interdependent societies, p. 187

culturally inclusive classrooms, p. 186

culturally relevant pedagogy, p. 190

culture, p. 160

discrimination, p. 171

English language learners (ELL), p. 184

ethnicity, p. 165

gender biases, p. 177

gender-role identity, p. 175

gender schemas, p. 176

Heritage Language Programs, p. 185

melting pot, p. 159

minority group, p. 166

monolinguals, p. 183

mosaic, p. 159

multicultural education, p. 159

participation structures, p. 189

prejudice, p. 170

race, p. 165

resilience, p. 190

resistance culture, p. 164

sexual identity, p. 174

socioeconomic status (SES), p. 162

sociolinguistics, p. 188

stereotype, p. 171

stereotype threat, p. 172

tracking, p. 164

BECOMING A PROFESSIONAL

Reflecting on the Chapter

Can you apply the ideas from this chapter on culture and community to solve the following problems of practice?

Preschool and Kindergarten

- You are surprised to overhear two of your students talking about two of their classmates in a prejudiced way. You cannot believe that young children could already hold such beliefs. You wonder where they are getting their ideas and what you can do to address them. How would you express your concerns to the children and, perhaps, their families?

Elementary and Middle School

- Several of your students live in a low-income housing complex in the district and clearly have fewer advantages than the other students in your class. You are concerned that these students never seem to work or play with the others in the class. What would you do?

- Every year, the number of non–English-speaking students in your class increases. This year, there are four different language groups represented—

and you know only about five words in each language. The school has little in the way of resources. Pick one topic and tell how you would teach it to accommodate the limited English-language proficiency of your students.

Junior High and High School

- One day you notice that the males are doing most of the talking in your classes, particularly the advanced classes. Just out of curiosity, you start to note each day how many girls and boys make contributions and ask questions. You are really surprised to see that your first impression was correct. What would you do to encourage more participation on the part of your female students?

- For some reason, this year there have been several racial incidents in your school. Each incident seems a bit nastier and more dangerous than the one before. What would you do in your classes to improve the situation?

Check Your Understanding

- Know the basic dimensions of multicultural education.

- Know the difference between prejudice and discrimination.

- Be familiar with the three propositions of culturally relevant pedagogy.

- Be familiar with research on differences in how teachers interact with male and female students.

Your Teaching Portfolio

- What is your stance on multicultural education? On tracking? Add these ideas in your philosophy of teaching statement for your portfolio.

- Include ideas for the integration of multicultural material in your portfolio.

Teaching Resources

Add Table 5.4 on page 186 to your teaching resources file.

Use the Family and Community Partnerships box on page 168 to brainstorm ideas for family involvement in helping your students "take their learning home."

Teachers' Casebook

What Would They Do?

Kate Whitton
MeadowView Public School
Addison, Ontario

Dynamics in any classroom can be a precarious balance, especially with middle-school students who are beginning to experience the responsibilities and freedoms of adulthood. Creating and building a "safe" but structured environment is crucial to establishing and maintaining a fully functioning class. This involves identifying both personal and group goals and emphasizing that to be an effective team the teacher and students will need to work together to find positive solutions for a productive year.

In this particular scenario, the cliques created are often a result of preconceived notions of another individual or group. These notions result in fear, and people naturally respond to the unknown by bunching together in safe groups. By focusing on team-building activities and cooperative learning situations, hopefully the students will begin to see that although there are differences among them, there are also similarities. With regard to group work, I would initially create their groups to encourage more interaction between the students. Although they usually balk at this, eventually they settle down and get the task completed.

Physical setup of the class is important as well; seating the students in a horseshoe shape allows everyone to see one another and also enables the teacher to try different arrangements. One approach is to allow students to sit by a friend for a few days to establish comfort within the class, and then rearrange them in order to facilitate socialization with other classmates.

With regard to Clarise, the emotionally disturbed student, I would put an IEP in place by having the school SERT (Special Education Review Team), parents, social skills worker, and board psychologist work together in order to establish an effective plan for her success.

In my experience, this type of exceptional student usually seeks attention and a purpose, and typically exhibits this through inappropriate behaviour. I sense that she would benefit immensely from realizing constructive success. Perhaps seeing the world through different eyes, in the form of a student with cerebral palsy, would give her an alternative perspective. With the above group of school personnel, I would develop the idea that Clarise could be responsible for working with the student who has cerebral palsy (along with the educational assistant). This would give her a meaningful purpose and goal.

Keep in mind that many other distinctive and subtle qualities make up "ethnic" groups—for example, their historical past, socioeconomic status, and religious beliefs—that may not be common knowledge. As far as the ethnic grouping issue, I would dispel myths and negative ideas through class participation, discussion, media presentations, group work, etc. Ideas include KWL charts (what we know, what we would like to know, what we have learned) about each culture with a comparison to Canadian culture, and documentaries (e.g., National Geographic, Discovery Channel) on culture with discussion. It's important to keep comments positive and encourage the idea that differences aren't necessarily bad—that it's okay to be different and to celebrate this diversity. We can learn so much from one another. One possible project is developing a class video that would be shown to the class and parents (or school) in a special "Celebrating Diversity" night. This medium is exciting for kids and also gives them a common goal. Each ethnic grouping, including the student with cerebral palsy, first develops a segment that focuses on traditional and present-day culture; then they all come together to create a segment based on their findings about their similarities and their diversity. This enables the class to develop their own distinct tapestry yet embrace their individual uniqueness. It's an approach that echoes the Canadian mosaic ideal as opposed to the "melting pot" stance.

Middle-school kids are a dynamic group. They want to articulate their ideas but also need to feel that they're part of the process, and in this way teachers can facilitate more appropriate responses—and actions instead of reactions.

Vicki Den Ouden
Learning Assistance Teacher
Surrey Christian School
Surrey, British Columbia

It is crucial to establish the right atmosphere in a classroom in order for successful learning to take place. Ideally, the students and teacher should feel mutual respect, trust, and acceptance. It is up to the teacher to develop this in her classroom. This can be done through carefully planned lessons and discussions. In this situation, since the teacher is already overwhelmed, she should team up with her colleagues and the school counsellor for some positive solutions.

One idea might be to teach a unit on multiculturalism, discrimination, or racism. Collaborative learning activities, peer teaching, and role playing should be included in the planning. This would allow the students to share their own views instead of feeling the teacher is just "preaching" at them. Of course, the teacher would need to carefully and sensitively guide the discussions. There are many excellent books and videos on these topics, some told from a teenager's point of view. The school librarian or school district resource centre can help locate such materials. The unit should culminate with a related project (e.g., posters, a play), thereby putting the words into action. Working together on a project can develop a sense of ownership, pride, and community among the students.

The student with cerebral palsy could participate fully in the activities with the help of his special education assistant, although some modifications to the assignments might be needed. The teacher should check his individualized education program (IEP) in this regard. If he is able or wishes to, the boy could eventually share his feelings about his disability or possible experiences of discrimination. (Taking his language/speech difficulties into consideration, the teacher may find that the boy chooses to share his views through a poem or a computer journal.) This could occur only once an atmosphere of trust and caring had been established. The student would need to feel safe in sharing such personal feelings. Once this had been achieved, the sharing could be a tremendously unifying force for the class.

Clarise's emotional/behavioural problems require some individual attention outside of the class. The school counsellor or resource teacher would be instrumental in this. Direct instruction in social skills would be most beneficial.

Also, the potential risk to Clarise's safety would need to be addressed immediately. The principal or school counsellor could be consulted on procedures to deal with bullying and conflict resolution. In addition, the teacher should find out how Clarise gets home. If possible, the teacher could either accompany Clarise to the bus or ensure she has a ride home until this matter was resolved.

6

BEHAVIOURAL VIEWS OF LEARNING

Playing Ball, 1999, Christian Pierre. Acrylic on canvas. © Christian Pierre/SuperStock.

Teachers' Casebook

What Would You Do?

You were hired in January to take over the class of a teacher who moved away. This is a great school. If you do well, you might be in line for a full-time opening next fall. As you are introduced around the school, you get a number of sympathetic looks and many—too many—offers of help: "Let me know if I can do anything for you."

As you walk toward your classroom, you begin to understand why so many teachers volunteered their help. You hear the screaming when you are still halfway down the hall. "Give it back, it's MINE!" "No way—come and get it!" "I hate you." A crashing sound follows as a table full of books hits the floor. The first day is a nightmare. Evidently, the previous teacher had no management system—no order. Several students walk around the room while you are talking to the class, interrupt you when you are working with a group, torment the class goldfish, and open their lunches (or other students') for a self-determined, mid-morning snack. Others listen, but ask a million questions off the topic. Simply taking roll and introducing the first activity takes an hour. You end the first day exhausted and discouraged, losing your voice and your patience.

Critical Thinking
How would you approach the situation? Which problem behaviours would you tackle first? Would giving rewards or administering punishments be useful in this situation? Why or why not?

Collaboration
With two other members of your class, role-play an orientation meeting between this new teacher and the mentor teacher assigned to help. How should the mentor prepare the new teacher for the assignment? What plans could be made to handle the situation?

We begin this chapter with a general definition of learning that takes into account the contrasting views of different theoretical groups. We will highlight one group, the behavioural theorists, in this chapter. In Chapters 7 and 8, we examine another major group, the cognitive theorists. Then, in Chapter 9, we look at social cognitive views and constructivism.

Our discussion in this chapter will focus on four behavioural learning processes—contiguity, classical conditioning, operant conditioning, and observational learning—with the greatest emphasis on the last two processes. After examining the implications of applied behaviour analysis for teaching, we look at two recent directions in behavioural approaches to learning: self-management and cognitive behaviour modification.

By the time you have completed this chapter, you should be able to answer these questions:

- *What is learning?*
- *What are the similarities and differences among contiguity, classical conditioning, and operant conditioning?*
- *What are examples of four different kinds of consequences that can follow any behaviour, and what effect is each likely to have on future behaviour?*
- *How could you use applied behaviour analysis (group consequences, contingency contracts, token economies or functional behavioural analysis) to solve common academic or behaviour problems?*
- *What and how can students learn through observation?*
- *What is cognitive behaviour modification, and how does it apply to teaching?*

UNDERSTANDING LEARNING

When we hear the word *learning,* most of us think of studying and school. We think about subjects or skills we intend to master, such as algebra, French, chemistry, or karate. But learning is not limited to school. We learn every day of our lives. Babies learn to kick their legs to make the mobile above their crib move, teenagers learn the lyrics to all their favourite songs, middle-aged people learn to change their diet and exercise patterns, and every few years we all learn to find a new style of dress attractive when the old styles (the styles we once loved) go out of fashion. This last example shows that learning is not always intentional. We don't try to like new styles and dislike old; it just seems to happen that way. We don't intend to become nervous when we see the dentist fill a syringe with Novocaine or when we step onto a stage, yet many of us do. So what is this powerful phenomenon called learning?

Learning: A Definition

In the broadest sense, **learning** occurs when experience causes a relatively permanent change in an individual's knowledge or behaviour. The change may be deliberate or unintentional, for better or for worse, and conscious or unconscious (Hill, 2002). To qualify as learning, this change must be brought about by experience—by the interaction of a person with his or her environment. Changes simply caused by maturation, such as growing taller or turning grey, do not qualify as learning. Temporary changes resulting from illness, fatigue, or hunger are also excluded from a general definition of learning. A person who has gone without food for two days does not learn to be hungry, and a person who is ill does not learn to run more slowly. Of course, learning plays a part in how we respond to hunger or illness.

Our definition specifies that the changes resulting from learning are in the individual's knowledge or behaviour. While most psychologists would agree with this statement, some tend to emphasize the change in knowledge, others the change in behaviour. Cognitive psychologists, who focus on changes in knowledge, believe that learning is an internal mental activity that cannot be observed directly. As you will see in the next chapter, cognitive psychologists studying learning are interested in unobservable mental activities such as thinking, remembering, and solving problems (Schwartz & Reisberg, 1991).

The psychologists discussed in this chapter, on the other hand, favour **behavioural learning theories.** The behavioural view generally assumes that the outcome of learning is a change in behaviour and emphasizes the effects of external events on the individual. Some early behaviourists such as J. B. Watson took the radical position that because thinking, intentions, and other internal mental events could not be seen or studied rigorously and scientifically, these "mentalisms," as he called them, should not even be included in an explanation of learning. Before we look in depth at behavioural explanations of learning, let's step into an actual classroom and note the possible results of learning.

Learning Is Not Always What It Seems

Elizabeth Chan was beginning her first day of solo teaching. After weeks of working with her cooperating teacher in a grade 8 social studies class, she was ready to take over. As she moved from behind the desk to the front of the room, she saw another adult approach the classroom door. It was B. J. Ross, her supervisor from the university. Elizabeth's neck and facial muscles suddenly became very tense and her hands trembled.

"I've stopped by to observe your teaching," Dr. Ross said. "This will be my first of six visits. I tried to reach you last night to tell you."

learning Process through which experience causes permanent change in knowledge or behaviour.

behavioural learning theories Explanations of learning that focus on external events as the cause of changes in observable behaviour.

Are there experiences in your "learning history" that have made you anxious about speaking in public or taking tests? How might behavioural principles of learning help explain the development of these anxieties?

Elizabeth tried to hide her reaction, but her hands trembled as she gathered the notes for the lesson.

"Let's start today with a kind of game. I will say some words, then I want you to tell me the first words you can think of. Don't bother to raise your hands. Just say the words out loud, and I will write them on the board. Don't all speak at once, though. Wait until someone else has finished to say your word. Okay, here is the first word: Métis."

"Red River." "Louis Riel." "Rebellion." The answers came very quickly, and Elizabeth was relieved to see that the students understood the game.

"All right, very good," she said. "Now try another one: Batoche."

"Duck Lake." "Fish Creek." "John A. Macdonald." "Big Mac." "Sir Ronald McDonald!" With this last answer, a ripple of laughter moved across the room.

"Ronald McDonald?" Elizabeth sighed wearily. "Get serious." Then she laughed too. Soon, all the students were laughing. "Okay, settle down," Elizabeth said. "These ideas are getting a little off base!"

"Off base? Baseball," shouted the boy who had first mentioned Ronald McDonald. He stood up and started throwing balls of paper to a friend in the back of the room, simulating the style of Roger Clemens.

"Red Sox." "No, the Blue Jays." "The Rogers Centre." "Hot dogs." "Popcorn." "Hamburgers." "Ronald McDonald." The responses now came too fast for Elizabeth to stop them. For some reason, the Ronald McDonald line got an even bigger laugh the second time around, and Elizabeth suddenly realized she had lost the class.

"Okay, since you know so much about the Rebellion, close your books and take out a pen," Elizabeth said, obviously angry. She passed out the worksheet that she had planned as a cooperative, open-book project. "You have 20 minutes to finish this test!"

"You didn't tell us we were having a test!" "This isn't fair!" "We haven't even covered this stuff yet!" "I didn't do anything wrong!" There were moans and disgusted looks, even from the most mellow students. "I'm reporting you to the principal; it's a violation of students' rights!"

This last comment hit hard. The class had just finished discussing human rights as preparation for this unit on the Northwest Rebellion. As she listened to the protests, Elizabeth felt terrible. How was she going to grade these "tests"? The first section of the worksheet involved facts about events leading up to the Northwest Rebellion, and the second section asked students to create a news-style program interviewing ordinary people touched by the war.

"All right, all right, it won't be a test. But you do have to complete this worksheet for a grade. I was going to let you work together, but your behaviour this morning tells me that you are not ready for group work. If you can complete the first section of the sheet working quietly and seriously, you may work together on the second section." Elizabeth knew that her students would like to work together on writing the script for the news interview program.

It appears, on the surface at least, that very little learning of any sort was taking place in Elizabeth's classroom. In fact, Elizabeth had some good ideas; but she also made some mistakes in her application of learning principles. We will return to this episode later in the chapter to analyze various aspects of what took place. To get us started, three events can be singled out, each possibly related to a different learning process.

First, Elizabeth's hands trembled when her university supervisor entered the room. Second, the students were able to associate the phrases *Red River* and *Louis Riel* with the word *Métis*. Third, one student continued to disrupt the class with inappropriate responses. The three learning processes represented are classical conditioning, contiguity, and operant conditioning. In the following pages, we will examine these three kinds of learning, starting with contiguity.

• Define learning.

Apply to Practice

• How will you explain to your students what you mean by learning?

EARLY EXPLANATIONS OF LEARNING: CONTIGUITY AND CLASSICAL CONDITIONING

One of the earliest explanations of learning came from Aristotle (384–322 BC). He said that we remember things together: (1) when they are similar, (2) when they contrast, and (3) when they are *contiguous*. This last principle is the most important, because it is included in all explanations of *learning by association*. The principle of **contiguity** states that whenever two or more sensations occur together often enough, they will become associated. Later, when only one of these sensations (a **stimulus**) occurs, the other will be remembered too (a **response**) (Rachlin, 1991; Wasserman & Miller, 1997).

Some results of contiguous learning were evident in Elizabeth's class. When she said *Métis*, students associated the words *Red River* and *Louis Riel*. They had heard these words together many times in a movie shown the day before. Other learning processes may also be involved when students learn these phrases, but contiguity is a factor. Contiguity also plays a major role in another learning process best known as *classical conditioning*.

If you are like Phil, thinking of French fries and fudge makes you salivate—a lot! Anita senses her stomach tightening with embarrassment when she remembers falling flat while doing a cartwheel in front of the whole high school. Nancy's jaw muscles tighten when she imagines hearing the dentist's drill. **Classical conditioning** focuses on how we learn *involuntary* emotional or physiological responses such as fear, increased heartbeat, salivation, or sweating. These responses are sometimes called **respondents** because they are automatic responses to stimuli. Through the process of classical conditioning, humans and animals can be trained to react involuntarily to a stimulus that previously had no effect—or a very different effect—on them. The stimulus comes to *elicit*, or bring forth, the response automatically.

Classical conditioning was discovered in the 1920s by Ivan Pavlov, a Russian physiologist trying to determine how long it took a dog to secrete digestive juices after it had been fed. At first, the dogs salivated in the expected manner while they were being fed. Then the dogs began to salivate as soon as they saw the food. Finally, they salivated as soon as they heard the scientist walking toward the lab. The sound of their footsteps *elicited* salivation. Pavlov decided to make a detour from his original experiments and examine these unexpected obstructions to his work.

In one of his first experiments, Pavlov began by sounding a tuning fork and recording a dog's response. As expected, there was no salivation. At this point, the sound of the tuning fork was a **neutral stimulus** because it brought forth no salivation. Then Pavlov fed the dog. The response was salivation. The food was an **unconditioned stimulus** (US) because no prior training or "conditioning" was needed to establish the natural connection between food and salivation. The salivation was an **unconditioned response** (UR), again because it occurred automatically—no conditioning was required.

Using these three elements—the food, the salivation, and the tuning fork—Pavlov demonstrated that a dog could be conditioned to salivate after hearing the tuning fork. He did this by contiguous pairing of the sound with food. At the beginning of the experiment, he sounded the fork and then quickly fed the dog.

contiguity Association of two events because of repeated pairing.

stimulus Event that activates behaviour.

response Observable reaction to a stimulus.

classical conditioning Association of automatic responses with new stimuli.

respondents Responses—generally automatic or involuntary—elicited by specific stimuli.

neutral stimulus Stimulus not connected to a response.

unconditioned stimulus (US) Stimulus that automatically produces an emotional or physiological response.

unconditioned response (UR) Naturally occurring emotional or physiological response.

conditioned stimulus (CS)
Stimulus that evokes an emotional or physiological response after conditioning.

conditioned response (CR)
Learned response to a previously neutral stimulus.

response generalization
Responding in the same way to similar stimuli.

stimulus discrimination
Responding differently to similar, but not identical, stimuli.

extinction Gradual disappearance of a learned response.

After Pavlov repeated this several times, the dog began to salivate after hearing the sound but before receiving the food. Now the sound had become a **conditioned stimulus (CS)** that could bring forth salivation by itself. The response of salivating after the tone was now a **conditioned response (CR)**.

Pavlov's work also identified three other processes in classical conditioning: *response generalization*, *stimulus discrimination*, and *extinction* (Hill, 2002). After the dogs learned to salivate in response to hearing one particular sound, they would also salivate after hearing similar tones that were slightly higher or lower. This process is called **response generalization** because the conditioned response of salivating generalized or occurred in the presence of similar stimuli. Pavlov could also teach the dogs **stimulus discrimination**—that is, responding to one tone but not to others that were similar—by making sure that food always followed only one tone, not any others. **Extinction** occurs when a conditioned stimulus (a particular tone) is presented repeatedly but is not followed by the unconditioned stimulus (food). The conditioned response (salivating) gradually fades away and finally is "extinguished"—it disappears altogether.

If you think Pavlov's model of classical conditioning is just something in the distant past, a contemporary news story described an advertising campaign for products aimed at "Gen Y," people born between 1977 and 1995:

> Mountain Dew executives have their own term for this [advertising strategy]: the Pavlovian connection. By handing out samples of the brand at surfing, skateboard and snowboard tournaments, "There's a Pavlovian connection between the brand and the exhilarating experience," says Dave Burwich, a top marketing executive at Pepsi, which makes Mountain Dew. (Horovitz, 2002, p. B2)

Studies of classical conditioning have implications for teachers as well as marketing executives because many of our emotional reactions may be learned this way. Physicians have a term, "white coat syndrome," that describes people whose blood pressure (an involuntary response) goes up when tested in the doctor's office, usually by someone in a white coat. In another example, Elizabeth's trembling hands when she saw her university supervisor might be traced to previous unpleasant experiences. Perhaps she had been embarrassed during past evaluations of her performance, and now just the thought of being observed elicits a pounding heart and sweaty palms. Remember that emotions and attitudes as well as facts and ideas are learned in classrooms. This emotional learning can sometimes interfere with academic learning. Procedures based on classical conditioning also can be used to help people learn more adaptive emotional responses, as the accompanying Guidelines suggest.

Check Your Knowledge

- How does a neutral stimulus become a conditioned stimulus?
- Compare and contrast response generalization and stimulus discrimination.

Apply to Practice

- After doing not too well on a series of quizzes in a biology course, you feel your heart rate increase when you open your biology textbook to read this week's assignment. Analyze this situation in terms of classical conditioning.

OPERANT CONDITIONING: TRYING NEW RESPONSES

So far, we have concentrated on the automatic conditioning of involuntary responses such as salivation and fear. Clearly, not all human learning is so automatic and unintentional. Most behaviours are voluntarily. People actively "operate" on their environment to produce different kinds of consequences. These deliberate actions are called **operants**. The learning process involved in operant

operants Voluntary (and generally goal-directed) behaviours emitted by a person or an animal.

GUIDELINES

APPLYING CLASSICAL CONDITIONING

Associate positive, pleasant events with learning tasks.

EXAMPLES

1. Emphasize group competition and cooperation over individual competition. Many students have negative emotional responses to individual competition that may generalize to other learning.

2. Make division drills fun by having students decide how to divide refreshments equally and then letting them eat the results.

3. Make voluntary reading appealing by creating a comfortable reading corner with pillows, colourful displays of books, and reading props such as puppets (see Morrow & Weinstein, 1986, for more ideas).

Help students risk anxiety-producing situations voluntarily and successfully.

EXAMPLES

1. Assign a shy student the responsibility of teaching two other students how to distribute materials for map study.

2. Devise small steps toward a larger goal. For example, give ungraded practice tests daily, and then weekly, to students who tend to "freeze" in test situations.

3. If a student is afraid of speaking in front of the class, let the student read a report to a small group while seated, then read it while standing, then give the report from notes instead of reading verbatim. Next, move in stages toward having the student give a report to the whole class.

Help students recognize differences and similarities among situations so that they can discriminate and generalize appropriately.

EXAMPLES

1. Explain that it is appropriate to avoid strangers who offer gifts or rides but safe to accept favours from adults when parents are present.

2. Assure students who are anxious about taking university entrance exams that these tests are like all the other achievement tests they have taken.

behaviour is called **operant conditioning** because we learn to behave in certain ways as we operate on the environment.

Edward L. Thorndike played a major role in developing the theory of operant conditioning. His (1913) early work involved cats that he placed in boxes. To escape the boxes and reach food outside, the cats had to pull out a bolt or perform some other task; they had to operate on their environment. During their frenzied movements after the box was closed, the cats would often accidentally make the correct movement to escape. After several escapes, the cats learned to make the correct response almost immediately. Thorndike thus defined the law of effect: Any act that produces a satisfying effect in a given situation will tend to be repeated in that situation.

The person most well known for developing the theory of operant learning is B. F. Skinner (1953). Skinner began with the belief that the principles of classical conditioning account for only a small portion of learned behaviour. Much human behaviour is operant, not respondent. Classical conditioning describes only how existing behaviour might be paired with new stimuli; it does not explain how new operant behaviour is acquired.

Behaviour, like response or action, is simply a word for what a person does in a particular situation. Conceptually, we may think of behaviour as sandwiched between two sets of environmental influences: those that precede it (its **antecedents**) and those that follow it (its **consequences**) (Skinner, 1950). This relationship can be shown very simply as antecedent–behaviour–consequence, or A–B–C. As behaviour unfolds, a given consequence becomes an antecedent for the next ABC sequence. Research in operant conditioning shows that operant behaviour can be altered by changes in the antecedents, the consequences, or both. Early work focused on consequences, often using rats or pigeons as subjects.

operant conditioning Learning in which voluntary behaviour is strengthened or weakened by consequences or antecedents.

B. F. Skinner's work on operant conditioning changed the way we think about consequences and learning.

antecedents Events that precede an action.

consequences Events that are brought about by an action.

Types of Consequences

According to the behavioural view, consequences determine to a great extent whether a person will repeat the behaviour that led to the consequences. The type and timing of consequences can strengthen or weaken behaviour. We will look first at consequences that strengthen behaviour.

Reinforcement.   While **reinforcement** is commonly understood to mean "reward," this term has a particular meaning in psychology. A **reinforcer** is any consequence that strengthens the behaviour it follows. So, by definition, *reinforced behaviour increases in frequency or duration*. Whenever you see a behaviour persisting or increasing over time, you can assume the consequences of that behaviour are reinforcers for the individual involved. The reinforcement process can be diagrammed as follows:

CONSEQUENCE   EFFECT

Behaviour   →   Reinforcer   →   Strengthened or repeated behaviour

We can be fairly certain that food will be a reinforcer for a hungry animal, but what about people? It may not be clear why an event acts as a reinforcer for an individual, but there are many theories about why reinforcement works. For example, some psychologists suggest that reinforcers satisfy needs, while other psychologists believe that reinforcers reduce tension or stimulate a part of the brain (Rachlin, 1991). Whether the consequences of any action are reinforcing depends on the individual's perception of the event and the meaning it holds for her or him. For example, students who repeatedly get themselves sent to the principal's office for misbehaving may be indicating that something about this consequence is reinforcing for them, even if it doesn't seem rewarding to you. By the way, Skinner did not speculate about why reinforcers increase behaviour. He believed it would undermine the science of behaviour to talk about "imaginary constructs" such as desires, reasons, and dislikes that could not be observed directly. Skinner simply described the tendency for a given operant to increase after certain consequences (Hill, 2002; Skinner, 1953, 1989).

Reinforcers are consequences that strengthen the associated behaviour (Skinner, 1953, 1989). There are two types of reinforcement: positive reinforcement and negative reinforcement. **Positive reinforcement** occurs when the behaviour produces a new stimulus. Examples include a peck on the red key producing food for a pigeon, wearing a new outfit producing many compliments, or checking out your improved muscle tone after a few months in the weight room.

Notice that positive reinforcement can occur even when the behaviour being reinforced (falling out of a chair) is not "positive" from the teacher's point of view. In fact, positive reinforcement of inappropriate behaviour often occurs unintentionally in many classrooms. Teachers inadvertently help maintain problem behaviour by reinforcing it. For example, Elizabeth may have unintentionally reinforced problem behaviour in her class by laughing when the boy answered, "Ronald McDonald." The problem behaviour may have persisted for other reasons, but the consequence of Elizabeth's laughter could have played a role.

When the consequence that strengthens behaviour is the *appearance* (addition) of a new stimulus, the situation is defined as positive reinforcement. In contrast, when the consequence that strengthens behaviour is the *disappearance* (subtraction) of a stimulus, the process is called **negative reinforcement**. If a particular action leads to stopping, avoiding, or escaping an **aversive** situation, the action is likely to be repeated in a similar situation. A common example is the car seat-belt buzzer. As soon as you attach your seat belt, the irritating buzzer stops. You are likely to repeat this action in the future because the behaviour made an aversive stimulus disappear. Consider students who continually "get sick" right before a test and are sent to the nurse's office. The behaviour allows the students to escape aversive situations—tests—so getting "sick" is being maintained, in part, through negative reinforcement. It is negative because the stimulus (the test) disappears; it

reinforcement Use of consequences to strengthen behaviour.

reinforcer Any event that follows behaviour and increases the chances that the behaviour will occur again.

Connect & Extend

TO REAL LIFE

To become aware of the prevalence of reinforcement in daily life, keep a log, noting every time you give or receive reinforcement. Look for positive and negative reinforcement and also record the kind of schedule on which it operates. Another possibility is to note reinforcement and schedules in a field placement classroom or even in university or college classes. What examples of reinforcement are present in your education classes?

positive reinforcement Strengthening behaviour by presenting a desired stimulus after the behaviour.

Connect & Extend

TO REAL LIFE

In some of his last writings, Skinner analyzed his own life in terms of his operant view of learning (Skinner, B. F. [1987]. *Upon further reflection*. Englewood Cliffs, NJ: Prentice Hall). He noted that the older scholar doesn't need frequent reinforcement if he has been reinforced through the years on a schedule that encourages persistence.

negative reinforcement Strengthening behaviour by removing an aversive stimulus.

aversive Irritating or unpleasant.

is reinforcement because the behaviour that caused the stimulus to disappear (getting "sick") increases or repeats. It is also possible that classical conditioning plays a role. The students may have been conditioned to experience unpleasant physiological reactions to tests.

The "negative" in negative reinforcement does not imply that the behaviour being reinforced is necessarily unrewarding. The meaning is closer to the meaning of the negative sign that indicates subtraction in arithmetic. Associate positive and negative reinforcement with adding or subtracting something following a specific behaviour.

Punishment. Negative reinforcement is often confused with punishment. The process of reinforcement (positive or negative) always involves strengthening behaviour. **Punishment**, on the other hand, always involves decreasing or suppressing behaviour. Behaviour followed by a "punisher" is less likely to be repeated in similar situations in the future. Again, it is the effect that defines a consequence as punishment, and different people have different perceptions of what is punishing. One student may find suspension from school punishing, while another student wouldn't mind at all. The process of punishment is diagrammed as follows:

CONSEQUENCE   EFFECT

Behaviour $\rightarrow$ Punisher $\rightarrow$ Weakened or decreased behaviour

Like reinforcement, punishment may take one of two forms. The first type has been called Type I punishment, but this name isn't very informative, so we use the term **presentation punishment**. It occurs when the appearance of a stimulus following the behaviour suppresses or decreases the behaviour. When teachers assign demerits, extra work, running laps, and so on, they are using presentation punishment. The other type of punishment (Type II punishment) we call **removal punishment** because it involves removing a stimulus. When teachers or parents take away privileges after a young person has behaved inappropriately, they are applying removal punishment. With both types, the effect is to decrease the behaviour that led to the punishment. Figure 6.1 summarizes the processes of reinforcement and punishment.

Connect & Extend

TO REAL LIFE
How can the principles of conditioning help explain the difficulty many people experience when they try to stop smoking? Outline a program for reducing or eliminating smoking behaviour.

punishment Process that weakens or suppresses behaviour.

presentation punishment Type of punishment that decreases the chances that a behaviour will occur again by presenting an aversive stimulus following the behaviour; also called Type I punishment.

removal punishment Type of punishment that decreases the chances that a behaviour will occur again by removing a pleasant stimulus following the behaviour; also called Type II punishment.

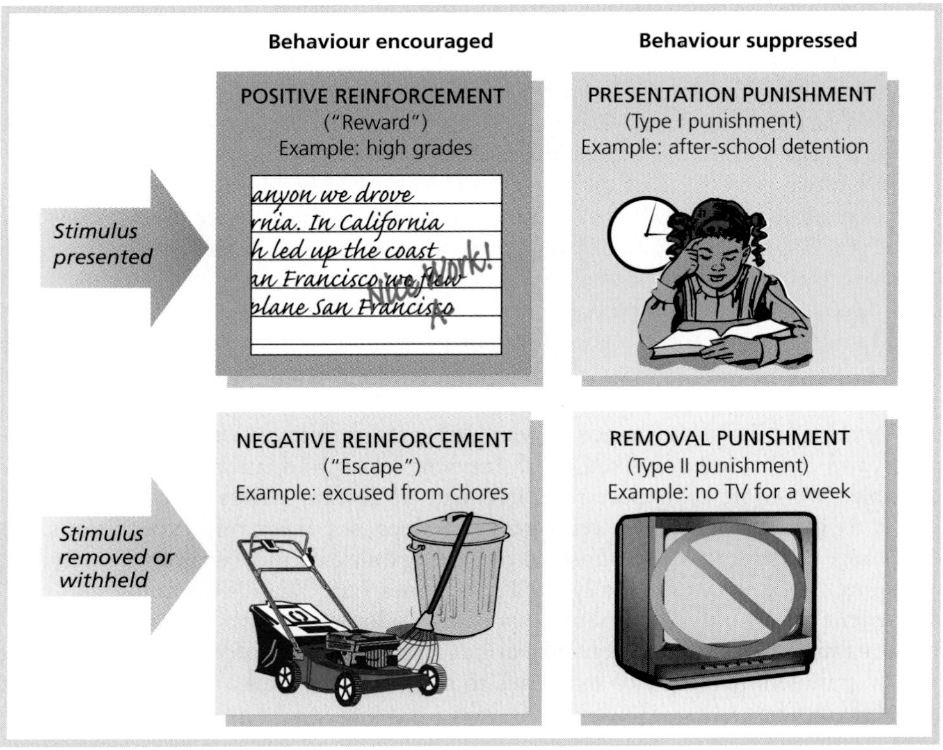

Figure 6.1 Kinds of Reinforcement and Punishment

Negative reinforcement and punishment are often confused. It may help you to remember that reinforcement is always associated with increases in behaviour, while punishment always involves decreasing or suppressing behaviour.

	Behaviour encouraged	**Behaviour suppressed**
Stimulus presented	POSITIVE REINFORCEMENT ("Reward") Example: high grades	PRESENTATION PUNISHMENT (Type I punishment) Example: after-school detention
Stimulus removed or withheld	NEGATIVE REINFORCEMENT ("Escape") Example: excused from chores	REMOVAL PUNISHMENT (Type II punishment) Example: no TV for a week

"HEY, WAIT A MINUTE!
YOU'RE CLEANING ERASERS
AS A PUNISHMENT? I'M
CLEANING ERASERS AS A
REWARD!"
(© 1991 Tony Saltzman)

Connect & Extend

TO YOUR TEACHING
Recall an instance of punishment that you experienced at some time during your life. What were your feelings when you were being punished? List the feelings. (Negative feelings, such as embarrassment, resentment, hurt, and anger, probably will account for 90 percent of the responses.) Does punishment work? What are some other negative effects of punishment? If punishment is ineffective and also produces negative side effects, why do so many teachers rely on it so much?

continuous reinforcement schedule Situation in which a reinforcer is presented after every appropriate response.

intermittent reinforcement schedule Situation in which a reinforcer is presented after some but not all responses.

interval schedule Reinforcement schedule based on a time interval between reinforcers.

ratio schedule Reinforcement schedule based on a number of responses between reinforcers.

Casino slot machines are a good example of the effectiveness of intermittent reinforcement: People "learn" to persist in losing their money on the chance that they will be rewarded with a jackpot.

Reinforcement Schedules

When people are first learning new behaviour, they will learn it faster if they are reinforced for every correct response. This is a **continuous reinforcement schedule**. Then, when the new behaviour has been mastered, they will maintain it best if they are reinforced intermittently rather than every time. An **intermittent reinforcement schedule** seems to help students maintain skills without expecting constant reinforcement.

There are two basic types of intermittent reinforcement schedules. One—called an **interval schedule**—is based on a time interval that passes between reinforcers. The other—a **ratio schedule**—is based on the number of responses learners make between reinforcers. Interval and ratio schedules may be either *fixed* (predictable) or *variable* (unpredictable). Table 6.1 summarizes the five possible reinforcement schedules (the continuous schedule and the four kinds of intermittent schedules).

What are the effects of different reinforcement schedules? Speed of performance depends on control. If reinforcement is based on the number of responses you make, you have more control over the reinforcement: the faster you accumulate the correct number of responses, the faster the reinforcer will come. A teacher who says, "As soon as you complete these 10 problems correctly, you may go to the student lounge," can expect higher rates of performance than a teacher who says, "Work on these 10 problems for the next 20 minutes. Then I will check your papers and those with 10 correct may go to the lounge."

Persistence in performance depends on predictability. Continuous reinforcement and both kinds of fixed reinforcement (ratio and interval) are quite predictable. We come to expect reinforcement at certain points and are generally quick to give up when the reinforcement does not meet our expectations. To encourage persistence of response, variable schedules are most appropriate. In fact, changing the schedule gradually until it becomes very "lean"—meaning that reinforcement occurs only after many responses or a long time interval—results in people learning to work for extended periods without any reinforcement at all. Just watch gamblers playing slot machines to see how powerful a lean reinforcement schedule can be.

TABLE 6.1 Reinforcement Schedules

Schedule	Definition	Example	Response Pattern	Reaction When Reinforcement Stops
Continuous	Reinforcement after every response	Turning on the television	Rapid learning of response	Very little persistence; rapid disappearance of response
Fixed-interval	Reinforcement after a set period of time	Weekly quiz	Response rate increases as time for reinforcement approaches, then drops after reinforcement	Little persistence; rapid drop in response rate when time for reinforcement passes and no reinforcer appears
Variable-interval	Reinforcement after varying lengths of time	Pop quizzes	Slow, steady rate of responding; very little pause after reinforcement	Greater persistence; slow decline in response rate
Fixed-ratio	Reinforcement after a set number of responses	Piece work Bake sale	Rapid response rate; pause after reinforcement	Little persistence; rapid drop in response rate when expected number of responses are given and no reinforcer appears
Variable-ratio	Reinforcement after a varying number of responses	Slot machines	Very high response rate; little pause after reinforcement	Greatest persistence; response rate stays high and gradually drops off

Reinforcement schedules influence how persistently we will respond when reinforcement is withheld. What happens when reinforcement is completely withdrawn?

Extinction.   In classical conditioning, we saw that the conditioned response was extinguished (disappeared) when the conditioned stimulus appeared but the unconditioned stimulus did not follow (tone, but no food). In operant conditioning, a person or an animal will not persist in certain behaviour if the usual reinforcer is withheld. The behaviour will eventually be extinguished (stop). For example, if you go for a week without selling even one magazine door to door, you may give up. Removal of reinforcement altogether leads to extinction. The process may take a while, however, as you know if you have tried to extinguish a child's tantrums by withholding your attention. Often the child wins—you give up ignoring and, instead of extinction, intermittent reinforcement occurs. This, of course, may encourage even more persistent tantrums in the future.

Antecedents and Behaviour Change

In operant conditioning, antecedents—the events preceding behaviour—provide information about which behaviour will lead to positive consequences and which to negative. Skinner's pigeons learned to peck for food when a light was on but not to bother when the light was off because no food followed pecking when the light was off. In other words, they learned to use the antecedent light as a cue to discriminate the likely consequence of pecking. The pigeons' pecking was under **stimulus control**, controlled by the discriminative stimulus of the light. You can see that this idea is related to discrimination in classical conditioning, but here we are talking about voluntary behaviour such as pecking, not reflexes such as salivating.

Connect & Extend

TO REAL LIFE
Positive reinforcement: Praise for good grades, bonus points on tests, a class pizza party when everyone makes above 85 on the weekly spelling test. *Negative reinforcement:* Removing a stone from your shoe; calling on a child who is madly waving his hand and shouting, "I know, I know!" (your behaviour is negatively reinforced because the noise stops); on trips, wearing a certain pair of shoes to avoid aching feet; saying "I'm really sorry" to your spouse to avoid his or her anger. *Presentation punishment:* Running extra laps; reprimands; bad grades; corporal punishment. *Removal punishment:* Fines; being grounded; missing recess; not being allowed to go on a field trip; getting fired.

stimulus control Capacity for the presence or absence of antecedents to regulate behaviour.

Connect & Extend

TO REAL LIFE

Examples of stimulus control: Anita more than once turned into her old office parking lot after her department moved across town. The old cues kept her heading automatically to the old office. Consider the supposedly true story of a getaway driver in a bank robbery who sped through town, only to be caught when she stopped at a red light. The stimulus of light exerted automatic control.

cueing Providing a stimulus that "sets up" desired behaviour.

Connect & Extend

TO YOUR TEACHING

Here are a few other examples of antecedents serving as cues about what behaviour will be rewarded in a particular situation:

Teacher giving lecture: Taking notes will be rewarded; reading a magazine will not.

Substitute teacher: Rule breaking may not be punished in this situation.

Desks in a circle: Discussion will be rewarded.

prompt A reminder that follows a cue to make sure the person reacts to the cue.

We all learn to discriminate—to "read" situations. When should you ask to borrow your roommate's car—after a major disagreement or after you both have had a great time at a hockey game? The antecedent cue of a school principal standing in the hall helps students discriminate the probable consequences of running or attempting to break into a locker. We often respond to such antecedent cues without fully realizing they are influencing our behaviour. But teachers can use cues deliberately in the classroom.

Cueing.   By definition, **cueing** is the act of providing an antecedent stimulus just before you want a particular behaviour to take place. Cueing is particularly useful in setting the stage for behaviour that must occur at a specific time but is easily forgotten. In working with young people, teachers often find themselves correcting behaviour after the fact. For example, they may ask students, "When are you going to start remembering to ...?" Such reminders often lead to irritation. The mistake is already made, and the young person is left with only two choices, to promise to try harder or to say, "Why don't you leave me alone?" Neither response is very satisfying. Presenting a non-judgmental cue before this happens can help prevent these negative confrontations. When a student performs the appropriate behaviour after a cue, the teacher can reinforce the student's accomplishment instead of punishing the student's failure.

Prompting.   Sometimes students need help in learning to respond to a cue in an appropriate way so that the cue becomes a discriminative stimulus. One approach is to provide an additional cue, called a **prompt**, following the first cue. There are two principles for using a cue and a prompt to teach new behaviour (Becker, Engelmann, & Thomas, 1975). First, make sure the environmental stimulus that you want to become a cue occurs immediately before the prompt you are using, so that students will learn to respond to the cue and not rely only on the prompt. Second, gradually use the prompt less and less—fade it—so that students do not become dependent on it.

An example of cueing and prompting is providing students with a checklist or reminder sheet. Figure 6.2 is a checklist for the steps in peer tutoring. Working in pairs is the cue; the checklist is the prompt. As students learn the procedures, the teacher may stop using the checklist, but may remind the students of the steps. When no written or oral prompts are necessary, the students have learned to respond appropriately to the environmental cue of working in pairs—they have learned how to behave in tutoring situations. But the teacher should continue to monitor the process, recognize and reinforce good work, and correct mistakes. Before a tutoring session, the teacher might ask students to close their eyes and "see" the checklist, focusing on each step. As students work, the teacher could listen to their interactions and continue to coach students as they improve their tutoring skills.

Check Your Knowledge

- What defines a consequence as a reinforcer? As a punisher?
- How are negative reinforcement and punishment different?
- How can you encourage persistence in behaviour?
- What is the difference between a prompt and a cue?

Apply to Practice

- How might you use reinforcement and punishment to improve the situation described at the beginning of the chapter?
- In what kinds of situations is cueing helpful?

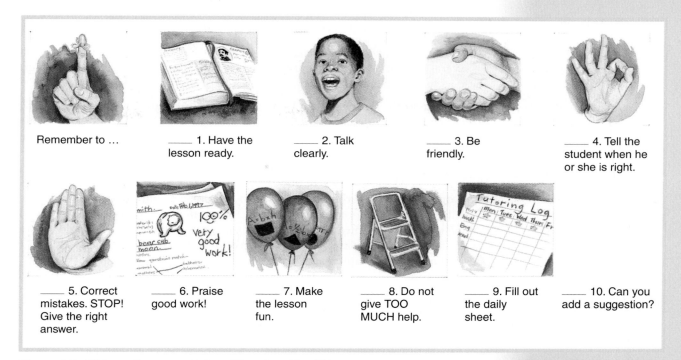

Figure 6.2 Written Prompts: A Peer-Tutoring Checklist

This checklist reminds students how to be effective tutors. As they become more proficient, the checklist may be less necessary.

Source: From Sulzer-Azaroff, B., & Mayer, G. R. (1994). *Achieving educational excellence: Behavior analysis for school personnel* (Figure, p. 89). San Marcos, CA: Western Image. Copyright © 1994 by Beth Sulzer-Azaroff and G. Roy Mayer. Reprinted by permission of the authors.

APPLIED BEHAVIOUR ANALYSIS

Applied behaviour analysis is the application of behavioural learning principles to change behaviour. The method is sometimes called **behaviour modification**, but this term has negative connotations for many people and is often misunderstood (Alberto & Troutman, 2003; Kaplan, 1991; Kazdin, 2001).

Ideally, applied behaviour analysis requires clear specification of the behaviour to be changed, careful recording of the behaviour, analysis of the antecedents and reinforcers that might be maintaining inappropriate or undesirable behaviour, interventions based on behavioural principles to change the behaviour, and careful measurement of changes. In research on applied behaviour analysis, a method or design called ABAB is common. That is, researchers take a baseline measurement of the behaviour (A), then apply the intervention (B), then stop the intervention to see if the behaviour goes back to the baseline level (A), and then reintroduce the intervention (B). If the behaviour during the B phases differs from the behaviour during the A phases, the consequences are effective.

In classrooms, teachers usually cannot follow all the ABAB steps, but they can do the following:

1. Clearly specify the behaviour to be changed and note the current level. For example, if a student is "careless," does this mean 2, 3, 4, or more computation errors for every 10 problems?

2. Plan a specific intervention using antecedents, consequences, or both. For example, offer the student one extra minute of computer time for every problem completed with no errors.

3. Keep track of the results, and modify the plan if necessary.

Let's consider some specific methods for accomplishing step 2—the intervention.

applied behaviour analysis Applying behavioural learning principles to understand and change behaviour.

behaviour modification Systematic application of antecedents and consequences to change behaviour.

Connect & Extend

TO YOUR TEACHING
Suggest the cues or prompts you would use to elicit the following behaviour: (1) the class looks at you to hear your directions; (2) the students open their books to the assigned page when the bell rings; (3) the students give you their full attention when you are making an important point; and (4) a student walks instead of runs to the door when the dismissal bell rings.

Connect & Extend

TO YOUR TEACHING

Mr. Stevens is a grade 2 teacher. He has been teaching for only a few weeks and is having problems. He has a class of 25 overeager children who consistently blurt and yell out their answers instead of waiting and raising their hands. He finds it difficult to respond to each student. He is pleased with their eagerness but needs a calmer setting. What would you do if you were Mr. Stevens?

Connect & Extend

TO THE RESEARCH

For an up-to-date look at applied behaviour analysis, see Kazdin, A. E. (2001). *Behavior modification in applied settings* (6th ed.). Belmont, CA: Wadsworth; and Alberto, P. A., & Troutman, A. C. (2003). *Applied behavior analysis for teachers* (6th ed.). Saddle River, NJ: Prentice Hall.

Connect & Extend

TO YOUR TEACHING

When a teacher decides to begin ignoring behaviour that he or she wants to extinguish, the behaviour frequently increases for a short time before it decreases. How do you explain this phenomenon?

Premack principle Principle stating that a more-preferred activity can serve as reinforcer for a less-preferred activity.

As we discussed earlier, to increase a particular behaviour, we reinforce it. There are several specific ways to encourage existing behaviour or teach new behaviour. These include praise, the Premack principle, shaping, and positive practice.

Reinforcing with Teacher Attention. Many psychologists advise teachers to "accentuate the positive"—liberally praise students for good behaviour while ignoring mistakes and misbehaviour. In fact, some researchers believe that "the systematic application of praise and attention may be the most powerful motivational and classroom management tool available to teachers" (Alber & Heward, 1997, p. 277; Alber & Heward, 2000). A related strategy is *differential reinforcement*, or ignoring inappropriate behaviours, while being sure to reinforce appropriate behaviours as soon as they occur. For example, if a student is prone to making irrelevant comments ("When is the game this Friday?"), you should ignore the off-task comment, but recognize a task-related contribution as soon as it occurs (Landrum & Kauffman, 2006).

This praise-and-ignore approach can be helpful, but we should not expect it to solve all classroom management problems. Several studies have shown that disruptive behaviour persists when teachers use positive consequences (mostly praise) as their only classroom management strategy (McGoey & DuPaul, 2000; Pfiffner & O'Leary, 1987; Sullivan & O'Leary, 199 Sullivan & O'Leary, 1990). Also, if peer attention is maintaining the problem behaviours, the teacher's ignoring them won't help much.

There is a second consideration in using praise. The positive results found in research occur when teachers *carefully* and *systematically* praise their students (Landrum & Kauffman, 2006). Unfortunately, praise is not always given appropriately and effectively. Merely "handing out compliments" will not improve behaviour. To be effective, praise must (1) be contingent on (immediately follow) the behaviour to be reinforced, (2) specify clearly the behaviour being reinforced, and (3) be believable (O'Leary & O'Leary, 1977). In other words, the praise should be sincere recognition of well-defined behaviour so that students understand what they did to warrant the recognition. Teachers who have not received special training often violate these conditions (Brophy, 1981). Ideas for using praise effectively, based on Brophy's extensive review of the subject, are presented in the accompanying Guidelines.

Some psychologists have suggested that teachers' use of praise tends to focus students on learning to win approval rather than on learning for its own sake. Perhaps the best advice is to be aware of the potential dangers of the overuse or misuse of praise and to navigate accordingly.

Selecting Reinforcers: The Premack Principle. In most classrooms, there are many readily available reinforcers other than teacher attention, such as the chance to talk to other students or feed the class animals. But teachers tend to offer these opportunities in a haphazard way. By making privileges and rewards directly contingent on learning and positive behaviour—just as with praise—the teacher may greatly increase both learning and desired behaviour.

A helpful guide for choosing the most effective reinforcers is the Premack principle, named for David Premack (1965). According to the **Premack principle**, high-frequency behaviour (a preferred activity) can be an effective reinforcer for low-frequency behaviour (a less-preferred activity). This is sometimes referred to as "Grandma's rule": First do what I want you to do, then you may do what you want to do. Elizabeth Chan used this principle in her class when she told students they could work together on their news program after they had quietly completed the first section of the worksheet on their own.

If students didn't have to study, what would they do? The answers to this question may suggest many possible reinforcers. For most students, talking, moving around the room, sitting near a friend, being exempt from assignments or tests,

USING PRAISE APPROPRIATELY

Be clear and systematic in giving praise.

EXAMPLES

1. Make sure that praise is tied directly to appropriate behaviour.
2. Make sure that the student understands the specific action or accomplishment that is being praised. Say, "You returned this poster on time and in good condition," not, "You were very responsible."

Recognize genuine accomplishments.

EXAMPLES

1. Reward the attainment of specified goals, not just participation.
2. Do not reward uninvolved students just for being quiet and not disrupting the class.
3. Tie praise to students' improving competence or to the value of their accomplishment. Say, "I noticed that you double-checked all your problems. Your score reflects your careful work."

Set standards for praise based on individual abilities and limitations.

EXAMPLES

1. Praise progress or accomplishment in relation to the individual student's past efforts.

2. Focus the student's attention on his or her own progress, not on comparisons with others.

Attribute the student's success to effort and ability so that the student will gain confidence that success is possible again.

EXAMPLES

1. Don't imply that the success may be based on luck, extra help, or easy material.
2. Ask students to describe the problems they encountered and ways in which they solved them.

Make praise really reinforcing.

EXAMPLES

1. Don't attempt to influence the rest of the class by singling out some students for praise. This tactic frequently backfires, since students know what's really going on. In addition, you risk embarrassing the student you have chosen to praise.
2. Don't give undeserved praise to students simply to balance failures. It is seldom consoling and calls attention to the student's inability to earn genuine recognition.

reading magazines, using the computer, or playing games are preferred activities. The best way to determine appropriate reinforcers for your students may be to watch what they do in their free time.

For the Premack principle to be effective, the low-frequency (less-preferred) behaviour must happen first. In the following dialogue, notice how the teacher loses a perfect opportunity to use the Premack principle:

Students: Oh, no! Do we have to work on grammar again today? The other classes got to discuss the film we saw in the auditorium this morning.

Teacher: But the other classes finished the lesson on sentences yesterday. We're almost finished too. If we don't finish the lesson, I'm afraid you'll forget the rules we reviewed yesterday.

Students: Why don't we finish the sentences at the end of the period and talk about the film now?

Teacher: Okay, if you promise to complete the sentences later.

Discussing the film could have served as a reinforcer for completing the lesson. As it is, the class may well spend the entire period discussing the film. Just as the discussion becomes fascinating, the teacher will have to end it and insist that the class return to the grammar lesson.

Remember, what works for one student may not be right for another. And students can get "too much of a good thing"—reinforcers can lose their potency if they are overused.

Shaping. What happens when students cannot gain reinforcement because they simply cannot perform a skill in the first place? Consider these examples:

- A grade 4 student looks at the results of the latest mathematics test. "No credit on almost half of the problems again because I made one dumb mistake in each problem. I hate math!"
- A grade 10 student tries each day to find some excuse for avoiding the softball game in gym class. The student cannot catch a ball and now refuses to try.

In both situations, the students are receiving no reinforcement for their work because the end product of their efforts is not good enough. A safe prediction is that the students will soon learn to dislike the class, the subject, and perhaps the teacher and school in general. One way to prevent this problem is the strategy of **shaping**, also called **successive approximations**. Shaping involves reinforcing progress instead of waiting for perfection.

In order to use shaping, the teacher must break down the final complex behaviour the student is expected to master into a number of small steps. One approach identifying the small steps is **task analysis**, originally developed by R. B. Miller (1962) to help the armed services train personnel. Miller's system begins with a definition of the final performance requirement, what the trainee (or student) must be able to do at the end of the program or unit. Then the steps that will lead to the final goal are specified. The procedure simply breaks down skills and processes into sub-skills and sub-processes.

Consider an example of task analysis in which students must write a position paper based on library research. If the teacher assigned the position paper without analyzing the task in this way, what could happen? Some of the students might not know how to do computer searching. They might search through one or two encyclopedias, then write a summary of the issues based only on the encyclopedia articles. Other students might know how to use computers, tables of contents, and indexes but might have difficulty reaching conclusions. They might hand in lengthy papers listing summaries of different ideas. Still others might be able to draw conclusions, but their written presentations might be so confusing and grammatically incorrect that the teacher could not understand what they were trying to say. Each of the groups would have failed in fulfilling the assignment, but for different reasons.

A task analysis gives a picture of the logical sequence of steps leading toward the final goal. An awareness of this sequence can help teachers make sure that students have the necessary skills before they move to the next step. In addition, when students have difficulty, the teacher can pinpoint problem areas.

Krumboltz and Krumboltz (1972) have described the following three methods of shaping: (1) reinforce each sub-skill, (2) reinforce improvements in accuracy, and (3) reinforce longer and longer periods of performance or participation.

Many behaviours can be improved through shaping, especially skills that require persistence, endurance, increased accuracy, greater speed, or extensive practice to master. Because shaping is a time-consuming process, however, it should not be used if success can be attained through simpler methods such as cueing.

Positive Practice. In **positive practice**, students replace one behaviour with another. This approach is especially appropriate for dealing with academic errors. When students make a mistake, they must correct it as soon as possible and practise the correct response (Gibbs & Luyben, 1985; Kazdin, 1984). The same principle can be applied when a student breaks classroom rules. Instead of being punished, the student might be required to practise the correct alternative action.

The following Guidelines summarize the approaches to encouraging positive behaviour.

shaping Reinforcing each small step of progress toward a desired goal or behaviour.

successive approximations Small components that make up complex behaviour.

task analysis System for breaking down a task hierarchically into basic skills and sub-skills.

positive practice Practising correct responses immediately after errors.

ENCOURAGING POSITIVE BEHAVIOURS

Make sure you recognize positive behaviour in ways that students value.

EXAMPLES

1. When presenting class rules, set up positive consequences for following rules as well as negative consequences for breaking rules.
2. Recognize honest admissions of mistakes by giving a second chance: "Because you admitted that you copied your paper from a book, I'm giving you a chance to rewrite it."
3. Offer desired rewards for academic efforts, such as extra recess time, exemptions from homework or tests, or extra credit on major projects.

When students are tackling new material or trying new skills, give plenty of reinforcement.

EXAMPLES

1. Find and comment on something right in every student's first life drawing.
2. Reinforce students for encouraging each other. "French pronunciation is difficult and awkward at first. Let's help each other by eliminating all giggles when someone is brave enough to attempt a new word."

After new behaviours are established, give reinforcement on an unpredictable schedule to encourage persistence.

EXAMPLES

1. Offer surprise rewards for good participation in class.
2. Start classes with a short, written extra-credit question. Students don't have to answer, but a good answer will add points to their total for the semester.
3. Make sure the good students get compliments for their work from time to time. Don't take them for granted.

Use the Premack principle to identify effective reinforcers.

EXAMPLES

1. Watch what students do with their free time.
2. Notice which students like to work together. The chance to work with friends is often a good reinforcer.

Use cueing to help establish new behaviours.

EXAMPLES

1. Put up humorous signs in the classroom to remind students of rules.
2. At the beginning of the year, as students enter class, call their attention to a list on the board of the materials they should have with them when they come to class.

Make sure that all students, even those who often cause problems, receive some praise, privileges, or other rewards when they do something well.

EXAMPLES

1. Review your class list occasionally to make sure all students are receiving some reinforcement.
2. Set standards for reinforcement so that all students will have a chance to be rewarded.
3. Check your biases. Are boys getting more opportunities for reinforcement than girls, or vice versa? How about students of different races?

Establish a variety of reinforcers.

EXAMPLES

1. Let students suggest their own reinforcers or choose from a "menu" of reinforcers with "weekly specials."
2. Talk to other teachers or parents about ideas for reinforcers.

Coping with Undesirable Behaviour

No matter how successful you are at accentuating the positive, there are times when you must cope with undesirable behaviour, either because other methods fail or because the behaviour itself is dangerous or calls for direct action. For this purpose, negative reinforcement, satiation, reprimands, and punishment all offer possible solutions.

Connect & Extend

TO THE CLASSROOM

Examples of negative reinforcement: A grade 10 teacher tells her class that those students who turn in sloppy, careless work will have to use their free-choice time to redo it. A grade 1 teacher tells an angry boy that he must sit by the tree until he feels able to rejoin the kickball game without arguing.

Connect & Extend

TO THE CLASSROOM

Satiation: A grade 6 teacher discovered one of his students making paper airplanes during an independent work time. He gave that student a stack of paper and told her to continue making airplanes until the stack of paper was gone. The student thought it was great fun for the first 10 minutes, but then she got weary and wanted to stop. After this experience, the student made better use of her independent work times.

satiation Requiring a person to repeat problem behaviour past the point of interest or motivation.

Negative Reinforcement.   Recall the basic principle of negative reinforcement: If an action stops or avoids something unpleasant, the action is likely to occur again in similar situations. Negative reinforcement was operating in Elizabeth Chan's classroom. When she gave in to the moans and complaints of her class and cancelled the test, her behaviour was being negatively reinforced. She escaped the unpleasant student comments by changing her assignment, but students may have learned to complain more in the future through negative reinforcement.

Negative reinforcement may also be used to enhance learning. To do this, you place students in mildly unpleasant situations so that they can "escape" when their behaviour improves. Consider these examples:

- *Teacher to a grade 3 class:* "When the supplies are put back in the cabinet and each of you is sitting quietly, we will go outside. Until then, we will miss our recess."
- *High school teacher to a student who seldom finishes in-class assignments:* "As soon as you complete the assignment, you may join the class in the auditorium. But until you finish, you must work in the study hall."

Actually, a strict behaviourist might object to predicting that these situations will become examples of negative reinforcement because too much student thinking and understanding is required to make them work. Teachers cannot treat students like lab animals, delivering a mild shock to their feet until they give a right answer, then turning off the shock briefly. But teachers can make sure that unpleasant situations improve when student behaviour improves.

You may wonder why these examples are not considered punishment. Surely staying in during recess or not accompanying the class to a special program is punishing. But the focus in each case is on strengthening specific behaviour (putting away supplies or finishing in-class assignments). The teacher strengthens (reinforces) the behaviour by removing something aversive *as soon as the desired behaviour occurs.* Because the consequence involves removing or "subtracting" a stimulus, the reinforcement is negative.

Negative reinforcement also gives students a chance to exercise control. Missing recess and staying behind in study hall are unpleasant situations, but in each case the students retain control. As soon as students perform the appropriate behaviour, the unpleasant situation ends. In contrast, punishment occurs after the fact, and a student cannot so easily control or terminate it.

There are several rules for negative reinforcement: Describe the desired change in a positive way. Don't bluff. Make sure you can enforce your unpleasant situation. Follow through despite complaints. Insist on action, not promises. If the unpleasant situation terminates when students promise to be better next time, you have reinforced making promises, not making changes (Alberto & Troutman, 2006; O'Leary, 1995).

Satiation.   Another way to stop problem behaviour is to insist that students continue the behaviour until they are tired of doing it. This procedure, called **satiation**, should be applied with care. Forcing students to continue some behaviour may be physically or emotionally harmful or even dangerous.

An example of an appropriate use of satiation is related by Krumboltz and Krumboltz (1972). In the middle of a grade 9 algebra class, the teacher suddenly noticed four students making all sorts of unusual motions. In response to persistent teacher questioning, the students finally admitted they were bouncing imaginary balls. The teacher pretended to greet this idea with enthusiasm and suggested the whole class do it. At first, there was a great deal of laughing and joking. After a minute this stopped, and one student even quit. The teacher, however, insisted that all the students continue. After five minutes and a number of exhausted sighs, the teacher allowed the students to stop. No one bounced an imaginary ball in that class again.

Teachers also may allow students to continue some action until they stop by themselves, if the behaviour is not interfering with the rest of the class. A teacher can do this by simply ignoring the behaviour. Remember that just responding to an ignorable behaviour may actually reinforce it.

In using satiation, a teacher must take care not to give in before the students do. It is also important that the repeated behaviour be the one you are trying to end. If the algebra teacher had insisted that the students write, "I will never bounce imaginary balls in class again" 500 times, the students would have become satiated with writing rather than with bouncing balls.

Reprimands. In the *Junction Journal*, Anita's daughter's elementary-school newspaper, the following lines appeared in a story called "Why I Like School," written by a grade 4 student: "I also like my teacher. She helps me understand and learn. She is nice to everyone.... I like it when she gets mad at somebody, but she doesn't yell at them in front of the class, but speaks to them privately."

Soft, calm, private **reprimands** are more effective than loud, public reprimands in decreasing disruptive behaviour (Landrum & Kauffman, 2006). Research has shown that when reprimands are loud enough for the entire class to hear, disruptions increase or continue at a constant level. Some students enjoy public recognition for misbehaviour, or they don't want classmates to see them "lose" to the teacher. Some students enjoy public recognition for misbehaviour. If reprimands are not used too often, and if the classroom is generally a positive, warm environment, students usually respond quickly (Kaplan, 1991; Van Houten & Doleys, 1983).

Response Cost. The concept of **response cost** is familiar to anyone who has ever paid a fine. For certain infractions of the rules, people must lose some reinforcer (money, time, privileges, pleasures). In a class, the concept of response cost may be applied in a number of ways. The first time a student breaks a class rule, the teacher gives a warning. The second time, the teacher makes a mark beside the student's name in the grade book. The student loses two minutes of recess for each mark accumulated. For older students, a certain number of marks might mean losing the privilege of working in a group or going on a class trip.

Social Isolation. One of the most controversial behavioural methods for decreasing undesirable behaviour is the strategy of **social isolation**, often called **time out** from reinforcement. The process involves removing a highly disruptive student from the classroom for 5 to 10 minutes. The student is placed in an empty, uninteresting room alone—the punishment of brief isolation from other people. A trip to the principal's office or confinement to a chair in the corner of the regular classroom does not have the same effect as sitting alone in an otherwise empty room.

Some Cautions. Punishment in and of itself does not lead to any positive behaviour. Harsh punishment communicates to students that "might makes right" and may encourage retaliation (Alberto & Troutman, 2006; Walker et al., 2004). Thus, whenever you consider the use of punishment, you should make it part of a two-pronged attack. The first goal is to carry out the punishment and suppress the undesirable behaviour. The second goal is to make clear what the student should be doing instead and to provide reinforcement for those desirable actions. Thus, while the problem behaviour is being suppressed, positive alternative responses are being strengthened. The Guidelines on page 218 give ideas for using punishment for positive purposes.

Connect & Extend

TO THE CLASSROOM
Soft reprimands: During reading in her grade 1 class, Ms. Chandler noticed that Kenny wasn't concentrating on his book. Ms. Chandler was working with a group at the time and could have called out, "Kenny, you'd better get back to work. You're not concentrating," but she decided that this would embarrass him as well as disturb the concentration of others. Instead, she walked over to him, asked him a couple of questions about the story, and asked him to let her know how the story ended. She achieved her goal without causing embarrassment, and she provided Kenny with an impetus and motive to concentrate on his story again.

reprimands Criticisms for misbehaviour; rebukes.

response cost Punishment by loss of reinforcers.

social isolation Removal of a disruptive student for 5 to 10 minutes.

time out Technically, the removal of all reinforcement; in practice, isolation of a student from the rest of the class for a brief time.

Connect & Extend

TO THE CLASSROOM
What are some forms of punishment used in public schools? In the long run, does the punishment decrease or extinguish the behaviour for which it is given? Think of times when punishment (according to the teacher's view) is experienced by the student as reinforcement.

USING PUNISHMENT

Try to structure the situation so that you can use negative reinforcement rather than punishment.

EXAMPLES

1. Allow students to escape unpleasant situations (completing additional workbook assignments, weekly test of math facts) when they reach a level of competence.

2. Insist on actions, not promises. Don't let students convince you to change terms of the agreement.

Be consistent in your application of punishment.

EXAMPLES

1. Avoid inadvertently reinforcing the behaviour you are trying to punish. Keep confrontations private, so that students don't become heroes for standing up to the teacher in a public showdown.

2. Let students know in advance the consequences of breaking the rules by posting major class rules for younger students or outlining rules and consequences in a course syllabus for older students.

3. Tell students that they will receive only one warning before punishment is given. Give the warning in a calm way, then follow through.

4. Make punishment as unavoidable and immediate as is reasonably possible.

Focus on the students' actions, not on the students' personal qualities.

EXAMPLES

1. Reprimand in a calm but firm voice.

2. Avoid vindictive or sarcastic words or tones of voice. You might hear your own angry words later when students imitate your sarcasm.

3. Stress the need to end the problem behaviour instead of expressing any dislike you might feel for the student.

4. Be aware that minority students and students of colour are disproportionately punished, sent to detention, and expelled from school—are your policies fair?

Adapt the punishment to the infraction.

EXAMPLES

1. Ignore minor misbehaviours that do not disrupt the class, or stop these misbehaviours with a disapproving glance or a move toward the student.

2. Make sure the punishment fits the crime—don't take away all the free time a student has earned for one infraction of the rules, for example (Landrum & Kauffman, 2006).

3. Don't use homework as a punishment for misbehaviours such as talking in class.

4. When a student misbehaves to gain peer acceptance, removal from the group of friends can be effective, since this is really time out from a reinforcing situation.

5. If the problem behaviours continue, analyze the situation and try a new approach. Your punishment may not be very punishing, or you may be inadvertently reinforcing the misbehaviour.

Functional Behavioural Assessment and Positive Behaviour Support

Teachers in both regular and special education classes have had success with a new approach that begins by asking, "What are students getting out of their problem behaviours—what functions do these behaviours serve?" The focus is on the *why* of the behaviour, not on the *what* (Lane, Falk, & Wehby, 2006). The reasons for problem behaviours generally fall into four categories (Barnhill, 2005; Maag & Kemp, 2003). Students act out to

1. receive attention from others—teachers, parent, or peers.

2. escape from some unpleasant situation—an academic or social demand.

3. get a desired item or activity.

4. meet sensory needs, such as stimulation from rocking or flapping arms for some children with autism.

If the reason for the behaviour is known, the teacher can devise ways of supporting positive behaviours that will serve the same "why" function. For example, Anita once worked with a middle-school principal who was concerned about a boy who had lost his father a few years earlier and was having trouble in a number of subjects, especially math. The student disrupted math class at least twice a week and ended up in the principal's office. When he arrived, the boy got the principal's undivided attention. After a scolding, they talked about sports because the principal liked the student and was concerned that he had no male role models. It is easy to spot the function of the classroom disruptions—they always led to (1) escape from math class (negative reinforcement) and (2) one-on-one time with the principal (positive reinforcement after a little bit of reprimanding). The principal, teacher, and Anita developed a way to support the student's positive behaviours in math by getting him some extra tutoring and by giving him time with the principal when he completed math problems instead of when he acted up in class. The new positive behaviours served many of the same functions as the old problem behaviours.

Positive Behavioural Supports.   There is in today's schools widespread acclaim for positive behavioural supports (PBS) for students with disabilities and those at-risk for special education placement. **Positive behavioural supports (PBS)** are interventions designed to replace problem behaviours with new actions that serve the same purpose for the student. The process of understanding the problem behaviour is known as a **functional behavioural assessment (FBA)**—"a collection of methods or procedures used to obtain information about antecedents, behaviors, and consequences to determine the reason or function of the behavior" (Barnhill, 2005, p. 132). With information from this assessment, teachers can develop an intervention package, as we did above with the math student.

Positive behaviour supports based on functional behavioural assessments can help students with disabilities succeed in inclusion classrooms. For example, the disruptive behaviour of a five-year-old boy with developmental disabilities was nearly eliminated in a relatively short time through a PBS intervention that was based on a functional assessment conducted by the regular teaching staff and the special education teacher. The intervention included making sure tasks assigned were at the right difficulty level, providing assistance with these tasks, teaching the student how to request assistance, and teaching the student how to request a break from assigned work (Soodak & McCarthy, 2006; Umbreit, 1995). But these approaches are not only for students with special needs. Research shows that disciplinary referrals decrease when the whole school uses these approaches for all students (Lewis, Sugai, & Colvin, 1998). Because about 5 percent of students account for half of the discipline referrals, it makes sense to develop interventions for those students. Positive behaviour interventions based on functional assessments can reduce these behaviour problems by 80 percent (Crone & Horner, 2003).

Doing Functional Behavioural Assessments.   Many different procedures might help you determine the functions of a behaviour. You can simply interview students about their behaviours. In one study, students were asked to describe what they did that got them in trouble in school, what happened just before, and what happened right after they acted out. Even though the students were not always sure why they acted out, they seemed to benefit from talking to a concerned adult who was trying to understand their situation, not just reprimand them (Murdock, O'Neill, & Cunningham, 2005). Teachers can also observe students with these questions in mind: When and where does the problem behaviour occur? What people or activities are involved? What happens right before—what do others do or say and what did the target student do or say? What happens right after the behaviour—what did you, other students, or the target student do or say? What does the target student gain or escape from—what changes after the student acts out? A more structured approach is shown in Figure 6.3 on the next page—an observation and planning worksheet for functional behavioural assessment.

positive behavioural supports (PBS) Interventions designed to replace problem behaviours with new actions that serve the same purpose for the student.

functional behavioural assessment (FBA) Procedures used to obtain information about antecedents, behaviours, and consequences to determine the reason or function of the behaviour.

Student Name: _____ **Date:** _____

Target behaviour: Operationally define the behaviour that most interferes with the student's functioning in the classroom. Include intensity (high, medium, or low), frequency, and duration.
_____
_____

When, where, with whom, and in what condition is the target behaviour *least* likely to occur?
_____

Setting Events or Context Variables (i.e., hunger, lack of sleep, medications, problems on bus):
_____

Immediate Antecedents & Consequences

Antecedents	*Problematic Settings*	*Consequences*
____ Demand/Request	____ Unstructured setting	____ behaviour ignored
____ Difficult task	____ Unstructured activity	____ Reprimanded
____ Time of day	____ Individual seat work	____ Verbal redirection
____ Interruption in routine	____ Group work	____ Time-out (duration: ____)
____ Peer tease/provoked	____ Specials	____ Loss of incentives
____ No materials/activities	____ Specific subject/task	____ Physical redirection
____ Could not get desired item	____ Crowded setting	____ Physical restraint
____ People _____	____ Noisy setting	____ Sent to office
____ Alone	____ Other _____	____ Suspension
____ Other _____	____ Other _____	____ Other _____

What function(s) does the target behaviour seem to serve for the student?

____ Escape from: ____ demand/request   ____ person   ____ activity/task   ____ school   ____ other _____

____ Attention from: ____ adult   ____ peer   ____ other _____

____ Gain desired: ____ item   ____ activity   ____ area   ____ other _____

____ Automatic sensory stimulation: _____

Hypothesis:

When _____ occurs in the context of _____
             (antecedent)   (problematic setting)

the student exhibits _____ in order to _____ .
                  (target behaviour)   (perceived function)

This behaviour is more likely to occur when_____ .
                                          (setting event/context variables)

Replacement or competing behaviour that could still serve the same function for the student:
_____

Is the replacement behaviour in the student's repertoire, or will it need to be taught directly?_____

If so, how will it be taught? _____

List some potential motivators for student: _____

Figure 6.3 A Structured Observation Guide for Functional Behavioural Analysis

Source: From Barnhill, G. P. (2005). Functional behavior assessment in schools. *Intervention in school and clinic, 40*, p. 138. Copyright © 2005 by PRO-ED, Inc. Reprinted with permission.

Check Your Knowledge

- What are the steps in applied behaviour analysis?
- How can the Premack principle help you identify reinforcers?
- When is shaping an appropriate approach?
- What are some limitations of punishment?
- How can functional behavioural assessment and positive behavioural supports be used to improve student behaviours?

Apply to Practice

- How could you use applied behavioural analysis to change some of your behaviour, such as exercising or studying?

BEHAVIOURAL APPROACHES TO TEACHING AND MANAGEMENT

The behavioural approach to learning has made several important contributions to instruction, including systems for specifying learning objectives (we will look at this topic in Chapter 12 when we discuss planning and teaching), mastery learning techniques, and class management systems such as group consequences, token economies, and contingency contracts. These approaches are useful when the goal is to learn *explicit information* or change *behaviour* and when the material is *sequential* and *factual*.

First, let's consider one element that is part of every behavioural learning program—specific practice of correct behaviours. Contrary to popular wisdom, practice does not make perfect. Instead, practice makes *permanent* the behaviours practised, so practising accurate behaviours is important. Describing Tiger Woods in a news article, Devin Gordon (2001) said,

> Tiger's habit of pounding golf ball after golf ball long into the twilight—often during tournament play—has already become part of his legend. During his so-called slump earlier this year, Woods claimed he was simply working on shots he would need for the Masters in April. People rolled their eyes. Until he won the Masters. (p. 45)

No doubt, Tiger has continued specific practice of the shots he would need for each tournament.

As an example of a behavioural approach, let's consider group consequences.

Group Consequences

A teacher can base reinforcement for the class on the cumulative behaviour of all members of the class, usually by adding each student's points to a class or a team total. The **good-behaviour game** is an example of this approach. A class is divided into two teams. Specific rules for good behaviour are cooperatively developed. Each time a student breaks one of the rules, that student's team is given a mark. The team with the fewest marks at the end of the period receives a special reward or privilege (longer recess, first to lunch, and so on). If both teams earn fewer than a pre-established number of marks, both teams receive the reward. Most studies indicate that even though the game produces only small improvements in academic achievement, it can produce definite improvements in the behaviour listed in the good-behaviour rules and prevent many behaviour problems (Embry, 2002).

You can also use **group consequences** without dividing the class into teams; that is, you can base reinforcement on the behaviour of the whole class. Wilson and Hopkins (1973) conducted a study using group consequences to reduce noise levels. Radio music served effectively as the reinforcer for students in a home economics class. Whenever noise in the class was below a predetermined level, students could listen to the radio; when the noise exceeded the level, the radio was turned off. Given the success of this simple method, such a procedure might be considered in any class where music does not interfere with the task at hand.

However, caution is needed in group approaches. The whole group should not suffer for the misbehaviour or mistakes of one individual if the group has no real influence over that person (Epanchin, Townsend, & Stoddard, 1994; Jenson, Sloane, & Young, 1988). Anita saw an entire class break into cheers when the teacher announced that one boy was transferring to another school. The chant "No more points! No more points!" filled the room. The "points" referred to the teacher's system of giving one point to the whole class each time anyone broke a rule. Every point meant five minutes of recess lost. The boy who was transferring had been responsible for many losses. He was not very popular to begin with, and the point system, though quite effective in maintaining order, had made the boy an outcast in his own class.

good-behaviour game Arrangement where a class is divided into teams and each team receives demerit points for breaking agreed-on rules of good behaviour.

group consequences Reinforcers or punishments given to a class as a whole for adhering to or violating rules of conduct.

Peer pressure in the form of support and encouragement, however, can be a positive influence. Group consequences are recommended for situations in which students care about the approval of their peers (Theodore et al., 2001). If the misbehaviour of several students seems to be encouraged by the attention and laughter of other students, group consequences could be helpful. Teachers might show students how to give support and constructive feedback to classmates. If a few students seem to enjoy sabotaging the system, those students may need separate arrangements.

Contingency Contract Programs

contingency contract A formal agreement, often written and signed, between the teacher and an individual student specifying what the student must do to earn a particular privilege or reward.

In a **contingency contract** program, the teacher draws up an individual contract with each student, describing exactly what the student must do to earn a particular privilege or reward. In some programs, students participate in deciding on the behaviour to be reinforced and the rewards that can be gained. The negotiating process itself can be an educational experience, as students learn to set reasonable goals and abide by the terms of a contract. And if students participate in setting the goals, they are often more committed to reaching them (Locke & Latham, 1990; Pintrich & Schunk, 2002).

An example of a contract for completing assignments that is appropriate for intermediate and upper-grade students is presented in Figure 6.4. This chart serves as a contract, assignment sheet, and progress record. Information about progress can support student motivation (Schunk, 2000). Something like this might even help you keep track of your assignments and due dates in college or university.

Figure 6.4 A Contingency Contract for Completing Assignments

The teacher and student agree on the due dates for each assignment, marking them in blue on the chart. Each time an assignment is turned in, the date of completion is marked in black on the chart. As long as the actual completion line is above the planned completion line, the student earns free time or other contracted rewards.

Source: From Sulzer-Azaroff, B., & Mayer, G. R. (1994). *Achieving educational excellence: Behavior analysis for school personnel* (Figure, p. 89). San Marcos, CA: Western Image. Copyright © 1994 by Beth Sulzer-Azaroff and G. Roy Mayer. Reprinted with permission.

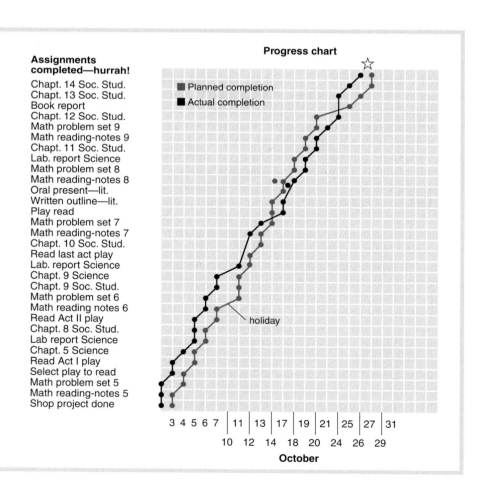

Token Reinforcement Programs

It is often difficult to provide positive consequences for all the students who deserve them. A **token reinforcement system** can help solve this problem by allowing all students to earn tokens for both academic work and positive classroom behaviour. The tokens may be points, checks, holes punched in a card, chips, play money, or anything else that is easily identified as the student's property. Periodically, the students exchange the tokens they have earned for some desired reward (Martin & Pear, 1992).

Depending on the age of the student, the rewards could be small toys, school supplies, free time, special class jobs, or other privileges. When a *token economy*, as this kind of system is called, is first established, the tokens should be given out on a fairly continuous schedule, with chances to exchange the tokens for rewards often available. Once the system is working well, however, tokens should be distributed on an intermittent schedule and saved for longer periods of time before they are exchanged for rewards.

Another variation is to allow students to earn tokens in the classroom and then exchange them for rewards at home. These plans are very successful when parents are willing to cooperate. Usually a note or report form is sent home daily or twice a week. The note indicates the number of points earned in the preceding time frame. The points may be exchanged for minutes of television viewing, access to special toys, or private time with parents. Points can also be saved up for larger rewards such as trips. Do not use this procedure, however, if you suspect the child might be severely punished for poor reports.

Token reinforcement systems are complicated and time-consuming. Generally, they should be used in only three situations: to motivate students who are completely uninterested in their work and have not responded to other approaches; to encourage students who have consistently failed to make academic progress; and to deal with a class that is out of control. Some groups of students seem to benefit more than others from token economies. Students who are developmentally disabled, slow learners, children who have failed often, students with few academic skills, and students with behaviour problems all seem to respond to the concrete, direct nature of token reinforcement.

Before you try a token system, you should be sure that your teaching methods and materials are right for the students. Sometimes, class disruptions or lack of motivation indicate that teaching practices need to be changed. Maybe the class rules are unclear or are enforced inconsistently. Maybe the text is too easy or too hard. Maybe the pace is wrong. If these problems exist, a token system may improve the situation temporarily, but the students will still have trouble learning the academic material.

Many of the systematic applications of behavioural principles focus on classroom management. For two examples that successfully applied behavioural principles to improve behaviours of students with special needs, see Reaching Every Student on page 224.

The few pages devoted here to contingency contracts and token reinforcement can offer only an introduction to these programs. If you want to set up a large-scale reward program in your classroom, you should probably seek professional advice. Often the school psychologist, counsellor, or principal can help.

token reinforcement system
System in which tokens earned for academic work and positive classroom behaviour can be exchanged for some desired reward.

Check Your Knowledge

- Describe the managerial strategies of group consequences, contracts, and token programs.

Apply to Practice

- How could you use one of these management approaches to handle the situation described at the beginning of the chapter?

STUDENTS WITH LEARNING AND BEHAVIOUR PROBLEMS

Students with severe behaviour problems provide some of the most difficult challenges for teachers. Two studies show how behavioural principles can be useful in helping these students.

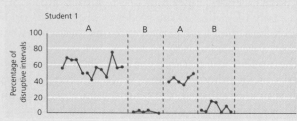

Student 1

Lisa Theodore and her colleagues (2001) worked with the teacher of five adolescent males who were diagnosed as having severe emotional disorders. A short list of clear rules was established (e.g., no obscene words, comply with teacher's requests within five seconds, no verbal put-downs). The rules were written on index cards taped to each student's desk. The teacher had a checklist on his desk with each student's name to note any rule breaking. This checklist was easily observable, so students could monitor their own and each others' performance. At the end of the 45-minute period, a student chose a "criterion" from a jar. The possible criteria were: performance of the whole group, student with the highest score, student with the lowest score, the average of all students, or a random single student. If the student or students selected to be the criterion had five checks or fewer for rule breaking, then the whole class got a reward, also chosen randomly from a jar. The possible rewards were things like a soda, a bag of chips, a candy bar, or a late-to-class pass. An ABAB design was used—baseline, two-week intervention, two-week withdrawal of intervention, and two-week

return to group consequences. All students showed clear improvement in following the rules when the reward system was in place, as you can see in this chart for one of the students. Students liked the approach and the teacher found it easy to implement.

In the second study, Kara McGoey and George DuPaul (2000) worked with teachers in three preschool classrooms to address problem behaviours of four students diagnosed as having attention-deficit hyperactivity disorder (ADHD). The teachers tried both a token reinforcement program (students earned small and large buttons on a chart for following class rules) and a response cost system (students began with five small buttons and one large button per activity each day and lost buttons for not following rules). Both procedures were effective in lowering rule-breaking, but the teachers found the response cost system easier to implement.

Source: For details of both of these approaches, see Theodore, L. A., Bray, M. A., Kehle, T. J., & Jenson, W. R. (2001). Randomization of group contingencies and reinforcers to reduce classroom disruptive behavior. *Journal of School Psychology, 39,* pp. 267–277; McGoey, K. E., & DuPaul, G. J. (2000). Token reinforcement and response cost procedures: Reducing disruptive behavior of preschool children with Attention-Deficit/Hyperactive Disorder. *School Psychology Quarterly, 15,* pp. 330–343.

THINKING ABOUT BEHAVIOUR: OBSERVATIONAL LEARNING AND COGNITIVE BEHAVIOUR MODIFICATION

In recent years, most behavioural psychologists have found that operant conditioning offers too limited an explanation of learning. Many have expanded their view of learning to include the study of cognitive processes that cannot be directly observed, such as expectations, thoughts, mental maps, and beliefs. Three examples of this expanded view are observational learning, self-management, and cognitive behaviour modification.

Observational Learning

Over 30 years ago, Albert Bandura noted that the traditional behavioural views of learning were accurate—but incomplete—because they gave only a partial explanation of learning and overlooked important elements, particularly social influences. His early work on learning was grounded in the behavioural principles of reinforcement and punishment, but he added a focus on *learning from observing others.* This expanded view was labelled **social learning theory**; it was considered a *neo-behavioural* approach (Bandura, 1977; Hill, 2002, Zimmerman & Schunk, 2003).

To explain some limitations of the behavioural model, Bandura distinguished between the *acquisition of knowledge* (learning) and the *observable performance based on that knowledge* (behaviour). In other words, Bandura suggested that we all may know more than we show. An example is found in one of Bandura's early studies (1965). Preschool children saw a film of a model kicking and punching an inflatable "Bobo" doll. One group saw the model rewarded for the aggression, another group saw the model punished, and a third group saw no consequences. When they were moved to a room with the Bobo doll, the children who had seen the punching and kicking reinforced on the film were the most aggressive toward the doll. Those who had seen the attacks punished were the least aggressive. But when the children were promised rewards for imitating the model's aggression, all of them demonstrated that they had learned the behaviour.

Thus, incentives can affect performance. Even though learning may have occurred, it may not be demonstrated until the situation is appropriate or there are incentives to perform. This might explain why some students don't perform "bad behaviours" such as swearing or smoking that they all see modelled by adults, peers, and the media. Personal consequences may discourage them from performing the behaviours. In other examples, children may have learned how to write the alphabet, but perform badly because their fine motor coordination is limited, or they may have learned how to simplify fractions, but perform badly on a test because they are anxious. In these cases, their performance is not an indication of their learning.

Recently, Bandura has focused on cognitive factors such as beliefs, self-perceptions, and expectations, so his theory is now called a social cognitive theory (Hill, 2002). **Social cognitive theory** (discussed more thoroughly in Chapters 9 and 10) distinguishes between enactive and vicarious learning. *Enactive learning* is learning by doing and experiencing the consequences of your actions. This may sound like operant conditioning all over again, but it is not, and the difference has to do with the role of consequences. Proponents of operant conditioning believe that consequences strengthen or weaken behaviour. In enactive learning, however, consequences are seen as providing information. Our interpretations of the consequences create expectations, influence motivation, and shape beliefs (Schunk, 2004). We will see many examples of enactive learning—learning by doing—throughout this book.

Vicarious learning is learning by observing others. People and animals can learn merely by observing another person or animal learn, and this fact challenges the behaviourist idea that cognitive factors are unnecessary in an explanation of learning. If people can learn by watching, they must be focusing their attention, constructing images, remembering, analyzing, and making decisions that affect learning. Thus, much is going on mentally before performance and reinforcement can even take place. Cognitive apprenticeships, discussed in Chapter 9, are examples of vicarious learning.

Elements of Observational Learning

Through **observational learning**, we learn not only how to perform a behaviour but also what will happen to us in specific situations if we do perform it. Observation can be a very efficient learning process. The first time children hold hairbrushes, cups, or tennis rackets, they usually brush, drink, or swing as well as they can, given their current muscle development and coordination. Let's take a closer look at how observational learning occurs. Bandura (1986) notes that observational learning includes four elements: *paying attention, retaining information or impressions, producing behaviours,* and *being motivated* to repeat the behaviours.

social learning theory Theory that emphasizes learning through observation of others.

Albert Bandura expanded on behavioural theories to emphasize observational learning.

social cognitive theory Theory that adds concern with cognitive factors such as beliefs, self-perceptions, and expectations to social learning theory.

Connect & Extend

TO THE RESEARCH
For a look at social cognitive theory and school achievement, see Schunk, D. H. (1999). Social-self interaction and achievement behavior. *Educational Psychologist, 34,* 219–227.

observational learning Learning by observation and imitation of others.

Attention.   In order to learn through observation, we have to pay attention. In teaching, you will have to ensure students' attention to the critical features of the lesson by making clear presentations and highlighting important points. In demonstrating a skill (for example, threading a sewing machine or operating a lathe), you may need to have students look over your shoulder as you work. Seeing your hands from the same perspective as they see their own directs their attention to the right features of the situation and makes observational learning easier.

Retention.   In order to imitate the behaviour of a model, you have to remember it. This involves mentally representing the model's actions in some way, probably as verbal steps ("Hwa-Rang, the eighth form in Tae Kwan Do karate, is a palm-heel block, then a middle riding stance punch, then..."), or as visual images, or both. Retention can be improved by mental rehearsal (imagining imitating the behaviour) or by actual practice. In the retention phase of observational learning, practice helps us remember the elements of the desired behaviour, such as the sequence of steps.

Production.   Once we "know" how a behaviour should look and remember the elements or steps, we still may not perform it smoothly. Sometimes we need a great deal of practice, feedback, and coaching about subtle points before we can reproduce the behaviour of the model. In the production phase, practice makes the behaviour smoother and more expert.

Motivation and Reinforcement.   As mentioned earlier, social learning theory distinguishes between acquisition and performance. We may acquire a new skill or behaviour through observation, but we may not perform that behaviour until there is some motivation or incentive to do so. Reinforcement can play several roles in observational learning. If we anticipate being reinforced for imitating the actions of a model, we may be more motivated to pay attention, remember, and reproduce the behaviours. In addition, reinforcement is important in maintaining learning. A person who tries a new behaviour is unlikely to persist without reinforcement (Ollendick, Dailey, & Shapiro, 1983; Schunk, 2004). For example, if an unpopular student adopted the dress of the "in" group, but was ignored or ridiculed, it is unlikely that the imitation would continue.

Bandura identifies three forms of reinforcement that can encourage observational learning. First, of course, the observer may reproduce the behaviours of the model and receive direct reinforcement, as when a gymnast successfully executes a front flip/round-off combination and the coach/model says, "Excellent!"

But the reinforcement need not be direct—it may be **vicarious reinforcement**. The observer may simply see others reinforced for a particular behaviour and then increase his or her production of that behaviour. For example, if you compliment two students on the attractive illustrations in their lab reports, several other students who observe your compliments may turn in illustrated lab reports next time. Most TV ads hope for this kind of effect. People in commercials become deliriously happy when they drive a particular car or drink a specific juice, and the viewer is supposed to do the same; the viewer's behaviour is reinforced vicariously by the actors' obvious pleasure. Punishment can also be vicarious: You may slow down on a stretch of highway after seeing several people get speeding tickets there.

The final form of reinforcement is **self-reinforcement**, or controlling your own reinforcers. This sort of reinforcement is important for both students and teachers. We want our students to improve not because it leads to external rewards, but because the students value and enjoy their growing competence. And as a teacher, sometimes self-reinforcement is all that keeps you going.

Factors That Influence Observational Learning.   What causes an individual to learn and perform modelled behaviours and skills? Several factors play a role, as shown in Table 6.2. The developmental level of the observer makes a difference in learning. As children grow older, they are able to focus attention for longer periods of time, use memory strategies to retain information, and motivate themselves

vicarious reinforcement Increasing the chances that we will repeat a behaviour by observing another person being reinforced for that behaviour.

self-reinforcement Controlling your own reinforcers.

Observational theories of learning consider the importance of learning by doing and learning by observing others.

to practise. A second influence is the status of the model. Children are more likely to imitate the actions of others who seem competent, powerful, prestigious, and enthusiastic, so parents, teachers, older siblings, athletes, action heroes, rock stars, or film personalities may serve as models, depending on the age and interests of the child. Third, by watching others, we learn about what behaviours are appropriate for people like ourselves, so models who are seen as similar are more readily imitated (Pintrich & Schunk, 2002). All students need to see successful, capable models who look and sound like them, no matter what their ethnicity, socioeconomic status, or gender.

Look at Table 6.2. The last three influences involve goals and expectations. If observers expect that certain actions of models will lead to particular outcomes

---

TABLE 6.2 Factors That Affect Observational Learning

Characteristic Effects of Modelling

Developmental Status	Improvements with development include longer attention and increased capacity to process information, use strategies, compare performances with memorial representations, and adopt intrinsic motivators.
Model Prestige and Competence	Observers pay greater attention to competent, high-status models. Consequences of modelled behaviours convey information about functional value. Observers attempt to learn actions they believe they will need to perform.
Vicarious Consequences	Consequences to models convey information about behavioural appropriateness and likely outcomes of actions. Valued consequences motivate observers. Similarity in attributes or competence signals appropriateness and heightens motivation.
Outcome Expectations	Observers are more likely to perform modelled actions they believe are appropriate and will result in rewarding outcomes.
Goal Setting	Observers are likely to attend to models who demonstrate behaviours that help observers attain goals.
Self-Efficacy	Observers attend to models when they believe they are capable of learning or performing the modelled behaviour. Observation of similar models affects self-efficacy ("If they can do it, I can too").

Source: From Schunk, D. H. (2004). *Learning theories: An education perspective* (4th ed.). Published by Prentice Hall. Copyright © 2004 by Prentice Hall. Reprinted by permission of Pearson Education, Inc., Upper Saddle River, NJ.

self-efficacy A person's sense of being able to deal effectively with a particular task.

Connect & Extend

TO OTHER CHAPTERS
Sense of self-efficacy is discussed more fully in **Chapter 10**, as is the related concept of teacher efficacy. *Background:* Two books by Bandura about self-efficacy: Bandura, A. (1997). *Self-efficacy: The exercise of control.* New York: Freeman. Bandura, A. (Ed.). (1995). *Self-efficacy in changing societies.* New York: Cambridge University Press.

"Dad, can you read?"

© The New Yorker Collection 1990 Peter Steiner from cartoonbank.com. All rights reserved.

What is this son learning by observing his father?

ripple effect "Contagious" spreading of behaviours through imitation.

modelling Changes in behaviour, thinking, or emotions that occur through observing another person—a model.

(such as particular practice regimens leading to improved athletic performance) and the observers value those outcomes or goals, then the observers are more likely to pay attention to the models and try to reproduce their behaviours. Finally, observers are more likely to learn from models if the observers have a high level of **self-efficacy**—that is, if they believe they are capable of doing the actions needed to reach the goals, or at least of learning how to do so (Bandura, 1997; Pintrich & Schunk, 2002). We will discuss goals, expectations, and self-efficacy in greater depth in Chapter 10 on motivation.

Observational Learning in Teaching

There are five possible outcomes of observational learning: directing attention, encouraging existing behaviours, changing inhibitions, teaching new behaviours and attitudes, and arousing emotions. Let's look at each of these as they occur in classrooms.

Directing Attention. By observing others, we not only learn about actions but also notice the objects involved in the actions. For example, in a preschool class, when one child plays enthusiastically with a toy that has been ignored for days, many other children may want to have the toy, even if they play with it in different ways or simply carry it around. This happens, in part, because the children's attention has been drawn to that particular toy.

Fine-Tuning Already-Learned Behaviours. All of us have had the experience of looking for cues from other people when we find ourselves in unfamiliar situations. Observing the behaviour of others tells us which of our already-learned behaviours to use: the proper fork for eating the salad, when to leave a gathering, what kind of language is appropriate, and so on. Adopting the dress and grooming styles of TV or music idols is another example of this kind of effect.

Strengthening or Weakening Inhibitions. If class members witness one student breaking a class rule and getting away with it, they may learn that undesirable consequences do not always follow rule breaking. If the rule breaker is a well-liked, high-status class leader, the effect of the modelling may be even more pronounced. This **ripple effect** (Kounin, 1970) can work for the teacher's benefit. When the teacher deals effectively with a rule breaker, especially a class leader, the idea of breaking this rule may be inhibited for the other students viewing the interaction. This does not mean that teachers must reprimand each student who breaks a rule, but once a teacher has called for a particular action, following through is an important part of capitalizing on the ripple effect.

Teaching New Behaviours. Modelling has long been used, of course, to teach dance, sports, and crafts, as well as skills in subjects such as food science, chemistry, and welding. Modelling can also be applied deliberately in the classroom to teach mental skills and to broaden horizons—to teach new ways of thinking. Teachers serve as models for a vast range of behaviours, from pronouncing vocabulary words, to reacting to the seizure of a student with epilepsy, to being enthusiastic about learning. For example, a teacher might model sound critical-thinking skills by thinking "out loud" about a student's question. Or a high school teacher concerned about girls who seem to have stereotyped ideas about careers might invite women with non-traditional jobs to speak to the class. Studies indicate that modelling can be most effective when the teacher makes use of all the elements of observational learning described in the previous section, especially reinforcement and practice.

Models who are the same age as the students may be particularly effective. For example, Schunk and Hanson (1985) compared two methods for teaching subtraction to grade 2 students who had difficulties learning this skill. One group of students observed other students learning the procedures, while another group watched a teacher's demonstration. Then both groups participated in the same instructional program. The students who observed peer models learning not only scored higher on tests of subtraction after instruction but also gained more confidence in their own ability to learn. For students who doubt their own abilities, a good model is a low-achieving student who keeps trying and finally masters the material (Schunk, 2004).

Abusing Emotion. Finally, through observational learning, people may develop emotional reactions to situations they have never experienced personally, such as flying or driving. A child who watches a friend fall from a swing and break an arm may become fearful of swings. After the terrible events of September 11, 2001, children may be anxious when they see airplanes flying close to the ground. News reports of shark attacks have many of us anxious about swimming in the ocean. Note that hearing and reading about a situation are also forms of observation. Some terrible examples of modelling occur with "copycat killings" in schools. When frightening things happen to people who are similar in age or circumstances to your students, they may need to talk about their emotions.

The following Guidelines will give you some ideas about using observational learning in the classroom.

GUIDELINES
USING OBSERVATIONAL LEARNING

Model behaviours and attitudes you want your students to learn.

EXAMPLES

1. Show enthusiasm for the subject you teach.
2. Be willing to demonstrate both the mental and the physical tasks you expect the students to perform. Anita once saw a teacher sit down in the sandbox while her four-year-old students watched her demonstrate the difference between "playing with sand" and "throwing sand."
3. When reading to students, model good problem solving. Stop and say, "Now let me see if I remember what happened so far," or "That was a hard sentence. I'm going to read it again."
4. Model good problem solving—think out loud as you work through a difficult problem.

Use peers, especially class leaders, as models.

EXAMPLES

1. In group work, pair students who do well with those who are having difficulties.
2. Ask students to demonstrate the difference between "whispering" and "silence—no talking."

Make sure students see that positive behaviours lead to reinforcement for others.

EXAMPLES

1. Point out the connections between positive behaviour and positive consequences in stories.
2. Be fair in giving reinforcement. The same rules for rewards should apply to the problem students as to the good students.

Enlist the help of class leaders in modelling behaviours for the entire class.

EXAMPLES

1. Ask a well-liked student to be friendly to an isolated, fearful student.
2. Let high-status students lead an activity when you need class cooperation or when students are likely to be reluctant at first. Popular students can model dialogues in foreign-language classes or be the first to tackle dissection procedures in biology.

For more information on observational learning, see **http://mentalhelp.net/psyhelp/chap4/chap4g.htm.**

Connect & Extend

TO OTHER CHAPTERS

Concern with self-management is not restricted to any one group or theory. Psychologists who study Vygotsky's ideas about cognitive development (**Chapter 2**) are involved, as are cognitive psychologists interested in learning strategies (**Chapters 7** and **8**), and motivational psychologists point to self-regulation as a critical factor in motivation (**Chapters 10** and **11**).

self-management Use of behavioural learning principles to change one's own behaviour.

Connect & Extend

TO THE CLASSROOM

Self-management can be used to encourage social behaviour. This self-recording form is taken from Jenson, W. R., Sloane, H. N., & Young, K. R. (1988). *Applied behavior analysis in education: A structured teaching approach* (p. 272). Englewood Cliffs, NJ: Prentice Hall.

SOCIAL SKILLS PRACTICE CARD

Name _____

Date _____

Things to remember:

Use your new skill. Take this card with you and mark it when you use the social skill.

Social skill: _____

WHERE?	How many times?
	1 2 3 4 5 6
1. In class	
2. On the playground	
3. At lunch	
4. At home	
5. Other	

Self-Management

If one goal of education is to produce people who are capable of educating themselves, students must learn to manage their own lives, set their own goals, and provide their own reinforcement. In adult life, rewards are sometimes vague and goals often take a long time to reach. Think how many small steps are required to complete an education and find your first job. Life is filled with tasks that call for this sort of **self-management** (Rachlin, 2000).

Students may be involved in any or all of the steps in implementing a basic behaviour-change program. They may help set goals, observe their own work, keep records of it, and evaluate their own performance. Finally, they can select and deliver reinforcement. Such involvement can help students master all the steps so that they can perform these tasks in the future (Kaplan, 1991).

Goal Setting. It appears that the goal-setting phase is very important in self-management (Pintrich & Schunk, 2002; Reeve, 1996). In fact, some research suggests that setting specific goals and making them public may be the critical elements of self-management programs. For example, S. C. Hayes and his colleagues identified college students who had serious problems with studying and then taught them how to set specific study goals. Students who set goals and announced them to the experimenters performed significantly better on tests covering the material they were studying than students who set goals privately and never revealed them to anyone (Hayes et al., 1985).

Higher standards tend to lead to higher performance (McLaughlin & Gnagey, 1981). Unfortunately, student-set goals have a tendency to slip lower and lower. Teachers can help students maintain high standards by monitoring the goals set and reinforcing high standards. In one study, a teacher helped grade 1 students raise the number of math problems they set for themselves to work on each day by praising them whenever they increased their objective by 10 percent. The students maintained their new, higher work standards, and the improvements even generalized to other subjects (Price & O'Leary, 1974).

Monitoring and Evaluating Progress. Students may also participate in the monitoring and evaluation phases of a behaviour-change program (Mace, Belfiore, & Hutchinson, 2002). Examples of behaviours that are appropriate for self-recording include the number of assignments completed, time spent practising a skill, number of books read, and number of times out of seat without permission. Tasks that must be accomplished without teacher supervision, such as homework or private study, are also good candidates for self-monitoring. Students keep a chart, diary, or checklist recording the frequency or duration of the behaviour in question. A progress record card can help older students break down assignments into small steps, determine the best sequence for completing the steps, and keep track of daily progress by setting goals for each day. The record card itself serves as a prompt that can be faded out.

Self-evaluation is somewhat more difficult than simple self-recording because it involves making a judgment about quality. Students can evaluate their behaviour with reasonable accuracy, especially if they learn standards for judging a good performance or product. For example, Sweeney, Salva, Cooper, and Talbert-Johnson (1993) taught secondary-school students how to evaluate their handwriting for size, slant, shape, and spacing. One key seems to be periodically checking students' self-evaluations and giving reinforcement for accurate judgments. Older students may learn accurate self-evaluation more readily than younger students. Again, bonus points can be awarded when the teachers' and students' evaluations match (Kaplan, 1991).

Self-correction can accompany self-evaluation. Students first evaluate, then alter and improve their work, and finally compare the improvements with the standards again (Mace, Belfiore, & Hutchinson, 2001).

Self-Reinforcement.　The last step in self-management is self-reinforcement. There is some disagreement, however, as to whether this step is actually necessary. Some psychologists believe that setting goals and monitoring progress alone are sufficient and that self-reinforcement adds nothing to the effects (Hayes et al., 1985). Others believe that rewarding yourself for a job well done can lead to higher levels of performance than simply setting goals and keeping track of progress (Bandura, 1986). If you are willing to be tough and really deny yourself something you want until your goals are reached, the promise of the reinforcer can provide extra incentive for work. With that in mind, you may want to think now of some way you can reinforce yourself when you finish reading this chapter. A similar approach helped us write the chapter in the first place.

At times, families can be enlisted to help their children develop self-management abilities. Working together, teachers and families can focus on a few goals and, at the same time, support the growing independence of the students. The Family and Community Partnerships box below gives some ideas.

Sometimes, teaching students self-management can solve a problem for teachers and provide fringe benefits as well. For example, the coaches of a competitive swim team with members aged 9 to 16 were having difficulty persuading swimmers to maintain high work rates. Then the coaches drew up four charts indicating the training program to be followed by each member and posted the charts near the pool. The swimmers were given the responsibility of recording their numbers of laps and completion of each training unit. Because the recording was public, swimmers could see their own progress and that of others, give and receive congratulations, and keep accurate track of the work units completed. Work output increased by 27 percent. The coaches also liked the system because swimmers could begin to work immediately without waiting for instructions (McKenzie & Rushall, 1974).

Connect & Extend

TO YOUR TEACHING
One student in your class is never prepared to do his work. He doesn't have a pencil, has misplaced his book, left his homework at home, doesn't understand the assignment, forgot to buy notebook paper, and so on. The result of all this is that he seldom hands in his homework assignments. How would you approach this problem? Develop several alternative strategies, such as reward and punishment, shaping, or self-management.

FAMILY AND COMMUNITY PARTNERSHIPS
STUDENT SELF-MANAGEMENT

Introduce the system to families and students in a positive way.

EXAMPLES

1. Invite family participation and stress possible benefits to all family members.

2. Consider starting the program just with volunteers.

3. Describe how you use self-management programs yourself.

Help families and students establish reachable goals.

EXAMPLES

1. Provide examples of possible self-management goals for students, such as starting homework early in the evening, or keeping track of books read.

2. Show families how to post goals and keep track of progress. Encourage everyone in the family to work on a goal.

Give families ways to record and evaluate their child's progress (or their own).

EXAMPLES

1. Divide the work into easily measured steps.

2. Provide models of good work where judgments are more difficult, such as in creative writing.

3. Give families a record form or checklist to keep track of progress.

Encourage families to check the accuracy of student records from time to time and to help their children develop forms of self-reinforcement.

EXAMPLES

1. Have many checkups when students are first learning and fewer later.

2. Have siblings check one another's records.

3. Where appropriate, test the skills that students are supposed to be developing at home and reward students whose self-evaluations match their test performances.

4. Have students brainstorm ideas with their families on how to reward themselves for jobs well done.

cognitive behaviour modification Procedures based on both behavioural and cognitive learning principles for changing one's own behaviour by using self-talk and self-instruction.

Connect & Extend

TO REAL LIFE

A study conducted by Mark Morgan (1985. Self-monitoring of attained subgoals in private study. *Journal of Educational Psychology, 77,* 623–630) combined goal setting, self-recording, and self-evaluation. Morgan taught self-monitoring strategies to all the education students in the required educational psychology course at his college. The students who set specific short-term objectives for each study unit and monitored their progress toward the objectives outperformed the students who simply monitored study time, even though the students who monitored their time actually spent more hours studying!

Connect & Extend

TO YOUR TEACHING

Here is a checklist, taken from Belfiore & Hornyak (1998), to help students manage their homework:

1. *Did I turn in yesterday's homework?*
2. Did I write all homework assignments in my notebook?
3. *Is all the homework in the homework folder?*
4. *Are all my materials to complete my homework with me?*
5. *Begin homework.*
6. *Are all homework papers completed?*
7. *Did someone check homework to make sure it was completed?*
8. *After checking, did I put all homework back in folder?*
9. *Did I give this paper to teacher? (p. 190).*

Cognitive Behaviour Modification and Self-Instruction

Self-management generally means getting students involved in the basic steps of a behaviour-change program. **Cognitive behaviour modification** adds an emphasis on thinking and self-talk. For this reason, many psychologists consider cognitive behaviour modification more a cognitive than a behavioural approach. We present it here because it serves as a bridge to Chapters 7 and 8 on cognitive learning.

As noted in Chapter 2, there is a stage in cognitive development when young children seem to guide themselves through a task using private speech. They talk to themselves, often repeating the words of a parent or teacher. In cognitive behaviour modification, students are taught directly how to use self-instruction. Meichenbaum (1977) outlined the steps:

1. An adult model performs a task while talking to him- or herself out loud (cognitive modelling).
2. The child performs the same task under the direction of the model's instructions (overt, external guidance).
3. The child performs the task while instructing him- or herself aloud (overt self-guidance).
4. The child whispers the instructions to him- or herself as he or she goes through the task (faded, overt self-guidance).
5. The child performs the task while guiding his or her performance via private speech (covert self-instruction). (p. 32)

Brenda Manning and Beverly Payne (1996) list four skills that can increase student learning: listening, planning, working, and checking. How might cognitive self-instruction help students develop these skills? One possibility is to use personal booklets or class posters that prompt students to "talk to themselves" about these skills. For example, one grade 5 class designed a set of prompts for each of the four skills and posted the prompts around the classroom. The prompts for listening included, "Does this make sense?" "Am I getting this?" "I need to ask a question now before I forget." "Pay attention!" "Can I do what he's saying to do?" Planning prompts were, "Do I have everything together?" "Do I have my friends tuned out for right now?" "Let me get organized first." "What order will I do this in?" "I know this stuff!" Posters for these and the other two skills, working and checking, are shown in Figure 6.5. Part of the power of this process is in getting students involved in thinking about and creating their own guides and prompts. Having the discussion and posting the ideas make students more self-aware and in control of their own learning.

Actually, cognitive behaviour modification as it is described by Meichenbaum and others has many more components than just teaching students to use self-instruction. Meichenbaum's methods also include dialogue and interaction between teacher and student, modelling, guided discovery, motivational strategies, feedback, careful matching of the task with the student's developmental level, and other principles of good teaching. The student is even involved in designing the program (Harris, 1990; Harris & Pressley, 1991). Given all this, it is no surprise that students do seem to generalize skills developed through cognitive behaviour modification to new learning situations (Harris, Graham, & Pressley, 1992).

Check Your Knowledge

- Distinguish between social learning and social cognitive theories.
- Distinguish between enactive and vicarious learning.
- What are the elements of observational learning?
- What are the steps in self-management?

Apply to Practice

- How could you use the elements of self-management to study in this course?

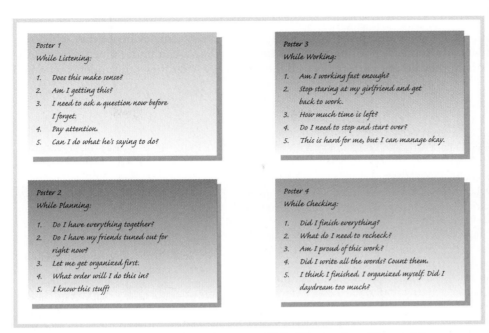

Figure 6.5 Posters to Remind Students to "Talk Themselves Through" Listening, Planning, Working, and Checking in School

These four posters were designed by a grade 5 class to help the students remember to use self-instruction. Some of the reminders reflect the special world of these preadolescents.

Source: From Manning, B. H., & Payne, B. D. (1996). *Self-talk for teachers and students: Metacognitive strategies for personal and classroom use* (p. 125). Boston: Allyn & Bacon. Copyright © 1996 by Allyn & Bacon. Adapted by permission.

PROBLEMS AND ISSUES

The preceding sections provide an overview of several strategies for changing classroom behaviour. However, you should be aware that these strategies are tools that may be used responsibly or irresponsibly. What, then, are some issues you should keep in mind?

Criticisms of Behavioural Methods

What Would You Say?

During your job interview, the principal asks, "A teacher last year got in trouble for bribing his students with homework exemptions to get them to behave in class. What do you think about using rewards and punishments in teaching?" What would you say?

While you think about your answer to this question, look at the Point/Counterpoint, "Should Students Be Rewarded for Learning?" on page 234 to see two different perspectives. Properly used, the strategies in this chapter can be effective tools to help students learn academically and grow in self-sufficiency. Effective tools, however, do not automatically produce excellent work, and behavioural strategies are often implemented haphazardly, inconsistently, incorrectly, or superficially (Landrum & Kauffman, 2006). The indiscriminate use of even the best tools can lead to difficulties.

Some psychologists fear that rewarding students for all learning will cause them to lose interest in learning for its own sake (Deci, 1975; Deci & Ryan, 1985; Kohn, 1993, 1996; Lepper & Greene, 1978; Lepper, Keavney, & Drake, 1996; Ryan & Deci, 1996). Studies have suggested that using reward programs with students who are already interested in the subject matter may, in fact, cause students to be less interested in the subject when the reward program ends, as you can see in the Point/Counterpoint box. In addition, there is some evidence that when students do succeed, praising them for being intelligent can undermine their motivation if they do not perform as well the next time. After they fail, students who had

POINT > < COUNTERPOINT

SHOULD STUDENTS BE REWARDED FOR LEARNING?

For years, educators and psychologists have debated whether students should be rewarded for school work and academic accomplishments. As an example, Judy Cameron and W. David Pierce (1996) of the University of Alberta published an article on reinforcement in the *Review of Educational Research* that precipitated extensive criticisms and rebuttals in the same journal from Mark Lepper, Mark Keavney, Michael Drake, Alfie Kohn, Richard Ryan, and Edward Deci. Earlier, Paul Chance and Alfie Kohn had exchanged opinions in several issues of *Phi Delta Kappan:* Kohn, A. (1991, March). Caring kids: The role of the schools; Chance, P. (1991, June). Backtalk: A gross injustice; Chance, P. (1992, November). The rewards of learning; Kohn, A. (1993, June). Rewards versus learning: A response to Paul Chance; Chance, P. (1993, June). Sticking up for rewards. What are the arguments?

> Point *Students are punished by rewards.*

Alfie Kohn (1993) argues that "Applied behaviorism, which amounts to saying, 'do this and you'll get that,' is essentially a technique for controlling people. In the classroom it is a way of doing things to children rather than working with them" (p. 784). Kohn goes on to contend that rewards are ineffective because when the praise and prizes stop, the behaviour stops too. "Rewards (like punishments) can get people to do what we want: buckle up, share a toy, read a book…. But they rarely produce effects that survive the rewards themselves…. They do not create an enduring commitment to a set of

values or to learning; they merely, and temporarily, change what we do" (p. 784).

The problem with rewards does not stop here. According to Kohn, rewarding students for learning actually makes them less interested in the material:

> All of this means that getting children to think about learning as a way to receive a sticker, a gold star, or a grade—or even worse, to get money or a toy for a grade, which amounts to an extrinsic motivator for an extrinsic motivator—is likely to turn learning from an end into a means. Learning becomes something that must be gotten through in order to receive the reward. Take the depressingly pervasive program by which children receive certificates for pizzas when they have read a certain number of books. John Nicholls of the University of Illinois comments, only half in jest, that the likely consequences of this program is "a lot of fat kids who don't like to read." (p. 785)

< Counterpoint *Learning should be rewarding.*

According to Paul Chance (1993),

> Behavioural psychologists in particular emphasize that we learn by acting on our environment. As B. F. Skinner put it: "[People] act on the world, and change it, and are changed in turn by the consequences of their actions." Skinner, unlike Kohn, understood that people learn best in a responsive environment. Teachers who praise or otherwise reward student performance provide such an environment…. If it is immoral to let students know they have answered questions correctly, to pat students on the back for a good effort, to show joy at a student's understanding of a concept, or to recognize the achievement of a goal by providing a gold star or a certificate—

if this is immoral, then count me a sinner. (p. 788)

Do rewards undermine interest? In their review of research, Cameron and Pierce (1996) concluded, "When tangible rewards (e.g., gold star, money) are offered contingent on performance on a task [not just participation] or are delivered unexpectedly, intrinsic motivation is maintained" (p. 49). Even psychologists such as Edward Deci and Mark Lepper, who suggest that rewards might undermine intrinsic motivation, agree that rewards can also be used positively. When rewards provide students with information about their growing mastery of a subject or when the rewards show appreciation for a job well done, then the rewards bolster confidence and make the task more interesting to the students, especially students who lacked ability or interest in the task initially. Nothing succeeds like success. If students master reading or mathematics with the support of rewards, they will not forget what they have learned when the praise stops. Would they have learned without the rewards? Some would, but some might not. Would you continue working for a company that didn't pay you, even though you liked the work? Will freelance writer Alfie Kohn, for that matter, lose interest in writing because he gets paid fees and royalties?

Source: From Chance, P. (1993, June). Sticking up for rewards. *Phi Delta Kappan,* pp. 787–790. Copyright © 1993 by Phi Delta Kappan. Reprinted with permission of *Phi Delta Kappan* and the author. From Kohn, A. (1993, June). Rewards versus learning: A response to Paul Chance. *Phi Delta Kappan,* pp. 784 and 785. Copyright © 1993 by Alfie Kohn. Reprinted from *Phi Delta Kappan* with the author's permission.

been praised for being smart may be less persistent and enjoy the task less compared with students who had been praised earlier for working hard (Mueller & Dweck, 1998).

Just as you must take into account the effects of a reward system on the individual, you must also consider the impact on other students. Using a reward program or giving one student increased attention may have a detrimental effect on the other students in the classroom. Is it possible that other students will learn to be "bad" in order to be included in the reward program? Most of the evidence on this question suggests that using individual adaptations such as reward programs does not have any adverse effects on students who are not participating if the teacher believes in the program and explains the reasons for using it to the non-participating students. After interviewing 98 students in grades 1 through 6, Cindy Fulk and Paula Smith (1995) concluded that "Teachers may be more concerned about equal treatment of students than students are" (p. 416). If the conduct of some students does seem to deteriorate when their peers are involved in special programs, many of the same procedures discussed in this chapter should help them return to previous levels of appropriate behaviour (Chance, 1992, 1993).

Ethical Issues

The ethical questions related to the use of the strategies described in this chapter are similar to those raised by any process that seeks to influence people. What are the goals? How do these goals fit with those of the school as a whole? What effect will a strategy have on the individuals involved? Is too much control being given to the teacher, or to a majority?

Goals. The strategies described in this chapter could be applied exclusively to teaching students to sit still, raise their hands before speaking, and remain silent at all other times (Winett & Winkler, 1972). This would certainly be an unethical use of the techniques. It is true that a teacher may need to establish some organization and order, but stopping with improvements in conduct will not ensure academic learning. On the other hand, in some situations, reinforcing academic skills may lead to improvements in conduct. Whenever possible, emphasis should be placed on academic learning. Academic improvements generalize to other situations more successfully than do changes in classroom conduct.

Strategies. Punishment can have negative side effects—it can serve as a model for aggressive responses, and it can encourage negative emotional reactions. Punishment is unnecessary and even unethical when positive approaches, which have fewer potential dangers, might work as well. When simpler, less restrictive procedures fail, more complicated procedures should be tried.

A second consideration in the selection of a strategy is the impact of the strategy on the individual student. For example, some teachers arrange for students to be rewarded at home with a gift or activities based on good work in school. But if a student has a history of being severely punished at home for bad reports from school, a home-based reinforcement program might be very harmful to that student. Reports of unsatisfactory progress at school could lead to increased abuse at home.

Check Your Knowledge

- What are the main criticisms of behavioural approaches?

Apply to Practice

- Is it ever appropriate to reward students for learning? Why or why not?

DIVERSITY AND CONVERGENCES IN BEHAVIOURAL LEARNING

Diversity

There is great *diversity* in the learning histories of students. Every person in your class will come to you with different fears and anxieties. Some students may be terrified of speaking in public or of failing in competitive sports. Others will be anxious around various animals. Different activities or objects will serve as reinforcers for some students, but not others. Some students will work for the promise of good grades—others couldn't care less. All your students will have learned from different models in their homes, neighbourhoods, or communities.

The research and theories presented in this chapter should help you understand how the learning histories of your students might have taught them to respond automatically to tests with sweaty palms and racing hearts—possible classical conditioning at work. Their learning histories might have included being reinforced for persistence or for whining—operant conditioning at work. The chance to work in a group may be a reinforcer for some students and a punisher for others. Some teachers use questionnaires such as the one in Table 6.3 to identify effective reinforcers for their students. Remember, what works for one student may not be right for another. And students can get "too much of a good thing"; reinforcers can lose their potency if they are overused.

In addition to providing a diversity of reinforcers, teachers, classrooms, and schools should provide a diversity of models because students learn through observation. Do students see themselves in the social studies and science texts? Are there characters and authors in literature that reflect the background and values of the students and the community? Whose work is posted in the room? Who gets the privileges and responsibilities?

Convergences

Even though your classroom will be filled with many different learning histories, there are some convergences—principles that apply to all people:

Connect & Extend

TO YOUR TEACHING PORTFOLIO
Use Table 6.3, "What Do You Like? Reinforcement Ideas from Students," to generate ideas for appropriate reinforcers for students you will teach and include these ideas in your portfolio.

TABLE 6.3 What Do You Like? Reinforcement Ideas from Students

Name _____ Grade _____ Date _____

Please answer all the questions as completely as you can.

1. The school subjects I like best are:
2. Three things I like most to do in school are:
3. If I had 30 minutes' free time at school each day to do what I really liked, it would be:
4. My two favourite snacks are:
5. At recess I like most to (three things):
6. If I had $1 to spend on anything, I would buy:
7. Three jobs I would enjoy in the class are:
8. The two people I most like to work with in school are:
9. At home I really enjoy (three things):

Source: From Blackman, G., and Silberman, A. (1979). *Modification of child and adolescent behavior* (3rd ed.). Published by Wadsworth, Belmont, CA. Copyright © 1979 by Wadsworth Publishing Co. Reprinted with permission of the publisher.

1. No one eagerly repeats behaviours that have been punished or ignored. Without some sense of progress, it is difficult to persist.

2. When actions lead to consequences that are positive for the person involved, those actions are likely to be repeated.

3. Teachers often fail to use reinforcement to recognize appropriate behaviour; they respond instead to inappropriate behaviours, sometimes providing reinforcing attention in the process.

4. To be effective, praise must be a sincere recognition of a real accomplishment.

5. Whatever their current level of functioning, students can learn to be more self-managing.

Check Your Knowledge

- "One person's treasure is another's trash." What key feature of behavioural learning theory does this statement illustrate?

Apply to Practice

- Sean repeatedly drops pencils, paper, and books, and every time he does you enforce the rule that he must pick up what he's dropped. Still, he persists. What's happening?

- How can you enlist students to help you identify opportunities to reinforce their appropriate behaviour?

SUMMARY

Understanding Learning
(pp. 201–203)

Define learning.

Although theorists disagree about the definition of learning, most would agree that learning occurs when experience causes a change in a person's knowledge or behaviour. Behavioural theorists emphasize the role of environmental stimuli in learning and focus on behaviour—that is, on observable responses. Behavioural learning processes include contiguity learning, classical conditioning, and operant conditioning.

Early Explanations of Learning: Contiguity and Classical Conditioning
(pp. 203–204)

How does a neutral stimulus become a conditioned stimulus?

In classical conditioning, which was discovered by Pavlov, a previously neutral stimulus is repeatedly paired with a stimulus that evokes an emotional or physiological response. Later, the previously neutral stimulus alone evokes the response—that is, the neutral stimulus is conditioned to bring forth a conditioned response. The neutral stimulus has become a conditioned stimulus.

Compare and contrast response generalization and stimulus discrimination.

Conditioned responses are subject to the processes of response generalization and stimulus discrimination. After animals or people learn to respond to one particular stimulus, they may also have similar responses to other stimuli that are similar to the original one. This process is called *response generalization* because the conditioned response has generalized or occurred in the presence of similar stimuli. Stimulus discrimination is learning to make distinctions—to respond to one stimulus but not to others that are similar.

Operant Conditioning: Trying New Responses
(pp. 204–211)

What defines a consequence as a reinforcer? As a punisher?

According to Skinner's theory of operant learning, people learn through the effects of their deliberate responses. For an individual, the effects of consequences following an action may serve as reinforcers or punishers. A consequence is a reinforcer if it strengthens or maintains the response that brought it about, while a consequence is a punisher if it decreases or suppresses the response that brought it about.

How are negative reinforcement and punishment different?

The process of reinforcement (positive or negative) always involves strengthening behaviour. The focus of negative reinforcement is strengthening specific behaviour (putting away supplies or finishing in-class assignments, etc.). The teacher strengthens (reinforces) the behaviour by removing something aversive *as soon as the desired behaviour occurs*. Because the consequence involves removing or "subtracting" a stimulus, the reinforcement is negative. Punishment, on the other hand, involves *decreasing or suppressing behaviour*. Behaviour followed by a "punisher" is *less* likely to be repeated in similar situations in the future. Negative reinforcement also gives students a chance to exercise control. As soon as they perform the appropriate behaviour, the unpleasant situation ends. In contrast, punishment occurs after the fact, and a student cannot so easily control or terminate it.

How can you encourage persistence in behaviour?

Ratio schedules (based on the number of responses) encourage higher rates of response, and variable schedules (based on varying numbers of responses or varying time intervals) encourage persistence of responses.

What is the difference between a prompt and a cue?

A cue is an antecedent stimulus just before particular behaviour is to take place. A prompt is an additional cue following the first cue. There are two principles for using a cue and a prompt to teach new behaviour. First, make sure that the environmental stimulus you want to become a cue occurs immediately before the prompt you are using, so that students will learn to respond to the cue and not rely only on the prompt. Second, fade the prompt as soon as possible so that students do not become dependent on it.

Applied Behaviour Analysis
(pp. 211–220)

What are the steps in applied behaviour analysis?

The steps are: (1) Clearly specify the behaviour to be changed and note the current level. (2) Plan a specific intervention using antecedents, consequences, or both. (3) Keep track of the results and modify the plan if necessary.

How can the Premack principle help you identify reinforcers?

The Premack principle states that high-frequency behaviour (a preferred activity) can be an effective reinforcer for a low-frequency behaviour (a less-preferred activity). This is sometimes referred to as "Grandma's rule": First do what I want you to do, then you may do what you want to do. The best way to determine appropriate reinforcers for your students may be to watch what they do in their free time. For most students, talking, moving around the room, sitting near a friend, being exempt from assignments or tests, reading magazines, or playing games are preferred activities.

When is shaping an appropriate approach?

Shaping helps students develop new responses a little at a time, so it is useful for building complex skills, working toward difficult goals, and increasing persistence, endurance, accuracy, or speed. Because shaping is a time-consuming process, however, it should not be used if success can be attained through simpler methods such as cueing.

What are some limitations of punishment?

Punishment in and of itself does not lead to any positive behaviour. Thus, whenever you consider the use of punishment, you should make it part of a two-pronged attack. The first goal is to carry out the punishment and suppress the undesirable behaviour. The second goal is to make clear what the student should be doing instead and to provide reinforcement for those desirable actions. Thus, while the problem behaviour is being suppressed, positive alternative responses are being strengthened.

How can functional behavioural assessment and positive behavioural supports be used to improve student behaviours?

In doing a functional behavioural assessment, a teacher studies the antecedents and consequences of problem behaviours to determine the reason or function of the behaviour. Then, positive behavioural supports are designed to replace problem behaviours with new actions that serve the same purpose for the student, but do not have the same problems.

Behavioural Approaches to Teaching and Management
(pp. 221–224)

Describe the managerial strategies of group consequences, contracts, and token programs.

Using group consequences involves basing reinforcement for the whole class on the behaviour of the whole class. In a contingency contract program, the teacher draws up an individual contract with each student, describing exactly what the student must do to earn a particular privilege or reward. In token programs, students earn tokens for both academic work and positive classroom behaviour. The tokens may be points, checks, holes punched in a card, chips, play money, or anything else that is easily identified as the student's property. Periodically, the students exchange the tokens they have earned for some desired reward. A teacher must use these programs with caution, emphasizing learning and not just "good" behaviour.

Thinking about Behaviour: Observational Learning and Cognitive Behaviour Modification
(pp. 224–233)

Distinguish between social learning and social cognitive theories.

Social learning theory was an early neo-behavioural theory that expanded behavioural views of reinforcement and punishment. In behavioural views, reinforcement and punishment directly affect behaviour. In social learning theory, seeing another person, a model, reinforced or punished can have similar effects on the observer's behaviour. Social cognitive theory expands social learning theory to include cognitive factors such as beliefs, expectations, and perceptions of self.

Distinguish between enactive and vicarious learning.

Enactive learning is learning by doing and experiencing the consequences of your actions. *Vicarious learning* is learning by observing, which challenges the behaviourist idea that cognitive factors are unnecessary in an explanation of learning. Much is going on mentally before performance and reinforcement can even take place.

What are the elements of observational learning?

In order to learn through observation, we have to pay attention to aspects of the situation that will help us learn. In order to imitate the behaviour of a model, we have to retain the information. This involves mentally representing the model's actions in some way, probably as verbal steps. In the production phase, practice makes the behaviour smoother and more expert. Sometimes we need a great deal of practice, feedback, and coaching about subtle points before we can reproduce the behaviour of the model. Finally, motivation shapes observational learning through incentives and reinforcement. We may not perform a learned behaviour until there is some motivation or incentive to do so. Reinforcement can focus attention, encourage reproduction or practice, and maintain the new learning.

What are the steps in self-management?

Students can apply behaviour analysis on their own to manage their own behaviour. Teachers can encourage the development of self-management skills by allowing students to participate in setting goals, keeping track of progress, evaluating accomplishments, and selecting and giving their own reinforcements. Teachers can also use cognitive behaviour modification, a behaviour-change program described by Meichenbaum in which students are directly taught how to use self-instruction.

Problems and Issues
(pp. 233–235)

What are the main criticisms of behavioural approaches?

The misuse or abuse of behavioural learning methods is unethical. Critics of behavioural methods also point out the danger that reinforcement could decrease interest in learning by overemphasizing rewards and could have a negative impact on other students. Guidelines do exist, however, for helping teachers use behavioural learning principles appropriately and ethically.

Diversity and Convergences in Behavioural Learning
(pp. 236–237)

"One person's treasure is another's trash." What key feature of behavioural learning theory does this statement illustrate?

According to behavioural learning theory, there is a difference between a reward and a reinforcer. A reinforcer is a consequence of behaviour that increases the frequency, intensity, or duration of that behaviour. There is a functional relationship between reinforcers and future behaviour. A reward, on the other hand, is a material object or an opportunity given to someone that we predict might function as a reinforcer for them—but it's not a sure thing. What might cause one person to treasure a keepsake—to reinforce whatever he or she does to preserve that keepsake—could cause another person to toss it in the trash. What the first person perceives as a reinforcer is just a reward. The second person doesn't value it at all.

KEY TERMS

antecedents,   p. 205

applied behaviour analysis,   p. 211

aversive,   p. 206

behaviour modification,   p. 211

behavioural learning theories,   p. 201

classical conditioning,   p. 203

cognitive behaviour modification,   p. 232

conditioned response (CR),   p. 204

conditioned stimulus (CS),   p. 204

consequences,   p. 205

contiguity,   p. 203

contingency contract,   p. 222

continuous reinforcement schedule,   p. 208

cueing,   p. 210

extinction,   p. 204

functional behavioural assessment (FBA),   p. 219

good-behaviour game,   p. 221

group consequences,   p. 221

intermittent reinforcement schedule,   p. 208

interval schedule,   p. 208

learning,   p. 201

modelling,   p. 228

negative reinforcement,   p. 206

neutral stimulus,   p. 203

observational learning,   p. 225

operant conditioning,   p. 205

BECOMING A PROFESSIONAL

Reflecting on the Chapter

Can you apply the ideas from this chapter on learning to solve the following problems of practice?

Preschool and Kindergarten

- A student in your class is terrified of the class's pet guinea pigs. The child won't get close to the cages and wants you to "give them away." How would you help the child overcome this fear?

Elementary and Middle School

- You want your students to improve their time management and self-management abilities so that they will be prepared for the increased demands of high school. What would you do?

Junior High and High School

- You have been assigned an emotionally disturbed student.

She seemed fine at first, but now you notice that when she encounters difficult work, she often interrupts or teases other students. How would you work with this student and the class to improve the situation?

- It takes you 10 minutes to get your class to settle down after the bell rings. Analyze this situation. What could be maintaining this problem? What could you do?

Check Your Understanding

- Understand the differences between reinforcers and punishers, and between negative reinforcement and punishment.
- Know how schedules of reinforcement affect behaviour.
- Be clear about how to use shaping to change behaviour.
- Know how to develop programs of teaching that apply

principles of behavioural models of learning.

Your Teaching Portfolio

What is your stance on using extrinsic reinforcement and punishment in teaching? Be prepared to answer questions about these issues in your interviews.

Teaching Resources

Use Table 6.3 ("What Do You Like? Reinforcement Ideas from Students," page 236) to generate ideas for appropriate reinforcers for students you will teach and include these ideas in your Portfolio.

Add Figures 6.2 ("Written Prompts: A Peer-Tutoring Checklist," page 211), 6.4 ("A Contingency Contract for Completing Assignments," page 222), and 6.5 ("Posters to Remind Students to 'Talk Themselves Through' Listening, Planning, Working, and Checking in School," page 233) to your Teaching Resources file.

Teachers' Casebook

What Would They Do?

Here is how two practising teachers responded to the teaching situation presented at the beginning of this chapter about a class out of control.

Janice Farrell Colby
St. Joseph School
Sydney, Nova Scotia

Accentuate the Positive—Eliminate the Negative

What goes on in our classrooms can be productive or destructive in relation to a child's self-image. I would like children to work with me in a cooperative, positive learning environment. I would use several strategies so that children learn such skills as responsibility, cooperation, and problem solving. These skills can help students come to terms with their own behaviour, knowing what they need to do rather than being told what to do.

I would use basic life skills in what I do every day. These skills are valuable ways to pass the ownership and responsibility of actions to each individual. Through a positive, cooperative learning plan, I would be flexible in my expectations while still adhering to some basic principles. These life skills are easily integrated in all subject areas. Working within this model, children would understand they are unique, important, and special and would develop their own self-worth and self-esteem. The strengths of each child would be emphasized.

Teachers shouldn't be afraid to be *human*. We assume many roles in a classroom but, most importantly, the roles of teacher and friend. We learn from one another; involving the students in decisions that affect them helps them feel important and worthwhile. Look on teaching as a daily adventure in humanity. Developing the basic life skills will help students prepare for the future.

Get to know your students and their strengths. Students and teachers should establish and achieve positive goals that will help promote a healthy learning environment. As educators, we all have the opportunity to plant a seed, but we must also be willing to nurture it so that each child will grow and develop to full potential in a safe and caring environment. Learning is ongoing, and as teachers we need to facilitate this learning process to encourage and develop the positive while making efforts to eliminate the negative. We must all try as teachers to remember that *the art of teaching lies in teaching from the heart!*

My Golden Rule   *by Janice Farrell Colby*

May I always have the strength
To stand tall and be ever so strong
So that the children I teach will realize
That I too can be wrong.
May I always have the insight
To not let the opportunity pass
To help the child that needs me
Each day within my class.
May I always have a sense of caring
Down deep within my heart
For each and every child I teach
So that I can always do my part.
May I always be ready to listen
And use love and guidance to try
To be there for my children
And to hear their gentle silent cry.
May I always value what they can offer
And know they may just need me near
To guide them along as they struggle
And help them ease away any fear.
May I always have the strength
To stand tall and be ever so strong
So that the children I teach will realize
That I too can be wrong.
May we always be ready to help one another
So that we can come to realize
When we walk along hand in hand
We all have our silent cries.

Rosemary Dixon
Retired
Ottawa, Ontario

This situation requires the use of both short- and long-term strategies. Positive behaviour must be rewarded immediately—by positive verbal statements and, initially, by a system of token rewards for which a larger reward, such as free time, will be given later. Whenever possible, negative behaviour must be ignored, as these children must be accepting negative attention as desirable.

Clear, explicit rules must be instituted immediately. These children should be involved in the making of these rules and in deciding on consequences for the infraction of rules. I would try to have as few rules as possible and insist that they be adhered to with absolute consistency. I would have to remind myself that learning would not take place in this class until the behaviour improved. I must not be afraid to stop the class at any time, send all the children to their seats, or call the children into a circle to discuss problems that are arising.

My first long-term strategy would be to get to know as many of the parents as possible. They could become invaluable allies. The teacher might have become a faceless name about whom horror stories were told. The parents would naturally feel more positive toward a friendly, concerned educator who had their children's best interests at heart and who was willing to involve them in the learning process.

How much help can I expect from my principal or vice-principal? It would be a good idea to find out if these colleagues would be willing to support my rewards program. A visit from the principal to the class or by the children to the principal's office so that praise and rewards could be given for appropriate behaviour would probably be a pleasant and reinforcing change. For these children, previous encounters with administration have been mostly negative.

Finally, I would take up offers of help from my colleagues. Perhaps my class, or groups from the class, could be involved in cooperative or friendly competitive activities with another class.

These strategies should lead to improved self-esteem, an improved reputation within the school, increased motivation, and a return to appropriate school behaviour.

Looking at a Star, 1999, © Christian Pierre/SuperStock.

Teachers' Casebook

What Would You Do?

The students in your senior history classes seem to equate understanding with memorizing. They prepare for each test by memorizing exact words in the textbook. Even the best students seem to think flash cards are the only learning strategy possible. In fact, when you try to get them to think about history by reading some original sources, debating issues in class, or examining art and music from the time period they are studying, they rebel. "Will this be on the test?" "Why are we looking at these pictures—will we have to know who painted them and when?" "What's this got to do with history?" Even students who participate in the debates seem to use words and phrases straight from the textbook without knowing what they are saying.

Critical Thinking

What do these students "know" about history? What are their beliefs and expectations, and how do these affect their learning? Why do you think they insist on using the rote memory approach? How would you teach your students to learn in this new way? How will these issues affect the grade levels you will teach?

Collaboration

With two or three other people in your class, talk about teachers you've had who helped you develop deep knowledge about a topic. How did they guide your thinking to move past memorizing to a more complete understanding?

In this chapter, we turn from behavioural theories of learning to the cognitive perspective. This means a shift from "viewing the learners and their behaviours as products of incoming environmental stimuli" to seeing the learners as "sources of plans, intentions, goals, ideas, memories, and emotions actively used to attend to, select, and construct meaning from stimuli and knowledge from experience" (Wittrock, 1982, pp. 1–2). We will begin with a discussion of the general cognitive approach to learning and memory and the importance of knowledge in learning. To understand memory, we will consider a widely accepted cognitive model, information processing, which suggests that information is manipulated in several storage systems. We will briefly consider an alternative to this model of information processing—depth of processing. Next we will explore metacognition, a field of study that may provide insights into individual and developmental differences in learning. Then we will turn to ideas about how teachers can help their students become more knowledgeable.

By the time you have completed this chapter, you should be able to answer these questions:

- *What is the role of knowledge in learning?*
- *What is the human information processing model of memory?*
- *How do perception, attention, schemas, and scripts influence learning and remembering?*
- *What are declarative, procedural, and conditional knowledge?*
- *Why do students forget what they have learned?*
- *What is the role of metacognition in learning and remembering?*
- *What are the stages in the development of cognitive skills?*

ELEMENTS OF THE COGNITIVE PERSPECTIVE

The cognitive perspective is both the oldest and the youngest member of the psychological community. It is old because discussions of the nature of knowledge, the value of reason, and the contents of the mind date back at least to the ancient Greek philosophers (Hernshaw, 1987). From the late 1800s until the late 20th century, however, cognitive studies fell from favour and behaviourism thrived. Then, several factors—research during the Second World War on the development of complex human skills; the computer revolution; and breakthroughs in understanding language development—all stimulated a resurgence in cognitive research. Evidence accumulated indicating that people do more than simply respond to reinforcement and punishment. For example, we plan our responses, use strategies to help us remember, and organize the material we are learning in our own unique ways (Miller, Galanter, & Pribram, 1960; Shuell, 1986). With the growing realization that learning is an active mental process, educational psychologists became interested in how people think, learn concepts, and solve problems (e.g., Ausubel, 1963; Bruner, Goodnow, & Austin, 1956).

Interest in concept learning and problem solving soon gave way, however, to interest in how knowledge is represented in the mind and particularly how it is remembered. Remembering and forgetting became major topics for investigation in cognitive psychology in the 1970s and 1980s, and the information processing model of memory dominated research.

Today, there is renewed interest in learning, thinking, and problem solving. The **cognitive view of learning** can be described as a generally agreed-upon philosophical orientation. This means that cognitive theorists share basic notions about learning and memory. Most importantly, cognitive psychologists assume that mental processes exist, that these processes can be studied scientifically, and that humans are active participants in their own acts of cognition (Ashcraft, 2006).

Comparing Cognitive and Behavioural Views

The cognitive and behavioural views differ in their assumptions about what is learned. According to the cognitive view, knowledge is learned, and changes in knowledge make changes in behaviour possible. In the behavioural view, the new behaviour itself is learned (Shuell, 1986). Both behavioural and cognitive theorists believe that reinforcement is important in learning, but for different reasons. Strict behaviourists maintain that reinforcement strengthens responses; cognitive theorists see reinforcement as a source of information that provides feedback about what is likely to happen if behaviour is repeated or changed.

The cognitive view sees learning as extending and transforming the understanding we already have, not simply writing associations on the blank slates of our brains (Greeno, Collins, & Resnick, 1996). Instead of being passively influenced by environmental events, people actively choose, practise, pay attention, ignore, reflect, and make many other decisions as they pursue goals. Older cognitive views emphasized the *acquisition* of knowledge, but newer approaches stress its *construction* (Anderson, Reder, & Simon, 1996; Greeno, Collins, & Resnick, 1996; Mayer, 1996).

The methods of cognitive and behavioural researchers also differ. Much work on behavioural learning principles has studied animals in controlled laboratory settings. The goal is to identify a few general laws of learning that apply to all higher organisms—including humans—regardless of age, intelligence, or other individual differences. Cognitive psychologists, on the other hand, study human learning in a wide range of situations. Because they focus on individual and developmental differences in cognition, they have not been as concerned with general laws of learning. This is one reason why there is no single cognitive model or theory of learning representative of the entire field.

Connect & Extend

TO OTHER CHAPTERS
Two different models of instruction based on principles of cognitive learning—Bruner's discovery learning and Ausubel's expository teaching—are described in **Chapter 8.**

cognitive view of learning A general approach that views learning as an active mental process of acquiring, remembering, and using knowledge.

The cognitive view sees people as active learners who initiate experiences, seek out information to solve problems, and reorganize what they already know to achieve new insights.

The Importance of Knowledge in Learning

Knowledge is the outcome of learning. If we learn a politician's name, the history of cognitive psychology, or the rules of tennis, we know something new. But knowledge is more than the end product of learning; it also guides new learning. The cognitive approach suggests that one of the most important elements in the learning process is what the individual brings to learning situations. What we already know is the foundation and frame for constructing all future learning. Knowledge determines to a great extent what we will pay attention to, perceive, learn, remember, and forget (Alexander, 1996; Bransford, Brown, & Cocking, 2000).

An Example Study. A study by Recht and Leslie (1988) shows the importance of knowledge in understanding and remembering new information. These psychologists identified junior high school students who were either very good or very poor readers, then tested the students on their knowledge of baseball. They found that knowledge of baseball was not related to reading ability. So the researchers were able to identify four groups of students: *good readers/high baseball knowledge*, *good readers/low baseball knowledge*, *poor readers/high baseball knowledge*, and *poor readers/low baseball knowledge*. Then all the students read a passage describing a baseball game and were tested in a number of ways to see if they understood and remembered what they had read.

The results demonstrated the power of knowledge. Poor readers who knew a lot about baseball remembered more than good readers with little baseball knowledge and almost as much as good readers who knew baseball. Poor readers who knew little about baseball remembered the least of what they had read. So a good basis of knowledge can be more important than good learning strategies in understanding and remembering—but extensive knowledge plus good strategies is even better.

General and Specific Knowledge. Knowledge in the cognitive perspective includes both subject or domain-specific understandings (math, music, soccer, etc.) and general cognitive abilities, such as planning, solving problems, and comprehending language (Greeno, Collins, & Resnick, 1996, p. 16). So, there are different kinds of knowledge. For example, **general knowledge** about how to read or write or use a word processor is useful in and out of school. **Domain-specific knowledge**, on the other hand, pertains to a particular task or subject. For example, knowing the shortstop plays between second and third base is specific to the domain of baseball. Of course, there is no absolute line between general and domain-specific knowledge. When you were first learning to read, you may have studied specific facts about the sounds of letters. At that time, knowledge about letter sounds was specific to the domain of reading. But now you can use both knowledge about sounds and the ability to read in more general ways (Alexander, 1992; Schunk, 2004).

What we know exists in our memory. To know something is to remember it over time and be able to recall it when you need it. Psychologists have studied memory extensively. Let's see what they have learned.

general knowledge Information that is useful in many different kinds of tasks; information that applies to many situations.

domain-specific knowledge Information that is useful in a particular situation or that applies only to one specific topic.

Check Your Knowledge

- Contrast cognitive and behavioural views of learning in terms of what is learned and the role of reinforcement.
- How does knowledge affect learning?

Apply to Practice

- What do you already know that will help you in learning the material in this chapter?

THE INFORMATION PROCESSING MODEL OF MEMORY

There are a number of theories of memory, but the most common are the **information processing** explanations (Ashcraft, 2006; Hunt & Ellis, 1999; Sternberg, 1999). We will use this well-researched framework for examining learning and memory.

information processing The human mind's activity of taking in, storing, and using information.

An Overview of the Information Processing Model

Early information processing views of memory used the computer as a model. Like the computer, the human mind takes in information, performs operations on it to change its form and content, stores the information, retrieves it when needed, and generates responses to it. Thus, processing involves gathering and representing information, or *encoding*; holding information, or *storage*; and getting at the information when needed, or *retrieval*. The whole system is guided by *control processes* that determine how and when information will flow through each part of the system.

For most cognitive psychologists, the computer model is only a metaphor for human mental activity. But other cognitive scientists, particularly those studying artificial intelligence, try to design and program computers to "think" and solve problems like human beings (Anderson, 1995a; Schunk, 2000). Some theorists suggest that the operation of the brain resembles a large number of very slow computers, all operating in parallel (at the same time), with each computer dedicated to a different, specific task (Ashcraft, 2006).

Figure 7.1 is a schematic representation of a typical information processing model of memory, derived from the ideas of several theorists (Atkinson & Shiffrin, 1968; R. M. Gagné, 1985). Other models have been suggested, but all of the models, despite their variations, resemble flow charts. To understand this model, let's examine each element.

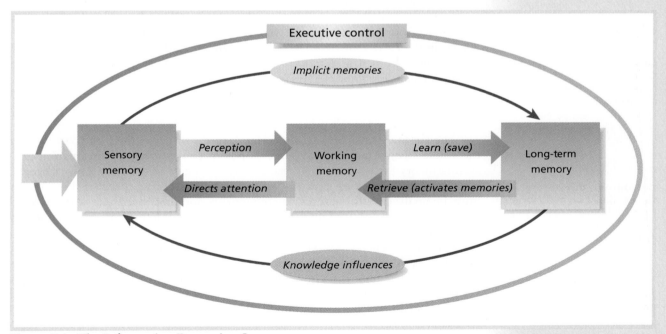

Figure 7.1 The Information Processing System

Information is encoded in the sensory register, where perception determines what will be held in working memory for further use. Thoroughly processed information becomes part of long-term memory and can be activated at any time to return to working memory.

Sensory Memory

Stimuli from the environment (sights, sounds, smells, etc.) constantly bombard our **receptors**, the body's mechanisms for seeing, hearing, tasting, smelling, and feeling. **Sensory memory** is the initial processing that transforms these incoming stimuli into information so that we can make sense of them. Even though sights and sounds may last only fractions of a second, the transformations (information) that represent these sensations are briefly held in the *sensory register* or *sensory information store* so that this initial processing can take place (Driscoll, 2005; Sperling, 1960).

receptors Parts of the human body that receive sensory information.

sensory memory System that holds sensory information very briefly.

Capacity, Duration, and Contents of Sensory Memory. The capacity of sensory memory is very large; sensory memory can take in more information than we can possibly handle at once. But this vast amount of sensory information is fragile—it lasts between one and three seconds.

If you wave a pencil (or your finger) back and forth before your eyes while you stare straight ahead, what do you see? You just experienced this brief holding of sensory information in your own sensory register. You can see a trace of the pencil after the actual stimulus has been removed (Lindsay & Norman, 1977). The information content of sensory memory resembles the sensations from the original stimulus. Visual sensations are coded briefly by the sensory register as images, almost like photographs. Auditory sensations are coded as sound patterns, similar to echoes. It may be that the other senses also have their own codes. Thus, for a second or so, a wealth of data from sensory experience remains intact. In these instants, we have a chance to select and organize information for further processing. Perception and attention are critical at this stage.

perception Detecting and interpreting sensory information.

Perception. The process of detecting a stimulus and assigning meaning to it is called **perception**. This meaning is constructed based on both objective reality and our existing knowledge. For example, consider these marks: 13. If asked what the letter is, you would say, "B." If asked what the number is, you would say, "13." The actual marks remain the same; the perception of them—their meaning—changes depending on whether you are asked to recognize a number or a letter. To a child without appropriate knowledge to perceive either a number or a letter, the marks would probably be meaningless (F. Smith, 1975).

Some of our present-day understanding of perception is based on studies conducted in the early 20th century, first in Germany and then on this continent, by psychologists known as *Gestalt theorists*. **Gestalt**, which means something like *pattern* or *configuration* in German, refers to people's tendency to organize sensory information into patterns or relationships. Instead of perceiving bits and pieces of unrelated information, we perceive organized, meaningful wholes. Figure 7.2 presents a few Gestalt principles.

Gestalt A pattern or whole; Gestalt theorists hold that people organize their perceptions into coherent wholes.

The Gestalt principles explain certain aspects of perception, but they are not the whole story. There are two other kinds of explanations in information processing theory for how we recognize patterns and give meaning to sensory events. The first is called *feature analysis,* or **bottom-up processing**, because the stimulus must be analyzed into features or components and assembled into a meaningful pattern "from the bottom up." For example, a capital letter "A" consists of two relatively straight lines joined at a 45-degree angle (/\) and a horizontal line (—) through the middle. Whenever we see these features, or anything close enough, including Λ, A, **A**, *A*, *A*, and A, we recognize an "A" (Anderson, 2005). Bottom-up processing mainly explains how we are able to read words written in other people's handwriting. We also have a **prototype** (a best example or classic case) of an "A" stored in memory to use along with features to help us detect the letter "A" (Driscoll, 2005).

bottom-up processing Perception based on noticing separate defining features and assembling them into a recognizable pattern.

prototype A best example or best representative of a category.

If all perception relied on feature analysis and prototypes, learning would be very slow. Luckily, humans are capable of another type of perception, based on knowledge and expectation, called **top-down processing**. To recognize patterns rapidly, in addition to noting features, we use what we already know about the

top-down processing Perceiving based on the context and the patterns you expect to occur in that situation.

Figure 7.2 Examples of Gestalt Principles

Gestalt principles of perception explain how we "see" patterns in the world around us.

Source: From Schunk, D. H. (1996). *Learning theories: An educational perspective* (2nd ed). Saddle River, NJ: Prentice Hall. Copyright © 1996. Adapted by permission of Prentice-Hall, Inc., Saddle River, NJ.

a. Figure–ground
What do you see? Faces or a vase? One is figure—the other is ground (background).

b. Proximity
You see these lines as three groups because of the proximity of lines.

c. Similarity
You see these lines as an alternating pattern because of the similarity in height of lines.

d. Closure
You perceive a circle instead of dotted curved lines.

situation—what we know about words or pictures or the way the world generally operates. For example, you would not have seen the marks on the previous page as the letter "A" if you had no knowledge of the Roman alphabet. So, what you know also affects what you are able to perceive. The role of knowledge in perception is represented by the arrows pointing left in Figure 7.1 (on page 247) from long-term memory (stored knowledge) to working memory and then to sensory memory.

The Role of Attention. If every variation in colour, movement, sound, smell, temperature, and so on, had to be perceived, life would be impossible. But **attention** is selective. By paying attention to certain stimuli and ignoring others, we select from all the possibilities what we will process. What we pay attention to is guided to a certain extent by what we already know and what we need to know, so attention is involved in and influenced by all three memory processes in Figure 7.1. Attention is also affected by what else is happening at the time, by the complexity of the task, and by your ability to control or focus your attention (Driscoll, 2005). Some students with attention-deficit disorder have great difficulty focusing attention or ignoring competing stimuli.

Attention is a very limited resource. We can pay attention to only one demanding task at a time (Anderson, 2005). For example, there was a time as Anita was learning to drive when she couldn't listen to the radio and drive at the same time. After some practice, she could listen, but had to turn the radio off when traffic was heavy. After years of practice, she can plan a class or talk on the phone as she drives. This is because many processes that initially require attention and concentration become automatic with practice. Actually, **automaticity** probably is a matter of degree—we are not completely automatic but rather more or less automatic in our performances depending on how much practice we have had and on features of the current situation (Anderson, 2005).

Attention and Teaching. The first step in learning is paying attention. Students cannot process something that they do not recognize or perceive (Lachter, Forster, & Ruthruff, 2004). Many factors in the classroom influence student attention. Eye-catching or startling displays or actions can draw attention at the beginning of a lesson. A teacher might begin a science lesson on air pressure by blowing up a balloon until it pops. Bright colours, underlining, highlighting of written or spoken words, calling students by name, surprise events, intriguing questions, variety in tasks and teaching methods, and changes in voice level, lighting, or pacing can

attention Focus on a stimulus.

automaticity The ability to perform thoroughly learned tasks without much mental effort.

Connect & Extend

TO THE RESEARCH
Flavell (1985) described four aspects of attention in developing children:

1. *Controlled*: Young children develop longer attention spans and ability to focus on important details, ignoring minor ones.

2. *Tailored to task*: Older children focus attention on most difficult material being learned (Berk, 1994).

3. *Directive*: Children develop a feel for cues (teacher's voice, gestures) telling them when/how to direct their attention.

4. *Self-monitoring*: Children learn to decide if they are using the right strategy and to change it if it's not working.

Connect & Extend

TO PRACTICE
Attention has an important place in instructional activities. What steps can a teacher take to gain and maintain student attention during instruction?

working memory The information that you are focusing on at a given moment.

all be used to focus attention. And students have to maintain attention—they have to stay focused on the important features of the learning situation. The Guidelines below offer additional ideas for capturing and maintaining students' attention.

Working Memory

The information in sensory memory is available for further processing as soon as it is noticed and transformed into patterns of images or sounds (or perhaps other types of sensory codes). **Working memory** is the "workbench" of the memory system, the component of memory where new information is held temporarily and combined with knowledge from long-term memory. Its *content* is activated information—what you are thinking about at the moment. For this reason, some

GUIDELINES

GAINING AND MAINTAINING ATTENTION

Use signals.

EXAMPLES

1. Develop a signal that tells students to stop what they are doing and focus on you. Some teachers move to a particular spot in the room, flick the lights, tap the table, or play a chord on the class piano. Mix visual and auditory signals.

2. Avoid distracting behaviours, such as tapping a pencil while talking, that interfere with both signals and attention to learning.

3. Give short, clear directions before, not during, transitions.

4. Be playful with younger children: Use a dramatic voice, sensational hat, or clapping game (Miller, 2005).

Reach out rather than call out (Miller, 2005).

EXAMPLES

1. Walk to the child, look into his or her eyes.

2. Speak in a firm but non-threatening voice.

3. Use child's name.

Make sure the purpose of the lesson or assignment is clear to students.

EXAMPLES

1. Write the goals or objectives on the board and discuss them with students before starting. Ask students to summarize or restate the goals.

2. Explain the reasons for learning, and ask students for examples of how they will apply their understanding of the material.

3. Tie the new material to previous lessons—show an outline or map of how the new topic fits with previous and upcoming material.

Incorporate variety, curiosity, and surprise.

EXAMPLES

1. Arouse curiosity with questions such as "What would happen if?"

2. Create shock by staging an unexpected event such as a loud argument just before a lesson on communication.

3. Alter the physical environment by changing the arrangement of the room or moving to a different setting.

4. Shift sensory channels by giving a lesson that requires students to touch, smell, or taste.

5. Use movements, gestures, and voice inflection—walk around the room, point, and speak softly and then more emphatically. (Anita's husband has been known to jump up on his desk to make an important point in his university classes!)

Ask questions and provide frames for answering.

EXAMPLES

1. Ask students why the material is important, how they intend to study, and what strategies they will use.

2. Give students self-checking or self-editing guides that focus on common mistakes or have them work in pairs to improve each other's work—sometimes it is difficult to pay attention to your own errors.

For more ideas about gaining student attention, see **www.inspiringteachers.com/tips/management/attention.html**.

Teachers must first be able to gain and maintain their students' attention, especially in learning situations that may be less inherently interesting. Lessons might be introduced with an eye-catching or startling display to "grab" students.

psychologists consider the working memory to be synonymous with "consciousness" (Sweller, van Merrienboer, & Paas, 1998). Unlike sensory memory or long-term memory, the capacity of working memory is very limited—something that many of your professors may forget as they race through a lecture while you work to hold and process the information.

You may have heard the term **short-term memory**. This was an earlier name for the brief memory component of the information processing system. Short-term memory is not exactly the same as working memory. Working memory includes both temporary storage and active processing. It is the workbench of memory where active mental effort is applied to new and old information. But short-term memory usually means just storage—the immediate memory for new information that can be held for about 15 to 20 seconds (Baddeley, 2001).

Early experiments suggested that the capacity of short-term memory was only about five to nine separate new items at once (Miller, 1956). Later we will see that this limitation can be overcome by using strategies such as chunking or grouping—but some limits on working memory do generally hold true in everyday life. It is quite common to remember a new phone number after looking it up, as you walk across the room to make the call. But what if you have two phone calls to make in succession? Two new phone numbers—20 digits in cities like Vancouver, where one has to dial the area code as well as the number—probably cannot be stored together.

A current view of working memory is that it is composed of at least three elements: the central executive that controls attention and other mental resources (the "worker" of working memory), the phonological loop that holds verbal and acoustical (sound) information, and the visuospatial sketchpad for visual and spatial information (Gathercole, Pickering, Ambridge, & Wearing, 2004).

The Central Executive. In solving the following problem from Ashcraft (2006, p. 190), pay attention to how you go about the process: $(4 + 5) \times 2\backslash3 + (12/4)$. The central executive of your working memory focused your attention on the facts that you needed (what is $4 + 5 = 9 \times 2 = 18$?), retrieved rules for which operations to do first, and recalled how to divide. The **central executive** supervises attention, makes plans, retrieves memories, and integrates information. Comprehending language, reasoning, rehearsing information to transfer to long-term memory—all these activities and more are handled by the central executive, as you can see in Figure 7.3 on page 252. Two systems help out and support the central executive— the phonological loop and the visuospatial sketchpad.

short-term memory Component of memory system that holds information for about 15 to 20 seconds.

central executive The part of working memory responsible for monitoring and directing attention and other mental resources.

Figure 7.3 Three Parts of Working Memory

The central executive system is the pool of mental resources for such cognitive activities as focusing attention, reasoning, and comprehension. The phonological loop holds verbal and sound information, and the visuospatial sketchpad holds visual and spatial information. The system is limited and can be overwhelmed if information is too much or too difficult.

Source: Adapted from Ashcraft, M. H. (2002). *Cognition* (3rd ed.). Upper Saddle River, NJ: Prentice-Hall. Copyright © by Prentice Hall. Reprinted by permission of Pearson Education, Inc., Upper Saddle River, NJ.

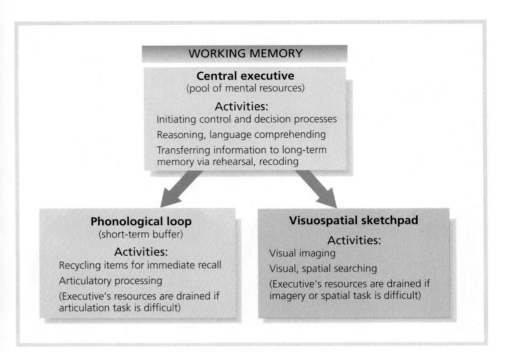

phonological loop Part of working memory; memory rehearsal system for verbal and sound information lasting about 1.5 to 2 seconds.

The Phonological Loop.   The **phonological loop** is a system for rehearsing words and sounds in short-term memory. It is the place where you put the "18" (4 + 5 = 9 × 2 = 18) from the top line of the problem above while you calculated the 3 + (12/4) on the bottom of the problem. Baddeley (1986, 2001) suggests that we can hold as much in the phonological loop as we can rehearse (say to ourselves) in 1.5 to 2 seconds. In cities like Ottawa, the seven-digit telephone number fits this limitation. But what if you tried to hold these seven words in mind: *disentangle appropriation gossamer anti-intellectual preventative foreclosure documentation* (Gray, 2002)? Besides being a mouthful, these words take longer than two seconds to rehearse and are more difficult to hold in working memory than seven single digits or seven short words.

Remember—put in your working memory—that we are discussing temporarily holding *new information*. In daily life, we certainly can hold more than five to nine bits or 1.5 seconds of information at once. While you are dialling that 7- or 10-digit phone number you just looked up, you are bound to have other things "on your mind"—in your memory—such as how to use a telephone, whom you are calling, and why. You don't have to pay attention to these things; they are not new knowledge. Some of the processes, such as dialling the phone, have become automatic. However, because of the working memory's limitations, if you were in a foreign country and were attempting to use an unfamiliar telephone system, you might very well have trouble remembering the phone number because your central executive was trying to figure out the foreign phone system at the same time. Even a few bits of new information can be too much to remember if the new information is very complex or unfamiliar or if you have to integrate several elements to make sense of a situation (Sweller, van Merrienboer, & Paas, 1998).

The Visuospatial Sketchpad.   Now try this problem from Gray (2002): If you rotate a *p* 180 degrees clockwise around its centre, do you get a *b* or a *d*? Most people answer this question by creating a visual image of a "p" and rotating it. The **visuospatial sketchpad** is the place where you manipulated the image (after your central executive retrieved the meaning of "180 degrees," of course). Working in the visuospatial sketchpad has some of the same aspects as actually looking at a picture or object. If you have to solve the "p" problem and also pay attention to an image on a screen, you will be slowed down just as you would be if you had to look back and forth between two different objects. But if you had to solve the "p"

visuospatial sketchpad Part of working memory; holding system for visual and spatial information.

problem while repeating digits, there is little slowdown. You can use your phonological loop and your visuospatial sketchpad at the same time, but each is quickly filled and easily overburdened. In fact, each kind of task—verbal and visual—appears to happen in different areas of the brain. As we will see later, there are some individual differences in the capacities of these systems as well (Ashcraft, 2006; Gray, 2002).

Duration and Contents of Working Memory.   The *duration* of information in working memory is short, about 5 to 20 seconds. (This is why some theories call working memory *short-term* memory instead.) It may seem to you that a memory system with a 20-second time limit is not very useful. But without this system, you would have already forgotten what you read in the first part of this sentence before you came to these last few words. This would clearly make understanding sentences difficult.

The *contents* of information in working memory may be in the form of images that resemble the perceptions in sensory memory, or the information may be structured more abstractly, based on meaning.

Retaining Information in Working Memory.   Because information in working memory is fragile and easily lost, it must be kept activated to be retained. Activation is high as long as you are focusing on information, but activation decays or fades quickly when attention shifts away. Holding information in working memory is like keeping a series of plates spinning on top of poles in a circus act. The performer gets one plate spinning, moves to the next plate, and the next, but has to return to the first plate before it slows down too much and falls off its pole. If we don't keep the information "spinning" in working memory—keep it activated—it will "fall off" (Anderson, 2005, 1995). When activation fades, forgetting follows, as shown in Figure 7.4. To keep information activated in working memory for longer than 20 seconds, most people keep rehearsing the information mentally.

There are two types of rehearsal (Craik & Lockhart, 1972). **Maintenance rehearsal** involves repeating the information in your mind—in the articulatory loop. As long as you repeat the information, it can be maintained in working

Connect & Extend

TO PRACTICE
To maximize learning during instructional activities, a teacher should be aware of the characteristics of working memory. Consider the techniques or tactics a teacher can employ that complement those characteristics.

maintenance rehearsal Keeping information in working memory by repeating it to yourself.

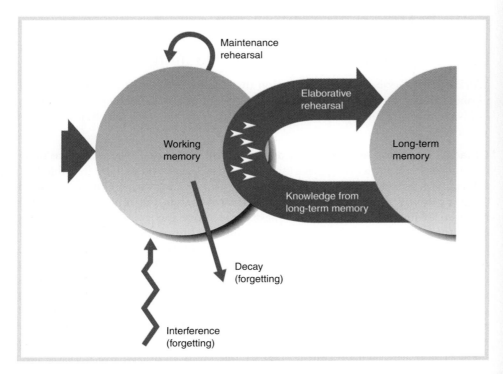

Figure 7.4 Working Memory

Information in working memory can be kept active through maintenance rehearsal, or it can be transferred into long-term memory by assembling it with information already in long-term memory (elaborative rehearsal).

elaborative rehearsal Keeping information in working memory by associating it with something else you already know.

chunking Grouping individual bits of data into meaningful larger units.

decay The weakening and fading of memories with the passage of time.

long-term memory Permanent store of knowledge.

memory indefinitely. Maintenance rehearsal is useful for retaining something you plan to use and then forget, such as a phone number or a location on a map.

Elaborative rehearsal involves connecting the information you are trying to remember with information you already know, which is retrieved from long-term memory. For example, if you meet someone at a party whose name is the same as your brother's, you don't have to repeat the name to keep it in memory—you just have to make the association. This kind of rehearsal not only retains information in working memory but helps move information to long-term memory. Rehearsal is thus an "executive control process" that affects the flow of information through the information processing system.

The limited capacity of working memory can also be somewhat circumvented by a process called **chunking**. Because the number of items of information, not the size of each item, is the limitation for working memory, you can retain more information if you can group individual items of information into one or several chunks. For example, if you have to remember the six digits 3, 5, 4, 8, 7, and 0, it is easier to put them together into three chunks of two digits each (35, 48, 70) or two chunks of three digits each (354, 870). With these changes, there are only two or three chunks of information rather than six digits to hold at one time. Chunking helps you remember a telephone number or a social insurance number (Driscoll, 2006).

Forgetting. Information may lose its place in working memory through interference or decay (see Figure 7.4 on page 253). Interference is fairly straightforward—remembering new information interferes with or gets in the way of remembering old information. The new thought replaces the old one. Information is also lost by **decay** over time. If you don't continue to pay attention to information, the activation level decays (weakens) and finally drops so low that the information cannot be reactivated—it disappears altogether.

Actually, forgetting is very useful. Without forgetting, people would quickly overload their working memories, and learning would cease. Also, it would be a problem if you remembered permanently every sentence you ever read or every picture you ever saw. Finding a particular bit of information in all that sea of knowledge would be impossible. It is helpful to have a system that "weeds out" some information from everything you experience.

We turn next to long-term memory. Because this is such an important topic for teachers, we will spend quite a bit of time on it.

Long-Term Memory: The Goal of Teaching

Working memory holds the information that is currently activated, such as a telephone number you have just found and are about to dial. **Long-term memory** holds the information that is well learned, such as all the other telephone numbers you know.

Capacity, Duration, and Contents of Long-Term Memory. There are five main differences between working and long-term memory, as you can see in Table 7.1. Information enters working memory quickly. To move information into long-term storage requires more time and a bit of effort. Whereas the capacity of working memory is limited, the capacity of long-term memory appears to be, for all practical purposes, unlimited. In addition, once information is securely stored in long-term memory, it can remain there permanently. Theoretically, we should be able to remember as much as we want for as long as we want. Of course, the problem is finding the right information when we need it. Our access to information in working memory is immediate because we are thinking about the information at that very moment. But access to information in long-term memory requires time and effort for search and retrieval. Recently, some psychologists have suggested that there are not two separate memory stores (working and long-term). So, working memory is more about processing than storage (Wilson, 2001).

TABLE 7.1 Working and Long-Term Memory

Type of Memory	Input	Capacity	Duration	Contents	Retrieval
Working	Very fast	Limited	Very brief: 5–20 sec.	Words, images, ideas, sentences	Immediate
Long-term	Relatively slow	Practically unlimited	Practically unlimited	Propositional networks, schemata, productions, episodes, perhaps images	Depends on representation and organization

Source: Adapted by permission of the author from Smith, F. (1975). *Comprehension and learning: A conceptual framework for teachers.* New York: Holt, Rinehart and Winston.

Allan Paivio (1971, 1986; Clark & Paivio, 1991) suggests that information is stored in long-term memory as either visual images or verbal units, or both. Psychologists who agree with this point of view believe that information coded both visually and verbally is easiest to learn (Mayer & Sims, 1994). This may be one reason why explaining an idea with words and representing it visually in a figure, as we do in textbooks, has proved helpful to students. (See the discussion of visual images on page 267.) Paivio's ideas have support, but critics contend that many images are actually stored as verbal codes and then translated into visual information when an image is needed (Driscoll, 2005).

Another recent addition to the information processing model is the notion of long-term working memory (Kintsch, 1998). **Long-term working memory** holds the retrieval structures and strategies that pull information from long-term memory that is needed at the moment. As you develop knowledge and expertise in an area, you create efficient long-term working memory structures for solving problems in that area. So long-term working memory involves a set of domain-specific access tools that improve as you gain expertise in that domain.

long-term working memory Memory that holds strategies for pulling information from long-term memory into working memory.

Contents of Long-Term Memory: Declarative, Procedural, and Conditional Knowledge.

What we know is stored in long-term memory. Earlier, we talked about general and specific knowledge. Another way to categorize knowledge is as declarative, procedural, or conditional (Paris & Cunningham, 1996; Paris, Lipson, & Wixson, 1983). **Declarative knowledge** is knowledge that can be declared, through words and symbol systems of all kinds—Braille, sign language, dance or musical notation, mathematical symbols, and so on (Farnham-Diggory, 1994). Declarative knowledge is "knowing that" something is the case. The history students in the opening "What Would You Do?" situation were focusing exclusively on declarative knowledge about history. The range of declarative knowledge is tremendous. You can know very specific facts (the atomic weight of gold is 196.967), or generalities (leaves of some trees change colour in autumn), or personal preferences (I don't like lima beans), or rules (to divide fractions, invert the divisor and multiply). Small units of declarative knowledge can be organized into larger units; for example, principles of reinforcement and punishment can be organized in your thinking into a theory of behavioural learning (Gagné, Yekovich, & Yekovich, 1993).

declarative knowledge Verbal information; facts; "knowing that" something is the case.

Procedural knowledge is "knowing how" to do something such as divide fractions or clean a carburetor—it is knowledge in action. Procedural knowledge must be demonstrated. Notice that repeating the rule "to divide fractions, invert the divisor and multiply" shows *declarative* knowledge—the student can state the rule. But to show *procedural* knowledge, the student must act. When faced with a fraction to divide, the student must divide correctly. Students demonstrate procedural

procedural knowledge Knowledge that is demonstrated when we perform a task; "knowing how."

conditional knowledge "Knowing when and why" to use declarative and procedural knowledge.

Connect & Extend

TO THE RESEARCH

Clark, J. M., & Paivio, A. (1991). Dual coding theory and education. *Educational Psychology Review, 3,* 149–210. This is a description of the dual coding theory.

explicit memory Long-term memories that involve deliberate or conscious recall.

implicit memory Knowledge that we are not conscious of recalling, but influences behaviour or thought without our awareness.

semantic memory Memory for meaning.

proposition The smallest unit of information that can be judged true or false.

propositional network Set of interconnected concepts and relationships in which long-term knowledge is held.

knowledge when they translate a passage into French, correctly categorize a geometric shape, or craft a coherent paragraph.

Conditional knowledge is "knowing when and why" to apply your declarative and procedural knowledge. Given the many kinds of math problems, it takes conditional knowledge to know when to apply one procedure and when to apply another to solve each problem. It takes conditional knowledge to know when to read every word in a text and when to skim. For many students, conditional knowledge is a stumbling block. They have the facts and can do the procedures, but they don't seem to understand how to apply what they know at the appropriate time.

Table 7.2 illustrates how declarative, procedural, and conditional knowledge can be either general or domain-specific.

Explicit and Implicit Long-Term Memory.   Most cognitive psychologists distinguish two categories of long-term memory, explicit and implicit, with subdivisions under each category, as shown in Figure 7.5. **Explicit memory** is knowledge from long-term memory that can be recalled and consciously considered. We are aware of these memories—we know we have remembered them. **Implicit memory**, on the other hand, is knowledge that we are not conscious of recalling, but that influences behaviour or thought without our awareness. These different kinds of memory are associated with different parts of the brain (Ashcraft, 2006).

Explicit Memories: Semantic and Episodic.   From Figure 7.5 you can see that explicit memories can be either semantic or episodic. **Semantic memory** is memory for meaning, including words, facts, theories, and concepts—declarative knowledge that is one primary goal of teaching. These memories are not tied to particular experiences and are stored as *propositions*, *images*, and *schemas*.

Propositions and Propositional Networks. A **proposition** is the smallest unit of information that can be judged true or false. The statement, "Ida borrowed the antique tablecloth" has two propositions:

1.   Ida borrowed the tablecloth.
2.   The tablecloth is an antique.

Propositions that share information, such as the two sentences above that share information about the tablecloth—Ida borrowed the tablecloth and the tablecloth is an antique—are linked in a **propositional network** of interconnected elements of information. It is meaning, not the exact words or word order, that is stored in the network. The same propositional network would apply to the sentence "The antique tablecloth was borrowed by Ida."

It is possible that most information is stored and represented in propositional networks. When we want to recall a bit of information, we may translate its meaning (as represented in the propositional network) into familiar phrases and sentences or into mental pictures. Also, because of the network, recall of one bit of information can trigger or *activate* recall of another. We are not aware of these

TABLE 7.2 Kinds of Knowledge

	General Knowledge	Domain-Specific Knowledge
Declarative	Hours the library is open	The definition of "hypotenuse"
	Rules of grammar	The lines of the poem, "The Raven"
Procedural	How to use your word processor	How to solve an oxidation-reduction equation
	How to drive	How to throw a pot on a potter's wheel
Conditional	When to give up and try another approach	When to use the formula for calculating volume
	When to skim and when to read carefully	When to rush the net in tennis

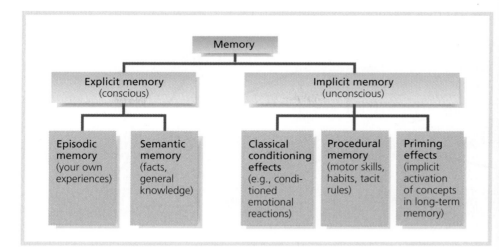

Figure 7.5 Explicit and Implicit Memory

Explicit and implicit memory systems follow different rules and involve different neural systems of the brain. The subdivisions of each kind of memory also may involve different neural systems.

Source: Gray, P. (2002). *Psychology* (4th ed.). New York: Worth Publishers. Copyright © 1991, 1994, 1999, 2002 by Worth Publishers. Adapted with permission of the publisher.

networks, for they are not part of our conscious memory (Anderson, 1995a). In much the same way, we are not aware of underlying grammatical structures when we form a sentence in our own language; we don't have to diagram a sentence to say it.

Images. **Images** are representations based on perceptions about the structure or appearance of the information (Anderson, 1995a). When we form images, as you did in the problem about rotating the letter "p," we try to remember or re-create the physical attributes and spatial structure of information. For example, when asked how many window panes are in their living room, most people call up an image of the room "in their mind's eye" and count the panes—the more panes, the longer it takes to respond. If the information were represented only in a proposition such as "my living room has seven window panes," then everyone would take about the same time to answer, whether the number was 1 or 24 (Mendell, 1971). However, as we saw earlier, researchers don't agree on exactly how images are stored in memory. Some psychologists believe that images are stored as pictures; others believe we store propositions in long-term memory and convert them to pictures in working memory when necessary.

images Representations based on the structure or physical appearance of information.

There probably are features of each process involved—some picture-copying memory and some memory for verbal or propositional descriptions of the image. Seeing images "in your mind's eye" is not exactly the same as seeing the actual image. It is more difficult to perform complicated transformations on mental images than on real images (Matlin & Foley, 1997). For example, if you had a plastic "p," you could very quickly rotate it. Nevertheless, images are useful in making many practical decisions, such as how a molecule of water is structured or how to line up a golf shot. Images may also be helpful in abstract reasoning. Physicists, such as Faraday and Einstein, have reported creating images to reason about complex problems. Einstein claimed that he was visualizing chasing a beam of light and catching up to it when the concept of relativity came to him (Kosslyn & Koenig, 1992).

Schemas. Propositions and images are fine for representing single ideas and relationships. But often our knowledge about a topic combines images and propositions. To explain this kind of complex knowledge, psychologists developed the idea of a schema (Gagné, Yekovich, & Yekovich, 1993, p. 81). Schemas (sometimes called *schemata*) are abstract knowledge structures that organize large amounts of information. A **schema** (the singular form) is a pattern or guide for understanding an event, concept, or skill. Figure 7.6 is a partial representation of a schema for knowledge about "reinforcement."

schema A basic structure for organizing information; concept.

The schema tells you what features are typical of a category, that is, what to expect. The pattern has "slots" that we fill with specific information as we

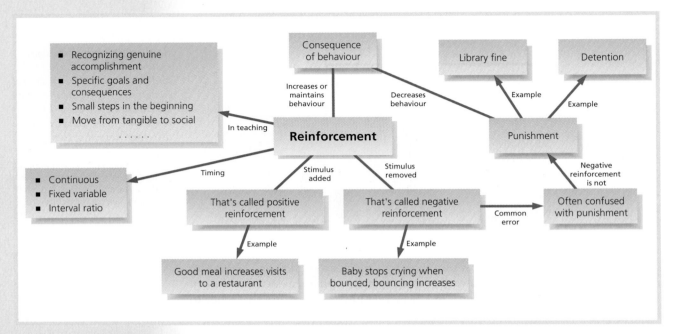

Figure 7.6 A Partial Schema for "Reinforcement"

The concept of "reinforcement" falls under the general category of "consequences." It is related to other concepts, such as eating in restaurants or bouncing babies on your lap, depending on the individual's experience.

story grammar The structure or organization—involving kinds of characters, major events, etc.—typical for a category of texts, such as mysteries or scientific reports.

script Schema or expected plan for the sequence of steps in a common event, such as buying groceries or ordering pizza.

apply the schema in a particular situation. Schemas are personal. For example, your schema of an antique may be less richly developed than an antique collector's schema. You encountered the very similar concept of scheme (note the "e" at the end) in the discussion of Piaget's theory of cognitive development in Chapter 2.

When you hear the sentence "Ida borrowed the antique tablecloth," you know even more about the two propositions. This is because you have schemas about borrowing, tablecloths, antiques, and maybe even Ida herself. You know without being told, for example, that the lender does not have the tablecloth now, because it is in Ida's possession, and that Ida has an obligation to return the tablecloth to the lender (Gentner, 1975). None of this information is explicitly stated, but it is part of our schema for understanding the meaning of "borrow." Other schemas allow you to infer that the cloth is not plastic (if it is a real antique) and that Ida has probably invited guests for a meal. Your schema about Ida may even allow you to predict how promptly the cloth will be returned and in what condition.

Another type of schema, a **story grammar** (sometimes called a schema for text or story structure), helps students understand and remember stories (Gagné, Yekovich, & Yekovich, 1993; Rumelhart & Ortony, 1977). A story grammar could be something like this: murder discovered, search for clues carried out, murderer's fatal mistake identified, trap set to trick suspect into confessing, murderer baited—mystery solved! In other words, a story grammar is a typical general structure that could fit many specific stories. To comprehend a story, we select a schema that seems appropriate. Then we use this framework to decide which details are important, what information to seek, and what to remember. It is as though the schema is a theory about what should occur in the story. The schema guides us in "interrogating" the text, filling in the specific information we expect to find so that the story makes sense. If we activate our "murder mystery schema," we may be alert for clues or a murderer's fatal mistake. Without the appropriate schema, trying to understand a story, textbook, or classroom lesson is a slow, difficult process, something like finding your way through a new town without a map. A schema representing the typical sequence of events in an everyday situation is called a **script** or an *event schema*. Children as young as age three have basic scripts for the familiar events in their lives (Nelson, 1986).

During your interview, the principal of an elementary school asks, "What is your script for a typical day? Tell me how a good day should go in terms of what you would plan and how much time you would give to each segment of your day." What is your response?

Storing knowledge of the world in schemas and scripts has advantages and disadvantages. A schema can be applied in many contexts, depending on what part of the schema is relevant. You can use what you know about antiques, for example, to plan trips, decide if a particular article is worth the price asked, or enjoy a museum display. Having a well-developed schema about Ida lets you recognize her (even as her appearance changes), remember many of her characteristics, and make predictions about her behaviour. But it also allows you to be wrong. You may have incorporated incorrect or biased information into your schema of Ida. For example, if Ida is a member of an ethnic group different from yours and if you believe that group is dishonest, you may assume that Ida will keep the tablecloth. In this way, racial and ethnic stereotypes can function as schemas that lead to misunderstanding individuals and in racial discrimination (Sherman & Bessenoff, 1999).

The second kind of explicit memory is episodic. We turn to that now.

Episodic Memory. Memory for information tied to a particular place and time, especially information about the events in your own life, is called **episodic memory**. Episodic memory keeps track of the order of events we have experienced. We often can explain *when* the event happened. In contrast, we usually can't describe when we acquired a semantic memory. For example, you may have a difficult time remembering when you developed semantic memories for the meaning of the word *injustice,* but you can easily remember a time when you felt unjustly treated. Episodic memory also keeps track of the order of things, so it is a good place to store jokes, gossip, or plots from films.

Memories for dramatic or emotional moments in your life are called **flashbulb memories**. These memories are vivid and complete, as if your brain demanded that you "record this moment." Under stress, more glucose energy goes to fuel brain activity, while stress-induced hormones signal the brain that something important is happening (Myers, 2005). So when we have strong emotional reactions, memories are stronger and more lasting. Many people have vivid memories of very positive or very negative events in school, winning a prize or being humiliated, for example. You probably know just where you were and what you were doing on 9/11. People over 35 have vivid memories of December 6, 1989, when 14 women were killed by Marc Lépine at Montreal's École Polytechnique.

Implicit Memories. Look back at Figure 7.5 on page 257. You see three kinds of implicit or out-of-awareness memories: classical conditioning, procedural memory, and priming effects. In classical conditioning, as you learned in Chapter 6, some out-of-awareness memories may cause you to feel anxious when you take a test or increase your heart rate if you hear a dentist's drill.

The second type of implicit memory is memory for skills, habits, and how to do things, called **procedural memory**. It may take a while to learn a procedure— such as how to write cursive letters, serve a tennis ball, or factor an equation—but once learned, this knowledge tends to be remembered for a long time. Procedural memories are represented as condition-action rules, sometimes called productions. **Productions** specify what to do under certain conditions: If A occurs, then do B. A production might be something like, "If you want to write smoothly, then relax your grip on the pencil" or "If your goal is to increase student attention, and a student has been paying attention a bit longer than usual, then praise the student." People can't necessarily state all their condition-action rules, but they act on them nevertheless. The more practised the procedure, the more automatic the action (Anderson, 1995a).

The final type of implicit memory involves **priming**, or activating information already in long-term memory through some out-of-awareness process. For example,

Connect & Extend

TO YOUR TEACHING
How can schemas we have about individuals' roles (teacher, younger sibling), groups (rural students), and social contexts (when there is a visitor in the classroom) affect how we interpret new information about people and situations?

episodic memory Long-term memory for information tied to a particular time and place, especially memory of the events in a person's life.

flashbulb memories Clear, vivid memories of emotionally important events in your life.

procedural memory Long-term memory for how to do things.

productions The contents of procedural memory; rules about what actions to take, given certain conditions.

priming Activating a concept in memory or the spread of activation from one concept to another.

fill in the blanks in the following word: ME __ __ __ __. If you wrote MEMORY instead of MENTOR, MEMBER, METEOR, or other ME____ words, then priming may have played a role because the word "memory" has occurred many times in this chapter. Priming may be the fundamental process in retrieval as associations are activated and spread through the memory system (Ashcraft, 2002).

Storing and Retrieving Information in Long-Term Memory

Connect & Extend

TO YOUR TEACHING

See the Teachers' Casebook for practising teachers' ideas about how to help students retain and retrieve information.

Just what is done to "save" information permanently—to create semantic, episodic, or procedural memories? How can we make the most effective use of our practically unlimited capacity to learn and remember? *The way you learn information in the first place*—the way you process it at the outset—seems to affect its recall later. One important requirement is that you integrate new material with information already stored in long-term memory as you construct an understanding. Here *elaboration, organization,* and *context* play a role.

elaboration Adding and extending meaning by connecting new information to existing knowledge.

Elaboration is adding meaning to new information by connecting it with already existing knowledge. In other words, we apply our schemas and draw on already existing knowledge to construct an understanding and frequently change our existing knowledge in the process. We often elaborate automatically. For example, a paragraph about a historic figure in the 17th century tends to activate our existing knowledge about that period; we use the old knowledge to understand the new.

Material that is elaborated when first learned will be easier to recall later. First, as we saw earlier, elaboration is a form of rehearsal. It keeps the information activated in working memory long enough for the information to have a chance at permanent storage in long-term memory. Second, elaboration builds extra links to existing knowledge. The more associations there are among elements or chunks of knowledge, the more routes there are to follow to get to the original bit. To put it another way, you have several "handles," or retrieval cues, by which you can recognize or "pick up" the information you might be seeking (Schunk, 2000).

Connect & Extend

TO YOUR TEACHING

Cognitivists emphasize roles that elaboration, organization, and context have in effectively encoding new information into long-term memory. What techniques in teaching your favourite subject make use of those processes?

The more students elaborate new ideas and the more their elaborations are precise and sensible, the deeper will be their understanding and the better will be their memory for the knowledge. We help students elaborate when we ask them to translate information into their own words, create examples, explain to a peer, draw the relationships, or apply the information to solve new problems. Of course, if students elaborate new information by making incorrect connections or developing misguided explanations, these misconceptions will be remembered too.

organization Ordered and logical network of relations.

Organization is a second element of processing that improves learning. Material that is well organized is easier to learn and to remember than separate bits of information, especially if the information is complex or extensive. Placing a concept in a structure will help you learn and remember either general definitions or specific examples. The structure serves as a guide back to the information when you need it. For example, Table 7.1 on page 255 gives an organized view of the input, capacity, duration, contents, and retrieval of information from working and long-term memory; Table 7.2 on page 256 organizes information about types of knowledge; and Figure 7.6 on page 258 organizes knowledge of reinforcement.

context The physical or emotional backdrop associated with an event.

Context is a third element of processing that influences learning. Aspects of physical and emotional context—places, rooms, how we are feeling on a particular day, who is with us—are learned along with other information. Later, if you try to remember the information, it will be easier if the current context is similar to the original one. This has been demonstrated in the laboratory. Students who learned material in one type of room performed better on tests taken in a similar room than they did on tests taken in a very different-looking room (Smith, Glenberg, & Bjork, 1978). So studying for a test under "testlike" conditions may result in improved performance. Of course, you can't always go back to the same or to a similar place to recall something. But by picturing the setting, the time of day, and your companions, you may eventually reach the information you seek.

Levels of Processing Theories. Craik and Lockhart (1972) of the University of Toronto first proposed their **levels of processing theory** as an alternative to short- and long-term memory models, but levels of processing theory is particularly related to the notion of elaboration described earlier. Craik and Lockhart suggested that what determines how long information is remembered is how completely the information is analyzed and connected with other information. The more completely information is processed, the better are our chances of remembering it. For example, according to the levels of processing theory, if you are asked to sort pictures of dogs based on the colour of their coats, you might not remember many of the pictures later. But if you are asked to rate each dog on how likely it is to chase you as you jog, you probably would remember more of the pictures. To rate the dogs you must pay attention to details in the pictures, relate features of the dogs to characteristics associated with danger, and so on. This rating procedure requires "deeper" processing and more focus on the meaning of the features in the photos.

levels of processing theory Theory that recall of information is based on how deeply it is processed.

Retrieving Information from Long-Term Memory. When we need to use information from long-term memory, we search for it. Sometimes the search is conscious, as when you see a person you met at a party last month and search for her name. At other times, locating and using information from long-term memory is automatic, as when you dial a telephone number or solve a math problem without having to search for each step. Think of long-term memory as a huge library full of tools and supplies ready to be brought to the workbench of working memory to accomplish a task. The library's shelves (long-term memory) store an incredible amount, but it may be hard to find quickly what you are looking for. The workbench (working memory) is small, but anything on it is immediately available. Because it is small, however, supplies (elements of information) sometimes are lost when the workbench overflows or when one bit of information covers (interferes with) another (E. D. Gagné, 1985).

Spreading Activation. The size of the memory network is huge, but only one small area is activated at any one time. Only the information we are currently thinking about is in working memory. Information is retrieved in this network through the **spread of activation.** When a particular proposition or image is active—when we are thinking about it—nearby (closely associated) knowledge can be activated as well, and activation can spread through the network (Anderson, 1993; Gagné, Yekovich, & Yekovich, 1993). Thus, if you focus on the propositions "I'd like to go for a drive to see the fall leaves today," related ideas such as "I should rake leaves" and "The car needs an oil change" come to mind. As activation spreads from the car trip to the oil change, the original thought, or active memory, disappears from working memory because of the limited space. So **retrieval** from long-term memory occurs partly through the spreading of activation from one bit of knowledge to related ideas in the network. We often use this spreading in reverse to retrace our steps in a conversation, as in, "Before we got onto the topic of where to get the oil changed, what were we talking about? Oh yes, seeing the leaves." The learning and retrieving processes of long-term memory are diagrammed in Figure 7.7 on page 262.

spread of activation Retrieval of pieces of information based on their relatedness to one another; remembering one bit of information activates (stimulates) recall of associated information.

retrieval Process of searching for and finding information in long-term memory.

Reconstruction. In long-term memory, information is still available even when it is not activated—that is, even when we are not thinking about it at the moment. If spreading activation does not "find" the information we seek, we might still come up with the answer through **reconstruction**, a problem-solving process that makes use of logic, cues, and other knowledge to *construct* a reasonable answer by filling in any missing parts (Koriat, Goldsmith, & Pansky, 2000). Sometimes reconstructed recollections are incorrect. For example, in 1932, F. C. Bartlett conducted a series of famous studies on remembering stories. He read a complex, unfamiliar Native North American tale to students at England's Cambridge University and, after various lengths of time, asked the students to recall the story. The stories that students recalled were generally shorter than the original and were translated into the concepts and language of the Cambridge student culture. The original story told of a seal hunt, for instance, but many students remembered a "fishing trip," an activity closer to their experiences and more consistent with their schemas.

reconstruction Re-creating information by using memories, expectations, logic, and existing knowledge.

Figure 7.7 Long-Term Memory

We activate information from long-term memory to help us understand new information in working memory. With mental work and processing (elaboration, organization, context), the new information can be stored permanently in long-term memory. Forgetting is caused by interference and time decay.

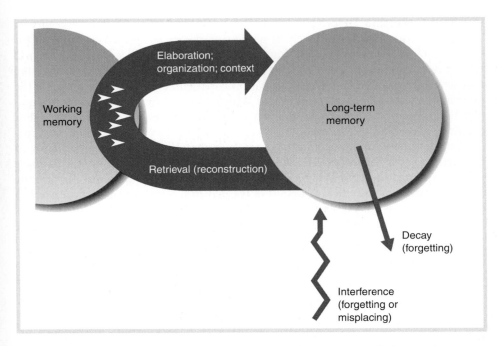

One area where reconstructed memory can play a major role is eyewitness testimony. Elizabeth Loftus and her colleagues have conducted a number of studies showing that misleading questions or other information during questioning can affect memory. For example, in a classic study, Loftus and Palmer (1974) showed subjects slides of a car accident. Later, the experimenters asked some subjects, "How fast were the cars going when they *hit* each other?"; other subjects who saw the same slides were asked, "How fast were the cars going when they *smashed* into each other?" The difference in verbs was enough to bias the subjects' memories—the "hit" subjects estimated that the cars were travelling an average of 55 kilometres per hour, but the "smashed" subjects estimated almost 66 kilometres per hour. And one week later, 32 percent of the "smashed" subjects remembered seeing broken glass at the scene of the wreck, while only 14 percent of the "hit" subjects remembered glass. (Broken glass was not visible in any of the slides.)

Forgetting and Long-Term Memory.   If information is lost from working memory, it truly disappears. No amount of effort will bring it back. But information stored in long-term memory may be available, given the right cues. Some researchers believe that nothing is ever lost from long-term memory; however, recent research casts doubts on this assertion (Schwartz, Wasserman, Robbins, 2002).

> **What Would You Say?**
>
> As part of your interview, the principal says, "We have to cover *so* much material to get our students ready for the provincial exams. What would you do to help students remember what they have learned in your classes?"

interference The effect that remembering certain information is hampered by the presence of other information.

Information appears to be lost from long-term memory through time decay and **interference**. For example, memory for French–English vocabulary decreases for about three years after a person's last course in French, then stays level for about 25 years, then drops again for the next 25 years. One explanation for this decline is that neural connections, like muscles, grow weak without use. After 25 years, it may be that the memories are still somewhere in the brain, but they are too weak to be reactivated (Anderson, 1995a, 1995b). Finally, newer memories may interfere with or obscure older memories, and older memories may interfere with memory for new material.

Even with decay and interference, long-term memory is remarkable. In a review of almost 100 studies of memory for knowledge taught in school, George

Semb and John Ellis (1994) concluded that, "contrary to popular belief, students retain much of the knowledge taught in the classroom" (p. 279). It appears that teaching strategies that encourage student engagement and lead to deeper levels of *initial* learning (such as frequent reviews and tests, elaborated feedback, high standards, mastery learning, and active involvement in learning projects) are associated with longer retention. The Guidelines below give applications of information processing to teaching.

GUIDELINES
USING INFORMATION PROCESSING IDEAS IN THE CLASSROOM

Make sure that you have the students' attention.

EXAMPLES

1. Develop a signal that tells students to stop what they are doing and focus on you. Make sure students respond to the signal—don't let them ignore it. Practise using the signal.

2. Move around the room, use gestures, and avoid speaking in a monotone.

3. Begin a lesson by asking a question that stimulates interest in the topic.

4. Regain the attention of individual students by walking closer to them, using their names, or asking them a question.

Help students separate essential from non-essential details and focus on the most important information.

EXAMPLES

1. Summarize instructional objectives to indicate what students should be learning. Relate the material you are presenting to the objectives as you teach: "Now I'm going to explain exactly how you can find the information you need to meet Objective 1 on the board—determining the tone of the story."

2. When you make an important point, pause, repeat, ask a student to paraphrase, note the information on the board in coloured chalk, or tell students to highlight the point in their notes or readings.

Help students make connections between new information and what they already know.

EXAMPLES

1. Review prerequisites to help students bring to mind the information they will need to understand new material: "Who can tell us the definition of a quadrilateral? Now, what is a rhombus? Is a square a quadrilateral? Is a square a rhombus? What did we say yesterday about how you can tell? Today we are going to look at some other quadrilaterals."

2. Use an outline or diagram to show how new information fits with the framework you have been developing. For example, "Now that you know the duties of the governor general, where would you expect to find the position in this diagram of the offices in the Canadian government?"

3. Give an assignment that specifically calls for the use of new information along with information already learned.

Provide for repetition and review of information.

EXAMPLES

1. Begin the class with a quick review of the homework assignment.

2. Give frequent, short tests.

3. Build practice and repetition into games or have students work with partners to quiz each other.

Present material in a clear, organized way.

EXAMPLES

1. Make the purpose of the lesson very clear.

2. Give students a brief outline to follow. Put the same outline on an overhead so that you can keep yourself on track. When students ask questions or make comments, relate these to the appropriate section of the outline.

3. Use summaries in the middle and at the end of the lesson.

Focus on meaning, not memorization.

EXAMPLES

1. In teaching new words, help students associate the new word to a related word they already understand: "*Enmity* is from the same base as *enemy*...."

2. In teaching about remainders, have students group 12 objects into sets of 2, 3, 4, 5, 6 and ask them to count the "leftovers" in each case.

Check Your Knowledge

- Compare declarative, procedural, and conditional knowledge.
- Give two explanations for perception.
- What is working memory, and what processes are applied there?
- How is information represented in long-term memory and what role do schemas play?
- What learning processes improve long-term memory?
- Why do we forget?

Apply to Practice

- A child from a large city has trouble understanding and remembering a story about endangered species in a national park. Explain this situation using information processing theory.

METACOGNITION

One question that intrigues many cognitive psychologists is why some people learn and remember more than others. For those who hold an information processing view, part of the answer lies in the concept of metacognition.

The executive control processes shown in Figure 7.1 on page 247 guide the flow of information through the information processing system. We have already discussed a number of control processes, including attention, maintenance rehearsal, elaborative rehearsal, organization, and elaboration. These **executive control processes** are sometimes called *metacognitive skills*, because the processes can be intentionally used to regulate cognition.

Metacognitive Knowledge and Regulation

Donald Meichenbaum and his colleagues at the University of Waterloo describe **metacognition** as people's "awareness of their own cognitive machinery and how the machinery works" (Meichenbaum et al., 1985, p. 5). Metacognition literally means cognition about cognition—or knowledge about knowledge. This knowledge is used to monitor and regulate cognitive processes—reasoning, comprehension, problem solving, learning, and so on (Metcalfe & Shimamura, 1994). Because people differ in their metacognitive knowledge and skills, they differ in how well and how quickly they learn (Brown, Bransord, Ferrara, & Campione, 1983; Morris, 1990).

Metacognition involves three kinds of knowledge. First, declarative knowledge describes yourself as a learner, factors that influence your learning and memory, and skills, strategies, and resources you believe are needed to perform a task. Second, knowing *what* to do—procedural knowledge—is knowing *how* to use the strategies. Third, conditional knowledge is critical to complete the task because it concerns knowing *when* and *why* to apply the strategies (Bruning, Schraw, & Ronning, 2004). Metacognition is the strategic application of this declarative, procedural, and conditional knowledge to accomplish goals and solve problems (Schunk, 2000).

Metacognitive knowledge is used to regulate thinking and learning (Brown, 1987; Nelson, 1996). Three essential skills allow us to do this: planning, monitoring, and evaluation. *Planning* involves deciding how much time to give to a task, which strategies to use, how to start, what resources to gather, what order to follow, what to skim and what to study intensely, and so on. *Monitoring* is the online awareness of "how I'm doing." Monitoring entails asking, "Is this making sense? Am I trying to go too fast? Have I studied enough?" *Evaluation* involves making judgments about the processes and outcomes of thinking and learning, such as

---

executive control processes Processes such as selective attention, rehearsal, elaboration, and organization that influence encoding, storage, and retrieval of information in memory.

metacognition Knowledge about our own thinking processes.

Connect & Extend

TO YOUR TEACHING
Bondy (1989) describes the importance of metacognitive processes, particularly monitoring comprehension, and lists nine suggestions for educators. (1) Have students keep a daily learning log. (2) Demonstrate and discuss appropriate metacognitive activity (such as estimating difficulty of task, choosing a strategy). (3) Provide opportunities for feedback. (4) Provide instruction in self-questioning. (5) Teach students to summarize material. (6) Teach students to rate their comprehension (e.g., "I understand well," "I sort of understand"). (7) Use model of learning as framework for planning instruction. (8) Teach students how to study. (9) Teach students to think aloud and systematically solve problems. (Thinking about thinking. In *Annual editions: Educational psychology* [pp. 83–86]. Guilford, CT: Duskin.)

"Should I change strategies? Get help? Give up for now? Is this paper (painting, model, poem, plan, etc.) finished?"

Of course, we don't have to be metacognitive all the time. Some actions become routine. Metacognition is most useful when tasks are challenging, but not too difficult. Then planning, monitoring, and evaluation can be helpful. And even when we are planning, monitoring, and evaluating, these processes are not necessarily conscious. Especially in adults, these processes can be automatic or implicit—we may use them without being aware of our efforts. Experts in a field may plan, monitor, and evaluate as second nature—they have difficulty describing their metacognitive knowledge and skills (Bargh & Chartrand, 1999; Reder, 1996). Conversely, students with learning disabilities may need to be taught these skills, as described in the Reaching Every Student feature.

Check Your Knowledge

- What are the three metacognitive skills?

Apply to Practice

- Give some examples of your own metacognitive abilities.

Now that we have examined the information processing explanation of how knowledge is represented and remembered, let's turn to the really important question: How can teachers support the development of knowledge?

Connect & Extend

TO THE RESEARCH
See the entire issue of *Learning and Individual Differences* (1996, #4) on individual differences in metacognition.

Metacognition involves three kinds of knowledge: First, declarative knowledge describes yourself as a learner; factors that influence your learning and memory; and skills, strategies, and resources you believe are needed to perform a task. Second, knowing what to do—procedural knowlege—is knowing how to use the strategies. Third, conditional knowledge is critical to complete the task because it concerns knowing when and why to apply the strategies (Bruning, Schraw, & Ronning, 2004). Metacognition is the strategic application of this declarative, procedural, and conditional knowledge to accomplish goals and solve problems (Schunk, 2000).

REACHING EVERY STUDENT

METACOGNITIVE STRATEGIES FOR STUDENTS WITH LEARNING DISABILITIES

For students with learning disabilities, executive control processes (that is, metacognitive strategies) such as planning, organizing, monitoring progress, and making adaptations are especially important, but often underdeveloped (Kirk et al., 2006). It makes sense to teach these strategies directly. Some approaches make use of mnemonics to remember the steps. For example, teachers can help older students use a writing strategy called DEFENDS (Deshler, Ellis, & Lenz, 1996):

- **D**ecide on audience, goals, and position.
- **E**stimate main ideas and details.
- **F**igure best order of main ideas and details.
- **E**xpress your position in the opening.
- **N**ote each main idea and supporting points.
- **D**rive home the message in the last sentence.
- **S**earch for errors and correct.

Of course, you have to do more than just tell students about the strategy—you have to teach it. Michael Pressley and his colleagues (1995) developed the Cognitive Strategies Model as a guide for teaching students to improve their metacognitive strategies. Here are their eight guidelines:

- Teach a few strategies at a time, intensively and extensively, as part of the ongoing curriculum.

- Model and explain new strategies.
- If parts of the strategy were not understood, model again and re-explain strategies in ways that are sensitive to those confusing or misunderstood aspects of strategy use.
- Explain to students where and when to use the strategy.
- Provide plenty of practice, using strategies for as many appropriate tasks as possible.
- Encourage students to monitor how they are doing when they are using strategies.
- Increase students' motivation to use strategies by heightening their awareness that they are acquiring valuable skills—skills that are at the heart of competent functioning.
- Emphasize reflective processing rather than speedy processing; do all possible to eliminate high anxiety in students; encourage students to shield themselves from distractions so they can attend to academic tasks.

For a list of strategies and how to teach them, see **www.unl.edu/csi/bank.html**.

Source: Adapted from Pressley, M., & Woloshyn, V. (1995). *Cognitive strategy instruction that really improves children's academic performance.* Cambridge, MA: Brookline Books, p. 18.

BECOMING KNOWLEDGEABLE: SOME BASIC PRINCIPLES

Understanding a concept such as "antique" involves declarative knowledge about characteristics and images and procedural knowledge about how to apply rules to categorize specific antiques. We will discuss the development of declarative and procedural knowledge separately, but keep in mind that real learning is a combination and integration of these elements.

Development of Declarative Knowledge

Within the information processing perspective, to learn declarative knowledge is really to integrate new ideas with existing knowledge and construct an understanding. As you have seen, people learn best when they have a good base of knowledge in the area they are studying. With many well-elaborated schemas and scripts to guide people's thinking, new material makes more sense to them, and there are many possible networks for connecting new information with old. But students don't always have a good base of knowledge. In the early phases of learning, students of any age must grope around the landscape a bit, searching for landmarks and direction. Even experts in an area must use learning strategies when they encounter unfamiliar material or new problems (Alexander, 1996, 1997; Garner, 1990; Perkins & Salomon, 1989; Shuell, 1990).

What are some possible strategies? Perhaps the best single method for helping students learn is to make each lesson as meaningful as possible.

Making It Meaningful. Meaningful lessons are presented in vocabulary that makes sense to the students. New terms are clarified through ties with more familiar words and ideas. Meaningful lessons are also well organized, with clear connections between the different elements of the lesson. Finally, meaningful lessons make natural use of old information to help students understand new information through examples or analogies.

The importance of meaningful lessons is emphasized in the following example presented by Smith (1975). Look at the three lines below. Begin by covering all but the first line. Look at it for a second, close the book, and write down all the letters you remember. Then repeat this procedure with the second and third lines.

1. KBVODUWGPJMSQTXNOGMCTRSO
2. READ JUMP WHEAT POOR BUT SEEK
3. KNIGHTS RODE HORSES INTO WAR

Each line has the same number of letters, but the chances are great that you remembered all the letters in the third line, a good number of letters in the second line, and very few in the first line. The first line makes no sense. There is no way to organize it in a brief glance. The second line is more meaningful. You do not have to see each letter because you bring prior knowledge of spelling rules and vocabulary to the task. The third line is the most meaningful. Just a glance and you can probably remember all of it because you bring to this task prior knowledge not only of spelling and vocabulary but also of rules about syntax and probably some historical information about knights (they didn't ride in tanks). This sentence is meaningful because you have existing schemas for assimilating it. It is relatively easy to associate the words and meaning with other information already in long-term memory (Sweller, van Merrienboer, & Paas, 1998).

The challenge for teachers is to make lessons less like learning the first line and more like learning the third line. Although this may seem obvious, think about the times when *you* have read a sentence in a text or heard an explanation from a professor that might just as well have been KBVODUWGPJMSQTXNOGMCTRSO. But remember, attempts to change the ways that students are used to learning—

moving from memorizing to meaningful activities, as in the chapter-opening "What Would You Do?" situation, are not always greeted with student enthusiasm. Students may be concerned about their grades; at least when memorization gains an A, they know what is expected. Meaningful learning can be riskier and more challenging. In Chapters 8, 9, and 12, we will examine a variety of ways in which teachers can support meaningful learning and understanding.

Visual Images and Illustrations.   Is a picture worth a thousand words in teaching? Richard Mayer (1999, 2001) has studied this question and found that the right combination of pictures and words can make a significant difference in students' learning. Mayer's cognitive theory of multimedia learning includes three ideas:

Dual Coding: Visual and verbal materials are processed in different systems (Clark & Paivio, 1991).

Limited Capacity: Working memory for verbal and visual material is severely limited (Baddeley, 2001).

Generative Learning: Meaningful learning happens when students focus on relevant information and generate or build connections (Mayer, 1999a).

The problem: How to build complex understandings that integrate information from visual (pictures, diagrams, graphs, films) and verbal (text, lecture) sources, given the limitations of working memory. The answer: Make sure the information is available at the same time or in focused small bites. Mayer and Gallini (1990) provide an example. They used three kinds of texts to explain how a bicycle pump works. One text used only words, the second had pictures that just showed the parts of the brake system and the steps, and the third (this one improved student learning and recall) showed both the "on" and the "off" states of the pumps with labels for each step, as in Figure 7.8.

The moral of the story? Give students multiple ways to understand—pictures *and* explanations. But don't overload working memory—"package" the visual and verbal information together in bite-size (or memory-size) pieces.

Another memory strategy that often makes use of images is mnemonics.

Mnemonics.   **Mnemonics** are systematic procedures for improving memory. Many mnemonic strategies use imagery (Atkinson et al., 1999; Levin, 1993).

The **loci method** derives its name from the plural of the Latin word *locus*, meaning "place." To use loci, you must first imagine a familiar place, such as your own house or apartment, and pick out particular locations. Every time you

mnemonics Techniques for remembering; also, the art of memory.

loci method Technique of associating items with specific places.

Figure 7.8 Images and Words that Help Students Understand

The right combination of pictures and words, like the labelled illustrations here, can make a significant difference in students' learning.

Source: Adapted from *The World Book Encyclopedia.* © 2003 World Book, Inc. By permission of the publisher. **www.worldbook.com**

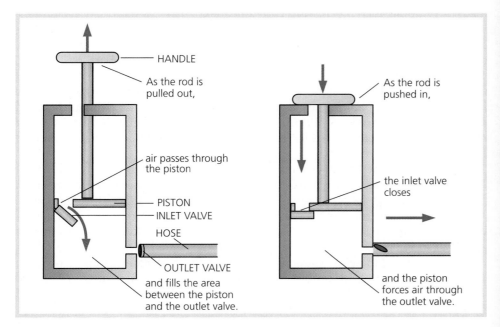

HANDLE

As the rod is pulled out,

As the rod is pushed in,

air passes through the piston

PISTON
INLET VALVE

HOSE

the inlet valve closes

OUTLET VALVE

and fills the area between the piston and the outlet valve.

and the piston forces air through the outlet valve.

peg-type mnemonics Systems of associating items with cue words.

acronym Technique for remembering names, phrases, or steps by using the first letter of each word to form a new, memorable word.

chain mnemonics Memory strategies that associate one element in a series with the next element.

keyword method System of associating new words or concepts with similar-sounding cue words and images.

To remember that the subdivision **angiosperms** includes the class **dicotyledons**, which in turn includes the three orders **rubales**, **sapindales**, and **rosales**, study the picture of the angel with the pet **dinosaur** that is walking up the **Rubik's cubes** so that he can lick the sweet **sap** that drips down from the **rose** tree.

Figure 7.9 Using Mnemonics to Promote Learning Complex Concepts

This illustration tells a story that provides a frame for remembering and pegs for hanging the concept names in the biological subdivision of angiosperms.

Source: Carney, R. N., & Levin, J. R. (2002). Pictorial illustrations still improve students' learning from text. *Educational Psychology Review*, 14. Copyright © 2002 by Kluwer Academic Publishers. Reprinted with permission of the publisher and authors.

have a list to remember, the same locations serve as "pegs" on which to "hang" memories. Simply place each item from your list in one of these locations. For instance, let's say you want to remember to buy milk, bread, butter, and cereal at the store. Imagine a giant bottle of milk blocking the entry hall, a lazy loaf of bread sleeping on the living-room couch, a stick of butter melting all over the dining-room table, and dry cereal covering the kitchen floor. When you want to remember the items, all you have to do is take an imaginary walk through your house. Other **peg-type mnemonics** use a standard list of words (one is bun, two is shoe ...) as pegs.

If you need to remember information for long periods of time, an acronym may be the answer. An **acronym** is a form of abbreviation—a word formed from the first letter of each word in a phrase, for example, NAFTA (North American Free Trade Agreement). Another method forms phrases or sentences out of the first letter of each word or item in a list, for example, Every Good Boy Does Fine to remember the lines on the G clef—E, G, B, D, F. Because the words must make sense as a sentence, this approach also has some characteristics of **chain mnemonics**, methods that connect the first item to be memorized with the second, the second item with the third, and so on. In one type of chain method, each item on a list is linked to the next through some visual association or story. Another chain-method approach is to incorporate all the items to be memorized into a jingle such as "*i* before *e* except after *c*," or "Thirty days hath September."

The mnemonic system that has been most extensively researched in teaching is the **keyword method**. Joel Levin and his colleagues use a mnemonic—the *3 Rs*—to teach the keyword mnemonic method:

- *Recode* the to-be-learned vocabulary item as a more familiar, concrete keyword—this is the keyword.
- *Relate* the keyword clue to the vocabulary item's definition through a sentence.
- *Retrieve* the desired definition.

For example, to remember that the English word *carlin* means *old woman*, you might recode *carlin* as the more familiar keyword *car*. Then make up a sentence such as *The old woman was driving a car*. When you are asked for the meaning of the word *carlin*, you think of the keyword *car*, which triggers the sentence about the car and the *old woman*, the meaning (Jones, Levin, Levin, & Beitzel, 2000).

The keyword method has been extensively applied in foreign-language learning. For example, the French word *carte* (meaning "map") sounds like the English word "cart." Cart becomes the keyword: you make a mental picture of a shopping cart being used to move a huge collection of old maps, or you make up a sentence such as, "The cart with all the maps tipped over" (Pressley, Levin, & Delaney, 1982). A similar approach has been used to help students connect artists with particular aspects of their paintings. For example, students are told to imagine that the heavy dark lines of paintings by Rouault are made with a *ruler* (Rouault) dipped in black paint (Carney & Levin, 2000). Figure 7.9 is an example of using mnemonic pictures as aids in learning complicated science concepts (Carney & Levin, 2002).

The keyword method does not work well if it is difficult to identify a keyword for a particular item. Many words and ideas that students need to remember do not lend themselves to associations with keywords (Hall, 1991; Pressley, 1991). Also, vocabulary learned with keywords may be more easily forgotten than vocabulary learned in other ways, especially if students are given keywords and images instead of being asked to supply the words and images. When the teacher provides the memory links, these associations may not fit the students' existing knowledge and may be forgotten or confused later, so that remembering suffers (Wang & Thomas, 1995; Wang, Thomas, & Ouellette, 1992). Younger students have some difficulty forming their own images. For them, memory aids that rely on auditory cues—rhymes such as "*i* before *e* except after *c*" and "Thirty days hath September"—seem to work better (Willoughby et al., 1999).

The last learning strategy for declarative knowledge involves *rote memorization* techniques, which help students remember information that may provide the basic building blocks for other learning.

Rote Memorization. *Very few things need to be learned by rote.* The greatest challenge teachers face is to help students think and understand, not just memorize. Unfortunately, many students—like those in the scenario at the opening of this chapter—see memorizing and learning as the same thing (Iran-Nejad, 1990). There are times, though, when we have to use **rote memorization**—to memorize something word for word, such as lines in a song, poem, or play.

If you must memorize, how would you do it? If you have tried to memorize a list of items that are all similar to one another, you may have found that you tended to remember items at the beginning and at the end of the list but forgot those in the middle. This is called the **serial-position effect**. Using **part learning**—breaking the list into smaller segments—can help prevent this effect, because breaking a list into several shorter lists means that there will be fewer middle items to forget.

Another strategy for memorizing a long selection or list is the use of **distributed practice.** A student who studies Hamlet's soliloquy intermittently throughout the weekend will probably do much better than a student who tries to memorize the entire speech on Sunday night. Studying straight through for an extended period is called **massed practice.** Distributed practice gives time for deeper processing and the chance to move information into long-term memory (Mumford, Costanza, Baughman, Threlfall, & Fleishman, 1994). What is forgotten after one session can be relearned in the next with distributed practice.

Until we have some knowledge to guide learning, it may help to use some mnemonic and rote memorization approaches to build vocabulary and facts. Not all educators agree, as is noted in the Point/Counterpoint feature on page 270.

Becoming an Expert: Development of Procedural and Conditional Knowledge

Experts in a particular field have a wealth of domain-specific knowledge, that is, knowledge that applies specifically to their area or domain. This includes *declarative knowledge* (facts and verbal information), *procedural knowledge* (how to perform various cognitive activities), and *conditional knowledge* (knowing when and why to apply what they know). In addition, it appears that experts have developed their *long-term working memories* in the domain and can quickly access relevant knowledge and strategies for solving problems in that domain.

Another characteristic distinguishes experts from novices in an area. Much of the expert's declarative knowledge has become "proceduralized," that is, incorporated into routines that can be applied automatically without making many demands on working memory. Skills that are applied without conscious thought are called **automated basic skills.** An example is shifting gears in a manual-transmission car. At first, you have to think about every step; as you become more expert, the procedure becomes automatic. But not all procedures (sometimes called *cognitive skills*) can be automatic, even for experts in a particular domain. For example, no matter how expert you are at driving, you still have to consciously

"HOW MANY TIMES MUST I TELL YOU—IT'S 'CAT' BEFORE 'TEMPLE' EXCEPT AFTER 'SLAVE.'"
(By permission of Bo Brown. From *Phi Delta Kappan*.)

rote memorization Remembering information by repetition without necessarily understanding the meaning of the information.

serial-position effect The tendency to remember the beginning and the end but not the middle of a list.

part learning Breaking a list of learning items into shorter lists.

distributed practice Practice that occurs in brief periods with rest intervals.

massed practice Practice for a single extended period.

Connect & Extend

TO YOUR TEACHING
What is the memory strategy used in each example?

a. To help children recall the symbol for the number eight, the teacher makes a snowman with the figure 8 and tells a story about the snowman with eight buttons who lives for eight days.

b. To help students remember how to spell "separate," the teacher says, "There is *a rat* in separate."

c. Columbus sailed the ocean blue in fourteen hundred and ninety-two.

d. To remember a grocery list, Pat imagines cheese on her TV, limes on the sofa, milk on the table, and beans in the wicker basket.

e. The teacher uses a timeline showing major events before, during, and after the War of 1812.

automated basic skills Skills that are applied without conscious thought.

WHAT'S WRONG WITH MEMORIZING?

For years, students have relied on memorization to learn vocabulary, procedures, steps, names, and facts. Is this a bad idea?

> Point *Rote memorization creates inert knowledge.*

Years ago, William James (1912) described the limitations of rote learning by telling a story about what can happen when students memorize but do not understand:

> A friend of mine, visiting a school, was asked to examine a young class in geography. Glancing at the book, she said: "Suppose you should dig a hole in the ground, hundreds of feet deep, how should you find it at the bottom—warmer or colder than on top?" None of the class replying, the teacher said: "I'm sure they know, but I think you don't ask the question quite rightly. Let me try." So, taking the book, she asked: "In what condition is the interior of the globe?" And received the immediate answer from half the class at once. "The interior of the globe is in a condition of igneous fusion." (p. 150)

The students had memorized the answer, but they had no idea what it meant. Perhaps they didn't understand the meaning of "interior," "globe," or "igneous fusion." At any rate, the knowledge was useful to them only when they were answering test questions, and only then when the questions were phrased exactly as they had been memorized. Students often resort to memorizing the exact words of definitions when they have no hope for actually understanding the terms or when teachers take off marks for definitions that are not exact.

Most recently, Howard Gardner has been a vocal critic of rote memorization and a champion of "teaching for understanding." In an interview in *Phi Delta Kappan* (Siegel & Shaughnessy, 1994), Gardner says:

> My biggest concern about education, particularly in America, is that even our better students in our better schools are just going through the motions of education. In *The Unschooled Mind,* I review ample evidence that suggests an absence of understanding—the inability of students to take knowledge, skills, and other apparent attainments and apply them successfully in new situations. In the absence of such flexibility and adaptability, the education that the students receive is worth little. (pp. 563–564)

< Counterpoint *Rote memorization can be effective.*

Memorization may not be such a bad way to learn new information that has little inherent meaning, such as foreign-language vocabulary. Alvin Wang, Margaret Thomas, and Judith Ouellette (1992) compared learning Tagalog (the national language of the Philippines) using either rote memorization or the keyword approach. The keyword method is a way of creating connections and meaning for associating new words with existing words and images. In their study, even though the keyword method led to faster and better learning initially, long-term forgetting was *greater* for students who had used the keyword method than for students who had learned by rote memorization.

There are times when students must memorize, and we do them a disservice if we don't teach them how. Every discipline has its own terms, names, facts, and rules. As adults, we want to work with physicians who have memorized the correct names for the bones and organs of the body or the drugs needed to combat particular infections. Of course, they can look up some information or research certain conditions, but they have to know where to start. We want to work with accountants who give us accurate information about the new tax codes, information they probably had to memorize because it changes from year to year in ways that are not necessarily rational or meaningful. We want to deal with computer sales people who have memorized their stock and know exactly which printers will work with our computer. Just because something was learned through memorization does not mean that it is inert knowledge. The real question, as Gardner points out above, is whether you can *use* the information flexibly and effectively to solve new problems.

---

watch the traffic around you. This kind of conscious procedure is called a *domain-specific strategy.* Automated basic skills and domain-specific strategies are learned in different ways (Gagné, Yekovich, & Yekovich, 1993).

What Would You Say?

As part of your interview, the department chair asks, "What are the basic skills for your students—the foundations of their more advanced learning—and how would you teach them?"

Automated Basic Skills. Most psychologists identify three stages in the development of an automated skill: cognitive, associative, and autonomous (Anderson, 1995; Fitts & Posner, 1967). At the **cognitive stage**, when we are first learning, we rely on declarative knowledge and general problem-solving strategies to accomplish our goal. For example, to learn to assemble a bookshelf, we might try to follow steps in the instruction manual, putting a check beside each step as we complete it to keep track of progress. At this stage we have to "think about" every step and perhaps refer back to the pictures of parts to see what a "1 cm metal bolt with lock nut" looks like. The load on working memory is heavy. There can be quite a bit of trial-and-error learning at this stage—for example, if the bolt we have chosen doesn't fit.

At the **associative stage**, individual steps of a procedure are combined or "chunked" into larger units. We reach for the right bolt and put it into the right hole. One step smoothly cues the next. With practice, the associative stage moves to the **autonomous stage**, where the whole procedure can be accomplished without much attention. So if you assemble enough bookshelves, you can have a lively conversation as you do, paying little attention to the assembly task. This movement from the cognitive to the associative to the autonomous stage holds for the development of basic cognitive skills in any area, but science, medicine, chess, and mathematics have been most heavily researched.

What can teachers do to help their students pass through these three stages and become more expert? In general, it appears that two factors are critical: *prerequisite knowledge* and *practice with feedback*. First, if students don't have the essential prior knowledge (schemas, skills, etc.), the load on working memory will be too great. To compose a poem in a foreign language, for example, you must know some of the vocabulary and grammar of that language, and you must have some understanding of poetry forms. To learn the vocabulary, grammar, *and* forms as you also try to compose the poem would be too much.

Second, practice with feedback allows you to form associations, recognize cues automatically, and combine small steps into larger condition-action rules or *productions*. Even from the earliest stage, some of this practice should include a simplified version of the whole process in a real context. Practice in real contexts helps students learn not only *how* to do a skill but also *why* and *when* (Collins, Brown, & Newman, 1989; Gagné, Yekovich, & Yekovich, 1993). Of course, as every athletic coach knows, if a particular step, component, or process is causing trouble, that element might be practised alone until it is more automatic, and then put back into the whole sequence, to lower the demands on working memory (Anderson, Reder, & Simon, 1996).

Domain-Specific Strategies. As we saw earlier, some procedural knowledge, such as monitoring the traffic while you drive, is not automatic because conditions are constantly changing. Once you decide to change lanes, the manoeuvre may be fairly automatic, but the decision to change lanes was conscious, based on the traffic conditions around you. **Domain-specific strategies** are these consciously applied skills of organizing thoughts and actions to reach a goal. To support this kind of learning, teachers need to provide opportunities for practice in many different situations—for example, they may have their students practise reading with newspapers, package labels, magazines, books, letters, operating manuals, and so on. In the next chapter's discussion of problem solving, we will examine other ways to help students develop domain-specific strategies. For now, let's turn to a consideration of diversity and convergence in cognitive learning.

Check Your Knowledge

- Describe three ways to develop declarative knowledge.
- Describe some procedures for developing procedural knowledge.

Apply to Practice

- How would you use the keyword method to teach about the exports of foreign countries?

cognitive stage Initial stage in learning an automated skill, when one relies on general problem-solving approaches to make sense of steps or procedures.

associative stage Middle stage in learning an automated skill, when individual steps of a procedure are combined or "chunked" into larger units.

autonomous stage Final stage in learning an automated skill, when the procedure is fine-tuned and becomes "automatic."

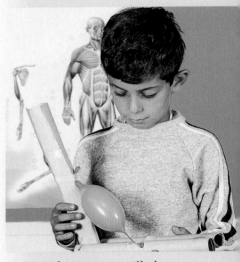

New information will be more meaningful to students, and thus will be learned more readily, if they can connect it to knowledge they already have. This student has made a model of an elbow using materials he is familiar with, such as balloons and construction paper.

domain-specific strategies Skills consciously applied to reach goals in a particular subject or problem area.

DIVERSITY AND CONVERGENCES IN COGNITIVE LEARNING

Many of the concepts and processes discussed in this chapter—the importance of knowledge in learning; the sensory, working, and long-term memory; metacognition—apply to all students. But there are developmental and individual differences in what students know and how their memory processes are used.

Diversity: Individual Differences and Working Memory

As you might expect, there are both developmental and individual differences in working memory. Let's examine a few. First, try this—read the following sentences and words in caps out loud once:

For many years my family and friends have been working on the farm. SPOT
Because the room was stuffy, Bob went outside for some fresh air. TRAIL
We were 50 kilometres out to sea before we lost sight of the land. BAND

Now cover the sentences and answer these questions (be honest): Name the words that were in all caps. Who was in the stuffy room? Who worked on the farm?

You have just taken a few items from a test of working memory span (Engle, 2001). The test required you to both process and store—process the meaning of the sentences and store the words (Ashcraft, 2006). How did you do?

Developmental Differences. Research indicates that young children have very limited working memories, but their memory span improves with age. Recent research shows that the three components of working memory—the central executive, phonological loop, and visuospatial sketchpad—all increase in capacity from ages four through adolescence (Gathercole et al., 2004). It is not clear whether these differences are the result of changes in memory *capacity* or improvements in *strategy* use. Case (1998) suggests that the total amount of "space" available for processing information is the same at each age, but young children must use quite a bit of this space to remember how to execute basic operations, such as reaching for a toy, finding the right word for an object, or counting. Using a new operation takes up a large portion of the child's working memory. Once an operation is mastered, however, there is more working memory available for short-term storage of new information. For very young children, biology may play a role, too. As the brain and neurological system of the child mature, processing may become more efficient so that more working-memory space is available (Bransford, Brown, & Cocking, 2000).

As children grow older, they develop more effective strategies for remembering information. At about age four, children begin to understand that "remembering" means recalling something from the past. Before age four, children think remembering means what they see or know now and forgetting means not knowing (Perner, 2000). Most children spontaneously discover rehearsal around age five or six. Siegler (1998) describes a nine-year-old boy who witnessed a robbery, then mentally repeated the licence number of the getaway car until he could give the number to the police. Younger children can be taught to rehearse, and will use the strategy effectively as long as they are reminded, but they will not apply the strategy spontaneously. Children are 10 to 11 years old before they have adult-like working memories.

According to Case (1998), young children often use reasonable but incorrect strategies to solve problems because of their limited memories. They try to simplify the task by ignoring important information or skipping steps to reach a correct solution. This puts less strain on memory. For example, when comparing quantities, young children may consider only the height of the water in a glass, not the diameter of the glass, because this approach demands less of their memory. According to Case, this explains young children's inability to solve the classic Piagetian conservation problem. (See Figure 2.2 on page 33.)

There are several developmental differences in how students use organization, elaboration, and knowledge to process information in working memory. Around age six, most children discover the value of using *organizational strategies* and by nine or ten, they use these strategies spontaneously. So, given the following words to learn,

couch, orange, rat, lamp, pear, sheep, banana, rug, pineapple, horse, table, dog

an older child or an adult might organize the words into three short lists of furniture, fruit, and animals. Younger children can be taught to use organization to improve memory, but they probably won't apply the strategy unless they are reminded. Children also become more able to use elaboration as they mature, but this strategy is developed late in childhood. Creating images or stories to remember ideas is more likely for older elementary school students and adolescents (Siegler, 1998).

Individual Differences.   Besides developmental differences, there are other individual variations in working memory, and these differences have implications for learning. For example, the correlation between scores on a test of working memory span (like the one you just took in the exercise on the previous page) and the verbal portion of the Scholastic Assessment Test (SAT) are about .59. But there is no correlation between the SAT and simple short-term memory span (repeating digits). Working-memory span is also related to scores on intelligence tests. If a task requires controlled attention or higher-level thinking, then working-memory span probably is a factor in performing that task (Ashcraft, 2006; Hambrick, Kane, & Engle, 2005; Ackerman, Beier, & Boyle, 2005; Unsworth & Engle, 2005).

Some people seem to have more efficient working memories than others (Cariglia-Bull & Pressley, 1990; DiVesta & Di Cintio, 1997; Jurden, 1995), and differences in working memory may be associated with giftedness in math and verbal areas. For example, subjects in one research study were asked to remember lists of numbers, the locations of marks on a page, letters, and words (Dark & Benbow, 1991). Subjects who excelled in mathematics remembered numbers and locations significantly better than subjects talented in verbal areas. The verbally talented subjects, on the other hand, had better memories for words. Based on these results, Dark and Benbow believe that basic differences in information processing abilities play a role in the development of mathematical and verbal talent.

There are several developmental differences in how students use process information in working and long-term memory.

Diversity: Individual Differences and Long-Term Memory

The major individual difference that affects long-term memory is knowledge. When students have more *domain-specific declarative* and *procedural knowledge,* they are better at learning and remembering material in that domain (Alexander, 1997). Think about what it is like to read a very technical textbook in an area you know little about. Every line is difficult. You have to stop and look up words or turn back to read about concepts you don't understand. It is hard to remember what you are reading because you are trying to understand and remember at the same time. But with a good basis of knowledge, learning and remembering become easier; the more you know, the easier it is to know more. This is true in part because having knowledge improves strategy use. Another factor is related to developing domain knowledge and remembering it: interest. To develop expert understanding and recall in a domain requires the "continuous interplay of skill (i.e., knowledge) and thrill (i.e., interest)" (Alexander, Kulikowich, & Schulze, 1994, p. 334).

People also differ in their abilities to use images in remembering. There are both developmental and individual differences. Children are more likely than adults to use images. As they mature cognitively, children may replace using images with using verbal propositions. As adults, some people are better than others at using imagery, but most people could improve their imagery abilities with practice (Schunk, 2004).

As we have seen throughout this book, because people grow up in different cultural contexts, they have different funds of knowledge (Moll, 1994; Nieto, 2004). Remember the baseball study earlier in this chapter—attention, learning, and memory are supported when teaching builds on the prior knowledge of students.

Individual Differences in Metacognition

Some differences in metacognitive abilities are the result of development. Younger children, for example, may not be aware of the purpose of a lesson—they may think the point is simply to finish. They also may not be good at gauging the difficulty of a task—they may think that reading for fun and reading a science book are the same (Gredler, 2005). As children grow older, they are more able to exercise executive control over strategies. For example, they are more able to determine if they have understood instructions (Markman, 1977, 1979) or if they have studied enough to remember a set of items (Flavell, Friedrichs, & Hoyt, 1970). Metacognitive abilities begin to develop around ages five to seven and improve throughout school (Flavell, Green, & Flavell, 1995; Garner, 1990). In her work with grade 1 and 2 students, Nancy Perry found that asking students two questions helped them become more metacognitive. The questions were "What did you learn about yourself as a reader/writer today?" and "What did you learn that you can do again and again and again?" When teachers asked these questions regularly during class, even young students demonstrated fairly sophisticated levels of metacognitive understanding and action (Perry et al., 2000).

Not all differences in metacognitive abilities have to do with age or maturation. There is great variability even among students of the same developmental level, but these differences do not appear to be related to intellectual abilities. In fact, superior metacognitive skills can compensate for lower levels of ability, so these metacognitive skills can be especially important for students who often have trouble in school (Schunk, 2004; Swanson, 1990).

Some individual differences in metacognitive abilities are probably caused by biological differences or by variations in learning experiences. Students can vary greatly in their ability to attend selectively to information in their environment. In fact, many students diagnosed as having learning disabilities actually have attention disorders (Hallahan & Kauffman, 2006), particularly with long tasks (Pelham, 1981). Other attention and behaviour difficulties associated with attention disorders may stem from sociocultural, emotional, developmental, cognitive, or educational sources, as indicated in Table 7.3.

Convergences: Connecting with Families

The last several sections of this chapter have described many ideas for helping students become knowledgeable—memory strategies, mnemonics, metacognitive skills such as planning or monitoring comprehension, and cognitive skills. Some students have an advantage in school because they learn these strategies and skills at home. One way to capitalize on this diversity is to connect with the family in support of the child's learning. The Family and Community Partnerships feature on page 276 gives ideas for working with families to give all your students more support and practice developing these skills.

TABLE 7.3 Questioning the Sources of Difficulties with Attention
If we take a holistic perspective on students, we can understand and capitalize on their differences.
In working with students diagnosed with ADHD, ask these questions:

Paradigm or Perspective	Key Question	Key Experts	Examples of Potential Assessments	Examples of Potential Interventions
Sociocultural	How much of the child's attention and behaviour difficulties results from cultural differences?	Culturally sensitive social worker, psychologist, teacher	Home visits; classroom observations	Provision of culturally sensitive curriculum; celebration of cultural diversity
Psychoaffective	How much of the child's attention and behaviour difficulties results from emotional trauma, anxiety/depression, or temperamental differences?	Clinical psychologist; psychiatrist; licensed counsellor	Assessments for depression, anxiety; temperament assessments	Psychotherapy; family therapy; provision of emotionally supportive classroom environment
Developmental	How much of the child's attention and behaviour difficulties results from a different pace of development?	Developmental pediatrician; child development specialist	Child development indexes; observation in natural settings	Provision of developmentally appropriate curriculum; readjustment of behavioural expectations
Cognitive	How much of the child's attention and behaviour difficulties results from creative behaviour or other positive cognitive differences?	Gifted and talented specialist; cognitive psychologist	Creativity instruments; cognitive style assessments	Use of expressive arts, creative curriculum, gifted and talented curriculum, and other creative approaches
Biological	How much of the child's attention and behaviour difficulties results from biological problems or neurobiological differences?	Family physician; medical specialist (e.g., neurologist, psychiatrist)	Medical examination; specialized medical tests	Medications (e.g., Ritalin); treatment for underlying physical problems
Educational	How much of the child's attention and behaviour difficulties results from learning differences?	Learning specialist; classroom teacher	Learning style inventories; multiple intelligences assessments, authentic assessments, portfolios of the child's work	Teaching strategies tailored to the child's individual learning style/multiple intelligences

Source: Adapted from Armstrong, T. *ADD/ADHD alternatives in the classroom* (p. 54). Copyright © 1999 by the Association for Supervision and Curriculum Development. Reprinted with permission from ASCD. All rights reserved. The Association for Supervision and Curriculum Development is a worldwide community of educators advocating sound policies and sharing best practices to achieve the success of each learner. To learn more, visit ASCD at **www.ascd.org**.

ORGANIZING LEARNING

Give families specific strategies to help their children practise and remember.

EXAMPLES

1. Develop "super learner" homework assignments that include material to be learned and a "parent coaching card" with a description of a simple memory strategy—appropriate for the material—that parents can teach their child.

2. Provide a few comprehension check questions so that a family member can review reading assignments and check the child's understanding.

3. Describe the value of distributed practice and give family members ideas for how and when to work skills practice into home conversations and projects.

Ask family members to share their strategies for organizing and remembering.

EXAMPLES

1. Create a family calendar.

2. Encourage planning discussions in which family members help students break large tasks into smaller jobs, identify goals, and find resources.

Discuss the importance of attention in learning.

EXAMPLES

1. Encourage families to create study spaces for children away from distractions.

3. Make sure that parents know the purpose of homework assignments.

Check Your Knowledge

- The expert needs no learning strategies—knowledge is power. True, false, or it depends? Elaborate.
- What factors can explain why students who know an effective strategy don't use it?

Apply to Practice

- What are some simple activities that create opportunities to investigate your students' abilities to use organizational strategies for learning?
- To help develop plans to make homework more effective, what questions could you ask students about how they do homework?

SUMMARY

Elements of the Cognitive Perspective
(pp. 245–246)

Contrast cognitive and behavioural views of learning in terms of what is learned and the role of reinforcement.

In the cognitive view, knowledge is learned, and changes in knowledge make changes in behaviour possible. In the behavioural view, the new behaviour itself is learned. Both behavioural and cognitive theorists believe that reinforcement is important in learning, but for different reasons. Strict behaviourists maintain that reinforcement strengthens responses; cognitive theorists see reinforcement as a source of feedback about what is likely to happen if behaviour is repeated—that is, as a source of information.

How does knowledge affect learning?

The cognitive approach suggests that one of the most important elements in the learning process is what the individual brings to the learning situation. What we already know determines to a great extent what we will pay attention to, perceive, learn, remember, and forget.

The Information Processing Model of Memory
(pp. 247–264)

Compare declarative, procedural, and conditional knowledge.

Declarative knowledge is knowledge that can be declared, usually in words or other symbols. Declarative knowledge is "knowing that" something is the case. Small units of declarative knowledge can be organized into larger units. Procedural knowledge is "knowing how" to do something; procedural knowledge must be demonstrated. Conditional knowledge is "knowing when and why" to apply your declarative and procedural knowledge.

Give two explanations for perception.

The Gestalt principles are valid explanations of certain aspects of perception, but there are two other kinds of explanations in information processing theory for how we recognize patterns and give meaning to sensory events. The first is called *feature analysis,* or *bottom-up processing,* because the stimulus must be analyzed into features or components and assembled into a meaningful pattern. The second type of perception, *top-down processing,* is based on knowledge and expectation. To recognize patterns rapidly, in addition to noting features, we use what we already know about the situation.

What is working memory, and what processes are applied there?

Working memory is both short-term storage in the phonological loop and visuospatial sketchpad, and processing guided by the central executive—it is the workbench of conscious thought. To keep information activated in working memory for longer than 20 seconds, people use maintenance rehearsal (mentally repeating information) and elaborative rehearsal (making connections with knowledge in long-term memory). Elaborative rehearsal also helps move new information to long-term memory. The limited capacity of working memory can also be somewhat circumvented by the control process of chunking.

How is information represented in long-term memory, and what role do schemas play?

Memories may be explicit (semantic or episodic) or implicit (procedural, classical conditioning, or priming). In long-term memory, bits of information may be stored and interrelated in terms of propositional networks or images and in schemas that are data structures that allow us to represent large amounts of complex information,

make inferences, and understand new information.

What learning processes improve long-term memory?

The way you learn information in the first place affects its recall later. One important requirement is to integrate new material with knowledge already stored in long-term memory using elaboration, organization, and context. Another view of memory is the levels of processing theory, in which recall of information is determined by how completely it is processed.

Why do we forget?

Information lost from working memory truly disappears, but information in long-term memory may be available, given the right cues. Information appears to be lost from long-term memory through time decay (neural connections, like muscles, grow weak without use) and interference (newer memories may obscure older memories, and older memories may interfere with memory for new material).

Metacognition
(pp. 264–265)

What are the three metacognitive skills?

The three metacognitive skills used to regulate thinking and learning are planning, monitoring, and evaluation. Planning involves deciding how much time to give to a task, which strategies to use, how to start, and so on. Monitoring is the online awareness of "how I'm doing." Evaluation involves making judgments about the processes and outcomes of thinking and learning and acting on those judgments.

Becoming Knowledgeable: Some Basic Principles
(pp. 266–271)

Describe three ways to develop declarative knowledge.

Declarative knowledge develops as we integrate new information with our existing understanding. The most useful and effective way to learn and remember is to understand and use new information. Making the information to be remembered meaningful is important and often is the greatest challenge for teachers. Mnemonics are memorization aids: They include peg-type approaches such as the loci method, acronyms, chain mnemonics, and the keyword method. A powerful but limiting way to accomplish this is rote memorization, which can best be supported by part learning and distributed practice.

Describe some methods for developing procedural knowledge.

Automated basic skills and domain-specific strategies—two types of procedural knowledge—are learned in different ways. There are three stages in developing an automated skill: cognitive (following steps or directions guided by declarative knowledge), associative (combining individual steps into larger units), and autonomous (where the whole procedure can be accomplished without much attention). Prerequisite knowledge and practice with feedback help students move through these stages. Domain-specific strategies are consciously applied skills of organizing thoughts and actions to reach a goal. To support this kind of learning, teachers need to provide opportunities for application in many different situations.

Diversity and Convergences in Cognitive Learning
(pp. 272–276)

The expert needs no learning strategies—knowledge is power. True, false, or it depends? Elaborate.

It depends. When the task or problem the expert faces is well within the expert's domain, the vast knowledge and skills the expert possesses will be enough to succeed. But when the expert's knowledge and skills are not enough to yield success—for example, when the problem is at the edge of domain knowledge—the expert, just like the novice, needs to draw on other resources in the form of learning strategies. Knowledge is power, but when tasks exceed knowledge, knowledge isn't powerful enough.

What factors can explain why students who know an effective strategy don't use it?

There are several answers to this question. One is that the student is cognitively overloaded, too busy with some parts of a task to be able to make use of a productive strat-egy. Working memory is over-loaded. Another is that the student simply doesn't recognize that a strategy is appropriate in a particular situation. Conditional knowledge is insufficient to set the strategy in motion. A third, which we'll explore more in the next chapter, is that the student judges the strategy as not worth the effort of applying it.

KEY TERMS

BECOMING A PROFESSIONAL

Reflecting on the Chapter

Can you apply the ideas from this chapter on cognitive views of learning to solve the following problems of practice?

Preschool and Kindergarten

- The grade 1 teachers believe that the kindergarten teachers could do a better job of preparing their students to "pay attention" in class. As a kindergarten teacher, what would you do? How would you justify your plans to the grade 1 teachers?

Elementary and Middle School

- Several students in your class are recent immigrants and have limited knowledge of the kinds of experiences described in your basal reader series (county fairs, zoos, trips to the beach, shopping malls, etc.). The students speak and read English, but they still have difficulty understanding and remembering what they read. What would you do?

Junior High and High School

- You have reached a complicated chapter in your text—one that is difficult for students every year. How would you make the highly abstract concepts (such as sovereignty and jurisprudence) understandable for your students?

Check Your Understanding

- Understand the role of prior knowledge in learning.
- Know what a schema is and how schemas affect attention, learning, and remembering.
- Know how metacognitive skills affect learning and remembering.
- Be familiar with some common mnemonic strategies.

Your Teaching Portfolio

Use the section on the differences between behavioural and cognitive approaches to learning to refine your teaching philosophy. How would you answer the job interview question, "What is your theory of learning and why?"

Teaching Resources

Use the section on mnemonics to generate ideas for helping your students learn key vocabulary in science or social studies subjects and include these ideas in your teaching resources file.

Teachers' Casebook

What Would They Do?

Here is how two practising teachers responded to the teaching situation presented at the beginning of this chapter about history students intent on memorizing.

Judith Rutledge
Eastern High School of Commerce
Toronto, Ontario

I'd recognize the importance of marks, first of all. Frequently, students have to produce a piece of writing that asks them for much more than memorized facts. While memorizing has many advantages, I'd also explore the limitations of using that as a primary learning strategy. In fact, for an interim period, I'd guarantee students their old marks and hold out the possibility of higher ones if they were willing to expand their ways of thinking.

People who are very concerned with marks often have high aspirations. They are also interested in other people who have achieved remarkable goals and in how they did it; it's not hard to demonstrate the advantages of creative and critical thinking and to set up some exercises that let the students experiment deliberately with a variety of thinking techniques. I'd explore the kind of thinking that goes on at the highest levels of human endeavour. We'd look at the factors that go into decision making, intellectual breakthroughs and discoveries, wise government, and good citizenship. Contemporary events invariably offer excellent case studies.

It's also interesting to examine the idea of what constitutes a "fact"—that is, what can be memorized with perfect assurance that it won't subsequently be challenged. Dividing the class into different groups and getting them to present the views of various people involved in a historical moment can be pretty illuminating. It provides an opportunity to think about who writes history; which views and values prevail; and whose voices are not heard at all. This kind of reflection can be very meaningful for students as they wonder about their own position and purpose in the world. They can see that it's fun and ultimately more useful and rewarding than attempting to simply memorize what one textbook has presented. They are in control of their learning, not just blind consumers.

Claire Frankel-Salama
Bishops College
St. John's, Newfoundland

Most students are motivated to obtain good marks and, for many, these have been achieved through rote learning. True learning through the association of ideas has not been part of their school experience. Why is this the case? Why is the rote memory approach still the favoured method of "learning"?

In many schools, teachers have to deal with the unpleasant logistical realities of extremely large classes, multiple preparations, heavy course loads, and extracurricular activities. In the interest of expedience, there is a strong emphasis on multiple-choice and factually strict questioning techniques that afford little room for independent thinking and development of good writing skills. In fact, the increased use of standardized testing has served only to exacerbate this problem by precluding more pedagogically sound qualitative forms of evaluation and feedback. Teachers feel increasingly pressured to prepare students for the exam rather than to develop keen, critical minds.

How can we, as educators, deal with these realities and still work toward a more synthetic approach to learning?

Certainly it is valuable to consider an interdisciplinary approach to teaching, especially at the high school level, where courses tend to be taught as separate units. Meetings between departments should take place, and multidisciplinary projects should be encouraged. For example, it may be possible to accommodate a history presentation or essay in a literature or even a science assignment. This should not be considered cheating; indeed, such an effort should have the co-operation of all departments involved. In this way, the student begins to realize the impact of science on literature, of music on history, of mathematics on art, etc. A co-directed paper on socialism in literature will surely have more intellectual impact than a simple research paper in one restricted area.

Another effective way to encourage analysis and synthesis involves the use of authentic documents and oral histories. A reading of Rabelais's recommendation of a good Renaissance education helps us question our own. The study of caricatures from different sources regarding the same historical event deepens understanding of different political viewpoints. A survivor's account of the Triangle Shirtwaist Factory fire helps us "feel" the need for labour reform. A study of socialist art and its relationship to an economic system will explain what the ideology is really about. The comprehension of contextualities will certainly deepen understanding.

Teachers should not despair nor think that these efforts will bear no fruit. After all, wisdom comes with age and experience. It is not unusual to receive visits or letters from former students thanking a teacher for introducing a particular author, some interesting paintings, a meaningful destination, or previously unheard music. Germination requires a confluence of several seemingly unrelated conditions. Eventually, some seeds will bloom, perhaps even beyond expectations.

8

COMPLEX COGNITIVE PROCESSES

Claude & Paloma, 1954. Pablo Picasso. © 2006 Estate of Pablo Picasso/Artists Rights Society (ARS), New York. Photo © SuperStock, Inc.

Teachers' Casebook

What Would You Do?

You know that your students need good study skills to do well in both their current and future classes. But many of the students just don't seem to know how to study. They can't read a longer assignment, understand it, and remember what they read. They have trouble completing larger projects—many wait until the last minute. They can't organize their work or decide what is most important. You are concerned because they will need all of these skills and strategies as they progress through their education. You have so much material to cover to meet curriculum guidelines, but many of your students are just drowning in the amount of work.

Critical Thinking

- What study skills do students need for your subject or class?
- What could you do to teach these skills, while still covering the material in the curriculum guidelines?

Collaboration

With three or four members of your class, identify the learning skills and study strategies that students will need in a grade you might teach. Then analyze the study skills necessary for your class using this text.

Think of a concept that you learned lately in a class. How did you learn it? If you learned from a text or a teacher, were examples provided? What kinds? Do you understand the concept well enough to define it in your own words? Can you apply it to solve a problem?

We focused on the development of knowledge—how people make sense of and remember information and ideas—in the previous chapter. In this chapter, we will focus on understanding, problem solving, and thinking. Understanding is more than memorizing. It is more than retelling in your own words. Understanding involves appropriately *transforming* and *using* knowledge, skills, and ideas. These understandings are considered "higher-level cognitive objectives" in a commonly used system of educational objectives (Anderson & Krathwohl, 2001; Bloom et al., 1956). We will focus on the implications of cognitive theories for the day-to-day practice of teaching, particularly for developing students' thinking and understanding.

Because the cognitive perspective is a philosophical orientation and not a unified theoretical model, teaching methods derived from it are varied. In this chapter, we will first examine four important areas in which cognitive theorists have made suggestions for learning and teaching: concept learning, problem solving, creativity, and learning strategies and tactics. Finally, we will explore the question of how to encourage the transfer of learning from one situation to another to make learning more useful.

By the time you have completed this chapter, you should be able to answer these questions:

- *What are characteristics of a good lesson for teaching a key concept in your subject area?*
- *What are steps in solving complex problems?*
- *What examples can you give of algorithms and heuristics for problem solving?*
- *How would you apply new learning strategies and tactics to prepare for tests and assignments in your current courses?*
- *How can teachers encourage creativity in their students?*
- *What are three ways a teacher might encourage positive transfer of learning?*

LEARNING AND TEACHING ABOUT CONCEPTS

Most of what we know about the world involves concepts and relations among concepts (Ashcraft, 2002). But what exactly is a concept? A **concept** is a category used to group similar events, ideas, objects, or people. When we talk about the concept *student*, for example, we refer to a category of people who are similar to one another—they all study a subject. The people may be old or young, in school or not, and they may be studying hockey or Bach, but they can all be categorized as students. Concepts are abstractions; they do not exist in the real world. Only individual examples of concepts exist. Concepts help us organize vast amounts of information into manageable units. For instance, there are about 7.5 million distinguishable differences in colours. By categorizing these colours into some dozen or so groups, we manage to deal with this diversity quite well (Bruner, 1973).

Views of Concept Learning

In early research, psychologists assumed that concepts are identified by a set of **defining attributes**, or distinctive features: for example, students all study; textbooks all contain pages that are bound together in some way. (But what about electronic "books"?) The defining attributes theory of concepts suggests that we recognize specific examples by noting key required features.

Since about 1970, however, these long-popular views about the nature of concepts have been challenged (Ashcraft, 2006). While some concepts, such as equilateral triangle, have clear-cut defining attributes, most concepts do not. Take the concept of *party*. What are the defining attributes? You might have difficulty listing these attributes, but you probably recognize a party when you see or hear one (unless, of course, we are talking about political parties, or the other party in a lawsuit, where the sound might not help you recognize the "party"). What about the concept of *bird*? Your first thought might be that birds are animals that fly. But is an ostrich a bird? What about a penguin? A bat?

Prototypes and Exemplars. Current conceptions of concept learning suggest that we have in our minds a prototype of a party and a bird—an image that captures the essence of each concept. A **prototype** is the best representative of its category. For instance, the best representative of the *birds* category for many Canadians might be a robin (Rosch, 1973). Other members of the category may be very similar to the prototype (sparrow) or similar in some ways but different in others (chicken, ostrich). At the boundaries of a category, it may be difficult to determine if a particular instance really belongs. For example, is a telephone a piece of "furniture"? Is an elevator a "vehicle"? Is an olive a "fruit"? Whether something fits into a category is a matter of degree. Thus, categories have fuzzy boundaries. Some events, objects, or ideas are simply better examples of a concept than others (Ashcraft, 2006).

Another explanation of concept learning suggests that we identify members of a category by referring to exemplars. **Exemplars** are our actual memories of specific birds, parties, furniture, and so on, that we use to compare with an item in question to see if that item belongs in the same category as our exemplar. For example, if you see a strange steel-and-stone bench in a public park, you may compare it with the sofa in your living room to decide if the uncomfortable-looking creation is still for sitting or if it has crossed a fuzzy boundary into "sculpture."

Prototypes are probably built from experiences with many exemplars. This happens naturally because episodic memories of particular events tend to blur together over time, creating an average or typical sofa prototype from all the sofa exemplars you have experienced (Schwartz & Reisberg, 1991).

Concepts and Schemas. In addition to prototypes and exemplars, a third element is involved when we recognize a concept—our schematic knowledge related to the

concept A general category of events, ideas, objects, or people whose members share certain properties.

Connect & Extend

TO YOUR TEACHING
According to Piaget, a person cannot think in abstract terms until the stage of formal operations is reached. How then can a child learn abstract concepts such as "yesterday" and "happy"?

defining attributes Distinctive features shared by members of a category.

prototype Best representative of a category.

exemplar A specific example of a given category that is used to classify an item.

"CITY CHILDREN HAVE
TROUBLE WITH THE CON-
CEPT OF HARVEST."
(© Martha Campbell. From *Phi
Delta Kappan.*)

concept. How do we know that counterfeit money is not "real" money, even though it perfectly fits our "money" prototype and exemplars? We know because of its history. It was printed by the "wrong" people. So our understanding of the concept of money is connected with such concepts as crime, forgery, and the Bank of Canada.

Jacob Feldman (2003) suggests a final aspect of concept learning—the simplicity principle. Feldman says that when people are confronted with examples, they induce the simplest category or rule that would cover all the examples. Sometimes it is easy to come up with a simple rule (triangles) and sometimes it is more difficult (fruit), but humans seek a simple hypothesis for collecting all the examples under one concept. Feldman suggests this simplicity principle is one of the oldest ideas in cognitive psychology: "Organisms seek to understand their environment by reducing incoming information to a simpler, more coherent, and more useful form" (p. 231). Does this remind you of the Gestalt principles of perception in Chapter 7?

What Would You Say?

You are being interviewed for a job in a school that serves many immigrant families. The principal asks, "How would you teach abstract concepts to a student who just arrived from Somalia and can't even read in her native language, much less English?"

Strategies for Teaching Concepts

Connect & Extend

TO YOUR TEACHING
Can abstract concepts be taught through the use of prototypes?

Both prototypes and defining attributes are important in learning. Children first learn many concepts in the real world from the best examples or prototypes, pointed out by adults (Tennyson, 1981). But when examples are ambiguous (is an olive a fruit?), we may consult the defining attributes to make a decision. Olives are foods with seeds in the edible parts, which matches the defining attributes for fruits, so they must be fruits, even though they are not typical or prototypic fruits (Schunk, 2004).

Like the learning of concepts, the teaching of concepts can combine both defining attributes and prototypes. One approach to teaching about concepts is called *concept attainment*—a way of helping students construct an understanding of specific concepts and practise thinking skills such as hypothesis testing (Joyce, Weil, & Calhoun, 2006; Klausmeier, 1992).

An Example Concept-Attainment Lesson. Here is how a grade 5 teacher helped his students learn about a familiar concept and practise thinking skills at the same time (Eggen & Kauchak, 1996, pp. 105–107). He placed two signs on a table—one said "Examples" and the other said "Non-examples." Then he placed an apple in front of the "Examples" sign. Next he put a rock in front of the "Non-examples" sign. He asked his students, "What do you think the idea might be?" "Things we eat" was the first suggestion. The teacher wrote "HYPOTHESES" on the board and, after a brief discussion of the meaning of "hypotheses," listed "things we eat" under this heading. Next, he asked for other hypotheses—"living things" and "things that grow on plants" came next. After some discussion about plants and living things, the teacher added a tomato to the "Examples" and a carrot to the "Non-examples." Animated reconsideration of all the hypotheses followed these additions and a new hypothesis—"red things"—was suggested. Through discussion of more examples (peach, squash, orange) and non-examples (lettuce, artichoke, potato), the students narrowed their hypothesis to "things with seeds in the parts you eat." The students had "constructed" the concept of "fruit"—foods we eat with seeds in the edible parts (or, a more advanced definition, any engorged ovary, such as a pea pod, nut, tomato, pineapple, or the edible part of the plant developed from a flower).

Lesson Components.   Whatever strategy you use for teaching concepts, you will need four components in any lesson: examples and non-examples, relevant and irrelevant attributes, the name of the concept, and a definition (Joyce, Weil, & Calhoun, 2006). In addition, visual aids such as pictures, diagrams, or maps can improve learning of many concepts (Anderson & Smith, 1987; Mayer, 2001).

1. *Examples:* More examples are needed in teaching complicated concepts and in working with younger or less-able students. Both examples and non-examples (sometimes called *positive* and *negative* instances) are necessary to make the boundaries of the category clear. So a discussion of why a bat (non-example) is not a bird will help students define the boundaries of the bird concept.

2. *Relevant and irrelevant attributes:* The ability to fly, as we've seen, is not a relevant attribute for classifying animals as birds. Even though many birds fly, some birds do not (ostrich, penguin), and some non-birds do (bats, flying squirrels). The ability to fly would have to be included in a discussion of the bird concept, but students should understand that flying does not define an animal as a bird.

3. *Name:* Simply learning a label does not mean that the person understands the concept, although the label is necessary for the understanding. In the example on the previous page, students probably already used the "fruit" name but may not have understood that squash and avocados are fruits.

4. *Definition:* A good definition has two elements: a reference to any *more general category* that the new concept falls into and a statement of the new concept's *defining attributes* (Klausmeier, 1976). For example, a fruit is food we eat (general category) with seeds in the edible parts (defining attributes). An equilateral triangle is a plane, simple, closed figure (general category) with three equal sides and three equal angles (defining attributes). This kind of definition helps place the concept in a schema of related knowledge.

In teaching some concepts, "a picture is worth a thousand words"—or at least a few hundred, as we saw in Chapter 7. Seeing and handling specific examples, or pictures of examples, helps young children learn concepts. For students of all ages, the complex concepts in history, science, and mathematics can often be illustrated in diagrams or graphs. For example, Anderson and Smith (1983) found that when the students they taught only read about the concept, just 20 percent could understand the role of reflected light in our ability to see objects. But when the students worked with diagrams such as the one in Figure 8.1 on page 286, almost 80 percent of them understood the concept.

Lesson Structure.   The fruit lesson described earlier is an example of good concept teaching for several reasons. First, examining examples and non-examples before discussing attributes or definitions appears to be the more effective method of teaching (Joyce, Weil, & Calhoun, 2000). Start your concept lesson with prototypes, or best examples, to help the students establish the category. The teacher began with the classic fruit example, an apple, then moved to less typical examples, such as tomatoes and squash. These examples show the wide range of possibilities the category includes and the variety of irrelevant attributes within a category. This information helps students avoid focusing on an irrelevant attribute as a defining feature. The peach example tells students that fruit can have one seed as well as many. The squash and avocado examples indicate that fruits do not have to be sweet. Including fruits of different colours that have one seed or many, a sweet taste or not, and thick or thin skin will prevent **undergeneralization**, or the exclusion of some foods from their rightful place in the fruit category.

Non-examples should be very close to the concept but miss by one or just a few critical attributes. For instance, sweet potatoes and rhubarb are not fruits, even though sweet potatoes are sweet and rhubarb is used to make pies. Including non-examples will prevent **overgeneralization**, or the inclusion of substances that are not fruits.

Connect and Extend

TO THE RESEARCH
Tennyson, R. D., & Cocchiarella, M. M. (1986). An empirically based instructional design theory for teaching concepts. *Review of Educational Research, 56,* 40–71.

Abstract
An instructional design theory views concept learning as a two-phase process: (a) formation of conceptual knowledge, and (b) development of procedural knowledge. Two fundamental components of the proposed theoretical model are content structure variables and instructional design variables. A rational combination of these components provides the means for the selection of one of four basic instructional design strategies. The theoretical model is described with reference to instructional methods and cognitive processes.

undergeneralization Exclusion of some true members from a category; limiting a concept.

overgeneralization Inclusion of non-members in a category; overextending a concept.

Figure 8.1 Understanding Complex Concepts

Illustrations can help students grasp a difficult concept.

Source: From Richardson-Koehler, V. (Ed.). (1987). *The educator's handbook: A research perspective.* New York: Longman. Copyright © 1987. Reprinted by permission of Addison-Wesley Educational Publishers, Inc.

Q. When sunlight strikes the tree, it helps the boy see the tree. How does it do this?

Q. When sunlight strikes the tree, it helps the boy see the tree. How does it do this?

A. Some of the light bounces (is reflected) off the tree and goes to the boy's eyes.

Connect & Extend

TO YOUR TEACHING
How can a teacher determine if a student has learned a concept?

After the students seem to have grasped the concept under consideration, it is useful to ask them to think about the ways in which they formed and tested their hypotheses. Thinking back helps students develop their metacognitive skills and shows them that different people approach problems in different ways (Joyce, Weil, & Calhoun, 2000). Table 8.1 summarizes the stages of concept teaching.

Extending and Connecting Concepts. Once students have a good sense of a concept, they should use it. This might mean writing, reading, explaining, doing exercises, solving problems, or engaging in any other activity that requires them to apply their new understanding. This will connect the concept into the students'

TABLE 8.1 Phases of the Concept Attainment Model

There are three main phases in concept attainment teaching. First, the teacher presents examples and non-examples and students identify the concept, then the teacher checks for understanding, and finally students analyze their thinking strategies.

Phase One: Presentation of Data and Identification of Concept	Phase Two: Testing Attainment of the Concept	Phase Three: Analysis of Thinking Strategies
Teacher presents labelled examples.	Students identify additional unlabelled examples as yes or no.	Students describe thoughts.
Students compare attributes in positive and negative examples.	Teacher confirms hypotheses, names concept, and restates definitions according to essential attributes.	Students discuss role of hypotheses and attributes.
Students generate and test hypotheses.	Students generate examples.	Students discuss type and number of hypotheses.
Students state a definition according to the essential attributes.		

Source: From Joyce, B. R., Weil, M., & Calhoun, E. (2000). *Models of teaching* (6th ed.). Boston: Allyn & Bacon. Copyright © 2000 by Allyn & Bacon. Reprinted by permission.

web of related schematic knowledge. One approach that you may see in texts and workbooks for students above the primary grades is **concept mapping** (Novak & Musonda, 1991). Students "diagram" their understanding of the concept, as Amy has in Figure 8.2. Amy's map shows a reasonable understanding of the concept of molecule but also indicates that Amy holds one misconception. She thinks that there is no space between the molecules in solids.

Teaching Concepts through Discovery

Jerome Bruner's early research on thinking (Bruner, Goodnow, & Austin, 1956) stirred his interest in educational approaches that encourage concept learning and the development of thinking. Bruner's work emphasized the importance of understanding the structure of a subject being studied, the need for active learning as the basis for true understanding, and the value of inductive reasoning in learning.

Structure and Discovery. *Subject structure* refers to the fundamental ideas, relationships, or patterns of the field—the essential information. Because structure does not include specific facts or details about the subject, the essential structure of an idea can be represented simply as a diagram, set of principles, or formula. According to Bruner, learning will be more meaningful, useful, and memorable for students if they focus on understanding the structure of the subject being studied.

To grasp the structure of information, Bruner believes, students must be active—they must identify key principles for themselves rather than simply accepting teachers' explanations. This process has been called **discovery learning**. In discovery learning, the teacher presents examples and the students work with the examples until they discover the interrelationships—the subject's structure. Thus, Bruner believes that classroom learning should take place through **inductive reasoning**, that is, by using specific examples to formulate a general principle.

concept mapping Student's diagram of his or her understanding of a concept.

Connect & Extend

TO YOUR TEACHING
For advice and additional information about the creation and use of concept maps, go to the Graphic Organizers website (**www.graphic.org/concept. html**).

discovery learning Students work on their own to discover basic principles.

inductive reasoning Formulating general principles based on knowledge of examples and details.

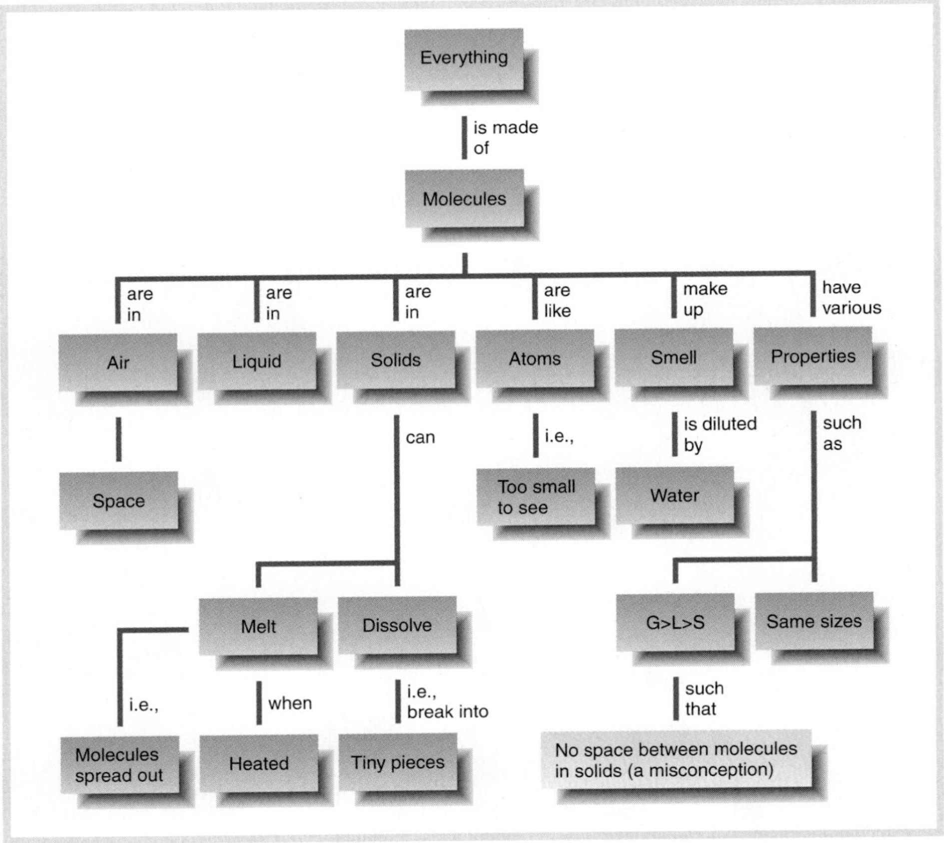

Figure 8.2 Amy's Molecule

Amy, in grade 8, has drawn a map to represent her understanding of the concept of "molecule." Her concept includes one misconception—that there is no space between molecules in solids.

Source: From Novak, J. D., & Musonda, D. (1991). A twelve-year longitudinal study of science concept learning. *American Educational Resource Journal, 28,* Figure p. 137. Copyright 1991 by the American Educational Research Association. Reprinted by permission of the publisher.

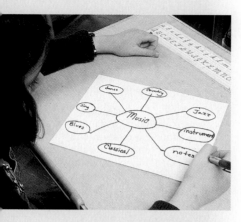

Concept mapping has students "diagram" their understanding of a concept. What are examples of the concept of music for this student?

intuitive thinking Making imaginative leaps to correct perceptions or workable solutions.

guided discovery An adaptation of discovery learning in which the teacher provides some direction.

Connect & Extend

TO YOUR TEACHING
See the **Teachers' Casebook** for ideas about how to develop lessons that promote the kinds of high-level cognitive skills that are central to developing understanding by comparing and contrasting concepts.

Bruner's ideas about discovery learning emphasize the importance of active learning as a basis for true understanding.

Discovery in Action. An inductive approach requires **intuitive thinking** on the part of students. Bruner suggests that teachers can nurture this intuitive thinking by encouraging students to make guesses based on incomplete evidence and then to confirm or disprove the guesses systematically (Bruner, 1960). After learning about ocean currents and the shipping industry, for example, students might be shown old maps of three harbours and asked to guess which one became a major port. Then students could check their guesses through systematic research. Unfortunately, educational practices often discourage intuitive thinking by punishing wrong guesses and rewarding safe but uncreative answers.

A distinction is usually made between discovery learning, in which the students work on their own to a great extent, and **guided discovery,** in which the teacher provides some direction. Reviewing 30 years of research on pure discovery learning, Richard Mayer (2004) concludes,

> Like some zombie that keeps returning from its grave, pure discovery continues to have its advocates. However, anyone who takes an evidence-based approach to educational practice must ask the same question: Where is the evidence that it works? In spite of calls for free discovery in every decade, the supporting evidence is hard to find. (p. 17)

Unguided discovery is appropriate for preschool children, but in a typical elementary or secondary classroom, unguided activities usually prove unmanageable and unproductive. For these situations, guided discovery is preferable. Students are presented with intriguing questions, baffling situations, or interesting problems, such as, Why does the flame go out when we cover it with a jar? Why does this pencil seem to bend when you put it in water? What is the rule for grouping these words together? Instead of explaining how to solve the problem, the teacher provides the appropriate materials and encourages students to make observations, form hypotheses, and test solutions. Feedback must be given at the optimal moment, when students can use it either to revise their approach or take it as encouragement to continue in the direction they've chosen. The accompanying Guidelines should help you apply Bruner's suggestions.

Teaching Concepts through Exposition

In contrast to Bruner, David Ausubel (1963, 1977, 1982) theorized that people acquire knowledge primarily by being exposed directly to it rather than through discovery. Concepts, principles, and ideas are understood using deductive reasoning—verbal information, ideas, and relationships among ideas, taken together.

APPLYING BRUNER'S IDEAS

Present both examples and non-examples of the concepts you are teaching.

EXAMPLES

1. In teaching about mammals, include people, kangaroos, whales, cats, dolphins, and camels as examples and chickens, fish, alligators, frogs, and penguins as non-examples.
2. Ask students for additional examples and non-examples.

Help students see connections among concepts.

EXAMPLES

1. Ask questions such as these: What else could you call this apple? (Fruit.) What do we do with fruit? (Eat.) What do we call things we eat? (Food.)
2. Use diagrams, outlines, and summaries to point out connections.

Pose a question and let students try to find the answer.

EXAMPLES

1. How could the human hand be improved?
2. What is the relation between the area of one tile and the area of the whole floor?

Encourage students to make intuitive guesses.

EXAMPLES

1. Instead of defining a word, say, "Let's guess what it might mean by looking at the words around it."
2. Give students a map of ancient Greece and ask where they think the major cities were.
3. Don't comment after the first few guesses. Wait for several ideas before giving the answer.
4. Use guiding questions to focus students when their discovery has led them too far astray.

Rote memorization is not meaningful learning, because material learned by rote is not *connected* with existing knowledge.

Advance Organizers.   Ausubel's strategy begins with an **advance organizer**. This is an introductory statement of a relationship or a high-level concept broad enough to encompass all the information that will follow. An advance organizer provides scaffolding, or support, for new information. It should direct attention to what is important in the coming material, highlight relationships among ideas that will be presented, and remind about relevant prior knowledge.

In general, advance organizers fall into one of two categories: *comparative* and *expository* (Mayer, 1984). Comparative organizers *activate* (bring into working memory) already existing schemas. They remind you of what you already know but may not realize is relevant. A comparative advance organizer for a history lesson on revolutions might be a statement that contrasts military uprisings with the physical and social changes involved in the Industrial Revolution; you could also compare the common aspects of the French, English, Mexican, Russian, Iranian, and American revolutions (Salomon & Perkins, 1989).

In contrast, *expository organizers* provide *new* knowledge that students will need to understand the upcoming information. In an English class, you might begin a large thematic unit on rites of passage in literature with a broad statement of the theme and why it has been so central in literature—something like, "A central character coming of age must learn to know himself or herself, often makes some kind of journey of self-discovery, and must decide what in the society is to be accepted and what rejected."

The general conclusion of research on advance organizers is that, under two conditions, they help students learn, especially when the material to be learned is quite unfamiliar, complex, or difficult (Corkill, 1992; Mayer, 1984; Shuell, Morin, & Miller, 1998). First, the students must process and understand information presented in the organizer. This was demonstrated dramatically in a study by Dinnel and Glover (1985). They found that instructing students to paraphrase an advance

Connect & Extend

TO PRACTICE
Many teachers, especially in mathematics and science, believe that meaningful learning in their areas is best supported by discovery learning. Be prepared to answer questions about the assumptions, techniques, strengths, and limitations of this instructional strategy.

advance organizer Statement of inclusive concepts to introduce and sum up material that follows.

Connect & Extend

TO PRACTICE
The advance organizer is an important element in many teacher-centred/expository approaches to instruction. Be able to explain the role of the advance organizer in these approaches and to identify the basic types of organizers.

Expository teaching methods present information to learners in an organized, "finished" form, rather than having them discover it themselves.

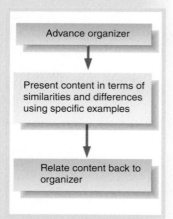

Figure 8.3 Phases of Expository Teaching

analogical instruction Teaching new concepts by making connections (analogies) with information that the student already understands.

organizer—which, of course, requires them to understand its meaning—increased the effectiveness of the organizer. Second, the organizer must really be an organizer: it must indicate relations among the basic concepts and terms that will be used. In other words, a true organizer isn't just a statement of historical or background information. No amount of student processing can make a bad organizer more effective. Concrete models, diagrams, or analogies seem to be especially good organizers (Robinson, 1998; Robinson & Kiewra, 1995).

Steps in an Expository Lesson. After presenting an advance organizer, the next step is to present content in terms of basic similarities and differences, using specific examples. It is important that students see not only the similarities between the material presented and what they already know but also the differences, so that interference—the confusion of old and new material—can be avoided.

Suppose you are teaching the coming-of-age theme in literature, and you choose *The Diary of Anne Frank* and *Paddle-to-the-Sea* as the basic material for the unit. As the students read the first book, you might ask them to compare the central character's growth, state of mind, and position in society with those of characters from other novels, plays, and films. When the class moves on to the second book, you can start by asking students to compare Anne Frank's inner journey with Paddle's journey through the Great Lakes to the Atlantic Ocean. As comparisons are made, whether within a single class lesson or during an entire unit, it is useful to underscore the goal of the lesson and occasionally to repeat the advance organizer (with amendments and elaborations).

Along with the comparisons, specific examples come into play so the specific elements of Paddle's and Anne Frank's dilemmas can become clear. Finally, when all the material has been presented, ask students to discuss how the examples can be used to expand on the original advance organizer. The phases of expository teaching are summarized in Figure 8.3.

Expository teaching is more developmentally appropriate for students at or above later elementary school, that is, around grades 5 or 6 (Luiten, Ames, & Ackerson, 1980). The accompanying Guidelines will help you follow the main steps in expository teaching.

Learning Disabilities and Concept Teaching

A recent approach to teaching concepts that also emphasizes links to prior knowledge is **analogical instruction** (Bulgren et al., 2000). This approach has proved helpful for teaching scientific or cultural knowledge in heterogeneous secondary classes that include students who are less academically prepared and students with learning disabilities. In secondary classrooms, as the amount and complexity of content increases, these students are especially at risk for failure. The goal of analogical instruction is to identify knowledge that these students already have and use it as a starting point for learning new, complex material by drawing analogies. Analogies have long been used in problem solving, as you will see in the next section, but until recently, studies of analogies in teaching content have been rare.

APPLYING AUSUBEL'S IDEAS

Use advance organizers.

EXAMPLES

1. English: Shakespeare used the social ideas of his time as a framework for his plays—*Julius Caesar, Hamlet,* and *Macbeth* deal with concepts of natural order, a nation as the human body, etc.
2. Social studies: Geography dictates economy in pre-industrialized regions or nations.
3. History: Important concepts during the Renaissance were symmetry, admiration of the classical world, and the centrality of the human mind.

Use a number of examples.

EXAMPLES

1. In mathematics class, ask students to point out all the examples of right angles that they can find in the room.

2. In teaching about islands and peninsulas, use maps, slides, models, postcards.

Focus on both similarities and differences.

EXAMPLES

1. In a history class, ask students to list the ways in which Canada was the same and different before and after Confederation.
2. In a biology class, ask students how they would transform spiders into insects or an amphibian into a reptile.

Check Your Knowledge

- Distinguish between prototypes and exemplars.
- What are the four elements needed in concept teaching?
- What are the key characteristics of Bruner's discovery learning?
- What are the stages of Ausubel's expository teaching?
- How can you teach concepts through analogies?

Apply to Practice

- What are the defining attributes of the concept of government? What attributes are irrelevant?

PROBLEM SOLVING

What Would You Say?

You're interviewing with the district superintendent for a position as a school psychologist. The man is known for his unorthodox interview questions. He hands you a pad of paper and a ruler and says, "Tell me, what is the exact thickness of a single sheet of paper?"

This is a true story. Anita was asked this problem in an interview years ago. The answer was to measure the thickness of the entire pad and divide by the number of pages in the pad. Anita got the answer and the job, but she experienced quite a tense moment before solving the problem.

A **problem** has an initial state, the current situation; a goal, the desired outcome; and a path for reaching the goal, including operations or activities that move you toward the goal. Problem solvers often have to set and reach subgoals as they move toward the final solution. For example, if your goal is to drive to the lake, but at the first stop sign you skid through the intersection, you may have to

problem Any situation in which you are trying to reach some goal and must find a means to do so.

problem solving Creating new solutions for problems.

Connect & Extend

TO THE RESEARCH
You might want to note that although interest in problem solving is great today, many of the early ideas of John Dewey are consistent with the recent emphasis on teaching students to be effective problem solvers. For a description, see Bredo, E. (2003). The development of Dewey's psychology. In B. J. Zimmerman & D. H. Schunk, *Educational psychology: A century of contributions* (pp. 81–111). Mahwah, NJ: Lawrence Erlbaum Associates.

reach a subgoal of fixing your brakes before you can continue toward the original goal (Schunk, 2000). Also, problems can range from well-structured to ill-structured, depending on how clear-cut the goal is and how much structure is provided for solving the problem. Most arithmetic problems are well-structured, but finding the right university major is ill-structured—many different solutions and paths to solutions are possible.

Problem solving is usually defined as formulating new answers, going beyond the simple application of previously learned rules to achieve a goal. Problem solving is what happens when no solution is obvious—when, for example, you can't afford new brakes (Mayer & Wittrock, 1996). Some psychologists suggest that most human learning involves problem solving (Anderson, 1993).

There is a debate about problem solving. Some psychologists believe that effective problem-solving strategies are specific to the problem area. That is, the problem-solving strategies in mathematics are unique to math, the strategies in art are unique to art, and so on. The other side of the debate claims that there are some general problem-solving strategies that can be useful in many areas.

Actually, there is evidence for both sides of the argument. In their research with 8- to 12-year-olds, Robert Kail and Lynda Hall (1999) found that both domain-specific and general factors affected performance on arithmetic word problems. The influences were *arithmetic knowledge*—assessed by the time needed and errors produced in solving simple addition and subtraction problems—and *general information processing skills,* including reading and information-processing time and, to a lesser extent, memory span.

It appears that people move between general and specific approaches, depending on the situation and their level of expertise. Early on, when we know little about a problem area or domain, we may rely on general learning and problem-solving strategies to make sense of the situation. As we gain more domain-specific knowledge (particularly procedural knowledge about how to do things in the domain), we need the general strategies less and less. But if we encounter a problem outside our current knowledge, we may return to relying on general strategies to attack the problem (Alexander, 1992, 1996; Shuell, 1990).

Let's consider general problem-solving strategies first. Think of a general problem-solving strategy as a beginning point, a broad outline. Such strategies usually have five stages (Derry, 1991; Derry & Murphy, 1986; Gallini, 1991; Gick, 1986). John Bransford and Barry Stein (1993) use the acronym IDEAL to identify the five steps:

I   Identify problems and opportunities.
D   Define goals and represent the problem.
E   Explore possible strategies.
A   Anticipate outcomes and Act.
L   Look back and Learn.

We will examine each of these steps because they are found in many approaches to problem solving.

Identifying: Problem Finding

The first step, identifying that a problem exists and treating the problem as an opportunity, begins the process. This is not always straightforward. There is a story describing tenants who were angry about the slow elevators in their building. Consultants hired to "fix the problem" reported that the elevators were no worse than average and that improvements would be expensive. Then one day, as the building supervisor watched people waiting impatiently for an elevator, he realized that the problem was not slow elevators but the fact that people were bored; they had nothing to do while they waited. When the problem was redefined as boredom and seen as an opportunity to improve the "waiting experience," the simple solution of installing a mirror on each floor eliminated complaints.

Identifying the problem is a critical first step. Research indicates that people often hurry through this important step and "leap" to naming the first problem that comes to mind ("The elevators are too slow!"). Experts in a field are more likely to spend time carefully considering the nature of the problem (Bruning, Schraw, & Ronning, 1999). Finding a solvable problem and turning it into an opportunity is the process behind thousands of successful inventions, including the ballpoint pen, appliance timer, alarm clock, self-cleaning oven, and garbage disposal. A walk through the kitchen section of Sears or Zellers will reveal problems someone turned into opportunities to sell you things you didn't know you needed—until you saw the creative solution!

Once a solvable problem is identified, what next? We will examine steps D, E, A, and L in some detail.

Defining Goals and Representing the Problem

Let's take a real problem: the machines designed to pick tomatoes are damaging the tomatoes. What to do? If we represent the problem as a faulty machine design, the goal is to improve the machine. But if we represent the problem as a faulty design of the tomatoes, the goal is to develop a tougher tomato. The problem-solving process follows two entirely different paths, depending on which representation and goal are chosen (Bransford & Stein, 1993). To represent the problem and set a goal, you have to focus on relevant information, understand the elements of the problem, and activate the right *schema* to understand the whole problem.

Focusing Attention. Representing the problem often requires finding the relevant information and ignoring the irrelevant details. For example, what information is relevant to solving this problem (adapted from Sternberg & Davidson, 1982): If you have black socks and white socks in your drawer, mixed in the ratio of four to five, how many socks will you have to take out to make sure that you have a pair the same colour? Did you realize that the information about the four-to-five ratio of black socks to white socks is irrelevant? As long as you have only two different colours of socks in the drawer, you will have to remove only three socks before two of them have to match.

Understanding the Words. The second task in representing a story problem is understanding the meaning of each sentence (Mayer, 1992). For example, the main stumbling block in representing many word problems is the students' understanding of *part–whole relations* (Cummins, 1991). Students have trouble figuring out what is part of what, as evident in this dialogue between a teacher and a grade 1 student:

Teacher: Pete has three apples; Ann also has some apples; Pete and Ann have nine apples altogether; how many apples does Ann have?

Student: Nine.

Teacher: Why?

Student: Because you just said so.

Teacher: Can you retell the story?

Student: Pete had three apples; Ann also had some apples; Ann had nine apples; Pete also has nine apples. (Adapted from De Corte & Verschaffel, 1985, p. 19)

The student interprets "altogether" (the whole) as "each" (the parts). Sometimes, students are taught to search for key words (more, less, greater, etc.), pick a strategy or formula based on the key words (more means "add"), and apply the formula. Actually, this gets in the way of forming a conceptual understanding of the whole problem.

Connect & Extend

TO PRACTICE
Be prepared to identify the steps in the general problem-solving process. Describe the techniques that students can employ to build useful representations of problems.

Connect & Extend

TO OTHER CHAPTERS
Piaget (**Chapter 2**) identified children's difficulties with part–whole relations years ago when he asked questions such as, "There are six daisies and two daffodils; are there more daisies or flowers?" Young children usually answer, "Daisies!"

Understanding the Whole Problem. The third task in representing a problem is to assemble all the relevant information and sentences into an accurate understanding or translation of the total problem. This means that students need to form a conceptual model of the problem—they have to understand what the problem is really asking (Jonassen, 2003). Consider the following example:

> Two train stations are 80 kilometres apart. At 2 p.m. one Saturday afternoon, two trains start toward each other, one from each station. Just as the trains pull out of the stations, a bird springs into the air in front of the first train and flies ahead to the front of the second train. When the bird reaches the second train, it turns back and flies toward the first train. The bird continues to do this until the trains meet. If both trains travel at the rate of 40 kilometres per hour and the bird flies at 160 kilometres per hour, how many kilometres will the bird have flown before the trains meet? (Posner, 1973)

Your interpretation of the problem is called a *translation* because you translate the problem into a schema that you understand. If you translate this as a *distance* problem and set a goal ("I have to figure out how far the bird travels before it meets the oncoming train and turns around, then how far it travels before it has to turn again, and finally add up all the trips back and forth ..."), then you have a very difficult task on your hands. But there is a better way to structure the problem. You can represent it as a question of *time* and focus on the time the bird is in the air. The solution could be stated like this:

> Because the stations are 80 kilometres apart and the trains are moving toward each other at the same speed, the trains will meet in the middle, 40 kilometres from each station. Because they are travelling 40 kilometres, it will take the trains one hour to reach the meeting point. In the one hour it takes the trains to meet, the bird will cover 160 kilometres because it is flying at 160 kilometres per hour. Easy!

Research shows that students can be too quick to decide what a problem is asking. Once a problem is categorized—"Aha, it's a distance problem!"—a particular schema is activated. The schema directs attention to relevant information and sets up expectations for what the right answer should look like (Kalyugaet et al., 2001; Reimann & Chi, 1989).

When students do not have the necessary schemas to represent problems, they often rely on surface features of the situation and represent the problem incorrectly—like the student who wrote "15 + 24 = 39" as the answer to the question, "Josée has 15 bonus points and Louise has 24. How many more does Louise have?" This student saw two numbers and the word "more," so he applied the *add to get more* procedure. When students use the wrong schema, they overlook critical information, use irrelevant information, and may even misread or misremember critical information so that it fits the schema. Errors in representing the problem and difficulties in solving it are the results. But when students use the proper schema for representing a problem, they are less likely to be confused by irrelevant information or tricky wording, such as *more* in a problem that really requires *subtraction* (Resnick, 1981). Figure 8.4 gives examples of different ways students might represent a simple mathematics problem.

Translation and Schema Training. How can students improve translation and schema selection? To answer this question, we often have to move from general to area-specific problem-solving strategies because schemas are specific to content areas. In mathematics, for example, it appears that students benefit from seeing many different kinds of example problems worked out correctly for them. The common practice of showing students a few examples, then having students work out many problems on their own, is less effective. Especially when problems are unfamiliar or difficult, worked-out examples are helpful (Cooper & Sweller, 1987). The most effective examples seem to be those that do not require students to integrate several sources of information, such as a diagram and a set of statements about the problem. This kind of attention splitting may put too much strain on the working memory. When students are learning, worked examples should

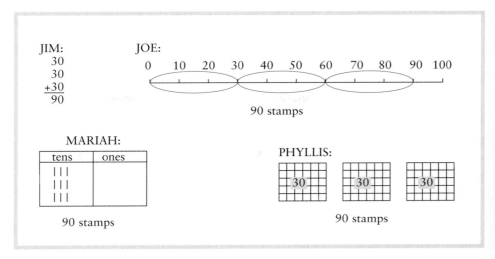

Figure 8.4 Four Different Ways to Represent a Problem

A teacher asks, "How many wildlife stamps will Jane need to fill her book if there are three empty pages and each page holds 30 stamps?" The teacher gives the students supplies such as squared paper, number lines, and place-value frames and encourages them to think of as many ways as possible to solve the problem. Here are four different solutions, based on four different but correct representations.

Source: From Schwartz, J. E., & Riedesel, C. A. (1994). *Essentials of classroom teaching: Elementary mathematics* (pp. 123–124). Boston: Allyn & Bacon. Copyright © 1994 by Allyn & Bacon. Reprinted by permission.

deal with one source of information at a time (Marcus, Cooper, & Sweller, 1996). Ask students to compare examples. What is the same about each solution? What is different? Why?

The same procedures may be effective in areas other than mathematics. Adrienne Lee and Laura Hutchinson (1998) found that undergraduate students learned more when they had examples of chemistry-problem solutions that were annotated to show an expert problem solver's thinking at critical steps. In Australia, Slava Kalyuga et al. (2001) found that worked examples helped apprentices learn about electrical circuits when the apprentices had less experience in the area. Asking students to reflect on the examples helped too, so explanation and reflection can make worked examples more effective. Some of the benefit from worked-out examples comes when students use the examples to explain to themselves what is happening at each step or to check their understanding by anticipating the next step; in this way, students have to be mentally engaged in making sense of the examples (Atkinson, Renkl, & Merrill, 2003).

Familiar examples can serve as analogies or models for solving new problems. But beware. Novices are likely to remember the surface features of an example or case instead of the deeper meaning or the structure. It is the meaning or structure, not the surface similarities, that help in solving new, analogous problems (Gentner, Lowenstein, & Thompson, 2003). We have heard students complain that the test preparation problems in their math classes were about river currents, but the test asked about wind speed. They protested, "There were no problems about boats on the test!" In fact, the problems on the test about wind were solved in exactly the same way as the "boat" problems, but the students were focusing only on the surface features. One way to overcome this tendency is to have students compare examples or cases so that they can develop a general problem-solving schema that captures the common structure, not the surface features, of the cases (Gentner et al., 2003).

How else might students develop the schemas they will need to represent problems in a particular subject area? Mayer (1983b) has recommended giving students practice in the following: (1) recognizing and categorizing a variety of problem types; (2) representing problems—either concretely in pictures, symbols, or graphs or in words; and (3) selecting relevant and irrelevant information in problems.

The Results of Problem Representation. There are two main outcomes of the problem representation stage of problem solving, as shown on the next page in Figure 8.5. If your representation of the problem suggests an immediate solution, your task is done. In the language of the cognitive scientist, you have activated the right schema, and the solution is apparent because it is part of the schema. In one sense, you haven't really solved a new problem; you have simply recognized the new problem as a "disguised" version of an old problem that you already know how to solve.

Connect & Extend

TO YOUR TEACHING
Guidelines for encouraging problem solving in children:

1. Provide problems, not just solutions.
2. Encourage viewing problems from different angles.
3. Make sure students have necessary background information.
4. Make sure students understand the problem.
   - Make accurate and useful representation.
   - Understand through associations and analogies.
5. Help students tackle the problem systematically.
   - Verbalize.
   - Describe and compare.
6. Practise with worked-out examples.

schema-driven problem solving Recognizing a problem as a "disguised" version of an old problem for which one already has a solution.

Mary Gick (1986) of Carleton University called this **schema-driven problem solving**, a kind of matching between the situation and your store of systems for dealing with different problems. In terms of Figure 8.5, you have taken the schema-activated route and proceeded directly to a solution. But what if you have no existing way of solving the problem or if your activated schema fails? Time to search for a solution!

Exploring Possible Solution Strategies

If you do not have existing schemas that suggest an immediate solution, you must take the *search-based route* indicated in Figure 8.5. Obviously, this path is not as efficient as activating the right schema, but sometimes it is the only way. In conducting your search for a solution, you have available two general kinds of procedures: algorithmic and heuristic.

algorithm Step-by-step procedure for solving a problem; prescription for solutions.

Algorithms. An **algorithm** is a step-by-step prescription for achieving a goal. It usually is domain-specific, that is, tied to a particular subject area. In solving a problem, if you choose an appropriate algorithm and implement it properly, a correct answer is guaranteed. Unfortunately, students often apply algorithms haphazardly. They try first this, then that. They may even happen on the right answer but not understand how they found it. For some students, applying algorithms haphazardly could be an indication that formal operational thinking and the ability to work through a set of possibilities systematically, as described by Piaget, are not yet developed.

Many problems cannot be solved by algorithms. What then?

heuristic General strategy used in attempting to solve problems.

Heuristics. A **heuristic** is a general strategy that might lead to the right answer. Because many of life's problems are fuzzy, with ill-defined problem statements and no apparent algorithms, the discovery or development of effective heuristics is important. Let's examine a few.

means-ends analysis Heuristic in which a goal is divided into subgoals.

In **means-ends analysis**, the problem is divided into a number of intermediate goals or subgoals, and then a means of solving each is figured out. For example, writing a 20-page term paper can loom as an insurmountable problem for some students. They would be better off breaking this task into several intermediate goals, such as selecting a topic, locating sources of information, reading and organizing the information, making an outline, and so on. As they attack a particular intermediate goal, they may find that other goals arise. For example, locating information may require that they find someone to refresh their memory about using the library computer search system. Keep in mind that psychologists have yet

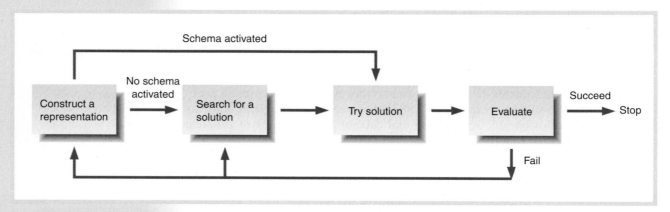

Figure 8.5 Diagram of the Problem-Solving Process
There are two paths to a solution. In the first, the correct schema is activated and the solution is apparent. But if no schema is available, searching and testing may become the path to a solution.
Source: From Gick, M. L. (1986). Problem-solving strategies. *Educational Psychologist, 21,* 101. Adapted by permission of the publisher and author.

to discover an effective heuristic for students who are just starting their term paper the night before it is due.

A second aspect of means-ends analysis is *distance reduction,* or pursuing a path that moves directly toward the final goal. People tend to look for the biggest difference between the current state of affairs and the goal and then search for a strategy that reduces the difference. We resist taking detours or making moves that are indirect as we search for the quickest way to reach the goal. So when you realize that reaching the goal of completing a term paper may require a detour of relearning the library computer search system, you may resist at first because you are not moving directly and quickly toward the final goal (Anderson, 1995b).

Some problems lend themselves to a **working-backward strategy**, in which you begin at the goal and move back to the unsolved initial problem. Working backward is sometimes an effective heuristic for solving geometry proofs. It can also be a good way to set intermediate deadlines ("Let's see, if I have to submit this chapter in three weeks, it has to be in the mail by the 28th, so I should have a first draft by the 11th").

Another useful heuristic is **analogical thinking** (Copi, 1961; Gentner et al., 2003), which limits your search for solutions to situations that have something in common with the one you currently face. When submarines were first designed, for example, engineers had to figure out how battleships could determine the presence and location of vessels hidden in the depths of the sea. Studying how bats solve an analogous problem of navigating in the dark led to the invention of sonar.

Analogical reasoning can lead to faulty problem solving too. When some people first learn to use a word processor, they use the analogy of the typewriter and fail to take advantage of the features of a computer. A common mistake is "typing" a return at the end of every line instead of using the word processor's wrap feature. It seems that people need knowledge both in the problem domain and the analogy domain to use an analogy effectively (Gagné, Yekovich, & Yekovich, 1993).

Putting your problem-solving plan into words and giving reasons for selecting it can lead to successful problem solving (Cooper & Sweller, 1987; Lee & Hutchinson, 1998). You may have discovered the effectiveness of this **verbalization** process accidentally, when a solution popped into your head as you were explaining a problem to someone else.

working-backward strategy Heuristic in which one starts with the goal and moves backward to solve the problem.

analogical thinking Heuristic in which a person limits the search for solutions to situations that are similar to the one at hand.

verbalization Putting your problem-solving plan and its logic into words.

One advantage of working in groups is the opportunity to explain your problem-solving strategy to someone else—putting solutions into words often improves problem solving.

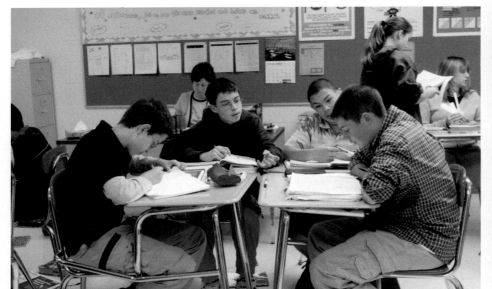

Anticipating, Acting, and Looking Back

What Would You Say?

You are being interviewed by a chair of the department. She asks, "What do you think about letting students use calculators and spell checkers? Do you think this is making learning too easy?"

After representing the problem and exploring possible solutions, the next step is to select a solution and *anticipate the consequences*. For example, if you decide to solve the damaged-tomato problem by developing a tougher tomato, how will consumers react? If you take time to learn a new graphics program to enhance your term paper (and your grade), will you still have enough time to finish the paper?

After you choose a solution strategy and implement it, evaluate the results by checking for evidence that confirms or contradicts your solution. Many people tend to stop working before reaching the best solution and simply accept an answer that works in some cases. In mathematical problems, evaluating the answer might mean applying a checking routine, such as adding to check the result of a subtraction problem or, in a long addition problem, adding the column from bottom to top instead of top to bottom. Another possibility is estimating the answer. For example, if the computation was 11×21, the answer should be around 200, since 10×20 is 200. A student who reaches an answer of 2311 or 23 or 562 should quickly realize that such an answer cannot be correct. Estimating an answer is particularly important when students rely on calculators or computers, because they cannot go back and spot an error in the figures. See the Point/Counterpoint feature for other views on using calculators in learning.

Factors That Hinder Problem Solving

Consider the following problem: You enter a room. There are two ropes suspended from the ceiling. You are asked by the experimenter to tie the two ends of the ropes

Connect & Extend

TO YOUR TEACHING
A student was given the following problem:
   Find the value of *x* and *y* that solves both equations:

   $8x + 4y = 28$
   $4x + 2y = 10$

The student quickly responded $x = 2$, $y = 3$, correctly addressing the first problem but neglecting to check the solution on the second. How could you help the student be more reflective?

POINT > < COUNTERPOINT
SHOULD STUDENTS BE ALLOWED TO USE CALCULATORS?

Not all educators believe that teachers should allow students to use calculators and other technical tools for performing mathematical operations.

> Point *Calculators are crutches that harm learning.*

We've heard many experienced teachers and principals express negative opinions about calculators. They assert, for example, "When students are given calculators to do math in the early grades, most of them never learn rudimentary mathematical concepts; they only learn to use the calculator." And, "To learn math, students need repetition and practice on the concepts to remember the operations—

calculators get in the way." David Gelernter (1998), a noted professor of computer science at Yale University, agrees. He believes that calculators should be completely eliminated from the classroom because if children use calculators to learn the basics of mathematics, they are doomed to being unable to do basic arithmetic as adults.

< Counterpoint *Calculators support learning.*

Some educators have different views. For instance, the *Report of the Expert Panel on Early Math in Ontario* (available online at **www.edu.gov.on.ca/eng/document/report/math**) proposes that "An

effective early mathematics program includes ... calculators that are available to enhance, rather than replace, mathematical learning." The Third International Mathematics and Science Study (1998) supports such views. The data show, on every test at the advanced level, that students who reported using calculators in daily math coursework performed much better than students who rarely or never used calculators. Rather than eroding basic skills, recent research has found that using calculators has positive effects on students' problem-solving skills and attitudes toward math (Waits & Demana, 2000).

together and are assured that the task is possible. On a nearby table are a few tools, including a hammer and pliers. You grab the end of one of the ropes and walk toward the other rope. You immediately realize that you cannot possibly reach the end of the other rope. You try to extend your reach using the pliers but still cannot grasp the other rope (Maier, 1933). What can you do?

Fixation. This problem can be solved by using an object in an unconventional way. If you tie the hammer or the pliers to the end of one rope and swing it like a pendulum, you will be able to catch it while you are standing across the room holding the other rope, as shown in Figure 8.6. You can use the weight of the tool to make the rope come to you instead of trying to stretch the rope. People often fail to solve this problem because they seldom consider unconventional uses for materials that have a specific function. This difficulty is called **functional fixedness** (Duncker, 1945). Problem solving requires seeing things in new ways. In your everyday life, you may often exhibit functional fixedness. Suppose a screw on a dresser-drawer handle is loose. Will you spend 10 minutes searching for a screwdriver? Or will you think to use another object not necessarily designed for this function, such as a ruler edge or a dime?

Another block to effective problem solving is **response set**, getting stuck on one way of representing a problem. Try this:

> In each of the four matchstick arrangements below, move only one stick to change the equation so that it represents a true equality such as V = V.

V=VII VI=XI XII=VII VI=II

You probably figured out how to solve the first example quite quickly. You simply move one matchstick from the right side over to the left to make VI = VI. Examples two and three can also be solved without too much difficulty by moving one stick to change the V to an X or vice versa. But the fourth example (taken from Raudsepp & Haugh, 1977) probably has you stumped. To solve this problem, you must change your response set or switch schemas, because what has worked for the first three problems will not work this time. The answer here lies in changing from Roman numerals to Arabic numbers and using the concept of square root. By overcoming response set, you can move one matchstick from the right to the left to form the symbol for square root; the solution reads $\sqrt{1} = 1$,

functional fixedness Inability to use objects, concepts, or tools in a new way.

response set Rigidity; tendency to respond in the most familiar way.

Figure 8.6 Overcoming Functional Fixedness

In the two-string problem, the subject must set one string in motion to tie both strings together.

which is simply the symbolic way of saying that the square root of 1 equals 1. Here are some other creative approaches. You could use any of the matchsticks to change the = sign to ≠. Then, the last example would be **V** ≠ **II** or 5 does not equal 2, an accurate statement. You also might move one matchstick to change = to < or >, and the statements would still be true (but not equalities as specified in the problem above). Can you come up with any other solutions?

Some Problems with Heuristics. We often apply heuristics automatically to make quick judgments; that saves us time in everyday problem solving. The mind can react automatically and instantaneously, but the price we often pay for this efficiency may be bad problem solving, and that can be costly. Making judgments by invoking stereotypes leads even smart people to make dumb decisions. For example, we might use **representativeness heuristic** to make judgments about possibilities based on our prototypes—what we think is representative of a category. Consider this: If you are asked whether a slim, short stranger who enjoys poetry is more likely to be a truck driver or a university classics professor, what would you say?

You might be tempted to answer based on your prototypes of truck drivers or professors. But consider the odds. Depending how you count, there are about 200 universities and colleges in Canada with perhaps an average of 2 or so classics professors per school. So, we have 400 professors. Say about 20 percent are both short and slim—that's 80; and half of those like poetry—we are left with 40. Suppose there are 200 000 truck drivers in Canada. If only 1 in every 1000 of those truck drivers were short, slim, poetry lovers, we have 200 truck drivers who fit the description. With 40 professors versus 200 truck drivers, it's 5 times more likely that our stranger is a truck driver.

Teachers and students are busy people, and they often base decisions on what they have in their minds at the time. When judgments are based on the availability of information in our memories, we are using the **availability heuristic**. If instances of events come to mind easily, we think they are common occurrences, but that is not necessarily the case; in fact, it is often wrong. People remember vivid stories and quickly come to believe that such events are the norm, but often they are wrong. For example, you may have been surprised to read in Chapter 4 that accelerating gifted students' pace through the grades does not undermine their social development. But **belief perseverance**, or the tendency to hold on to our beliefs, even in the face of contradictory evidence, may make us resist change.

The **confirmation bias** is the tendency to search for information that confirms our ideas and beliefs: this arises from our eagerness to get a good solution. You have often heard the saying "Don't confuse me with the facts." This aphorism captures the essence of the confirmation bias. Most people seek evidence that supports their ideas more readily than they search for facts that might refute them (Myers, 2005). For example, once you decide to buy a certain car, you are likely to notice reports about the good features of the car you chose, not the good news about the cars you rejected. Our automatic use of heuristics to make judgments, our eagerness to confirm what we like to believe, and our tendency to explain away failure combine to generate *overconfidence*. Students are usually overconfident about how fast they can get their papers written; it typically takes twice as long as they estimate (Buehler, Griffith, & Ross, 1994). In spite of their underestimation of their completion time, they remain overly confident of their next prediction.

The Importance of Flexibility. Functional fixedness, response set, and belief perseverance point to the importance of flexibility in understanding problems. If you get started with an inaccurate or inefficient representation of the true problem, it will be difficult—or at least very time-consuming—to reach a solution (Wessells, 1982). Sometimes it is helpful to play with the problem. Ask yourself: "What do I know? What do I need to know to answer this question? Can I look at this problem in other ways?" Try to think conditionally rather than rigidly and divergently rather than convergently. Ask, "What could this be?" instead of "What is it?" (Benjafield, 1992).

representativeness heuristic Judging the likelihood of an event based on how well the events match your prototypes—what you think is representative of the category.

availability heuristic Judging the likelihood of an event based on what is available in your memory, assuming those easily remembered events are common.

belief perseverance The tendency to hold onto beliefs, even in the face of contradictory evidence.

confirmation bias Seeking information that confirms our choices and beliefs, while disconfirming evidence.

If you open your mind to multiple possibilities, you may have what the Gestalt psychologists called an insight. Insight is the sudden reorganization or reconceptualization of a problem that clarifies the problem and suggests a feasible solution. The supervisor described earlier, who suddenly realized that the problem in his building was not slow elevators but impatient, bored tenants, had an insight that allowed him to reach the solution of installing mirrors by the elevators.

Effective Problem Solving: What Do the Experts Do?

Most psychologists agree that effective problem solving is based on an ample store of knowledge about the problem area. To solve the matchstick problem, for example, you had to understand Roman and Arabic numbers as well as the concept of square root. You also had to know that the square root of 1 is 1. Let's take a moment to examine this notion of expert knowledge.

Expert Knowledge. The modern study of expertise began with investigations of chess masters (Simon & Chase, 1973). Results indicated that masters can quickly recognize about 50 000 different arrangements of chess pieces. They can look at one of these patterns for a few seconds and remember where every piece on the board was placed. It is as though they have a "vocabulary" of 50 000 patterns. Michelene Chi (1978) demonstrated that chess experts in grades 3 through 8 had a similar ability to remember chess-piece arrangement. For all the masters, patterns of pieces are like words. If you were shown any word from your vocabulary store for just a few seconds, you would be able to remember every letter in the word in the right order (assuming you could spell the word).

But a series of letters arranged randomly is hard to remember, as you saw in Chapter 7. An analogous situation holds for chess masters. When chess pieces are placed on a board randomly, masters are no better than average players at remembering the positions of the pieces. The master's memory is for patterns that make sense or could occur in a game.

A similar phenomenon occurs in other fields. There may be an intuition about how to solve a problem based on recognizing patterns and knowing the "right moves" for those patterns. Experts in physics, for example, organize their knowledge around central principles, whereas beginners organize their smaller amounts of physics knowledge around the specific details stated in the problems. For instance, when asked to sort physics problems from a textbook in any way they wanted, novices sorted based on superficial features such as the kind of apparatus mentioned—a lever or a pulley—while the experts grouped problems according to the underlying physics principle needed to solve the problem, such as Boyle's or Newton's laws (Hardiman, Dufresne, & Mestre, 1989). And the experts can recognize the patterns needed to solve a particular problem very quickly, so they literally don't have to think as hard.

In addition to representing a problem very quickly, experts know what to do next. They have a large store of productions or condition-action schemas about what action to take in various situations. Thus, the steps of understanding the problem and choosing a solution happen simultaneously and fairly automatically (Ericsson & Charness, 1999). Of course, this means that they must have many, many schemas available. A large part of becoming an expert is simply acquiring a great store of *domain knowledge* or knowledge that is particular to a field (Alexander, 1992). To do this, you must encounter many different kinds of problems in that field, see problems solved by others, and practise solving many yourself. Some estimates are that it takes 10 years or 10 000 hours of study to become an expert in most fields (Simon, 1995).

Experts' rich store of knowledge is *elaborated* and *well practised,* so that it is easy to retrieve from long-term memory when needed (Anderson, 1995b). Experts can use their extensive knowledge to *organize* information for easier learning and retrieval. Among grade 4 students, those who were soccer experts learned and

Connect & Extend

TO YOUR TEACHING
The following five heuristics that might help students solve post-secondary math problems are from Schoenfeld (1979):

1. Draw a diagram, if possible.

2. If the problem has an "N" that takes on integer values, try substituting numbers such as 1, then 2, then 3, then 4 for the "N," and look for a pattern in the results.

3. If you are trying to prove a statement, for example, "If X is true, then Y is true," try proving the contrapositive, "If X is false, then Y is false," or try assuming the statement you want to prove is false and look for a contradiction.

4. Try solving a similar problem with fewer variables.

5. Try to set up subgoals.

remembered far more new soccer terms than those with little knowledge of soccer, even though the abilities of the two groups to learn and remember non-soccer terms were the same. The soccer experts organized and clustered the soccer terms to aid in recall (Schneider & Bjorklund, 1992). Even very young children who are experts on a topic can use strategies to organize their knowledge. A good example of using category knowledge about dinosaurs was provided by Anita's nephews (only three and four years old at the time), who promptly ran down the list of large and small plant- and meat-eating dinosaurs, from the well-known stegosaurus (large plant-eater) to the less familiar ceolophysis (small meat-eater).

With organization comes planning and monitoring. Experts spend more time analyzing problems, drawing diagrams, breaking large problems down into sub-problems, and making plans. While a novice might begin immediately—writing equations for a physics problem or drafting the first paragraph of a paper, experts plan out the whole solution and often make the task simpler in the process. As they work, experts monitor progress, so time is not lost pursuing dead ends or weak ideas (Gagné et al., 1993).

Chi, Glaser, and Farr (1988) summarize the superior capabilities of experts. Experts (1) perceive large, meaningful patterns in given information, (2) perform tasks quickly and with few errors, (3) deal with problems at a deeper level, (4) have superior short- and long-term memories, (5) take a great deal of time to analyze a given problem, and (6) are better at monitoring their performance. When the area of problem solving is fairly well defined, such as chess or physics or computer programming, these skills of expert problem solvers hold fairly consistently. But when the problem-solving area is less well-defined and has fewer clear underlying principles, such as problem solving in economics or psychology, the differences between experts and novices are not as clear-cut (Alexander, 1992).

Expert Teachers. Studies of expert teachers identify many of the characteristics just described. Expert teachers have a sense of what is typical in classrooms, of what to expect during certain activities or times of the day. Many of their teaching routines have become automatic—they don't even have to think about how to distribute materials, take roll, move students in and out of groups, or assign grades. This gives the teachers more mental and physical energy for being creative and focusing on their students' progress. For example, one study found that expert math teachers could go over the previous day's work with the class in two or three minutes, compared with 15 minutes for novices (Leinhardt, 1986).

Expert teachers work from integrated sets of principles instead of dealing with each new event as a new problem. They look for patterns revealing similarities in situations that seem quite different at first glance. Experts focus more than beginners on analyzing a problem and mentally applying different principles to develop a solution. In one study of solutions to discipline problems, the expert teachers spent quite a bit of time framing each problem, forming questions, deciding what information was necessary, and considering alternatives (Swanson, O'Conner, & Cooney, 1990).

Expert teachers have a deep and well-organized knowledge of the subjects they teach. A study by François Tochon of the Université de Sherbrooke and Hugh Munby of Queen's University (1993) clearly showed that expert teachers, in contrast to novices, deliberately avoid rigid plans. Expert teachers improvise lessons on the spot to accommodate the needs of their students in ways such as inventing explanations and generating additional examples (see also Borko & Livingston, 1989; Sabers, Cushing, & Berliner, 1991). And as we saw in Chapter 1, expert teachers also know a great deal about their students, the curriculum, teaching strategies, and ways to make the curriculum understandable and accessible to the students.

Novice Knowledge. Studies of the differences between experts and novices in particular areas have revealed surprising information about how novices understand and misunderstand a subject. Physics again provides many examples. Most beginners approach physics with a great deal of misinformation, partly because many of their intuitive ideas about the physical world are wrong. Most elementary-school children believe that light helps us see by brightening the area around objects. They do not realize that we see an object because the light is reflected by the object to our eyes. This concept does not fit with the everyday experience of turning on a light and "brightening" the dark area. Researchers found that even after completing a unit on light in which materials explicitly stated the idea of reflected light and vision, most grade 5 students—about 78 percent—continued to cling to their intuitive notions. But when new materials were designed that directly confronted the students' misconceptions, only about 20 percent of the students failed to understand (Eaton, Anderson, & Smith, 1984).

It seems quite important for science teachers to understand their students' intuitive models of basic concepts. If the students' intuitive model includes misconceptions and inaccuracies, the students are likely to develop inadequate or misleading representations of a problem. (You should note that some researchers don't use the term "misconception" but refer to *naive* or *intuitive conceptions* to describe students' beginning knowledge in an area.) To learn new information and solve problems, students must sometimes "unlearn" common-sense ideas (Joshua & Dupin, 1987). Changing your intuitive ideas about concepts involves motivation too. Pintrich, Marx, and Boyle (1993) suggest that four conditions are necessary for people to change basic concepts: (1) Students have to be dissatisfied with the current concept; that is, their existing concept must be seen as inaccurate, incomplete, or not useful. (2) Students must understand the new concept. (3) The new concept must be plausible—it must fit in with what the students already know. (4) The new concept must be fruitful—it must be seen as useful in solving problems or answering questions.

The Guidelines on page 304 give some ideas for helping students become expert problem solvers.

Check Your Knowledge

- What are the steps in the general problem-solving process?
- Why is the representation stage of problem solving so important?
- Describe factors that can interfere with problem solving.
- How do misconceptions and heuristics interfere with learning?
- What are the differences between expert and novice knowledge in a given area?

Apply to Practice

- What are some common misconceptions about being an expert?

Connect & Extend

TO YOUR TEACHING
Brainstorm about intuitive models in other fields besides science and mathematics. What are some common misconceptions about cultural differences, history, government, or educational psychology?

Connect & Extend

TO THE RESEARCH
Joshua, S., & Dupin, J. J. (1987). Taking into account student conceptions in instructional strategy: An example in physics. *Cognition and Instruction, 4,* 117–135.

Abstract
Several studies have emphasized the predominant influence of students' conceptions in the learning process in physics. But, more often than not, these conceptions are somehow considered in a negative way, as "errors." This article describes taking students' conceptions as an active basis for scientific reasoning in real class situations with groups of students aged approximately 12 and 14 years.

The subject matter taught was basic electricity. The article shows how pre-instruction conceptions were actually used (or not used) by the students to explain the electricity phenomena and how these conceptions subsequently changed, increasing in internal consistency, without moving closer to scientific conceptions. Analogical explanation helped overcome this situation.

Teachers can help students develop strategies and tactics for accomplishing learning goals—in this case, by writing a story.

PROBLEM SOLVING

Ask students if they are sure they understand the problem.

EXAMPLES

1. Can they separate relevant from irrelevant information?
2. Are they aware of the assumptions they are making?
3. Encourage them to visualize the problem by diagramming or drawing it.
4. Ask them to explain the problem to someone else. What would a good solution look like?

Encourage attempts to see the problem from different angles.

EXAMPLES

1. Suggest several different possibilities yourself and then ask students to offer some.
2. Give students practice in taking and defending different points of view on an issue.

Help students develop systematic ways of considering alternatives.

EXAMPLES

1. Think out loud as you solve problems.

2. Ask, "What would happen if ...?"
3. Keep a list of suggestions.

Teach heuristics.

EXAMPLES

1. Ask students to explain the steps they take as they solve problems.
2. Use analogies to solve the problem of limited parking in the downtown area. How are other "storage" problems solved?
3. Use the working-backward strategy to plan a party.

Let students do the thinking; don't just hand them solutions.

EXAMPLES

1. Offer individual problems as well as group problems, so that each student has the chance to practise.
2. Give partial credit if students have good reasons for "wrong" solutions to problems.
3. If students are stuck, resist the temptation to give too many clues. Let them think about the problem overnight.

CREATIVITY AND CREATIVE PROBLEM SOLVING

Consider this student. He had severe dyslexia—a learning disability that made reading and writing exceedingly difficult. He described himself as an "underdog." In school, he knew that if the reading assignment would take others an hour, he had to allow two or three hours. He knew that he had to keep a list of all his most frequently misspelled words in order to be able to write at all. He spent hours alone in his room. Would you expect his writing to be creative? Why or why not?

The student is John Irving, celebrated author of what one critic called "wildly inventive" novels such as *The World According to Garp, The Cider House Rules,* and *A Prayer for Owen Meany* (Amabile, 2001). How do we explain his amazing creativity? What is creativity?

Defining Creativity

Let's start with what creativity is not. Here are four myths about creativity (Plucker, Beghetto, & Dow, 2004):

1. *People are born creative.* Actually, years of research show that creativity can be developed, enhanced, and supported by the individual's or group's environment.

2. *Creativity is intertwined with negative qualities.* It is true that some creative people are nonconforming or some may have mental or emotional problems, but many non-creative people do, too. The danger with this myth is that teachers may expect creative students to be troublemakers and treat these students in a biased way (Scott, 1999).

3. *Creativity is a fuzzy, soft construct.* In contrast to seeing a creative person as mentally unbalanced, some people think creative individuals are New Age hippies. Actually, even though creative people may be open to new experiences and be generally nonconforming, they also may be focused, organized, and flexible.

4. *Creativity is enhanced within a group.* It is true that brainstorming in a group can lead to creative ideas, but these group efforts tend to be more creative if individuals brainstorm on their own first.

So what is creativity? **Creativity** is the ability to produce work that is original, but still appropriate and useful (Berk, 2005). Most psychologists agree that there is no such thing as "all-purpose creativity"; people are creative *in a particular area,* as John Irving is in writing fiction. But to be creative, the "invention" must be intended. An accidental spilling of paint that produces a novel design is not creative unless the artist recognizes the potential of the "accident" or uses the spilling technique intentionally to create new works (Weisberg, 1993). Although we frequently associate the arts with creativity, any subject can be approached in a creative manner.

creativity Imaginative, original thinking or problem solving.

A definition that combines many aspects of creativity (Plucker et al., 2004) highlights that creativity:

- often involves more than one person,
- happens when people apply their abilities as part of a helpful process in a supportive environment, and
- results in an identifiable product that is new and useful in a particular culture or situation.

What Are the Sources of Creativity?

Creativity requires knowledge, flexibility, motivation, and persistence; social support plays an important role as well.

Researchers have studied cognitive processes, personality factors, motivational patterns, and background experiences to explain creativity (Simonton, 2000). But to truly understand creativity, we must look at the social environment too. Both intrapersonal (cognition, personality) and social factors support creativity (Amabile, 1996, 2001; Simonton, 2000). Teresa Amabile (1996) proposes a three-component model of creativity. Individuals or groups must have:

1. *Domain-relevant skills,* including talents and competencies that are valuable for working in the domain. One example is Michelangelo's skills in shaping stone, developed when he lived with a stonecutter's family as a child.

2. *Creativity-relevant processes,* including work habits and personality traits such as John Irving's habit of working 10-hour days to write and rewrite and rewrite until he perfected his stories.

3. *Intrinsic task motivation* or a deep curiosity and fascination with the task. This aspect of creativity can be greatly influenced by the social environment (as we will see in Chapter 10), and by supporting autonomy, stimulating curiosity, encouraging fantasy, and providing challenge.

Another social factor that influences creativity is whether the field is ready and willing to acknowledge the creative contribution (Nakamura & Csikszentmihalyi, 2001). History is filled with examples of creative breakthroughs rejected at the time (for example, Galileo's theory of the sun at the centre of the solar system) and of rivalries between creators that led each to push the edges of creativity (the friendly and productive rivalry between Picasso and Matisse).

restructuring Conceiving of a problem in a new or different way.

Creativity and Cognition. Having a rich store of knowledge in an area is the basis for creativity, but something more is needed. For many problems, that "something more" is the ability to break set—**restructuring** the problem to see things in a new way, which leads to a sudden insight. Often this happens when a person has struggled with a problem or project, then sets it aside for a while. Some psychologists believe that time away from the problem allows for *incubation,* a kind of unconscious working through the problem. It is more likely that leaving the problem for a time interrupts rigid ways of thinking so that you can restructure your view of the situation (Gleitman, Fridlund, & Reisberg, 1999). So it seems that creativity requires extensive knowledge, flexibility, and the continual reorganizing of ideas. And we saw that motivation, persistence, and social support play important roles in the creative process as well.

Assessing Creativity

Like the author John Irving, Paul Torrance also had a learning disability; he became interested in educational psychology when he was a high school English teacher (Neumeister & Cramond, 2004). Torrance was known as the "father of creativity." He developed two types of creativity tests: verbal and graphic (Torrance, 1972; Torrance & Hall, 1980). In the verbal test, you might be instructed to think up as many uses as possible for a brick or asked how a particular toy might be changed to make it more fun. On the graphic test, you might be given 30 circles and asked to create 30 different drawings, with each drawing including at least one circle. Figure 8.7 shows the creativity of an eight-year-old girl in completing this task.

divergent thinking Coming up with many possible solutions.

convergent thinking Narrowing possibilities to a single answer.

These tests require **divergent thinking**, an important component of many conceptions of creativity. Divergent thinking is the ability to propose many different ideas or answers. **Convergent thinking** is the more common ability to identify only one answer. Responses to all these creativity tasks are scored for originality, fluency, and flexibility, three aspects of divergent thinking. *Originality* is usually determined statistically. To be original, a response must be given by fewer than 5 or 10 people out of every 100 who take the test. *Fluency* is the number of different responses. *Flexibility* is generally measured by the number

Figure 8.7 A Graphic Assessment of the Creativity of an Eight-Year-Old

The titles she gave her drawings, from left to right, are as follows: "Dracula," "one-eyed monster," "pumpkin," "Hula-Hoop," "poster," "wheelchair," "earth," "moon," "planet," "movie camera," "sad face," "picture," "stoplight," "beach ball," "the letter O," "car," "glasses."

Source: From Torrance, E. P. (1986, 2000). A graphic assessment of the creativity of an eight-year-old. *The Torrance Test of Creative Thinking,*. Reprinted with permission of Scholastic Testing Service, Inc., Bensonville, IL 60106 USA.

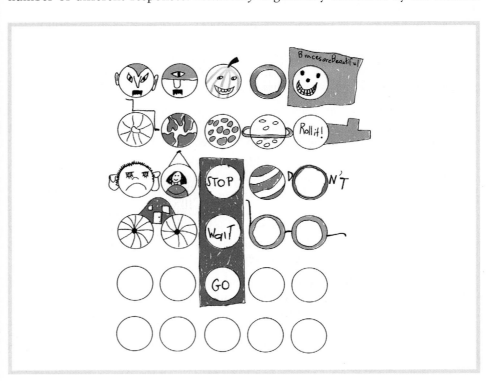

AGNES IS ABLE TO THINK DIVERGENTLY.
(*Agnes*, May 24, 2002. © Tony Cochran. Reprinted with permission of the Creators Syndicate.)

of different categories of responses. For instance, if you were asked to list the uses of a brick and each of your 20 responses involved building something, your fluency score might be high, but your flexibility score would be low. Of the three measures, fluency—the number of responses—is the best predictor of divergent thinking, but there is more to real-life creativity than divergent thinking (Plucker et al., 2004).

Teachers are not always the best judges of creativity. In fact, Torrance (1972) reports data from a 12-year follow-up study indicating no relationship between teachers' judgments of their students' creative abilities and the actual creativity these students revealed in their adult lives. A few possible indicators of creativity in your students are curiosity, concentration, adaptability, high energy, humour (sometimes bizarre), independence, playfulness, nonconformity, risk taking, attraction to the complex and mysterious, willingness to fantasize and daydream, intolerance for boredom, and inventiveness (Sattler, 1992).

Creativity in the Classroom

Today's and tomorrow's complex problems require creative solutions. And creativity is important for an individual's psychological, physical, social, and career success (Plucker et al., 2004). How can teachers promote creative thinking? All too often, in the crush of day-to-day classroom life, teachers stifle creative ideas without realizing what they are doing. Teachers are in an excellent position to encourage or discourage creativity through their acceptance or rejection of the unusual and imaginative. The Guidelines on page 308, which were adapted from Fleith (2000) and Sattler (1992), describe other possibilities for encouraging creativity.

Brainstorming. In addition to encouraging creativity through everyday interactions with students, teachers can try brainstorming. The basic tenet of **brainstorming** is to separate the process of creating ideas from the process of evaluating them because evaluation often inhibits creativity (Osborn, 1963). Evaluation, discussion, and criticism are postponed until all possible suggestions have been made. In this way, one idea inspires others; people do not withhold potentially creative solutions out of fear of criticism. John Baer (1997, p. 43) gives these rules for brainstorming:

Connect & Extend

TO YOUR TEACHING/ PORTFOLIO
For a wonderful story of a first-year teacher with truly creative ideas, see Codell, E. R. (2001). *Educating Esme: Diary of a teacher's first year.* Chapel Hill, NC: Algonquin Books.

brainstorming Generating ideas without stopping to evaluate them.

DILBERT

DILBERT LEADS HIS CO-WORKERS IN BRAINSTORMING.
(*Dilbert*, February 21, 2002. Copyright © 2002 Scott Adams. Reprinted with permission of United Features Syndicate, Inc.)

ENCOURAGING CREATIVITY

Accept and encourage divergent thinking.

EXAMPLES

1. During class discussion, ask: "Can anyone suggest a different way of looking at this question?"
2. Reinforce attempts at unusual solutions to problems, even if the final product is not perfect.
3. Offer choices in topics for projects or modes of presentation (written, oral, visual or graphic, using technology).

Tolerate dissent.

EXAMPLES

1. Ask students to support dissenting opinions.
2. Make sure nonconforming students receive an equal share of classroom privileges and rewards.

Encourage students to trust their own judgment.

EXAMPLES

1. When students ask questions you think they can answer, rephrase or clarify the questions and direct them back to the students.
2. Give ungraded assignments from time to time.

Emphasize that everyone is capable of creativity in some form.

EXAMPLES

1. Avoid describing the feats of great artists or inventors as if they were superhuman accomplishments.

2. Recognize creative efforts in each student's work. Have a separate grade for originality on some assignments.

Provide time, space, and materials to support creative projects.

EXAMPLES

1. Collect "found" materials for collages and creations—buttons, stones, shells, paper, fabric, beads, seeds, drawing tools, clay—try flea markets and friends for donations. Have mirrors and pictures for drawing faces.
2. Make a well-lighted space available where children can work on projects, leave them, and come back to finish them.
3. Follow up on memorable occasions (field trips, news events, holidays) with opportunities to draw, write, or make music.

Be a stimulus for creative thinking.

EXAMPLES

1. Use a class brainstorming session whenever possible.
2. Model creative problem solving by suggesting unusual solutions for class problems.
3. Encourage students to delay judging a particular suggestion for solving a problem until all the possibilities have been considered.

See **http://ceep.crc.uiuc.edu/eecearchive/digests/1995/edward95.html** for more ideas.

Connect & Extend

TO THE RESEARCH
For recent research on brainstorming, see Brown, V. R., & Paulus, P. B. (2002). Making group brainstorming more effective: Recommendations from an associative memory perspective. *Current Directions in Psychological Science, 11*, 208–212.

1. Defer judgment.
2. Avoid ownership of ideas. When people feel that an idea is "theirs," egos sometimes get in the way of creative thinking. They are likely to be more defensive later when ideas are critiqued, and they are less willing to allow their ideas to be modified.
3. Feel free to "hitchhike" on other ideas. This means that it's okay to borrow elements from ideas already on the table, or to make slight modifications of ideas already suggested.
4. Encourage wild ideas. Impossible, totally unworkable ideas may lead someone to think of other, more possible, more workable ideas. It's easier to take a wildly imaginative bad idea and tone it down to fit the constraints of reality than to take a boring bad idea and make it interesting enough to be worth thinking about.

Individuals as well as groups may benefit from brainstorming. In writing this book, for example, Anita has sometimes found it helpful to list all the different topics that could be covered in a chapter, then leave the list and return to it later to evaluate the ideas.

Take Your Time—and Play!   Years ago, Sigmund Freud (1959) linked creativity and play: "Might we not say that every child at play behaves like a creative writer, in that he creates a world of his own, or, rather, rearranges the things of his world in a new way which pleases him? The creative writer does the same as the child at play. He creates a world of phantasy which he takes very seriously—that is, which he invests with large amounts of emotion" (pp. 143–144). There is some evidence that preschool children who spend more time in fantasy and pretend play are more creative. In fact, playing before taking a creativity test resulted in higher scores on the test for the young students in one study (Berk, 2001; Bjorklund, 1989). Teachers can encourage students of all ages to be more reflective—to take time for ideas to grow, develop, and be restructured.

The Big C: Revolutionary Innovation

Ellen Winner (2000) describes the "big-C creativity" or innovation that establishes a new field or revolutionizes an old one. Even child prodigies do not necessarily become adult innovators. Prodigies have mastered well-established domains very early, but innovators change the entire domain. "Individuals who ultimately make creative breakthroughs tend from their earliest days to be explorers, innovators, and tinkerers. Often this adventurousness is interpreted as insubordination, though more fortunate tinkerers receive from teachers or peers some form of encouragement for their experimentation" (Gardner, 1993, pp. 32–33). What can parents and teachers do to encourage these potential creators? Winner (2000) lists four dangers to avoid:

1. Avoid pushing so hard that the child's intrinsic passion to master a field becomes a craving for extrinsic rewards.

2. Avoid pushing so hard that the child later looks back on a missed childhood.

3. Avoid freezing the child into a safe, technically perfect way of performing that has led to lavish rewards.

4. Be aware of the psychological wounds that can follow when the child who can perform perfectly becomes the forgotten adult who can do nothing more than continue to perform perfectly—without ever creating something new.

Finally, teachers and parents can encourage students with outstanding abilities and creative talents to give back to the society that has provided the extra support and resources that they needed. Service learning, discussed in Chapter 11, is one opportunity.

We may not all be revolutionary in our creativity, but we all can be experts in one area—learning.

Check Your Knowledge

- What are some myths about creativity?
- What is creativity and how is it assessed?
- What can teachers do to support creativity in the classroom?

Apply to Practice

- How could you turn a test of divergent thinking into a learning activity that invites students to expand their views about the role of creativity in learning?

BECOMING AN EXPERT STUDENT: LEARNING STRATEGIES AND STUDY SKILLS

What Would You Say?

As part of your interview, the department chair asks, "Many of our students go to high-pressure universities and don't seem to know how to study when they don't have daily homework deadlines. How would you help them prepare to handle the heavy workload at those institutions?"

Most teachers will tell you that they want their students to "learn how to learn." Years of research indicate that using good learning strategies helps students learn and that these strategies can be taught (Hamman et al., 2000). But were you ever taught how to learn? Powerful and sophisticated learning strategies and study skills are seldom taught directly, even in high school or university. So students have little practice with these powerful strategies. In contrast, students usually discover repetition and rote learning by themselves early on, so they have extensive practice with these strategies. And, unfortunately, some teachers think that memorizing is sufficient for learning (Hofer & Pintrich, 1997; Woolfolk Hoy & Murphy, 2001). This may explain why many students cling to flash cards and brute maintenance rehearsal—they don't know what else to do to learn (Willoughby et al., 1999).

As we saw in Chapter 7, the way something is learned in the first place greatly influences how readily we remember and how appropriately we can apply the knowledge later. First, students must be *cognitively engaged* to learn—they have to focus attention on the relevant or important aspects of the material. Second, they have to *invest effort,* make connections, elaborate, translate, organize, and reorganize in order to *think and process deeply*—the greater the practice and processing, the stronger the learning. Finally, students must *regulate and monitor* their own learning—keep track of what is making sense and notice when a new approach is needed. The emphasis today is on helping students develop effective learning strategies and tactics that *focus attention and effort, process information deeply, and monitor understanding.* Some students will develop good strategies for organizing and learning on their own, but most need help.

Learning Strategies and Tactics

Learning strategies are ideas for accomplishing learning goals, a kind of overall plan of attack. **Learning tactics** are the specific techniques that make up the plan (Winne & Perry, 1994). Your use of strategies and tactics reflects metacognitive knowledge. Using learning strategies and study skills is related to higher GPAs in high school and staying in school in university (Robbins et al., 2004). Researchers have identified several important principles:

1. Students must be exposed to a number of *different strategies,* not only general learning strategies but also specific tactics, such as the graphic strategies described later in this chapter.

2. *Teach conditional knowledge* about when, where, and why to use various strategies (Pressley, 1986). Although this may seem obvious, teachers often neglect this step, either because they do not realize its significance or because they assume that students will make inferences on their own. A strategy is more likely to be maintained and employed if students know when, where, and why to use it.

3. Students may know when and how to use a strategy, but unless they also *develop the desire to employ these skills,* general learning ability will not improve. Several learning strategy programs (Borkowski, Johnston, & Reid, 1986;

Connect & Extend

TO THE RESEARCH
Willoughby, T., Porter, L., Belsito, L., & Yearsley, T. (1999). Use of elaboration strategies by grades two, four, and six. *Elementary School Journal, 99,* 221–231.

This study tested the effectiveness of verbal elaboration (answer why each fact is true), imagery (create a metal picture), and keyword (create a mental picture using the keywords provided) in helping Canadian grade 2, 4, and 6 students remember information from stories. Verbal elaboration worked for all three grades, especially when the students had some prior knowledge related to the stories. Imagery was more helpful than elaborations for older students when the students lacked prior knowledge about the story content, but grade 2 students needed support to use imagery.

learning strategies General plans for approaching learning tasks.

learning tactics Specific techniques for learning, such as using mnemonics or outlining a passage.

Connect & Extend

TO YOUR TEACHING
For suggestions about the effective use of learning strategies, take a look at the study skills site developed by the Virginia Polytechnic Institute (**www.ucc.vt.edu/stdysk/stdyhlp.html**), and also see **www.studygs.net** for more ideas.

Dansereau, 1985) include a motivational training component. In Chapters 10 and 11, we look more closely at this important issue of motivation.

4. *Direct instruction in schematic knowledge* is often an important component of strategy training. To identify main ideas—a critical skill for a number of learning strategies—you must have an appropriate schema for making sense of the material. Table 8.2 summarizes several tactics for learning declarative (verbal) knowledge and procedural skills (Derry, 1989).

The recommendations about study skills described in this section apply to everyone who wishes to become an expert learner and involve the metacognitive abilities and executive control processes discussed in Chapter 7.

Deciding What Is Important. You can see from the first entry in Table 8.2 that learning begins with focusing attention—deciding what is important. But distinguishing the main idea from less important information is not always easy. Often, students focus on the "seductive details" or the concrete examples, perhaps because these are more interesting (Dole et al., 1991; Gardner et al., 1992). You may have had the experience of remembering a joke or an intriguing example from a lecture but not being clear about the larger point the professor was trying to make. Finding the central idea is especially difficult if students lack prior knowledge in an area and the amount of new information provided is extensive. Teachers can give students practice using signals in texts such as headings, bold words, outlines, or other indicators to identify key concepts and main ideas. Teaching students to summarize material can be helpful too (Lorchet et al., 2001).

Summaries. Creating summaries can help students learn, but students have to be taught how to summarize (Byrnes, 1996; Dole et al., 1991; Palincsar & Brown, 1984). Jeanne Ormrod (1999, p. 333) summarizes these suggestions for helping students create summaries:

Connect & Extend

TO YOUR TEACHING
Use Table 8.2 plus the section titled "Learning Strategies and Tactics" on pages 310–312 to generate ideas for appropriate learning strategies and tactics for the students you will teach.

TABLE 8.2 Examples of Learning Tactics

	Examples	Use When?
Tactics for learning verbal information	1. Attention focusing • Making outlines, underlining • Looking for headings and topic sentences	 With easy, structured materials; for good readers For poorer readers; with more difficult materials
	2. Schema building • Story grammars • Theory schemas • Networking and mapping	 With poor text structure, goal is to encourage active comprehension
	3. Ideal elaboration • Self-questioning • Imagery	 To understand and remember specific ideas
Tactics for learning procedural information	1. Pattern learning • Hypothesizing • Identifying reasons for actions	 To learn attributes of concepts To match procedures to situations
	2. Self-instruction • Comparing own performance to expert model	 To tune, improve complex skills
	3. Practice • Part practice • Whole practice	 When few specific aspects of a performance need attention To maintain and improve skill

Source: Based on Derry, S. (1989). Putting learning strategies to work. *Educational Leadership, 47*(5), 5–6.

- Begin doing summaries of short, easy, well-organized readings. Introduce longer, less organized, and more difficult passages gradually.
- For each summary, ask students to
  - find or write a *topic sentence* for each paragraph or section;
  - identify *big ideas* that cover several specific points;
  - find some *supporting information* for each big idea; and
  - delete any *redundant information* or unnecessary details.

Ask students to compare their summaries and discuss what ideas they thought were important and why—what's their evidence?

Two other study strategies that are based on identifying key ideas are *underlining* texts and *taking notes*.

Underlining and Highlighting. Do you underline or highlight key phrases in textbooks? Underlining and note taking are probably two of the most commonly used strategies among university and college students. Yet few students receive any instruction in the best ways to underline, so it is not surprising that many students use ineffective strategies. One common problem is that students underline or highlight too much. It is better to be selective. In studies where students have had limits placed on how much they could underline—for example, only one sentence per paragraph—learning has improved (Snowman, 1984).

In addition to being selective, you also should actively transform information into your own words as you underline. Don't rely on the words of the book. Build connections between what you are reading and other knowledge you already have. Draw diagrams to illustrate relationships. Finally, look for organizational patterns in the material and use them to guide your underlining and transformations of what you underline into notes (Irwin, 1991; Kiewra, 1988).

Taking Notes. As you sit in class, filling your notebook with words or furiously trying to keep up with a lecturer, you may wonder if taking notes makes a difference. It does—if it is used well.

- Taking notes focuses attention during class and helps encode information so that it has a chance of making it to long-term memory. When you record key ideas in your own words, you translate, connect, elaborate, and organize. Even if students don't review notes before a test, taking notes in the first place appears to aid learning, especially for those who lack prior knowledge in the topic. Of course, if taking notes distracts you from actually listening to and making sense of the lecture, then note taking may not be effective (Di Vesta & Gray, 1972; Kiewra, 1989; Van Metter, Yokoi, & Pressley, 1994).
- Notes provide extended external storage that allows you to return and review. Students who use their notes to study tend to perform better on tests, especially if they take many high-quality notes—more is better as long as you are capturing key ideas, concepts, and *relationships*, not just intriguing details (Kiewra, 1985, 1989).
- Expert students match notes to their anticipated use and modify note-taking strategies after tests or assignments, use personal codes to flag material that is unfamiliar or difficult, fill in holes by consulting relevant sources (including other students in the class), and record information verbatim only when a verbatim response will be required. In other words, they are strategic about taking and using notes (Van Meter, Yokoi, & Pressley, 1994).

To help students organize note taking, some teachers provide matrices or maps. When students are first learning to use these maps, you might fill in some of the spaces for them. If you use such an approach with your students, you might encourage students to exchange their filled-in maps and explain their thinking to each other.

Connect & Extend

TO YOUR TEACHING
Weinstein, C., Ridley, D. S., Dahl, T., & Weber, E. S. (1988/1989). Helping students develop strategies for effective learning. Educational Leadership, 46(4), 17–19.

The authors give many examples of elaboration strategies. For example:
- What is the main idea of this story?
- If this principle were not true, what would that imply?
- What does this remind me of?
- How could I use this information in the project I am working on?
- How could I represent this in a diagram?
- How do I feel about the author's opinion?
- How could I put this in my own words?
- What might be an example of this?
- If I were going to interview the author, what would I ask her?
- How does this apply to my life?

Visual Tools for Organizing

To use underlining and note taking effectively, you must identify main ideas. In addition, effective use of underlining and note taking depends on understanding the organization of the text or lecture—the connections and relationships among ideas. Some visual strategies have been developed to help students with this key element. There is evidence that creating graphic organizers such as maps or charts is more effective than outlining in learning from texts (Robinson, 1998; Robinson & Kiewra, 1995). "Mapping" these relationships by noting causal connections, comparison-and-contrast connections, and examples improves recall. Davidson (1982) suggested that students compare one another's "maps" and discuss the differences. The map in Figure 8.8 below is a complex web about Holden Caulfield, the main character of J. D. Salinger's *Catcher in the Rye,* developed using Inspiration software. Amy's molecule (Figure 8.2 on page 287) is a hierarchical graphic depiction of the relationships among concepts. Other ways to visualize organization include *Venn diagrams,* which show how ideas or concepts overlap, and *tree diagrams,* which show how ideas branch off each other. *Timelines* organize information in sequence and are useful in classes such as history or geology.

An exciting possibility is **Cmap,** a software tool for creating concept maps that is available for downloading at no cost. Computer Cmaps can be linked to the internet, and students in different classrooms and schools all over the world can collaborate on them. The homepage of the Cmap tools is shown in Figure 8.9 on page 314.

Cmaps Tools for concept mapping developed by the Institute for Human Machine Cognition that are connected to many knowledge maps and other resources on the internet.

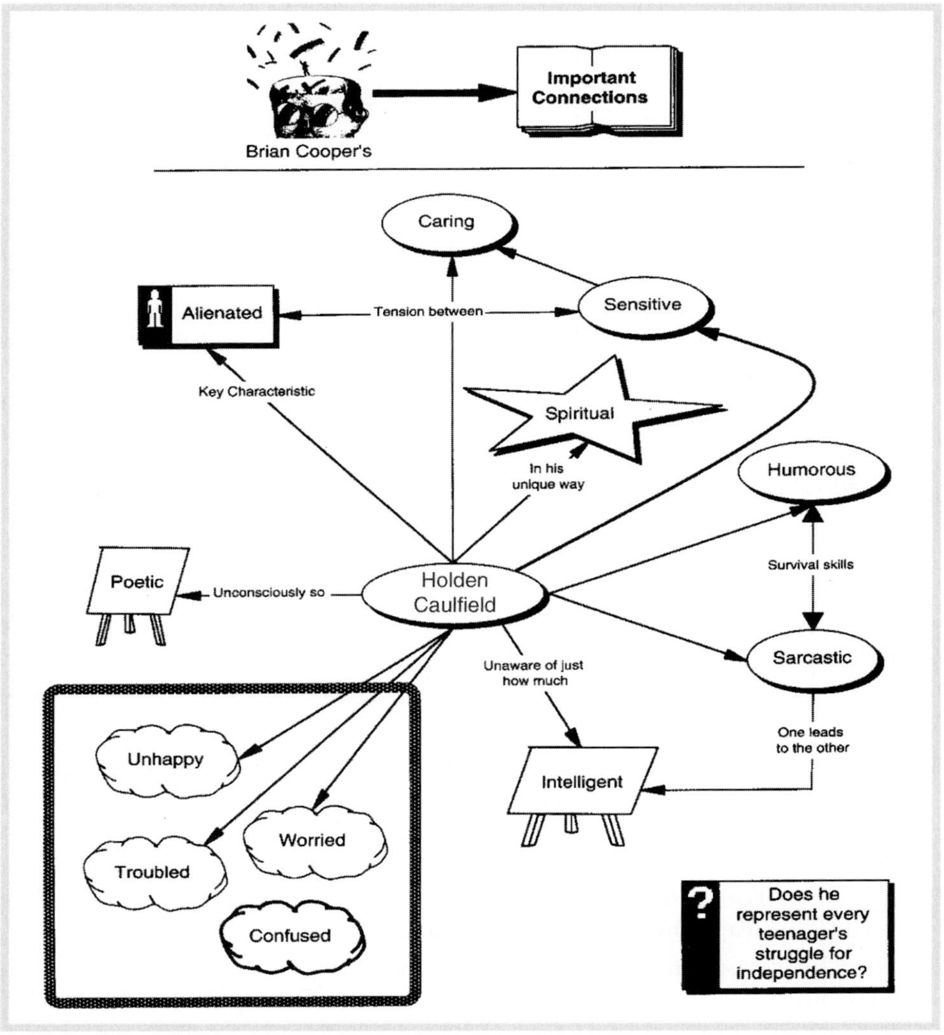

Figure 8.8 A Map to Organize Studying and Learning

This map represents one student's (Brian Cooper's) analysis of Catcher in the Rye. *The map was produced using software called Inspiration.*

Source: From Helfgott, D., Westhaver, M., & Hoof, B. (1992). *Inspiration software: User's guide manual.* Inspiration Software Inc., 1-800-877-4792.

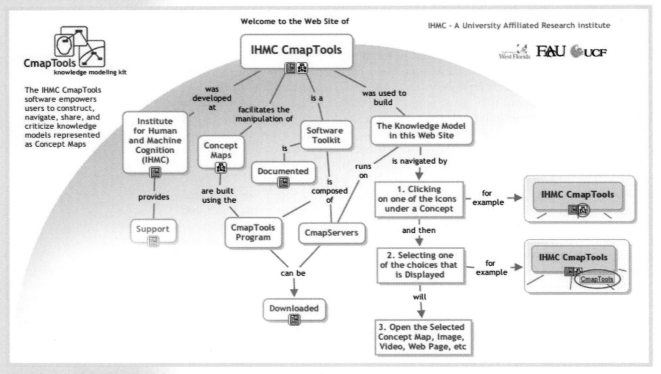

Figure 8.9 The Website for the Institute for Human Machine Cognition Cmap Tools at http://cmap.ihmc.us
At this site, you can download concept mapping tools to construct, share, and criticize knowledge on any subject.

Reading Strategies

READS A five-step reading strategy: *Review* headings; *Examine* boldface words; *Ask*, "What do I expect to learn?"; *Do* it—Read; *Summarize* in your own words.

Connect & Extend

TO THE RESEARCH
See Peterson, D., & Van Der Wege, C. (2002). Guiding children to be strategic readers. *Phi Delta Kappan, 83,* 437–440.

PQ4R A method for studying text that involves six steps: *Preview, Question, Read, Reflect, Recite, Review.*

As we saw earlier, effective learning strategies and tactics should help students focus attention; invest effort (elaborate, organize, summarize, connect, translate) so that they process information deeply; and monitor their understanding. There are a number of strategies that support these processes in reading. Many use mnemonics to help students remember the steps involved. For example, one strategy for any grade above later elementary is **READS:**

R *Review* headings and subheadings.

E *Examine* boldface words.

A *Ask*, "What do I expect to learn?"

D *Do* it—Read!

S *Summarize* in your own words. (Friend & Bursuck, 1996)

READS is similar to a well-known strategy you might have encountered in school, called **PQ4R** (Thomas & Robinson, 1972). In this system, the extra *R* is for reflection, and the *P* stands for preview. So the acronym stands for preview, question, read, reflect, recite, and review. To use PQ4R to study this chapter, you would:

1. *Preview.* Survey the major sections—the overview, objectives, headings and subheadings, and the summary, if there is one. Set goals for reading: What are key ideas or events? What is the author's bias? These procedures activate schemas for interpreting and remembering what you read.

2. *Question.* For each major section, write questions related to your reading goals. One way is to turn the headings and subheadings into questions.

3. *Read.* Pay attention to signals in the text: bold terms, references to figures and previous material, phrases like "In contrast to ..." and "A critical part ...."

Adjust your reading speed to suit the difficulty of the material and your goals for reading.

4. *Reflect.* While you are reading, try to think of examples or create images of the material. Elaborate and try to make connections between what you are reading and what you already know.

5. *Recite.* After reading each section, sit back and think about your initial purposes and questions. Can you answer the questions without looking at the book? Did you meet your goals? Reciting helps you monitor your understanding.

6. *Review.* Effective review incorporates new material more thoroughly into long-term memory. As study progresses, review should be cumulative, including the sections and chapters you read previously.

A strategy that can be used in reading literature is **CAPS**:

C Who are the *characters*?
A What is the *aim* of the story?
P What *problem* happens?
S How is the problem *solved*?

CAPS A strategy that can be used in reading literature: *Characters*, *Aim* of story, *Problem*, *Solution*.

Many cooperating teachers we work with use a strategy called **KWL** to guide reading and inquiry in general. This general framework can be used with most grade levels. The steps are:

K What do I already *know* about this subject?
W What do I *want* to know?
L At the end of the reading or inquiry, what have I *learned*?

KWL A strategy to guide reading and inquiry: Before—What do I already *know*? What do I *want* to know? After—What have I *learned*?

See the Reaching Every Student box on page 316 for an example of how learning strategies can be highlighted in a lesson to make sure that students understand them.

Anderson (1995a) suggests several reasons why strategies such as READS and PQ4R are effective. First, following the steps makes students more aware of the organization of a given chapter. How often have you skipped reading headings entirely and thus missed major clues to the way the information was organized? Next, these steps require students to study the chapter in sections instead of trying to learn all the information at once. This makes use of distributed practice. Creating and answering questions about the material forces students to process the information more deeply and with greater elaboration (Doctorow, Wittrock, & Marks, 1978; Hamilton, 1985).

As you may have guessed, methods such as PQ4R are more appropriate for older children. Teaching study skills to students in the early elementary grades, however, is probably difficult because these skills require cognitive and metacognitive tools that are quite difficult for very young children to use (Winne, 1997). And, of course, young children are still focusing much of their attention on learning the basics of word recognition.

The Guidelines on page 317 provide a summary of ideas about studying.

Applying Learning Strategies

Assuming students have a repertoire of powerful learning strategies, will they use them? Several conditions must be met (Ormrod, 2004). First, of course, the learning task must be appropriate. Why would students use more complex learning strategies when the task set by the teacher is to "learn and return" the exact words of the text or lecture? With these tasks, memorizing will be rewarded and the best strategies involve distributed practice and perhaps mnemonics (described in Chapter 7). But we hope that there are few of these kinds of tasks in contemporary teaching, so if the task is understanding, not memorizing, what else is necessary?

Connect & Extend

TO OTHER CHAPTERS
The guidelines for study skills apply to everyone who wishes to become an expert learner and involve the metacognitive abilities and executive control processes discussed in **Chapter 7**. See Chapter 7 for a discussion of declarative, procedural, and conditional knowledge.

SUPPORTING STUDENTS' USE OF STRATEGIES

No matter what strategies you use, students have to be taught how to use them. Direct teaching, explanation, modelling, and practice with feedback are necessary. Here is how one teacher participating in Nancy's research supports her students' use of strategies.

Tanya teaches grade 2 and 3 students and strategies are an important part of her instructional repertoire. For example, Tanya observed her grade 2 students were welded to one strategy for solving addition problems. They were depending on "counting on" when they could use more effective and efficient strategies for getting the correct answer (e.g., doubles, near doubles, make 10, two apart). Tanya taught the students several new strategies and posted them on a bulletin board in the classroom. Then she gave the students many opportunities to practise using the strategies to solve addition problems (i.e., addition facts to 20).

One day when Nancy visited the class, Tanya asked the students to work with a partner to practise addition strategies and addition facts. She gave each pair of students a pair of dice with numbers on the. She instructed the students to take turns throwing the dice and adding the numbers. One partner was the learner. The other partner was the coach. Tanya prompted the coaches to ask questions and offer encouragement to the learners. "Ask learners how they solved the problem. Ask them what strategy they used?" On that particular day, Tanya asked students to use at least three different strategies to solve addition facts and to be prepared to talk about the strategies they used. At the end of the lesson, all the students gathered on the carpet with Tanya and discussed the strategies they used, and how and why the strategies worked. Also, they talked about how they supported and offered encouragement to one another.

Tanya asked, "What can you say to offer encouragement?"

The students chimed, "Don't give up!"

In this lesson, the students in Tanya's class were developing a repertoire of strategies for solving addition problems as well as learning how to offer support and encouragement for one another's learning.

Connect & Extend

TO YOUR TEACHING
The teacher in the Reaching Every Student box uses both examples and non-examples to teach the concept of KWL. This is consistent with what you learned about teaching concepts earlier in this chapter.

Valuing Learning.   The second condition for using sophisticated strategies is that students must care about learning and understanding. They must have goals that can be reached using effective strategies (Zimmerman & Schunk, 2001). Anita was reminded of this one semester when she enthusiastically shared with her educational psychology class a newspaper article about study skills. The gist of the article was that students should continually revise and rewrite their notes from a course, so that by the end, all their understanding could be captured in one or two pages. Of course, the majority of the knowledge at that point would be reorganized and connected well with other knowledge. "See," she told the class, "these ideas are real—not just trapped in texts. They can help you study smarter in college." After a heated discussion, one of the best students said in exasperation, "I'm carrying 18 credits—I don't have time to *learn* this stuff!" She did not believe that her goal—to survive the semester—could be reached by using time-consuming study strategies.

Effort and Efficacy.   The student above also was concerned about effort. The third condition for applying learning strategies is that students must believe that the effort and investment required to apply the strategies are *reasonable*, given the likely return (Winne, 2001). And of course, students must believe that they are capable of using the strategies; that is, they must have self-efficacy for using the strategies to learn the material in question (Schunk, 2004). This is related to another condition. Students must have a base of knowledge and/or experience in the area. No learning strategies will help students accomplish tasks that are completely beyond their current understandings.

Epistemological Beliefs.   Finally, what students believe about knowledge and learning (their epistemological beliefs) will influence the kinds of strategies that they use.

How would you answer these questions (taken from Chan & Sachs, 2001)?

BECOMING AN EXPERT STUDENT

Make sure that you have the necessary declarative knowledge (facts, concepts, ideas) to understand new information.

EXAMPLES

1. Keep definitions of key vocabulary available as you study.
2. Review required facts and concepts before attempting new material.

Find out what type of test the teacher will give (essay, short answer) and study the material with that in mind.

EXAMPLES

1. For a test with detailed questions, practise writing answers to possible questions.
2. For a multiple-choice test, use mnemonics to remember definitions of key terms.

Make sure that you are familiar with the organization of the materials to be learned.

EXAMPLES

1. Preview the headings, introductions, topic sentences, and summaries of the text.
2. Be alert for words and phrases that signal relationships, such as *on the other hand, because, first, second, however, since.*

Know your own cognitive skills and use them deliberately.

EXAMPLES

1. Use examples and analogies to relate new material to something you care about and understand well, such as sports, hobbies, or films.

2. If one study technique is not working, try another—the goal is to stay involved and be as effective as you can, not to use any particular strategy.

Study the right information in the right way.

EXAMPLES

1. Be sure that you know exactly what topics and readings the test will cover.
2. Spend your time on the important, difficult, and unfamiliar material that will be required for the test or assignment.
3. Keep a list of the parts of the text that give you trouble and spend more time on those pages.
4. Process the important information thoroughly by using mnemonics, forming images, creating examples, answering questions, making notes in your own words, and elaborating on the text. Do not try to memorize the author's words—use your own.

Monitor your own comprehension.

EXAMPLES

1. Use questioning to check your understanding.
2. When reading speed slows down, decide if the information in the passage is important. If it is, note the problem so that you can reread or get help to understand. If it is not important, ignore it.
3. Check your understanding by working with a friend and quizzing one another.

Source: Adapted from Armbruster, B. B., & Anderson. T. H. (1981). Research synthesis on study skills. *Educational Leadership, 39,* 154–156. Reprinted by permission of the Association for Supervision and Curriculum Development. Copyright © 1981 by ASCD. All rights reserved.

1. The most important thing in learning math is to: (a) remember what the teacher has taught you, (b) practise lots of problems, (c) understand the problems you work on.

2. The most important thing you can do when trying to do science is (a) faithfully do the work the teacher tells you, (b) try to see how the explanation makes sense, (c) try to remember everything you are supposed to know.

3. If you wanted to know everything there is about something, say animals, how long would you have to study it? (a) Less than a year if you study hard, (b) about one or two years, (c) forever.

Connect & Extend

TO THE RESEARCH
See the Winter 2004 special issue of the *Educational Psychologist* on "Personal Epistemology: Paradigmatic Approaches to Understanding Students' Beliefs about Knowledge and Knowing" (Vol. 39, No. 1). Guest Editor: Barbara K. Hofer.

epistemological beliefs Beliefs about the structure, stability, and certainty of knowledge and how knowledge is best learned.

4. As you learn more and more about something, (a) the questions get more and more complex, (b) the questions get easier and easier, (c) the questions all get answered.

Using questions such as these, researchers have identified several dimensions of **epistemological beliefs** (Chan & Sachs, 2001; Schommer, 1997; Schommer-Aikins, 2002; Schraw & Olafson, 2002). For example,

- *Structure of Knowledge:* Is knowledge in a field a simple set of facts or a complex structure of concepts and relationships?
- *Stability/Certainty of Knowledge:* Is knowledge fixed or evolving over time?
- *Ability to Learn:* Is the ability to learn fixed (based on innate ability) or changeable?
- *Speed of Learning:* Can we gain knowledge quickly or does it take time to develop knowledge?
- *Nature of Learning:* Does learning mean memorizing facts passed down from authorities and keeping the facts isolated, or developing your own integrated understandings?

Students' beliefs about knowing and learning affect their use of learning strategies. For example, if you believe that knowledge should be gained quickly, you are likely to try one or two quick strategies (read the text once, spend two minutes trying to solve the word problem) and then stop. If you believe that learning means developing integrated understandings, you will process the material more deeply, connect to existing knowledge, create your own examples, or draw diagrams, and generally elaborate the information to make it your own (Hofer & Pintrich, 1997; Kardash & Howell, 2000). In one study, elementary-school students (grades 4 and 6), who believed that learning is understanding, processed science texts more deeply than students who believed that learning is reproducing facts (Chan & Sachs, 2001). The preceding questions about learning were used in that study to assess the students' beliefs. The answers associated with a belief in complex, evolving, knowledge that takes time to understand and grows from active learning are 1c, 2b, 3c, and 4a.

Here is an important question: What is the purpose of all that studying if you never use the knowledge—if you never transfer it to new situations?

Check Your Knowledge

- Distinguish between learning strategies and tactics.
- What key functions do learning strategies perform?
- Describe some procedures for developing learning strategies.
- When will students apply learning strategies?

Apply to Practice

- How would you use study skills to study this chapter?
- How could you improve your strategies for taking notes?

TEACHING FOR TRANSFER

Connect & Extend

TO YOUR TEACHING
Successful transfer of learning from the school to other contexts is evidence of superior instruction. What can teachers do to optimize transfer of knowledge and skills to the broader world?

Think back for a moment to a class in one of your high school subjects that you did not go on to study in university. Imagine the teacher, the room, the textbook. Now remember what you actually studied in class. If it was a science class, what were some of the formulas you learned? Oxidation reduction? If you are like most of us, you may remember that you learned these things, but you will not be quite sure exactly what you learned. Were those hours wasted? These questions are about the transfer of learning.

Whenever something previously learned influences current learning, or when solving an earlier problem affects how you solve a new problem, **transfer** has occurred (Mayer & Wittrock, 1996). If students learn a mathematical principle in first block and use it to solve a physics problem in third block, positive transfer has taken place. Even more rewarding for teachers is when a math principle learned in October is applied to a physics problem in March. However, the effect of past learning on present learning is not always positive. *Functional fixedness* and *response set* are examples of negative transfer because they involve the attempt to apply familiar but *inappropriate* strategies to a new situation.

The Many Views of Transfer

Transfer has been a focus of research in educational psychology for over 100 years. After all, the productive use of knowledge, skills, and motivations across a lifetime is a fundamental goal of education (De Corte, 2003). Early work focused on specific transfer of skills and the general transfer of mental discipline gained from studying rigorous subjects such as Latin or mathematics. But in 1924, E. L. Thorndike demonstrated that there was no mental discipline benefit from learning Latin. Learning Latin just helped you learn more Latin. So, thanks to Thorndike, you were not required to take Latin in high school. Other researchers looked at positive and negative transfer, such as the appropriate and inappropriate uses of heuristics in solving problems.

More recently, researchers have distinguished between the automatic, direct use of skills such as reading or writing in everyday applications and the extraordinary transfer of knowledge and strategies to arrive at creative solutions to problems (Bereiter, 1995; Bransford & Schwartz, 1999; Salomon & Perkins, 1989). Gavriel Salomon and David Perkins (1989) describe two kinds of transfer, termed *low-road* and *high-road transfer*. **Low-road transfer** "involves the spontaneous, automatic transfer of highly practised skills, with little need for reflective thinking" (p. 118). The key to low-road transfer is practising a skill often, in a variety of situations, until your performance becomes automatic. So if you worked one summer for a temporary secretarial service and were sent to many different offices to work on several kinds of software, by the end of the summer you probably would be able to handle most software tools easily. Your practice with many machines would let you transfer your skill automatically to a new situation. Bransford and Schwartz (1999) refer to this kind of transfer as *direct-application transfer*.

High-road transfer, on the other hand, involves consciously applying abstract knowledge learned in one situation to a different situation. This can happen in one of two ways. First, you may learn a principle or a strategy, intending to use it in the future. This is *forward-reaching transfer*. For example, if you plan to apply what you learn in anatomy class this semester to work in an art course you will take next semester, you may search for principles about human proportions, muscle definition, and so on. Second, suppose you are working on a problem and you look back on what you had learned in other situations to find help. This is *backward-reaching transfer*. Analogical thinking is an example of this kind of transfer. You search for other, related situations that might provide clues to the current problem. Bransford and Schwartz (1999) consider this kind of high-road transfer to be *preparation for future learning*.

The key to high-road transfer is *mindful abstraction*, or the deliberate identification of a principle, main idea, strategy, or procedure that is not tied to one specific problem or situation but could apply to many. Such an abstraction becomes part of your metacognitive knowledge, available to guide future learning and problem solving. Table 8.3 on the next page summarizes low-road and high-road transfer.

transfer Influence of previously learned material on new material.

Connect & Extend

TO YOUR TEACHING
What transfer in learning the sound "o" could be expected from learning to read the following words?
First group: does oh Spot good dog
Second group: hot stop clock pop Tom
Which group of words is more likely to be found in a grade 1 basal reading program?

low-road transfer Spontaneous and automatic transfer of highly practised skills.

high-road transfer Application of abstract knowledge learned in one situation to a different situation.

TABLE 8.3 Kinds of Transfer

	Low-Road Transfer (Direct Application)	High-Road Transfer (Preparation for Future Learning)
Definition	Automatic transfer of highly practised skill	Conscious application of abstract knowledge to a new situation
		Productive use of cognitive tools and motivations
Key Conditions	Extensive practice	Mindful focus on abstracting a principle, main idea, or procedure that can be used in many situations
	Variety of settings and conditions	
	Overlearning to automaticity	Learning in powerful teaching–learning environments
Examples	Driving many different cars	Applying KWL or READS strategies
	Finding your gate in an airport	Applying procedures from math in designing a page layout for the school newspaper

Teaching for Positive Transfer

Connect & Extend

TO YOUR TEACHING
What principles do you anticipate teaching that could be expected to transfer?

Years of research and experience show that students will master new knowledge, problem-solving procedures, and learning strategies, but they will not use them unless prompted or guided. For example, studies of real-world mathematics show that people do not always apply math procedures learned in school to solve practical problems in their homes or grocery stores (Lave, 1988; Lave & Wenger, 1991). This is because learning is *situated*; that is, learning happens in specific situations. We learn solutions to particular problems, not general all-purpose solutions that can fit any problem. Because we learn knowledge as a tool for solving particular problems, we may not realize that it is relevant when we encounter a problem that seems different, at least on the surface (Driscoll, 2000; Singley & Anderson, 1989). How can you make sure that your students will use what they learn, even when situations change?

What Is Worth Learning?　First, you must answer the question, "What is worth learning?" Learning basic skills such as reading, writing, computing, cooperating, and speaking will definitely transfer to other situations because these skills are necessary for later work both in and out of school—writing job applications, reading novels, paying bills, working on a team, locating and evaluating health care services, among others. All later learning depends on positive transfer of these basics to new situations.

Connect & Extend

TO YOUR TEACHING/ PORTFOLIO
"The greatest enemy of understanding is coverage. As long as you are determined to cover everything, you actually ensure that most kids are not going to understand." Howard Gardner in Brandt, R. (1993). On teaching for understanding: A Conversation with Howard Gardner. *Educational Leadership, 50*(7), 7.

Teachers must also be aware of what the future is likely to hold for their students, both as a group and as individuals. What will society require of them as adults? What will their careers require of them? As a child, Anita studied nothing about computers. Now she spends hours at her word processor. Computer programming and word processing were not part of her high school curriculum, but using a slide rule was. Now calculators and computers have made this skill obsolete. Undoubtedly, changes as extreme and unpredictable as these await the students you will teach. For this reason, the general transfer of principles, attitudes, learning strategies, and problem solving will be just as important to your students as the specific transfer of basic skills.

How Can Teachers Help?　For basic skills, greater transfer can also be ensured by **overlearning**, practising a skill past the point of mastery. Many of the basic facts students learn in elementary school, such as the multiplication tables, are traditionally overlearned. Overlearning helps students retrieve the information quickly and automatically when it is needed.

overlearning Practising a skill past the point of mastery.

For higher-level transfer, students must first learn and understand. Students will be more likely to transfer knowledge to new situations if they have been actively involved in the learning process. They must be encouraged to form abstractions that they will apply later. Erik De Corte (2003) believes that teachers support transfer, the productive use of cognitive tools and motivations, when they create powerful teaching-learning environments using these design principles:

- The environments should support constructive learning processes in all students.
- The environments should encourage the development of student self-regulation, so that teachers gradually give over more and more responsibilities to the students.
- Learning should involve interaction and collaboration.
- Learners should deal with problems that have personal meaning for them, problems like the ones they will face in the future.
- The classroom culture should encourage students to become aware of and develop their cognitive and motivational processes. In order to be productive users of these tools, students must know about and value them.

There is one last kind of transfer that is especially important for students—the transfer of the learning strategies we encountered in the previous section. Learning strategies and tactics are meant to be applied across a wide range of situations, but this often does not happen, as you will see below.

Stages of Transfer for Strategies. Gary Phye (1992, 2001; Phye & Sanders, 1994) suggests that we think of the transfer of learning strategies as a tool to be used in a "mindful" way to solve academic problems. He describes three stages in developing strategic transfer. In the *acquisition phase,* students should not only receive instruction about a strategy and how to use it, but they should also rehearse the strategy and practise being aware of when and how they are using it. In the *retention phase,* more practice with feedback helps students hone their strategy use. In the *transfer phase,* the teacher should provide new problems that can be solved with the same strategy, even though the problems appear different on the surface. To enhance motivation, point out to students how using the strategy will help them solve many problems and accomplish different tasks. These steps help build both procedural and conditional knowledge—how to use the strategy as well as when and why.

Newly mastered concepts, principles, and strategies must be practised and applied in a wide variety of situations. Positive transfer is encouraged when skills are used under authentic conditions, similar to those that will exist when the skills are needed later. Students can learn to write by corresponding with email pen pals in other countries. They can learn historical research methods by researching their own families. Some of these applications should involve complex, ill-defined, unstructured problems, because many of the problems to be faced in later life, in school and out, will not come to students complete with instructions, and applications should include situations outside school. The Family and Community Partnerships box on page 322 gives ideas for enlisting the support of families in encouraging transfer.

Check Your Knowledge

- What is transfer?
- Distinguish between low-road and high-road transfer.

Apply to Practice

- Why is it important to ask students to apply new knowledge to both well-defined and ill-defined problems?

A challenge for all learners and educators is to be sure that knowledge acquired in school will be applicable to real-life situations or problems. Will this girl's technology skills be applicable years from now?

Connect & Extend

TO LIFE
Why is information that is overlearned resistant to forgetting? Do we overlearn all information that is practised and rehearsed?

Connect & Extend

TO THE RESEARCH
Garner, R. (1990). When children and adults do not use learning strategies: Toward a theory of settings. *Review of Educational Research, 60,* 517–530.

PROMOTING TRANSFER

Keep families informed about their child's curriculum so that they can support learning.

EXAMPLES

1. At the beginning of units or major projects, send a letter summarizing the key goals, a few of the major assignments, and some common problems students have in learning the material for that unit.

2. Ask parents for suggestions about how their child's interests could be connected to the curriculum topics.

3. Invite parents to school for an evening of "strategy learning"—have the students teach their family members one of the strategies they have learned in school.

Give families ideas for how they might practise, extend, or apply learning from school.

EXAMPLES

1. To extend writing, ask parents to encourage their children to write letters or to email companies or civic organizations asking for information or free products. Provide a shell letter form for structure and ideas and include addresses of companies that provide free samples or information.

2. Ask family members to include their children in some projects that require measurement, halving or doubling recipes, or estimating costs.

3. Suggest that students work with senior family members to create a family memory book. Combine historical research and writing.

Show connections between learning in school and life outside.

EXAMPLES

1. Ask families to talk about and show how they use the skills their children are learning in jobs, hobbies, or community involvement projects.

2. Ask family members to come to class to demonstrate how they use reading, writing, science, math, or other knowledge in their work.

Make families partners in practising learning strategies.

EXAMPLES

1. Focusing on one learning tactic at a time, ask families to simply remind their children to use study tactics with homework that week.

2. Develop a lending library of books and videotapes to teach families about learning strategies.

3. Give parents a copy of the "Becoming an Expert Student" Guidelines on page 317, rewritten for your grade level.

DIVERSITY AND CONVERGENCES IN COMPLEX COGNITIVE PROCESSES

This chapter has covered quite a bit of territory, partly because the cognitive perspective has so many implications for instruction. Although these principles are varied, most of the cognitively based ideas for teaching concepts, creative problem solving, and learning strategies emphasize the role of students' prior knowledge and the need for active, mindful learning.

Diversity

Concept learning, problem solving, and strategy-learning processes may be similar for all students, but the prior knowledge, beliefs, and skills they bring to the classroom are bound to vary, based on their experience and culture. For example, Chen and his colleagues (2004) wondered if university students might use familiar folk tales—one kind of cultural knowledge—as analogies to solve problems. That is just what happened. Chinese students were better at solving a problem of weighing a statue because the problem was similar to their folk tale about how to weigh an elephant (by water displacement). American students were better at solving a problem of finding the way out of a cave (leaving a trail) by using an analogy to *Hansel and Gretel*, a common folk tale familiar to American students. In another study in Australia, Volet (1999) found that some culturally based knowledge and motivation of Asian students—such as high achievement motivation, a deep processing and effortful approach to learning, and a recognition of the benefits of collaboration—transferred well to Western-oriented schools. Other culturally based beliefs, such as valuing rote memorization or solitary learning, might cause conflicts with the expectations of some schools. For example, we saw in Chapter 5 that the native Hawaiian style of interacting was seen as interrupting by non-Hawaiian teachers until the teachers learned more about the family communication styles of their students.

Creativity and Diversity.   Even though creativity has been studied for centuries, "Psychologists still have a long way to go before they come anywhere close to understanding creativity in women and minorities" (Simonton, 2000, p. 156). The focus of creativity research and writing over the years has been white males. Patterns of creativity in other groups are complex—sometimes matching and sometimes diverging from patterns found in traditional research.

In another connection between creativity and culture, research suggests that being on the outside of mainstream society, being bilingual, or being exposed to other cultures might encourage creativity (Simonton, 1999, 2000). In fact, true innovators often break rules. "Creators have a desire to shake things up. They are restless, rebellious, and dissatisfied with the status quo" (Winner, 2000, p. 167).

Convergences

As you have seen throughout this chapter, in the beginning, as students learn problem solving or try to transfer cognitive tools to new situations, there is a tendency to focus on surface features. For all novices, their challenge is to grasp the abstractions: underlying principles, structures, strategies, or big ideas. It is those larger ideas that lead to understanding and serve as a foundation for future learning (Chen & Mo, 2004).

A second convergence: For all students, there is a positive relationship between using learning strategies and academic gains such as high school GPA and retention in university (Robbins, Le, & Lauver, 2005). Some students will learn productive strategies on their own, but all students can benefit from direct teaching, modelling, and practice of learning strategies and study skills. This is one important way to prepare all your students for their futures.

Check Your Knowledge

- What kinds of individual differences can interfere with problem solving and creativity?
- What is a common fault when students face situations that call for transferring knowledge?

Apply to Practice

- Generate a shell letter your students could use to write for information and free products, and match it to feedback you could provide that would promote transfer to writing in general.

SUMMARY

Learning and Teaching about Concepts
(pp. 283–291)

Distinguish between prototypes and exemplars.

Concepts are categories used to group similar events, ideas, people, or objects. A prototype is the best representative of its category. For instance, the best representative of the "birds" category for many Canadians might be a robin. Exemplars are our actual memories of specific birds and so on that we use to compare with an item in question to see if that item belongs in the same category as our exemplar. We probably learn concepts from prototypes or exemplars of the category, understand in terms of our schematic knowledge, and then refine concepts through our additional experience of relevant and irrelevant features.

What are the four elements needed in concept teaching?

Lessons about concepts include four basic components: concept examples (along with non-examples), relevant and irrelevant attributes, name, and definition. The concept attainment model is one approach to teaching concepts that asks students to form hypotheses about why particular examples are members of a category and what that category (concept) might be.

What are the key characteristics of Bruner's discovery learning?

In discovery learning, the teacher presents examples and the students work with the examples until they discover the interrelationships—the subject's structure. Bruner believes that classroom learning should take place through inductive reasoning; that is, by using specific examples to formulate a general principle.

What are the stages of Ausubel's expository teaching?

Ausubel believes that learning should progress deductively: from the general to the specific, or from the rule or principle to examples. After presenting an advance organizer, the next step in a lesson using Ausubel's approach is to present content in terms of basic similarities and differences, using specific examples. Finally, when all the material has been presented, ask students to discuss how the examples can be used to expand on the original advance organizer.

How can you teach concepts through analogies?

By identifying known information that relates to a new concept, teachers and students can map the analogies between the known and the new, then summarize an understanding of the new concept by explaining the similarities and differences between the known and the new concepts.

Problem Solving
(pp. 291–304)

What are the steps in the general problem-solving process?

Problem solving is both general and domain-specific. The five stages of problem solving are contained in the acronym IDEAL: *I*dentify problems and opportunities; *D*efine goals and represent the problem; *E*xplore possible strategies; *A*nticipate outcomes and *A*ct; *L*ook back and *L*earn.

Why is the representation stage of problem solving so important?

To represent the problem accurately, you must understand both the whole problem and its discrete elements. Schema training may improve this ability. The problem-solving process follows entirely different paths, depending on what representation and goal are chosen. If your representation of the problem suggests an immediate solution, the task is done; the new problem is recognized as a "disguised" version of an old problem with a clear solution. But if there is no existing way of solving the problem or if the activated schema fails, then students must search for a solution. The application of algorithms and heuristics—such as means-ends analysis, analogical thinking, working backward, and verbalization—may help students solve problems.

Describe factors that can interfere with problem solving.

Factors that hinder problem solving include functional fixedness or rigidity (response set). These disallow the flexibility needed to represent problems accurately and to have insight into solutions. Also, as we make decisions and judgments, we may overlook important information because we base judgments on what seems representative of a category (representativeness heuristic) or what is available in memory (availability heuristic), then pay attention only to information that confirms our choices (confirmation bias) so that we hold on to beliefs, even in the face of contradictory evidence (belief perseverance).

How do misconceptions and heuristics interfere with learning?

If the students' intuitive model includes misconceptions and inaccuracies, then the students are likely to develop inadequate or misleading representations of a problem. In order to learn new information and solve problems, students must sometimes "unlearn" common-sense ideas.

What are the differences between expert and novice knowledge in a given area?

Expert problem solvers have a rich store of declarative, procedural, and conditional knowledge. They organize this knowledge around general principles or patterns that apply to large classes of problems. They work faster, remember relevant information, and monitor their progress better than novices.

Creativity and Creative Problem Solving
(pp. 304–309)

What are some myths about creativity?

These four statements are completely or partly wrong: Creativity is determined at birth. Creativity comes with negative personality traits. Creative people are disorganized hippie types. Working in a group enhances creativity. The facts are: Creativity can be developed. A few but not all creative people are nonconforming or have emotional problems. Many creative people are focused, organized, and part of the mainstream. Finally, groups can limit as well as enhance creativity.

What is creativity and how is it assessed?

Creativity is a process that involves independently restructuring problems to see things in new, imaginative ways. Creativity is difficult to measure, but tests of divergent thinking can assess originality, fluency, and flexibility. Originality is usually determined statistically. To be original, a response must be given by fewer than 5 or 10 people out of every 100 who take the test. Fluency is the number of different responses. The number of different categories of responses measures flexibility.

What can teachers do to support creativity in the classroom?

Teachers can encourage creativity in their interactions with students by accepting unusual, imaginative answers, modelling divergent thinking, using brainstorming, and tolerating dissent.

Becoming an Expert Student: Learning Strategies and Study Skills
(pp. 310–318)

Distinguish between learning strategies and tactics.

Learning strategies are ideas for accomplishing learning goals, a kind of overall plan of attack. Learning tactics are the specific techniques that make up the plan. A strategy for learning might include several tactics such as mnemonics to remember key terms, skimming to identify the organization, and then writing answers to possible essay questions. Use of strategies and tactics reflects metacognitive knowledge.

What key functions do learning strategies perform?

Learning strategies help students *become cognitively engaged*—focus attention on the relevant or important aspects of the material. Second, they encourage students to *invest effort,* make connections, elaborate, translate, organize, and reorganize in order to *think and process deeply*—the greater the practice and processing, the stronger the learn-

ing. Finally, strategies help students *regulate and monitor* their own learning—keep track of what is making sense and notice when a new approach is needed.

Describe some procedures for developing learning strategies.

Expose students to a number of different strategies, not only general learning strategies but also very specific tactics, such as the graphic strategies. Teach conditional knowledge about when, where, and why to use various strategies. Develop motivation to use the strategies and tactics by showing students how their learning and performance can be improved. Provide direct instruction in content knowledge needed to use the strategies.

When will students apply learning strategies?

If they have appropriate strategies, students will apply them if they are faced with a task that requires good strategies, value doing well on that task, think the effort to apply the strategies will be worthwhile, and believe that they can succeed using the strategies. Also, to apply deep processing strategies, students must assume that knowledge is complex and takes time to learn and that learning requires their own active efforts.

Teaching for Transfer
(pp. 318–322)

What is transfer?

Transfer occurs when a rule, fact, or skill learned in one situation is applied in another situation; for example, applying rules of punctuation to write a job application letter. Transfer also involves applying to new problems the principles learned in other, often dissimilar situations.

Distinguish between low-road and high-road transfer.

Transfer involving spontaneity and automaticity in familiar situations has been called *low-road transfer.*

High-road transfer involves reflection and conscious application of abstract knowledge to new situations. Learning environments should support active constructive learning, self-regulation, collaboration, and awareness of cognitive tools and motivational processes. In addition, students should deal with problems that have meaning in their lives. Teachers can help students transfer learning strategies by teaching strategies directly, providing practice with feedback, and then expanding the application of the strategies to new and unfamiliar situations.

Diversity and Convergences in Complex Cognitive Processes
(pp. 322–323)

What kinds of individual differences can interfere with problem solving and creativity?

Cultural beliefs about the nature of creativity, problem solving, and their relative roles in tasks or learning can ignite or dampen how these are used.

What is a common fault when students face situations that call for transferring knowledge?

Students often focus on surface features of the situation and are misled to overlook larger ideas that are keys to learning.

KEY TERMS

BECOMING A PROFESSIONAL

Reflecting on the Chapter

Can you apply the ideas from this chapter on complex cognitive processes to solve the following problems of practice?

Preschool and Kindergarten

- Several students in your class still have trouble discriminating between simple shapes. What would you do to help them understand?

Elementary and Middle School

- Students in your class are having a really hard time with the concepts of heat and energy. What would you do?

Junior High and High School

- Students in your math class can solve problems for homework, but they become confused on tests that cover several chapters. They don't seem to know when to apply one procedure and when to use another. How would you help them?

- You decide to give an essay test that requires original thinking and creativity. Your students perform very poorly and protest loudly that the test is "unfair." They want to use the definitions and facts they have so carefully memorized. What would you do?

Check Your Understanding

- Know the basic features of concept teaching.

- Know the common steps in problem solving.

- Be familiar with techniques for promoting creativity.

- Be familiar with a range of learning strategies and tactics.

- Know how to promote students' transfer.

Your Teaching Portfolio

Use Table 8.2 ("Examples of Learning Tactics," page 311) plus the section titled "Learning Strategies and Tactics" on pages 310–312 to generate ideas for appropriate learning strategies and tactics for the students you will teach, and include these ideas in your portfolio.

Teaching Resources

Add Figures 8.4 ("Four Different Ways to Represent a Problem," page 295) and 8.8 ("A Map to Organize Studying and Learning," page 313), and Table 8.2 on page 311 to your file of teaching resources.

Use the Family and Community Partnerships box on page 322 in this chapter to brainstorm ideas for family involvement in helping your students take their learning home.

Teachers' Casebook

What Would They Do?

Here is how two practising teachers responded to the teaching situation presented at the beginning of this chapter about teaching learning tactics and strategies.

Barbara McKinley
Secondary Science Teacher
Argyle Secondary School
North Vancouver, British Columbia

The study skills that students were taught in elementary school need to be reinforced and expanded as they enter middle and high school. Initially, I try to guide my students at each grade level by recommending a specific amount of time to be spent on homework and review. We discuss the things in their lives they must make time for and map out a tentative schedule that allows them to see how, through organization and time management, they can get a number of things done in a day, a weekend, or a week.

Early in the year, in order to teach learning strategies, I photocopy a piece of high-interest science news from the paper that is at a reading level slightly below the class level. Using "think alouds," I show students how to identify what is important in the article. If students are having trouble deciphering the main ideas, we look for signals in the article such as headings and captions.

I also use this time to teach how to underline and take notes. I limit the amount of underlining that they can use. I then show the class how to write out the important information in note form. Students' first instinct is often to copy down sentences from the article verbatim, so I emphasize the importance of putting the concepts into their own words. As we are taking notes, I encourage students to build connections between the material in the article and what they have already learned. We discuss the main scientific principles and where else they have seen them applied and hypothesize about other situations where they could also be used. With sufficient practice, these skills can be transferred to their science text.

As we move through the first unit, I break it into manageable chunks to help their comprehension and, again, we discuss why some things are more important than others, so, eventually, they can make this distinction themselves. After each of the initial chapters, I demonstrate how to write summaries in chart form. I show students how to focus on the big ideas under each chapter heading and how to find the supporting ideas. Students compare ideas in groups and then as a whole class. I clarify correct answers to ensure that students are not copying incorrect responses.

Jill Brindle
Secondary English Teacher
St. Catharines, Ontario

As students move into their senior years of high school, they face longer reading assignments that are to be completed more independently. At this stage, they are also expected to create essay responses to their readings, with developed arguments and precise documentation.

The task of reading a novel and then writing an argumentative essay about the novel can appear daunting to students. To lessen this anxiety and the resulting temptation of students to procrastinate, I provide students with a schematic time frame, showing that the large project is actually accomplished through completion of smaller tasks, each carried out within a reasonable period of time, each with its own value, and each a step towards the completion of the whole.

At the beginning of the unit on the novel, I first engage students in discussion of a human-interest story or news item that relates to an issue explored by the author in the novel. We discuss potential questions and diverging viewpoints that the issue can raise. After presenting a short introduction on the author's background and interests, I encourage students to build connections to the work they are about to study, to ask questions about the characters and the story, and questions about the author's methods and messages. Students begin this questioning with a short, silent survey of the novel, during which students can survey the table of contents, read the introduction, preface, part of the first chapter, and so on. I ask students to jot down any questions that come to them about the story or its technique. When we pause to share and discuss the questions, I point out that the broad range of questions typifies the many aspects of a novel that can be explored.

After students have completed an assigned reading of the first chapter, I review six elements of the novel (plot, characterization, setting, mood, diction, and theme). This discussion reinforces and expands upon terms taught in earlier grades. We discuss the pertinent questions we might ask ourselves when examining each of these elements of a novel.

Using these six elements as headings, I demonstrate how to make notes on important information and ideas drawn from the chapter readings. Together, we fill out the chart, on the basis of our previous reading. During the progress of their reading of the novel, students continue to complete charts for the other chapters in a more independent fashion. I encourage students to read a chapter first before jotting down the relevant information. I also emphasize the need to keep the notes brief, to review a chapter after making notes for it, to check that the notes are accurate, and to provide page references for examples.

During this novel unit, the chapter notes remain useful for several interrelated assignments. Student groups are required to prepare presentations on assigned chapters. To do so, the members of each group first compare their notes, and then synthesize concepts. Each group, in its presentation, must focus on a particular topic that I assign to it. There is, then, a transfer of ideas as the group members relate their concepts to the assigned topic. I also ask the group members to build some connections in their presentations between the literary issue they are discussing and the real issues of the world. During class question-and-answer portions of the presentations, the presenters and the other students compare ideas and use the opportunity to add key points to their notes. I correct any inaccuracies to make sure information being recorded is sound.

There is another aspect of transfer that occurs in these group presentations. The outline I give students for organizing their presentations is really a simple version of the standard pattern of the essay format. Therefore, as students organize for their presentations, they are also practising an organizational pattern that they will transfer to the writing of the essay at a later point in the unit. In the process of writing that essay, the students will also again be able to use their chapter notes to assist them in remembering and retrieving the details they will need to support their arguments.

9

SOCIAL COGNITIVE AND CONSTRUCTIVIST VIEWS OF LEARNING

Brighton Beach, Edward Henry Potthast. Oil on wood panel © Christie's Images/
SuperStock.

Teachers' Casebook

What Would You Do?

You have finally landed a job teaching English and writing in a high school. The first day of class, you discover that many of your students are learning English as a second language. You make a mental note to meet with them to determine how much and what kind of reading they can handle. To get a sense of the class's interest, you ask them to write a review of the last book they read, as if they were on TV doing a "book beat" program. There is a bit of grumbling, but the students seem to be writing, so you take a few minutes to try to talk with one of the students who seems to have trouble with English.

That night, you look over the book reviews. Either the students are giving you a hard time, or no one has read anything lately. Several students mention a text from another class, but their reviews are one-sentence evaluations—usually containing the words *lame* or *useless* (often misspelled). In stark contrast are the papers of three students—they are a pleasure to read, worthy of publication in the school literary magazine (if there were one), and they reflect a fairly sophisticated understanding of some good literature.

Critical Thinking

- How would you adapt your plans for this group?
- What will you do tomorrow?
- What teaching approaches do you think will work with this class?
- How will you work with the three students who are more advanced and the students who are just learning English?

Collaboration

With two or three other students in your class, redesign the assignment to get students more engaged. How could you prepare them to use what they know to succeed on this assignment?

In the preceding three chapters, we analyzed different aspects of learning. We considered behavioural and information processing explanations of what and how people learn. We examined complex cognitive processes such as concept learning and problem solving. These explanations of learning focus on the individual and what is happening in his or her "head." Recent perspectives have called attention to two other aspects of learning that are critical—social and cultural factors. In this chapter, we look at the role of other people and the cultural context in learning.

Two general theoretical frames include social and cultural factors as major elements. The first, social cognitive theory, has its roots in Bandura's early social learning theories of observational learning and vicarious reinforcement. You read about these early versions in Chapter 6. The second, sociocultural constructivist theories, have roots in cognitive perspectives, but have moved well beyond these early explanations. Rather than debating the merits of each approach, we will consider the contributions of these different models of instruction, grounded in different theories of learning. Don't feel that you must choose the "best" approach—there is no such thing. Even though theorists argue about which model is best, excellent teachers apply all the approaches as appropriate.

By the time you have completed this chapter, you should be able to answer these questions:

- *What is reciprocal determinism and what role does it play in social cognitive theory?*

- *What is self-efficacy, and how does it affect learning in school?*

- *What is teachers' sense of efficacy?*
- *How can teachers support the development of self-efficacy and self-regulated learning?*
- *What are three constructivist perspectives on learning?*
- *How could you incorporate inquiry, problem-based learning, instructional conversations, and cognitive apprenticeships in your teaching?*
- *What dilemmas do constructivist teachers face?*

SOCIAL COGNITIVE THEORY

As we saw in Chapter 6, in the early 1960s, Albert Bandura demonstrated that people can learn by observing the actions and consequences of others. Bandura's **social learning theory** emphasized observation, modelling, and vicarious reinforcement. Over time, Bandura's explanations of learning included more attention to cognitive factors such as expectations and beliefs in addition to the social influences of models. His current perspective is called **social cognitive theory.**

Reciprocal Determinism

In social cognitive theory, both internal and external factors are important. Environmental events, personal factors, and behaviours are seen as interacting in the process of learning. Personal factors (beliefs, expectations, attitudes, and knowledge), the physical and social environment (resources, consequences of actions, other people, and physical settings), and behaviour (individual actions, choices, and verbal statements) all influence and are influenced by each other. Bandura calls this interaction of forces **reciprocal determinism.**

Figure 9.1 shows the interaction of person, environment, and behaviours in learning settings (Schunk, 2004). Social factors such as models, instructional strategies, or feedback (elements of the *environment* for students) can affect student *personal* factors such as goals, sense of efficacy for the task (described in the next section), attributions (beliefs about causes for success and failure), and processes of self-regulation such as planning, monitoring, and controlling distractions. For example, teacher feedback can lead students to set higher goals. Social influences in the environment and personal factors encourage the *behaviours* that lead to achievement such as persistence and effort (motivation) and learning. But these behaviours also reciprocally impact personal factors. As students achieve,

social learning theory Theory that emphasizes learning through observation of others.

social cognitive theory Theory that adds concern with cognitive factors such as beliefs, self-perceptions, and expectations to social learning theory.

reciprocal determinism An explanation of behaviour that emphasizes the mutual effects of the individual and the environment on each other.

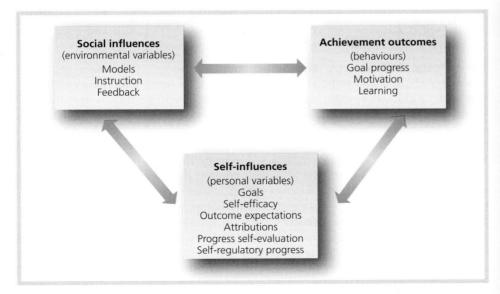

Figure 9.1 Reciprocal Influences

All three forces—personal, social/environmental, and behavioural—are in constant interaction. They influence and are influenced by each other.

Source: From Schunk, D. H. (1999). Social-self interaction and achievement behaviour. *Educational Psychologist, 34,* p. 221. Adapted with permission of Lawrence Erlbaum Associates, Inc. and the author.

their confidence and interest increase, for example. And behaviours also affect the social environment. For example, if students do not persist or if they seem to misunderstand, teachers may change instructional strategies or feedback.

Think for a minute about the power of reciprocal determinism in classrooms. If personal factors, behaviours, and the environment are in constant interaction, then cycles of events are progressive and self-perpetuating. Suppose a student who is new to the school walks into class late because he got lost in the unfamiliar building. The student has a tattoo and several visible body piercings. The student is actually anxious about his first day and hopes to do better at this new school, but the teacher's initial reaction to the late entry and dramatic appearance is a bit hostile. The student feels insulted and responds in kind, so the teacher begins to form expectations about the student and acts more vigilant, less trusting. The student senses the distrust. He decides that this school will be just as worthless as his previous one—and wonders why he should bother to try. The teacher sees the student's disengagement, invests less effort in teaching him, and the cycle continues.

This complex interplay of forces can be positive, too. Imagine the same scenario unfolding with just one important change at the beginning. Instead of the teacher reacting as she did in the first scenario, she says, "Oh, hi. What's your name?" After the student replies, "Gregor," the teacher says, "Gregor, welcome! Let's do this, everyone. Carly, would you and your group please make a spot for Gregor at your table and bring him up to date on what we're doing? People in the other groups: your job is to develop a five-sentence summary of where we are in our discussion. When we reconvene in eight minutes—I'm setting my watch—let's compare notes to see if we're all on the same page this morning." In this different way, the reciprocity between people and environment takes a whole different shape.

Self-Efficacy

Connect & Extend

TO OTHER CHAPTERS
Sense of self-efficacy is discussed again in **Chapter 10**. *Background:* Two books by Bandura about self-efficacy: Bandura, A. (1997). *Self-efficacy: The exercise of control.* New York: Freeman. Bandura, A. (Ed.). (1995). *Self-efficacy in changing societies.* New York: Cambridge University Press.

self-efficacy A person's sense of being able to deal effectively with a particular task.

What Would You Say?

The last question in your interview for the grade 8 position is, "We have some pretty discouraged students and parents because our provincial test scores were so low last year. What would you do to help students believe in their ability to learn?"

Albert Bandura (1986, 1997) suggests that predictions about possible outcomes of behaviour are critical for learning because they affect motivation. "Will I succeed or fail? Will I be liked or laughed at?" "Will I be more accepted by teachers in this new school?" These predictions are affected by **self-efficacy**—our beliefs about our personal competence or effectiveness *in a given area.* Bandura (1997) defines self-efficacy as "beliefs in one's capabilities to organize and execute the courses of action required to produce given attainments" (p. 3).

Self-Efficacy, Self-Concept, and Self-Esteem. Most people assume that self-efficacy is the same as self-concept or self-esteem. It isn't. Self-efficacy is future-oriented, "a context-specific assessment of competence to perform a specific task" (Pajares, 1997, p. 15). Self-concept is a more global construct that involves many perceptions about the self, including self-efficacy. Self-concept is developed as a result of external and internal comparisons, using other people or other aspects of one's self as frames of reference. But self-efficacy focuses on *your* ability to successfully accomplish a particular task with no need for comparisons—the question is whether *you* can do it, not whether others would be successful. Another difference is that self-efficacy beliefs are strong predictors of behaviour, but self-concept has weaker predictive power (Bandura, 1997).

Compared with self-esteem, self-efficacy is concerned with judgments of personal capabilities; self-esteem is concerned with judgments of self-worth. There is no direct relationship between self-esteem and self-efficacy. It is possible to feel highly efficacious in one area and still not have a high level of self-esteem, or vice versa (Valentine, DuBois, & Cooper, 2004). For example, Phil has a very low self-efficacy for singing, but his self-esteem is not affected, probably because his life does not require singing. But if his self-efficacy for teaching a particular class started dropping after several bad experiences, his self-esteem would suffer.

Sources of Self-Efficacy. Bandura identified four sources of self-efficacy expectations: mastery experiences, physiological and emotional arousal, vicarious experiences, and social persuasion. **Mastery experiences** are our own direct experiences—the most powerful source of efficacy information. Successes usually raise efficacy beliefs, while failures usually lower efficacy. Level of **arousal** affects self-efficacy, depending on how the arousal is interpreted. As you face the task, are you anxious and worried (lowers efficacy) or excited and "psyched" (raises efficacy) (Bandura, 1997; Pintrich & Schunk, 2002)?

In **vicarious experiences**, someone else models accomplishments. The more closely a student identifies with the model, the greater the impact on self-efficacy will be. When the model performs well, the student's efficacy is enhanced, but when the model performs poorly, efficacy expectations decrease. Although mastery experiences generally are acknowledged as the most influential source of efficacy beliefs in adults, Keyser and Barling (1981) found that children (grade 6 students in this study) rely more on **modelling** as a source of self-efficacy information.

Social persuasion can be a "pep talk" or specific performance feedback. Social persuasion alone can't create enduring increases in self-efficacy, but a persuasive boost in self-efficacy can lead a student to make an effort, attempt new strategies, or try hard enough to succeed (Bandura, 1982). Social persuasion can counter occasional setbacks that might have instilled self-doubt and interrupted persistence. The potency of persuasion depends on the credibility, trustworthiness, and expertise of the persuader (Bandura, 1997).

Check Your Knowledge

- Distinguish between social learning and social cognitive theories.
- What is reciprocal determinism?
- What is self-efficacy, and how is it different from other self-schemas?
- What are the sources of self-efficacy?

Apply to Practice

- Describe how observational learning and modelling might be used in helping the students described at the beginning of the chapter write better book reviews.

APPLYING SOCIAL COGNITIVE THEORY

Self-efficacy and self-regulated learning are two key elements of social cognitive theory that are especially important in learning and teaching.

Self-Efficacy and Motivation

Let's assume your sense of efficacy is around 90 out of 100 for completing this chapter today. Greater efficacy leads to greater effort and persistence in the face of setbacks, so even if you are interrupted in your reading, you are likely to return to the task. Self-efficacy also influences motivation through goal setting. If we have a high sense of efficacy in a given area, we will set higher goals, be less afraid of failure, and find new strategies when old ones fail. If your sense of efficacy for reading this chapter is high, you are likely to set high goals for completing the chapter—maybe you will take some notes, too. If your sense of efficacy is low,

mastery experiences Our own direct experiences—the most powerful source of efficacy information.

arousal Physical and psychological reactions causing a person to feel alert, excited, or tense.

vicarious experiences Accomplishments that are modelled by someone else.

modelling Changes in behaviour, thinking, or emotions that happen through observing another person—a model.

social persuasion A "pep talk" or specific performance feedback—one source of self-effi-

Self-efficacy refers to the knowledge of one's own ability to successfully accomplish a particular task with no need for comparisons with others' ability—the question is, "Can I do it?" not, "Are others better than I am?"

however, you may avoid the reading altogether or give up easily if problems arise (Bandura, 1993, 1997; Zimmerman, 1995).

What is the most motivating level of efficacy? Should students be accurate, optimistic, or pessimistic in their predictions? There is evidence that a higher sense of self-efficacy supports motivation, even when the efficacy is an overestimation. Children and adults who are optimistic about the future are more mentally and physically healthy, less depressed, and more motivated to achieve (Flammer, 1995). After examining almost 140 studies of motivation, Sandra Graham concluded that these qualities characterize many minority students. They had strong self-concepts and high expectations, even in the face of difficulties (Graham, 1994, 1995).

As you might expect, there are dangers in underestimating abilities because then students are more likely to put out a weak effort and give up easily. But there are dangers in continually overestimating performance as well. Students who think they are better readers than they actually are may not be motivated to go back and repair misunderstandings as they read. They don't discover that they did not really understand the material until it is too late (Pintrich & Zusho, 2002).

Research indicates that performance in school is improved and self-efficacy is increased when students (a) adopt short-term goals, so it is easier to judge progress; (b) are taught to use specific learning strategies such as outlining or summarizing that help them focus attention; and (c) receive rewards based on achievement, not just engagement, because achievement rewards signal increasing competence (Graham & Weiner, 1996).

Teachers' Sense of Efficacy

Much of Anita's research has focused on a particular kind of self-efficacy—teachers' sense of efficacy (Hoy & Woolfolk, 1990, 1993; Tschannen-Moran & Woolfolk Hoy, 2001; Tschannen-Moran, Woolfolk Hoy, & Hoy, 1998; Woolfolk & Hoy, 1990; Woolfolk Hoy & Burke-Spero, 2005). **Teachers' sense of efficacy**, a teacher's belief that he or she can reach even difficult students to help them learn, appears to be one of the few personal characteristics of teachers that is correlated with student achievement. Self-efficacy theory predicts that teachers with a high sense of efficacy work harder and persist longer even when students are difficult to teach, in part because these teachers believe in themselves and in their students. Also, they are less likely to experience burnout (Fives, Hamman, & Olivarez, 2005).

Anita and her colleagues have found that prospective teachers tend to increase in their personal sense of efficacy as a consequence of completing student teaching. But sense of efficacy may go down after the first year as a teacher, perhaps because support that was there for you in student teaching is gone (Woolfolk Hoy & Burke-Spero, 2005). Teachers' sense of efficacy is higher in schools where the other teachers and administrators have high expectations for students *and* where teachers receive help from their principals in solving instructional and management problems (Capa, 2005; Hoy & Woolfolk, 1993). Another important conclusion from this research is that efficacy grows from real success with students, not just from the moral support or cheerleading of professors and colleagues. Any experience or training that helps you succeed in the day-to-day tasks of teaching will give you a foundation for developing a sense of efficacy in your career.

As with any kind of efficacy, there may be both benefits and dangers in overestimating abilities. Optimistic teachers probably set higher goals, work harder, reteach when necessary, and

teachers' sense of efficacy A teacher's belief that he or she can reach even the most difficult students and help them learn.

Research shows that teachers' sense of efficacy grows from real success with students. Experience or training that helps teachers succeed in the day-to-day tasks of teaching will contribute to their sense of efficacy.

persist in the face of problems. But some benefits might follow from having doubts about your efficacy. Doubts might foster reflection, motivation to learn, greater responsiveness to diversity, productive collaboration, and the kind of disequilibrium described by Piaget that motivates change (Wheatley, 2002). It seems reasonable that a sense of efficacy for learning to teach would be necessary to respond to doubts in these positive ways, but it is true that persistent high efficacy perceptions in the face of poor performance can produce avoidance rather than action.

Self-Regulated Learning

Phil and his colleague at the University of Victoria, Allyson Hadwin (Winne & Hadwin, 1998), define **self-regulation** as intentional and strategic adaptation of cognition, motivation, and behaviour to reach goals. When the goals involve learning, we talk about self-regulated learning.

Today, people change jobs an average of seven times before they retire. Many of these career changes require new learning that must be self-initiated and self-directed (Martinez-Pons, 2002; Weinstein, 1994). Thus, one goal of teaching should be to free students from the need for teachers so that the students can continue to learn independently throughout their lives. To continue learning independently throughout life, you must be a self-regulated learner. Self-regulated learners have a combination of academic learning skills and self-control that makes learning easier, which in turn makes them more motivated; in other words, they have the *skill* and the *will* to learn (McCombs & Marzano, 1990; Murphy & Alexander, 2000). Self-regulated learners transform their mental abilities, whatever they are, into academic skills and strategies (Winne, 1995; Zimmerman, 2002). Many studies link strategy use to different measures of academic achievement, especially for middle school and high school students (Fredricks et al., 2004).

What Influences Self-Regulation? The concept of self-regulated learning integrates much of what is known about effective learning and motivation. As you can see from the processes described above, three factors influence skill and will: knowledge, motivation, and self-discipline or volition.

To be self-regulated learners, students need *knowledge* about themselves, the subject, the task, strategies for learning, and the contexts in which they will apply their learning. "Expert" students know about *themselves* and how they learn best. For example, they know what is easy and what is hard for them; how to cope with the difficult parts; what their interests and talents are; and how to use their strengths (see Chapter 4 of this book). These experts also know quite a bit about the *subject* being studied—and the more they know, the easier it is to learn more (Alexander, 2006). They probably understand that different *learning tasks* require different approaches on their part. A simple memory task, for example, might require a mnemonic strategy (see Chapter 7), whereas a complex comprehension task might be approached by means of concept maps of the key ideas (see Chapter 8). Also, these self-regulated learners know that learning is often difficult and knowledge is seldom absolute; there usually are different ways of looking at problems as well as different solutions (Pressley, 1995; Winne, 1995).

These expert students not only know what each task requires but can also apply the *strategy* needed. They can skim or read carefully. They can use memory strategies or reorganize the material. As they become more knowledgeable in a field, they apply many of these strategies automatically. In short, they have mastered a large, flexible repertoire of learning strategies and tactics (see Chapter 8).

Finally, expert learners think about the *contexts* in which they will apply their knowledge—when and where they will use their learning—so they can set motivating goals and connect present work to future accomplishments (Wang & Palincsar, 1989; Weinstein, 1994; Winne, 1995).

Self-regulated learners are *motivated* to learn (see Chapter 10). They find many tasks in school interesting because they value learning, not just performing

self-regulation Process of activating and sustaining thoughts, behaviours, and emotions in order to reach goals.

Connect & Extend

TO YOUR TEACHING
Take a look at The Learning Base (**www.allkindsofminds. org/library/challenges/ GTPSelfregulatingLearning. htm**) for tips to help students develop the goals, metacognitive skills, and self-regulatory practices that can support a lifelong devotion to learning.

Self-regulated learners have a combination of academic learning skills and self-control that makes learning easier; they have the skill and the will to learn.

volition Will power; self-discipline; work styles that protect opportunities to reach goals by applying self-regulated learning.

self-regulated learning A view of learning as skills and will applied to analyzing learning tasks, setting goals, and planning how to do the task, applying skills, and especially making adjustments about how learning is carried out.

agency The capacity to coordinate learning skills, motivation, and emotions to reach your goals.

well in the eyes of others. But even if they are not intrinsically motivated by a particular task, they are serious about getting the intended benefit from it. They know *why* they are studying, so their actions and choices are self-determined and not controlled by others. However, knowledge and motivation are not always enough. Self-regulated learners need volition or self-discipline. "Where motivation denotes commitment, volition denotes follow-through" (Corno, 1992, p. 72).

It is late Thursday morning. Nancy has been writing almost all day every day since last weekend. Because she's skimped on her exercise, her back is hurting but she wants to keep writing because the deadline for an article is very near. She has knowledge and motivation, but to keep going she needs a good dose of *volition.* **Volition** is an old-fashioned word for will power. The technical definition for volition is *protecting opportunities* to reach goals by applying self-regulated learning. Self-regulated learners know how to protect themselves from distractions—where to study, for example, so they are not interrupted. They know how to cope when they feel anxious, drowsy, or lazy (Corno, 1992, 1995; Snow, Corno, & Jackson, 1996). And they know what to do when tempted to stop working and have another cup of tea or play with their eager dog.

Obviously, not all your students will be expert self-regulated learners when it comes to academics. In fact, some psychologists suggest that you think of this capacity as one of many characteristics that distinguish individuals (Snow, Corno, & Jackson, 1996). Some students are much better at it than others. How can you help more students become self-regulated learners in school? What is involved in being self-regulated?

Models of Self-Regulated Learning and Agency. Models of **self-regulated learning** describe how learners—like you!—make choices among the skills they use to learn and how they manage factors that affect learning. There are several models (Puustinen & Pulkkinen, 2001). Let's look at one Phil and his colleague Allyson Hadwin developed (Winne & Hadwin, 1998), depicted in Figure 9.2. It has many facets, as it should when the topic at hand is how you manage your academic life.

This model is based on the position that learners are agents. **Agency** is the capacity to coordinate learning skills, motivation, and emotions to reach your goals. Agents are not puppets on strings held by teachers, textbook authors, or webpage designers. Instead, agents control many factors that influence how they learn. Self-regulating learners exercise agency as they engage in a cycle of four main stages: analyzing the task, setting goals and designing plans, engaging in learning, and adjusting their approach to learning.

1. *Analyzing the learning task.* You are familiar with this stage of self-regulated learning. What do you do when a professor announces there will be a test? You ask about conditions you believe will influence how you'll study. Is it essay or multiple choice? Is my best friend more up to date than I am? In general, learners examine whatever information they think is relevant in order to construct a sense of what the task is about, what resources to bring to bear, and how they feel about the work to be done.

2. *Setting goals and devising plans.* Knowing conditions that influence work on tasks provides information that learners use to create goals for learning. Then, plans can be developed about how to reach those goals. What goals for studying might you set for a quiz covering only one chapter that counts as just 3 percent of your course grade? Would your goals change if the test covered the last six chapters and counted as 30 percent of your course grade? What targets are identified in these goals—repeating definitions, being able to discuss how a teacher could apply findings from key research studies described in the textbook, or critiquing theoretical positions? Choosing goals affects the shape of a learner's plans for how to study. Is cramming (massed practice) the best approach? Is a better plan to study a half-hour each day, overlapping content a bit from one day to the next (distributed practice)?

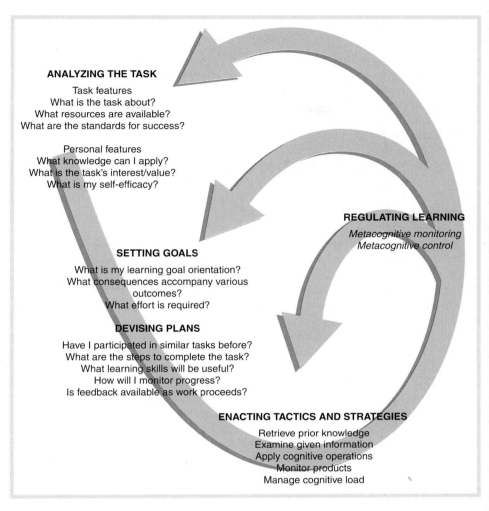

Figure 9.2 The Cycle of Self-Regulated Learning

ANALYZING THE TASK

Task features
What is the task about?
What resources are available?
What are the standards for success?

Personal features
What knowledge can I apply?
What is the task's interest/value?
What is my self-efficacy?

REGULATING LEARNING

Metacognitive monitoring
Metacognitive control

SETTING GOALS

What is my learning goal orientation?
What consequences accompany various outcomes?
What effort is required?

DEVISING PLANS

Have I participated in similar tasks before?
What are the steps to complete the task?
What learning skills will be useful?
How will I monitor progress?
Is feedback available as work proceeds?

ENACTING TACTICS AND STRATEGIES

Retrieve prior knowledge
Examine given information
Apply cognitive operations
Monitor products
Manage cognitive load

3. *Enacting tactics and strategies to accomplish the task.* Self-regulated learners are especially alert during this stage as they monitor how well the plan is working. This is metacognitive monitoring (see Chapter 7). Are you reaching your goals? Is the approach you take to learning too effortful for the results you are achieving? Is your progress rate fast enough to be prepared for the test?

4. *Regulating learning.* In this stage of self-regulated learning, learners make decisions about whether changes are needed in any of the three preceding stages. For example, if learning is slow: Should you study with your best friend? Do you need to review some prior material that provides foundations for the content you are now studying?

An Individual Example of Self-Regulated Learning. Students today are faced with constant distractions. Barry Zimmerman (2002, p. 64) describes Tracy, a high-school student who is devoted to MTV:

> An important mid-term math exam is two weeks away, and she had begun to study while listening to popular music "to relax her." Tracy has not set any study goals for herself—instead she simply tells herself to do as well as she can on the test. She uses no specific learning strategies for condensing and memorizing important material and does not plan out her study time, so she ends up cramming for a few hours before the test. She has only vague self-evaluative standards and cannot gauge her academic preparation accurately. Tracy attributes her learning difficulties to an inherent lack of mathematical ability and is very defensive about her poor study methods. However, she does not ask for help from others because she is afraid of "looking stupid," or seek out supplementary materials from the library because she "already has too much to learn."

She finds studying to be anxiety-provoking, has little self-confidence in achieving success, and sees little intrinsic value in acquiring mathematical skill.

Clearly, Tracy is unlikely to do well on the test. What would help? For an answer, let's consider Zimmerman's cycle of self-regulated learning. His cycle has three phases and is similar to the Winne and Hadwin model just described. In phase 1, the *forethought phase* (like Winne and Hadwin's steps 1 and 2 of analyzing the task and setting goals), Tracy needs to set clear, reasonable goals and plan a few strategies for accomplishing those goals. And Tracy's beliefs about motivation make a difference at this point too. If Tracy had a sense of self-efficacy for applying the strategies that she planned, if she believed that using those strategies would lead to math learning and success on the test, if she saw some connections between her own interests and the math learning, and if she were trying to master the material—not just look good or avoid looking bad—then she would be on the road to self-regulated learning.

Moving to phase 2, from the forethought to the *performance phase* (similar to Winne and Hadwin's step 3 of enacting the strategies), brings new challenges. Now Tracy must have a repertoire of self-control (volitional) and learning strategies, including using imagery, mnemonics, attention focusing, and other techniques such as those described in Chapters 7 and 8 (Kiewra, 2002). She will also need to self-observe, that is, monitor how things are going so that she can change strategies if needed. Actual recording of time spent, problems solved, or pages written may provide clues about when or how to make the best use of study time. Turning off the music would help, too.

Finally, Tracy needs to move to phase 3, similar to Winne and Hadwin's step 4 of regulating learning, by looking back on her performance and *reflecting* on what happened. It will help her develop a sense of efficacy if she attributes successes to effort and good strategy use and avoids self-defeating actions and beliefs such as making weak efforts, pretending not to care, or assuming she is "no good at math."

Both Zimmerman's and Winne and Hadwin's models emphasize the cyclical nature of self-regulated learning: Each phase flows into the next, and the cycle continues as students encounter new learning challenges. Both models begin with being informed about the task so that you can set good goals. Having a repertoire of learning strategies and tactics is also necessary in both models. And self-monitoring of progress followed by modifying plans if needed are critical to both. Notice also that the way students think about the task and their ability to do it—their sense of efficacy for self-regulation—is key as well.

A Classroom Example of Self-Regulated Learning.   Students differ in their self-regulation knowledge and skills. But teachers must work with an entire classroom, and still reach every student. Here is an example of a real situation where teachers did just that.

Lynn Fuchs and her colleagues (2003) assessed the value of incorporating self-regulated learning strategies into math problem-solving lessons in real classrooms. The researchers worked with 24 teachers. All the teachers taught the same content in their grade 3 classes. Some of these teachers (randomly chosen) taught in their usual way. Another randomly chosen group incorporated strategies to encourage problem-solving *transfer*—using skills and knowledge learned in the lessons to solve problems in other situations and classes. The third group of teachers added transfers and self-regulated learning strategies to their units on math problem solving. Here are a few of the transfer and self-regulated learning strategies taught:

- Using a key, students scored their homework and gave it to a homework collector (a peer).
- Students graphed their completion of homework on a class report.

- Students used individual thermometer graphs that were kept in folders to chart their daily scores on individual problems.
- At the beginning of each session, students inspected their previous charts and set goals to beat their previous scores.
- Students discussed with partners how they might apply problem-solving strategies outside class.
- Before some lessons, students reported to the group about how they had applied problem-solving skills outside class.

Both transfer and self-regulated learning strategies helped students learn mathematical problem solving and apply this knowledge to new problems. The addition of self-regulated learning strategies was especially effective when students were asked to solve problems that were very different from those they encountered in the lessons. Students at every achievement level as well as students with learning disabilities benefited from learning the strategies.

Families and Self-Regulated Learning. Children begin to learn self-regulation in their homes. Parents can teach and support self-regulated learning through modelling, encouragement, facilitation, rewarding of goal setting, good strategy use, and other processes described in the next section (Martinez-Pons, 2002). The following Guidelines give some ideas for helping students become more self-regulating.

GUIDELINES
SUPPORTING SELF-REGULATION

Emphasize the value of encouragement.

EXAMPLES

1. Teach students to encourage each other.
2. Tell parents about the areas that are most challenging for their child—the areas that will be the most in need of encouragement.

Model self-regulation.

EXAMPLES

1. Target small steps for improving an academic skill. Tailor goals to the student's current achievement level.
2. Discuss with your students how you set goals and monitor progress.
3. Ask parents to show their children how they set goals for the day or week, write to-do lists, or keep appointment books.

Make families a source of good strategy ideas.

EXAMPLES

1. Have short, simple materials describing a "strategy of the month" that students can practise at home.

2. Create a lending library of books about goal setting, motivation, learning, and time-management strategies for students.
3. Encourage families to help their children focus on problem-solving processes and not turn immediately to the answers at the back of the book when doing homework.

Provide self-evaluation guidelines.

EXAMPLES

1. Develop rubrics for self-evaluation with students (see Chapter 13). Model how to use them.
2. Provide record-keeping sheets for assignments early in the year, then gradually have students develop their own.
3. Encourage parents to model self-evaluation as they focus on areas they want to improve.
4. For parent conferences, have examples of materials other families have successfully used to keep track of progress.

For more ideas to share with parents, see - **www.pbs.org/wholechild/parents/building.html.**

Teaching toward Self-Efficacy and Self-Regulated Learning

Most teachers agree that students need to develop skills and attitudes for independent, life-long learning (self-regulated learning and a sense of efficacy for learning). Fortunately, there is a growing body of research that offers guidance about how to design tasks and structure classroom interactions to support students' development of and engagement in self-regulated learning (Neuman & Roskos, 1997; Perry, 1998; Turner, 1995; Wharton-McDonald et al., 1997; Zimmerman, 2002). This research indicates that students develop academically effective forms of self-regulated learning (SRL) and a sense of efficacy for learning when teachers involve them in complex meaningful tasks that extend over long periods of time, much like the constructivist activities described later in this chapter. Also, to develop self-regulated learning and self-efficacy for learning, students need to have some control over their learning processes and products—they need to make choices. And because self-monitoring and self-evaluation are key to effective SRL and a sense of efficacy, teachers can help students develop SRL by involving them in setting criteria for evaluating their learning processes and products, then giving them opportunities to make judgments about their progress using those standards. Finally, it helps to work collaboratively with peers and seek feedback from them. Let's examine each of these more closely.

To develop self-regulated learning and self-efficacy for learning, students need to have some control over their learning processes and products; teachers can help by involving students in evaluating their learning processes, products, and progress.

Complex Tasks. Teachers don't want to assign students tasks that are too difficult and that lead to frustration. This is especially true when students have learning difficulties or disabilities. In fact, research indicates that the most motivating and academically beneficial tasks for students are those that challenge, but don't overwhelm them (Rohrkemper & Corno, 1988; Turner, 1997); complex tasks need not be overly difficult for students.

The term *complex* refers to the design of tasks, not their level of difficulty. From a design point of view, tasks are complex when they address multiple goals and involve large chunks of meaning, such as projects and thematic units. Furthermore, complex tasks extend over long periods of time, engage students in a variety of cognitive and metacognitive processes, and allow for the production of a wide range of products (Perry et al., 2002; Wharton-McDonald et al., 1997). For example, a study of Egyptian pyramids might result in the production of written reports, maps, diagrams, and models.

Even more important, complex tasks provide students with information about their learning progress. These tasks require them to engage in deep, elaborative thinking and problem solving. In the process, students develop and refine their cognitive and metacognitive strategies. Furthermore, succeeding at such tasks increases students' self-efficacy and intrinsic motivation (McCaslin & Good, 1996; Turner, 1997). Rohrkemper and Corno (1988) advised teachers to design complex tasks that provide opportunities for students to modify the learning conditions in order to cope with challenging problems.

Learning to cope with stressful situations and make adaptations is an important educational goal. Remember from Chapter 4 that, according to Sternberg, one aspect of intelligence is choosing or adapting environments so that you can succeed.

Control. Teachers can share control with students by giving them choices. When students have choices (e.g., about what to produce, how to produce it, where to work, who to work with), they are more likely to anticipate a successful outcome (increased self-efficacy) and consequently increase effort and persist when difficulty arises (Turner & Paris, 1995). Also, by involving students in making decisions, teachers invite them to take responsibility for learning by planning, setting goals, monitoring progress, and evaluating outcomes (Turner, 1997). These are qualities of highly effective, self-regulating learners.

Giving students choices creates opportunities for them to adjust the level of challenge that particular tasks present (e.g., they can choose easy or more challenging reading materials, determine the nature and amount of writing in a report, supplement writing with other expressions of learning). But what if students make poor academic choices? Highly effective, high-SRL teachers carefully consider the choices they give to students. They make sure students have the knowledge and skills they need to operate independently and make good decisions (Perry & Drummond, 2002). For example, when students are learning new skills or routines, teachers can offer choices with constraints (e.g., students must write a minimum of four sentences/paragraphs/pages, but they can choose to write more; they must demonstrate their understanding of an animal's habitat, food, and babies, but they can write, draw, or speak their knowledge).

Highly effective teachers also teach and model good decision making. For example, when students are choosing partners, these teachers ask them to consider what they need from their partner (e.g., shared interest and commitment, perhaps knowledge or skills that they need to develop). When students are making choices about how best to use their time, these teachers ask, "What can you do when you're finished? What can you do if you're waiting for my help?" Often, lists are generated and posted so that students can refer to them while they work. Finally, highly effective teachers give students feedback about the choices they make and tailor the choices they give to suit the unique characteristics of particular learners. For example, they might encourage some students to select research topics for which resources are readily available and written at a level that is accessible to the learner. Alternatively, they might encourage some students to work collaboratively versus independently to ensure they have the support they need to be successful.

Self-Evaluation.   Evaluation practices that support SRL are non-threatening. They are embedded in ongoing activities, emphasize process as well as products, focus on personal progress, and help students interpret errors as opportunities for learning to occur. In these contexts, students enjoy and actually seek challenging tasks because the cost of participation is low (Paris & Ayres, 1994). Involving students in generating evaluation criteria and evaluating their own work also reduces the anxiety that often accompanies assessment by giving students a sense of control over the outcome. Students can judge their work in relation to a set of qualities that both they and their teachers identify as "good" work. They can consider the effectiveness of their approaches to learning and alter their behaviours in ways that enhance it (Winne & Perry, 2000).

In high-SRL classrooms, there are both formal and informal opportunities for students to evaluate their learning. For example, in a study Nancy did with colleagues, one student teacher asked grade 4 and 5 students to submit reflections journals describing the games they designed with a partner or small group of collaborators in a probability and statistics unit (Perry, Phillips, & Dowler, 2004). Their journals explained their contribution to the group's process and product, and described what they learned from participating. The student teacher took these reflections into account when she evaluated the games. More informally, teachers ask students, "What have you learned about yourself as a writer today?" "What do good researchers and writers do?" "What can we do that we couldn't do before?" Questions like these, posed to individuals or embedded in class discussions, prompt students' metacognition, motivation, and strategic action—the components of SRL.

Collaboration.   The *Committee on Increasing High School Students' Motivation to Learn* (2004) concluded that when students can put their heads together, they are more receptive to challenging assignments—the very kind of complex task that develops self-regulation. The Committee added,

> Collaborative work also can help students develop skills in cooperation. Furthermore, it helps create a community of learners who have responsibility for each other's learning, rather than a competitive environment, which is alienating to many students, particularly those who do not perform as well as their classmates. (p. 51)

The most effective uses of cooperative/collaborative relationships to support SRL are those that reflect a climate of community and shared problem solving (Perry & Drummond, 2002; Perry et al., 2002). In these contexts, teachers and students actually co-regulate one another's learning (McCaslin & Good, 1996), offering support, whether working alone, in pairs, or small groups. This support is instrumental to individuals' development and use of metacognition, intrinsic motivation, and strategic action (e.g., sharing ideas, comparing strategies for solving problems, identifying *everyone's* area of expertise). High-SRL teachers spend time at the start of each school year teaching routines and establishing norms of participation (e.g., how to give constructive feedback and how to interpret and respond to peers' suggestions). As you will see in Chapter 12, developing useful management and learning procedures and routines takes time in the beginning of the year, but it is time well spent. Once routines and patterns of interaction are established, students can focus on learning and teachers can attend to teaching academic skills and the curriculum.

The last element of teaching for self-regulation, collaboration, is an important ingredient in constructivist learning. We will spend the rest of the chapter exploring more closely this important and very current perspective.

Check Your Knowledge

- How does efficacy affect motivation?
- What is teacher's sense of efficacy?
- What factors are involved in self-regulated learning?
- What is the self-regulated learning cycle?
- How can teachers support the development of self-efficacy and self-regulated learning?

Apply to Practice

- How can you use questioning to help students become more effective at self-regulating learning?
- What kinds of information could you include in feedback on students' assignments to promote self-regulated learning?

COGNITIVE AND SOCIAL CONSTRUCTIVISM

Consider this situation:

> A young child who has never been to hospital is in her bed in the pediatric wing. The nurse at the station down the hall calls over the intercom above the bed, "Hi Chelsea, how are you doing? Do you need anything?" The girl looks puzzled and does not answer. The nurse repeats the question with the same result. Finally, the nurse says emphatically, "Chelsea, are you there? Say something!" The little girl responds tentatively, "Hello wall—I'm here."

Connect & Extend

TO THE RESEARCH
The 2000 Yearbook of the National Society for the Study of Education (NSSE) is devoted to the examination of constructivism. Phillips, D. C. (Ed.) (2000). *Constructivism in education: Opinions and second opinions on controversial issues.* Chicago, IL: University of Chicago Press.

Chelsea encountered a new situation—a talking wall. The wall is persistent. It sounds like a grown-up wall. She shouldn't talk to strangers, but she is not sure about walls. She uses what she knows and what the situation provides to construct meaning and to act.

Here is another example of constructing meaning taken from Berk (2001, p. 31). This time, a father and his four-year-old son co-construct understandings as they walk along a beach, collecting litter after a busy day:

Ben: (*running ahead and calling out*) Some bottles and cans. I'll get them.

Mel: If the bottles are broken, you could cut yourself, so let me get them. (*Catches up and holds out the bag as Ben drops items in*)

Ben: Dad, look at this shell. It's a whole one, really big. Colors all inside!

Mel: Hmmm, might be an abalone shell.

Ben:	What's abalone?
Mel:	Do you remember what I had in my sandwich on the wharf yesterday? That's abalone.
Ben:	You eat it?
Mel:	Well, you can. You eat a meaty part that the abalone uses to stick to rocks.
Ben:	Ewww. I don't want to eat it. Can I keep the shell?
Mel:	I think so. Maybe you can find some things in your room to put in it. (*Points to the shell's colors*) Sometimes people make jewelry out of these shells.
Ben:	Like mom's necklace?
Mel:	That's right. Mom's necklace is made out of a kind of abalone with a very colorful shell—pinks, purples, blues. It's called Paua. When you turn it, the colors change.
Ben:	Wow! Let's look for Paua shells!
Mel:	You can't find them here, only in New Zealand.
Ben:	Where's that? Have you been there?
Mel:	No, someone brought Mom the necklace as a gift. But I'll show you New Zealand on the globe. It's far away, halfway around the world.

Look at the knowledge being co-constructed about sea creatures and their uses for food or decoration; safety; environmental responsibility; and even geography. Constructivist theories of learning focus on how people make meaning, both on their own like Chelsea and in interaction with others like Ben.

Constructivist Views of Learning

Constructivism is a broad term used by philosophers, curriculum designers, psychologists, educators, and others. Ernst Von Glasersfeld calls it "a vast and woolly area in contemporary psychology, epistemology, and education" (1997, p. 204). Constructivist perspectives are grounded in the research of Piaget, Vygotsky, the Gestalt psychologists, Bartlett, and Bruner as well as the philosophy of John Dewey, to mention just a few intellectual roots.

There is no one constructivist theory of learning, but "most constructivists share two main ideas: that learners are active in constructing their own knowledge and

constructivism View that emphasizes the active role of the learner in building understanding and making sense of information.

Constructivist theories are based on the ideas that learners actively develop their knowledge, rather than passively receive it, in package form, from teachers or outside sources.

that social interactions are important to knowledge construction" (Bruning et al., 2004, p. 195). Constructivism views learning as more than receiving and processing information transmitted by teachers or texts. Rather, learning is the active and personal construction of knowledge (de Kock, Sleegers, and Voeten, 2004). Thus, many theories in cognitive science include some kind of constructivism because these theories assume that individuals construct their own cognitive structures as they interpret their experiences in particular situations (Palincsar, 1998). There are constructivist approaches in science and mathematics education, in educational psychology and anthropology, and in computer-based education. Even though many psychologists and educators use the term *constructivism*, they often mean very different things (Driscoll, 2005; McCaslin & Hickey, 2001; Phillips, 1997).

One way to organize constructivist views is to talk about two forms of constructivism: psychological and social construction (Palincsar, 1998; Phillips, 1997). We could oversimplify a bit and say that psychological constructivists focus on how individuals use information, resources, and even help from others to build and improve their mental models and problem-solving strategies. In contrast, social constructivists see learning as increasing our abilities to participate with others in activities that are meaningful in the culture (Windschitl, 2002). Let's look a bit closer at each type of constructivism.

Psychological/Individual Constructivism. Psychological constructivists "are concerned with how *individuals* build up certain elements of their cognitive or emotional apparatus" (Phillips, 1997, p. 153). These constructivists are interested in individual knowledge, beliefs, self-concept, or identity, so they are sometimes called *individual* constructivists or *cognitive* constructivists; they all focus on the inner psychological life of people. When Chelsea talked to the wall in the previous section, she was making meaning using her own individual knowledge and beliefs about how to respond when someone (or something) talks to you. She was using what she knew to impose intellectual structure on her world (Piaget, 1971; Windschitl, 2002).

Using these standards, the most recent information processing theories are constructivist (Mayer, 1996). Information processing approaches to learning regard the human mind as a symbol processing system. This system converts sensory input into symbol structures (propositions, images, or schemas), and then processes (rehearses or elaborates) those symbol structures so that knowledge can be held in memory and retrieved. The outside world is seen as a source of input, but once the sensations are perceived and enter working memory, the important work is assumed to be happening "inside the head" of the individual (Schunk, 2000; Vera & Simon, 1993). Some psychologists, however, believe that information processing is "trivial" or "weak" constructivism because the individual's only constructive contribution is to build accurate representations of the outside world (Derry, 1992; Garrison, 1995; Marshall, 1996; Windschitl, 2002).

In contrast, Piaget's psychological (cognitive) constructivist perspective is less concerned with "correct" representations and more interested in meaning as constructed by the individual. As we saw in Chapter 2, Piaget proposed a sequence of cognitive stages that all humans pass through. Thinking at each stage builds on and incorporates previous stages as it becomes more organized and adaptive and less tied to concrete events. Piaget's special concern was with logic and the construction of universal knowledge that cannot be learned directly from the environment—knowledge such as conservation or reversibility (Miller, 2002). Such knowledge comes from reflecting on and coordinating our own cognitions or thoughts, not from mapping external reality. Piaget saw the social environment as an important factor in development, but did not believe that social interaction was the main mechanism for changing thinking (Moshman, 1997). Some educational and developmental psychologists have referred to Piaget's kind of constructivism as **first wave constructivism** or "solo" constructivism, with its emphasis on individual meaning-making (De Corte, Greer, and Verschaffel, 1996; Paris, Byrnes, & Paris, 2001).

At the extreme end of individual constructivism is the notion of **radical constructivism**. This perspective holds that there is no reality or truth in the world,

first wave constructivism A focus on the individual and psychological sources of knowing, as in Piaget's theory.

radical constructivism Knowledge is assumed to be the individual's construction; it cannot be judged right or wrong.

only the individual's perceptions and beliefs. Each of us constructs meaning from our own experiences, but we have no way of understanding or "knowing" the reality of others (Woods & Murphy, 2002). A difficulty with this position is that, when pushed to the extreme of relativism, all knowledge and all beliefs are equally valid (or wrong!) because they are individual perceptions. There are problems with this thinking for educators. First, teachers have a professional responsibility to emphasize some values, such as honesty or justice, over others, such as bigotry and deception. All perceptions and beliefs are not equal in our culture. As teachers, we ask students to work hard to learn. If learning cannot advance understanding because all understandings are equally acceptable, then, as David Moshman (1997) notes, "we might just as well let students continue to believe whatever they believe" (p. 230) and let education go by the boards. Also, it appears that some knowledge, such as counting and one-to-one correspondence, is not constructed, but universal. Knowing one-to-one correspondence is part of being human (Geary, 1995; Schunk, 2000).

"Maybe it's not a wrong answer—maybe it's just a different answer."

"MAYBE IT'S NOT A WRONG ANSWER—MAYBE IT'S JUST A DIFFERENT ANSWER."
© The New Yorker Collection 2001 Barbara G. Smaller from cartoonbank.com. All rights reserved. Reprinted by permission.

Vygotsky's Social Constructivism. As you also saw in Chapter 2, Vygotsky believed that social interaction, cultural tools, and activity shape individual development and learning, just as Ben's interactions on the beach with his father shaped Ben's learning about sea creatures, safety, environmental responsibility, and geography. By participating in a broad range of activities with others, learners **appropriate** (internalize or take for themselves) the outcomes produced by working together; these outcomes could include both new strategies and knowledge. Putting learning in social and cultural context is **second wave constructivism** (Paris, Byrnes, & Paris, 2001).

Because Vygotsky's theory relies heavily on social interactions and the cultural context to explain learning, most psychologists classify him as a social constructivist (Palincsar, 1998; Prawat, 1996). However, some theorists categorize him as a psychological constructivist because he was primarily interested in development within the individual (Moshman, 1997; Phillips, 1997). In a sense, Vygotsky was both. One advantage of his theory of learning is that it gives us a way to consider both the psychological and the social: He bridges both camps. For example, Vygotsky's concept of the zone of proximal development—the area where a child can solve a problem with the help (scaffolding) of an adult or more able peer—has been called a place where culture and cognition create each other (Cole, 1985). Culture creates cognition when the adult uses tools and practices from the culture (language, maps, computers, looms, or music) to guide the child toward goals the culture values (reading, writing, weaving, dance). Cognition creates culture as the adult and child together generate new practices and problem solutions to add to the cultural group's repertoire (Serpell, 1993). One way of integrating individual and social constructivism is to think of knowledge as individually constructed and socially mediated (Windschitl, 2002).

The term *constructionism* is sometimes used to talk about how public knowledge is created. Although this is not our main concern in educational psychology, it is worth a quick look.

Constructionism. Social constructionists do not focus on individual learning. Their concern is how public knowledge in disciplines such as science, math, economics, and history is constructed in the public sphere. Beyond this kind of academic knowledge, constructionists are also interested in how common-sense ideas, everyday beliefs, and commonly held understandings about people and the world are communicated to new members of a sociocultural group (Gergen, 1997; Phillips, 1997). Questions raised might include who determines what constitutes history, what is the proper way to behave in public, or how to get elected class

appropriate Internalize or take for yourself knowledge and skills developed in interaction with others or with cultural tools.

second wave constructivism A focus on the social and cultural sources of knowing, as in Vygotsky's theory.

president. In this view, all knowledge is socially constructed, and, more important, some people have more power than others to define what constitutes such knowledge. Relationships between and among teachers, students, families, and the community are the central issues. Collaboration to understand diverse viewpoints is encouraged, and traditional bodies of knowledge often are challenged (Gergen, 1997). The philosophies of Jacques Derrida and Michel Foucault are important sources for constructionists. Vygotsky's theory, with its attention to how cognition creates culture, has some elements in common with constructionism.

These different perspectives on constructivism raise some general questions, and disagree on the answers. These questions can never be fully resolved, but different theories tend to favour different positions. Let's consider the questions.

How Is Knowledge Constructed?

One tension among different approaches to constructivism is based on *how* knowledge is constructed. Moshman (1982) describes three explanations:

1. *The realities and truths of the external world direct knowledge construction.* Individuals *reconstruct* outside reality by building accurate mental representations such as propositional networks, concepts, cause-and-effect patterns, and condition-action production rules that reflect "the way things really are." The more the person learns, the deeper and broader his or her experience is, the closer that person's knowledge will reflect objective reality. Information processing holds this view of knowledge (Cobb & Bowers, 1999).

2. *Internal processes such as Piaget's organization, assimilation, and accommodation direct knowledge construction.* New knowledge is abstracted from old knowledge. Knowledge is not a mirror of reality, but rather an abstraction that grows and develops with cognitive activity. Knowledge is not true or false; it just grows more internally consistent and organized with development.

3. *Both external and internal factors direct knowledge construction.* Knowledge grows through the *interactions* of internal (cognitive) and external (environmental and social) factors. Vygotsky's description of cognitive development through the appropriation and use of cultural tools such as language is consistent with this view (Bruning et al., 2004). Another example is Bandura's theory of reciprocal interactions among people, behaviours, and environments (Schunk, 2000). Table 9.1 summarizes the three general explanations about how knowledge is constructed.

TABLE 9.1 How Knowledge Is Constructed

Type	Assumptions about Learning and Knowledge	Example Theories
External Direction	Knowledge is acquired by constructing a representation of the outside world. Direct teaching, feedback, and explanation affect learning. Knowledge is accurate to the extent that it reflects the "way things really are" in the outside world.	Information processing
Internal Direction	Knowledge is constructed by transforming, organizing, and reorganizing previous knowledge. Knowledge is not a mirror of the external world, even though experience influences thinking and thinking influences knowledge. Exploration and discovery are more important than teaching.	Piaget
Both External and Internal Direction	Knowledge is constructed based on social interactions and experience. Knowledge reflects the outside world filtered through and influenced by culture, language, beliefs, interactions with others, direct teaching, and modelling. Guided discovery, teaching, models, and coaching as well as the individual's prior knowledge, beliefs, and thinking affect learning.	Vygotsky

Knowledge: Situated or General?

A second question that cuts across many constructivist perspectives is whether knowledge is internal, general, and transferable; or whether it is bound to the time and place in which it is constructed. Psychologists who emphasize the social construction of knowledge and situated learning affirm Vygotsky's notion that learning is inherently social and tied to a particular cultural setting (Cobb & Bowers, 1999). What is true in one time and place—such as the "fact" before Columbus's time that the earth was flat—becomes false in another time and place. Particular ideas may be useful within a specific **community of practice**, such as 15th-century navigation, but useless outside that community. What counts as new knowledge is determined in part by how well the new idea fits with current accepted practice. Over time, the current practice may be questioned and even overthrown, but until such major shifts occur, current practice will shape what is considered valuable.

Situated learning emphasizes that learning in the real world is not like studying in school. It is more like an apprenticeship where novices, with the support of an expert guide and model, take on more and more responsibility until they are able to function independently. Proponents of this view believe that situated learning explains learning in factories, around the dinner table, in high school halls, in street gangs, in the business office, and on the playground.

Situated learning is often described as "enculturation," which means adopting the norms, behaviours, skills, beliefs, language, and attitudes of a particular community. The community might be mathematicians or gang members or writers or students in your grade 8 class or soccer players—any group that has particular ways of thinking and doing. Knowledge is seen *not* as individual cognitive structures but as a creation of the community over time. The practices of the community—the ways of interacting and getting things done, as well as the tools the community has created—constitute the knowledge of that community. Learning means becoming more able to participate in those practices, use the tools, and take on the identity of a member of the community (Derry, 1992; Garrison, 1995; Greeno, Collins, & Resnick, 1996; Rogoff, 1998).

At the most basic level, "situated learning emphasizes the idea that much of what is learned is specific to the situation in which it is learned" (Anderson, Reder, & Simon, 1996, p. 5). Thus, some would argue, learning to do calculations in school may help students do more school calculations, but it may not help them balance a chequebook, because the skills can be applied only in the context in which they were learned, namely school (Lave, 1997; Lave & Wenger, 1991). But it also appears that knowledge and skills can be applied across contexts that were not part of the initial learning situation, as when you use your ability to read and calculate to do your income taxes, even though income tax forms were not part of your high school curriculum (Anderson, Reder, & Simon, 1996).

Learning that is situated in school does not have to be doomed or irrelevant (Bereiter, 1997). As you saw in Chapter 8, a major question in educational psychology and education in general concerns the *transfer* of knowledge from one situation to another. How can you encourage this transfer? Help is on the way in the next section.

Common Elements of Constructivist Perspectives

We have looked at some areas of disagreement among the constructivist perspectives, but what about areas of agreement? All constructivist theories assume that knowing develops as learners, like Chelsea and Ben, try to make sense of their experiences. "Learners, therefore, are not empty vessels waiting to be filled, but rather active organisms seeking meaning" (Driscoll, 2005, p. 487). These learners construct mental models or schemas and continue to revise them to make better sense of their experiences. Their constructions do not necessarily resemble external reality; rather, they are the unique interpretations of the learner, like Chelsea's friendly, persistent wall. This doesn't mean that all constructions are equally useful

community of practice Social situation or context in which ideas are judged useful or true.

situated learning The idea that skills and knowledge are tied to the situation in which they were learned and difficult to apply in new settings.

Connect & Extend

TO THE RESEARCH
For more on constructivism and education, see Marshall, H. H. (Ed.) (1992). *Redefining student learning: Roots of educational change*. Norwood, NJ: Ablex.

Constructivist approaches recommend that educators emphasize complex, realistic, and relevant learning environments, as well as the importance of social interactions in the learning process. For example, the students here are collaborating to create a household budget.

or viable. Learners test their understandings against experience and the understandings of other people—they negotiate and co-construct meanings, as Ben did with his father.

Constructivists share similar goals for learning. They emphasize knowledge in use rather than the storing of inert facts, concepts, and skills. Learning goals include developing abilities to find and solve ill-structured problems, critical thinking, inquiry, self-determination, and openness to multiple perspectives (Driscoll, 2005).

Even though there is no single constructivist theory, many constructivist approaches recommend five conditions for learning:

1. Embed learning in complex, realistic, and relevant learning environments.
2. Provide for social negotiation and shared responsibility as a part of learning.
3. Support multiple perspectives and use multiple representations of content.
4. Nurture self-awareness and an understanding that knowledge is constructed.
5. Encourage ownership in learning. (Driscoll, 2005; Marshall, 1992)

Before we discuss particular teaching approaches, let's look more closely at these dimensions of constructivist teaching.

Complex Learning Environments and Authentic Tasks.   Constructivists believe that students should not be given stripped-down, simplified problems and basic skills drills, but instead should encounter **complex learning environments** that deal with authentic, "fuzzy," ill-structured problems. The world beyond school presents few simple problems or step-by-step directions, so schools should be sure that *every* student has experience solving problems like these. Complex problems are not simply difficult ones; they have many parts. There are multiple, interacting elements in complex problems and multiple solutions are possible. There is no one right way to reach a conclusion, and each solution may bring a new set of problems. These complex problems should be embedded in real tasks and activities, the kinds of situations that students will face as they apply what they are learning to the real world (Needles & Knapp, 1994). Students may need support as they work on these complex problems, with teachers helping them find resources, keeping track of their progress, breaking larger problems down into smaller ones, and so on. This aspect of constructivist approaches is consistent with self-regulation and situated learning in emphasizing learning in *situations* where the learning will be applied.

complex learning environments Problems and learning situations that mimic the ill-structured nature of real life.

Social Negotiation. Many constructivists share Vygotsky's belief that higher mental processes develop through **social negotiation** and interaction, so collaboration in learning is valued. The Language Development and Hypermedia Group (1992) suggests that a major goal of teaching is to develop students' abilities to establish and defend their own positions while respecting the positions of others and working together to negotiate or co-construct meaning. To accomplish this exchange, students must talk and listen to each other. It is a challenge for children in cultures that are individualistic and competitive, such as Canada and the United States, to adopt what has been called an **intersubjective attitude**—a commitment to build shared meaning by finding common ground and exchanging interpretations.

Multiple Perspectives and Representations of Content. When students encounter only one model, one analogy, one way of understanding complex content, they often oversimplify as they try to apply that one approach to every situation. Anita saw this happen in her educational psychology class when six students were presenting an example of guided discovery learning. The students' presentation was a near copy of a guided discovery demonstration given earlier in the semester, but with some major misconceptions. Anita's students knew only one way to represent discovery learning. Resources for the class should have provided **multiple representations of content** using different analogies, examples, and metaphors.

Rand Spiro and his colleagues (1991) suggest that "revisiting the same material, at different times, in rearranged contexts, for different purposes, and from different conceptual perspectives is essential for attaining the goals of advanced knowledge acquisition" (p. 28). This idea is consistent with Jerome Bruner's (1966) **spiral curriculum**, a structure for teaching that introduces the fundamental structure of all subjects—the "big ideas"—early in the school years, then revisits the subjects in more and more complex forms over time.

Understanding the Knowledge Construction Process. Constructivist approaches emphasize making students aware of their own role in constructing knowledge (Cunningham, 1992). The assumptions we make, our beliefs, and our experiences shape what each of us comes to "know" about the world. Different assumptions and different experiences lead to different knowledge. If students are aware of the influences that shape their thinking, they will be more able to choose, develop, and defend positions in a self-critical way while respecting the positions of others.

Student Ownership of Learning. "While there are several interpretations of what [constructivist] theory means, most agree that it involves a dramatic change in the focus of teaching, putting the students' own efforts to understand at the center of the educational enterprise" (Prawat, 1992, p. 357). Student ownership does not mean that the teacher abandons responsibility for instruction. Because the design of teaching is a central issue in this book, we will spend the rest of this chapter discussing examples of ownership of learning and student-centred instruction.

Check Your Knowledge

- Describe two kinds of constructivism, and distinguish these from constructionism.
- In what ways do constructivist views differ about knowledge sources, accuracy, and generality?
- What are some common elements in most constructivist views of learning?

Apply to Practice

- Explain how a constructivist approach might be used to help the students described at the beginning of the chapter write better book reviews.

---

social negotiation Aspect of learning process that relies on collaboration with others and respect for different perspectives.

intersubjective attitude A commitment to build shared meaning with others by finding common ground and exchanging interpretations.

multiple representations of content Considering problems using various analogies, examples, and metaphors.

spiral curriculum Bruner's design for teaching that introduces the fundamental structure of all subjects early in the school years, then revisits the subjects in more and more complex forms over time.

Connect & Extend

TO PRACTICE
Many of the major initiatives to reform content-area curricula (e.g., science, mathematics) emphasize student-centred/constructivist approaches to learning. Describe the major principles of these approaches and explain how they differ from teacher-centred approaches.

APPLYING CONSTRUCTIVIST PERSPECTIVES

Connect & Extend

TO THE RESEARCH

Confrey, J. (1990). What constructivism implies for teaching. In R. Davis, C. Maher, & N. Noddings (Eds.), *Constructivist views on the teaching and learning of mathematics* (pp. 107–122). Monograph 4 of the National Council of Teachers of Mathematics, Reston, VA.

Even though there are many applications of constructivist views of learning, we can recognize constructivist approaches by the activities of the teacher and the students. Mark Windschitl (2002) suggests that the following activities encourage meaningful learning:

- Teachers elicit students' ideas and experiences in relation to key topics, then fashion learning situations that help students elaborate on or restructure their current knowledge.
- Students are given frequent opportunities to engage in complex, meaningful, problem-based activities.
- Teachers provide students with a variety of information resources as well as the tools (technological and conceptual) necessary to mediate learning.
- Students work collaboratively and are given support to engage in task-oriented dialogue with one another.
- Teachers make their own thinking processes explicit to learners and encourage students to do the same through dialogue, writing, drawings, or other representations.
- Students are routinely asked to apply knowledge in diverse and authentic contexts, to explain ideas, interpret texts, predict phenomena, and construct arguments based on evidence, rather than to focus exclusively on the acquisition of predetermined "right answers."
- Teachers encourage students' reflective and autonomous thinking in conjunction with the conditions listed above.
- Teachers employ a variety of assessment strategies to understand how students' ideas are evolving and to give feedback on the processes as well as the products of their thinking. (p. 137)

In this section, we will examine three specific teaching approaches that put the student at the centre: inquiry and problem-based learning, dialogue and instructional conversations, and cognitive apprenticeships. Two other approaches consistent with constructivism are cooperative learning, presented in Chapter 11, and conceptual change, discussed in Chapter 12.

Inquiry and Problem-Based Learning

inquiry learning Approach in which the teacher presents a puzzling situation and students solve the problem by gathering data and testing their conclusions.

John Dewey described the basic **inquiry learning** format in 1910. There have been many adaptations of this strategy, but the form usually includes the following elements (Echevarria, 2003; Lashley, Matczynski, & Rowley, 2002). The teacher presents a puzzling event, question, or problem. The students

- formulate hypotheses to explain the event or solve the problem,
- collect data to test the hypotheses,
- draw conclusions, and
- reflect on the original problem and the thinking processes needed to solve it.

Connect & Extend

TO PRACTICE

Inquiry learning is a student-centred approach to learning that predates many "traditional" forms of instruction. Describe the basic structure of this approach to learning. What are its strengths and limitations? What roles does the teacher have?

Examples of Inquiry.   In one kind of inquiry, teachers present a problem and students ask yes/no questions to gather data and test hypotheses. This allows the teacher to monitor students' thinking and guide the process. Here is an example:

1. *Teacher presents discrepant event* (after clarifying ground rules). The teacher blows softly across the top of an 8 ½" × 11" sheet of paper, and the paper rises. She tells students to figure out why it rises.

2. *Students ask questions* to gather more information and to isolate relevant variables. Teacher answers only "yes" or "no." Students ask if temperature is important (no). They ask if the paper is of a special kind (no). They ask if air pressure has anything to do with the paper rising (yes). Questions continue.

3. *Students test causal relationships.* In this case, they ask if the nature of the air on top causes the paper to rise (yes). They ask if the fast movement of the air results in less pressure on the top (yes). Then they test out the rule with other materials—for example, thin plastic.

4. *Students form a generalization* (principle): "If the air on the top moves faster than the air on the bottom of a surface, then the air pressure on top is lessened, and the object rises." Later lessons expand students' understanding of the principles and physical laws through further experiments.

5. *The teacher leads students in a discussion of their thinking processes.* What were the important variables? How did you put the causes and effects together? and so on. (Pasch et al., 1991, pp. 188–189)

Shirley Magnusson and Annemarie Palincsar have developed a teachers' guide for planning, implementing, and assessing different phases of inquiry science units (Palincsar et al., 1998). The model, called *Guided Inquiry Supporting Multiple Literacies,* or GIsML, is shown in Figure 9.3.

The teacher first identifies a curriculum area and some general guiding questions, puzzles, or problems. For example, an elementary teacher chooses communication as the area and asks this general question: "How and why do humans and animals communicate?" Next, several specific focus questions are posed. "How do whales communicate?" "How do gorillas communicate?" The focus questions have to be carefully chosen to guide students toward important understandings. One key idea in understanding animal communication is the relationship among the animal's structures, survival functions, and habitat. Animals have specific structures such as large ears or echo-locators, which function to find food or attract mates or identify predators, and these structures and functions are related to the animals' habitats. Thus, focus questions must ask about animals with different structures for communication, different functional needs for survival, and different habitats. Questions about animals with the same kinds of structures or the same habitats would not be good focus points for inquiry (Magnusson & Palincsar, 1995).

The next phase is to engage students in the inquiry, perhaps by playing different animal sounds, having students make guesses and claims about communication, and asking the students questions about their guesses and claims. Then, the

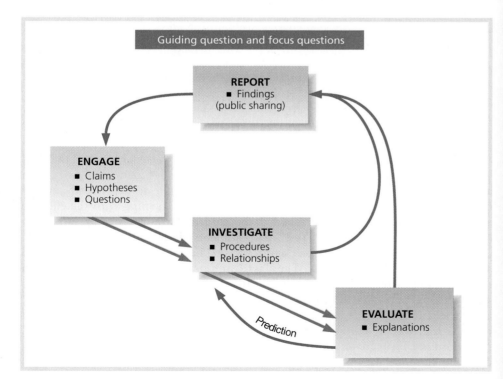

Figure 9.3 A Model to Guide Teacher Thinking about Inquiry-Based Science Instruction

The straight lines show the sequence of phases in instruction and the curved lines show cycles that might be repeated during instruction.

Source: From Palincsar, A. S., Magnusson, S. J., Marano, N., Ford, D., and Brown, N. (1998). Designing a community of practice: Principles and practices of the GisML community. *Teaching and Teacher Education, 14,* p. 12. Adapted with permission.

students conduct both first-hand and second-hand investigations. First-hand investigations are direct experiences and experiments, for example, measuring the size of bats' eyes and ears in relation to their bodies (using pictures or videos—not real bats!). In second-hand investigations, students consult books, the internet, interviews with experts, and other resources to find specific information or get new ideas. As part of their investigating, the students begin to identify patterns. The curved line in Figure 9.3 shows that cycles can be repeated. In fact, students might go through several cycles of investigating, identifying patterns, and reporting results before moving on to constructing explanations and making final reports. Another possible cycle is to evaluate explanations before reporting by making and then checking predictions, applying the explanation to new situations.

Inquiry teaching allows students to learn content and process at the same time. In the examples we've discussed, students learned about the effects of air pressure, how airplanes fly, how animals communicate, and how structures are related to habitats. In addition, they learned the inquiry process itself—how to solve problems, evaluate solutions, and think critically.

problem-based learning Methods that provide students with realistic problems that don't necessarily have "right" answers.

Problem-Based Learning. The goals of **problem-based learning** are to help students develop flexible knowledge that can be applied in many situations, in contrast to inert knowledge. Inert knowledge is information that is memorized but seldom applied (Cognition and Technology Group at Vanderbilt [CTGV], 1996; Whitehead, 1929). Other goals of problem-based learning are to enhance intrinsic motivation and skills in problem solving, collaboration, and self-directed life-long learning. In problem-based learning, students are confronted with a problem that launches their inquiry as they collaborate to find solutions. The process of problem-based learning is similar to the GIsML, shown in Figure 9.3. The students are confronted with a problem scenario; they identify and analyze the problem based on the facts from the scenario; and then they begin to generate hypotheses about solutions. As they suggest hypotheses, they identify missing information—what do they need to know to test their solutions? This launches a phase of self-directed learning and research. Then, students apply their new knowledge, evaluate their problem solutions, recycle to research again if necessary, and finally reflect on the knowledge and skills they have gained (Hmelo-Silver, 2004).

In true problem-based learning, the problem is real and the students' actions matter. In one example, a teacher capitalized on current affairs to encourage student reading, writing, and social studies problem solving:

> Cathie's elementary class learned about the Alaskan oil spill. She brought a newspaper article to class that sequenced in logbook fashion the events of the oil spill in Prince William Sound. To prepare her students to understand the article, she had her students participate in several background-building experiences. First, they used a world map, an encyclopedia, and library books to gather and share relevant information. Next, she simulated an oil spill by coating an object with oil. By then, the class was eager to read the article. (Espe, Worner, & Hotkevich, 1990, p. 45)

After they read and discussed the newspaper article, the teacher asked the class to imagine how the problem might have been prevented. Students had to explain and support their proposed solutions. The next week, the students read another newspaper article about how people in their state were helping with the cleanup efforts in Alaska. The teacher asked if the students wanted to help, and they replied with an enthusiastic "Yes!" The students designed posters and made speeches requesting donations of clean towels to be used to clean the oil-soaked animals in Prince William Sound. The class sent four large bags of towels to Alaska to help in the cleanup. The teacher's and the students' reading, writing, research, and speaking were directed toward solving a real-life problem (Espe, Worner, & Hotkevich, 1990). Other authentic problems that might be the focus for student projects are reducing pollution in local rivers, resolving student conflicts in school, raising money for tsunami or hurricane relief, or building a playground for young children. The teacher's role in problem-based learning is summarized in Table 9.2.

TABLE 9.2 The Teacher's Role in Problem-Based Learning

Phase	Teacher Behaviour
Phase 1 Orient students to the problem	Teacher goes over the objectives of the lesson, describes important logistical requirements, and motivates students to engage in self-selected problem-solving activity.
Phase 2 Organize students for study	Teacher helps students define and organize study tasks related to the problem.
Phase 3 Assist independent and group investigation	Teacher encourages students to gather appropriate information, conduct experiments, and search for explanations and solutions.
Phase 4 Develop and present artifacts and exhibits	Teacher assists students in planning and preparing appropriate artifacts such as reports, videos, and models and helps them share their work with others.
Phase 5 Analyze and evaluate the problem-solving process	Teacher helps students to reflect on their investigations and the processes they used.

Source: From Arends, R. I. (1997). *Classroom instruction and management* (p. 161). Published by McGraw-Hill. Copyright © 1997 by McGraw-Hill. Reprinted with permission of The McGraw-Hill Companies.

Some problems are not authentic in the sense that they affect the students' lives, but they are engaging. For example, the Cognition and Technology Group at Vanderbilt University (1990, 1993) has developed a videodisc-based learning environment that focuses on mathematics instruction for grades 5 and 6. The series, called *The Adventures of Jasper Woodbury,* presents students with complex situations that require problem finding; subgoal setting; and the application of mathematics, science, history, and literature concepts to solve problems. Even though the situations are complex and lifelike, the problems can be solved using data embedded in the stories presented. Often the adventures have real-life follow-up problems that build on the knowledge developed. For example, after designing a playground for a hypothetical group of children in one Jasper adventure, students can tackle building a real playhouse for a preschool class.

The Vanderbilt group calls its problem-solving approach **anchored instruction.** The *anchor* is the rich, interesting situation. This anchor provides a focus—a reason for setting goals, planning, and using mathematical tools to solve problems. The intended outcome is to develop knowledge that is useful and flexible, not inert. Project-based science is another approach similar to problem-based learning. Table 9.3 on page 354 compares these three approaches to learning that are situated in problem-solving experiences.

anchored instruction A type of problem-based learning that uses a complex interesting situation as an anchor for learning.

Research on Inquiry and Problem-Based Learning. Inquiry methods are similar to discovery learning and share some of the same problems, so inquiry must be carefully planned and organized, especially for less-prepared students who may lack the background knowledge and problem-solving skills needed to benefit. Some research has shown that discovery methods are ineffective and even detrimental for lower-ability students (Corno & Snow, 1986; Mayer, 2004). When Ted Bredderman (1983) analyzed the results of 57 comparisons of activity-based learning and more traditional approaches for teaching science, he concluded that activity-based methods were superior to content-based traditional approaches in terms of students' understanding of the scientific method and creativity, but about the same for learning science content.

TABLE 9.3 Three Approaches to Learning Situated in Problem-Solving Experiences

Problem-based learning (PBL), anchored instruction, and project-based science all begin with problems to be solved.

	PBL	Anchored Instruction	Project-Based Science
Problem	Realistic ill-structured problem	Video-based narrative ending with complex problem	Driving question
Role of problem	Focus for learning information and reasoning strategies	Provide shared experience so that students can understand how knowledge can support problem solving Video supports problem comprehension	Focus for scientific inquiry process leading to artifact production
Process	Identify facts, generate ideas and learning issues, SDL, revisit, and reflect	Guided planning and subgoal generation	Prediction, observation, explanation cycles
Role of teacher	Facilitate learning process and model reasoning	Engage students' prior knowledge, model problem-solving strategies, provide content instruction when needed by students	Introduce relevant content before and during inquiry
Collaboration	Negotiation of ideas Individual students bring new knowledge to group for application to problem	Negotiation of ideas and strategies within small groups and whole class	Guides inquiry process Negotiation of ideas with peers and local community members
Tools	Structured whiteboard Student-identified learning resources	Video controller Problem-specific tools (e.g., maps, compasses)	Computer-based tools that support planning, data collection and analysis, modelling, and information-gathering

Source: From Hmelo-Silver, C. E. (2004). Problem-based learning: What and how do students learn? *Educational Psychology Review, 16,* p. 238. Plenum Publishing Corporation, 2004.

In 1993, a similar comparison was made of problem-based instruction in medical school. Students learning through problem-based instruction were better at clinical skills such as problem formation and reasoning, but they were worse in their basic knowledge of science and felt less prepared in science (Albanese & Mitchell, 1993). In another study, MBA students who learned a concept using problem-based methods were better at explaining the concept than students who had learned the concept from lecture and discussion (Capon & Kuhn, 2004). Students who are better at self-regulation may benefit more from problem-based methods (Evensen, Salisbury-Glennon, & Glenn, 2001), but using problem-based methods over time can help students to develop self-directed learning skills.

In terms of the goals of problem-based learning listed earlier, Cindy Hmelo-Silver (2004) reviewed the research and found good evidence that problem-based learning supports the construction of flexible knowledge and the development of problem-solving and self-directed learning skills, but there is less evidence that participating in problem-based learning is intrinsically motivating or that it teaches students to collaborate. In addition, most of the research has been done in higher education, especially medical schools.

The best approach in elementary and secondary schools may be a balance of content-focused and inquiry or problem-based methods (Arends, 2004). For example, Eva Toth, David Klahr, and Zhe Chen (2000) tested a balanced approach for teaching grade 4 students how to use the controlled variable strategy in science to design good experiments. The method had three phases: (1) in small groups, students conducted exploratory experiments to identify variables that made a ball roll farther down a ramp; (2) the teacher led a discussion, explained the controlled variable strategy, and modelled good thinking about experiment design; and (3) the students designed and conducted application experiments to isolate which variables caused the ball to roll farther. The combination of inquiry, discussion, explanation, and modelling was successful in helping the students understand the concepts.

Another constructivist approach that relies heavily on interaction is instructional conversations.

Dialogue and Instructional Conversations

One implication of Vygotsky's theory of cognitive development is that important learning and understanding require interaction and conversation. Students need to grapple with problems in their zone of proximal development, and they need the scaffolding provided by interaction with a teacher or other students. Here is a good definition of scaffolding that emphasizes the knowledge that both teacher and student bring—both are experts on something: "Scaffolding is a powerful conception of teaching and learning in which teachers and students create meaningful connections between teachers' cultural knowledge and the everyday experience and knowledge of the student" (McCaslin & Hickey, 2001, p. 137). Look back at the beach conversation between Ben and his father on pages 342–343. Notice how the father used the abalone sandwich and the necklace—connections to Ben's experience and knowledge—to scaffold Ben's understanding.

Instructional conversations are *instructional* because they are designed to promote learning, but they are *conversations,* not lectures or traditional discussions. Here is a segment of conversation from a literature group in a bilingual grade 3 classroom (Moll & Whitmore, 1993). The conversation shows how the participants mediate each other's learning through dialogue about the shared experience.

Connect & Extend

TO PRACTICE
Engaging discussions and instructional conversations are often students' most memorable and valuable learning experiences. Understand the principles involved in using conversations and dialogue as an instructional strategy.

instructional conversation Situation in which students learn through interactions with teachers and/or other students.

T:	*Sylvester and the Magic Pebble.* What did you think about this story?
Rita:	I think they cared a lot for him.
T:	What do you mean? You mean his parents?
Rita:	Yes.
T:	What made you think that when you read the story?
Rita:	Because they really worried about him.
T:	Who else wants to share something? I'd like to hear everybody's ideas. Then we can decide what we want to talk about. Sarah?
Sarah:	I think he got the idea of it when he was little, or maybe one of his friends got lost or something?
T:	What do you mean, he got the idea?
Sarah:	He got the idea for his parents to think that Sylvester got lost.
T:	You're talking about where William Steig might have gotten his ideas.
Sarah:	Yes.
T:	That maybe something like this happened to him or someone he knew. A lot of times authors get their ideas from real life things, don't they? Jon, what did you think about this story?
Jon:	It was like a moral story. It's like you can't wish for everything. But, in a sense, everything happened to him when he was panicking.
T:	When did you think he panicked?
Jon:	Well, when he saw the lion, he started to panic.
Richard:	And he turned himself into a rock.
Jon:	Yeah. He said, "I wish I were a rock."

T: Right. And it happened, didn't it?

Richard: It was stupid of him.

T: So maybe he wasn't thinking far enough ahead? What would you have wished instead of a rock? (pp. 24–25)

The conversation continues as the students contribute different levels of interpretation of the story. The teacher notes these interpretations in her summary: "Look at all the different kinds of things you had to say. Rita talked about the characters in the story and what they must be feeling. Sarah took the author's point of view. And you saw it as a particular kind of story, Jon, a moral story."

In instructional conversations, the teacher's goal is to keep everyone cognitively engaged in a substantive discussion. In the above conversation, the teacher takes almost every other turn. As the students become more familiar with this learning approach, we would expect them to talk more among themselves with less teacher talk. These conversations do not have to be long. Even taking up lunch money can be an opportunity for an instructional conversation:

> During the first few minutes of the day, Ms. White asked how many children wanted hot lunches that day. Eighteen children raised their hands. Six children were going to eat cold lunches. Ms. White asked, "How many children are going to eat lunch here today?"
>
> By starting with 18 and counting on, several children got to the answer of 24. One child got out counters and counted out a set of 18 and another set of 6. He then counted all of them and said "24."
>
> Ms. White then asked, "How many more children are eating hot lunch than are eating cold lunch?"
>
> Several children counted back from 18 to 12. The child with the blocks matched 18 blocks with 6 blocks and counted the blocks left over.
>
> Ms. White asked the children who volunteered to tell the rest of the class how they got the answer. Ms. White continued asking for different solutions until no one could think of a new way to solve the problem. (Peterson, Fennema, & Carpenter, 1989, p. 45)

This teacher is creating an environment in which students can make sense of mathematics and use mathematics to make sense of the world. To accomplish these goals, teaching begins with the student's current understanding. Teachers can capitalize on the natural use of counting strategies to see how many different ways students can solve a problem. The emphasis is on mathematical thinking, not on math "facts" or on learning the one best (teacher's) way to solve the problem. The teacher is a guide, helping students construct their own understandings through dialogue (Putnam & Borko, 1997).

Table 9.4 summarizes the elements of productive instructional conversations.

Cognitive Apprenticeships

Cognitive apprenticeship approaches may use knowledgeable guides or "masters" to provide models, demonstrations, and corrections in learning tasks, as well as a personal bond that is motivating to younger or less experienced "apprentices" as they perform and perfect the tasks.

Over the centuries, apprenticeships have proved to be an effective form of education. By working alongside a master and perhaps other apprentices, young people have learned many skills, trades, and crafts. Knowledgeable guides provide models, demonstrations, and corrections, as well as a personal bond that is motivating. The performances required of the learner are real and important and grow more complex as the learner becomes more competent (Collins, Brown, & Holum, 1991; Collins, Brown, & Newman, 1989; Hung, 1999). With *guided participation* in real tasks comes *participatory appropriation*—students appropriate the knowledge, skills, and values involved in doing the tasks (Rogoff, 1995, 1998). In addition, both the newcomers to learning and the old-timers contribute to the community of practice by mastering and remastering skills—and sometimes improving these skills in the process (Lave & Wenger, 1991).

Allan Collins and his colleagues (1989) suggest that knowledge and skills learned in school have become too separated from their use in the world beyond school. To correct this imbalance, some educators recommend that schools adopt many of the features of apprenticeships. But rather than learning to sculpt or dance

TABLE 9.4 Elements of the Instructional Conversation

Good instructional conversations must have elements of both instruction and conversation.

Instruction	Conversation
1. *Thematic focus.* Teacher selects a theme on which to focus the discussion and has a general plan for how the theme will unfold, including how to "chunk" the text to permit optimal exploration of the theme.	6. *Fewer "known-answer" questions.* Much of the discussion centres on questions for which there might be more than one correct answer.
2. *Activation and use of background knowledge.* Teacher either "hooks into" or provides students with pertinent background knowledge necessary for understanding a text, weaving the information into the discussion.	7. *Responsiveness to student contributions.* While having an initial plan and maintaining the focus and coherence of the discussion, teacher is also responsive to students' statements and the opportunities they provide.
3. *Direct teaching.* When necessary, teacher provides direct teaching of a skill or concept.	8. *Connected discourse.* The discussion is characterized by multiple, interactive, connected turns; succeeding utterances build on and extend previous ones.
4. *Promotion of more complex language and expression.* Teacher elicits more extended student contributions by using a variety of elicitation techniques: invitation to expand, questions, restatements, and pauses.	9. *Challenging, but non-threatening, atmosphere.* Teacher creates a challenging atmosphere that is balanced by a positive affective climate. Teacher is more collaborator than evaluator and students are challenged to negotiate and construct the meaning of the text.
5. *Promotion of bases for statements or positions.* Teacher promotes students' use of text, pictures, and reasoning to support an argument or position, by gently probing: "What makes you think that?" or "Show us where it says ____."	10. *General participation, including self-selected turns.* Teacher does not hold exclusive right to determine who talks; students are encouraged to volunteer or otherwise influence the selection of speaking turns.

Source: From Goldenberg, Claude. (1991). *Instructional conversations and their classroom application* (p. 7). Santa Cruz, CA and Washington, DC: National Center for Research on Cultural Diversity and Second Language Learning. Copyright © 1991 by National Center for Research on Cultural Diversity and Second Language Learning. Reprinted with permission.

or build a cabinet, apprenticeships in school would focus on cognitive objectives, such as reading comprehension, writing, or mathematical problem solving. There are many **cognitive apprenticeship** models, but most share six features:

cognitive apprenticeship A relationship in which a less experienced learner acquires knowledge and skills under the guidance of an expert.

- Students observe an expert (usually the teacher) *model* the performance.
- Students get external support through *coaching* or tutoring (including hints, feedback, models, and reminders).
- Students receive conceptual *scaffolding,* which is then gradually faded as the student becomes more competent and proficient.
- Students continually *articulate* their knowledge—putting into words their understanding of the processes and content being learned.
- Students *reflect* on their progress, comparing their problem solving with an expert's performance and to their own earlier performances.
- Students are required to *explore* new ways to apply what they are learning— ways that they have not practised at the master's side.

As students learn, they are challenged to master more complex concepts and skills and to perform them in many different settings (Roth & Bowen, 1995; Shuell, 1996).

How can teaching provide cognitive apprenticeships? Mentoring in teaching is one example. Another is cross-age grouping. In one inner-city elementary school, students of different ages work side by side for part of every day on a "pod" designed to have many of the qualities of an apprenticeship. The pods might focus on a craft or a discipline. Examples include gardening, architecture, and "making money." Many levels of expertise are evident in the students of different ages, so students can move at a comfortable pace, but still have the model of a master available. Community volunteers, including many parents, visit to demonstrate a skill that is related to the pod topic.

Connect & Extend

TO YOUR TEACHING

A nearly universal goal of educational programs across the country is the development of thinking skills. Describe what a teacher can do to cultivate these skills in the classroom. Read *Teaching Thinking Skills* (**www.nwrel.org/scpd/sirs/6/cu11.html**) for a concise overview of research, issues, and key factors related to this topic.

Connect & Extend

TO THE RESEARCH

Perkins, D., Jay, E., & Tishman, S. (1993). New conceptions of thinking: From ontology to education. *Educational Psychologist, 28,* 67–85; see also Tishman, S., Perkins, D., and Jay, E. (1995). *The thinking classroom: Learning and teaching in a culture of thinking.* Boston: Allyn and Bacon.

stand-alone thinking skills programs Programs that teach thinking skills directly without need for extensive subject matter knowledge.

THINK

VANSELOW

"WE DID THAT LAST YEAR—HOW COME WE HAVE TO DO IT AGAIN THIS YEAR?"
© W. A. Vanslow—From *Phi Delta Kappan.* Reprinted by permission.

A Cognitive Apprenticeship in Learning Mathematics. Schoenfeld's (1989, 1994) teaching of mathematical problem solving is another example of the cognitive apprenticeship instructional model. Schoenfeld found that novice problem solvers began ineffective solution paths and continued on these paths even though they were not leading toward a solution. In comparison, expert problem solvers moved toward solutions using various cognitive processes such as planning, implementing, and verifying, altering their behaviour based on judgments of the validity of their solution processes.

To help students become more expert problem solvers, Schoenfeld asks students three important questions: What are you doing? Why are you doing it? and How will success in what you are doing help you find a solution to the problem? These questions help students control the processes they use and build their metacognitive awareness. Here is an example:

> Problem sessions begin when I hand out a list of questions.... Often one student has an "inspiration."... My task is not to say yes or no, or even to evaluate the suggestion. Rather it is to raise the issue for discussion.... Typically a number of students respond [that they haven't made sense of the problem]. When we have made sense of the problem, the suggestion [X] simply doesn't make sense.... When this happens, I step out of my role as moderator to make the point to the whole class: If you make sure you understand the problem before you jump into a solution, you are less likely to go off on a wild goose chase. (Schoenfeld, 1987, p. 201)

This monitoring of the understanding of a problem and the problem-solving process help students begin to think and act as mathematicians. Throughout this process, Schoenfeld repeats his three questions (What are you doing? Why? How will this help?). Each of these components is essential in helping students to be aware of and to regulate their behaviours.

Apprenticeships in Thinking

Many educational psychologists believe that good thinking can and should be developed in school. But teaching thinking entails much more than the typical classroom practices of answering "thought" questions at the end of the chapter or participating in teacher-led discussions. What else is needed? One approach has been to focus on the development of *thinking skills,* either through stand-alone programs that teach skills directly, or through indirect methods that embed development of thinking in the regular curriculum. The advantage of **stand-alone thinking skills programs** is that students do not need extensive subject matter knowledge to master the skills. Students who have had trouble with the traditional curriculum may achieve success—and perhaps an enhanced sense of self-efficacy—through these programs. The disadvantage is that the general skills are often not used outside the program unless teachers make a concerted effort to show students how to apply the skills in specific subjects (Mayer & Wittrock, 1996; Prawat, 1991).

Developing Thinking in Every Class. Another way to develop students' thinking is to provide cognitive apprenticeships in analysis, problem solving, and reasoning through the regular lessons of the curriculum. David Perkins and his colleagues (Perkins, Jay, & Tishman, 1993) propose that teachers do this by creating a culture of thinking in their classrooms. This means that there is a spirit of inquisitiveness and critical thinking, a respect for reasoning and creativity, and an expectation that students will learn and understand. In such a classroom, education is seen as *enculturation,* a broad and complex process of acquiring knowledge and understanding consistent with Vygotsky's theory of mediated learning. Just as our home culture taught us lessons about the use of language, the culture of a classroom can teach lessons about thinking by giving us models of good thinking; providing direct instruction in thinking processes; and encouraging practice of those thinking processes through interactions with others.

Many educational psychologists believe good thinking can and should be developed in school and that thinking skills can be taught through stand-alone programs that teach thinking skills directly.

Critical Thinking. Critical **thinking** skills are useful in almost every life situation—even in evaluating the media ads that constantly bombard us. When you see a group of gorgeous people extolling the virtues of a particular brand of orange juice as they frolic in skimpy bathing suits, you must decide if sex appeal is a relevant factor in choosing a fruit drink. (Remember Pavlovian advertising from Chapter 6.) As you can see in the Point/Counterpoint feature on page 360, educators don't agree about the best way to foster creative thinking in schools.

No matter what approach you use to develop critical thinking, it is important to follow up with additional practice. One lesson is not enough. For example, if your class examined a particular historical document to determine if it reflected bias or propaganda, you should follow up by analyzing other written historical documents, contemporary advertisements, or news stories. Until thinking skills become overlearned and relatively automatic, they are not likely to be transferred to new situations. Instead, students will use these skills only to complete the lesson in social studies, not to evaluate the claims made by friends, politicians, toy manufacturers, or diet plans. Table 9.5 provides a representative list of critical thinking skills.

critical thinking Evaluating conclusions by logically and systematically examining the problem, the evidence, and the solution.

Connect & Extend

TO YOUR TEACHING
List all the different words related to thinking that you hear during one of your university classes. You might contrast the "thinking language" in a class that seems to challenge you to think with that of a class that focuses on skills and facts.

TABLE 9.5 Examples of Critical Thinking Skills

Defining and Clarifying the Problem	Judging Information Related to the Problem	Solving Problems/Drawing Conclusions
1. Identify central issues or problems.	5. Distinguish among fact, opinion, and reasoned judgment.	11. Recognize the adequacy of data.
2. Compare similarities and differences.	6. Check consistency.	12. Predict probable consequences.
3. Determine which information is relevant.	7. Identify unstated assumptions.	
4. Formulate appropriate questions.	8. Recognize stereotypes and clichés.	
	9. Recognize bias, emotional factors, propaganda, and semantic slanting.	
	10. Recognize different value systems and ideologies.	

Source: From Kneedler, P. (1985). California assesses critical thinking. In A. Costa (Ed.), *Developing minds: A resource book for teaching thinking*, p. 277. Copyright © 1985 by the Association for Supervision and Curriculum Development and author. Reprinted with permission of the ASCD. All rights reserved.

SHOULD SCHOOLS TEACH CRITICAL THINKING AND PROBLEM SOLVING?

The question of whether schools should focus on process or content, problem-solving skills or core knowledge, higher-order thinking skills or academic information has been debated for years. Some educators suggest that students must be taught how to think and solve problems, while other educators assert that students cannot learn to "think" in the abstract. They must be thinking about something—some content. Should teachers focus on knowledge or thinking?

> Point *Problem solving and higher-order thinking can and should be taught.*

An article in the April, 28, 1995, issue of the *Chronicle of Higher Education* makes this claim:

> Critical thinking is at the heart of effective reading, writing, speaking, and listening. It enables us to link together mastery of content with such diverse goals as self-esteem, self-discipline, multicultural education, effective cooperative learning, and problem solving. It enables all instructors and administrators to raise the level of their own teaching and thinking. (p. A-71)

How can students learn to think critically? Some educators recommend teaching thinking skills directly with widely used techniques such as the Productive Thinking Program or CoRT (Cognitive Research Trust). Other researchers argue that learning computer programming languages such as LOGO will improve students' minds and teach them how to think logically. For example, Papert (1980) believes that when children learn through discovery how to give instructions to computers in LOGO, "powerful intellectual skills are developed in the process" (p. 60). Finally, because expert readers automatically apply certain metacognitive strategies, many educators and psychologists recommend directly teaching novice or poor readers how to apply these strategies. Michael Pressley's Good Strategy User model and Palincsar and Brown's (1984) reciprocal teaching approach are successful examples of direct teaching of metacognitive skills. Research on these approaches generally shows improvements in achievement and comprehension for students of all ages who participate (Pressley, Barkowski, & Schneider, 1987; Rosenshine & Meister, 1994).

< Counterpoint *Thinking and problem-solving skills do not transfer.*

According to E. D. Hirsch, a vocal critic of critical thinking programs,

> But whether such direct instruction of critical thinking or self-monitoring does in fact improve performance is a subject of debate in the research community. For instance, the research regarding critical thinking is not reassuring. Instruction in critical thinking has been going on in several countries for over a hundred years. Yet researchers found that students from nations as varied as Israel, Germany, Australia, the Philippines, and the United States, including those who have been taught critical thinking, continue to fall into logical fallacies. (1996, p. 136)

The CoRT program has been used in over 5000 classrooms in 10 nations. But Polson and Jeffries (1985) report that "after 10 years of widespread use we have no adequate evidence concerning the effectiveness of the program" (p. 445). In addition, Mayer and Wittrock (1996) note that field studies of problem solving in real situations show that people often fail to apply the mathematical problem-solving approaches they learn in school to actual problems encountered in the grocery store or home.

Even though educators have been more successful in teaching metacognitive skills, critics still caution that there are times when such teaching hinders rather than helps learning. Robert Siegler (1993) suggests that teaching self-monitoring strategies to low-achieving students can interfere with the students' development of adaptive strategies. Forcing students to use the strategies of experts may put too much burden on working memory as the students struggle to use an unfamiliar strategy and miss the meaning or content of the lesson. For example, rather than teach students strategies for figuring out words from context, it may be helpful for students to focus on learning more vocabulary words.

The Language of Thinking. The language of thinking consists of natural language terms that refer to mental processes and mental products—"words like *think, believe, guess, conjecture, hypothesis, evidence, reasons, estimate, calculate, suspect, doubt,* and *theorize*—to name just a few" (Tishman, Perkins, & Jay, 1995, p. 8). The classroom should be filled with a clear, precise, and rich vocabulary of thinking. Rather than saying, "What do you think about Jamie's answer?" the teacher might ask questions that expand thinking, such as, "What evidence can you give to refute or support Jamie's answer?" "What assumptions is Jamie making?" "What are some alternative explanations?" Students surrounded by a rich language of thinking are more likely to think deeply about thinking. Students learn more when they engage in talk that is interpretive and that analyzes and gives explanations. Talk that just describes is less helpful in learning than talk that explains, give reasons, identifies parts, makes a case, defends a position, or evaluates evidence (Palincsar, 1998).

An Integrated Constructivist Program: Fostering Communities of Learners

Fostering communities of learners (FCL) is "a system of interacting activities that results in a self-consciously active and reflective learning environment" (Brown & Campione, 1996, p. 292). This is an entire instructional program grounded in constructivist learning theories.

It is tempting to reduce the complex processes and understandings of FCL to a simple set of steps or procedures. But the inventors, Ann Brown and Joseph Campione, caution that in considering FCL, our emphasis should be on philosophy and principles, not procedures and steps. At the heart of FCL is a three-part process: Students engage in independent and group research on one aspect of the class inquiry topic—for example, animal adaptation and survival. The goal is for the entire class to develop a deep understanding of the topic. Because the material is complex, class mastery requires that students become experts on different aspects of the larger topic and share their expertise. The sharing is motivated by a consequential task—a performance that matters. The task may be a traditional test or it may be a public performance, service project, or competition. Thus, the heart of FCL is *research,* in order to *share* information, in order to *perform* a consequential task (Brown, 1997; Brown & Campione, 1996).

This inquiry cycle may not seem that new, but what sets FCL apart, among other things, is having a variety of research-based ways of accomplishing each phase and paying careful attention to teaching students how to benefit intellectually and socially from each step. *Research* can take many forms, such as reading, studying, research seminars, guided writing, consulting with experts face to face or electronically, or peer and cross-age tutoring. In order to do research, students are taught and coached in powerful comprehension-monitoring and comprehension-extending strategies such as summarizing and predicting for younger students, and for older students, forming analogies, giving causal explanations, providing evidence, and making sound arguments and predictions. Students are taught explicitly how to *share* information by asking for and giving help, majoring (developing special interest and expertise in an area), learning from each others' exhibitions, participating in cooperative groups, and joining in whole-class cross-talk sessions to check the progress of the research groups. *Performing* consequential tasks includes publishing; designing; creating solutions to real problems; setting up exhibitions; staging performances; and taking tests, quizzes, and authentic assessments that can hardly be distinguished from ongoing teaching.

Thoughtful reflection and deep disciplinary content surround and support the *research, share, perform* cycle. FCL teachers create a culture of thinking—self-conscious reflection about important and complex disciplinary units. As Brown and Campione (1996) point out, we "cannot expect students to invest intellectual curiosity and disciplined inquiry on trivia" (p. 306). In FCL classrooms, the teachers' main ploy is to "trap students into thinking deeply" about complex content (Brown & Campione, 1996, p. 302).

Dilemmas of Constructivist Practice

Years ago, Larry Cremin (1961) observed that progressive, innovative pedagogies require infinitely skilled teachers. Today, the same could be said about constructivist teaching. We have already seen that there are many varieties of constructivism and many practices that flow from these different conceptions. We also

fostering communities of learners (FCL) A system of interacting activities that results in a self-consciously active and reflective learning environment, and uses a research, share, perform learning cycle.

Connect & Extend

TO YOUR TEACHING
John Cronin lists these four common misconceptions about authentic learning:

Misconception #1: If you can't take 'em to Spain, they might as well not learn Spanish at all. The fact that living with native speakers is the best way to learn Spanish does not make using the language in classroom conversations a poor alternative. Look for the small and obvious ways to make learning more authentic—especially if you can't take 'em to Spain.

Misconception #2: If you don't have your chef's licence, then you'll have to starve. You don't need special training or materials to create authentic instruction. Good teachers have been doing it for years.

Misconception #3: If it isn't real fun, then it isn't real. Important learning and valuable life skills are not always fun to learn or fun to use. Self-discipline is part of growing up authentically.

Misconception #4: If you want to learn to play the piano, you must start with mastering Chopin. Not all learning has to be complicated; some important life skills are simple. From Cronin, J. F. (1993). Four misconceptions about authentic learning. *Educational Leadership, 50*(7), 78–80.

know that all teaching today happens in a context of high-stakes testing and accountability. In these situations, constructivist teachers face many challenges. Mark Windschitl (2002) identified four teacher dilemmas of constructivism in practice, summarized in Table 9.6. The first is conceptual: How do I make sense of cognitive versus social conceptions of constructivism and reconcile these different perspectives with my practice? The second dilemma is pedagogical: How do I teach in truly constructivist ways that both honour my students' attempts to think for themselves, but still ensure that they learn the academic material? Third are cultural dilemmas: What activities, cultural knowledge, and ways of talking will build a community in a diverse classroom? Finally, there are political dilemmas:

TABLE 9.6 Teachers' Dilemmas of Constructivism in Practice

Teachers face conceptual, pedagogical, cultural, and political dilemmas as they implement constructivist practices. Here are explanations of these dilemmas and some representative questions that teachers face as they confront them.

Teachers' Dilemma Category	Representative Questions of Concern
I. *Conceptual dilemmas:* Grasping the underpinnings of cognitive and social constructivism; reconciling current beliefs about pedagogy with the beliefs necessary to support a constructivist learning environment.	Which version of constructivism is suitable as a basis for my teaching? Is my classroom supposed to be a collection of individuals working toward conceptual change or a community of learners whose development is measured by participation in authentic disciplinary practices? If certain ideas are considered correct by experts, should students internalize those ideas instead of constructing their own?
II. *Pedagogical dilemmas:* Honouring students' attempts to think for themselves while remaining faithful to accepted disciplinary ideas; developing deeper knowledge of subject matter; mastering the art of facilitation; managing new kinds of discourse and collaborative work in the classroom.	Do I base my teaching on students' existing ideas rather than on learning objectives? What skills and strategies are necessary for me to become a facilitator? How do I manage a classroom where students are talking to one another rather than to me? Should I place limits on students' construction of their own ideas? What types of assessments will capture the learning I want to foster?
III. *Cultural dilemmas:* Becoming conscious of the culture of your classroom; questioning assumptions about what kinds of activities should be valued; taking advantage of experiences, discourse patterns, and local knowledge of students with varied cultural backgrounds.	How can we contradict traditional, efficient classroom routines and generate new agreements with students about what is valued and rewarded? How do my own past images of what is proper and possible in a classroom prevent me from seeing the potential for a different kind of learning environment? How can I accommodate the worldviews of students from diverse backgrounds while at the same time transforming my own classroom culture? Can I trust students to accept responsibility for their own learning?
IV. *Political dilemmas:* Confronting issues of accountability with various stakeholders in the school community; negotiating with key others the authority and support to teach for understanding.	How can I gain the support of administrators and parents for teaching in such a radically different and unfamiliar way? Should I make use of approved curriculums that are not sensitive enough to my students' needs, or should I create my own? How can diverse problem-based experiences help students meet specific state and local standards? Will constructivist approaches adequately prepare my students for high-stakes testing for college admissions?

Source: Windschitl, M. (2002). Framing constructivism in practice as the negotiation of dilemmas: An analysis of the conceptual, pedagogical, cultural, and political challenges facing teachers. *Review of Educational Research, 72,* p. 133. Copyright © 2002 by the American Educational Research Association. Reproduced with permission of the publisher.

How can I teach for deep understanding and critical thinking, but still satisfy the accountability demands of parents and of the curriculum?

Check Your Knowledge

- Distinguish between inquiry methods and problem-based learning.
- What are instructional conversations?
- Describe six features that most cognitive apprenticeship approaches share.
- What is meant by thinking as enculturation?
- What is critical thinking?
- What is FCL?

Apply to Practice

- Give an example of inquiry learning.
- How does the teacher's role in problem-based learning compare with the role in cognitive apprenticeship?

DIVERSITY AND CONVERGENCES IN THEORIES OF LEARNING

What Would You Say?

As part of your interview for a job in a large district, the superintendent asks, "What is your conception of learning? How do students learn?"

Diversity

The power and value of diversity is part of the theoretical frameworks of social cognitive and constructivist theories of learning. Social cognitive theory describes the unique reciprocal interactions among personal, environmental, and behavioural factors that shape the individual's learning and motivation. Culture, social context, personal history, ethnicity, language, and racial identity—to name only a few factors—all shape personal characteristics such as knowledge and beliefs, environmental features such as resources and challenges, and behavioural actions and choices. And a major tenet of constructivist theories is that knowing is socially constructed—shaped by the culture and the families in which the knowers learn, develop, and create their identities.

One of the political dilemmas for teachers indicated in Table 9.6 is that families often question and criticize educational reforms. Many teachers using nontraditional approaches to learning find that they must explain these approaches to students' families.

The Family and Community Partnerships feature on page 364 gives ideas for communicating with parents about innovative constructivist teaching and learning.

For the past four chapters, we have examined different aspects of learning. We considered behavioural, information processing, social cognitive, constructivist, and situated learning explanations of what people learn and how they learn it. Table 9.7 on page 365 presents a summary of several of these perspectives on learning.

Convergences

Rather than debating the merits of different approaches, consider their contributions to understanding learning and improving teaching. Don't feel that you must choose the "best" approach—there is no such thing. Chemists, biologists, and nutritionists rely on different theories to explain and improve health. Different views of learning can be used together to create productive learning environments for the diverse students you will teach. Behavioural theory helps us understand the

Connect & Extend

TO YOUR TEACHING
Use the Family and Community Partnerships feature to brainstorm ideas for how you would explain your teaching innovations to families. Experiment by drafting a newsletter.

Connect & Extend

TO YOUR TEACHING
Can different formats, such as lecture or seatwork, be used in the service of different models, such as direct instruction or constructivist approaches?

FAMILY AND COMMUNITY PARTNERSHIPS
COMMUNICATING ABOUT INNOVATIONS

Be confident and honest.

EXAMPLES

1. Write out your rationale for the methods you are using—consider likely objections and craft your responses.

2. Admit mistakes or oversights—explain what you have learned from them.

Treat parents as equal partners.

EXAMPLES

1. Listen carefully to parents' objections, take notes, and follow up on requests or suggestions—remember, you both want the best for the child.

2. Give parents the telephone number of an administrator who will answer their questions about a new program or initiative.

3. Invite families to visit your room or assist in the project in some way.

Communicate effectively.

EXAMPLES

1. Use plain language and avoid jargon. If you must use a technical term, define it in accessible ways. Use your best teaching skills to educate parents about the new approach.

2. Encourage local newspapers or television stations to feature stories about the "great learning" going on in your classroom or school.

3. Create a lending library of articles and references about the new strategies.

Have examples of projects and assignments available for parents when they visit your class.

EXAMPLES

1. Encourage parents to try math activities. If they have trouble, show them how your students (and their child) are successful with the activities and highlight the strategies the students have learned.

2. Keep a library of students' favourite activities to demonstrate for parents.

Develop family involvement packages.

EXAMPLES

1. Once a month, send families, via their children, descriptions and examples of the math, science, or language skills to be learned in the upcoming unit. Include activities children can do with their parents.

2. Make the family project count, for example, as a homework grade.

Source: From Meyer, M., Delgardelle, M., & Middleton, J. (1996). Addressing parents' concerns over curriculum reform. *Educational Leadership, 53*(7). Copyright © 1996 by the American Association for Supervision and Curriculum Development. Reprinted with permission from ASCD. All rights reserved. The Association for Supervision and Curriculum Development is a worldwide community of educators advocating sound policies and sharing best practices to achieve the success of each learner. To learn more, visit ASCD at **www.ascd.org**.

Connect & Extend

TO YOUR TEACHING
Use Table 9.7, "Four Views of Learning," to think about your own philosophy of learning. Would you incorporate elements from different theoretical approaches into your personal conception of learning?

role of cues in setting the stage for behaviours and the role of consequences and practice in encouraging or discouraging behaviours. But much of humans' lives and learning is more than behaviours. Language and higher-order thinking require complex information processing and memory—something the cognitive models of the thinker-as-computer have helped us understand. And what about the person as a creator and constructor of knowledge, not just a processor of information? Here, constructivist perspectives have much to offer.

The three main learning theories in Table 9.7 can be thought of as three pillars for teaching. Students must first understand and make sense of the material (constructivist); then they must remember what they have understood (cognitive—information processing); and then they must practise and apply (behavioural) their new skills and understanding to make them more fluid and automatic—a permanent part of their repertoire. Failure to attend to any part of the process means lower-quality learning.

Check Your Knowledge

- What are basic similarities and differences between cognitive and constructivist views of learning?

Apply to Practice

- What are some objections parents might have against constructivist approaches to teaching and learning? How would you reply to these concerns?

TABLE 9.7 Four Views of Learning

There are variations within each of these views of learning that differ in emphasis. There is also an overlap in constructivist views.

	Behavioural	Cognitive Information Processing	Constructivist Psychological/Individual	Social Situated
	Skinner	J. Anderson	Piaget	Vygotsky
Knowledge	Fixed body of knowledge to acquire	Fixed body of knowledge to acquire	Changing body of knowledge, individually constructed in social world	Socially constructed knowledge
	Stimulated from outside	Stimulated from outside	Built on what learner brings	Built on what participants contribute, construct together
		Prior knowledge influences how information is processed		
Learning	Acquisition of facts, skills, concepts	Acquisition of facts, skills, concepts, and strategies	Active construction, restructuring prior knowledge	Collaborative construction of socially defined knowledge and values
	Occurs through drill, guided practice	Occurs through the effective application of strategies	Occurs through multiple opportunities and diverse processes to connect to what is already known	Occurs through socially constructed opportunities
Teaching	Transmission	Transmission	Challenge, guide thinking toward more complete understanding	Co-construct knowledge with students
	Presentation (telling)	Guide students toward more "accurate" and complete knowledge		
Role of teacher	Manager, supervisor	Teach and model effective strategies	Facilitator, guide	Facilitator, guide
	Correct wrong answers	Correct misconceptions	Listen for student's current conceptions, ideas, thinking	Co-participant
				Co-construct different interpretation of knowledge; listen to socially constructed conceptions
Role of peers	Not usually considered	Not necessary but can influence information processing	Not necessary but can stimulate thinking, raise questions	Ordinary part of process of knowledge construction
Role of student	Passive reception of information	Active processor of information, strategy user	Active construction (within mind)	Active co-construction with others and self
	Active listener, direction-follower	Organizer and reorganizer of information	Active thinker, explainer, interpreter, questioner	Active thinker, explainer, interpreter, questioner
		Rememberer		Active social participator

Source: From Marshall, H. H. (1992). *Reconceptualizing learning for restructured schools.* Paper presented at the Annual Meeting of the American Educational Research Association, April 1992. Copyright © Hermine H. Marshall. Adapted with permission.

SUMMARY

Social Cognitive Theory
(pp. 331–333)

Distinguish between social learning and social cognitive theories.

Social learning theory expanded behavioural views of reinforcement and punishment. In behavioural views, reinforcement and punishment directly affect behaviour. In social learning theory, seeing another person, a model, reinforced or punished can have similar effects on the observer's behaviour. Social cognitive theory expands social learning theory to include cognitive factors such as beliefs, expectations, and perceptions of self.

What is reciprocal determinism?

Personal factors (beliefs, expectations, attitudes, and knowledge), the physical and social environment (resources, consequences of actions, other people, and physical settings), and behaviour (individual actions, choices, and verbal statements) all influence and are influenced by each other.

What is self-efficacy, and how is it different from other self-schemas?

Self-efficacy is distinct from other self-schemas in that it involves judgments of capabilities *specific to a particular task*. Self-concept is a more global construct that contains many perceptions about the self, including self-efficacy. Compared with self-esteem, self-efficacy is concerned with judgments of personal capabilities; self-esteem is concerned with judgments of self-worth.

What are the sources of self-efficacy?

Four sources are mastery experiences (direct experiences), level of arousal as you face the task, vicarious experiences (accomplishments are modelled by someone else), and social persuasion (a "pep talk" or specific performance feedback).

Applying Social Cognitive Theory
(pp. 333–342)

How does efficacy affect motivation?

Greater efficacy leads to greater effort, persistence in the face of setbacks, higher goals, and finding new strategies when old ones fail. If sense of efficacy is low, however, people may avoid a task altogether or give up easily when problems arise.

What is teacher's sense of efficacy?

One of the few personal characteristics of teachers related to student achievement is a teacher's efficacy belief that he or she can reach even difficult students to help them learn. Teachers with a high sense of efficacy work harder, persist longer, and are less likely to experience burnout. Teachers' sense of efficacy is higher in schools where the other teachers and administrators have high expectations for students and where teachers receive help from their principals in solving instructional and management problems. Efficacy grows from real success with students, so any experience or training that helps you succeed in the day-to-day tasks of teaching will give you a foundation for developing a sense of efficacy in your career.

What factors are involved in self-regulated learning?

One important goal of teaching is to prepare students for life-long learning. To reach this goal, students must be self-regulated learners; that is, they must have a combination of the knowledge, motivation to learn, and volition that provides the skill and will to learn independently and effectively. Knowledge includes an understanding of self, subject, task, learning strategy, and contexts for application. Motivation to learn

provides the commitment, and volition is the follow-through that combats distraction and protects persistence.

What is the self-regulated learning cycle?

There are several models of self-regulated learning. Winne and Hadwin describe a four-phase model: analyzing the task, setting goals and designing plans, enacting tactics to accomplish the task, and regulating learning. Zimmerman notes three similar phases: forethought (which includes setting goals, making plans, self-efficacy, and motivation); performance (which involves self-control and self-monitoring); and reflection (which includes self-evaluation and adaptations, leading to the forethought/planning phase again).

How can teachers support the development of self-efficacy and self-regulated learning?

Teachers should involve students in complex meaningful tasks that extend over long periods of time; provide them control over their learning processes and products—they need to make choices. Involve students in setting criteria for evaluating their learning processes and products, then give them opportunities to make judgments about their progress using those standards. Finally, encourage students to work collaboratively with and seek feedback from peers.

Cognitive and Social Constructivism
(pp. 342–349)

Describe two kinds of constructivism, and distinguish these from constructionism.

Psychological constructivists such as Piaget are concerned with how *individuals* make sense of their world, based on individual knowledge, beliefs, self-concept, or identity—also called *first wave constructivism*. *Social* constructivists such as Vygotsky believe that social interaction, cultural tools, and activity shape individual development and learning—also called *second wave constructivism*. By participating in a broad range of activities with others, learners appropriate the outcomes produced by working together; they acquire new strategies and knowledge of their world. Finally, constructionists are interested in how public knowledge in academic disciplines is constructed as well as how everyday beliefs about the world are communicated to new members of a sociocultural group.

In what ways do constructivist views differ about knowledge sources, accuracy, and generality?

Constructivists debate whether knowledge is constructed by mapping external reality, by adapting and changing internal understandings, or by an interaction of external forces and internal understandings. Most psychologists posit a role for both internal and external factors, but differ in how much they emphasize one or the other. Also, there is discussion about whether knowledge can be constructed in one situation and applied to another or whether knowledge is situated, that is, specific and tied to the context in which it was learned.

What are some common elements in most constructivist views of learning?

Even though there is no single constructivist theory, many constructivist approaches recommend complex, challenging learning environments and authentic tasks; social negotiation and co-construction; multiple representations of content; understanding that knowledge is constructed; and student ownership of learning.

Applying Constructivist Perspectives
(pp. 350–363)

Distinguish between inquiry methods and problem-based learning.

The inquiry strategy begins when the teacher presents a puzzling event, question, or problem. The students ask questions (only yes-no questions in some kinds of inquiry) and then formulate hypotheses to explain the event or solve the problem; collect data to test the hypotheses about casual relationships; form conclusions and generalizations; and reflect on the original problem and the thinking processes needed to solve it. Problem-based learning may follow a similar path, but the learning begins with an authentic problem—one that matters to the students. The goal is to learn math or science or history or some other important subject while seeking a real solution to a real problem.

What are instructional conversations?

Instructional conversations are *instructional* because they are designed to promote learning, but they are *conversations*, not lectures or traditional discussions. They are responsive to students' contributions, challenging but not threatening, connected, and interactive—involving all the students. The teacher's goal is to keep everyone cognitively engaged in a substantive discussion.

Describe six features that most cognitive apprenticeship approaches share.

Students observe an expert (usually the teacher) *model* the performance; get external support through *coaching* or tutoring; and receive conceptual *scaffolding*, which is then gradually faded as the student becomes more competent and proficient. Students continually *articulate* their knowledge—putting into words their understanding of the

processes and content being learned. They *reflect* on their progress, comparing their problem solving to an expert's performance and to their own earlier performances. Finally, students *explore* new ways to apply what they are learning—ways that they have not practised at the master's side.

What is meant by thinking as enculturation?

Enculturation is a broad and complex process of acquiring knowledge and understanding consistent with Vygotsky's theory of mediated learning. Just as our home culture taught us lessons about the use of language, the culture of a classroom can teach lessons about thinking by giving us *models* of good thinking; providing *direct instruction* in thinking processes; and encouraging *practice* of those thinking processes through *interactions* with others.

What is critical thinking?

Critical thinking skills include defining and clarifying the problem, making judgments about the consistency and adequacy of the information related to a problem, and drawing conclusions. No matter what approach you use to develop critical thinking, it is important to follow up activities with additional practice. One lesson is not enough.

What is FCL?

Fostering Communities of Learners is an approach to organizing classrooms and schools. The heart of FCL is *research*, in order to *share* information, in order to *perform* a consequential task that involves deep disciplinary content. Students engage in independent and group research so the entire class can develop an understanding of the topic. Because the material is complex, class mastery requires that students become experts on different aspects of the larger topic and share their expertise. The sharing is motivated by a consequential task—a performance that matters.

Diversity and Convergences in Theories of Learning
(pp. 363–365)

What are basic similarities and differences between cognitive and constructivist views of learning? Knowledge is viewed as relatively fixed in the cognitive view but as changeable in constructivist views.

Learning in constructivist views involves the learner much more in thinking about how learning should happen. Teaching from the cognitive view is mostly presentation, whereas according to constructivists it is more a question of engaging students. The roles of teachers are modestly different, but both views consider learners as needing access to information if they have wrong or incomplete information. Peers are essential only to the social/situated facet of the constructivist view of learning. While all three views emphasize that learners are active, the constructivist views highlight the learner as an interpreter of information.

KEY TERMS

agency, p. 336

anchored instruction, p. 353

appropriate, p. 345

arousal, p. 333

cognitive apprenticeship, p. 357

community of practice, p. 347

complex learning environments, p. 348

constructivism, p. 343

critical thinking, p. 359

first wave constructivism, p. 344

fostering communities of learners (FCL), p. 361

instructional conversation, p. 355

inquiry learning, p. 350

intersubjective attitude, p. 349

mastery experiences, p. 333

modelling, p. 333

multiple representations of content, p. 349

problem-based learning, p. 352

radical constructivism, p. 344

reciprocal determinism, p. 331

second wave constructivism, p. 345

self-efficacy, p. 332

self-regulated learning, p. 336

self-regulation, p. 335

situated learning, p. 347

social cognitive theory, p. 331

social learning theory, p. 331

social negotiation, p. 349

social persuasion, p. 333

spiral curriculum, p. 349

stand-alone thinking skills programs, p. 358

teachers' sense of efficacy, p. 334

vicarious experiences, p. 333

volition, p. 336

BECOMING A PROFESSIONAL

Reflecting on the Chapter

Can you apply the ideas from this chapter on social cognitive and constructivist views of learning to solve the following problems of practice?

Preschool and Kindergarten

- One of your students is very fearful of taking risks or attempting any task that does not have a right answer. The child tries to tell other students "the right way" to do everything. How would you help the student tolerate uncertainty and take risks in her thinking?

Elementary and Middle School

- How would you help grade 3 students understand negative numbers?

Junior High and High School

- Your school librarian wants to help all the history classes learn to use the print and database resources in the library. How would you take advantage of this opportunity?

- Brainstorm ways to "understand your students' understanding" in a particular content area. What would you do before, during, and after a class to make your students' knowledge and thinking processes visible to both you and them?

Check Your Understanding

- Know elements of observational learning.

- Know the five common teaching recommendations shared by most constructivist views.

- Be able to recognize examples of inquiry, problem-based learning, cognitive apprenticeships, instructional conversations, and fostering communities of learners.

Your Teaching Portfolio

Use Table 9.7 on page 365 to think about your own philosophy of learning. Would you incorporate elements from different theoretical approaches into your personal conception of learning?

Teaching Resources

Use the Family and Community Partnerships box on page 364 to brainstorm ideas for how you would explain your teaching innovations to families. Experiment by drafting a newsletter.

Add Table 9.4, "Elements of the Instructional Conversation" on page 357, and Figure 9.3, "A Model to Guide Teacher Thinking about Inquiry-Based Science Instruction" on page 351, to your teaching resources file.

Teachers' Casebook

What Would They Do?

Here is how some practising teachers responded to the awful book reviews.

Elaine A. Tan
Lakeview Elementary School
Burnaby, British Columbia

As a new teacher myself, I understand the initial excitement this teacher was feeling. Rather than feel helpless at this point, remember that these reviews reflect only one type of assessment—the written form. Today's multi-ability-level classrooms require a variety of assessment methods to address diverse backgrounds and learning styles and to give students more opportunities to demonstrate progress. The key here is to focus less on what needs to be covered and more on how it will be covered—process over content!

The first assignment might have caused some students to feel incapable because they lacked English grammar and writing skills and had an underdeveloped vocabulary. The key for ESL students is to provide lower-language and higher-interest visuals; for example, to use key words that connect ideas, sentence frames, or line maps. All students will benefit from vocabulary building. Select key vocabulary in each lesson and have students discuss, use, and apply those words.

The teacher should also adapt various instructional methods. For example, supplement long novels with videos or short stories written at appropriate levels to access different learning styles and means of understanding; integrate fine art to access another learning style. Try the same activity again by grouping students in twos and threes, providing each with an interesting article she or he can relate to and write about. Prepare in advance a set of sentence frames to be completed for the students' articles.

Make use of the capable students, since all students benefit from shared learning experiences. Assign these three students as peer tutors in small groups. Cooperative learning groups assist with the inherent behavioural management challenge and help reduce the isolation, boredom, and fear of sharing some students feel. Small groups also provide the ESL learner with a fluent English speaker while simultaneously building the confidence and self-esteem of the peer tutor.

Where possible, assign world literature selections based on students' countries of origin to heighten interest and attention span. ESL students may want to write responses in their first languages. Have peer tutors assist in translating ideas into English. This provides major language and interpersonal benefits for both groups of students, along with challenges for the advanced students.

Lesley Peterson
Sister High School
Winnipeg, Manitoba

The first thing to determine is whether this writing task was a reasonably reliable diagnostic tool. Did you check that the students were familiar with the conventions of the review form, or fail to make your expectations clear? It might be worth assigning another writing task before deciding that the students whose papers were lacking in coherence were, in fact, unable to write coherent papers. However, in my experience, weak students tend to interpret every writing task as an invitation to retell the story. If these students have failed to do even that coherently, the problem is probably a real one.

How to proceed with the very weak students, then, assuming that their weaknesses are real, requires reference to the program policy and course outline. Also, if the course is required for university entrance or is a prerequisite for such a course, you cannot solely grade on effort and improvement. There must be standards. You should be prepared to differentiate your teaching in terms of the material that students read, the assignments they may choose, and the criteria by which they are evaluated. Differentiating instruction is still a good strategy for the standards-driven curriculum while retaining the same evaluation criteria for all students.

Central to the design of courses like this is a strong emphasis on the writing process. You should plan to teach writing, reading, and revision strategies that will be helpful to all or most students. If this is your goal, however, I strongly suggest changing this first assignment. Instead, ask the students to write reviews of the "best" book they have ever read. Knowing what they consider the "best" is invaluable for planning a wide range of readings that engage students' interest. If you're well and widely read in world literature, you'll be able to find novels, short stories, and poems that intersect with what engages students. It's that old basic principle of teaching: Find out where they are, then meet them, and take them forward from there.

If this is a university-entrance course, you should gather more data on the students who appear weak. Check their final marks in the prerequisite course and talk to previous English teachers. If you still feel a stu-dent does not have the reading, writing, and thinking skills necessary for success in this course, consider conferencing with the student's parents. Advise them that this course will be a struggle for their child. An early recommendation to see a guidance counsellor or to change a timetable can be a real favour to the student. Better that the student enrol in an appropriate course now than sit in the wrong one, have her or his self-esteem battered for months, and then drop the course.

As for the really advanced writers, they need to be recognized, supported, and challenged. Nurture and challenge their love of literature and writing. Easy assignments can hurt self-esteem and lead to under-achievement (not to mention boredom). Encourage these students to get involved in whatever writing communities are available. If there isn't a school magazine, encourage them to start one. Many cities have organizations similar to the Manitoba Writers' Guild, which sponsors readings and open-microphone sessions, organizes workshops, etc.

Teaching a separate gifted program for three students is more work than most English teachers have time for. But there are community resources you can access. Does your town library or college have a writer in residence? If your school has a work experience coordinator, can she hook up these students with a professional journalist? Our local theatre gave one of my students a volunteer position reading and making recommendations on scripts. It changed her life.

Find out what kind of writing these students are most interested in and introduce them to other people who care about it as much as they do. You definitely shouldn't punish them for their ability by giving them extra work. It might be possible for them to earn a separate credit for their extra involvement—talk to a guidance counsellor, work experience coordinator, or administrator to find out what's available. And have the grace to admit that these students might learn more if you let them spend part of your class time in the library. They'll respect you more for it, not less.

10 MOTIVATION IN LEARNING AND TEACHING

Two Girls at the Piano, 1892. Auguste Renoir. Photo: Erich Lessing/Art Resource, New York.

Teachers' Casebook

What Would You Do?

It is July and you have finally gotten a teaching position. The district wasn't your first choice, but job openings were really tight, so you're pleased to have a job in your field.

You are discovering that the teaching resources in your school are slim to none; the only resources are some aging texts and the workbooks that go with them. Every idea you have suggested for software, simulation games, visual aids, or other more active teaching materials has been greeted with the same response, "There's no money in the budget for that." As you look over the texts and workbooks, you wonder how the students could be anything but bored by them. To make matters worse, the texts look pretty high-level for grade 3. But the objectives in the workbooks are important. Besides, the district curriculum requires these units, and students will be tested on them in district-wide assessments next spring.

Critical Thinking

How would you arouse student curiosity and interest about the topics and tasks in the workbooks? How would you establish the value of learning this material? How would you handle the difficulty level of the texts? What do you need to know about motivation to solve these problems?

Collaboration

With two or three other members of your class, brainstorm what you could do to motivate your students.

Most educators agree that motivating students is a critical task of teaching. To learn, students must be cognitively, emotionally, and behaviourally engaged in productive class activities. We begin with the question, "What is motivation?" and examine some answers that have been proposed, including a discussion of intrinsic and extrinsic motivation and four general theories of motivation: behavioural, humanistic, cognitive, and sociocultural. Next, we consider more closely several personal factors that frequently appear in discussions of motivation: needs, goal orientations; interests and emotions, including the important concept of self-efficacy. How do we put all this information together in teaching? How do we create environments, situations, and relationships that encourage motivation? First, we consider how the personal influences on motivation come together to support motivation to learn. We then examine how motivation is influenced by the academic work of the class, the value of the work, and the setting in which the work must be done. Finally, we discuss a number of strategies for developing motivation as a constant state in your classroom and as a permanent trait in your students.

By the time you have completed this chapter, you should be able to answer these questions:

- *What examples can you give of intrinsic and extrinsic motivation and of motivation to learn?*

- *How is motivation defined in the behavioural, humanistic, cognitive, and sociocultural points of view?*

- *What are the possible motivational effects of success and failure, and how do these effects relate to beliefs about ability?*

- *What are the roles of goals, interests, emotions, and beliefs about the self in motivation?*

- *What is your strategy for teaching your subject to an uninterested student?*

- *What are the potential effects of teachers' expectations on students?*

WHAT IS MOTIVATION?

Motivation is usually defined as an internal state that arouses, directs, and maintains behaviour. Psychologists studying motivation have focused on five basic questions (Graham & Weiner, 1996; Pintrich, Marx, & Boyle, 1993):

1. *What choices do people make about their behaviour?* Why do some students, for example, focus on their homework, while others watch television?

2. *How long does it take to get started?* Why do some students choose to start their homework right away, while others procrastinate?

3. *What is the intensity or level of involvement in the chosen activity?* Once the book bag is opened, is the student absorbed and focused or just going through the motions?

4. *What causes a person to persist or to give up?* For example, will a student read the entire Shakespeare assignment or just a few pages?

5. *What is the individual thinking and feeling while engaged in the activity?* Is the student enjoying Shakespeare or worrying about an upcoming test?

Answering these questions about real students in classrooms is a challenge. As you will see in this chapter and the next, many factors influence motivation.

Intrinsic and Extrinsic Motivation

We all know how it feels to be motivated, to move energetically toward a goal or to work hard, even if we are not fascinated by the task. What energizes and directs our behaviour? The explanation could be drives, needs, incentives, fears, goals, social pressure, self-confidence, interests, curiosity, beliefs, values, expectations, and more. Some psychologists have explained motivation in terms of personal *traits* or persistent individual characteristics. Certain people, so the theory goes, have a strong need to achieve, a fear of tests, or an enduring interest in art, so they behave accordingly. They work hard to achieve, avoid tests, or spend hours in art galleries. Other psychologists see motivation more as a *state,* a temporary situation. If, for example, you are reading this paragraph because you have a test tomorrow, you are motivated (at least for now) by the situation. Actually, the motivation we experience at any given time is a combination of trait and state. You may be studying because you value learning *and* because your professor gives pop quizzes.

As you can see, some explanations of motivation rely on internal, personal factors such as needs, interests, curiosity, and enjoyment. Other explanations point to external, environmental factors—rewards, social pressure, or punishment, for example. Motivation that stems from internal factors is called **intrinsic motivation.** Intrinsic motivation is the tendency to seek out and persist with challenges as we pursue personal interests and exercise our capabilities (Deci & Ryan, 1985, 2002; Reeve, 1996). When we are intrinsically motivated, we do not need external incentives or punishments—*the activity itself is rewarding.* We're motivated to do something when we don't have to do it.

In contrast, when we do something to earn a grade or reward, avoid punishment, please the teacher, or for some other reason that has little to do with the task itself, we experience **extrinsic motivation.** We are not really interested in the activity for its own sake; we care only about what we gain by doing it.

You can't tell just by looking if a behaviour is motivated intrinsically or extrinsically. The essential difference between the two types of motivation is the student's reason for acting, that is, whether the location or **locus of causality** for the action is internal or external—inside or outside the person. Students who read or practise their backstroke or paint landscapes may be reading or swimming or painting because they freely chose the activity based on personal interests (*internal locus* of

motivation An internal state that arouses, directs, and maintains behaviour.

Connect & Extend

TO THE RESEARCH

For a thorough discussion of the many terms and concepts related to motivation, see Murphy, P. K., & Alexander, P. A. (2000). A motivated exploration of motivation terminology. *Contemporary Educational Psychology, 25,* 3–53.

Connect & Extend

TO THE RESEARCH

Weiner, B. (1990). History of motivational research in education. *Journal of Educational Psychology, 82,* 616–622.

Focus Questions: How are the behavioural and cognitive views of learning reflected in the various theories of motivation? What is the current conception of motivation?

intrinsic motivation Motivation associated with activities that are their own reward.

extrinsic motivation Motivation created by external factors such as rewards and punishments.

locus of causality The location—internal or external—of the cause of behaviour.

"WHAT DO I GET FOR JUST NEATNESS?"
(© Glenn Bernhardt)

causality/intrinsic motivation) or because someone or something else outside is influencing them (*external locus* of causality/extrinsic motivation) (Reeve, 1996).

Is your motivation for reading this chapter intrinsic or extrinsic? Is your locus of causality internal or external? You probably realize that these all-or-nothing descriptions are too simple. Our activities are jointly *self-determined* (internal locus of causality/intrinsic motivation) and *determined by others* (external locus of extrinsic motivation). Students may freely choose to work hard on activities they don't find particularly enjoyable because they believe that these activities are important for reaching a valued goal. You may spend hours studying motivation to become a great teacher. Is this intrinsic or extrinsic motivation? Actually it is in between— you freely choose to respond to outside causes such as requirements of the teaching profession. You have *internalized an external cause*.

Recently, the notion of intrinsic and extrinsic motivation as two ends of a continuum has been challenged. An alternative explanation is that just as motivation can include both trait and state factors, it can also include both intrinsic and extrinsic factors. Intrinsic and extrinsic tendencies are two independent possibilities; at any given time, we can be motivated by some of each (Covington & Mueller, 2001). In school, both intrinsic and extrinsic motivation are useful. Teaching can encourage students' intrinsic motivation by stimulating their curiosity and making them feel more competent as they learn. But this won't work all the time. Did you find long division or grammar inherently interesting? Was your curiosity piqued by the provinces and their capitals? Teachers will be disappointed if they count on intrinsic motivation to energize every student all the time. In some situations, incentives and external supports are necessary. Teachers must encourage and nurture intrinsic motivation while making sure that extrinsic motivation supports learning (Brophy, 1988, 2003; Deci, Koestner, & Ryan, 1999; Ryan & Deci, 1996). To do this, they need to know about factors that influence motivation.

A basic question in motivation is "Where does it come from—within or outside the individual?" Why does this girl raise her hand in class— because she is interested in the subject or because she wants to earn a good grade? The answer is probably much more complicated than either alternative.

Check Your Knowledge

- Define motivation.
- What is the difference between intrinsic and extrinsic motivation?
- How does locus of causality apply to motivation?

Apply to Practice

- It is sometimes suggested that one way of improving education would be to pay students for successful school achievement. What would be the likely effects of doing this?

FOUR GENERAL APPROACHES TO MOTIVATION

Motivation is a vast, complicated subject encompassing many theories. Some theories were developed through work with animals in laboratories. Others are based on research with humans in situations that used games or puzzles. Some theories grow out of work done in clinical or industrial psychology. Our examination of the field is necessarily selective.

Behavioural Approaches to Motivation

According to the behavioural view, to understand student motivation, you should begin with a careful analysis of what students perceive as incentives and rewards in their classroom. A **reward** is an object or event supplied as a consequence of a particular behaviour that *we* think is attractive. For example, a chemistry teacher might believe that bonus points are rewards for students who

reward An object or event that we think is attractive and provide as a consequence of a behaviour.

make neat sketches of lab apparatus in their notebooks. An **incentive** is an object or event that actually motivates a person's behaviour. Students who value bonus points view points as an incentive. Receiving bonus points will motivate these students—they will make neat sketches in their lab reports. According to the behavioural view, then, understanding student motivation requires probing what students count as incentives and distinguishing these from what we may think of as rewards.

incentive An object or event that encourages or discourages behaviour.

If we are consistently reinforced for certain behaviour, we may develop habits or tendencies to act in certain ways. If a student is regularly reinforced by social recognition and school letters in volleyball but receives little recognition for studying, that student will probably work longer and harder on perfecting her serve than on understanding geometry. Providing grades for learning—or demerits for misbehaviour—is an attempt to motivate students by extrinsic means. Whether this works depends on whether grades are incentives. Of course, in any individual case, other factors can affect how a student behaves.

Humanistic Approaches to Motivation

In the 1940s, proponents of humanistic psychology such as Abraham Maslow and Carl Rogers believed that neither behavioural nor Freudian psychology adequately explained why people act as they do.

Humanistic interpretations of motivation emphasize such intrinsic sources of motivation as people's needs for "self-actualization" (Maslow, 1968, 1970), the inborn "actualizing tendency" (Rogers & Freiberg, 1994), or "self-determination" (Deci et al., 1991). From the humanistic perspective, motivating students means encouraging their inner resources—their sense of competence, self-esteem, autonomy, and self-actualization.

humanistic interpretation Approach to motivation that emphasizes personal freedom, choice, self-determination, and striving for personal growth.

Maslow's Hierarchy. Abraham Maslow (1970) suggested that people have a **hierarchy of needs** and that, by satisfying these, they reach **self-actualization**, his term for realizing personal potential. Lower-order needs must be met before higher-order needs can be addressed. Four lower-order needs—for survival, safety, belongingness and love, and esteem—are categorized as **deficiency needs** because when these needs are satisfied, the motivation for fulfilling them decreases. Three higher-order needs—for knowing and understanding, aesthetic appreciation, and ultimately self-actualization—are called **being needs**. As these needs are partially satisfied, people strive for more and continue striving because these needs can never be completely satisfied. For example, the more successful you are in your efforts to develop as a teacher, the harder you are likely to strive for even greater improvement.

hierarchy of needs Maslow's model of seven levels of human needs, from basic physiological requirements to the need for self-actualization.

self-actualization Fulfilling one's potential.

deficiency needs Maslow's four lower-order needs, which must be satisfied first.

being needs Maslow's three higher-order needs, sometimes called growth needs.

Maslow's theory has been criticized because people do not always behave as it predicts. Most of us move back and forth among different types of needs and may even be motivated by many different needs at the same time. For example, some people deny themselves lower-order safety needs or friendship needs to achieve knowledge or understanding.

Criticisms aside, Maslow's theory does invite looking at the whole person, whose physical, emotional, and intellectual needs are interrelated. It helps us understand that, if school is a fearful, unpredictable place, students are likely to be more concerned with safety and less with needs to know and understand. Belonging to a social group and maintaining self-esteem within that group, for example, are important to students. If doing what the teacher says conflicts with group rules, students may choose to ignore the teacher's wishes or even defy the teacher.

A more recent approach to motivation that focuses on human needs is self-determination theory (Deci & Ryan, 2002), discussed later in this chapter.

Connect & Extend

TO THE RESEARCH
See the entire September 2002 issue of *Educational Leadership* (60[1]) for 14 articles addressing the question, "Do Students Care about Learning?" These articles discuss how to create enthusiasm, excitement, and investment in learning.

Cognitive and Social Approaches to Motivation

In cognitive theories, people are seen as active and curious searchers for information to solve personally relevant problems. Thus, cognitive theories of motivation emphasize intrinsic motivation. Cognitive theorists hold that behaviour is determined by our thinking, not simply by whether we have been reinforced or punished (Stipek, 2002). Behaviour is initiated and regulated by mental plans (Miller, Galanter, & Pribram, 1960), goals (Locke & Latham, 1990), schemas (Ortony, Clore, & Collins, 1988), expectations (Vroom, 1964), and attributions (Weiner, 1992).

We will look at goals and attributions later in this chapter.

Expectancy × Value Theories. Theories that blend behaviourists' focus on behaviour with cognitivists' attention to thinking are **expectancy × value theories**. In these theories, motivation originates with two main factors: the individual's expectation of reaching a goal and the value of that goal. "If I try hard, can I succeed?" "If I succeed, is the outcome valuable or rewarding to me?" Motivation is a product of both factors. If either factor is zero, there is no motivation to work toward the goal. For example, if Cindy believes that she has a good chance of winning a prize in the science fair (high expectation), and if that prize is very important to her (high value), her motivation should be strong. But if either factor is near zero (she believes she hasn't much chance of winning, or she couldn't care less about science fair prizes), her motivation will be nil (Tollefson, 2000).

Phil adds the element of *cost* to the expectancy × value model (Winne, 1997; Winne & Marx, 1989). Values have to be considered in relation to the cost of pursuing them. For example, people may ask themselves, "How much energy will be required?" "What could I be doing instead?" "What are the risks if I fail?" "Will I look stupid?" (Wigfield & Eccles, 1992; Wigfield & Eccles, 2000). Albert Bandura's social cognitive theory, discussed later in this chapter, is another example of an expectancy × value approach to motivation (Feather, 1982; Pintrich & Schunk, 2002).

Sociocultural Conceptions of Motivation

Sociocultural conceptions of motivation emphasize participation in communities of practice. People engage in activities to develop knowledge as they maintain their identities and their interpersonal relations within a community. In this view, students will be motivated to learn if they are members of a community, a classroom, or school that values learning. Just as we learn to speak and dress and conduct ourselves in museums or theatres by watching and learning from capable members of our culture, students learn how to be students by watching and learning from classmates and peers in school. In other words, we learn by the company we keep (Greeno, Collins, & Resnick, 1996; Rogoff, Turkanis, & Bartlett, 2001).

The concept of identity is central in sociocultural views of motivation. When students see themselves as budding computer scientists or violinists or newspaper editors, they have an identity within a group. Part of socialization is moving from being a member or participant on the edge or periphery of these groups to a central place in the group's activities. The concept of **legitimate peripheral participation** means that beginners are genuinely involved in the work of the group, even if their abilities are undeveloped and their contributions are small at first. Each task is a piece of the real work of the expert. The novice computer scientist learns about surfing the web before learning how to code elegant webpages, just as the novice teacher learns to tutor one child before working with a whole class. The identities of both the novice and the expert are bound up in their participation in the community. To strengthen their identities as community members, they are motivated to learn the values and carry out the practices of their community (Lave & Wenger, 1991).

According to Maslow's hierarchy, when the needs for love and belongingness are met, individuals can then address the so-called higher-order needs of intellectual achievement and self-actualization.

expectancy × value theories Explanations of motivation that emphasize individuals' expectations for success combined with their valuing of the goal.

Connect & Extend

TO YOUR TEACHING
Based on expectancy × value theories, predict the level of motivation in each of the following situations:

a. Perceived probability of success under minimum effort is high; incentive value is high.

b. Perceived probability of success under maximum effort is high; incentive value is moderate.

c. Perceived probability of success under maximum effort is low; incentive value is moderate.

sociocultural views of motivation Perspectives that emphasize participation, identities, and interpersonal relations within communities of practice.

legitimate peripheral participation Genuine involvement in the work of the group, even if one's abilities are undeveloped and contributions small.

TABLE 10.1 Four Views of Motivation

	Behavioural	Humanistic	Cognitive	Sociocultural
Source of motivation	Extrinsic	Intrinsic	Intrinsic	Intrinsic
Important influences	Reinforcers, rewards, incentives, and punishers	Need for self-esteem, self-fulfillment, and self-determination	Beliefs, attributions for success and failure, expectations	Engaged participation in learning communities; maintaining identity through participation in activities of group
Key theorists	Skinner	Maslow Deci	Weiner Graham	Lave Wenger

Some classrooms are designed as learning communities. For example, Brown and Campione (1996) developed learning communities for middle school students around research projects in science. Scardamalia and Bereiter (1996), colleagues at the University of Toronto, designed a learning community where students use a computer system, called Knowledge Forum, that supports collaboration among students about questions, hypotheses, methods of inquiry, and findings in communal projects. The challenge in designs for learning communities is to be sure that all students can progress from positions of legitimate peripheral participation to become full participants in the community. Daniel Hickey (2003) says it this way: Engagement is "meaningful participation in a context where to-be-learned knowledge is valued and used" (p. 411)

The behavioural, humanistic, cognitive, and sociocultural approaches to motivation are summarized in Table 10.1. These theories differ in their answers to the question, "What is motivation?" but each contributes in its own way to a comprehensive understanding.

Check Your Knowledge

- What are key factors in motivation according to a behavioural viewpoint? A humanistic viewpoint? A cognitive viewpoint? A sociocultural viewpoint?
- Distinguish between deficiency needs and being needs in Maslow's theory.
- What are expectancy × value theories?
- What is legitimate peripheral participation?

Apply to Practice

- Use Maslow's theory to explain why a student who is upset about events in his or her family might not be motivated to study.
- How does participation and identity in a group affect your motivation?

NEEDS: COMPETENCE, AUTONOMY, AND RELATEDNESS

We have already seen one motivation theory that focused on needs—Maslow's hierarchy of needs. Other early research in psychology conceived of motivation in terms of trait-like needs or consistent personal characteristics. Three of the main needs studied extensively were the needs for achievement, power, and affiliation (Pintrich, 2003). We will look at one recent theory that emphasizes similar needs through a focus on self-determination.

Self-Determination

Self-determination theory suggests that we all need to feel competent and capable in our interactions in the world. We also need to have some choices and a sense of control over our lives, and to be connected to others—to belong to a social group. Notice that these are similar to conceptions of basic needs: competence (achievement), autonomy and control (power), and relatedness (affiliation).

Need for autonomy is central to self-determination because it is the desire to have our own wishes, rather than external rewards or pressures, determine our actions (Deci & Ryan, 2002; Reeve, Deci, & Ryan, 2004; Ryan & Deci, 2000). People strive to be in charge of their own behaviour. They constantly struggle against pressure from external controls such as the rules, schedules, deadlines, orders, and limits imposed by others. Sometimes, even help is rejected so that the individual can remain in command (deCharms, 1983).

Self-Determination in the Classroom.

Classroom environments that support student self-determination and autonomy are associated with greater student interest, sense of competence, creativity, conceptual learning, and preference for challenge. These relationships appear to hold from grade 1 through graduate school (Deci & Ryan, 2002; Williams et al., 1993). When students can make choices, they are more likely to believe that the work is important, even if it is not "fun." Thus, they tend to internalize educational goals and take them as their own.

In contrast to autonomy-supporting classrooms, controlling environments tend to improve performance only on rote recall tasks. When students are pressured to perform, they often seek the quickest, easiest solution. One discomforting finding, however, is that both students and parents seem to prefer more controlling teachers, even though the students learn more when their teachers support autonomy (Flink, Boggiano, & Barrett, 1990). Assuming you are willing to risk going against popular images, how can you support student autonomy? One answer is to focus on *information*, not *control*, in your interactions with students.

Information and Control.

Many things happen to students throughout the school day. They are praised or criticized, reminded of deadlines, assigned grades, given choices, lectured about rules, and on and on. **Cognitive evaluation theory** (Deci & Ryan, 2002; Ryan & Deci, 2000) explains how these events can influence the students' intrinsic motivation by affecting their sense of self-determination and competence. According to this theory, all events have two aspects: controlling and informational. If an event is highly controlling, that is, if it pressures students to act or feel a certain way, then students will experience less control and their *intrinsic motivation* will be diminished. If, on the other hand, the event provides information that increases the students' sense of competence, then intrinsic motivation will increase. Of course, if the information provided makes students feel less competent, it is likely that motivation will decrease (Pintrich, 2003).

For example, a teacher might praise a student by saying, "Good for you! You got an A because you finally followed my instructions correctly." This is a highly controlling statement, giving the credit to the teacher and thus undermining the student's sense of self-determination and intrinsic motivation. The teacher could praise the same work by saying, "Good for you! Your understanding of the author's use of metaphors has improved tremendously. You earned an A." This statement provides information about the student's growing competence and should increase intrinsic motivation.

What can teachers do to support student needs for autonomy and competence? An obvious first step is to limit their controlling messages to their students and make sure the information they provide highlights students' growing competence. The accompanying Guidelines give ideas.

The Need for Relatedness.

The need for relatedness is the desire to establish close emotional bonds and attachments with others. When teachers and parents

Connect & Extend

TO YOUR TEACHING
Understand how self-determination can boost or diminish motivation, and describe practical steps that teachers can take to establish a sense of self-determination in students.

need for autonomy The desire to have our own wishes, rather than external rewards or pressures, determine our actions.

Connect & Extend

TO THE RESEARCH
To capture the difference between self- and other-determination, Richard deCharms (1976, 1983) used the metaphor of people as "origins" and "pawns." Origins perceive themselves as the origin or source of their intention to act in a certain way. As pawns, people see themselves as powerless participants in a game controlled by others. When people feel like pawns, play becomes work, leisure feels like obligation, and intrinsic motivation becomes extrinsic motivation. For example, you may have had the experience of a real option to wash the car, only to have your motivation dampened by a parent who insists that you tackle the chore. Your chance to be an origin seems spoiled by outside attempts at control. You don't want to wash the car any more because your sense of self-determination is taken away. DeCharms observed that students are too little governed by their own intrinsic motivation and too powerless over external controls. To deal with the issue, he developed programs to help teachers support student self-determination. The programs emphasized setting realistic goals, personal planning of activities to reach the goals, personal responsibility for actions, and feelings of self-confidence.

cognitive evaluation theory Suggests that events affect motivation through the individual's perception of the events as controlling behaviour or providing information.

SUPPORTING SELF-DETERMINATION AND AUTONOMY

Allow and encourage students to make choices.

EXAMPLES

1. Design several different ways to meet a learning objective (e.g., a paper, a compilation of interviews, a test, a news broadcast) and let students choose one. Encourage them to explain the reasons for their choice.

2. Appoint student committees to make suggestions about streamlining procedures such as caring for class pets or distributing equipment.

3. Provide time for independent and extended projects.

Help students plan actions to accomplish self-selected goals.

EXAMPLES

1. Experiment with goal cards. Students list their short- and long-term goals and then record three or four specific actions that will move them toward the goals. Goal cards are personal—like credit cards.

2. Encourage middle- and high-school students to set goals in each subject area, record them in a goal book or on a floppy disk, and check progress toward the goals on a regular basis.

Hold students accountable for the consequences of their choices.

EXAMPLES

1. If students choose to work with friends and do not finish a project because too much time was spent socializing, grade the project as it deserves and help the students see the connection between lost time and poor performance.

2. When students choose a topic that captures their imagination, discuss the connections between their investment in the work and the quality of the products that follow.

Provide rationales for limits, rules, and constraints.

EXAMPLES

1. Explain reasons for rules.

2. Respect rules and constraints in your own behaviour.

Acknowledge that negative emotions are valid reactions to teacher control.

EXAMPLES

1. Communicate that it is okay (and normal) to feel bored waiting for a turn, for example.

2. Communicate that sometimes important learning involves frustration, confusion, weariness.

Use non-controlling, positive feedback.

EXAMPLES

1. See poor performance or behaviour as a problem to be solved, not a target of criticism.

2. Avoid controlling language, for example "should," "must," "have to."

For more information on self-determination theory, see **www.psych.rochester.edu/SDT**.

Source: From Raffini, P. (1996). *150 ways to increase intrinsic motiviation in the classroom.* Published by Allyn and Bacon, Boston, MA. Copyright © 1996 by Pearson Education; Reeve, Johnmarshall (1996). *Motivating others: nurturing inner motivational resources.* Published by Allyn and Bacon, Boston, MA. Copyright © 1996 by Pearson Education. Adapted by permission of the publisher.

are responsive and demonstrate that they care about the children's interests and well-being, the children show high intrinsic motivation. But when children are denied the interpersonal involvement they seek from adults—when adults, for example, are unresponsive to their needs—the children lose intrinsic motivation (Solomon et al., 2000). Students who feel a sense of relatedness to teachers, parents, and peers are more emotionally engaged in school (Furrer & Skinner, 2003). In addition, emotional and physical problems—ranging from eating disorders to suicide—are more common among people who lack social relationships (Baumeister & Leary, 1995). Relatedness is similar to a sense of belonging, discussed in Chapter 3.

Needs: Lessons for Teachers

From infancy to old age, people want to be both competent and connected. Students are more likely to participate in activities that help them grow more competent and less likely to engage in activities that cause them to fail. This means that the students need appropriately challenging tasks—not too easy, but not impossible either. They also benefit from ways of watching their competence grow, perhaps through self-monitoring systems or portfolios. To be connected, students need to feel that people in school care about them and can be trusted to help them learn.

What else matters in motivation? Many theories include goals as key elements.

Check Your Knowledge

- What are the basic needs and how do they affect motivation?
- How can feedback actually undermine motivation?

Apply to Practice

- When you assign students to groups to collaborate on a project, what guidance could you give them about how to interact with one another in their work to sustain or increase their motivation?

GOAL ORIENTATION AND MOTIVATION

goal What an individual strives to accomplish.

A **goal** is an outcome or attainment that an individual is striving to accomplish (Locke & Latham, 1990). When students strive to understand a math problem or make a 4.0 grade-point average, this is *goal-directed behaviour.* In pursuing goals, students are generally aware of some current condition ("I haven't even opened my book!"), some ideal condition ("I have read and understood every page"), and the discrepancy between the current and ideal situations. Goals motivate people to act to reduce the discrepancy between where they are and where they want to be.

Goal setting is usually effective for most people. It is often a good idea to set goals for each day. For example, "Today, I intend to review this chapter, gather library references for my history paper, and jog."

According to Locke and Latham (1990), there are four main reasons why goal setting improves performance. Goals

Connect & Extend

TO THE RESEARCH

For a synthesis of the research on goals from two founders of the theory, see Locke, E. A., & Latham, G. P. (2002). Building a practically useful theory of goal setting and task motivation: A 35-year odyssey. *American Psychologist, 57,* 705–717.

1. Direct our attention to tasks at hand. If your mind wanders while reviewing the chapter, your goal helps direct your attention back to the task.

2. Mobilize effort. The harder the goal, up to a point, the greater the effort.

3. Increase persistence. When we have a clear goal, we are less likely to be distracted or to give up until we reach the goal.

4. Promote developing new strategies when old strategies fall short. If your goal is making an A and you don't reach that goal on your first quiz, you might drop the strategy of reviewing once a month and try a new approach to studying, such as explaining the key points every week to peers in your study group.

Types of Goals and Goal Orientations

The types of goals we set influence our motivation. Goals that are specific, moderately difficult, and likely to be reached in the relatively near future tend to enhance motivation and persistence (Pintrich & Schunk, 2002; Stipek, 2002). Specific goals provide clearer standards for judging performance. If performance falls short, we keep going. For example, instead of working on an entire essay, you may decide to write an introduction. Because it is clear when you are finished (your introduction is done), you know when you have met the goal. Anything short of finishing the introduction means "keep working." Moderate difficulty provides a challenge but not an unreasonable one. You can finish your introduction if you stay with it. Finally, goals that can be reached fairly soon are not likely to be pushed aside by more immediate concerns. Self-help groups that encourage their members to make progress "one day at a time" are aware of this property of short-term goals.

Four Goal Orientations in School. Goals are specific targets. **Goal orientations** are patterns of beliefs about goals related to achievement in school. Goal orientations include the reasons we pursue goals and the standards we use to evaluate progress toward those goals. Students categorize goals in terms of one of four main orientations: mastery (learning), performance (looking good), work-avoidance, and social (Murphy & Alexander, 2000; Pintrich & Schunk, 2002).

The most common distinction in research on students' goals is between mastery goals (sometimes called *task goals* or *learning goals*) and performance goals (also termed *ability goals* or *ego goals*). The point of a **mastery goal** is to improve, to learn, regardless of mistakes you make or how awkward you appear. Students who set mastery goals tend to seek challenges and persist when they encounter difficulties. Because they focus on the task at hand and are not worried about how their performance "measures up" compared with others in the class, these students have been called **task-involved learners** (Nicholls & Miller, 1984). We often say these people get "lost in their work." In addition, task-involved learners are more likely to seek appropriate help, and they report using deeper cognitive processing strategies and better study strategies (Butler & Neuman, 1995; Midgley, 2001; Young, 1997).

The second kind of goal is a performance goal. Students who hold a **performance goal** care about demonstrating their ability to others. They may be focused on getting good grades. Or they may be more concerned with winning and outdoing other students than with what they learn (Wolters, Yu, & Pintrich, 1996). Students holding performance goals undermine learning by doing things just to look smart, such as reading easy books to "read the most books" (Young, 1997). If success seems impossible, they may adopt defensive, failure-avoiding strategies—they pretend not to care, make a show of "not really trying," cheat, or may simply give up (Pintrich & Schunk, 1996). These students have been referred to as **ego-involved learners** because they are preoccupied with themselves. Deborah Stipek (2002) lists several behaviours that can indicate that a student is too ego-involved with school work:

- Cheats, copies from classmates' papers, or uses shortcuts to finish ahead of others.
- Seeks attention for good performance.
- Works hard only on graded assignments.
- Is upset by and hides papers with low grades.
- Compares grades with classmates.
- Chooses tasks most likely to result in positive evaluations.
- Is uncomfortable with assignments that have unclear evaluation criteria.

Wait—Are Performance Goals Always Bad? Performance goals sound pretty dysfunctional, don't they? Earlier research indicated that performance goals generally were detrimental to learning. But like extrinsic motivation, a performance goal orientation may not be all bad all the time. In fact, some research indicates that both mastery and performance goals are associated with using active learning strategies and high self-efficacy (Midgley, Kaplan, Middleton, 2001; Stipek, 2002). And, as with intrinsic and extrinsic motivation, students can and often do pursue mastery and performance goals at the same time.

To account for these recent findings, educational psychologists have added the distinction of approach versus avoidance to the mastery versus performance

goal orientations Patterns of beliefs about goals related to achievement in school.

mastery goal A personal intention to improve abilities and understand, no matter how performance suffers.

task-involved learners Students who focus on mastering the task or solving the problem.

performance goal A personal intention to seem competent or perform well in the eyes of others.

ego-involved learners Students who focus on how well they are performing and how they are judged by others.

Connect & Extend

TO YOUR TEACHING
Are students with learning goals more likely to: (1) be internal or external in locus of control; (2) have internal and stable or internal and unstable attributions; (3) be failure avoiders or success seekers?

If this girl's goal is to improve and not worry about mistakes, she may attempt more difficult pieces and welcome criticism. If her goal is to simply look good, she may avoid difficulty and criticism.

work-avoidant learners Students who don't want to learn or to look smart but just want to avoid work.

social goals A wide variety of needs and motives to be connected to others or to be part of a group.

distinction. In other words, students may be motivated to either approach mastery or avoid misunderstanding. They may approach performance or avoid looking dumb. Look at Table 10.2 for an example of each kind of goal orientation and the effects of each. Where do you see the most problems? Do you agree that the real problems are with avoidance? Students who fear misunderstanding (mastery avoid) may be perfectionistic—focused on getting it exactly right. Students who avoid looking dumb (performance avoid) may adopt defensive, failure-avoiding strategies (Jagacinski & Nicholls, 1987; Pintrich & Schunk, 2002).

Beyond Mastery and Performance.   Some students don't want to learn or to look smart; they just want to avoid work. These students try to complete assignments and activities as quickly as possible without exerting much effort (Pintrich & Schunk, 2002). Nicholls called these students **work-avoidant learners**—they feel successful when they don't have to try hard, when the work is easy, or when they can "goof off."

The final category of goals, **social goals**, becomes more important as students get older. As students move into adolescence, their social networks change to include more peers. Non-academic activities such as athletics, dating, and "hanging out" compete with school work (Urdan & Maehr, 1995). Social goals include a wide variety of needs and motives with different relationships to learning. Some help, but others hinder learning. For example, adolescents' goal of maintaining friendly relations in a cooperative learning group can interfere with learning if group members don't challenge friends' wrong answers or misconceptions because they are afraid to hurt their feelings (Anderson, Holland, & Palincsar, 1997). Certainly, pursuing goals such as having fun with friends or avoiding being labelled a "nerd" can get in the way of learning. But goals of bringing honour to your family or team by working hard can support learning (Urdan & Maehr, 1995). Social goals that include being a part of peer groups that value academics certainly can support learning (Pintrich, 2003; A. Ryan, 2001).

We talk about goals in separate categories, but students have to coordinate their goals as they decide what to do and how to act. Sometimes social and academic goals are incompatible. For example, academic failure may be interpreted positively by some minority-group students because non-compliance with the majority culture's norms and standards is seen as an accomplishment. Thus it would be impossible to simultaneously succeed in both school and the peer group (Ogbu, 1987; Wentzel, 1999). And succeeding in the peer group is important—the need for social relationships is basic and strong for most people.

TABLE 10.2 Goal Orientations

Students may have either an approach focus or an avoidance focus for mastery and performance goal orientations.

Goal Orientation	Approach Focus	Avoidance Focus
Mastery	*Focus*: Mastering the task, learning, understanding	*Focus*: Avoiding misunderstanding or not mastering the task
	Standards used: Self-improvement, progress, deep understanding (task-involved)	*Standards used*: Just don't be wrong, don't do it incorrectly
Performance	*Focus*: Being superior, winning, being the best	*Focus*: Avoiding looking stupid, avoid losing
	Standards used: Normative—getting the highest grade, winning the competition (ego-involved)	*Standards used*: Normative—don't be the worst, get the lowest grade, or be the slowest (ego-involved)

Source: Pintrich, P., & Schunk, D. (2002). *Motivation in education: Theory, research, and applications* (2nd ed.). Upper Saddle River, NJ: Prentice Hall. Copyright © 2002 by Prentice Hall. Reprinted by permission of Pearson Education, Inc., Upper Saddle River, NJ.

Feedback and Goal Acceptance

Besides having specific goals and creating supportive social relationships, there are two additional factors that make goal-setting in the classroom effective. The first is *feedback*. To be motivated to resolve a discrepancy between where you are and where you want to be, you need an accurate sense of where you are and how far you have to go. When feedback tells a student that current efforts fall short of the goal, and if the feedback describes how to do better, the student can exert more effort or has an idea of what to do (Butler & Winne, 1995). When feedback describes accomplishment in relation to goals, the student can feel satisfied and competent, and he or she may even set a slightly higher goal for the future. In one study, feedback to some adults emphasized that they had accomplished 75 percent of the standards set; other adults were told they had fallen short of the standards by 25 percent. When the feedback highlighted accomplishment, the subjects' self-confidence, analytic thinking, and performance were all enhanced (Bandura, 1997).

The second factor affecting motivation to pursue a goal is *goal acceptance*. If students reject goals set by others or refuse to set their own goals, motivation suffers. Generally, students are more willing to adopt goals that others set when the goals seem realistic, reasonably difficult, and meaningful—and if good reasons are given for the value of the goals (Grolnick et al., 2002). Commitment matters—the relationship between higher goals and better performance is strongest when people are committed to the goals (Locke & Latham, 2002).

Goals: Lessons for Teachers

Students are more likely to work toward goals that are clear, specific, reasonable, moderately challenging, and attainable within a relatively short time frame. If teachers overstress student performance, high grades, competition, and achievement, they may encourage students to set performance goals. This undermines students' learning and task involvement (Anderman & Maehr, 1994). Students may not yet be expert at setting their own goals or keeping these goals in mind, so encouragement and accurate feedback are necessary. If you use a reward system, be sure that the goal you set is to *learn and improve,* not just to perform well or look smart. And be sure that the goal is not too difficult. Students, like adults, are more likely to stick with tasks or respond well to teachers who make them feel secure and competent.

Check Your Knowledge

- What kinds of goals are the most motivating?
- Describe mastery, performance, work-avoidant, and social goals.
- What makes goal setting effective in the classroom?

Apply to Practice

- A teacher says to the class, "I want all of you to study hard so you can make good scores on the provincial exams next June." Predict the effects of this goal-setting statement. Are students likely to be motivated by the goal? Why or why not?

What else do we know about motivation? Feelings matter.

INTERESTS AND EMOTIONS

How do you feel about learning? Excited, bored, curious, fearful? Today, researchers emphasize that learning involves not only the *cold cognition* of reasoning and problem solving. Learning and information processing also involve emotion, invitingly called *hot cognition* (Miller, 1993; Pintrich, Marx, & Boyle, 1993). Students are more likely to pay attention to, learn, and remember material that provokes appropriate emotional responses (Alexander & Murphy, 1998; Cowley & Underwood, 1998; Reisberg & Heuer, 1992) or that relates to their personal interests (Renninger, Hidi, & Krapp, 1992). How can we use these findings to support learning in school?

Tapping Interests

What Would You Say?

As part of your interview for a job in a large high school, the principal asks, "How would you get students interested in learning? Could you tap their interests?"

When Walter Vispoel and James Austin (1995) surveyed over 200 middle school students, lack of interest in the topic was rated highest as an explanation for failures. Interest was second only to effort as the explanation for successes. It seems logical that learning experiences should be related to the interests of students, and that interests increase when students feel competent. Even if students are not initially interested in a subject or activity, they may develop interest as they experience success (Stipek, 2002).

There are two kinds of interests—personal and situational—the trait and state distinction again. *Personal interests* are more enduring aspects of the person, such as an interest in astronomy, music, or ancient history. *Situational interests* are more short-lived aspects of the activity, text, or materials that catch and keep the student's attention. Both personal and situational interests are related to learning from texts—the more interest, the more deep processing and remembering of the material (Ainley, Hidi, & Berndorf, 2002; Pintrich, 2003; Schraw & Lehman, 2001).

Catching and Holding Interests. Whenever possible, it helps to connect academic content to students' enduring personal interests. But given that the content you will teach is not fully yours to control, it will be difficult to tailor lessons to each student's personal interests. You will have to rely more on situational interest. Here, the challenge is to not only *catch* but also *hold* students' interest (Pintrich, 2003). For example, Mathew Mitchell (1993) found that using computers, groups, and puzzles caught students' interest in secondary mathematics classes, but the interests did not hold. Lessons that held interests over time included math

Students' interest in and excitement about what they're learning is one of the most important factors in education.

activities that were related to real-life problems and active participation in laboratory activities and projects. However, there are cautions in responding to students' interests, as you can see in the Point/Counterpoint.

Another source of interest is fantasy. For example, Cordova and Lepper (1996) found that students learned more math facts during a computer exercise when they were challenged, as captains of starships, to navigate through space by solving math problems. The students got to name their ships, stock the (imaginary) galley with their favourite snacks, and name all the crew members after their friends.

The Guidelines on page 386 give other ideas for building on students' interests in the classroom.

POINT > < COUNTERPOINT

DOES MAKING LEARNING FUN MAKE FOR GOOD LEARNING?

When many beginning teachers are asked about how to motivate students, they often mention making learning fun. It is true that connecting to students' interests, stimulating curiosity, and using fantasy all encourage motivation and engagement. But is it necessary for learning to be fun?

> Point *Teachers should make learning fun.*

When Phil searched "making learning fun" on Google.ca, he found more than 20 000 hits. Clearly, there is interest in making learning fun. In 1987, Thomas Malone and Mark Lepper wrote a chapter titled "Making Learning Fun: A Taxonomy of Intrinsic Motivations for Learning." Research shows that passages in texts that are more interesting are remembered better (Pintrich & Schunk, 2002). For example, students who read books that interested them spent more time reading, read more words in the books, and felt more positive about reading (Guthrie & Alao, 1997).

Games and simulations can also make learning more fun. For example, in a school Anita knows, all the students in grade 8 spent three days playing a game. Students were divided into groups and formed their own "countries." Each country had to choose a name, symbol, national flower, and bird. They wrote and sang a national anthem and elected government officials. The teachers allocated different resources to the countries. To obtain all the materials needed to complete assigned projects, the countries had to establish trade with one another. There was a monetary system and a stock market. Students had to work with their fellow citizens to complete cooperative learning assignments. Some countries "cheated" in their trades with other nations, and this allowed debate about international relations, trust, and war. The students reported that they had fun. They also said that they learned how to work in a group without the teacher's supervision and gained a deeper understanding of world economics and international conflicts.

< Counterpoint *Fun can get in the way of learning.*

As far back as the early 1900s, educators warned about the dangers of focusing on fun in learning. None other than John Dewey, who wrote extensively about the role of interest in learning, cautioned that you can't make boring lessons interesting by mixing in fun like you can make bad chili good by adding some spicy hot sauce. Dewey wrote, "When things have to be made interesting, it is because interest itself is wanting. Moreover, the phrase itself is a mis-nomer. The thing, the object, is no more interesting than it was before" (Dewey, 1913, pp. 11–12).

There is a good deal of research now indicating that adding interest by adding fascinating but irrelevant details actually gets in the way of learning the important information. These "seductive details" divert the readers' attention from the less interesting main ideas (Harp & Mayer, 1998). For example, students who read biographies of historical figures remembered more very interesting but unimportant information compared with interesting main ideas (Wade et al., 1993). Shannon Harp and Richard Mayer (1998) found similar results with high school science texts. These texts added emotional interest and seductive details about swimmers and golfers who are injured by lightning to a lesson on the process of lightning. They concluded that "in the case of emotional interest versus cognitive interest, the verdict is clear. Adjuncts aimed at increasing emotional interest failed to improve understanding of scientific explanations" (p. 100). The seductive details may have disrupted students' attempts to follow the logic of the explanations and thus interfered with comprehending the text. Harp and Mayer conclude that "the best way to help students enjoy a passage is to help them understand it" (p. 100).

BUILDING ON STUDENTS' INTERESTS

Relate content objectives to student experiences.

EXAMPLES

1. With a teacher in another school, city, or province, establish pen pals across the classes. Through writing letters or email messages, students exchange personal experiences, photos, drawings, written work, and ask and answer questions ("Have you learned cursive writing yet?" "What are you doing in math now?" "What are you reading?"). Letters can be mailed in one large mailer to save stamps.

2. Identify classroom experts for different assignments or tasks. Who knows how to use the computer for graphics? How to search the internet? How to cook? How to use an index?

3. Have a "Switch Day" when each student exchanges roles with a member of the school staff or a support person. Students must research the role by interviewing their staff members, prepare for the job, dress the part for the day they take over, and then evaluate their success after the switch.

Identify student interests, hobbies, and extracurricular activities that can be incorporated into class lessons and discussions.

EXAMPLES

1. Have students design and conduct interviews and surveys to learn about each other's interests.

2. Keep the class library stocked with books that connect to students' interests and hobbies.

Support instruction with humour, personal experiences, and anecdotes that show the human side of the content.

EXAMPLES

1. Share your own hobbies, interests, and favourites.

2. Tell students that there will be a surprise visitor, then dress up as the author of a story and tell about "yourself" and your writing.

Use original source material with interesting content or details.

EXAMPLES

1. In history classes, use letters and diaries.

2. In biology, use, for example, Darwin's notes.

Create surprise and curiosity.

EXAMPLES

1. Have students predict what will happen in an experiment, then show them why they are wrong.

2. Provide famous quotations by historical figures and ask students to guess the author.

Source: Adapted from Raffini, J. P. (1996). *150 ways to increase intrinsic motivation in the classroom.* Boston: Allyn & Bacon. Copyright © 1996 by Allyn & Bacon.

However, there are cautions about responding to students' interests. Ruth Garner (1992) found that "seductive details" can hinder learning. Seductive details are interesting bits of information that are not central to the curriculum. Some examples might be details about the life of a scientist that do not help you understand her theories. Interesting puzzles or manipulatives that don't directly support learning objectives can also be seductive. The research is quite clear: students remember these seductive details at the expense of the curriculum they should know.

Arousal: Excitement and Anxiety in Learning

arousal Physical and psychological reactions causing a person to be alert, attentive, wide awake.

We all know what it is like to be excited and aroused—we feel alert, wide awake, even excited. **Arousal** involves both psychological and physical reactions—changes in brainwave patterns, blood pressure, heart rate, and breathing rate. To understand the effects of arousal on motivation, think of two extremes. Imagine that it is late at night, and you are struggling for the third time to understand a chapter (hopefully not ours!), but you are so sleepy. Your attention drifts and your eyes droop—but you're not done with the reading. You decide to go to bed and get up early to study (a plan you know seldom works). At the other extreme, imagine a scholarship exam scheduled for tomorrow. As you try to go to sleep, you worry about doing well. You know that you need a good night's sleep, but you are wide awake. In the first case, arousal is too low; in the second, it's too high.

We've known for a century that there is an optimum level of arousal for most activities (Yerkes & Dodson, 1908). Generally, moderately high arousal is helpful on new tasks that are relatively simple or tasks where thinking is automated. Lower levels of arousal are better for complex tasks. Let's look for a moment at how to increase arousal by arousing curiosity.

Curiosity: Novelty and Complexity. Psychologists suggested 40 years ago that individuals are naturally motivated to seek novelty, surprise, and complexity (Pintrich, 2003). Research has since found that variety in teaching approaches and diversity in tasks can support learning (Brophy & Good, 1986; Stipek, 2002). For younger students, the chance to manipulate and explore objects, provided they are relevant to objectives, is an effective way to stimulate curiosity. For older students, well-constructed questions, logical puzzles, and paradoxes can have the same effect. Consider this example. Ranchers killed the wolves on their land; the following spring, their sheep population was smaller—how could this be, since wolves hunt sheep but fewer wolves means more sheep? Searching to solve this paradox, students learn about ecological systems: without wolves to eliminate weaker and sicker sheep, the sheep population exceeds the winter food supply needed to sustain the flocks. Many sheep died of starvation.

George Lowenstein (1994) suggests that gaps in knowledge can "produce the feeling of deprivation labelled *curiosity*. The curious person is motivated to obtain the missing information to reduce or eliminate the feeling of deprivation" (p. 87). This idea is similar to Piaget's concept of disequilibrium, discussed in Chapter 2, and has several implications for teaching. First, students need some base of knowledge before they can experience gaps in knowledge that spark curiosity. Second, students must be aware of those gaps for curiosity to result. Asking students to make guesses and then providing feedback can help them recall what they know and expose gaps. Also, mistakes, if appropriately handled, can stimulate curiosity by pointing to missing knowledge. Finally, the more we learn about a topic, the more curious we may become about it. As Maslow (1970) predicted, the need for more knowledge is often stimulated by learning.

As we noted earlier, sometimes arousal is too high, not too low. Because classrooms are places where students are tested and graded, anxiety can also be a factor in classroom motivation.

Anxiety in the Classroom. At one time or another, everyone has experienced **anxiety**, or a general uneasiness, a feeling of self-doubt, a sense of tension. Over the entire last century, "researchers have consistently reported a negative correlation between virtually every aspect of school achievement and a wide range of anxiety measures" (Covington & Omelich, 1987, p. 393). Anxiety can be both a cause and an effect of school failure—students do poorly because they are anxious, and their poor performance further increases their anxiety. Anxiety is probably both a trait and a state. Some students tend to be anxious in many situations (*trait anxiety*), but some situations are especially anxiety-provoking (*state anxiety*) (Covington, 1992; Zeidner, 1998).

Anxiety has both cognitive and affective components. The cognitive side includes worry and negative thoughts—for example, thinking about how bad it would be to fail and worrying (predicting) that you will. The affective side involves physiological elements such as sweaty palms, upset stomach, and racing heartbeat, as well as emotional reactions such as fear (Pintrich & Schunk, 2002; Zeidner, 1995, 1998). Whenever pressures to perform are coupled with severe consequences for failure, and when competitive comparisons are emphasized, anxiety may be elevated (Wigfield & Eccles, 1989). Also, research with school-age children

Connect & Extend

TO THE RESEARCH
Lowenstein, G. (1994). The psychology of curiosity: A review and reinterpretation. *Psychological Bulletin, 117,* 75–98. This article connects curiosity to perceived gaps in information.

anxiety General uneasiness; a feeling of tension.

Connect & Extend

TO THE RESEARCH
Meece, J. L., Wigfield, A., & Eccles, J. (1990). Predictors of math anxiety and its influence on young adolescents' course enrolment intentions and performance in mathematics. *Journal of Educational Psychology, 92*, 6–70. This study found that math anxiety was most directly related to students' math ability perceptions, performance expectancies, and value perceptions. Students' performance expectancies predicted subsequent math grades, whereas their value perception predicted course enrolment intentions.

Connect & Extend

TO PRACTICE
The Test Taking and Anxiety site (**www.ulrc.psu.edu/studyskills/ test_taking.html**) provides tips and insights into addressing the problems associated with test anxiety. (These tips might be useful for doing well on your own exams!)

shows a relationship between the quality of sleep (how quickly and how well you sleep) and anxiety. Better-quality sleep is associated with positive arousal or an "eagerness" to learn. Poor-quality sleep, on the other hand, was related to debilitating anxiety and decreased school performance. You may have discovered these relationships for yourself in your own school career (Meijer & van den Wittenboer, 2004).

How Does Anxiety Interfere with Achievement? Anxiety interferes at three points: focusing attention, learning, and demonstrating learning on tests. When students are learning new material, they must pay attention to it. Highly anxious students divide their attention between new material and nervous feelings. Instead of concentrating on a lecture or on what they are reading, they keep noticing their laboured breathing and think, "I'm so tense, I'll never understand this stuff!" Much of their attention is taken up with thoughts about performing poorly, being criticized, and feeling embarrassed. From the beginning, anxious students may miss much of the information they are supposed to learn because their thoughts are focused on their own worries (Cassady & Johnson, 2002; Paulman & Kennelly, 1984).

But the problems do not end here. Even if they are paying attention, many anxious students have trouble learning material that is somewhat disorganized and difficult—material that requires them to rely on their memory. Unfortunately, much material in school is just like this. In addition, many highly anxious students have poor study habits. Simply learning to be more relaxed will not automatically improve these students' performance; their learning strategies and study skills must be improved as well (Naveh-Benjamin, 1991).

Finally, anxious students often know more than they can demonstrate on a test. They may lack useful test-taking skills, or they may have learned the materials but "freeze and forget." Thus, anxiety can interfere at one or all three points: attention, learning, and testing (Naveh-Benjamin, McKeachie, & Lin, 1987).

Coping with Anxiety. When students face stressful situations in school, they can use three kinds of coping strategies—problem solving, emotional management, and avoidance. Problem-focused strategies include planning a study schedule, borrowing good notes, or finding a protected place to study. Emotion-focused strategies are attempts to reduce anxious feelings—for example, by using relaxation exercises or describing the feelings to a friend. Of course, the latter might become an avoidance strategy, along with going out for pizza or suddenly launching an all-out desk-cleaning attack—"Can't study until you get organized!" Different strategies are helpful at different points—for example, problem solving before and emotion management during an exam. Different strategies fit different people and situations (Zeidner, 1995, 1998).

Some students, particularly those with learning disabilities or emotional disorders, may be especially anxious in school. Teachers should guide anxious students to set realistic short- and long-term goals. Anxious students left on their own often select either extremely difficult or extremely easy tasks. In the first case, they are likely to fail, which will increase their sense of hopelessness and anxiety about school. In the second case, they will probably succeed on the easy tasks, but they will miss the sense of satisfaction that could encourage greater effort, ease their fears about school work, and nurture a sense of self-efficacy. Goal cards, progress charts, or goal-planning journals may help here.

Interests and Emotions: Lessons for Teachers

Try to keep the level of arousal right for the task at hand. If students are going to sleep, energize them by introducing variety, piquing their curiosity, surprising them, or giving them a brief chance to be physically active. Learn about their interests and incorporate interests into lessons and assignments. If arousal is too great, follow the accompanying Guidelines for dealing with anxiety.

GUIDELINES

COPING WITH ANXIETY

Use competition carefully.

EXAMPLES

1. Monitor activities to make sure that no students are being put under undue pressure.
2. During competitive games, make sure that all students involved have a reasonable chance of succeeding.
3. Experiment with cooperative learning activities.

Avoid situations in which highly anxious students will have to perform in front of large groups.

EXAMPLES

1. Ask anxious students questions that can be answered with a simple yes or no or some other brief reply.
2. Give anxious students practice in speaking before smaller groups.

Make sure that all instructions are clear. Uncertainty can lead to anxiety.

EXAMPLES

1. Write test instructions on the board or on the test itself instead of giving them orally.
2. Check with students to make sure that they understand. Ask several students how they would do the first question, exercise, or sample question on a test. Correct any misconceptions.
3. If you are using a new format or starting a new type of task, give students examples or models to show how it is done.

Avoid unnecessary time pressures.

EXAMPLES

1. Give occasional take-home tests.
2. Make sure that all students can complete classroom tests within the period given.

Remove some of the pressures from major tests and exams.

EXAMPLES

1. Teach test-taking skills; give practice tests; provide study guides.
2. Avoid basing most of a report-card grade on one test.
3. Make extra-credit work available to add points to course grades.
4. Use different types of items in testing because some students have difficulty with particular formats.

Develop alternatives to written tests.

EXAMPLES

1. Try oral, open-book, or group tests.
2. Have students do projects, organize portfolios of their work, make oral presentations, or create a finished product.

Teach students self-regulation strategies (see Schutz & Davis, 2000).

EXAMPLES

1. Before the test, encourage students to see the test as an important and challenging task, one for which they can prepare. Help students stay focused on obtaining as much information as possible about the test.
2. During the test, remind students that the test is important (but not overly important). Encourage task focus—for example, tell the students to pick out the main idea in the question, slow down, stay relaxed.
3. After the test, think back about what went well and what could be improved. Focus on controllable attributions—study tactics, effort, careful reading of questions, relaxation techniques.

Check Your Knowledge

- How do interests and emotions affect learning?
- What is the role of arousal in learning?
- How does anxiety interfere with learning?

Apply to Practice

- How would you use students' interests in sports or films to motivate learning?
- Name some sources of anxiety in typical classroom situations.

BELIEFS AND SELF-SCHEMAS

Thus far, we have examined goals, interests, and emotions, but there is another factor that must be considered in explaining motivation. What do students believe about themselves? Let's start with a basic question: What do they believe about abilities?

Beliefs about Ability

Some of the most powerful beliefs affecting motivation in school are beliefs about *ability*. By examining these beliefs and how they affect motivation, we can understand why some people set inappropriate, unmotivating goals, why some students adopt self-defeating strategies, and why some students seem to give up altogether.

entity view of ability Belief that ability is a fixed characteristic that cannot be changed.

incremental view of ability Belief that ability is a set of skills that can be changed.

Adults use two basic concepts of ability (Dweck, 1999, 2002). An **entity view of ability** assumes that ability is a stable, uncontrollable trait—a characteristic of the individual that cannot be changed. According to this view, some people have more ability than others, but the amount that each person has is set. An **incremental view of ability**, on the other hand, suggests that ability is unstable and controllable—"an ever-expanding repertoire of skills and knowledge" (Dweck & Bempechat, 1983, p. 144). By hard work, study, or practice, knowledge can be increased and thus ability can be improved.

Young children tend to hold an exclusively incremental view of ability. Through the early elementary grades, most students believe effort is the same as intelligence. Smart people try hard, and trying hard makes you smart. If you fail, you aren't smart and you didn't try hard (Dweck, 2000; Stipek, 2002). Children are 11 or 12 years old before they begin to differentiate among effort, ability, and performance. About this time, they come to believe that someone who succeeds without working at all must be really smart. This is when beliefs about ability begin to influence motivation (Anderman & Maehr, 1994).

Students who hold an entity view of intelligence tend to set performance goals to avoid looking bad in others' eyes. They seek situations where they can look smart and protect their self-esteem. They keep doing what they can do well without expending too much effort or risking failure, because either one—working hard or failing—indicates (to them) low ability. To work hard but still fail would be devastating. Students with learning disabilities are more likely to hold an entity view.

Teachers who hold entity views are quicker to form judgments about students and slower to modify their opinions when confronted with contradictory evidence (Stipek, 2002). Teachers who hold incremental views, in contrast, tend to set learning goals and seek situations in which they can improve their skills, since improvement means getting smarter. Failure is not devastating; it simply indicates more work is needed. Ability is not threatened. Incremental theorists tend to set moderately difficult goals, the kind that we have seen are the most motivating.

Beliefs about ability are related to other beliefs about what you can and cannot control in learning.

Beliefs about Causes and Control: Attribution Theory

One well-known explanation of motivation assumes that we try to make sense of our own behaviour and the behaviour of others by searching for explanations and causes. To understand our successes and failures, particularly unexpected ones, we all ask "Why?" Students ask themselves, "Why did I flunk my midterm?" or "Why did I do so well this grading period?" They may attribute their successes and failures to ability, effort, mood, knowledge, luck, help, interest, clarity of instructions, the interference of others, unfair policies, and so on. To understand the successes and failures of others, we also make attributions—that the others are smart or lucky or work hard, for example. **Attribution theories** of motivation describe how the individual's explanations, justifications, and excuses about self or others influence motivation.

Bernard Weiner is one of the main educational psychologists responsible for relating attribution theory to school learning (Weiner, 1979, 1986, 1992, 1994a, 1994b, 2000; Weiner & Graham, 1989). According to Weiner, most of the attributed causes for successes or failures can be characterized in terms of three dimensions:

1. *locus* (location of the cause—internal or external to the person),
2. *stability* (whether the cause is likely to stay the same in the near future or can change), and
3. *controllability* (whether the person can control the cause).

Every cause for success or failure can be categorized on these three dimensions. For example, luck is external (locus), unstable (stability), and uncontrollable (controllability). Table 10.3 shows some common attributions for success or failure on a test. Notice that ability is usually considered stable and uncontrollable, but incremental theorists (described above) would argue that ability is unstable and controllable. Weiner's locus and controllability dimensions are closely related to Deci's concept of *locus of causality*.

Weiner believes that these three dimensions have important implications for motivation because they affect expectancy and value. The *stability* dimension, for example, seems to be closely related to expectations about the future. If students attribute their failure to stable factors such as the difficulty of the subject, they will expect to fail in that subject in the future. But if they attribute the outcome to unstable factors such as mood or luck, they can hope for better outcomes next time. The *internal/external locus* seems to be closely related to feelings of self-esteem (Weiner, 2000). If success or failure is attributed to internal factors, success will lead to pride and increased motivation, whereas failure will diminish self-esteem. The *controllability* dimension is related to emotions such as anger, pity, gratitude, or shame. If we feel responsible for our failures, we may feel guilt; if we feel responsible for successes, we may feel proud. Failing at a task we cannot control can lead to shame or anger.

Also, feeling in control of your learning seems to be related to choosing more difficult academic tasks, putting out more effort, using better strategies, and

attribution theories Descriptions of how individuals' explanations, justifications, and excuses influence their motivation and behavior.

Connect & Extend

TO YOUR TEACHING
Go to the *Encyclopedia of Psychology* (**www.psychology.org/ links/Environment_Behavior_ Relationships/Motivation**) and follow its link for Attribution Theory to learn more about using principles derived from this theory to boost intrinsic motivation to learn.

TABLE 10.3 Weiner's Theory of Causal Attribution

There are many explanations students can give for why they fail a test. Below are eight reasons representing the eight combinations of locus, stability, and responsibility in Weiner's model of attributions.

Dimension Classification	Reason for Failure
Internal-stable-uncontrollable	Low aptitude
Internal-stable-controllable	Never studies
Internal-unstable-uncontrollable	Sick the day of the exam
Internal-unstable-controllable	Did not study for this particular test
External-stable-uncontrollable	School has hard requirements
External-stable-controllable	Instructor is biased
External-unstable-uncontrollable	Bad luck
External-unstable-controllable	Friends failed to help

Source: From Weiner, B. (1992). *Human motivation: Metaphors, theories and research.* Published by Sage Publications, Newbury Park, CA. Copyright © 1992 by Sage Publications. Adapted with permission of the publisher.

Connect & Extend

*TO YOUR TEACHING/
PORTFOLIO*

Clifford, M. M. (1990). Students need challenge, not easy success. *Educational Leadership, 48*(1), 22–26. Evaluate Clifford's claim that students need some experience with failure. For whom is this experience most needed?

persisting longer in school work (Schunk, 2000; Weiner, 1994a, 1994b). Factors such as continuing discrimination against women, ethnic minorities, and individuals with special needs can affect these individuals' perceptions of their ability to control their lives (Beane, 1991; van Laar, 2000).

Attributions in the Classroom.   When usually successful students fail, they often make internal, controllable attributions: They misunderstood the directions, lacked the necessary knowledge, or simply did not study hard enough, for example. As a consequence, they usually focus on strategies for succeeding next time. This response often leads to achievement, pride, and a greater feeling of control (Ames, 1992; Stipek, 2002).

The greatest motivational problems arise when students attribute failures to stable, uncontrollable causes. Such students may seem resigned to failure, depressed, helpless—what we generally call "unmotivated" (Weiner, 2000). These students respond to failure by focusing even more on their own inadequacy; their attitudes toward school work may deteriorate even further (Ames, 1992). Apathy is a logical reaction to failure if students believe the causes are stable, unlikely to change, and beyond their control. In addition, students who view their failures in this light are less likely to seek help; they believe nothing and no one can help (Ames & Lau, 1982).

Teacher Actions and Student Attributions.   How do students determine the causes of their successes and failures? Remember, we also make attributions about the causes of other people's successes and failures. When teachers assume that student failure is attributable to forces beyond the students' control, the teachers tend to respond with sympathy and avoid giving punishments. If, however, the failures are attributed to a controllable factor such as lack of effort, the teacher's response is more likely to be irritation or anger, and reprimands may follow. These tendencies seem to be consistent across time and cultures (Weiner, 1986, 2000).

What do students make of these reactions from their teachers? Sandra Graham (1991, 1996) gives some surprising answers. There is evidence that when teachers respond to students' mistakes with pity, praise for a "good try," or unsolicited help, the students are more likely to attribute their failure to an uncontrollable cause—usually lack of ability. For example, Graham and Barker (1990) asked people of various ages to rate the effort and ability of two boys viewed on a videotape. On the tape, a teacher circulated around the class while students worked. The teacher stopped to look at the two boys' papers, did not make any comments to the first boy, but said to the second, "Let me give you a hint. Don't forget to carry your tens." The second boy had not asked for help and did not appear to be stumped by the problem. All the age groups watching the tapes, even the youngest, perceived the boy who received help as being lower in ability than the boy who did not get help. It is as if the subjects read the teacher's behaviour as saying, "You poor child, you just don't have the ability to do this hard work, so I will help."

Does this mean teachers should be critical and withhold help? Of course not! But it is a reminder that "praise as a consolation prize" for failing (Brophy, 1985) or over-solicitous help can give unintended messages.

Beliefs about Self-Efficacy and Learned Helplessness

Connect & Extend

TO THE RESEARCH

Graham, S. (1991). A review of attribution theory in achievement contexts. *Educational Psychology Review, 3,* 5–39. This article reviews several major principles of attribution theory as they relate to achievement strivings, including the antecedents to particular self-ascriptions, the emotional consequences of causal attributions for success and failure, help-seeking and help-giving, peer acceptance and rejection, achievement evaluation, and attributional process in African American populations.

We have already examined one of the most important self beliefs affecting motivation: self-efficacy. **Self-efficacy** is our belief about our personal competence or effectiveness *in a given area*. Bandura (1997) defines self-efficacy as "beliefs in one's capabilities to organize and execute the courses of action required to produce given attainments" (p. 3). In schools, we are particularly interested in self-efficacy for learning mathematics, writing, history, science, sports, and other subjects, as well as for using learning strategies and for the many other challenges that classrooms present. Because it is a key concept in social cognitive theory, we discussed self-efficacy in depth in Chapter 9.

self-efficacy Beliefs about personal competence in a particular situation.

Self-efficacy and attributions affect each other. If success is attributed to internal or controllable causes such As ability or effort, then self-efficacy is enhanced. But if success is attributed to luck or to the intervention of others, then self-efficacy may not be strengthened. And efficacy affects attributions, too. People with a strong sense of self-efficacy for a given task ("I'm good at math") tend to attribute their failures to lack of effort ("I should have double-checked my work"). But people with a low sense of self-efficacy ("I'm terrible at math") tend to attribute their failures to lack of ability ("I'm just dumb"). So having a strong sense of self-efficacy for a certain task encourages controllable attributions, and controllable attributions increase self-efficacy. You can see that if a student held an entity view (ability cannot be changed) and a low sense of self-efficacy, motivation would be destroyed when failures were attributed to lack of ability ("I just can't do this and I'll never be able to learn") (Bandura, 1997; Pintrich & Schunk, 2002).

Whatever the label, most theorists agree that a sense of efficacy, control, or self-determination is critical if people are to feel intrinsically motivated. When people come to believe that the events and outcomes in their lives are mostly uncontrollable, they have developed **learned helplessness** (Seligman, 1975). To understand the power of learned helplessness, consider this experiment (Hiroto & Seligman, 1975): Subjects receive either solvable or unsolvable puzzles. In the next phase of the experiment, all subjects are given a series of solvable puzzles. The subjects who struggled with unsolvable problems in the first phase of the experiment usually solve significantly fewer puzzles in the second phase. They have learned that they cannot control the outcome, so why even try?

Learned helplessness appears to cause three types of deficits: motivational, cognitive, and affective. Students who feel hopeless will be unmotivated and reluctant to attempt work. They expect to fail, so why should they even try—thus motivation suffers. Because they are pessimistic about learning, these students miss opportunities to practise and improve skills and abilities, so they develop cognitive deficits. Finally, they often suffer from affective problems such as depression, anxiety, and listlessness (Alloy & Seligman, 1979). Once established, it is very difficult to reverse the effects of learned helplessness.

Beliefs about Self-Worth

What are the connections between attributions for success and failure and beliefs about ability, self-efficacy, and self-worth? Covington and his colleagues suggest these factors come together in three kinds of motivational sets, shown in Table 10.4 on page 394: *mastery-oriented*, *failure-avoiding*, and *failure-accepting* (Covington, 1992; Covington & Mueller, 2001).

Mastery-oriented students tend to value achievement and see ability as improvable (an incremental view). They focus on learning goals to increase their skills and abilities. They are not fearful of failure because failing does not threaten their sense of competence and self-worth. This allows them to set moderately difficult goals, take risks, and cope constructively with failure. They generally attribute success to their own effort and thus they assume responsibility for learning and have a strong sense of self-efficacy. They perform very well in competitive situations, learn quickly, have more self-confidence and energy, are more aroused, welcome concrete feedback (it does not threaten them), and are eager to learn "the rules of the game" so that they can succeed. All these factors make for persistent, successful learning (Covington & Mueller, 2001; McClelland, 1985).

Failure-avoiding students tend to hold an entity view of ability. They set performance goals. They lack a strong sense of competence and self-worth, and they base these beliefs only on how well they perform. They feel only as smart as their last test grade, so they do not develop a solid sense of self-efficacy. To feel competent, they must protect themselves (and their self-images) from failure. If they have been generally successful, they may avoid failure by taking few risks and sticking with what they know. If, on the other hand, they have experienced some successes but also

Connect & Extend

TO THE RESEARCH
A recent study found that anxiety played a significant role in judging self-efficacy for middle-school students. See Klassen, R. M. (2002). *Motivational beliefs for Indo-Canadian and Anglo-Canadian early adolescents: A cross-cultural investigation of self and collective efficacy.* Dissertation. Simon Fraser University.

Self-efficacy is a factor in motivation. This student likely attributes at least part of her success to internal factors such as her own ability and effort.

learned helplessness The expectation, based on previous experiences with a lack of control, that all one's efforts will lead to failure.

mastery-oriented students Students who focus on learning goals because they value achievement and see ability as improvable.

failure-avoiding students Students who avoid failure by sticking to what they know, by not taking risks, or by claiming not to care about their performance.

TABLE 10.4 Mastery-Oriented, Failure-Avoiding, and Failure-Accepting Students

	Need for Achievement	Goals Set	Attributions	View of Ability	Strategies
Mastery-oriented	High need for achievement; low fear of failure	Learning goals: moderately difficult and challenging	Effort, use of right strategy, sufficient knowledge is cause of success	Incremental; improvable	Adaptive strategies: e.g., try another way, seek help, practise/study more
Failure-avoiding	High fear of failure	Performance goals; very hard or very easy	Lack of ability is cause of failure	Entity; set	Self-defeating strategies: e.g., make a feeble effort, pretend not to care
Failure-accepting	Expectation of failure; depression	Performance goals or no goals	Lack of ability is cause of failure	Entity; set	Learned helplessness; likely to give up

many failures, they may adopt strategies such as procrastination, feeble efforts, setting very low or ridiculously high goals, or claiming not to care. Just before a test, a student might say, "I didn't study at all!" or "All I want to do is pass." Then, any grade above passing is a success. Procrastination is another self-protective strategy. Low grades do not imply low ability if the student can claim, "I did okay considering I didn't start the term paper until last night." Some evidence suggests that blaming anxiety for poor test performance can also be a self-protective strategy (Covington & Omelich, 1987). Of course, even though these strategies may help students avoid the negative implications of failure, very little learning is going on.

Unfortunately, failure-avoiding strategies generally lead to the very failure students were trying to avoid. If failure continues and excuses wear thin, these students may finally decide that they are incompetent. This is what they feared in the first place. Now they come to accept it. Their sense of self-worth and self-efficacy deteriorate. They give up and become **failure-accepting students**. As we saw earlier, students who attribute failure to low ability and believe that ability is fixed are likely to become depressed, apathetic, and helpless. They have little hope for change.

failure-accepting students Students who believe that their failures are due to low ability and that there is little they can do about it.

Teachers may be able to prevent some failure-avoiding students from becoming failure-accepting by helping them to set new and more realistic goals. Also, some students may need support in aspiring to higher levels in the face of gender or ethnic stereotypes about what they "should" want or what they "should not" be able to do well. This kind of support could make all the difference. Instead of pitying or excusing these students, teach them tactics for learning and then hold them accountable. This will help the students develop a sense of self-efficacy for learning and avoid learned helplessness.

Beliefs and Self-Schemas: Lessons for Teachers

If students believe that they lack ability to deal with a subject, they will probably act on this belief even if their actual abilities are well above average. These students are likely to have little motivation to tackle advanced topics because they expect to do poorly in these areas. If students believe that failing means they are stupid, they are likely to adopt self-protective, but also self-defeating, strategies. Simply telling students to "try harder" is not particularly effective. Students need real evidence that effort will pay off, that setting a higher goal will not lead to failure, that they can improve, and that abilities change. They need authentic mastery experiences. The accompanying Guidelines offer ideas for encouraging self-efficacy and self-worth.

How can we put together all this information about motivation? How can teachers create environments, situations, and relationships that encourage motivation? We address these questions next.

Motivation to Learn in School

Teachers are concerned about developing a particular kind of motivation in their students—the motivation to learn. Jere Brophy (1988) describes **motivation to learn** as "a student tendency to find academic activities meaningful and worthwhile and to try to derive the intended academic benefits from them. Motivation to learn can be construed as both a general trait and a situation-specific state" (pp. 205–206). Motivation to learn involves more than just wanting or intending to learn. It includes positive views about learning *plus* thoughtful, active study strategies, such as summarizing, elaborating the basic ideas, outlining in your own words, or drawing graphs of the key relationships (Brophy, 1988).

What makes student motivation to learn a challenge in classrooms? In an interview, Jere Brophy listed five obstacles:

> First, school attendance is compulsory and curriculum content and learning activities are selected primarily on the basis of what society believes students need to learn, not on the basis of what students would choose to do if given the opportunity.... Second, teachers usually work with classes of 20 or more students and therefore cannot always meet each individual's needs, so some students are often bored and others are often confused or frustrated. Third, classrooms are social settings in which much that occurs is public, so that failures often produce not only personal disappointment but public embarrassment.

Connect & Extend

TO YOUR TEACHING
Think about your philosophy of teaching, a question you will be asked at most job interviews. What do you believe about motivating hard-to-reach students? How can you support the development of genuine and well-founded self-efficacy in your students? (Consult the Guidelines for ideas.)

motivation to learn The tendency to find academic activities meaningful and worthwhile and to try to benefit from them.

GUIDELINES
ENCOURAGING SELF-EFFICACY AND SELF-WORTH

Emphasize students' progress in a particular area.

EXAMPLES

1. Return to earlier material in reviews and show how "easy" it is now.
2. Encourage students to improve projects when they have learned more.
3. Keep examples of particularly good work in portfolios.

Make specific suggestions for improvement and revise grades when improvements are made.

EXAMPLES

1. Return work with comments noting what the students did right, what they did wrong, and why they might have made the mistakes.
2. Experiment with peer editing.
3. Show students how their revised, higher grade reflects greater competence and raises their class average.

Stress connections between past efforts and past accomplishments.

EXAMPLES

1. Have individual goal-setting and goal-review conferences with students in which you ask students to reflect on how they solved difficult problems.
2. Confront self-defeating, failure-avoiding strategies directly.

Set learning goals for your students and model a mastery orientation for them.

EXAMPLES

1. Recognize progress and improvement.
2. Share examples of how you have developed your abilities in a given area and provide other achievement models who are similar to your students—no supermen or superwomen whose accomplishments seem unattainable.
3. Read stories about students who overcame physical, mental, or economic challenges.
4. Don't excuse failure because a student has problems outside school. Help the student succeed inside school.

Fourth, students are graded, and periodic reports are sent home to their parents. Finally, teachers and students often settle into familiar routines that become the "daily grind." School reduces to covering content (for the teachers) and completing assignments (for the students). (Gaedke & Shaughnessy, 2003, pp. 206–207)

In this challenging context, it would be wonderful if all our students came to us filled with the motivation to learn, but they don't. As teachers, we have three major goals. The first is to get students productively involved with the work of the class; in other words, to create a *state* of motivation to learn. The second and longer-term goal is to develop in our students the *trait* of being motivated to learn so they will be able "to educate themselves throughout their lifetime" (Bandura, 1993, p. 136). And finally, we want our students to be cognitively engaged—to think deeply about what they study. In other words, we want them to be *thoughtful* (Blumenfeld, Puro, & Mergendoller, 1992).

In this chapter we examined the roles of intrinsic and extrinsic motivation, attributions, goals, interests, emotions, and self-schemas in motivation. Table 10.5 shows how each of these factors contributes to motivation to learn.

The central questions for the remainder of the chapter are: What can teachers do to encourage and support motivation to learn? How can teachers use knowledge about attributions, goals, interests, beliefs, and self-schemas to increase motivation to learn? To organize our discussion, we will use the TARGET model.

Check Your Knowledge

- How do beliefs about ability affect motivation?
- What are the three dimensions of attributions in Weiner's theory?
- What is self-efficacy, and how does it relate to learned helplessness?
- How does self-worth influence motivation?
- Define motivation to learn.

Apply to Practice

- Explain how beliefs about the nature of ability might be associated with students' self-protective, self-defeating behaviour such as procrastination or not trying.
- Describe the development of learned helplessness. What kinds of goals would a student set if the student felt helpless?

TABLE 10.5 Building a Concept of Motivation to Learn

Motivation to learn is encouraged when the following six elements come together:

	Optimum Characteristics of Motivation to Learn	Characteristics That Diminish Motivation to Learn
Source of Motivation	*Intrinsic:* Personal factors such as needs, interests, curiosity, enjoyment	*Extrinsic:* Environmental factors such as rewards, social pressure, punishment
Type of Goal Set	*Learning goal:* Personal satisfaction in meeting challenges and improving; tendency to choose moderately difficult and challenging goals	*Performance goal:* Desire for approval for performance in others' eyes; tendency to choose very easy or very difficult goals
Type of Involvement	*Task-involved:* Concerned with mastering the task	*Ego-involved:* Concerned with self in others' eyes.
Achievement Motivation	Motivation to *achieve:* Mastery orientation	Motivation to *avoid failure:* Prone to anxiety
Likely Attributions	Successes and failures attributed to *controllable* effort and ability	Success and failures attributed to *uncontrollable* causes
Beliefs about Ability	*Incremental view:* Belief that ability can be improved through hard work and added knowledge and skills	*Entity view:* Belief that ability is a stable, uncontrollable trait

ON TARGET FOR LEARNING

Connect & Extend

TO THE RESEARCH
Vispoel, W. P., & Austin, J. R. (1995). Success and failure in junior high school: A critical incident approach to understanding students' attributional beliefs. *American Educational Research Journal, 32,* 377–412.

Carol Ames (1990, 1992) identified six areas of teachers' decisions that influence student motivation to learn: the *task* set for students; the *autonomy* students are allowed in working; how students are *recognized* for accomplishments; *grouping* practices; *evaluation* procedures; and how *time* is scheduled in classes. Epstein (1989) coined the acronym TARGET for these six areas that are summarized in Table 10.6 on page 398. Let's examine each area more closely.

Tasks for Learning

To understand how an **academic task** can affect students' motivation, we need to analyze the task. Tasks can be interesting or boring for students. And tasks have different values for students.

academic tasks The work the student must accomplish, including the content covered and the mental operations required.

Task Value. As you probably recall, many theories suggest the strength of our motivation in a particular situation is determined by both our *expectation* that we can succeed and the *value* of that success to us. Students' beliefs about the value of a task seem to predict the choices they make, such as whether to enrol in advanced science classes or join a team. Efficacy expectations predict achievement in doing the task—how well the students actually perform in the advance science class or on the team (Wigfield & Eccles, 2002b).

We can think of a task value as having four components: importance, interest, utility, and cost (Eccles & Wigfield, 2001; Eccles, Wigfield, & Schiefele, 1998). **Importance or attainment value** is the significance of doing well on the task; this is closely tied to the needs of the individual (for example, the need to be well-liked, athletic, etc.). For instance, if someone has a strong need to appear smart and believes that a high grade on a test shows you are smart, then the test has high attainment value for that person. A second component is **interest or intrinsic value**. This is simply the enjoyment one gets from the activity itself. Some people like the experience of learning. Others enjoy the feeling of hard physical effort or the challenge of solving puzzles. Tasks also can have **utility value**; that is, they help us achieve a short-term or long-term goal such as earning a degree. Finally, tasks have costs—negative consequences that might follow from doing the task such as not having time to do other things or looking awkward as you perform the task. You see from our discussion of task value that personal and environmental influences on motivation interact constantly. The task we ask students to accomplish is an aspect of the environment; it is external to the student. But the value of accomplishing the task is bound up with the internal needs, beliefs, and goals of the individual.

attainment value The importance of doing well on a task; how success on the task meets personal needs.

intrinsic or interest value The enjoyment a person gets from a task.

utility value The contribution of a task to meeting one's goals.

Authentic Tasks. Recently, there has been a great deal written about using authentic tasks in teaching. **Authentic tasks** have some connection to the real-life problems and situations students will face outside the classroom, now and in the future. If you ask students to memorize definitions they will never use, to learn the material only because it is on the test, or to repeat work they already understand, then there likely will be little motivation to learn. But if the tasks are authentic, students are more likely to see the genuine utility value of the work and are also more likely to find the tasks meaningful and interesting.

authentic tasks Tasks that have some connection to real-life problems the students will face outside the classroom.

Problem-based learning is one example of teaching using authentic tasks. In problem-based learning, according to Stepien and Gallagher (1993), "Students meet an ill-structured problem before they receive any instruction. In place of covering the curriculum, learners probe deeply into issues searching for connections, grappling with complexity, and using knowledge to fashion solutions" (p. 26). Teachers act as coaches and tutors, asking questions, modelling thinking, helping students organize and monitor their problem solving. One example of such a problem appropriate for grade 7 or 8 students is, "Where should we locate a new

TABLE 10.6 The TARGET Model for Supporting Student Motivation to Learn

Teachers make decisions in many areas that can influence motivation to learn. The TARGET acronym highlights task, autonomy, recognition, grouping, evaluation, and time.

TARGET Area	Focus	Objectives	Examples of Possible Strategies
Task	How learning tasks are structured—what the student is asked to do	Enhance intrinsic attractiveness of learning tasks Make learning meaningful	Encourage instruction that relates to students' backgrounds and experience Avoid payment (monetary or other) for attendance, grades, or achievement Foster goal setting and self-regulation
Autonomy/responsibility	Student participation in learning/school decisions	Provide optimal freedom for students to make choices and take responsibility	Give alternatives in making assignments Ask for student comments on school life—and take them seriously Encourage students to take initiatives and evaluate their own learning Establish leadership opportunities for *all* students
Recognition	The nature and use of recognition and reward in the school setting	Provide opportunities for all students to be recognized for learning Recognize progress in goal attainment Recognize challenge seeking and innovation	Foster "personal best" awards Reduce emphasis on "honour rolls" Recognize and publicize a wide range of school-related activities of students
Grouping	The organization of school learning and experiences	Build an environment of acceptance and appreciation of all students Broaden the range of social interaction, particularly of at-risk students Enhance social skills development	Provide opportunities for cooperative learning, problem solving, and decision making Encourage multiple group membership to increase range of peer interaction Eliminate ability-grouped classes
Evaluation	The nature and use of evaluation and assessment procedures	Grade to promote positive motivation Define goals and standards to emphasize productive attributions	Reduce emphasis on social comparisons of achievement Give students opportunities to improve their performance (e.g., study skills, classes) Establish grading/reporting practices that portray student progress in learning Encourage student participation in the evaluation process
Time	The scheduling of the school day	Allow the learning task and student needs to dictate scheduling Provide opportunities for extended and significant student involvement in learning tasks	Allow students to progress at their own rate whenever possible Encourage flexibility in the scheduling of learning experiences Give teachers greater control over time usage through, for example, block scheduling

Source: Adapted from Maehr, M. L., & Anderman, E. M. (1993). Reinventing schools for early adolescents: Emphasizing task goals. *The Elementary School Journal, 93,* 604–605. Copyright © 1993. Adapted by permission of The University of Chicago Press.

landfill?" Students would research the situation, perhaps interview experts, and develop recommendations to present to their municipal council. The novelty of the problem, its challenge, the opportunity to pursue diverse solutions, and its real-life meaning help motivate students.

Supporting Autonomy and Recognizing Accomplishment

The second area in the TARGET model concerns how much choice and autonomy students are allowed. Choice is not the norm in schools. Students spend thousands of hours in schools where other people decide what will happen. Yet, as we saw earlier, self-determination and an internal locus of causality are keys to intrinsic motivation. What can teachers do to support choice without inviting chaos?

Supporting Choices. Like totally unguided discovery learning, unstructured or unguided choice can be counterproductive for learning (Garner, 1998). For example, Dyson (1997) found that children became anxious and upset if their teachers asked them to draw or write about anything they wanted in any way they wanted. Unbounded choice was perceived as a "scary void." Even graduate students in our classes find it disconcerting if we ask them to design a final project that will determine their grade, just as we panic when asked to give a talk on "whatever you want."

The alternative is bounded choice—giving students a range of options that set valuable tasks for them but also allow them to follow personal interests. The balance must be just right: "too much autonomy is bewildering and too little is boring" (Guthrie et al., 1998, p. 185). Guthrie describes how a grade 5 student exercised her choices about researching and writing. The class was studying the life cycle of the Monarch butterfly. Each child worked in a heterogeneous team and each team had a chrysalis to observe as it grew. The class had organized a library of multilevel expository books, trade books, literary books, reference books, maps, electronic databases, and other resources. The teacher had taught specific skills that would be needed—using an index and table of contents, setting goals, and writing summaries—but the students were able to choose topics and appropriate resources for crafting their own chapter.

Students also can exercise autonomy about feedback from the teacher or classmates. Figure 10.1 on the next page illustrates a strategy called "Check It Out." Students specify a set of skills that they want evaluated in a particular assignment. Over a unit, all the skills have to be "checked out," but students can choose when each skill is evaluated. How else can teachers support student self-determination? According to a study by Reeve, Bolt, and Cai (1999), compared with controlling teachers, autonomy-supporting teachers listened more, resisted solving problems for students, gave fewer directives, and asked more questions about what students wanted to do.

Connect & Extend

TO PROFESSIONAL JOURNALS
See the April 1993 special issue of *Educational Leadership* devoted to "authentic learning."

Connect & Extend

TO THE RESEARCH
Graham, S., & Golan, S. (1991). Motivational influences on cognition: Task involvement, ego involvement, and depth of information processing. *Journal of Educational Psychology, 83,* 187–194.

Connect & Extend

TO THE RESEARCH
Maehr, M. L., & Anderman, E. M. (1993). Reinventing schools for early adolescents: Emphasizing task goals. *Elementary School Journal, 93,* 593–610. This article describes how the TARGET model can be used to reform middle schools to support learning goals.

Connect & Extend

TO THE RESEARCH
The January 1988 issue of *Elementary School Journal* is devoted to the topic of school work and academic tasks.

CALVIN AND HOBBES © 1991 Watterson. Dist. by Universal Press Syndicate. Reprinted with permission. All rights reserved.

Calvin and Hobbes
by Bill Watterson

Students may differ in the degree to which they are willing to take risks in both classroom and social situations.

Connect & Extend

TO THE RESEARCH
The June 1998 issue of *Educational Psychology Review*, edited by Karen Harris and Pat Alexander, has a series of articles describing models of integrated teaching that include student choice. One article by Ruth Garner (pp. 227–238) describes the power of bounded choices.

Recognizing Accomplishment. The third TARGET area is *recognition*. Students should be recognized for improving on their own personal best, for tackling difficult tasks, for persistence, and for creativity—not just for performing better than others. In Chapter 6, we described authentic praise that focuses on progress, growing competence, and independence. At times, praise can have paradoxical effects. Some students may view a teacher's feedback, whether praise or criticism, as a cue about capabilities: "Praise means I'm not very smart—when I succeed, the teacher has to recognize it. Criticism means my teacher thinks I'm smart and I could do better" (Stipek, 1996).

What sort of recognition leads to engagement? In a study by Ruth Butler (1987), grade 5 and 6 students were given interesting divergent thinking tasks followed by either individual comments, standardized praise ("very good"), grades, or no feedback. Interest, performance, attributions to effort, and task involvement were higher after personal comments. Ego-involved motivation (the desire to look good or do better than others) was greater after grades and standard praise. We recommend recognizing students for self-referenced improvement, for tackling difficult tasks, for persistence, and for creativity.

Grouping, Evaluation, and Time

You may remember a teacher who made you want to work hard—someone who made a subject come alive. Or you may remember how many hours you spent practising as a member of a team, orchestra, choir, or theatre troupe. If you do, then you know the motivational power of relationships with other people.

Grouping and Goal Structures. Motivation can be greatly influenced by the ways in which we relate to the other people who are also involved in accomplishing a particular goal (Johnson & Johnson, 1999). This interpersonal factor is the

Figure 10.1 Student Autonomy: "Check It Out"

Using this technique to support student autonomy, the teacher decides on a set of skills that will be developed over a unit, but the student decides which skill(s) will be evaluated on any given assignment. Over the course of the unit, all the skills have to be "checked out." This student has indicated that she wants the teacher to "check out" her creativity and verb tense.

Source: From Raffini, J. P. (1996). 150 ways to increase intrinsic motivation in the classroom (pp. 33–34). Boston: Allyn & Bacon. Copyright © Allyn & Bacon, Inc. Adapted with permission.

☐ Capitals
☐ Punctuation
☐ Complete Sentences
☑ Creativity

☐ Spelling
☐ Commas
☑ Tense
☐ Semicolons

On a bittery col̶ December morning, Jack set out to find the perfect cup of coffee. He had nothing in the house but instant, a gift from his mother, who was visiting over th̶ holidays

goal structure of the task. There are three such structures: cooperative, competitive, and individualistic, as shown in Figure 10.2.

When the task involves complex learning and problem-solving skills, co-operation leads to higher achievement than competition, especially for students with lower abilities. Students learn to set attainable goals and negotiate. They become more altruistic. The interaction with peers that students enjoy so much becomes a part of the learning process. The result? The need for belonging described by Maslow is more likely to be met and motivation is increased (Stipek, 2002; Webb & Palincsar, 1996).

Bette Chambers and Philip Abrami (1991) of Concordia University in Montreal found that members of successful teams learned more than members of unsuccessful teams, and were also happier about the outcome and rated their ability higher than members of losing teams. For low-achieving students who tend to be anxious, failure-accepting, or helpless, being on a losing team could make matters worse. Chambers and Abrami suggest experimenting with cooperation both within and between teams. For example, the whole class might earn recognition if each team reaches a specified level of learning.

Table 10.6 on page 398 gives ideas for fostering motivation through peer relations. Besides the use of cooperative learning, ideas include allowing time and opportunity for peer interaction in school, using project-based learning, and encouraging the development of teams and "schools within schools."

The nature of the goal structure—cooperative, competitive, or individualistic—has implications for the next two TARGET areas, *evaluation* and *time*.

Evaluation. The greater the emphasis on competitive evaluation and grading, the more students will focus on performance goals rather than mastery. In addition, low-achieving students who have little hope of mastering the tasks may simply want to get them over with. In a study of grade 1 students, low-achieving students made up answers, filled in the page with patterns, or copied from other students, just to get through their seatwork. As one student said when she finished a word-definition matching exercise, "I don't know what it means, but I did it" (Anderson et al., 1985, p. 132). On closer examination, the researchers found that the work was much too hard for these students, so they connected words and definitions at random.

How can teachers avoid these negative effects? De-emphasize grades and emphasize learning. Students should understand the value of their work. Instead

goal structure The way in which students relate to others who are also working toward a particular goal.

Connect & Extend

TO THE RESEARCH
For a thorough review of research on different forms of cooperative learning, see O'Donnell, A. M., & O'Kelly, J. (1994). Learning from peers: Beyond the rhetoric of positive results. *Educational Psychology Review, 6*, 321–350.

Figure 10.2 Different Goal Structures

Each goal structure is associated with a different relationship between the individual and the group. This relationship influences motivation to reach the goal.

Source: From Johnson, D., & Johnson, R. (1999). *Learning together and alone: Cooperation, competition, and individualization* (5th ed.). Published by Allyn and Bacon, Boston, MA. Copyright © 1999 by Pearson Education. Adapted by permission of the publisher.

	Cooperative	Competitive	Individualistic
Definition	Students believe that their goal is attainable only if other students will also reach the goal.	Students believe that they will reach their goal if and only if other students do not reach the goal.	Students believe that their own attempt to reach a goal is not related to other students' attempts to reach the goal.
Examples	Team victories—each player wins only if all the team members win; a relay race; a quilting bee; a barn raising; a symphony; a play.	Golf tournament, singles tennis match, a 100-metre dash; valedictorian.	Lowering your handicap in golf; jogging; learning a new language; enjoying a museum; losing or gaining weight; stopping smoking.

Connect & Extend

TO YOUR TEACHING
Design a lesson plan using a cooperative learning format. The assignment should consist of (1) a description of how to prepare the students for this lesson; (2) a summary of the expected results; (3) the topic of the lesson and the information that would be given to members of the groups; and (4) the actual test or means of assessment that would be used to determine learning. If possible, you should actually teach the lesson in a school classroom.

of saying, "You will need to know this for the test," tell students that what they learn will be useful in solving problems they want to solve. Suggest that the lesson will answer some interesting questions. Communicate that understanding is more important than finishing. Unfortunately, many teachers do not follow this advice. Jere Brophy (1988) reports that when he and several colleagues spent about 100 hours observing how six teachers introduced their lessons, they found that most introductions were routine, apologetic, or unenthusiastic. The introductions described procedures, made threats, emphasized finishing, or promised tests on the material.

One way to emphasize learning rather than grades is to use self-evaluation. This strategy also supports autonomy. For example, the sheet for self-evaluating and goal planning in Figure 10.3 could be adapted for almost any grade.

Time. Most experienced teachers know that there is too much work and not enough time in the school day. Students can seldom stick with an activity. Even if they become engrossed in a project, they must stop and turn to another subject when the block is over or the schedule demands. Furthermore, students must progress as a group. If some individuals can move faster or if they need more time, they still have to follow the pace of the whole group. Scheduling often interferes with motivation by making students move faster or slower than is appropriate or

Figure 10.3 Self-Evaluation and Goal Planning

By completing this form, students evaluate their own work in relation to their goals and set new goals for the future.

Source: From Raffini, J. P. (1996). *150 ways to increase intrinsic motivation in the classroom* (p. 67). Boston: Allyn & Bacon. Copyright © 1996 Allyn & Bacon. Adapted with permission.

Name _____   Advisor _____

Subject _____   Quarter _____

1. Self-Evaluation

a. How am I doing in this course? _____
_____

b. What difficulties have I been having? _____
_____

c. How much time and effort have I been spending in this course? _____

d. Do I need more help in this course? If yes, how have I tried to get it? _____
_____

2. Academic Goal

a. My goal to achieve before the end of the quarter is _____
_____

b. I want to work on this goal because _____
_____

c. I will achieve this goal by _____
_____

3. Behaviour or Social Goal

a. My goal to achieve before the end of the quarter is _____
_____

b. I want to work on this goal because _____
_____

c. I will achieve this goal by _____
_____

Variations
Advisors may choose to use this activity at the beginning of each quarter and adapt self-evaluation and goal planning sheets to specific grade levels. Follow-up conferences are also useful for helping students evaluate their plans.

by interrupting their involvement. It is difficult to develop persistence and a sense of self-efficacy in the face of these conditions. One challenge for you as a teacher will be to schedule time for engaged and persistent learning. Some elementary classrooms have time for DEAR—Drop Everything And Read—to give extended periods when everyone, even the teacher, reads. Some middle schools and high schools have teachers work in teams to plan larger blocks of time when students pursue interdisciplinary projects.

We can see how these motivational elements come together in real classrooms. Sara Dolezal and her colleagues observed and interviewed grade 3 teachers in eight Catholic schools and determined if their students were low, moderate, or high in their level of motivation (Dolezal, Welsh, Pressley, & Vincent, 2003). Table 10.7 on pages 404–405 summarizes the dramatic differences in these classrooms between strategies that support motivation and those that undermine it. Students in the low-engagement classes were restless and chatty as they faced their easy, undemanding seatwork. The classrooms were bare, unattractive, and filled with management problems. Instruction was disorganized. The class atmosphere was generally negative. The moderately engaged classrooms were organized to be "student friendly," with reading areas, group work area, posters, and student artwork. The teachers were warm and caring, and they connected lessons to students' background knowledge. Management routines were smooth and organized, and the class atmosphere was positive. The teachers were good at catching student attention and encouraging students to become more self-regulating, but they had trouble holding attention, probably because the tasks were too easy. Highly engaging teachers had all the positive qualities of student-friendly classrooms—positive atmosphere, smooth management routines, support for student self-regulation, and effective instruction—but they added more challenging tasks along with the support to succeed. These excellent motivators did not rely on one or two approaches to motivate their students; they applied a large repertoire of strategies from Table 10.7.

Check Your Knowledge

- What does TARGET stand for?
- How do tasks and task value affect motivation?
- Distinguish between bounded and unbounded choices.
- How can recognition undermine motivation and a sense of self-efficacy?
- List three goal structures and distinguish among them.
- How does evaluative climate affect goal setting?
- What are some effects of time on motivation?

Apply to Practice

- Name some ways other than problem-based learning to make learning tasks more authentic.
- Why would providing rationales for class rules help students feel more autonomous?
- Describe a cooperative learning structure that is designed to support student motivation.
- How can evaluation procedures help create a learning-oriented classroom?

Connect & Extend

TO THE RESEARCH
Chambers, B., & Abrami, P. C. (1991). The relationship between student team learning outcomes and achievement, causal attributions, and affect. *Journal of Educational Psychology, 83,* 140–146.

Connect & Extend

TO YOUR TEACHING
A recent addition to the list of cooperative learning techniques is Cooperative Integrated Reading and Composition (CIRC). This system supports the traditional approach of using ability-based reading groups. Students are assigned to teams made up of pairs from each reading group in the class. While the teacher works with one reading group, the teams work in their pairs using many of the methods of reciprocal teaching described in Chapter 12—reading aloud, making predictions, asking questions, summarizing, and writing about the stories they are reading. Team members help each other prepare for tests, write and edit work, and often "publish" team books. Teams are rewarded based on the average performance of all their members on all the reading and writing assignments. Thus, there is equal opportunity for success, group support for learning, and individual accountability for final performance. These three elements are characteristic of many cooperative learning strategies (Slavin, 1995).

TABLE 10.7 Strategies That Support and Undermine Motivation in the Classroom

A Few Strategies That Support Motivation

Strategy	Example
Messages of accountability and high expectations	The teacher asks students to have parents review and sign some assignments.
Teacher communicates importance of work	"We need to check it for at least one minute, which means looking over it carefully."
Clear goals/directions	The teacher explains exactly how the students are to separate into groups and complete their nominations for their favourite book.
Connections across the curriculum	The teacher relates the concept of ratios in math to compare/contrast skills in reading.
Opportunities to learn about and practise dramatic arts	After studying about historical figures, students write and produce their own plays.
Attributions to effort	During a word game, the teacher says to a student, "Did you study last night?" The student nods. "See how it helps?"
Encouraging risk-taking	"I need a new shining face. Someone I haven't called on yet. I need a risk-taker."
Uses games and play to reinforce concept or review material	During a math lesson using balance, students spend five minutes weighing the favourite toy they were asked to bring in that day.
Home–school connections	As part of math science unit, a recycling activity asks families to keep a chart of everything they recycle in a week.
Multiple representations of a task	The teacher uses four ways to teach multiplication: "magic multipliers," sing-along multiplication facts, whole-class flash card review, "Around-the-World" game.
Positive classroom management, praise, private reprimands	"Thumbs up when you are ready to work. Table 7 has thumbs up, table 7. I like the way table 7 is waiting patiently."
Stimulating creative thought	"We are going to use our imaginations today. We are going to take a trip to an imaginary theatre in our heads."
Opportunities for choice	Students can choose to use prompts for their journal writing or pick their own topic.
Teacher communicates to students that they can handle challenging tasks	"This is hard stuff and you are doing great. I know adults who have trouble with this."
Value students—communicate caring	The teacher allows a new student to sit with a buddy for the day.

DIVERSITY AND CONVERGENCES IN MOTIVATION TO LEARN

We have seen that motivation to learn grows from the individual's needs, goals, interests, emotions, beliefs, and attributions in interaction with the tasks set, autonomy and recognition provided, grouping structures, evaluation procedures, and time allowed.

Diversity in Motivation

Because students differ in terms of language, culture, economic privilege, personality, knowledge, and experience, they will also differ in their needs, goals, inter-

A Few Strategies That Undermine Motivation

Strategy	Example
Attributions to intellect rather than effort	When students remark during a lesson, "I'm stupid" or "I'm a dork," the teacher says nothing, then replies, "Let's have someone who is smart."
Teacher emphasizes competition rather than working together	The teacher conducts a poetry contest where students read poems to class and the class members hold up cards with scores rating how well each student performed.
Few displays of student work	Public bulletin boards are used for posting grades.
No scaffolding for learning a new skill	The teacher is loud and critical when students have trouble: "Just look back in the glossary and don't miss it because you are too lazy to look it up."
Ineffective/negative feedback	"Does everyone understand?" A few students say yes and the teacher moves on.
Lack of connections	On Remembrance Day, the teacher leads a brief discussion of World War I, then the remainder of the activities are about 9/11.
Easy tasks	The teacher provides easy work and "fun" activities that teach little.
Negative class atmosphere	"Excuse me, I said the page number. If you follow and listen, you would know."
Punitive classroom management	The teacher threatens bad grades if students do not look up words in the glossary.
Work that is much too difficult	The teacher assigns independent math work that only one or two students can do.
Slow pacing	The pace is set for the slowest students—others finish and have nothing to do.
Emphasis on finishing, not learning	The teacher communicates the purpose is to finish, not learn or use the vocabulary.
Sparse, unattractive classroom	There are no decorated bulletin boards, maps, charts, or displays of student work.
Poor planning	Missing handouts force the teacher to have large instead of smaller work groups.
Public punishment	All students stand, and the teacher reads a list of those who finished the assignment and they sit down. The teacher gives public lecture on responsibility to those left standing.

Source: Adapted from Dolezal, S. E., Welsh, L. M., Pressley, M., & Vincent, M. (2003). How do nine third-grade teachers motivate their students? *Elementary School Journal, 103,* pp. 247–248.

ests, and beliefs. For example, self-efficacy is a central concept in motivation because it is strong predictor of academic performance. But there are cultural differences as well. Males and are more likely to be overconfident in their academic abilities, so their predictions of future achievement are less accurate than the predictions of Asian students and female students who are much less likely to express overconfidence in their abilities. Gifted male students are less likely to be overconfident, and gifted female students are likely to underestimate their abilities, whereas students with disabilities tend to be overconfident in their sense of efficacy (Pajares, 2000).

Taking this diversity into account when designing tasks, supporting autonomy, recognizing accomplishments, grouping, making evaluations, and managing time can encourage motivation to learn. Take interest, for example. Embedding student writing tasks in cultural contexts is one way to *catch* and *hold* situational interest

(Alderman, 2004; Bergin, 1999). When immigrant students in junior-high classes moved from writing using worksheets and standard assignments to writing about such topics as immigration, bilingualism, and gang life—factors that were important to them and to their families—their papers got longer and the writing quality was better (Rueda & Moll, 1994).

Language is a central factor in students' connections with the school. When bilingual students are encouraged to draw on both English and their heritage language, motivation and participation can increase. Robert Jimenez (2000) found in his study of bilingual Latin American students that successful readers saw reading as a process of making sense; they used both of their languages to understand the material. For instance, they might look for Spanish word parts in English words to help them translate. Less-successful students had a different goal. They believed that reading just meant saying the words correctly in English. It is likely that their interest and sense of efficacy for reading in English would be less, too.

Convergences: Strategies to Encourage Motivation and Thoughtful Learning

Connect & Extend

TO YOUR TEACHING
For a set of practical tips, guidelines, and suggestions for boosting and maintaining motivation to learn, go to Increasing Student Engagement and Motivation: From Time-on-Task to Homework (**www.nwrel.org/request/oct00/textonly.html**).

Until four basic conditions are met, no motivational strategies will succeed. First, the classroom must be relatively organized and free from constant interruptions and disruptions. (Chapter 11 will give you the information you need to make sure this requirement is met.) Second, the teacher must be a patient, supportive person who never embarrasses students for their mistakes. Everyone in the class should see mistakes as opportunities for learning (Clifford, 1990, 1991). Third, the work must be challenging but reasonable. If work is too easy or too difficult, students will have little motivation to learn. They will focus on finishing, not on learning. Finally, the learning tasks must be authentic as much as possible (Brophy 1983; Brophy & Kher, 1986; Stipek, 1993).

Once these four basic conditions are met, students' motivation to learn in a particular situation can be summarized in three questions: Can I succeed at this task? Do I want to succeed? What do I need to do to succeed? (Eccles & Wigfield, 1985). We want students to have confidence in their ability so that they will approach learning with energy and enthusiasm. We want them to see value in tasks they undertake and the work they do to learn, not just try to get the grade or get finished. We want students to believe that success will come when they apply good learning strategies instead of believing that their only option is to use self-defeating, failure-avoiding, face-saving strategies. When things get difficult, we want students to stay focused on the task and not get so worried about failure that they "freeze."

Can I Do It? Building Confidence and Positive Expectations. No amount of encouragement or "cheerleading" will substitute for real accomplishment. To ensure genuine progress,

1. *Begin work at the students' level and move in small steps.* The pace should be brisk, but not so fast that students have to move to the next step before they understand the previous one. This may require assigning different tasks to different students. One possibility is to have very easy and very difficult questions on every test and assignment, so that all students are both successful and challenged. When grades are required, make sure that all the students in class have a chance to make at least a C if they work hard.

2. *Make sure that learning goals are clear, specific, and possible to reach in the near future.* When long-term projects are planned, break the work into subgoals and help students feel a sense of progress toward the long-term goal. If possible, give students a range of goals at different levels of difficulty and let them choose.

3. *Stress self-comparison, not comparison with others.* Help students see the progress they are making by showing them how to use self-management strategies such as those described in Chapter 6. Give specific feedback and corrections. Tell students what they are doing right as well as what is wrong and *why* it is wrong. Periodically, give students a question or problem that was once hard for them but now seems easy. Point out how much they have improved.

4. *Communicate to students that academic ability is improvable* and specific to the task at hand. In other words, the fact that a student has trouble in algebra doesn't necessarily mean that geometry will be difficult or that he or she is a bad English student. Don't undermine your efforts to stress improvement by displaying only the 100 percent papers on the bulletin board.

5. *Model good problem solving,* especially when *you* have to try several approaches to get a solution. Students need to see that learning is not smooth and error-free, even for the teacher.

Do I Want to Do It? Seeing the Value of Learning.   Teachers can use intrinsic and extrinsic motivation strategies to help students see the value of the learning task.

Attainment and Intrinsic Value. To establish attainment value, *connect the learning task with the needs of the students.* First, it must be possible for students to meet their needs for safety, belonging, and achievement in their classes. The classroom should not be a frightening or lonely place. Second, be sure that gender or ethnic stereotypes do not interfere with motivation. For example, make it clear that both women and men can be high achievers in all subjects and that no subjects are the territory of only one sex. It is not "unfeminine" to be strong in mathematics, science, shop, or sports. It is not "unmasculine" to be good in literature, art, music, or French.

There are many strategies for encouraging *intrinsic* (interest) motivation. Several of the following are taken from Brophy (1988):

1. *Tie class activities to the students' interests* in sports, music, current events, pets, common problems or conflicts with family and friends, fads, television and cinema personalities, or other significant features of their lives (Schiefele, 1991). But be sure that you know what you are talking about. For example, if you use a verse from a Shania Twain song to make a point, you had better have some knowledge of the music and the performer. When possible, give students choices of research paper or reading topics so that they can follow their own interests.

2. *Arouse curiosity.* Point out puzzling discrepancies between students' beliefs and the facts. For example, Stipek (1993) describes a teacher who asked her grade 5 class if there were "people" on some of the other planets. When the students said yes, the teacher asked if people needed oxygen to breathe. Since the students had just learned this fact, they responded yes to this question also. Then the teacher told them that there is no oxygen in the atmosphere of the other planets. This surprising discrepancy between what the children knew about oxygen and what they believed about life on other planets led to a rousing discussion of the atmospheres of other planets, the kinds of beings that could survive in these atmospheres, and so on. A straight lecture on the atmosphere of the planets might have put the students to sleep, but this discussion led to real interest in the subject.

3. *Make the learning task fun.* Many lessons can be taught through simulations or games, as you saw in the Point/Counterpoint on making learning fun (page 385). Used appropriately so that the activity connects with learning, these experiences can be very worthwhile and fun too.

4. *Make use of novelty and familiarity.* Don't overuse a few teaching approaches or motivational strategies. We all need some variety. Varying the goal structures of tasks (cooperative, competitive, individualistic) can help, as can using different teaching media. When the material being covered in class is abstract or

unfamiliar to students, try to connect it to something they know and understand. For example, talk about the size of a large area, such as the Acropolis in Athens, in terms of football fields. Brophy (1988) describes one teacher who read a brief passage from *Spartacus* to personalize the unit on slavery in the ancient world.

Instrumental Value. Sometimes it is difficult to encourage intrinsic motivation, and so teachers must rely on the utility or *instrumental* value of tasks. That is, it is important to learn many skills because they will be needed in more advanced classes or because they are necessary for life outside school.

1. When these connections are not obvious, you should *explain the connections to your students.* Jeanette Abi-Nader (1991) describes one project, the PLAN program, that makes these connections come alive for Hispanic high school students. The three major strategies used in the program to focus students' attention on their future are: (1) working with mentors and models—often PLAN graduates—who give advice about how to choose courses, budget time, take notes, and deal with cultural differences at college and university; (2) storytelling about the achievements of former students (sometimes the college term papers of former students are posted on PLAN bulletin boards); and (3) filling the classroom with future-oriented talk such as "When you go to college, you will encounter these situations ..." or, "You're at a parents' meeting—you want a good education for your children—and you are the ones who must speak up; that's why it is important to learn public speaking skills" (p. 548).

2. In some situations, teachers can *provide incentives and rewards for learning* (see Chapter 6). Remember, though, that giving rewards when students are already interested in the activity may undermine intrinsic motivation.

3. Use *ill-structured problems that can be solved in a variety of ways and authentic tasks* in teaching. Connect problems in school to real problems outside.

What Do I Need to Do to Succeed? Staying Focused on the Task. When students encounter difficulties, as they must if they are working at a challenging level, they need to keep their attention on the task. If the focus shifts to worries about performance, fear of failure, or concern with looking smart, then motivation to learn is lost. Here are some ideas for keeping the focus on learning:

1. *Give students frequent opportunities to respond* through questions and answers, short assignments, or demonstrations of skills. Make sure to check the students' answers so that you can correct problems quickly. You don't want students to practise errors too long. Computer learning programs give students the immediate feedback they need to correct errors before they become habits.

2. When possible, *have students create a finished product.* They will be more persistent and focused on the task when the end is in sight. We have all experienced the power of the need for closure.

3. *Avoid heavy emphasis on grades and competition.* An emphasis on grades forces students to be ego-involved rather than task-involved. Anxious students are especially hard hit by highly competitive evaluation.

4. *Reduce task risk without oversimplifying the task.* When tasks are risky (failure is likely and the consequences of failing are grave), student motivation suffers. For difficult, complex, or ambiguous tasks, provide students with plenty of time, support, resources, help, and the chance to revise or improve work.

5. *Model motivation to learn for your students.* Talk about your interest in the subject and about how you deal with difficult learning problems.

6. *Teach the particular learning tactics* that students will need to master the material being studied. Show students how to learn and remember so that they won't be forced to fall back on self-defeating strategies or rote memory.

Connect & Extend

TO THE RESEARCH
Abi-Nader, J. (1991). Creating a vision of the future: Strategies for motivating minority students. *Phi Delta Kappan, 72,* 546–549. *Focus Questions:* Why do minority-group students sometimes find schooling unmotivating? What can be done?

Connect & Extend

TO THE RESEARCH
Thorkildsen, T. A., Nolen, S. B., & Fournier, J. (1994). What is fair? Children's critiques of practices that influence motivation. *Journal of Educational Psychology, 86,* 475–486. In this study, children aged 7–12 years were interviewed about the fairness of selected practices for influencing motivation to learn.

MOTIVATION TO LEARN

Understand family goals for children.

EXAMPLES

1. In an informal setting, around a coffee pot or snacks, meet with families individually or in small groups to listen to what they want for their children.
2. Mail out questionnaires or send response cards home with students, asking what skills the families believe their children most need to work on. Pick one goal for each child and develop a plan for working toward the goal both inside and outside school. Share the plan with the families and ask for feedback.

Identify student and family interests that can be related to goals.

EXAMPLES

1. Ask a member of the family to share a skill or hobby with the class.
2. Identify "family favourites"—favourite foods, music, vacations, sports, colours, activities, hymns, movies, games, snacks, recipes, memories. Tie class lessons to interests.

Give families a way to track progress toward goals.

EXAMPLES

1. Provide simple "progress charts" or goal cards that can be posted on the refrigerator.
2. Ask for feedback (and mean it) about parents' perceptions of your effectiveness in helping students reach goals.

Work with families to build confidence and positive expectations.

EXAMPLES

1. Avoid comparing one child in a family with another during conferences and discussions with family members.

2. Ask family members to highlight strong points of homework assignments. They might attach a note to assignments describing the three best aspects of the work and one element that could be improved.

Make families partners in showing the value of learning.

EXAMPLES

1. Invite family members to the class to demonstrate how they use mathematics or writing in their work.
2. Involve family members in identifying skills and knowledge for the children to learn in school that could be applied at home and prove helpful to the family right now, for example, keeping records on service agencies, writing letters of complaint to department stores or landlords, or researching vacation destinations.

Provide resources that build skill and will for families.

EXAMPLES

1. Give family members simple strategies for helping their children improve study skills.
2. Involve older students in a "homework hotline" telephone network for helping younger students with class assignments.

Have frequent celebrations of learning.

EXAMPLES

1. Invite families to a "museum" at the end of a unit on dinosaurs. Students create the museum in the auditorium, library, or cafeteria. After visiting the museum, families go to the classroom to examine their child's portfolio for the unit.
2. Place mini-exhibits of student work at local grocery stores, libraries, or community centres.

The support of families can be helpful as you design strategies for your students. The Family and Community Partnerships box above gives ideas for working with families.

Check Your Knowledge

- What four conditions must exist in a classroom so that motivational strategies can be successful?
- What else can teachers do to motivate students?

Apply to Practice

- What can teachers do to motivate students?

SUMMARY

What Is Motivation?
(pp. 373–374)

Define motivation.

Motivation is an internal state that arouses, directs, and maintains behaviour. The study of motivation focuses on how and why people initiate actions directed toward specific goals, how long it takes them to get started in the activity, how intensively they are involved in the activity, how persistent they are in their attempts to reach these goals, and what they are thinking and feeling along the way.

What is the difference between intrinsic and extrinsic motivation?

Intrinsic motivation is the natural tendency to seek out and conquer challenges as we pursue personal interests and exercise capabilities—it is motivation to do something when we don't have to. Extrinsic motivation is based on factors not related to the activity itself. We are not really interested in the activity for its own sake; we care only about what it will gain us.

How does locus of causality apply to motivation?

The essential difference between intrinsic and extrinsic motivation is the person's reason for acting, that is, whether the locus of causality for the action is inside or outside the person. If the locus is internal, the motivation is intrinsic; if the locus is external, the motivation is extrinsic. Most motivation has elements of both. In fact, intrinsic and extrinsic motivation may be two separate tendencies—both can operate at the same time in a given situation.

Four General Approaches to Motivation
(pp. 374–377)

What are the key factors in motivation according to a behavioural viewpoint? A humanistic viewpoint? A cognitive viewpoint? A sociocultural viewpoint?

Behaviourists tend to emphasize extrinsic motivation caused by incentives, rewards, and punishment. Humanistic views stress the intrinsic motivation created by the need for personal growth, fulfillment, and self-determination. Cognitive views stress a person's active search for meaning, understanding, and competence, and the power of the individual's attributions and interpretations. Sociocultural views emphasize legitimate engaged participation and identity within a community.

Distinguish between deficiency needs and being needs in Maslow's theory.

Maslow called the four lower-level needs—survival, safety, belonging, and self-esteem—deficiency needs. When these needs are satisfied, the motivation for fulfilling them decreases. He labelled the three higher-level needs—intellectual achievement, aesthetic appreciation, and self-actualization—being needs. When they are met, a person's motivation increases to seek further fulfillment.

What are expectancy × value theories?

Expectancy × value theories suggest that motivation to reach a goal is the product of our expectations for success and the value of the goal to us. If either is zero, our motivation is zero also.

What is legitimate peripheral participation?

Legitimate peripheral participation means that beginners are genuinely involved in the work of the group, even if their abilities are undeveloped and their contributions are small. The identities of the novice and the expert are bound up in their participation in the community. They are motivated to learn the values and practices of the community to keep their identity as community members.

Needs: Competence, Autonomy, and Relatedness
(pp. 377–380)

What are the basic needs and how do they affect motivation?

Self-determination theory suggests that motivation is affected by the need for competence, autonomy and control, and relatedness. When students experience self-determination, they are intrinsically motivated—they are more interested in their work, have a greater sense of self-esteem, and learn more. Whether students experience self-determination depends in part on if the teacher's communications with students provide information or seek to control them. In addition, teachers must acknowledge the students' perspective, offer choices, provide rationales for limits, and treat poor performance as a problem to be solved rather than a target for criticism.

How can feedback actually undermine motivation?

When students perceive feedback as too controlling—for example, about what needs improvement and how to do it—it may be conveying that students can't exercise their own abilities to determine what when wrong and to figure out how to improve their work.

Goal Orientation and Motivation
(pp. 380–383)

What kinds of goals are the most motivating?

Goals increase motivation if they are specific, moderately difficult, and able to be reached in the near future.

Describe mastery, performance, work-avoidant, and social goals.

A mastery goal is the intention to gain knowledge and master skills, leading students to seek challenges and persist when they encounter difficulties. A performance goal is the intention to get good grades or to appear smarter or more capable than others, leading students to be preoccupied with themselves and how they appear (ego-involved learners). Students can approach or avoid these two kinds of goals—the problems are greatest with avoidance. Another kind of avoidance is evident with work-avoidant learners, who simply want to find the easiest way to handle the situation. Students with social goals can be supported or hindered in their learning, depending on the specific goal (i.e., have fun with friends or bring honour to the family).

What makes goal setting effective in the classroom?

In order for goal setting to be effective in the classroom, students need accurate feedback about their progress toward goals and they must accept the goals set. Generally, students are more willing to adopt goals that seem realistic, reasonably difficult, and meaningful, and for which good reasons are given for the value of the goals.

Interests and Emotions
(pp. 383–389)

How do interests and emotions affect learning?

Learning and information processing are influenced by emotion. Students are more likely to pay attention to, learn, and remember events, images, and readings that provoke emotional responses or that are related to their personal interests. However, there are cautions in responding to students' interests. "Seductive details," interesting bits of information that are not central to the learning, can hinder learning.

What is the role of arousal in learning?

There appears to be an optimum level of arousal for most activities. Generally speaking, a higher level of arousal is helpful on simple tasks, but lower levels of arousal are better for complex tasks. When arousal is too low, teachers can stimulate curiosity by pointing out gaps in knowledge or using variety in activities. Severe anxiety is an example of arousal that is too high for optimal learning.

How does anxiety interfere with learning?

Anxiety can be the cause or the result of poor performance; it can interfere with attention to, learning of, and retrieval of information. Many anxious students need help in developing effective test-taking and study skills.

Beliefs and Self-Schemas
(pp. 390–396)

How do beliefs about ability affect motivation?

When people hold an entity theory of ability—that is, they believe that ability is fixed—they tend to set performance goals and strive to protect themselves from failure. When they believe ability is improvable (an incremental theory), however, they tend to set mastery goals and handle failure constructively.

What are the three dimensions of attributions in Weiner's theory?

According to Weiner, most of the attributed causes for successes or failures can be characterized in terms of three dimensions: *locus* (location of the cause internal or external to the person), *stability* (whether the cause stays the same or can change), and *responsibility* (whether the person can control the cause). The greatest motivational problems arise when students attribute failures to stable, uncontrollable causes. These students may seem resigned to failure, depressed, helpless—what we generally call "unmotivated."

What is self-efficacy, and how does it relate to learned helplessness?

Self-efficacy is a belief about personal competence in a particular situation such as learning or teaching fractions. A sense of efficacy, control, or self-determination is critical if people are to feel intrinsically motivated. When people come to believe that the events and outcomes in their lives are mostly uncontrollable, they have developed learned helplessness, which is associated with three types of deficits: motivational, cognitive, and affective. Students who feel hopeless will be unmotivated and reluctant to attempt work. They miss opportunities to practise and improve skills and abilities, so they develop cognitive deficits and they often suffer from affective problems such as depression, anxiety, and listlessness.

How does self-worth influence motivation?

Mastery-oriented students tend to value achievement and see ability as improvable, so they focus on mastery goals, take risks, and cope with failure constructively. A low sense of self-worth seems to be linked with the failure-avoiding and failure-accepting strategies intended to protect the individual from the consequences of failure. These strategies may seem to help in the short term, but are damaging to motivation and self-esteem in the long run.

Define motivation to learn.

Teachers are interested in a particular kind of motivation—student motivation to learn. Student motivation to learn is both a trait and a state. It involves taking academic work seriously, trying to get the most from it, and applying appropriate learning strategies in the process.

On TARGET for Learning
(pp. 397–404)

What does TARGET stand for?
TARGET is an acronym for the six areas where teachers make decisions that can influence student motivation to learn: the nature of the *task* that students are asked to do, the *autonomy* students are allowed in working, how students are *recognized* for their accomplishments, *grouping* practices, *evaluation* procedures, and the scheduling of *time* in the classroom.

How do tasks and task value affect motivation?
The tasks that teachers set affect motivation. When students encounter tasks that are related to their interests, stimulate their curiosity, or are connected to real-life situations, the students are more likely to be motivated to learn. Tasks can have attainment, intrinsic, or utility value for students. Attainment value is the importance to the student of succeeding. Intrinsic value is the enjoyment the student gets from the task. Utility value is determined by how much the task contributes to reaching short-term or long-term goals.

Distinguish between bounded and unbounded choices.
Like totally unguided discovery or aimless discussions, unstructured or unbounded choices can be counterproductive for learning. The alternative is bounded choice—giving students a range of options that set out valuable tasks for them, but also allowing them to follow personal interests. The balance must be just right so that students are not bewildered by too much choice or bored by too little room to explore.

How can recognition undermine motivation and a sense of self-efficacy?
Recognition and reward in the classroom will support motivation to learn if the recognition is for personal progress rather than competitive victories. Praise and rewards should focus on students' growing competence. At times, praise can have paradoxical effects when students use the teacher's praise or criticism as cues about capabilities.

List three goal structures and distinguish among them.
How students relate to their peers in the classroom is influenced by the goal structure of the activities. Goal structures can be competitive, individualistic, or cooperative. Cooperative goal structures can encourage motivation and increase learning, especially for low-achieving students.

How does evaluative climate affect goal setting?
The more competitive the grading, the more students set performance goals and focus on "looking competent," that is, the more they are ego-involved. When the focus is on performing rather than learning, students often see the goal of classroom tasks as simply finishing, especially if the work is difficult.

What are some effects of time on motivation?
In order to foster motivation to learn, teachers should be flexible in their use of time in the classroom. Students who are forced to move faster or slower than they should or who are interrupted as they become involved in a project are not likely to develop persistence for learning.

Diversity and Convergences in Motivation to Learn
(pp. 404–409)

What four conditions must exist in a classroom so that motivational strategies can be successful?
Before any strategies to encourage motivation can be effective, four conditions must exist in the classroom. The classroom must be organized and free from constant disruption, the teacher must be a supportive person who never embarrasses students for making mistakes, the work must be neither too easy nor too difficult, and the tasks set for students must be authentic—not busy work.

What else can teachers do to motivate students?
Once these conditions are met, teachers can use strategies that help students feel confident in their abilities to improve (e.g., set challenging but reachable goals, stress self—not other—comparisons, communicate that ability is improvable), strategies that highlight the value of the learning tasks (e.g., tie tasks to student interests, arouse curiosity, show connections to the future and to real-world problems, provide incentives), and strategies that help students stay involved in the learning process without being threatened by fear of failure (e.g., provide opportunities to create a finished product, teach learning tactics, model motivation to learn for students, avoid emphasizing grades, reduce risk without oversimplifying the task).

BECOMING A PROFESSIONAL

Reflecting on the Chapter

Can you apply the ideas from this chapter on motivation to solve the following problems of practice?

Preschool and Kindergarten

- How could you help young students build a foundation for self-efficacy in school?

- What would you do to help students develop persistence without discouraging spontaneity and enthusiasm?

Elementary and Middle School

- Several of your students seem to have given up in science. They almost expect to fail. This is especially troubling because a number of the students are girls who believe "girls are no good in science." What would you do?

- How would you respond to mistakes without communicating to students that their mistakes are the result of low ability? You also want to avoid being unrealistic about

what they can do or implying that the material is "easy."

- You are talking to the parents of one of your lower-achieving students. You really like the student, but he seems not to apply himself to the work. Suddenly, the boy's mother says, "We think our son is doing badly in your class because you don't like him. You just seem to expect him to fail!" What would you do?

Junior High and High School

- You are the faculty advisor for the student newspaper. Your students have grand ideas for stories and features, but they seem to run out of steam and never quite finish. The production of the paper is always last-minute and rush-rush. How would you help the students stay motivated and work steadily?

- As the time to take provincial exams nears, a few of your students are becoming so anxious that you wonder if they

will make it through the tests. What can you do to help them?

- You want to prepare your senior classes for the kind of independent work they will face in university, so you assign a research project. As soon as you have set the assignment, the questions begin: "How many sources?" "How many pages?" "What exactly do you mean by 'support your conclusions with evidence'?" "What kind of evidence?" How do you make the assignment clear without spoon-feeding?

Check Your Understanding

- Be clear about the kinds of goals that are most motivating.

- Make sure you understand the difference between intrinsic and extrinsic motivation.

- Understand the elements of attribution theory.

- Know ways to enhance self-efficacy in students.

- Know about the role of choice in motivation.
- Understand the difference between a self-fulfilling prophecy and a sustaining expectation effect.
- Be familiar with several approaches to cooperative learning.

Your Teaching Portfolio

Think about your philosophy of teaching, a question you will be asked at most job interviews. What do you believe about motivating hard-to-reach students? How can you support the development of genuine and well-founded self-efficacy in your students? (Consult the Guidelines titled "Supporting Self-Determination and Autonomy" on page 379 for ideas.)

Add some ideas for parent involvement from this chapter to your portfolio.

Use the section on the TARGET model to refine your teaching philosophy. How will you answer the job interview question, "What would you do to motivate difficult-to-reach students?"

Teaching Resources

Adapt all the Guidelines from the chapter for the age group you plan to teach.

Use the TARGET model (Table 10.6 on page 398) to generate motivational strategies for the grade you will teach.

Teachers' Casebook

What Would They Do?

Here is how two practising teachers responded to the teaching situation presented at the beginning of this chapter about motivating students.

Michael Landis
James R. Henderson Public School
Kingston, Ontario

As a teacher coming into a new classroom and grade, you'll encounter insufficient resources more often than not. Money will always be a problem with education, especially considering how quickly the world changes, making it hard to keep up with the most current resources. Yet in this case I believe the teacher is lucky. Many times you're faced with no resources at all—new or old! In this situation the teacher has a base to start from. Not having even that could be overwhelming.

The district school board uses these units to evaluate their students; therefore, they can be seen as an asset, a tool to prepare students for the district-wide assessments. Students will know what to expect, and in some board-wide assessments teachers don't have that knowledge. As well, even though you may feel that the texts are at a high grade 3 level, you at least know the level your district school board is striving for.

Having this base, your job is now to expand it into a full, up-to-date grade 3 program. Your love of learning and exploring and your good humour will be your number one motivators. Your second motivator will be your hard work. You'll need to create and/or find resources (using the teachers' resource centre, library, internet, etc.) and connect with district colleagues to prepare daily activities and projects, locate videos, book guest speakers from the community, buy computer programs, organize field trips, etc. Most of these you'll be able to produce with only your time, others with small funds, and a few through parent and student fundraisers.

This varied learning program will touch all the different styles of learning (auditory, visual, etc.). You'll also touch the different academic levels in the class by modifying the activities' levels of difficulty in order to gear the learning to individual student needs. Have fun with the activities—this will motivate your students to enjoy learning, not only for the year they spend with you, but also for life!

Kate Whitton
MeadowView Public School
Addison, Ontario

Part of the reality of teaching today is that there never seems to be enough funds for stimulating material. As a result, teachers have had to become even more creative and versatile with the resources that are available. As well, many excellent free resources can be found outside the school. I would begin by searching within the local community for guest speakers and for free programs and materials offered by government and private agencies and at public libraries. Sometimes local industry can offer products, such as paper, that would otherwise be discarded. Other wonderful sources are the internet, the Board Learning Resources centres, and inter-school swaps.

By experiencing concrete results students will begin to comprehend the concept of the value of learning, so these results have to be meaningful for them. Creating assignments that integrate the various learning styles in the classroom will initiate and maintain student interest. One possible approach is to find a common theme that incorporates the objectives in the workbooks and then develop problem-solving projects or assignments based on this theme. The Stability strand in science, for example, could be combined with the social studies Pioneers strand by having students create a 3-D model of pioneer life that includes components of language (skit, written report, brochure) and math (geometry, measurement, and number sense).

Breaking down material into smaller chunks helps students understand it without feeling overwhelmed. Going on to apply it in a more concrete, hands-on way will extend and solidify their knowledge. The project approach gives students a goal to work toward and acts as an incentive to work through some of the more "boring" workbook material. Furthermore, everyone can be successful on some level with a multi-faceted project. Kids love to problem-solve; however, they do require parameters within which to work, and as they become accustomed to this style of learning these parameters can become less stringent. Another advantage of this approach is that teachers can continue making more connections with other curriculum requirements. The key is to remain flexible and open-minded in altering your own "gems," even at the last minute!

Motivation is highly individualistic. Setting realistic goals and hooking students on some level will enable them to work through most difficult areas, especially when they can bring their own visions and experiences to a project or assignment. Kids usually enjoy working in groups or pairs as they apply concepts in a more active and creative manner. In short, rather than dictating to students, teaching should be more facilitative.

11 CREATING LEARNING ENVIRONMENTS

Booker T. Washington Legend, c. 1944–45. William H. Johnson. Photo: Smithsonian American Art Museum, Washington, DC/Art Resource, New York.

Teachers' Casebook

What Would You Do?

Two boys in your classroom are terrorizing another student. They are larger, stronger, and older than the boy being victimized, who is small and shy. There are incidents on the bus before and after school, in the gym, and at lunch, including intimidation, extortion of lunch money, tripping, shoving, and verbal taunts—"fag" is a favourite chant. The other students in your class see what is going on and know you are aware of the problem too.

Critical Thinking

How do you handle this situation? What if the bullies were not in your classroom? What if the bullies and victim were girls? How will these issues affect the grade levels you will teach?

Collaboration

With two or three other members of your class, consider how you might structure your classrooms to help students get along together. How would you involve them in finding a solution to this problem?

This chapter looks at the ways that teachers create social and physical environments for learning by examining classroom management—one of the main concerns of teachers, particularly beginning teachers. The very nature of classes, teaching, and students makes good management a critical ingredient of success; we will investigate why this is true. Successful managers create more time for learning, involve more students, and help students to become self-managing.

A positive learning environment must be established and maintained throughout the year. One of the best ways to do this is to try to prevent problems from occurring at all. But when problems arise—as they always do—an appropriate response is important. What will you do when students challenge you openly in class, when one student asks your advice on a difficult personal problem, or when another withdraws from all participation? We will examine the ways in which teachers can communicate effectively with their students in these and many other situations.

By the time you have completed this chapter, you should be able to answer these questions:

- *What are the special managerial demands of classrooms, and how do they relate to the needs of students of different ages?*

- *How will you establish a list of rules and procedures for a class?*

- *How will you arrange the physical environment of your classroom to fit your learning goals and teaching methods?*

- *How will you manage computers in your classroom to fit your learning goals and teaching methods?*

- *What are Jacob Kounin's suggestions for preventing management problems?*

- *How would you respond to a student who seldom completes work?*

- *What are two different approaches for dealing with a conflict between teacher and student?*

THE NEED FOR ORGANIZATION

In study after study of the factors related to student achievement, classroom management stands out as the variable with the largest impact (Marzano & Marzano, 2003). Knowledge and expertise in classroom management are marks of expertise in teaching; stress and exhaustion from managerial difficulties are precursors of burnout in teaching (Emmer & Stough, 2001). Why is classroom management so critical?

Classes are particular kinds of environments. They have distinctive features that influence their inhabitants no matter how the students or the desks are organized or what the teacher believes about education (Doyle, 1986, 2006). Classrooms are *multidimensional*. They are crowded with people, tasks, and time pressures. Many individuals, all with differing goals, preferences, and abilities, must share resources, accomplish various tasks, use and reuse materials without losing them, move in and out of the room, and so on. In addition, actions can have multiple effects. Calling on students of/with low ability may encourage their participation and thinking but may slow the discussion and lead to management problems if the students cannot answer. And events occur *simultaneously*—everything happens at once, and the *pace is fast*. Teachers have literally hundreds of exchanges with students during a single day.

In this rapid-fire existence, events are *unpredictable*. Even when plans are carefully made, the overhead projector is in place, and the demonstration is ready, the lesson can still be interrupted by a burned-out bulb in the projector or a loud, angry discussion right outside the classroom. Because classrooms are *public*, the way the teacher handles these unexpected intrusions is seen and judged by all. Students are always noticing if the teacher is being "fair." Is there favouritism? What happens when a rule is broken? Finally, classrooms have *histories*. The meaning of a particular teacher's or student's actions depends in part on what has happened before. The fifteenth time a student arrives late requires a different response from the teacher than the first late arrival. In addition, the history of the first few weeks of school affects life in the class all year.

The Basic Task: Gain Their Cooperation

No productive activity can take place in a group without the cooperation of all members. This obviously applies to classrooms. Even if some students don't participate, they must allow others to do so. (You have probably seen one or two

Connect & Extend

TO YOUR OWN PHILOSOPHY

Some educators object to the metaphor of teacher as manager. These critics suggest that the image brings with it notions of manipulation and detachment. Is the metaphor of manager an appropriate choice? What other metaphors can you suggest for teachers acting to maintain order and discipline? Anita's research in this area suggests that images of group leaders (coaches, guides, etc.), problem solvers (physicians, chess players), and nurturers (mothers, fathers, gardeners) are common for beginning teachers.

So much is happening at any given moment in a typical classroom that a teacher needs to be "on" at every moment of the day.

students bring an entire class to a halt.) So the basic management task for teachers is to achieve order and harmony by gaining and maintaining student cooperation in class activities (Doyle, 2006). Given the multidimensional, simultaneous, immediate, unpredictable, public, and historical nature of classrooms, this is quite a challenge.

Gaining student cooperation means much more than dealing effectively with misbehaviour. It means planning activities, having materials ready, making appropriate behavioural and academic demands on students, giving clear signals, accomplishing transitions smoothly, foreseeing problems and stopping them before they start, selecting and sequencing activities so that flow and interest are maintained—and much more. Also, different activities require different managerial skills. For example, a new or complicated activity may be a greater threat to classroom management than a familiar or simple activity. And appropriate student participation varies across different activities. For example, loud student comments during a hip-hop reading of *Green Eggs and Ham* in an urban classroom are indications of engagement and cooperation, not disorderly call-outs (Doyle, 2006).

Obviously, gaining the cooperation of kindergartners is not the same task as gaining the cooperation of students in grade 12. Jere Brophy and Carolyn Evertson (1978) have identified four general stages of classroom management, defined by age-related needs. During kindergarten and the first few years of elementary school, direct teaching of classroom rules and procedures is important because these students are still learning how to behave in school. For children in the middle elementary years, many school and classroom routines have become relatively automatic, but new rules and procedures for a particular activity may need to be taught directly, and the entire system still needs monitoring and maintenance.

Toward the end of elementary school and middle school and the beginning of high school, some students begin to test and defy authority. The management challenges at this stage are to deal productively with these disruptions and to motivate students who are becoming less concerned with teachers' opinions and more interested in their social lives. By the end of high school, the challenges are to manage the curriculum, fit academic material to students' interests and abilities, and help students become more self-managing. The first few classes each semester may be devoted to teaching particular procedures for using materials and equipment or for keeping track of and submitting assignments. However, most students know what is expected.

The Goals of Classroom Management

The aim of **classroom management** is to maintain a positive, productive learning environment. But order for its own sake is an empty goal. As we discussed in Chapter 6, it is unethical to use class management techniques just to keep students docile and quiet. What, then, is the point of working so hard to manage classrooms? There are at least three reasons why management is important.

More Time for Learning. If you were to use a stopwatch to time the commercials during a TV quiz show, you'd likely find that almost half of the program was devoted to commercials. Then, if you timed all the "small talk," you'd find that very little quizzing takes place. If you used a similar approach in classrooms, timing all the different activities throughout the day, you might be surprised by how little actual teaching takes place. Many minutes are lost each day through interruptions, disruptions, late starts, and rough transitions (Karweit, 1989; Karweit & Slavin, 1981).

Obviously, students will learn only the material they have a chance to learn. Almost every study examining time and learning has found a significant relationship between time spent on content and student learning (Berliner, 1988). In fact, the correlations between content studied and student learning are usually larger than the correlations between specific teacher behaviour and student learning

Connect & Extend

TO YOUR TEACHING
Many computer programs exist to help teachers manage their own activities inside and outside the classroom. Having standard forms available, such as IEPs, student reports, and letters to parents, is a tremendous help, as is having access to databases, electronic mail, and schedules. Complete classroom management systems and computer-managed instruction (CMI) are also available. For more information, see Bitter, G. G., & Pierson, M. E. (1999). *Using technology in the classroom* (3rd ed.). Boston: Allyn & Bacon.

classroom management Techniques used to maintain a healthy learning environment, relatively free of behaviour problems.

allocated time Time set aside for learning.

engaged time/time on task Time spent actively engaged in the learning task at hand.

academic learning time Time when students are actually succeeding at the learning task.

(Rosenshine, 1979). So one important goal of classroom management is to expand the sheer number of minutes available for learning. This time is sometimes called **allocated time.**

Simply making more time available for learning will not automatically lead to achievement. To be valuable, time must be used effectively. As you saw in the chapters on cognitive learning, how students process information is a central factor in what they learn and remember. Basically, students will learn what they practise and think about (Doyle, 1983). The time spent actively involved in specific learning tasks is often called **engaged time,** or sometimes **time on task.**

Again, however, engaged time doesn't guarantee learning. Students may be struggling with material that is too difficult or using the wrong learning strategies. When students are working with a high rate of success—really learning and understanding—we call the time spent **academic learning time.** A second goal of class management is to increase academic learning time by keeping students *actively engaged in worthwhile, appropriate learning activities.* Figure 11.1 shows how the 1000+ hours of time mandated for school can become only about 333 hours of high-quality academic learning time for a typical student.

Getting students engaged in learning early in their school careers can make a big difference. Several studies have shown that teachers' rating of students' on-task, persistent engagement in grade 1 predicts achievement test score gains and grades through grade 4, as well as the decision to drop out of high school (Fredricks, Blumenfeld, & Paris, 2004).

Access to Learning.   Each classroom activity has its own rules for participation. Sometimes these rules are clearly stated by the teacher, but often they are implicit and unstated. Teacher and students may not even be aware that they are following different rules for different activities (Berliner, 1983). The differences are sometimes quite subtle. For example, in a reading group students may have to raise their hands to make a comment, but in a show-and-tell circle in the same class they may simply have to catch the teacher's eye.

As we saw in Chapter 5, the rules defining who can talk; what they can talk about; and when, to whom, and how long they can talk are often called

Figure 11.1 Who Knows Where the Time Goes?

The over 1000 hours per year of instruction students receive can represent only 300 or 400 hours of high-quality academic learning time.

Source: From Weinstein, C. S., & Mignano, A. J., Jr. (2003). *Elementary classroom management* (3rd ed.). New York: McGraw-Hill. Copyright © 2003 by The McGraw-Hill Companies. Adapted with permission.

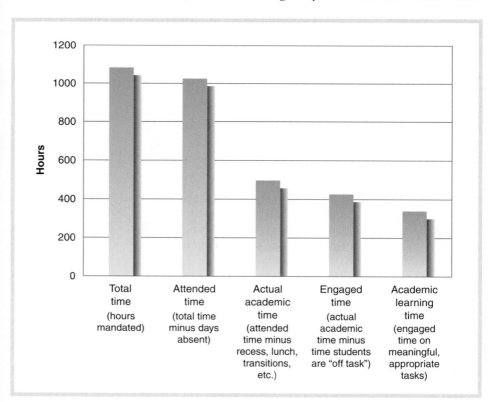

participation structures. In order to participate successfully in a given activity, students must understand the participation structure. Some students, however, seem to come to school less able to participate than others. The participation structures they learn at home in interactions with siblings, parents, and other adults do not match the participation structures of school activities (Tharp, 1989). Teachers are not necessarily aware of this conflict. Instead, the teachers may see that a child doesn't quite fit in, always seems to say the wrong thing at the wrong time, or is very reluctant to participate, and they are not sure why.

What can we conclude? To reach the second goal of classroom management—giving all students access to learning—you must make sure that everyone knows *how to participate* in each specific activity. The key is awareness. What are your rules and expectations? Are they understandable, given your students' cultural backgrounds and home experiences? What unspoken rules or values may be operating? Are you clear and consistent in signalling to students how to participate? For some students, particularly those with behavioural and emotional challenges, direct teaching and practice of the important behaviours may be required (Emmer & Stough, 2001).

An example of being sensitive to participation structures was documented by Adrienne Alton-Lee and her colleagues in a classroom in New Zealand (2001). As a critical part of a unit on children in hospitals, the teacher, Ms. Nikora, planned to have one of her students, a Maori girl named Huhana, describe a recent visit to the hospital. Huhana agreed. But when the time came and the teacher asked her to come to the front of the class and share her experiences, Huhana looked down and shook her head. Rather than confront or scold Huhana, the teacher simply said, "All right. If we sit in a circle ... Huhana might be able to tell us about what happened." When students were in a circle, the teacher said, "All right, Huhana, after Ms. Nikora called your mum and she ... Where did she take you to?" As Huhana began to share her experience, the teacher scaffolded her participation by asking questions, providing reminders of details the teacher had learned in previous conversations with Huhana, and waiting patiently for the student's responses. Rather than perceiving the *child* as lacking competence, the teacher saw the *situation* as hindering competent expression.

Management for Self-Management.   The third goal of any management system is to help students become better able to manage themselves. If teachers focus on student compliance, they will spend much of the teaching/learning time monitoring and correcting. Students come to see the purpose of school as just following rules, not constructing deep understanding of academic knowledge. And complex learning structures such as cooperative or problem-based learning require student self-management. Compliance with rules is not enough to make these learning structures work (McCaslin & Good, 1998).

The movement from demanding obedience to teaching self-regulation and self-control is a fundamental shift in discussions of classroom management today (Weinstein, 1999). Tom Savage (1999) says simply, "the most fundamental purpose of discipline is the development of self-control. Academic knowledge and technological skill will be of little consequence if those who possess them lack self-control" (p. 11). Through self-control, students demonstrate *responsibility*—the ability to fulfill their own needs without interfering with the rights and needs of others (Glasser, 1990). Students learn self-control by making choices and dealing with the consequences, setting goals and priorities, managing time, collaborating to learn, mediating disputes and making peace, and developing trusting relations with trustworthy teachers and classmates (Bear, 2005; Rogers & Frieberg, 1994).

Encouraging **self-management** requires extra time, but teaching students how to take responsibility is an investment well worth the effort. When elementary and secondary teachers have effective class management systems but neglect to set student self-management as a goal, their students often have trouble working independently after graduating from these "well-managed" classes.

participation structures Rules defining how to participate in different activities.

Connect & Extend

TO YOUR TEACHING
Are there cultural differences in the verbal and non-verbal ways that students show respect, pay attention, and bid for a turn in conversation? How can cultural differences in interaction styles and expectations make classroom management more challenging?

self-management Management of your own behaviour and acceptance of responsibility for your own actions.

Check Your Knowledge

• What are the challenges of classroom management?
• What are the goals of good classroom management?

Apply to Practice

• How would you increase academic learning time in your classroom?

CREATING A POSITIVE LEARNING ENVIRONMENT

In making plans for your class, much of what you have already learned in this book should prove helpful. You know, for example, that problems are prevented when student development and diversity, as was discussed in Chapters 2 through 5, are taken into account in instructional planning. Sometimes students become disruptive because the work assigned is too difficult. And students who are bored by lessons well below their ability levels may be interested in finding more exciting activities to fill their time.

In one sense, teachers prevent discipline problems whenever they make an effort to motivate students. A student involved in learning is usually not involved in a clash with the teacher or other students at the same time. All plans for motivating students are steps toward preventing problems.

Some Research Results

What else can teachers do to be good managers? For several years, educational psychologists at the University of Texas at Austin studied classroom management quite thoroughly (Emmer & Stough, 2001; Emmer, Evertson, & Anderson, 1980; Emmer & Gerwels, 2006). Their general approach was to study a large number of classrooms, making frequent observations during the first weeks of school and less frequent visits later in the year. After several months, there were dramatic differences among the classes. Some had very few management problems, while others had many. The most and least effective teachers were identified on the basis of the quality of classroom management and student achievement later in the year.

Next, the researchers looked at their observation records of the first weeks of class to see how the effective teachers got started. Other comparisons were made between the teachers who ultimately had harmonious, high-achieving classes and those whose classes were fraught with problems. On the basis of these comparisons, management principles were developed. The researchers then taught these principles to a new group of teachers; the results were quite positive. Teachers who applied the principles had fewer problems, their students spent more time learning and less time disrupting, and achievement was higher. The findings of these studies formed the basis for two books on classroom management (Emmer, Evertson, & Worsham, 2006; Evertson, Emmer, & Worsham, 2006). Many of the ideas in the following pages are from these books.

Rules and Procedures Required

At the elementary-school level, teachers must lead 20 to 30 students of varying abilities through many different activities each day. Without efficient rules and procedures, a great deal of time is wasted answering the same question over and over. "My pencil broke. How can I do my math?" "I'm finished with my story. What should I do now?" "Steven hit me!" "I left my homework in my locker."

At the secondary-school level, teachers must deal daily with more than 100 students who use dozens of materials and often change rooms for each class. Secondary-school students are also more likely to challenge teachers' authority. The

---

Connect & Extend

TO OTHER CHAPTERS

In **Chapter 12**, you will learn about the importance of careful planning and clear objectives. Good planning is an important aspect of classroom management.

Connect & Extend

TO OTHER CHAPTERS

Motivation and classroom management are closely related. The motivational strategies described in **Chapter 10** are good first steps in effective class management.

effective teachers studied by Emmer, Evertson, and their colleagues had planned procedures and rules for coping with these situations.

Procedures. How will materials and assignments be distributed and collected? Under what conditions can students leave the room? How will grades be determined? What are the special routines for handling equipment and supplies in science, art, or vocational classes? **Procedures** (often called routines) describe how activities are accomplished in classrooms, but they are seldom written down; they are simply the ways of getting things done in class. Carol Weinstein and Andy Mignano, at the University of Texas, recommend that teachers establish procedures to cover the following areas (Weinstein, 2003; Weinstein & Mignano, 2003):

1. *Administrative routines*, such as taking attendance.
2. *Student movement*, such as entering and leaving or going to the bathroom.
3. *Housekeeping*, such as watering plants or storing personal items.
4. *Routines for accomplishing lessons*, such as how to collect assignments or return homework.
5. *Interactions between teacher and student*, such as how to get the teacher's attention when help is needed.
6. *Talk among students*, such as giving help or socializing.

You might use these six areas as a framework for planning your class procedures and routines. The Guidelines on page 424 should help you as you plan.

As you've seen, different activities often require different rules, which can be confusing for elementary students until they have thoroughly learned all the rules. To prevent confusion, you might consider making signs that list the rules for each activity. Then, before the activity, you can post the appropriate sign as a reminder and review the rules. This reminder provides clear and consistent cues about participation structures so that all students, not just the "well-behaved," know what is expected. Of course, these rules must be explained and discussed before the signs can have their full effect.

Rules. **Rules** specify expected and forbidden actions in the class. They are the dos and don'ts of classroom life. Unlike procedures, rules are often written down and posted. In establishing rules, Jack Martin and Jeff Sugarman (1993) at Simon Fraser University in B.C. recommend considering what kind of atmosphere you want to create. What student behaviour will help you teach effectively? What limits do the students need to guide their behaviour? The rules you set should be consistent with school rules and also in keeping with principles of learning. For example, we know from the research on small-group learning that students benefit when they explain work to peers. They learn as they teach. A rule that forbids students to help each other may be inconsistent with good learning principles. Or a rule that says "No erasures when writing" may make students focus more on preventing mistakes than on communicating clearly in their writing (Burden, 1995; Emmer & Stough, 2001; Weinstein & Mignano, 2003).

Rules should be positive and observable (raise your hand to be recognized). Having a few general rules that cover many specifics is better than listing all the dos and don'ts. But if specific actions, such as chewing gum in class or smoking in the bathrooms, are forbidden, a rule should make this clear.

Rules for Elementary School. Evertson and her colleagues (2006) give four examples of general rules for elementary-school students:

1. *Respect and be polite to all people.* Give clear explanations of what you mean by "polite," including not hitting, fighting, or teasing. Examples of polite behaviour include waiting your turn, saying "please" and "thank you," and not calling names. This applies to behaviour toward adults (including substitute teachers) and children.

procedures Prescribed steps for an activity.

rules Statements specifying expected and forbidden behaviour; dos and don'ts.

Connect & Extend

TO YOUR TEACHING
Visit elementary-school classes and note the rules posted by different teachers at the same grade level. Identify rules that are common to all or most classes, as well as those that are unusual.

Determine procedures for student upkeep of desks, classroom equipment, and other facilities.

EXAMPLES

1. Some teachers set aside a cleanup time each day or once a week in self-contained classes.

2. You might demonstrate and have students practise how to push chairs under the desk, take and return materials stored on shelves, sharpen pencils, use the sink or water fountain, assemble lab equipment, and so on.

3. In some classes, a rotating monitor is in charge of equipment or materials.

Decide how students will be expected to enter and leave the room.

EXAMPLES

1. How will students know what they should do as soon as they enter the room? Some teachers have a standard assignment ("Have your homework out and be checking it over").

2. Under what conditions can students leave the room? When do they need permission?

3. If students are late, how do they gain admission to the room?

4. Many teachers require students to be in their seats and quiet before they can leave at the end of class. The teacher, not the bell, dismisses class.

Establish a signal and teach it to your students.

EXAMPLES

1. In the classroom, some teachers flick the lights, sound a chord on a piano or recorder, move to the podium and stare silently at the class, use a phrase such as "Eyes, please," take out their grade books, or move to the front of the class.

2. In the halls, a raised hand, one clap, or some other signal may mean "Stop."

3. On the playground, a raised hand or whistle may mean "Line up."

Set procedures for student participation in class.

EXAMPLES

1. Will you have students raise their hands for permission to speak or simply require that they wait until the speaker has finished?

2. How will you signal that you want everyone to respond at once? Some teachers raise a cupped hand to an ear. Others preface the question with "Everyone."

3. Make sure that you are clear about differences in procedures for different activities: reading group, learning centre, discussion, teacher presentation, seatwork, film, peer learning group, library, and so forth.

4. How many students at a time can be at the pencil sharpener, teacher's desk, learning centre, sink, bookshelves, reading corner, or bathroom?

Determine how you will communicate, collect, and return assignments.

EXAMPLES

1. Some teachers reserve a particular corner of the board for listing assignments. Others write assignments in coloured chalk. For younger students, it may be better to prepare assignment sheets or folders, colour-coding them for math workbook, reading packet, and science kit.

2. Some teachers collect assignments in a box or bin; others have a student collect work while they introduce the next activity.

2. *Be prompt and prepared.* This rule highlights the importance of the academic work in the class. Being prompt includes the beginning of the day and transitions between activities.

3. *Listen quietly while others are speaking.* This applies to the teacher and other students, in both large-class lessons or small-group discussions.

4. *Obey all school rules.* This reminds students that all school rules apply in your classroom. Then students cannot claim, for example, that they thought it was okay to chew gum or listen to a radio in your class, even though these are against school rules, "because you never made a rule against it for us."

Whatever the rule, students need to be taught the behaviour that the rule includes and excludes. Examples, practice, and discussion will be needed before learning is complete.

Rules for Secondary School. Emmer and colleagues (2006) suggest six examples of rules for secondary-school students:

1. *Bring all needed materials to class.* The teacher must specify the type of pen, pencil, paper, notebook, texts, and so on.

2. *Be in your seat and ready to work when the bell rings.* Many teachers combine this rule with a standard beginning procedure for the class, such as a warm-up exercise on the board or a requirement that students have paper with a proper heading ready when the bell rings.

3. *Respect and be polite to everyone.* This rule covers fighting, verbal abuse, and general troublemaking.

4. *Respect other people's property.* This means property belonging to the school, the teacher, or other students.

5. *Listen and stay seated while someone else is speaking.* This applies when the teacher or other students are talking.

6. *Obey all school rules.* As with the elementary-class rules, this covers a variety of behaviour and situations, so you do not have to repeat every school rule for your class. It also reminds the students that you will be monitoring them inside and outside your class. Make sure that you know all the school rules. Some secondary students are adept at convincing teachers that their misbehaviour "really isn't against the rules."

Consequences. As soon as you decide on your rules and procedures, you must consider what you will do when a student breaks a rule or does not follow a procedure. It is too late to make this decision after the rule has been broken. For many infractions, the logical consequence is having to go back and "do it right." Students who run in the hall may have to return to where they started and walk properly. Incomplete papers can be redone. Materials left out should be put back (Charles, 2002b). You can use **natural or logical consequences** to support social/emotional development by doing the following (Elias & Schwab, 2006):

- Your response should separate the deed from the doer—the problem is the behaviour, not the student.
- Emphasize to students that they have the power to choose their actions and thus avoid losing control.
- Encourage student reflection, self-evaluation, and problem solving—avoid teacher lecturing.
- Help students identify and give a rationale for what they could do differently next time in a similar situation.

natural/logical consequences Instead of punishing, have students redo, repair, or in some way face the consequences that naturally flow from their actions.

The main point here is that decisions about penalties (and rewards) must be made early on, so that students know before they break a rule or use the wrong procedure what this will mean for them. Anita encourages her student teachers to get a copy of the school rules and their cooperating teacher's rules, and then plan their own. Sometimes, consequences are more complicated. In their case studies of four expert elementary-school teachers, Weinstein and Mignano (2003) found that the teachers' negative consequences fell into seven categories, as shown in Table 11.1 on the next page.

Who Sets the Rules and Consequences? In Chapter 1, we described Ken, an expert teacher who worked with his students to establish a students' and teacher's "Bill of Rights" instead of defining rules. These "rights" cover most situations that might require a "rule" and help the students move toward the goal of becom-

TABLE 11.1 Seven Categories of Consequences for Students

1. *Expressions of disappointment.* If students like and respect their teacher, then a serious, sorrowful expression of disappointment may cause students to stop and think about their behaviour.

2. *Loss of privileges.* Students can lose free time. If they have not completed homework, for example, they can be required to do it during a free period or recess.

3. *Exclusion from the group.* Students who distract their peers or fail to cooperate can be separated from the group until they are ready to cooperate. Some teachers give a student a pass for 10 to 15 minutes. During this time, the student goes to another class or study hall, where the other students and teachers ignore them. Some students may perceive this consequence as a reward.

4. *Written reflections on the problem.* Students can write in journals, write essays about what they did and how it affected others, or write letters of apology—if this is appropriate. Another possibility is to ask students to describe objectively what they did; then the teacher and the student can discuss and sign and date this statement. These records are available if parents or administrators need evidence of the students' behaviour.

5. *Detentions.* Detentions can be very brief meetings after school, during a free period, or at lunch. The main purpose is to talk about what has happened. (In high school, detentions are often used as punishments; suspensions and expulsions are available as more extreme measures.)

6. *Visits to the principal's office.* Expert teachers tend to use this consequence rarely, but they do use it when the situation warrants. Some schools require students to be sent to the office for certain offences, such as fighting. If you tell a student to go to the office and the student refuses, you might call the office saying that the student has been sent. Then the student has the choice of either going to the office or facing the principal's penalty for "disappearing" on the way.

7. *Contact with parents.* If problems become a repeated pattern, most teachers contact the student's family. This is done to seek support for helping the student, not to blame the parents or punish the student.

Source: From Weinstein, C. S., & Mignano, A. J., Jr. (2003). *Elementary classroom management* (3rd ed.). New York: McGraw-Hill. Copyright © 2003 by The McGraw-Hill Companies. Adapted with permission.

ing self-managing. The rights for one recent year's class are listed in Table 11.2. Developing rights and responsibilities rather than rules makes a very important point to students. "Teaching children that something is wrong because there is a rule against it is not the same as teaching them that there is a rule against it because it is wrong, and helping them to understand why this is so" (Weinstein,

Consequences for breaking rules are posted in this classroom. How about consequences for following the rules?

TABLE 11.2 A Bill of Rights for Students and Teachers

Students' Bill of Rights

Students in this class have the following rights:

To whisper when the teacher isn't talking or asking for silence.

To celebrate authorship or other work at least once a month.

To exercise outside on days there is no physical education class.

To have two-minute breaks.

To have healthy snacks during snack time.

To participate in choosing a table.

To have privacy. Get permission to touch anyone else's possessions.

To be comfortable.

To chew gum without blowing bubbles or making a mess.

To make choices about the day's schedule.

To have free work time.

To work with partners.

To talk to the class without anyone else talking.

To work without being disturbed.

Teacher's Bill of Rights

The teacher has the following rights:

To talk without anyone else talking, moving about, or disturbing the class.

To work without being disturbed.

To have everyone's attention while giving directions.

To punish someone who is not cooperating.

To send someone out of the group or room, or to the office.

Source: From Weinstein, C. S., & Mignano, A. J., Jr. (2003). *Elementary classroom management* (3rd ed.). New York: McGraw-Hill. Copyright © 2003 by The McGraw-Hill Companies. Adapted with permission.

1999, p. 154). Students should understand that the rules are developed so that everyone can work and learn together. It should be noted that when Ken has had some very difficult classes, he and his students have had to establish some "laws" that protect students' rights.

If you are going to involve students in setting rules or creating a constitution, you may need to wait until you have established a sense of community in your classroom. Before students can contribute meaningfully to the class rules, they need to trust the teacher and the situation (Elias & Schwab, 2006).

Another kind of planning that affects the learning environment is designing the physical arrangement of the class furniture, materials, and learning tools.

Planning Spaces for Learning

Spaces for learning should invite and support the activities you plan in your classroom, and they should respect the inhabitants of the space. This respect begins at the classroom door for young children by helping them identify their class. One school that has won awards for its architecture paints each classroom door a different bright colour so that young children can find their "home" (Herbert, 1998). Once inside, spaces can be created that invite quiet reading, group collaboration, or independent research. If students are to use materials, they should be able to

Connect & Extend

TO PROFESSIONAL JOURNALS
See the September 1998 issue of *Educational Leadership* for several articles on the topic of "Realizing a Positive School Climate." There are descriptions of ways to improve school climate through architecture and design, school meetings, cooperative learning, violence prevention, parent involvement, and other approaches.

action zone Area of a classroom where the greatest amount of interaction takes place.

reach them. In an interview with Marge Scherer (1999), Herb Kohl describes how he creates a positive environment in his classes:

> What I do is put up the most beautiful things I know—posters, games, puzzles, challenges—and let the children know these are provocations. These are ways of provoking them into using their minds. You have to create an environment that makes kids walk in and say, "I really want to see what's here. I would really like to look at this." (p. 9)

In terms of classroom arrangement, there are two basic ways of organizing space: one focusing on personal territories and one focusing on interest areas.

Personal Territories. Can the physical setting influence teaching and learning in classrooms organized by territories? Front-seat location does seem to increase participation for students who are predisposed to speak in class, whereas a seat in the back will make it more difficult to participate and easier to sit back and daydream (Woolfolk & Brooks, 1983). But the **action zone**, where participation is greatest, may be in other areas, such as on one side or near a particular learning centre (Good, 1983a; Lambert, 1994). To "spread the action around," Weinstein and Mignano (2003) suggest that teachers move around the room when possible, establish eye contact with and direct questions to students seated far away, and vary the seating so that the same students are not always consigned to the back.

Horizontal rows share many of the advantages of the traditional row and column arrangements. Both are useful for independent seatwork and teacher, student, or media presentations; they encourage students to focus on the presenter and simplify housekeeping. Horizontal rows also permit students to work more easily in pairs. However, this is a poor arrangement for large-group discussion.

Clusters of four or circle arrangements are best for student interaction. Circles are especially useful for discussions but still allow for independent seatwork. Clusters permit students to talk, help one another, share materials, and work on group tasks. Both arrangements, however, are poor for whole-group presentations and may make class management more difficult.

The fishbowl, or stack, special formation, where students sit close together near the focus of attention (the back row may even be standing), should be used only for short periods of time, because it is not comfortable and can lead to discipline problems. On the other hand, the fishbowl can create a feeling of group cohesion and is helpful when the teacher wants students to watch a demonstration, brainstorm on a class problem, or see a small visual aid.

Interest Areas. The design of interest areas can influence the way the areas are used by students. For example, working with a classroom teacher, Weinstein (1977) was able to make changes in interest areas that helped the teacher meet her objectives of having more girls involved in the science centre and having all students experiment more with a variety of manipulative materials. In a second study, changes in a library corner led to more involvement in literature activities throughout the class (Morrow & Weinstein, 1986). If you design areas of interest for your class, keep the accompanying Guidelines in mind.

Personal territories and interest areas are not mutually exclusive; many teachers use a design that combines these types of organizations. Individual students' desks—their territories—are placed in the centre, with interest areas in the back or around the periphery of the room. This allows the flexibility needed for both large- and small-group activities. Figure 11.2 on page 430 shows an elementary classroom that combines interest area and personal territory arrangements.

Planning for Computer Uses

Many classrooms today have computers. Some classes have only one, others have several, and some classes are labs with a computer for every student. Using computers productively brings with it management challenges. Computers can be used

DESIGNING LEARNING SPACES

Note the fixed features and plan accordingly.

EXAMPLES

1. Remember that the audiovisual centre and computers need an electrical outlet.
2. Keep art supplies near the sink; keep small-group work by a blackboard.

Create easy access to materials and a well-organized place to store them.

EXAMPLES

1. Make sure that materials are easy to reach and visible to students.
2. Have enough shelves so that materials need not be stacked.

Provide students with clean, convenient surfaces for studying.

EXAMPLES

1. Put bookshelves next to the reading area and games by the game table.
2. Prevent fights by avoiding crowded work spaces.

Make sure that work areas are private and quiet.

EXAMPLES

1. Make sure that there are no tables or work areas in the middle of traffic lanes; a person should not have to pass through one area to get to another.
2. Keep noisy activities as far as possible from quiet ones. Increase the feeling of privacy by placing partitions, such as bookcases or pegboards, between areas or within large areas.

Arrange things so that you can see your students and they can see all instructional presentations.

EXAMPLES

1. Make sure that you can see over partitions.
2. Design seating so that students can see instruction without moving their chairs or desks.

Avoid dead spaces and "racetracks."

EXAMPLES

1. Don't have all the interest areas around the outside of the room, leaving a large dead space in the middle.
2. Avoid placing a few items of furniture right in the middle of this large space, creating a "racetrack" around the furniture.

Provide choices and flexibility.

EXAMPLES

1. Establish private work spaces (e.g., cubicles for individual work); open tables for group work; and cushions on the floor for whole-class meetings.
2. Give students a place to keep their personal belongings. This is especially important if students don't have personal desks.

Try new arrangements, then evaluate and improve.

EXAMPLES

1. Have a "two-week arrangement," then evaluate.
2. Enlist the aid of your students. They have to live in the room too, and designing a classroom can be a very challenging educational experience.

to connect to powerful knowledge bases around the world; to act as tools for writing, drawing, calculating, and designing; to simulate scientific experiments or life in other times and places; to collaborate and communicate with people across the hall or across the ocean; to publish work or make presentations; and to keep track of appointments, assignments, or grades. To get the greatest benefits from computers in your classroom, teachers must have good management systems. Table 11.3 on page 431 summarizes strategies for managing computer labs. The Guidelines on page 432 discuss using computers in regular classrooms.

Getting Started: The First Weeks of Class

Determining a room design, rules, and procedures are first steps toward having a well-managed class, but how do effective teachers gain students' cooperation in

Figure 11.2 An Elementary Classroom Arrangement

This grade 4 teacher had designed a space that allows teacher presentations and demonstrations, small-group work, computer interactions, math manipulatives activities, informal reading, art project, and other activities without requiring constant rearrangement.

Source: From Weinstein, C. S., & Mignano, A. J., Jr. (2003). *Elementary classroom management* (3rd ed.). New York: McGraw-Hill. Copyright © 2003 by The McGraw-Hill Companies. Reproduced with permission of The McGraw-Hill Companies.

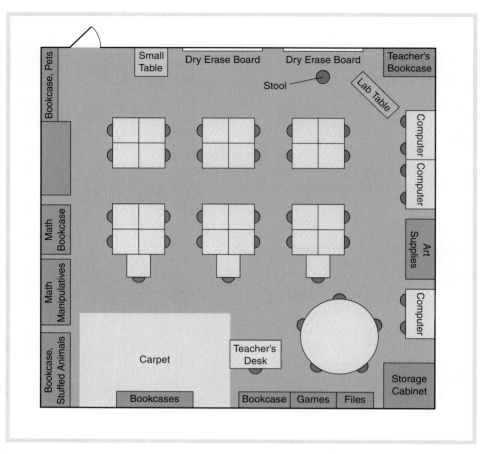

those first critical days and weeks? One study carefully analyzed the first weeks' activities of effective and ineffective elementary teachers and found striking differences (Emmer, Evertson, & Anderson, 1980). By the second or third week of school, students in the ineffective teachers' classrooms were more and more disruptive, less and less on task.

Effective Managers for Elementary Students. In the effective teachers' classrooms, the very first day was well organized. Name tags were ready. There was something interesting for each child to do right away. Materials were set up. The teachers had planned carefully to avoid any last-minute tasks that might take them away from their students. These teachers dealt with the children's pressing concerns first. "Where do I put my things?" "How do I pronounce my teacher's name?" "Can I whisper to my neighbour?" "Where is the washroom?" The effective teachers had a workable, easily understood set of rules and taught the students the most important rules right away. They taught the rules as they would any other subject, with lots of explanation, examples, and practice.

Throughout the first weeks, the effective teachers continued to spend quite a bit of time teaching rules and procedures. Some used guided practice to teach procedures; others used rewards to shape behaviour. Most taught students to respond to a bell or some other signal to gain their attention. These teachers worked with the class as a whole on enjoyable academic activities. They did not rush to get students into small groups or to get them started in readers. This whole-class work gave the teachers a better opportunity to continue monitoring all students' learning of the rules and procedures. Misbehaviour was stopped quickly and firmly, but not harshly.

In the poorly managed classrooms, the first weeks were quite different. Rules were not workable; they were either too vague or very complicated. For example, one teacher made a rule that students should "be in the right place at the right

TABLE 11.3 Tips for Managing a Computer Lab

All these ideas are from Cheryl Bolick and James Cooper (2006).

- Always run through a technology lesson before presenting it to the class—and always have a backup lesson prepared in case the technology fails.

- Type directions for frequently used computer operations—opening programs, inserting clip art, printing documents, and so on—on index cards, laminate them, and connect them with a circle ring. Keep a set next to each computer.

- Have students turn off their monitors when you're giving directions.

- Appoint classroom technology managers. Consider an Attendance Manager, who takes attendance and serves as a substitute teacher helper when necessary; a Materials Manager, who passes out materials and runs errands; a Technical Manager, who helps resolve printer and computer issues; and an End-of-Class Manager, who makes sure work areas are neat—keyboards pushed in, mice straight, and programs closed—before students are dismissed.

- If you have classes filtering in and out of a computer lab each day and have little or no time to set up between classes, arrange for older students to help. Simply end your lesson five minutes early and walk the older students through the process of setting up for the next class.

- When working on lengthy technology projects, print out step-by-step instructions. Include some that say "Save your work; do not go any further until you help your neighbours reach this point." This helps less-proficient students solve problems more quickly, keeps the class at roughly the same point in the project, and fosters collaborative learning.

- Make it a class rule that students can help one another but cannot ever touch another student's computer. That way, you can be sure that learning occurs even when students help one another.

- Keep a red plastic cup at each computer. When students need help, have them place the highly visible cups on top of their monitors.

- Before students leave class, have them turn their mice upside down so that the trackballs are showing. You'll lose fewer trackballs that way.

- Place different coloured sticker dots on the left and the right bottom corners of each monitor. Use these to indicate which side of the screen you are talking about—very helpful when using certain programs, such as the new Kid Pix—and to determine whose turn it is if students share a computer.

- Plug all speakers into a main power bar. Turn the bar off when you're teaching and turn it on when students are working. If the room becomes too noisy, turn off the power bar to get students' attention.

- Use a Video Out card to project a monitor display onto a television screen.

- Type PLEASE WAIT FOR INSTRUCTIONS on 8 by 11 papers, laminate them, and tape one sheet to the top of every monitor. Students flip the signs to the back of the monitor after you've given directions.

- Create a folder in the Start menu and place any programs you use with students in that folder. Students never have to click Programs—everything they use is in one folder.

- When working in a computer lab, assign each student a computer. Students can line up in "computer lab order" in their classrooms. Seating goes very quickly when they get to the lab.

- If you're working on a network, ask your technology coordinator to set up a shared folder for internet resources. Then, when you're planning an internet lesson, simply save a shortcut to the website in that folder. During lab time, students can go to the shared folder, double click the link, and go right to the site without typing the URL. This saves time and stress for both students and teachers.

Source: From Bolick, C. M., & Cooper, J. M. (2006). "Tips for Managing a Computer Lab," Classroom management and technology. In C. Evertson & C. Weinstein (Eds.), *Handbook for classroom management: Research, practice, and contemporary issues*. Reprinted by permission of Lawrence Erlbaum Associates, Inc. and Cheryl Mason Bolick, Ph.D.

time." Students were not told what this meant, so their behaviour could not be guided by the rule. Neither positive nor negative behaviour had clear, consistent consequences. After students broke a rule, ineffective teachers might give a vague criticism, such as "Some of my children are too noisy," or issue a warning, but not follow through with the threatened consequence.

USING COMPUTERS: MANAGEMENT ISSUES

If you have only one computer in your classroom:
Provide convenient access.

EXAMPLES

1. Find a central location if the computer is used to display material for the class.
2. Find a spot on the side of the room that allows seating and view of the screen, but does not crowd or disturb other students if the computer is used as a workstation for individuals or small groups.

Be prepared.

EXAMPLES

1. Check to be sure software needed for a lesson or assignment is installed and working.
2. Make sure instructions for using the software or doing the assignment are in an obvious place and clear.
3. Provide a checklist for completing assignments.

Create "trained experts" to help with computers.

EXAMPLES

1. Train student experts, and rotate experts.
2. Use adult volunteers—parents, grandparents, or older siblings.

Develop systems for using the computer.

EXAMPLES

1. Make up a schedule to ensure that all students have access to the computer and no students monopolize the time.
2. Create standard ways of saving student work.

If you have more than one computer in your classroom:
Plan the arrangement of the computers to fit your instructional goals.

EXAMPLES

1. For cooperative groups, arrange seating so that students can cluster around their group's computer.
2. For different projects at different computer stations, allow for easy rotation from station to station.

Experiment with other models for using computers.

EXAMPLES

1. Navigator Model—four students per computer: One student is the (mouse and keyboard) driver, another is the "navigator." "Back-seat driver 1" manages the group's progress and "back-seat driver 2" serves as the timekeeper. The navigator attends a 10-minute to 20-minute training session in which the facilitator provides an overview of the basics of particular software. Navigators cannot touch the mouse. Driver roles are rotated.
2. Facilitator Model—six students per computer: the facilitator has more experience, expertise, or training—serves as the guide or teacher.
3. Collaborative Group Model—seven students per computer: Each small group is responsible for creating some component of the whole group's final product. For example, one part of the group writes a report, another creates a map, and a third uses the computer to gather and graph census data.

For more ideas, see **www.internet4classrooms. com/one_computer.htm**.

In the poorly managed classes, procedures for accomplishing routine tasks varied from day to day and were never taught or practised. Instead of dealing with these obvious needs, ineffective teachers spent time on procedures that could have waited. For example, one teacher had the class practise for a fire drill the first day, but left unexplained other procedures that would be needed every day. Students wandered aimlessly and had to ask each other what they should be doing. Often, the students talked to one another because they had nothing productive to do. Ineffective teachers frequently left the room. Many became absorbed in paperwork or in helping just one student. They had not made plans for how to deal with late-arriving students or other interruptions. One ineffective teacher tried to teach students to respond to a bell as a signal for attention but later let the students ignore it. All in all, the first weeks in these classrooms were disorganized and filled with surprises for teachers and students alike.

Effective Manager for Secondary Students.   What about getting started in a secondary-school class? It appears that many of the differences between effective and ineffective elementary-school teachers hold at the secondary level as well. Again, effective teachers focus on establishing rules, procedures, and expectations on the first day of class. These standards for academic work and class behaviour are clearly communicated to students and consistently enforced during the first weeks of class. Student behaviour is closely monitored, and infractions of the rules are dealt with quickly. In classes with students of lower ability, work cycles are shorter; students are not required to spend long, unbroken periods on one type of activity. Instead, during each period, they are moved smoothly through several different tasks. In general, effective teachers carefully follow each student's progress so that students cannot avoid work without facing consequences (Emmer & Evertson, 1982).

With all this close monitoring and consistent enforcement of the rules, you may wonder if effective secondary teachers have to be grim and humourless. Not necessarily. The effective teachers in one study also smiled and joked more with their students (Moskowitz & Hayman, 1976). As any experienced teacher can tell you, there is much more to smile about when the class is cooperative.

Check Your Knowledge

- Distinguish between rules and procedures.
- Distinguish between personal territories and interest-area spatial arrangements.
- What management issues do computers raise in the classroom?
- Contrast the first school week of effective and ineffective classroom managers.

Apply to Practice

- What basic rules would you use for your students and how would you teach them?
- How can the physical arrangement of the room promote learning?

CREATING A LEARNING COMMUNITY

Nel Noddings (1992, 1995) has written about the need to create caring educational environments where students take more responsibility for governing their school and classroom. As we saw in Chapter 10 when we discussed the need for relatedness, students are more intrinsically motivated when they feel that their teachers care about them (Grolnick, Ryan, & Deci, 1991). When Blakeburn Elementary School in Port Coquitlam, British Columbia, opened in 2000, one of its school-wide goals was to develop supportive, caring relationships among colleagues, with parents, and among students (Laidlaw, 2001). The school focused on helping students become socially responsible. This required consistency and modelling at all levels, and the students learned the language of solving problems, respecting diversity, and contributing to the classroom and the school. In interviews, students talked about feeling safe, included, and happy to be at school. Parents said, "There is a different atmosphere at this school.... There is a sense of mutual trust. The expectation is that the kids will manage and get along, and they do" (Laidlaw, 2001, p. 1). Historically, however, North American schools have emphasized regulating students' behaviour through rules, not through relationships.

Classroom Community

David and Roger Johnson (1999b) describe three C's for developing the kind of caring and mutually trusting community that exists at Blakeburn Elementary: cooperative community, constructive conflict resolution, and civic values. At the heart of the community is the idea of positive interdependence—individuals working together to achieve mutual goals. Constructive conflict resolution is essential in the community because conflicts are inevitable and even necessary for learning. Piaget's theory of development and the research on conceptual change teaching tell us that true learning requires cognitive conflict. And individuals trying to exist in groups will have interpersonal conflicts; these can lead to learning too. Table 11.4 shows how academic and interpersonal conflicts can be positive forces in a learning community.

The last C stands for civic values—the understandings and beliefs that hold the community together. Values are learned through direct teaching, modelling, literature, group discussions, and the sharing of concerns. Some teachers have a "Concerns Box," where students can put written concerns and comments. The box is opened once a week at a class meeting, and the concerns are discussed. Johnson and Johnson (1999) give the example of a class meeting about respect. One student told her classmates that she felt hurt during recess the day before because no one listened when she was trying to teach them the rules to a new game. The students discussed what it means to be respectful and why respect is important. Then the students shared personal experiences of times when they felt respected versus not respected.

Getting Started on Community

Whether you are working as an individual or as part of a school-wide team, creating the kind of community that is now visible in the day-to-day routines at Blakeburn Elementary School does not happen automatically (Laidlaw, 2001, p. 4). It involves input from many different levels to develop a philosophy and participation structures that will foster self-control and social responsibility on the part of students. At Blakeburn, the "leadership team" met first and talked about how to create a caring and socially responsible learning community. Team members used the provincial ministry's Performance Standards for Social Responsibility as a framework for developing a common language and set of expectations. Then they involved the children and their families. The first week of school was devoted to the articulation of what it means (for all members) to be part of a

TABLE 11.4 Academic and Interpersonal Conflict and Learning

Conflict, if handled well, can support learning. Academic conflicts can lead to critical thinking and conceptual change. Conflicts of interest are unavoidable, but they can be handled so that no one is the loser.

Academic Controversy	Conflicts of Interest
One person's ideas, information, theories, conclusions, and opinions are incompatible with those of another, and the two seek to reach an agreement.	The actions of one person attempting to maximize benefits prevent, block, or interfere with those of another person maximizing her or his benefits.
Controversy Procedure	*Integrative (Problem-Solving) Negotiations*
Research and prepare positions	Describe wants
Present and advocate positions	Describe feelings
Refute opposing position and refute attacks on own position	Describe reasons for wants and feelings
Reverse perspectives	Take other's perspective
Synthesize and integrate best evidence and reasoning from all sides	Invent three optional agreements that maximize joint outcomes
	Choose one and formalize agreement

Source: From Johnson, D., & Johnson, R. (1999). The three C's of school and classroom management. In H. J. Freiberg (Ed.), *Beyond behaviorism: Changing the classroom management paradigm* (p. 133). Boston: Allyn & Bacon. Copyright © 1999 by Pearson Education. Reprinted by permission of the publisher.

socially responsible community. Students participated in multi-aged "family" groups on relevant activities. Throughout this process, the staff recognized that this work must be multifaceted and integrated in all the curricula and interactions in their classrooms and at the school. They realized that creating positive classroom and school climates requires more than the implementation of prepackaged programs at a scheduled time in the day. It involves "living the principles of inclusion and responsibility ... all day, every day" (Laidlaw, 2001, p. 4).

Check Your Knowledge

- What are Johnson and Johnson's three C's of establishing a classroom community?

Apply to Practice

- How would you introduce the idea of community to the students you will teach?

MAINTAINING A GOOD ENVIRONMENT FOR LEARNING

A good start is just that—a beginning. Effective teachers build on this beginning. They maintain their management system by preventing problems and keeping students motivated and engaged in productive learning activities. We have discussed several ways to keep students motivated and engaged. In Chapter 10, for example, we considered stimulating curiosity, relating lessons to student interests, encouraging cooperative learning, establishing learning goals instead of performance goals, and having positive expectations. What else can teachers do?

Encouraging Engagement

The format of a lesson affects student involvement. In general, as teacher supervision increases, students' engaged time also increases (Emmer & Evertson, 1981). For example, one study found that elementary students working directly with a teacher were on task 97 percent of the time, while students working on their own were on task only 57 percent of the time (Frick, 1990). This does not mean that teachers should eliminate independent work for students. It simply means that this type of activity usually requires careful monitoring.

When the task provides continuous cues for the student about what to do next, involvement will be greater. Activities with clear steps are likely to be more absorbing, because one step leads naturally to the next. When students have all the materials they need to complete a task, they tend to stay involved. If their curiosity is piqued, students will be motivated to continue seeking an answer. And, as you now know, students will be more engaged if they are involved in authentic tasks—activities that have connections to real life. Also, activities are more engaging when the level of challenge is higher and when students' interests are incorporated into the tasks (Emmer & Gerwels, 2006).

Of course, teachers can't supervise every student all the time, or rely on curiosity. Something else must keep students working on their own. In their study of elementary and secondary teachers, Evertson, Emmer, and their colleagues found that effective class managers at both levels had well-planned systems for encouraging students to manage their own work (Emmer, Evertson, & Worsham, 2006; Evertson, Emmer, & Worsham, 2006). The Guidelines on page 436 are based on their findings.

Prevention Is the Best Medicine

Martin and Sugarman (1993) note that "many difficulties in classroom management can be prevented by effective teaching" (p. 51) that interests students, avoids

KEEPING STUDENTS ENGAGED

Make basic work requirements clear.

EXAMPLES

1. Specify and post the routine work requirements for headings, paper size, pen or pencil use, and neatness.

2. Establish and explain rules about late or incomplete work and absences. If a pattern of incomplete work begins to develop, deal with it early; speak with parents if necessary.

3. Make due dates reasonable and stick to them unless the student has a very good excuse for lateness.

Communicate the specifics of assignments.

EXAMPLES

1. With younger students, have a routine procedure for giving assignments, such as writing them on the board in the same place each day. With older students, assignments may be dictated, posted, or given in a syllabus.

2. Remind students of coming assignments.

3. With complicated assignments, give students a sheet describing what to do, what resources are available, due dates, and so on. Explain your grading criteria to older students.

4. Demonstrate how to do the assignment, do the first few questions together, or provide a sample worksheet.

Monitor work in progress.

EXAMPLES

1. When you set an in-class assignment, make sure that each student gets started correctly. If you check only students who raise their hands for help, you will miss those who think they know what to do but don't really understand, those who are too shy to ask for help, and those who don't plan to do the work at all.

2. Check progress periodically. In discussions, make sure that everyone has a chance to respond.

Give frequent academic feedback.

EXAMPLES

1. Elementary students should get papers back the day after they are handed in.

2. Good work can be displayed in class and graded papers sent home to parents each week.

3. Students of all ages can keep records of grades, projects completed, and extra credits earned.

4. For older students, break up long-term assignments into several phases, giving feedback at each point.

confusion, and keeps activities moving. In a classic study, Jacob Kounin (1970) examined classroom management by comparing effective teachers, whose classes were relatively free of problems, with ineffective teachers, whose classes were continually plagued by chaos and disruption. Observing both groups in action, Kounin found that the teachers were not very different in the way they handled discipline once problems arose. The difference was that the successful teachers were much better at preventing problems. Kounin concluded that effective classroom teachers were especially skilled in four areas: "*withitness*," *overlapping activities*, *group focusing*, and *movement management* (Doyle, 1977). More recent research confirms the importance of these factors (Emmer & Stough, 2001; Evertson, 1988).

withitness According to Jacob Kounin, awareness of everything happening in a classroom.

Withitness. Withitness means communicating to students that you are aware of everything that is happening in the classroom, that you aren't missing anything. "With-it" teachers seem to have eyes in the backs of their heads. They avoid becoming absorbed or interacting with only a few students, since such behaviour encourages the rest of the class to wander. They are always scanning the room, making eye contact with individual students, so that the students know they are being monitored (Brooks, 1985; Charles, 2002a).

These teachers prevent minor disruptions from becoming major. They also know who instigated the problem, and they make sure that the right people are dealt with. In other words, they do not make what Kounin called timing errors (waiting too long before intervening) or target errors (blaming the wrong student and letting the real perpetrators escape responsibility for their behaviour).

If two problems occur at the same time, effective teachers deal with the more serious one first. For example, a teacher who tells two students to stop whispering but ignores even a brief shoving match at the pencil sharpener communicates to students a lack of awareness. Students begin to believe that they can get away with almost anything if they are clever (Charles, 2002b).

Overlapping and Group Focus. **Overlapping** means keeping track of and supervising several activities at the same time. For example, a teacher may have to check the work of an individual and at the same time keep a small group working by saying, "Right, go on," and stop an incident in another group with a quick "look" or reminder (Burden, 1995; Charles, 2002b).

Maintaining a **group focus** means keeping as many students as possible involved in appropriate class activities and avoiding narrowing in on just one or two students. All students should have something to do during a lesson. For example, the teacher might ask everyone to write the answer to a question, then call on individuals to respond while the other students compare their answers. Choral responses might be required while the teacher moves around the room to make sure everyone is participating (Charles, 2002b). For example, during a grammar lesson the teacher might say, "Everyone who thinks the answer is *have run*, hold up the red side of your card. If you think the answer is *has run*, hold up the green side" (Hunter, 1982). This is one way teachers can ensure that all students are involved and that everyone understands the material.

Movement Management. Movement management means keeping lessons and the group moving at an appropriate (and flexible) pace, with smooth transitions and variety. The effective teacher avoids abrupt transitions, such as announcing a new activity before gaining the students' attention or starting a new activity in the middle of something else. In these situations, one-third of the class will be doing the new activity, many will be working on the old lesson, several will be asking other students what to do, some will be taking the opportunity to have a little fun, and most will be confused. Another transition problem Kounin noted is the *slow-down*, or taking too much time to start a new activity. Sometimes teachers give too many directions. Problems also arise when teachers have students work one at a time while the rest of the class waits and watches.

Caring Relationships: Connections with School. When students and teachers have positive, trusting relationships, many management problems never develop. Students respect teachers who maintain their authority without being rigid, harsh,

overlapping Supervising several activities at once.

group focus The ability to keep as many students as possible involved in activities.

movement management Keeping lessons and the group moving at an appropriate (and flexible) pace, with smooth transitions and variety.

While this teacher is talking to a group of students, does she know what else is happening in the class? Can she "overlap" activities and still be "with it"?

or unfair and who use creative instructional practices to "make learning fun." Students also value teachers who show academic and personal caring by acting like real people (not just as teachers), sharing responsibility, minimizing the use of external controls, including everyone, searching for students' strengths, communicating effectively, and showing an interest in their students' lives and pursuits (Elias & Schwab, 2006; Woolfolk Hoy & Weinstein, 2006). All efforts at building positive relationships and classroom community are steps toward preventing management problems. Students who feel connected with school are happier, more self-disciplined, and less likely to engage in dangerous behaviours such as substance abuse, violence, and early sexual activity (Freiberg, 2006; McNeely, Nonnemaker, & Blum, 2002).

Student Social Skills as Prevention.　But what about the students? What can they do? When students lack social and emotional skills such as being able to share materials, read the intentions of others, or handle frustration, classroom management problems often follow. So all efforts to teach social and emotional self-regulation are steps for preventing management problems. Over the short term, educators can teach and model these skills, then give students feedback and practise using them in a variety of settings. Over the long term, teachers can help to change attitudes that value aggression over cooperation and compromise (Elias & Schwab, 2006). Chapter 3 gave ideas for teaching social and emotional skills and competencies.

Dealing with Discipline Problems

What Would You Say?

You are being interviewed for a job in a high school that has been in the news lately in relation to its policy of zero tolerance for violence. The principal asks, "So what do you think about zero tolerance?" What is your position?

In 2005, *Phi Delta Kappan* published the 37th annual Gallup Poll of the public's attitude toward public schools. From 1969 until 1999, "lack of discipline" was named as the number one problem facing the schools almost every year (Rose & Gallup, 1999). Beginning in 2000, lack of financial support took over the number one place, but lack of discipline remained a close second or third every year. Clearly, the public sees discipline as an important challenge for teachers.

Being an effective manager does not mean publicly correcting every minor infraction of the rules. This kind of public attention may actually reinforce the misbehaviour, as we saw in Chapter 6. Teachers who frequently correct students do not necessarily have the best behaved classes (Irving & Martin, 1982). The key is being aware of what is happening and knowing what is important so that you can prevent problems.

Most students comply quickly when the teacher gives a desist order (a "stop doing that") or redirects behaviour. But some students are the targets of more than their share of desists. One study found that these disruptive students seldom complied with the first teacher request to stop. Often, the disruptive students responded negatively, leading to an average of four to five cycles of teacher desists and student responses before the student complied (Nelson & Roberts, 2000). Emmer and colleagues (2006) and Levin and Nolan (2000) suggest seven simple ways to stop misbehaviour quickly, moving from least to most intrusive:

- *Make eye contact* with, or move closer to, the offender. Other non-verbal signals, such as pointing to the work students are supposed to be doing, might be helpful. Make sure the student actually stops the inappropriate behaviour and gets back to work. If you do not, students will learn to ignore your signals.

- *Try verbal hints* such as "name-dropping" (simply insert the student's name into the lecture), asking the student a question, or making a humorous (not sarcastic) comment such as, "I must be hallucinating. I swear I heard someone shout out an answer, but that can't be because I haven't called on anyone yet!"
- Ask students *if they are aware* of the negative effects of their actions or send an "I message," described later in the chapter.
- If they are not performing a class procedure correctly, *remind the students* of the procedure and have them follow it correctly. You may need to quietly collect a toy, comb, magazine, or note that is competing with the learning activities, while privately informing the students that their possessions will be returned after class.
- In a calm, unhostile way, *ask the student to state the correct rule or procedure* and then to follow it. Glasser (1969) proposes three questions: "What are you doing? Is it against the rules? What should you be doing?"
- Tell the student in a clear, assertive, and unhostile way to *stop the misbehaviour*. (Later in the chapter we will discuss assertive messages to students in more detail.) If students "talk back," simply repeat your statement.
- *Offer a choice.* For example, when a student continued to call out answers no matter what the teacher tried, the teacher said, "John, you have a choice. Stop calling out answers immediately and begin raising your hand to answer or move your seat to the back of the room and you and I will have a private discussion later. You decide" (Levin & Nolan, 2000, p. 177).

Many teachers prefer the use of logical consequences, described earlier, as opposed to penalties. For example, if one student has harmed another, you can require the offending student to make an "Apology of Action," which includes a verbal apology plus somehow repairing the damage done. This helps offenders develop empathy and social perspective-taking as they think about what would be an appropriate "repair" (Elias & Schwab, 2006).

If you must impose penalties, the Guidelines on page 440, taken from Weinstein (2003) and Weinstein and Mignano (2003), give ideas about how to do it. The examples are taken from the actual words of the expert teachers described in their book.

There is a caution about penalties. Never use lower achievement status (moving to a lower reading group, giving a lower grade, giving excess homework) as a punishment for breaking class rules. These actions should be done only if the benefit of the action outweighs the possible risk of harm. As Carolyn Orange (2000) notes, "Effective, caring teachers would not use low achievement status, grades, or the like as a means of discipline. This strategy is unfair and ineffective. It only serves to alienate the student" (p. 76).

Special Problems with Secondary Students

Many secondary students never complete their work. Besides encouraging student responsibility, what else can teachers do to deal with this frustrating problem? Because students at this age have many assignments and teachers have many students, both teachers and students may lose track of what has and has not been completed. It often helps to teach students how to use a daily planner. In addition, the teacher must keep accurate records. The most important thing is to enforce the established consequences for incomplete work. Do not pass a student because you know that he or she is "bright enough" to pass. Make it clear to these students that the choice is theirs: they can do the work and pass, or they can refuse to do the work and face the consequences.

There is also the problem of students who continually break the same rules— always forgetting materials, for example, or getting into fights. What should you do? Seat these students away from others who might be influenced by them. Try

IMPOSING PENALTIES

Delay the discussion of the situation until you and the students involved are calmer and more objective.

EXAMPLES

1. Say calmly to a student, "Sit there and think about what happened. I'll talk to you in a few minutes," or "I don't like what I just saw. Talk to me during your free period today."

2. Say, "I'm really angry about what just happened. Everybody take out journals; we are going to write about this." After a few minutes of writing, the class can discuss the incident.

Impose consequences privately.

EXAMPLES

1. Make arrangements with students privately. Stand firm in enforcing arrangements.

2. Resist the temptation to "remind" students in public that they are not keeping their side of the bargain.

3. Move close to a student who must be disciplined and speak so that only the student can hear.

After imposing a consequence, re-establish a positive relationship with the student immediately.

EXAMPLES

1. Send the student on an errand or ask him or her for help.

2. Compliment the student's work or give a real or symbolic "pat on the back" when the student's behaviour warrants. Look hard for such an opportunity.

Set up a graded list of penalties that will fit many occasions.

EXAMPLE

1. For not turning in homework: (1) receive reminder; (2) receive warning; (3) hand homework in before close of school day; (4) stay after school to finish work; (5) participate in a teacher–student–parent conference to develop an action plan.

Connect & Extend

TO YOUR TEACHING
What is a teacher's responsibility if he or she finds out that a pupil is involved in illegal acts such as selling drugs or stealing?

to catch them before they break the rules, but if rules are broken, be consistent in applying established consequences. Do not accept promises to do better next time (Levin & Nolan, 2000). Teach the students how to monitor their own behaviour; some of the self-management techniques described in Chapter 6 should be helpful. Finally, remain friendly with the students. Try to catch them in a good moment so that you can talk to them about something other than their rule breaking.

A defiant, hostile student can pose serious problems. If there is an outbreak, try to get out of the situation as soon as possible; everyone loses in a public power struggle. One possibility is to give the student a chance to save face and cool down by saying, "It's your choice to cooperate or not. You can take a minute to think about it." If the student complies, the two of you can talk later about controlling the outbursts. If the student refuses to cooperate, you can tell him or her to wait in the hall until you get the class started on work, then step outside for a private talk. If the student refuses to leave, send another class member for the assistant principal. Again, follow through. If the student complies before help arrives, do not let him or her off the hook. If outbursts occur frequently, you might have a conference with the counsellor, parents, or other teachers. If the problem is an irreconcilable clash of personalities, the student should be transferred to another teacher. There is quite a bit of discussion today about zero tolerance for rule breaking in the schools. Is this a good idea? The accompanying Point/Counterpoint feature looks at both sides.

It is sometimes useful to keep records of the incidents by logging the student's name, words and actions, date, time, place, and teacher's response. These records may help identify patterns and can prove useful in meetings with administrators,

IS ZERO TOLERANCE A GOOD IDEA?

With the very visible violence in schools today, some districts have instituted "zero-tolerance" policies for rule breaking.

One result? A five-year-old student in Toronto was threatened with suspension because he allegedly violated the school's sexual harassment policy. His offence was showing affection toward his classmates (*National Post*, September 13, 2004).

Do zero-tolerance policies make sense?

> Point *Zero tolerance is necessary for now.*

The arguments for zero tolerance focus on school safety and the responsibilities of schools and teachers to protect the students and themselves, especially since the much-publicized school shootings in Littleton, Colorado, and even Taber, Alberta (April 29, 1999). Of course, many of the incidents reported in the news seem to be overreactions to childhood pranks, or worse, overzealous applications of zero tolerance to innocent mistakes or lapses of memory. But how do school officials separate the innocent from the dangerous? For example, it has been widely reported that Andy Williams (the boy who killed two classmates in Santee, California) assured his friends before the shootings that he was only joking about "pulling a Columbine."

On January 13, 2003, Gregg Toppo wrote an article for *USA Today* in which he described how a grade 2 student used his shoe to attack his teacher; a kindergartner hit a pregnant teacher in the stomach; and an eight-year-old threatened to use gasoline to burn down his suburban elementary school. Toppo noted, "Elementary school principals and safety experts say they're seeing more violence and aggression than ever among their youngest students, pointing to what they see as an alarming rise in assaults and threats to classmates and teachers" (p. A2).

Incidents such as these have pressed schools to take a hard line on aggressive behaviour, and their response has often been to adopt the so-called zero-tolerance policy.

< Counterpoint *Zero tolerance means zero common sense.*

An internet search using the keywords *zero tolerance* and *schools* will locate a wealth of information about the policy—much of it against. For example, in the August 29, 2001, issue of *Salon* magazine, Johanna Wald wrote an article entitled "The Failure of Zero Tolerance." Here is one of the examples she cites:

> A 17-year-old honors student in Arkansas begins his senior year with an even more ominous cloud over his head. His college scholarship is in danger because of a 45-day sentence to an alternative school. His offense? An arbitrary search of his car by school officials in the spring revealed no drugs, but a scraper and pocketknife that his father had inadvertently left there the night before when he was fixing the rearview mirror. Despite anguished pleas of extenuating circumstances by the

desperate father, the school system has so far adamantly insisted that automatic punishments for weapon possession in school are inviolate.

Mary Hall, director of Safe Schools Manitoba and adjunct professor at the University of Manitoba, argues that despite their extensive use, zero-tolerance policies are drawing considerable criticism for a number of reasons (2005, April 26, personal communication). According to Hall, whose dissertation research was on the topic of violence in schools,

> These policies treat minor and major incidents of violence with equal severity regardless of extenuating circumstances. [Also], they are deemed to be too prescriptive. Most cases of student violence are too complex to be reduced to a programmed response. [Moreover], the policies are highly punitive. Rigid, punitive responses by schools can destroy educator–student relationships—a key element of resiliency. Such responses can fuel frustration and anger of troubled students, contributing to their disfranchisement from school. Since the introduction of zero-tolerance policies into Canadian school systems, there has been a rapid and alarming increase in student suspensions. In numerous cases, adherence to zero-tolerance policies has led to negative and often ludicrous consequences [as we saw in the previous examples]. Finally, the root causes of the problems are not addressed by zero-tolerance policies and they do not allow for the professional judgment of educators who understand the various factors that contribute to problematic behaviour.

parents, or special services personnel (Burden, 1995). Some teachers have students sign each entry to verify the incidents.

Violence or destruction of property is a difficult and potentially dangerous problem. The first step is to send for help and get the names of participants and witnesses. Then get rid of any crowd that may have gathered; an audience will only make things worse. Make sure that the school office is aware of the incident and follow the school policy in dealing with the situation.

- How can teachers encourage engagement?
- Explain the factors identified by Kounin that prevent management problems in the classroom.
- Describe seven levels of intervention in misbehaviour.

Apply to Practice

- Will you use consequences in your class when students violate rules? What kinds?
- Give an example of a strategy to
  1. build student confidence;
  2. show the value of learning;
  3. help students stay focused on the task.

THE NEED FOR COMMUNICATION

Communication between teacher and students is essential when problems arise. Communication is more than "teacher talks—student listens." It is more than the words exchanged between individuals. We communicate in many ways. Our actions, movements, voice tone, facial expressions, and other non-verbal behaviour send messages to our students. Many times, the messages we intend to send are not the messages our students receive.

Message Sent—Message Received

Teacher: Carl, where is your homework?

Carl: I left it in my dad's car this morning.

Teacher: Again? You'll have to bring me a note tomorrow from your father saying that you actually did the homework. No grade without the note.

Message Carl receives: I can't trust you. I need proof that you did the work.

Teacher: Sit at every other desk. Put all your things under your desk. Jane and Laurel, you're sitting too close together. One of you move!

Message Jane and Laurel receive: I expect you two to cheat on this test.

A new student comes to Ms. Tung's kindergarten. The child is messy and unwashed. Ms. Tung puts her hand lightly on the girl's shoulder and says, "I'm glad you're here." Her muscles tense, and she leans away from the child.

Message student receives: I don't like you. I think you are bad.

In all interactions, a message is sent and a message is received. Sometimes teachers believe that they are sending one message, but their voices, body positions, choices of words, and gestures may communicate a different message.

Students may hear the hidden message and respond to it. For example, a student may respond with hostility if she or he feels insulted by the teacher (or by another student), but may not be able to say exactly where the feeling of being insulted came from. Perhaps it was in the teacher's tone of voice, not the words actually spoken. In such cases, the teacher may feel attacked for no reason. "What did I say? All I said was ..." The first principle of communication is that people respond to what they think was said or meant, not necessarily to the speaker's intended message or actual words.

There are many exercises for practising sending and receiving messages accurately. Students in Anita's classes have told her about one instructor who encourages accurate communication by using the **paraphrase rule**. Before any participant, including the teacher, is allowed to respond to any other participant in a class discussion, he or she must summarize what the previous speaker said. If the summary

paraphrase rule Policy whereby listeners must accurately summarize what a speaker has said before being allowed to respond.

is wrong, indicating that the speaker was misunderstood, the speaker must explain again. The respondent then tries again to paraphrase. The process continues until the speaker agrees that the listener has heard the intended message.

Paraphrasing is more than a classroom exercise. It can be the first step in communicating with students. Before teachers can deal appropriately with any student problem, they must know what the real problem is. A student who says, "This book is really dumb! Why did we have to read it?" may really be saying, "The book was too difficult for me. I couldn't read it, and I feel dumb."

Diagnosis: Whose Problem Is It?

As a teacher, you may find some student behaviour unacceptable, unpleasant, or troubling. It is often difficult to stand back from these problems, take an objective look, and decide on an appropriate response. According to Thomas Gordon (1981), the key to good teacher–student relationships is determining why you are troubled by a particular behaviour and whose problem it is. The teacher must begin by asking who "owns" the problem. The answer to this question is critical. If it is really the student's problem, the teacher must become a counsellor and supporter, helping the student find his or her own solution. But if the teacher "owns" the problem, it is the teacher's responsibility to find a solution through problem solving with the student.

One of the challenges of managing elementary-school children is to deal effectively with disruptive behaviour and achieve a positive outcome. In some cases, it might be appropriate to involve a student's family.

Diagnosing who owns the problem is not always straightforward. Let's look at three troubling situations to get some practice in this skill:

1. A student writes obscene words and draws sexually explicit illustrations in a school encyclopedia.
2. A student tells you that his parents had a bad fight and he hates his father.
3. A student quietly reads a newspaper in the back of the room.

Why is this behaviour troubling? If you cannot accept the student's behaviour because it has a serious effect on you as a teacher—if you are blocked from reaching your goals by the student's action—then you own the problem. It is your responsibility to confront the student and seek a solution. A teacher-owned problem appears to be present in the first situation described above—the young pornographer—because teaching materials are damaged.

If you feel annoyed by the behaviour because it is getting in the student's own way or because you are embarrassed for the child, but the behaviour does not directly interfere with your teaching, it is probably the student's problem. The test question is: Does this student's action tangibly affect you or prevent you from fulfilling your role as a teacher? The student who hates his father would not prevent you from teaching, even though you might wish the student felt differently. The problem is really the student's, and he must find his own solution.

Situation 3 is more difficult to diagnose. There have been lengthy debates about whose problem it is when a student reads a newspaper in class. One argument is that the teacher is not interfered with in any way, so it is the student's problem. Another argument is that teachers might find reading the paper distracting during a lecture, so it is their problem, and they must find a solution. In a grey area such as this, the answer probably depends on how the teacher actually experiences the student's behaviour. After deciding who owns the problem, it is time to act.

Counselling: The Student's Problem

Let's pick up the situation in which the student found the reading assignment "dumb." How might a teacher handle this positively?

> *Student:* This book is really dumb! Why did we have to read it?
>
> *Teacher:* You're pretty upset. This seemed like a worthless assignment to

you. [Teacher paraphrases the student's statement, trying to hear the emotions as well as the words.]

Student: Yeah! Well, I guess it was worthless. I mean, I don't know if it was. I couldn't exactly read it.

Teacher: It was just too hard to read, and that bothers you.

Student: Sure, I felt really dumb. I know I can write a good report, but not with a book this tough.

Teacher: I think I can give you some hints that will make the book easier to understand. Can you see me after school today?

Student: Okay.

empathetic listening Hearing the intent and emotions behind what another says and reflecting them back by paraphrasing.

Here the teacher used **empathetic listening** to allow the student to find a solution. (As you can see, this approach relies heavily on paraphrasing.) By trying to hear the student and by avoiding the tendency to jump in too quickly with advice, solutions, criticisms, reprimands, or interrogations, the teacher keeps the communication lines open. Here are a few *unhelpful* responses the teacher might have made:

- I chose the book because it is the best example of this author's style in our library. You will need to have read it before your IB English class next year. (The teacher justifies the choice; this prevents the student from admitting that this "important" assignment is too difficult.)
- Did you really read it? I bet you didn't do the work, and now you want out of the assignment. (The teacher accuses; the student hears, "The teacher doesn't trust me!" and must defend herself or himself or accept the teacher's view.)
- Your job is to read the book, not ask me why. I know what's best. (The teacher pulls rank, and the student hears, "You can't possibly decide what is good for you!" The student can rebel or passively accept the teacher's judgment.)

Empathetic, active listening can be a helpful response when students bring problems to you. You must reflect back to the student what you hear him or her saying. This reflection is more than a parroting of the student's words; it should capture the emotions, intent, and meaning behind them. Sokolove, Garrett, Sadker, and Sadker (1986, p. 241) have summarized the components of active listening: (1) blocking out external stimuli; (2) attending carefully to both the verbal and non-verbal messages; (3) differentiating between the intellectual and the emotional content of the message; and (4) making inferences regarding the speaker's feelings.

When students realize that they really have been heard and not evaluated negatively for what they have said or felt, they feel freer to trust the teacher and to talk more openly. Sometimes the true problem surfaces later in the conversation.

Confrontation and Assertive Discipline

Now let's assume that a student is doing something that actively interferes with teaching. The teacher decides that the student must stop. The problem is the teacher's. Confrontation, not counselling, is required.

"I" message Clear, non-accusatory statement of how something is affecting you.

"I" Messages.   Gordon (1981) recommends sending an **"I" message** in order to intervene and change a student's behaviour. Basically, this means telling a student in a straightforward, assertive, and non-judgmental way what she or he is doing, how it affects you as a teacher, and how you feel about it. The student is then free to change voluntarily, and often does so. Here are two "I" messages:

- If you leave your book bags in the aisles, I might trip and hurt myself.
- When you all call out, I can't concentrate on each answer, and I'm frustrated.

assertive discipline Clear, firm, unhostile response style.

Assertive Discipline.   Lee and Marlene Canter (1992; Canter, 1996) suggest other approaches for dealing with a teacher-owned problem. They call their method **assertive discipline.** Teachers are assertive when they make their expectations clear and follow through with established consequences. Students then have a straightforward choice: they can follow the rules or accept the consequences. Many teachers are ineffective with students because they are either wishy-washy and passive or hostile and aggressive (Charles, 2002a).

Instead of telling the student directly what to do, teachers with a *passive response style* tell, or often ask, the student to try or to think about the appropriate action. Such a teacher may comment on the problem behaviour without actually telling the child what to do differently: "Why are you doing that? Don't you know the rules?" or "Sam, are you disturbing the class?" Or teachers may clearly state what should happen, but never follow through with the established consequences, giving the students "one more chance" every time. Finally, teachers may ignore behaviour that should receive a response or may wait too long before responding.

A *hostile response style* involves different mistakes. Teachers may make "you" statements that condemn the student without stating clearly what the student should be doing: "You should be ashamed of the way you're behaving!" or "You never listen!" or "You're acting like a baby!" Teachers may also threaten students angrily but follow through too seldom, perhaps because the threats are too vague—"You'll be very sorry you did that when I get through with you!"—or too severe. For example, a teacher tells a student in a physical education class that he will have to "sit on the bench for *three weeks*." A few days later the team is short one member and the teacher allows the student to play, never returning him to the bench to complete the three-week sentence. Often, a teacher who has been passive becomes hostile and explodes when students persist in misbehaving.

In contrast to both the passive and hostile styles, an *assertive response* communicates to the students that you care too much about them and the process of learning to allow inappropriate behaviour to persist. Assertive teachers clearly state what they expect. To be most effective, the teachers often look into a student's eyes when speaking and address the student by name. Assertive teachers' voices are calm, firm, and confident. They are not sidetracked by accusations such as "You just don't understand!" or "You don't like me!" Assertive teachers do not get into a debate about the fairness of the rules. They expect changes, not promises or apologies.

Not all educators believe that assertive discipline is useful. Earlier critics questioned the penalty-focused approach and emphasized that assertive discipline undermined student self-management (Render, Padilla, & Krank, 1989). John Covaleskie (1992) observed, "What helps children become moral is not knowledge of the rules, or even obedience to the rules, but discussions about the reasons for acting in certain ways" (p. 56). These critics have had an impact. More recent versions of assertive discipline focus on teaching students "in an atmosphere of respect, trust, and support, how to behave responsibly" (Charles, 2002a, p. 47).

Confrontations and Negotiations. If "I" messages or assertive responses fail and a student persists in misbehaving, teacher and student are in a conflict. Several pitfalls now loom. The two individuals become less able to perceive each other's behaviour accurately. Research has shown that the angrier you get with another person, the more you see the other as the villain and yourself as an innocent victim. Because you feel that the other person is in the wrong, and he or she feels just as strongly that the conflict is all your fault, very little mutual trust is possible. A cooperative solution to the problem is almost impossible. In fact, by the time the discussion has gone on a few minutes, the original problem is lost in a sea of charges, countercharges, and self-defence (Baron & Byrne, 2003).

There are three methods of resolving a conflict between teacher and student. One is for the teacher to impose a solution. This may be necessary during an emergency, as when a defiant student refuses to go to the hall to discuss a public outbreak, but it is not a good solution for most conflicts. The second method is for the teacher to give in to the student's demands. You might be convinced by a particularly compelling student argument, but again, this method should be used

Connect & Extend

TO PROFESSIONAL DEBATES
Read Canter, L. (1989). Assertive discipline—More than names on the board and marbles in a jar. *Phi Delta Kappan, 71*(1), 41–56. Evaluate Canter's claims for his "assertive discipline" approach. What are the similarities between the criticism of behavioural approaches to learning and the criticisms of assertive discipline? A special feature on discipline can be found in the 1989 issue of *Educational Leadership, 46*(6), 72–83. This feature presents a debate between supporters and critics of assertive discipline.

Connect & Extend

TO THE RESEARCH
Carter, S. P., & Stewin, L. L. (1999). School violence in the Canadian context: An overview and model for intervention. *International Journal for the Advancement of Counselling, 21,* 267–277.

Abstract
School violence and the incidence of violent crimes among Canadian youth are seen to be increasing. While more research is being conducted in the area of school violence, little has previously been done to examine psychopathology as a possible factor influencing violent student behaviour. A recent study conducted by S. P. Carter using the Behavior Assessment System for Children and a structured interview showed a high incidence of psychopathology among violent junior high male students. A comprehensive model for intervention is described in which several factors are presented.

Handling conflict can be difficult for young people. Studies have shown that many conflicts among middle and high school students are resolved in destructive ways or never at all.

sparingly. It is generally a bad idea to be talked out of a position, unless the position was wrong in the first place. Problems arise when either the teacher or the student gives in completely.

Gordon (1981) recommends a third approach, which he calls the "no-lose method." Here the needs of both the teacher and the students are taken into account in the solution. No one person is expected to give in completely; all participants retain respect for themselves and each other. The no-lose method is a six-step, problem-solving strategy:

1. *Define the problem.* What exactly is the behaviour involved? What does each person want? (Use active listening to help students pinpoint the real problem.)

2. *Generate many possible solutions.* Brainstorm, but remember to not allow any evaluations of ideas yet.

3. *Evaluate each solution.* Any participant may veto any idea. If no solutions are found to be acceptable, brainstorm again.

4. *Make a decision.* Choose one solution through consensus, not voting. In the end, everyone must be satisfied with the solution.

5. *Determine how to implement the solution.* What will be needed? Who will be responsible for each task? What is the timetable?

6. *Evaluate the success of the solution.* After trying the solution for a while, ask, "Are we satisfied with our decision? How well is it working? Should we make some changes?"

Many of the conflicts in classrooms are between students and can involve violence. It is important to be prepared should this occur.

Violence in the Schools

Violence in Canadian schools is a serious and growing concern among students, parents, and teachers. In the year of the Canadian Research Institute for Law and the Family's school violence survey, Sillars (1995, p. 37) reported that nearly one-third of junior and senior high school students in Calgary carried a weapon to school. Four-fifths claimed that they had been struck, threatened, or had something stolen at school, and more than half admitted to committing seriously delinquent acts. This problem has many causes; it is a challenge for every element of society. What can the schools do? Teachers and students need to know the warning signs of potential dangers. Table 11.5 describes two kinds of signs: immediate warning and potential problems. Table 11.6 offers some ideas for handling a potentially explosive situation should one arise.

Prevention. The best answer to school violence is prevention. As a teacher, you may have little to say about violence on television or in video games, but you have much to say about the way students treat each other and the sense of community created in your classes. You can teach acceptance and compassion and create a culture of belongingness for all your students.

Some gang members have reported that they turned to gang activities when their teachers insulted them, called them names, humiliated them publicly, belittled their culture, ignored them in class, or blamed all negative incidents on particular students. These students reported joining gangs for security and to escape teachers who treated them badly or expected little of them because they were members of minority groups (Padilla, 1992; Parks, 1995). Other studies have found that gang members respected teachers who insisted on academic performance in a caring way (Huff, 1989). Anita once asked a teacher in an urban high school which teachers were most effective with the really tough students. He said that there are two kinds: teachers who can't be intimidated or fooled and expect their students to learn and teachers who really care about the students. When asked, "Which kind are you?" he answered, "Both!"

TABLE 11.5 Recognizing the Warning Signs of Violence

The following lists were developed by the American Psychological Association. Other resources are available at **http://helping.apa.org/warningsigns**.

If you see these immediate warning signs, violence is a serious possibility:

- loss of temper on a daily basis
- frequent physical fighting
- significant vandalism or property damage
- increase in use of drugs or alcohol
- increase in risk-taking behaviour
- detailed plans to commit acts of violence
- announcing threats or plans for hurting others
- enjoying hurting animals
- carrying a weapon

If you notice the following signs over a period of time, the potential for violence exists:

- a history of violent or aggressive behaviour
- serious drug or alcohol use
- gang membership or strong desire to be in a gang
- access to or fascination with weapons, especially guns
- threatening others regularly
- trouble controlling feelings like anger
- withdrawal from friends and usual activities
- feeling rejected or alone
- having been a victim of bullying
- poor school performance
- history of discipline problems or frequent run-ins with authority
- feeling constantly disrespected
- failing to acknowledge the feelings or rights of others

Source: From "Warning Signs." Copyright © 1999 by the American Psychological Association. Adapted with permission of the APA. For more information, consult the website **http://apahelpcenter.org/featuredtopics/feature.php?id=38**.

TABLE 11.6 Handling a Potentially Explosive Situation

Here are some ideas for dealing with potential danger.

- Move slowly and deliberately toward the problem situation.
- Speak privately, quietly, and calmly. Do not threaten. Be as matter-of-fact as possible.
- Be as still as possible. Avoid pointing or gesturing.
- Keep a reasonable distance. Do not crowd the student. Do not get "in the student's face."
- Speak respectfully. Use the student's name.
- Establish eye-level position.
- Be brief. Avoid long-winded statements or nagging.
- Stay with the agenda. Stay focused on the problem at hand. Do not get sidetracked. Deal with less severe problems later.
- Avoid power struggles. Do not get drawn into "I won't, you will" arguments.
- Inform the student of the expected behaviour and the negative consequence as a choice or decision for the student to make. Then withdraw from the student and allow some time for the student to decide. ("Michael, you need to return to your desk, or I will have to send for the principal. You have a few seconds to decide." Then move away, perhaps attending to other students. If Michael does not choose the appropriate behaviour, deliver the negative consequences. "You are choosing to have me call the principal.") Follow through with the consequence.

Source: From Weinstein, C. S. (2003). *Secondary classroom management: Lessons from research and practice* (3rd ed.). New York: McGraw-Hill. Copyright © 2003 by McGraw-Hill. Adapted with permission from The McGraw-Hill Companies.

Besides prevention, schools can also establish mentoring programs, conflict resolution training, social skills training, more relevant curricula, and parent and community involvement programs (Padilla, 1992; Parks, 1995). For example, peer mediation has been successful with older students and those with serious problems (Sanchez & Anderson, 1990). In one program, selected gang members were given mediation training, then all members were invited to participate voluntarily in the mediation process, supervised by school counsellors. Strict rules governed the process leading to written agreements signed by gang representatives. Sanchez and Anderson (1990) found that gang violence in the school was reduced to a bare minimum—"The magic of the mediation process was communication" (p. 56).

Respect and Protect. One system that has been developed to combat violence in the schools is Respect and Protect from the Johnson Institute in Minneapolis, Minnesota. The program is founded on five ideas. First, everyone is obliged to respect and protect the rights of others. Second, violence is not acceptable. Third, the program targets the violence-enabling behaviours of staff, students, and parents such as denying, rationalizing, justifying, or blaming others for violence. Fourth, there is a clear definition of what constitutes violence that distinguishes two kinds of violence: bully—victim violence and violence that arises from normal conflicts. Finally, the program has both adult-centred prevention that improves the school climate and student-centred interventions that give students choices and clear consequences (Rembolt, 1998). Table 11.7 gives an overview of the levels of choices and consequences.

Check Your Knowledge

- What is meant by "empathetic listening"?
- Distinguish among assertive, passive, and hostile response styles.
- What are some options for dealing with student–student and student–teacher conflicts?

Apply to Practice

- Describe how you might use Gordon's problem-solving approach to handle a classroom problem you have witnessed.

LEARNING ENVIRONMENTS FOR ALL STUDENTS

What Would You Say?

You are being interviewed for a job to take over a class in the middle of the school year. The principal asks, "In your experience with students in any capacity, what was your most challenging discipline problem so far, and how did you handle it?"

We have examined a number of approaches to classroom student discipline. Are some better than others? Research provides some guidance.

Research on Different Management Approaches

Emmer and Aussiker (1990) conducted a meta-analysis of three general perspectives on management: influencing students through listening and problem solving, as described by Gordon (1981, 1991); group management through class meetings and student discussion, as advocated by Glasser (1969, 1990); and control through rewards and punishments, as exemplified by Canter and Canter (1992). No clear conclusions could be drawn about the impact of these approaches on student behaviours. However, some evaluations have found positive effects for Freiberg's (1999) Consistency Management program and for programs that use rewards and punishments (Lewis, 2001).

TABLE 11.7 Respect and Protect: Overview of Choices, Consequences, and Contracts Intervention Process

Violence Level	Level One	Level Two	Level Three	Level Four	Level Five
Violation	Rule violation (minor infraction)	Misuse of power (repeat violation)	Abuse of power (serious)	Continued abuse (severe)	Pathology (intractable)
Staff action	Confront behaviour Stop violence Deal with problem File intervention report Review "no violence" rule Suggest anger management, conflict resolution, peer mediation, or class meeting	Confront behaviour Stop violence Refer to office File intervention report Try to assess type of conflict Evaluate for talk with parent	Confront behaviour Stop violence Refer to office File intervention report Try to assess type of conflict Parent conference Suggest parenting program	Confront behaviour Stop violence Refer to office File intervention report Assess type of conflict Do psychosocial evaluation Hold parent conference Mandate parenting program Suggest family counselling	Confront behaviour Stop violence Refer to office File intervention report Follow psychosocial recommenda-tions Hold parent conference Mandate parenting program Suggest intensive therapy or treatment for student
Student consequences	Review of activity for violence Parent** notified (optional) Restitution Legal action	Office referral Life skills worksheet Parent notified Restricted until worksheet finished Restitution Legal action	Office referral Parent notified Minimum time-out Violence Group Anger management Connections Empowerment Restitution Legal action	Office referral Parent notified Maximum time-out Violence Group Reconnections Restitution Legal action	Office referral Parent notified Maximum time-out Placement into an alternative setting Restitution Legal action
Contracts*	Verbal promise	Simple contract	Turf contract I	Turf contract II	Bottom-line contract

Students are placed at Levels One to Five depending on the frequency and severity of their violent behaviour. Students may stay at a particular level as the situation warrants. Any violent act that is racial, sexual, involves physical fighting, or is committed against staff results in the student being placed immediately at Level Three or higher. The program manual provides lists of behaviours that correlate with each level of violence.

* See source for a complete description of the different contracts.
** In this table, the term *parent* includes guardians and primary caregivers.

Source: Adapted from Rembolt, C. (1998). Making violence unacceptable. *Educational Leadership*, 56(1), 36. Copyright © 1998 by Educational Leadership. Adapted with permission. The Association for Supervision and Curriculum Development is a worldwide community of educators advocating sound policies and sharing best practices to achieve the success of each learner. To learn more, visit ASCA at www.ascd.org.

In a study conducted in Australia, Ramon Lewis (2001) found that recognizing and rewarding appropriate student behaviours, talking with students about how their behaviour affects others, involving students in class discipline decisions, and providing non-directive hints and descriptions about unacceptable behaviours were associated with students taking greater responsibility for their own learning. It is interesting that these interventions represent all three of the general approaches reviewed by Emmer and Aussiker—influence, group management, and control. Lewis also concluded that teachers sometimes find using these interventions difficult when students are aggressive—and most in need of the approaches. When teachers feel threatened, it can be difficult to do what students need, but that may be the most important time to act positively.

Culturally Responsive Management

Research on discipline shows that students from minority groups may be disciplined for behaviours they never meant to be disruptive or disrespectful because of a lack of cultural synchronization between teachers and students. For example, studies involving African Americans, especially males, indicate that these students are punished more often and more harshly than other students. These students lose time from learning as they spend more hours in detention or suspension (Ferguson, 2000; Monroe & Obidah, 2002; Skiba et al., 2000). Why?

The notion that African American and Latin American students are punished more because they commit more serious offences is not supported by the data. Instead, these students are punished more severely for minor offences such as rudeness or defiance—words and actions that are interpreted by teachers as meriting severe punishment. One explanation is a lack of cultural synchronization between teachers and students. "The language, style of walking, glances, and dress of black children, particularly males, have engendered fear, apprehension, and overreaction among many teachers and school administrators" (Irvine, 1990, p. 27). According to Joyce Barakett of Concordia University, teachers in Canada also "call upon cultural differences" to explain students' behaviour (Barakett, 1986, p. 98). In interviews, teachers reported that children from Yugoslavia "posed problems of control" and Greek children were more motivated (Barakett, 1986, p. 99). The teachers who seem to be most effective with African American students practise **culturally responsive management** and have been called "**warm demanders**" (Irvine & Armento, 2001; Irvine & Fraser, 1998). See the Reaching Every Student box for an example. Sometimes these warm demanders appear harsh to outside observers (Burke-Spero, 1999; Burke-Spero & Woolfolk Hoy, 2002).

Communicating with Families about Classroom Management

As we have seen throughout this book, families are important partners in education. This statement applies to classroom management as well. When parents and teachers share the same expectations and support each other, they can create a more positive classroom environment and more time for learning. The accompanying Family and Community Partnerships box gives ideas for working with families and the community.

Check Your Knowledge

- What does research say about different discipline approaches?
- How does culture affect classroom management?

Apply to Practice

- How will you involve families in creating a learning community in your classroom?

culturally responsive management Taking cultural meanings and styles into account when developing management plans and responding to students.

warm demanders Effective teachers who show both high expectations and great caring for their students.

Carla Monroe and Jennifer Obidah (2002) studied Ms. Simpson, a grade 8 science teacher. She described herself as having high expectations for academics and behaviour in her classes—so much so that she believed that her students perceived her as "mean." Yet, she often used humour and dialect to communicate her expectations, as in the following exchange:

Ms. Simpson [addressing the class]:

> If you know you're going to act the fool just come to me and say, "I'm going to act the fool at the pep rally," so I can go ahead and send you to wherever you need to go. [Class laughs.]

Ms. Simpson: I'm real serious. If you know you're having a bad day, you don't want anybody touching you, you don't want nobody saying nothing to you, somebody bump into you you're going to snap—you need to come up to me and say, "I'm going to snap and I can't go to the pep rally." [The students start to call out various comments.]

Ms. Simpson: Now, I just want to say I expect you to have the best behavior because you're the most mature students in the building ... don't make me stop the pep rally and ask the 8th graders to leave.

Edward: We'll have silent lunch won't we? [Class laughs.]

Ms. Simpson: You don't want to dream about what you're going to have. [Class laughs.] Ok, 15 minutes for warm-ups. [The students begin their warm-up assignment.]

CLASSROOM MANAGEMENT

Make sure that families know the expectations and rules of your class and school.

EXAMPLES

1. At a Family Fun Night, have your students do skits showing the rules—how to follow them and what breaking them "looks like" and "sounds like."

2. Make a poster for the refrigerator at home that describes, in a light way, the most important rules and expectations.

3. For older students, give families a list of due dates for the major assignments, along with tips about how to encourage high-quality work by pacing the effort—avoiding last-minute panic.

4. Communicate in appropriate ways; for example, use the family's first language when possible. Tailor messages to the reading level of the home.

Make families partners in recognizing good citizenship.

EXAMPLES

1. Send positive notes home when students, especially students who have had trouble with classroom management, work well in the classroom.

2. Give ideas for ways in which any family, even one with few economic resources, can celebrate accomplishment—a favourite food; the chance to choose a movie to rent; a comment to a special person such as an aunt, grandparent, or minister; the chance to read to a younger sibling.

Identify talents in the community to help build a learning environment in your class.

EXAMPLES

1. Have students write letters to carpet and furniture stores asking for donations of remnants to carpet a reading corner.

2. Find family members who can build shelves or room dividers, paint, sew, laminate manipulatives, write stories, repot plants, or network computers.

3. Contact businesses for donations of computers, printers, or other equipment.

Seek cooperation from families when behaviour problems arise.

EXAMPLES

1. Talk to families over the phone or in their home. Have good records about the problem behaviour.

2. Listen to family members and solve problems with them.

The Need for Organization
(pp. 418–422)

What are the challenges of classroom management?

Classrooms are by nature multidimensional, full of simultaneous activities, fast-paced and immediate, unpredictable, public, and affected by the history of students' and teachers' actions. A teacher must juggle all these elements every day. Productive classroom activity requires students' cooperation. Maintaining cooperation involves different things for each age group. Young students are learning how to "go to school" and need to learn the general procedures of school. Older students need to learn the specifics required for working in different subjects. Working with adolescents requires teachers to understand the power of the adolescent peer group.

What are the goals of good classroom management?

The goals of effective classroom management are to make ample time for learning; improve the quality of time use by keeping students actively engaged; make sure that participation structures are clear, straightforward, and consistently signalled; and encourage student self-management, self-control, and responsibility.

Creating a Positive Learning Environment
(pp. 422–433)

Distinguish between rules and procedures.

Rules are the specific dos and don'ts of classroom life. They usually are written down or posted. Procedures cover administrative tasks, student movement, housekeeping, routines for running lessons, interactions between students and teachers, and interactions among students. Rules can be written in terms of rights,

and students may benefit from participating in establishing these rules. Consequences should be established for following and breaking the rules and procedures, so that the teacher and the students know what will happen.

Distinguish between personal territories and interest-area spatial arrangements.

There are two basic kinds of spatial organization: personal territories (the traditional classroom arrangement) and functional arrangements (dividing space into interest or work areas). Flexibility is often the key, and many teachers use a design that combines both kinds of spaces. Important considerations in the teacher's choice of physical arrangements include access to materials, convenience, privacy when needed, ease of supervision, and a willingness to re-evaluate plans.

What management issues do computers raise in the classroom?

Clear procedures are especially important when there are computers in the classroom. Whether teachers have one, several, or a room full of computers, they need to think through what students will need to know, teach procedures, and provide easy-to-find and follow written instructions for common tasks. Students or parent volunteers can be trained as expert support. Different role structures make management of computer tasks easier.

Contrast the first school week of effective and ineffective classroom managers.

Effective classroom managers spent the first days of class teaching a workable, easily understood set of rules and procedures by using lots of explanation, examples, and practice. Students were occupied with organized, enjoyable activities and learned to function cooperatively in the group. Quick, firm, clear, and consistent responses to infractions

of the rules characterized effective teachers. The teachers had planned carefully to avoid any last-minute tasks that might have taken them away from their students. These teachers dealt with the children's pressing concerns first.

Creating a Learning Community
(pp. 433–435)

What are Johnson and Johnson's three C's of establishing a classroom community?

The three C's are cooperative community, constructive conflict resolution, and civic values. Classroom management begins by establishing a community based on cooperative learning. At the heart of the community is the idea of positive interdependence—individuals working together to achieve mutual goals. Constructive conflict resolution is essential in the community because conflicts are inevitable and even necessary for learning. The last C stands for civic values—the understandings and beliefs that hold the community together. Values are learned through direct teaching, modelling, literature, group discussions, and the sharing of concerns.

Maintaining a Good Environment for Learning
(pp. 435–442)

How can teachers encourage engagement?

The format of a lesson affects student involvement. In general, as teacher supervision increases, students' engaged time also increases. When the task provides continuous cues for the student about what to do next, involvement will be greater. Activities with clear steps are likely to be more absorbing, since one step leads naturally to the next. Making work requirements clear and specific, providing needed materials, and monitoring activities all add to engagement.

Explain the factors identified by Kounin that prevent management problems in the classroom.

To create a positive environment and prevent problems, teachers must take student differences into account, maintain student motivation, and reinforce positive behaviour. Successful problem preventers are skilled in four areas described by Kounin: "withitness," overlapping, group focusing, and movement management. When penalties have to be imposed, teachers should impose them calmly and privately.

Describe seven levels of intervention in misbehaviour.

The teacher can first make eye contact with the student or use other non-verbal signals, then try verbal hints, such as simply inserting the student's name into the lecture. Next, the teacher can ask if the offender is aware of the negative effects of the actions, then remind the student of the procedure and have her or him follow it correctly. If this does not work, the teacher can ask the student to state the correct rule or procedure and then to follow it, and then move to telling the student in a clear, assertive, and unhostile way to stop the misbehaviour. If this fails too, the teacher can offer a choice—stop the behaviour or meet privately to work out the consequences.

The Need for Communication
(pp. 442–448)

What is meant by "empathetic listening"?

Communication between teacher and student is essential when problems arise. All interactions between people, even silence or neglect, communicate some meaning. Empathetic, active listening can be a helpful response when students bring problems to teachers. Teachers must reflect back to the students what they hear them saying. This reflection is more than a parroting of words; it should capture the emotions, intent, and meaning behind them.

Distinguish among assertive, passive, and hostile response styles.

The passive response style can take several forms. Instead of telling the student directly what to do, the teacher simply comments on the behaviour, asks the student to think about the appropriate action, or threatens but never follows through. In a hostile response style, teachers may make "you" statements that condemn the student without stating clearly what the student should be doing. An assertive response communicates to the students that the teacher cares too much about them and the process of learning to allow inappropriate behaviour to persist. Assertive teachers clearly state what they expect.

What are some options for dealing with student–student and student–teacher conflicts?

Students need guidance in resolving conflicts. Different strategies are useful, depending on whether the goal, the relationship, or both are important to those experiencing conflict. It can help to reverse roles and see the situation through the eyes of the other. In dealing with serious problems, prevention and peer mediation might be useful. No matter what the situation, the cooperation of families can help create a positive learning environment in the classroom and school.

Learning Environments for All Students
(pp. 448–451)

What does research say about different discipline approaches?

A combination of recognition for appropriate behaviour, hints about what is unacceptable, discussion about how behaviour affects others, and student involvement in discipline decisions encourages student responsibility, but these approaches are difficult when students are aggressive.

How does culture affect classroom management?

Students from minority cultures may be disciplined for behaviours they never intended to be disruptive or disrespectful. Cultural differences in behavioural expression can be the basis for misunderstandings in classroom management.

KEY TERMS

academic learning time, p. 420

action zone, p. 428

allocated time, p. 420

assertive discipline, p. 444

classroom management, p. 419

culturally responsive management, p. 450

empathetic listening, p. 444

engaged time/time on task, p. 420

group focus, p. 437

"I" message, p. 444

movement management, p. 437

natural/logical consequences, p. 425

overlapping, p. 437

paraphrase rule, p. 442

participation structures, p. 421

procedures, p. 423

rules, p. 423

self-management, p. 421

warm demanders, p. 450

withitness, p. 436

BECOMING A PROFESSIONAL

Reflecting on the Chapter

Can you apply the ideas from this chapter on creating learning environments to solve the following problems of practice?

Preschool and Kindergarten

- Your class is larger than ever this year, and it is very difficult to get everyone dressed for play outside. How would you handle the situation?

Elementary and Middle School

- It takes your class 15 minutes to settle down each morning and begin work. What would you do?

- A few students in your class always seem to be out of step with the rest of the class. They call out answers when they shouldn't, interrupt others, and get up and walk around when they should be seated and working. What would you do?

Junior High and High School

- You tell a student to put away a CD player, and she says, "Try and make me!" What would you do?

- One of your bright and able students has stopped doing homework. What would you do?

Check Your Understanding

- Be familiar with Kounin's terms of *withitness*, *overlapping activities*, *group focusing*, and *movement management*.

- Know the basic room arrangements of rows, circles, clusters, and horseshoes and the activities for which each is best suited.

- Understand a range of consequences for minor to major misbehaviour.

- Be familiar with alternatives for communicating with students, such as empathetic listening, "I" messages, and problem solving.

Your Teaching Portfolio

Think about your philosophy of teaching, a question you will be asked at most job interviews. What is your philosophy of classroom management? What rules will you set, and how will you establish them? (Consult the Guidelines on establishing class procedures for ideas.)

Add some ideas for parent involvement from this chapter to your portfolio.

Teaching Resources

Adapt the rules on pages 423 to 425 for students you will teach.

Add the floor plan from Figure 11.2 (page 430) to your teaching resources file.

Add Table 11.6 (page 447) on graduated responses to school violence to your teaching resources file.

Teachers' Casebook

What Would They Do?

William Wallace
Western Technical and Commercial School
Toronto, Ontario

You cannot wish bullying away; intervention is essential. Action takes several forms. There are many ways of thinking about how to act, and one way is to think about three steps: being preventative, being proactive, and being persistent.

First is prevention. I work quickly at the beginning of each semester to develop relationships with my students so that as issues, academic or behavioural, arise, I can deal with them as one human being to another. Dealing with bullying is easier if there are relationships in place where each student knows that he or she is seen as a whole human being. When conflict arises, and it will, you can focus on the behaviour without judging the person. It's very hard to get to the person through the negative behaviour. As well, the culture of caring and mutual respect is something that needs to be nurtured and developed in the classroom and in the school. It's not enough to assume that it should be in place. Opportunities for leadership, mentorship, stewardship, and cooperation need to be a part of everyday life at a school. A place where student contributions are not highly valued is a place where bullying is more likely to arise.

Second is being proactive. If there's a one-off incident, I address it with the students involved and, where appropriate, use it in a generic way to discuss broader issues with my classes, for example, homophobia and gay-bashing. If I have any sense that this one incident is serious, or part of a broader pattern, then I immediately involve other teachers who know and work with the students involved, particularly the teachers in guidance, who often have an excellent knowledge of the history of students who might be prone to bullying or to being bullied. If the incidents are ongoing, I would work to develop a joint strategy with my colleagues for how to address them; for example, when to involve parents, the administration, social workers, and so on.

Third is persistence. Bullying and being bullied are usually symptomatic of underlying problems. It pro-vides an opportunity for teachers and schools to respond to the signal students are sending. Checking in with the students involved, and providing opportunities for discussion as well as for the students' personal success, are ways of contributing to a positive outcome from a bullying incident. In addressing bullying directly, we send a strong message that it is not acceptable behaviour; we indicate our concern for the individuals involved, both bullies and bullied; and we help chart a course within the school community to build and strengthen a positive culture.

As you will have gathered, I have talked very little about discipline. Discipline has its place, but wrongly used it will simply alienate the bullies, making them harder to reach. There is no replacement for relationship building, and this is certainly an idea that the bullies themselves need to embrace.

Keith J. Boyle
Dunellen High School
Dunellen, NJ

Errant behaviour throughout the middle school may be indicative of future behavioural problems and, as many things in life, the more this misbehaviour is allowed to exist, the longer it will have a chance to thrive. In this case of a child being continually bullied by two other children (gender having no bearing in this situation), the knowledge of this wrongdoing must not be ignored or isolated. I would interview both the victim and the bullies, separately, to glean as much information as possible. If this were a singular incident, I would attempt to handle it myself via contact with the pertinent parents. However, if this were a recurring problem, the administration must be made aware. Any administrator will acknowledge that to be left in the dark about a serious situation within the environs of his/her responsibility is precarious. The appropriate guidance counsellor should also be involved. The gravity of abusive behaviour toward fellow students must be emphasized to the offenders. Significant punitive action is integral in order to send a message to the entire community that their school is indeed a haven in which one can feel the uninhibited freedom to learn.

Claude Drawing, Francoise and Paloma. May 17, 1954. Valauris. Pablo Picasso. Oil on canvas, 116 × 89 cm. Inv.: MP 209. Photo: J. G. Berizzi. © 2006 Estate of Pablo Picasso/Artist Rights Society (ARS), New York. Photo: Réunion des Musées Nationaux/Art Resource, New York.

12 TEACHING FOR LEARNING

Teachers' Casebook

What Would You Do?

Your school district has adopted a new student-centred curriculum for grades K through 6. Quite a bit of time and money was spent on workshops for teachers; buying levelled books and good children's literature; developing manipulatives for mathematics; building comfortable reading corners; making costumes, puppets, and other reading props; designing science projects; and generally supporting the innovations. Students and teachers are mostly pleased with the program. Many students appear to be more engaged in learning—but some students seem lost. The students' written work is longer and more creative. However, standardized tests indicate a drop in scores. The principal is clearly getting worried—this was her big project, and she had to work hard to "sell it" to some members of the parent advisory committee and school board. Several parents of students in your class are complaining that they have had to hire tutors or buy commercial programs to teach their children basic skills.

Critical Thinking

As a teacher, what would you do about the parents' complaints? Would you make any changes in your approach? What information would you need to make good decisions? Who should be involved in these decisions?

Collaboration

With three or four other students in your class, role-play a staff meeting in which the principal has asked whether the move toward more student-centred teaching was hasty and needs to be reconsidered. How do you and your colleagues respond?

Much of this text has been about learning and learners. In this chapter, we focus on teachers and teaching. We look first at characteristics of effective teachers and at how teachers' expectations for and interactions with students can influence achievement. Next, we examine how teachers plan, including how they use taxonomies of learning objectives or themes as a basis for planning.

With a sense of how to set goals and make plans, we move to a consideration of some general teacher-centred strategies: direct instruction, seatwork, homework, questioning, recitation, and group discussion. The next section focuses on student-centred approaches to teaching in different subjects. These reflect the constructivist views of learning described in Chapter 9. Finally, we discuss how teachers can support self-regulated learning in their classrooms—the highly effective approach to learning also described in Chapter 9.

In addition to reading about strategies for teaching described in this chapter, we encourage you to review strategies for meeting the diverse needs of learners in inclusive classrooms that we discussed in Chapter 4.

By the time you have completed this chapter, you should be able to answer these questions:

- *What are the characteristics of effective teachers?*

- *How can teachers' expectations affect student learning?*

- *When and how should teachers use instructional objectives and themes for planning?*

- *In what situations would each of the following formats be most appropriate: lecture, seatwork and homework, questioning, and group discussion?*

- *How does the teacher's role vary in direct and student-centred approaches to teaching?*

- *What are the merits of student-centred approaches to teaching reading, mathematics, and science?*
- *How can teachers promote self-regulated learning in their classrooms?*

CHARACTERISTICS OF EFFECTIVE TEACHERS

Some of the earliest research on effective teaching focused on the personal qualities of the teachers themselves. Results revealed some lessons about three teacher characteristics: knowledge, clarity, and warmth.

Teachers' Knowledge

Do teachers who know more about their subject have a more positive impact on their students? It depends on the subject. High-school students appear to learn more mathematics from teachers with degrees or significant coursework in mathematics (Wayne & Youngs, 2003). However, when we look at teachers' knowledge of facts and concepts, as measured by test scores and university grades, the relationship to student learning is unclear and may be indirect. Teachers who know more facts about their subject do not necessarily have students who learn more. But teachers who know more may make clearer presentations and recognize student difficulties more readily. They are ready for any student questions and do not have to be evasive or vague in their answers. Thus, knowledge is necessary because being more knowledgeable helps teachers be clearer and more organized; however, such knowledge may not be sufficient in itself for effective teaching.

Clarity and Organization

When Barak Rosenshine and Norma Furst (1973) reviewed about 50 studies of teaching, they concluded that clarity was the most promising teacher behaviour for future research on effective teaching. Teachers who provide clear presentations and explanations tend to have students who learn more and who rate their teachers more positively (Hines, Cruickshank, & Kennedy, 1985; Land, 1987). Teachers with more knowledge of the subject tend to be less vague in their explanations to the class. The less vague the teacher, the more the students learn (Berliner, 1987; Evertson et al., 2003; Land, 1987). See the accompanying Guidelines for ideas about how to be clear and organized in your teaching.

Warmth and Enthusiasm

As you are well aware, some teachers are much more enthusiastic than others. Some studies have found that ratings of teachers' enthusiasm for their subject are correlated with student achievement gains (Rosenshine & Furst, 1973). Warmth, friendliness, and understanding seem to be the teacher traits most strongly related to student attitudes (Murray, 1983; Ryans, 1960; Soar & Soar, 1979). In other words, teachers who are warm and friendly tend to have students who like them and the class in general. But note that these are correlational studies. The results do not tell us that teacher enthusiasm causes student learning or that warmth causes positive attitudes, only that the two variables tend to occur together. Teachers trained to demonstrate their enthusiasm have students who are more attentive and involved, but not necessarily more successful on tests of content (Gillett & Gall, 1982). The Guidelines include some ideas for communicating warmth and enthusiasm.

Check Your Knowledge

- What are some general characteristics of effective teachers?

Apply to Practice

- Identify one of your teachers who exemplifies good teaching.

Organize your lessons carefully.

EXAMPLES

1. Provide objectives that help students focus on the purpose of the lesson.
2. Begin lessons by writing a brief outline on the board, or work on an outline with the class as part of the lesson.
3. If possible, break the presentation into clear steps or stages.
4. Review periodically.

Anticipate and plan for difficult parts in the lesson.

EXAMPLES

1. Plan a clear introduction to the lesson that tells students what they are going to learn and how they are going to learn it.
2. Do the exercises and anticipate student problems—consult the teachers' manual for ideas.
3. Have definitions ready for new terms, and prepare several relevant examples for concepts.
4. Think of analogies that will make ideas easier to understand.
5. Organize the lesson in a logical sequence; include checkpoints that incorporate oral or written questions or problems to make sure the students are following the explanations.

Strive for clear explanations.

EXAMPLES

1. Avoid vague words and ambiguous phrases. Steer clear of "the somes"—*something, someone, sometime, somehow;* "the not verys"—*not very much, not very well, not very hard, not very often;* and other unspecific fillers, such as *most, not all, sort of, and so on, of course, as you know, I guess, in fact, or whatever, and more or less.*
2. Use specific (and, if possible, colourful) names instead of *it, them,* and *thing.*

3. Refrain from using pet phrases such as *you know, like, and Okay?.* Another idea is to record a lesson on tape to check yourself for clarity.
4. Give explanations at several levels so that all students, not just the brightest, will understand.
5. Focus on one idea at a time and avoid digressions.

Make clear connections by using explanatory links such as because, if ... then, or therefore.

EXAMPLES

1. "Explorers found it difficult to get to the west coast of Canada because it was so hard to cross the Rockies."
2. Explanatory links are also helpful in labelling visual material such as graphs, concept maps, or illustrations.

Signal transitions from one major topic to another with phrases.

EXAMPLES

1. *"The next area ...,"* *"Now we will turn to ...,"* or *"The second step is...."*
2. Outline topics by listing key points, drawing concept maps on the board, or using an overhead projector.

Communicate an enthusiasm for your subject and the day's lesson.

EXAMPLES

1. Tell students why the lesson is important. Have a better reason than "This will be on the test" or "You will need to know it next year." Emphasize the value of the learning itself.
2. Be sure to make eye contact with the students.
3. Vary your pace and volume in speaking. Use silence for emphasis.

Teachers' beliefs about students also affect students' learning. For this reason, we turn to teacher expectations next.

TEACHER EXPECTATIONS

Pygmalion effect Exceptional progress by a student as a result of high teacher expectations for that student; named for the mythological king Pygmalion, who made a statue, then caused it to be brought to life.

self-fulfilling prophecy A groundless expectation that is confirmed because it has been expected.

sustaining expectation effect An effect that occurs when student performance is maintained at a certain level because teachers don't recognize improvements.

Two kinds of expectation effects can occur in classrooms. The first has been referred to as the **Pygmalion effect** (Rosenthal & Jacobson, 1968), or self-fulfilling prophecy. When teachers' beliefs about students' abilities have no basis in fact, but student behaviour comes to match the initially inaccurate expectation, the outcome may be explained as a **self-fulfilling prophecy**. The second kind of expectation effect occurs when teachers are fairly accurate in their initial reading of students' abilities and respond to students appropriately. There is nothing wrong with forming and acting on accurate estimates of student ability. The problems arise when students show some improvement but teachers do not alter their expectations to take account of the improvement. This is called a **sustaining expectation effect**, because the teacher's unchanging expectation sustains the student's achievement at the expected level. The chance to raise expectations, provide more appropriate teaching, and thus encourage greater student achievement is lost. In practice, self-fulfilling prophecy effects seem to be stronger in the early grades and sustaining effects are more likely in the later grades (Kuklinski & Weinstein, 2001). And some students are more likely than others to be the recipients of sustaining expectations. For example, children who are withdrawn provide little information about themselves, so teachers may sustain their expectations about these children for lack of new input (Jones & Gerig, 1994).

Sources of Expectations

Research indicates that there can be many sources of teachers' expectations (Van Matre, Valentine, & Cooper, 2000). Intelligence test scores are an obvious source, especially if teachers do not interpret the scores appropriately. Gender also influences teachers; most teachers expect more behaviour problems from boys than from girls and may have higher academic expectations for girls. The notes from previous teachers and the medical or psychological reports found in students' permanent record files are another obvious source of expectations. Knowledge of ethnic background also seems to have an influence, as does knowledge of older brothers and sisters. Teachers hold higher expectations for attractive students. Previous achievement, socioeconomic class, and the actual behaviours of the student are also often used as sources of information. Even the student's after-school activities can be a source of expectations. Teachers tend to hold higher expectations for students who participate in extracurricular activities than for students who do nothing after school.

Expectations and beliefs focus attention and organize memory, so teachers may pay attention to and remember the information that fits the initial expectations (Fiske, 1993; Hewstone, 1989). Even when student performance does not fit expectations, the teacher may rationalize and attribute the performance to external causes beyond the student's control. For example, a teacher may assume that the student who is typically low achieving but who did well on a test must have cheated and that the typically high-achieving student who failed must have been upset that day. In both cases, behaviour that seems out of character is dismissed. It may take many instances of supposedly uncharacteristic behaviour to change the teacher's beliefs about a particular student's abilities. Thus, expectations often remain in the face of contradictory evidence (Brophy, 1982, 1998).

Do Teachers' Expectations Really Affect Students' Achievement?

The answer to this question is more complicated than it might seem. There are two ways to investigate the question. One is to give teachers unfounded expectations about their students and note if these baseless expectations have any effects. The other approach is to identify the naturally occurring expectations of teachers and study the effects of these expectations. The answer to the question of whether teacher expectations affect student learning depends in part on which approach is taken to study the question.

Rosenthal and Jacobson used the first approach—giving teachers groundless expectations and noting the effects. The study was heavily criticized for the experimental and statistical methods used (Elashoff & Snow, 1971; Snow, 1995; Weinberg, 1989). A careful analysis of the results revealed that even though grade 1 through 6 students participated in the study, the self-fulfilling prophecy effects could be traced to just five students in grades 1 to 2 who changed dramatically. When other researchers tried to replicate the study, they did not find evidence of a self-fulfilling prophecy effect, even for children in these lower grades (Claiborn, 1969; Wilkins & Glock, 1973). After reviewing the research on teacher expectations, Raudenbush (1984) concluded that these expectations have only a small effect on student IQ scores (the outcome measure used by Rosenthal and Jacobson) and only in the early years of a new school setting—in the first years of elementary school and then again in the first years of junior high school.

But what about the second approach—naturally occurring expectations? Research shows that teachers do indeed form beliefs about students' capabilities. Many of these beliefs are accurate assessments based on the best available data and are corrected as new information is collected. Even so, some teachers do favour certain students (Babad, 1995; Rosenthal, 1987). For example, in a study of 110 students followed from age 4 to age 18, Jennifer Alvidrez and Rhona Weinstein (1999) found that teachers tended to overestimate the abilities of preschool children they rated as independent and interesting and underestimate the abilities of children seen as immature and anxious. Teachers' judgments of student ability at age 4 predicted student grade-point average at age 18. The strongest predictions were for students whose abilities were *underestimated*. If teachers decide that some students are less able, and if the teachers lack effective strategies for working with lower-achieving students, then students may experience a double threat—low expectations and inadequate teaching (Good & Brophy, 2003). The power of the expectation effect depends on the age of the students (generally speaking, younger students are more susceptible) and on how differently a teacher treats students for whom he or she has high and low expectations, an issue we turn to next (Kuklinski & Weinstein, 2001).

Instructional Strategies. As we saw in Chapter 4, different grouping processes may well have a marked effect on students. And some teachers leave little to the imagination; they make their expectations all too clear. For example, Alloway (1984) recorded comments such as these directed to low-achieving groups:

"I'll be over to help you slow ones in a minute." "The blue group will find this hard."

In these remarks, the teacher not only tells the students that they lack ability but also communicates that finishing the work, not understanding, is the goal.

Once teachers assign students to ability groups, they usually assign different learning activities. To the extent that teachers choose activities that challenge students and increase achievement, these differences are probably necessary. Activities become inappropriate, however, when students who are ready for more challenging work are not given the opportunity to try it because teachers believe that they cannot handle it. This is an example of a sustaining expectation effect and can result in underachievement on the part of students, since they are not expanding their knowledge and skills, or boredom.

Teacher–Student Interactions. However the class is grouped and whatever the assignments, the quantity and the quality of teacher–student interactions are likely to affect the students. Students who are expected to achieve tend to be asked more and harder questions, to be given more chances and a longer time to respond, and to be interrupted less often than students who are expected to do poorly. Teachers also give these students cues and prompts, communicating their belief that the students can answer the question (Allington, 1980; Good & Brophy, 2003; Rosenthal, 1995).

When an answer on a test is "almost right," the teacher is more likely to give the benefit of the doubt (and thus the better grade) to students who are high achieving (Finn, 1972). Teachers tend to smile at these students more often and show greater warmth through such non-verbal responses as leaning toward the students and nodding their heads as the students speak (Woolfolk & Brooks, 1983, 1985).

In contrast, teachers ask easier questions, allow less time for answering, and are less likely to give prompts to students for whom they hold low expectations. Teachers are more likely to respond with sympathetic acceptance or even praise to inadequate answers from students who are low achieving but criticize them for wrong answers. Even more disturbing, students who are low achieving receive less praise than students who are high achieving for similar correct answers. This inconsistent feedback can be very confusing for low-ability students. Imagine how hard it would be to learn if your wrong answers were sometimes praised, sometimes ignored, and sometimes criticized and your right answers received little recognition (Good 1983a, 1983b).

Of course, not all teachers form inappropriate expectations or act on their expectations in unconstructive ways (Babad, Inbar, & Rosenthal, 1982). But avoiding the problem may be more difficult than it seems. In general, students for whom teachers' expectations are low also tend to be the most disruptive students. (Of course, low expectations can reinforce their desire to disrupt or misbehave.) Teachers may call on these students less, wait a shorter time for their answers, and give them less praise for right answers, partly to avoid the wrong, careless, or silly answers that can cause disruptions, delays, and digressions (Cooper, 1979). The challenge is to deal with these very real threats to classroom management without communicating low expectations to some students or fostering their own low expectations of themselves. And sometimes, low expectations become part of the culture of the school—beliefs shared by teachers and administrators alike (Weinstein, Madison, & Kuklinski, 1995). The accompanying Guidelines may help you avoid some of these problems.

Check Your Knowledge

- What are some sources of teacher expectations?
- What are the two kinds of expectation effects, and how do they happen?
- What are the different avenues for communicating teacher expectations?

Apply to Practice

- How have teachers communicated their expectations to you in the past? What behaviours have you found most encouraging?

Next, we describe how teachers can effectively plan and implement instruction to support students' learning.

PLANNING: THE FIRST STEP IN EFFECTIVE TEACHING

Greta Morine-Dershimer (2006) asks which of the following are true about teacher planning:

Time is of the essence.	A little planning goes a long way.
Plans are made to be broken.	You can do it yourself.
Don't look back.	One size fits all.

When you thought about the What Would You Do? challenge at the beginning of this chapter, you were planning. In the past few years, educational researchers have become very interested in teachers' planning. They have interviewed teachers about how they plan, asked teachers to "think out loud" while planning or to keep

AVOIDING THE NEGATIVE EFFECTS OF TEACHER EXPECTATIONS

Use information about students from tests, cumulative folders, and other teachers very carefully.

EXAMPLES

1. Some teachers avoid reading cumulative folders at the beginning of the year.
2. Be critical and objective about the reports you hear from other teachers.

Be flexible in your use of grouping strategies.

EXAMPLES

1. Review work of students often and experiment with new groupings.
2. Use different groups for different subjects.
3. Use mixed-ability groups in cooperative exercises.

Make sure that all the students are challenged.

EXAMPLES

1. Don't say, "This is easy; I know you can do it."
2. Offer a wide range of problems and encourage all students to try a few of the harder ones for extra credit. Find something positive about these attempts.

Be especially careful about how you respond to low-achieving students during class discussions.

EXAMPLES

1. Give them prompts, cues, and time to answer.
2. Give ample praise for good answers.
3. Call on low achievers as often as high achievers.

Use materials that show a wide range of ethnic groups.

EXAMPLES

1. Check readers and library books. Is there ethnic diversity?
2. If few materials are available, ask students to research and create their own, based on community or family sources.

Make sure that your teaching does not reflect racial, ethnic, or sexual stereotypes or prejudice.

EXAMPLES

1. Use a checking system to be sure you call on and include all students.

2. Monitor the content of the tasks you assign. Do boys get the "hard" math problems to work at the board? Do you avoid having students with limited English give oral presentations?

Be fair in evaluation and disciplinary procedures.

EXAMPLES

1. Make sure that equal offences receive equal punishment. Find out from students in an anonymous questionnaire whether you seem to be favouring certain individuals.
2. Try to grade student work without knowing the identity of the student. Ask another teacher to give you a second opinion from time to time.

Communicate to all students that you believe they can learn—and mean it.

EXAMPLES

1. Return papers that do not meet standards with specific suggestions for improvements.
2. If students do not have the answers immediately, wait, probe, and then help them think through an answer.

Involve all students in learning tasks and in privileges.

EXAMPLES

1. Use some system to make sure that you give each student practice in reading, speaking, and answering questions.
2. Keep track of who gets to do what job. Are some students always on the list while others seldom make it?

Monitor your non-verbal behaviour.

EXAMPLES

1. Do you lean away or stand farther away from some students? Do some students get smiles when they approach your desk while others get only frowns?
2. Does your tone of voice vary with different students?

journals describing their plans, and even studied teachers intensively for months at a time. What have they found?

First, planning influences what students will learn, since planning transforms the available time and curriculum materials into activities, assignments, and tasks for students—*time is the essence* of planning. When a teacher decides to devote seven hours to language arts and 15 minutes to science in a given week, the students in that class will learn more language than science. In fact, differences as dramatic as this do occur, with some classes dedicating twice as much time as others to certain subjects (Clark & Yinger, 1988; Karweitt, 1989). Planning done at the beginning of the year is particularly important because many routines and patterns, such as time allocations, are established early. So *a little planning does go a long way* in terms of what will be taught and what will be learned.

Second, teachers engage in several levels of planning—by the year, term, unit, week, and day. All the levels must be coordinated. Accomplishing the year's plan requires breaking the work into terms, the terms into units, and the units into weeks and days. Planning done at the beginning of the year is particularly important, because many routines and patterns are established early. For experienced teachers, unit planning seems to be the most important level, followed by weekly and then daily planning. As you gain experience in teaching, it will become easier to coordinate these levels of planning (Morine-Dershimer, 2006).

Third, plans reduce—but do not eliminate—uncertainty in teaching. Even the best plans cannot (and should not) control everything that happens in class; planning must allow flexibility. There is some evidence that when teachers "overplan"—when they fill every minute and stick to the plan no matter what—their students do not learn as much as students whose teachers are flexible (Shavelson, 1987). So *plans are not made to be broken*—but sometimes they need to be bent a bit.

In order to plan creatively and flexibly, teachers need to have wide-ranging knowledge about students, their interests, and abilities; the subjects being taught; alternative ways to teach and assess understanding; working with groups; the expectations and limitations of the school and community; how to apply and adapt materials and texts; and how to pull all this knowledge together into meaningful activities. The plans of beginning teachers sometimes don't work because the teachers lack knowledge about the students or the subject—they can't estimate how long it will take students to complete an activity, for example, or they stumble when asked for an explanation or a different example (Calderhead, 1996).

In planning, you can *do it yourself*—but *collaboration* is better. Working with other teachers and sharing ideas is one of the best experiences in teaching. But even great lesson plans taken from a terrific website on science have to be adapted to your situation. Some of the adaptation comes before you teach and some comes after. In fact, much of what experienced teachers know about planning comes from looking back—reflecting—on what worked and what didn't, so *do look back* on your plans and grow professionally in the process.

Finally, there is no one model for effective planning. *One size does not fit all* in planning. For experienced teachers, planning is a creative problem-solving process. Experienced teachers know how to accomplish many lessons and segments of lessons. They know what to expect and how to proceed, so they don't necessarily continue to follow the detailed lesson-planning models they learned during their teacher-preparation programs. Planning is more informal—"in their heads." However, many experienced teachers think it was helpful to learn this detailed system as a foundation (Clark & Peterson, 1986).

No matter how you plan, you must have a learning goal in mind. In the next section, we consider the range of goals you might have for your students.

"AND THEN, OF COURSE, THERE'S THE POSSIBILITY OF BEING JUST THE SLIGHTEST BIT TOO ORGANIZED."
(By permission of Glen Dines. From *Phi Delta Kappan*.)

Objectives for Learning

We hear quite a bit today about visions, goals, outcomes, and standards. At a very general, abstract level are the grand goals society may have for graduates of public schools (e.g., that all graduates have effective communication and problem-solving skills). However, very general goals are meaningless as potential guidelines for instruction. Therefore, many provinces (e.g., British Columbia, Manitoba, Ontario) are developing standards that provide more specific descriptions of how students will demonstrate progress toward the attainment of grand goals (e.g., students will develop the concept of fractions, mixed numbers, and decimals and use models to relate fractions to decimals and to find equivalent fractions). Sometimes the standards are turned into indicators such as "representing equivalent fractions" (Anderson & Krathwohl, 2001, p. 18). At this level, the indicators are close to being instructional objectives.

Norman Gronlund (2004) defines **instructional objectives** as intended learning outcomes, or the types of performance students will demonstrate after instruction to show what they have learned. Although there are many different approaches to writing objectives, each assumes that the first step in teaching is to decide what changes should take place in the learner—what is the goal of teaching. When people with behavioural views write objectives, they focus on observable and measurable changes in the learner. **Behavioural objectives** use terms such as *list*, *define*, *add*, or *calculate*. **Cognitive objectives**, on the other hand, emphasize thinking and comprehension, so they are more likely to include words such as *understand*, *recognize*, *create*, or *apply*. Let us look more closely at two different methods of writing instructional objectives: one that reflects behaviourist views of learning and another based on cognitive views of learning.

instructional objectives Clear statement of what students are intended to learn through instruction.

behavioural objectives Instructional objectives stated in terms of observable behaviour.

cognitive objectives Instructional objectives stated in terms of higher-level thinking operations.

Mager: Start with the Specific.   Robert Mager has developed a very influential system for writing instructional objectives (Mager, 1975). Mager's idea is that objectives ought to describe what students will be doing when demonstrating their achievement and how you will know they are doing it. Mager's objectives are generally regarded as *behavioural*. According to Mager, a good objective has three parts. First, it describes the intended student behaviour—what must the student do? Second, it lists the conditions under which the behaviour will occur—how will this behaviour be recognized or tested? Third, it gives the criteria for acceptable performance on the test. This system, with its emphasis on final behaviour, requires a very explicit statement. Mager contends that often students can teach themselves if they are given well-stated objectives.

Gronlund: Start with the General.   Norman Gronlund (2004) offers a different approach, often used for writing cognitive objectives. He believes that an objective should be stated first in general terms (*understand, solve, appreciate*, etc.). Then the teacher should clarify by listing examples of behaviour that would provide evidence that the student has attained the objective. Look at the example in Table 12.1 on page 466. The goal here is presenting and defending a research project. A teacher could never list all the behaviours that might be involved in "presenting and defending," but stating an initial, general objective along with specific examples makes the purpose clear.

The most recent research on instructional objectives tends to favour approaches similar to Gronlund's. James Popham (2005), a former proponent of very specific objectives, makes this recommendation:

> Strive to come up with a half dozen or so truly salient, broad, yet measurable instructional objectives for your own classroom. Too many small-scope, hyperspecific objectives will be of scant value to you because, if you're at all normal, you'll soon disregard [them]. On the other hand, a small number of intellectually manageable, broad, yet measurable objectives will not only prove helpful to you instructionally but will also help you answer the what-to-assess question. (pp. 104–105)

Connect & Extend

TO YOUR OWN PHILOSOPHY
What is your reaction to the following statement? "Behavioural objectives often may be appropriate for training (an end in itself) but are seldom appropriate for education (which is concerned with understanding)."

TABLE 12.1 Gronlund's Combined Method for Creating Objectives
General Objective
Presents and defends the research project before a group.
Specific Examples
1. Describes the project in a well-organized manner.
2. Summarizes the findings and their implications.
3. Uses display materials to clarify ideas and relationships.
4. Answers group members' questions directly and completely.
5. Presents a report that reflects careful planning.
6. Displays sound reasoning ability through presentation and answers to questions.
Source: Gronlund, N. Gronlund's combined method for creating objectives. *How to write and use instructional objectives* (6th ed.) © 2000. Adapted by permission of Pearson Education, Inc., Upper Saddle River, NJ.

Flexible and Creative Plans—Using Taxonomies

taxonomy Classification system.

Fifty years ago, a group of experts in educational evaluation led by Benjamin Bloom set out to improve college and university examinations. The impact of their work has touched education at all levels around the world (Anderson & Sosniak, 1994). Bloom and his colleagues developed a **taxonomy**, or classification system, of educational objectives. Objectives were divided into three domains: cognitive, affective, and psychomotor. A handbook describing the objectives in each area was eventually published. In real life, of course, behaviour from these three domains occurs simultaneously. While students are writing (psychomotor), they are also remembering or reasoning (cognitive), and they are likely to have some emotional response to the task as well (affective).

cognitive domain In Bloom's taxonomy, memory and reasoning objectives.

The Cognitive Domain.   Six basic objectives are listed in Bloom's taxonomy of the thinking or **cognitive domain** (Bloom et al., 1956):

Planning involves designating learning goals, making decisions about how to help students achieve them, and assessing their success. Tactics may or may not involve written tasks.

1. *Knowledge:* Remembering or recognizing something without necessarily understanding, using, or changing it.
2. *Comprehension:* Understanding the material being communicated without necessarily relating it to anything else.
3. *Application:* Using a general concept to solve a particular problem.
4. *Analysis:* Breaking something down into its parts.
5. *Synthesis:* Creating something new by combining different ideas.
6. *Evaluation:* Judging the value of materials or methods as they might be applied in a particular situation.

It is common in education to consider these objectives as a hierarchy, each skill building on those below, but such a view is not entirely accurate. Some subjects, such as mathematics, do not fit this structure very well (Kreitzer & Madaus, 1994). Still, you will hear many references to *lower-level* and *higher-level objectives,* with knowledge, comprehension, and application considered lower level and the other categories considered higher level. As a rough way of thinking about objectives, this classification can be helpful (Gronlund, 2004).

The taxonomy of objectives can also be helpful in planning assessments because different procedures are appropriate for objectives at the various levels. Gronlund (2004) suggests that factual knowledge objectives can best be measured by true/false, short-answer, matching, or multiple-choice tests. Such tests also work with the comprehension, application, and analysis levels of the taxonomy. For measuring synthesis and evaluation objectives, however, essays, reports, projects, and portfolios are more appropriate. Essay tests also work at the middle levels of the taxonomy.

Bloom 2001. Bloom's taxonomy has guided educators for over 50 years and is considered among the most significant educational writings of the 20th century (Anderson & Sosniak, 1994). In 2001, a group of educational researchers met to discuss revising the taxonomy (Anderson & Krathwohl, 2001). The new version retains the six basic levels in a slightly different order, but the names of three levels have been changed to indicate the cognitive processes involved. The six cognitive processes are remembering (knowledge), understanding (comprehension), applying, analyzing, evaluating, and creating (synthesizing). In addition, the revisers have added a new dimension to the taxonomy to recognize that cognitive processes must process something—you have to remember or understand or apply some form of knowledge. Table 12.2 summarizes the resulting model by showing that six processes—the cognitive acts of remembering, understanding, applying, analyzing, evaluating, and creating—act on four kinds of knowledge—factual, conceptual, procedural, and metacognitive.

Consider how this revised taxonomy might suggest objectives for a social studies/language arts class. For example, an objective that targets *analysis of conceptual knowledge* might be:

> After reading a historical account of the framing of Canada's Constitution, students will be able to recognize the author's point of view or bias.

An objective for evaluating metacognitive knowledge might be:

> Students will reflect on their strategies for identifying the biases of the author.

The Affective Domain. The objectives in the taxonomy of the **affective domain,** or domain of emotional response, have not yet been revised from the original version. They range from least committed to most committed (Krathwohl, Bloom, & Masia, 1964). At the lowest level, students simply pay attention to a certain idea. At the highest level, students adopt an idea or a value and act consistently with that idea. There are five basic objectives in the affective domain:

affective domain Realm of attitudes and feelings.

1. *Receiving:* Being aware of or attending to something in the environment. This is the "I'll-listen-to-the-concert-but-I-won't-promise-to-like-it" level.

2. *Responding:* Showing some new behaviour as a result of experience. At this level, a person might applaud after the concert or hum some of the music the next day.

TABLE 12.2 A Revised Taxonomy in the Cognitive Domain

The Knowledge Dimension	The Cognitive Process Dimension					
	1. Remember	2. Understand	3. Apply	4. Analyze	5. Evaluate	6. Create
A. Factual Knowledge						
B. Conceptual Knowledge						
C. Procedural Knowledge						
D. Metacognitive Knowledge						

Source: From Anderson, L. W., & Krathwohl, D. R. (Eds.). (2001). *A taxonomy for learning, teaching, and assessing: A revision of Bloom's taxonomy of educational objectives.* New York: Addison-Wesley Longman. Copyright © 2000 by Addison-Wesley Longman. Adapted with permission.

3. *Valuing:* Showing some definite involvement or commitment. At this point, a person might choose to go to a concert instead of a film.

4. *Organization:* Integrating a new value into one's general set of values, giving it some ranking among one's general priorities. This is the level at which a person would begin to make long-range commitments to concert attendance.

5. *Characterization by value:* Acting consistently with the new value. At this highest level, a person would be firmly committed to a love of music and demonstrate it openly and consistently.

Like the basic objectives in the cognitive domain, these five objectives are very general. To write specific learning objectives, you must state what students will actually be doing when they are receiving, responding, valuing, and so on. For example, an objective for a nutrition class at the valuing level (showing involvement or commitment) might be stated as follows: "After completing the unit on food contents and labelling, at least 50 percent of the class will commit to a junk-food boycott project by giving up candy for a month."

psychomotor domain Realm of physical ability and coordination objectives.

The Psychomotor Domain. Until recently, the **psychomotor domain,** or the realm of physical ability objectives, has been mostly overlooked by teachers not directly involved with physical education. There are several taxonomies in this domain (e.g., Harrow, 1972; Simpson, 1972) that generally move from basic perceptions and reflex actions to skilled, creative movements. James Cangelosi (1990) provides a useful way to think about objectives in the psychomotor domain either as voluntary muscle capabilities that require endurance, strength, flexibility, agility, and speed or as the ability to perform a specific skill.

Objectives in the psychomotor domain should be of interest to a wide range of educators, including those in fine arts, vocational-technical education, and special education. Many other subjects, such as chemistry, physics, and biology, also require specialized movements and well-developed hand and eye coordination. Using lab equipment, the mouse on a computer, or art materials means learning new physical skills. Here are two examples of psychomotor objectives:

Four minutes after completing a 1.6-kilometre run in eight minutes or under, your heart rate will be below 120.

Use a computer mouse effectively to "drag and drop" files.

Whatever your instructional objectives for your students, Terry TenBrink (2006, p. 57) suggests the following four criteria. Objectives should be

1. Student-oriented (emphasis on what the student is expected to do).

2. Descriptive of an appropriate learning *outcome* (both developmentally appropriate and appropriately sequenced, with more complex objectives following prerequisite objectives).

3. Clear and understandable (not too general or too specific).

4. Observable (avoid outcomes you can't see such as "appreciating" or "realizing").

The accompanying Guidelines should help you whether you use objectives for every lesson or for just a few assignments.

Another View: Planning from a Constructivist Perspective

constructivist approach View that emphasizes the active role of the learner in building understanding and making sense of information.

Traditionally, it has been the teacher's responsibility to do most of the planning for instruction, but new ways of planning are developing. In **constructivist approaches,** planning is shared and negotiated. The teacher and students together make decisions about content, activities, and approaches. Rather than having specific student behaviour and skills as objectives, the teacher has overarching goals—"big ideas"—that guide planning. These goals are understandings or abilities that the teacher returns to again and again.

USING INSTRUCTIONAL OBJECTIVES

Avoid "word magic"—phrases that sound noble and important but say very little, such as, "Students will become deep thinkers."

EXAMPLES

1. Keep the focus on specific changes that will take place in the students' knowledge of skills.

2. Ask students to explain the meaning of the objectives. If they can't give specific examples of what you mean, the objectives are not communicating your intentions to your students.

Suit the activities to the objectives.

EXAMPLES

1. If the goal is the memorization of vocabulary, give the students memory aids and practice exercises.

2. If the goal is the ability to develop well-thought-out positions, consider position papers, debates, projects, or mock trials.

3. If you want students to become better writers, give many opportunities for writing and rewriting.

Make sure that your tests are related to your objectives.

EXAMPLES

1. Write objectives and rough drafts for tests at the same time. Revise these drafts of tests as the units unfold and objectives change.

2. Weight the tests according to the importance of the various objectives and the time spent on each.

An Example of Constructivist Planning. Vito Perrone (1994) has these goals for his secondary history students. He wants his students to be able to

- use primary sources, formulate hypotheses, and engage in systematic study;
- handle multiple points of view;
- be close readers and active writers;
- pose and solve problems.

The next step in the planning process is to create a learning environment that allows students to move toward these goals in ways that respect their individual interests and abilities. Perrone (1994) suggests identifying "those ideas, themes, and issues that provide the depth and variety of perspective that help students develop significant understandings" (p. 12). For a secondary history course, a theme might be "democracy and revolution" or "fairness concerning land claims." A theme in math or music might be "patterns"; in literature, "personal identity." Perrone suggests mapping the topic as a way of thinking about how the theme can generate learning and understanding. An example of a topic map, using the theme of ecology, is shown in Figure 12.1 on page 470.

With this topic map as a guide, teacher and students can work together to identify activities, materials, projects, and performances that will support the development of the students' understanding and abilities—the overarching goals of the class. The teacher spends less time planning specific presentations and assignments and more time gathering a variety of resources and facilitating students' learning. The focus is not so much on students' products as on the processes of learning and the thinking behind the products.

Integrated and Thematic Plans. Perrone's planning map shows a way to use the theme of ecology to integrate issues in a science class. Today, teaching with themes and with integrated content are major elements in planning and designing lessons and units, from kindergarten (Roskos & Neuman, 1998) through high school (Clarke & Agne, 1997). For example, middle school teachers Elaine Homestead and Karen McGinnis and college professor Elizabeth Pate (Pate, McGinnis, & Homestead, 1995) designed a unit, "Human Interactions," that included studying racism, world hunger, pollution, and air and water quality. Students researched issues by

Figure 12.1 Planning with a Topic Map

With this map of the topic "ecology," a grade 6 teacher can identify themes, issues, and ideas for study. Rather than "cover" the whole map, the teacher can examine a few areas in depth.

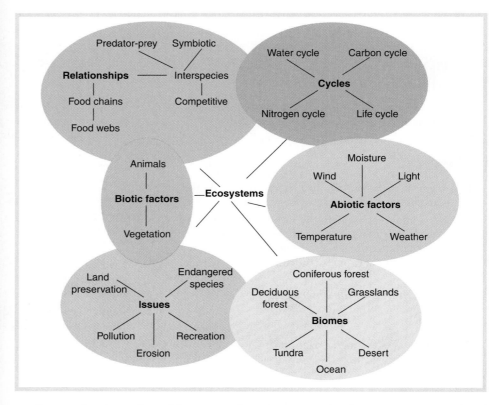

reading textbooks and outside sources, learning to use databases, interviewing local officials, and inviting guest speakers into class. Students had to develop knowledge in science, mathematics, and social studies. They learned to write and speak persuasively, and in the process raised money for hunger relief in Africa.

Elementary-age students can benefit from integrated planning too. There is no reason to work on spelling skills, then listening skills, then writing skills, and then social studies or science. All these abilities can be developed together if students work to solve authentic problems. Themes for younger children can include, for example, people, pets, gardens as habitats, communities, and patterns. Possibilities for older children are given in Table 12.3.

Check Your Knowledge

- What are the levels of planning, and how do they affect teaching?
- What is an instructional objective?
- Describe the three taxonomies of educational objectives.
- Describe teacher-centred and student-centred planning.

Apply to Practice

- Identify a cognitive, affective, and psychomotor objective for yourself for this week.
- Name a theme that could organize your planning for a grade you might teach.

TABLE 12.3 Some Themes for Integrated Planning for Older Children

General Systems Theory	Graphical Representations of Patterns
The Politics of Biology	Field-Based Research
Cause and Effect	Probability and Prediction
Levels of Analysis	Diversity and Variation
Conditional and Enabling Relations	Stewardship
Darwinism	Conservation of Energy and Matter

Let's assume you and your students have valuable and interesting plans and learning objectives. What next? You still need to decide what is happening on Monday. You need to design tasks and activities for teaching and learning that are appropriate for the objectives. You have an idea of *what* you want students to understand, but *how* do you teach to encourage understanding?

TEACHER-DIRECTED INSTRUCTION

What Would You Say?

In your interview for the last remaining opening in the district of your dreams, the principal asks, "What is the best lesson you have taught so far? Tell me all about it and especially about what made it so good."

In this section, we turn to examining a variety of strategies that reflect teacher-led, or teacher-directed, formats for turning objectives into action in the classroom. These strategies are not complete models of teaching, but rather building blocks that can be used to construct lessons and units. We begin with the strategy many people associate most directly with teaching: explanation and direct instruction.

Explanation and Direct Instruction

Some studies have found that teacher-led instruction takes up one-sixth to one-fourth of all classroom time. Teacher explanation is appropriate for communicating a large amount of material to many students in a short period of time, introducing a new topic, giving background information, or motivating students to learn more on their own. Teacher-led instruction is therefore most appropriate for cognitive and affective objectives at the lower levels of the taxonomies described earlier: for remembering, understanding, applying, receiving, responding, and valuing (Arends, 2001; Kindsvatter, Wilen, & Ishler, 1992). Student-centred approaches that rely heavily on students' active construction of meaning are more appropriate for higher levels of learning and self-regulated learning. These will be described in the next main section.

Direct Instruction. In the 1970s and 1980s, there was an explosion of research that focused on effective teaching. The results of all this work identified a model of teaching that was related to improved student learning. Barak Rosenshine calls this approach **direct instruction** (1979) or **explicit teaching** (1986). Tom Good (1983a) uses the term **active teaching** for a similar approach.

The direct instruction model fits a specific set of circumstances because it was derived from a particular approach to research. Researchers identified the elements of direct instruction by comparing teachers whose students learned more than expected (based on entering knowledge) with teachers whose students performed at an expected or average level. The researchers focused on existing practices in American classrooms. Because the focus was on traditional forms of teaching, the research could not identify successful innovations. Effectiveness was usually defined as average improvement in standardized test scores for a whole class or school. So the results hold for large groups, but not necessarily for every student in the group. Even when the average achievement of a group improves, the achievement of some individuals may decline (Brophy & Good, 1986; Good, 1996; Shuell, 1996).

Given these conditions, direct instruction applies best to the teaching of **basic skills**—clearly structured knowledge and essential skills, such as science facts, mathematics computations, reading vocabulary, and grammar rules (Rosenshine & Stevens, 1986). These skills involve tasks that are relatively unambiguous; they can be taught step-by-step and tested objectively. Direct instruction is not necessarily appropriate for objectives such as helping students write creatively, solve

direct instruction/explicit teaching Systematic instruction for mastery of basic skills, facts, and information.

active teaching Teaching characterized by high levels of teacher explanation, demonstration, and interaction with students.

basic skills Clearly structured knowledge that is needed for later learning and that can be taught step by step.

complex problems, or mature emotionally. Weinert and Helmke (1995) describe effective direct instruction as having the following features:

(a) the teacher's classroom management is especially effective and the rate of student interruptive behaviors is very low; (b) the teacher maintains a strong academic focus and uses available instructional time intensively to initiate and facilitate students' learning activities; (c) the teacher insures that as many students as possible achieve good learning progress by carefully choosing appropriate tasks, clearly presenting subject-matter information and solution strategies, continuously diagnosing each student's learning progress and learning difficulties, and providing effective help through remedial instruction. (p. 138)

But how exactly can teachers ensure that their direct instruction has these characteristics and is effective in practice?

Rosenshine's Six Teaching Functions.   Rosenshine and his colleagues (Rosenshine, 1988; Rosenshine & Stevens, 1986) have identified six teaching functions based on the research on effective instruction. These can serve as a checklist or framework for teaching basic skills.

1. *Review and check the previous day's work.* Reteach if students misunderstood or made errors.

2. *Present new material.* Make the purpose clear, teach in small steps, and provide many examples and non-examples.

3. *Provide guided practice.* Question students, give practice problems, and listen for misconceptions and misunderstandings. Reteach if necessary. Continue guided practice until students answer about 80 percent of the questions correctly.

4. *Give feedback and correctives* based on student answers. Reteach if necessary.

5. *Provide independent practice.* Let students apply the new learning on their own, in seatwork, cooperative groups, or homework. The success rate during independent practice should be about 95 percent. This means that students must be well prepared for the work by the presentation and guided practice and that assignments must not be too difficult. The point is for the students to practise until the skills become overlearned and automatic—until the students are confident. Hold students accountable for the work they do—check it.

6. *Review weekly and monthly* to consolidate learning. Include some review items as homework. Test often, and reteach material missed on the tests.

These six functions are not steps to be followed in a particular order, but all of them are elements of effective instruction. For example, feedback, review, or reteaching should occur whenever necessary and should match the abilities of the students. Also, keep in mind the age and prior knowledge of your students. The younger or the less prepared your students, the briefer your explanations should be. Use more and shorter cycles of presentation, guided practice, feedback, and correctives.

Why Does Direct Instruction Work? What aspects of direct instruction might explain its success? Linda Anderson (1989b) suggests that lessons that help students perceive links among main ideas help them construct accurate understandings. Well-organized presentations, clear explanations, the use of explanatory links, and reviews can all help students perceive connections among ideas. If done well, therefore, a direct instruction lesson may be a resource that students use to construct understanding. For example, reviews activate prior knowledge, so that students are ready to understand. Brief, clear presentations and guided practice avoid overloading the students' information processing systems and taxing their working memories. Numerous examples and explanations give many pathways and associations for building networks of concepts. Guided practice can also give the teacher a snapshot of the students' thinking as well as their misconceptions,

Connect & Extend

TO THE RESEARCH
For another perspective, read Berg, C. A., & Clough, M. (1991). Hunter lesson design: The wrong one for science teaching. *Educational Leadership, 48*(4), 73–78. *Focus Questions*: Why do Berg and Clough believe that the Hunter design is the wrong one for science teaching? How do you think Hunter would react? Then read Hunter, M. (1991). Hunter design helps achieve the goals of science instruction. *Educational Leadership, 48*(4), 79–81. *Focus Questions*: Evaluate Hunter's defence of her model. Do you agree that the Hunter approach can achieve the goals of science instruction?

IS HOMEWORK A VALUABLE USE OF TIME?

Like so many methods in education, homework has moved in and out of favour. In the early 1900s, homework was seen as an important path to mental discipline, but by the 1940s, homework was criticized as too much drill and low-level learning. Then in the 1950s, homework was rediscovered as a way for North American children to catch up with the Soviet Union in science and mathematics, only to be seen as too much pressure on students during the more laid-back 1960s. By the 1980s, homework was viewed as necessary for our students to compete with students around the world (Cooper & Valentine, 2001b). Everyone has done homework—were those hours well spent?

> Point Homework does not help students learn.

No matter how interesting an activity is, students will eventually get bored with it—so why give them work both in and out of school?

They will simply grow weary of learning. And important opportunities are lost for community involvement or leisure activities that would create well-rounded citizens. When parents help with homework, they can do more harm than good—sometimes confusing their children or teaching them incorrectly. And students from poorer families often must work, so they miss doing the homework; then the learning discrepancy between the rich and poor grows even greater. Besides, the research is inconsistent about the effects of homework. For example, one study found that in-class work was better than homework in helping elementary students learn (Cooper & Valentine, 2001b).

< Counterpoint Well-planned homework can work for many students.

Harris Cooper and Jeffrey Valentine reviewed many studies of homework and concluded that there is little

relationship between homework and learning for young students, but that the relationship between homework and achievement grows progressively stronger for older students. There is recent evidence that students in high school who do more homework (and watch less television after school) have higher grades, even when other factors such as gender, grade level, ethnicity, socioeconomic status, and amount of adult supervision are taken into consideration (Cooper & Valentine, 2001b; Cooper et al., 1999). Consistent with these findings, the National PTA in the United States makes these recommendations:

> For children in grades K–2, homework is most effective when it does not exceed 10–20 minutes each day; older students, in grades 3–6, can handle 30–60 minutes a day; in junior and senior high school, the amount of homework will vary by subject. (Henderson, 1996, p. 1)

is especially important for homework assignments because students may have no one at home to consult if they have problems with the assignment. A second way to keep students involved is to hold them accountable for completing the work correctly, not just for filling in the page. This means the work should be checked, the students given a chance to correct the errors or revise work, and the results counted toward the class grade (Brophy & Good, 1986). Expert teachers often have ways of correcting homework quickly during the first minutes of class by having students check each other's or their own work.

Making Seatwork and Homework Valuable. Seatwork in particular requires careful monitoring. Being available to students doing seatwork is more effective than offering students help before they ask for it. To be available, you should move around the class and avoid spending too much time with one or two students. Short, frequent contacts are best (Brophy & Good, 1986; Rosenshine, 1977). Sometimes you may be working with a small group while other students do seatwork. In these situations, it is especially important for students to know what to do if they need help. Nancy has observed in classrooms where students follow a rule, "Ask three, then me." Students have to consult three classmates before seeking help from the teacher. Teachers in these classrooms spend time early in the year showing students *how* to help each other—how to ask questions and how to explain.

What about monitoring homework? If students get stuck on homework, they need help at home, someone who can scaffold their work without just "giving the answer" (Pressley, 1995). But many family members don't know how to help

(Hoover-Dempsey et al., 2001; Hoover-Dempsey, Bassler, & Burow, 1995). The Family and Community Partnerships box below includes ideas for helping families help with homework.

Questioning and Recitation

Teachers pose questions; students answer. This form of teaching, sometimes called *recitation,* has been with us for many years (Stodolsky, 1988). The teacher's questions develop a framework for the subject matter involved. The students' answers are often followed by reactions from the teacher, such as praise, correction, or requests for further information. The pattern from the teacher's point of view consists of *initiation* (teacher asks questions), *response* (student answers), and *reaction* (praising, correcting, probing or expanding) or IRE (Burbules & Bruce, 2001). These steps are repeated over and over.

Let us consider the heart of recitation, the initiation, or *questioning,* phase. Effective questioning techniques may be among the most powerful tools teachers

---

FAMILY AND COMMUNITY PARTNERSHIPS

HOMEWORK

Make sure that families know what students are expected to learn.

EXAMPLES

1. At the beginning of a unit, send home a list of the main objectives, examples of major assignments, key due dates, homework "calendar," and a list of resources available free at libraries or on the internet.

2. Provide a clear, concise description of your homework policy—how homework is counted toward class grades; consequences for late, forgotten, or missing homework; etc.

Help families find a comfortable and helpful role in their child's homework.

EXAMPLES

1. Remind families that "helping with homework" means encouraging, listening, monitoring, praising, discussing, brainstorming—not necessarily teaching and never doing the work for their child.

2. Encourage families to set aside a quiet time and place for everyone in the family to study. Make this time a regular part of the daily routine.

3. Have some homework assignments that are fun and involve the whole family—puzzles, family albums, watching a television program together and doing a "review."

4. At parent–teacher conferences, ask families what they need to play a helpful role in their child's homework.

Solicit and use suggestions from families about homework.

EXAMPLES

1. Find out what responsibilities the child has at home—how much time is available for homework.

2. Periodically, have a "homework hotline" for call-in questions and suggestions.

If no one is at home to help with homework, set up other support systems.

EXAMPLES

1. Assign study buddies who can be available over the phone.

2. If students have computers, provide lists of internet help lines.

3. Locate free help in public libraries and make these resources known.

Take advantage of family and community "funds of knowledge" to connect homework with life in the community and life in the community with lessons in school (Moll et al., 1992).

EXAMPLES

1. Create a lesson about how family members use math and reading in sewing and in housing construction (Epstein & Van Voorhis, 2001).

2. Design interactive homework projects that families do together to evaluate needed products for their home; for example, deciding on the best buy on shampoo or paper towels.

employ during lessons. An essential element of innovations such as cognitive apprenticeships, peer learning techniques, authentic learning activities, and nearly all other contemporary learning techniques is keeping students cognitively engaged—and that is where skilful questioning strategies are especially effective. Questions play several roles in cognition. They can help students rehearse information for effective recall. They can work to identify gaps in their knowledge base and provoke curiosity and long-term interest. They can initiate cognitive conflict and promote the disequilibrium that results in a changed knowledge structure. They can serve as cues, tips, or reminders. And students as well as teachers should learn to question effectively. We tell our students that the first step in doing a good research project is asking a good question.

For now, we will focus on teachers' questions, to make them as helpful as possible for students. Many beginning teachers are surprised to discover how valuable good questions can be and how difficult they are to create.

Kinds of Questions.   Some educators have estimated that the typical teacher asks between 30 and 120 questions an hour, or about 1 500 000 questions over a teaching career (Sadker & Sadker, 2006). What are these questions like? Many can be categorized in terms of Bloom's taxonomy of objectives in the cognitive domain. Table 12.5 on page 478 offers examples of questions at the different taxonomic levels.

Another way to categorize questioning is in terms of **convergent questions** (only one right answer) or **divergent questions** (many possible answers). Questions about concrete facts are convergent: "Who ruled England in 1540?" "Who wrote the original *Peter Pan*?" Questions dealing with opinions or hypotheses are divergent: "In this story, which character is most like you and why?" "In 100 years, which of the past five prime ministers will be most admired?"

Quite a bit of space in education textbooks has been devoted to urging teachers to ask a greater number of higher-level (analysis, synthesis, and evaluation) and divergent questions. Is this really a better way of questioning? Research has provided several surprises.

Fitting the Questions to the Students.   Both high- and low-level questions can be effective (Barden, 1995; Redfield & Rousseau, 1981), although whether a question is actually high- or low-level depends on the student's knowledge (Winne, 1979). Different patterns seem to be better for different students, however. The best pattern for younger students and for lower-ability students of all ages is simple questions that allow a high percentage of correct answers, ample encouragement, help when the student does not have the correct answer, and praise. For high-ability students, the successful pattern includes harder questions at both higher and lower levels and more critical feedback (Berliner, 1987; Good, 1988).

Whatever their age or ability, all students should have some experience with thought-provoking questions and, if necessary, help in learning how to answer them. As we saw in Chapter 8, to master critical thinking and problem-solving skills, students must have a chance to practise the skills. They also need time to think about their answers. But research shows that teachers wait an average of only one second for students to answer (Rowe, 1974). Consider the following slice of classroom life (Sadker & Sadker, 2006, pp. 130–131):

Teacher: Who wrote the poem "Stopping by Woods on a Snowy Evening"? Tom?

Tom: Robert Frost.

Teacher: Good. What action takes place in the poem? Sally?

Sally: A man stops his sleigh to watch the woods get filled with snow.

Teacher: Yes. Emma, what thoughts go through the man's mind?

Emma: He thinks how beautiful the woods are ... (*She pauses for a second.*)

Teacher: What else does he think about? Joe?

convergent questions Questions that have a single correct answer.

divergent questions Questions that have no single correct answer.

TABLE 12.5 Classroom Questions for Objectives in the Cognitive Domain

Thinking at different levels of Bloom's taxonomy in the cognitive domain can be encouraged by different questions. Of course, the thinking required depends on what has gone before in the discussion.

Category	Type of Thinking Expected	Examples
Knowledge (recognition)	Recalling or recognizing information as learned	Define ... What is the capital of ...? What did the text say about ...?
Comprehension	Demonstrating understanding of the materials; transforming, reorganizing, or interpreting	Explain in your own words ... Compare ... What is the main idea of ...? Describe what you saw ...
Application	Using information to solve a problem with a single correct answer	Which principle is demonstrated in ...? Calculate the area of ... Apply the rule of ... to solve ...
Analysis	Critical thinking; identifying reasons and motives; making inferences based on specific data; analyzing conclusions to see if supported by evidence	What influenced the writings of ...? Why was Ottawa chosen ...? Which of the following are facts and which are opinions ...? Based on your experiment, what is the chemical ...?
Synthesis	Divergent, original thinking; original plan, proposal, design, or story	What's a good name for ...? How could we raise money for ...? What would Canada be like if the Bloc Québécois were the official opposition?
Evaluation	Judging the merits of ideas, offering opinions, applying standards	Which prime minister was the most effective? Which painting do you believe to be better? Why? Why would you favour ...?

Source: Adapted from Sadker, M., & Sadker, D. (1986). Questioning skills. In J. Cooper (Ed.), *Classroom teaching skills: A Handbook* (3rd ed., pp. 143–160). Boston: D. C. Heath. Adapted by permission of D. C. Heath.

Joe: He thinks how he would like to stay and watch. (Pauses for a second.)

Teacher: Yes—and what else? Rita? (*Waits half a second.*) Come on, Rita, you can get the answer to this. (*Waits half a second.*) Well, why does he feel he can't stay there indefinitely and watch the woods and the snow?

Sarah: Well, I think it might be ... (*Pauses for a second.*)

Teacher: Think, Sarah. (*Teacher waits for half a second.*) All right then— Mike? (*Waits again for half a second.*) John? (*Waits half a second.*) What's the matter with everyone today? Didn't you do the reading?

Very little thoughtful responding can take place in this situation. When teachers learn to pose a question, then wait at least three to five seconds before calling on a student to answer, students tend to give longer answers; more students are likely to participate, ask questions, and volunteer appropriate answers; student comments involving analysis, synthesis, inference, and speculation tend to increase; and the students generally appear more confident in their answers (Berliner, 1987; Rowe, 1974; Sadker & Sadker, 2006).

This seems to be a simple improvement in teaching, but five seconds of silence is not that easy to handle. It takes practice. You might try asking students to jot down ideas or even to discuss the question with another student and formulate an answer together. This makes the wait more comfortable and gives students a chance to think. Of course, if it is clear that students are lost or don't understand the question, waiting longer will not help. When your question is met with blank stares, rephrase the question or ask if anyone can explain the confusion. Also, there is some evidence that extending wait times does not affect learning in university classes (Duell, 1994), so with advanced high school students, you may want to conduct your own evaluation of wait time.

Finally, if you call only on volunteers when selecting students to answer questions, you may get the wrong idea about how well students understand the material. Also, the same people volunteer over and over again. Many expert teachers have some systematic way of making sure that they call on everyone; they may pull names from a jar or check names off a list as each student speaks (Weinstein, 2003; Weinstein & Mignano, 2003). Another possibility is to put each student's name on an index card, then shuffle the cards and go through the deck as you call on people. You can use the card to make notes about students' answers or extra help they may need.

Responding to Student Answers.   What do you do after the student answers? The most common response, occurring about 50 percent of the time in most classrooms, is simple acceptance—"Okay" or "Uh-huh" (Sadker & Sadker, 2006). But there are better reactions, depending on whether the student's answer is correct, partly correct, or wrong. If the answer is quick, firm, and correct, simply accept the answer or ask another question. If the answer is correct but hesitant, give the student feedback about why the answer is correct: "That's right, Chris, the Governor General is the Queen's representative in Canada." This allows you to explain the material again. If this student is unsure, others may be confused as well. If the answer is partially or completely wrong but the student has made an honest attempt, you should probe for more information, give clues, simplify the question, review the previous steps, or reteach the material. If the student's wrong answer is silly or careless, however, it is better simply to correct the answer and go on (Good, 1988; Rosenshine & Stevens, 1986).

Group Discussion

Group discussion is in some ways similar to the recitation strategy described in the previous section but should be more like the instructional conversations described in Chapter 9 (Tharp & Gallimore, 1991). A teacher may pose questions, listen to student answers, react, and probe for more information, but in a true group discussion, the teacher does not have a dominant role. Students ask questions, answer each other's questions, and respond to each other's answers (Beck et al., 1996; Burbules & Bruce, 2001; Parker & Hess, 2001).

There are many advantages to group discussions. The students are directly involved and have the chance to participate. Group discussion helps students learn to express themselves clearly, to justify opinions, and to tolerate different views. Group discussion also gives students a chance to ask for clarification, examine their own thinking, follow personal interests, and assume responsibility by taking leadership roles in the group. Thus, group discussions help students evaluate ideas and synthesize personal viewpoints. Discussions are also useful when students are trying to understand difficult concepts that go against common sense. As we saw in Chapters 8 and 9, many scientific concepts, such as the role of light in vision or Newton's laws of motion, are difficult to grasp because they contradict common sense notions. By thinking together, challenging each other, and suggesting and evaluating possible explanations, students are more likely to reach a genuine understanding.

Of course, there are disadvantages. Class discussions are quite unpredictable and may easily digress into exchanges of ignorance. Some members of the group may have great difficulty participating and may become anxious if forced to speak. In addition, you may have to do a good deal of preparation to ensure that participants have a background of knowledge on which to base the discussion. And large

group discussion Conversation in which the teacher does not have the dominant role; students pose and answer their own questions.

groups are often unwieldy. In many cases, a few students will dominate the discussion while the others daydream (Arends, 2004; Freiberg & Driscoll, 2005). The Guidelines below give some ideas for facilitating a productive group discussion.

Check Your Knowledge

- What is direct instruction?
- Distinguish between convergent and divergent questions and between high-level and low-level questions.
- How can wait time affect student learning?
- What are the uses and disadvantages of group discussion?

Apply to Practice

- What are some alternatives to seatwork?
- Give examples of convergent and divergent questions in your subject area.

GUIDELINES
PRODUCTIVE GROUP DISCUSSIONS

Invite shy children to participate.

EXAMPLES

1. "What's your opinion, Joel? We need to hear from some other students."
2. Don't wait until there is a deadly silence to ask shy students to reply. Most people, even those who are confident, hate to break a silence.

Direct student comments and questions back to another student.

EXAMPLES

1. "That's an unusual idea, Steve. Kim, what do you think of Steve's idea?"
2. "That's an important question, John. Maura, do you have any thoughts about how you'd answer that?"
3. Encourage students to look at and talk to one another rather than wait for your opinion.

Make sure you understand what a student has said. If you are unsure, other students may be unsure as well.

EXAMPLES

1. Ask a second student to summarize what the first student said; then the first student can try again to explain if the summary is incorrect.
2. "Jasdev, I think you're saying …. Is that right, or have I misunderstood?"

Probe for more information.

EXAMPLES

1. "That's a strong statement. Do you have any evidence to back it up?"
2. "Tell us how you reached that conclusion. What steps did you go through?"

Bring the discussion back to the subject.

EXAMPLES

1. "Let's see, we were discussing … and Sarah made one suggestion. Does anyone have a different idea?"
2. "Before we continue, let me try to summarize what has happened so far."

Give time for thought before asking for responses.

EXAMPLE

1. "How would your life be different if television had never been invented? Jot down your ideas on paper, and we will share reactions in a minute." After a minute: "Hiromi, will you tell us what you wrote?"

When a student finishes speaking, look around the room to judge reactions.

EXAMPLES

1. If other students look puzzled, ask them to describe why they are confused.
2. If students are nodding assent, ask them to give an example of what was just said.

We have been looking at instructional planning and some basic teaching formats associated with teacher-led, or direct, instruction. Now we turn to formats associated with teaching that is student-centred.

STUDENT-CENTRED TEACHING: EXAMPLES IN READING, MATHEMATICS, AND SCIENCE

What do we know about good teaching in student-centred instruction? Table 12.6 lists some student-centred teaching practices, which reflect constructivist views of learning described earlier in this chapter and in Chapter 9. It is clear that a teacher's knowledge of the subject is critical for teaching (Ball, Lubienski, & Mewborn, 2001; Borko & Putnam, 1996). Part of that knowledge is pedagogical content knowledge, or knowing how to teach a subject to your particular students (Shulman, 1987). In the past decade, researchers have made great progress in understanding how students learn, or construct understandings, about different subjects (Mayer, 1992b; 1999). Below we describe approaches to teaching reading, mathematics, and science that are based on these recent research findings.

Learning and Teaching Reading and Writing

For years, educators have debated whether students should be taught to read and write through code-based (phonics, skills) approaches that relate letters to sounds and sounds to words or through meaning-based (whole language, literature-based, emergent literacy) approaches that do not dissect words and sentences into pieces but instead focus on the meaning of the text (Barr, 2001; Carlisle, Stahl, &

Connect & Extend

TO YOUR TEACHING

If you have observed in a primary grade, would you say the teacher made good use of direct, teacher-led approaches to instruction? Why or why not?

Connect & Extend

TO YOUR OWN PHILOSOPHY

Can different formats, such as lecture or seatwork, be used in the service of different models, such as direct instruction or constructivist approaches?

TABLE 12.6 Constructivist Teaching Practices

Constructivist teachers should

1. encourage and accept student autonomy and initiative;
2. use raw data and primary sources, along with manipulative, interactive, and physical materials;
3. use cognitive terminology when framing tasks—e.g., "classify," "analyze," "predict," and "create";
4. allow student responses to drive lessons, shift instructional strategies, and alter content;
5. inquire about students' understandings of concepts before sharing their own understandings of those concepts;
6. encourage students to engage in dialogue, both with the teacher and with one another;
7. encourage student inquiry by asking thoughtful, open-ended questions and encouraging students to ask questions of each other;
8. seek elaboration of students' initial responses;
9. engage students in experiences that might engender contradictions to their initial hypotheses and then encourage discussion;
10. allow wait time after posing questions;
11. provide time for students to discover relationships and create metaphors.

Source: Adapted from Brooks, J. G., & Brooks, M. G. Becoming a constructivist teacher. In J. G. Brooks & M. G. Brooks. (1995). *In search of understanding: The case for constructivist classrooms* (pp. 101–118). Alexandria, VA: Association for Supervision and Curriculum Development. Copyright © 1995 by ASCD. Reprinted with permission.

Birdyshaw, 2004; Goodman & Goodman, 1990; Smith, 1994; Stahl & Miller, 1989; Symons, Woloshyn, & Pressley, 1994). Now the consensus is that the best approach to teaching reading and writing balances strategies from both code-based and meaning-based approaches. After all, we want our students to be both fluent and enthusiastic readers and writers.

Focus on Meaning.   Informed by theory and research in the fields of emergent literacy and developmental psychology, advocates of meaning-based approaches, such as whole language, believe that becoming literate is a natural process—much like mastering your native language—that begins long before children enter school. Also, consistent with cognitive and constructivist views of learning, whole language advocates believe that children actively create understandings of what it really means to read and to write by engaging in authentic reading and writing activities. Finally, they stress social aspects of learning to read and write. They emphasize how important it is for parents and teachers to model literate behaviour for developing readers and writers. From this **whole language perspective**, learning to read and write during the elementary-school years is part of a continuum of learning that begins at birth and continues through adulthood (Chapman, 1997). Teachers have to be astute observers of students' literacy development to determine the supports or resources students need to learn.

whole language perspective
A philosophical approach to teaching and learning that stresses learning through authentic, real-life tasks; it emphasizes using language to learn, integrating learning across skills and subjects, and respecting the language abilities of student and teacher.

In many whole language classrooms, teachers and students set goals and design curriculum together. In writing, for instance, students and teachers identify a purpose and an audience. For example, students might decide to write letters to the mayor of their city about her recycling policy. Using such activities is consistent with Lev Vygotsky's (1978) view that "writing should be incorporated into a task that is necessary and relevant for life. Only then can we be certain that it will develop not as a matter of hand and finger habits but as a really new and complex form of speech" (p. 118). Marilyn Chapman, at the University of British Columbia, agrees: "Children develop knowledge about writing primarily in the context of its purposeful use" (1997, p. 31). She also observes that the two main purposes for writing are to communicate with others and to facilitate students' thinking and learning.

Another hallmark of meaning-based approaches to instruction is their emphasis on integrating language processes—speaking, listening, reading, writing—across curricula and on teaching language and literacy skills in the context of meaningful curricular activities. Whole language advocates design instruction according to the belief that speaking, listening, reading, and writing processes are "integrated, mutually reinforcing … activities" (Gunderson, 1997, p. 226) that develop concurrently (Chapman, 1997). They also hold that specific skills are better taught in a context of meaningful activities rather than in isolation.

Clearly, whole language approaches to instruction have much to commend them. John Shapiro (1994), at the University of British Columbia, argues that children who experience whole language approaches do become effective readers and writers:

> Their vocabulary increases, they employ varied strategies in word recognition, their comprehension abilities range from simple literal recall to more sophisticated judgments about authors' intent, they read for pleasure and information, and, perhaps more importantly, they have positive attitudes toward reading [and writing]. (pp. 458–459)

But is whole language the whole story?

Students Need Knowledge about the Code.   There are now two decades of research demonstrating that skill in recognizing sounds and words supports reading. Keith Stanovich, at the Ontario Institute for Studies in Education, has conducted numerous studies that show that being able to identify many words as you read does not depend on using context to guess meaning (Stanovich, 1993/1994; Stanovich, West, & Freeman, 1984). In fact, it is almost the other way around— knowing words helps you make sense of context. Identifying words as you read is

Contemporary learning theories have sought to understand how students learn different subjects in different ways and how teaching methods might be adapted to these differences.

a highly automatic process. The more fluent and automatic you are in identifying words, the more effective you will be in getting meaning from context (Vandervelden & Siegel, 1995). It is the poorest readers who resort to using context to help them understand meaning (Pressley, 1996).

Many studies support the code-based position. For example, three different groups reported in the *Journal of Educational Psychology* (December 1991) that alphabetic coding and awareness of letter sounds are essential skills for acquiring word identification, so some direct teaching of the alphabet and phonics is helpful in learning to read. Stanovich (1993/1994) acknowledges that it is possible to "overdo the teaching of phonics," but he also contends that "some children in whole language classrooms do not pick up the alphabetic principle through simple immersion in print and writing activities, and such children need explicit instruction in alphabetic coding" (p. 285).

Being Sensible about Reading and Writing.   The results of high-quality studies indicate that

- Whole language approaches to reading and writing are most effective in preschool and kindergarten. Whole language gives children a good conceptual basis for reading and writing. The social interactions around reading and writing—reading big books, writing shared stories, examining pictures, discussing meaning—are activities that support literacy and mirror the early home experiences of children who come to school prepared to learn. Whole language approaches seem to improve students' motivation, interest, and attitude toward reading and help children understand the nature and purposes of reading and writing (Graham & Harris, 1994; Shapiro, 1994).
- Phonemic awareness—the sense that words are composed of separate sounds and that sounds are combined to say words—in kindergarten and grade 1 predicts literacy in later grades. If children do not have phonemic awareness in the early grades, direct teaching can dramatically improve their chances of long-term achievement in literacy (Pressley, 1996).
- Excellent primary school teachers balance their explicit teaching of decoding skills and their whole language instruction (Adams, Treiman, & Pressley, 1998; Vellutino, 1991; Wharton-McDonald, Pressley, & Mistretta, 1996). The Center for the Improvement of Early Reading Achievement (CIERA) has generated 10 research-based principles regarding early literacy development. These are outlined in Table 12.7 on page 484.

If students need help cracking the code, give them what they need. Don't let ideology get in the way. You will just send more students to private tutors—if their families can afford it. But don't forget that reading and writing are for a purpose. Surround students with good literature and create a community of readers and writers.

The above discussion applies to reading and writing in the early grades, but what about the later years when comprehending texts becomes more demanding? Here reciprocal teaching (Chapter 9) and study skills (Chapter 8) can be helpful.

Learning and Teaching Mathematics

Some of the most compelling support for constructivist approaches to teaching comes from mathematics education. Critics of direct instruction believe that traditional mathematics instruction often teaches students an unintended lesson—that they "cannot understand mathematics," or worse, that mathematics doesn't have to make sense, you just have to memorize the formulas. Arthur Baroody and Herbert Ginsburg (1990, p. 62) give this example (which follows on page 485):

TABLE 12.7 Improving Early Reading Achievement

CIERA (the Center for the Improvement of Early Reading Achievement) has reviewed the research on learning to read and distilled the best findings into these 10 principles. You can read the expanded version of the principles online at **www.ciera.org/library/instresrc/principles.**

1. **Home language and literacy experiences** support the development of key print concepts, and a range of knowledge prepares students for school-based learning. Programs that help families initiate and sustain these experiences show positive benefits for children's reaching achievement.

   Examples: Joint reading with a family member, parental modelling of good reading habits, monitoring homework and television viewing.

2. **Preschool programs** are particularly beneficial for children who do not experience informal learning opportunities in their homes. Such preschool experiences lead to improved reading achievement, with some effects lasting through grade 3.

   Examples: Listening to and examining books, saying nursery rhymes, writing messages, and seeing and talking about print.

3. **Skills that predict later reading success** can be promoted in kindergarten and grade 1. The two most powerful of these predictors are letter-name knowledge and phonemic awareness. Instruction in these skills has demonstrated positive effects on primary-grade reading achievement, especially when it is coupled with letter-sound instruction.

   Examples: Hearing and blending sound through oral renditions of rhymes, poems, and songs, as well as writing messages and in journals.

4. **Primary-level instruction** that supports successful reading acquisition is consistent, well-designed, and focused.

   Examples: Systematic word recognition instruction on common, consistent letter-sound relationships and important but often unpredictable high-frequency words, such as *the* and *what;* teaching children to monitor the accuracy of their reading as well as their understanding of texts through strategies such as predicting, inferencing, clarifying misunderstandings, and summarizing; promoting word recognition and comprehension through repeated reading of text, guided reading and writing, strategy lessons, reading aloud with feedback, and conversations about texts children have read.

5. **Primary-level classroom environments** in successful schools provide opportunities for students to apply what they have learned in teacher-guided instruction to everyday reading and writing.

   Examples: Teachers read books aloud and hold follow-up discussions, children read independently every day, and children write stories and keep journals. These events are monitored frequently by teachers, ensuring that time is well spent and that children receive feedback on their efforts. Teachers design and revise these events based on information from ongoing assessment of children's strengths and needs.

6. **Cultural and linguistic diversity** among children reflects the variations within their communities and homes. This diversity is manifest in differences in the children's dispositions toward and knowledge about topics, language, and literacy.

   Examples: Effective instruction includes assessment, integration, and extension of relevant background knowledge and the use of texts that recognize diverse backgrounds. Build on the children's language when children are learning to speak, listen to, write, and read English. When teachers capitalize on the advantages of bilingualism or biliteracy, second-language reading acquisition is significantly enhanced.

7. **Children who are identified as having reading disabilities** profit from the same sort of well-balanced instructional programs that benefit all children who are learning to read and write, including systematic instruction *and* meaningful reading and writing.

   Examples: Intensive one-on-one or small-group instruction; attention to both comprehension and word recognition processes; thoroughly individualized assessment and instructional planning; extensive experiences with many types of texts.

8. **Proficient reading in grade 3 and above** is sustained and enhanced by programs that adhere to four fundamental features:

   Features: (1) deep and wide opportunities to read; (2) acquiring new knowledge and vocabulary, through wide reading and through explicit instruction about networks of new concepts; (3) emphasizing the influence on understanding of kinds of text (e.g., stories versus essays) and the ways writers organize particular texts; and (4) assisting students in reasoning about text.

9. **Professional opportunities** to improve reading achievement are prominent in successful schools and programs.

   Examples: Opportunities for teachers and administrators to analyze instruction, assessment, and achievement; to set goals for improvement; to learn about effective practices; and to participate in ongoing communities that deliberately try to understand both successes and persistent problems.

10. **Entire school staffs**, not just grade 1 teachers, are involved in bringing children to high levels of achievement.

    Examples: In successful schools, reading achievement goals are clear, expectations are high, instructional means for attaining goals are articulated, and shared assessments monitor children's progress. Even though they might use different materials and technologies, successful schools maintain a focus on reading and writing and have programs to involve family members in their children's reading and homework. Community partnerships, including volunteer tutoring programs, are common.

Source: Adapted from CIERA. (2002). Improving the reading achievement of America's children: 10 research-based principles. Retrieved April 1, 2005, from **www.ciera.org/library/instresrc/principles.** Copyright © Center for the Improvement of Early Reading Achievement, University of Michigan School of Education. Reprinted with permission.

Sherry, a junior high student, explained that her math class was learning how to convert measurements from one unit to another. The interviewer gave Sherry the following problem:

> To feed data into the computer, the measurements in your report have to be converted to one unit of measurement: metres. Your first measurement, however, is 150 centimetres. What are you going to feed into the computer?

Sherry recognized immediately that the conversion algorithm taught in school applied. However, because she really did not understand the rationale behind the conversion algorithm, Sherry had difficulty in remembering the steps and how to execute them. After some time she came up with an improbable answer (it was less than 1 m). Sherry knew she was in trouble and became flustered. At this point, the interviewer tried to help by asking her if there was any other way of solving the problem. Sherry responded sharply, "No!" She explained, "That's the way it has to be done." The interviewer tried to give Sherry a hint: "Look at the numbers in the problem, is there another way we can think about them that might help us figure out the problem more easily?" Sherry grew even more impatient, "This is the way I learned in school, so it has to be the way."

Sherry believed that there was only one way to solve a problem. Though Sherry knew that 100 centimetres was 1 metre and that shifting the "invisible" decimal at the end of 150 to the left increased the unit size in metric measurements, she did not use this knowledge to solve the problem informally and quickly. Her beliefs prevented her from effectively using her existing mathematical knowledge to solve the problem. Sherry had probably been taught to memorize the steps to convert one measurement to another. How would a constructivist approach teach the same material?

The following excerpt shows how a grade 3 teacher, Ms. Coleman, uses a constructivist approach to teach negative numbers. Notice the use of dialogue and the way the teacher asks students to justify and explain their thinking. The class has been considering one problem: $-10 + 10 = ?$ A student, Marta, has just tried to explain, using a number line, why $-10 + 10 = 0$:

Teacher: Marta says that negative ten plus ten equals zero, so you have to count ten numbers to the right. What do you think, Harold?

Harold: I think it's easy, but I don't understand how she explained it.

Teacher: OK. Does anybody else have a comment or a response to that? Tessa? (Peterson, 1992, p. 165)

As the discussion progresses, Ms. Coleman encourages students to talk directly to each other:

Teacher: You said you don't understand what she is trying to say?

Chang: No.

Teacher: Do you want to ask her?

Chang: What do you mean by counting to the right?

This dialogue reveals three things about learning and teaching in a constructivist classroom: the thinking processes of the students are the focus of attention; one topic is considered in depth rather than attempting to "cover" many topics; and assessment is ongoing and mutually shared by teacher and students. Conducting these kinds of productive dialogues about mathematics concepts is not easy. You have to continually monitor the dialogue, have a good idea where the discussion is going and if it is productive, and learn when to step in and out of the discussion (Nathan & Knuth, 2003).

Jere Confrey (1990b) analyzed an expert mathematics teacher in a class for high school girls who had difficulty with mathematics. Confrey identified five components in a model of this teacher's approach to teaching. These components are summarized in Table 12.8 on the next page.

TABLE 12.8 A Constructivist Approach to Mathematics: Five Components

1. Promote students' autonomy and commitment to their answers.

   Examples:

   - Question both right and wrong student answers.
   - Insist that students at least try to solve a problem and be able to explain what they tried.

2. Develop students' reflective processes.

   Examples:

   - Question students to guide them to try different ways to resolve the problem.
   - Ask students to restate the problem in their own words; to explain what they are doing and why; and to discuss what they mean by the terms they are using.

3. Construct a case history of each student.

   Examples:

   - Note general tendencies in the way the student approaches problems, as well as common misconceptions and strengths.

4. If the student is unable to solve a problem, intervene to negotiate a possible solution with the student.

   Examples:

   - Based on the case study and your understanding of how the student is thinking about a problem, guide the student to think about a possible solution.
   - Ask questions such as, "Is there anything you did in the last one that will help you here?" or "Can you explain your diagram?"
   - If the student is becoming frustrated, ask more direct, product-oriented questions.

5. When the problem is solved, review the solution.

   Examples:

   - Encourage students to reflect on what they did and why.
   - Note what students did well and build confidence.

Source: From Confrey, J. (1990). What constructivism implies for teaching. In R. Davis, C. Maher, & N. Noddings (Eds.), *Constructivist views on the teaching and learning of mathematics.* Monograph 4 of the National Council of Teachers of Mathematics, Reston, VA. Copyright © 1990 National Council of Teachers of Mathematics. Adapted with permission.

Connect & Extend

TO OTHER RESEARCH

Gersten, R., & Chard, D. (1999). Number sense: Rethinking arithmetic instruction for students with mathematical disabilities. *Journal of Special Education, 33,* 18–28.

Peterson, P., Fennema, E., & Carpenter, T. (1989). Using knowledge of how students think about mathematics. *Educational Leadership, 46*(4), 42–46.

Klein, P. D. (2000). Elementary students' strategies for writing-to-learn in science. *Cognition and Instruction, 18,* 317–348.

There is a caution, however. Some studies have found that students with learning disabilities and lower-achieving students benefit more from explicit instruction in mathematics problem-solving strategies (teacher explanation and modelling, practice with feedback) than from constructivist teaching that encourages students to discuss and discover strategies. But both explicit instruction and constructivist methods were better than traditional instruction in at least one study (Kroesbergen, Van Luit, & Maas, 2004).

Learning and Teaching Science

We have seen a number of times that by high school many students have "learned" some unfortunate lessons in school. Like Sherry, described in the preceding section, they have learned that math is impossible to understand and that you just have to apply the rules to get the answers. Or they may have developed misconceptions about the world, such as the belief that the Earth is warmer in the summer because it is closer to the sun.

Many educators note that the key to understanding in science is for students to directly examine their own theories and confront the shortcomings (Hewson, Beeth, & Thorley, 1998). For conceptual change to take place, students must go through six stages: initial discomfort with their own ideas and beliefs; attempts to explain away inconsistencies between their theories and evidence presented to them; attempts to adjust measurements or observations to fit personal theories; doubt; vacillation; and finally conceptual change (Nissani & Hoefler-Nissani, 1992). You can see Piaget's notions of assimilation, disequilibrium, and accommodation operating here. Students try to make new information fit existing ideas (assimilation), but when the fit simply won't work and disequilibrium occurs, then accommodation or changes in cognitive structures follow.

The goal of **conceptual change teaching in science** is to help students pass through these six stages of learning. The two central features of conceptual change teaching are:

- Teachers are committed to teaching for student understanding rather than "covering the curriculum."
- Students are encouraged to make sense of science using their current ideas—they are challenged to describe, predict, explain, justify, debate, and defend the adequacy of their understanding. Dialogue is key. Only when intuitive ideas prove inadequate can new learning take hold (Anderson & Roth, 1989).

Conceptual change teaching has much in common with cognitive apprenticeships, inquiry learning, and reciprocal teaching described in Chapter 9—with scaffolding and dialogue playing key roles (Shuell, 1996). The Guidelines below, adapted from Hewson, Beeth, and Thorley (1998), give some ideas for promoting conceptual change.

How would these guidelines look in practice? One answer comes from Michael Beeth's study of a grade 5 classroom. Table 12.9 on page 488 is a list of learning goals that the teacher presented to her students. In this classroom, the teacher typically began instruction with questions such as, "Do you have ideas? Can you talk about them? Bring them out into the open? Why do you like your ideas? Why are you attracted to them?" (Beeth, 1998, p. 1095).

conceptual change teaching in science A method that helps students understand (rather than memorize) concepts in science by using and challenging the students' current ideas.

GUIDELINES

TEACHING FOR CONCEPTUAL CHANGE

Encourage students to make their ideas explicit.

EXAMPLES

1. Ask students to make predictions that might contradict their naive conceptions.
2. Ask students to state their ideas in their own words, including the attractions and limitations of the ideas for them.
3. Have students explain their ideas using physical models or illustrations.

Help students see the differences among ideas.

EXAMPLES

1. Have students summarize or paraphrase each other's ideas.
2. Encourage comparing ideas by presenting and comparing evidence.

Encourage metacognition.

EXAMPLES

1. Give a pretest before starting a unit, then have students discuss their own responses to the pretest. Group similar pretest responses together and ask students to discover a more general concept underlying the responses.

2. At the end of lessons, ask students, "What did you learn?" "What do you understand?" "What do you believe about the lesson?" "How have your ideas changed?"

Explore the status of ideas. Status is an indication of how much students know and accept ideas and find them useful.

EXAMPLES

1. Ask direct questions about how intelligible, plausible, and fruitful an idea is. That is, "Do you know what the idea means?" "Do you believe it?" "Can you achieve some valuable outcome using the idea?"
2. Plan activities and experiments that support and question the students' ideas, such as showing successful applications or pointing out contradictions.

Ask students for justifications of their ideas.

EXAMPLES

1. Teach students to use terms such as *logical, consistent, inconsistent,* and *coherent* in giving justifications.
2. Ask students to share and analyze each other's justifications.

Conceptual change teaching in science focuses teachers' and students' attention on students' understanding rather than on "covering the curriculum." Dialogue is key.

During her teaching, she constantly asked questions that required explanation and justifications. She summarized the students' answers and sometimes challenged, "But do you really believe what you say?" Studies of the students in the teacher's classroom over the years showed that they had a sophisticated understanding of science concepts.

Canadian researchers Wolf-Michael Roth and Michelle McGinn add that a key to unlocking opportunities for students to construct understandings in science (and mathematics) is posing better problems (Roth & McGinn, 1997). Usually, the problems students are given to solve are uncluttered with the complexities that enrich the real world. Too often, problems have prefigured answers where "students' tasks are to disclose what the texts (or problems) hide … as *the* solution" (pp. 19–20) rather than learn how to do science. Roth and McGinn suggest that teachers invite students to bring problems from outside school into the classroom. Then, teachers should support students as students frame hypotheses and explore methods to investigate them. This places problems in context so that students' experiences from outside school are joined with experiences of doing

---

TABLE 12.9 One Teacher's Learning Goals for Conceptual Change Teaching

The teacher in a grade 5 class gives these questions to her students to support their thinking about science:

1. Can you state your own ideas?
2. Can you talk about why you are attracted to your ideas?
3. Are your ideas consistent?
4. Do you realize the limitations of your ideas and the possibility they might need to change?
5. Can you try to explain your ideas using physical models?
6. Can you explain the difference between understanding an idea and believing in an idea?
7. Can you apply the words *intelligible* and *plausible* as standards for evaluating your ideas?

Source: Adapted from Beeth, M. E. (1998). Teaching science in fifth grade: Instructional goals that support conceptual change. *Journal of Research in Science Teaching, 35,* 1093.

science. This model, called *open inquiry,* transforms what students do to resemble what scientists do. The result? Students construct understandings about science that are genuine rather than textbookish (Roth & Bowen, 1995; Roth & Roychoudhury, 1993).

Evaluating Constructivist Approaches to Subject Teaching

Constructivist approaches have done much to correct the excesses of tell-and-drill teaching. Some positive outcomes from constructivist teaching are better understanding of the material, greater enjoyment of literature, more positive attitudes toward school, better problem solving, and greater motivation (Harris & Graham, 1996; Palincsar, 1998). But we have noted that total reliance on constructivist approaches that ignores direct teaching of skills can be detrimental for some children (e.g., young children and children with learning disabilities).

Ernst von Glasersfeld (1995), a strong advocate of constructivist teaching in mathematics, believes that it is a misunderstanding of constructivism to say that memorization and rote learning are always useless. "There are, indeed, matters that can and perhaps must be learned in a purely mechanical way" (p. 5). Classrooms that integrate constructivist teaching with needed direct teaching of skills are especially good learning environments for students with special needs. Careful ongoing assessment of each student's abilities, knowledge, and motivations, followed by appropriate support, should ensure that no students are lost or left behind (Graham & Harris, 1994). Again, it seems that balance is the key to successful learning and teaching.

Check Your Knowledge

- What is a balanced approach to teaching reading and writing?
- Describe constructivist approaches to mathematics and science teaching.

Apply to Practice

- How would you assess students' conceptions about the science topics you will teach?

BEYOND THE DEBATES TOWARD OUTSTANDING TEACHING

In spite of the criticisms and debates, there is no one best way to teach. Different goals require different methods. Direct instruction leads to better performance on achievement tests, whereas the open, informal methods such as discovery learning or inquiry approaches are associated with better performance on tasks requiring creativity, abstract thinking, problem solving, and self-regulated learning. In addition, the open methods are better for improving attitudes toward school and for stimulating curiosity, cooperation among students, and lower absence rates (Walberg, 1990). According to these conclusions, when the goals of teaching involve problem solving, creativity, understanding, and mastering processes, many approaches besides direct instruction should be effective. This view is in keeping with Tom Good's conclusion that teaching should become less direct as students mature and when the goals involve affective development and problem solving or critical thinking (Good, 1983a).

Below we describe teaching practices that promote self-regulated learning, a highly effective form of learning that was introduced in Chapter 9.

Connect & Extend

TO THE RESEARCH
White, B. Y. (1993). TinkerTools: Causal models, conceptual change, and science education. *Cognition and Instruction, 10,* 1–100.

Lapadat, J. C. (2000). Construction of science knowledge: Scaffolding conceptual change through discourse. *Journal of Classroom Instruction, 35,* 1–14.

Teaching toward Self-Regulated Learning

Most teachers agree that students need to develop skills and attitudes for independent, lifelong learning—that is, self-regulated learning, or SRL. Fortunately, there is a growing body of research that offers guidance on how to design tasks and structure classroom interactions to support students' development of and engagement in SRL (Neuman & Roskos, 1997; Many et al., 1996; Perry, 1998; Tuner, 1995; Wharton-McDonald et al., 1997). This research indicates that students develop academically effective forms of SRL when teachers involve them in complex, meaningful tasks that extend over long periods of time, much like the math and science activities we described in the previous section on student-centred, constructivist approaches to teaching. Also, to develop SRL, students need to have some degree of control over their learning processes and products (e.g., choices), and it helps them if they work collaboratively with and seek feedback from peers. Finally, since self-monitoring and self-evaluation are key to effective SRL, teachers can help students develop SRL by involving them in setting criteria for evaluating their learning processes and products and giving them opportunities to make judgments about their progress toward those standards.

Complex Tasks. We use the term *complex* to refer to the design of tasks, not their level of difficulty. From a design point of view, tasks are complex when they address multiple goals and involve large chunks of meaning, as projects and thematic units do. Furthermore, complex tasks that extend over long periods of time engage students in a variety of cognitive and metacognitive processes and allow for the production of a wide range of products (Perry et al., 2002; Wharton-McDonald et al., 1997). For example, a study of Egyptian pyramids might result in the production of written reports, maps, diagrams, and models.

Research indicates that the most motivating and academically beneficial tasks for students are those that challenge but don't overwhelm them (Rohrkemper & Corno, 1988; Turner, 1997). Complex tasks need not be overly difficult for students. See the accompanying Reaching Every Student box for a description of how one student who is low achieving benefited from her engagement with complex, meaningful tasks.

Importantly, complex tasks provide students with information about their learning progress, require them to engage in deep, elaborative processing and problem solving, and help them develop and refine cognitive and metacognitive strategies (Bruning, Schraw, & Ronning, 1995; McCaslin & Good, 1996; Turner, 1997). Furthermore, succeeding at such tasks increases students' self-efficacy and intrinsic motivation (McCaslin & Good, 1996). Rohrkemper and Corno (1988) advised teachers to design complex tasks that provide students with opportunities to modify the learning conditions or themselves to cope with challenging problems: "[L]earning to cope with and modify stressful situations ... is an important outcome of education; its deliberate promotion in a supportive classroom environment is a valuable educational goal" (p. 299).

Control. Teachers can share control with students by giving them choices. When students have choices (e.g., about what to produce, how to produce it, where to work, who to work with), they are more likely to predict a successful outcome and consequently increase effort and persist when difficulty arises (Turner & Paris, 1995). Also, by involving students in making decisions, teachers invite them to take responsibility for learning by planning, setting goals, monitoring progress, and evaluating outcomes (Turner, 1997). These are qualities of highly effective, self-regulating learners.

Giving students choices creates opportunities for them to adjust the degree of challenge particular tasks present (e.g., they can choose easy or more challenging reading materials, determine the nature and amount of writing in a report, supplement writing with other expressions of learning). But what if students make poor academic choices? Highly effective teachers who support self-

FROM OTHER-REGULATION TO SELF-REGULATION

Carol, a grade 2 student, had diffi-culty finding facts and then trans-forming those facts into meaningful prose. Carol's teacher, Lynn, also characterized her as "a very weak writer." Carol had problems with the mechanics of writing, which, accord-ing to Lynn, held her back.

Over the course of the school year, Lynn involved her grade 2 and 3 students in three writing projects about animals. Through these proj-ects, she wanted students to learn how to: (a) do research, (b) write expository text, (c) edit and revise their writing, and (d) use the computer as a tool for researching and writing. For the first report, the class worked on one topic together (chip-munks). Students did the fact finding and writing together because Lynn needed to show them how to do research and write a report. Also, the class developed frameworks for working collaboratively as a commu-nity of learners. When students wrote the second report (on penguins), Lynn offered them many more choices and encouraged them to depend more on themselves and on one another. Finally, for the third report, stu-dents conducted a self-regulated research project and wrote about an animal of their choos-ing. Now that they knew how to do research and write a report, they could work alone or together and be successful at this complex task.

Carol worked with a student in grade 3 who was doing research on a related topic. He showed Carol how to use a table of contents and offered advice about how to phrase ideas in her report. Also, Carol underlined words she thought were misspelled so that she could check them later when she met with Lynn to edit her report. Unlike many stu-dents who are low achieving, Carol was engaging with meaningful tasks and content and learning strategies for SRL. Carol was not afraid to attempt challenging tasks, and she was confident about her ability to develop as a writer. Reflecting on her progress across the school year, Carol said, "I learned a lot from when I was in grade 1 because I had a lot of trouble then."

Source: Perry, N., & Drummond, L. (2003). Helping young stu-dents become self-regulated researchers and writers. *The Reading Teacher, 56,* 298–310.

regulated learning carefully consider the choices they give to students. They make sure that students have the knowledge and skills they need to operate independently and make good decisions (Perry & Drummond, 2002). For example, when students are learning new skills or routines, teachers can offer choices with constraints (e.g., students must write a minimum of four para-graphs, but they can choose to write more; they must demonstrate their under-standing of an animal's habitat, food, and babies, but they can write, draw, or speak their knowledge).

Also, highly effective teachers teach and model good decision making. For example, when students are choosing partners, teachers ask them to consider what they need from their partner (e.g., shared interest and commitment, perhaps knowledge or skills that they need to develop). When students are making choices about how best to use their time, teachers ask, "What can you do when you're fin-ished?" "What can you do if you are waiting for my help?" Often, lists are gener-ated and posted, so that students can refer to these while they work. Finally, highly effective teachers give students feedback about the choices they make and tailor the choices they give to suit the unique characteristics of particular learners. For exam-ple, they might encourage some students to select research topics for which resources are readily available and written at a level that is accessible to them. Or they might encourage some students to work collaboratively to ensure that they have the support they need to be successful.

Collaboration.   Nancy has observed that the most effective uses of cooperative/ collaborative relationships to support SRL are those that reflect a climate of community and shared problem solving (Perry & Drummond, 2003; Perry et al., 2002). In these contexts, teachers and students actually co-regulate one another's learning (McCaslin & Good, 1996), offering support to each other, whether working alone, in pairs, or small groups. This support is instrumental to individuals' development and use of metacognition, intrinsic motivation, and strategic action (e.g., sharing ideas, comparing strategies for solving problems, identifying *everyone's* area of expertise). Importantly, teachers who support self-regulated learning spend time at the start of each school year teaching routines and establishing norms of participation (e.g., how to give constructive feedback and how to interpret and respond to peers' suggestions). One teacher Nancy worked with said that instruction aimed at SRL "takes a lot of time but it is time well spent." Once routines and patterns of interaction are established, students can focus on learning, and teachers can attend to teaching academic skills and the curriculum.

Self-Evaluation. Evaluation practices that support SRL are non-threatening. They are embedded in ongoing activities, emphasize process as well as products, focus on personal progress, and help students interpret errors as opportunities for learning to occur. In these contexts, students actually seek challenging tasks because the cost of participation is low (Paris & Ayres, 1994). Involving students in generating evaluation criteria and in evaluating their work also reduces anxiety that often accompanies assessment, since it gives students a sense of control over the outcome. Students can judge their work in relation to a set of qualities they and their teachers identify as "good" work. They can consider the effectiveness of their approaches to learning and alter their behaviours in ways that enhance learning (Winne & Perry, 2000).

In classrooms where teachers support SRL, Nancy has observed both formal and informal opportunities for students to evaluate their learning. One student teacher asked grade 4/5 students to submit reflections journals with the games they designed with a partner or small group of collaborators in a probability and statistics unit (Perry, Phillips, & Dowler, 2004). These journals described students' contributions to their group's process and product and included reflections on what the students learned from participating. The student teacher took these reflections into account when she evaluated the games. More informally, teachers ask students, "What have you learned about yourself as a writer today?" "What do good researchers and writers do?" "What can we do that we couldn't do before?" Questions such as these, posed to individuals or embedded in class discussions, prompt students' metacognition, motivation, and strategic action, the components of SRL.

Check Your Knowledge

- How can teachers support self-regulated learning in their classrooms?

Apply to Practice

- Plan a complex task and then identify the opportunities it presents for students to engage in SRL.

Teaching toward SRL incorporates many of the beliefs and behaviours associated with highly effective teachers. Moreover, more than a quarter century of research indicates that SRL leads to success in school and beyond.

SUMMARY

Characteristics of Effective Teachers
(pp. 458–459)

What are some general characteristics of good teachers?

Teacher knowledge of the subject is necessary but not sufficient for effective teaching; being more knowledgeable helps teachers be clearer and more organized. Teachers who provide clear presentations and explanations tend to have students who learn more and who rate their teachers more positively. Teacher warmth, friendliness, and understanding seem to be the traits most strongly related to positive student attitudes.

Teacher Expectations
(pp. 460–462)

What are some sources of teacher expectations?

Sources include intelligence test scores, sex, notes from previous teachers and the medical or psychological reports found in cumulative folders, ethnic background, knowledge of older brothers and sisters, physical characteristics, previous achievement, socioeconomic class, and the actual behaviours of the student.

What are the two kinds of expectation effects, and how do they happen?

The first is the self-fulfilling prophecy, which occurs when the teacher's beliefs about the students' abilities have no basis in fact, but student behaviour comes to match the initially inaccurate expectation. The second is a sustaining expectation effect, which occurs when teachers are fairly accurate in their initial reading of students' abilities and respond to students appropriately. The problems arise when students show some improvement but teachers do not alter their expectations to take account of the improvement. When this happens, the teacher's unchanging expectation can sustain the students' achievement at the expected level. In practice, sustaining effects are more common than self-fulfilling prophecy effects.

What are the different avenues for communicating teacher expectations?

Some teachers tend to treat students differently, depending on their own views of how well the students are likely to do. Differences in treatment toward low-expectation students may include setting less challenging tasks, focusing on lower-level learning, giving fewer choices, providing inconsistent feedback, and communicating less respect and trust. Students may behave accordingly, fulfilling teachers' predictions or staying at an expected level of achievement.

Planning: The First Step in Effective Teaching
(pp. 462–471)

What are the levels of planning, and how do they affect teaching?

Teachers engage in several levels of planning—by the year, term, unit, week, and day. All the levels must be coordinated. Accomplishing the year's plan requires breaking the work into terms, the terms into units, and the units into weeks and days. The plan determines how time and materials will be turned into activities for students. There is no single model of planning, but all plans should allow for flexibility. Planning is a creative problem-solving process. Experienced teachers know how to accomplish many lessons and segments of lessons. They know what to expect and how to proceed, so they may not continue to follow the detailed lesson-planning models they learned during their teacher-preparation programs. Their planning may appear less formal. However, effective teachers plan for instruction.

What is an instructional objective?

An instructional objective is a clear and unambiguous description of your educational intentions for your students. Mager's influential system for writing behavioural objectives states that objectives ought to describe what students will be doing when demonstrating their achievement and how you will know they are doing it. A good objective has three parts—the intended student behaviour, the conditions under which the behaviour will occur, and the criteria for acceptable performance. Gronlund's alternative approach suggests that an objective should be stated first in general terms, then the teacher should clarify by listing sample behaviour that would provide evidence that the student has attained the objective. The most recent research on instructional objectives tends to favour approaches similar to Gronlund's.

Describe the three taxonomies of educational objectives.

Bloom and others have developed taxonomies categorizing basic objectives in the cognitive, affective, and psychomotor domains. In real life, of course, behaviour from these three domains occurs simultaneously. A taxonomy encourages systematic thinking about relevant objectives and ways to evaluate them. Six basic objectives are listed in the cognitive domain: knowledge, comprehension, application, analysis, synthesis, and evaluation. A recent revision of this taxonomy keeps the same cognitive processes but adds that these processes can act on four kinds of knowledge—factual, conceptual, procedural, and metacognitive. Objectives in the affective domain run from least committed to most committed. At the lowest level, students simply pay attention to a certain idea. At the highest level, students adopt an idea or a value and act consistently with that idea. Objectives in the psychomotor domain generally move from basic perceptions and reflex actions to skilled, creative movements.

Describe teacher-centred and student-centred planning.

In teacher-centred approaches, teachers select learning objectives and plan how to get students to meet those objectives. Teachers control the "what" and "how" of learning. In contrast, planning is shared and negotiated in student-centred, or constructivist, approaches. Rather than having specific student behaviours as objectives, the teacher has overarching goals or "big ideas" that guide planning. Integrated content and teaching with themes are often part of the planning. Assessment of learning is ongoing and mutually shared by teacher and students.

Teacher-Directed Instruction
(pp. 471–481)

What is direct instruction?

Direct instruction is appropriate for teaching basic skills and explicit knowledge. It includes the teaching functions of review/overview, presentation, guided practice, feedback and correctives (with reteaching if necessary), independent practice, and periodic reviews. The younger or less able the students, the shorter the presentation should be, with more cycles of practice and feedback.

Distinguish between convergent and divergent questions and between high-level and low-level questions.

Convergent questions have only one right answer. Divergent questions have many possible answers. High-level questions require analysis, synthesis, and evaluation—students have to think for themselves. Low-level questions assess remem-

bering, understanding, and applying. The best pattern for younger students and for lower-ability students of all ages is simple questions that allow a high percentage of correct answers, ample encouragement, help when the student does not have the correct answer, and praise. For high-ability students, the successful pattern includes harder questions at both higher and lower levels and more critical feedback. Whatever their age or ability, all students should have some experience with thought-provoking questions and, if necessary, help in learning how to answer them.

How can wait time affect student learning?

Teacher responses to answers should not be too hasty in most cases and should provide appropriate feedback. When teachers learn to pose a question, then wait at least three to five seconds before calling on a student to answer, students tend to give longer answers; more students are likely to participate, ask questions, and volunteer appropriate answers; student comments involving analysis, synthesis, inference, and speculation tend to increase; and the students generally appear more confident in their answers.

What are the uses and disadvantages of group discussion?

Group discussion helps students participate directly, express themselves clearly, justify opinions, and tolerate different views. Group discussion also gives students a chance to ask for clarification, examine their own thinking, follow personal interests, and assume responsibility by taking leadership roles in the group. Thus, group discussions help students evaluate ideas and synthesize personal viewpoints. By thinking together, challenging each other, and suggesting and evaluating possible explanations, students are more likely to reach a genuine understanding. However, discussions are quite unpredictable and

may easily digress into exchanges of ignorance.

Student-Centred Teaching: Examples in Reading, Mathematics, and Science
(pp. 481–489)

What is a balanced approach to reading and writing?

The best approach to teaching reading and writing balances strategies from both code-based and meaning-based approaches. There is extensive research indicating that skill in recognizing sounds and words—phonemic awareness—is fundamental in learning to read. Research also indicates that children are motivated to learn when they are surrounded by good literature and read and write for authentic purposes. Highly effective primary teachers use a balanced approach combining authentic reading and writing with skills instruction when needed.

Describe constructivist approaches to mathematics and science teaching.

Constructivist approaches to teaching mathematics and science emphasize deep understanding of concepts (as opposed to memorization), discussion and explanation, and exploration of students' implicit understandings. Many educators note that the key to understanding in science is for students to directly examine their own theories and confront the shortcomings. For change to take place, students must go through six stages: initial discomfort with their own ideas and beliefs; attempts to explain away inconsistencies between their theories and evidence presented to them; attempts to adjust measurements or observations to fit personal theories; doubt; vacillation; and finally conceptual change.

Beyond the Debates toward Outstanding Teaching
(pp. 489–492)

How can teachers support self-regulated learning in their classrooms?

Students develop academically effective forms of SRL when teachers involve them gin complex, meaningful tasks. Such tasks present opportunities for students to control their learning processes and products (e.g., by embedding choices) and monitor and evaluate their progress toward learning objectives. Teachers can support students' SRL by asking questions that require students to think deeply about learning and by teaching and modelling effective learning strategies. Also, working with and receiving feedback from peers supports SRL.

KEY TERMS

active teaching,   p. 471

affective domain,   p. 467

basic skills,   p. 471

behavioural objectives,   p. 465

cognitive domain,   p. 466

cognitive objectives,   p. 465

conceptual change teaching in science,   p. 487

constructivist approach,   p. 468

convergent questions,   p. 477

direct instruction/explicit teaching,   p. 471

divergent questions,   p. 477

group discussion,   p. 479

instructional objectives,   p. 465

psychomotor domain,   p. 468

Pygmalion effect,   p. 460

scripted cooperation,   p. 473

seatwork,   p. 474

self-fulfilling prophecy,   p. 460

sustaining expectation effect,   p. 460

taxonomy,   p. 466

whole language perspective,   p. 482

BECOMING A PROFESSIONAL

Reflecting on the Chapter

Can you apply the ideas from this chapter on teaching to solve the following problems of practice?

Preschool and Kindergarten

- You have a well-supplied science corner in your class, but your students seldom visit it. When they do, they don't seem to take advantage of the learning possibilities available with the manipulatives. How would you help students benefit from the materials?

Elementary and Middle School

- Your school administrator wants sample lesson plans for each of the subjects you teach. What would you include in the plans to make them useful for you?

- You are given a math workbook and text series and told that you must use these materials as the basis for your math teaching. What would you do to incorporate these materials into lessons that help students understand mathematical thinking and problem solving?

Junior High and High School

- Identify three instructional objectives for a lesson in your subject to be used in a mixed-ability grade 10 class. How would you make these learning objectives clear to your students?

Check Your Understanding

- Be familiar with Bloom's taxonomy in the cognitive domain, including examples of verbs that fit each level of the domain.

- Be familiar with the teaching functions of direct instruction.

- Know the differences between convergent and divergent questions and between high- and low-level questions.

Your Teaching Portfolio

Think about your philosophy of teaching, a question you will be asked at most job interviews.

What is your approach to planning? How will you match teaching approaches to learning goals?

Add some ideas for family involvement in homework from this chapter to your portfolio.

Teaching Resources

Include a summary of the cognitive, affective, and psychomotor taxonomies in your teaching resources file.

Add Table 12.2 ("A Revised Taxonomy in the Cognitive Domain," page 467) to your file.

Include Table 12.4 ("Active Learning and Teacher Presentations," page 473) in your file.

If you will teach elementary school, include Table 12.7 ("Improving Early Reading Achievement," page 484) in your file.

Teachers' Casebook

What Would They Do?

Here is how two practising teachers responded to the teaching situation presented at the beginning of this chapter about implementing a student-centred curriculum.

Carole Thomas Mandel
Whitney Public School
Toronto, Ontario

A student-centred curriculum is one that develops knowledge, skills, and independent thinking. In the student-centred classroom the teacher acknowledges the different ways children learn. The key to understanding and implementing a truly student-centred curriculum lies in achieving a balance between child-initiated and teacher-directed experiences. With diverse teaching materials and learning practices in place, and with parents and others acting as partners in the children's education, teachers and administrators can readily respond to parental complaints and other issues that have arisen about the new curriculum.

The good news is that there's a lot to celebrate. Many students appear to be more engaged in learning. However, some appear lost. As in any classroom, there can be a number of reasons why some students experience learning challenges. And so, rather than oppose a new curriculum that's been well planned in terms of both time and money, these reasons need to be carefully investigated. The school support team, including non-teaching professionals and parents, is the first place to seek guidance in helping a student who's experiencing unusual or exceptional difficulty. Modifications and adaptations to the curriculum (perhaps formalized in an Individual Education Plan) and remedial support during classroom time are normally suggested and then implemented by the classroom and sometimes resource room teachers.

Students' written work is now longer and more creative, an achievement everyone should celebrate. This hallmark, however, is set against a drop in standardized test scores, which tends to dismay parents. But parents need to be informed that standardized tests are only one method of evaluation and assessment. Equally valid—and for many educators even more valid, since standardized tests tend to assess what a student knows, or has memorized, on a given day—are the many other methods of evaluation and assessment in which classroom teachers are continually engaged. There needs to be a balance, then, between standardized tests and the ongoing and often more authentic classroom assessments. These assess-

ments include, for example, clearly delineated rubrics attached to assignments (so that students and parents have a clear understanding of what's required to successfully complete them) and opportunities for student self-evaluation. They also involve regular reporting to parents in the form of oral and written reports that include anecdotal comments and achievement levels. However, with parents complaining that they have to hire private tutors or buy commercial programs to help teach their children the basics, more needs to be done beyond a fair and balanced approach in the use of different types of assessment.

The lower standardized test scores have to be addressed by implementing ways for students to improve without detracting from student-centred learning. After the test results are received, teachers should be encouraged to use this information as they plan their future test-preparation lessons. They can also make sure that students know how to use all the test material. Teachers need to provide opportunities to model, practise, and solve test-type questions throughout the year and for practice tests to be completed before testing. During information or curriculum evenings, teachers can map out what they've identified as areas of weakness. Homework that's at least partially reflective of the type of work that appears on standardized tests can be assigned, with a note to parents indicating this and encouraging home support. Hopefully, as test scores improve they'll be viewed as a valuable but incidental index that effective student-centred education is taking place.

Parental concerns about children not getting the basics also need to be validated. For students to successfully progress year by year, they need the basics, which usually refer to such knowledge and essential skills as science facts, grammar rules, reading vocabulary, and math computations. And since these are often included in standardized tests, improving test scores and giving greater attention to effective, perhaps more step-by-step instruction of the basics are by no means mutually exclusive. A consistent, school-wide approach to teaching the basics could easily be implemented, and could include something as straightforward as all teachers using the same math textbook series and support materials (just as levelled books were initially purchased with the goal of progress and consistency). Extra assistance in the classrooms can come from parent volunteers, and home support can also be sought. Teachers' websites can further communicate with parents and students, with reminders, for example, to review basic facts on a regular basis. As always, a balance must be maintained among teacher-directed instruction, the usually more open-ended student-initiated projects, and learning experiences that lend themselves readily to parental support (such as learning multiplication facts).

The planning and purchase of materials for the new student-centred classroom are parts of effective teaching and learning, but they are not the whole. Teachers have received professional development by taking workshops and much has been invested in quality children's literature, math manipulatives, and reading corners, etc. These are all good things. However, all good teachers know that in order to deliver the most effective, student-centred curriculum, a middle ground needs to be found. This includes open and positive responses to issues in education today, including a plan to improve standardized test results. Implicit in the student-centred curriculum is the belief that all children can learn but that sometimes support is needed; the need to implement a variety of instructional as well as assessment methods; and the acknowledgment that teachers must connect with parents and others involved in the school community as partners in the children's education.

Shannon Smith
Algonquin Public School
Brockville, Ontario

I would communicate with the parents and indicate to them my commitment to providing a positive learning experience for their children. I would welcome parents into my classroom and ensure that they are well informed of the educational processes taking place. In addition, I would take the parents' complaints directly to my principal and ensure that she is aware that parents are expressing concern about the new curriculum. The principal and the staff of the school should be involved in these decisions. I would back my principal and demonstrate my strong commitment to student learning and to the school as a whole.

Past experiences have given me the opportunity to implement creative educational strategies. As a teacher, I hope to motivate students by ascertaining their inner strengths and abilities and discovering what truly inspires them, and to create knowledge with students rather than simply passing it on. I believe in hands-on learning experiences. Through my teaching experience thus far, I have found facilitating, rather than dictating, to be a highly beneficial style of teaching. Students should be given power over their own education. If students construct their own learning experiences, they will not only retain the information longer, but they will also become more confident in their abilities.

Through my commitment to learning, I hope to improve on my teaching skills to effectively teach and encourage children. I would reflect on my program by using numerous assessment techniques and then modify my program according to the needs of my students. I would make time for students who require additional instruction. In the past I have assisted students during lunch and recess to ensure that concepts are fully understood. I adapt materials, teaching techniques, and activities to meet the particular needs of my students. I hope to instill a love of learning through providing challenging and creative learning experiences.

13 CLASSROOM ASSESSMENT AND GRADING

Dancing Girl—Fin d'arabesque. 1877. Edgar Dégas. Pastel, essence and oil on paper, 65 × 36 cm. Photo: Réunion des Musées Nationaux/Art Resource, New York.

Teachers' Casebook

What Would You Do?

Your school requires you to assign letter grades to students in your class. You can use any method you prefer, as long as an A, B, C, D, or F appears for each subject area on every student's report card, every grading period. Some teachers base their grades on worksheets, quizzes, homework, and tests. Others assign group work and portfolios. A few teachers individualize standards by grading on progress and effort more than final achievement. Some are trying contract approaches and experimenting with long-term projects, while others rely almost completely on daily class work. Two teachers who use group work are considering giving credit toward grades for being a "good group member" or competitive bonus points for the top-scoring group. Others are planning to use improvement points for class rewards but not for grades. Your only experience with grading was providing written comments and a mastery approach that rated each student as making satisfactory or unsatisfactory progress toward particular objectives. You want a system that is fair and manageable but also encourages learning, not just performance.

Critical Thinking

What would be your major graded assignments and projects? Would you include credit for such behaviour as group participation or effort? How would you put all the elements together to assign one grade to each student for every marking period? How would you justify your system to the principal and to your students' families? How will these issues affect the grade levels that you teach?

Collaboration

With two or three other members of your class, develop a section of a class handbook that describes your grading policy. Be prepared to defend the policy.

Connect & Extend

TO YOUR TEACHING
Because assessment is essential to good teaching—and so important to students—teachers and everyone else in the educational system must be fully aware of how assessment can be done fairly and usefully. To meet this need, nine national associations representing educators, psychologists, teachers, counsellors, and school administrators, as well as representatives from all the provincial and territorial ministries, developed the *Principles for Fair Student Assessment Practices for Education in Canada.* Based on the premise that assessments depend on professional judgment, the *Principles* document identifies issues to consider in exercising your professional judgment to ensure fair and equitable assessment of all students. Download your own copy of the *Principles* from - **www.education.ualberta.ca/ educ/psych/crame/files/ eng_prin.pdf.**

In this chapter, you will look at tests and grades, focusing on the effects these are likely to have on students, as well as practical means of developing more efficient methods for testing and grading.

We begin by considering the many types of tests teachers prepare each year and factors that affect test scores and interpretations, as well as some new approaches to assessment. Then we examine the effects that grades are likely to have on students. Because there are so many grading systems, we also spend some time identifying advantages and disadvantages of one system over another. Finally, we turn to the very important topic of communication with students and their families, including the important topic of justifying grades you give.

By the time complete this chapter, you should be able to answer these questions:

- *How are test scores interpreted in relation to norms and criteria?*

- *What are examples of criterion-referenced and norm-referenced grading systems?*

- *How can you judge whether evidence provided by tests is appropriate for evaluating students' achievements?*

- *How would you plan a test of students' work on a unit of the curriculum?*

- *How can you evaluate tests that accompany textbooks and teachers' manuals?*

- *How should you create multiple-choice and essay test items for your subject area?*

- *How can you use authentic assessment approaches, including portfolios, performances, exhibitions, and scoring rubrics?*

- *What are potential positive and negative effects of grades on students?*

EVALUATION, MEASUREMENT, AND ASSESSMENT

Teaching involves making many kinds of judgments—decisions based on values: "Should we use a different text this year?" "Is the film appropriate for my students?" "Will Sarah do better if she repeats grade 1?" "Should Terry get a B– or a C+ on the project?" In the process of **evaluation**, we compare information we gather to standards, and then we make judgments.

Measurement is quantitative—it is a numeric description of an event or characteristic. Measurement tells how much, how often, or how well by providing scores, ranks, or ratings. Instead of saying vaguely, "Sarah doesn't seem to understand addition," a teacher using measurements might say, "Sarah answered only 6 of the 15 problems correctly in her addition homework." Measurement, when done *properly*, allows a teacher to compare one student's performance on one particular task with a standard of performance or to compare a student's performance with other students' performances. The teacher might say, "Compared with provincial standards, Sarah's understanding of math rates as 'needs significant improvement.'" Or, "Sarah ranks 20th in her class of 24 classmates."

Not all the evaluative decisions teachers make involve measurement. Some are based on information that is difficult to express numerically: student interest, information about family support, previous experiences, even intuition. Nonetheless, measurement plays a large role in many classroom decisions and, again, when properly done, it provides unbiased and useful data for evaluations.

Increasingly, evaluation and measurement specialists are using the term **assessment** to describe the process of gathering information about students' learning. It is a broader undertaking than testing and measurement. Assessments can be formal, such as unit tests or lab reports; or they can be informal, such as observing who emerges as a leader in group work. Assessments can be designed by classroom teachers or by local, provincial, national, and even international agencies. Today, assessments go well beyond paper-and-pencil exercises to methods for observing performances, frameworks for developing portfolios, and guidelines for creating artifacts (Gronlund & Cameron, 2004; Popham, 2005).

In the first part of this chapter, we focus on formal assessments designed by groups and agencies outside the classroom. These assessments usually involve paper-and-pencil tests and reports of scores on those tests. So, we start by examining two types of tests that are differentiated on the basis of an important principle. Read carefully, now: Any score on any type of test has *no* meaning by itself. To interpret test results, we must make some kind of comparison. There are two basic types of comparison, as we describe next.

Norm-Referenced Tests

In **norm-referenced testing**, a sample of people who have taken the test provides *norms* for determining the meaning of other people's scores. Think of norms as scores that describe typical levels of performance for one particular group, the norm group. By comparing an individual's raw score (the actual number of correct answers) with norms, we can determine where that person's score falls in relation to scores in the norm group.

At least three types of **norm groups** are used as reference points for interpreting an individual's score on a test. Often, the norm group is the class or the several classes at that grade in the school. Norm groups may also be drawn from wider areas such as a school district. In this case, a student's score is compared with scores of all the students at their grade level throughout the district. Finally, some tests have national or even international norm groups. When students take an examination of this sort, their scores are compared with the scores of students all over the country and around the world.

Norm-referenced achievement tests usually make a trade-off. An advantage is that they cover a wide range of general objectives. A disadvantage is that they are

evaluation Decision making about student performance and about appropriate teaching strategies based on comparing data with standards.

measurement An evaluation expressed in quantitative (number) terms.

assessment Procedures used to obtain information about student performance.

Connect & Extend

TO YOUR TEACHING
Both subjective judgments and objective measurements are inevitably involved in evaluating students. Are both equally justified? When might one prevail over the other?

norm-referenced testing Testing in which individual scores are compared with the average performance of others.

norm group A group whose average score serves as a standard for evaluating any student's score on a test.

usually poor for assessing specific objectives. So, norm-referenced achievement tests are especially useful in measuring overall achievement when students have studied a large amount of complex material by different routes. Most norm-referenced tests used in Canada are tests of achievement in a subject over a whole grade or measures of intelligence, or tests that measure transferable capabilities, such as auditory discrimination. Norm-referenced tests are almost always supplements to other information. For example, norm-referenced grade 12 provincial exams in British Columbia are combined with marks a teacher assigns in a 40-to-60 ratio to determine overall achievement in many grade 12 subjects. If a teacher is concerned that a student may have a learning disability or a special talent, norm-referenced tests contribute to the decision about whether that student should participate in instruction that complements or replaces regular classroom teaching.

Norm-referenced measurement has several limitations. The results of a norm-referenced test do not tell you where students are in a program or a curriculum. For instance, knowing that a student is in the top 3 percent of the class based on district norms on a test of algebraic concepts will not tell you if he or she is ready to move on to trigonometry or even what exactly the student knows about algebra. Some students clearly understand more than others, but everyone in the class may have a rather limited understanding of particular algebraic concepts.

Norm-referenced tests are not typically appropriate for measuring affective and psychomotor objectives. To measure individuals' psychomotor learning, you need a clear description of standards. (Even though the best gymnast in school performs certain exercises better than others, he needs specific guidance about how to improve.) In affective areas, attitudes and values are personal; comparisons among individuals are not really appropriate. For example, how could we measure an "average" level of liberalism or support for private schools? Finally, norm-referenced tests tend to encourage competition and comparison of scores. Some students compete to be the best. Others, realizing that being the best seems impossible for them, may compete to be the worst (a dubious but nonetheless sometimes valued distinction). Either goal has its casualties.

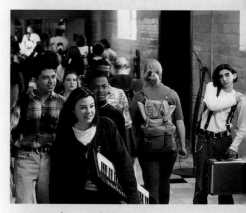

Norm-referenced testing compares an individual's score with the average score of others in a larger group. The group could be a particular classroom, school district, or international sample.

Criterion-Referenced Tests

When test scores are compared not with other students' scores but with a given criterion or standard of performance, this is **criterion-referenced testing**. To decide who should be allowed to drive a car, it is important to determine just what standard of performance is appropriate for licensing safe drivers. It does not matter how your test results compare with others'. If your performance on the test was in the top 10 percent but you consistently ran through red lights and bumped cars while parking, you would be a poor candidate for receiving a licence, even though your score was high.

Criterion-referenced tests measure the degree of mastery of very specific objectives. The results of a criterion-referenced test should tell the teacher exactly what a student can and cannot do under certain conditions (with or without access to the book, for example). A criterion-referenced test would be useful in measuring the ability to add three-digit numbers. A test could be designed with 20 different and representative problems, and the standard for mastery could be set at 17 correct out of 20. If two students receive scores of 7 and 11, it does not matter that one student did better than the other, since neither met the standard of 17. Both need more help with addition.

In teaching basic skills, there are many instances where comparison with a preset standard is more important than comparison with the performance of others. It is not very comforting to know, as a parent, that your child is better in reading than most of the students in class if none of the students are able to read material suited for their grade level. Sometimes standards for meeting the criterion must be set at 100-percent correct. You would not like to have your appendix removed by a surgeon who left surgical instruments inside the body *only* 10 percent of the time.

criterion-referenced testing
Testing in which individuals' scores are compared with a pre-defined standard of performance.

Connect & Extend

TO THE RESEARCH
Berk, R. A. (1986). A consumer's guide to setting performance standards on criterion-referenced tests. *Review of Educational Research, 56,* 137–172.
   This review identifies 38 methods for setting standards or adjusting error rates. Ten criteria for technical adequacy and practicability are proposed to evaluate these methods, and specific recommendations are offered for classroom teachers.

Connect & Extend

TO YOUR TEACHING

A student in your grade 4 class does poorly in the letter decoding subtest of a test that was standardized on a national sample of American students in grade 4. How would your interpretation of these results differ if the test were a criterion-referenced score versus a norm-referenced score? Explain.

standardized tests Tests administered under uniform conditions and scored according to uniform procedures.

Connect & Extend

TO YOUR TEACHING

Giving accurate feedback to families is part of a teacher's job. When talking with a parent about a child's abilities, do you think the use of norm-referenced or criterion-referenced test results is more desirable?

achievement tests Tests measuring how much students have learned in a given content area.

aptitude Capability for learning knowledge or skills in a particular setting.

aptitude tests Tests meant to predict future performance.

But criterion-referenced tests are not appropriate for every situation. Some subjects cannot be analyzed into a set of specific objectives on which most educators would agree. Moreover, although standards are important in criterion-eferenced testing, they can sometimes seem arbitrary. When deciding whether a student has mastered the addition of three-digit numbers comes down to the difference between 16 or 17 correct answers, it seems difficult to justify one particular standard over another—why 17? Why not 16 or even 18? Finally, at times, it is valuable to know how students in your class compare with other students at their grade level locally, provincially, and beyond. Table 13.1 below offers a comparison of norm-referenced and criterion-referenced tests. You can see that each type of test is well suited for certain situations, but each also has its limitations.

Standardized Tests

During their lives in school, almost all Canadian students will take **standardized tests**. These tests have two special qualities. First, they are administered to students under precisely defined and carefully controlled conditions. That is, the administration of the test is standardized. Second, students' test answers are scored in a consistent and reliable way. Thus, scoring is standardized. When both conditions are met, different people's scores can be interpreted in terms of the same benchmark.

Standardized tests don't have to originate with big testing companies or a province's Education Ministry. If teachers who teach the same subject at the same grade use the same test items, agree how they will administer the test, score it identically, and agree how to report scores, they are using a standardized test, whether they realize it or not. In fact, the intent behind some district grading policies is to approximate a standardized test. School staff want to be able to compare students' marks for a subject such as grade 8 math when students are in different classes in the same school or change schools.

There are three main kinds of standardized tests used in Canadian schools. When properly administered and expertly interpreted, each can contribute to a fuller understanding about a student.

Achievement Tests. Almost every standardized **achievement test** used in Canada is criterion-referenced. This is a significant difference from standardized achievement tests that are prominent in other countries, particularly the United States, where norm-referenced interpretations dominate. A good example of criterion-referenced standardized achievement tests are British Columbia's provincial examinations, which you can download from the internet at **www.bced.gov.bc.ca/assessment/fsa**.

Aptitude Tests. An **aptitude** is a capability for learning knowledge or skills in a relatively specific situation, for example, in classrooms or on the job. **Aptitude tests** are intended to provide a score that, along with other information, helps pre-

---

TABLE 13.1 Two Kinds of Test Interpretations

Norm-referenced tests may work best when you are	Criterion-referenced tests may work best when you are
• Measuring general ability in certain areas, such as English, algebra, general science, or Canadian history.	• Measuring mastery of basic skills.
• Assessing the range of abilities in a large group.	• Providing evidence students have met learning standards.
• Selecting top candidates when only a few openings are available.	• Determining if students have prerequisites to start a new unit.
	• Assessing affective and psychomotor objectives.
	• Grouping students for instruction.

dict how well, how fast, or how accurately a student can learn. Almost all standardized aptitude tests are norm-referenced, so it is essential to know characteristics of the **norming sample** of students and whether these characteristics correspond to a particular student whose score you are interpreting. A common aptitude test used in Canada's schools is the Stanford-Binet Intelligence Scales.

Psychoeducational Diagnostic Tests.   A **diagnosis** describes a student's current knowledge, skill, or ability. In manuals that accompany **diagnostic tests**, relatively narrow bands of scores are sometimes matched to descriptions of problems or cognitive processing deficiencies that might cause the diagnosis. To take a specific example, the Woodcock-Johnson Tests of Achievement, Basic Reading Skills cluster is a commonly used diagnostic test that includes measures of letter-word identification and word attack. Scores describe the quality of performance a student would be expected to show on tasks at a known level of difficulty.

norming sample A large sample of students with published characteristics who serve as a comparison group for interpreting scores on norm-referenced standardized tests.

diagnosis Description of a student's current knowledge, skills, or ability.

diagnostic tests Individually administered tests to identify special learning problems.

Check Your Knowledge

- Distinguish among evaluation, measurement, and assessment.
- Distinguish between norm-referenced and criterion-referenced tests.
- Describe the key features of a standardized test.

Apply to Practice

- The counsellor tells you that your musical aptitude is below average on a test about careers. What would you like to know about the norming sample?
- Would you prefer a criterion-referenced or norm-referenced measure of your blood pressure? Why?

INTERPRETING TEST SCORES

What Would You Say?

As part of the interview process for a job in a high school, you are asked the following: "How would you interpret the test scores of recent immigrant students?"

It is alarming that many people in and outside schools misinterpret test scores. One reason this happens is that not everyone who should know about the shortcomings of tests does know about them. One all-too-common misunderstanding about test scores is that numbers are precise measurements of a student's ability, attitude, or anything else. No test provides a perfectly accurate description of a student's achievement or aptitude. First of all, a test is only one small sample of behaviour. Two factors are important in developing good tests and interpreting results: reliability and validity.

Reliability

If you took a test on Monday, took the same test again a week later, and received about the same score each time, you would have reason to believe the score was reliable. If 100 people took the test one day, repeated it the following week, and each individual's score on the test had about the same rank both times, you would be even more convinced the scores were reliable. (Of course, this assumes that no one looks up answers or studies before the second test.) When a score has **reliability**, it represents a consistent and stable "reading" about a person's characteristic from one occasion to the next—assuming the characteristic remains the same. A reliable thermometer works similarly, giving you a reading of 100°C each time you measure the temperature of boiling water. Measuring a score's reliability in this way, by giving the test on two different occasions, indicates *stability*—or, as it is

reliability Consistency of test results.

often called, *test-retest reliability*. If a group of people takes two comparable versions or forms of a test and the scores on both tests are comparable, this is called *alternate-form reliability*.

Reliability can also refer to the internal consistency of items on a test or the precision of a score on a test. The *split-half reliability* is an internal consistency type of reliability. It is calculated by comparing performance on half of the test questions with performance on the other half. If, for example, a student did quite well on all the odd-numbered items and not at all well on the even-numbered items, we could assume the items were not very consistent or precise in measuring what they were intended to measure.

There are several ways to compute reliability, but all of them give numbers between 0.0 and 1.0, like a correlation coefficient. Above .90 is considered very reliable, .80 to .90 is good, and below .80 is not very good reliability for making important decisions (Haladyna, 2002). The simplest way to improve reliability is to add more appropriate items to a test or more observations to records of students' behaviour. Generally speaking, having more items or observations that are consistent with the original set improves the reliability of a score or description.

True Score. All tests imperfectly estimate the qualities or skills we try to measure with a test. There are errors in every testing situation. Sometimes the errors are in your favour, and you score higher than your ability or interest or skills warrant. This can occur when you just happen to review a key section just before a pop quiz or when your guesses are lucky. Sometimes the errors go against you. You don't feel well on the day of the examination, you have just received bad news from home, or you focused on the wrong material in your review. But if you could be tested over and over again without becoming tired and without memorizing the answers, the randomness of good luck and bad luck would even out. The average of your test scores would be very close to a true score for you. In other words, we can think of a student's **true score** as the average of all the scores that student would receive if the test were repeated an infinite number of times.

Most times, students take a test only once. The score each student receives is highly unlikely to be 100 percent accurate. Alternatively, we can view any single score as being made up of the hypothetical true score as well as some error, either plus or minus. How can error be reduced so that the actual score is a closer reflection of the true score? As you might guess, this returns us to the question of reliability. The more reliable the test, the less error in the score actually obtained. On standardized tests, test developers take this into consideration and make estimations of how much students' scores would probably vary due to unreliability. This estimate is called the **standard error of measurement**. It represents how variable a student's scores may be because a single number generated in one testing session has too much variability to place trust in it. Thus, a reliable test can also be defined as a test with a small standard error of measurement. As teachers and others interpret *any* test score, they *must* take into consideration the margin for error.

Confidence Interval. Because every test score is unreliable to some degree, teachers should not base a judgment of a student's ability, motivation, or achievement on just one test score or just one observation. A more reasonable view of any test result is to consider it as one point inside a **confidence interval** or "standard error band" that shows how widely the student's scores vary around the particular score the student received. Viewing scores as a range is better because no measurement process—a test, an observation, a rating—is perfectly reliable. Scores always vary due to random influences, that is, unreliability.

Suppose, for instance, that two students in an International Baccalaureate chemistry class take a standardized achievement test. One student receives a score of 77; the other, a score of 85. At first glance, these scores seem quite different. But consider the standard error bands around each of these scores. Suppose the standard error of measurement for this test is 3 points. First, calculate the length of a "leg" of the standard error band by multiplying the value of the standard error by

Connect & Extend

TO YOUR TEACHING
There are many sources of error in testing: personal (e.g., illness, anxiety, misreading directions, reviewing wrong material); test-related (e.g., unclear directions, excessive length, too-high reading level); and context-related (too-competitive situation, noise, mistakes by test administrator).

true score Hypothetical average of an individual's scores if repeated testing under ideal conditions were possible.

standard error of measurement A measure of unreliability representing how much variability there is in an average student's test scores around the student's true score.

confidence interval A range of scores within which a student's particular score is likely to fall.

two: $2 \times 3 = 6$. Now, subtract this result from each score to find the lower endpoint of each score's standard error band; then, add six to each student's score to find the upper endpoint of the standard error band. The standard error band for the student who scored 77 is $77 - 6 = 71$ to $77 + 6 = 83$. This student's true score on the test is somewhere in this confidence interval with about 95 percent confidence. The other student's standard error band is $85 - 6 = 79$ to $85 + 6 = 91$, so the true score is somewhere between 79 and 91 with about 95 percent confidence. As you can see, these confidence intervals overlap. It's possible that the student who scored 85 might have a true score that's actually less than that of the student who obtained the score of 77. If these two students took the test again, they might even switch ranks.

Any significant decision about a student should take into account that every test result has some degree of unreliability. Standard error bands are a useful method for gauging that uncertainty. When selecting students for special programs, no child should be rejected simply because one obtained score missed the cut-off by a few points. The student's true score might well be on the other side of the cut-off point.

Validity of Interpretations

If a test is sufficiently reliable, the next question is whether judgments and decisions based on the test are valid. A test itself never has validity. Only people's decisions and interpretations have some degree of validity.

To have **validity**, judgments or decisions based on a test score must be supported by *evidence* that stands in relation to a particular use or purpose for the test score (Linn & Gronlund, 2000). There are different kinds of evidence to support a particular judgment. If the purpose of a test is to measure the skills covered in a particular course or unit, we would hope to see test questions on all the important topics and none on extraneous topics. If this holds true, the condition of **curriculum alignment** is satisfied, and we have *content-related evidence of validity*. Have you ever taken a test that dealt only with a few ideas from one lecture or just a few chapters of the whole textbook? If so, decisions based on that test (your grade, for instance) lacked content-related evidence of validity.

Some tests are designed to predict outcomes. The LSATs (Law School Admission Tests), for example, are intended to predict performance in law school. If LSAT scores correlate with academic performance as measured by, say, grade-point average in the first year, then we have *criterion-related evidence of validity* for the use of the LSAT in admissions decisions. In other words, the test scores are fairly accurate predictors of the criterion—how well the student will do in law school.

Most standardized tests are designed to measure some psychological characteristic or "construct" such as reasoning ability, reading comprehension, achievement motivation, intelligence, creativity, and so on. It is a bit more difficult to gather *construct-related evidence of validity*, yet this is a critical requirement.

Construct-related evidence of validity is gathered over many years. It is indicated by a pattern of scores. For example, older children can answer more questions on intelligence tests than younger children. This fits with our construct of intelligence. If the average 5-year-old answered as many questions correctly on a test as the average 13-year-old, we would doubt that the test really measured intelligence. Construct-related evidence of validity can also be demonstrated when the results of a test correlate with the results of other well-established measures of the same construct.

Today, many educational psychologists suggest that concerns about evidence for construct-related validity form the broadest category. In their view, gathering content- and criterion-related evidence is another way of determining if the test measures the construct that it was designed to measure. But new questions are being raised about validity. What are the consequences of using a particular assessment procedure for teaching and learning? Forty years ago, Sam Messick (1975)

validity Degree to which a particular use of a test score is justified by evidence.

curriculum alignment The quality and degree to which an achievement test's items correspond to the curriculum that students are taught in school.

Connect & Extend

TO THE RESEARCH
Moss, P. A. (1992). Shifting conceptions of validity in educational measurement: Implications for performance assessment. *Review of Educational Research, 62*, 229–258.

Connect & Extend

TO YOUR TEACHING
What makes any test or measurement procedure a good predictor? Consider the relevance of the test or measurement procedure to the outcome, absence of bias, reliability, convenience, and cost.

TO YOUR TEACHING

Can you answer these questions (adapted from Popham, W. J. [1988]. *Educational evaluation* [2nd ed., p. 127]. Englewood Cliffs, NJ: Prentice Hall)?

Indicate which of the following types of validity is being gathered.

a. Subject matter experts have been summoned to rate the consonance of a test's items with the objectives the test is supposed to measure.

b. A correlation is computed between a new test of student self-esteem and a previously validated and widely used test of student self-esteem.

c. Scores on a screening test (used to assign grade 10 students to standard or enriched English classes) are correlated with English competence of first-year university students (as reflected by grades assigned at the end of first-year English).

Answers: a. content b. construct c. criterion

assessment bias Qualities of an assessment instrument that offend or unfairly penalize a group of students because of the students' gender, SES, race, ethnicity, etc.

raised two important questions to consider in making any decisions about using a test: Is the test a good measure of the characteristic it is assumed to assess? Should the test be used for the proposed purpose? The first question is about construct-related validity; the second is about ethics and values (Moss, 1992).

A number of factors may interfere with the validity of interpretations based on tests given in classroom situations. One problem has already been mentioned—a poorly planned test with weak relation to the important topics; that is, poor curriculum alignment. Standardized achievement tests must be designed so that items on the test measure knowledge actually gained in school. This match is absent more often than we might assume. Also, students must have the necessary skills to take the test. If students score low on a science test not because they lack knowledge about science but because they have difficulty reading the questions, do not understand the directions, or do not have enough time to finish, the test is not valid for measuring science achievement for those students.

A test must be reliable to be valid. For example, if, over a few months, an intelligence test yields different results each time it is given to the same child, then by definition it is not reliable. Certainly, it couldn't be the basis for valid interpretations about intelligence because intelligence is assumed to be fairly stable, at least over a short time span. However, reliability will not guarantee valid interpretations. If that intelligence test gave the same score every time for a particular child but didn't predict school achievement, rate of learning, or other characteristics associated with intelligence, then performance on the test would not be a valid indicator of intelligence. The test would be reliable—but invalid. The accompanying Guidelines should help you increase the reliability and validity of the standardized tests you give.

Absence of Bias

Reliability and validity have long been criteria for judging assessments. But over the past few decades, educators and psychologists realized that another criterion should be added—absence of bias. **Assessment bias** refers to "qualities of an assessment instrument that offend or unfairly penalize a group of students because of the students' gender, ethnicity, socioeconomic status, religion, or other such group-defining characteristic" (Popham, 2005, p. 77). Biases are aspects of the test such as content, language, or examples that might distort the performance of a group—either for better or for worse. For example, if a reading test used passages that described scenarios about milking cows, we might expect students living in farming communities, on average, to do better than those from a city because the former have more exposure to this activity.

Two forms of assessment bias are unfair penalization and offensiveness. A reading comprehension test with heavy emphasis on some sports content is an example of *unfair penalization*—some students may be penalized for their lack of knowledge. *Offensiveness* occurs when a particular group might be insulted by the content of the assessment. Offended, angry students may not perform at their best.

Check Your Knowledge

- What is test score reliability?
- How do you judge the validity of the interpretation of a test score?

Apply to Practice

- Suppose that all grade 12 students in your province take a well-designed, standardized international test of science. The average score on the test for students around the world is 70. If the standard error of measurement for this test is 4 points, would you describe a student who scored 80 as well above average?
- Every time you check your weight on your bathroom scale and at the gym, you weigh 0.5 kg more than you do on your scale at home. Is your weight reliable? Is it valid to say you're over- or underweight?

INCREASING SCORE RELIABILITY AND VALIDITY OF INTERPRETATIONS

Make sure that the test actually covers the content of the unit of study.

EXAMPLES

1. Compare test questions with course objectives. A behaviour-content matrix (described later in this chapter) is useful for doing this.
2. Use local achievement tests and local norms if norm-referenced interpretations are appropriate.
3. Check to see if the test is long enough and is aligned with the curriculum.
4. Are there any difficulties your students experience with the test, such as not enough time, level of reading, and so on? If so, discuss these problems with appropriate school personnel.

Make sure that students know how to use all the test materials.

EXAMPLES

1. Several days before a test, do a few practice questions that have a similar format.
2. If the test has separate answer sheets, show students how to use them.
3. Check with new students, shy students, students whose achievement lags behind the class, and students who have difficulty reading to make sure that they understand the questions.
4. Make sure that students know if and when guessing is appropriate.

Follow instructions for administering the test exactly.

EXAMPLES

1. Practise giving the test before you actually use it.
2. If there are time limits, follow them exactly for every student taking the test.

Make students as comfortable as possible during testing.

EXAMPLES

1. Do not create anxiety by making the test seem like the most important event of the year.
2. Help the class relax before beginning the test, perhaps by telling a joke or having everyone take a few deep breaths. Don't be tense yourself!
3. Make sure that the room is quiet.
4. Discourage cheating by monitoring the room. Don't become absorbed in your own paperwork.

Remember that no test scores are perfect.

EXAMPLES

1. Interpret scores using confidence intervals instead of just one point on the scale.
2. Ignore small differences between scores.

FORMATIVE AND SUMMATIVE ASSESSMENT

As a teacher, you may or may not help in designing the grading system for your school or your class. Many school districts have a standard approach to grading. Still, you will have choices about how you use your district's grading system and how you assess your students' learning. Will you give tests? How many? What kinds? Will students do projects or keep portfolios of their work? How will homework influence grades? Will you grade on students' current academic performance or on their degree of improvement? How will you use the information from standardized student assessments?

There are two general uses or functions for assessment: formative and summative. **Formative assessment** occurs before or during instruction. It has two basic purposes: to guide the teacher in planning and to help students identify areas that need work. In other words, formative assessment helps shape or form instruction. Often, students are given a formative test prior to instruction, a **pretest** that helps the teacher determine what students already know. Sometimes a test is given

formative assessment Ungraded testing used before or during instruction to aid in planning and diagnosis.

pretest Formative test for assessing students' knowledge, readiness, and abilities.

Connect & Extend

TO YOUR TEACHING

What are some specific ways in which formative evaluations can be implemented in the classroom?

data-based instruction Assessment method using frequent probes of specific-skill mastery.

curriculum-based assessment (CBA) Evaluation method using frequent tests of specific skills and knowledge.

summative assessment Testing that follows instruction and assesses achievement.

Connect & Extend

TO THE RESEARCH

For a description of the different models of curriculum-based assessment and ideas for how it can be used with mainstreamed students, see Shapiro, E. S., & Ager, C. (1992). Assessment of special education students in regular education programs: Linking assessment to instruction. *Elementary School Journal*, *92*, 283–296.

Testing is formative or summative depending on what is done with the results: If the results are used to plan future instruction, it is formative. If they're used to determine a final evaluation of a student, it is summative.

during instruction to see what areas of weakness remain so that teaching can be directed toward those. This is generally called a diagnostic test but should not be confused with the standardized diagnostic tests of more general learning abilities. A classroom diagnostic test identifies a student's areas of achievement and weakness in a particular subject. Older students are often able to apply the information from diagnostic tests to "reteach" themselves. For example, if a test on types of interpretations for test scores revealed you were fuzzy on norm-referenced interpretations, you could review the material about norm-referenced tests.

Pretests and diagnostic tests are not part of grades. And since formative tests do not count toward the final grade, students who tend to be very anxious on "real" tests may find this low-pressure practice in test taking especially helpful.

A variation of formative measurement is ongoing measurement, often called **data-based instruction** or **curriculum-based assessment (CBA)**. This approach uses frequent "probes," brief tests of specific skills and knowledge drawn from the curriculum, to give a precise picture of a student's current performance. Actually, CBA is not just one approach but a whole family of approaches for linking teaching and assessment. CBA is "any set of measurement procedures that use direct observation and recording of a student's performance in the local curriculum as a basis for gathering information to make instructional decisions" (Deno, 1987, p. 41). This method has been used primarily with students who have learning problems because it provides systematic assessment of both student performance and the teaching methods used. The assessment probes check to see if the difficulty level and the pace of instruction are right for the student. If a student shows inadequate progress on the assessment probes, the teacher should consider modifying or switching instructional strategies or pacing (Shapiro & Ager, 1992).

Summative assessment occurs at the end of instruction. Its purpose is to let the teacher and the students know the level of accomplishment attained. Summative assessment, therefore, provides a summary of accomplishment. The final exam is a classic example.

The distinction between formative and summative assessment is based on how results are used. The same assessment procedure often can be used for either purpose. If the goal is to obtain information about student learning for planning purposes, the assessment is formative. If the purpose is to determine final achievement (and help determine a course grade), the assessment is summative.

Check Your Knowledge

- What are two kinds of classroom assessment?

Apply to Practice

- What is the most important consideration in deciding whether to use a test that comes with the text for your class?

GETTING THE MOST FROM TRADITIONAL ASSESSMENT APPROACHES

What Would You Say?

In an interview with the principal of a school where you hope to get a job, the principal asks, "How would you justify using multiple-choice tests to parents who complain that these tests are old-fashioned and just test memorization?"

When most people think of assessment, they usually think of testing. As you will see shortly, teachers today have many other options, but testing is still a significant activity in most classrooms. Let's consider your options for assessing students using the traditional testing approach. In this section, we will examine how to plan effective tests, how to evaluate the tests that accompany standard curriculum materials, and how to write your own test questions.

Planning for Testing

Instruction and assessment are most effective when they are well organized and thoroughly planned. Because today's classes are populated with very diverse students, one essential part of planning is taking steps to accommodate students with special needs. In Reaching Every Student on page 510, we provide a list of the most common issues to be considered in this regard.

Creating a behaviour-content matrix is helpful in planning for tests. A behaviour-content matrix is a table that lists behaviour or skills as columns and key areas of the curriculum as rows. It is like a road map to the objectives you use to plan teaching and plan tests. A behaviour-content matrix offers a better way to judge whether the content of tests aligns with the objectives you create for your curriculum.

Using a Behaviour-Content Matrix. How might you use a behaviour-content matrix to design a unit test? First, decide how many items students can complete during the testing period. Divide this total into cells of a behaviour-content matrix so that more important skills and more important elements of content have more items (Berliner, 1987).

An example of a behaviour-content matrix that might be appropriate for planning a 40-question unit test on government is given in Table 13.2 below.

In this plan, you can see that this teacher decided that the most important topic is major political issues and accordingly allotted a total of 15 questions to it.

TABLE 13.2 Behaviour-Content Matrix for a Unit on Government

In making a test plan, begin by deciding on the total number of questions for each topic and for each kind of objective (the numbers in bold) and then allocate the number of questions to each particular combination of objective (behaviour) and topic (content).

Topics	Skills Tested				
	Understanding Concepts	Making Generalizations	Locating Information	Interpreting Graphs	Total Questions
Social Trends	4	4	1	1	10
National Political Events	2	3	3	2	10
Methods of Inquiry	1	1	2	1	5
Major Political Issues	3	6	4	2	15
Total Questions	10	14	10	6	4

ACCOMMODATIONS IN TESTING

Accommodations in testing may be made in the setting of the test, timing and scheduling, test presentation, and student response modes. Schools have to keep good records about what is done, because these accommodations have to be documented. Here are some examples of possible accommodations taken from Spinelli (2002, pp. 151–152).

Examples of Setting Accommodations

Conditions of Setting

- Minimal distractive elements (e.g., books, artwork, window views)
- Special lighting
- Special acoustics
- Adaptive or special furniture
- Individual student or small group of students rather than large group

Location

- Study carrel
- Separate room (including special education classroom)
- Seat closest to test administrator (teacher, proctor, etc.)
- Home
- Hospital
- Correctional institution

Examples of Timing Accommodations

Duration

- Changes in duration can be applied to selected subtests of an assessment or to the assessment overall
- Extended time (i.e., extra time)
- Unlimited time

Organization

- Frequent breaks during parts of the assessment (e.g., during subtests)
- Extended breaks between parts of assessment (e.g., subtests) so that assessments can be administered in several sessions

Examples of Scheduling Accommodations

Time

- Specific time of day (e.g., morning, midday, afternoon, after ingestion of medication)
- Specific day of week
- Over several days

Organization

- Present items in a different order from that used for most students (e.g., longer subtest first, shorter later; math first, English later)
- Omit questions that cannot be adjusted for an accommodation (e.g., graph reading for student using Braille) and adjust for missing scores

The least important topic is methods of inquiry. Also, the teacher wanted to focus on students' abilities to make generalizations (14 questions) while giving considerable attention to understanding concepts and locating information. Interpreting graphs is the least important objective, but it is not overlooked.

Once the behaviour-content matrix is filled in, write test items appropriate to each combination of skill and content. Note that this same process applies to writing objectives for the unit. Using the same behaviour-content matrix helps ensure that your tests are validly aligned to the curriculum you teach.

When to Test? Frank Dempster (1991) examined the research on reviews and tests and reached these useful conclusions for teachers:

1. Frequent testing encourages the retention of information and appears to be more effective than a comparable amount of time spent reviewing and studying the material.

2. Tests are especially effective in promoting learning if you give students a test on the material soon after they learn it, then retest on the material later. The retests should be spaced further and further apart.

3. Using cumulative questions on tests is a key to effective learning. Cumulative questions ask students to apply information learned in previous units to solve a new problem.

Examples of Presentation Accommodations

Format Alterations

- Braille edition
- Large-print version
- Larger bubbles on answer sheet
- One complete sentence per line in reading passage
- Bubbles to side of choices in multiple-choice exams
- Key words or phrases highlighted
- Increased spacing between lines
- Fewer items per page

Procedural Changes

- Use sign language to give directions to student
- Reread directions
- Write helpful verbs in directions on board or on separate piece of paper
- Simplify language, clarify or explain directions
- Provide extra examples
- Prompt student to stay focused on test, move ahead, read entire item
- Explain directions to student during test

Assistive Devices

- Audiotape of directions
- Computer that reads directions and/or items
- Magnification device
- Amplification device (e.g., hearing aid)

- Noise buffer
- Templates to reduce visible print
- Markers or masks to maintain place
- Dark or raised lines
- Pencil grips

Examples of Response Accommodations

Format Alterations

- Allow marking responses in test booklet rather than recording them on a separate page
- Allow responding on different paper, such as graph paper, wide-lined paper, paper with wide margins

Procedural Changes

- Use reference materials (e.g. dictionary, arithmetic tables)
- Give response in different mode (e.g., pointing, oral response to tape recorders, sign language)

Assistive Devices

- Word processor or computer to record responses
- Amanuensis (proctor-scribe writes student responses)
- Slant board or wedge
- Calculator or abacus
- Brailler
- Other communication device (e.g., symbol board)
- Spell checker

Unfortunately, the curriculum in many schools is so full that there is little time for frequent tests and reviews. Dempster argues that students will learn more if we "teach them less," that is, if the curriculum includes fewer topics, but explores those topics in greater depth and allows more time for review, practice, testing, and feedback (Dempster, 1993).

Judging Textbook Tests.   Most elementary and secondary school texts today come complete with supplemental materials such as teaching manuals, handout masters, and ready-made tests. Using these tests can save time, but is this good teaching practice? The answer depends on your objectives for your students, the way you taught the material, and the quality of the tests provided (Airasian, Engemann, & Gallagher, 2007). If the textbook test matches your testing plan and the instruction you actually provided for your students, then it may be the right test to use. Table 13.3 on the next page gives key points to consider in evaluating textbook tests.

What if no tests are available for the material you want to cover, or the tests provided in your teacher's manuals are not appropriate for your students? Then it's time for you to create your own tests. We will consider the two major kinds of tests—objective and essay.

Connect & Extend

TO THE RESEARCH
Dempster, F. N. (1991). Synthesis of research on reviews and tests. *Educational Leadership,* *48*(7), 71–76. *Focus Question:* How can tests and reviews be used to encourage student learning?

Connect & Extend

TO THE RESEARCH
Dempster, F. N. (1993). Exposing our students to less should help them learn more. *Phi Delta Kappan, 74,* 432–437.

TABLE 13.3 Key Points to Consider in Judging Textbook Tests

The decision to use a textbook test must come after a teacher identifies the objectives that he or she taught and now wants to assess.

Textbook tests are designed for the typical classroom, but since few classrooms are typical, most teachers deviate somewhat from the text in order to accommodate their pupils' needs.

The more classroom instruction deviates from the textbook objectives and lesson plans, the less valid the textbook tests are likely to be.

The main consideration in judging the adequacy of a textbook test is the match between its test questions and what pupils were taught in their classes:

- Are questions similar to the teacher's objectives and instructional emphases?
- Do questions require pupils to perform the behaviour they were taught?
- Do questions cover all or most of the important objectives taught?
- Is the language level and terminology appropriate for pupils?
- Does the number of items for each objective provide a sufficient sample of pupil performance?

Source: From Airasian, P. (1996). *Assessment in the classroom* (p. 190). New York: McGraw-Hill. Copyright © 1996 by The McGraw-Hill Companies. Adapted with permission of The McGraw-Hill Companies.

Objective Testing

objective testing The kind of tests that do not require interpretation in scoring, such as multiple-choice, true/false, short-answer, and fill-in.

Multiple-choice questions, matching exercises, true/false statements, and short-answer or fill-in items are all types of **objective testing**. The word *objective* in relation to testing means "not open to many interpretations," or "not subjective." The scoring of these types of items is relatively straightforward compared with the scoring of essay questions because the answers are more clear-cut than essay answers.

The guiding principle for deciding which item format is best is to use the format that gives you the most direct measure of the learning outcome you intended for your students (Gronlund & Cameron, 2004). In other words, if you want to see how well students can write a letter, have them write a letter; don't ask multiple-choice questions about letters. But if many different item formats will work equally well, use multiple-choice questions because they are easier to score fairly and can cover many topics. Switch to other formats if writing good multiple-choice items for the material is not possible. For example, if related concepts need to be linked, such as terms and definitions, then a matching item is a better format than multiple-choice. If it is difficult to come up with several wrong answers for a multiple-choice item, try a true/false question instead. Alternatively, ask the student to supply a short answer that completes a statement (fill in the blank). Variety in objective testing can lower students' anxiety because the entire grade does not depend on one type of question that a particular student may find difficult. Here we look closely at the multiple-choice format because it is the most versatile—and the most difficult to use well.

Connect & Extend

TO OTHER CHAPTERS
See **Chapter 12** for a discussion of Bloom's taxonomy of objectives in the cognitive domain and a recent revision of this taxonomy.

Using Multiple-Choice Tests. People often assume that multiple-choice items are appropriate only for asking factual questions. But multiple-choice items can test higher-level objectives as well, although writing higher-level items is difficult. A multiple-choice item can assess more than recall and recognition if it requires the student to deal with new material by applying or analyzing the concept or principle being tested (Gronlund & Cameron, 2004; Popham, 2005). For example, the following multiple-choice item is designed to assess students' ability to recognize unstated assumptions, one of the skills involved in analyzing an idea:

A teacher's plan for improving classroom management includes making statements such as, "That's great cooperation!" and "Now that's what I call a polite way to debate." Which of the following assumptions is the teacher making?

1. Students are too often not attentive to their own behaviour. 2. Rewarding statements function as positive reinforcers. (correct answer) 3. Punishers don't have to be aversive. 4. Group work is naturally motivating.

Writing Multiple-Choice Questions. All test items require skilful construction, but good multiple-choice items are a real challenge. Some students jokingly refer to multiple-choice tests as "multiple-guess" tests—a sign that these tests are often poorly designed. Your goal in writing test items is to design them so that they measure student achievement, not test-taking and guessing skills.

The **stem** of a multiple-choice item is the part that asks the question or poses the problem. The choices that follow are called alternatives. The wrong answers are called **distractors** because their purpose is to distract students who have only a partial understanding of the material. If there were no good distractors, students with only a vague understanding would have no difficulty in finding the right answer.

The Guidelines on pages 514–515, adapted from Gronlund and Cameron (2004), Popham (2005), and Smith, Smith, & De Lisi (2001), should make writing multiple-choice and other objective test questions easier.

stem The question part of a multiple-choice item.

distractors Wrong answers offered as choices in a multiple-choice item.

Evaluating Objective Test Items

How will you evaluate the quality of the objective tests you give? One way is to conduct an item analysis to identify items that are performing well and those that should be changed or eliminated. There are many techniques for item analysis, but one basic approach is to calculate a difficulty index and a discrimination index for each item on the test. The difficulty index (symbolized p) of any item is simply the proportion or percentage of people who answered that item correctly. (Note that, although p is called the difficulty index, it actually shows how easy an item is. A p of 1.00 describes an item that everyone answers correctly and a p of 0.00 identifies an item that no one could answer.) For tests where you want to have the best chance to identify differences among people, items with difficulty indices of around .50 are best. A simple way of calculating the difficulty index of an item when you have a large class is shown in Table 13.4 on page 516.

The discrimination index (d) tells you how well each test item differentiates between people who performed well overall on the test versus those who did poorly. The assumption here is that a test item is a better item if people who answered that item correctly also did better on the entire test, and, conversely, students who missed that item got lower scores on the test. A test item that was passed more often by the low scorers than by the high scorers would be suspect. Table 13.4 shows an uncomplicated way to estimate the discrimination index of a test item.

Essay Testing

Some learning objectives are best measured by requiring students to create answers on their own. An essay question is appropriate in these cases. The most difficult part of essay testing is judging the quality of the answers, but writing good, clear questions is not particularly easy either. We will look at writing, administering, and grading essay tests, with most of the specific suggestions taken from Gronlund and Cameron (2004). We will also consider factors that can bias the scoring of essay questions and ways you can overcome these problems.

WRITING OBJECTIVE TEST ITEMS

The stem should be clear and simple, and it should present only a single problem. Unessential details should be left out.

POOR
There are several different kinds of standard or derived scores. An IQ score is especially useful because ...

BETTER
An advantage of an IQ score is ...

The problem in the stem should be stated in positive terms. Negative language is confusing. If you must use words such as not, no, or except, underline them or type them in all-capitals.

POOR
Which of the following is not a standard score?

BETTER
Which of the following is NOT a standard score?

Do not expect students to make extremely fine discrimination among answer choices.

POOR
The percentage of area in a normal curve falling between +1 and −1 standard deviations is about:
    a. 66%. b. 67%. c. 68%. d. 69%.

BETTER
The percentage of area in a normal curve falling between +1 and −1 standard deviations is about:
    a. 14%. b. 34%. c. 68%. d. 95%.

As much wording as possible should be included in the stem so that phrases will not have to be repeated in each alternative.

POOR
A percentage score

a. indicates the percentage of items answered correctly.
b. indicates the percentage of correct answers divided by the percentage of wrong answers.
c. indicates the percentage of people who scored at or above a given raw score.
d. indicates the percentage of people who scored at or below a given raw score.

BETTER
A percentage score indicates the percentage of

a. items answered correctly.
b. correct answers divided by the percentage of wrong answers.
c. people who scored at or above a given raw score.
d. people who scored at or below a given raw score.

Each alternative answer should fit the grammatical form of the stem, so that no answers are obviously right or wrong.

POOR
The Stanford-Binet test yields an

a. IQ score.
b. vocational preference.
c. reading level.
d. mechanical aptitude.

BETTER
The Stanford-Binet is a test of

a. intelligence.
b. reading level.
c. vocational preference.
d. mechanical aptitude.

Constructing Essay Tests. Because answering essays takes time, true essay tests necessarily cover less material than objective tests. Thus, for efficiency, essay tests should be limited to assessing the more complex learning outcomes.

An essay question should give students a clear and precise task and should indicate the elements to be covered in the answer. Gronlund and Cameron (2003, p. 125) suggest the following as an example of an essay question that might appear in an educational psychology course to measure an objective at the synthesis level of Bloom's taxonomy in the cognitive domain:

> For a course that you are teaching or expect to teach, prepare a complete plan for assessing student achievement. Be sure to include the procedures you would follow, the instruments you would use, and the reasons for your choices.

Categorical words such as always, all, only, or never should be avoided unless they can appear consistently in all the alternatives. Most smart test-takers know that categorical answers signalled by these kinds of words are usually wrong.

POOR
A student's true score on a standardized test is

a. never equal to the obtained score.
b. always very close to the obtained score.
c. always determined by the standard error of measurement.
d. usually within a band that extends from +1 to –1 standard errors of measurement on each side of the obtained score.

BETTER
Which one of these statements would most often be correct about a student's true score on a standardized test?

a. It equals the obtained score.
b. It is very close to the obtained score.
c. It is determined by the standard error of measurement.
d. It could be above or below the obtained score.

You should also avoid including two distractors that have the same meaning. If only one answer can be right and if two answers are the same, these two must both be wrong. This narrows down the choices considerably.

POOR
The most frequently occurring score in a distribution is called the

a. mode.
b. median.
c. arithmetical average.
d. mean.

BETTER
The most frequently occurring score in a distribution is called the

a. mode.
b. median.
c. standard deviation.
d. mean.

Avoid using the exact wording found in the textbook. Poor students may recognize the answers without knowing what they mean.

Avoid overuse of all of the above *and* none of the above. *Such choices may be helpful to students who are simply guessing. In addition, using* all of the above *may trick a quick student who sees that the first alternative is correct and does not read on to discover that the others are correct too.*

Obvious patterns on a test also aid students who are guessing. The position of the correct answer should be varied, as should its length.

This question requires students to apply information and values derived from course material to produce a complex new product.

Students should be given ample time for answering. If more than one essay is being completed in the same class period, you may want to suggest time limits for each. Remember, however, that time pressure increases anxiety and may interfere with accurate assessment of some students. Whatever your approach, do not try to make up for the limited amount of material an essay test can cover by including a large number of essay questions. It would be better to plan more frequent testing than to include more than two or three essay questions in a single class period. Combining an essay question with a number of objective items is one way to avoid the problem of limited sampling of course material (Gronlund & Cameron, 2004).

TABLE 13.4 Calculating the Difficulty and Discrimination Indices for Test Items

To estimate the Difficulty Index (p) for each item,

- Rank the scores on the test from highest to lowest.
- Identify the people in the top one-third (the high-scoring group, or HSG) and the people in the bottom one-third (the low-scoring group, or LSG).
- For each item, count the number of people who answered correctly in the HSG and the LSG combined and divide by the total in the two groups. The formula is:

$$\text{Difficulty Index of an item} = \frac{\text{number correct in HSG} + \text{number correct in LSG}}{\text{number in HSG} + \text{number in LSG}}$$

This calculation is a reasonable estimate of the proportion of students in the whole class who answered correctly. Ideally, most of the items on a norm-referenced test would have difficulty indices of .40 to .59, with only a few hard (.00 to .25) or easy (.75 to 1.00) items. To estimate the Discrimination Index (d) for each item,

- Rank the scores on the test from highest to lowest.
- Identify the people in the top one-third of the scores (high-scoring group, or HSG) and the people in the bottom one-third (low-scoring group, or LSG).
- Subtract the percentage of students in the LSG who answered correctly from the percentage of students in the HSG who answered correctly. The formula is:

$$\text{Discrimination Index of an item} = \text{percentage correct in HSG} - \text{percentage correct in LSG}$$

The meaning of the discrimination index for any item is as follows:

$d = +.60$ to 1.00	*Very strong* discriminator between high- and low-scoring students
$d = +.40$ to $.59$	*Strong* discriminator between high- and low-scoring students
$d = +.20$ to $.39$	*Moderate* discriminator between high- and low-scoring students (improve the item)
$d = -.19$ to $.19$	*Does not* discriminate between high- and low-scoring students (improve or eliminate the item)
$d = -.20$ to -1.00	*Strong negative* discriminator between high- and low-scoring students (check item for problems: miskeyed? two right answers? etc.)

Source: Adapted with permission from Linden, K. (1992). *Cooperative learning and problem solving* (pp. 207–209). Prospect Heights, IL: Waveland Press.

Connect & Extend

TO YOUR TEACHING
One reason students prefer essay tests is that they can write down something, even if it doesn't answer the question, and receive at least partial credit for it. Do you think that granting partial credit is a common grading practice among teachers? Considering that essay questions sample only a limited amount of material, does giving partial credit seem commendable or defensible?

Evaluating Essays: Dangers. In 1912, Starch and Elliot began a series of classic experiments that shocked educators into critical consideration of subjectivity in testing. These researchers wanted to find out the extent to which teachers were influenced by personal values, standards, and expectations in scoring essay tests. For their initial study, they sent copies of English examination papers written by two high school students to English teachers in 200 high schools. Each teacher was asked to score the papers according to his or her school's standards. A percentage scale was to be used, with 75 percent as a passing grade.

The results? Neatness, spelling, punctuation, and communicative effectiveness were all valued to different degrees by different teachers. The scores on one of the papers ranged from 64 to 98 percent, with a mean of 88.2. The average score for the other paper was 80.2, with a range between 50 and 97. The following year, Starch and Elliot (1913a, 1913b) published similar findings in a study involving history and geometry papers. The most important result of these studies was the discovery that the problem of subjectivity in grading was not confined to any particular subject area. The main difficulties were the individual standards of the grader and the unreliability of scoring procedures.

Certain qualities of an essay may influence grades. Teachers may reward quantity rather than quality in essays. In a series of studies described by Fiske (1981), many high school and university English teachers rated pairs of student essays that were identical in every way but linguistic style. One essay was quite verbose, with flowery language, complex sentences, and passive verbs. The other essay was written in the simple, straightforward language most teachers claim is the goal for students of writing. The teachers consistently rated the verbose essay higher.

Evaluating Essays: Methods. Phil designs essay items so that each one targets three to five key ideas. Generally, a key idea is something that requires a paragraph or two to describe. He also provides some opportunity to include a few connected supplementary ideas. To prepare for marking, Phil first writes out the essential parts of each key idea that every student's essay should include. Then he adds a list of other points that supplement those key ideas but aren't absolutely essential to a full and accurate answer. For each key idea, he scores a 0 if the idea is missing or wrongly described, +1 if it is mentioned but otherwise not developed, +2 if the idea is fairly well described and yet missing something small but important or is slightly off target, and +3 if the idea is fully and accurately presented. Next, he scores supplements to key ideas using the same scale of 0, +1, or +2 for each one. Because these are supplements rather than key ideas, the maximum score for all the supplements is set at approximately a quarter or a third of the maximum score for key ideas, about four to five points overall. Next, Phil makes a judgment about the overall quality and organization of the student's essay, scoring this feature from 0 to +3. Then he adds up the points for key ideas, supplements, and quality. Finally, as a check that the marks make "good sense," he lays out students' papers on the floor in order of their total score. He compares close papers and, if necessary, makes scoring adjustments to be fair. This method has several advantages. It makes most essay test questions about the same "size." It reduces subjectivity by limiting the range of points assigned to any one part. It rewards students for elaborations that enrich the focus of an item. Last but not least, it recognizes that students' answers can have quality beyond just content.

There are special cautions in evaluating essay tests. The challenges are to be clear with students about the criteria for grading and then to apply those criteria fairly and consistently.

Gronlund and Cameron (2004) suggest several other good strategies for avoiding problems of subjectivity and inaccuracy in marking essays. When grading essay tests with several questions, it makes sense to grade all responses to one question before moving on to the next. This helps prevent the quality of a student's answer to one question from influencing your reaction to the student's other answers. After you finish reading and scoring the first question, shuffle the papers so that no students end up having all their questions graded first, last, or in the middle.

You may achieve greater objectivity if you ask students to put their names on the back of the paper, so that grading is anonymous. A final check on your fairness as a grader is to have another teacher who is equally familiar with your goals and subject matter grade your tests without knowing what grades you assigned. This can give you valuable insights into areas of bias in your grading practices.

Now that we have examined both objective and essay testing, we can compare the two approaches. Table 13.5 on page 518 presents a summary of the important characteristics of each.

Connect & Extend

TO THE RESEARCH
Writing evaluation: Examining four teachers' holistic analytic scores. *Elementary School Journal, 90,* 88–95.

Check Your Knowledge

- How should teachers plan for assessment?
- Describe two kinds of traditional testing.

Apply to Practice

- Would an objective test or an essay test be more appropriate under the following circumstances?
  1. You wish to test the students' knowledge of the terminology used in lab experiments.
  2. The test must be given and graded in the two days before the end of the six-week grading period.
  3. You want to test the students' ability to present a logical argument.
  4. Your aim is to balance subjective judgments with a highly reliable measure.
  5. You are seeking to test student understanding of a few major principles.
  6. You have limited time to construct the test.

TABLE 13.5 Comparing Objective and Essay Tests

Objective tests include any tests that ask the student to select the answer from a set of choices (multiple choice, true/false, matching).

	Selection-Type Items	Essay Questions
Learning outcomes measured	Good for measuring outcomes at the knowledge, comprehension, and application levels of learning; inadequate for organizing and expressing ideas.	Inefficient for measuring knowledge outcomes; best for ability to organize, integrate, and express ideas.
Sampling of content	The use of a large number of items results in broad coverage, which makes representative sampling of content feasible.	The use of a small number of items limits coverage, which makes representative sampling of content infeasible.
Preparation of items	Preparation of good items is difficult and time consuming.	Preparation of good items is difficult but easier than selection-type items.
Scoring	Objective, simple, and highly reliable.	Subjective, difficult, and less reliable.
Factors distorting scores	Reading ability and guessing.	Writing ability and bluffing.
Probable effect on learning	Encourages students to remember, interpret, and use the ideas of others.	Encourages students to organize, integrate, and express their own ideas.

Source: From Gronlund, N. E. (1993). *How to make achievement tests and assessments* (5th ed., p. 83). Boston: Allyn & Bacon. Copyright © 1996 by Pearson Education. Reprinted by permission of the publisher.

INNOVATIONS IN ASSESSMENT

Connect & Extend

TO THE RESEARCH
For ideas about making classroom assessment better, see Stiggins, R. J. (2001). Assessment crisis: The absence of assessment FOR learning, *Phi Delta Kappan, 83,* 758–765. Available online at www.pdkintl.org/kappan/k0206sti.htm.

We have been considering how to make traditional testing more effective; now let's look at a few new approaches to classroom assessment. One of the main criticisms of standardized tests—that they control the curriculum, emphasizing recall of facts instead of thinking and problem solving—is a major criticism of classroom tests as well. Few teachers would dispute these criticisms. Even if you follow the guidelines we have been discussing, traditional testing can be limiting. What can be done? Should innovations in classroom assessment make traditional testing obsolete? The accompanying Point/Counterpoint feature addresses this question.

One solution that has been proposed to solve the testing dilemma is to apply the concept of authentic assessment to classroom testing.

Authentic Classroom Tests

What Would You Say?

In your interview with the search team in an elementary school known for innovation, one of the teachers asks, "What do you know about using portfolios, performances, projects, and rubrics to assess learning?"

authentic assessments Assessment procedures that test skills and abilities as they would be applied in real-life situations.

Authentic assessments ask students to apply skills and abilities as they would in real life. For example, they might use fractions to enlarge or reduce recipes. The argument in favour of authentic assessments goes like this:

> If tests determine what teachers actually teach and what students will study for—and they do—then the road to reform is a straight but steep one: test those capabilities and habits we think are essential, and test them in context. Make [tests] replicate, within

POINT > < COUNTERPOINT
TO TEST OR NOT TO TEST

Are traditional multiple-choice and essay tests useful in classroom assessment?

> Point *Traditional tests are a poor basis for classroom assessment.*

In his article "Standards, Not Standardization: Evoking Quality Student Work," Grant Wiggins (1991) makes a strong case for giving students standards of excellence against which they can judge their accomplishments. But these standards should not be higher scores on multiple-choice tests. When scores on traditional tests become the standard, the message to students is that only right answers matter and the thinking behind the answers is unimportant. Wiggins notes,

> We do not judge Xerox, the Boston Symphony, the Cincinnati Reds, or Dom Perignon vineyards on the basis of indirect, easy to test, and common indicators. Nor would the workers in those places likely produce quality if some generic, secure test served as the only measure of their success in meeting a standard. Demanding and getting quality, whether from students or adult workers, means framing standards in terms of the work that we undertake and value. And it means framing expectations about that work which make quality a necessity, not an option. Consider:
>
> - the English teacher who instructs peer-editors to mark the place in a student paper where they lost

interest in it or found it slapdash and to hand it back for revision at that point;
> - the professor who demands that all math homework be turned in with another student having signed off on it, where one earns the grade for one's work and the grade for the work that each person (willingly!) countersigned. (p. 22)

In a more recent article, Wiggins continues to argue for assessment that makes sense, that tests knowledge as it is applied in real-world situations. Understanding cannot be measured by tests that ask students to use skills and knowledge out of context. "In other words, we cannot be said to understand something unless we can employ our knowledge wisely, fluently, flexibly, and aptly in particular and diverse contexts" (Wiggins, 1993, p. 200).

< Counterpoint *Traditional tests can play an important role.*

Most psychologists and educators would agree with Wiggins that setting clear, high, authentic standards is important, but many also believe that traditional tests are useful in this process. Learning may be more than knowing the right answers, but right answers are important. While schooling is about learning to think and solve problems, it is also about knowledge. Students must have something to think about—facts,

ideas, concepts, principles, theories, explanations, arguments, images, opinions. Well-designed traditional tests can evaluate students' knowledge effectively and efficiently (Airasian, Engemann, & Gallagher, 2007; Kirst, 1991).

Some educators believe that traditional testing should play an even greater role than it currently does. Educational policy analysts suggest that North American students, compared with students in many other developed countries, lack essential knowledge because North American schools emphasize process—critical thinking, self-esteem, problem solving—more than content. In order to teach more about content, teachers will need to determine how well their students are learning the content, and traditional testing provides useful information about content learning.

Tests are also valuable in motivating and guiding students' learning. There is research evidence that frequent testing encourages learning and retention (Nungester & Duchastel, 1982). In fact, students generally learn more in classes with more rather than fewer tests (Dempster, 1991).

Source: From Wiggins, G. (1991). Standards, not standardization. *Educational Leadership, 48*(5), 18–25. Copyright © 1991 by the Association for Supervision and Curriculum Development. Reprinted with permission.

reason, the challenges at the heart of each academic discipline. Let them be—authentic. (Wiggins, 1989, p. 41)

Wiggins goes on to say that if our instructional goals for students include the abilities to write, speak, listen, create, think critically, do research, solve problems, or apply knowledge, then our tests should ask students to write, speak, listen, create, think, research, solve, and apply. How can this happen?

Many educators suggest that we look to the arts and sports for analogies to solve this problem. If we think of the "test" as being the recital, exhibition, game, mock court trial, or other performance, then teaching to the test is just fine. All coaches, artists, and musicians eagerly "teach" to these "tests" because performing well on these tests is the whole point of instruction. Authentic assessment asks

Connect & Extend

TO YOUR OWN PHILOSOPHY
The emphasis on student-centred learning has been accompanied by an emphasis on authentic assessments. What do you think are the purposes, values, and advantages and disadvantages of these forms of assessment?

Connect & Extend

TO PROFESSIONAL JOURNALS
Aschbacher, P. (1997). New directions in student assessment (special issue). *Theory into Practice*, 36(4), 194–272. *Focus Question:* What makes assessments "authentic"?

students to perform. The performances may be thinking performances, physical performances, creative performances, or other forms.

It may seem odd to talk of thinking as a performance, but there are many parallels. Serious thinking is risky because real-life problems are not well defined. Often, the outcomes of our thinking are public—our ideas are evaluated by others. Like a dancer auditioning for a theatre show, we must cope with the consequences of being evaluated. Like a sculptor looking at a lump of clay, a student facing a difficult problem must experiment, observe, redo, imagine and test solutions, apply both basic skills and inventive techniques, make interpretations, decide how to communicate results to the intended audience, and often accept criticism and improve the solution (Wolf et al., 1991). Table 13.6 lists some characteristics of authentic assessments.

Performance in Context: Portfolios and Exhibitions

The concern with authentic assessment has led to the development of several new approaches based on the goal of performance in context. Instead of circling answers to "factual" questions about non-existent situations, students are required to solve real problems. Facts are used in a context where they apply—for example,

---

TABLE 13.6 Characteristics of Authentic Assessments

A. Structure and Logistics

1. Are more appropriately public; involve an audience, a panel, and so on.
2. Do not rely on unrealistic and arbitrary time constraints.
3. Offer known, not secret, questions or tasks.
4. Are more like portfolios or a season of games (not one-shot).
5. Require some collaboration with others.
6. Recur—and are worth practising for, rehearsing, and retaking.
7. Make assessment and feedback to students so central that school schedules, structures, and policies are modified to support them.

B. Intellectual Design Features

1. Are "essential"—not needlessly intrusive, arbitrary, or contrived to "shake out" a grade.
2. Are "enabling"—constructed to point the student toward more sophisticated use of the skills or knowledge.
3. Are contextualized, complex intellectual challenges, not "atomized" tasks, corresponding to isolated "outcomes."
4. Involve the student's own research or use of knowledge, for which "content" is a means.
5. Assess student habits and repertoires, not mere recall or plug-in skills.
6. Are representative challenges—designed to emphasize depth more than breadth.

7. Are engaging and educational.
8. Involve somewhat ambiguous ("ill-structured") tasks or problems.

C. Grading and Scoring Standards

1. Involve criteria that assess essentials, not easily counted (but relatively unimportant) errors.
2. Are graded not on a "curve" but in reference to performance standards (criterion-referenced, not norm-referenced).
3. Involve demystified criteria of success that appear to students as inherent in successful activity.
4. Make self-assessment a part of the assessment.
5. Use a multifaceted scoring system instead of one aggregate grade.
6. Exhibit harmony with shared school-wide aims—a standard.

D. Fairness and Equity

1. Ferret out and identify (perhaps hidden) strengths.
2. Strike a constantly examined balance between honouring achievement and native skill or fortunate prior training.
3. Minimize needless, unfair, and demoralizing comparisons.
4. Allow appropriate room for student learning styles, aptitudes, and interests.
5. Can be—should be—attempted by all students, with the test "scaffolded up," not "dumbed down," as necessary.

Source: From Wiggins, G. (1989). Teaching to the authentic test. *Educational Leadership*, 46(7), 44. Reprinted by permission of the Association of Supervision and Curriculum Development. Copyright © 1989 by ASCD. All rights reserved.

---

the student uses grammar facts to write a persuasive letter to a software company requesting donations for the class computer centre.

In Ontario's 2006 language curriculum guide (Ontario Ministry of Education, 2006), elementary students are expected to "have opportunities to use available technologies to create media texts of different types" (p. 13). Here's an example we created of a performance assessment and exhibition linked to this objective for grade 6 students:

> As you probably know, a lot of kids begin smoking at about your age. And you also probably know that smoking is a big threat to health, not to mention how much it costs a smoker to sustain a cigarette habit. Your assignment is to write a script for a TV "commercial" that will convince kids your age not to start smoking. Then, you and your team will produce your commercial using our classroom's video equipment—you'll create a setting for your ad and shoot actors (you!) to make your point. At the end of the month, we'll have a kind of Gemini Awards where we'll view each team's commercial and, as a class, we'll consider how to judge the effectiveness of messages like your TV commercials.

Students completing this "test" will need to use several language-related skills, such as thinking critically and writing persuasively, as they develop a script concerning this real-life issue. Group discussion skills can be examined as the team plans the script and produces the video. In their acting roles, students can demonstrate other communication skills, such as using tone of voice and gestures to persuade others. As well, students' skills in using modern communication tools, such as video cameras, and in helping one another can be observed during the shoot. When the class has its exhibition, you can evaluate students' use of high-level skills as they synthesize a method to judge the social impact of TV messages.

Test items such as this performance assessment, and portfolios and exhibitions, are new approaches to assessment that require performance in context. With these new approaches, it is difficult to tell where instruction stops and assessment starts because the two processes are interwoven.

Portfolios. For years, photographers, artists, models, and architects have had portfolios to display their skills and often to get jobs. A **portfolio** is a systematic collection of work, often including work in progress, revisions, student self-analyses, and reflections on what the student has learned (Popham, 2005). One student's self-reflection is presented in Figure 13.1 on page 522.

Written work or artistic pieces are common contents of portfolios, but students might also include graphs, diagrams, snapshots of displays, peer comments, audio- or videotapes, laboratory reports, computer programs—anything that demonstrates learning in the area being taught and assessed (Belanoff & Dickson, 1991; Camp, 1990; Wolf et al., 1991).

There is a distinction between process portfolios and final or "best works" portfolios. The distinction is similar to the difference between formative and summative evaluation. Process portfolios document learning and show progress. Best works portfolios showcase final accomplishments (Johnson & Johnson, 2002). Table 13.7 on page 522 shows some examples for both individuals and groups. The Guidelines on page 523 give some ideas for using portfolios in your teaching.

Exhibitions. An **exhibition** is a performance test that has two additional features. First, it is public, so students preparing exhibitions must take the audience into account; communication and understanding are essential. Second, an exhibition often requires many hours of preparation, because it is the culminating experience of a whole program of study. Thomas Guskey and Jane Bailey (2001) suggest that exhibits help students understand the qualities of good work and recognize those qualities in their own productions and performances. Students also benefit when they select examples of their work to exhibit and articulate their reasons for the selections. Being able to judge quality can encourage student motivation by setting clear goals.

Connect & Extend

TO PROFESSIONAL JOURNALS
Paulson, F. L., Paulson, P. R., & Meyer, C. A. (1991). What makes a portfolio a portfolio? *Educational Leadership, 48*(5), 60–63.

Focus Question: Describe five entries that teachers might include in portfolios for their students.

portfolio A collection of the student's work in an area, showing growth, self-reflection, and achievement.

Connect & Extend

TO PRACTICE
For a discussion of the advantages, limitations, design, and implementation of portfolio programs, and to examine samples of portfolio checklists, go to Teachervision.com (**www.teachervision.fen. com/teaching-methods-and-management/experimental-education/4536.html**).

exhibition A performance test or demonstration of learning that is public and usually takes an extended time to prepare.

Figure 13.1 A Student Reflects on Learning: Self-Analysis of Work in a Portfolio

Not only has this student's writing improved, but the student has become a more self-aware and self-critical writer.

Source: From Paulson, F. L., Paulson, P., & Meyer. C. (1991). What makes a portfolio a portfolio? *Educational Leadership, 48*(5), 63. Reprinted with permission of the Association of Supervision and Curriculum Development. Copyright © 1991 by ASCD. All rights reserved.

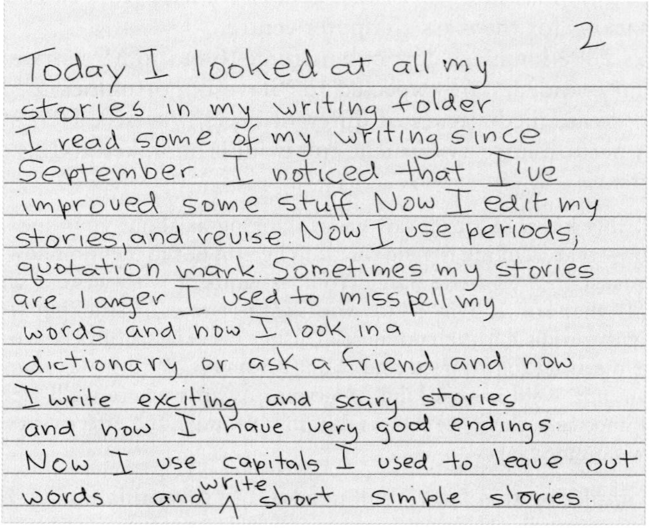

> 2
>
> Today I looked at all my stories in my writing folder I read some of my writing since September. I noticed that I've improved some stuff. Now I edit my stories, and revise. Now I use periods, quotation mark. Sometimes my stories are longer I used to misspell my words and now I look in a dictionary or ask a friend and now I write exciting and scary stories and now I have very good endings. Now I use capitals I used to leave out words and write short simple stories.

TABLE 13.7 Process and Best Works Portfolios for Individuals and Groups

Here are a few examples of how to use portfolios in different subjects.

The Process Portfolio

Subject Area	Individual Student	Cooperative Group
Science	Documentation (running records or logs) of using the scientific method to solve a series of laboratory problems	Documentation (observation checklists) of using the scientific method to solve a series of laboratory problems
Mathematics	Documentation of mathematical reasoning through double-column mathematical problem solving (computations on the left side and running commentary explaining thought processes on the right side)	Documentation of complex problem solving and use of higher-level strategies
Language arts	Evolution of compositions from early notes through outlines, research notes, response to others' editing, and final draft	Rubrics and procedures developed to ensure high-quality peer editing

The Best Works Portfolio

Subject Area	Individual Student	Cooperative Group
Language arts	The best compositions in a variety of styles—expository, humour/satire, creative (poetry, drama, short story), journalistic (reporting, editorial columnist, reviewer), and advertising copy	The best dramatic production, video project, TV broadcast, newspaper, advertising display
Social studies	The best historical research paper, opinion essay on historical issue, commentary on current event, original historical theory, review of a historical biography, account of academic controversy participated in	The best community survey, paper resulting from academic controversy, oral history compilation, multidimensional analysis of historical event, press corps interview with historical figure
Fine arts	The best creative products such as drawings, paintings, sculptures, pottery, poems, thespian performance	The best creative products such as murals, plays written and performed, inventions thought of and built

Source: From Johnson, D. W., & Johnson, R. T. (2002). *Meaningful assessment: A meaningful and cooperative process.* Boston, MA: Allyn & Bacon. Copyright © 2002 by Pearson Education. Adapted by permission of the publisher.

CREATING PORTFOLIOS

Students should be involved in selecting the pieces that will make up the portfolio.

EXAMPLES

1. During the unit or semester, ask each student to select work that fits certain criteria, such as "my most difficult problem," "my best work," "my most improved work," or "three approaches to..."

2. For their final submissions, ask students to select pieces that best show how much they have learned.

A portfolio should include information that shows student self-reflection and self-criticism.

EXAMPLES

1. Ask students to include a rationale for their selections.

2. Have each student write a "guide" to his or her portfolio, explaining how strengths and weaknesses are reflected in the work included.

3. Include self- and peer critiques, indicating specifically what is good and what might be improved.

4. Model self-criticism of your own productions.

The portfolio should reflect the students' activities in learning.

EXAMPLES

1. Include a representative selection of projects, writings, drawings, and so forth.

2. Ask students to relate the goals of learning to the contents of their portfolios.

The portfolio can serve different functions at different times of the year.

EXAMPLES

1. Early in the year, the portfolio might hold unfinished work or "problem pieces."

2. At the end of the year, the portfolio should contain only what the student is willing to make public.

Portfolios should show growth.

EXAMPLES

1. Ask students to make a "history" of their progress along certain dimensions and to illustrate points in their growth with specific works.

2. Ask students to include descriptions of activities outside class that reflect the growth illustrated in the portfolio.

Teach students how to create and use portfolios.

EXAMPLES

1. Keep models of very well-done portfolios as examples, but stress that each portfolio is an individual statement.

2. Examine your students' portfolios frequently, especially early in the year when they are just getting used to the idea. Give constructive feedback.

Evaluating Portfolios and Performances

Checklists, rating scales, and scoring rubrics are helpful when you assess performances because assessments of performances, portfolios, and exhibitions are criterion-referenced, not norm-referenced. In other words, the students' products and performances are compared with established public standards, not ranked in relation to other students' work (Cambourne & Turbill, 1990; Wiggins, 1991). For example, Figure 13.2 on page 524 gives three alternatives—numerical, graphic, and descriptive—for rating an oral presentation.

Scoring Rubrics. A checklist or rating scale gives specific feedback about elements of a performance. **Scoring rubrics** are more general descriptions of overall performance. For example, a rubric describing an excellent oral presentation might be:

> Pupil consistently faces audience, stands straight, and maintains eye contact; voice projects well and clearly; pacing and tone variation appropriate; well-organized; points logically and completely presented; brief summary at end. (Airasian, Engemann, & Gallagher, 2007, p. 155)

Connect & Extend

TO PROFESSIONAL JOURNALS
For a description of one school's graduation exhibitions and a thoughtful analysis of the use of exhibitions in teaching, see McDonald, J. P. (1993). Three pictures of an exhibition: Warm, cool, and hard. *Phi Delta Kappan, 74*, 480–485.

scoring rubrics Rules that are used to determine the quality of a student performance.

Figure 13.2 Three Ways of Rating an Oral Presentation

Source: From Airasian, P. W. (1996). *Assessment in the classroom* (p. 153). New York: McGraw-Hill. Copyright © 1996 by The McGraw-Hill Companies. Reproduced with permission of The McGraw-Hill Companies.

Numerical Rating Scale

Directions: Indicate how often the pupil performs each behaviour while giving an oral presentation. For each behaviour, circle 1 if the pupil always performs the behaviour, 2 if the pupil usually performs the behaviour, 3 if the pupil seldom performs the behaviour, and 4 if the pupil never performs the behaviour.

Physical Expression

A. Stands straight and faces audience.

1   2   3   4

B. Changes facial expression with change in the tone of the presentation.

1   2   3   4

Graphic Rating Scale

Directions: Place an X on the line that shows how often the pupil did each behaviour listed while giving an oral presentation.

Physical Expression

A. Stands straight and faces the audience.

| always | usually | seldom | never |

B. Changes facial expressions with change in tone of the presentation.

| always | usually | seldom | never |

Descriptive Rating Scale

Directions: Place an X on the line at the place that best describes the pupil's performance on each behaviour.

Physical Expression

A. Stands straight and faces audience.

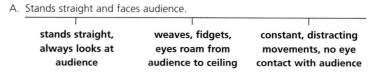

| **stands straight, always looks at audience** | **weaves, fidgets, eyes roam from audience to ceiling** | **constant, distracting movements, no eye contact with audience** |

B. Changes facial expressions with change in tone of the presentation.

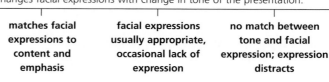

| **matches facial expressions to content and emphasis** | **facial expressions usually appropriate, occasional lack of expression** | **no match between tone and facial expression; expression distracts** |

It is often helpful to have students join in developing rating scales and scoring rubrics. When students participate, they are challenged to decide what quality work looks or sounds like in a particular area. They know in advance what is expected. As students gain practice in designing and applying scoring rubrics, their work and their learning often improve. Figure 13.3 shows an evaluation form for self- and peer assessment of contributions to cooperative learning groups.

Performance assessment requires careful judgment on the part of teachers and clear communication to students about what is good and what needs improving. In some ways, the approach is similar to the clinical method first introduced by Binet to assess intelligence: It is based on observing the student perform a variety of tasks and comparing his or her performance with a standard. Just as Binet never wanted to assign a single number to represent the child's intelligence, teachers who use authentic assessments do not try to assign one score to the student's performance. Even if rankings, ratings, and grades have to be given, these judgments are

STUDENT SELF- AND PEER EVALUATION FORM

This form will be used to assess the members of your learning group. Fill one form out on yourself. Fill one form out on each member of your group. During the group discussion, give each member the form you have filled out on them. Compare the way you rated yourself with the ways your groupmates have rated you. Ask for clarification when your rating differs from the ratings given you by your groupmates. Each member should set a goal for increasing his or her contribution to the academic learning of all group members.

Person Being Rated: _____

Write the number of points earned by the group member:
(4=Excellent, 3=Good, 2=Poor, 1=Inadequate)

___ On time for class.
___ Arrives prepared for class.
___ Reliably completes all assigned work on time.
___ Work is of high quality.
___ Contributes to groupmates' learning daily.
___ Asks for academic help and assistance when it is needed.

___ Gives careful step-by-step explanations (doesn't just tell answers).
___ Builds on others' reasoning.
___ Relates what is being learned to previous knowledge.
___ Helps draw a visual representation of what is being learned.
___ Voluntarily extends a project.

Figure 13.3 Self- and Peer Evaluating of Group Learning

Source: From Johnson, D. W., & Johnson, R. T. (1996). The role of cooperative learning in assessing and communicating student learning. In T. Guskey (Ed.), *ASCD 1996 Yearbook: Communicating student learning* (p. 41). Arlington, VA: Association of Supervision and Curriculum Development. Reprinted by permission of the Association for Supervision and Curriculum Development. Copyright © 1996 by ASCD. All rights reserved.

not the ultimate goals—improvement of learning is. The Guidelines below for developing rubrics are taken from Goodrich (1997) and Johnson and Johnson (2002).

Reliability, Validity, Generalizability. Because judgment plays such a central role in evaluating performances, issues of reliability, validity, and equity are critical considerations. Research clearly indicates that judges assessing portfolios often do not agree on ratings, so reliability may not be adequate. When raters are experienced and scoring rubrics are well developed and refined, however,

GUIDELINES
STEPS IN DEVELOPING A RUBRIC

1. *Look at models:* Show students examples of good and not-so-good work. Identify the characteristics that make the good ones good and the bad ones bad.

2. *List criteria:* Use the discussion of models to begin a list of what counts in high-quality work.

3. *Articulate gradations of quality:* Describe the best and worst levels of quality, then fill in the middle levels based on your knowledge of common problems and the discussion of not-so-good work.

4. *Practise on models:* Have students use the rubrics to evaluate the models you gave them in Step 1.

5. *Use self- and peer assessment:* Give students their task. As they work, stop them occasionally for self- and peer assessment.

6. *Revise:* Always give students time to revise their work based on the feedback they get in Step 5.

7. *Use teacher assessment:* Assess students' work using the same rubrics they used in Step 4.

Step 1 may be necessary only when you are asking students to engage in a task with which they are unfamiliar. Steps 3 and 4 are useful but time-consuming; you can do these on your own, especially when you've been using rubrics for a while. A class experienced in rubric-based assessment can streamline the process so that it begins with listing criteria, after which the teacher writes out the gradations of quality, checks them with the students, makes revisions, then uses the rubric for self-, peer, and teacher assessment.

A number of websites provide examples of rubrics in different subjects and grades or will allow teachers to generate their own rubrics. Three of these are **http://rubistar.4teachers.org**, **www.teachnology.com/web_tools/rubrics**, and **http://pareonline.net** (where you can choose "keywords" from the clickable menu and type "rubric" in the search box to search this site).

To prepare for this performance, these students may have conducted historical research, written scripts, and negotiated their roles in the oral presentation. How will the teacher assess individual learning?

| Connect & Extend

TO THE RESEARCH
Boudett, K. P., Murnane, R. J., City, E., & Moody, L. (2005). Teaching educators how to use student assessment data to improve instruction. *Phi Delta Kappa, 86,* 700–706.

informal assessments Ungraded (formative) assessments that gather information from multiple sources to help teachers make decisions.

reliability may improve (Herman & Winters, 1994; LeMahieu, Gitomer, & Eresh, 1993). Some of this improvement in reliability occurs because a rubric focuses the raters' attention on a few dimensions of the work and gives limited scoring levels to choose from. If scorers can give only a rating of 1, 2, 3, or 4, they are more likely to agree than if they could score based on a 100-point scale. So the rubrics may achieve reliability not because they capture underlying agreement among raters, but because the rubrics limit options and thus limit variability in scoring (Mabry, 1999).

In terms of validity, there is some evidence that students who are classified as "master" writers on the basis of portfolio assessment are judged less capable using standard writing assessment. Which form of assessment is the best reflection of enduring qualities? There is so little research on this question, it is hard to say (Herman & Winters, 1994). In addition, when rubrics are developed to assess specific tasks, the results of applying the rubrics may not predict performance on anything except very similar tasks, so what do we actually know about students' learning more generally (Haertel, 1999; MacMillan, 2004)?

Diversity and Equity in Performance Assessment. Equity is an issue in all assessment and no less so with performances and portfolios. With a public performance, there could be bias effects based on a student's appearance and speech or the student's access to expensive audio, video, or graphic resources. Performance assessments have the same potential as other tests to discriminate unfairly against students who are not wealthy or who are culturally different (McDonald, 1993). And the extensive group work, peer editing, and out-of-class time devoted to portfolios provides opportunities for some students to access more extensive networks of support and outright help. Many students in your classes will have families with sophisticated computer graphics and desktop publishing capabilities. Others may have little support from home. These differences can be sources of bias and inequity.

Informal Assessments

Informal assessments are ungraded (formative) assessments that gather information from multiple sources to help teachers make decisions (Banks, 2006). Early on in the unit, assessments should be formative (provide feedback, but not count toward a grade), saving the actual graded assessments for later in the unit when all students have had the chance to learn the material (Tomlinson, 2005a). Some examples of informal assessment are student observations and checklists, questioning, journals, and student self-assessment.

Journals are very flexible and widely used informal assessments. Students usually have personal or group journals and write in them on a regular basis. In their study, Michael Pressley and his colleagues (2001) found that excellent grade 1 literacy teachers used journalling for three purposes:

- As communication tools that allowed students to express their own thoughts and ideas.
- As an opportunity to apply what they have learned.
- As an outlet to encourage fluency and creative expression in language usage.

Teachers may use journals to learn about their students in order to better connect their teaching to the students' concerns and interests. But often journals focus on academic learning, usually through responses to prompts. For example, Banks (2006) describes one high school physics teacher who asked his students to respond to these three questions in their journals:

1. How can you determine the coefficient of friction if you know only the angle of the inclined plane?

2. Compare and contrast some of the similarities and the differences between magnetic, electronic, and gravitational fields.

3. If you were to describe the physical concept of sound to your best friend, what music would you use to demonstrate this concept?

When he read the students' journals, the teacher realized that many of the students' basic assumptions about friction, acceleration, and velocity came from personal experiences and not from scientific reasoning. His approach to teaching had to change to reach the students. The teacher never would have known to make the changes without reading the journals (Banks, 2005).

There are many other kinds of informal assessments—keeping notes and observations about student performance, rating scales, and checklists. Every time teachers ask questions or watch students perform skills, the teachers are conducting informal assessments. Look at Table 13.8. It summarizes the possibilities and limitations of aligning different assessment tools with their targets. One major message in this chapter is to match the type of assessment tools used to the target—what is being assessed.

Involving Students in Assessments

One way to connect teaching and assessment while developing students' sense of efficacy for learning is to involve the students in the assessment process. Students

TABLE 13.8 Aligning Different Assessment Tools with Their Targets

Different learning outcomes require different assessment methods.

Assessment Method

Target to Be Assessed	Selected Response	Essay	Performance Assessment	Personal Communication
Knowledge mastery	Multiple choice, true/false, matching, and fill-in can sample mastery of elements of knowledge	Essay exercises can tap understanding of relationships among elements of knowledge	Not a good choice for this target—three other options preferred	Can ask questions, evaluate answers, and infer mastery—but a time-consuming option
Reasoning proficiency	Can assess understanding of basic patterns of reasoning	Written descriptions of complex problem solutions can provide a window into reasoning proficiency	Can watch students solve some problems and infer about reasoning proficiency	Can ask student to "think aloud" or can ask follow-up questions to probe reasoning
Skills	Can assess mastery of the prerequisites of skilful performance—but cannot tap the skill itself	Can assess mastery of the prerequisites of skilful performance—but cannot tap the skill itself	Can observe and evaluate skills as they are being performed	Strong match when skill is oral communication proficiency; also can assess mastery of knowledge prerequisite to skilful performance
Ability to create products	Can assess mastery of knowledge prerequisite to the ability to create quality products—but cannot assess the quality of products themselves	Can assess mastery of knowledge prerequisite to the ability to create quality products—but cannot assess the quality of products themselves	A strong match can assess: (a) proficiency in carrying out steps in product development and (b) attributes of the product itself	Can probe procedural knowledge and knowledge of attributes of quality products—but not product quality

Source: From Stiggins, R. J. Where is our assessment future and how can we get there? In R. W. Lissitz, W. D. Schafer (Eds.), *Meaningful assessment: A meaningful and cooperative process.* Published by Allyn & Bacon, Boston, MA. Copyright © 2002 by Pearson Education. Adapted by permission of the publisher.

Connect & Extend

TO THE RESEARCH
For more ideas about making classroom assessment better, see: Black, P., Harrison, C., Lee, C., Marshall, B., & Wiliam, D. (2004). Working inside the black box: Assessment for learning in the classroom. *Phi Delta Kappan, 86*, 8–21; Stiggins, R. (2004). New assessment beliefs for a new school mission. *Phi Delta Kappan, 86*, 22–37.

can keep track of their own progress and assess their improvement. Table 13.9 gives ideas for how to help students judge their own work and participate in assessing their own learning.

Assessing Learning Potential: Dynamic Assessment

One criticism of traditional forms of ability testing is that such tests are merely samples of performance at one particular point in time; they fail to capture the child's potential for future learning. An alternative view of cognitive assessment is based on the assumption that the goal of assessment is to reveal potential for learning and

---

TABLE 13.9 Involving Students in Classroom Assessment

Here are a dozen ways of using assessment in the service of student learning.

1. Engage students in reviewing strong and weak samples to determine attributes of a good performance or product.

2. Before a discussion or conference with the teacher or peer, students identify their own perceptions of strengths and weaknesses on a specific aspect of their work.

3. Students practise using criteria to evaluate anonymous strong and weak work.

4. Students work in pairs to revise an anonymous weak-work sample they have just evaluated.

5. Students write a process paper, detailing the process they went through to create a product or performance. In it they reflect on problems they encountered and how they solved them.

6. Students develop practice test plans based on their understanding of the intended learning targets and essential concepts in material to be learned.

7. Students generate and answer questions they think might be on the test, based on their understanding of the content/processes/skills they were responsible for learning.

8. A few days before a test, students discuss or write answers to questions such as "Why am I taking this test? Who will use the results? How?" "What is it testing?" "How do I think I'll do?" "What do I need to study?" "With whom might I work?"

9. Teacher arranges items on a test according to specific learning targets, and prepares a "test analysis" chart for students, with three boxes: "My strengths," "Quick review," and "Further study." After handing back the corrected test, students identify learning targets they have mastered and write them in the "My strengths" box. Next, students categorize their wrong answers as either "simple mistake" or "further study." Then, students list the simple mistakes in the "Quick review" box. Last, students write the rest of the learning targets represented by wrong answers in the "Further study" box.

10. Students review a collection of their work over time and reflect on their growth: "I have become a better reader this quarter. I used to ..., but now I ..."

11. Students use a collection of their self-assessments to summarize their learning and set goals for future learning: "Here is what I have learned ... Here is what I need to work on ..."

12. Students select and annotate evidence of achievement for a portfolio.

Source: From Stiggins, R., and Chappuis, J. Using student-involved classroom assessment to close achievement gaps. *Theory Into Practice, 44,* 2005, p. 16. Reprinted with permission of Lawrence Erlbaum Associates, Inc. and R. Stiggins.

to identify the psychological and educational interventions that will help the person realize this potential. Procedures developed by Joe Campione and Ann Brown give graduated prompts as a child works to solve a problem. The prompts are scripted, beginning with a general hint and ending with a detailed instruction for how find the answer. The way the child uses the prompt and learns within the testing situation gives evidence of learning potential (Feuerstein, 1979; Kozulin & Falik, 1995).

Campione and Brown's techniques reflect Vygotsky's ideas about the zone of proximal development—the range of functioning where a child cannot solve problems independently but can benefit from guidance. Results of these tests offer a thought-provoking and radically different approach to testing. Rather than focusing on where a child is, these approaches point toward where the child could go and give guidance for the journey (Grigorenko & Sternberg, 1998).

Check Your Knowledge

- What is authentic assessment?
- Describe portfolios and exhibitions.
- What is learning potential assessment?

Apply to Practice

- How would you ensure reliability, validity, and equity in your use of authentic assessment tasks?
- How can checklists and rating scales be used to assess student portfolios and exhibitions?

EFFECTS OF GRADES AND GRADING ON STUDENTS

When we think of grades, we often think of competition. Highly competitive classes may be particularly hard on anxious students, students who lack self-confidence, and students who are less prepared. So, although high standards and competition do tend to be generally related to increased academic learning, it is clear that a balance must be struck between high standards and a reasonable chance to succeed. Rick Stiggins and Jan Chappuis (2005) observe:

> From their very earliest school experiences, our students draw life-shaping conclusions about themselves as learners on the basis of the information we provide to them as a result of their teachers' classroom assessments. As the evidence accumulates over time, they decide if they are capable of succeeding or not. They decide whether the learning is worth the commitment it will take to attain it. They decide ... whether to risk investing in the schooling experience. These decisions are crucial to their academic well-being. (p. 11)

Effects of Failure

It may sound as though low grades and failure should be avoided in school. But the situation is not that simple.

The Value of Failing?   After reviewing many years of research on the effects of failure from several perspectives, Margaret Clifford (1990, 1991) concluded that failure can have both positive and negative effects on subsequent performance, depending on the situation and the personality of the students involved.

For example, one study required subjects to complete three sets of problems. On the first set, the experimenters arranged for subjects to experience 0, 50- or 100 percent success. On the second set, it was arranged for all subjects to fail completely. On the third set of problems, the experimenters merely recorded how well the subjects performed. Those who had succeeded only 50 percent of the time before the failure experience performed the best. It appears that a history of

Connect & Extend

TO YOUR OWN PHILOSOPHY
Classroom evaluation is frequently referred to as the "grading game." What aspects of grading resemble a game from the student's point of view?

Connect & Extend

TO PROFESSIONAL JOURNALS

Harvard Graduate School of Education. (1999, January/February). Retention vs. social promotion: Schools search for alternatives. *Harvard Education Newsletter, 15*(1), 1–3.

Focus Question: What are the effects of retention on students? Can you propose alternatives?

Connect & Extend

TO PROFESSIONAL JOURNALS

Here are several studies on grade retention: Mantzicopoulos, P., & Morrison, D. (1992). Kindergarten retention: Academic and behavioral outcomes through the end of second grade. *American Educational Research Journal, 29*, 182–198. Pierson, L. H., & Connell, J. P. (1992). Effect of grade retention on self-system processes, school engagement, and academic performance. *Journal of Educational Psychology, 84*, 300–307. Shepard, L. A., & Smith, M. L. (1990). Synthesis of research on grade retention. *Educational Leadership, 47*(8), 84–88. McCoy, A. R., & Reynolds, A. J. (1999). Grade retention and school performance: An extended investigation. *Journal of School Psychology, 37*, 273–298. Vitaro, F., Brendgen, M., & Tremblay, R. E. (1999). Prevention of school dropout through the reduction of disruptive behaviors and school failure in elementary school. *Journal of School Psychology, 37*, 205–226.

complete failure or 100 percent success may be bad preparation for learning to cope with failure, something we must all learn. Some level of failure may be helpful for most students, especially if teachers help the students see connections between improvement and hard work that strives to repair faults in knowledge. Efforts to protect students from failure and guarantee success may be counterproductive. Clifford (1990) gives this advice to teachers:

> It is time for educators to replace easy success with challenge. We must encourage students to reach beyond their intellectual grasp and allow them the privilege of learning from mistakes. There must be a tolerance for error-making in every classroom, and gradual success rather than continual success must become the yardstick by which learning is judged. (p. 23)

The more able your students, the more challenging and important it will be to help them learn to "fail successfully" (Foster, 1981). Carol Tomlinson, an expert on differentiated instruction, puts it this way: "Students whose learning histories have caused them to believe that excellence can be achieved with minimal effort do not learn to expend effort, and yet perceive that high grades are an entitlement for them" (2005b, p. 266).

Retention in Grade. So far, we have been talking about the effects of failing a test or perhaps a course. But what about the effect of failing an entire grade—that is, of being "held back"? In some U.S. jurisdictions, almost 20 percent of grade 12 students have repeated at least one grade since kindergarten, usually in the earlier grades (Kelly, 1999). Retained students are more likely to be male, members of minority groups, and living in poverty (Beebe-Frankenberger et al., 2004).

Most research finds that grade retention is associated with poor long-term outcomes such as dropping out of school, higher arrest rates, fewer job opportunities, and lower self-esteem (Grissom & Shepard, 1989; Jimerson, Anderson, & Whipple, 2002). In their view, students generally do better academically when they are promoted. For example, in a longitudinal study of 29 retained and 50 low-achieving but promoted students, Shane Jimerson (1999) found that years later, the retained students had poorer educational and employment outcomes than the promoted students. The retained students dropped out more often, had lower-paying jobs, and received lower competence ratings from employers. In addition, the low-achieving but promoted students were comparable to a control group in all employment outcomes at age 20.

Retention assumes that the students just need more time and that they have the abilities needed to catch up. But one study found that the students retained after grade 2 had the same average IQ score as those targeted for more intensive interventions under special education requirements. In addition, about 20 percent of the retained group had IQ scores in the range that would qualify as having developmental disabilities (Beebe-Frankenberger et al., 2004), so it was probably wrong to assume that these students would benefit from the same teaching. Primary-grade students who benefit from retention tend to be more emotionally immature than their peers, but have average or above average ability (Kelly, 1999; Pierson & Connell, 1992). Even with this group, the advantage may not last. In one study that followed many students for several years, children who could have been retained, but who were promoted, did about as well as similar children who were held back, and sometimes better (Reynolds, 1992).

No matter what, students who have trouble should get help, whether they are promoted (this is often called "social promotion") or retained. Just covering the same material again in the same way won't solve the students' academic or social problems. As Jeannie Oakes (1999) has said, "No sensible person advocates social promotion as it is currently framed—simply passing incompetent students on to the next grade" (p. 8). The best approach may be to promote the students along with their peers, but to give them special remediation during the summer or the next year (Mantzicopoulos & Morrison, 1992; Shepard & Smith, 1989). An even better approach would be to prevent the problems before they occur by differentiating instruction early.

Effects of Feedback

The results of several studies of feedback fit well with the notion of "successful" or constructive failure. These studies have concluded that it is more helpful to tell students why they are wrong so that they can learn more appropriate strategies (Bangert-Drowns et al., 1991). Students often need help figuring out why their answers are incorrect and help understanding how learning skills should be applied (Butler & Winne, 1995). Without such feedback, they are likely to make the same mistakes again. Yet this type of feedback is rarely given. In one study, only about 8 percent of the teachers noticed a consistent type of error in a student's arithmetic computation and informed the student (Bloom & Bourdon, 1980).

What are the identifying characteristics of effective written feedback? With older students (late elementary through high school), written comments are most helpful when they are personalized and when they provide constructive criticism. This means that the teacher should make specific comments on errors or faulty strategies, but balance this criticism with suggestions about how to improve and with comments on the positive aspects of the work (Butler & Nisan, 1986; Elawar & Corno, 1985). Working with grade 6 teachers, Elawar and Corno (1985) found that feedback was dramatically improved when the teachers used these four questions as a guide: "What is the key error? What is the probable reason the student made this error? How can I guide the student to avoid the error in the future? What did the student do well that could be noted?" (p. 166). Here are some examples of teachers' written comments that proved helpful (Elawar & Corno, 1985, p. 164):

> Juan, you know how to get a percent, but the computation is wrong in this instance ... Can you see where? (Teacher has underlined the location of errors.)

> You know how to solve the problem—the formula is correct—but you have not demonstrated that you understand how one fraction multiplied by another can give an answer that is smaller than either (1/2 × 1/2 × 1/4).

Extensive written comments may be inappropriate for younger students, but brief written comments are a different matter. Comments should help students correct errors and should recognize good work, progress, and increasing skill.

Grades and Motivation

If you are relying on grades to motivate students, you had better think again (Smith, Smith, & De Lisi, 2001). The assessments you give should support students' motivation to learn—not just to work for a grade.

Is there really a difference between working for a grade and working to learn? The answer depends in part on how a grade is determined. As a teacher, you can use grades to motivate the kind of learning you intend students to achieve in your class. If you test only at a simple but detailed level of knowledge, you may force students to choose between higher aspects of learning and a good grade. But when a grade reflects meaningful learning, working for a grade and working to learn become the same thing. Finally, while high grades may have some value as rewards or incentives for meaningful engagement in learning, low grades generally do not encourage greater efforts. Students receiving low grades are more likely to withdraw, blame others, decide that the work is "dumb," or feel responsible for the low grade but helpless to make improvements. Rather than give a failing grade, you might consider the work incomplete and give students support in revising or improving. Maintain high standards and give students a chance to reach them (Guskey, 1994; Guskey & Bailey, 2001). The Guidelines on page 532 offer ideas on how to minimize detrimental effects that grades can have on students.

Connect & Extend

TO YOUR OWN PHILOSOPHY
What are some of your experiences in receiving feedback on papers and tests? Is it fair to give a student less than an A without indicating where improvement needs to be made?

Connect & Extend

TO OTHER CHAPTERS
See **Chapter 6** for a discussion of how to use praise effectively. These guidelines apply to written feedback as well.

Connect & Extend

TO YOUR OWN PHILOSOPHY
Given the various roles of evaluation, what is the disadvantage of a teacher giving a test and not returning the results until several weeks later? What is the disadvantage of merely posting the grade without returning the actual test? What is the disadvantage of returning the students' scored answer sheets without reviewing the correct answers?

TO YOUR OWN PHILOSOPHY
Can grades be used as motivators for all students? What determines whether a grade is motivation? How can a teacher use grades so that they tend to be motivating instead of discouraging?

MINIMIZING DETRIMENTAL EFFECTS OF GRADES

Avoid reserving high grades and high praise for answers that conform to your ideas or to those in the textbook.

EXAMPLES

1. Give extra points for correct and creative answers.
2. Withhold your opinions until all sides of an issue have been explored.
3. Reinforce students for disagreeing in a rational, productive manner.
4. Give partial credit for partly correct answers.

Make sure that each student has a reasonable chance to be successful, especially at the beginning of a new task.

EXAMPLES

1. Pretest students to make sure that they have prerequisite abilities.
2. When appropriate, provide opportunities for students to retest to raise their grades, but make sure that the retest is as difficult as the original.
3. Consider failing efforts as "incomplete" and encourage students to revise and improve.

Balance written and oral feedback.

EXAMPLES

1. Consider giving short, lively, written comments for younger students and more extensive written comments for older students.
2. When the grade on a paper is lower than the student might have expected, be sure that the reason for the lower grade is clear.
3. Tailor comments to the individual student's performance; avoid writing the same phrases over and over.
4. Note specific errors, possible reasons for errors, ideas for improvement, and work done well.

Make grades as meaningful as possible.

EXAMPLES

1. Tie grades to the mastery of important objectives.
2. Give ungraded assignments to encourage exploration.
3. Experiment with performances and portfolios.

Base grades on more than just one criterion.

EXAMPLES

1. Use essay questions as well as multiple-choice items on a test.
2. Grade oral reports and class participation.

Mistakes on tests can help students learn if appropriate feedback from teachers is provided so that the students can figure out why their answers were incorrect; they will be less likely to repeat the same mistake again if they know what was wrong and why.

Check Your Knowledge

- How can failure support learning?
- Which is better, social promotion or being "held back"?
- Can feedback, including grades, promote learning and motivation?

Apply to Practice

- How would you assess the value of the feedback you are receiving in your classes?

GRADING AND REPORTING: NUTS AND BOLTS

In determining a final grade, the teacher must make a major decision. Should a student's grade reflect the amount of material learned and how well it has been learned, or should the grade reflect the student's status in comparison with the rest of the class? In other words, should grading be criterion-referenced or norm-referenced?

Criterion-Referenced versus Norm-Referenced Grading

In **criterion-referenced grading**, the grade represents the quality of accomplishments. If clear objectives have been set for the course, the grade may represent a certain number of objectives met satisfactorily. When a criterion-referenced system is used, criteria for each grade generally are spelled out in advance. It is then up to the student to earn the grade that she or he wants to receive. Theoretically, in this system, all students can achieve an A if they reach the criteria.

In **norm-referenced grading**, the major influence on a grade is the student's standing in comparison with others who also took the course. If a student studies very hard and almost everyone else does too, the student may receive a disappointing grade, perhaps a C.

Criterion-Referenced Systems. Criterion-referenced grading has the advantage of relating judgments about a student to the achievement of clearly defined instructional goals. Some school districts have developed reporting systems where report cards list objectives along with judgments about the student's attainment of each. Reporting is done at the end of each unit of instruction. The junior high report card shown in Figure 13.4 on the next page demonstrates the relationship between assessment and the goals of the unit.

In practice, many school systems would look suspiciously at a teacher who turned in a roster filled with A's and explained that all the students had reached the class objectives. Administrators might say that if all the objectives could be so easily attained by all the students, more or tougher objectives would be needed. Nevertheless, with effective teaching, a criterion-referenced system could well yield just such results and may be acceptable in some schools.

Norm-Referenced Systems. One common type of norm-referenced grading is called **grading on the curve**. In grading on the curve, the middle of the normal distribution, or "average" performance, becomes the anchor on which grading is based. In other words, teachers look at the average level of performance, assign what they consider an "average grade" for this performance, and then grade superior performances higher and inferior performances lower. How you feel about this approach probably depends on where your grades generally fell along that "curve." There is good evidence that this type of grading damages the relationships among students and between teachers and students (Krumboltz & Yeh, 1996). When you think about it, if the curve arbitrarily limits the number of good grades that can be given, then, in the game of grading, most students will be losers (Guskey & Bailey, 2001; Haladyna, 2002; Kohn, 1996). Over 25 years ago, Benjamin Bloom (of Bloom's taxonomy) and his colleagues (1981) pointed out the fallacy of grading on the curve:

Connect & Extend

TO YOUR OWN PHILOS-OPHY
What would school be like for students if all testing were eliminated? Would most students still be motivated to learn and complete assignments?

criterion-referenced grading Assessment of each student's mastery of each course objective.

norm-referenced grading Assessment of students' achievement in relation to one another or a defined group.

grading on the curve Norm-referenced grading that compares students' performance with an average level.

Connect & Extend

TO PROFESSIONAL JOURNALS
Hills, J. R. (1991). Apathy concerning grading and testing. *Phi Delta Kappan, 72*(7), 540–545.

MACKENZIE ELEMENTARY SCHOOL
GRADE 5

Student _____ Teacher _____ Principal _____Muriel Simms_____ Quarter 2 3 4

E = Excellent   S = Satisfactory   P = Making Progress   N = Needs improvement

READING PROGRAM
Materials Used: _____

_____

_____

___ Reads with understanding
___ Is able to write about what is read
___ Completes reading group work accurately and on time
___ Shows interest in reading

Reading Skills
___ Decodes new words
___ Understands new words

Independent Reading Level
Below   At Grade Level   Above

LANGUAGE ARTS
___ Uses oral language effectively
___ Listens carefully
___ Masters weekly spelling

Writing Skills
___ Understands writing as process
___ Creates a rough draft
___ Makes meaningful revisions
___ Creates edited, legible final draft

Editing Skills
___ Capitalizes
___ Punctuates
___ Uses complete sentences
___ Uses paragraphs
___ Demonstrates dictionary skills

Writing Skill Level
Below   At Grade Level   Above

MATHEMATICS
Problem Solving
___ Solves teacher-generated problems
___ Solves self-/student-generated problems
___ Can create story problems

Interpreting Problems
___ Uses appropriate strategies
___ Can use more than one strategy
___ Can explain strategies in written form
___ Can explain strategies orally

Math Concepts
   Understands Base Ten
Beginning Developing Sophisticated
   Multiplication, Basic Facts
Beginning Developing Sophisticated
   2-digit Multiplication
Beginning Developing Sophisticated
   Division
Beginning Developing Sophisticated
   Geometry
Beginning Developing Sophisticated
Overall Math Skill Level
Beginning Developing Sophisticated

Attitude/Work Skills
___ Welcomes a challenge
___ Persistent
___ Takes advantage of learning from others
___ Listens to others
___ Participates in discussion

It Figures
Is working on: _____
Goals: _____
Is working on achieving goal: _____

SOCIAL STUDIES
___ Understands subject matter
___ Shows curiosity and enthusiasm
___ Contributes to class discussions
___ Uses map skills
___ Demonstrates control of reading skills by interpreting text
Topics covered: individual cultures, Columbus–first English colonies

SCIENCE
___ Shows curiosity about scientific subject matter
___ Asks good scientific questions
___ Shows knowledge of scientific method
___ Uses knowledge of scientific method to help set up and run experiment(s)
___ Makes good scientific observations
___ Has researched scientific topic(s)
Topic(s) _____

I Wonder
Is currently working on_____

WORKING SKILLS
___ Listens carefully
___ Follows directions
___ Works neatly and carefully
___ Checks work
___ Completes work on time
___ Uses time wisely
___ Works well independently
___ Works well in a group
___ Takes risks in learning
___ Welcomes a challenge

HOMEWORK
___ Self-selects homework
___ Completes work accurately
___ Completes work on time

PRESENTATIONS/PROJECTS
_____

_____

HUMAN RELATIONS
___ Shows courtesy
___ Respects rights of others
___ Shows self-control
___ Interacts well with peers
___ Shows a cooperative and positive attitude in class
___ Shows a cooperative attitude when asked to work with other students
___ Is willing to help other students
___ Works well with other adults (subs, student teacher, parents, etc.)

Attendance

	1st	2nd	3rd	4th
Present				
Absent				
Tardy				

Placement for next year: _____

Figure 13.4 A Criterion-Referenced Report Card

This is one example of a criterion-referenced report card. Other forms are possible, but all criterion-referenced reports indicate student progress toward specific goals.

Source: From Lake, K., & Kafka, K. (1996). Reporting methods in grades K–8. In T. Guskey (Ed.), *ASCD 1996 Yearbook: Communicating student learning* (p. 104). Arlington, VA: Association of Supervision and Curriculum Development. Reprinted by permission of the Association for Supervision and Curriculum Development. Copyright © 1996 by ASCD. All rights reserved.

There is nothing sacred about the normal curve. It is the distribution most appropriate to chance and random activity. Education is a purposeful activity, and we seek to have students learn what we have to teach. If we are effective in our instruction, the distribution of achievement should be very different from the normal curve. In fact, we may even insist that our educational efforts have been *unsuccessful* to the extent that the distribution of achievement approximates the normal distribution. (pp. 52–53)

Table 13.10 compares descriptions of a student's performance using criterion-referenced and norm-referenced standards and suggests a way to translate these descriptions into grades.

TABLE 13.10 Comparing Norm-Referenced and Criterion-Referenced Standards for Grading

Norm-referenced systems use the performance of the rest of the class as the standard for determining grades. Criterion-referenced systems use standards of subject mastery and learning to determine grades.

Grade	Criterion-referenced	Norm-referenced
A	Firm command of knowledge domain High level of skill development Exceptional preparation for later learning	Far above class average
B	Command of knowledge beyond the minimum Advanced development of most skills Has prerequisites for later learning	Above class average
C	Command of only the basic concepts of knowledge Demonstrated ability to use basic skills Lacks a few prerequisites for later learning	At the class average
D	Lacks knowledge of some fundamental ideas Some important skills not attained Deficient in many of the prerequisites for later learning	Below class average
F	Most of the basic concepts and principles not learned Most essential skills cannot be demonstrated Lacks most prerequisites needed for later learning	Far below class average

Source: From Frisbie, D. A., & Waltman, K. K. (1992). Developing a personal grading plan. *Educational Measurement: Issues and Practice, 11*(3), 37. Copyright © 1992 by the National Council on Measurement in Education. Reprinted by permission of the publisher.

The Point System

One popular system for combining grades from many assignments is a point system. Each test or assignment is given a certain number of total points, depending on its importance. A test worth 40 percent of the grade could be worth 40 points. A paper worth 20 percent could be worth 20 points. Points are then awarded on the test or paper based upon specific criteria. An A+ paper, one that meets all the criteria, could be given the full 20 points; an average paper might be given 10 points. If tests of comparable importance are worth the same number of points, are equally difficult, and cover a similar amount of material, just add together the points each student accumulates. But when tests vary quite a bit on one or several of these characteristics, use judgment to consider how much each test should contribute to the total.

Let us assume that a grade book indicates the scores shown in Table 13.11 on page 536. How would you assign grades to students for this unit? The most common way is to find the total number of points for each student and rank the students. Assign grades by looking for natural gaps of several points or imposing a curve (a certain percentage of A's, B's, and so on).

Percentage Grading

There is another approach to assigning grades to a group of students like those in Table 13.11. Using **percentage grading**, the teacher can assign grades based on how

Connect & Extend

TO YOUR OWN PHILOSOPHY

What type of grading orientation—norm-referenced or criterion-referenced—could be best understood by parents and other family members? Which would they generally favour? Would the choices vary depending on the grade level concerned?

percentage grading System of converting class performances to percentage scores and assigning grades based on predetermined cut-off points.

TABLE 13.11 Points Earned on Five Assignments

Student	Test 1 20% 20 points	Test 2 20% 20 points	Unit Test 30% 30 points	Homework 15% 15 points	Portfolio 15% 15 points	Total
Amy	10	12	16	6	7	——
Larry	12	10	14	7	6	——
Lee	20	19	30	15	13	——
Ming	18	20	25	15	15	——
Étienne	6	5	12	4	10	——
Francine	10	12	18	10	9	——
Seiko	13	11	22	11	10	——
Harv	7	9	12	5	6	——
Ivory	14	16	26	12	12	——
Nalini	20	18	28	10	15	——
Keith	19	20	25	11	12	——
Linda	14	12	20	13	9	——
Marki	15	13	24	8	10	——
Naomi	8	7	12	8	6	——
Olivia	11	12	16	9	10	——
Carlos	7	8	11	4	8	——

Connect & Extend

TO PROFESSIONAL JOURNALS

For a summary of the considerations in developing a grading plan, see Frisbie, D. A., & Waltman, K. K. (1992). Developing a personal grading plan. *Educational Measurement: Issues and Practice 11*(3), 35–42. Washington, DC: National Council on Measurement in Education.

much knowledge each student has mastered—what percentage of the total knowledge he or she understands. To do this, the teacher might score tests and other classwork with percentage scores (based on how much is correct—50 percent, 85 percent, etc.) and then average these scores to reach a course score. These scores can then be converted into letter grades according to predetermined cut-off points. Any number of students can earn any grade. This procedure is very common; you may have experienced it yourself as a student. Let us look at it more closely, because it has some frequently overlooked problems.

The grading symbols of A, B, C, D, and F are probably the most popular means of reporting. School systems often establish equivalent percentage categories for each of these letter grades. The percentages vary from school district to school district, but two typical ones are these:

District 1

90 – 100% = A
80 – 89% = B
70 – 79% = C
60 – 69% = D
below 60% = F

District 2

94 – 100% = A
85 – 93% = B
76 – 83% = C
70 – 75% = D
below 70% = F

As you can see, although both districts have an A to F grading system, the average achievement required for each grade is different.

Can we really say what is the total amount of knowledge available in, for example, grade 8 science? Can we accurately measure what percentage of this body of knowledge each student has attained? Does it matter which parts of the science curriculum a student knows and doesn't know, a feature that is camouflaged by a single percentage score?

Another problem with percentage grading is the way an overall percentage is created. As we noted before, most teachers simply average percentage grades from a set of assignments, even though the assignments can vary considerably in "size" and importance. In this system, every percentage score is treated as if it measured learning on an assignment that is the same "size" and importance as every other assignment. Note that the point system we just described and illustrate in Table 13.11 completely avoids this particular problem.

And don't be confused—a percentage grade is not a criterion-referenced grade, even though it may look like one. Moreover, as the examples just given illustrate, teachers assign grades according to cut-offs in percentage grade systems as if measurement were so accurate that a one-point difference was meaningful: "In spite of decades of research in educational and psychological measurement, which has produced more defensible methods, the concept [of percentage grading], once established, has proved remarkably resistant to change" (Zimmerman, 1981, p. 178).

Any grading system prescribed or suggested by the school can be influenced by particular concerns of the teacher. So don't be fooled by the seeming security of absolute percentages. Your own grading philosophy will continue to evolve, even in this system. Because there is more concern today with specifying objectives and criterion-referenced assessment, especially at the elementary grade levels, several alternative methods for evaluating student progress against predetermined criteria have evolved. We will look at one: the contract system.

The Contract System and Grading Rubrics

When applied to the whole class, the **contract system** indicates the type, quantity, and quality of work required for each number or letter grade in the system. Rubrics describe the performance expected for each level. Students agree, or "contract," to work for particular grades by meeting the specified requirements and performing at the level specified. For example, the following standards might be established:

F: Not coming to class regularly or not turning in the required work.
D: Coming to class regularly and turning in the required work on time.
C: Coming to class regularly, turning in the required work on time, and receiving a check mark on all assignments to indicate they are satisfactory.
B: Coming to class regularly, turning in the required work on time, and receiving a check mark on all assignments except at least three that achieve a check-plus, indicating superior achievement.
A: As above, plus a successful oral or written report on one of the books listed for supplementary reading.

This example calls for more subjective judgment than would be ideal. However, contract systems reduce student anxiety about grades. The contract system can be applied to individual students, in which case it functions much like an independent study plan.

Unfortunately, the system can lead to overemphasis on the quantity of work. Teachers may be too vague about the standards that differentiate acceptable from unacceptable work. This is where scoring rubrics for each assignment can be helpful. If clear and well-developed rubrics describe the performances expected for each assignment, and if students learn to use the rubrics to evaluate their own work, then quality, not quantity, will be at the centre of grading.

A teacher can modify the contract system by including a **revise option**. For example, a check mark might be worth 75 points and a check-plus, 90 points; a check-plus earned after revision could be worth 85 points—more than a check but less than a check-plus earned the first time around. This system allows students to improve their work but also rewards getting it right the first time. Some quality control is possible because students earn points not just for quantity but also for quality. In addition, the teacher may be less reluctant to judge a project unsatisfactory because students can improve their work (King, 1979). But beware, if a school system requires a five-point grading scale and all students contract for and achieve the highest grade (before or after revising), the teacher will wish that the principal had been consulted about the system before the grades came out.

contract system System in which each student works for a particular grade according to agreed-upon standards.

Connect & Extend

TO YOUR OWN PHILOSOPHY
How would you solve the following problem? You are using a contract system in one of your classes. One of the requirements for an A is "to write a book report." However, some students are reporting on books that you think they read last year, and some are handing in short, superficial reports. How can you structure the contract system so that the students will produce better-quality work?

revise option In a contract system, the chance to revise and improve work.

Connect & Extend

TO OTHER CHAPTERS
See **Chapter 6** for a discussion of behaviour management contracts.

Grading on Effort and Improvement

Grading on effort and improvement should not be a complete grading system but rather a theme that can run through most grading methods. Should teachers grade students based on how much they learn or on the final level of learning? One problem with using improvement as a standard for grading is that the best students improve the least, because they are already the most competent. Do you want to penalize these students because they knew quite a bit initially, and because teaching and testing have limited how much learning they can demonstrate? After all, unless you assign extra work, these students will run out of opportunities to demonstrate their potential (Airasian, Engemann, & Gallager, 2007; Guskey & Bailey, 2001).

Many teachers try to include some judgment of effort in final grades, but effort is difficult to assess. Are you certain that your perception of each student's effort is correct? Clement (1978) suggests a system called the **dual marking system** that includes a judgment about effort in the final grade. Students are assigned two grades. One, usually a letter, indicates the actual level of achievement. The other, a number, indicates the relationship of the achievement to the student's ability and effort. For example, a grade of B could be qualified as follows (Clement, 1978, p. 51):

> B1: Outstanding effort, better achievement than expected, good attitude; B2: Average effort, satisfactory in terms of ability; B3: Lower achievement than ability would indicate, poor attitude.

Of course, this system assumes that the teacher can adequately judge both true ability and effort. A grade of D1, D2, or F2 could be quite insulting. A grade of A3 or F1 should not be possible. But the system does have the advantage of recognizing hard work and giving feedback about a seeming lack of effort. An A2 or B2 might tell very bright students: "You're doing well, but I know you could do better." This could help the students to expect more of themselves and not slip by on high ability. The overall grade—A, B, C—still reflects achievement and is not changed (or biased) by teachers' subjective judgment of effort.

Some teachers use the **individual learning expectation** (ILE) system. Students earn improvement points on tests or assignments for scoring above their personal base (average) score or for making a perfect score. The teacher can count these improvement points when figuring a final grade or simply use them as a basis for giving other classroom rewards.

Cautions: Being Fair

The attributions a teacher makes about the causes of student successes or failures can affect the grades that students receive. Teachers are more likely to give higher grades for students' effort (a controllable factor) than for ability (an uncontrollable factor). Lower grades are more likely when teachers attribute a student's failure to lack of effort instead of lack of ability (Weiner, 1979). It is also possible that grades can be influenced by a **halo effect**—that is, the tendency to view particular aspects of a student based on a general impression, either positive or negative. As a teacher, you may find it difficult to avoid being affected by positive and negative halos. A very pleasant student who seems to work hard and causes little trouble may be given the benefit of the doubt (B– instead of C+), whereas a very difficult student who seems to refuse to try might be a loser at grading time (D instead of C–). There is another aspect of fairness. If students' grades are affected by unclear directions, difficulty reading the test or assignment questions, low grades for missing homework, a test that did not measure what was taught, time pressures, or other factors that are not related to the skills being assessed, then "grade pollution" has occurred. When flowery language or an artistic cover inflates a student's grade, we have more grade pollution. Grades should reflect what a student knows,

---

dual marking system System of assigning two grades, one reflecting achievement and the other effort, attitude, and actual ability.

individual learning expectation (ILE) Personal average score.

halo effect The tendency for a general impression of a person to influence our perception of any aspect of that person.

"I HOPE THIS ISN'T ANOTHER PLOY TO UP YOUR GRADE, HASKELL."
(© Art Bouthillier)

understands, or can do related to the learning objective specified (Tomlinson, 2005b). The following Guidelines give ideas for using any grading system in a fair and reasonable way.

GUIDELINES
USING ANY GRADING SYSTEM

Explain your grading policies to students early in the course and remind them of the policies regularly.

EXAMPLES

1. Give older students a handout describing the assignments, tests, grading criteria, and schedule.
2. Explain to younger students in a low-pressure manner how their work will be evaluated.

Set reasonable standards.

EXAMPLES

1. Discuss workload and grading standards with more experienced teachers.
2. Give a few formative tests to get a sense of your students' abilities before you give a graded test.
3. Take tests yourself first to gauge the difficulty of the test and to estimate the time your students will need.

Base your grades on as much objective evidence as possible.

EXAMPLES

1. Plan in advance how and when you will test.
2. Keep a portfolio of student work. This may be useful in conferences with students and their families.

Be sure that students understand test directions.

EXAMPLES

1. Outline the directions on the board.
2. Ask several students to explain the directions.
3. Go over a sample question first.

Correct, return, and discuss test questions as soon as possible.

EXAMPLES

1. Have students who wrote good answers read their responses for the class; make sure that they are not the same students each time.
2. Discuss why wrong answers, especially popular wrong choices, are incorrect.

3. As soon as students finish a test, give them the answers to questions and the page numbers where answers are discussed in the text.

As a rule, do not change a grade.

EXAMPLES

1. Make sure that you can defend the grade in the first place.
2. DO change any clerical or calculation errors.

Guard against bias in grading.

EXAMPLES

1. Ask students to put their names on the backs of their papers.
2. Use an objective point system or model papers when grading essays.

Keep pupils informed of their standing in the class.

EXAMPLES

1. Write the distribution of scores on the board after tests.
2. Schedule periodic conferences to go over work from previous weeks.

Give students the benefit of the doubt. All measurement techniques involve error.

EXAMPLES

1. Unless there is a very good reason not to, give the higher grade in borderline cases.
2. If a large number of students miss the same question in the same way, revise the question for the future and consider throwing it out for that test.

Source: From Drayer, A. M. (1979). *Problems in middle and high school teaching: A handbook for student teachers and beginning teachers* (pp. 182–187). Boston: Allyn & Bacon. Copyright © 1979 by Allyn & Bacon. Adapted by permission of the author and publisher.

Connect & Extend

TO THE RESEARCH
Munk, D. D., & Bursuck, W. D. (2001). Preliminary findings on personalized grading plans for middle school students with learning disabilities. *Exceptional Children, 67*, 211–234.

Diversity and Grading

In assigning and reporting grades, how do you make accommodations for students with special needs? Table 13.12 gives some options.

It may be up to you as the teacher to decide how to calculate the grades of students with special needs and students whose first language is not English, but be sure to check whether there are school or district policies in place.

Check Your Knowledge

- Describe two kinds of grading.
- What are the point and percentage systems?
- Describe some alternatives to traditional grading.
- What are some sources of bias in grading?

Apply to Practice

- What grading systems are you experiencing right now in the classes you are taking?
- What are the advantages and disadvantages of contract grading? Percentage grading? Grading on the curve?

TABLE 13.12 Possible Grading Accommodations for Students with Special Needs

Adaptation	Example
Change Grading Criteria	
Vary grading weights assigned to different activities or products.	Increase credit for participation in classroom group activities and decrease credit for essay examinations.
Grade on improvement by assigning extra points.	Change a C to a B if the student's total points have increased significantly from the previous marking period.
Modify or individualize curriculum expectations.	Indicate in the IEP that the student will work on subtraction while the other students work on division.
Use contracts and modified course requirements for quality, quantity, and timelines.	State in the contract that student will receive a B for completing all assignments at 80% quantity, within specific timelines and with a particular degree of accuracy, attending all classes, and completing one extra-credit report.
Provide Supplemental Information	
Add written comments to clarify details about the criteria used.	Write on the report card that the student's grade reflects performance on IEP objectives and not on the regular classroom curriculum.
Add information from student activity log.	Note that while the student's grade was the same this marking period, daily records show that the student completed math assignments with less teacher assistance.
Add information about effort, progress, and achievement from portfolios or performance-based assignments.	State that the student's written language showed an increase in word variety, sentence length, and quality of ideas.
Use Other Grading Options	
Use checklists of skills and show the number or percentage of objectives met.	Attach a checklist to the report card indicating that during the marking period, the student mastered addition facts, two-digit addition with regrouping, and counting change to one dollar.
Use pass/fail grades.	Students receive a "pass" for completing 80% of daily work with at least 70% accuracy and attending 90% of class sessions.

Source: From Guskey, T. R., & Bailey, J. M. (2001). *Developing grading and reporting systems for student learning* (p. 118). Thousand Oaks, CA: Corwin Press. Copyright © 2001. Reprinted by permission of Corwin Press, Inc.

BEYOND GRADING: COMMUNICATION WITH FAMILIES

What Would You Say?

During your interview for a job in a district with a very diverse student population, the principal asks you, "How will you communicate with families about your homework and grading policies?"

No number or letter grade conveys the totality of a student's experience in a class or course. Students, parents, and teachers sometimes become too focused on the end point—the grade. But communicating with families should involve more than just sending home grades. There are a number of ways to communicate with and report to families. Many teachers have a beginning-of-the-year newsletter or student handbook that communicates homework, behaviour, and grading policies to families. Other options described by Guskey & Bailey (2001) are

- Notes attached to report cards
- Phone calls, especially "good news" calls
- School open houses
- Conferences, including student-led conferences
- Portfolios or exhibits of student work
- Homework hotlines
- School or class webpages
- Home visits

Here is an example of a "good news call" that makes use of cell phone technology taken from Guskey and Bailey (2001). An elementary school principal carries her phone with her as she walks through the hallways, visits the cafeteria, supervises the playground, and observes teachers' classes. When she sees a student performing well in class, assisting a classmate, or helping to improve the school, she immediately calls that student's parent or guardian on her phone and announces, "Hello, this is Ms. Johnson, the principal at Judd Elementary School. I just saw Tonya ..." After explaining what she observed and complimenting the child, she hands the phone to the child so that he or she can talk briefly with the parent or guardian. Everyone leaves with a big smile. One caution—if a family member didn't answer, it would be a bad idea to leave a call back message because the message recipients might fear that their children were sick or injured.

When asked about calls to parents concerning student problems, Ms. Johnson explains, "Those I save for after school. Often, I have to think more carefully about what I'm going to say and what strategies I'm going to recommend. When I see a child doing something wonderful, however, I want to let the parents know about that right away. And I never have to weigh my words. Plus, I think it means more to the child."

The principal's phone calls have completely altered the culture of this school. Parent involvement and participation in school events is at an all-time high, and their regard for Ms. Johnson and the school staff is exceptionally positive. It's a small thing, but it has made a big difference.

Conferences with family members are often expected of teachers in elementary school and can be equally important in junior high and high school. Schedule conferences at a time convenient for families; confirm appointments in writing or by phone. The conference should not be a time for lecturing family members or students. As the professional, the teacher needs to take a leadership role and yet remain sensitive to the needs of the other participants. The atmosphere should be friendly and unrushed. Any observations about the student should be factual, based on first-hand observation or information from assignments. Information gained from a student or a family member should be kept confidential. Listening and problem-solving skills such as those discussed in Chapter 11 can be particularly important when you are dealing with family members or students who are

The success of a parent–teacher conference depends largely on the teacher's communication skills. Listening is an important element.

angry or upset. Make sure that you really hear the concerns of the participants, not just their words. The Family and Community Partnerships box below offers some helpful ideas for planning and conducting conferences.

You should be aware that parents and guardians have the right to view all information about their child in your files and in the school's record. In some provinces, parents and guardians can decide who else, other than their child's classroom teacher or principal, can access this material. And, in other cases, students 16 years old or older can have access to all this information. If the records contain information that students or family members believe is incorrect, they can challenge such entries and have the information removed if they win the challenge. This means that the information in a student's records must be based on firm, defensible evidence. Tests must be valid and reliable. Your grades, assessments, observations, and notes must be justified by thorough testing and observation. Comments and anecdotes about students must be accurate and fair.

Check Your Knowledge

- How can communication with families support learning?

Apply to Practice

- Evaluate a parent conference you have seen.

FAMILY AND COMMUNITY PARTNERSHIPS

CONFERENCES

Plan ahead.

EXAMPLES
What are your goals?
- Are there specific problems you hope to solve?
- Are you sharing test results? For what purpose?
- Are there particular questions that you want answered?
- Is there information you want to share? Emphasize the positive.
- Are you describing your "next steps" in the classroom?
- Will you be making suggestions for use at home?

Begin with a positive statement.

EXAMPLES

"Howard has a great sense of humour."
"Giselle really enjoys materials that deal with animals."
"Sandy is sympathetic when somebody has a problem."

Listen actively.

EXAMPLES

Empathize with the family members.
Accept their feelings: "You seem to feel frustrated when Lee doesn't listen."

Establish a partnership.

EXAMPLES
Ask family members to follow through on class goals at home: "If you ask to see the homework checklist and go over it at home with Iris, I'll review it and chart her progress at school."

Plan follow-up contacts.

EXAMPLES

Write notes or make phone calls to share successes.
Keep families informed before problems develop.

End with a positive statement.

EXAMPLES

"José has made several friends this year."
"Courtney should be a big help in the social studies play that her group is developing."

Source: From Fromberg, D. P., & Driscoll, M. (1985). *The successful classroom: Management strategies for regular and special education teachers* (p. 181). New York: Teachers College Press. Copyright © 1985 by Teachers College Press. Adapted with permission.

Evaluation, Measurement, and Assessment
(pp. 500–503)

Distinguish among evaluation, measurement, and assessment.

In the process of evaluation, we compare information with criteria and then make judgments. Measurement is evaluation put in quantitative terms. Assessment includes measurement but is broader because it includes all kinds of ways to sample and observe students' skills, knowledge, and abilities.

Distinguish between norm-referenced and criterion-referenced tests.

In norm-referenced tests, a student's performance is compared with the average performance of others. In criterion-referenced tests, scores are compared with a pre-established standard. Norm-referenced tests cover a wide range of general objectives and are appropriate when only the top few candidates can be admitted to a program. However, results of norm-referenced tests do not tell whether students are ready for advanced material, and they are not appropriate for affective and psychomotor objectives. Criterion-referenced tests measure the mastery of very specific objectives—they tell the teacher exactly what the students can and cannot do, but they cannot compare students with others at their grade level either locally or nationally.

Describe the key features of a standardized test.

Three kinds of standardized tests are commonly used. Standardized criterion-referenced achievement tests provide good models for some aspects of classroom assessment and often are used to gauge the overall effectiveness of education. In some provinces, these tests scores are combined with classroom test scores to form grades in grade 12. Aptitude tests are used mainly to predict future performance. Psychoeducational diagnostic tests are used to describe a student's current capabilities or difficulties as a basis for designing more effective instruction. Aptitude and diagnostic tests both measure achievement, but items on them are often quite different from everyday school tasks and do not align with particular elements in a curriculum.

Interpreting Test Scores
(pp. 503–507)

What is test score reliability?

Every test score is only an estimate of a student's hypothetical true score. Some test scores are more reliable than others; that is, they reflect more stable and consistent estimates of true score. The standard error of measurement highlights that a score is imprecise. A confidence interval based on the standard error of measurement is a helpful way to depict test reliability.

How do you judge the validity of the interpretation of a test score?

The most important consideration about a test is the validity of interpretations and decisions based on the test's results. Some interpretations are more valid than others because there is stronger evidence for the interpretation or decision. Evidence that contributes to making valid interpretations can be related to the content tested, a criterion to be predicted, or a construct that the test is supposed to reflect. Construct-related evidence of validity is the broadest category and encompasses the other two categories of content and criterion. Tests must be reliable to be valid, but reliability does not guarantee validity.

Formative and Summative Assessment
(pp. 507–509)

What are two kinds of classroom assessment?

Most teachers must assess students and assign grades. Many schools have policies about testing and grading practices, but individual teachers decide how these practices will be carried out. In the classroom, assessment may be formative (ungraded, diagnostic) or summative (graded). Formative assessment helps form instruction, and summative assessment summarizes students' accomplishments.

Getting the Most from Traditional Assessment Approaches
(pp. 509–518)

How should teachers plan for assessment?

Assessment requires planning. Learning is supported when teachers test frequently using cumulative questions that ask students to apply and integrate knowledge. With clear goals for assessment, teachers are in a better position to design their own tests or evaluate the tests provided by textbook publishers.

Describe two kinds of traditional testing.

Two traditional formats for testing are the objective test and the essay test. Objective tests, which can include multiple-choice, true/false, fill-in, and matching items, should be written with specific guidelines in mind. Writing and scoring essay questions requires careful planning and clear criteria for scoring answers that discourage bias. Essay tests are susceptible to biases such as grading essays higher when they are longer or written in elaborate prose.

Innovations in Assessment
(pp. 518–529)

What is authentic assessment?

Critics of traditional testing believe that teachers should use authentic assessments. Authentic assessments require students to perform tasks and solve problems similar to real-life performances that will be expected of them outside of school.

Describe portfolios and exhibitions.

Portfolios and exhibitions are two examples of potentially authentic assessment. A portfolio is a collection of a student's work often chosen to represent growth or improvement or to feature "best work." Exhibitions are public displays of the student's understandings. With portfolios and exhibitions, there is an emphasis on carrying out real-life tasks in meaningful contexts. Evaluating alternative assessments requires careful judgment and attention to validity, reliability, generalizability, and equity, just as with other kinds of assessment.

What is learning potential assessment?

An alternative goal of assessment is to reveal potential for learning and identify the psychological and educational interventions that will help the individual realize this potential. Procedures give graduated prompts as a child works to solve a problem—beginning with a general hint and ending with a detailed instruction for how to find the answer. The way the child uses the prompt and learns within the testing situation gives evidence of learning potential.

Effects of Grades and Grading on Students
(pp. 529–533)

How can failure support learning?

Students need experience in coping with failure, so standards must be high enough to encourage effort.

Students who don't learn how to cope with failure by persisting at learning may give up too quickly when their first efforts are unsuccessful. Occasional failure can be positive, provided that appropriate feedback is given.

Which is better, social promotion or being "held back"?

Neither retaining nor promoting a student who is having difficulty guarantees that the student will learn. Unless the student is very young or emotionally immature compared with classmates, the best approach may be to promote and provide extra support such as tutoring or summer school sessions.

Can feedback, including grades, promote learning and motivation?

Written or oral feedback should include specific comments on errors or faulty strategies. Learning improves when this criticism is balanced with suggestions about how to improve, along with comments on the positive aspects of the work. Grades can encourage students' motivation to learn if they are tied to meaningful learning.

Grading and Reporting: Nuts and Bolts
(pp. 533–540)

Describe two kinds of grading.

Grading can be either criterion-referenced or norm-referenced. Criterion-referenced report cards usually indicate how well each of several objectives has been met by the student. One popular norm-referenced system is grading on the curve, based on a ranking of students in relation to the average performance level.

What are the point and percentage systems?

In a point system, each assignment contribution to a grade is allocated a number of points based on each part's importance. Points are added across assignments, then students are rank ordered by total points as a guide to assigning grades. Many schools use percentage grading systems in which scores of percent correct or percent mastered are averaged across assignments. This system has flaws because it treats every assignment as having the same importance.

Describe some alternatives to traditional grading.

Alternatives to traditional grading are the contract and dual marking approaches. Whatever system you use, you have to decide whether you want to grade on effort, improvement, or some combination and whether you want to limit the number of good grades available.

What are some sources of bias in grading?

Many factors besides quality of work can influence grades: the teacher's beliefs about the student's ability or effort or the student's general classroom behaviour, for example.

Beyond Grading: Communication with Families
(pp. 541–542)

How can communication with families support learning?

Not every communication from the teacher needs to be tied to a grade. Communication with students and family members can be important in helping a teacher understand students and present effective instruction by creating a consistent learning environment. Students and parents or guardians have a legal right to see all the information in the students' records; the contents of files must be appropriate, accurate, and supported by evidence.

KEY TERMS

BECOMING A PROFESSIONAL

Reflecting on the Chapter

Can you apply the ideas from this chapter on classroom assessment and grading to solve the following problems of practice?

Preschool and Kindergarten

- The parents of several children in your class want a report about how their daughters and sons are "progressing" in pre-school. How would you respond to their requests? What kind of assessment and reporting would be helpful for your young students?

Elementary and Middle School

- During a parent–teacher conference, a mother and father accuse you of playing favourites and giving their child low grades "just because he's different." How would you respond?

Junior High and High School

- Several students are very unhappy with the grades on their term projects. They come to you for an explanation and to try to get you to raise their grades. What would you do?

- Your school requires percentage grading, but you would prefer a different system. How would you make a case for your alternative?

Check Your Understanding

- Know the differences between formative and summative assessments.

- Understand the characteristics of authentic assessment.

- Be familiar with different ways of determining grades.

Your Teaching Portfolio

Think about your philosophy of teaching. What do you believe about testing and grading? How will you assign grades? (Consult the Guidelines in this chapter for ideas.)

Develop a grading plan for the grade level you want to teach and add it to your portfolio.

Add some ideas for family involvement from this chapter to your portfolio.

Teaching Resources

Adapt the Guidelines for developing rubrics (page 525) for the age group you plan to teach.

Add Table 13.3 ("Key Points to Consider in Judging Textbook Tests," page 512) and Table 13.6 ("Characteristics of Authentic Assessments," page 520) to your teaching resources file.

Add Figure 13.2 ("Three Ways of Rating an Oral Presentation," page 524) and Figure 13.3 ("Self- and Peer Evaluation of Group Learning," page 525) to your teaching resources file.

Teachers' Casebook

What Would They Do?

Here is how two practising teachers responded to the teaching situation presented at the beginning of this chapter about setting up a system to give letter grades.

Marci Green
H. J. Alexander Community School
Toronto, Ontario

The Ontario curriculum for grades 1 to 8 was introduced into my school in 1998. Previously, the teachers who worked in my Board of Education did not use letter grades for report cards. It has taken some time to adjust to this new system of grading and to ensure that the students are assessed fairly.

The provincial report card states that teachers must use letter grades from "A to R." The letter grade A represents the highest level of achievement that exceeds the provincial standard. The letter grade R represents "below 50," which means that a student has not been able to demonstrate the required knowledge and skills.

In order to implement a grading system that is fair and manageable, I would initially review the Health and Physical Education curriculum for grades 1 to 8. By reviewing this curriculum, I would ensure that I was teaching the required material. Then I would determine the units I would teach for each term, ensuring I had a balanced program that incorporated the requirements from the curriculum. For each unit I would develop a grid, or rubric, which would represent the expectations for each letter grade. These expectations would reflect the skills to be taught and would be clearly stated to the students, parents, and administrators before the grading period began. Posting the rubric in the gym or classroom is helpful in reminding the students of the expectations for their report cards.

There are many ways to assess students' achievements. These consist of anecdotal records, checklists, observations, participation, and effort and tracking sheets. The students are given an appropriate amount of time to learn and practise skills before they are assessed. It is important that a variety of instructional approaches be used to ensure that students have the opportunity to learn and perform to their potential. I would make program modifications for any students with any exceptionalities. The evaluation process should be ongoing throughout the school year.

Also, reviewing the students' previous report cards may help in determining their progress or achievements throughout the school year. Once a letter grade is assigned to a student, it is important to retain any checklists, observations, etc., to help in assessing the strengths, weaknesses, and next-steps sections of the report card. It is also important to retain the information for parent–teacher interviews in case a letter grade is questioned.

Paula Brown
Bialik Hebrew Day School
Toronto, Ontario

Whether a teacher uses "A, B, C, D" grades, achievement levels (i.e., "beginning to develop," "developing," "developed," or "highly developed"), or anecdotal reporting, the results are the same. The teacher is judging or evaluating a child's work. Most important is to have a clear understanding of the purpose of the evaluation, to know what you are evaluating, and to provide a learning environment that will foster the student's growth academically and emotionally.

In order to understand what you are evaluating, it is important to consistently review current curriculum guidelines.

Creating a learning environment that fosters growth for all students is a challenge. I need to provide a wide variety of experiences and opportunities for learning so that each student can demonstrate an understanding of concepts.

I believe the process of learning is more important than the final product. For this reason, I like to include a self-evaluation or student's response to a peer's work. I have found that a clearly delineated rubric is a wonderful tool for encouraging and evaluating the learning process. I attach it to the assignment when it is first handed out. This way the student, the parents, and I have a clear understanding of the steps needed to successfully complete the task. When used as an evaluation tool, the rubric gives immediate, relevant feedback to the student on his or her progress and helps provide a meaningful learning experience. This, after all, is the most important purpose of evaluation.

GLOSSARY

"I" message Clear, non-accusatory statement of how something is affecting you.

academic learning time Time when students are actually succeeding at the learning task.

academic tasks The work the student must accomplish, including the content covered and the mental operations required.

accommodation Altering existing schemes or creating new ones in response to new information.

achievement tests Tests measuring how much students have learned in a given content area.

acronym Technique for remembering names, phrases, or steps by using the first letter of each word to form a new, memorable word.

action research Systematic observations or tests of methods conducted by teachers or schools to improve teaching and learning for their students.

action zone Area of a classroom where the greatest amount of interaction takes place.

active teaching Teaching characterized by high levels of teacher explanation, demonstration, and interaction with students.

adaptation Adjustment to the environment.

adolescent egocentrism Assumption that everyone else is interested in one's thoughts, feelings, and concerns.

advance organizer Statement of inclusive concepts to introduce and sum up material that follows.

affective domain Realm of attitudes and feelings.

agency The capacity to coordinate learning skills, motivation, and emotions to reach your goals.

algorithm Step-by-step procedure for solving a problem; prescription for solutions.

allocated time Time set aside for learning.

analogical instruction Teaching new concepts by making connections (analogies) with information that the student already understands.

analogical thinking Heuristic in which a person limits the search for solutions to situations that are similar to the one at hand.

anchored instruction A type of problem-based learning that uses a complex interesting situation as an anchor for learning.

anorexia nervosa Eating disorder characterized by very limited food intake.

antecedents Events that precede an action.

anxiety General uneasiness; a feeling of tension.

applied behaviour analysis Applying behavioural learning principles to understand and change behaviour.

appropriate Internalize or take for yourself knowledge and skills developed in interaction with others or with cultural tools.

aptitude Capability for learning knowledge or skills in a particular setting.

aptitude tests Tests meant to predict future performance.

arousal Physical and psychological reactions causing a person to feel alert, excited, or tense.

articulation disorders Any of a variety of pronunciation difficulties.

assertive discipline Clear, firm, unhostile response style.

assessment Procedures used to obtain information about student performance.

assessment bias Qualities of an assessment instrument that offend or unfairly penalize a group of students because of the students' gender, SES, race, ethnicity, etc.

assimilation Fitting new information into existing schemes.

assisted learning Learning by having strategic help provided in the initial stages; the help gradually diminishes as students gain independence.

assistive technology Devices, systems, and services that support and improve the capabilities of individuals with disabilities.

associative stage Middle stage in learning an automated skill, when individual steps of a procedure are combined or "chunked" into larger units.

attainment value The importance of doing well on a task; how success on the task meets personal needs.

attention Focus on a stimulus.

attention-deficit/hyperactivity disorder (ADHD) Current term for disruptive behaviour disorders marked by overactivity, excessive difficulty sustaining attention, or impulsiveness.

attribution theories Descriptions of how individuals' explanations, justifications, and excuses influence their motivation and behavior.

authentic assessments Assessment procedures that test skills and abilities as they would be applied in real-life situations.

authentic tasks Tasks that have some connection to real-life problems the students will face outside the classroom.

autism/autism spectrum disorders Developmental disability significantly affecting verbal and non-verbal communication, social interaction, and imaginative creativity, generally evident before age three and ranging from mild to major.

automated basic skills Skills that are applied without conscious thought.

automaticity The result of learning to perform a behaviour or thinking process so thoroughly that the performance is automatic and does not require effort.

autonomous stage Final stage in learning an automated skill, when the procedure is fine-tuned and becomes "automatic."

autonomy Independence.

availability heuristic Judging the likelihood of an event based on what is available in your memory, assuming those easily remembered events are common.

aversive Irritating or unpleasant.

basic skills Clearly structured knowledge that is needed for later learning and that can be taught step by step.

behaviour modification Systematic application of antecedents and consequences to change behaviour.

behavioural learning theories Explanations of learning that focus on external events as the cause of changes in observable behaviour.

behavioural objectives Instructional objectives stated in terms of observable behaviour.

being needs Maslow's three higher-order needs, sometimes called growth needs.

belief perseverance The tendency to hold onto beliefs, even in the face of contradictory evidence.

between-class ability grouping System of grouping in which students are assigned to classes based on their measured ability or their achievements.

bilingualism The ability to speak two languages fluently.

bioecological model Bronfenbrenner's theory describing the nested social and cultural contexts that shape development. Every person develops within a *microsystem*, inside a *mesosystem*, embedded in an *exosystem*, all of which are a part of the *macrosystem* of the culture.

blended families Parents, children, and stepchildren merged into families through remarriages.

bottom-up processing Perception based on noticing separate defining features and assembling them into a recognizable pattern.

brainstorming Generating ideas without stopping to evaluate them.

bulimia Eating disorder characterized by overeating, then getting rid of the food by self-induced vomiting or laxatives.

Canadian Charter of Rights and Freedoms Legislation that protects the rights of all Canadians and, in particular, Canadians who are members of minority groups, including Canadians with disabilities.

CAPS A strategy that can be used in reading literature: *Characters, Aim* of story, *Problem, Solution.*

case study Intensive study of one person or one situation.

central executive The part of working memory responsible for monitoring and directing attention and other mental resources.

cerebral palsy Condition involving a range of motor or coordination difficulties due to brain damage.

chain mnemonics Memory strategies that associate one element in a series with the next element.

chunking Grouping individual bits of data into meaningful larger units.

classical conditioning Association of automatic responses with new stimuli.

classification Grouping objects into categories.

classroom management Techniques used to maintain a healthy learning environment, relatively free of behaviour problems.

Cmaps Tools for concept mapping developed by the Institute for Human Machine Cognition that are connected to many knowledge maps and other resources on the internet.

co-constructed Constructed through a social process in which people interact and negotiate (usually verbally) to create an understanding or to solve a problem; the final product is shaped by all participants.

cognitive apprenticeship A relationship in which a less experienced learner acquires knowledge and skills under the guidance of an expert.

cognitive behaviour modification Procedures based on both behavioural and cognitive learning principles for changing one's own behaviour by using self-talk and self-instruction.

cognitive development Gradual, orderly changes by which mental processes become more complex and sophisticated.

cognitive domain In Bloom's taxonomy, memory and reasoning objectives.

cognitive evaluation theory Suggests that events affect motivation through the individual's perception of the events as controlling behaviour or providing information.

cognitive objectives Instructional objectives stated in terms of higher-level thinking operations.

cognitive stage Initial stage in learning an automated skill, when one relies on general problem-solving approaches to make sense of steps or procedures.

cognitive view of learning A general approach that views learning as an active mental process of acquiring, remembering, and using knowledge.

collective monologue Form of speech in which children in a group talk but do not really interact or communicate.

collective self-esteem The sense of the value of a group, such as an ethnic group, to which one belongs.

collectivist/interdependent societies Societies in which it is more important to connect with others than distinguish yourself.

community of practice Social situation or context in which ideas are judged useful or true.

compensation The principle that changes in one dimension can be offset by changes in another dimension.

complex learning environments Problems and learning situations that mimic the ill-structured nature of real life.

components In an information processing view, basic problem-solving processes underlying intelligence.

concept A general category of events, ideas, objects, or people whose members share certain properties.

concept mapping Student's diagram of his or her understanding of a concept.

conceptual change teaching in science A method that helps students understand (rather than memorize) concepts in science by using and challenging the students' current ideas.

concrete operations Mental tasks tied to concrete objects and situations.

conditional knowledge "Knowing when and why" to use declarative and procedural knowledge.

conditioned response (CR) Learned response to a previously neutral stimulus.

conditioned stimulus (CS) Stimulus that evokes an emotional or physiological response after conditioning.

confidence interval A range of scores within which a student's particular score is likely to fall.

confirmation bias Seeking information that confirms our choices and beliefs, while disconfirming evidence.

consequences Events that are brought about by an action.

conservation Principle that some characteristics of an object remain the same despite changes in appearance.

constructivism View that emphasizes the active role of the learner in building understanding and making sense of information.

constructivist approach View that emphasizes the active role of the learner in building understanding and making sense of information.

context The physical or emotional backdrop associated with an event.

contiguity Association of two events because of repeated pairing.

contingency contract A formal agreement, often written and signed, between the teacher and an individual student specifying what the student must do to earn a particular privilege or reward.

continuous reinforcement schedule Situation in which a reinforcer is presented after every appropriate response.

contract system System in which each student works for a particular grade according to agreed-upon standards.

convergent questions Questions that have a single correct answer.

convergent thinking Narrowing possibilities to a single answer.

cooperative teaching Collaboration between regular and special education teachers.

correlation Statistical description of how closely two variables are related.

creativity Imaginative, original thinking or problem solving.

criterion-referenced grading Assessment of each student's mastery of each course objective.

criterion-referenced testing Testing in which individuals' scores are compared with a pre-defined standard of performance.

critical thinking Evaluating conclusions by logically and systematically examining the problem, the evidence, and the solution.

cross-sectional studies Studies that focus on groups of subjects at different ages rather than following the same group for many years.

crystallized intelligence Ability to apply culturally approved problem-solving methods.

cueing Providing a stimulus that "sets up" desired behaviour.

cultural tools The real tools (computers, scales, etc.) and symbol systems (numbers, language, graphs, etc.) that allow people in a society to communicate, think, solve problems, and create knowledge.

culturally inclusive classrooms Classrooms in which procedures, rules, grouping strategies, attitudes, and teaching methods do not cause conflicts with the students' culturally influenced ways of learning and interacting.

culturally relevant pedagogy Excellent teaching for students from visible minorities that includes academic success and developing/maintaining cultural competence and critical consciousness to challenge the status quo.

culturally responsive management Taking cultural meanings and styles into account when developing management plans and responding to students.

culture The knowledge, rules, traditions, attitudes, and values that guide the behaviour of a group of people and allow them to solve the problems of living in their environment.

curriculum alignment The quality and degree to which an achievement test's items correspond to the curriculum that students are taught in school.

curriculum-based assessment (CBA) Evaluation method using frequent tests of specific skills and knowledge.

data-based instruction Assessment method using frequent probes of specific-skill mastery.

decay The weakening and fading of memories with the passage of time.

decentring Focusing on more than one aspect at a time.

declarative knowledge Verbal information; facts; "knowing that" something is the case.

deficiency needs Maslow's four lower-order needs, which must be satisfied first.

defining attributes Distinctive features shared by members of a category.

descriptive studies Studies that collect detailed information about specific situations, often using observation, surveys, interviews, recordings, or a combination of these methods.

development Orderly, adaptive changes that humans (or animals) go through from conception to death.

developmental crisis A specific conflict whose resolution prepares the way for the next stage.

developmental disabilities Significantly below-average intellectual and adaptive social behaviour evident before the age of 18.

deviation IQ Score based on statistical comparison of individuals' performance with the average performance of others in that age group.

diagnosis Description of a student's current knowledge, skills, or ability.

diagnostic tests Individually administered tests to identify special learning problems.

direct instruction/explicit teaching Systematic instruction for mastery of basic skills, facts, and information.

disability The inability to do something specific, such as walk or hear.

discovery learning Students work on their own to discover basic principles.

discrimination Treating particular categories of people unequally.

disequilibrium In Piaget's theory, the "out-of-balance" state that occurs when a person realizes that his or her current ways of thinking are not working to solve a problem or understand a situation.

distractors Wrong answers offered as choices in a multiple-choice item.

distributed practice Practice that occurs in brief periods with rest intervals.

distributive justice Beliefs about how to divide materials or privileges fairly among members of a group; follows a sequence of development from equality to merit to benevolence.

divergent questions Questions that have no single correct answer.

divergent thinking Coming up with many possible solutions.

domain-specific knowledge Information that is useful in a particular situation or that applies only to one specific topic.

domain-specific strategies Skills consciously applied to reach goals in a particular subject or problem area.

dual marking system System of assigning two grades, one reflecting achievement and the other effort, attitude, and actual ability.

education or school act Provincial or territorial legislation that governs education in elementary and secondary schools.

educational psychology The discipline concerned with teaching and learning processes; applies the methods and theories of psychology and has its own as well.

educationally blind Needing Braille materials in order to learn.

ego-involved learners Students who focus on how well they are performing and how they are judged by others.

ego integrity Sense of self-acceptance and fulfillment.

egocentric Assuming that others experience the world the way you do.

elaboration Adding and extending meaning by connecting new information to existing knowledge.

elaborative rehearsal Keeping information in working memory by associating it with something else you already know.

emotional and behavioural disorders Behaviours or emotions that deviate so much from the norm that they interfere with the child's own growth and development and/or the lives of others—inappropriate behaviours, unhappiness or depression, fears and anxieties, and trouble with relationships.

empathetic listening Hearing the intent and emotions behind what another says and reflecting them back by paraphrasing.

engaged time/time on task Time spent actively engaged in the learning task at hand.

English language learners (ELL) Students whose primary or heritage language is not English.

entity view of ability Belief that ability is a fixed characteristic that cannot be changed.

epilepsy Disorder marked by seizures and caused by abnormal electrical discharges in the brain.

episodic memory Long-term memory for information tied to a particular time and place, especially memory of the events in a person's life.

epistemological beliefs Beliefs about the structure, stability, and certainty of knowledge and how knowledge is best learned.

equilibration Search for mental balance between cognitive schemes and information from the environment.

ethnic pride A positive self-concept about one's racial or ethnic heritage.

ethnicity A cultural heritage shared by a group of people.

ethnography A descriptive approach to research that focuses on life within a group and tries to understand the meaning of events to the people involved.

evaluation Decision making about student performance and about appropriate teaching strategies based on comparing data with standards.

exceptional students Students who have high abilities in particular areas or disabilities that impact learning and may require special education or other services.

executive control processes Processes such as selective attention, rehearsal, elaboration, and organization that influence encoding, storage, and retrieval of information in memory.

exemplar A specific example of a given category that is used to classify an item.

exhibition A performance test or demonstration of learning that is public and usually takes an extended time to prepare.

expectancy × value theories Explanations of motivation that emphasize individuals' expectations for success combined with their valuing of the goal.

experimentation Research method in which variables are manipulated and the effects recorded.

expert teachers Experienced, effective teachers who have developed solutions for common classroom problems. Their knowledge of teaching process and content is extensive and well organized.

explicit memory Long-term memories that involve deliberate or conscious recall.

extinction Gradual disappearance of a learned response.

extrinsic motivation Motivation created by external factors such as rewards and punishments.

failure-accepting students Students who believe that their failures are due to low ability and that there is little they can do about it.

failure-avoiding students Students who avoid failure by sticking to what they know, by not taking risks, or by claiming not to care about their performance.

finger spelling Communication system that "spells out" each letter with a hand position.

first wave constructivism A focus on the individual and psychological sources of knowing, as in Piaget's theory.

flashbulb memories Clear, vivid memories of emotionally important events in your life.

flexible grouping Grouping and regrouping students based on learning needs.

fluid intelligence Mental efficiency that is culture-free and non-verbal and is grounded in brain development.

Flynn effect Because of better health, smaller families, increased complexity in the environment, and more and better schooling, IQ test scores are steadily rising.

formal operations Mental tasks involving abstract thinking and coordination of a number of variables.

formative assessment Ungraded testing used before or during instruction to aid in planning and diagnosis.

fostering communities of learners (FCL) A system of interacting activities that results in a self-consciously active and reflective learning environment, and uses a research, share, perform learning cycle.

functional behavioural assessment (FBA) Procedures used to obtain information about antecedents, behaviours, and consequences to determine the reason or function of the behaviour.

functional fixedness Inability to use objects, concepts, or tools in a new way.

gender biases Different views of males and females, often favouring one gender over the other.

gender-role identity Beliefs about characteristics and behaviour associated with one gender as opposed to the other.

gender schemas Organized networks of knowledge about what it means to be male or female.

general knowledge Information that is useful in many different kinds of tasks; information that applies to many situations.

generalized seizure A seizure involving a large portion of the brain.

generativity Sense of concern for future generations.

Gestalt A pattern or whole; Gestalt theorists hold that people organize their perceptions into coherent wholes.

gifted student A very bright, creative, and talented student.

goal What an individual strives to accomplish.

goal-directed actions Deliberate actions toward a goal.

goal orientations Patterns of beliefs about goals related to achievement in school.

goal structure The way in which students relate to others who are also working toward a particular goal.

good-behaviour game Arrangement where a class is divided into teams and each team receives demerit points for breaking agreed-on rules of good behaviour.

grading on the curve Norm-referenced grading that compares students' performance with an average level.

group consequences Reinforcers or punishments given to a class as a whole for adhering to or violating rules of conduct.

group discussion Conversation in which the teacher does not have the dominant role; students pose and answer their own questions.

group focus The ability to keep as many students as possible involved in activities.

guided discovery An adaptation of discovery learning in which the teacher provides some direction.

halo effect The tendency for a general impression of a person to influence our perception of any aspect of that person.

handicap A disadvantage in a particular situation, sometimes caused by a disability.

Heritage Language Programs Programs that offer opportunities for students to receive instruction in their own language.

heuristic General strategy used in attempting to solve problems.

hierarchy of needs Maslow's model of seven levels of human needs, from basic physiological requirements to the need for self-actualization.

high-road transfer Application of abstract knowledge learned in one situation to a different situation.

hostile aggression Bold, direct action that is intended to hurt someone else; unprovoked attack.

humanistic interpretation Approach to motivation that emphasizes personal freedom, choice, self-determination, and striving for personal growth.

hyperactivity Behaviour disorder marked by atypical, excessive restlessness and inattentiveness.

hypothetico-deductive reasoning A formal-operations problem-solving strategy in which an individual begins by identifying all the factors that might affect a problem and then deduces and systematically evaluates specific solutions.

identity The complex answer to the question, "Who am I?" The principle that a person or object remains the same over time.

identity achievement Strong sense of commitment to life choices after free consideration of alternatives.

identity diffusion Uncentredness; confusion about who one is and what one wants.

identity foreclosure Acceptance of other life choices without consideration of options.

images Representations based on the structure or physical appearance of information.

implicit memory Knowledge that we are not conscious of recalling, but influences behaviour or thought without our awareness.

incentive An object or event that encourages or discourages behaviour.

inclusion The practice of integrating exceptional students into regular education classrooms; the emphasis is on participation rather than placement.

incremental view of ability Belief that ability is a set of skills that can be changed.

individual learning expectation (ILE) Personal average score.

individualized education program (IEP) Annually revised program for an exceptional student detailing present achievement level, goals, and strategies, drawn up by teachers, family members, specialists, and (if possible) the student.

inductive reasoning Formulating general principles based on knowledge of examples and details.

industry Eagerness to engage in productive work.

informal assessments Ungraded (formative) assessments that gather information from multiple sources to help teachers make decisions.

information processing The human mind's activity of taking in, storing, and using information.

initiative Willingness to begin new activities and explore new directions.

inquiry learning Approach in which the teacher presents a puzzling situation and students solve the problem by gathering data and testing their conclusions.

insight The ability to deal effectively with novel situations.

instructional conversation Situation in which students learn through interactions with teachers and/or other students.

instructional objectives Clear statement of what students are intended to learn through instruction.

instrumental aggression Strong actions aimed at claiming an object, place, or privilege—not intended to harm, but may lead to harm.

integration The practice of having exceptional students participate in activities with their non-exceptional peers.

intelligence Ability or abilities to acquire and use knowledge for solving problems and adapting to the world.

intelligence quotient (IQ) Score comparing mental and chronological ages.

interference The effect that remembering certain information is hampered by the presence of other information.

intermittent reinforcement schedule Situation in which a reinforcer is presented after some but not all responses.

internalize To adopt external standards as one's own.

intersubjective attitude A commitment to build shared meaning with others by finding common ground and exchanging interpretations.

interval schedule Reinforcement schedule based on a time interval between reinforcers.

intrinsic motivation Motivation associated with activities that are their own reward.

intrinsic or interest value The enjoyment a person gets from a task.

intuitive thinking Making imaginative leaps to correct perceptions or workable solutions.

keyword method System of associating new words or concepts with similar-sounding cue words and images.

KWL A strategy to guide reading and inquiry: Before—What do I already *know*? What do I *want* to know? After—What have I *learned*?

lateralization The specialization of the two hemispheres (sides) of the brain cortex.

learned helplessness The expectation, based on previous experiences involving lack of control, that all one's efforts will lead to failure.

learning Process through which experience causes permanent change in knowledge or behaviour.

learning disability Problem with acquisition and use of language; may show up as difficulty with reading, writing, reasoning, or math.

learning preferences Individual preferences for particular learning environments (e.g., quiet versus loud).

learning strategies General plans for approaching learning tasks.

learning styles An individual's characteristic approaches to learning and studying, usually involving deep or superficial processing of information.

learning tactics Specific techniques for learning, such as using mnemonics or outlining a passage.

least restrictive placement The practice of placing exceptional students in the most regular educational settings possible while ensuring that they are successful and receive support appropriate to their special needs.

legitimate peripheral participation Genuine involvement in the work of the group, even if one's abilities are undeveloped and contributions small.

levels of processing theory Theory that recall of information is based on how deeply it is processed.

loci method Technique of associating items with specific places.

locus of causality The location—internal or external—of the cause of behaviour.

long-term memory Permanent store of knowledge.

long-term working memory Memory that holds strategies for pulling information from long-term memory into working memory.

longitudinal studies Studies that document changes that occur in subjects over time, often many years.

low-road transfer Spontaneous and automatic transfer of highly practised skills.

low vision Vision limited to close objects.

maintenance rehearsal Keeping information in working memory by repeating it to yourself.

massed practice Practice for a single extended period.

mastery experiences Our own direct experiences—the most powerful source of efficacy information.

mastery goal A personal intention to improve abilities and understand, no matter how performance suffers.

mastery-oriented students Students who focus on learning goals because they value achievement and see ability as improvable.

maturation Genetically programmed, naturally occurring changes over time.

means-ends analysis Heuristic in which a goal is divided into subgoals.

measurement An evaluation expressed in quantitative (number) terms.

melting pot A metaphor for the absorption and assimilation of immigrants into the mainstream of society so that ethnic differences vanish.

mental age In intelligence testing, a score based on average abilities for that age group.

metacognition Knowledge about our own thinking processes.

metalinguistic awareness Understanding about one's own use of language.

microgenetic studies Detailed observation and analysis of changes in a cognitive process as the process unfolds over several days or weeks.

minority group A group of people who have been socially disadvantaged—not always a minority in actual numbers.

mnemonics Techniques for remembering; also, the art of memory.

modelling Changes in behaviour, thinking, or emotions that happen through observing another person—a model.

monolinguals Individuals who speak only one language.

moral dilemmas Situations in which no single choice is clearly and indisputably right.

moral realism Stage of development wherein children see rules as absolute.

moral reasoning The thinking process involved in judgments about questions of right and wrong.

morality of cooperation Stage of development wherein children realize that people make rules and people can change them.

moratorium Identity crisis; suspension of choices because of struggle.

mosaic The idea that individuals can maintain their culture and identity while still being a respected part of the larger society.

motivation An internal state that arouses, directs, and maintains behaviour.

motivation to learn The tendency to find academic activities meaningful and worthwhile and to try to benefit from them.

movement management Keeping lessons and the group moving at an appropriate (and flexible) pace, with smooth transitions and variety.

multicultural education Education that teaches the value of cultural diversity.

multiple intelligences In Gardner's theory of intelligence, a person's eight separate abilities: logical-mathematical, linguistic, musical, spatial, bodily-kinesthetic, interpersonal, intrapersonal, and naturalist.

multiple representations of content Considering problems using various analogies, examples, and metaphors.

myelination The process by which neural fibres are coated with a fatty sheath called *myelin* that makes message transfer more efficient.

natural/logical consequences Instead of punishing, have students redo, repair, or in some way face the consequences that naturally flow from their actions.

need for autonomy The desire to have our own wishes, rather than external rewards or pressures, determine our actions.

negative correlation A relationship between two variables in which a high value on one is associated with a low value on the other. Example: height and distance from top of head to the ceiling.

negative reinforcement Strengthening behaviour by removing an aversive stimulus.

neo-Piagetian theories More recent theories that integrate findings about attention, memory, and strategy use with Piaget's insights about children's thinking and the construction of knowledge.

neurons Nerve cells that store and transfer information.

neutral stimulus Stimulus not connected to a response.

non-graded elementary school/Joplin Plan Arrangement wherein students are grouped by ability in particular subjects, regardless of their ages or grades.

norm-referenced grading Assessment of students' achievement in relation to one another or a defined group.

norm-referenced testing Testing in which individual scores are compared with the average performance of others.

norm group A group whose average score serves as a standard for evaluating any student's score on a test.

norming sample A large sample of students with published characteristics who serve as a comparison group for interpreting scores on norm-referenced standardized tests.

object permanence The understanding that objects have a separate, permanent existence.

objective testing The kind of tests that do not require interpretation in scoring, such as multiple-choice, true/false, short-answer, and fill-in.

observational learning Learning by observation and imitation of others.

operant conditioning Learning in which voluntary behaviour is strengthened or weakened by consequences or antecedents.

operants Voluntary (and generally goal-directed) behaviours emitted by a person or an animal.

operations Actions that a person carries out by thinking them through instead of literally performing them.

organization Ongoing process of arranging information and experience into mental systems or categories. Ordered and logical network of relations.

overgeneralization Inclusion of non-members in a category; overextending a concept.

overlapping Supervising several activities at once.

overlearning Practising a skill past the point of mastery.

overt aggression A form of hostile aggression that involves physical attack.

paraphrase rule Policy whereby listeners must accurately summarize what a speaker has said before being allowed to respond.

parenting styles The ways of interacting with and disciplining children.

part learning Breaking a list of learning items into shorter lists.

partial seizure or absence seizure A seizure involving only a small part of the brain.

participant observation A method for conducting descriptive research in which the researcher becomes a participant in the situation in order to better understand life in that group.

participation structures The formal and informal rules for how to take part in a given activity.

peg-type mnemonics Systems of associating items with cue words.

percentage grading System of converting class performances to percentage scores and assigning grades based on predetermined cut-off points.

perception Detecting and interpreting sensory information.

performance goal A personal intention to seem competent or perform well in the eyes of others.

perspective-taking ability Understanding that others have different feelings and experiences.

phonological loop Part of working memory; memory rehearsal system for verbal and sound information lasting about 1.5 to 2seconds.

physical development Changes in body structure that take place as one grows.

plasticity The brain's tendency to remain somewhat adaptable or flexible.

portfolio A collection of the student's work in an area, showing growth, self-reflection, and achievement.

positive behavioural supports (PBS) Interventions designed to replace problem behaviours with new actions that serve the same purpose for the student.

positive correlation A relationship between two variables in which the two increase or decrease together. Example: calorie intake and weight gain.

positive practice Practising correct responses immediately after errors.

positive reinforcement Strengthening behaviour by presenting a desired stimulus after the behaviour.

PQ4R A method for studying text that involves six steps: *Preview, Question, Read, Reflect, Recite, Review.*

pragmatics Knowledge about how to use language—when, where, how, and to whom to speak.

prejudice Prejudgment, or irrational generalization about an entire category of people.

Premack principle Principle stating that a more-preferred activity can serve as reinforcer for a less-preferred activity.

preoperational The stage of development before a child masters logical mental operations.

presentation punishment Type of punishment that decreases the chances that a behaviour will occur again by presenting an aversive stimulus following the behaviour; also called Type I punishment.

pretest Formative test for assessing students' knowledge, readiness, and abilities.

priming Activating a concept in memory or the spread of activation from one concept to another.

principle Established relationship between factors.

private speech Children's self-talk, which guides their thinking and action; eventually, these verbalizations are internalized as silent inner speech.

problem Any situation in which you are trying to reach some goal and must find a means to do so.

problem-based learning Methods that provide students with realistic problems that don't necessarily have "right" answers.

problem solving Creating new solutions for problems.

procedural knowledge Knowledge that is demonstrated when we perform a task; "knowing how."

procedural memory Long-term memory for how to do things.

procedures Prescribed steps for an activity.

productions The contents of procedural memory; rules about what actions to take, given certain conditions.

prompt A reminder that follows a cue to make sure the person reacts to the cue.

proposition The smallest unit of information that can be judged true or false.

propositional network Set of interconnected concepts and relationships in which long-term knowledge is held.

prototype Best representative of a category.

psychomotor domain Realm of physical ability and coordination objectives.

psychosocial Describing the relation of the individual's emotional needs to the social environment.

puberty The physiological changes during adolescence that lead to the ability to reproduce.

punishment Process that weakens or suppresses behaviour.

Pygmalion effect Exceptional progress by a student as a result of high teacher expectations for that student; named for the mythological king Pygmalion, who made a statue, then caused it to be brought to life.

race A group of people who share common biological traits that are seen as self-defining by the people of the group.

radical constructivism Knowledge is assumed to be the individual's construction; it cannot be judged right or wrong.

random Without any definite pattern; following no rule.

ratio schedule Reinforcement schedule based on a number of responses between reinforcers.

READS A five-step reading strategy: *Review* headings; *Examine* boldface words; *Ask*, "What do I expect to learn?"; *Do* it—Read; *Summarize* in your own words.

receptors Parts of the human body that receive sensory information.

reciprocal determinism An explanation of behaviour that emphasizes the mutual effects of the individual and the environment on each other.

reconstruction Re-creating information by using memories, expectations, logic, and existing knowledge.

reflective Thoughtful and inventive. Reflective teachers think back over situations to analyze what they did and why, and to consider how they might improve learning for their students.

reinforcement Use of consequences to strengthen behaviour.

reinforcer Any event that follows behaviour and increases the chances that the behaviour will occur again.

relational aggression A form of hostile aggression that involves verbal attacks and other actions meant to harm social relationships.

reliability Consistency of test results.

removal punishment Type of punishment that decreases the chances that a behaviour will occur again by removing a pleasant stimulus following the behaviour; also called Type II punishment.

representativeness heuristic Judging the likelihood of an event based on how well the events match your prototypes—what you think is representative of the category.

reprimands Criticisms for misbehaviour; rebukes.

resilience The ability to adapt successfully in spite of difficult circumstances and threats to development.

resistance culture Group values and beliefs about refusing to adopt the behaviour and attitudes of the majority culture.

resource room Classroom with special materials and a specially trained teacher.

respondents Responses—generally automatic or involuntary—elicited by specific stimuli.

response Observable reaction to a stimulus.

response cost Punishment by loss of reinforcers.

response generalization Responding in the same way to similar stimuli.

response set Rigidity; tendency to respond in the most familiar way.

restructuring Conceiving of a problem in a new or different way.

retrieval Process of searching for and finding information in long-term memory.

reversibility A characteristic of Piagetian logical operations—the ability to think through a series of steps, then mentally reverse the steps and return to the starting point; also called reversible thinking.

reversible thinking Thinking backward, from the end to the beginning.

revise option In a contract system, the chance to revise and improve work.

reward An object or event that we think is attractive and provide as a consequence of a behaviour.

ripple effect "Contagious" spreading of behaviours through imitation.

rote memorization Remembering information by repetition without necessarily understanding the meaning of the information.

rules Statements specifying expected and forbidden behaviour; dos and don'ts.

satiation Requiring a person to repeat problem behaviour past the point of interest or motivation.

scaffolding Support for learning and problem solving; the support could be clues, reminders, encouragement, breaking the problem down into steps, providing an example, or anything else that allows the student to grow in independence as a learner.

schema A basic structure for organizing information; concept.

schema-driven problem solving Recognizing a problem as a "disguised" version of an old problem for which one already has a solution.

schemes Mental systems or categories of perception and experience.

scoring rubrics Rules that are used to determine the quality of a student performance.

script Schema or expected plan for the sequence of steps in a common event, such as buying groceries or ordering pizza.

scripted cooperation Learning strategy in which two students take turns summarizing material and criticizing the summaries.

seatwork Independent classroom work.

second wave constructivism A focus on the social and cultural sources of knowing, as in Vygotsky's theory.

self-actualization Fulfilling one's potential.

self-concept Individuals' knowledge and beliefs about themselves—their ideas, feelings, attitudes, and expectations.

self-efficacy A person's sense of being able to deal effectively with a particular task.

self-esteem The value each of us places on our own characteristics, abilities, and behaviour.

self-fulfilling prophecy A groundless expectation that is confirmed because it has been expected.

self-management Management of your own behaviour and acceptance of responsibility for your own actions. Use of behavioural learning principles to change one's own behaviour.

self-regulated learning A view of learning as skills and will applied to analyzing learning tasks, setting goals, and planning how to do the task, applying skills, and especially making adjustments about how learning is carried out.

self-regulation Process of activating and sustaining thoughts, behaviours, and emotions in order to reach goals.

self-reinforcement Controlling your own reinforcers.

semantic memory Memory for meaning.

semiotic function The ability to use symbols—language, pictures, signs, or gestures—to represent actions or objects mentally.

sensorimotor Involving the senses and motor activity.

sensory memory System that holds sensory information very briefly.

serial-position effect The tendency to remember the beginning and the end but not the middle of a list.

seriation Arrangement of objects in sequential order according to one aspect, such as size, weight, or volume.

sexual identity A complex combination of beliefs and orientations about gender roles and sexual orientation.

shaping Reinforcing each small step of progress toward a desired goal or behaviour.

short-term memory Component of memory system that holds information for about 15 to 20 seconds.

sign language Communication system of hand movements that symbolize words and concepts.

single-subject experimental studies Systematic interventions to study effects with one person, often by applying and then withdrawing a treatment.

situated learning The idea that skills and knowledge are tied to the situation in which they were learned and difficult to apply in new settings.

social and emotional development Changes over time in the ways in which one relates to others and the self.

social cognitive theory Theory that adds concern with cognitive factors such as beliefs, self-perceptions, and expectations to social learning theory.

social goals A wide variety of needs and motives to be connected to others or to be part of a group.

social isolation Removal of a disruptive student for 5 to 10 minutes.

social learning theory Theory that emphasizes learning through observation of others.

social negotiation Aspect of learning process that relies on collaboration with others and respect for different perspectives.

social persuasion A "pep talk" or specific performance feedback—one source of self-efficacy.

sociocultural theory Theory that emphasizes the role in development of cooperative dialogues between children and more knowledgeable members of society; children learn the culture of their community (ways of thinking and behaving) through these interactions.

sociocultural views of motivation Perspectives that emphasize participation, identities, and interpersonal relations within communities of practice.

socioeconomic status (SES) Relative standing in the society based on income, power, background, and prestige.

sociolinguistics The study of formal and informal rules for how, when, about what, to whom, and how long to speak in conversations within cultural groups.

spasticity Overly tight or tense muscles, characteristic of some forms of cerebral palsy.

speech impairment Inability to produce sounds effectively for speaking.

speech reading Using visual cues to understand language.

spiral curriculum Bruner's design for teaching that introduces the fundamental structure of all subjects early in the school years, then revisits the subjects in more and more complex forms over time.

spread of activation Retrieval of pieces of information based on their relatedness to one another; remembering one bit of information activates (stimulates) recall of associated information.

stand-alone thinking skills programs Programs that teach thinking skills directly without need for extensive subject matter knowledge.

standard error of measurement A measure of unreliability representing how much variability there is in an average student's test scores around the student's true score.

standardized tests Tests administered under uniform conditions and scored according to uniform procedures.

statistically significant Not likely to be a chance occurrence.

stem The question part of a multiple-choice item.

stereotype Schema that organizes knowledge or perceptions of a category.

stereotype threat The extra emotional and cognitive burden that one's performance in an academic situation might confirm a stereotype that others hold.

stimulus Event that activates behaviour.

stimulus control Capacity for the presence or absence of antecedents to regulate behaviour.

stimulus discrimination Responding differently to similar, but not identical, stimuli.

story grammar The structure or organization—involving kinds of characters, major events, etc.—typical for a category of texts, such as mysteries or scientific reports.

stuttering Repetitions, prolongations, and hesitations that block flow of speech.

subjects People or animals participating in a study.

successive approximations Small components that make up complex behaviour.

summative assessment Testing that follows instruction and assesses achievement.

sustaining expectation effect An effect that occurs when student performance is maintained at a certain level because teachers don't recognize improvements.

synapses The tiny space between neurons; chemical messages are sent across these gaps.

syntax The order of words in phrases or sentences.

tacit knowledge Knowing *how* rather than knowing *that*—knowledge that is more likely to be learned during everyday life than through formal schooling.

task-involved learners Students who focus on mastering the task or solving the problem.

task analysis System for breaking down a task hierarchically into basic skills and sub-skills.

taxonomy Classification system.

teachers' sense of efficacy A teacher's belief that he or she can reach even the most difficult students and help them learn.

theory Integrated statement of principles that attempts to explain a phenomenon and make predictions.

theory of mind An understanding that other people are people too, with their own minds, thoughts, feelings, beliefs, desires, and perceptions.

time out Technically, the removal of all reinforcement; in practice, isolation of a student from the rest of the class for a brief time.

token reinforcement system System in which tokens earned for academic work and positive classroom behaviour can be exchanged for some desired reward.

top-down processing Perceiving based on the context and the patterns you expect to occur in that situation.

tracking Assignment to different classes and academic experiences based on achievement.

transfer Influence of previously learned material on new material.

transition programming Gradual preparation of exceptional students to move from high school into further education or training, employment, or community involvement.

triarchic theory of intelligence A three-part description of the mental abilities (thinking processes, coping with new experiences, and adapting to context) that lead to more or less intelligent behaviour.

true score Hypothetical average of an individual's scores if repeated testing under ideal conditions were possible.

unconditioned response (UR) Naturally occurring emotional or physiological response.

unconditioned stimulus (US) Stimulus that automatically produces an emotional or physiological response.

undergeneralization Exclusion of some true members from a category; limiting a concept.

universal design Considering the needs of all users in the design of new tools, learning programs, or websites.

utility value The contribution of a task to meeting one's goals.

validity Degree to which a particular use of a test score is justified by evidence.

verbalization Putting your problem-solving plan and its logic into words.

vicarious experiences Accomplishments that are modelled by someone else.

vicarious reinforcement Increasing the chances that we will repeat a behaviour by observing another person being reinforced for that behaviour.

visuospatial sketchpad Part of working memory; holding system for visual and spatial information.

voicing problems Speech impairments involving inappropriate pitch, quality, loudness, or intonation.

volition Will power; self-discipline; work styles that protect opportunities to reach goals by applying self-regulated learning.

warm demanders Effective teachers who show both high expectations and great caring for their students.

whole language perspective A philosophical approach to teaching and learning that stresses learning through authentic, real-life tasks; it emphasizes using language to learn, integrating learning across skills and subjects, and respecting the language abilities of student and teacher.

within-class ability grouping System of grouping in which students in a class are divided into two or three groups based on ability in an attempt to accommodate student differences.

withitness According to Jacob Kounin, awareness of everything happening in a classroom.

work-avoidant learners Students who don't want to learn or to look smart but just want to avoid work.

working-backward strategy Heuristic in which one starts with the goal and moves backward to solve the problem.

working memory The information that you are focusing on at a given moment.

zone of proximal development Phase at which a child can master a task if given appropriate help and support.

References

ABA recommends dropping "zero tolerance" in schools. (2001, February 21). Retrieved March 15, 2005, from http://archives.cnn.com/2001/fyi/teachers.ednews/02/21/zero.tolerance.ap.

Abi-Nader, J. (1991). Creating a vision of the future: Strategies for motivating minority students. *Phi Delta Kappan, 72,* 546–549.

Aboud, F., & Skerry, S. (1984). The development of ethnic identification: A critical review. *Journal of Cross-Cultural Psychology, 15,* 3–34.

Aboud, F. E. (2003). The formation of in-group favoritism and out-group prejudice in young children: Are they distinct attitudes? *Developmental Psychology, 39,* 48–60.

Acker, S., & Oatley, K. (1993). Gender issues in education for science and technology: Current situation and prospects for change. *Canadian Journal of Education, 18,* 255–272.

Ackerman, B. P., Brown, E. D., & Izard, C. E. (2004). The relations between contextual risk, earned income, and the school adjustment of children from economically disadvantaged families. *Developmental Psychology, 40,* 204–216.

Ackerman, P. L., Beier, M. E., & Boyle, M. O. (2005). Working memory and intelligence: The same or different constructs? *Psychological Bulletin, 131,* 30–60.

Adams, M. J., Treiman, R., & Pressley, M. (1998). Reading, writing, and literacy. In W. Damon, I. Sigel, & A. Renninger (Eds.), *Handbook of child psychology* (5th ed.), *Child psychology in practice* (Vol. 4, pp. 275–355). New York: Wiley.

Airasian, P. W. (1996). *Assessment in the classroom.* New York: McGraw-Hill.

Airasian, P. W. (2001). *Classroom assessment: Concepts and applications* (4th ed.). New York: McGraw-Hill.

Albanese, M. A., & Mitchell, S. A. (1993). Problem-based learning: A review of literature on its outcomes and implementation issues. *Academic Medicine, 68,* 52–81.

Alberto, P., & Troutman, A. C. (1990). *Applied behavior analysis for teachers: Influencing student performance* (3rd ed.). Columbus, OH: Merrill.

Alberto, P., & Troutman, A. (2003). *Applied behavior analysis for teachers* (6th ed.). Columbus, OH: Prentice-Hall-Merrill.

Alderman, M. K. (1985). Achievement motivation and the preservice teacher. In M. Alderman & M. Cohen (Eds.), *Motivation theory and practice for preservice teachers* (pp. 37–49). Washington, DC: ERIC Clearinghouse on Teacher Education.

Alderman, M. K. (2004). *Motivation for achievement: Possibilities for teaching and learning.* Mahwah, NJ: Lawrence Erlbaum.

Alexander, P. A. (1992). Domain knowledge: Evolving themes and emerging concerns. *Educational Psychologist, 27,* 33–51.

Alexander, P. A. (1996). The past, present, and future of knowledge research: A reexamination of the role of knowledge in learning and instruction. *Educational Psychologist, 31,* 89–92.

Alexander, P. A. (1997). Mapping the multidimensional nature of domain learning: The interplay of cognitive, motivational, and strategic forces. *Advances in Motivation and Achievement, 10,* 213–250.

Alexander, P. A. (2006). *Psychology in learning and instruction.* Upper Saddle River, NJ: Merrill/Prentice-Hall.

Alexander, P. A., Kulikowich, J. M., & Schulze, S. K. (1994). How subject-matter knowledge affects recall and interest. *American Educational Research Journal, 31,* 313–337.

Alexander, P. A., & Murphy, P. K. (1998). The research base for APA's Learner-Centered Psychological Principles. In N. Lambert & B. McCombs (Eds.), *How students learn: Reforming schools through learner-centered education* (pp. 25–60). Washington, DC: American Psychological Association.

Allington, R. (1980). Teacher interruption behaviors during primary-grade oral reading. *Journal of Educational Psychology, 71,* 371–377.

Alloy, L. B., & Seligman, M. E. P. (1979). On the cognitive component of learned helplessness and depression. *The Journal of Learning and Motivation, 13,* 219–276.

Altermatt, E. R., Pomerantz, E. M., Ruble, D. N., Frey, K. S., & Greulich, F. K. (2002). Predicting changes in children's self-perceptions of academic competence: A naturalistic examination of evaluative discourse among classmates. *Developmental Psychology, 38,* 903–917.

Alton-Lee, A., Diggins, C., Klenner, L., Vine, E., & Dalton, N. (2001). Teacher management of the learning environment during a social studies discussion in a new-entrant classroom in New Zealand. *The Elementary School Journal, 101,* 549–566.

Alvidrez, J., & Weinstein, R. S. (1999). Early teacher perceptions and later student academic achievement. *Journal of Educational Psychology, 91,* 731–746.

Alwin, D., & Thornton, A. (1984). Family origins and schooling processes: Early versus late influence of parental characteristics. *American Sociological Review, 49,* 784–802.

Amabile, T. M. (1996). *Creativity in context.* Boulder, CO: Westview Press.

Amabile, T. M. (2001). Beyond talent: John Irving and the passionate craft of creativity. *American Psychologist, 56,* 333–336.

Amato, L. F., Loomis, L. S., & Booth, A. (1995). Parental divorce, marital conflict, and offspring well-being during early adulthood. *Social Forces, 73,* 895–915.

American Psychiatric Association. (2000). *The diagnostic and statistical manual of mental disorders* (DSM-IV-TR). Washington, DC: APA.

American Association for the Advancement of Science (AAAS). (1993). *Benchmarks for science literacy.* Washington, DC: Author.

Ames, C. (1990). Motivation: What teachers need to know. *Teachers College Record, 91,* 409–421.

Ames, C. (1992). Classrooms: Goals, structures, and student motivation. *Journal of Educational Psychology, 84,* 261–271.

Ames, R., & Lau, S. (1982). An attributional analysis of student help-seeking in academic settings. *Journal of Educational Psychology, 74,* 414–423.

Anderman, E. M., & Maehr, M. L. (1994). Motivation and schooling in the middle grades. *Review of Educational Research, 64,* 287–310.

Anderman, E. M., & Midgley, C. (2004). Changes in self-reported academic cheating across the transition from middle school to high school. *Contemporary Educational Psychology, 29,* 499–517.

Anderson, C. W., Holland, J. D., & Palincsar, A. S. (1997). Canonical and sociocultural approaches to research and reform in science education: The story of Juan and his group. *The Elementary School Journal, 97,* 359–384.

Anderson, C. W., & Roth, K. J. (1989). Teaching for meaningful and self-regulated learning of science. In J. Brophy (Ed.), *Advances in research on teaching* (Vol. 1, pp. 265–306). Greenwich, CT: JAI Press.

Anderson, C. W., & Smith, E. L. (1983, April). *Children's conceptions of light and color: Developing the concept of unseen rays.*

Paper presented at the annual meeting of the American Educational Research Association, Montreal.

Anderson, C. W., & Smith, E. L. (1987). Teaching science. In V. Richardson-Koehler (Ed.), *Educators' handbook: A research perspective* (pp. 84–111). New York: Longman.

Anderson, J. (1995). Listening to parents' voices: Cross cultural perceptions of learning to read and write. *Reading Horizons, 35,* 394–413.

Anderson, J., & Gunderson, L. (1997). Literacy learning from a multicultural perspective. *The Reading Teacher, 50,* 514–516.

Anderson, J. R. (1993). Problem solving and learning. *American Psychologist, 48,* 35–44.

Anderson, J. R. (1995a). *Cognitive psychology and its implications* (4th ed.). New York: Freeman.

Anderson, J. R. (1995b). *Learning and memory.* New York: John Wiley & Sons.

Anderson, J. R. (2005). *Cognitive psychology and its implications* (6th ed.). New York: Worth.

Anderson, J. R., Reder, L. M., & Simon, H. A. (1995). Applications and misapplication of cognitive psychology to mathematics education. Unpublished manuscript.

Anderson, J. R., Reder, L. M., & Simon, H. A. (1996). Situated learning and education. *Educational Researcher, 25,* 5–11.

Anderson, L. M. (1985). What are students doing when they do all that seatwork? In C. Fisher & D. Berliner (Eds.), *Perspectives on instructional time.* New York: Longman.

Anderson, L. M. (1989a). Learners and learning. In M. Reynolds (Ed.), *Knowledge base for beginning teachers* (pp. 85–100). New York: Pergamon.

Anderson, L. M. (1989b). Classroom instruction. In M. Reynolds (Ed.), *Knowledge base for beginning teachers* (pp. 101–116). New York: Pergamon.

Anderson, L. M., Brubaker, N. L., Alleman-Brooks, J., & Duffy, G. G. (1985). A qualitative study of seatwork in first-grade classrooms. *Elementary School Journal, 86,* 123–140.

Anderson, L. W., & Krathwohl, D. R. (Eds.). (2001). *A taxonomy for learning, teaching, and assessing: A revision of Bloom's taxonomy of educational objectives.* New York: Addison-Wesley Longman.

Anderson, L. W., & Sosniak, L. A. (Eds.). (1994). *Bloom's taxonomy: A forty-year retrospective.* Ninety-third yearbook for the National Society for the Study of Education, Part II. Chicago: University of Chicago Press.

Anderson, P. J., & Graham, S. M. (1994). Issues in second-language phonological acquisition among children and adults. *Topics in Language Disorders, 14,* 84–100.

Anderson, R., Hiebert, E., Scott, J., & Wilkinson, I. (1985). *Becoming a nation of readers: The report of the commission on reading.* Washington, DC: National Institute of Education.

Anderson, R. C., et al. (2001). The snowball phenomenon: Spread of ways of talking and ways of thinking across groups of children. *Cognition and Instruction, 19,* 1–46.

Anderson, S. M., Klatzky, R. L., & Murray, J. (1990). Traits and social stereotypes: Efficiency differences in social information processing. *Journal of Personality and Social Psychology, 59,* 192–201.

Angier, N., & Chang, K. (2005, January 24). Gray matter and the sexes: Still a scientific gray area. *The New York Times,* A1+.

Anyon, J. (1980). Social class and the hidden curriculum of work. *Journal of Education, 162,* 67–92.

Archer, S. L., & Waterman, A. S. (1990). Varieties of identity diffusions and foreclosures: An exploration of the subcategories of the identity statuses. *Journal of Adolescent Research, 5,* 96–111.

Arends, R. I. (2001). *Learning to teach* (5th ed.). New York: McGraw-Hill.

Arends, R. I. (2004). *Learning to teach* (6th ed.). New York: McGraw-Hill.

Arlin, M. (1984). Time, equality, and mastery learning. *Review of Educational Research, 54,* 65–86.

Arnold, M. L. (2000). Stage, sequence, and sequels: Changing conceptions of morality, post-Kohlberg. *Educational Psychology Review, 12,* 365–383.

Aronson, E. (2000). *Nobody left to hate: Teaching compassion after Columbine.* New York: Worth.

Aronson, J., Fried, C. B., & Good, C. (2002). Reducing the effects of stereotype threat on African American college students by shaping theories of intelligence. *Journal of Experimental Social Psychology, 38(2),* 113–125.

Aronson, J., & Inzlicht, M. (2004) The ups and downs of attributional ambiguity: Stereotype vulnerability and the academic self-knowledge of African American college students. *Psychological Science, 15,* 829–836.

Aronson, J., Lustina, M. J., Good, C., Keough, K., Steele, C. M., & Brown, J. (1999). When White men can't do math: Necessary and sufficient factors in stereotype threat. *Journal of Experimental Social Psychology, 35,* 29–46.

Aronson, J., & Salinas, M. F. (1998). Stereotype threat, attributional ambiguity, and Latino underperformance. Unpublished manuscript, University of Texas at Austin.

Aronson, J., Steele, C. M., Salinas, M. F., & Lustina, M. J. (1999). The effect of stereotype threat on the standardized test performance of college students. In E. Aronson (Ed.), *Readings about the social animal* (8th ed.). New York: Freeman.

Artman, L., & Cahan, S. (1993). Schooling and the development of transitive inference. *Developmental Psychology, 29,* 753–759.

Ashcraft, M. H. (2002). *Cognition* (3rd ed.). Upper Saddle River, NJ: Prentice-Hall.

Ashcraft, M. H. (2006). *Cognition* (4th ed.). Upper Saddle River, NJ: Prentice-Hall.

Ashton, P. T. (1978). Cross-cultural Piagetian research: An experimental perspective. *Harvard Educational Review* (Reprint Series No. 13), 475–506.

Association for the Gifted. (2001). *Diversity and developing gifts and talents: A national action plan.* Arlington, VA: Author.

Atkinson, R. C., & Shiffrin, R. M. (1968). Human memory: A proposed system and its control processes. In K. Spence & J. T. Spence (Eds.), *The psychology of learning and motivation* (Vol. 2). Oxford, UK: Academic Press.

Atkinson, R. K., Levin, J. R., Kiewra, K. A., Meyers, T., Atkinson, L. A., Renandya, W. A., & Hwang, Y. (1999). Matrix and mnemonic text-processing adjuncts: Comparing and combining their components. *Journal of Educational Psychology, 91,* 242–257.

Au, K. H. (1980). Participation structures in a reading lesson with Hawaiian children: Analysis of a culturally appropriate instructional event. *Anthropology and Education Quarterly, 11,* 91–115.

Ausubel, D. P. (1963). *The psychology of meaningful verbal learning.* New York: Grune and Stratton.

Ausubel, D. P. (1977). The facilitation of meaningful verbal learning in the classroom. *Educational Psychologist, 12,* 162–178.

Ausubel, D. P. (1982). Schemata, advance organizers, and anchoring ideas: A reply to Anderson, Spiro, and Anderson. *Journal of Structural Learning, 7,* 63–73.

Babad, E. (1995). The "teachers' pet" phenomenon, students' perceptions of differential behavior, and students' morale. *Journal of Educational Psychology, 87,* 361–374.

Babad, E. Y., Inbar, J., & Rosenthal, R. (1982). Pygmalion, Galatea, and the Golem: Investigations of biased and unbiased teachers. *Journal of Educational Psychology, 74,* 459–474.

Baddeley, A. D. (1986). *Working memory.* Oxford, UK: Claredon Books.

Baddeley, A. D. (2001). Is working memory still working? *American Psychologist, 56,* 851–864.

Baer, J. (1997). *Creative teachers, creative students.* Boston: Allyn & Bacon.

Bailey, S. M. (1993). The current status of gender equity research in American Schools. *Educational Psychologist, 28,* 321–339.

Baillargeon, R., & De Vos, J. (1991). Object permanence in young infants: Further evidence. *Child Development, 62,* 1227–1246.

Baker, C. (1993). *Foundations of bilingual education and bilingualism.* Clevedon, England: Multilingual Matters.

Baker, D. (1986). Sex differences in classroom interaction in secondary science. *Journal of Classroom Interaction, 22,* 212–218.

Bakerman, R., Adamson, L. B., Koner, M., & Barr, R. G. (1990). !Kung infancy: The social context of object exploration. *Child Development, 61,* 794–809.

Ball, D. L. (1997). What do students know? Facing challenges of distance, context, and desire in trying to hear children. In B. J. Biddle, T. L. Good, & I. F. Goodson (Eds.), *The international handbook of teachers and teaching* (pp. 769–818). Dordrecht, the Netherlands: Kluwer.

Ball, D. L., Lubienski, S. T., & Mewborn, D. S. (2001). Research on teaching mathematics: The unsolved problem of teachers' mathematical knowledge. In V. Richardson (Ed.), *Handbook of research on teaching* (4th ed., pp. 433–456). Washington, DC: American Educational Research Association.

Bandura, A. (1965). Influence of models' reinforcement contingencies on the acquisition of imitative responses. *Journal of Personality and Social Psychology, 1,* 589–595.

Bandura, A. (1977). *Social learning theory.* Englewood Cliffs, NJ: Prentice-Hall.

Bandura, A. (1982). Self-efficacy mechanisms in human agency. *American Psychologist, 37,* 122–147.

Bandura, A. (1986). *Social foundations of thought and action.* Englewood Cliffs, NJ: Prentice-Hall.

Bandura, A. (1993). Perceived self-efficacy in cognitive development and functioning. *Educational Psychologist, 28,* 117–148.

Bandura, A. (1997). *Self-efficacy: The exercise of control.* New York: Freeman.

Bandura, A., Ross, D., & Ross, S. A. (1963). Vicarious reinforcement and imitative learning. *Journal of Abnormal and Social Psychology, 67,* 601–607.

Bangert-Drowns, R. L., Kulik, C. C., Kulik, J. A., & Morgan, M. (1991). The instructional effect of feedback in test-like events. *Review of Educational Research, 61,* 213–238.

Banks, J. A. (1994). *Multiethnic education: Theory and practice.* Boston: Allyn & Bacon.

Banks, J. A. (1997). *Teaching strategies for ethnic studies* (6th ed.). Boston: Allyn & Bacon.

Banks, J. A. (1999). *An introduction to multicultural education* (2nd ed.). Boston: Allyn & Bacon.

Banks, J. A. (2002). *An introduction to multicultural education* (3rd ed.). Boston: Allyn & Bacon.

Banks, J. A. (2006). *Cultural diversity and education: Foundations, curriculum, and teaching* (5th ed.). Boston: Allyn and Bacon.

Banks, S. R. (2005). *Classroom assessment: Issues and practice.* Boston: Allyn and Bacon.

Barakett, J. M. (1986). Teachers' theories and methods in structuring routine activities in an inner city school. *Canadian Journal of Education, 11*(2), 91–108.

Barden, L. M. (1995). Effective questioning and the ever-elusive higher-order question. *American Biology Teacher, 57,* 423–426.

Bargh, J. A., & Chartrand, T. L. (1999). The unbearable automaticity of being. *American Psychologist, 54,* 462–479.

Bargh, J. A., McKenna, K. Y. A., & Fitzsimons, G. M. (2002). Can you see the real me? Activation and expression of the "true self" on the Internet. *Journal of Social Issues, 58*(1), 33–48.

Barnhill, G. P. (2005). Functional behavioral assessment in schools. *Intervention in School and Clinic, 40,* 131–143.

Baron, R. A. (1998). *Psychology* (4th ed.). Boston: Allyn & Bacon.

Baron, R. A., & Byrne, D. (2003). *Social psychology* (10th ed.). Boston: Allyn & Bacon.

Baroody, A. R., & Ginsburg, H. P. (1990). Children's learning: A cognitive view. In R. Davis, C. Maher, & N. Noddings (Eds.), *Constructivist views on the teaching and learning of mathematics* (pp. 51–64). Monograph 4 of the National Council of Teachers of Mathematics, Reston, VA.

Bartlett, F. C. (1932). *Remembering: A study in experimental and social psychology.* New York: Macmillan.

Barton, E. J. (1981). Developing sharing: An analysis of modeling and other behavioral techniques. *Behavior Modification, 5,* 386–398.

Batschaw, M. L. (1997). *Children with disabilities* (4th ed.). Baltimore, ML: Brookes.

Battistich, V., Solomon, D., & Delucci, K. (1993). Interaction processes and student outcomes in cooperative groups. *Elementary School Journal, 94,* 19–32.

Baumeister, R. F., & Leary, M. R. (1995). The need to belong: Desire for interpersonal attachments as a fundamental human motivation. *Psychological Bulletin, 117,* 497–529.

Baumrind, D. (1991). Effective parenting during early adolescent transitions. In P. A. Cowan & M. Hetherington (Eds.), *Family transitions* (pp. 111–165). Hillsdale, NJ: Lawrence Erlbaum.

BC College of Teachers. (2004, May). *Standards for the education, competence and professional conduct of educators in British Columbia* (2nd ed.). Retrieved February 18, 2005, from http://www.bcct.ca/standards/default.aspx.

BCTF. (2001). New advertising campaign. Retrieved April 5, 2005, from http://www.bctf.ca/Publications/ezine/Archive/2001-2002/2001-09/support/07Advertising.html.

BCTF. (2003). Summary Analysis of the BC College of Teachers' Standards for the education competence and professional conduct of educators in BC. Retrieved 19 May 2005, from www.bctf.ca/education/CoT/standardsanalysis.html.

Beane, J. A. (1991). Sorting out the self-esteem controversy. *Educational Leadership, 49*(1), 25–30.

Bear, G. G. (with Cavalier, A. R., & Manning, M. A.). (2005). *Developing self-discipline and preventing and correcting misbehavior.* Boston: Allyn & Bacon.

Beck, C., Hart, D., & Kosnik, C. (2002). The teaching standards movement and current teaching practices. *Canadian Journal of Education, 27,* 175–194.

Beck, I. L., McKeown, M. G., Worthy, J., Sandora, C. A., & Kucan, L. (1996). Questioning the author: A yearlong classroom implementation to engage students with text. *The Elementary School Journal, 96,* 385–414.

Becker, W. C., Engelmann, S., & Thomas, D. R. (1975). *Teaching 1: Classroom management.* Chicago: Science Research Associates.

Bee, H. (1981). *The developing child* (3rd ed.). New York: Harper & Row.

Bee, H. (1992). *The developing child* (6th ed.). New York: Harper & Row.

Beebe-Frankenberger, M., Bocian, K. L., MacMillan, D. L., & Gresham, F. M. (2004). Sorting second grade students with academic deficiencies: Characteristics differentiating those retained in grade from those promoted to third grade. *Journal of Educational Psychology, 96,* 204–215.

Beeth, M. E. (1998). Teaching science in fifth grade: Instructional goals that support conceptual change. *Journal of Research in Science Teaching, 35,* 1091–1101.

Belanoff, P., & Dickson, M. (1991). *Portfolios: Process and product.* Portsmouth, NH: Heinemann, Boynton/Cook.

Belfiore, P. J., & Hornyak, R. S. (1998). Operant theory and the application of self-monitoring to adolescents. In D. Schunk & B. Zimmerman (Eds.), *Self-regulated learning: From theory to self-reflective practice* (pp. 184–202). New York: Guilford.

Benenson, J. F. (1993). Greater preference among females than males for dyadic interaction in early childhood. *Child Development, 64*, 544–555.

Benjafield, J. G. (1992). *Cognition.* Englewood Cliffs, NJ: Prentice-Hall.

Bennett, C. I. (1995). *Comprehensive multicultural education: Theory and practice* (3rd ed.). Boston: Allyn & Bacon.

Bennett, C. I. (1999). *Comprehensive multicultural education: Theory and practice* (4th ed.). Boston: Allyn & Bacon.

Bereiter, C. (1995). A dispositional view of transfer. In A. McKeough, J. Lupart, & A. Marini (Eds.), *Teaching for mastery: Fostering generalization in learning* (pp. 21–34). Mahwah, NJ: Lawrence Erlbaum.

Bereiter, C. (1997). Situated cognition and how I overcome it. In D. Kirshner & J. A. Whitson (Eds.), *Situated cognition: Social, semiotic, and psychological perspectives* (pp. 281–300). Mahwah, NJ: Lawrence Erlbaum.

Berg, C. A., & Clough, M. (1991). Hunter lesson design: The wrong one for science teaching. *Educational Leadership, 48*(4), 73–78.

Berger, K. S. (2004). *Development through the lifespan.* New York: Worth.

Berger, K. S. (2003). *The developing person through childhood and adolescence* (6th ed.). New York: Worth Publishers.

Berger, K. S. (2006). *The developing person through childhood and adolescence* (7th ed.). New York, NY: Worth Publishers.

Berger, K. S., & Thompson, R. A. (1995). *The developing person through childhood and adolescence.* New York: Worth.

Bergin, D. (1999). Influences on classroom interest. *Educational Psychologist, 34*, 87–98.

Berk, L. E. (2002). *Infants, children, and adolescents* (4th ed.). Boston: Allyn & Bacon.

Berk, L. E. (2005). *Infants, children, and adolescents* (5th ed.). Boston: Allyn and Bacon.

Berk, L. E. (1994). *Child development* (3rd ed.). Boston: Allyn & Bacon.

Berk, L. E. (2000). *Child development* (5th ed.). Boston: Allyn & Bacon.

Berk, L. E. (2001). *Awakening children's minds: How parents and teachers can make a difference.* New York: Oxford University Press.

Berk, L. E., & Spuhl, S. T. (1995). Maternal interaction, private speech, and task performance in preschool children. *Early Childhood Research Quarterly, 10*, 145–169.

Berliner, D. C. (2002). Educational research: The hardest science of all. *Educational Researcher, 31*(8), 18–20.

Berliner, D. (1993). The 100-year journey of educational psychology: From interest to disdain to respect for practice. In T. K. Faigin & G. R. VandenBos (Eds.), *Exploring applied psychology: Origins and critical analyses* (pp. 39–78). Washington DC: American Psychological Association.

Berliner, D. (1983). Developing concepts of classroom environments: Some light on the T in studies of ATI. *Educational Psychologist, 18*, 1–13.

Berliner, D. (1987). But do they understand? In V. Richardson-Koehler (Ed.), *Educators' handbook: A research perspective* (pp. 259–293). New York: Longman.

Berliner, D. (1988). Simple views of effective teaching and a simple theory of classroom instruction. In D. Berliner & B. Rosenshine (Eds.), *Talks to teachers* (pp. 93–110). New York: Random House.

Berlyne, D. (1966). Curiosity and exploration. *Science, 153*, 25–33.

Betancourt, H., & Lopez, S. R. (1993). The study of culture, ethnicity, and race in American psychology. *American Psychologist, 48*, 629–637.

Bhatia, T. K., & Richie, W. C. (1999). The bilingual child: Some issues and perspectives. In W. C. Richie & T. K. Bhatia (Eds.), *Handbook of child language acquisition.* San Diego: Academic Press.

Bialystok, E. (1999). Cognitive complexity and attentional control in the bilingual child. *Child Development, 70*, 636–644.

Biemiller, A. (1993, December). Students differ: So address differences effectively. *Educational Researcher, 22*(9), 14–15.

Biggs, J. (2001). Enhancing learning: A matter of style of approach. In R. Sternberg & L. Zhang (Eds.), *Perspectives on cognitive, learning, and thinking styles* (pp. 73–102). Mahwah, NJ: Lawrence Erlbaum.

Bivens, J. A., & Berk, L. E. (1990). A longitudinal study of elementary school children's private speech. *Merrill-Palmer Quarterly, 36*, 443–463.

Bjorklund, D. F. (1989). *Children's thinking: Developmental function and individual differences.* Pacific Grove, CA: Brooks/Cole.

Block, J. (1983). Differential premises arising from differential socialization of the sexes: Some conjectures. *Child Development, 54*, 1335–1354.

Block, J. H., & Anderson, L. W. (1975). *Mastery learning in classroom instruction.* New York: Macmillan.

Bloom, B. S. (1968). *Learning for mastery. Evaluation Comment, 1*(2). Los Angeles: University of California, Center for the Study of Evaluation of Instructional Programs.

Bloom, B. S. (1981). *All our children learning: A primer for parents, teachers, and other educators.* New York: McGraw-Hill.

Bloom, B. S., Engelhart, M. D., Frost, E. J., Hill, W. H., & Krathwohl, D. R. (1956). *Taxonomy of educational objectives: Handbook I. Cognitive domain.* New York: David McKay.

Bloom, R., & Bourdon, L. (1980). Types and frequencies of teachers' written instructional feedback. *Journal of Educational Research, 74*, 13–15.

Blumenfeld, P. C., Puro, P., & Mergendoller, J. R. (1992). Translating motivation into thoughtfulness. In H. Marshall (Ed.), *Redefining student learning: Roots of educational change* (pp. 207–240). Norwood, NJ: Ablex.

Bolick, C. M., & Cooper J. M. (2006). Classroom management and technology. In C. Evertson & C. S. Weinstein (Eds.), *Handbook for classroom management: Research, practice, and contemporary issues.* Mahwah, NJ: Lawrence Erlbaum.

Boom, J., Brugman, D., & van der Heijden, P. G. (2001). Hierarchical structure of moral stages assessed by a sorting task. *Child Development, 72*, 535–548.

Borko, H. (1989). Research on learning to teach: Implications for graduate teacher preparation. In A. Woolfolk (Ed.), *Research perspectives on the graduate preparation of teachers* (pp. 69–87). Boston: Allyn & Bacon.

Borko, H., & Livingston, C. (1989). Cognition and improvisation: Differences in mathematics instruction by expert and novice teachers. *American Educational Research Journal, 26*, 473–498.

Borko, H., & Putnam, R. (1996). Learning to teach. In D. Berliner & R. Calfee (Eds.), *Handbook of educational psychology* (pp. 673–708). New York: Macmillan.

Borkowski, J. G., Johnston, M. B., & Reid, M. K. (1986). Metacognition, motivation, and the transfer of control processes. In S. J. Ceci (Ed.), *Handbook of cognition: Social and neurological aspects of learning disabilities.* Hillsdale, NJ: Erlbaum.

Borman, G. D., & Overman, L. T. (2004). Academic resilience in mathematics among poor and minority students. *The Elementary School Journal, 104*, 177–195.

Bos, C. S., & Reyes, E. I. (1996). Conversations with a Latina teacher about education for language-minority students with special needs. *The Elementary School Journal, 96*, 344–351.

Bosworth, K. (1995). Caring for others and being cared for. *Phi Delta Kappan, 76*(9), 686–693.

Brannon, L. (2002). *Gender: Psychological perspectives* (3rd ed.). Boston: Allyn & Bacon.

Bransford, J. D., Brown, A. L., & Cocking, R. R. (2000). *How people learn: Brain, mind, experience, and school.* Washington, DC: National Academy Press.

Bransford, J.D., & Schwartz, D. (1999). Rethinking transfer: A simple proposal with multiple implications. In A. Iran-Nejad & P. D. Pearson (Eds.), *Review of research in education* (Vol. 24

pp. 61–100). Washington, DC: American Educational Research Association.

Bransford, J. D., & Stein, B. S. (1993). *The IDEAL problem solver: A guide for improving thinking, learning, and creativity* (2nd ed.). New York: Freemen.

Bransford, J. D., Stein, B. S., Vye, N. J., Franks, J. J., Auble, P. M., Mezynski, K. J., & Perfetto, G. A. (1982). Differences in approaches to learning: An overview. *Journal of Experimental Psychology: General, 111,* 390–398.

Bredderman, T. (1983). Effects of activity-based elementary science on student outcomes: A qualitative synthesis. *Review of Educational Research, 53,* 499–518.

Bretherton, I., & Waters, E. (1985). Growing points of attachment theory and research. *Monographs of the Society for Research in Child Development, 50*(1, 2, Serial No. 209).

British Columbia Ministry for Children and Families. (1998). *The BC handbook for action on child abuse and neglect.* Victoria, BC: Crown Publications.

British Columbia Ministry of Education. (1996). *Gifted education: A resource guide for teachers.* BC: Author.

British Columbia Ministry of Education. (1998). *English as a second language: Policy framework* [draft document]. Victoria, BC: Author.

British Columbia Special Education Branch. (1995). *Special education services: A manual of policies, procedures, and guidelines.* Victoria, BC: Author.

Brody, L. (1999). *Gender, emotion, and the family.* Cambridge, MA: Harvard University Press.

Bronfenbrenner, U. (1989). Ecological systems theory. In R. Vasta (Ed.), *Annals of child development* (Vol. 6, pp.187–249). Boston: JAI Press, Inc.

Bronfenbrenner, U., & Evans, G. W. (2000): Developmental science in the 21st century: Emerging theoretical models, research designs, and empirical findings. *Social Development, 9,* 115–125.

Bronfenbrenner, U., McClelland, P., Wethington, E., Moen, P., & Ceci, S. (1996). *The state of Americans: This generation and the next.* New York: Free Press.

Brooks, D. (1985). Beginning the year in junior high: The first day of school. *Educational Leadership, 42,* 76–78.

Brooks-Gunn, J. (1988). Antecedents and consequences of variations in girls' maturational timing. In M. D. Levin & E. R. McAnarney (Eds.), *Early adolescent transitions* (pp. 101–121). Lexington, MA: Lexington Books.

Brophy, J. (1998). *Motivating students to learn.* New York: McGraw-Hill.

Brophy, J. E. (2003). An interview with Jere Brophy by B. Gaedke, & M. Shaughnessy. *Educational Psychology Review, 15,* 199–211.

Brophy, J. E. (1981). Teacher praise: A functional analysis. *Review of Educational Research, 51,* 5–21.

Brophy, J. E. (1982, March). *Research on the self-fulfilling prophecy and teacher expectations.* Paper presented at the annual meeting of the American Educational Research Association, New York.

Brophy, J. E. (1983). Conceptualizing student motivation to learn. *Educational Psychologist, 18,* 200–215.

Brophy, J. E. (1985). Teacher-student interaction. In J. Dusek (Ed.), *Teacher expectancies.* Hillsdale, NJ: Erlbaum.

Brophy, J. E. (1988). On motivating students. In D. Berliner & B. Rosenshine (Eds.), *Talks to teachers* (pp. 201–245). New York: Random House.

Brophy, J. E., & Evertson, C. (1978). Context variables in teaching. *Educational Psychologist, 12,* 310–316.

Brophy, J. E., & Good, T. (1986). Teacher behavior and student achievement. In M. Wittrock (Ed.), *Handbook of research on teaching* (3rd ed., pp. 328–375). New York: Macmillan.

Brophy, J. E., & Kher, N. (1986). Teacher socialization as a mechanism for developing student motivation to learn. In R. Feldman (Ed.), *Social psychology applied to education* (pp. 256–288). New York: Cambridge University Press.

Brown, A. (1987). Metacognition, executive control, self-regulation, and other more mysterious mechanisms. In F. Weinert & R. Kluwe (Eds.), *Metacognition, motivation, and understanding* (pp. 65–116). Hillside, NJ: Erlbaum.

Brown, A. (1997). Transforming schools into communities of thinking and learning about serious matters. *American Psychologist, 52,* 399–413.

Brown, A. L., Bransford, J., Ferrara, R., & Campione, J. (1983). Learning, remembering, and understanding. In P. Mussen (Ed.), *Handbook of child psychology* (Vol. 3). New York: Wiley.

Brown, A. L., & Campione, J. C. (1996). Psychological theory and the design of innovative learning environments: On procedures, principles, and systems. In L. Schauble & R. Glasser (Eds.), *Innovations in learning: New environments for education* (pp. 289–325). Mahwah, NJ: Lawrence Erlbaum Associates.

Bruer, John T. (1999). In search of . . . brainbased education. *Phi Delta Kappan, 80,* 648–657.

Bruner, J. S. (1960). *The process of education.* New York: Vintage Books.

Bruner, J. S. (1966). *Toward a theory of instruction.* New York: Norton.

Bruner, J. S. (1973). *Beyond the information given: Studies in the psychology of knowing.* New York: Norton.

Bruner, J. S., Goodnow, J. J., & Austin, G. A. (1956). *A study of thinking.* New York: Wiley.

Bruning, R. H., Schraw, G. J., Norby, M. M., & Ronning, R. R. (2004). *Cognitive psychology and instruction* (4th ed.). Columbus, OH: Merrill.

Bruning, R. H., Schraw, G. J., & Ronning, R. R. (1995). *Cognitive psychology and instruction* (2nd ed.). Englewood Cliffs, NJ: Merrill/Prentice-Hall.

Bruning, R. H., Schraw, G. J., & Ronning, R. R. (1999). *Cognitive psychology and instruction* (3rd ed.). Columbus, OH: Merrill.

Buehler, R., Griffin, D., & Ross, M. (1994). Exploring the "planning fallacy": Why people underestimate their task completion times. *Journal of Personality and Social Psychology, 67,* 366–381.

Bulgren, J. A., Deshler, D. D., Schumaker, J. B., & Lenz, B. K. (2000). The use and effectiveness of analogical instruction in diverse secondary content classrooms. *Journal of Educational Psychology, 92,* 426–441.

Burbules, N. C., & Bruce, B. C. (2001). Theory and research on teaching as dialogue. In V. Richardson (Ed.), *Handbook of research on teaching* (4th ed., pp. 1102–1121). Washington, DC: American Educational Research Association.

Burden, P. R. (1995). *Classroom management and discipline: Methods to facilitate cooperation and instruction.* White Plains, NY: Longman.

Bureau of Reproductive and Child Health. (1999). Suicide. Retrieved February 9, 2005, from http://www.canadian-health-network.ca.

Burke-Spero, R. (1999). Toward a model of "civitas" through an ethic of care: A qualitative study of preservice teachers' perceptions about learning to teach diverse populations (Doctoral dissertation, The Ohio State University, 1999). *Dissertation Abstracts International, 60,* 11A, 3967.

Burke-Spero, R., & Woolfolk Hoy, A. (2002). *The need for thick description: A qualitative investigation of developing teacher efficacy.* Unpublished manuscript, University of Miami.

Burton, R. V. (1963). The generality of honesty reconsidered. *Psychological Review, 70,* 481–499.

Bus, A. G., & van Ijzendoorn, M. H. (1999). Phonological awareness and early reading: a meta-analysis of experimental training studies. *Journal of Educational Psychology, 91,* 403–414.

Buss, D. M. (1995). Psychological sex differences: Origin through sexual selection. *American Psychologist, 50,* 164–168.

Butler, D. L. (1998). A strategic content learning approach to promoting self-regulated learning by students with learning disabilities. In D. H. Schunk & B. J. Zimmerman (Eds.), *Self-regulated learning:*

From teaching to self-reflective practice (pp. 160–183). NY: Guilford Press.

Butler, D. L. (2002). Individualized instruction in self-regulated learning. *Theory into Practice, 41*, 81–92.

Butler, D. L., & Winne, P. H. (1995). Feedback and self-regulated learning: A theoretical synthesis. *Review of Educational Research, 65*, 245–281.

Butler, R. (1987). Task-involving and ego-involving properties of evaluation: Effects of different feedback conditions on motivational perceptions, interest, and performance. *Journal of Educational Psychology, 79*, 474–482.

Butler, R., & Neuman, O. (1995). Effects of task and ego achievement goals on help-seeking behaviors and attitudes. *Journal of Educational Psychology, 87*, 261–271.

Butler, R., & Nisan, M. (1986). Effects of no feedback, task-related comments, and grades on intrinsic motivation and performance. *Journal of Educational Psychology, 78*, 210–224.

Byrne, B. M. (2002). Validating the measurement and structure of self-concept: Snapshots of past, present, and future research. *American Psychologist, 57*, 897–909.

Byrne, B. M., & Shavelson, R. J. (1996). On the structure of social self-concept for pre-, early, and late adolescents: A test of the Shavelson model. *Journal of Personality and Social Psychology, 70*, 599–613.

Byrne, B. M., & Worth Gavin, D. A. (1996). The Shavelson model revisited: Testing for structure of academic self concept across pre-, early, and late adolescents. *Journal of Educational Psychology, 88*, 215–229.

Byrnes, J. P. (1996). *Cognitive development and learning in instructional contexts.* Boston: Allyn & Bacon.

Byrnes, J. P. (2003). Factors predictive of mathematics achievement in White, Black, and Hispanic 12th graders. *Journal of Educational Psychology, 95*, 316–326.

Byrnes, J. P., & Fox, N. A. (1998). The educational relevance of research in cognitive neuroscience. *Educational Psychology Review, 10*, 297–342.

Caine, R. N., & Caine, G. (1991). *Making connections: Teaching and the human brain.* Alexandria, VA: Association for Supervision and Curriculum Development.

Calderhead, J. (1996). Teacher: Beliefs and knowledge. In D. Berliner & R. Calfee (Eds.), *Handbook of educational psychology* (pp. 709–725). New York: Macmillan.

Callahan, C. M., Tomlinson, C. A., & Plucker, J. (1997). *Project START using a multiple intelligences model in identifying and promoting talent in high-risk students* (University of Connecticut Technical Report). Storrs, CT: National Research Center for Gifted and Talented.

Cambourne, B., & Turbill, J. (1990). Assessment in whole-language classrooms: Theory into practice. *Elementary School Journal, 90*, 337–349.

Cameron, J., & Pierce, W. D. (1996). The debate about rewards and intrinsic motivation: Protests and accusations do not alter the results. *Review of Educational Research, 66*, 39–52.

Camp, R. (1990, Spring). Thinking together about portfolios. *The Quarterly of the National Writing Project, 27*, 8–14.

Campaign 2000. (2004). *One million too many: Implementing solutions to child poverty in Canada.* Retrieved February 24, 2005, from http://www.campaign2000.ca/rc/index.html.

Canadian Centre on Substance Abuse. (2007). *Substance abuse in Canada: Youth in focus.* Retrieved October 9, 2007, from http://www.ccsa.ca/NR/rdonlyres/5D418288-5147-4CAC-A6E4-6D09EC6CBE13/0/ccsa0115212007e.pdf.

Canadian Teachers' Federation & Ontario Women's Directorate. (1992). *The better idea book: A resource book on gender, culture, science and schools.* Ottawa, ON: Canadian Teachers' Federation.

Cangelosi, J. S. (1990). *Designing tests for evaluating student achievement.* New York: Longman.

Canter, L. (1989). Assertive discipline—More than names on the board and marbles in a jar. *Phi Delta Kappan, 71*(1), 41–56.

Canter, L. (1996). First the rapport—then the rules. *Learning, 24*(5), 12+.

Canter, L., & Canter, M. (1992). *Lee Canter's Assertive Discipline: Positive behavior management for today's classroom.* Santa Monica: Lee Canter and Associates.

Capa, Y. (2005). *Novice teachers' sense of efficacy.* Doctoral dissertation, The Ohio State University, Columbus, OH.

Capon, N., & Kuhn, D. (2004). What's so good about problem-based learning? *Cognition and Instruction, 22*, 61–79.

Carey, S., & Gellman, R. (Eds.). (1991). *The epigenesis of mind: Essays on biology and cognition.* Cambridge, MA: MIT Press.

Cariglia-Bull, T., & Pressley, M. (1990). Short-term memory differences between children predict imagery effects when sentences are read. *Journal of Experimental Child Psychology, 49*, 384–398.

Carlisle, J. F., Stahl, S. A., & Birdyshaw, D. (Eds.). (2004, November). Lessons from research at the Center for the Improvement of Early Reading Achievement [Special Issue]. *The Elementary School Journal, 105*(2).

Carnegie Council on Adolescent Development. (1995). *Great transitions: Preparing adolescents for a new century.* New York: Carnegie Corporation of New York.

Carney, R. N., & Levin, J. R. (2000). Mnemonic instruction, with a focus on transfer. *Journal of Educational Psychology, 92*, 783–790.

Carpendale, J. I. M. (2000). Kohlberg and Piaget on stages and moral reasoning. *Developmental Review, 20*, 181–205.

Carroll, J. (1993). *Human cognitive abilities: A survey of factor analytic studies.* Cambridge, England: Cambridge University Press.

Carroll, J. B. (1997). The three-stratum theory of cognitive abilities. In D. P. Flanagan, J. L. Genshaft, & P. L. Harrison (Eds.), *Contemporary intellectual assessment: Theories, tests, and issues* (pp. 122–130). New York: Guilford.

Casanova, U. (1987). Ethnic and cultural differences. In V. Richardson-Koehler (Ed.), *Educators' handbook: A research perspective* (pp. 370–393). New York: Longman.

Case, R. (1985a). *Intellectual development: Birth to adulthood.* New York: Academic Press.

Case, R. (1985b). A developmentally-based approach to the problem of instructional design. In R. Glaser, S. Chipman, & J. Segal (Eds.), *Teaching thinking skills* (Vol. 2, pp. 545–562). Hillsdale, NJ: Erlbaum.

Case, R. (1992). *The mind's staircase: Exploring the conceptual underpinnings of children's thought and knowledge.* Mahwah, NJ: Lawrence Erlbaum.

Case, R. (1998). The development of conceptual structures. In D. Kuhn & R. S. Siegler (Eds.), *Handbook of child psychology: Vol. 2. Cognition, perception, and language* (pp. 745–800). New York: Wiley.

Cassady, J. C., & Johnson, R. E. (2002). Cognitive anxiety and academic performance. *Contemporary Educational Psychology, 27*, 270–295.

Castellano, J. A., & Diaz, E. I. (Eds.). (2002). *Reaching new horizons. Gifted and talented education for culturally and linguistically diverse students.* Boston: Allyn and Bacon.

Castle, S., Deniz, C. B., & Tortora, M. (2005). Flexible grouping and student learning in a high-needs school. *Education and Urban Society, 37*, 139–150.

Cattell, R. B. (1963). Theory of fluid and crystallized intelligence: A critical experiment. *Journal of Educational Psychology, 54*, 1–22.

Cauley, K., & Tyler, B. (1989). The relationship of self-concept to prosocial behavior in children. *Early Childhood Research Quarterly, 4*, 51–60.

Ceci, S. J. (1991). How much does schooling influence intelligence and its cognitive components? A reassessment of the evidence. *Developmental Psychology, 27*, 703–720.

Ceci, S. J., & Roazzi, A. (1994). The effects of context on cognition: Postcards from Brazil. In R. J. Sternberg (Ed.), *Mind in context* (pp. 74–101). New York: Cambridge University Press.

Chambers, B., & Abrami, P. C. (1991). The relationship between student team learning outcomes and achievement, causal attributions, and affect. *Journal of Educational Psychology, 83,* 140–146.

Chamot, A. U., & O'Malley, J. M. (1996). The Cognitive Academic Language Learning Approach: A model for linguistically diverse classrooms. *The Elementary School Journal, 96,* 259–274.

Chan, C. K., & Sachs, J. (2001). Beliefs about learning in children's understanding of science texts. *Contemporary Educational Psychology, 26,* 192–210.

Chance, P. (1991). Backtalk: A gross injustice. *Phi Delta Kappan, 72,* 803.

Chance, P. (1992). The rewards of learning. *Phi Delta Kappan, 73,* 200–207.

Chance, P. (1993). Sticking up for rewards. *Phi Delta Kappan, 74,* 787–790.

Chapman, M. L. (1997). *Weaving webs of meaning: Writing in the elementary school.* Toronto: ITP Nelson.

Chapman, J. W., Tunmer, W. E., & Prochnow, J. E. (2000). Early reading-related skills and performance, reading self-concept, and the development of academic self-concept: A longitudinal study. *Journal of Educational Psychology, 92,* 703–708.

Charach, A., Pepler, D. J., & Ziegler, S. (1995). Bullying at school: A Canadian perspective. *Education Canada, 35,* 12–18.

Charles, C. M. (1985). *Building classroom discipline: From models to practice* (2nd ed.). New York: Longman.

Charles, C. M. (2002a). *Essential elements of effective discipline.* Boston: Allyn & Bacon.

Charles, C. M. (2002b). *Building classroom discipline* (7th ed.). Boston: Allyn & Bacon.

Chen, Z., & Mo, L. (2004). Schema induction in problem solving: A multidimensional analysis. *Journal of Experimental Psychology: Learning, Memory, and Cognition, 30,* 583–600.

Chen, Z., Mo, L., & Honomichl, R. (2004). Having the memory of an elephant: long-term retrieval and the use of analogues in problem solving. *Journal of Experimental Psychology: General, 133,* 415–433.

Chi, M. T. H. (1978). Knowledge structures and memory development. In R. Siegler (Ed.), *Children's thinking: What develops?* (pp. 73–96). Hillsdale, NJ: Erlbaum.

Chi, M. T. H., Glaser, R., & Farr, M. (Eds.). (1988). *The nature of expertise.* Hillsdale, NJ: Earlbaum.

Claiborn, W. L. (1969). Expectancy effects in the classroom: A failure to replicate. *Journal of Education Psychology, 60,* 377–383.

Clark, C. M., Gage, N. L., Marx, R. W., Peterson, P. L., Staybrook, N. G., & Winne, P. H. (1979). A factorial experiment on teacher structuring, soliciting, and reacting. *Journal of Educational Psychology, 71,* 534–550.

Clark, C. M., & Peterson, P. L. (1986). Teachers' thought processes. In M. Wittrock (Ed.), *Handbook of research on teaching* (3rd ed., pp. 255–296). New York: Macmillan.

Clark, C. M., & Yinger, R. (1988). Teacher planning. In D. Berliner & B. Rosenshine (Eds.), *Talks to teachers* (pp. 342–365). New York: Random House.

Clark, J. M., & Paivio, A. (1991). Dual coding theory and education. *Educational Psychology Review, 3,* 149–210.

Clark, K., & Clark, M. (1939). The development of consciousness of self and the emergence of racial identification in Negro preschool children. *Journal of Social Psychology, 10,* 591–599.

Clarke, J. H., & Agne, R. M. (1997). *Interdisciplinary high school teaching.* Boston: Allyn & Bacon.

Clement, S. L. (1978). Dual marking system: Simple and effective. *American Secondary Education, 8,* 49–52.

Clifford, M. M. (1984). Educational psychology. In *Encyclopedia of Education* (pp. 413–416). New York: Macmillan.

Clifford, M. M. (1990). Students need challenge, not easy success. *Educational Leadership, 48*(1), 22–26.

Clifford, M. M. (1991). Risk taking: Empirical and educational considerations. *Educational Psychologist, 26,* 263–298.

Cobb, P., & Bowers, J. (1999). Cognitive and situated learning: Perspectives in theory and practice. *Educational Researcher, 28*(2), 4–15.

Codell, E. R. (2001). *Educating Esme: Diary of a teacher's first year.* Chapel Hill, NC: Algonquin Books.

Coffield, F. J., Moseley, D. V., Hall, E., & Ecclestone, K. (2004). *Learning styles and pedagogy in post–16 learning: A systematic and critical review.* London: Learning and Skills Research Centre/University of Newcastle upon Tyne.

Cognition and Technology Group at Vanderbilt. (1990). Anchored instruction and its relations to situated cognition. *Educational Researcher, 19*(6), 2–10.

Cognition and Technology Group at Vanderbilt. (1993). Anchored instruction and situated learning revisited. *Educational Technology, 33*(3), 52–70.

Cognition and Technology Group at Vanderbilt. (1996). Looking at technology in context: A framework for understanding technology and educational research. In D. Berliner & R. Calfee (Eds.), *Handbook of educational psychology* (pp. 807–840). New York: Macmillan.

Cohen, E. G. (1986). *Designing groupwork: Strategies for the heterogeneous classroom.* New York: Teachers College Press.

Coie, J. D., & Dodge, K. A. (1998). Aggression and antisocial behavior. In N. Eisenberg (Ed.), *Handbook of child psychology: Vol. 3. Social, emotional, and personality development* (5th ed., pp. 779–862). New York: Wiley.

Coie, J. D., Terry, R., Lenox, K., Lochman, J., & Hyman, C. (1995). Childhood peer rejection and aggression as predictors of stable patterns of adolescent disorder. *Development and Psychopathology, 7,* 697–714.

Cokley, K. O. (2002). Ethnicity, gender, and academic self-concept: A preliminary examination of academic disidentification and implications for psychologists. *Cultural Diversity and Ethnic Minority Psychology, 8,* 378–388.

Cole, D. A., Martin, J. M., Peeke, L. A., Seroczynski, A. D., & Fier, J. (1999). Children's over- and underestimation of academic competence: A longitudinal study of gender differences, depression, and anxiety. *Child Development, 70,* 459–473.

Cole, M. (1985). The zone of proximal development: Where culture and cognition create each other. In J. V. Wertsch (Ed.), *Culture, communication, and cognition: Vygotskian perspectives* (pp. 146–161). Cambridge, England: Cambridge University Press.

Coleman, J. S. (1966). *Equality of educational opportunity.* Washington, DC: US Government Printing Office.

Collins, A., Brown, J. S., & Holum, A. (1991). Cognitive apprenticeship: Making thinking visible. *American Educator, 15*(3), 38–39.

Collins, A., Brown, J. S., & Newman, S. E. (1989). Cognitive apprenticeship: Teaching the crafts of reading, writing, and mathematics. In L. B. Resnick (Ed.), *Knowing, learning, and instruction: Essays in honor of Robert Glaser* (pp. 453–494). Hillsdale, NJ: Lawrence Earlbaum.

Comer, J. P., Haynes, N., M., & Joyner, E. T. (1996). The School Development Program. In J. P. Comer, N. M. Haynes, E. T. Joyner, & M. Ben-Avie (Eds.), *Rallying the whole village: The Comer process for reforming education* (pp. 1–26). New York: Teachers College Press.

Committee on Increasing High School Students' Engagement and Motivation to Learn. (2004). *Engaging schools: Fostering high school students' motivation to learn.* Washington, DC: The National Academies Press.

Confrey, J. (1990a). A review of the research on students' conceptions in mathematics, science, and programming. *Review of Research in Education, 16,* 3–56.

Confrey, J. (1990b). What constructivism implies for teaching. In R. Davis, C. Maher, & N. Noddings (Eds.), *Constructivist views on the teaching and learning of mathematics* (pp. 107–122). Monograph 4 of the National Council of Teachers of Mathematics, Reston, VA.

Conger, R. D., Conger, K. J., & Elder, G. (1997). Family economic hardship and adolescent academic performance: Mediating and moderating processes. In G. Duncan & J. Brooks-Gunn (Eds.), *Consequences of growing up poor* (pp. 288–310). New York: Russell Sage Foundation.

Connell, R. W. (1996). Teaching the boys: New research on masculinity, and gender strategies for schools. *Teachers College Record, 98,* 206–235.

Controversies. (1993). *Current Directions in Psychological Science* [Special section of issue 2], 1–12.

Conway, P. F., & Clark, C. M. (2003). The journey inward and outward: A re-examination of Fuller's concerns-based model of teacher development. *Teaching and Teacher Education 19,* 465–482.

Cook, J. L., & Cook, G. (2005). *Child development: Principles and perspectives.* Boston: Allyn and Bacon.

Cooke, B. L., & Pang, K. C. (1991). Recent research on beginning teachers: Studies of trained and untrained novices. *Teaching and Teacher Education, 7,* 93–110.

Cooper, C. R. (1998). *The weaving of maturity: Cultural perspectives on adolescent development.* New York: Oxford University Press.

Cooper, G., & Sweller, J. (1987). Effects of schema acquisition and rule automation on mathematical problem-solving transfer. *Journal of Educational Psychology, 79,* 347–362.

Cooper, H. (1979). Pygmalion grows up: A model for teacher expectation communication and performance influence. *Review of Educational Research, 49,* 389–410.

Cooper, H., & Valentine, J. C. (Eds.). (2001a). Homework [Special issue]. *Educational Psychologist, 36(3).*

Cooper, H., & Valentine, J. C. (2001b). Using research to answer practical questions about homework. *Educational Psychologist, 36(3),* 143–153.

Cooper, H. M, Valentine, J. C., Nye, B., & Lindsay, J. J. (1999). Relationships between five after-school activities and academic achievement. *Journal of Educational Psychology, 91,* 369–683.

Copi, I. M. (1961). *Introduction to logic.* New York: Macmillan.

Coplan, R. J., Prakash, K., O'Neil, K., & Armer, M. (2004). Do you "want" to play? Distinguishing between conflicted shyness and social disinterest in early childhood. *Developmental Psychology, 40,* 244–258.

Cordova, D. I., & Lepper, M. R. (1996). Intrinsic motivation and the process of learning: Beneficial effects of contextualization, personalization, and choice. *Journal of Educational Psychology, 88,* 715–730.

Corenblum, B., & Annis, R. C. (1987). Racial identity and preference among Canadian Indian and White children: Replication and extension. *Canadian Journal of Behavioural Science, 19,* 254–265.

Corkill, A. J. (1992). Advance organizers: Facilitators of recall. *Educational Psychology Review, 4,* 33–67.

Corno, L. (1992). Encouraging students to take responsibility for learning and performance. *The Elementary School Journal, 93,* 69–84.

Corno, L. (1995). Comments on Winne: Analytic and systemic research are both needed. *Educational Psychologist, 30,* 201–206.

Corno, L. (2000). Looking at homework differently. *Elementary School Journal, 100,* 529–548.

Corno, L. (2004). Introduction to the special issue. *Work habits and work styles: Volition in education. Teachers College Record, 106(9),* 1669–1694.

Corno, L., & Snow, R. E. (1986). Adapting teaching to individual differences in learners. In M. Wittrock (Ed.), *Handbook of research on teaching* (3rd ed.) (pp. 605–629). New York: Macmillan.

Cota-Robles, S., Neiss, M., & Rowe, D. C. (2002). The role of puberty in violent and nonviolent delinquency among Anglo American, Mexican American and African American boys. *Journal of Adolescent Research, 17,* 364–376.

Cothran, D. J., & Ennis, C. D. (2000). Building bridges to student engagement: Communicating respect and care for students in urban high school. *Journal of Research and Development in Education, 33(2),* 106–117.

Covaleskie, J. F. (1992). Discipline and morality: Beyond rules and consequences. *The Educational Forum, 56(2),* 56–60.

Covington, M., & Omelich, C. (1987). "I knew it cold before the exam": A test of the anxiety-blockage hypothesis. *Journal of Educational Psychology, 79,* 393–400.

Covington, M. V. (1992). *Making the grade: A self-worth perspective on motivation and school reform.* New York: Holt, Rinehart & Winston.

Covington, M. V., & Mueller, K. J. (2001). Intrinsic versus extrinsic motivation: An approach/avoidance reformulation. *Education Psychology Review, 13,* 157–176.

Cowley, G., & Underwood, A. (1998, June 15). Memory. *Newsweek, 131(24),* 48–54.

Craig, W. M., & Pepler, D. J. (1997). Observations of bullying and victimization in the school yard. *Canadian Journal of School Psychology, 13,* 41–60.

Craig, W. M., & Pepler, D. J. (1998). Observations of aggressive and nonaggressive children on the school playground. *Merrill-Palmer Quarterly, 44,* 55-76.

Craig, W. M., Peters, R. D., & Konarski, R. (1998, October). *Bullying and victimization among Canadian school children* (Working Paper Series W-98-28E). Hull, QC: Applied Research Branch of Strategic Policy, Human Resources and Development Canada.

Craik, F. I. M., & Lockhart, R. S. (1972). Levels of processing: A framework for memory research. *Journal of Verbal Learning and Verbal Behavior, 11,* 671–684.

Crawford, J. (1997). *Best evidence: Research foundations of the Bilingual Education Act.* Washington, DC: National Clearinghouse for Bilingual Education.

Crealock, C., & Bachor, D. G. (1995). *Instructional strategies for students with special needs* (2nd ed.). Scarborough, ON: Allyn & Bacon Canada.

Cremin, L. (1961). *The transformation of the school: Progressivism in American education, 1876–1957.* New York: Vintage.

Crick, N. R., Casas, J. F., & Mosher M. (1997). Relational and overt aggression in preschool. *Developmental Psychology, 33,* 579–588.

Crisci, P. E. (1986). The Quest National Center: A focus on prevention of alienation. *Phi Delta Kappan, 67,* 440–442.

Crone, D. A., & Horner, R. H. (2003) *Building positive behavior support systems in schools: Functional behavioral assessment.* New York: The Guilford Press.

Cubberly, E. P. (1919). *Public education in the United States; A study and interpretation of American educational history.* Boston: Houghton Mifflin Company.

Cummins, D. D. (1991). Children's interpretation of arithmetic word problems. *Cognition and Instruction, 8,* 261–289.

Cummins, J. (1984). *Bilingualism and special education.* San Diego: College Hill Press.

Cummins, J. (1989). A theoretical framework for bilingual special education. *Exceptional Children, 56,* 111–119.

Cummins, J. (1994). *The acquisition of English as a second language.* In K. Spangenberg-Urbschat & R. Prichard (Eds.), *Kids come in all languages: Reading instruction for ESL students* (pp. 36–62). Newark, DE: International Reading Association.

Cunningham, D. J. (1992). Beyond educational psychology: Steps toward an educational semiotic. *Educational Psychology Review, 4,* 165–194.

Daley, T. C., Whaley, S. E., Sigman, M. D., Espinosa, M. P., & Neumann, C. (2003). IQ on the rise: The Flynn Effect in rural Kenyan children. *Psychological Science, 14(3),* 215–219.

Damon, W. (1994). Fair distribution and sharing: The development of positive justice. In B. Puka (Ed.), *Fundamental research in moral development. Moral development: A compendium* (Vol. 2, pp. 189–254). New York: Garland Publishing.

Dansereau, D. F. (1985). Learning strategy research. In J. Segal, S. Chipman, & R. Glaser (Eds.), *Thinking and learning skills: Vol. 1. Relating instruction to research*). Hillsdale, NJ: Erlbaum.

Darcey, J. S., & Travers, J. F. (2006). *Human development across the lifespan* (6th ed.). New York: McGraw-Hill.

Dark, V. J., & Benbow, C. P. (1991). Differential enhancement of working memory with mathematical versus verbal precocity. *Journal of Educational Psychology, 83,* 48–60.

Darling-Hammond, L. (2000). Teacher quality and student achievement: A review of state policy evidence. *Educational Policy Analysis Archives, 8,* 1–48. Retrieved January 20, 2002, from http://epaa. asu.edu/epaa/v8n1/.

Das, J. P. (1995). Some thought on two aspects of Vygotsky's work. *Educational Psychologist, 30,* 93–97.

Davidson, J. (1982). The group mapping activity for instruction in reading and thinking. *Journal of Reading, 26,* 52–56.

Davis, H. A. (2003). Conceptualizing the role and influence of student–teacher relationships on children's social and cognitive development, *Educational Psychologist, 38,* 207–234.

Davis, J. K. (1991). Educational implications of field-dependence—independence. In S. Wapner & J. Demick (Eds.), *Field-dependence—independence: Cognitive styles across the life span* (pp. 149–176). Hillsdale, NJ: Lawrence Erlbaum.

Davis, R. B., Maher, C. A., & Noddings, N. (Eds.). (1990). Constructivist views on the teaching and learning of mathematics. Monograph 4 of the National Council of Teachers of Mathematics, Reston, VA.

Davis-Kean, P. E., & Sandler, H. M. (2001). A meta-analysis of measures of self-esteem for young children: A framework for future measurers. *Child Development, 72,* 887–906.

Deaux, K. (1993). Commentary: Sorry, wrong number: A reply to Gentile's call. *Psychological Science, 4,* 125–126.

DeCecco, J., & Richards, A. (1974). *Growing pains: Uses of school conflicts.* New York: Aberdeen.

deCharms, R. (1976). *Enhancing motivation.* New York: Irvington.

deCharms, R. (1983). Intrinsic motivation, peer tutoring, and cooperative learning: Practical maxims. In J. Levine & M. Wang (Eds.), *Teacher and student perceptions: Implications for learning* (pp. 391–398). Hillsdale, NJ: Erlbaum.

Deci, E. (1975). *Intrinsic motivation.* New York: Plenum.

Deci, E., Vallerand, R. J., Pelletier, L. G., & Ryan, R. M. (1991). Motivation and education: The self-determination perspective. *Educational Psychologist, 26,* 325–346.

Deci, E. L., Koestner, R., & Ryan, R. M. (1999). A meta-analytic review of experiments examining the effects of extrinsic rewards on intrinsic motivation. *Psychological Bulletin, 125,* 627–668.

Deci, E. L., & Ryan, R. M. (1985). *Intrinsic motivation and self-determination in human behavior.* New York: Plenum.

Deci, E. L., & Ryan, R. M. (Eds.). (2002). *Handbook of self-determination research.* Rochester: University of Rochester Press.

De Corte, E. (2003). Transfer as the productive use of acquired knowledge, skills, and motivations. *Current Directions in Psychological Research, 12,* 142–146.

De Corte, E., Greer, B., Verschaffel, L. (1996). Mathematics learning and teaching. In D. Berliner & R. Calfee (Eds.), *Handbook of educational psychology* (pp. 491–549). New York: Macmillan.

De Corte, E., & Verschaffel, L. (1985). Beginning first graders' initial impression of arithmetic word problems. *Journal of Mathematical Behavior, 4,* 3–21.

De Kock, A., Sleegers, P., & Voeten, J. M. (2004). New learning and the classification of learning environments in secondary education. *Review of Educational Research, 74,* 141–170.

Dee, J. R., & Henkin, A. B. (2002). Assessing dispositions toward cultural diversity among preservice teachers. *Urban Education, 37*(1), 22–40.

Delpit, L. (1995). *Other people's children: Cultural conflict in the classroom.* New York: The New York Press.

Dempster, F. N. (1991). Synthesis of research on reviews and tests. *Educational Leadership, 48*(7), 71–76.

Dempster, F. N. (1993). Exposing our students to less should help them learn more. *Phi Delta Kappan, 74,* 432–437.

Derry, S. (1991). Beyond symbolic processing: Expanding horizons for educational psychology. *Journal of Educational Psychology, 84,* 413–418.

Derry, S. J. (1989). Putting learning strategies to work. *Educational Leadership, 47*(5), 4–10.

Derry, S. J. (1992). Beyond symbolic processing: Expanding horizons for educational psychology. *Journal of Educational Psychology, 84,* 413–419.

Derry, S. J., & Murphy, D. A. (1986). Designing systems that train learning ability: From theory to practice. *Review of Educational Research, 56,* 1–39.

Deshler, D., Ellis, E. S., & Lenz, B. K. (1996). *Teaching adolescents with learning disabilities: Strategies and methods* (2nd ed.). Denver: Love Publishing.

Dewey, J. (1910). *How we think.* Boston: D. C. Heath.

Dewey, J. (1913). *Interest and effort in education.* Cambridge, MA: Houghton-Mifflin.

Diamond, M., & Hobson, J. (1998). *Magic trees of the mind.* New York: Dutton.

Diaz, R. M., & Berk, L. E. (Eds.). (1992). *Private speech: From social interaction to self-regulation.* Hillsdale, NJ: Erlbaum.

Diaz-Rico, L. T., & Weed, K. Z. (2002). *The crosscultural, language, and academic development handbook* (2nd ed.). Boston: Allyn & Bacon.

Dinnel, D., & Glover, J. A. (1985). Advance organizers: Encoding manipulations. *Journal of Educational Psychology, 77,* 514–522.

Di Vesta, F. J., & Di Cintio, M. J. (1997). Interactive effects of working memory span and text comprehension on reading comprehension and retrieval. *Learning and Individual Differences, 9,* 215–231.

Di Vesta, F. J., & Gray, G. S. (1972). Listening and notetaking. *Journal of Educational Psychology, 63,* 8–14.

Dochy, F., Segers, M., & Buehl, M. M. (1999). The relation between assessment practices and outcome studies: The case of research on prior knowledge. *Review of Educational Research, 69,* 145–186.

Doctorow, M., Wittrock, M. C., & Marks, C. (1978). Generative processes in reading comprehension. *Journal of Educational Psychology, 70,* 109–118.

Dodge, K. A., & Somberg, D. R. (1987). Hostile attributional biases among aggressive boys are exacerbated under conditions of threats to the self. *Child Development, 58,* 213–224.

Dole, J. A., Duffy, G. G., Roehler, L. R., & Pearson, P. D. (1991). Moving from the old to the new: Research on reading comprehension instruction. *Review of Educational Research, 61,* 239–264.

Dolezal, S. E., Welsh, L. M., Pressley, M., & Vincent, M. (2003). How do nine third-grade teachers motivate their students? *Elementary School Journal, 103,* 239–267.

Doll, B., Zucker, S., & Brehm, K. (2005). *Resilient classrooms: Creating healthy environments for learning.* New York: Guilford.

Doyle, A., & Aboud, F. (1995). A longitudinal study of White children's racial prejudice as a social cognitive development. *Merrill-Palmer Quarterly, 41,* 213–223.

Doyle, W. (1977). The uses of nonverbal behaviors: Toward an ecological model of classrooms. *Merrill-Palmer Quarterly, 23,* 179–192.

Doyle, W. (1983). Academic work. *Review of Educational Research, 53,* 159–200.

Doyle, W. (1986). Classroom organization and management. In M. C. Wittrock (Ed.), *Handbook of research on teaching* (3rd ed., pp. 392–431). New York: Macmillan.

Doyle, W. (2006). Ecological approaches to classroom management. In C. Evertson & C. S. Weinstein (Eds.), *Handbook for classroom* management: Research, practice, and contemporary issues. Mahwah, NJ: Lawrence Erlbaum.

Driscoll, M. P. (1994). Psychology of learning for instruction. Boston: Allyn & Bacon.

Driscoll, M. P. (2000). Psychology of learning for instruction (2nd ed.). Boston: Allyn & Bacon.

Driscoll, M. P. (2005). Psychology of learning for instruction (3rd ed.). Boston: Allyn and Bacon.

Duckitt, J. (1992). Psychology and prejudice: A historical analysis and integrative framework. American Psychologist, 47, 1182–1193.

Duckitt, J. (1994). The social psychology of prejudice. Westport, CN: Praeger.

Duell, O. K. (1994). Extended wait time and university student achievement. American Educational Research Journal, 31, 397–414.

Duncan, G. J., & Brooks-Gunn, J. (2000). Family poverty, welfare reform, and child development. Child Development, 71, 188–196.

Duncan, R. M., & Cheyne, J. A. (1999). Incidence and functions of self-reported private speech in young adults: A self-verbalization questionnaire. Canadian Journal of Behavioural Sciences, 31, 133–136.

Duncker, K. (1945). On solving problems. Psychological Monographs, 58(5, Whole No. 270).

Dunn, K., & Dunn, R. (1978). Teaching students through their individual learning styles. Reston, VA: National Council of Principals.

Dunn, K., & Dunn, R. (1987). Dispelling outmoded beliefs about student learning. Educational Leadership, 44(6), 55–63.

Dunn, R. (1987). Research on instructional environments: Implications for student achievement and attitudes. Professional School Psychology, 2, 43–52.

Dunn, R., Beaudry, J. S., & Klavas, A. (1989). Survey of research on learning styles. Educational Leadership, 47(7), 50–58.

Dunn, R., Dunn, K., & Price, G. E. (1984). Learning Style Inventory. Lawrence, KS: Price Systems.

Dweck, C. (1999). Self-theories: Their role in motivation, personality, and development. Philadelphia: Psychology Press.

Dweck, C. (2000). Self-theories: Their role in motivation, personality, and development. Philadelphia: Routledge Press.

Dweck, C. (2002). The development of ability conceptions. In A. Wigfield & J. Eccles (Eds.), The development of achievement motivation (pp. 57–88). San Diego, CA: Academic Press.

Dweck, C. S., & Bempechat, J. (1983). Children's theories on intelligence: Consequences for learning. In S. Paris, G. Olson, & W. Stevenson (Eds.), Learning and motivation in the classroom (pp. 239–256). Hillsdale, NJ: Erlbaum.

Dworet, D., & Rathgeber, R. (1999). Behaviour Disorders in Canada: Confusion reigns. Exceptionality Education Canada, 8, 3–19.

Dyson, A. H. (1997). Writing superheroes: Contemporary childhood, popular culture, and classroom literacy. New York: Teachers College Press.

Eaton, J. F., Anderson, C. W., & Smith, E. L. (1984). Students' misconceptions interfere with science learning: Case studies of fifth-graders. Elementary School Journal, 84, 365–379.

Eccles, J., & Wigfield, A. (1985). Teacher expectations and student motivation. In J. Dusek (Ed.), Teacher expectancies (pp. 185–226). Hillsdale, NJ: Erlbaum.

Eccles, J., Wigfield, A., & Schiefele, U. (1998). Motivation to succeed. In W. Damon (Series Ed.) & N. Eisenberg (Vol. Ed.), Handbook of child psychology: Vol. 3. Social, emotional, and personality development (5th ed., pp. 1017–1095). New York: Wiley.

Echevarria, M. (2003). Anomalies as a catalyst for middle school students' knowledge construction and scientific reasoning during science inquiry. Journal of Educational Psychology, 95, 357–374.

Edelman, G. M. (1992). Bright air, brilliant fire: On the matter of the mind. New York: Basic Books.

Egan, S. K., Monson, T. C., & Perry, D. G. (1998). Social-cognitive influences on change in aggression over time. Developmental Psychology, 34, 996–1006.

Eggen, P. D., & Kauchak, D. P. (1996). Strategies for teachers: Teaching content and thinking skills (3rd ed.). Boston: Allyn & Bacon.

Eisenberg, N., & Fabes, R. A. (1998). Prosocial development. In W. Damon (Series Ed.) & N. Eisenberg (Vol. Ed.), Handbook of child psychology: Vol. 3. Social, emotional, and personality development (5th ed., pp. 701–778). New York: Wiley.

Eisenberg, N., Martin, C. L., & Fabes, R. A. (1996). Gender development and gender effects. In D. Berliner & R. Calfee (Eds.), Handbook of educational psychology (pp. 358–396). New York: Macmillan.

Eisenberg, N., Shell, R., Pasernack, J., Lennon, R., Beller, R., & Mathy, R. M. (1987). Prosocial development in middle childhood: A longitudinal study. Developmental Psychology, 23, 712–718.

Elashoff, J. D., & Snow, R. E. (1971). Pygmalion reconsidered. Worthington, OH: Charles A. Jones.

Elawar, M. C., & Corno, L. (1985). A factorial experiment in teachers' written feedback on student homework: Changing teacher behavior a little rather than a lot. Journal of Educational Psychology, 77, 162–173.

Elias, M. J., & Schwab, Y. (2006). From compliance to responsibility: Social and emotional learning and classroom management. In C. Evertson & C. S. Weinstein (Eds.), Handbook for classroom management: Research, practice, and contemporary issues. Mahwah, NJ: Lawrence Erlbaum.

Elkind, D. (1981). Obituary: Jean Piaget (1896–1980). American Psychologist, 36, 911–913.

Elkind, D. (1991). Formal education and early childhood education: An essential difference. In K. M. Cauley, F. Linder, & J. H. MacMillan (Eds.), Annual Editions: Educational Psychology 91/92 (pp. 27–37). Guilford, CT: Duskin.

Ellis, A. K., & Fouts, J. T. (1993). Research on educational innovations. Princeton, NJ: Eye on Education.

Elrich, M. (1994). The stereotype within. Educational Leadership, 51(8), 12–15.

Emerson, M. J., & Miyake, A. (2003). The role of inner speech in task switching: A dual-task investigation. Journal of Memory and Language, 48, 148–168.

Emmer, E. T., & Aussiker, A. (1990). School and classroom discipline problems: How well do they work? In O. Moles (Ed.), Student discipline strategies: Research and practice (pp. 129–165). Albany, NY: SUNY Press.

Emmer, E. T., & Evertson, C. M. (1981). Synthesis of research on classroom management. Educational Leadership, 38, 342–345.

Emmer, E. T., & Evertson, C. M. (1982). Effective classroom management at the beginning of the school year in junior high school classes. Journal of Educational Psychology, 74, 485–498.

Emmer, E. T., Evertson, C. M., & Anderson, L. M. (1980). Effective classroom management at the beginning of the school year. Elementary School Journal, 80, 219–231.

Emmer, E. T., Evertson, C. M., & Worsham, M. E. (2003). Classroom management for secondary teachers (6th ed.). Boston: Allyn & Bacon.

Emmer, E. T., Evertson, C. M., & Worsham, M. E. (2006). Classroom management for secondary teachers (7th ed.). Boston: Allyn and Bacon.

Emmer, E. T., & Gerwels, M. C. (2006). Classroom management in middle school and high school classrooms. In C. Evertson & C. S. Weinstein (Eds.), Handbook for classroom management: Research, practice, and contemporary issues. Mahwah, NJ: Lawrence Erlbaum.

Emmer, E. T., & Stough, L. M. (2001). Classroom management: A critical part of educational psychology with implications for teacher education. Educational Psychologist, 36, 103–112.

Engelmann, S., & Engelmann, T. (1981). *Give your child a superior mind*. New York: Cornerstone.

Engle, R. W. (2001). What is working memory capacity? In H. Roediger, J. Nairne, I. Neath, & A. Suprenant (Eds.), *The nature of remembering: Essays in honor of Robert G. Crowder* (pp. 297–314). Washington, DC: American Psychological Association.

Entwisle, D. R., & Alexander, K. L. (1998). Facilitating the transition to first grade: The nature of transition and research on factors affecting it. *The Elementary School Journal, 98*, 351–364.

Epanchin, B. C., Townsend, B., & Stoddard, K. (1994). *Constructive classroom management: Strategies for creating positive learning environments*. Pacific Grove, CA: Brooks/Cole.

Epstein, H. (1978). Growth spurts during brain development: Implications for educational policy and practice. In J. Chall & A. Mirsky (Eds.), *Education and the brain*. Seventy-seventh yearbook of the National Society for the Study of Education, Part II. Chicago: University of Chicago Press.

Epstein, H. (1980). EEG developmental stages. *Developmental Psychobiology, 13*, 629–631.

Epstein, J. L. (1989). Family structure and student motivation. In R. E. Ames & C. Ames (Eds.), *Research on motivation in education: Vol 3. Goals and cognitions* (pp. 259–295). New York: Academic Press.

Epstein, J. L. (1995). School/family/community partnerships: Caring for the children we share. *Phi Delta Kappan, 76*, 701–712.

Epstein, J. L., & Van Voorhis, F. L. (2001). More than minutes: Teachers' roles in designing homework. *Educational Psychologist, 36*, 181–193.

Erez, M., & Zidon, I. (1984). Effects of goal acceptance on the relationship of goal difficulty to performance. *Journal of Applied Psychology, 69*, 69–78.

Erickson, F., & Shultz, J. (1982). *The counselor as gatekeeper: Social interaction in interviews*. New York: Academic Press.

Ericsson, K. A., & Charness, N. (1999). Expert performance: Its structure and acquisition. In S. J. Ceci & W. M. Williams (Eds.), *The nature-nurture debate: The essential readings* (pp. 199–255). Malden, MA: Blackwell.

Erikson, E. (1963). *Childhood and society* (2nd ed.). New York: Norton.

Erikson, E. H. (1968). *Identity, youth, and crisis*. New York: Norton.

Erikson, E. H. (1980). *Identity and the life cycle* (2nd ed.). New York: Norton.

Espe, C., Worner, C., & Hotkevich, M. (1990). Whole language—What a bargain. *Educational Leadership, 47*(6), 45.

Evans, E. D., & Craig, D. (1990). Adolescent cognitions for academic cheating as a function of grade level and achievement status. *Journal of Adolescent Research, 5*, 325–345.

Evans, G. W. (2004). The environment of childhood poverty. *American Psychologist, 59*, 77–92.

Evans, L., & Davies, K. (2000). No sissy boys here: A content analysis of the representation of masculinity in elementary school reading texts. *Sex Roles, 42*, 255–270.

Evensen, D. H., Salisbury-Glennon, J. D., & Glenn, J. (2001). A qualitative study of six medical students in a problem-based curriculum: Toward a situated model of self-regulation. *Journal of Educational Psychology, 93*, 659–676.

Evertson, C. M. (1988). Managing classrooms: A framework for teachers. In D. Berliner & B. Rosenshine (Eds.), *Talks to teachers* (pp. 54–74). New York: Random House.

Evertson, C. M., Emmer, E. T., & Worsham, M. E. (2003). *Classroom management for elementary teachers* (6th ed.). Boston: Allyn & Bacon.

Evertson, C. M., Emmer, E. T., & Worsham, M. E. (2006). *Classroom management for secondary teachers* (7th ed.). Boston: Allyn and Bacon.

Fagot, B. I., & Hagan, R. (1991). Observations of parent reactions to sex-stereotyped behaviors: Age and sex effects. *Child Development, 62*, 617–628.

Fagot, B. I., Hagan, R., Leinbach, M. D., & Kronsberg, S. (1985). Differential reactions to assertive and communicative acts of toddler boys and girls. *Child Development, 56*, 1499–1505.

Fantuzzo, J., Davis, G., & Ginsburg, M. (1995). Effects of parent involvement in isolation or in combination with peer tutoring on student self-concept and mathematics achievement. *Journal of Educational Psychology, 87*, 272–281.

Farnaham-Diggory, S. (1994). Paradigms of knowledge and instruction. *Review of Educational Research, 64*, 463–477.

Feather, N. T. (1982). *Expectations and actions: Expectancy-value models in psychology*. Hillsdale, NJ: Lawrence Erlbaum.

Feiman-Nemser, S. (1983). Learning to teach. In L. Shulman & G. Sykes (Eds.), *Handbook of teaching and policy* (pp. 150–170). New York: Longman.

Feldman, J. (2003). The simplicity principle in human concept learning. *Current Directions in Psychological Science, 12*, 227–232.

Feldman, R. S. (2004). *Child development* (3rd ed.). Upper Saddle River, NJ: Prentice-Hall.

Fennema, E., & Peterson, P. (1988). Effective teaching for boys and girls: The same or different? In D. Berliner & B. Rosenshine (Eds.), *Talks to teachers* (pp. 111–127). New York: Random House.

Ferguson, A. A. (2000). *Bad boys: Public schools and the making of Black masculinity*. Ann Arbor, MI: University of Michigan Press.

Ferguson, D. L., Ferguson, P. M., & Bogdan, R. C. (1987). If mainstreaming is the answer, what is the question? In V. Richardson-Koehler (Ed.), *Educators' handbook: A research perspective* (pp. 394–419). New York: Longman.

Feuerstein, R. (1979). *The dynamic assessment of retarded performers: The Learning Potential Assessment Device, theory, instruments, and techniques*. Baltimore: University Park Press.

Feuerstein, R. (1990). The theory of structural cognitive modifiability. In B. Presseisen (Ed.), *Learning and thinking styles: Classroom interaction* (pp. 68–134). Washington, DC: National Education Association.

Fiedler R. L. (2002). WebQuests: A Critical Examination In Light of Selected Learning Theories. Retrieved from http://www.beckyfiedler.com/wq/fiedler.pdf.

Finkel, D., Reynolds, C. A., McArdle, J. J., Gatz, M., & Pedersen, N. L. (2003). Latent growth curve analyses of accelerating decline in cognitive abilities in adulthood. *Developmental Psychology, 39*, 535–550.

Finn, J. (1972). Expectations and the educational environment. *Review of Educational Research, 42*, 387–410.

Fischer, K. W., & Pare-Blagoev, J. (2000). From individual differences to dynamic pathways of development. *Child Development, 71*, 850–853.

Fiske, E. B. (1981, October 27). Teachers reward muddy prose, study finds. *The New York Times*, p. C1.

Fitts, P. M., & Posner, M. I. (1967). *Human performance*. Belmont, CA: Brooks Cole.

Fitzgerald, J. (1995). English-as-a-second-language learners' cognitive reading process: A review of the research in the United States. *Review of Educational Research, 62*, 145–190.

Fives, H. R., Hamman, D., & Olivarez, A. (2005, April). *Does burnout begin with student teaching? Analyzing efficacy, burnout, and support during the student-teaching semester*. Paper presented at the Annual Meeting of the America Educational Research Association, Montreal, CA.

Flammer, A. (1995). Developmental analysis of control beliefs. In A. Bandura (Ed.), *Self-efficacy in changing societies* (pp. 69–113). New York: Cambridge University Press.

Flavell, J. H. (1985). *Cognitive development* (2nd ed.). Englewood Cliffs, NJ: Prentice-Hall.

Flavell, J. H., Friedrichs, A. G., & Hoyt, J. D. (1970). Developmental changes in memorization processes. *Cognitive Psychology, 1,* 324–340.

Flavell, J. H., Green, F. L., & Flavell, E. R. (1995). Young children's knowledge about thinking. *Monographs of the Society for Research in Child Development,* 60(1, Serial No. 243).

Flavell, J. H., Miller, P. H., & Miller, S. A. (2002). *Cognitive development* (4th ed.). Upper Saddle River, NJ: Prentice-Hall.

Fleith, D. (2000). Teacher and student perceptions of creativity in the classroom environment. *Roeper Review, 22,* 148–153.

Flink, C. F., Boggiano, A. K., & Barrett, M. (1990). Controlling teaching strategies: Undermining children's self-determination and performance. *Journal of Personality and Social Psychology, 59,* 916–924.

Floden, R. E., & Klinzing, H. G. (1990). What can research on teacher thinking contribute to teacher preparation? A second opinion. *Educational Researcher,* 19(4), 15–20.

Forness, S. R., & Knitzer, J. (1992). A new proposed definition and terminology to replace "Serious Emotional Disturbance" in Individuals with Disabilities Education Act. *School Psychology Review, 21,* 12–20.

Foster, W. (1981, August). *Social and emotional development in gifted individuals.* Paper presented at the Fourth World Conference on Gifted and Talented, Montreal.

Fox, L. H. (1981). Identification of the academically gifted. *American Psychologist, 36,* 1103–1111.

Frable, D. E. S. (1997). Gender, Racial, ethnic, and class identities. In J. T. Spence, J. M. Darley, & D. J. Foss (Eds.), *Annual Review of Psychology* (pp. 139–162). Palo Alto, CA: Annual Reviews.

Frank, S. J., Pirsch, L. A., & Wright, V. C. (1990). Late adolescents' perceptions of their parents: Relationships among deidealization, autonomy, relatedness, and insecurity and implications for adolescent adjustment and ego identity status. *Journal of Youth and Adolescence, 19,* 571–588.

Frederiksen, N. (1984). Implications of cognitive theory for instruction in problem solving. *Review of Educational Research 54,* 363–407.

Fredricks, J. A., Blumenfeld, P. C., & Paris, A. H. (2004). School engagement: Potential of the concept, state of the evidence. *Review of Educational Research, 74,* 59–109.

Freiberg, H. J. (1999). Sustaining the paradigm. In H. J. Freiberg (Ed.), *Beyond behaviorism: Changing the classroom management paradigm* (pp. 164–173). Boston: Allyn & Bacon.

Freiberg, H. J., & Driscoll, A. (1996). *Universal teaching strategies* (2nd ed.). Boston: Allyn & Bacon.

Freiberg, H. J., & Driscoll, A. (2005). *Universal teaching strategies* (4th ed.). Boston: Allyn and Bacon.

Freiberg, J. (2006). Research-based programs for preventing and solving discipline problems. In C. Evertson & C. S. Weinstein (Eds.), *Handbook for classroom management: Research, practice, and contemporary issues.* Mahwah, NJ: Lawrence Erlbaum.

Freud, S. (1959). Creative writers and daydreaming. In J. Strachey (Ed.), *The standard edition of the complete psychological works of Sigmund Freud* (Vol. 9). London: Hogarth Press.

Frick, T. W. (1990). Analysis of patterns in time: A method of recording and quantifying temporal relations in education. *American Educational Research Journal, 27,* 180–204.

Friend, M. (2006). *Special education: Contemporary perspectives for school professionals.* Boston: Allyn and Bacon.

Friend, M., & Bursuck, W. (1996). *Including students with special needs: A practical guide for classroom teachers.* Boston: Allyn & Bacon.

Friend, M., & Bursuck, W. D. (2002). *Including students with special needs* (3rd ed.). Boston: Allyn & Bacon.

Friend, M., Bursuck, W., & Hutchinson, N. (1998). *Including exceptional students: A practical guide for classroom teachers.* Scarborough, ON: Allyn & Bacon Canada.

Fuchs, L. S., Fuchs, D., Hamlett, C. L., & Karns, K. (1998). High-achieving students' interactions and performance on complex mathematical tasks as a function of homogeneous and heterogeneous pairings. *American Educational Research Journal, 35,* 227–268.

Fulk, C. L., & Smith, P. J. (1995). Students' perceptions of teachers' instructional and management adaptations for students with learning or behavior problems. *The Elementary School Journal, 95,* 409–419.

Fuller, F. G. (1969). Concerns of teachers: A developmental conceptualization. *American Educational Research Journal, 6,* 207–226.

Furrer, C, & Skinner, E. (2003). Sense of relatedness as a factor in children's academic engagement and performance. *Journal of Educational Psychology,* 95(11), 148–161.

Furstenberg, F. F., & Cherlin, A. J. (1991). *Divided families.* Cambridge, MA: Harvard University Press.

Gaedke, B., & Shaughnessy, M. F. (2003). An interview with Jere Brophy. *Educational Psychology Review, 15,* 199–211.

Gage, N. L. (1991). The obviousness of social and educational research results. *Educational Researcher,* 20(1), 10–16.

Gagné, E. D. (1985). *The cognitive psychology of school learning.* Boston: Little, Brown.

Gagné, E. D., Yekovich, C. W., & Yekovich, F. R. (1993). *The cognitive psychology of school learning* (2nd ed.). New York: HarperCollins.

Gagné, R. M. (1977). *The conditions of learning* (3rd ed.). New York: Holt, Rinehart & Winston.

Gagné, R. M. (1985). *The conditions of learning and theory of instruction* (4th ed.). New York: Holt, Rinehart & Winston.

Gagné, R. M., & Driscoll, M. P. (1988). *Essentials of learning for instruction* (2nd ed.). Englewood Cliffs, NJ: Prentice-Hall.

Galambos, S. J., & Goldin-Meadow, S. (1990). The effects of learning two languages on metalinguistic development. *Cognition, 34,* 1–56.

Gallini, J. K. (1991). Schema-based strategies and implications for instructional design in strategy training. In C. McCormick, G. Miller, & M. Pressley (Eds.), *Cognitive strategies research: From basic research to educational applications.* New York: Springer-Verlag.

Garcia, E. E. (1992). "Hispanic" children: Theoretical, empirical, and related policy issues. *Educational Psychology Review, 4,* 69–94.

Garcia, R. L. (1991). *Teaching in a pluralistic society: Concepts, models, and strategies.* New York: HarperCollins.

Gardner, H. (1982). *Developmental psychology* (2nd ed.). Boston: Little, Brown.

Gardner, H. (1983). *Frames of mind: The theory of multiple intelligences.* New York: Basic Books.

Gardner, H. (1993). *Creating minds: An anatomy of creativity seen through the lives of Freud, Einstein, Picasso, Stravinsky, Elliot, Graham, and Gandhi.* New York: Basic Books.

Gardner, H. (1998). Reflections on multiple intelligences: Myths and messages. In A. Woolfolk (Ed.), *Readings in educational psychology* (2nd ed., pp. 61–67). Boston: Allyn & Bacon.

Gardner, H. (1999, August). *Who owns intelligence?* Invited address at the Annual Meeting of the American Psychological Association, Boston.

Gardner, H. (2003, April 21). *Multiple intelligence after twenty years.* Paper presented at the American Educational Research Association, Chicago, Illinois.

Gardner, R., Brown, R., Sanders, S., & Menke, D. J. (1992). "Seductive details" in learning from text. In K. A. Renninger, S. Hidi, & A. Krapp (Eds.), *The role of interest in learning and development* (pp. 239–254). Hillsdale, NJ: Erlbaum.

Garmon, A., Nystrand, M., Berends, M., & LePore, P. C. (1995). An organizational analysis of the effects of ability grouping. *American Educational Research Journal, 32,* 687–715.

Garner, P. W., & Spears, F. M. (2000). Emotion regulation in low-income preschool children. *Social Development, 9,* 246–264.

Garner, R. (1990). When children and adults do not use learning strategies: Toward a theory of settings. *Review of Educational Research, 60,* 517–530.

Garner, R. (1992). Learning from school tests. *Educational Psychologist, 27,* 53–63.

Garner, R. (1998). Choosing to learn and not-learn in school. *Educational Psychology Review, 10,* 227–238.

Garnets, L. (2002). Sexual orientations in perspective. *Cultural Diversity and Ethnic Minority Psychology, 8,* 115–129.

Garrison, J. (1995). Deweyan pragmatism and the epistemology of contemporary social constructivism. *American Educational Research Journal, 32,* 716–741.

Garrod, A., Beal, C., & Shin, P. (1990). The development of moral orientation in elementary school children. *Sex Roles, 22,* 13–27.

Gathercole, S. E., Pickering, S. J., Ambridge, B., & Wearing, H., (2004). The structure of working memory from 4 to 15 years of age. *Developmental Psychology, 40,* 177–190.

Geary, D. C. (1995). Sexual selection and sex differences in spatial cognition. *Learning and Individual Differences, 7,* 289–303.

Geary, D. C. (1998). What is the function of mind and brain? *Educational Psychologist, 10,* 377–388.

Geary, D. C., & Bjorklund, D. F. (2000). Evolutionary developmental psychology. *Child Development, 7,* 57–65.

Gehlbach, H. (2004). A new perspective on perspective taking: A multidimensional approach to conceptualizing an aptitude. *Educational Psychology Review, 16,* 207–234.

Gelernter, D. (1998, October). Kick calculators out of class. *Reader's Digest, 153,* 136–137.

Gelman, R. (1979). Preschool thought. *American Psychologist, 34,* 900–905.

Gelman, R. (2000). The epigenesis of mathematical thinking. *Journal of Applied Developmental Psychology, 21,* 27–37.

Gelman, R., & Baillargeon, R. (1983). A review of some Piagetian concepts. In P. Mussen (Ed.), *Carmichael's manual of child psychology: Vol. 3. Cognitive development* (E. Markman & J. Flavell, Vol. Eds.). New York: Wiley.

Gelman, R., & Cordes, S. A. (2001). Counting in animals and humans. In E. Dupoux (Ed.), *Essay in honor of Jacques Mehler.* Cambridge, MA: MIT Press.

Gelman, S. A., & Ebeling, K. S. (1989). Children's use of nonegocentric standards in judgments of size. *Child Development, 60,* 920–932.

Gentner, D. (1975). Evidence for the psychological reality of semantic components: The verbs of possession. In D. Norman & D. Rumelhart (Eds.), *Explorations in cognition.* San Francisco: Freeman.

Gentner, D., Loewenstein, J., & Thompson, L. (2003). Learning and transfer: A general role for analogical encoding. *Journal of Educational Psychology, 95,* 393–408.

Gerbner, G., Gross, L. Signorelli, N., & Morgan, M. (1986). *Television's mean world: Violence Profile No. 14–15.* Philadelphia: Annenberg School of Communication, University of Pennsylvania.

Gergen, K. J. (1997). Constructing constructivism: Pedagogical potentials. *Issues in Education: Contributions from Educational Psychology, 3,* 195–202.

Gersten, R. (1996a). The language-minority students in transition: Contemporary instructional research. *The Elementary School Journal, 96,* 217–219.

Gersten, R. (1996b). Literacy instruction for language-minority students: The transition years. *The Elementary School Journal, 96,* 225–244.

Gersten, R., & Woodward, J. (1994). The language minority student and special education: Issues, trends and paradoxes. *Exceptional Children, 60,* 310–322.

Gibbs, J. W., & Luyben, P. D. (1985). Treatment of self-injurious behavior: Contingent versus noncontingent positive practice overcorrection. *Behavior Modification, 9,* 3–21.

Gick, M. L. (1986). Problem-solving strategies. *Educational Psychologist, 21,* 99–120.

Gillett, M., & Gall, M. (1982, March). *The effects of teacher enthusiasm on the at-task behavior of students in the elementary grades.* Paper presented at the annual meeting of the American Educational Research Association, New York.

Gilligan, C. (1982). *In a different voice: Psychological theory and women's development.* Cambridge, MA: Harvard University Press.

Gilligan, C., & Attanucci, J. (1988). Two moral orientations: Gender differences and similarities. *Merrill-Palmer Quarterly, 34,* 223–237.

Gilstrap, R. L., & Martin, W. R. (1975). *Current strategies for teachers: A resource for personalizing education.* Pacific Palisades, CA: Goodyear.

Ginsburg, H., & Opper, S. (1988). *Piaget's theory of intellectual development* (3rd ed.). Englewood Cliffs, NJ: Prentice-Hall.

Girls' math achievement: What we do and don't know. (1986, January). *Harvard Education Letter, 2*(1), 1–5.

Glaser, R. (1981). The future of testing: A research agenda for cognitive psychology and psychometrics. *American Psychologist, 36,* 923–936.

Glasgow, K. L., Dornbusch, S. M., Troyer, L., Steinberg, L., & Ritter, P. L. (1997). Parenting styles, adolescents' attributions, and educational outcomes in nine heterogeneous high schools. *Child Development, 68,* 507–523.

Glasser, W. (1969). *Schools without failure.* New York: Harper & Row.

Glasser, W. (1990). *The quality school: Managing students without coercion.* New York: Harper & Row.

Glassman, M. (2001). Dewey and Vygotsky: Society, experience, and inquiry in educational practice. *Educational Researcher, 30*(4), 3–14.

Gleitman, H., Fridlund, A. J., & Reisberg, D. (1999). *Psychology* (5th ed.). New York: Norton.

Goldenberg, C. (1996). The education of language-minority students: Where are we, and where do we need to go? *The Elementary School Journal, 96,* 353–361.

Goldman, S. R., Lawless, K., Pellegrino, J. W., & Plants, R. (2006). Technology for teaching and learning with understanding. In J. Cooper (Ed.), *Classroom teaching skills* (8th ed., pp. 104–150). Boston: Houghton-Mifflin.

Goleman, D. (1988, April 10). An emerging theory on blacks' IQ scores. *The New York Times* (Education Life Section), pp. 22–24.

Goleman, D. (1995). *Emotional intelligence.* New York: Bantam.

Gollnick, D. A., & Chinn, P. C. (1994). *Multicultural education in a pluralistic society* (4th ed.). New York: Merrill.

Good, T. (1996). Teaching effects and teacher evaluation. In J. Sikula (Ed.), *Handbook of research on teacher education* (pp. 617–665). New York: Macmillan.

Good, T., & Brophy, J. (2003). *Looking in classrooms* (9th ed.). Boston: Allyn & Bacon.

Good, T. L. (1983a). Classroom research: A decade of progress. *Educational Psychologist, 18,* 127–144.

Good, T. L. (1983b). Research on classroom teaching. In L. Shulman & G. Sykes (Eds.), *Handbook of teaching and policy* (pp. 42–80). New York: Longman.

Good, T. L. (1988). Teacher expectations. In D. Berliner & B. Rosenshine (Eds.), *Talks to teachers* (pp. 159–200). New York: Random House.

Good, T. L., & Brophy, J. E. (1997). *Looking in classrooms* (7th ed.). New York: Longman.

Good, T. L., & Marshall, S. (1984). Do students learn more in heterogeneous or homogeneous groups? In P. Peterson, L. C. Wilkinson, & M. Hallinan (Eds.), *The social context of instruction: Group organization and group processes* (pp. 15–38). Orlando, FL: Academic Press.

Goodman, K. S. (1986). *What's whole in whole language: A parent–teacher guide.* Portsmouth, NH: Heinemann.

Goodrich, H. (1997). Understanding rubrics. *Educational Leadership, 54*(4), 14–17.

Gordon, D. (2001, June 18). The dominator. *Newsweek,* pp. 42–47.

Gordon, E. W. (1991). Human diversity and pluralism. *Educational Psychologist, 26,* 99–108.

Gordon, T. (1981). Crippling our children with discipline. *Journal of Education, 163,* 228–243.

Grabe, M., & Latta, R. M. (1981). Cumulative achievement in a mastery instructional system: The impact of differences in resultant achievement motivation and persistence. *American Educational Research Journal, 18,* 7–14.

Graber, J. A, & Brooks-Gunn, J. (1996). Transitions and turning points: Navigating the passage from childhood through adolescence. *Developmental Psychology, 32,* 768–776.

Graham, S. (1991). A review of attribution theory in achievement contexts. *Educational Psychology Review, 3,* 5–39.

Graham, S. (1994). Motivation in African Americans. *Review of Educational Research, 64,* 55–117.

Graham, S. (1995). Narrative versus meta-analytic reviews of race differences in motivation. *Review of Educational Research, 65,* 509–514.

Graham, S. (1996). How causal beliefs influence the academic and social motivation of African-American children. In G. G. Brannigan (Ed.), *The enlightened educator: Research adventures in the schools* (pp. 111–126). New York: McGraw-Hill.

Graham, S. (1998). Self-blame and peer victimization in middle school: An attributional analysis. *Developmental Psychology, 34,* 587–599.

Graham, S., & Barker, G. (1990). The downside of help: An attributional developmental analysis of helping behavior as a low ability cue. *Journal of Educational Psychology, 82,* 7–14.

Graham, S., & Harris, K. R. (1994). The effects of whole language on children's writing: A review of the literature. *Educational Psychologist, 29,* 187–192.

Graham, S., & Weiner, B. (1996). Theories and principles of motivation. In D. Berliner & R. Calfee (Eds.), *Handbook of educational psychology* (pp. 63–84). New York: Macmillan.

Gray, P. (2002). *Psychology* (4th ed.). New York: Worth.

Gredler, M. E. (2005). *Learning and instruction: Theory into practice* (5th ed.). Boston: Allyn and Bacon.

Greeno, J. G., Collins, A. M., & Resnick, L. B. (1996). Cognition and learning. In D. Berliner & R. Calfee (Eds.), *Handbook of educational psychology* (pp. 15–46). New York: Macmillan.

Greenough, W. T., Black, J. E., & Wallace, C. S. (1987). Experience and brain development. *Child Development, 58,* 539–559.

Gregorc, A. F. (1982). *Gregorc Style Delineator: Development, technical, and administrative manual.* Maynard, MA: Gabriel Systems.

Gresham, F. (1981). Social skills training with handicapped children. *Review of Educational Research, 51,* 139–176.

Grigorenko, E. L., & Sternberg, R. J. (1998). Dynamic testing. *Psychological Bulletin, 124,* 75–111.

Grigorenko, E. L., & Sternberg, R. J. (2001). Analytical, creative, and practical intelligence as predictors of self-reported adaptive functioning: A case study in Russia. *Intelligence, 29,* 57–73.

Grinder, R. E. (1981). The "new" science of education: Educational psychology in search of a mission. In F. H. Farley & N. J. Gordon (Eds.), *Psychology and education: The state of the union.* Berkeley, CA: McCutchan.

Grissom, J. B., & Shepard, L. A. (1989). Repeating and dropping out of school. In L. A. Shepard & M. L. Smith (Eds.), *Flunking grades: Research and policies on retention* (pp. 34–63). New York: Falmer.

Grissom, J. B., & Smith, L. A. (1989). Repeating and dropping out of school. In L. Shepard & M. Smith (Eds.), *Flunking grades: Research and policies on retention* (pp. 34–63). Philadelphia: Falmer Press.

Grolnick, W. S., Ryan, R. M., & Deci, E. L. (1991). Inner resources for school achievement: Motivational mediators of children's perceptions of their parents. *Journal of Educational Psychology, 83,* 508–517.

Gronlund, N. E. (2000). *How to write and use instructional objectives* (6th ed.). Columbus, OH: Merrill.

Gronlund, N. E. (2004). *Writing instructional objectives for teaching and assessment* (7th ed.). Upper Saddle River, NJ: Prentice-Hall.

Gronlund, N. E., & Cameron, I. J. (2003). *Assessment of student achievement.* Toronto: Pearson Education Canada.

Gross, E. F., Juvonen, J., & Gable, S. L. (2002). Internet use and well-being in adolescence. *Journal of Social Issues 58*(1), 75–90.

Gross, M. U. M. (1992). The use of radical acceleration in cases of extreme intellectual precocity. *Gifted Child Quarterly, 36,* 91–99.

Grossman, H., & Grossman, S. H. (1994). *Gender issues in education.* Boston: Allyn & Bacon.

Grotevant, H. D. (1998). Adolescent development in family contexts. In N. Eisenberg (Ed.), *Handbook of child psychology: Vol 3. Social, emotional, and personality development* (5th ed., pp. 1097–1149). New York: Wiley.

Guilford, J. P. (1988). Some changes in the Structure-of-Intellect model. *Educational and Psychological Measurement, 48,* 1–4.

Gunderson, L. (1997). Whole language approaches to reading and writing. In S. A. Stahl & D. H. Hayes (Eds.), *Instructional models in reading* (pp. 221–247). Hillsdale, NJ: Erlbaum.

Gurian, M., & Henley, P. (2001). *Boys and girls learn differently: A guide for teachers and parents.* San Francisco: Jossey-Bass.

Guskey, T. (1990). Making the grade: What benefits students? *Educational Leadership, 52*(2), 14–21.

Guskey, T. R., & Bailey, J. M. (2001). *Developing grading and reporting systems for student learning.* Thousand Oaks, CA: Corwin Press.

Guskey, T. R., & Gates, S. L. (1986). Synthesis of research on mastery learning. *Education Leadership, 43,* 73–81.

Gustafsson, J.-E., & Undheim, J. O. (1996). Individual differences in cognitive functioning. In D. Berliner & R. Calfee (Eds.), *Handbook of educational psychology* (pp. 186–242). New York: Macmillan.

Guthrie, J. T., & Alao, S. (1997). Designing contexts to increase motivations of reading. *Educational Psychologist, 32,* 95–105.

Guthrie, J. T., Cox, K. E., Anderson, E., Harris, K., Mazzoni, S., & Rach, L. (1998). Principles of integrated instruction for engagement in reading. *Educational Psychology Review, 10,* 227–238.

Gutman, L. M., Sameroff, A., & Cole, R. (2003). Academic growth curve trajectories from 1st grade to 12th grade: effects of multiple social risk factors and preschool child factors. *Developmental Psychology, 39,* 777–790.

Haertel, E. H. (1999). Performance assessment and educational reform. *Phi Delta Kappan, 80,* 662–666.

Hakuta, K. (1986). *Mirror of language: The debate on bilingualism.* New York: Basic Books.

Hakuta, K., & Garcia, E. E. (1989). Bilingualism and education. *American Psychologist, 44,* 374–379.

Hakuta, K., & Gould, L. J. (1987). Synthesis of research on bilingual education. *Educational Leadership, 44*(6), 38–45.

Haladyna, T. H. (2002). *Essentials of standardized achievement testing: Validity and accountability.* Boston: Allyn & Bacon.

Hall, J. W. (1991). More on the utility of the keyword method. *Journal of Educational Psychology, 83,* 171–172.

Hallahan, D. P., & Kauffman, J. M. (2000). *Exceptional learners: Introduction to special education* (8th ed.). Boston: Allyn & Bacon.

Hallahan, D. P., & Kauffman, J. M. (2003). *Exceptional learners: Introduction to special education* (9th ed.). Boston: Allyn and Bacon

Hallahan, D. P., & Kauffman, J. M. (2006). *Exceptional learners: Introduction to special education* (10th ed.). Boston: Allyn and Bacon.

Hallahan, D. P., Kauffman, J. M., & Lloyd, J. W. (1999). *Introduction to learning disabilities* (4th ed.). Boston: Allyn & Bacon.

Hallahan, D. P., Lloyd, J. W., Kauffman, J. M., Weiss, M. P., & Martinez, E. A. (2005). *Introduction to learning disabilities* (5th ed.). Boston: Allyn and Bacon.

Hallowell, E. M., & Ratey, J. J. (1994). *Driven to distraction.* New York: Pantheon Books.

Halpern, D. F. (2000). *Sex differences in cognitive abilities.* Mahwah, NJ: Lawrence Erlbaum.

Halpern, D. F. (2004). A cognitive-process taxonomy for sex differences n cognitive abilities. *Current Directions in Psychological Science, 13*, 135–139.

Halpern, D. F., & LaMay, M. L. (2000). The smarter sex: A critical review of sex differences in intelligence. *Educational Psychology Review, 12*, 229–246.

Hambrick, D. Z., Kane, M. J., & Engle, R. W. (2005). The role of working memory in higher-level cognition. In R. Sternberg & J. E. Pretz (Eds.), *Cognition and intelligence: Identifying the mechanisms of the mind* (pp. 104–121). New York: Cambridge University Press.

Hamilton, R. J. (1985). A framework for the evaluation of the effectiveness of adjunct questions and objectives. *Review of Educational Research, 55*, 47–86.

Hamman, D., Berthelot, J., Saia, J., & Crowley, E. (2000). Teachers' coaching of learning and its relation to students' strategic learning. *Journal of Educational Psychology, 92*, 342–348.

Hamre, B. K., & Pianta, R. C. (2001). Early teacher–child relationships and the trajectory of children's school outcomes through eighth grade. *Child Development, 72*, 625–638.

Hardiman, P. T., Dufresne, R., & Mestre, J. P. (1989). The relation between problem categorization and problem solving among experts and novices. *Memory and Cognition, 17*, 627–638.

Hardman, M. L. (1994). *Inclusion: Issues of educating students with disabilities in regular educational settings.* A booklet to accompany Hardman, M. L., Drew, C. J., Egan, M. W., & Wolf, B. (1993). *Human exceptionality: Society, school, and family* (4th ed.). Boston: Allyn & Bacon.

Hardman, M. L., Drew, C. J., & Egan, M. W. (1996). *Human exceptionality: Society, school, and family* (5th ed.). Boston: Allyn & Bacon.

Hardman, M. L., Drew, C. J., & Egan, M. W. (1999). *Human exceptionality: Society, school, and family* (6th ed.). Boston: Allyn & Bacon.

Hardman, M. L., Drew, C. J., & Egan, M. W. (2005). *Human exceptionality: Society, school, and family* (8th ed.). Boston: Allyn & Bacon.

Harp, S. F., & Mayer, R. E. (1998). How seductive details do their damage: A theory of cognitive interest in science learning. *Journal of Educational Psychology, 90*, 414–434.

Harris, J. R. (1998). *The nurture assumption: Why children turn out the way they do; parents matter less than you think and peers matter more.* New York: Free Press.

Harris, K. R. (1990). Developing self-regulated learners: The role of private speech and self-instruction. *Educational Psychologist, 25*, 35–50.

Harris, K. R., & Graham, S. (1996). Memo to constructivist: Skills count too. *Educational Leadership, 53*(5), 26–29.

Harris, K. R., Graham S., & Pressley, M. (1992). Cognitive-behavioral approaches in reading and written language: Developing self-regulated learners. In N. N. Singh & I. L. Beale (Eds.), *Learning disabilities: Nature, theory, and treatment* (pp. 415–451). New York: Springer-Verlag.

Harris, K. R., & Pressley, M. (1991). The nature of cognitive strategy instruction: Interactive strategy construction. *Exceptional Children, 57*, 392–404.

Harrow, A. J. (1972). *A taxonomy of the psychomotor domain: A guide for developing behavior objectives.* New York: David McKay.

Harter, S. (1990). Issues in the assessment of self-concept of children and adolescents. In A. LaGreca (Ed.), *Through the eyes of a child* (pp. 292–325). Boston: Allyn & Bacon.

Harter, S. (1998). The development of self-representations. In N. Eisenberg (Ed.), *Handbook of child psychology: Vol 3. Social, emotional, and personality development* (5th ed., pp. 553–618). New York: Wiley.

Harter, S. (2003). The development of self-representation during childhood and adolescence. In M. R. Leary & J. P. Tangney (Eds.), *Handbook of self and identity* (pp. 610–642). New York: Guilford.

Hartup, W. W., & Stevens, N. (1999). Friendships and adaptation across the lifespan. *Current Directions in Psychological Science, 8*, 76–79.

Hayes, S. C., Rosenfarb, I., Wulfert, E., Munt, E. D., Korn, Z., & Zettle, R. D. (1985). Self-reinforcement effects: An artifact of social standard setting? *Journal of Applied Behavior Analysis, 18*, 201–214.

Health Canada. *Summary of results of the 2004–05 Youth Smoking Survey.* Retrieved October 9, 2007, from http://www.hc-sc.gc.ca/hl-vs/tobac-tabac/research-recherche/stat/survey-sondage/2004-2005/result_e.html.

Heath, N. (1996). The emotional domain: Self-concept and depression in children with learning disabilities. *Advances in Learning and Behavioural Disabilities, 10*, 47–75.

Heath, N. L., & Ross, S. (2000). The prevalence and expression of depressive symptomatology in children with and without learning disabilities. *Learning Disability Quarterly, 23*, 24–36.

Henderson, M. (1996). *Helping your students get the most of homework* [Brochure]. Chicago: National Parent–Teacher Association.

Herbert, E. A. (1998). Design matters: How school environment affects children. *Educational Leadership, 56*(1), 69–71.

Herman, J. (1997). Assessing new assessments: How do they measure up? *Theory into Practice, 36*, 197–204.

Herman, J., & Winters, L. (1994). Portfolio research: A slim collection. *Educational Leadership, 52*(2), 48–55.

Hernshaw, L. S. (1987). *The shaping of modern psychology: A historical introduction from dawn to present day.* London: Routledge & Kegan Paul.

Hess, R., Chih-Mei, C., & McDevitt, T. M. (1987). Cultural variation in family beliefs about children's performance in mathematics: Comparisons among People's Republic of China, Chinese-American, and Caucasian-American families. *Journal of Educational Psychology, 79*, 179–188.

Hess, R., & McDevitt, T. (1984). Some cognitive consequences of maternal intervention techniques. A longitudinal study. *Child Development, 55*, 1902–1912.

Hess, R. D., & Shipman, V. C. (1965). Early experience and the socialization of cognitive modes in children. *Child Development, 36*, 869–886.

Hetherington, E. M. (1999). Should we stay together for the sake of the children? In E. Hetherington (Ed.), *Coping with divorce, single-parenting, and remarriage: A risk and resilience perspective* (pp. 93–116). Hillsdale, NJ: Lawrence Erlbaum.

Heward, W. L., & Orlansky, M. D. (1992). *Exceptional children* (4th ed.). Columbus, OH: Charles E. Merrill.

Hewson, P. W., Beeth, M. E., & Thorley, N. R. (1998). Teaching for conceptual change. In B. J. Fraserr & K. G. Tobin (Eds.), *International handbook of science education* (pp. 199–218). New York: Kluwer.

Hewstone, M. (1989). Changing stereotypes with disconfirming information. In D. Bar-Tal, C. Graumann, A. Kruglanski, & W. Stroebe (Eds.), *Stereotyping and prejudice: Changing conceptions* (pp. 207–223). New York: Springer-Verlag.

Hilgard, E. R. (1996). History of educational psychology. In R. Calfee & D. Berliner (Eds.), *Handbook of educational psychology* (pp. 990–1004). New York: Macmillan.

Hilgard, E. R., Atkinson, R. L., & Atkinson, R. C. (1979). *Introduction to psychology* (7th ed.). New York: Harcourt Brace Jovanovich.

Hill, K. T., & Wigfield, A. (1984). Test anxiety: A major educational problem and what can be done about it. *Elementary School Journal, 85*, 105–126.

Hill, W. F. (2002). *Learning: A survey of psychological interpretations* (7th ed.). Boston: Allyn & Bacon.

Hines, C. V., Cruickshank, D. R., & Kennedy, J. J. (1985). Teacher clarity and its relation to student achievement and satisfaction. *American Educational Research Journal, 22*, 87–99.

Hiroto, D. S., & Seligman, M. E. P. (1975). Generality of learned helplessness in man. *Journal of Personality and Social Psychology, 31*, 311–327.

Hirsch, E. D., Jr. (1996). *The schools we need—And why we don't have them.* New York: Doubleday.

Hmelo-Silver, C. E. (2004). Problem-based learning: What and how do students learn? *Educational Psychology Review, 16*, 235–266.

Hodges, E. V. E., & Perry, D. G. (1999). Personal and interpersonal antecedents and consequences of victimization by peers. *Journal of Personality and Social Psychology, 76*, 677–685.

Hofer, B. K., & Pintrich, P. R. (1997). The development of epistemological theories: Beliefs about knowledge and knowing and their relation to learning. *Review of Educational Research, 67*, 88–140.

Hoffman, L. W. (1984). Work, family, and the socialization of the child. In R. Parke (Ed.), *Review of child development research* (Vol. 7, pp. 223–282). Chicago: University of Chicago Press.

Hoffman, M. L. (2000). *Empathy and moral development.* New York: Cambridge University Press.

Hoffman, M. L. (2001). A comprehensive theory of prosocial moral development. In A. Bohart & D. Stipek (Eds.), *Constructive and destructive behavior* (pp. 61–86). Washington, DC: American Psychological Association.

Hogan, T., Rabinowitz, M., & Craven, J. A. III. (2003). Representation in teaching: Inferences from research of expert and novice teachers. *Educational Psychologist, 38*, 235–247.

Hoge, D. R., Smit, E. K., & Hanson, S. L. (1990). School experiences predicting changes in self-esteem of sixth- and seventh-grade students. *Journal of Educational Psychology, 82*, 117–126.

Hoover-Dempsey, K. V., Bassler, O. C., & Burow, R. (1995). Parents' reported involvement in students' homework: Strategies and practices. *The Elementary School Journal, 95*, 435–450.

Hoover-Dempsey, K. V., Battiato, A. C., Walker, J. M. T., Reed, R. P., DeJong, J. M., & Jones, K. P. (2001). Parental involvement in homework, *Educational Psychologist, 36*, 195–209.

Horgan, D. D. (1995). *Achieving gender equity: Strategies for the classroom.* Boston: Allyn & Bacon.

Horn, J. L. (1998). A basis for research on age differences in cognitive capabilities. In J. J. McArdle & R. W. Woodcock (Eds.), *Human cognitive theories in theory and practice* (pp. 57–87). Mahwah, NJ: Lawrence Erlbaum.

Horovitz, B. (2002, April 22). Gen Y: A tough crowd to sell. *USA Today*, pp. B1–2.

Hoy, W. K., & Woolfolk, A. E. (1990). Organizational socialization of student teachers. *American Educational Research Journal, 27*, 279–300.

Hoy, W. K., & Woolfolk, A. E. (1993). Teachers' sense of efficacy and the organizational health of schools. *Elementary School Journal, 93*, 355–372.

Huessman, L. R., Eron, L. D., Klein, R., Brice, P., & Fischer, P. (1983). Mitigating the imitation of aggressive behaviors by changing children's attitudes about media violence. *Journal of Personality and Social Psychology, 44*, 899–910.

Huesmann, L. R., Moise-Titus, J., Podolski, C. P., & Eron, L. D. (2003). Longitudinal relations between children's exposure to TV violence and their aggressive and violent behavior in young adulthood: 1977–1992. *Developmental Psychology, 39*, 201–221.

Huff, C. R. (1989). Youth gangs and public policy. *Crime Del, 35*, 524–537.

Hughes, D. R. (1998). *Kids online: Protecting your children in cyberspace.* Grand Rapids, MI: Fleming H. Revell.

Hung, D. W. L. (1999). Activity, apprenticeship, and epistemological appropriation: Implications from the writings of Michael Polanyi. *Educational Psychologist, 34*, 193–205.

Hunt, E. (2000). Let's hear it for crystallized intelligence. *Learning and Individual Differences, 12*, 123–129.

Hunt, J. M. (1961). *Intelligence and experience.* New York: Ronald.

Hunt, N., & Marshall, K. (2002). *Exceptional children and youth: An introduction to special education* (3rd ed.). Boston: Houghton Mifflin.

Hunt, R. R., & Ellis, H. C. (1999). *Fundamentals of cognitive psychology* (6th ed.). New York: McGraw-Hill College.

Hunter, M. (1982). *Mastery teaching.* El Segundo, CA: TIP Publications.

Hutchinson, N. L. (2002). *Inclusion of exceptional learners in Canadian schools.* Toronto: Prentice-Hall.

Hutchinson, N. L. (2007). *Inclusion of exceptional learners in Canadian schools.* (2nd ed.). Toronto: Prentice-Hall.

Hutchinson, N. L., Wintermute, J., Munby, H., Versnel, J., Chin, P., & Dalgarno, N. (2005, April). Negotiating accommodations so that work-based education facilitates career development for youth with disabilities. Paper presented at the annual meeting of the American Educational Research Association, Montreal.

International Reading Association & National Association for the Education of Young Children. (1998). Learning to read and write: Developmentally appropriate practices for young children. *The Reading Teacher, 52*, 193–216.

Iran-Nejad, A. (1990). Active and dynamic self-regulation of learning processes. *Review of Educational Research, 60*, 573–602.

Irvine, J. J. (1990). *Black students and school failure: Policies, practices, and prescriptions.* New York: Praeger.

Irvine, J. J., & Armento, B. J. (2001). *Culturally responsive teaching: Lesson planning for elementary and middle grades.* New York: McGraw-Hill.

Irvine, J. J., & Fraser, J. W. (1998, May). Warm demanders. *Education Week*. Retrieved May 10, 2005, from http://www.edweek.org/ew/ewstory.cfm?slug=35irvine.h17&keywords=Irvine.

Irving, O., & Martin, J. (1982). Withitness: The confusing variable. *American Educational Research Journal, 19*, 313–319.

Irwin, J. W. (1991). *Teaching reading comprehension* (2nd ed.). Boston: Allyn & Bacon.

Isabella, R., & Belsky, J. (1991). Interactional synchrony and the origins of infant-mother attachment: A replication study. *Child Development, 62*, 373–384.

Jacklin, C. N., DiPietro, J. A., & Maccoby, E. E. (1984). Sex-typing behavior and sex-typing pressure in child-parent interactions. *Sex Roles, 13*, 413–425.

Jacobs, J. E., Lanza, S., Osgood, D. W., Eccles, J. S., & Wigfield, A. (2002). Changes in children's self-competence and values: Gender and domain differences across grades one through twelve. *Child Development, 73*, 509–527.

Jagacinski, C. M., & Nicholls, J. G. (1987). Competence and affect in task involvement and ego involvement: The impact of social comparison information. *Journal of Educational Psychology, 76*, 107–114.

James, W. (1890). *The principles of psychology* (Vol. 2). New York: Henry Holt.

James, W. (1912). *Talks to teachers on psychology: And to students on some of life's ideals.* New York: Holt.

Jarrett, R. (1995). Growing up poor: The family experiences of socially mobile youth in low-income African American neighborhoods. *Journal of Adolescent Research, 10*, 111–135.

Jensen, L. A., Arnett, J. J., Feldman, S. S., & Cauffman, E. (2002). It's wrong but everybody does it: Academic dishonesty among high school and college students. *Contemporary Educational Psychology, 27,* 209–228.

Jenson, W. R., Sloane, H. N., & Young, K. R. (1988). *Applied behavior analysis in education: A structured teaching approach.* Englewood Cliffs, NJ: Prentice-Hall.

Jimenez, R. (2000). Literacy and identity development of Latina/o students who are successful English readers: Opportunities and obstacles. *American Educational Research Journal, 37,* 971–1000.

Jimerson, S. R. (1999). On the failure of failure: Examining the association between early grade retention and education and employment outcomes during late adolescence. *Journal of School Psychology, 37,* 243–272.

Jimerson, S. R., Anderson, G. E., & Whipple, A. D. (2002). Winning the battle and losing the war: Examining the relation between grade retention and dropping out of high school. *Psychology in the Schools, 39,* 441–457.

Johnson, D., & Johnson, R. (1985). Motivational processes in cooperative, competitive, and individualistic learning situations. In C. Ames & R. Ames (Eds.), *Research on motivation in education: Vol. 2. The classroom milieu* (pp. 249–286). New York: Academic Press.

Johnson, D., & Johnson, R. (1994). *Learning together and alone: Cooperation, competition, and individualization* (4th ed.). Boston: Allyn & Bacon.

Johnson, D. W., & Johnson, R. (1999). The three Cs of school and classroom management. In H. J. Freiberg (Ed.), *Beyond behaviorism: Changing the classroom management paradigm* (pp. 119–144). Boston: Allyn & Bacon.

Johnson, D. W., Johnson, R., Dudley, B., Ward, M., & Magnuson, D. (1995). The impact of peer mediation training on the management of school and home conflicts. *American Educational Research Journal, 32,* 829–844.

Johnson, D. W., & Johnson, R. T. (2002). *Meaningful assessment: A meaningful and cooperative process.* Boston: Allyn & Bacon.

John-Steiner, V., & Mahn, H. (1996). Sociocultural approaches to learning and development: A Vygotskian framework. *Educational Psychologist, 31,* 191–206.

Johnston, L. D., O'Malley, P. M., Bachman, J. G., & Schulenberg, J. E. (December 21, 2004). *Overall teen drug use continues gradual decline; but use of inhalants rises.* University of Michigan News and Information Services: Ann Arbor, MI. [On-line]. Available: www.monitoringthefuture.org; accessed 03/22/05.

Jones, D. C. (2004). Body image among adolescent girls and boys: A longitudinal study. *Developmental Psychology, 40,* 823–835.

Jones, E. D., & Southern, W. T. (1991). Conclusions about acceleration: Echoes of a debate. In W. Southern & E. Jones (Eds.), *The academic acceleration of gifted children* (pp. 223–228). New York: Teachers College Press.

Jones, M. G., & Gerig, T. M. (1994). Silent sixth-grade students: Characteristics, achievement, and teacher expectations. *Elementary School Journal, 95,* 169–182.

Jones, M. S., Levin, M. E., Levin, J. R., & Beitzel, B. D. (2000). Can vocabulary-learning strategies and pair-learning formats be profitably combined? *Journal of Educational Psychology, 92,* 256–262.

Jones, S. M., & Dindia, K. (2004). A meta-analytic perspective on sex equity in the classroom. *Review of Educational Research, 74,* 443–471.

Jordan, N., & Goldsmith-Phillips, J. (1994). *Assessment of learning disabilities.* Boston: Allyn & Bacon.

Joshua, S., & Dupin, J. J. (1987). Taking into account students conceptions in instructional strategy: An example in physics. *Cognition and Instruction, 4,* 117–135.

Joyce, B., & Weil, M. (1988). *Models of teaching* (3rd ed.). Englewood Cliffs, NJ: Prentice-Hall.

Joyce, B. R., Weil, M., & Calhoun, E. (2000). *Models of teaching* (6th ed.). Boston: Allyn & Bacon.

Jurden, F. H. (1995). Individual differences in working memory and complex cognition. *Journal of Educational Psychology, 87,* 93–102.

Kagan, S. (1983). Social orientation among Mexican-American children: A challenge to traditional classroom structures. In E. Garcia (Ed.), *The Mexican-American child: Language, cognition, and social development.* Tempe, AZ: Center for Bilingual Education.

Kail, R., & Hall, L. K. (1999). Sources of developmental change in children's word-problem performance. *Journal of Educational Psychology, 91,* 600–668.

Kalyuga, S., Chandler, P., Tuovinen, J., & Sweller, J. (2001). When problem solving is superior to studying worked examples. *Journal of Educational Psychology, 93,* 579–588.

Kamaya, T., Scullin, M.H., & Ceci, S. J. (2003). The Flynn effect and U.S. policies: The impact of rising IQ scores on American society via mental retardation diagnoses. *American Psychologist, 58,* 1–13.

Kanfer, F. H., & Gaelick, L. (1986). Self-management methods. In F. Kanfer & A. Goldstein (Eds.), *Helping people change: A textbook of methods* (3rd ed.). New York: Pergamon.

Kaplan, J. S. (1991). *Beyond behavior modification* (2nd ed.). Austin, TX: Pro-Ed.

Kardash, C. M., & Howell, K. L. (2000). Effects of epistemological beliefs and topic-specific beliefs on undergraduates' cognitive and strategic processing of dual-positional text. *Journal of Educational Psychology, 92,* 524–535.

Karpov, Y. V., & Bransford, J. D. (1995). L. S. Vygotsky and the doctrine of empirical and theoretical learning. *Educational Psychologist, 30,* 61–66.

Karpov, Y. V., & Haywood, H. C. (1998). Two ways to elaborate Vygotsky's concept of mediation implications for instruction. *American Psychologist, 53,* 27–36.

Karweit, N. (1989). Time and learning: A review. In R. E. Slavin (Ed.), *School and classroom organization.* Hillsdale, NJ: Erlbaum.

Karweit, N., & Slavin, R. (1981). Measurement and modeling choices in studies of time and learning. *American Educational Research Journal, 18,* 157–171.

Katz, P. A. (2003). Racists or tolerant multiculturalists? How do they begin? *American Psychologist, 58,* 897–909.

Kazdin, A. E. (1984). *Behavior modification in applied settings.* Homewood, IL: Dorsey Press.

Kazdin, A. E. (2001). *Behavior modification in applied settings* (6th ed.). Belmont, CA: Wadsworth.

Keating, D. P. (1990). Charting pathways to the development of expertise. *Educational Psychologist, 25,* 243–267.

Keating, D. P. (1991). Curriculum options for the developmentally advanced: A developmental alternative for gifted education. *Exceptionality Education Canada, 1,* 53–83.

Keefe, J. W. (1982). Assessing student learning styles: An overview. In *Student learning styles and brain behavior.* Reston, VA: National Association of Secondary School Principals.

Keefe, J. W., & Monk, J. S. (1986). *Learning style profile examiner's manual.* Reston, VA: National Association of Secondary School Principals.

Keenan, T., Ruffman, T., & Olson, D. R. (1994). When do children begin to understand logical inference as a source of knowledge? *Cognitive Development, 9,* 331–353.

Kelly, K. (1999). Retention vs. social promotion: Schools search for alternatives. *Harvard Education Letter, 15*(1), 1–3.

Keogh, B. K., & MacMillan, D. L. (1996). Exceptionality. In D. Berliner & R. Calfee (Eds.), *Handbook of educational psychology* (pp. 311–330). New York: Macmillan.

Keyser, V., & Barling, J. (1981). Determinants of children's self-efficacy beliefs in an academic environment. *Cognitive Therapy and Research, 5,* 29–40.

Kiewra, K. A. (1985). Investigating notetaking and review: A depth of processing alternative. *Educational Psychologist, 20,* 23–32.

Kiewra, K. A. (1988). Cognitive aspects of autonomous note taking: Control processes, learning strategies, and prior knowledge. *Educational Psychologist, 23,* 39–56.

Kiewra, K. A. (1989). A review of note-taking: The encoding storage paradigm and beyond. *Educational Psychology Review, 1,* 147–172.

Kiewra, K. A. (2002). How classroom teachers can help students learn and teach them how to learn. *Theory Into Practice, 41,* 71–80.

Kindsvatter, R., Wilen, W., & Ishler, M. (1988). *Dynamics of effective teaching.* New York: Longman.

Kindsvatter, R., Wilen, W., & Ishler, M. (1992). *Dynamics of effective teaching* (2nd ed.). New York: Longman.

King, A. (1990). Enhancing peer interaction and learning in the classroom through reciprocal questioning. *American Educational Research Journal, 27,* 664–687.

King, A. (1994). Guiding knowledge construction in the classroom: Effects of teaching children how to question and how to explain. *American Educational Research Journal, 31,* 338–368.

King, A. (2002). Structuring peer interactions to promote high-level cognitive processing. *Theory into Practice, 41,* 31–39.

King, G. (1979, June). Personal communication. University of Texas at Austin.

Kintsch, W. (1998). *Comprehension: A paradigm for cognition.* New York: Cambridge University Press.

Kirk, S., Gallagher, J. J., Anastasiow, N. J., & Coleman, M. R. (2006). *Educating exceptional children* (11th ed.). Boston: Houghton Mifflin.

Kirk, S., & Gallagher, J. J., & Anastasiow, N. J. (1993). *Educating exceptional children* (7th ed.). Boston: Houghton Mifflin.

Kirst, M. (1991). Interview on assessment issues with James Popham. *Educational Researcher, 20*(2), 24–27.

Klahr, D., & Nigam, M. (2004). The equivalence of learning paths in early science. Effects of direct instruction and discovery learning. *Psychological Science, 15,* 661–667.

Klausmeier, H. J. (1976). Instructional design and the teaching of concepts. In J. Levin & V. Allen (Eds.), *Cognitive learning in children: Theories and strategies.* New York: Academic Press.

Klausmeier, H. J. (1992). Concept learning and concept teaching. *Educational Psychologist, 27,* 267–286.

Klein, P. (2002). Multiplying the problem of intelligence by eight. In L. Abbeduto (Ed.), *Taking sides: Clashing on controversial issues in educational psychology* (pp. 219–232). Guilford, CT: McGraw-Hill/Duskin.

Kling, K. C., Hyde, J. S., Showers, C. J., & Buswell, B. N. (1999). Gender differences in self-esteem: A meta-analysis. *Psychological Bulletin, 125,* 470–500.

Knapp, M., Turnbull, B. J., & Shields, P. M. (1990). New directions for educating children of poverty. *Educational Leadership, 48*(1), 4–9.

Kneedler, R. (1984). *Special education for today.* Englewood Cliffs, NJ: Prentice-Hall.

Kogan, N. (1983). Stylistic variation in childhood and adolescence: Creativity, metaphor, and cognitive style. In P. Mussen (Ed.), *Handbook of child psychology* (4th ed., Vol. 3, pp. 630–706). New York: Wiley.

Kohlberg, L. (1963). The development of children's orientations toward moral order: Sequence in the development of moral thought. *Vita Humana, 6,* 11–33.

Kohlberg, L. (1975). The cognitive-developmental approach to moral education. *Phi Delta Kappan, 56,* 670–677.

Kohlberg, L. (1981). *The philosophy of moral development.* New York: Harper & Row.

Kohlberg, L. (1984). *Essays on moral development.* San Francisco: Harper & Row.

Kohlberg, L., Yaeger, J., & Hjertholm, E. (1969). Private speech: Four studies and a review of theories. *Child Development, 39,* 691–736.

Kohn, A. (1991). Caring kids: The role of the schools. *Phi Delta Kappan, 72,* 496–506.

Kohn, A. (1993). Rewards versus learning: A response to Paul Chance. *Phi Delta Kappan, 74,* 783–787.

Kohn, A. (1996). By all available means: Cameron and Pierce's defense of extrinsic motivators. *Review of Educational Research, 66,* 1–4.

Kokko, K., & Pulkkinen, L. (2000). Aggression in childhood and long-term unemployment in adulthood: A cycle of maladaptation and some protective factors. *Developmental Psychology, 36,* 463–472.

Kolb, G., & Whishaw, I. Q. (1998). Brain plasticity and behavior. In J. T. Spence, J. M. Darley, & D. J. Foss (Eds.), *Annual Review of Psychology* (pp. 43–64). Palo Alto, CA: Annual Reviews.

Korenman, S., Miller, J., & Sjaastad, J. (1995). Long-term poverty and child development in the United States: Results from the NLSY. *Children and Youth Services Review, 17,* 127–155.

Koriat, A., Goldsmith, M., & Pansky, A. (2000). Toward a psychology of memory accuracy. In S. Fiske (Ed.), *Annual review of psychology* (pp. 481–537). Palo Alto, CA: Annual Reviews.

Kounin, J. (1970). *Discipline and group management in classrooms.* New York: Holt, Rinehart & Winston.

Kounin, J. S., & Doyle, P. H. (1975). Degree of continuity of a lesson's signal system and task involvement of children. *Journal of Educational Psychology, 67,* 159–164.

Kozulin, A. (1990). *Vygotsky's psychology: A biography of ideas.* Cambridge, MA: Harvard University Press.

Kozulin, A. (Ed.). (2003). *Vygotsky's educational theory in cultural context.* Cambridge, U. K.: Cambridge University Press.

Kozulin, A., & Falik, L. (1995). Dynamic cognitive assessment of the child. *Current Directions, 4,* 192–195.

Kozulin, A., & Presseisen, B. Z. (1995). Mediated learning experience and psychological tools: Vygotsky's and Feuerstein's perspectives in a study of student learning. *Educational Psychologist, 30,* 67–75.

Krashen, S. D. (1981). Bilingual education and second language acquisition theory. In *Schooling and language minority students: A theoretical framework.* Developed by the California State Department of Education, Office of Bilingual Bicultural Education. Los Angeles, CA: Evaluation, Dissemination, and Assessment Center, California State University.

Krathwohl, D. R., Bloom, B. S., & Masia, B. B. (1964). *Taxonomy of educational objectives: Handbook II. Affective domain.* New York: David McKay.

Kreitzer, A. E., & Madaus, G. F. (1994). Empirical investigations of the hierarchical structure of the taxonomy. In L. W. Anderson & L. A. Sosniak (Eds.), *Bloom's taxonomy: A forty-year retrospective.* Ninety-third yearbook for the National Society for the Study of Education, Part II (pp. 64–81). Chicago: University of Chicago Press.

Kroesbergen, E. H., Van Luit, J. E. H., & Maas, C. J. M. (2004). Effectiveness of explicit and constructivist mathematics for low-achieving students in the Netherlands. *The Elementary School Journal, 104,* 233–251.

Kroger, J. (1995). The differentiation of "firm" and "developmental" foreclosure identity statuses: A longitudinal study. *Journal of Adolescent Research, 10,* 317–337.

Kroger, J. (2000). *Identity development: Adolescence through adulthood.* Thousand Oaks, CA: Sage.

Krumboltz, J. D., & Krumboltz, H. B. (1972). *Changing children's behavior.* Englewood Cliffs, NJ: Prentice-Hall.

Krumboltz, J. D., & Yeh, C. J. (1996). Competitive grading sabotages good teaching. *Phi Delta Kappan, 78,* 324–326.

Kuhn, M. H., & McPartland, T. S. (1954). An empirical investigation of self-attitudes. *American Sociological Review, 19,* 68–76.

Kuklinski, M. R., & Weinstein, R. S. (2001). Classroom and developmental differences in a path model of teacher expectancy effects. *Child Development, 72,* 1554–1578.

Kulik, C. L., Kulik, J. A., & Bangert-Drowns, R. L. (1990). Effectiveness of mastery learning programs: A meta-analysis. *Review of Educational Research, 60,* 265–299.

Kulik, J. A., & Kulik, C. C. (1984). Effects of accelerated instruction on students. *Review of Educational Research, 54,* 409–425.

van Laar, C. (2000). The paradox of low academic achievement but high self-esteem in African American students: An attributional account. *Educational Psychology Review, 12,* 33–61.

Ladson-Billings, G. (1990). Like lightning in a bottle: Attempting to capture the pedagogical excellence of successful teachers of Black students. *Qualitative Studies in Education, 3,* 335–344.

Ladson-Billings, G. (1992). Culturally relevant teaching: The key to making multicultural education work. In C.A. Grant (Ed.), *Research and multicultural education* (pp. 106–121). London: Falmer Press.

Ladson-Billings, G. (1994). *The dream keepers.* San Francisco: Jossey-Bass.

Ladson-Billings, G. (1995). But that is just good teaching! The case for culturally relevant pedagogy. *Theory into Practice, 34,* 159–165.

Ladson-Billings, G. (2004). Landing on the wrong note: The price we paid for Brown. *Educational Researcher, 33*(7), 3–13.

Lambert, A. J. (1995). Stereotypes and social judgment: The consequences of group variability. *Journal of Personality and Social Psychology, 68,* 388–403.

Lambert, N. M. (1994). Seating arrangement in classrooms. *The International Encyclopedia of Education* (2nd ed., Vol. 9, pp. 5355–5359).

Land, M. L. (1987). Vagueness and clarity. In M. Dunkin (Ed.), *The international encyclopedia of teaching and teacher education* (pp. 392–397). New York: Pergamon.

Landrum, T. J., & Kauffman, J. M. (2006). Behavioral approaches to classroom management. In C. M. Evertson & C. S. Weinstein (Eds.), *Handbook of classroom management: Research, practice, and contemporary issues.* Mahwah, NJ: Erlbaum.

Lane, K., Falk, K., & Wehby, J. (2006). Classroom management in special education classrooms and resource rooms. In C. M. Evertson & C. S. Weinstein (Eds.), *Handbook of classroom management: Research, practice, and contemporary issues.* Mahwah, NJ: Erlbaum.

Language Development and Hypermedia Group (1992). "Open" software design: A case study. *Educational Technology, 32,* 43–55.

Laosa, L. (1984). Ethnic, socioeconomic, and home language influences on early performance on measures of ability. *Journal of Educational Psychology, 76,* 1178–1198.

Larrivee, B. (1985). *Effective teaching behaviors for successful mainstreaming.* New York: Longman.

Lashley, T. J., II, Matczynski, T. J., & Rowley, J. B. (2002). *Instructional models: Strategies for teaching in a diverse society* (2nd ed.). Belmont, CA: Wadsworth/Thomson Learning.

Lave, J. (1988). *Cognition in practice: Mind, mathematics, and culture in everyday life.* New York: Cambridge University Press.

Lave, J. (1997). The culture of acquisition and the practice of understanding. In D. Kirshner & J. A. Whitson (Eds.), *Situated cognition: Social, semiotic, and psychological perspectives* (pp. 17–35). Mahwah, NJ: Lawrence Erlbaum.

Lave, J., & Wenger, E. (1991). *Situated learning: Legitimate peripheral participation.* Cambridge, MA: Cambridge University Press.

Leaper, C. (2002). Parenting girls and boys. In M. H. Bornstein (Ed.), *Handbook of parenting, Vol. 1: Children and parenting* (2nd ed., pp. 127–152). Mahwah, NJ: Lawrence Erlbaum.

Learning Disabilities Association of Canada. (2002). *LD defined.* Retrieved September 30, 2007, from http://www.Idac-taac.ca/index-e.asp.

Learning Disabilities Association of Ontario. (2001, May 25). *Learning disabilities: A new definition.* Retrieved from http://www.ldao.on.ca/pei/defdraft.html.

Lee, R. M. (2005). Resilience against discrimination: Ethnic identity and other-group orientation as protective factors for Korean Americans. *Journal of Counseling Psychology, 52,* 36–44.

Lee, A. Y., & Hutchinson, L. (1998). Improving learning from examples through reflection. *Journal of Experimental Psychology: Applied, 4,* 187–210.

Lehman, D. R., & Nisbett, R. E. (1990). A longitudinal study of the effects of undergraduate training on reasoning. *Developmental Psychology, 26,* 952–960.

Leinhardt, G. (2001). Instructional explanations: A commonplace for teaching and location for contrasts. In V. Richardson (Ed.), *Handbook of research on teaching* (4th ed., pp. 333–357). Washington, DC: American Educational Research Association.

Leinhardt, G. (1986). Expertise in mathematics teaching. *Educational Leadership, 43,* 28–33.

Leinhardt, G. (1988). Situated knowledge and expertise in teaching. In J. Calderhead (Ed.), *Teachers' professional learning.* London: Farmer Press.

Leinhardt, G. (2001). Instructional explanations: A commonplace for teaching and location for contrasts. In V. Richardson (Ed.), *Handbook of research on teaching* (4th ed., pp. 333–357). Washington, DC: American Educational Research Association.

LeMahieu, P., Gitomer, D. H., & Eresh, J. T. (1993). *Portfolios in large-scale assessment: Difficult but not impossible.* Unpublished manuscript, University of Delaware.

Leming, J. S. (1981). Curriculum effectiveness in value/moral education. *Journal of Moral Education, 10,* 147–164.

Lepper, M. R., & Greene, D. (1978). *The hidden costs of rewards: New perspectives on the psychology of human motivation.* Hillsdale, NJ: Erlbaum.

Lepper, M. R., Keavney, M., & Drake, M. (1996). Intrinsic motivation and extrinsic reward: A commentary on Cameron and Pierce's meta-analysis. *Review of Educational Research, 66,* 5–32.

Lerner, R. M., & Galambos, N. L. (1998). Adolescent development: Challenges and opportunities for research, programs, and policies. In J. T. Spence, J. M. Darley, & D. J. Foss (Eds.), *Annual Review of Psychology* (pp. 413–446). Palo Alto, CA: Annual Reviews.

Levin, J. R. (1993). Mnemonic strategies and classroom learning: A twenty-year report card. *Elementary School Journal, 94,* 235–254.

Levin, J. R., & Nolan, J. F. (2000). *Principles of classroom management: A professional decision-making model.* Boston: Allyn & Bacon.

Lewinsohn, P. M., Rohde, P., & Seeley, J. R. (1994). Psychological risk factors for future attempts. *Journal of Consulting and Clinical Psychology, 62,* 297–305.

Lewis, R. (2001). Classroom discipline and student responsibility: The students' view. *Teaching and Teacher Education, 17,* 307–319.

Lewis, T. J., Sugai, G., & Colvin, G. (1998). Reducing problem behavior through a school-wide system of effective behavioral support: Investigation of a school-wide social skills training program and contextual interventions. *School Psychology Review, 27,* 446–459.

Liben, L. S., & Signorella, M. L. (1993). Gender-schematic processing in children: the role of initial interpretations of stimuli. *Developmental Psychology, 29,* 141–149.

Lindsay, P. H., & Norman, D. A. (1977). *Human information processing: An introduction to psychology* (2nd ed.). New York: Academic Press.

Linn, M. C., & Hyde, J. S. (1989). Gender, mathematics, and science. *Educational Researcher, 18,* 17–27.

Linn, R. L., & Gronlund, N. E. (2000). *Measurement and assessment in education* (8th ed.). Columbus, OH: Merrill.

Lipps, G., & Frank, J. (1997). *The national longitudinal survey of children and youth, 1994–95: Initial results from the school component* (Cat. no. 81-003-XPB, Vol. 4[2]).Ottawa: Statistics Canada.

Lipscomb, T. J., MacAllister, H. A., & Bregman, N. J. (1985). A developmental inquiry into the effects of multiple models on children's generosity. *Merrill-Palmer Quarterly, 31,* 335–344.

Liu, W. M., Ali, S. R., Soleck, G., Hopps, J., Dunston, K., & Pickett, T., Jr. (2004). Using social class in counseling psychology research. *Journal of Counseling Psychology, 51,* 3–18.

Locke, E. A., & Latham, G. P. (1990). *A theory of goal setting and task performance.* Englewood Cliffs, NJ: Prentice-Hall.

Loftus, E., & Palmer, J. C. (1974). Reconstruction of automobile destruction: An example of the interaction between language and memory. *Journal of Verbal Learning and Verbal Behavior, 13,* 585–589.

Lorch, R. F., Lorch, E. P., Ritchey, K., McGovern, L., & Coleman, D. (2001). Effects of headings on text summarization. *Contemporary Educational Psychology, 26,* 171–191.

Lord, J. (1991). *Lives in transition: The process of personal empowerment.* Kitchener, ON: Centre for Research and Education in Human Services.

Lord, S., Eccles, J., & McCarthy, K. (1994). Surviving the junior high school transition: Family processes and self-perceptions as protective factors. *Journal of Early Adolescence, 14,* 162–199.

Louis, B., Subotnik, R. F., Breland, P. S., & Lewis, M. (2000). Establishing criteria for high ability versus selective admission to gifted programs: Implications for policy and practice. *Educational Psychology Review, 12,* 295–314.

Loveless, T. (1998). The tracking and ability grouping debate. *Fordham Report, 2*(88), 1–27.

Lovett, M. W., et al. (2000). Components of effective remediation for developmental disabilities: Combining phonological and strategy-based instruction to improve outcomes. *Journal of Educational Psychology, 92,* 263–283.

Lowenstein, G. (1994). The psychology of curiosity: A review and reinterpretation. *Psychological Bulletin, 117,* 75–98.

Lucyshyn, J. M., Horner, R. H., Dunlap, G., Albin, R. W., & Ben, K. R. (2002). Positive behavior support with families. In J. M. Lucyshyn, G. Dunlap, & R. W. Albin (Eds.), *Families and positive behavior support: Addressing problem behavior in family contexts* (pp. 3–43). Baltimore: Paul H. Brookes.

Luiten, J., Ames, W., & Ackerson, G. (1980). A meta-analysis of the effects of advance organizers on learning and retention. *American Educational Research Journal, 17,* 211–218.

Lupart, J., & Barva, C. (1998). Promoting female achievement in the sciences: Research and implications. *International Journal for the Advancement of Counselling, 20,* 319–338.

Lupart, J. L., & Pyryt, M. C. (1996). "Hidden gifted" students: Underachiever prevalence and profile. *Journal for the Education of the Gifted, 20*(1), 36–53.

Lupart, J., & Timmons, V. (2003). Preamble. *Exceptionality Education Canada, 13,* 5–7.

Ma, X., & Kishor, N. (1997). Attitude toward self, social factors, and achievement in mathematics: A meta-analytic review. *Educational Psychology Review, 9,* 89–120.

Maag, J. W., & Kemp, S. E. (2003). Behavioral intent of power and affiliation: Implications for functional analysis. *Remedial and Special Education, 24,* 57–64.

Mabry, L. (1999). Writing to the rubrics: Lingering effects of traditional standardized testing on direct writing assessment. *Phi Delta Kappan, 80,* 673–679.

Maccoby, E. E. (1998). *The two sexes: Growing up apart, coming together.* Cambridge, MA: Belknap/Harvard University Press.

Maccoby, E. E., & Jacklin, C. N. (1974). *The psychology of sex differences.* Stanford, CA: Stanford University Press.

Mace, F. C., Belfiore, P. J., & Hutchinson, J. M. (2001). Operant theory and research on self-regulation. In B. Zimmerman & D. Schunk (Eds.), *Self-regulated learning and academic achievement: Theoretical perspectives* (2nd ed.). Mahwah, NJ: Lawrence Erlbaum.

Macionis, J. J. (1991). *Sociology* (3rd ed.). Englewood Cliffs, NJ: Prentice-Hall.

Macionis, J. J. (1994). *Sociology* (4th ed.). Englewood Cliffs, NJ: Prentice-Hall.

Macionis, J. J. (2003). *Sociology* (9th ed.). Upper Saddle River, NJ: Prentice-Hall.

MacKay, A. W. (1986). The Charter's equality provisions and education: A structural analysis. *Canadian Journal of Education, 11,* 293–312.

Macrae, C. N., Milne, A. B., & Bodenhausen, C. V. (1994). Stereotypes as energy-saving devices: A peek inside the cognitive toolbox. *Journal of Personality and Social Psychology, 66,* 37–47.

Maczewski, M. (2002). Exploring identities through the Internet: Youth Experiences Online. *Child and Youth Care Forum, 31*(2), pp. 111–129.

Madsen, C. H., Becker, W. C., & Thomas, D. R. (1968). Rules, praise, and ignoring: Elements of elementary classroom control. *Journal of Applied Behavior Analysis, 1,* 139–150.

Madsen, C. H., Becker, W. C., Thomas, D. R., Koser, L., & Plager, E. (1968). An analysis of the reinforcing function of "sit down" commands. In R. K. Parker (Ed.), *Readings in educational psychology.* Boston: Allyn & Bacon.

Mager, R. (1975). *Preparing instructional objectives* (2nd ed.). Palo Alto, CA: Fearon.

Magnusson, S. J., & Palincsar, A. S. (1995). The learning environment as a site of science reform. *Theory into Practice, 34,* 43–50.

Maier, N. R. F. (1933). An aspect of human reasoning. *British Journal of Psychology, 24,* 144–155.

Major, B., & Schmader, T. (1998). Coping with stigma through psychological disengagement. In J. Swim & C. Stangor (Eds.), *Stigma: The target's perspective* (pp. 219–241). New York: Academic Press.

Maker, C. J. (1987). Gifted and talented. In V. Richardson-Koehler (Ed.), *Educators' handbook: A research perspective* (pp. 420–455). New York: Longman.

Malone, T. W., & Lepper, M. (1987). Making learning fun: A taxonomy of intrinsic motivations for learning. In R. E. Snow & M. J. Farr (Eds.), *Aptitude, learning and instruction: Vol. 3. Cognitive and affective process analysis* (pp. 223–253). Hillsdale, NJ: Lawrence Erlbaum.

Mangione, P. L., & Speth, T. (1998). The transition to elementary school: A framework for creating early childhood continuity through home, school, and community partnerships. *The Elementary School Journal, 98,* 381–397.

Manning, B. H. (1991). *Cognitive self-instruction of classroom processes.* Albany, NY: SUNY Press.

Manning, B. H., & Payne, B. D. (1996). *Self-talk for teachers and students: Metacognitive strategies for personal and classroom use.* Boston: Allyn & Bacon.

Mantzicopoulos, P., & Morrison, D. (1992). Kindergarten retention: Academic and behavioral outcomes through the end of second grade. *American Educational Research Journal, 29,* 182–198.

Many, J. E., Fyfe, R., Lewis, G., & Mitchell, E. (1996). Traversing the topical landscape: Exploring students' self-directed reading-writing-research processes. *Reading Research Quarterly, 31,* 12–35.

Marcia, J. (1980). Ego identity development. In J. Adelson (Ed.), *The handbook of adolescent psychology.* New York: Wiley.

Marcia, J. (1987). The identity status approach to the study of ego identity development. In T. Honess & K. Yardley (Eds.), *Self and identity: Perspectives across the life span.* London: Routledge & Kagan Paul.

Marcia, J. E. (1991). Identity and self development. In R. Lerner, A. Peterson, & J. Brooks-Gunn (Eds.), *Encyclopedia of adolescence* (Vol. 1). New York: Garland.

Marcia, J. E. (1994). The empirical study of ego identity. In H. Bosma, T. Graafsma, H. Grotebanc, & D. DeLivita (Eds.), *The identity and development.* Newbury Park, CA: Sage.

Marcia, J. (1999). Representational thought in ego identity, psychotherapy, and psychosocial development. In I. E. Sigel (Ed.), *Development of mental representation: Theories and applications.* Mahwah, NJ: Lawrence Erlbaum.

Marcus, N., Cooper, M., & Sweller, J. (1996). Understanding instructions. *Journal of Educational Psychology, 88,* 49–63.

Marinova-Todd, S., Marshall, D., & Snow, C. (2000). Three misconceptions about age and L2 learning. *TESOL Quarterly, 34*(1), 9–34.

Markman, E. M. (1977). Realizing that you don't understand: A preliminary investigation. *Child Development, 48*, 986–992.

Markman, E. M. (1979). Realizing that you don't understand: Elementary school children's awareness of inconsistencies. *Child Development, 50*, 643–655.

Markman, E. (1992). Constraints on word learning: Speculations about their nature, origins, and domain specificity. In M. Gunnar & M. Maratsos (Eds.), *Minnesota symposium on child psychology* (Vol. 25, pp. 59–101). Hillsdale, NJ: Lawrence Erlbaum.

Markstrom-Adams, C. (1992). A consideration of intervening factors in adolescent identity formation. In G. R. Adams, R. Montemayor, & T. Gullotta (Eds.), *Advances in adolescent development: Vol. 4. Adolescent identity formation* (pp. 173–192). Newbury Park, CA: Sage.

Marsh, H. W. (1987). The big-fish-little-pond effect on academic self-concept. *Journal of Educational Psychology, 79*, 280–295.

Marsh, H. W. (1990). Influences of internal and external frames of reference on the formation of math and English self-concepts. *Journal of Educational Psychology, 82*, 107–116.

Marsh, H. W. (1994). Using the National Longitudinal Study of 1988 to evaluate theoretical models of self-concept: The Self-Description Questionnaire. *Journal of Educational Psychology, 86*, 439–456.

Marsh, H. W., & Ayotte, V. (2003). Do multiple dimensions of self-concept become more differentiated with age? The differential distinctiveness hypothesis. *Journal of Educational Psychology, 95*, 687–706.

Marsh, H. W., & Craven, R. (2002). The pivotal role of frames of reference in academic self-concept formation: The Big Fish Little Pond Effect. In F. Pajares & T. Urdan (Eds.), *Adolescence and Education* (Volume II, pp. 83–123). Greenwich, CT: Information Age.

Marsh, H. W., & Hau, K-T. (2003). Big-Fish-Little-Pond effect on academic self-concept. *American Psychologist, 58*, 364–376.

Marsh, H. W., & Holmes, I. W. M. (1990). Multidimensional self-concepts: Construct validation of responses by children. *American Educational Research Journal, 27*, 89–118.

Marsh, H. W., Kong, C., & Hau, K. (2000). Longitudinal multilevel models of the big-fish-little-pond effect on academic self-concept: Counterbalancing contrast and reflected-glory effects in Hong Kong schools. *Journal of Personality & Social Psychology, 78*, 337–349.

Marsh, H. W., Walker, R., & Debus, R. (1991). Subject-specific components of academic self-concept and self-efficacy. *Contemporary Educational Psychology, 16*, 331–345.

Marsh, H. W., & Yeung, A. S. (1997). Coursework selection: Relation to academic self-concept and achievement. *American Educational Research Journal, 34*, 691–720.

Marshall, H. (1996). Implications of differentiating and understanding constructivist approaches. *Journal of Educational Psychology, 31*, 235–240.

Marshall, H. H. (1987). Motivational strategies of three fifth-grade teachers. *Elementary School Journal, 88*, 135–150.

Marshall, H. H. (Ed.). (1992). *Redefining student learning: Roots of educational change*. Norwood, NJ: Ablex.

Martin, C. L. (1989). Children's use of gender-related information in making social judgments. *Developmental Psychology, 25*, 80–88.

Martin, C. L., & Little, J. K. (1990). The relation of gender understanding to children's sex-typed preferences and gender stereotypes. *Child Development, 61*, 1427–1439.

Martin, G., & Pear, J. (1992). *Behavior modification: What it is and how to do it* (4th ed.). Englewood Cliffs, NJ: Prentice-Hall.

Martin, J., & Sugarman, J. (1993). *Models of classroom management: Principles, applications and critical perspectives* (2nd ed.). Calgary: Detselig.

Martinez-Pons, M. (2002). A social cognitive view of parental influence on student academic self-regulation. *Theory into Practice, 61*, 126–131.

Marzano, R. J., & Marzano, J. S. (2003, September). The key to classroom management. *Educational Leadership, 61*(1), 6–13.

Maslow, A. H. (1968). *Toward a psychology of being* (2nd ed.). New York: Van Nostrand.

Maslow, A. H. (1970). *Motivation and personality* (2nd ed.). New York: Harper and Row.

Mason, D. A., & Good, T. L. (1993). Effects of two-group and whole-class teaching on regrouped elementary students' mathematics achievement. *American Educational Research Journal, 30*, 328–360.

Maté, G. (2000). *Scattered minds: A new look at the origins and healing of attention deficit disorder*. Toronto: Alfred A. Knopf Canada.

Matlin, M. W., & Foley, H. J. (1997). *Sensation and perception* (4th ed.). Boston: Allyn & Bacon.

Matthews (1996). Giftedness at adolescence: Diverse educational options required. *Exceptionality Education Canada, 6*, 25–49.

Mautone, P. D., & Mayer, R. E. (2001). Signaling as a cognitive guide in multimedia learning. *Journal of Educational Psychology, 93*, 377–389.

Mayer, R. E. (1979). Can advance organizers influence meaningful learning? *Review of Educational Research, 49*, 371–383.

Mayer, R. E. (1982). Memory for algebra story problems. *Journal of Educational Psychology, 74*, 199–216.

Mayer, R. E. (1983a). Can you repeat that? Qualitative and quantitative effects of repetition and advance organizers on learning from science prose. *Journal of Educational Psychology, 75*, 40–49.

Mayer, R. E. (1983b). *Thinking, problem solving, cognition*. San Francisco: Freeman.

Mayer, R. E. (1984). Twenty-five years of research on advance organizers. *Instructional Science, 8*, 133–169.

Mayer, R. E. (1992a). Cognition and instruction: Their historic meeting within educational psychology. *Journal of Educational Psychology, 84*, 405–412.

Mayer, R. E. (1992b). *Thinking, problem solving, and cognition* (2nd ed.). New York: Freeman.

Mayer, R. E. (1996). Learners as information processors: Legacies and limitations of educational psychology's second metaphor. *Journal of Educational Psychology, 31*, 151–161.

Mayer, R. E. (1999). Multimedia aids to problem-solving transfer. *International Journal of Educational Research, 31*, 611–623.

Mayer, R. E. (2001). *Multimedia learning*. New York: Cambridge University Press.

Mayer, R. E. (2004). Should there be a three-strikes rule against discovery learning? A case for guided methods of instruction. *American Psychologist, 59*, 14–19.

Mayer, R. E., & Gallini, J. K. (1990). When is an illustration worth ten thousand words? *Journal of Educational Psychology, 82*, 715–726.

Mayer, R. E., & Sims, V. K. (1994). For whom is a picture worth a thousand words? Extensions of a dual-coding theory of multimedia learning. *Journal of Educational Psychology, 86*, 389–401.

Mayer, R. E., & Wittrock, M. C. (1996). Problem-solving transfer. In D. Berliner & R. Calfee (Eds.), *Handbook of educational psychology* (pp. 47–62). New York: Macmillan.

McCafferty, S. G. (2004). Introduction. *International Journal of Applied Linguistics, 14*(1), 1–6.

McCaslin, M., & Good, T. L. (1998). Moving beyond management as sheer compliance: Helping students to develop goal coordination strategies. *Educational Horizons, 76*, 169–176.

McCaslin, M., & Good, T. L. (1996). The informal curriculum. In D. Berliner, & R. Calfee (Eds.), *Handbook of educational psychology* (pp. 622–670). New York: Macmillan.

McCaslin, M., & Hickey, D. T. (2001). Self-regulated learning and academic achievement: A Vygotskian view. In B. Zimmerman & D. Schunk (Eds.), *Self-regulated learning and academic achievement: Theoretical perspectives* (2nd ed., pp. 227–252). Mahwah, NJ: Lawrence Erlbaum.

McClelland, D. (1985). *Human motivation.* Glenview, IL: Scott, Foresman.

McClelland, D. C. (1993). Intelligence is not the best predictor of job performance. *Current Directions in Psychological Science, 2,* 5–6.

McCombs, B. L., & Marzano, R. J. (1990). Putting the self in self-regulated learning: The self as agent in integrating skill and will. *Educational Psychologist, 25,* 51–70.

McCreary Centre Society. (1993). *Adolescent health survey: Province of British Columbia.* Vancouver, BC: The McCreary Centre Society.

McDevitt, T. M., & Ormrod, J. E. (2002). *Child development and education.* Upper Saddle River, NJ: Merrill/Prentice-Hall.

McDonald, J. P. (1993). Three pictures of an exhibition: Warm, cool, and hard. *Phi Delta Kappan, 74,* 480–485.

McGoey, K. E., & DuPaul, G. J. (2000). Token reinforcement and response cost procedures: Reducing disruptive behavior of children with attention-deficit/hyperactivity disorder. *School Psychology Quarterly, 15,* 330–343.

McKenzie, T. L., & Rushall, B. S. (1974). Effects of self-recording on attendance and performance in a competitive swimming training environment. *Journal of Applied Behavior Analysis, 7,* 199–206.

McLaughlin, T. F., & Gnagey, W. J. (1981, April). *Self-management and pupil self-control.* Paper presented at the annual meeting of the American Educational Research Association, Los Angeles.

McLoyd, V. C. (1998). Economic disadvantage and child development. *American Psychologist, 53,* 185–204.

McNemar, Q. (1964). Lost: Our intelligence? Why? *American Psychologist, 19,* 871–882.

Media Awareness Network (2005). Young Canadians in a Wired World, Phase 2: Student Survey Report. Retrieved from the World Wide Web: http://www.media-awareness.ca/english/research/YCWW/phaseII/upload/YCWWII_Student_Survey.pdf.

Mediascope. (1996). National television violence study: Executive summary 1994–1995. Studio City, CA: Author.

Medley, D. M. (1979). The effectiveness of teachers. In P. Peterson & H. Walberg (Eds.), *Research on teaching: Concepts, findings, and implications* (pp. 11–27). Berkeley, CA: McCutchan.

Meece, J. L. (1997). *Child and adolescent development for educators.* New York: McGraw-Hill.

Meece, J. L. (2002). *Child and adolescent development for educators* (2nd ed.). New York: McGraw-Hill.

Meichenbaum, D. (1977). *Cognitive behavior modification: An integrative approach.* New York: Plenum.

Meichenbaum, D. (1986). Cognitive behavior modification. In F. Kanfer & A. Goldstein (Eds.), *Helping people change: A textbook of methods* (3rd ed., pp. 346–380). New York: Pergamon.

Meichenbaum, D., Burland, S., Gruson, L., & Cameron, R. (1985). Metacognitive assessment. In S. Yussen (Ed.), *The growth of reflection in children.* Orlando, FL: Academic Press.

Mendell, P. R. (1971). Retrieval and representation in long-term memory. *Psychonomic Science, 23,* 295–296.

Messick, S. (1975). The standard problem: Meaning and values in measurement and evaluation. *American Psychologist, 35,* 1012–1027.

Messick, S. (1994). The matter of style: Manifestations of personality in cognition, learning, and teaching. *Educational Psychologist, 29,* 121–136.

Metcalfe, B. (1981). Self-concept and attitude toward school. *British Journal of Educational Psychology, 51,* 66–76.

Metcalfe, J., & Shimamura, A. P. (Eds.). (1994). *Metacognition: Knowledge about knowing.* Cambridge, MA: MIT Press.

Mickleburgh, R. (1999, February 1). Parents put heat on BC schools: Asian immigrants behind latest drive for more structured, back-to-basics education. *Globe and Mail,* p. A3.

Midgley, C. (2001). A goal theory perspective on the current status of middle level schools. In T. Urdan & F. Pajares (Eds.), *Adolescence and education* (Vol. 1, pp. 33–59). Greenwich, CT: Information Age Publishing.

Midgley, C., Kaplan, A., & Middleton, M. (2001). Performance-approach goals: Good for what, for whom, under what circumstances, and at what cost? *Journal of Educational Psychology, 93,* 77–86.

Mifflin, M. (1999, December 13). Singing the pink blues. Mothers who think. Retrieved March 16, 2002, from http://www.salon.com/mwt/feature/1999/12/13/toys.

Miller, E. (1994). Peer mediation catches on, but some adults don't. *Harvard Education Letter, 10*(3), 8.

Miller, G. A. (1956). The magical number seven, plus or minus two: Some limits on our capacity for processing information. *Psychological Review, 63,* 81–97.

Miller, G. A., Galanter, E., & Pribram, K. H. (1960). *Plans and the structure of behavior.* New York: Holt, Rinehart & Winston.

Miller, K., & Gelman, R. (1983). The child's representation of number: A multidimensional scaling analysis. *Child Development, 54,* 1470–1479.

Miller, P. H. (1993). *Theories of developmental psychology* (3rd ed.). New York: Freeman.

Miller, P. H. (2002). *Theories of developmental psychology* (4th ed.). New York: Worth.

Miller, R. B. (1962). Analysis and specification of behavior for training. In R. Glaser (Ed.), *Training research and education: Science edition.* New York: Wiley.

Miller, S. A. (2005). Tips for getting children's attention. *Early Childhood Today,* 19.

Mills, J. R., & Jackson, N. E. (1990). Predictive significance of early giftedness: The case of precocious reading. *Journal of Educational Psychology, 82,* 410–419.

Mitchell, M. (1993). Situational interest: Its multifaceted structure in the secondary school mathematics classroom. *Journal of Educational Psychology. 85,* 424–436.

Moll, L. C., Amanti, C., Neff, D., & Gonzalez, N. (1992). Funds of knowledge: Using a qualitative approach to connect homes and classrooms. *Theory into Practice, 31,* 132–141.

Moll, L. C., & Whitmore, K. F. (1993). Vygotsky in classroom practice: Moving from individual transmission to social transaction. In E. Forman, N. Minick, & C. A. Stone (Eds.), *Contexts for learning: Sociocultural dynamics in children's development* (pp. 19–42). New York: Oxford University Press.

Monroe, C. R., & Obidah, J. E. (2002, April). *The impact of cultural synchronization on a teacher's perceptions of disruption: A case study of an African American middle school classroom.* Paper presented at the American Educational Research Association, New Orleans, LA.

Monteleone, J. A. (1998). *Child abuse.* St. Louis, MO: G. W. Medical Publisher.

Morin, V. A., & Miller, S. P. (1998). Teaching multiplication to middle school students with mental retardation. *Education & Treatment of Children, 21,* 22–36.

Morine-Dershimer, G. (2006). Instructional planning. In J. Cooper (Ed.), *Classroom teaching skills* (7th ed., pp. 20–54). Boston: Houghton-Mifflin.

Morris, C. G. (1991). *Psychology: An introduction* (7th ed.). Englewood Cliffs, NJ: Prentice-Hall.

Morris, P. F. (1990). Metacognition. In M. W. Eysenck (Ed.), *The Blackwell dictionary of cognitive psychology* (pp. 225–229). Oxford, UK: Basil Blackwell.

Morrow, L. (1983). Home and school correlates of early interest in literature. *Journal of Educational Research, 76,* 221–230.

Morrow, L., & Weinstein, C. (1986). Encouraging voluntary reading: The impact of a literature. *Reading Research Quarterly, 21,* 330–346.

Moshman, D. (1982). Exogenous, endogenous, and dialectical constructivism. *Developmental Review, 2,* 371–384.

Moshman, D. (1997). Pluralist rational constructivism. *Issues in Education: Contributions from Educational Psychology, 3,* 229–234.

Moskowitz, G., & Hayman, M. L. (1976). Successful strategies of inner-city teachers: A year-long study. *Journal of Educational Research, 69,* 283–289.

Moss, P. A. (1992). Shifting conceptions of validity in educational measurement: Implications for performance assessment. *Review of Educational Research, 62,* 229–258.

Mueller, C. M., & Dweck, C. S. (1998). Praise for intelligence can undermine children's motivation and performance. *Journal of Personality and Social Psychology, 75,* 33–52.

Mumford, M. D., Costanza, D. P., Baughman, W. A., Threlfall, V., & Fleishman, E. A. (1994). Influence of abilities on performance during practice: Effects of massed and distributed practice. *Journal of Educational Psychology, 86,* 134–144.

Murdock, T. B., Hale, N. M., & Weber, M. J. (2001). Predictors of cheating among early adolescents: Academic and social motivations. *Contemporary Educational Psychology, 26,* 96–115.

Murdock, T. B., & Miller, A. (2003). Teachers as sources of middle school students' motivational identity: Variable-centered and person-centered analytic approaches. *Elementary School Journal, 103,* 383–399.

Murdock, S. G., O'Neill, R. E., & Cunningham, E. (2005). A comparison of results and acceptability of functional behavioral assessment procedures with a group of middle school students with emotional/behavioral disorders (E/BD). *Journal of Behavioral Education, 14,* 5–18.

Murphy, P. K., & Alexander, P. A. (2000). A motivated exploration of motivation terminology. *Contemporary Educational Psychology, 25,* 3–53.

Murray, H. G. (1983). Low inference classroom teaching behavior and student ratings of college teaching effectiveness. *Journal of Educational Psychology, 75,* 138–149.

Mussen, P., Conger, J. J., & Kagan, J. (1984). *Child development and personality* (6th ed.). New York: Harper & Row.

Muth, K. D., & Alverman, D. E. (1999). *Teaching and learning in the middle grades.* Boston: Allyn & Bacon.

Myers, D. G. (2005). *Exploring psychology* (6th ed. in modules). New York: Worth.

Nakamura, J., & Csikszentmihalyi, M. (2001). Catalytic creativity: The case of Linus Pauling. *American Psychologist, 56,* 337–341.

Nathan, M. J., & Knuth, E. J. (2003). A study of whole class mathematical discourse and teacher change. *Cognition and Instruction, 21,* 175–207.

National Council of Teachers of Mathematics (NCTM) (1989). *Curriculum and evaluation standards for school mathematics.* Reston, VA: Author.

National Science Foundation. (1988). *Women and minorities in science and engineering* (NSF 88–301). Washington, DC: National Science Foundation.

Naveh-Benjamin, M. (1991). A comparison of training programs intended for different types of test-anxious students: Further support for an information-processing model. *Journal of Educational Psychology, 83,* 134–139.

Naveh-Benjamin, M., McKeachie, W. J., & Lin, Y. (1987). Two types of test-anxious students: Support for an information processing model. *Journal of Educational Psychology, 79,* 131–136.

Needles, M., & Knapp, M. (1994). Teaching writing to children who are undeserved. *Journal of Educational Psychology, 86,* 339–349.

Neimark, E. (1975). Intellectual development during adolescence. In F. D. Horowitz (Ed.), *Review of child development research* (Vol. 4). Chicago: University of Chicago Press.

Neisser, U., Boodoo, G., Bouchard, A., Boykin, W., Brody, N., Ceci, S. J., Halpern, D. F., Loehlin, J. C., Perloff, R., Sternberg, R. J., & Urbina, S. (1996). Intelligence: Knowns and unknowns. *American Psychologist, 51,* 77–101.

Nelson, C. A. (2001). The development and neural bases of face recognition. *Infant and Child Development, 10,* 3–18.

Nelson, G. (1993). Risk, resistance, and self-esteem: A longitudinal study of elementary school-aged children from mother-custody and two-parent families. *Journal of Divorce and Remarriage, 19,* 99–119.

Nelson, K. (1986). *Event knowledge.* Hillsdale, NJ: Erlbaum.

Nelson, R., & Roberts, M. L. (2000). Ongoing reciprocal teacher-student interactions involving disruptive behaviors in general education classrooms. *Journal of Emotional and Behavioral Disorders, 4,* 147–161.

Nelson, T. O. (1996). Consciousness and metacognition. *American Psychologist, 51,* 102–116.

Neuman, S. B. & Roskos, K. (1997). Literacy knowledge in practice: Contexts of participation for young writers and readers. *Reading Research Quarterly, 32,* 10–32.

Neumeister, K. L. S., & Cramond, B. (2004). E. Paul Torrance (1915–2003). *American Psychologist, 59,* 179.

Newcombe, N., & Baenninger, M. (1990). The role of expectations in spatial test performance: A meta-analysis. *Sex Roles, 16,* 25–37.

Newstead, S. E., Franklyn-Stokes, A., & Armstead, P. (1996). Individual differences in student cheating. *Journal of Educational Psychology, 88,* 229–241.

Nicholls, J., Cobb, P., Wood, T., Yachel, E., & Patashnick, M. (1990). Assessing student's theories of success in mathematics: Individual and classroom differences. *Journal for Research in Mathematics Education, 21,* 109–122.

Nicholls, J. G., & Miller, A. (1984). Conceptions of ability and achievement motivation. In R. Ames & C. Ames (Eds.), *Research on motivation in education: Vol. 1. Student motivation* (pp. 39–73). New York: Academic Press.

Nieto, S. (2004). *Affirming diversity: The sociopolitical context of multicultural education* (4th ed.). Boston: Allyn & Bacon.

Nissani, M., & Hoefler-Nissani, D. M. (1992). Experimental studies of belief dependence of observations and of resistance to conceptual change. *Cognition and Instruction, 9,* 97–111.

Noddings, N. (1990). Constructivism in mathematics education. In R. Davis, C. Maher, & N. Noddings (Eds.), *Constructivist views on the teaching and learning of mathematics* (pp. 7–18). Monograph 4 of the National Council of Teachers of Mathematics, Reston, VA.

Noddings, N. (1992). *The challenge to care in schools: An alternative approach to education.* New York: Teachers College Press.

Noddings, N. (1995). Teaching themes of care. *Phi Delta Kappan, 76,* 675–679.

Novak, J. D., & Musonda, D. (1991). A twelve-year longitudinal study of science concept learning. *American Educational Research Journal, 28,* 117–154.

Noguera, P. (2005). The racial achievement gap: How can we assume an equity of outcomes. In L. Johnson, M. E. Finn, & R. Lewis (Eds.), *Urban education with an attitude.* Albany, NY: SUNY Press.

Nucci, L. (1987). Synthesis of research on moral development. *Educational Leadership, 44*(5), 86–92.

Nucci, L. P. (2001). *Education in the moral domain.* New York: Cambridge Press.

Nungester, R. J., & Duchastel, P. C. (1982). Testing versus review: Effects on retention. *Journal of Educational Psychology, 74,* 18–22.

Nurmi, J. (2004). Socialization and self-development: Channeling, selection, adjustment, and reflection. In R. Lerner & L. Steinberg (Eds.), *Handbook of adolescent psychology.* New York: Wiley.

Nylund, D. (2000). *Treating Huckleberry Finn: A new narrative approach to working with kids diagnosed ADD/ADHD.* San Francisco: Jossey-Bass.

Oakes, J. (1990). *Multiplying inequities: The effects of race, social class, and tracking on opportunities to learn mathematics and science.* Santa Monica, CA: Rand.

Oakes, J. (1999). Promotion or retention: Which one is social? *Harvard Education Letter, 15*(1), 8.

Oakes, J., & Wells, A. S. (1998). Detracking for high student achievement. *Educational Leadership, 55*(6), 38–41.

Oakes, J., & Wells, A. S. (2002). Detracking for high student achievement. In L. Abbeduto (Ed.), *Taking sides: Clashing views and controversial issues in educational psychology* (2nd ed., pp. 26–30). Guilford, CT: McGraw-Hill Duskin.

O'Boyle, M. W., & Gill, H. S. (1998). On the relevance of research findings in cognitive neuroscience to educational practice. *Educational Psychology Review, 10*, 397–410.

O'Donnell, A. (Ed.). (2002, Winter). Promoting thinking through peer learning [Special issue]. *Theory into Practice, 61*(1).

O'Donnell, A. M., & O'Kelly, J. (1994). Learning from peers: Beyond the rhetoric of positive results. *Educational Psychology Review, 6*, 321–350.

Ogbu, J. (1987). Variability in minority school performance: A problem in search of an explanation. *Anthropology and Education Quarterly, 18*, 312–334.

Ogbu, J. U. (1997). Understanding the school performance of urban blacks: Some essential background knowledge. In H. Walberg, O. Reyes, & R. P. Weissberg (Eds.), *Children and youth: Interdisciplinary perspectives* (pp. 140–190). Norwood, NJ: Ablex.

Ogden, J. E., Brophy, J. E., & Evertson, C. M. (1977, April). *An experimental investigation of organization and management techniques in first-grade reading groups.* Paper presented at the annual meeting of the American Educational Research Association, New York.

Okagaki, L. (2001). Triarchic model of minority children's school achievement. *Educational Psychologist, 36*, 9–20.

O'Leary, K. D. (1980). Pills or skills for hyperactive children? *Journal of Applied Behavior Analysis, 13*, 191–204.

O'Leary, K. D., Kaufman, K. F., Kass, R. E., & Drabman, R. S. (1970). The effects of loud and soft reprimands on the behavior of disruptive students. *Exceptional Children, 37*, 145–155.

O'Leary, K. D., & O'Leary, S. (Eds.). (1977). *Classroom management: The successful use of behavior modification* (2nd ed.). Elmsford, NY: Pergamon.

O'Leary, K. D., & Wilson, G. T. (1987). *Behavior therapy: Application and outcome.* Englewood Cliffs, NJ: Prentice-Hall.

O'Leary, S. (1995). Parental discipline mistakes. *Current Directions in Psychological Science, 4*, 11–13.

O'Leary, S. G., & O'Leary, K. D. (1976). Behavior modification in the schools. In H. Leitenberg (Ed.), *Handbook of behavior modification and behavior therapy.* Englewood Cliffs, NJ: Prentice-Hall.

Ollendick, T. H., Dailey, D., & Shapiro, E. S. (1983). Vicarious reinforcement: Expected and unexpected effects. *Journal of Applied Behavior Analysis, 16*, 485–491.

Olson, D. R. (2004). The triumph of hope over experience in the search for "what works": A response to Slavin. *Educational Researcher, 33*(1), 24–26.

Omi, M., & Winant, H. (1994). *Racial formation in the United States: From the 1960s to the 1990s* (2nd ed.). New York: Routledge.

O'Neil, J. (1990). Link between style, culture proves divisive. *Educational Leadership, 48*, 8.

Onslow, M. (1992). Choosing a treatment program for early stuttering: Issues and future directions. *Journal of Speech and Hearing Research, 35*, 983–993.

Ontario Ministry of Education. (1995). *Consultation to validate: Categories of exceptionalities.* Toronto: Author.

Ontario Ministry of Education & Training. (1997). *Language: The Ontario curriculum, grades 1–8.* Retrieved March 17, 1999, from http://www.edu.gov.on.ca/eng/document/curricul/curr971.html

Ontario Ministry of Education & Training. (1999). *For the love of learning* (Vol. 2). Retrieved March 1999, from http://edu.gov.on.ca/eng/general/absc/rcom/full/volume2/chapter10.html

Orange, C. (2000). *25 biggest mistakes teachers make and how to avoid them.* Thousand Oaks, CA: Corwin.

Orlando L., & Machado, A. (1996). In defense of Piaget's theory: A reply to 10 common criticisms. *Psychological Review, 103*, 143–164.

Ormrod, J. E. (2004). *Human learning* (4th ed.). Columbus, OH: Merrill/Prentice-Hall.

Ormrod, J. E. (1999). *Human learning* (3rd ed.). Upper Saddle River, NJ: Merrill/Prentice-Hall.

Ortony, A., Clore, G. L., & Collins, A. (1988). *The cognitive structure of emotions.* Cambridge, England: Cambridge University Press.

Osborn, A. F. (1963). *Applied imagination* (3rd ed.). New York: Scribner's.

Osborne, J. W. (2001). Testing stereotype threat: Does anxiety explain race and sex differences in achievement? *Contemporary Educational Psychology, 26*, 291–310.

Ovando, C. J. (1989). Language diversity and education. In J. Banks & C. McGee Banks (Eds.), *Multicultural education: Issues and perspectives* (pp. 208–228). Boston: Allyn & Bacon.

Owens, R. (1999). *Language disorders: A functional approach to assessment and intervention* (3rd ed.). Boston: Allyn and Bacon.

Owens, R. E. (1995). *Language disorders* (2nd ed.). Boston: Allyn & Bacon.

Padilla, F. M. (1992). *The gang as an American enterprise.* New Brunswick, NJ: Rutgers University Press.

Page, E. B. (1958). Teacher comments and student performances: A 74-classroom experiment in school motivation. *Journal of Educational Psychology, 49*, 173–181.

Pai, Y., & Adler, S. A. (2001). *Cultural foundations of education* (3rd ed.). Upper Saddle River, NJ: Merrill.

Paivio, A. (1971). *Imagery and verbal processes.* New York: Holt, Rinehart & Winston.

Paivio, A. (1986). *Mental representations: A dual-coding approach.* New York: Oxford University Press.

Pajares, F. (2000, April). *Seeking a culturally attentive educational psychology.* Paper presented at the annual meeting of the American Educational Research Association, New Orleans, LA. Available online at http://www.emory.edu/EDUCATION/mfp.

Pajares, F. (1997). Current directions in self-efficacy research. In M. L. Maehr & P. R. Pintrich (Eds.), *Advances in motivation and achievement* (Vol. 10, pp. 1–49). Greenwich, CT: JAI Press.

Pajares, F., & Schunk, D. H. (2001). Self-beliefs and school success: Self-efficacy, self-concept, and school achievement. In R. Riding & S. Rayner (Eds.), *Perception* (pp. 239–266). London: Ablex Publishing.

Palincsar, A. S. (1996). Language-minority students: Instructional issues in school cultures and classroom social systems. *Elementary School Journal, 96*, 221–226.

Palincsar, A. S. (1998). Social constructivist perspectives on teaching and learning. In J. T. Spence, J. M. Darley, & D. J. Foss (Eds.), *Annual Review of Psychology* (pp. 345–375). Palo Alto, CA: Annual Reviews.

Palincsar, A. S., & Brown, A. L. (1984). Reciprocal teaching of comprehension-fostering and monitoring activities. *Cognition and Instruction, 1*, 117–175.

Palincsar, A. S., & Herrenkohl, L. R. (2002). Designing collaborative learning contexts. *Theory into Practice, 61*, 26–32.

Palincsar, A. S., Magnusson, S. J., Marano, N., Ford, D., & Brown, N. (1998). Designing a community of practice: Principles and practices of the GIsML community. *Teaching and Teacher Education, 14*, 5–19.

Pallas, A. M., & Alexander, K. (1983). Sex differences in quantitative SAT performance: New evidence on the differential coursework hypothesis. *American Educational Research Journal, 20,* 165–182.

Pape, S. J., & Smith, C. (2002). Self-regulating mathematics skills. *Theory into Practice, 41,* 93–101.

Papert, S. (1980). *Mindstorms: Children, computers, and powerful ideas.* New York: Basic Books.

Paris, S. G., & Ayres, L. R. (1994). *Becoming reflective students and teachers with portfolios and authentic assessment.* Washington, DC: American Psychological Association.

Paris, S. G., Byrnes, J. P., & Paris, A. H. (2001). Constructing theories, identities, and actions of self-regulated learners. In B. J. Zimmerman & D. H. Schunk (Eds.), *Self-regulated learning and academic achievement: Theoretical perspectives* (2nd ed., pp. 253–287). Mahwah, NJ: Lawrence Erlbaum.

Paris, S. G., & Cunningham, A. E. (1996). Children becoming students. In D. Berliner & R. Calfee (Eds.), *Handbook of educational psychology* (pp. 117–146). New York: Macmillan.

Paris, S. G., Lipson, M. Y., & Wixson, K. K. (1983). Becoming a strategic reader. *Contemporary Educational Psychology, 8,* 293–316.

Parker, W. C., & Hess, D. (2001). Teaching with and for discussion. *Teaching and Teacher Education, 17,* 273–289.

Parks, C. P. (1995). Gang behavior in the schools: Myth or reality? *Educational Psychology Review, 7,* 41–68.

Pasch, M., Sparks-Langer, G., Gardner, T. G., Starko, A. J., & Moody, C. D. (1991). *Teaching as decision making: Instructional practices for the successful teacher.* New York: Longman.

Pate, P. E., McGinnis, K., & Homestead, E. (1995). Creating coherence through curriculum integration. In M. Harmin (1994), *Inspiring active learning: A handbook for teachers* (pp. 62–70). Alexandria, VA: Association for Supervision and Curriculum Development.

Patterson, C. (1995). Go to http://www.apa.org/pi/parent.html; downloaded 2/7/2005.

Paulman, R. G., & Kennelly, K. J. (1984). Test anxiety and ineffective test taking: Different names, same construct? *Journal of Educational Psychology, 76,* 279–288.

Pelham, W. E. (1981). Attention deficits in hyperactive and learning-disabled children. *Exceptional Education Quarterly, 2,* 13–23.

Pellegrini, A. D., Bartini, M., & Brooks, F. (1999). School bullies, victims, and aggressive victims: Factors relating to group affiliation and victimization in early adolescence. *Journal of Educational Psychology, 91,* 216–224.

Peneul, W. R., & Wertsch, J. V. (1995). Vygotsky and identity formation: A sociocultural approach. *Educational Psychologist, 30,* 83–92.

Peng, S., & Lee, R. (1992, April). *Home variables, parent-child activities, and academic achievement: A study of 1988 eighth graders.* Paper presented at the annual meeting of the American Educational Research Association, San Francisco.

Pepler, D. J., & Sedighdeilami, F. (1998, October). *Aggressive girls in Canada* (Working Paper Series W-98-30E). Hull, QC: Applied Research Branch of Strategic Policy, Human Resources and Development Canada.

Perkins, D., Jay, E., & Tishman, S. (1993). New conceptions of thinking: From ontology to education. *Educational Psychologist, 28,* 67–85.

Perkins, D. N., & Salomon, G. (1989). Are cognitive skills context-bound? *Educational Researcher, 18,* 16–25.

Perner, J. (2000). Memory and theory of mind. In E. Tulving & F. I. M. Craik (Eds.), *The Oxford handbook of memory* (pp. 297–312). New York: Oxford.

Perrone, V. (1994). How to engage students in learning. *Educational Leadership, 51*(5), 11–13.

Perry, N. E. (1998). Young children's self-regulated learning and contexts that support it. *Journal of Educational Psychology, 90,* 715–729.

Perry, N. E., & Drummond, L. (2003). Helping young students become self-regulated researchers and writers. *The Reading Teacher, 56,* 298–310.

Perry, N. E., McNamara, J. K., & Mercer, K. L. (2002). Principles, policies, and practices in special education in British Columbia. *Exceptionality Education Canada.*

Perry, N. E., Phillips, L., & Dowler, J. (2004). Examining features of tasks and their potential to promote self-regulated learning. *Teachers College Record, 106,* 1854–1878.

Perry, N. E., VandeKamp, K. O., & Mercer, L. K. (2000, April). *Investigating teacher-student interactions that foster self-regulated learning.* In N. E. Perry (Chair), Symposium conducted at the meeting of the American Educational Research Association, New Orleans.

Perry, N. E., VandeKamp, K. O., Mercer, L. K., & Nordby, C. J. (2002). Investigating teacher-student interactions that foster self-regulated learning. *Educational Psychologist, 37,* 5–15.

Peterson, J. L., & Newman, R. (2000). Helping to curb youth violence: The APA-MTV "Warning Signs" initiative. *Professional Psychology: Research & Practice, 31,* 509–514.

Peterson, P., Fennema, E., & Carpenter, T. (1989). Using knowledge of how students think about mathematics. *Educational Leadership, 46*(4), 42–46.

Peterson, P. L. (1992). Revising their thinking: Keisha Coleman and her third-grade mathematics class. In H. Marshall (Ed.), *Redefining student learning: Roots of educational change* (pp. 151–176). Norwood, NJ: Ablex.

Peterson, P. L., & Comeaux, M. A. (1989). Assessing the teacher as a reflective professional: New perspectives on teacher evaluation. In A. Woolfolk (Ed.), *Research perspectives on the graduate preparation of teachers* (pp. 132–152). Englewood Cliffs, NJ: Prentice-Hall.

Petrill, S. A., & Wilkerson, B. (2000). Intelligence and achievement: A behavioral genetic perspective. *Educational Psychology Review, 12,* 185–199.

Pettigrew, T. (1998). Intergroup contact theory. In J. T. Spence, J. M. Darley, & D. J. Foss (Eds.), *Annual Review of Psychology* (pp. 65–85). Palo Alto, CA: Annual Reviews.

Pfeffer, C. R. (1981). Developmental issues among children of separation and divorce. In I. Stuart & L. Abt (Eds.), *Children of separation and divorce.* New York: Van Nostrand Reinhold.

Pfiffner, L. J., & O'Leary, S. G. (1987). The efficacy of all positive management as a function of the prior use of negative consequences. *Journal of Applied Behavior Analysis, 20,* 265–271.

Pfiffner, L. J., Rosen, L. A., & O'Leary, S. G. (1985). The efficacy of an all-positive approach to classroom management. *Journal of Applied Behavior Analysis, 18,* 257–261.

Phelan, P., Davidson, A. L., & Cao, H. T. (1992). Speaking up: Students' perspectives on school. *Phi Delta Kappan, 73*(9), 695–704.

Phillips, D. (1997). How, why, what, when, and where: Perspectives on constructivism and education. *Issues in Education: Contributions from Educational Psychology, 3,* 151–194.

Phillips, D., & Zimmerman, M. (1990). The developmental course of perceived competence and incompetence among competent children. In R. Sternberg & J. Kolligian (Eds.), *Competence considered* (pp. 41–66). New Haven, CT: Yale University Press.

Phye, G. D. (1992). Strategic transfer: A tool for academic problem solving. *Educational Psychology Review, 4,* 393–421.

Phye, G. D. (2001). Problem-solving instruction and problem-solving transfer: The correspondence issue. *Journal of Educational Psychology, 93,* 571–578.

Phye, G. D., & Sanders, C. E. (1994). Advice and feedback: Elements of practice for problem solving. *Contemporary Educational Psychology, 17,* 211–223.

Piaget, J. (1954). *The construction of reality in the child* (M. Cook, Trans.). New York: Basic Books.

Piaget, J. (1962). *Comments on Vygotsky's critical remarks concerning "The language and thought of the child" and "Judgment and reasoning in the child."* Cambridge, MA: MIT Press.

Piaget, J. (1963). *Origins of intelligence in children*. New York: Norton.

Piaget, J. (1964). Development and learning. In R. Ripple & V. Rockcastle (Eds.), *Piaget rediscovered* (pp. 7–20). Ithaca, NY: Cornell University Press.

Piaget, J. (1965). *The moral judgment of the child*. New York: Free Press.

Piaget, J. (1965/1995). *Sociological studies*. New York: Routledge. (Original work published in 1965.)

Piaget, J. (1969). *Science of education and the psychology of the child*. New York: Viking.

Piaget, J. (1970a). Piaget's theory. In P. Mussen (Ed.), *Handbook of child psychology* (3rd ed.). New York: Wiley.

Piaget, J. (1970b). *The science of education and the psychology of the child*. New York: Orion Press.

Piaget, J. (1971). *Biology and knowledge*. Edinburgh, UK: Edinburgh Press.

Piaget, J. (1974). *Understanding causality* (D. Miles & M. Miles, Trans.). New York: Norton.

Piaget, J. (1985). *The equilibrium of cognitive structures: The central problem of intellectual development*. (T. Brown & K. L. Thampy, Trans.). Chicago: University of Chicago Press.

Pierson, L. H., & Connell, J. P. (1992). Effect of grade retention on self-system processes, school engagement, and academic performance. *Journal of Educational Psychology, 84*, 300–307.

Pigge, F. L., & Marso, R. N. (1997). A seven year longitudinal multi-factor assessment of teaching concerns development through preparation and early years of teaching, *Teaching and Teacher Education, 13*, 225–235.

Pintrich, P. R. (2000). Educational psychology at the millennium: A look back and a look forward. *Educational Psychologist, 35*, 221–226.

Pintrich, P. R. (2003). A motivational science perspective on the role of student motivation in learning and teaching. *Journal of Educational Psychology, 95*, 667–686.

Pintrich, P. R., Marx, R. W., & Boyle, R. A. (1993). Beyond cold conceptual change: The role of motivational beliefs and classroom contextual factors in the process of conceptual change. *Review of Educational Research, 63*(2), 167–199.

Pintrich, P., & Schrauben, B. (1992). Students' motivational beliefs and their cognitive engagement in academic tasks. In D. Schunk & J. Meece (Eds.), *Students' perceptions in the classroom: Causes and consequences* (pp. 149–183). Hillsdale, NJ: Erlbaum.

Pintrich, P. R., & Schunk, D. H. (1996). *Motivation in education: Theory, research, and applications*. Columbus, OH: Merrill.

Pintrich, P. R., & Schunk, D. H. (2002). *Motivation in education: Theory, research, and applications* (2nd ed.). Upper Saddle River, NJ: Merrill/Prentice-Hall.

Pintrich, P. R., & Zusho, A. (2002). The development of academic self-regulation: The role of cognitive and motivational factors. In A. Wigfield & J. Eccles (Eds.), *Development of achievement motivation* (pp. 249–284). San Diego: Academic Press.

Pisha, B., & Coyne, P. (2001). Smart for the start: The promise of universal design for learning. *Remedial and Special Education, 22*, 197–203.

Pitts, J. M. (1992). Constructivism: Learning rethought. In J. B. Smith & J. C. Coleman, Jr. (Eds.), *School Library Media Annual* (Vol. 10, pp. 14–25). Englewood, CO: Libraries Unlimited.

Plucker, J. A., Beghetto, R. A., & Dow, G. T. (2004). Why isn't creativity more important to educational psychologists? Potential pitfalls and future directions in creativity research. *Educational Psychology, 39*(2), 83–96.

Polson, P. G., & Jeffries, R. (1985). Instruction in general problem-solving skills: An analysis of four approaches. In J. Segal, S. Chipman, & R. Glaser (Eds.), *Thinking and learning skills* (Vol. 1, pp. 417–455). Mahwah, NJ: Erlbaum.

Popham, W. J. (2002). *Classroom assessment: What teachers need to know*. (3rd ed.). Boston: Allyn & Bacon.

Popham, W. J. (2005). *Classroom assessment : What teachers need to know* (4th ed.). Boston, MA: Allyn and Bacon.

Porath, M. (1996). Narrative performance in verbally gifted children. *Journal for the Education of the Gifted, 19*, 276–292.

Porath, M. (1997). A developmental model of artistic giftedness in middle childhood. *Journal for the Education of the Gifted, 20*, 201–223.

Porath, M. (2001). Young girls' social understanding: Emergent interpersonal expertise. *High Ability Studies, 12*, 113–126.

Porath, M. (2003). Social understanding in the first years of school. *Early Childhood Research Quarterly, 18(4)*, 468–484.

Posada, G., Jacobs, A., Richmond, M., Carbonell, O. A., Alzate, G., Bustamante, M. R., & Quiceno, J. (2002). Maternal care giving and infant security in two cultures. *Developmental Psychology, 38*, 67–78.

Posner, M. I. (1973). *Cognition: An introduction*. Glenview, IL: Scott, Foresman.

Prawat, R. S. (1991). The value of ideas: The immersion approach to the development of thinking. *Educational Researcher, 20*, 3–10.

Prawat, R. S. (1992). Teachers beliefs about teaching and learning: A constructivist perspective. *American Journal of Education, 100*, 354–395.

Prawat, R. S. (1996). Constructivism, modern and postmodern. *Issues in Education: Contributions from Educational Psychology, 3*, 215–226.

Premack, D. (1965). Reinforcement theory. In D. Levine (Ed.), *Nebraska symposium on motivation* (Vol. 13). Lincoln, NE: University of Nebraska Press.

Pressley, M. (1986). The relevance of the good strategy user model to the teaching of mathematics. In J. Levin & M. Pressley (Eds.), *Educational Psychologist, 21* [Special issue on learning strategies], 139–161.

Pressley, M. (1991). Comparing Hall (1988) with related research on elaborative mnemonics. *Journal of Educational Psychology, 83*, 165–170.

Pressley, M. (1995). More about the development of self-regulation: Complex, long-term, and thoroughly social. *Educational Psychologist, 30*, 207–212.

Pressley, M. (1996, August). *Getting beyond whole language: Elementary reading instruction that makes sense in light of recent psychological research*. Paper presented at the Annual meeting of the American Psychological Association, Toronto.

Pressley, M. (1998). *Reading instruction that works: The case for balanced teaching*. New York: The Guilford Press.

Pressley, M., Barkowski, J. G., & Schneider, W. (1987). Cognitive strategies: Good strategy users coordinate metacognition and knowledge. In R. Vasta & G. Whitehurst (Eds.), *Annals of Child Development: Vol. 4*. Greenwich, CT: JAI Press.

Pressley, M., Levin, J., & Delaney, H. D. (1982). The mnemonic keyword method. *Review of Research in Education, 52*, 61–91.

Pressley, M., & Roehrig A.D. (2003). Educational psychology in the modern era: 1960 to the present. In B. J. Zimmerman & D. H. Schunk (Eds.), *Educational psychology: A Century of Contributions* (pp. 333–366). Mahwah, NJ: Lawrence Erlbaum.

Pressley, M., & Woloshyn, V. (1995). *Cognitive strategy instruction that really improves children's academic performance*. Cambridge, MA: Brookline Books.

Price, G., & O'Leary, K. D. (1974). *Teaching children to develop high performance standards*. Unpublished manuscript, State University of New York at Stony Brook.

Price, L. F. (2005). The biology of risk taking. *Educational Leadership, 62*(7), 22–27.

Price, W. F., & Crapo, R. H. (2002). *Cross-cultural perspectives in introductory psychology* (4th ed.). Pacific Grove, CA: Wadsworth.

Putnam, R., & Borko, H. (2000). What do new views of knowledge and thinking have to say about research on teacher learning? *Educational Researcher, 29*(1), 4–15.

Putnam, R. T., & Borko, H. (1997). Teacher learning: Implications of new views of cognition. In B. J. Biddle, T. L. Good, & I. F. Goodson (Eds.), *The international handbook of teachers and teaching* (Vol. 2, pp. 1223–1296). Dordrecht, the Netherlands: Kluwer.

Putnam, R. T., & Borko, H. (1998). Teacher learning: Implications of new views of cognition. In B. J. Biddle, T. L. Good, & I. F. Goodson (Eds.), *The international handbook of teachers and teaching.* Dordrecht, the Netherlands: Kluwer.

Puustinen, M., & Pulkkinen, L. (2001). Models of self-regulated learning: A review. *Scandinavian Journal of Educational Research, 45(3),* 269–286.

Pyryt, M. C., & Mendaglio, S. (2004, Fall). Understanding self-concept processes in gifted students. *Keeping in Touch: Canadian Council for Exceptional Children Newsletter,* pp. 7–8.

Rachlin, H. (1991). *Introduction to modern behaviorism* (3rd ed.), New York: W. H. Freeman.

Raffini, J. P. (1996). *150 ways to increase intrinsic motivation in the classroom.* Boston: Allyn & Bacon.

Randhawa, B. S., & Randhawa, J. S. (1993). Understanding differences in the components of mathematics achievement. *Psychological Reports, 73,* 435–444.

Range, L. M. (1993). Suicide prevention: Guidelines for schools. *Educational Psychology Review, 5,* 135–154.

Rathus, S. A. (1988). *Understanding child development.* New York: Holt, Rinehart & Winston.

Raudenbush, S. (1984). Magnitude of teacher expectancy effects on pupil IQ as a function of the credibility of expectancy induction: A synthesis of findings from 18 experiments. *Journal of Educational Psychology, 76,* 85–97.

Raudsepp, E., & Haugh, G. P. (1977). *Creative growth games.* New York: Harcourt Brace Jovanovich.

Recht, D. R., & Leslie, L. (1988). Effect of prior knowledge on good and poor readers' memory of text. *Journal of Educational Psychology, 80,* 16–20.

Reder, L. M. (1996). Different research programs on metacognition: Are the boundaries imaginary? *Learning and Individual Differences, 8,* 383–390.

Redfield, D. L., & Rousseau, E. W. (1981). A meta-analysis of experimental research on teacher questioning behavior. *Review of Educational Research, 51,* 181–193.

Reeve, J. (1996). *Motivating others: Nurturing inner motivational resources.* Boston: Allyn & Bacon.

Reeve, J., Bolt, E., & Cai, Y. (1999). Autonomy-supportive teachers: How they teach and motivate students. *Journal of Educational Psychology, 91,* 537–548.

Reeve, J., Deci, E. L., & Ryan, R. M. (2004). *Self-determination theory: A dialectical framework for understanding the sociocultural influences on motivation and learning: Big theories revisited* (Vol. 4, pp. 31–59). Greenwich, CT: Information Age Press.

Reich, P. A. (1986). *Language development.* Englewood Cliffs, NJ: Prentice-Hall.

Reimann, P., & Chi, M. T. H. (1989). Human expertise In K. J. Gilhooly (Ed.), *Human and machine problem solving* (pp. 161–191). New York: Plenum Press.

Reis, S. M., Kaplan, S. N., Tomlinson, C. A., Westberg, K. L., Callahan, C. M., & Cooper, C. R. (2002). Equal does not mean identical. In L. Abbeduto (Ed.), *Taking sides: Clashing on controversial issues in educational psychology* (pp. 31–35). Guilford, CT: McGraw-Hill/Duskin.

Reisberg, D., & Heuer, F. (1992). Remembering the details of emotional events. In E. Winograd & U. Neisser (Eds.), *Affect and accuracy in recall: Studies of "flashbulb" memories.* Cambridge, England: Cambridge University Press.

Rembolt, C. (1998). Making violence unacceptable. *Educational Leadership, 56(1),* 32–38.

Render, G. F., Padilla, J. N. M., & Krank, H. M. (1989). What research really shows about assertive discipline. *Educational Leadership, 46(6),* 72–75.

Rennie, L. J., & Parker, L. H. (1987). Detecting and accounting for gender differences in mixed-sex and single-sex groupings in science lessons. *Educational Review, 39(1),* 65–73.

Renninger, K. A., Hidi, S., & Krapp, A. (Eds.). (1992). *The role of interest in learning and development.* Hillsdale, NJ: Lawrence Erlbaum.

Renzulli, J. S., & Reis, S. M. (1991). The schoolwide enrichment model: A comprehensive plan for the development of creative productivity. In N. Colangelo & G. Davis (Eds.), *Handbook of gifted education* (pp. 111–141). Boston: Allyn & Bacon.

Renzulli, J. S., & Reis, S. M. (2003). The schoolwide enrichment model: Developing creative and productive giftedness. In N. Colangelo & G. A. Davis (Eds.). *Handbook of gifted education* (pp. 184–203). Boston: Allyn & Bacon.

Renzulli, J. S., & Smith, L. H. (1978). *The Learning Styles Inventory: A measure of student preferences for instructional techniques.* Mansfield Center, CT: Creative Learning Press.

Resnick, L. (1987). Learning in school and out. *Educational Researcher, 16(9),* 13–20.

Resnick, L. B. (1981). Instructional psychology. *Annual Review of Psychology, 32,* 659–704.

Reynolds, A. (1992). Grade retention and school adjustment: An explanatory analysis. *Educational Evaluation and Policy Analysis, 14(2),* 101–121.

Reynolds, M. C., & Birch, J. W. (1988). *Adaptive mainstreaming: A primer for teachers and principals* (3rd ed.). New York: Longman.

Reynolds, W. M. (1980). Self-esteem and classroom behavior in elementary school children. *Psychology in the Schools, 17,* 273–277.

Ricciardelli, L. A. (1992). Bilingualism and cognitive development: Relation to threshold theory. *Journal of Psycholinguistic Research, 21,* 301–316.

Rice, F. P., & Dolgin, K. G. (2002). *The adolescent: Development, relationships, and culture* (10th ed.). Boston: Allyn & Bacon.

Richardson, T. M., & Benbow, C. P. (1990). Long-term effects of acceleration on the social-emotional adjustment of mathematically precocious youths. *Journal of Educational Psychology, 82,* 464–470.

Rideout, V., Roberts, D. F., Foehr, U. G. (2005). *Generation M: Media in the Lives of 8–18 year-olds: Executive Summary.* Kaiser Family Foundation.

Robbins, S. B., Le, L., & Lauver, K. (2005). Promoting successful college outcomes for all students: Reply to Weissberg and Owen (2005). *Psychological Bulletin, 131,* 410–411.

Roberts, D. F., Foehr, U. G., & Ridout, V. (2005, March). *Generation M: Media in the lives of 8–18 year olds.* A Kaiser Foundation Study. Retrieved July 15, 2007, from http://www.kff.org/entmedia/entmedia030905pkg.cfm.

Robinson, A., & Clinkenbeard, P. R. (1998). Giftedness: An exceptionality examined. In J. T. Spence, J. M. Darley, & D. J. Foss (Eds.), *Annual Review of Psychology* (pp. 117–139). Palo Alto, CA: Annual Reviews.

Robinson, D. H. (1998). Graphic organizers as aids to test learning. *Reading Research and Instruction, 37,* 85–105.

Robinson, D. H., & Kiewra, K. A. (1995). Visual argument: Graphic outlines are superior to outlines in improving learning form text. *Journal of Educational Psychology, 87,* 455–467.

Roderick, M. (1994). Grade retention and school dropout: Investigating an association. *American Educational Research Journal, 31,* 729–760.

Rogers, C. R., & Freiberg, H. J. (1994). *Freedom to learn* (3rd ed.). Columbus, OH: Charles E. Merrill.

Rogoff, B. (1990). *Apprenticeship in thinking: Cognitive development in social context.* New York: Oxford University Press.

Rogoff, B. (1995). Observing sociocultural activity on three planes: Participatory appropriation, guided participation, and apprenticeship. In J. Wertsch, P. del Rio, & A. Alverez (Eds.), *Sociocultural studies of mind* (pp. 139–164). Cambridge, England: Cambridge University Press.

Rogoff, B. (1998). Cognition as a collaborative process. In W. Damon (Series Ed.) & D. Kuhn & R. S. Siegler (Vol. Eds.), *Handbook of child psychology: Vol. 2.* (5th ed., pp. 679–744). New York: Wiley.

Rogoff, B. (2003). *The cultural nature of human development.* New York: Oxford University Press.

Rogoff, B., & Chavajay, P. (1995). What's become of the research on the cultural basis of cognitive development? *American Psychologist, 50,* 859–877.

Rogoff, B., & Morelli, G. (1989). Perspectives on children's development from cultural psychology. *American Psychologist, 44,* 343–348.

Rogoff, B., Turkanis, C. G., & Bartlett, L. (2001). *Learning together: Children and adults in a school community.* New York: Oxford.

Rohrkemper, M., & Corno, L. (1988). Success and failure on classroom tasks: Adaptive learning and classroom teaching. *Elementary School Journal, 88,* 297–312.

Roid, G. H. (2003). *Stanford-Binet Intelligence Scales, Fifth Edition.* Itasca, IL: Riverside Publishing.

Rop, C. (1997/1998). Breaking the gender barrier in the physical sciences. *Educational Leadership, 55*(4), 58–60.

Rosch, E. H. (1973). On the internal structure of perceptual and semantic categories. In T. Moore (Ed.), *Cognitive development and the acquisition of language.* New York: Academic Press.

Rose, L. C., & Gallup, A. M. (2001). The 33rd annual Phi Delta Kappa/Gallup Poll of the public's attitude toward the public schools. *Phi Delta Kappan, 83*(1), 41–58.

Rosen, L. A., O'Leary, S. G., Joyce, S. A., Conway, G., & Pfiffner, L. J. (1984). The importance of prudent negative consequences for maintaining the appropriate behavior of hyperactive students. *Journal of Abnormal Child Psychology, 12,* 581–604.

Rosen, N. (2004). Background report and recommendations for setting up adult Michif language classes. Unpublished Technical Report.

Rosenshine, B. (1977, April). *Primary grades instruction and student achievement.* Paper presented at the annual meeting of the American Educational Research Association, New York.

Rosenshine, B. (1979). Content, time, and direct instruction. In P. Peterson & H. Walberg (Eds.), *Research on teaching: Concepts, findings, and implications* (pp. 28–56). Berkeley, CA: McCutchan.

Rosenshine, B. (1986). Synthesis of research on explicit teaching. *Educational Leadership, 43*(7), 60–69.

Rosenshine, B. (1988). Explicit teaching. In D. Berliner & B. Rosenshine (Eds.), *Talks to teachers* (pp. 75–92). New York: Random House.

Rosenshine, B., & Furst, N. (1973). The use of direct observation to study teaching. In R. Travers (Ed.), *Second handbook of research on teaching.* Chicago: Rand McNally.

Rosenshine, B., & Meister, C. (1992, April). *The uses of scaffolds for teaching less structured academic tasks.* Paper presented at the annual meeting of the American Educational Research Association, San Francisco.

Rosenshine, B., & Meister, C. (1994). Reciprocal teaching: A review of the research. *Review of Educational Research, 64,* 479–530.

Rosenshine, B., & Stevens, R. (1986). Teaching functions. In M. Wittrock (Ed.), *Handbook of research on teaching* (3rd ed., pp. 376–391). New York: Macmillan.

Rosenthal, R. (1987). Pygmalion effects: Existence, magnitude and social importance. A reply to Wineburg. *Educational Researcher, 16,* 37–41.

Rosenthal, R. (1995). Critiquing Pygmalion: A 25-year perspective. *Current Directions in Psychological Science, 4,* 171–172.

Rosenthal, R., & Jacobson, L. (1968). *Pygmalion in the classroom.* New York: Holt, Rinehart & Winston.

Roskos, K., & Neuman, S. B. (1993). Descriptive observation of adults' facilitation of literacy in young children's play. *Early Childhood Research Quarterly, 8,* 77–98.

Roskos, K., & Neuman, S. B. (1998). Play as an opportunity for literacy. In O. N. Saracho & B. Spodek (Eds.), *Multiple perspectives on play in early childhood education* (pp. 100–115). Albany: SUNY Press.

Rosser, R. (1994). *Cognitive development: Psychological and biological perspectives.* Boston: Allyn & Bacon.

Roth, W.-M., & Bowen, G. M. (1995). Knowing and interacting: A study of culture, practices, and resources in a grade 8 open-inquiry science guided by an apprenticeship metaphor. *Cognition and Instruction, 13,* 73–128.

Roth, W.-M., & McGinn, M. K. (1997). Toward a new perspective on problem solving. *Canadian Journal of Education, 22,* 18–32.

Roth, W.-M., & Roychoudhury, A. (1993). The development of science process skills in authentic contexts. *Journal of Research on Science Teaching, 30,* 127–152.

Rotherham-Borus, M. J. (1994). Bicultural reference group orientations and adjustment. In M. Bernal & G. Knight (Eds.), *Ethnic identity.* Albany, NY: SUNY Press.

Rowe, M. B. (1974). Wait-time and rewards as instructional variables: Their influence on language, logic, and fate control: Part 1. Wait-time. *Journal of Research in Science Teaching, 11,* 81–94.

Rudolph, K. D., Lambert, S. F., Clark, A. G., & Kurlakowsky, K. D. (2001). Negotiating the transition to middle school: The role of self-regulatory processes. *Child Development, 72,* 926–946.

Rueda, R., & Moll, L. C. (1994) A sociocultural perspective on motivation. In F. O'Neil Jr. & M. Drillings (Eds.), *Motivation: Theory and research (*pp. 117–137). Hillsdale, NJ: Lawrence Erlbaum.

Rumelhart, D., & Ortony, A. (1977). The representation of knowledge in memory. In R. Anderson, R. Spiro, & W. Montague (Eds.), *Schooling and the acquisition of knowledge.* Hillsdale, NJ: Erlbaum.

Ryan, A. (2001). The peer group as a context for development of young adolescents' motivation and achievement. *Child Development, 72,* 1135–1150.

Ryan, R. M., & Deci, E. L. (1996). When paradigms clash: Comments on Cameron and Pierce's claim that rewards do not undermine intrinsic motivation. *Review of Educational Research, 66,* 33–38.

Ryan, R. M., & Deci, E. L. (2000). Intrinsic and extrinsic motivation: Classic definitions and new directions. *Contemporary Educational Psychology, 25,* 54–67.

Ryan, R. M., & Grolnick, W. S. (1986). Origins and pawns in the classroom: Self-report and projective assessments of individual differences in the children's perceptions. *Journal of Personality and Social Psychology, 50,* 550–558.

Ryans, D. G. (1960). *Characteristics of effective teachers, their descriptions, comparisons and appraisal: A research study.* Washington, DC: American Council on Education.

Saarni, C. (2002). *The development of emotional competence.* New York: Guilford.

Sabers, D. S., Cushing, K. S., & Berliner, D. C. (1991). Differences among teachers in a task characterized by simultanity, multidimensionality, and immediacy. *American Educational Research Journal, 28,* 68–87.

Sadker, M., & Sadker, D. (1994). *Failing at fairness: How America's schools cheat girls.* New York: Scribner.

Sadker, M., & Sadker, D. (1995). *Failing at fairness: How America's schools cheat girls.* New York: Touchstone Press.

Sadker, M., & Sadker, D. (2003). Questioning skills. In J. Cooper (Ed.), *Classroom teaching skills* (7th ed., pp. 101–147). Boston: Houghton-Mifflin.

Sadker, M., & Sadker, D. (2006). Questioning skills. In J. Cooper (Ed.), *Classroom teaching skills* (8th ed., pp. 104–150). Boston: Houghton-Mifflin.

Sadker, M., Sadker, D., & Klein, S. (1991). The issue of gender in elementary and secondary education. *Review of Research in Education, 17,* 269–334.

Salomon, G., & Perkins, D. N. (1989). Rocky roads to transfer: Rethinking mechanisms of a neglected phenomenon. *Educational Psychologist, 24,* 113–142.

Sanchez, F., & Anderson, M. L. (1990, May). Gang mediation: A process that works. *Principal, 54–56.*

Sanders, W. L., & Rivers, J. C. (1996). *Cumulative and residual effects of teachers on student academic achievement.* Knoxville, TN: University of Tennessee Value-Added Research and Assessment Center.

Sandrock, J. W. (1996). *Adolescence.* Dubuque, IA: Brown & Benchmark.

Sattler, J. (1992). *Assessment of children* (Rev. 3rd ed.). San Diego: Jerome M. Sattler.

Sattler, J. M. (2001). *Assessment of children: Cognitive applications* (4th ed.). San Diego, CA: Jerome M. Sattler.

Savage, T. V. (1999). *Teaching self-control through management and discipline.* Boston: Allyn & Bacon.

Savin-Williams, R. C., & Diamond, L. M. (2004). Sex. In R. M. Lerner & L. Steinberg (Eds.), *Handbook of adolescent psychology* (2nd ed., pp. 189–231). New York: John Wiley & Sons.

Sawyer, R. J., Graham, S., & Harris, K. R. (1992). Direct teaching, strategy instruction, and strategy instruction with explicit self-regulation: Effects on the composition skills and self-efficacy of learning disabled students. *Journal of Educational Psychology, 84,* 340–352.

Scardamalia, M., & Bereiter, C. (1996). Adaptation and understanding: A case for new cultures of schooling. In S. Vosniado, E. De Corte, R. Glasse, & H. Mandl (Eds.), *International perspectives on the design of technology-supported learning environments* (pp. 149–163). Hillsdale, NJ: Lawrence Erlbaum.

Scarr, S., & Carter-Saltzman, L. (1982). Genetics and intelligence. In R. Sternberg (Ed.), *Handbook of human intelligence.* New York: Cambridge University Press.

Scherer, M. (1993). On savage inequalities: A conversation with Jonathan Kozol. *Educational Leadership, 50*(4), 4–9.

Schiefele, U. (1991). Interest, learning, and motivation. *Educational Psychologist, 26,* 299–324.

Schneider, W., & Bjorklund, D. F. (1992). Expertise, aptitude, and strategic remembering. *Child Development, 63,* 416–473.

Schoenfeld, A. H. (1987). What's all the fuss about metacognition? In A. H. Schoenfeld (Ed.), *Cognitive science and mathematics education* (pp. 189–215). Hillsdale, NJ: Lawrence Erlbaum.

Schoenfeld, A. H. (1989). Teaching mathematical thinking and problem solving. In L. B. Resnick & L. E. Klopfer (Eds.), *Toward the thinking curriculum: Current cognitive research* (pp. 83–103). Alexandria, VA: ASCD.

Schoenfeld, A. H. (1994). *Mathematics thinking and problem solving.* Hillsdale, NJ: Lawrence Erlbaum.

Schofield, J. W. (1991). School desegregation and intergroup relations. *Review of Research in Education, 17,* 235–412.

Schommer, M. (1997). The development of epistemological beliefs among secondary students: A longitudinal study. *Journal of Educational Psychology, 89,* 37–40.

Schommer-Aikins, M. (2002). An evolving theoretical framework for an epistemological belief system. In B. K. Hofer & P. R. Pintrich (Eds.), *Personal epistemology: The psychology of beliefs about knowledge and knowing* (pp. 103–118). Mahwah, NJ: Lawrence Erlbaum.

Schonert-Reichl, K. A. (1994). Gender differences in depressive symptomatology and egocentrism in adolescence. *Journal of Early Adolescence, 14,* 49–65.

Schraw, G., & Lehman, S. (2001). Situational interest: A review of the literature and directions for future research. *Educational Psychology Review, 13,* 23–52.

Schraw, G., & Olafson, L. (2002). Teachers epistemological world views and educational practices. *Issues in Education, 8,* 99–148.

Schunk, D. H. (1987). Peer models and children's behavioral change. *Review of Educational Research, 57,* 149–174.

Schunk, D. H. (1996). *Learning theories: An educational perspective* (2nd ed.). Columbus, OH: Merrill.

Schunk, D. H. (1999). Social-self interaction and achievement behavior. *Educational Psychologist, 34,* 219–227.

Schunk, D. H. (2000). *Learning theories: An educational perspective* (3rd ed.). Columbus, OH: Merrill/Prentice-Hall.

Schunk, D. H. (2004). *Learning theories: An educational perspective* (4th ed.). Columbus, OH: Merrill/Prentice-Hall.

Schunk, D. H., & Hanson, A. R. (1985). Peer models: Influence on children's self-efficacy and achievement. *Journal of Educational Psychology, 77,* 313–322.

Schutz, P. A., & Davis, H. A. (2000). Emotions and self-regulations during test-taking. *Educational Psychologist, 35,* 243–256.

Schwartz, B., & Reisberg, D. (1991). *Learning and memory.* New York: Norton.

Schwartz, B., Wasserman, E. A., & Robbins, S. J. (2002). *Psychology of learning and behavior* (5th ed.). New York: W. W. Norton.

Scott, C. L. (1999). Teachers' biases toward creative children. *Creativity Research Journal, 12,* 321–337.

Seddon, G. M. (1978). The properties of Bloom's taxonomy of educational objectives for the cognitive domain. *Review of Educational Research, 48,* 303–323.

Seiber, J. E., O'Neil, H. F., & Tobias, S. (1977). *Anxiety, learning, and instruction.* Hillsdale, NJ: Erlbaum.

Seligman, M. E. P. (1975). *Helplessness: On depression, development, and death.* San Francisco: Freeman.

Selman, R. L. (1980). *The growth of interpersonal understanding.* New York: Academic Press.

Semb, G. B., & Ellis, J. A. (1994). Knowledge taught in school: What is remembered? *Review of Educational Research, 64,* 253–286.

Serbin, L., & O'Leary, D. (1975, January). How nursery schools teach girls to shut up. *Psychology Today,* pp. 56–58.

Serpell, R. (1993). Interface between sociocultural and psychological aspects of cognition. In E. Forman, N. Minick, & C. A. Stone (Eds.), *Contexts for learning: Sociocultural dynamics in children's development* (pp. 357–368). New York: Oxford University Press.

Shapiro, E. S., & Ager, C. (1992). Assessment of special education students in regular education programs: Linking assessment to instruction. *The Elementary School Journal, 92,* 283–296.

Shapiro, J. (1994). Research perspectives on whole language. In V. Froese (Ed.), *Whole language: Practice and theory* (pp. 433–470). Scarborough, ON: Allyn & Bacon Canada.

Shapka, J.D. & Keating, D.P. (2003). Effects of a girls-only curriculum during adolescence: Performance, persistence, and engagement in mathematics and science. *American Education Research Journal, 40,* 929–960.

Shapka, J. D., & Keating, D. P. (2005). Structure and change in self-concept during adolescence. *Canadian Journal of Behavioural Sciences, 37,* 83–96.

Shavelson, R. J. (1987). Planning. In M. Dunkin (Ed.), *The international encyclopedia of teaching and teacher education* (pp. 483–486). New York: Pergamon Press.

Sheets, R. H. (2005). *Diversity pedagogy: Examining the role of culture in the teaching-learning process.* Boston: Allyn and Bacon.

Shepard, L. A., & Smith, M. L. (1989). Academic and emotional effects of kindergarten retention. In L. Shepard & M. Smith (Eds.), *Flunking grades: Research and policies on retention* (pp. 79–107). Philadelphia: Falmer Press.

Shaywitz, B. A. et al. (2004). Development of left occipitotemporal systems for skilled reading in children after a phonologically-based intervention. *Biological Psychiatry, 55,* 926–933.

Sherman, A. (1994). *Wasting America's future: The Children's Defense Fund report on the costs of child poverty.* Boston: Beacon Press.

Sherman, J. G., Ruskin, R. S., & Semb, G. B. (Eds.). (1982). *The Personalized System of Instruction: 48 seminal papers.* Lawrence, KS: TRI Publications.

Sherman, J. W., & Bessenoff, G. R. (1999). Stereotypes as source-monitoring cues: On the interaction between episodic and semantic memory. *Psychological Science, 10,* 106–110.

Shields, P., Gordon, J., & Dupree, D. (1983). Influence of parent practices upon the reading achievement of good and poor readers. *Journal of Negro Education, 52,* 436–445.

Shuell, T. (1996). Teaching and learning in a classroom context. In D. Berliner & R. Calfee (Eds.), *Handbook of educational psychology* (pp. 726–764). New York: Macmillan.

Shuell, T. J. (1986). Cognitive conceptions of learning. *Review of Educational Research, 56,* 411–436.

Shuell, T. J. (1990). Phases of meaningful learning. *Review of Educational Psychology, 60,* 531–548.

Shulman, L. S. (1987). Knowledge and teaching: Foundations of the new reform. *Harvard Educational Review, 19*(2), 4–14.

Shultz, J., & Florio, S. (1979). Stop and freeze: The negotiation of social and physical space in a kindergarten/first grade classroom. *Anthropology and Education Quarterly, 10,* 166–181.

Siegel, J., & Shaughnessy, M. F. (1994). Educating for understanding: An interview with Howard Gardner. *Phi Delta Kappan, 75,* 536–566.

Siegel, L. S. (1989). IQ is irrelevant to the definition of learning disabilities. *Journal of Learning Disabilities, 22,* 469–479.

Siegel, L. S. (1999). Issues in the definition and diagnosis of learning disabilities. *Journal of Learning Disabilities, 32,* 304–319.

Siegler, R. S. (1993). Adaptive and non-adaptive characteristics of low-income children's mathematical strategy use. In B. Penner (Ed.), *The challenge in mathematics and science education: Psychology's response* (pp. 341–366). Washington, DC: American Psychological Association.

Siegler, R. S. (1998). *Children's thinking* (3rd ed.). Upper Saddle River, NJ: Prentice-Hall.

Siegler, R. S., & Crowley, K. (1991). The microgenetic method: A direct means for studying cognitive development. *American Psychologist, 56,* 606–620.

Sillars, L. (1995). Studying crime in school. *Alberta Report, 22*(25), 37.

Simon, D. P., & Chase, W. G. (1973). Skill in chess. *American Scientist, 61,* 394–403.

Simon, H. A. (1995). The information-processing view of mind. *American Psychologist, 50,* 507–508.

Simonton, D. K. (1999). Creativity from a historiometric perspective. In R. J. Sternberg (Ed.), *Handbook of creativity* (pp. 116–133). New York: Cambridge University Press.

Simonton, D. K. (2000). Creativity: Cognitive, personal, developmental, and social aspects. *American Psychologist, 55,* 151–158.

Simpson, E. J. (1972). The classification of educational objectives in the psychomotor domain. *The Psychomotor Domain, 3.*

Singley, K., & Anderson, J. R. (1989). *The transfer of cognitive skill.* Cambridge, MA: Harvard University Press.

Sisk, D. A. (1988). Children at risk: The identification of the gifted among the minority. *Gifted Education International, 5,* 138–141.

Skiba, R. J., Michael, R. S., Nardo, A. C., & Peterson, R. (2000). *The color of discipline: Sources of racial and gender disproportionality in school punishment* (Report #SRS1). Bloomington, IN: Indiana Education Policy Center.

Skinner, B. F. (1950). Are theories of learning necessary? *Psychological Review, 57,* 193–216.

Skinner, B. F. (1953). *Science and human behavior.* New York: Macmillan.

Skinner, B. F. (1989). The origins of cognitive thought. *American Psychologist, 44,* 13–18.

Skoe, E. E. A. (1998). The ethic of care: Issues in moral development. In E. E. A. Skoe & A. L. von der Lippe (Eds.), *Personality development in adolescence* (pp. 143–171). London: Routledge.

Slaby, R. G., Roedell, W. C., Arezzo, D., & Hendrix, K. (1995). *Early violence prevention.* Washington, DC: National Association for the Education of Young Children.

Slater, L. (2002, February 3). The trouble with self-esteem. *The New York Times Magazine,* pp. 44–47.

Slavin, R. E. (2002). Evidence-based education policies: Transforming education practice and research. *Educational Researcher, 31*(7), 15–21.

Slavin, R. E. (1987). Ability grouping and student achievement in elementary schools: A best-evidence synthesis. *Review of Educational Research, 57,* 293–336.

Slavin, R. E. (1990). Achievement effects of ability grouping in secondary schools: A best-evidence synthesis. *Review of Educational Research, 60,* 471–500.

Slavin, R. E. (1995). *Cooperative learning* (2nd ed.). Boston: Allyn & Bacon.

Sleeter, C. E. (1995). Curriculum controversies in multicultural education. In E. Flaxman & H. Passow (Eds.), *94th yearbook of the national society for the study of education: Part II: Changing populations, changing schools* (pp. 162–185). Chicago: University of Chicago Press.

Smetana, J. G. (2000). Middle-class African American adolescents' and parents' conceptions of parental authority and parenting practices: A longitudinal investigation. *Child Development, 71,* 1672–1686.

Smetana, J. G., & Braeges, J. L. (1990). The development of toddlers' moral and conventional judgments. *Merrill-Palmer Quarterly, 36,* 329–346.

Smith, C. B. (Moderator). (1994). *Whole language: The debate.* Bloomington, IN: EDINFO Press.

Smith, D. D. (1998). *Introduction to special education: Teaching in an age of challenge* (3rd ed.). Boston: Allyn & Bacon.

Smith, F. (1975). *Comprehension and learning: A conceptual framework for teachers.* New York: Holt, Rinehart & Winston.

Smith, J. D., & Caplan, J. (1988). Cultural differences in cognitive style development. *Developmental Psychology, 24,* 46–52.

Smith, J. K., Smith, L. F., & De Lisi, R. (2001). *Natural classroom assessment: Designing seamless instruction and assessment.* Thousand Oaks, CA: Corwin Press.

Smith, M. (1993). Some school-based violence prevention strategies. *NASSP Bulletin, 77*(557), 70–75.

Smith, S. M., Glenberg, A., & Bjork, R. A. (1978). Environmental context and human memory. *Memory and Cognition, 6,* 342–353.

Snider, V. E. (1990). What we know about learning styles from research in special education. *Educational Leadership, 48*(2), 53.

Snow, C. E. (1987). Beyond conversation: Second language learners' acquisition of description and explanation. In J. P. Lantolf & A. Labarca (Eds.), *Research in second language learning: Focus on the classroom* (pp. 3–16). Norwood, NJ: Ablex.

Snow, C. E. (1993). Families as social contexts for literacy development. In C. Daiute (Ed.), *New directions for child development* (No. 61, pp. 11–24). San Francisco: Jossey-Bass.

Snow, R. E. (1995). Pygmalion and intelligence. *Current Directions in Psychological Science, 4,* 169–171.

Snow, R. E., Corno, L., & Jackson, D. (1996). Individual differences in affective and cognitive functions. In D. Berliner & R. Calfee (Eds.), *Handbook of educational psychology* (pp. 243–310). New York: Macmillan.

Snowman, J. (1984). Learning tactics and strategies. In G. Phye & T. Andre (Eds.), *Cognitive instructional psychology.* Orlando, FL: Academic Press.

Soar, R. S., & Soar, R. M. (1979). Emotional climate and management. In P. Peterson & H. Walberg (Eds.), *Research on teaching: Concepts, findings, and implications.* Berkeley, CA: McCutchan.

Sobesky, W. E. (1983). The effects of situational factors on moral judgment. *Child Development, 54,* 575–584.

Sokolove, S., Garrett, J., Sadker, D., & Sadker, M. (1986). Interpersonal communications skills. In J. Cooper (Ed.), *Classroom teaching skills: A handbook.* Lexington, MA: D. C. Heath.

Solomon, D., Battistich, V., Watson, M., Schaps, E., & Lewis, C. (2000). A six-district study of educational change: Direct and mediated effects of the Child Development Project. *Social Psychology of Education, 4,* 3–51.

Solomon, D., Watson, M. S., & Battistich, V. A. (2001). Teaching and schooling effects on moral/prosocial development. In V. Richardson (Ed.), *Handbook of research on teaching* (4th ed., pp. 566–603). Washington, DC: American Educational Research Association.

Soodak, L. C., & McCarthy, M. R. (2006). Classroom management in inclusive settings. In C. M. Evertson & C. S. Weinstein (Eds.), *Handbook of classroom management: Research, practice, and contemporary issues.* Mahwah, NJ: Erlbaum.

Spearman, C. (1927). *The abilities of man: Their nature and measurement.* New York: Macmillan.

Spector, J. E. (1992). Predicting progress in beginning reading: Dynamic assessment of phonemic awareness. *Journal of Educational Psychology, 84,* 353–363.

Spence, J. T., & Buckner, C. E. (2000). Instrumental and expressive traits, trait stereotypes, and sexist attitudes: What do they signify? *Psychology of Women Quarterly, 24,* 44–62.

Spencer, M. B., & Markstrom-Adams, C. (1990). Identity processes among racial and ethnic-minority children in America. *Child Development, 61,* 290–310.

Spencer, M. B., Noll, E., Stoltzfus, J., & Harpalani, V. (2001). Identity and school adjustment: Questioning the "Acting White" assumption. *Educational Psychologist, 36*(1), 21–30.

Spencer, S. J., Steele, C. M., & Quinn, D. M. (1999). Stereotype threat and women's math performance. *Journal of Experimental Social Psychology, 35,* 4–28.

Spinelli, C. G. (2002). *Classroom assessment for students with special needs in inclusive classrooms.* Upper Saddle River, NJ: Merrill/Prentice-Hall.

Spiro, R. J., Feltovich, P. J., Jacobson, M. L., & Coulson, R. L. (1991). Cognitive flexibility, constructivism, and hypertext: Random access instruction for advanced knowledge acquisition in ill-structured domains. *Educational Technology, 31*(5), 24–33.

Sprague, J., & Walker, H. (2000). Early identification and intervention for youth with antisocial and violent behavior. *Exceptional Children, 66,* 367–379.

Sprenger, M. (2005). In side Amy's brain. *Educational Leadership, 62*(7), 28–32.

Stahl, S. A. (2002). Different strokes for different folks? In L. Abbeduto (Ed.), *Taking sides: Clashing on controversial issues in educational psychology* (pp. 98–107). Guilford, CT: McGraw-Hill/Duskin.

Stahl, S. A., & Miller, P. D. (1989). Whole language and language experience approaches for beginning reading: A quantitative research synthesis. *Review of Educational Research, 59,* 87–116.

Stanovich, K. (1993/1994). Romance and reality. *The Reading Teacher, 47,* 280–291.

Stanovich, K. E. (1992). *How to think straight about psychology* (3rd ed.). Glenview, IL: Scott, Foresman.

Stanovich, K. E. (1998). Cognitive neuroscience and educational psychology: What season is it? *Educational Psychology Review, 10,* 419–426.

Stanovich, K. E., West, R. F., & Freeman, D. J. (1984). A longitudinal study of sentence context effects in second-grade children: Tests of an interactive-compensatory model. *Journal of Experimental Child Psychology, 32,* 185–199.

Stanovich, P. J. (1999). Conversations about inclusion. *Teaching Exceptional Children, 31*(6), 54–58.

Stanovich, P. J., & Jordan, A. (1998). Canadian teachers' and principals' beliefs about inclusive education as predictors of effective teaching in heterogeneous classrooms. *Elementary School Journal, 98,* 221–238.

Starch, D., & Elliot, E. C. (1912). Reliability of grading high school work in English. *Scholastic Review, 20,* 442–457.

Starch, D., & Elliot, E. C. (1913a). Reliability of grading work in history. *Scholastic Review, 21,* 676–681.

Starch, D., & Elliot, E. C. (1913b). Reliability of grading work in mathematics. *Scholastic Review, 21,* 254–259.

Starr, R. H., Jr. (1979). Child abuse. *American Psychologist, 34,* 872–878.

Statistics Canada. (1996). Single family households. *Canadian Census.* Retrieved March 1999, from http://www.statcan.ca/People/Families/famil51a.htm

Statistics Canada. (1998a). Average hours per week of television viewing. Retrieved March 1999, from http://www.statcan.ca/english/Pgdb/People/Culture/arts23.htm

Statistics Canada. (1998b). Family violence in Canada: A statistical profile. Retrieved April 5, 2005, from http://www.statcan.ca:80/Daily/English/980528/d980528.htm#ART1

Statistics Canada. (2000, September 28). Divorces: 1998. Retrieved April 5, 2005, from http://www.statcan.ca/Daily/English/000928/d000928b.htm

Statistics Canada. (2001). *Canada's ethnocultural portrait: The changing mosaic.* Retrieved March 2, 2005, from http://www12.statcan.ca/english/census01/products/analytic/companion/etoimm/pdf/96F0030XIE2001008.pdf

Statistics Canada. (2005, March 9). Divorces: 2003. Retrieved July 10, 2007, from http://www.statcan.ca/Daily/English/050309/d050309b.htm

Steele, C. (1992). Race and the schooling of African-Americans. *Atlantic Monthly, 269*(4), 68–78.

Steele, C. M., & Aronson, J. (1995). Stereotype threat and the intellectual test performance of African Americans. *Journal of Personality and Social Psychology, 69,* 797–811.

Stein, B. S., Littlefield, J., Bransford, J. D., & Persampieri, M. (1984). Elaboration and knowledge acquisition. *Memory and Cognition, 12,* 522–529.

Steinberg, L. (1996). *Beyond the classroom: Why schools are failing and what parents need to do.* New York: Simon & Schuster.

Steinberg, L. (1998). Standards outside the classroom. In D. Ravitch (Ed.), *Brookings papers on educational policy* (pp. 319–358). Washington, DC: Brookings Institute.

Steinberg, L. (2005). *Adolescence* (7th ed.). New York: McGraw-Hill.

Stephen, J., Fraser, E., & Marcia, J. E. (1992). Moratorium achievement (Mama) cycles in life span identity development: Vale orientations and reasoning system correlates. *Journal of Adolescence, 15,* 283–300.

Stepien, W., & Gallagher, S. (1993). Problem-based learning: As authentic as it gets. *Educational Leadership, 50*(7), 25–28.

Sternberg, R. (1985). *Beyond IQ: A triarchic theory of human intelligence.* New York: Cambridge University Press.

Sternberg, R. (1990). *Metaphors of mind: Conceptions of the nature of intelligence.* New York: Cambridge University Press.

Sternberg, R., & Davidson, J. (1982, June). The mind of the puzzler. *Psychology Today,* pp. 37–44.

Sternberg, R. J. (1999). *Cognitive psychology* (2nd ed.). Fort Worth, TX: Harcourt Brace.

Sternberg, R. J. (2000). *Handbook of human intelligence.* New York: Cambridge University Press.

Sternberg, R. J. (2002). Raising the achievement of all students: Teaching for successful intelligence. *Educational Psychology Review, 14,* 383–393.

Sternberg, R. J. (2004). Culture and intelligence. *American Psychologist, 59,* 325–338.

Sternberg, R. J., & Detterman, D. L. (Eds.). (1986). *What is intelligence? Contemporary viewpoints on its nature and definition.* Norwood, NJ: Ablex.

Sternberg, R. J., & Kaufman, J. C. (1998). Human abilities. In J. T. Spence, J. M. Darley, & D. J. Foss (Eds.), *Annual Review of Psychology* (pp. 479–502). Palo Alto, CA: Annual Reviews.

Sternberg, R. J., & Wagner, R. K. (1993). The g-ocentric view of intelligence and job performance is wrong. *Current Directions in Psychological Science, 2,* 1–5.

Sternberg, R. J., Wagner, R. K., Williams, W. M., & Horvath, J. A. (1995). Testing common sense. *American Psychologist, 50,* 912–927.

Stevenson, H. W., & Stigler, J. (1992). *The learning gap.* New York: Summit Books.

Stice, E., & Shaw, H. (2004). Eating disorder prevention programs: A meta-analytic review. *Psychological Bulletin, 130,* 206–227.

Stigler, J. W., Lee, S., & Stevenson, H. W. (1987). Mathematics classrooms in Japan, Taiwan, and the United States. *Child Development, 58,* 1272–1285.

Stinson, S. W. (1993). Meaning and value: Reflections on what students say about school. *Journal of Curriculum and Supervision, 8*(3), 216–238.

Stipek, D. J. (1993). *Motivation to learn* (2nd ed.). Boston: Allyn & Bacon.

Stipek, D. J. (1996). Motivation and Instruction. In D. Berliner & R. Calfee (Eds.), *Handbook of educational psychology* (pp. 85–109). New York: Macmillan.

Stipek, D. J. (2002). *Motivation to learn: Integrating theory and practice* (4th ed.). Boston: Allyn & Bacon.

Stodolsky, S. S. (1988). *The subject matters: Classroom activity in math and social studies.* Chicago: University of Chicago Press.

Stormshak, E. A., Bierman, K. L., Bruschi, C., Dodge, K. A., Coie, J. D., et al. (1999). The relation between behavior problems and peer preference in different classrooms. *Child Development, 70,* 169–182.

Stumpf, H. (1995). Gender differences on test of cognitive abilities: Experimental design issues and empirical results. *Learning and Individual Differences, 7,* 275–288.

Sullivan, M. A., & O'Leary, S. G. (1990). Maintenance following reward and cost token programs. *Behavior Therapy, 21,* 139–149.

Sulzby, E., & Teale, W. (1991). Emergent literacy. In R. Barr, M. L. Kamil, P. B. Mosenthal, & P. D. Pearson (Eds.), *Handbook of reading research* (Vol. 2, pp. 727–758). New York: Longman.

Svoboda, J. S. (2001). Review of *Boys and girls learn differently.* The Men's Resource Network. Retrieved May 18, 2002 from http://www.themenscenter.com/mensight/reviews/Svoboda/boysandgirls.htm.

Swanson, H. L. (1990). The influence of metacognitive knowledge and aptitude on problem solving. *Journal of Educational Psychology, 82,* 306–314.

Swanson, H. L., O'Conner, J. E., & Cooney, J. B. (1990). An information processing analysis of expert and novice teachers' problem solving. *American Educational Research Journal, 27,* 533–556.

Sweeney, W. J., Salva, E., Cooper, J. O., & Talbert-Johnson, C. (1993). Using self-evaluation to improve difficult to read handwriting for secondary students. *Journal of Behavioral Education, 3,* 427–443.

Sweller, J., van Merrienboer, J. J. G., & Paas, F. G. W. C. (1998). Cognitive architecture and instructional design. *Educational Psychology Review, 10,* 251–296.

Symons, S., Woloshyn, V., & Pressley, M. (1994). The scientific evaluation of the whole language approach to literacy development [Special issue]. *Educational Psychologist, 29*(4).

Tait, H., & Entwistle, N. J. (1998). Identifying students at risk through ineffective study strategies. *Higher Education.*

Talbot, M. (2002, February 24). Girls just want to be mean. *The New York Times Magazine,* pp. 24–29+.

Taylor, E. (1998). Clinical foundation of hyperactivity research. *Behavioural Brain Research, 94,* 11–24.

TenBrink, T. D. (2006). Assessment. In J. Cooper (Ed.), *Classroom teaching skills* (8th ed., pp. 55–78). Boston: Houghton-Mifflin.

TenBrink, T. D. (2003). Assessment. In J. Cooper (Ed.), *Classroom teaching skills* (7th ed., pp. 311–353). Boston: Houghton-Mifflin.

Tennyson, R. D. (1981, April). *Concept learning effectiveness using prototype and skill development presentation forms.* Paper presented at the annual meeting of the American Educational Research Association, Los Angeles.

Terman, L. M., Baldwin, B. T., & Bronson, E. (1925). Mental and physical traits of a thousand gifted children. In L. M. Terman (Ed.), *Genetic studies of genius* (Vol. 1). Stanford, CA: Stanford University Press.

Terman, L. M., & Oden, M. H. (1947). The gifted child grows up. In L. M. Terman (Ed.), *Genetic studies of genius* (Vol. 4). Stanford, CA: Stanford University Press.

Terman, L. M., & Oden, M. H. (1959). The gifted group in mid-life. In L. M. Terman (Ed.), *Genetic studies of genius* (Vol. 5). Stanford, CA: Stanford University Press.

Tesser, A., Stapel, D. A., & Wood, J. V. (2002). *Self and motivation: Emerging psychological perspectives.* Washington, DC: American Psychological Association.

Tharp, R. G. (1989). Psychocultural variables and constants: Effects on teaching and learning in schools. *American Psychologist, 44,* 349–359.

Tharp, R. G., & Gallimore, R. (1988). *Rousing minds to life: Teaching, learning, and schooling in social context.* New York: Cambridge University Press.

Tharp, R. G., & Gallimore, R. (1991). *The instructional conversation: Teaching and learning in social activity.* Washington, DC: National Center for Research on Cultural Diversity and Second Language Learning.

Theodore, L. A., Bray, M. A., Kehle, T. J., & Jenson, W. R. (2001). Randomization of group contingencies and reinforcers for reduced classroom disruptive behavior. *Journal of School Psychology, 39,* 267–277.

Third International Mathematics and Science Study. (1998). Washington, DC: National Center for Educational Statistics. Retrieved April 5, 2005, from http://nces.ed.gov/timss.

Thomas, E. L., & Robinson, H. A. (1972). *Improving reading in every class: A sourcebook for teachers.* Boston: Allyn & Bacon.

Thompson, R. A., & Wyatt, J. M. (1999). Current research on child maltreatment: Implications for educators. *Educational Psychology Review, 11,* 173–202.

Thorndike, E. L. (1913). Educational psychology. In *The psychology of learning* (Vol. 2). New York: Teachers College, Columbia University.

Thorndike, R., Hagen, E., & Sattler, J. (1986). *The Stanford-Binet Intelligence Scale* (4th ed.). Chicago: Riverside.

Tierney, R. J., Readence, J. E., & Dishner, E. K. (1990). *Reading strategies and practices: A compendium* (3rd ed.). Boston: Allyn & Bacon.

Timmer, S. G., Eccles, J., & O'Brien, K. (1988). How children use time. In F. Juster & F. Stafford (Eds.), *Time, goods, and well-being.* Ann Arbor, MI: Institute for Social Research, University of Michigan.

Tishman, S., Perkins, D., & Jay, E. (1995). *The thinking classroom: Learning and teaching in a culture of thinking.* Boston: Allyn & Bacon.

Tobin, K. (1987). The role of wait time in higher cognitive learning. *Review of Educational Research, 56,* 69–95.

Tochon, F., & Munby, H. (1993). Novice and expert teachers' time epistemology: A wave function from didactics to pedagogy. *Teaching and Teacher Education, 9,* 205–218.

Tollefson, N. (2000). Classroom applications of cognitive theories of motivation. *Education Psychology Review, 12,* 63–83.

Tomasello, M., Kruger, A. C., & Ratner, H. H. (1993). Cultural learning. *Behavioral and Brain Sciences, 16,* 495–552.

Tomlinson, C. A. (2005a). Grading and differentiation: Paradox or good practice? *Theory Into Practice, 44,* 262–269.

Tomlinson, C. A. (2005b, Summer). Differentiating instruction. *Theory Into Practice, 44*(3).

Torrance, E. P. (1972). Predictive validity of the Torrance tests of creative thinking. *Journal of Creative Behavior, 6,* 236–262.

Torrance, E. P. (1986). Teaching creative and gifted learners. In M. Wittrock (Ed.), *Handbook of research on teaching* (3rd ed., pp. 630–647). New York: Macmillan.

Torrance, E. P., & Hall, L. K. (1980). Assessing the future reaches of creative potential. *Journal of Creative Behavior, 14,* 1–19.

Toth, E., Klahr, D., & Chen, Z. (2000). Bridging research and practice: A cognitively based classroom intervention for teaching experimentation to elementary school children. *Cognition and Instruction, 18,* 423–459.

Tremblay, R. E., Boulerice, B., Harden, P. W., McDuff, P., Perusse, D., Pihl, R. O., & Zoccolillo, M. (1996). Do children in Canada become more aggressive as they approach adolescence? In *Growing up in Canada: National Longitudinal Survey of Children and Youth.* Ottawa: Statistics Canada, Human Resources Development.

Tschannen-Moran, M., & Woolfolk Hoy, A. (2001). Teacher efficacy: Capturing an elusive construct. *Teaching and Teacher Education, 17,* 783–805.

Tschannen-Moran, M., Woolfolk Hoy, A., & Hoy, W. K. (1998). Teacher efficacy: Its meaning and measure. *Review of Educational Research, 68,* 202–248.

Turiel, E. (1983). *The development of social knowledge: Morality and convention.* New York: Cambridge University Press.

Turiel, E. (1998). The development of morality. In W. Damon (Series Ed.) & N. Eisenberg (Vol. Ed.), *Handbook of child psychology: Vol. 3. Social, emotional, and personality development* (5th ed., pp. 863–932). New York: Wiley.

Turner, J. C. (1995). The influence of classroom contexts on young children's motivation for literacy. *Reading Research Quarterly, 30,* 410–441.

Turner, J. C. (1997). Starting right: Strategies for engaging young literacy learners. In J. T. Guthrie & A. Wigfield (Eds.), *Reading engagement: Motivating readers through integrated instruction* (pp. 183–204). Newark, DL: International Reading Association.

Turner, J. C., & Paris, S. G. (1995). How literacy tasks influence students' motivation for literacy. *The Reading Teacher, 48,* 662–673.

Uline, C. L., & Johnson, J. F. (2005). Closing the achievement gap: What will it take? Special Issue of *Theory Into Practice, 44*(1), Winter.

Umbreit, J. (1995). Functional analysis of disruptive behavior in an inclusive classroom. *Journal of Early Intervention, 20*(1), 18–29.

Unsworth, N., & Engle, R. W. (2005). Working memory capacity and fluid abilities: Examining the correlation between Operation Span and Raven. *Intelligence, 33,* 67–81.

Urdan, T. C., & Maehr, M. L. (1995). Beyond a two-goal theory of motivation and achievement: A case for social goals. *Review of Educational Research, 65,* 213–243.

Valentine, J. C., DuBois, D. L., & Cooper, H. (2004). The relations between self-beliefs and academic achievement: A systematic review. *Educational Psychologist, 39,* 111–133.

Valenzuela, A. (1999). *Subtractive schooling: U.S.-Mexican youth and the politics of caring.* Albany: SUNY Press.

Valkenburg, P. M., Schouten, A. P., & Peter, J. (2005). Adolescents' identity experiments on the internet. *New Media & Society, 7*(3), 383–402.

Vandervelden, M. C., & Siegel, L. S. (1995). Phonological recoding and phoneme awareness in early literacy: A developmental approach. *Reading Research Quarterly, 30,* 854–875.

Van Houten, R., & Doleys, D. M. (1983). Are social reprimands effective? In S. Axelrod & J. Apsche (Eds.), *The effects of punishment on human behavior.* San Diego: Academic Press.

van Laar, C. (2000). The paradox of low academic achievement but high self-esteem in African American students: An attributional account. *Educational Psychology Review, 12,* 33–61.

Van Matre, J. C., Valentine, J. C., & Cooper, H. (2000). Effect of students' after-school activities on teachers' academic expectations. *Contemporary Educational Psychology, 25,* 167–183.

Van Metter, P., Yokoi, L., & Pressley, M. (1994). College students' theory of note-taking derived from their perceptions of note-taking. *Journal of Educational Psychology, 86,* 323–338.

Veenman, S. (1984). Perceived problems of beginning teachers. *Review of Educational Research, 54,* 143–178.

Veenman, S. (1997). Combination classes revisited. *Educational Research and Evaluation, 65*(4), 319–381.

Vellutino, F. R. (1991). Introduction to three studies on reading acquisition: Convergent findings on theoretical foundations of code-oriented versus whole-language approaches to reading instruction. *Journal of Educational Psychology, 83,* 437–443.

Vera, A. H., & Simon, H. A. (1993). Situated action: A symbolic interpretation. *Cognitive Science, 17,* 7–48.

Vispoel, W. P. (1995). Self-concept in artistic domains: An extension of the Shavelson, Hubmner, and Stanton (1976) model. *Journal of Educational Psychology, 87,* 134–153.

Vispoel, W. P., & Austin, J. R. (1995). Success and failure in junior high school: A critical incident approach to understanding students' attributional beliefs. *American Educational Research Journal, 32,* 377–412.

Volet, S. (1999). Learning across cultures: Appropriateness of knowledge transfer. *International Journal of Educational Research, 31,* 625–643.

von Glaserfeld, E. (1995). A constructivist approach to teaching. In L. Steffe & J. Gale (Eds.), *Constructivism in education* (p. 5). Hillsdale, NJ: Lawrence Erlbaum.

von Glaserfeld, E. (1997). Amplification of a constructivist perspective. *Issues in Education: Contributions from Educational Psychology, 3,* 203–210.

Vroom, V. (1964). *Work and motivation.* New York: Wiley.

Vygotsky, L. S. (1978). *Mind in society: The development of higher mental process.* Cambridge, MA: Harvard University Press.

Vygotsky, L. S. (1986). *Thought and language.* Cambridge, MA: MIT Press.

Vygotsky, L. S. (1987). *Problems of general psychology.* New York: Plenum.

Vygotsky, L. S. (1993). *The collected works of L. S. Vygotsky: Vol. 2.* (J. Knox & C. Stevens, Trans.). New York: Plenum.

Vygotsky, L. S. (1997). *Educational psychology* (R. Silverman, Trans.). Boca Raton, FL: St. Lucie.

Vygotsky, L. S., Rieber, R. W., & Carton, A. S. (1987). *The collected works of L. S. Vygotsky, Vol. 1: Problems of general psychology.* New York, NY: Plenum Press.

Wade, S. E., Schraw, G., Buxton, W. M., & Hayes, M. T. (1993). Seduction of the strategic reader: Effects of interest on strategies and recall. *Reading Research Quarterly, 28,* 3–24.

Wadsworth, B. J. (1978). *Piaget for the classroom teacher.* Oxford, UK: Longman.

Waits, B. K., & Demana, F. (2000). Calculators in mathematics teaching and learning: Past, present, future. In M. J. Burke & F. R. Curcio (Eds.), *Learning mathematics for a new century: NCTM 2000 Yearbook* (pp. 51–66). Reston, VA: National Council of Teachers of Mathematics.

Walberg, H. J. (1984). Improving the productivity of America's schools. *Educational Leadership, 41,* 19–27.

Walberg, H. J. (1990). Productive teaching and instruction: Assessing the knowledge base. *Phi Delta Kappan, 72,* 470–478.

Wald, J. (2001, August 29). The failure of zero tolerance. *Salon Magazine.*

Walker, L. J. (1991). Sex differences in moral reasoning. In W. M. Kurtines & J. L. Gewirtz (Eds.), *Handbook of moral behavior and development* (Vol. 2, pp. 333–362). Hillsdale, NJ: Erlbaum.

Walker, L. J., & Pitts, R. C. (1998). Naturalistic conceptions of moral maturity. *Developmental Psychology, 34,* 403–419.

Walker, L. J., Pitts, R. C., Hennig, K. H., & Matsuba, M. K. (1995). Reasoning about morality and real-life moral problems. In M. Killen & D. Hart (Eds.), *Morality in everyday life: Developmental perspectives* (pp. 371–407). Cambridge, England: Cambridge University Press.

Walker, V. S. (1996). *Their highest potential.* Chapel Hill: University of North Carolina Press.

Walton, G. (1961). *Identification of the intellectually gifted children in the public school kindergarten.* Unpublished doctoral dissertation, University of California, Los Angeles.

Wang, A. Y., & Thomas, M. H. (1995). Effects of keywords on long-term retention: Help or hindrance? *Journal of Educational Psychology, 87,* 468–475.

Wang, A. Y., Thomas, M. H., & Ouellette, J. A. (1992). Keyword mnemonic and retention of second-language vocabulary words. *Journal of Educational Psychology, 84,* 520–528.

Wang, M. C., & Palincsar, A. S. (1989). Teaching students to assume an active role in their learning. In M. Reynolds (Ed.), *Knowledge base for the beginning teacher* (pp. 71–84). New York: Pergamon.

Ward, L. M. (2004). Wading through the stereotypes: Positive and negative associations between media use and Black adolescents' conception of self. *Developmental Psychology, 40,* 284–294.

Wasserman, E. A., & Miller, R. R. (1997). What's elementary about associative learning. In J. T. Spence, J. M. Darley, & D. J. Foss (Eds.), *Annual Review of Psychology* (pp. 573–607). Palo Alto, CA: Annual Reviews.

Waterman, A. S. (1992). Identity as an affect of optimal psychological functioning. In G. Adams, T. Gullota, & R. Montemayoor (Eds.), *Adolescent identity formation.* Newbury Park, CA: Sage.

Waters, H. F. (1993, July 12). Networks under the gun. *Newsweek,* pp. 64–66.

Wayne, A. J., & Youngs, P. (2003). Teacher characteristics and student achievement gains: A review. *Review of Educational Research, 73,* 89–122.

Webb, N. (1985). Verbal interaction and learning in peer-directed groups. *Theory into Practice, 24,* 32–39.

Webb, N. M., Farivar, S. H., & Mastergeorge, A. M. (2002). Productive helping in cooperative groups. *Theory into Practice, 41,* 13–20.

Webb, N., & Palincsar, A. (1996). Group processes in the classroom. In D. C. Berliner & R. C. Calfee (Eds.), *Handbook of educational psychology* (pp. 841–876). New York: Macmillan.

Weiland, A., & Coughlin, R. (1979). Self-identification and preferences: A comparison of White and Mexican-American first- and third-graders. *Journal of Cross-Cultural Psychology, 10,* 356–365.

Weinberg, R. A. (1989). Intelligence and IQ. *American Psychologist, 44,* 98–104.

Weiner, B. (1979). A theory of motivation for some classroom experiences. *Journal of Educational Psychology, 71,* 3–25.

Weiner, B. (1980). The role of affect in rational (attributional) approaches to human motivation. *Educational Researcher, 9,* 4–11.

Weiner, B. (1986). *An attributional theory of motivation and emotion.* New York: Springer.

Weiner, B. (1992). *Human motivation: Metaphors, theories, and research.* Newbury Park, CA: Sage.

Weiner, B. (1994a). Ability versus effort revisited: The moral determinants of achievement evaluation and achievement as a moral system. *Educational Psychologist, 29,* 163–172.

Weiner, B. (1994b). Integrating social and persons theories of achievement striving. *Review of Educational Research, 64,* 557–575.

Weiner, B. (2000). Interpersonal and intrapersonal theories of motivation from an attributional perspective. *Educational Psychology Review, 12,* 1–14.

Weiner, B., & Graham, S. (1989). Understanding the motivational role of affect: Lifespan research from an attributional perspective. *Cognition and Emotion, 4,* 401–419.

Weiner, B., Russell, D., & Lerman, D. (1978). Affective consequences of causal ascriptions. In J. H. Harvey, W. J. Ickes, & R. F. Kidd (Eds.), *New directions in attribution research* (Vol. 2). Hillsdale, NJ: Erlbaum.

Weinert, F. E., & Helmke, A. (1995). Learning from wise mother nature or big brother instructor: The wrong choice as seen from an educational perspective. *Educational Psychologist, 30,* 135–143.

Weinstein, C. E. (1994). Learning strategies and learning to learn. In *Encyclopedia of Education.*

Weinstein, C. S. (1977). Modifying student behavior in an open classroom through changes in the physical design. *American Educational Research Journal, 14,* 249–262.

Weinstein, C. S. (1999). Reflections on best practices and promising programs: Beyond assertive classroom discipline. In H. J. Freiberg (Ed.), *Beyond behaviorism: Changing the classroom management paradigm* (pp. 147–163). Boston: Allyn & Bacon.

Weinstein, C. S. (2003). *Secondary classroom management: Lessons from research and practice* (2nd ed.). New York: McGraw-Hill.

Weinstein, C. S., & Mignano, A. J., Jr. (1997). *Elementary classroom management: Lessons from research and practice* (2nd ed.). New York: McGraw-Hill.

Weinstein, C. S., & Mignano, A. (2003). *Elementary classroom management: Lessons from research and practice* (3rd ed.). New York: McGraw-Hill.

Weinstein, R. S., Madison, S. M., & Kuklinski, M. R. (1995). Raising expectations in schools: Obstacles and opportunities for change. *American Educational Research Journal, 32,* 121–159.

Weisberg, R. W. (1993). *Creativity: Beyond the myth of genius.* New York: W. H. Freemen.

Wellman et al. (2002). Thought bubbles help children with autism acquire an alternative to a theory of mind. *Autism, 6,* 343–363.

Wentzel, K. R. (1997). Student motivation in middle school: The role of perceived pedagogical caring. *Journal of Educational Psychology, 89*(3), 411–419.

Wentzel, K. R. (1999). Social-motivational processes and interpersonal relations: Implications for understanding motivation in school. *Journal of Educational Psychology, 91,* 76–97.

Wentzel, K. R., Barry, C. M., & Caldwell, K. A. (2004). Friendships in middle school: Influences on motivation and school adjustment. *Journal of Educational Psychology, 96,* 195–203.

Wertsch, J., & Tulviste, P. (1992). L. S. Vygotsky and contemporary developmental psychology. *Developmental Psychology, 28,* 548–557.

Wertsch, J. V. (1991). *Voices of the mind: A sociocultural approach to mediated action.* Cambridge, MA: Harvard University Press.

Wessells, M. G. (1982). *Cognitive psychology.* New York: Harper & Row.

Westberg, K. L., Archambault, F. X., Dobyns, S. M., & Slavin, T. J. (1993). The classroom practices observation study. *Journal of the Education of the Gifted, 16*(2), 120–146.

Wharton-McDonald, R., Pressley, M., & Mistretta, J. (1996). *Outstanding literacy instruction in first grade: Teacher practices and student achievement.* Albany, NY: National Reading Research Center.

Wharton-McDonald, R., Pressley, M., Rankin, J., Mistretta, J., Yokoi, L., & Ettenberger, S. (1997). Effective primary-grades literacy instruction = Balanced literacy instruction. *The Reading Teacher, 50,* 518–521.

Wheatley, K. F. (2002). The potential benefits of teacher efficacy doubts for educational reform. *Teaching and Teacher Education, 18,* 5–22.

Whitaker, S. D. (2000). Mentoring beginning special education teachers and the relationship to attrition. *Exceptional Children, 66,* 546–566.

White, K. R. (1982). The relation between socioeconomic status and academic achievement. *Psychological Bulletin, 91*(3), 461–481.

White, S., & Tharp, R. G. (1988, April). *Questioning and wait-time: A cross cultural analysis.* Paper presented at the annual meeting of the American Educational Research Association, New Orleans.

Whitehead, A. N. (1929). *The aims of education.* New York: Macmillan.

Whitehurst, G. J., Epstein, J. N., Angell, A. L., Payne, A. C., Crone, D. A., & Fischel, J. E. (1994). Outcomes of an emergent literacy program in headstart. *Journal of Educational Psychology, 86,* 542–555.

Wigfield, A., & Eccles, J. (1989). Test anxiety in elementary and secondary school students. *Educational Psychologist, 24,* 159–183.

Wigfield, A., & Eccles, J. (1992). The development of achievement task values: A theoretical analysis. *Developmental Review, 12*(3), 265–310.

Wigfield, A., & Eccles, J. S. (2000). Expectancy-value theory of achievement motivation. *Contemporary Educational Psychology, 25,* 68–81.

Wigfield, A., & Eccles, J. S. (2002a). Students' motivation during the middle school years. In J. Aronson (Ed.), *Improving academic development: Impact of psychological factors in education* (pp. 159–184). San Diego, CA: Academic Press.

Wigfield, A., & Eccles, J. (2002b). The development of competence beliefs, expectancies of success, and achievement values from childhood through adolescence. In A. Wigfield & J. Eccles (Eds.), *Development of achievement motivation* (pp. 91–120). San Diego: Academic Press.

Wigfield, A., Eccles, J., MacIver, D., Rueman, D., & Midgley, C. (1991). Transitions at early adolescence: Changes in children's domain-specific self-perceptions and general self-esteem across the transition to junior high school. *Developmental Psychology, 27,* 552–565.

Wigfield, A., Eccles, J. S., & Pintrich, P. R. (1996). Development between the ages of 11 and 25. In D. Berliner & R. Calfee (Eds.), *Handbook of educational psychology* (pp. 148–185). New York: Macmillan.

Wiggins, G. (1989). Teaching to the authentic test. *Educational Leadership, 46*(7), 41–47.

Wiggins, G. (1991). Standards, not standardization: Evoking quality student work. *Educational Leadership, 48*(5), 18–25.

Wiggins, G. (1993). Assessment, authenticity, context, and validity. *Phi Delta Kappan, 75,* 200–214.

Wiig, E. H. (1982). Communication disorders. In H. Haring (Ed.), *Exceptional children and youth.* Columbus, OH: Charles E. Merrill.

Wilgenbusch, T., & Merrell, K. W. (1999). Gender differences in self-concept among children and adolescents: A meta-analysis of multidimensional studies. *School Psychology Quarterly, 14,* 101–120.

Wilkins, W. E., & Glock, M. D. (1973). *Teacher expectations and student achievement: A replication and extension.* Ithaca, NY: Cornell University Press.

Willerman, L. (1979). *The psychology of individual and group differences.* San Francisco: Freeman.

Williams, C., & Bybee, J. (1994). What do children feel guilty about? Developmental and gender differences. *Developmental Psychology, 30,* 617–623.

Williams, G. C., Wiener, M. W., Markakis, K. M., Reeve, J., & Deci, E. L. (1993). Medical student motivation for internal medicine. *Annals of Internal Medicine.*

Williams, J. (2002). Using the Theme Scheme to improve story comprehension. In C. C. Block & M. Pressley (Eds.), *Comprehension instruction: Research-based best practices* (pp. 126–139). New York: Guilford.

Williams, W., Blythe, T., White, N., Li, J., Sternberg, R., & Gardner, H. (1996). *Practical intelligence in school.* New York: HarperCollins.

Willis, P. (1977). *Learning to labor.* Lexington, MA: D. C. Heath.

Willoughby, T., Porter, L., Belsito, L., & Yearsley, T. (1999). Use of elaboration strategies by grades two, four, and six. *Elementary School Journal, 99,* 221–231.

Wilson, C. W., & Hopkins, B. L. (1973). The effects of contingent music on the intensity of noise in junior high home economics classes. *Journal of Applied Behavior Analysis, 6,* 269–275.

Wilson, M. (2001). The case for sensorimotor coding in working memory. *Psychonomic Bulletin and Review, 8,* 44–57.

Windschitl, M. (2002). Framing constructivism in practice as the negotiation of dilemmas; An analysis of the conceptual, pedagogical, cultural, and political challenges facing teachers. *Review of Educational Research, 72,* 131–175.

Winett, R. A., & Winkler, R. C. (1972). Current behavior modification in the classroom: Be still, be quiet, be docile. *Journal of Applied Behavior Analysis, 15,* 499–504.

Wingate, N. (1986). Sexism in the classroom. *Equity and Excellence, 22,* 105–110.

Wink, J., & Putney, L. (2002). *A vision of Vygotsky.* Boston: Allyn & Bacon.

Winne, P. H. (1979). Experiments relating teachers' use of higher cognitive questions to student achievement. *Review of Educational Research, 49,* 3–50.

Winne, P. H. (1995). Inherent details in self-regulated learning. *Educational Psychologist, 30,* 173–188.

Winne, P. H. (1997). Experimenting to bootstrap self-regulated learning. *Journal of Educational Psychology, 89,* 397–410.

Winne, P. H. (2001). Self-regulated learning viewed from models of information processing. In B. J. Zimmerman & D. H. Schunk (Eds.), *Self-regulated learning and academic achievement: Theoretical perspectives* (2nd ed., pp. 153–189). Mahwah, NJ: Lawrence Erlbaum.

Winne, P. H., & Hadwin, A. F. (1998). Studying as self-regulated learning. In D. J. Hacker, J. Dunlosky, & A. C. Graesser (Eds.), *Metacognition in educational theory and practice* (pp. 277–304). Mahwah, NJ: Lawrence Erlbaum.

Winne, P. H., & Marx, R. W. (1989). A cognitive processing analysis of motivation within classroom tasks. In C. Ames & R. Ames (Eds.), *Research on motivation in education* (Vol. 3, pp. 223–257). Orlando, FL: Academic Press.

Winne, P. H., & Perry, N. E. (1994). Educational psychology. In V. Ramachandran (Ed.), *Encyclopedia of human behavior* (Vol. 2, pp. 213–223). San Diego, CA: Academic Press.

Winne, P. H. & Perry, N. E. (2000). Measuring self-regulated learning. In P. Pintrich, M. Boekaerts, & M. Zeidner (Eds.), *Handbook of self-regulation* (pp. 531–566). Orlando, FL: Academic Press.

Winner, E. (2000). The origins and ends of giftedness. *American Psychologist, 55,* 159–169.

Winsler, A., Carlton, M. P., & Barry, M. J. (2000). Age-related changes in preschool children's systematic use of private speech in a natural setting. *Journal of Child Language, 27,* 665–687.

Winsler, A., & Naglieri, J. A. (2003). Overt and covert verbal problem-solving strategies: Developmental trends in use, awareness, and relations with task performance in children age 5 to 17. *Child Development, 74,* 659–678.

Winzer, M. A. (1999). *Children with exceptionalities in Canadian classrooms* (5th ed.). Scarborough, ON: Prentice-Hall.

Winzer, M. A. (2006). *Children with exceptionalities in Canadian classrooms* (6th ed.). Toronto, ON: Prentice-Hall.

Winzer, M. A., & Mazurek, K. (1998). *Special education in multicultural contexts.* Columbus, OH: Merrill.

Witkin, H. A., Moore, C. A., Goodenough, D. R., & Cox, R. W. (1977). Field-dependent and field-independent cognitive styles and their educational implications. *Review of Educational Research, 47,* 1–64.

Wittrock, M. (Ed.). (1986). *Handbook of research on teaching* (3rd ed.). New York: Macmillan.

Wittrock, M. C. (1978). The cognitive movement in instruction. *Educational Psychologist, 13,* 15–30.

Wittrock, M. C. (1982, March). *Educational implications of recent research on learning and memory.* Paper presented at the annual meeting of the American Educational Research Association, New York.

Wittrock, M. C. (1992). An empowering conception of educational psychology. *Educational Psychologist, 27,* 129–142.

Wolf, D., Bixby, J., Glenn, J., III, & Gardner, H. (1991). To use their minds well: New forms of student assessment. *Review of Research in Education, 17,* 31–74.

Wolters, C. A., Yu, S. L., & Pintrich, P. R. (1996). The relation between goal orientation and students' motivational beliefs and self-regulated learning. *Learning and Individual Differences, 8,* 211–238.

Wong, B. Y. L. (1996). *The ABCs of learning disabilities.* San Diego, CA: Academic Press.

Wong, B. Y. L., Harris, K. R., Graham, S., & Butler, D. L. (2003). Cognitive strategies instruction research in learning disabilities. In H. L. Swanson, K. R. Harris, & S. Graham (Eds.), *Handbook of learning disabilities* (pp. 383–402). New York: Guilford Press.

Wong, L. (1987). Reaction to research findings: Is the feeling of obviousness warranted? *Dissertation Abstracts International, 48/12,* 3709B (University Microfilms #DA 8801059).

Wood, D., Bruner, J., & Ross, S. (1976). The role of tutoring in problem solving. *British Journal of Psychology, 66,* 181–191.

Wood, E. R. G., & Wood, S. E. (1999). *The world of psychology.* Boston: Allyn & Bacon.

Wood, S. E., Wood, E. G., & Boyd, D. (2005). *The world of psychology* (5th ed.). Boston: Allyn & Bacon.

Woods, B. S., & Murphy, P. K. (2002). Thickening the discussion: What can William James tell us about constructivism? *Educational Theory, 52,* 443–449.

Woolfolk, A. E., & Brooks, D. (1983). Nonverbal communication in teaching. In E. Gordon (Ed.), *Review of research in education* (Vol. 10, pp. 103–150). Washington, DC: American Educational Research Association.

Woolfolk, A. E., & Brooks, D. (1985). The influence of teachers' nonverbal behaviors on students' perceptions and performance. *Elementary School Journal, 85,* 514–528.

Woolfolk, A. E., & Hoy, W. K. (1990). Prospective teachers' sense of efficacy and beliefs about control. *Journal of Educational Psychology, 82,* 81–91.

Woolfolk, A. E., Rosoff, B., & Hoy, W. K. (1990). Teachers' sense of efficacy and their beliefs about managing students. *Teaching and Teacher Education, 6,* 137–148.

Woolfolk, A. E., & Woolfolk, R. L. (1974). A contingency management technique for increasing student attention in a small group. *Journal of School Psychology, 12,* 204–212.

Woolfolk Hoy, A., & Burke-Spero, R. (2005). Changes in teacher efficacy during the early years of teaching: A comparison of four measures. *Teaching and Teacher Education, 21,* 343–356.

Woolfolk Hoy, A., & Murphy, P. K. (2001). Teaching educational psychology to the implicit mind. In R. Sternberg & B. Torff (Eds.), *Understanding and teaching the implicit mind* (pp. 145–185). Mahwah, NJ: Lawrence Erlbaum.

Woolfolk Hoy, A., Pape, S., & Davis, H. (2006). Teachers' knowledge, beliefs, and thinking. In P. A. Alexander & P. H, Winne (Eds.), *Handbook of educational psychology* (2nd ed.). Mahwah, NJ: Lawrence Erlbaum.

Woolfolk Hoy, A., & Tschannen-Moran, M. (1999). Implications of cognitive approaches to peer learning for teacher education. In A. O'Donnell & A. King (Eds.), *Cognitive perspectives on peer learning* (pp. 257–284). Mahwah, NJ: Erlbaum.

Woolfolk Hoy, A., & Weinstein, C. S. (2006). Students' and teachers' perspectives about classroom management. In C. Evertson & C. S. Weinstein (Eds.), *Handbook for classroom management: Research, practice, and contemporary issues.* Mahwah, NJ: Lawrence Erlbaum.

Wright, S. C., & Taylor, D. M. (1995). Identity and the language of the classroom: Investigating the impact of heritage versus second language instruction on personal and collective self-esteem. *Journal of Educational Psychology, 87,* 241–252.

Wyler, R. S. (1988). Social memory and social judgment. In P. Solomon, G. Goethals, C. Kelly, & B. Stephans (Eds.), *Perspectives on memory research.* New York: Springer-Verlag.

Yarhouse, M. A. (2001). Sexual identity development: The influence of valuative frameworks on identity synthesis. *Psychotherapy, 38* (3), 331–341

Ybarra, M. L., & Mitchell, K. J. (2004). Youth engaging in online harassment: associations with caregiver-child relationships, Internet use, and personal characteristics. *Journal of Adolescence, 27,* 319–336.

Yee, A. H. (1992). Asians as stereotypes and students: Misperceptions that persist. *Educational Psychology Review, 4,* 95–132.

Yeung, A. S., McInerney, D. M., Russell-Bowie, D., Suliman, R., Chui, H., & Lau, I. C. (2000). Where is the hierarchy of academic self-concept? *Journal of Educational Psychology, 92,* 556–567.

Yerkes, R. M., & Dodson, J. D. (1908). The relation of strength of stimulus to rapidity of habit formation. *Journal of Comparative Neurology, 18,* 459–482.

Young, A. J. (1997). I think, therefore I'm motivated: The relations among cognitive strategy use, motivational orientation, and classroom perceptions over time. *Learning and Individual Differences, 9,* 249–283.

Zeidner, M. (1995). Adaptive coping with test situations. *Educational Psychologist, 30,* 123–134.

Zeidner, M. (1998). *Test anxiety: The state of the art.* New York: Plenum.

Zelli, A., Dodge, K. A., Lochman, J. E., & Laird, R. D. (1999). The distinction between beliefs legitimizing aggression and deviant processing of social cues: Testing measurement validity and the hypothesis that biased processing mediates the effects of beliefs on aggression. *Journal of Personality and Social Psychology, 77,* 150–166.

Zentall, S. S. (1993). Research on the educational implications of attention deficit hyperactivity disorder. *Exceptional Children, 60,* 143–153.

Zimmerman, B. J. (1990). Self-regulated learning and academic achievement: An overview. *Educational Psychologist, 21,* 3–18.

Zimmerman. B. J. (1995). Self-efficacy and educational development. In A. Bandura (Ed.), *Self-efficacy in changing societies* (pp. 202–231). New York: Cambridge University Press.

Zimmerman, B. J. (2002). Becoming a self-regulated learner: An overview. *Theory Into Practice, 41,* 64–70.

Zimmerman, B. J., & Schunk, D. H. (Eds.). (1989). *Self-regulated learning and academic achievement: Theory, research, and practice.* New York: Springer-Verlag.

Zimmerman, B. J., & Schunk, D. H. (Eds.). (2001). *Self-regulated learning and academic achievement: Theoretical perspectives* (2nd ed.). Mahwah, NJ: Lawrence Erlbaum.

Zimmerman, B. J., & Schunk, D. H. (Eds). (2003). *Educational psychology: A century of contributions* [A Project of Division 15 (Educational Psychology) of the American Psychological Association]. Mahwah, NJ: Erlbaum.

Zimmerman, D. W. (1981). On the perennial argument about grading "on the curve" in college courses. *Educational Psychologist, 16,* 175–178.

Name Index

Subject Index

in preschool years, 66
supporting, 399
autonomy versus shame and doubt, 66
availability heuristic, 300
aversive situation, 206–207

B

basic skills, teaching of, 471
behaviour-content matrix, 509–510
behaviour, coping with undesirable,
216–217
see also punishment
cautions, 217
negative reinforcement, 216
reprimands, 217
response cost, 217
satiation, 216–217
social isolation, 217
behaviour encouragement methods,
212–214
guidelines, 215
positive practice, 214
Premack Principle, 212–214
reinforcing with teacher attention,
212
shaping, 214
behaviour modification. *See* applied
behavioural analysis
behavioural and emotional disorders,
134–138
defined, 134–135
drug abuse, 137–138
suicide, 136–137
teaching, 135–136
behavioural approaches to motivation,
374–375
behavioural approaches to teaching and
management, 221–223
contingency contract programs, 222
group consequences, 221–222
importance of, 221
for learning and behaviour problems,
224
token reinforcement programs, 223
behavioural objectives, 465
behavioural views of learning, 201, 365
see also applied behavioural analysis;
observational learning; operant
conditioning; self-management
classical conditioning, 203–204
cognitive behaviour modification,
232
versus cognitive view, 245
contiguity, 203
criticisms of, 233–235
diversity and convergence, 236–237
ethical issues, 235
being needs, 375
belief perseverance, 300
beliefs and self-schemas, 390–396
about ability, 390
about causes and control, 390–392
lessons for teachers, 394
motivation to learn in school,
395–396
about self-efficacy and learned helplessness, 392–393
about self-worth, 393–394
"best works" portfolios, 521, 522

between-class ability grouping,
117–118
bias
see also stereotype(s)
assessment bias, 506
in performance assessments, 526
"Big-Fish-Little-Pond Effect (BFLP)",
84
bilingual education
ideas for promoting, 186
research on bilingual programs, 185
bilingualism, 51–53, 182–185
becoming bilingual, 182–183
demographics and, 182
education, 184–185, 186
meaning of, 182
myths about bilingual students, 183
recognizing gifted bilingual students,
183–184
Bill C-37, 76
"Bill of Rights" for students and teachers, 427
bioecological model. *See* Bronfenbrenner's bioecological model
blended families, 71
Bloom's taxonomies, 466–468
affective domain, 467
cognitive domain, 466–467
psychomotor domain, 468
bottom-up processing, 248
Boys and Girls Learn Differently (Gurian
and Henley), 181
brain
and intelligence, 108
structure of, 22–23
brain development, 23–26
see also Piaget's theory of cognitive
development
of adolescents, 64
adverse factors of, 24
cerebral cortex, 24–25
implications for teachers, 26
and information-processing skills,
36
instruction and, 26
neurons, 23–24
overview of, 22–23
specialization and integration, 25
and stage model of development, 38
brain hemispheres, 25
brain injury, 139
brainstorming, 307–309
Bronfenbrenner's bioecological model,
described, 70–71
see also families and individual development; peers; teachers and individual development
Brown v. Topeka Board of Education,
169
Bruner's discovery learning. *See* discovery
learning
bulimia, 63
bullying, 76–77
cyberbullying, 78

C

calculators, use of, 298
Canada
bilingualism, 182

bullying, 76
child abuse, 80
children's television viewing statistics,
76
commitment of teachers, 16
cultural diversity of, 159, 160–161,
166
discrimination, 172
divorce rate, 71
multiple languages among immigrants, 51
poverty rates, 162
substance abuse among youth, 138
suicide rates, 137
victim statistics, 77
visually impaired students, 141
*Canadian Charter of Rights and Free-
doms*, 144, 159
Canadian *Criminal Code*, 76
Canadian Human Rights Act, 159
Canadian Multiculturalism Act, 159
CAPS strategy, 315
caring relationships, 438
case study, 10
Catcher in the Rye (Salinger), 313
causation, 11
cause and effect, 11
central executive, 251
cerebellum, 23
cerebral cortex, 23, 24–25
cerebral palsy, 139, 140
chain mnemonics, 268
cheating, 99
child abuse, 80–81
indicators of, 81
safety on the internet, 80
*Child, Family, and Community Service
Act* (British Columbia), 81
Childhood and Society (Erikson), 64
children
see also elementary school years;
peers; middle school years; preschool years
cognitive tools of, 38
developmental differences of working
memory, 272–273
effect of divorce on, 71
media and, 75–76
parenting styles and, 73
private self-talk, 42–44
and self-concept, 82
chronic health impairments, 139, 140
chunking, 254
class inclusion, 45
classical conditioning, 203–205
classification, 31–32
classroom(s)
see also culturally inclusive classrooms; gender in the classroom;
learning communities; learning
environments; multicultural classrooms
attributions in, 392
creativity in, 307–309
moral versus conventional domains,
96–97
self-determination in, 378
self-regulated learning example,
338–339

classroom community, 433–434
classroom management, 9, 419–421
    see also learning communities; learn-
      ing environments; learning spaces
classroom supports
    for Asperger students, 143
    for exceptional learning needs,
      146–148
    for students with behaviour disorders,
      135–136
    for visually impaired students, 142
Cmap, 313–314
co-construction of mental processes, 40
cognition
    and anxiety, 387
    creativity and, 306
    and culture, 345
cognitive and social approaches to moti-
    vation, 376
cognitive and social constructivism,
    342–349, 365
    see also constructivist approaches to
      learning
    common elements of, 347–349
    construction of knowledge, 346
    constructivist views of learning,
      343–346
    knowledge: situated versus general,
      347
    overview of, 342–343
cognitive apprenticeships, 356–358
cognitive behaviour modification, 232
cognitive development
    see also brain development; Piaget's
      theory of cognitive development;
      Vygotsky's sociocultural theory
    acceleration of, 48
    the brain and, 22–23
    culture and, 37–38
    defined, 22
    microgenetic studies, 12
cognitive domain (in Bloom's taxonomy),
    466–467
    classroom questions for objectives in,
      478
cognitive evaluation theory, 378
cognitive objectives, 465
Cognitive Research Trust(CoRT), 360
cognitive stage (of learning an automated
    skill), 271
Cognitive Strategies Model, 265
cognitive views of learning, 201, 365
    see also complex cognitive processes;
      information processing model of
      memory; metacognition
    background of, 245
    versus behavioural views, 245
    connecting with families, 274, 276
    importance of knowledge in learning,
      246
collaboration in self-regulated learning,
    341–342, 491–492
collaborative consultation, 147–148
collaborative learning, 47
collective monologue, 31
collective self-esteem, 88–90
collectivist societies, 187
Columbine school shooting, 441
communication disorders, 132–133

language disorders, 133
    speech impairments, 132
communication (teacher-student),
    442–446
    see also violence
    confrontation and assertive discipline,
      444–446
    diagnosing ownership of problem,
      443
    empathetic listening, 444
    miscommunication of messages,
      442–443
community of practice, 347
comparative organizers, 289
compensation (principle), 31
complex cognitive processes
    see also concept learning and teach-
      ing; creativity; learning strategies;
      problem solving
    diversity and convergences in,
      322–323
complex learning environments, 348
complex tasks, 340, 348, 490
components of information processing,
    112–113
computer-managed instruction, 419
computer use
    management issues, 432
    managing a lab, 431
    planning for, 428–429
concept, 283
concept learning and teaching,
    283–290
    concept, 283
      through discovery, 287–288, 289
    diversity and convergences,
      322–323
      through exposition, 288–290,
      291
    learning disabilities and, 290
    strategies for teaching, 284–287
    views of concept learning, 283–284
concept mapping, 287
concept teaching strategies, 284–287
    example concept-attainment lesson,
      284
    extending and connecting concepts,
      286–287
    lesson components, 285
    lesson structure, 285–286
    stages of teaching, 286
conceptual change teaching in science,
    486–489
concrete-operation, 31
concrete-operational stage of cognitive
    development, 31–33, 34
conditional knowledge, 269–271
    automated basic skills and, 271
    defined, 256, 264
    domain-specific strategies and, 271
    teaching of, 310
conditioned response (CR), 204
conditioned stimulus (CS), 204
conduct disorders. *See* behavioural and
    emotional disorders
confidence interval, 504–505
confirmation bias, 300
conflict

confrontation and negotiations,
    445–446
    and learning, 434
    resolution, between teacher and stu-
      dent, 445–446
consequences of behaviour, 205–209
    defined, 205
    extinction, 209–214
    punishment, 207
    reinforcement, 206–207
    reinforcement schedules, 208–209
    rules and procedures and, 425, 426
conservation, 30–31
    among cultures, 48
    solving, 31
Consistency Management program,
    448
constructionism, 345–346
constructivism. *See* cognitive and social
    constructivism
constructivist approaches to learning,
    350–363
    see also cooperative learning
    apprenticeships in thinking,
      358–360
    cognitive apprenticeships, 356–358
    dialogue and instructional conversa-
      tions, 355–356, 357
    dilemmas of, 361–363, 362
    fostering communities of learners,
      361
    inquiry learning, 350–352, 353–355
    overview of, 350
    problem-based learning, 352–355
constructivist approaches to planning,
    468–470
    example of, 469
    integrated and thematic plans,
      469–470
constructivist approaches to teaching,
    481
    evaluation of, 489
    mathematics instruction, 483–486
constructivist views of learning,
    343–346
    constructionism, 345–346
    diversity and convergences in,
      363–364
    overview of, 343–344
    psychological/individual construc-
      tivism, 344–345
    Vygotsky's social constructivism,
      345
context, 260
contiguity, 203
contingency contract, 222
continuous reinforcement schedule, 208
contract system and grading rubrics,
    537
control
    and intrinsic motivation, 378
    sharing, 340–341
conventional moral reasoning, 93
convergent questions, 477
convergent thinking, 306
cooperation, gaining, 418–419
cooperative learning, 118, 401
    see also classroom management

safety guidelines, 80
intersubjective attitude, 349
interval schedule, 208
intimacy versus isolation, 68
intrinsic motivation, 373–374
intrinsic value of task, 397
intuitive thinking, 288
Inuit, 42, 89
IQ test(s)
    group versus individual, 114, 115
    history of, 113–114
    and identification of gifted students, 122
    individual, 115
    Stanford-Binet test, 114
IQ test scores
    and achievement, 115–116
    for developmental disabilities, 134
    Flynn effect, 114–115
    interpreting, 115
    meaning of, 114

J

Joplin Plan, 117–118
journals, special and general, 136
juvenile arthritis, 139

K

keyword method, 268
knowledge
    see also conditional knowledge; declarative knowledge; procedural knowledge
    constructing, 46–47, 346, 349
    expert, 301–302
    importance in learning, 246
    metacognitive, 264–265
    novice, 302–303
    and self-regulation, 335
    situated versus general, 347
    teachers', 458
knowledge development
    declarative knowledge, 266–269
    procedural and conditional knowledge, 269–271
Kohlberg's theory of moral development, 93–94, 95
Kpelle people (Africa), 38
KWL strategy, 315, 316

L

labelling of disabled/gifted. See language and labelling
language
    see also bilingualism; private talk
    and child development, 47–48
    and cultural diversity, 42
language and labelling, 106
    disabilities and handicaps, 106
    people-first language, 106
language development, 51–54
    age factor, 53
    dual language, 51–53
    milestones in first six years, 52
    overview of, 51
    partnerships with families, 54, 55
    in the school years, 53–54
    synaptic pruning and, 23
language disorders, 133

lateralization, 25
Latin Americans. See Hispanic Americans
lead poisoning, 164
learned helplessness, 127, 393
learning, 200–202
    see also learning theories; objectives for learning; TARGET model for learning
    access to, 420–421
    assisted, 48–49
    cognitive development and, 44–45
    as a constructive process, 46–47
    defined, 200–201
    example of three kinds of, 201–202
    scaffolding, 48–49, 50
    self-talk and, 43
    student ownership of, 349
    time for, 419–420
    viewpoints on "making learning fun", 385
learning communities, 377, 433–439
    classroom community, 433–434
    discipline problems, 438–439
    encouraging engagement, 435, 436
    getting started, 434–435
    importance of, 433
    prevention, 435–438
    special problems with secondary students, 439–441
learning disabilities, 124–128
    and concept teaching, 290
    described, 124–125
    metacognitive strategies for students with, 265
    problems and habits of students with, 126–127
    teaching students with, 127–128
    Theme Identification Program, 128
learning environments
    see also communication (teacher-student); learning spaces; organization; rules (and procedures)
    culturally responsive management, 450
    different management approaches, 448–450
    family communication, 450, 451
    importance of positive, 422
    managing the first weeks of class, 429–433
    research results, 422
learning preferences. See learning styles and preferences
learning spaces, 427–428
    computer management, 428–429, 431, 432
    designing guidelines, 429
    importance of, 427–428
    interest areas, 428
    personal territories, 428
learning strategies, 310–318
    application of, 315–318
    diversity and convergences of, 322–323
    guidelines to become an expert student, 317
    importance of, 310
    modelling, 316
    reading strategies, 314–315

    and tactics, 310–312
    visual tools for organizing, 313
learning styles and preferences, 119–120
    cautions about, 120
    cautions about research on, 188
    cultural values and, 187–188
    learning preferences, 119–120
    learning styles, 119
learning tactics, 310
    see also learning strategies
learning theories
    see also behavioural views of learning; cognitive view of learning; constructivist views of learning
    four views of learning, 365
least restrictive placement, 144–145
left hemisphere of brain, 25
legislation
    child protection, 81
    exceptional education and inclusion, 144
    on multiculturalism, 159
    violent crimes among children, 76
legitimate peripheral participation, 376
lessons, meaningful, 266–267
levels of processing theories, 261
literacy promotion, 54–55
loci method, 267–268
locus of causality, 373–374
LOGO, 360
long-term memory, 254–263
    capacity, duration, and contents of, 254–255
    declarative, procedural, and conditional knowledge, 255–256
    explicit: semantic and episodic, 256–259
    forgetting, 262–263
    implicit, 256, 259
    individual differences and, 273–274
    levels of processing theories, 261
    retrieving information from, 261–262
    storing information in, 260
    versus working memory, 255
longitudinal studies, 12
low-incidence disabilities, 138–143
    autism spectrum disorders, 142–143
    chronic health concerns, 140
    deaf and hard of hearing, 141
    described, 138, 139
    low vision and blindness, 141–142
    making a referral, 143
low-road transfer, 319
low vision and blindness, 141–142

M

macrosystem, 71
Mager's objectives for learning, 465
maintenance rehearsal, 253
Maslow's hierarchy, 375
massed practice, 269
mastery experiences, 333
mastery goal, 381
mastery-oriented students, 393
mathematics
    cognitive learning approach to, 358
    learning and teaching, 483–486

peer cultures, 73–74
peers, 73–78
    aggression, 75–76
    bullying, 76–77
    and cognitive development, 47–48
    cyberbullying, 78
    importance of, 73
    peer cultures, 73–74
    relational aggression, 77
    resistance cultures, 164
    students likely to have problems with, 74–75
    victims, 77–78
peg-type mnemonics, 268
penalties. *See* punishment
people-first language, 106, 107
percentage grading, 535–537
perception, 248
performance goals, 381–382
Performance Standards for Social Responsibility, 434
permissive parents, 73
personal-social development
    see also Bronfenbrenner's bioecological model; Erikson's stages of individual development supporting, 98
personal territories, 428
perspective-taking ability, 91
petit mal, 140
phonics, 482–483
phonological loop, 252
physical development, 22, 24, 62–64
    adolescents, 63–64
    brain and adolescent development, 64
    elementary school years, 62
    preschool children, 62
Piaget's stages of cognitive development, 28–36
    concrete-operational stage, 31–33, 34
    formal-operational stage, 33–36, 37
    limitations of, 37–38
    preoperational stage, 30–31, 32
    sensorimotor stage, 29–30
    summary of, 29
Piaget's theory of cognitive development, 26–28
    see also Piaget's stages of cognitive development
    adaptation, 28
    basic tendencies in thinking, 27–28
    equilibration, 28
    implications for teachers, 45–47
    influences on development, 27
    information processing and neo-Piagetian views, 36
    limitations of, 37–38
    organization, 27
    private speech, 42–43, 44
    role of learning and development, 44–45
plasticity, 24
play, value of, 47
point system, 535
portfolio and performance assessment, 523–526
    diversity and equity in, 526

methods of, 523
    reliability, validity, generalizability, 525–526
    scoring rubrics, 523–525
portfolios and exhibitions, 520–521
    see also portfolio and performance assessment
    background of, 520–521
    exhibitions, 521
    portfolios, 521–522, 523
Positive Behaviour Support (PBS), 130, 135
positive behavioural support, 218–219
positive correlation, 10
positive practice, 214
positive reinforcement, 206
postconventional moral reasoning, 93–94
poverty
    health, environment and stress, 163–164
    home environment and resources, 165
    low expectations and self-esteem, 164
    peer influences and resistance cultures, 164
    retained students, 530
    and school achievement, 162–165, 169
    tracking of students, 165
PQ4R strategy, 314–315
practical/contextual intelligence, 113
pragmatics, 54
praise, 212
preconventional moral reasoning, 93
prefrontal cortex and impulse control, 24–25
prejudice, 170–171
Premack Principle, 212–214
preoperational stage of cognitive development, 30–31, 32
prerequisite knowledge, 271
preschool years
    belief about ability, 390
    classroom management, 419
    cognitive tools of, 38
    gender-role identity, 175–177
    reading/writing strategies, 483, 484
    teaching learning disabled, 127
preschool years development
    moral development, 92–93
    physical development, 62
    Piaget's developmental stage, 30–31
    theory of mind and intention, 91
    trust, autonomy and initiative (Erikson), 65–66
presentation punishment, 207
pretest, 507–508
prevention, 435–438, 446–448
priming, 260
principle, 14
private speech
    and learning, 43
    Vygotsky and Piaget's views compared, 42–43, 44
    and zone of proximal development, 44
problem, 291

problem-based learning, 352–355, 397
problem solving, 291–303
    see also creativity
    anticipating, acting, and looking back, 298
    calculator use, 298
    diversity and convergences in, 322–323
    expert versus novice knowledge, 301–303
    exploring solution strategies, 296–297
    factors that hinder, 298–301
    guidelines, 304
    identification of problem, 292–293
    mathematical, 358
    overview of, 291–292
    representing the problem, 293–295
    viewpoints on teaching, 360
procedural knowledge, 269–271, 273
    automated basic skills and, 271
    defined, 255–256
    domain-specific strategies and, 271
procedural memory, 259
procedures. *See* rules (and procedures)
process portfolios, 521, 522
prodigies, 309
production phase (observational learning), 226
productions (of procedural memory), 259
productive conferences, 149
Productive Thinking Program, 360
prompting, 210
pronunciation, 53
proposition, 256
propositional network, 256
prototype, 248, 283
psychoeducational diagnostic tests, 503
psychomotor domain in Bloom's taxonomy, 468
psychosocial theory. *See* Erikson's stages of individual development
psychostimulant medications, 130
puberty, 63
punishment
    described, 207
    group consequences, 221–222
    guidelines for using, 218
    imposing penalties, 440
    zero tolerance, 441
Pygmalion effect, 460

Q

questioning and recitation
    fitting questions to students, 477–479
    kinds of questions, 477
    overview of, 476–477
    responding to student answers, 479

R

race, 165–166
radical constructivism, 344–345
random assignment, 11
ratio schedule, 208
reading strategies, 314–315
reading/writing, learning and teaching, 481–483

Credits

Text Credits

p. 83, From Marsh, H. W., & Shavelson, R. J. (1985). Self-concept: Its multifaceted, hierarchical structure. *Educational Psychologist*, 20, no.3, p. 114. Adapted by permission of the publisher and authors; p. 91, From Saarni, C. (2002). The development of emotional competence. New York: Guilford Publications. Copyright © 2002 by Guilford Publications, Inc. Adapted with permission of the publisher; p. 107, Adapted from the Office for Disability Issues, *A Way with Words: Guidelines and Appropriate Terminology for the Portrayal of Persons with Disabilities* (Human Resources and Social Development Canada). Reproduced with the permission of Her Majesty the Queen in Right of Canada 2007; p. 124, Copyright © Province of British Columbia. All rights reserved. Reprinted with permission from the Province of British Columbia. www.ipp.gov.bc.ca; p. 125–126, Adopted by the Learning Disabilities Association of Canada, January 30, 2002; p. 131, *Teaching Young Children and Adolescents: A Canadian Casebook*, N.L. Hutchinson, 2004, p. 201. Toronto: Prentice Hall, reprinted with permission by Pearson Education Canada Inc.; p. 131, Adapted with permission of John Wiley & Sons, Inc.; p. 163, Source: "Children from highest socio-economic status families are most likely to be near the top of their class," adapted from the Statistics Canada publication "Education Quarterly Review," Catalogue 81-003, vol. 04 no. 02, released September 29, 1997, page 55, URL: http://www.statcan.ca/english/freepub/81-003-XIB/0029781-003-XIB.pdf; p. 166, Source: "Recent Immigrants by Country of Last Residence," adapted from the Statistics Canada CANSIM database, http://cansim2. statcan.ca, Table 051-0006. Available at http://cansim2.statcan.ca/cgi-win/CNSMCGI.EXE.table051-006; p. 170, British Columbia College of Teachers. (2004, Winter). Aboriginal education initiatives: From parents clubs to teacher education. Connected, 9–11; p. 434, Johnson, D., & Johnson, R. (1999). The three C's of school and classroom management. In H. J. Freiberg (Ed.), Beyond behaviorism: Changing the classroom management paradigm (p. 133). Boston: Allyn & Bacon; p. 536, Frisbie, D. A., & Waltman, K. K. (1992). Developing a personal grading plan. Educational Measurement: Issues and Practice, 11(3), 37. Copyright © 1992 by the National Council on Measurement in Education. Reprinted with permission from Blackwell Publishing.

Photo Credits

Note: Cartoon credits appear with the cartoons.

p. 7, Ray Boudreau; p. 12, Will Faller; p. 27, Anderson/Monkmeyer; p. 29, Brian Smith; p. 39, James V. Wertsch/Washington University; p. 41, Owen Franklen/Stock Boston; p. 44, © Robert Harbinson; p. 49, (top) Kelly Hoy, Arlington Writers, (bottom) Courtesy of VIDEO-DISCOVERY; p. 53, © Charles Gupton/CORBIS; p. 65, © Ted Streshinsky/CORBIS; p. 74, © Ellen Senisi/The Image Works; p. 76, © David Young-Wolff/PhotoEdit; p. 80, © Nancy Richmond/The Image Works; p. 86, © Michael Newman/PhotoEdit; p. 95, Courtesy of Carol Gilligan; p. 112, Birgitte Nielsen; p. 113, Lyrl Ahern; p. 116, © Bob Daemmrich/The Image Works; p. 120, Will Hart; p. 121, Digital Vision; pp. 128, 133, Will Hart; p. 150, © Jeff Greenberg/Omni-Photo Communications; p. 165, Andy Sacks/Getty Images; p. 167, Bill Bachman/MaXx Images Inc.; p. 170, (top) Time Inc., (bottom) Courtesy of Gwen Point; p. 177, © John Boykin/PhotoEdit; p. 179, Will Hart; p. 185, Kindra Clineff/MaXx Images; p. 188, Lindfors Photography; p. 201, Ray Boudreau; p. 206, Falk/Monkmeyer; p. 208, AP Wide World Photos; p. 225, Stanford University News Service Library; p. 227, © Tony Freeman/PhotoEdit; p. 245, Li-Hua Lan/Syracuse Newspapers; p. 251, Lindfors Photography; p. 271, Stephen Frisch/ Stock Boston; p. 273, © Laura Dwight/PhotoEdit; p. 288, (top) Will Hart, (bottom) Al Harvey/The Slide Farm; p. 290, © Syracuse Newspapers/Michelle Gabeel/The Image Works; p. 297, © Frank Siteman; p. 303, Will Faller; p. 305, AP Wide World Photos; p. 321, Lindfors Photography; p. 333, © Dimitri Lundt/Bettman/Corbis; pp. 334, 336, © Frank Siteman; p. 340, © Marty Heitner/The Image Works; p. 343, © Michael Newman/PhotoEdit; p. 348, © Robert Harbinson; p. 357, © Nancy Sheenan Photography; p. 359, © Frank Siteman; p. 374, Kelly Hoy, Arlington Writers; p. 376, © Bob Daemmrich/The Image Works; p. 382, Andy Sacks/Stone/Getty Images; p. 384, © Robert Harbinson; p. 393, © Michael Newman/PhotoEdit; p. 400, © Bill Bachman/The Image Works; p. 418, © Michelle Bridwell/PhotoEdit; p. 426, Will Hart; p. 437, Birgitte Nielsen; p. 443, © Frank Siteman/PhotoEdit; p. 446, © Nancy Richmond/The Image Works; p. 466, Brian Smith; p. 474, Dick Hemingway; p. 482, Ernest Braun/Stone/Getty Images; p. 488, Will Hart; p. 491, Kelly Hoy, Arlington Writers; p. 501, Richard Clintsman/Stone/Getty Images; p. 508, Birgitte Nielsen; p. 510, © Nancy Richmond/The Image Works; p. 517, © Bob Daemmrich/The Image Works; p. 526, Ray Boudreau; p. 532, © Mary Kate Denny/PhotoEdit; p. 543, Robert E. Daemmrich/Stone/Getty Images.